International Business Strategy

With stagnated demand in many home economies, the need to internationalize and exploit foreign market opportunities has never been more paramount for businesses to succeed at a global level. However, this process raises a number of questions, such as: Can firms use their knowledge of one market in the next? Can firms pursue internationalization on several fronts at the same time? How should firms handle cultural and institutional differences between markets?

This textbook provides students with the core research in international business strategy, including organization, efficiency, external relationships and the challenges found in an increasingly multicultural world. Each part begins with a presentation of the issues and controversies faced in that particular area, followed by a synthesis of the research, which provides avenues for future research. To facilitate and encourage further debate and learning, each part also includes at least one original case study.

Compiled by two world-leading scholars of international business, and supplemented with critical commentaries and a range of integrative case studies, this comprehensive textbook provides advanced students of international business strategy with a resource that will be invaluable in their studies and beyond.

Peter J Buckley is Professor of International Business at the University of Leeds, UK.

Pervez N Ghauri is Professor of International Business at Kings College London, UK.

International Business Strategy

Theory and practice

Edited by
Peter J Buckley and Pervez N Ghauri

Routledge
Taylor & Francis Group

LONDON AND NEW YORK

First published 2015
by Routledge
2 Park Square, Milton Park, Abingdon, Oxon OX14 4RN

and by Routledge
711 Third Avenue, New York, NY 10017

Routledge is an imprint of the Taylor & Francis Group, an informa business

British Library Cataloguing in Publication Data
A catalogue record for this book is available from the British Library.

Library of Congress Cataloging in Publication Data
International business strategy: theory and practice/edited by Peter J. Buckley and Pervez Ghauri.
    pages cm
    1. International business enterprises–Management–Cross-cultural
    studies–Case studies. 2. International trade–Case studies. I. Buckley, Peter J.,
    II. Ghauri, Pervez N.,
    HD62.4.I5496 2014
    658'.049–dc23   2014024753

ISBN: 978-0-415-62469-5 (hbk)
ISBN: 978-0-415-62470-1 (pbk)
ISBN: 978-1-315-84836-5 (ebk)

Typeset in Times New Roman
by Sunrise Setting Ltd, Paignton, UK

Contents

Figures

Tables

Contributors

Christoph Barmeyer *(University of Passau, Germany)*

Ulf Elg *(Lund University, Sweden)*

Jens Gammelgaard *(Copenhagen Business School, Denmark)*

Sylvie Hertrich *(EM Strasbourg, University of Strasbourg, France)*

Michel Kalika *(Dauphine University, France)*

Thomas Kotulla *(ESCP Europe, Germany)*

Ulrike Mayrhofer *(IAE Lyon, France)*

Surender Munjal *(Leeds University, UK)*

Janina Schaumann *(Lund University, Sweden)*

Stefan Schmid *(ESCP Europe, Germany)*

Dennis J. Wurster *(ESCP Europe, Germany)*

Part I

Basic concepts of international business

1 Introduction

What is international business?

At its simplest, international business is easily defined: doing business across international frontiers. As this book will show, in practice this is far from simple. There are many methods (modes) for companies to engage in business internationally and the management and co-ordination of these complex activities has become a specialized field of study as "international management".

The academic subject of international business approaches the empirical phenomena of doing business across borders at a variety of levels of analysis, using a variety of theoretical frameworks (Buckley and Lessard, 2005). The most important levels of analysis are:

- the individual manager;
- the firm;
- the industry;
- the country;
- the global economy.

In each category, there is great heterogeneity.

Over the history of international business, different phases of research dominance have led to one level or another being privileged in order to give clarity to the analysis. For instance, internalization theory (Chapter 6) and the product cycle hypothesis (Chapter 3) privilege the level of the firm. Analyses of global strategy emphasize the industry level and institutional analysis has the macro-environment as its core. Individual managers, too, have been studied, investigating their decision-making (Chapter 11) and often the impact of national cultures on their attitudes and style (Chapters 25 and 26).

In order to reconcile these differing levels of analysis, the international business research community has often focussed on a "big question". This has included explaining the flows of foreign direct investment (FDI), exploring the existence, strategy and organization of multi-national enterprises (MNEs) and understanding and predicting the development of the internationalization of firms and globalization. It is arguable that the current (2014) big question is the rise of emerging economies, particularly the BRIC countries (Brazil, Russia, India and China) and the impact this has on the international economy, not least by their outward FDI. All these themes are examined in this book.

The domain of international business research is given by its empirical subject matter. "International" implies comparative. It is the international heterogeneity and variance of business activity that gives the subject matter its inherent interest and importance; international business is imbued with comparative method. The key comparators are: geographical, across space; historical, across time; counterfactual, a thought experiment comparing different (hypothetical) conditions of the world.

The geographical comparison is the most obvious for international business; comparisons across nations are fundamental to its *raison d'être*. This has great advantages for the research area and for its central factor, the multinational enterprise, because this is a single firm operating in more than one country. The MNE performs an experimental function holding "firm" constant and varying "context". We can see that a firm (and its managers) may behave differently, respond to different stimuli and take different decisions according to the geographical space in which it is operating. This type of analysis need not only operate at the national level; it is important, for instance, in comparing cities, often the key factor in location decisions.

The second key comparison is historical time. Firms that are "successful" in time (t) are not necessarily successful in time (t+l) and "loss of competitiveness" over time is a major issue for countries, regions, cities, firms and economic blocs. Concepts of growth, development, decline and loss all have a temporal element. Combining analyses of firms and industries over space and time are key contributors of international business theory.

Examining counterfactual positions is a challenging process. What would have happened if Nissan had not invested in the UK? Nothing? An investment by another foreign company? An investment by a UK company? The UK market being served by exports from Japan rather than a local output of cars? All these are theoretical possibilities and the judgement and analysis of the researcher is required to specify which is the most feasible alternative. On this judgement hangs our view of whether Nissan's investment was a "good thing" (because it created new economic activity in the UK) or a "bad thing" (because it diverted productive capacity from UK ownership to foreign ownership). Note that the judgement here depends on whose welfare we are considering: the UK, Japan, the firm, Nissan, local workers, the consumers of cars and the British and Japanese governments are just some of the actors on whom we may analyse the impact of the investment.

It will have been noted that the analysis of international business requires an interdisciplinary approach. Not only are social sciences, such as economics and sociology, necessary to encompass the impacts of international business, but so too are history and geography. Understanding and reducing complexity is an important task for the international business scholar.

International trade and investment

International business has centred on the actions and outcomes of decisions by firms operating across borders. There is a long tradition of international economics examining trade: flows of goods and services exported and imported across national frontiers. This tradition largely abstracted from the institution of the firm. It was a focus on the firm as an institution that undertakes not only trade but also investment across borders that created international business as a distinct subject. This was allied to the distinction between direct foreign investment where the firm owns and controls an entity in the host country (the one receiving the investment), thus giving the source countries (investing) parent firm control over part of a foreign country's economic activity as distinct from portfolio foreign investment, where a source country entity simply acquires a non-controlling share of a foreign firm. This distinction (first made by Stephen Hymer in 1960, published 1976) propelled the firm and its major international competitive weapon – foreign direct investment – to centre stage in the global economy.

From this sharp distinction between FDI and portfolio foreign investment, grew a literature on foreign entry and development analysis at the level of the firm. This strand of research compares exporting, FDI and foreign licensing as means of competing in the world economy. The choice of "foreign entry modes" is made up of the interaction between two critical decisions. These are: where is an activity to be located and how is the activity to be controlled? We should remember that firms coordinate far more activities than just production and service performance. They also carry out marketing, financing, research and development (R&D), human resource management (HRM) amongst others. All these activities have (different) optimal locations and means of control that change over time, meaning the MNE is the major dynamic factor in the world economy.

The use by firms of trade (exporting and importing) and foreign investment raises the strategic issue of the means (often called modes of international operation) by which firms service foreign markets. This must be preceded by the question of *why* firms venture abroad.

Why firms engage in international business

The reason firms venture abroad is simple: they do so to obtain things that are not available at home. Firms import goods and services, labour, technology, skills and inputs that are unavailable or more expensive at home. The analogue of this is that firms export a similar portfolio of goods, services and assets because foreigners cannot obtain these things at all or as cheaply at home.

It has become traditional to examine the motives for foreign direct investment into:

- market seeking;
- resource seeking (more generally, locationally fixed input seeking);
- efficiency (lower cost) seeking;
- asset seeking.

This represents a set of factors that are not transferable from the foreign country, they are locationally fixed. If they were not locationally fixed then they could be transferred internationally by trade or licence and there would be no need to undertake foreign investment. Moreover, foreign *direct* investment is preferred because this allows the investor to control the resources. Markets, natural resources or inputs, cheap labour (or a lower tax rate) and certain types of locationally fixed assets are the target and control of these is the key reason for FDI.

So far, we have considered only a two-country world (home and foreign). FDI becomes more complicated when we add a third country (or third countries more generally) because we can then consider an "offshore base" which is neither the home country (source country from which the investment comes) or target market. It may be considered an entrepôt where activities are carried out on behalf of Country 1 with a target market that may be Country 1 or 2. Offshore bases in large countries (for example, China) may also service their own market as well.

Dynamics are extremely important in global strategies. As cost and market conditions shift and are affected by a myriad of causes, including wage rates, transportation rates, exchange rates, tax rates, so do location decisions. Over time, we observe shifts of whole industries and types of activity between locations. This affects the welfare of home, host, third countries and the international economy. The shifting of locations, in particular in response to changes in tax rates, are a significant source of political controversy.

How firms engage in international business: modes of doing business abroad

There are three basic (or generic) modes of doing business internationally: exporting, foreign licensing and foreign direct investment. Each of these modes has a variety of sub-types including direct exporting, exporting through an agent or distributor, licensing, franchising, turn-key operations, assembly, sales subsidiary and production subsidiary.

This is further complicated by the ownership dimension: should these activities be wholly owned or jointly owned with others? Joint ownership includes joint ventures (equity or non-equity), alliances (which may imply joint equity shares or no ownership commitment) or minority joint ventures.

Initial entry into the foreign market may be by acquisition, often referred to as "mergers and acquisitions" (M&A) even though the number of mergers – two companies joining together – is rare in practice, or by "greenfield ventures" where a *de novo* entry is made, all the required assets are put together from scratch. Further development in the foreign market may be by acquisition or organic growth.

"Entry and development" strategy is complex and has several dimensions: ownership strategy, entry strategy and growth strategy. All are predicated on picking the optimal location. Where this ceases to be optimal, MNEs will require exit strategies involving disinvestment.

Internationalization (and de-internationalization) has a time dimension, a dynamic, a sequencing of strategic moves that is complex and subject to a wide range of influences from the firm itself and from its environment. Analyses of internationalization have to take cognizance of this complexity either by simplification (in a theoretical context) or by "thick description" in insightful case studies.

The first part of this collection covers key articles, introducing basic concepts that have had a fundamental effect on subsequent research and writing.

The first reading in this volume, Chapter 2, is an abridgement (by Peter Buckley) of Yair Aharoni's 1966 study of the foreign investment decision process. The foreign investment decision is analysed as a complex social process which is influenced by social relationships within and outside the firm. Aharoni provides a rich description of individual and organizational behaviour over time and shows the crucial effect of perception and uncertainty in the course of this process. A holistic understanding of all the stages is necessary to comprehend the decision. Although Aharoni analyses the decision as a succession of stages, he is at pains to point out that in real life these stages are ill-defined and messy. This piece emphasizes the importance of the initiating force and explains many elements that may be wrongly labelled "irrational". Aharoni's work laid a firm foundation for studies of decision processes in multinational firms.

Chapter 3 is a work which can justly claim the epithet "seminal", Raymond Vernon's 1966 article "International investment and international trade in the product cycle". The argument of this paper is that firms are highly stimulated by their local environment and are more likely to innovate when their immediate surroundings are more conducive to the creation of (particular) new techniques or products. For internationalization to occur, these innovations must be transferable to other economies. In adapting to its market, the firm moves through stages from innovation to standardization and maturity according to the developing forces of supply and demand for its product. This model of sequential decision-making has had a great influence on internationalization theory. The model was originally developed to explain US investment in Europe and in cheap labour countries. Its usefulness goes beyond Vernon's reappraisal of its efficacy under changed world conditions (1979) or the sting of its critics (for example, Giddy, 1978). Its relevance arises from the fact that the dynamic of the model lies in the interaction of the evolving forces of demand (taste) patterns and production possibilities. In some ways, its powerful, yet simple, dynamic resting on the changing equilibria of demand and supply over time, has never been bettered. The twin rationales of cost imperatives and market pull are simply explained in Vernon's model. Its programmatic nature may have strait jacketed later analyses into a unilinear internationalization path. Although its validity for the explanation of the behaviour of modern multinationals may be questioned, this article spawned much of the empirical literature on international marketing.

Chapter 4 is Johanson and Vahlne's 2009 revisiting of the Uppsala internationalization process model. The original model, published in 1977 (Johanson and Vahlne, 1977), was reproduced in earlier versions of this book (Buckley and Ghauri (eds.) 1993, 1999). In the original piece the authors examined the internationalization process by investigating the development of knowledge and the building of a commitment within the firm to foreign markets. The twin notions of increasing knowledge of foreign markets as a means of reducing uncertainty and the creation of a commitment to foreign ventures had been examined in a key study by Aharoni (1966) (see Chapter 2) and the authors tied these notions to the framework of the behavioural theory of the firm. Internationalization is again envisaged as the product of a series of incremental decisions. Decisions taken at a point in time affect subsequent steps in the process. Psychic distance is invoked and is defined as "the sum of the factors preventing the flow of information from and to the market". The decision-making process is dependent on the firm's previous experience. Again, the empirical evidence is based on a small number of companies. Four Swedish companies are examined from Johanson and Wiedersheim-Paul (1975), a case study of the Swedish pharmaceutical firm Pharmacia is introduced and other industry studies are quoted (special steel, pulp and paper and nine further cases). Casual empirical evidence from other countries is also adduced. The two notions of market commitment and market knowledge entered the literature as key elements of internationalization. The updated 2009 paper emphasizes the international business environment as a "web of relationships, a network, rather than as a neoclassical market with many independent suppliers and customers". The root of uncertainty is "outsidership" to these networks rather than psychic distance (see Chapter 27). Trust-building and knowledge-creation are added to commitment-building and opportunity-development as critical change mechanisms. The celebrated establishment chain is felt to have declining validity in the context of extended (international) business networks. The establishment chain was introduced when Johanson and Wiedersheim-Paul (1975) examined the internationalization of four Swedish firms. For this small sample, they found a regular process of gradual incremental change. The firm progresses from no regular exports to export through independent representatives and the establishment of sales subsidiaries to the establishment of production facilities. Flows of information between the firm and the market are (as in Vernon's model) crucial in this process and the cultural distance between spatially separated units of the firm is termed psychic distance. The establishment profiles of the four firms were mapped across a number of countries in time and the gradualist pattern was confirmed. Johanson and Wiedersheim-Paul's path-breaking article gave rise to considerable controversy centred on the general applicability of the findings and the underlying theory. Suggestions were made that experienced firms can "jump" stages and transfer learning from one market to another without having to go through each stage in each foreign market. The knowledge collection and planning processes of large multinationals can, some authors feel, obviate the need for incremental learning. Some empirical findings suggest a less gradualist and one-directional expansion path. The theory has also been questioned in its classification of stage or stages of involvement ranked in order of "depth". Is a licensing deal a deeper form of involvement than a foreign agency agreement? Methodologically, looking back in time a successful firm eliminates firms that have failed at an earlier stage, i.e. it induces a bias towards longer routes of establishment. More carefully designed experiments are required to establish the conditions under which a stages approach is valid. Here, the authors draw parallels and contrasts with internalization theory (see Chapter 6) and the eclectic paradigm (see Chapter 5). The most recent version of the Uppsala School has strong parallels with the analysis of the global factory (Chapter 8) although readers will be able to identify the contrasts of the two approaches.

John Dunning has produced a large corpus of work in international business (see the encyclopaedic Dunning and Lundan, 2008). From them, we have chosen a piece originally written in 2000 (Chapter 5), which presents the key elements of Dunning's "eclectic paradigm". This approach uses three sets of explanatory factors to analyse international business issues: locational factors, internalization factors and ownership factors. Firms transfer their ownership-specific assets to combine with the most favourable sets of traditionally fixed elements in the global economy, and they do this, where appropriate, internally, in order to retain control of the revenue generation. Later versions of the eclectic approach refined this position and extended its taxonomy and it has become familiar to many generations of researchers and students as a set of key organizing principles in international business.

The dominant paradigm in research on the multinational firm is the internalization approach. Chapter 6 is a summary and review of the theoretical work in this tradition by Buckley and Casson whose book, the *Future of the Multinational Enterprise* (1976), was a basic contribution. The basic theory explains the division of national markets (and therefore of the world market) between domestic firms and foreign multinationals. It does so by reference to two effects: the location effect and the internalization decisions of firms. The location effect determines where value adding activities take place and the internalization effect explains who owns and controls those activities. The concepts of least cost location and growth by internalization of markets are introduced to internationalization theory. Firms grow by replacing the (imperfect) external market and earn a return from so doing until the point at which the benefits of further internalization are outweighed by the costs. The types of benefit and cost of growth by internalization are listed and it is suggested that certain types of market are more likely to be internalized than others, given the configuration of the world economy. These ideas were expanded in Buckley and Casson (1985), Casson (1987) and Buckley (1988, 1989, 1990). The direction of internationalization can be predicted by predicting changes in cost and market conditions. These factors are classified as industry specific, region specific, firm specific and nation specific. The current piece, from 2009, reviews the research agenda pursued by Buckley and Casson in the forty years since the 1976 book. This agenda has become progressively more wide-ranging, covering joint ventures (see also Chapters 16 and 17), innovation and the role of culture (see also Part V).

Chapter 8 was one of the first pieces to introduce the theoretical structure "The Global Factory" (Buckley, 2004, 2007, 2009, 2010, 2011a, 2011b). It points to the importance (and re-emergence) of spatial issues in international business theorizing and focusses on the two key decisions for multinationals: locational spread and the extent of control, mirroring the essential concepts of optimal location, and internalization and externalization decisions that determine the boundaries of the firm. The more flexible boundaries of the global factory focus attention on offshoring (a locational choice) and outsourcing (an externalization decision) and provide links with literatures on these two important trends (references) and on the cognate literature on "global value chains" (Gereffi and Memedovic, 2003; Gereffi et al., 2005).

References

Aharoni, Y. 1966. *The foreign investment decision process*. Cambridge, Mass: Harvard Business School Press.

Buckley, P.J. 1988. Organisational firms and multinational companies. In Wright, M. and S. Thompson, (Eds.), *Internal organisation, efficiency and profit*. Oxford: Philip Allan.

Buckley, P.J. 1989. Foreign direct investment by small and medium-sized enterprises: The theoretical background. *Small Business Economics*, 1(2): 89–100.

Buckley, P.J. 1990. Problems and developments in the core theory of international business. *Journal of International Business Studies*, 21(4): 657–65.

Buckley, P.J. 2004. The role of China in the global strategy of multinational enterprises. *Journal of Chinese Economic and Business Studies*, 2/1, 1–25.

Buckley, P.J. 2007. The strategy of multinational enterprises in the light of the rise of China. *Scandinavian Journal of Management*, 23/2, 107–26.

Buckley, P.J. 2009. The impact of the global factory on economic development. *Journal of World Business*, 44/2, 131–43.

Buckley, P.J. 2010. The role of headquarters in the global factory. In U. Andersson and U. Holm (Eds.), *Managing the contemporary multinational* (pp. 60–84). Cheltenham: Edward Elgar.

Buckley, P.J. 2011a. (Ed.) *Globalization and the global factory*. Cheltenham: Edward Elgar, p. 634.

Buckley, P.J. 2011b. International integration and coordination in the global factory. *Management International Review*, 51/2, 269–83.

Buckley P.J. and Casson, M. 1976. *The future of the multinational enterprise*. London: Macmillan.

Buckley, P.J. and Casson, M. 1985. *The economic theory of the multinational enterprise*. London: Macmillan and New York: St Martin's Press, 1985.

Buckley, P.J. and Ghauri, P.N. 1993. (Eds.) *The internationalisation of the firm: A reader*. London: Academic Press, p. 371.

Buckley, P.J. and Ghauri, P.N. 1999. (Eds.) *The global challenge for multinational enterprises. Managing increasing interdependence*. Oxford: Elsevier Science, p. 525.

Buckley, P.J. and Lessard, D.R. 2005. Regaining the edge for international business research. *Journal of International Business Studies*, 36(6): 595–9.

Casson, M. 1987. Transaction costs and the theory of the multinational enterprise. In P.J. Buckley and M. Casson (Eds.) *The economic theory of the multinational enterprise*. London: Macmillan, pp. 113–43.

Dunning, J.H. and Lundan, S.M. 2008. *Multinational enterprises and the global economy*. Cheltenham: Edward Elgar.

Gereffi, G. and Memedovic, O. 2003. *The global apparel value chain: What prospects for upgrading by developing countries?* Vienna: UNIDO.

Gereffi, G., Humphrey J. and Sturgeon T. 2005. The governance of global value chains. *Review of International Political Economy*, 12(1): 78–104.

Giddy, I.H. 1978. The demise of the product cycle model in international business theory. *Columbia Journal of World Business*, 13(Spring): 90–7.

Hymer, S. 1976. 1960. *The international operations of national firms: A study of direct foreign investment*. Cambridge, Mass.: MIT Press.

Johanson, J. and Vahlne, J.E. 1977. The internationalisation process of the firm – A model of knowledge development and increasing foreign market commitments. *Journal of International Business Studies*, 8(1): 23–32.

Johanson, J. and Vahlne, J.E. 2009. The Uppsala internationalization process model revisited: From liability of foreignness to liability of outsidership. *Journal of International Business Studies*, 40(9): 1411–31.

Johanson, J. and Wiedersheim-Paul, F. 1975. The internationalisation process of the firm: Four Swedish cases. *Journal of Management Studies*, 12(3): 305–22.

2 The foreign investment decision process*

Yair Aharoni

Elements in the decision process

In any decision process the following elements can be delineated: first, any one choice made in the organization depends on the *social system* in which the process takes place; second, the process, although not each of the decisions from which it is composed, takes a long *time*; third, decisions are made under *uncertainty*; fourth, organizations have *goals*; and finally, there are many *constraints* on the freedom of action of the decision-makers to be reckoned with.

A system is a set of interrelated parts. Any organization is a system of individuals, grouped in subsystems according to their role definitions, mutually influencing each other through a continual process of interactions. However, every participant in the organization is not only an involved member of the organization. They are intimately connected with the wider variety of other systems of which they are a part, and which they cannot ignore. The organization as a whole is also part of superordinate systems: the industry, the community in which it operates, the cultural environment of which it is a part. All these influence the way problems are defined, alternatives are perceived and selected, and opinions are formulated. 'In order to survive, an organization must achieve what is called "symbiosis" (i.e., the mutually beneficial living together of two dissimilar organizations) with a variety of external systems.'

The first element in the analysis of any decision process is therefore the **organization and environment** in which it takes individuals, each with his own goals and aspirations, and which influnces place. The decision is made within an organization which has established strategy, procedures and standard operating policies, which is composed of different individuals, each with his own goals and aspirations, and which is influenced by other, superordinate systems. The organization has devised an established 'way of doing things' according to agreed-upon goals and past experience; these rules and specifications influence the behavior of its members, the information gathered by them and their adaptive reactions to the environment. Moreover, individuals within the organization. These relations will influence any specific decision.

Those making the decision will have to continue acting for the same organization and interacting with various people in and outside it long after any specific decision is made or implemented. Consciously or unconsciously, they will weigh these future relations throughout the decision process. For example, one may choose a certain course of action because somebody else, to whom one feels an obligation for a favour done in the *past*, prefers it.

One may also take a course of action because one feels that another decision will harm *future* relations with someone else inside or outside the organization. These future relations

*Aharoni, Y. (1966), The foreign investment decision process. The Int. Exec., 8: 13–14, Wiley.

are not necessarily important in terms of the specific decision being considered. They are relevant only if we look at any one specific decision as part of a whole spectrum; the whole stream of past, present and future events in the organization. Interdependence is a well-known phenomenon in the theory of oligopoly: the decision-making of any one entrepreneur depends on his evaluation of his competitors' activities in the past and a projection of his reactions in the future. The same phenomenon, however, is common in all walks of life, among friends and collaborators as well as among competitors. The rationality of behavior is seen only if we observe the whole system instead of concentrating our attention on one isolated phase of it. For example, the officials of a bank decide to lend money to a company despite their disapproval of a specific deal, because they 'look at the total picture' of relations with this specific customer. The executives of a company decide to invest in a certain country against their own business judgement because they were asked to do so by the company's largest supplier. They feel that a refusal might hamper their future relations with the supplier with regard to totally different business deals.

The manner of handling a problem depends strongly on the other activities of the organization. A problem may be considered important enough for immediate investigation during an inactive period, but its solution may be delayed indefinitely if many other activities are going on at the same time. An organization's executives might not explore a profitable opportunity for investment because they were busy with other affairs at the time the opportunity presented itself. The same executives would have vigorously investigated this opportunity at other, less hectic times. As individuals choose to focus their attention on a problem at one time and ignore it at another, depending on their frame of mind or other preoccupations. The priorities set on one's time become an important factor in the decision of what issues should get attention.

A second important element in the decision process that should be explicitly emphasized is the **time dimension**. One of the major arguments to be developed in this book is that this dimension plays a very important role in the way any one decision made at a specific point in time. Rather, there is a long *process*, spread over a considerable period of time and involving many people at different echelons of various organizations. Throughout this process, numerous 'subdecisions' have to be made. These subdecisions usually reduce the degree of freedom of the decision-making unit, thereby influencing the final outcome of the process. Throughout the process, the persons involved change their perception of different variables, numerous shifts in the environment occur, and many changes in other activities of the organization take place. The decision to invest or reject an investment possibility is the final one. Any attempt to 'fold' this time element into a 'point decision' would create grave distortions in the understanding of the process.

A third element to be reckoned with is **uncertainty**. Businessmen are not endowed with the faculty of blissful prescience. They operate in a world of uncertainty. Uncertainty creates anxiety, and anxiety, we are told by psychologists, is a situation human beings try to avoid. It is not surprising, therefore, to find that businessmen try to avoid uncertainty as much as possible. They impose plans, standard operating procedures, industry tradition and uncertainty absorption contracts on that environment. They achieve a reasonable manageable decision situation by avoiding planning where plans depend on predictions of uncertain future events and by emphasizing planning where the plans can be made self-confirming through some control device.

Businessmen not only shy away from uncertainty, they also are not willing to take more than a certain degree of risk. The risk taken depends on the organization and on role-definition, for executives are willing to assume only what they consider to be 'normal business risks'.

From our point of view, the avoidance of risk and uncertainty is a very important factor. For a person or an organization unfamiliar with foreign investments the uncertainty involved is quite large. Therefore, it seems advisable to pause momentarily and examine the meaning of these terms.

The first attempt to distinguish between risk and uncertainty was made by Frank H. Knight in 1921 as part of his treatment of profits. 'Risk' for Knight is a situation in which the probabilities of alternative outcomes are known. For example, contingencies that can be insured constitute risk. Uncertainty, on the other hand, is unmeasurable.

This definition, however, begs the question: what exactly constitutes 'a quantity susceptible of measurement?' For example, is it legitimate to measure probabilities on subjective beliefs or should only objective phenomena be gauged? Does it make sense to talk about the probability of a unique event or can probability be measured only when the experiment is repetitive? These and related questions have been debated for centuries by those dealing with probability and they are still unsolved. It is often argued that objective probability is a pure mathematical concept that cannot be found in real life. Therefore, only subjective probabilities must be used. However, when subjective probabilities are used, the distinction between risk and uncertainty loses much of its sharpness. Indeed, the Bayesian statisticians have developed theories in which management is conceived as assigning subjective probabilities to uncertain events, changing these probabilities when additional information becomes available. Thus, the decision is transformed into one under risk.

For our purposes it seems useful to distinguish between a subjective probability and the degree of belief in it. We shall therefore define 'risk' as the proportion of cases in a subjective joint probability distribution that falls below a subjectively defined expected minimum. Uncertainty will be used to refer to the degree of confidence in the correctness of the estimated subjective probability distribution; the lesser the confidence, the higher the uncertainty.

Note that this definition of risk is not commensurate with the one generally used in economics. Economists define risk as an estimate of a dispersion of a probability distribution; the greater the dispersion, the greater the risk. Our definition is nearer the day-to-day use of the word. Risk is the chance of injury, damage or loss, compared with some previous standard. Uncertainty, on the other hand, is a feeling of doubt and unreliability.

When businessmen talk about risk, they use this word to include both the subjective probability of loss, either in absolute terms or in relation to some expectations, and the amount the company may lose. The loss referred to may be a monetary one, the waste of management time, or the inability to achieve a specific objective of the company other than profits (for example, the risk of losing control). When a businessman says that 'the political risks abroad are high', he may be referring to the possibility of losing his freedom of decision-making because of a high degree of government regulation. Political risks may mean to him a high subjective probability of total or partial loss of the investment itself because of expropriation, nationalization, or war; they may mean that the unsettled conditions put the very basis of planning in question and make the work of management more difficult; or they may be any combination of all these factors.

The subjective evaluation of risk stems from uncertainty. Uncertainty is affected mainly by two factors; ignorance and perceived changes. Ignorance may prevail either because of lack of information (i.e., the information is not available at any cost), or because of lack of knowledge (i.e., the information exists but the decision-maker does not avail themself of it, either because they do not know of its existence, or because they do not want or are not able to spend the resources needed to get it). Perceived changes are conditions where there is a high subjective probability of unsettled or insecure conditions, which would question the very basis of consistent information.

Uncertainty exists not only in regard to the consequences of alternatives; there is also uncertainty about the alternatives themselves. Indeed, some authorities on economic development feel that lack of knowledge about opportunities abroad is a major obstacle to such investments. The responses of others in the organization and of competitors, governments and other outsiders are also unknown. Still, there is always *some* information on similar events that the decision-maker considers similar. Using this information, decision-makers reach some judgement about the future state of affairs and their effects. Therefore, one should learn how people behave in the face of uncertainty, how judgements are formulated when knowledge is inadequate, and when a decision-maker will acquire more information. Obviously, information on every possible opportunity is not available, and even if it were, one would have to be interested in such information in order to focus one's attention on it and to spend such scarce resources as time and energy to digest it. This brings us back to the question of priorities.

In any given business situation, few of the variables are known with precision. There are always many factors which are not subject to mathematical analysis. Many others can be analyzed mathematically only on the basis of subjectively arrived at figures. Because of uncertainty, we deal with perceptions and subjective estimates. No quantitative prediction can be made in an exact, objective manner. To predict a rate of return, one has to estimate investment costs, production cost, sales volume and prices, advertising cost etc. All these are unknown and many of them can be only subjectively estimated. Subjective estimates vary by nature; they also change because of changing expectations of the kind of pay-off associated with various possible errors. If an executive feels that the punishment for an error resulting in a loss will be much greater than a reward for success, he will tend to bias his estimates on the pessimistic side. On the other hand, if he feels that the rewards for success will be much greater than the penalty for failure, he will have a bias on the optimistic side.

One reacts to facts as one perceives them and to what one infers from this perception. Two businessmen with the same motives and the same information may infer different things and reach different conclusions. The following two quotations from the interviews with two businessmen manufacturing the same product will suffice to illustrate this point:

> I know we shall have competition in India. However, you must realize that India is a fast growing market and one of the largest markets in the world.

> Sure, India has a larger population, but they are starving. It will take them another ten years before they will need another plant.

Needless to say, India is the same country, with the same number of inhabitants and the same size of gross national product in both cases. It is the perceptions of the two businessmen about the size of the market in India and the way they evaluate the factual data that are different.

Not only do subjective estimates and perceptions vary, they are also modified with time. Pay-off expectations and subjective estimates of facts are changed during investigation and to a large extent because of it. Here again, the time dimension becomes a crucial factor in the decision process.

Additional information can be purchased before a conclusion is reached. Getting additional information may change perception and subjective estimates, but it costs money and time. Therefore, it will be bought only if the cost of obtaining it is deemed justified by some crude test. Decisions to buy more information are based on 'hunches' and intuition. The intuition is based on beliefs held and on information already available. Because of this, the *sequence* of steps in the investigation is a very crucial variable in the decision process. For example, businessmen evaluate risk at a very early stage of the investigation. They have a 'threshold' for risk and abandon any further consideration of a project that is deemed to be 'too risky'. They do not compensate for risk by higher profits for the simple reason that they evaluate risk at an early stage, when even cursory and precarious calculations of rate of return are still unavailable.

A fourth important element is **goals**. Any normative analysis must presuppose some model of behavior, based on certain assumptions about the goals to be achieved by the decision-makers. However, our approach in this book is descriptive rather than normative. We do not intend to eulogize or condemn any behavior, or to label it as rational or irrational. Our aim is to show how businessmen actually behave in order to predict their behavior rather than to prescribe how they should behave. Because of this, we do not think it is necessary for us to probe into the question of goals and motivations. We should add that we do not feel it possible to explain our data on the basis of one narrow, rigid or inimutable motivating force. In fact, our field research revealed clearly the existence of a multitude of objectives. The interaction of the various goals of individuals executives, of the different divisions, and of the organization as a whole in the process of formulating the decision created a situation that may seem to those looking for one objective as inconsistent and lacking transitivity.

Fifth are the **constraints**. Any major decision in business involves a multitude of variables that could be investigated. A decision to build a plant in a foreign country necessitates search in many directions and the checking of a host of details. For instance, it involves an evaluation of the general political environment, the attitude of the foreign government, and the concessions that may be granted. It necessitates some knowledge of the legal system, the size of the market, the sociological and cultural backgrounds of the population, and the way this background influences its habits. It requires an evaluation of the location and the size of plant to be erected and of the production methods to be used. A decision must be made about which components should be procured and which should be produced. Land prices, wages, firing benefits, behavior of trade unions and productivity of the workers, must all be evaluated. The best 'product mix' should be examined from technological and marketing points of view. A captilaization scheme should be worked out and sources of funds must be tapped. Personnel should be checked and its availability ensured, etc.

Some of these variables – the political environment of the foreign country, for example – must, from the investor's point of view, be taken as given. Many can be changed at will. Many other variables may be changed after negotiations. Investors often negotiate such factors as special tax concessions, relaxation of various legal requirements, size of loans and the rate of interest to be paid on these loans, various guarantees, special rates of exchange, ban on imports or high custom duties on the product to be manufactured, etc. The total number of plausible permutations and combinations of all these variables is almost infinite and each one of these combinations may give a different picture.

Some investments may seem unprofitable if new machines are required, but they could be expected to show high profits if used machines are available: a highly mechanized process of production may create problems, but a labor-intensive process might be the answer. The size of the market could seem to be too small for a very large plant, but a smaller plant might be used and the profits could be high, even though the loss in larger scale economies might result in higher costs; or negotiations with the government might lead to a levy imposed on imports, thus making even a small-scale plant highly profitable.

But investigation costs money and management time. We have already pointed out that because of these factors businessmen are compelled to decide on the basis of crude indicators whether more thorough investigation may be worthwhile. Another plausible method to save money and management time is to assume some variables to be fixed, i.e., as having assigned values or a range of values. Instead of checking all possible permutations, only some crucial variables might be investigated and only incremental changes considered. No explicit recognition is given to the possibility of changes in some variables, such as size of plant. Thus, the decision-maker atones for gaps in his information and for the finiteness of his computational capacity by adopting 'strategies', 'decision rules', and policies, and by assuming some variables to be fixed.

Cyert and March (1963) have demonstrated that organizations accept precedents as binding and look at standard operating procedures as constraints in any problem-solving situation. This was also found to be true in the case of the foreign investment decision process. First, many organizations lacking the precedent of a foreign investment experience would refuse to consider such a possibility. Second, when such a possibility is considered, many previous 'policies' are taken as given and become constraints in the decision process. Under certain circumstances, however, certain constraints will not be binding and changes will be considered. The constraints and the conditions under which they will be changed are therefore another element in the decision process.

The foreign investment decision

Investments in foreign countries are not within the sphere of interest of the overwhelming majority of businessmen in the United States. The possibility of looking for investment opportunities outside the United States (and Canada) simply does not occur to them. This way of thinking manifests itself in such expressions as: 'There are enough profitable opportunities in the United States. Why bother to go abroad?' When a foreign investment opportunity is brought before management, the burden of proof that such an opportunity should be considered (let alone decided upon) is on the proposer. It is not enough to show that the expected value of profits is high, it must be proved that 'it is worthwhile to go abroad'.

Investment decisions in business are based on the alternatives which are known to exist, or those which have emerged from previous activities of the business unit (such as those that are a result of research and development activities). Except for companies that already have made direct foreign investments, investments abroad are very rarely included in these alternatives.

Our analysis leads us to conclude that the most important question is: 'Who and what event posed the problem initially?' The first foreign investment decision is to a large extent a trip to the unknown. It is an innovation and development of a new dimension, and a major breakthrough in the normal course of events. There should be some strong force, some drastic experience that will trigger and push the organization into this new path. This trigger compels the organization to shift the focus of its attention and to look at investment possibilities abroad. It creates a situation that leads the decision-maker to feel that an investment abroad may help him solve some urgent problem or carry on some activity that he has committed himself to maintain, or simply that such an investment may fulfill some important needs. The types of initiating forces are listed below.

Generally, the decision to look abroad is actually a specific one. It is a decision to look at the possibilities of a specific investment in a specific country, not a general resolution to look around the globe for investment opportunities. The most crucial decision is taken when the first venture abroad is considered. At this stage, the organization has had no experience in the complicated field of foreign investment, although it often has had export experience. No standard operating procedure exists to give some guidelines in dealing with the problem. No-one in the organization is explicitly responsible for dealing with this type of problem. In all these cases, quite a strong push is needed for making the decision to look abroad. When subsequent foreign investment decision processes are carried through, the company will benefit from its experience in previous investigations.

The initiating forces

The forces leading an organization to consider the possibility of launching a project outside the United States might be classified into those arising within the organization and those exogenous to it, stemming from its environment. In the first category are forces arising from a strong interest by one or several high-ranking executives inside the organization. In the second, we include the following:

1   An outside proposal, provided it comes from a source that cannot be easily ignored. The most frequent sources of such proposals are foreign governments, the distributors of the company's products, and its clients.
2   Fear of losing a market.
3   The 'band wagon' effect: very successful activities abroad of a competing firm in the same line of business, or a general belief that investment in some area is 'a must'.
4   Strong competition from abroad in the home market.

In any specific case it is generally very difficult, if not impossible, to pin down one reason for a decision to look abroad, or to find out precisely who was the initiator of a project. The decision results from a chain of events, incomplete information, activities of different persons (not necessarily in connection with the particular project) and a combination of several motivating forces, some of them working in favor of such a decision, some against it. The existence or the emergence of any one of these initiating forces might be looked upon as a necessary but not sufficient condition for the decision to look abroad. There is no simple functional relationship between any one force and such a decision; a company may lose a market and still not decide to look abroad. The impact of any one of these forces depends on the social system it encounters. It depends on various feelings and social and organizational structures, on previous events in the company's history, and on other problem areas facing the company at the time this force is encountered. In general, the decision to look abroad is brought about by the interaction of several forces – partly environmental and partly inside the organization – influencing different persons at different times. Generally, a decision to look abroad means only that an investigation will be made of some possibility abroad; it does not mean that an investment will follow. This decision means only that the investment will be considered on its own merits and will not be rejected *a priori* simply because it is an investment *abroad*. It also means that money, and what is usually even more important, management time, energy and attention will be spent on investigation and data gathering. The next logical step is, therefore, *investigation*. The process of investigation is generally geared to a purpose. Individual investment opportunities are considered on their own merits, rather than as choices among many alternatives. The sequence of the investigation, the variables assumed as fixed, the nature of the data collected and their evaluation, depend to a large extent on the impact of the initiating force. In some cases, the force may have been so strong as to lead to an immediate decision to invest. In these cases the purpose of the investigation is to find a sufficiently good way to implement and execute this earliest decision. In other situations, there will be only a tentative decision to check possibilities. In some instances, much of the relevant data will be presented by the outsider who suggested the investment in the first place. If this is the case, information is collected to evaluate both the data presented and the person presenting them.

The investigation is generally carried out in stages and with various 'check points' built into the process. Depending on the strength of the force which initiated it, the investigation might be stopped at any time when one of these early benchmarks is perceived as unsatisfactory from the organization's point of view, or it might be carried on to find ways to circumvent this unsatisfactory sign. If this second alternative is followed, many conditions that were considered 'given' (such as production methods and techniques, size of the plant, or majority of control) or as *sine qua non* for the investment (such as monopoly in the market) might be changed.

The order of the investigation has therefore a crucial importance. Our field research shows that the first check point will be the 'risk involved'. Risks may be considered excessive because of a multitude of reasons, such as fear of war, a strong belief that the attitude of the foreign government is 'unfriendly to business', fear of expropriation, exchange restrictions, lack of adequate basic services or labor problems.

Because of the lack of knowledge of foreign countries in general, and the lack of interest in direct foreign investments in particular, there is a general belief that the risks involved in foreign investments, particularly in the less developed countries, are excessive, that the probability of making mistakes is very high and that such investments would require 'too much' management time. Often, the risks abroad are not specified. When they are enumerated, this is done in general terms and not in terms of their impact on a specific business situation.

If the risks are perceived to be too high and the force triggering the investigation is a weak one, the investigation is stopped. Otherwise, the next step will be taken: some crude idea of the size of the market will be developed. Again, depending on the investigator's perception about the size of the market on the one hand and the evaluation of the strength of the initiating force on the other hand, the investigation may or may not be carried on to check such other variables as cost, availability of labor, and so on.

Because information is not readily available, and because its acquisition is costly, decision-makers are compelled to reach tentative conclusions, to operate on the basis of assumptions, and to be ready to alter their line of action or redefine the problem when more information becomes available. Partly because of past history, partly because of this necessarily roundabout way of looking at a problem, the decision-maker finds themself engulfed by commitments they themself created, albeit unintentionally. Thus involved and getting in deeper and deeper, they seek the best way out. The way commitments are created are now briefly discussed.

The decision to invest

It is natural to assume that after the investigation is completed, a report is written and a decision is reached as to whether an investment should be made. Unfortunately, things are not as simple as that. In general, it is virtually impossible to find out at what point and by whom a decision to invest was made. Even in those cases in which such a point can be defined, the decision to invest is not necessarily the last in a chain of decisions, nor is it always the outcome of the investigation process. Sometimes, as we have seen, the decision is made before the investigation begins and the investigation is carried out with the specific aim of finding an optimal way of implementing it. Quite often, the investigation reveals additional facts, the original decision is changed or problems are redefined. The investigation usually takes a long time and conditions may change both inside the company and in its environment, although not necessarily in direct connection with the specific project considered. These changes influence the decision process.

Creation of commitments during the investigation

The very fact that an organization is making an investigation creates new commitments. Some of these emerge because money and time are spent; executives apparently find it hard to look at this investment of scarce resources as a sunk cost. They resist the idea of abandoning the project. They feel an urge to persist, to find ways to overcome difficulties and 'to make a go of it'.

One executive, when asked to estimate the cost of investigation, a foreign investment, added the following revealing comment:

> When the negotiations become complicated, you get in deeper and deeper. You want to protect your initial investment, so you continue. . . . By that time you are stuck and have to go on. You have spent $25,000 and you do not want to lose it, so you invest another $10,000 to continue the negotiations, and then you are in even deeper.

In another case, a concern investigating an investment possibility found it would have to face a welter of problems if it wanted to invest: detailed examination revealed the existence of strong competition, and the foreign government did not agree to any one of the original proposals suggested. The respondent telling the history of the project was frustrated and exasperated. Still, it was crucially important to him to find some way to complete a deal. According to him: 'We had spent a lot of time on this thing and also money from our own pockets, and, having committed so much time and money, we decided to be stubborn.'

Commitments are created not only by financial investments. They may also emerge because of a psychic or social investment. The fact that a certain group of people – inside or outside the investigating organization – knows that an investigation is being carried on may also cause a feeling of commitment. It may be felt that once an investigation has begun, a decision to reject the investment proposal may create some psychologically or socially undesirable effects. The investigator may feel this will be interpreted as a failure; he may think this will hamper his relations with these people or his social standing among them, or will destroy further deals. The following examples may help to elucidate this point.

Consider first the case of the executive who felt his company should invest in Japan and finally got permission to investigate this possibility. It was only natural that he felt committed to negotiate conditions that would make investment in Japan acceptable to his organization.

An American Jewish businessman was approached by a friend and was asked to join in an investment in Israel. The businessman felt that he could not turn his friend down and began to investigate the details of the project. In the meantime, the friend decided not to go along with the project. The Jewish businessman, however, had made it known in his community that he was considering an investment in Israel. He was frequently asked by his Jewish friends about it. According to him, he simply felt he could not tell them that he had decided to pull out after his friend left. Therefore, he decided to persevere.

In other cases, commitments emerged from negotiations with prospective partners or with financial institutions. When a decision is made by an organization, additional entangling situations are created by prior commitments of the organization as a whole and interrelationships among its various members. Each one of the organization's members has to take into account feelings, actions, powers, values and commitments of orders that are not necessarily related to the specific opportunity considered. Modifications have to be made not only to satisfy individual commitments, but also to assuage various members of the organization and to take a host of environmental factors into account. Somebody in the organization decides to invest, usually on the basis of the most cursory information. He tries to influence others by writing reports on or arguing orally the points that rationalize and support his conclusions. Depending upon relationships in the organization, others may or may not agree, often posing several more restraints as conditions for their agreement. Then, an effort is made to incorporate these new requests and point of view into the program. Often, the conclusion is a tentative one: it is agreed to open negotiations with a foreign government, prospective partners, financial institutions – or executives in the company itself – to hammer out a modified version of a project that, again, will help the organization keep as many commitments as possible. The negotiations may create new commitments and new problems, and a new round of bargaining inside and outside the organization.

When a decision is sought concerning a second foreign investment, the experience gained in the first decision process comes to bear. Gradually, the organization gains experience in foreign operations, and some persons in the organization are assigned roles in a newly created international division. The very creation of a particular division in an organization devoting all its time and energy to international operations creates forces that will drive the organization toward increasing involvement and expansion of this field. An analysis of a decision cannot be separated from the history of the organization, from the personalities and roles of the various participants, or from the continuing stream of activities. It is a stream of events in many dimensions and therefore should be analyzed in terms of a total system that includes the self systems of various persons, the impact of the environment and the characteristics of the organizational system.

Summary

In summary, a foreign investment decision process is a very complicated social process, involving an intricate structure of attitudes and opinions, social relationships both in and outside the firm, and the way such attitudes, opinions and social relations are changing. It contains various elements of individual and organizational behavior, influenced by the past and the perception of the future as well as by the present. It is composed of a large number of decisions, made by different people at different points in time. The understanding of the final outcome of such a process depends on an understanding of all its stages and parts. The breakdown of this process into neat stages is done just for the convenience of presentation. The reader should keep in mind that in real-life situations these stages are not well defined. They may be blended one into the other; several investigations could be made at the same time by different people, or the same person may continue other activities and thus find himself unable to devote as much time as he would like to this specific investigation; there may be discontinuities in the process, etc. Only if we fully grasp the meaning of all the elements involved and discard any stereotyped notion of a simplified model of decision making can we proceed to observe how actual investment decisions in a busy organization emerge. Only if all the factors in the system are kept in mind can we hope to find some order and logic in what might seem at first glance to be totally chaotic, and thus labeled as hopelessly 'irrational'. It should be reiterated that human beings are not a mathematical programming machines. They have limited faculties and limited ability to focus their attention. A multiplicity of reasonable alternatives always exists. Their priorities in dividing their time and attention among them depend on many factors. The first question that should be posed is therefore: What factors make an organization veer off its 'normal' path and look abroad?

Reference

Cyert, R.M. and March, J.G. 1963. *A behavioral theory of the firm*. Englewood Cliffs, NJ: Prentice-Hall.

3 International investment and international trade in the product cycle*

Raymond Vernon

Anyone who has sought to understand the shifts in international trade and international invest-ment over the past twenty years has chafed from time to time under an acute sense of the inad-equacy of the available analytical tools. While the comparative cost concept and other basic concepts have rarely failed to provide some help, they have usually carried the analyst only a little way toward adequate understanding. For the most part, it has been necessary to formulate new concepts in order to explore issues such as the strengths and limitations of import substitu-tion in the development process, the implications of common market arrangements for trade and investment, the underlying reasons for the Leontief paradox and other critical issues of the day.

As theorists have searched for some more efficient tools, there has been a flowering in inter-national trade and capital theory. But the proliferation of theory has increased the urgency of the search for unifying concepts. It is doubtful that we shall find many propositions that can match the simplicity, power and universality of application of the theory of comparative advantage and the international equilibrating mechanism; but unless the search for better tools goes on, the usefulness of economic theory for the solution of problems in international trade and capital movements will probably decline.

This chapter deals with one promising line of generalization and synthesis which seems to me to have been somewhat neglected by the mainstream of trade theory. It puts less emphasis upon comparative cost doctrine and more upon the timing of innovation, the effects of scale econo-mies, and the roles of ignorance and uncertainty in influencing trade patterns. It is an approach with respectable sponsorship, deriving bits and pieces of its inspiration from the writings of such persons as Williams, Kindleberger, Hoffmeyer, MacDougall and Burenstam-Linder.[1]

Emphases of this sort seem first to have appeared when economists were searching for an explanation of what looked like a persistent, structural shortage of dollars in the world. When the shortage proved ephemeral in the late 1950s, many of the ideas that the shortage had stim-ulated were tossed overboard as prima facie wrong.[2] Nevertheless, one cannot be exposed to the main currents of international trade for very long without feeling that any theory which neglected the roles of innovation, scale, ignorance and uncertainty would be incomplete.

Location of new products

We begin with the assumption that the enterprises in any one of the advanced countries of the world are not distinguishably different from those in any other advanced country, in terms of

*Raymond Vernon, 'International Investment and International Trade in the Product Cycle', The Quarterly Journal of Economics (1966) 80 (2): pp. 190–207. By permission of Oxford University Press.

their access to scientific knowledge and their capacity to comprehend scientific principles.[3] All of them, we may safely assume, can secure access to the knowledge that exists in the physical, chemical and biological sciences. These sciences at times may be difficult, but they are rarely occult.

It is a mistake to assume, however, that equal access to scientific principles in all the advanced countries means equal probability of the application of these principles in the generation of new products. There is ordinarily a large gap between the knowledge of a scientific principle and the embodiment of the principle in a marketable product. An entrepreneur usually has to intervene to accept the risks involved in testing whether the gap can be bridged.

If all entrepreneurs, wherever located, could be presumed to be equally conscious of and equally responsive to all entrepreneurial opportunities, wherever they arose, the classical view of the dominant role of price in resource allocation might be highly relevant. There is good reason to believe, however, that the entrepreneur's consciousness of and responsiveness to opportunity are a function of ease of communication; further, that ease of communication is a function of geographical proximity.[4] Accordingly, we abandon the powerful simplifying notion that knowledge is a universal free good and introduce it as an independent variable in the decision to trade or to invest.

The fact that the search for knowledge is an inseparable part of the decision-making process and that relative ease of access to knowledge can profoundly affect the outcome are now reasonably well established through empirical research.[5] One implication of that fact is that producers in any market are more likely to be aware of the possibility of introducing new products in that market than producers located elsewhere would be.

The United States market offers certain unique kinds of opportunities to those who are in a position to be aware them. First, it consists of consumers with an average income which is higher (except for a few anomalies like Kuwait) than that in any other national market; twice as high as that of Western Europe, for instance. Wherever there was a chance to offer a new product responsive to wants at high levels of income, this chance would presumably first be apparent to someone in a position to observe the United States market. Second, it is characterized by high unit labour costs and relatively unrationed capital compared with practically all other markets. This is a fact which conditions the demand for both consumer goods and industrial products. In the case of consumers goods, for instance, the high cost of laundresses contributes to the origins of the drip-dry shirt and the home washing machine. In the case of industrial goods, high labour cost leads to the early development and use of the conveyor belt, the fork-lift truck and the automatic control system. It seems to follow that wherever there was a chance successfully to sell a new product responsive to the need to conserve labour, this chance would be apparent first to those in a position to observe the United States market.

Assume, then, that entrepreneurs in the United States are first aware of opportunities to satisfy new wants associated with high income levels or high unit labour costs. Assume further that the evidence of an unfilled need and the hope of some kind of monopoly windfall for the early starter both are sufficiently strong to justify the initial investment that is usually involved in converting an abstract idea into a marketable product. Here we have a reason for expecting a consistently higher rate of expenditure on product development to be undertaken by United States producers than by producers in other countries, at least in lines which promise to substitute capital for labour or which promise to satisfy high-income wants. Therefore, if United States firms spend more than their foreign counterparts on new product development (often misleadingly labelled 'research'), this may be due not to some obscure sociological drive for innovation but to more effective communication between the potential market and the potential supplier of the market. This explanation is consistent with the pioneer appearance in the United States (conflicting claims of the Soviet Union notwithstanding) of the sewing machine, the typewriter, the tractor, etc.

At this point in the exposition, it is important to emphasize that the discussion so far relates only to innovation in certain kinds of products, namely to those associated with high income and those which substitute capital for labour. Our hypothesis says nothing about industrial innovation in general; this is a larger subject than we have tackled here. There are very few countries that have failed to introduce at least a few products; there are some, such as Germany and Japan, which have been responsible for a considerable number of such introductions. For example, Germany's outstanding successes in the development and use of plastics may have been due to a traditional concern with her lack of a raw materials base and a recognition that a market might exist in Germany for synthetic substitutes.[6]

Our hypothesis asserts that United States producers are likely to be the first to spy an opportunity for high-income or labour-saving new products.[7] But it goes on to assert that the first producing facilities for such products will be located in the United States. This is not a self-evident proposition. Under the calculus of least cost, production need not automatically take place at a location close to the market, unless the product can be produced and delivered from that location at lowest cost. Besides, now that most major United States companies control facilities situated in one or more locations outside of the United States, the possibility of considering a non-United States location is even more plausible than it might once have been.

If prospective producers were to make their locational choices on the basis of least-cost considerations, the United States would not always be ruled out. For example, the costs of international transport and United States import duties might be so high as to argue for such a location. My guess is, however, that the early producers of a new product intended for the United States market are attracted to a United States location by forces which are far stronger than relative factor-cost and transport considerations. For the reasoning on this point, one has to take a long detour away from comparative cost analysis into areas which fall under the rubrics of communication and external economies.

By now, a considerable amount of empirical work has been done on the factors affecting the location of industry.[8] Many of these studies try to explain observed locational patterns in conventional cost-minimizing terms, by implicit or explicit reference to labour cost and transportation cost. But some explicitly introduce problems of communication and external economies as powerful locational forces. These factors were given special emphasis in the analyses which were a part of the New York Metropolitan Region Study of the 1950s. At the risk of oversimplifying, I shall try to summarize what these studies suggested.[9]

In the early stages of introduction of a new product, producers were usually confronted with a number of critical, albeit transitory, conditions. For one thing, the product itself may be quite unstandardized for a time; its inputs, its processing, and its final specifications may cover a wide range. Contrast the great variety of automobiles produced and marketed before 1910 with the thoroughly standardized product of the 1930s, or the variegated radio designs of the 1920s with the uniform models of the 1930s. The unstandardized nature of the design at this early stage carries with it a number of locational implications.

First, producers at this stage are particularly concerned with the degree of freedom they have in changing their inputs. Of course, the cost of the inputs is also relevant. But as long as the nature of these inputs cannot be fixed in advance with assurance, the calculation of cost must take into account the general need for flexibility in any locational choice.[10]

Second, the price elasticity of demand for the output of individual firms is comparatively low. This follows from the high degree of production differentiation, or the existence of monopoly in the early stages.[11] One result is that small cost differences count less in the calculations of the entrepreneur than they are likely to count later on.

Third, the need for swift and effective communication on the part of the producer with customers, suppliers, and even competitors is especially high at this stage. This is a corollary of the fact that a considerable amount of uncertainly remains regarding the ultimate dimensions of the market, the efforts of rivals to pre-empt that market, the specifications of the inputs needed for production and the specifications of the products likely to be most successful in the effort.

All of these considerations tend to argue for a location in which communication between the market and the executives directly concerned with the new product is swift and easy, and in which a wide variety of potential types of input that might be needed by the production unit are easily come by. In brief, the producer who sees a market for some new product in the United States may be led to select a United States location for production on the basis of national locational considerations which extend well beyond simple factor cost analysis plus transport considerations.

The maturing product[12]

As the demand for a product expands, a certain degree of standardization usually takes place, which is not to say that efforts at product differentiation come to an end. Such efforts may even intensify, as competitors try to avoid the full brunt of price competition. Moreover, variety may appear as a result of specialization. Radios, for instance, ultimately acquired such specialized forms as clock radios, automobile radios, portable radios, etc. Nevertheless, though the subcategories may multiply and the efforts at product differentiation increase, a growing acceptance of certain general standards seems to be typical.

Once again, the change has locational implications. First, the need for flexibility declines. A commitment to some set of product standards opens up technical possibilities for achieving economies of scale through mass output, and encourages long-term commitments to some given process and some fixed set of facilities. Second, concern about production cost begins to take the place of concern about product characteristics. Even if increased price competition is not yet present, the reduction of the uncertainties surrounding the operation enhances the usefulness of cost projections and increases the attention devoted to cost.

The empirical studies to which I referred earlier suggest that, at this stage in an industry's development, there is likely to be considerable shift in the location of production facilities at least as far as internal United States locations are concerned. The empirical materials on international locational shifts simply have not yet been analysed sufficiently to tell us very much. A little speculation, however, indicates some hypotheses worth testing.

Picture an industry engaged in the manufacture of the high-income or labour-saving products that are the focus of our discussion. Assume that the industry has begun to settle down in the United States to some degree of large-scale production. Although the first mass market may be located in the United States, some demand for the product begins almost at once to appear elsewhere. For example, although heavy fork-lift trucks in general may have a comparatively small market in Spain because of the relative cheapness of unskilled labour in that country, some limited demand for the product will appear there almost as soon as the existence of the product is known.

If the product has a high income elasticity of demand or if it is a satisfactory substitute for high-cost labour, the demand in time will begin to grow quite rapidly in relatively advanced countries such as those of Western Europe. Once the market expands in such an advanced country, entrepreneurs will begin to ask themselves whether the time has come to take the risk of setting up a local producing facility.[13]

How long does it take to reach this stage? An adequate answer must surely be a complex one. Producers located in the United States, weighing the wisdom of setting up a new production facility in the importing country, will feel obliged to balance a number of complex considerations. As long as the marginal production cost plus the transport cost of the goods exported from the United States is lower than the average cost of prospective production in the market of import, United States producers will presumably prefer to avoid an investment. But that calculation depends on the producer's ability to project the cost of production in a market in which factor costs and the appropriate technology differ from those at home.

Now and again, the locational force which determined some particular overseas investment is so simple and so powerful that one has little difficulty in identifying it. Otis Elevator's early proliferation of production facilities abroad was quite patently a function of the high cost of shipping assembled elevator cabins to distant locations and the limited scale advantages involved in manufacturing elevator cabins at a single location.[14] Singer's decision to invest in Scotland as early as 1867 was also based an considerations of a sort sympathetic with our hypothesis.[15] It is not unlikely that the overseas demand for its highly standardized product was already sufficiently large at that time to exhaust the obvious scale advantages of manufacturing in a single location, especially if that location was one of high labour cost.

In an area as complex and 'imperfect' as international trade and investment, however, one ought not to anticipate that any hypothesis will have more than a limited explanatory power. United States airplane manufacturers surely respond to many 'non-economic' locational forces, such as the desire to play safe in problems of military security. Producers in the United States who have a protected patent position overseas presumably take that fact into account in deciding whether or when to produce abroad. Other producers often are motivated by considerations too complex to reconstruct readily, such as the fortuitous timing of a threat of new competition in the country of import, the level of tariff protection anticipated for the future, the political situation in the country of prospective investment and so on.

We arrive, then, at the stage at which United States producers have come around to the establishment of production units in the advanced countries. Now a new group of forces is set in train. In an idealized form, Figure 3.1 suggests what may be anticipated next.

As far as individual United States producers are concerned, the local markets will be filled from local production units set up abroad. Once these facilities are in operation, however, more ambitious possibilities for their use may be suggested. When comparing a United States producing facility and a facility in another advanced country, the obvious production-cost differences between the rival producing areas are usually differences due to scale and labour costs. If the producer is an international firm with producing locations in several countries, its costs of financing capital at the different locations may not be sufficiently different to matter very much. If economies of scale are being fully exploited, the principal differences between any two locations are likely to be labour costs.[16] Accordingly, it may prove wise for the international firm to begin servicing third-country markets from the new location. If labour cost differences are large enough to offset transport costs then exports back to the United States may become a possibility as well.

Any hypothesis based on the assumption that the United States entrepreneur will react rationally when offered the possibility of a lower-cost location abroad is, of course, somewhat suspect. The decision-making sequence that is used in connection with international investments, according to various empirical studies, is not a model of the rational process.[17] But there is one theme that emerges again and again in such studies. Any threat to the established

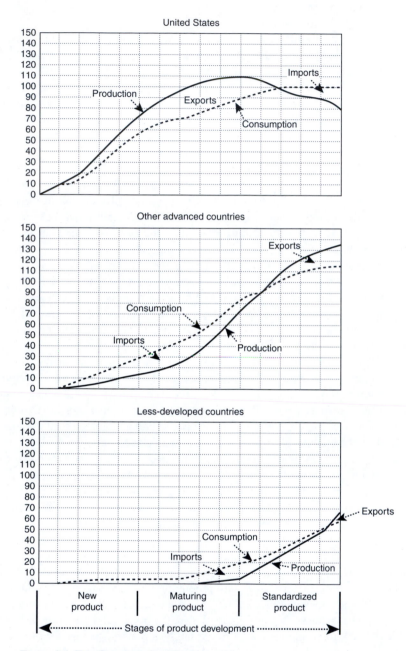

Figure 3.1 Development of production units.

position of an enterprise is a powerful galvanizing force to action; in fact, if I interpret the empirical work correctly, threat in general is a more reliable stimulus to action than opportunity is likely to be.

In the international investment field, threats appear in various forms once a large-scale export business in manufactured products has developed. Local entrepreneurs located in the countries which are the targets of these exports grow restive at the opportunities they are missing. Local governments concerned with generating employment or promoting growth or balancing their trade accounts begin thinking of ways and means to replace the imports. An international investment by the exporter, therefore, becomes a prudent means of forestalling the loss of a market. In this case, the yield on the investment is seen largely as the avoidance of a loss of income to the system.

The notion that a threat to the status quo is a powerful galvanizing force for international investment also seems to explain what happens after the initial investment. Once such an investment is made by a United States producer, other major producers in the United States sometimes see it as a threat to the status quo. They see themselves as losing position relative to the investing company, with vague intimations of further losses to come. Their 'share of the market' is imperilled, viewing 'share of the market' in global terms. At the same time, their ability to estimate the production-cost structure of their competitors, operating far away in an unfamiliar foreign area, is impaired; this is a particularly unsettling state because it conjures up the possibility of a return flow of products to the United States and a new source of price competition, based on cost differences of unknown magnitude. The uncertainly can be reduced by emulating the pathfinding investor and by investing in the same area; this may not be an optimizing investment pattern and it may be costly, but is disturbing to the status quo.

Pieces of this hypothetical pattern are subject to empirical tests of a sort. So far, at any rate, the empirical tests have been reassuring. The office machinery industry, for instance, has seen repeatedly the phenomenon of the introduction of a new product in the United States, followed by United States exports,[18] followed still later by United States imports (we have still to test whether the timing of the commencement of overseas production by United States subsidiaries fits into the expected pattern). In the electrical and electronic products industry, those elements in the pattern which can be measured show up nicely.[19] A broader effort is now under way to test the United States trade patterns of a group of products with high income elasticities; here too, the preliminary results are encouraging.[20] On a much more general basis, it is reassuring for our hypothesis to observe that the foreign manufacturing subsidiaries of the United States have been increasing their exports to third countries.

It will have occurred to the reader by now that the pattern envisaged here also may shed some light on the Leontief paradox.[21] Leontief, it will be recalled, seemed to confound comparative cost theory by establishing the fact that the ratio of capital to labour in United States exports was lower, not higher, than the like ratio in the United States production which had been displaced by competitive imports. The hypothesis suggested in this chapter would have the United States exporting high-income and labour-saving products in the early stages of their existence, and importing them later on.[22] In the early stages, the value-added contribution of industries engaged in producing these items probably contains an unusually high proportion of labour cost, This is not so much because the labour is particularly skilled, as is so often suggested. More likely, it is due to a quite different phenomenon. At this stage, the standardization of the manufacturing process has not got very far; that is to come later, when the volume of output is high enough and the degree of uncertainty low enough to justify investment in relatively inflexible, capital-intensive facilities. As a result, the production process relies relatively heavily on labour inputs at a time when the United States commands an export position; and the process relies more heavily on capital at a time when imports become important.

This, of course, is an hypothesis which has not yet been subjected to any really rigorous test. But it does open up a line of inquiry into the structure of United States trade which is well worth pursuing.

The standardized product

Figure 3.1 carries a panel which suggests that, at an advanced stage in the standardization of some products, the less-developed countries may offer competitive advantages as a production location.

This is a bold projection, which seems on first blush to be wholly at variance with the Heckscher-Ohlin theorem. According to that theorem, one presumably ought to anticipate that the exports of the less-developed countries would tend to be relatively labour-intensive products.

One of the difficulties with the theorem, however, is that it leaves marketing considerations out of account. One reason for the omission is evident. As long as knowledge is regarded as a free good, instantaneously available, and as long as individual producers are regarded as atomistic contributors to the total supply, marketing problems cannot be expected to find much of a place in economic theory. In projecting the patterns of export from less-developed areas, however, we cannot afford to disregard the fact that information comes at a cost; and that entrepreneurs are not readily disposed to pay the price of investigating overseas markets of unknown dimensions and unknown promise. Neither are they eager to venture into situations which they know will demand a constant flow of reliable marketing information from remote sources.

If we can assume that highly standardized products tend to have a well-articulated, easily accessible international market and to sell largely on the basis of price (an assumption inherent in the definition), then it follows that such products will not pose the problem of market information quite so acutely for the less-developed countries. This establishes a necessary if not a sufficient condition for investment in such industries.

Of course, foreign investors seeking an optimum location for a captive facility may not have to concern themselves too much with questions of market information; presumably, they are thoroughly familiar with the marketing end of the business and are looking for a low-cost captive source of supply. In that case, the low cost of labour may be the initial attraction drawing the investor to less-developed areas. But other limitations in such areas, according to our hypothesis, will bias such captive operations toward the production of standardized items. The reasons in this case turn on the part played in the production process by external economies. Manufacturing processes which receive significant inputs from the local economy, such as skilled labour, repairmen, reliable power, spare parts, industrial materials processed according to exacting specification, and so on, are less appropriate to the less-developed areas than those that do not have such requirements. Unhappily, most industrial processes require one or another ingredient of this difficult sort, however, the industries which produce a standardized product are in the best position to avoid the problem, by producing on a vertically-integrated self-sustaining basis.

In speculating about future industrial exports from the less-developed areas, therefore, we are led to think of products with a fairly clear-cut set of economic characteristics.[23] Their production function is such as to require significant inputs of labour; otherwise there is no reason to expect a lower production cost in less-developed countries. At the same time, they are products with a high price elasticity of demand for the output of individual firms; otherwise, there is no strong incentive to take the risks of pioneering with production in a new area. In addition, products whose production process did not rely heavily upon external economies would be more obvious candidates than those which required a more elaborate industrial environment. The implications of remoteness also would be critical; products which could be precisely described by standardized specifications and which could be produced for inventory without fear of obsolescence would be more relevant than those which had less precise specifications and which could not easily be ordered from remote locations. Moreover, high-value items capable of absorbing significant freight costs would be more likely to appear than bulky items low in value by weight. Standardized textile products are, of course, the illustration par excellence of the sort of product that meets the criteria. But other products come to mind such as crude steel, simple fertilizers, newsprint, etc.

Speculation of this sort draws some support from various interregional experiences in industrial location. In the United States, for example, the 'export' industries which moved to the low-wage south in search of lower costs tended to be industries which had no greater need for a sophisticated industrial environment and which produced fairly standardized products. In the textile industry, it was the grey goods, cotton sheetings and men's shirt plants that went south: producers of high-style dresses or other unstandardized items were far more reluctant to move. In the electronics industry, it was the mass producers of tubes, resistors and other standardized high-volume components that showed the greatest disposition to move south: custom-built and research-oriented production remained closer to markets and to the main industrial complexes. A similar pattern could be discerned in printing and in chemicals production.[24]

In other countries, a like pattern is suggested by the impressionistic evidence. The underdeveloped south of Italy and the laggard north of Britain and Ireland both seem to be attracting industry with standardized output and self-sufficient process.[25]

Once we begin to look for relevant evidence of such investment patterns in the less-developed countries proper, however, only the barest shreds of corroboratory information can be found. One would have difficulty in thinking of many cases in which manufacturers of standardized products in the more advanced countries had made significant investments in the less-developed countries with a view of exporting such products from those countries. Other types of foreign investment are not uncommon in the less-developed countries, such as investments in import-replacing industries which were made in the face of a threat of import restriction. But there are only a few export-oriented cases similar to that of Taiwan's foreign-owned electronics plants and Argentina's new producing facility, set up to manufacture and export standard sorting equipment for computers.

If we look to foreign trade patterns, rather than foreign investment patterns, to learn something about the competitive advantage of the less-developed countries, the possibility that they are an attractive locus for the output of standardized products gains slightly more support. The Taiwanese and Japanese trade performances are perhaps the most telling ones in support of the projected pattern; both countries have managed to develop significant overseas markets for standardized manufactured products. According to one major study of the subject (a study stimulated by the Leontief paradox), Japanese exports are more capital-intensive than is the Japanese production which is displaced by imports;[26] this is what one might expect if the hypothetical patterns suggested by Figure 3.1 were operational. Apart from these cases, however, all that one sees are a few provocative successes such as some sporadic sales of newsprint from Pakistan, the successful export of sewing machines from India, etc. Even in these cases, one cannot be sure that they are consistent with the hypothesis unless more empirical investigation has been carried out.

The reason why so few relevant cases come to mind may be that the process has not yet advanced far enough. Or it may be that such factors as extensive export constraints and over-valued exchange rates are combining to prevent the investment and exports that otherwise would occur.

If there is one respect in which this discussion may deviate from classical expectations, it is in the view that the overall scarcity of capital in the less-developed countries will not prevent investment in facilities for the production of standardized products.

There are two reasons why capital costs may not prove a barrier to such investment. First, according to our hypotheses, the investment will occur in industries which require some significant labour inputs in the production process; but they will be concentrated in that subsector of the industry which produces highly standardized products capable of self-contained production establishments. The net of these specifications is indeterminate so far as capital-intensiveness is concerned. A standardized textile item may be more or less capital-intensive than a plant for unstandardized petro-chemicals.

Besides, even if the capital requirements for a particular plant are heavy, the cost of the capital need not prove a bar. The assumption that capital costs come high in the less-developed countries requires a number of fundamental qualifications. The reality, to the extent that it is known, is more complex.

One reason for this complexity is the role played by the international investor. Producers of chemical fertilizers, when considering whether to invest in a given country, may be less concerned with the going rate for capital in that country than with their opportunity costs as they see such costs. For such investors the alternatives to be weighed are not the full range of possibilities calling for capital but only a very restricted range of alternatives, such as the possibilities offered by chemical fertilizer investment elsewhere. The relevant capital cost for a chemical fertilizer plant, therefore, may be fairly low if the investor is an international entrepreneur.

Moreover, the assumption that finance capital is scarce and that interest rates are high in a less-developed country may prove inapplicable to the class of investors who concern us here.[27] The capital markets of the less-developed countries typically consist of a series of water-tight, insulated, submarkets in which wholly different rates prevail and between which arbitrage opportunities are limited. In some countries, the going figures may vary from 5 to 40 per cent, on grounds which seem to have little relation to issuer risk or term of loan (in some economies, where inflation is endemic, interest rates which in effect represent a negative real cost are not uncommon).

These internal differences in interest rates may be due to a number of factors: the fact that funds generated inside the firm usually are exposed to a different yield test than external borrowings; the fact that government loans are often floated by mandatory levies on banks and other intermediaries; and the fact that funds borrowed by governments from international sources are often re-loaned in domestic markets at rates which are linked closely to the international borrowing rate, however irrelevant that may be. Moreover, one has to reckon with the fact that public international lenders tend to lend at near-uniform rates, irrespective of the identity of the borrower and the going interest rate in his country. Access to capital on the part of underdeveloped countries, therefore, becomes a direct function of the country's capacity to propose plausible projects to international lenders. If a project can plausibly be shown to 'pay its own way' in balance-of-payment and output terms at 'reasonable' interest rates, the largest single obstacle to obtaining capital at such rates has usually been overcome.

Accordingly, one may say that from the entrepreneur's viewpoints certain systematic and predictable 'imperfections' of the capital markets may reduce or eliminate the capital-shortage handicap which is characteristic of the less-developed countries; and, further, that as a result of the reduction or elimination such countries may find themselves in a position to compete effectively in the export of certain standardized capital-intensive goods. This is not the statement of another paradox; it is not the same as to say that the capital-poor countries will develop capital-intensive economies. All we are concerned with here is a modest fraction of the industry of such countries, which in turn is a minor fraction of their total economic activity. It may be that the anomalies such industries represent are systematic enough to be included in our normal expectations regarding conditions in the less-developed countries.

Like the other observations which have preceded, these views about the likely patterns of exports by the less-developed countries are attempts to relax some of the constraints imposed by purer and simpler models. Here and there, the hypotheses take on plausibility because they jibe with the record of past events. But, for the most part, they are still speculative in nature, having been subjected to tests of a very low order of rigorousness. What is needed, obviously, is continued probing to determine whether the 'imperfections' stressed so strongly in these pages deserve to be elevated out of the footnotes into the main text of economic theory.

Notes

The preparation of this article was financed in part by a grant from the Ford Foundation to the Harvard Business School to support a study of the implications of United States foreign direct investment. This paper is a by-product of the hypothesis-building stage of the study.

1 J. H. Williams, 'The Theory of International Trade Reconsidered', reprinted as Chap. 2 in his *Postwar Monetary Plans and Other Essays'* (Oxford: Basil Blackwell, 1947); C. P. Kindleberger. *The Dollar Shortage* (New York: Wiley, 1950); Erik Hoffmeyer, *Dollar Shortage* (Amsterdam: North-Holland, 1958); Sir Donald MacDougall, *The World Dollar Problem* (London: Macmillan, 1957); Staffan Burenstam-Linder, *An Essay on Trade and Transformation* (Uppsala: Almqvist & Wicksell, 1961).

2 The best summary of the state of trade theory that has come to my attention truncated in recent years is J. Bhagwati, 'The Pure Theory of International Trade', *Economic Journal*, LXXIV (Mar. 1964), 1–84. Bhagwati refers obliquely to some of the theories which concern us here; but they receive much less attention than I think they deserve.

3 Some of the account that follows will be found in greatly truncated form in my 'The Trade Expansion Act in Perspective', in *Emerging Concepts in Marketing*. Proceedings of the American Marketing Association, December 1962. pp. 384–9. The elaboration here owes a good deal to the perceptive work of Se've Hirsch, summarized in his unpublished doctoral thesis, Location of Industry and International Competitiveness, Harvard Bussiness School, 1965.

4 Note C. P. Kindleberger's reference to the 'horizon' of the decision-maker, and the view that he can only be rational within that horizon; see his *Foreign Trade and the National Economy* (New Haven: Yale University Press, 1962), p. 15 *passim*.

5 See, for instance, Richard M. Cyert and James G. March, *A Behavioral Theory off the Firm* (Englewood Cliffs, N.J.: Prentice-Hall, 1963), esp. Chap. 6; and Yair Aharoni, *The Foreign Investment Decision Process*, to be published by the Division of Research of the Harvard Business School, 1966.

6 See two excellent studies: C. Freeman, 'The Plastics Industry: A Comparative Study of Research and Innovation', in *National Institute Economic Review*, No. 26 (Nov. 1963), p. 22 *et seq.*: G. C. Hufbauer, *Synthetic Material and the Theory of International Trade* (London: Gerald Duckworth, 1965). A number of links in the Hufbauer arguments are remarkably similar to some in this paper; but he was not aware of my writings nor I of his until after both had been completed.

7 There is a kind of first-cousin relationship between this simple notion and the 'entrained want' concept defined by H. G. Barnett in *Innovation: The Basis of Culture Change* (New York McGraw-Hill, 1953), p. 148. Albert O. Hirschman, *The Strategy of Economic Development* (New Haven: Yale University Press, 1958), p. 68, also finds the concept helpful in his effort to explain certain aspects of economic development.

8 For a summary of such work, together with a useful bibliography, see John Meyer, 'Regional Economics: A Survey', in the *American Economic Review*, LIII (Mar. 1963), pp. 19–54.

9 The points that follow are dealt with at length in the following publications: Raymond Vernon, *Metropolis, 1985* (Cambridge: Harvard University Press, 1960), pp. 38–85: Max Hell (ed.), *Made in New York* (Cambridge: Harvard University Press, 1959), pp. 3–8, 19 *passim*: Robert M. Lichtenberg, *One-Tenth of a Nation* (Cambridge: Harvard University Press, 1960), pp. 31–70.

10 This is, of course, a familiar point elaborated in George F. Stigler, 'Production and Distribution in the Short Run', *Journal of Political Economy*, XLVII (June 1939), 305, *et seq.*

11 Hufbauer, *op. cit.*, suggests that the low price elasticity of demand in the first stage may be due simply to the fact that the first market may be a 'captive market' unresponsive to price changes; but that later, in order to expand the use of the new product, other markets may be brought in which are more price responsive.

12 Both Hirsch, *op. cit.*, and Freeman, *op. cit.*, make use of a three-stage product classification of the sort used here.

13 M. V. Posner, 'International Trade and Technical Change', *Oxford Economic Paper*, Vol. 13 (Oct. 1961), p. 323, *et seq.*, presents a stimulating model purporting to explain such familiar trade phenomena as the exchange of machine tools between the United Kingdom and Germany. In the process he offers some particularly helpful notions concerning the size of the 'imitation lag' in the responses of competing nations.

14 Dudley M. Phelps, *Migration of Industry in South America* (New York: McGraw-Hill, 1963), p. 4.

15 John H. Dunning, *American Investment in British Manufacturing Industry* (London: George Allen & Unwin, 1958), p. 18. The Dunning book is filled with observations that lend casual support to the main hypotheses of this paper.

16 Note the interesting finding of Mordecai Kreinin in his 'The Leontief Scarce-Factor Paradox', *The American Economic Review*, LV (Mar. 1965), 131–9. Kreinin finds that the higher cost of labour in the United States is not explained by a higher rate of labour productivity in this country.

17 Aharoni, *op. cit.*, provides an excellent summary and exhaustive bibliography of the evidence on this point.

18 Reported in U.S. Senate, Interstate and Foreign Commerce Committee, *Hearings on Foreign Commerce*, 1960, pp. 130–9.

19 See Hirsch, *op. cit.*

20 These are to appear in a forthcoming doctoral thesis at the Harvard Business School by Louis T. Wells, tentatively entitled 'International Trade and Business Policy'.

21 See Wassily Leontief, 'Domestic Production and Foreign Trade: The American Capital Position Reexamined', *Proceedings of the American Philosophical Society*: Vol. 97 (Sept. 1953), and 'Factor Proportions and the Structure of American Trade: Further Theoretical and Empirical Analysis', *Review of Economic and Statistics*, XXXVIII (Nov. 1956).

22 Of course, if there were some systematic trend in the inputs of new products – for example, if the new products which appeared in the 1960s were more capital-intensive than the new products which appeared in the 1950s – then the tendencies suggested by our hypotheses might be swamped by such a trend. As long as we do not posit offsetting systematic patterns of this sort, however, the Leontief findings and the hypotheses offered here seem consistent.

23 The concepts sketched out here are presented in more detail in my 'Problems and Prospects in the Export of Manufactured Products from the Less-developed Countries', UX Conference on Trade and Development. Dec. 16, 1963 (mimeo).

24 This conclusion derives largely from the industry studies conducted in connection with the New York Metropolitan Region study. There have been some excellent more general analyses of shifts in industrial location among the regions of the United States. See, e.g., Victor R. Fuchs, *Changes in the Location of Manufacturing in the United States Since 1929* (New Haven: Yale University Press, 1962). Unfortunately, however, none has been designed, so far as I know, to test hypotheses relating locational shifts to product characteristics such as price elasticity of demand and degree of standardization.

25 This statement, too, is based on only impressionistic materials. Among the more suggestive, illustrative of the best of the available evidence, see, J. N. Toothill, *Inquiry into the Scottish Economy* (Edinburgh: Scottish Council, 1962).

26 M. Tatemoto and S. Ichimura. 'Factor Proportions and Foreign Trade: the Case of Japan', *Review of Economics and Statistics*, XLI (Nov. 1959), 442–6.

27 See George Rosen, *Industrial Change in India* (Glencoe, IL: Free Press, 1958), Rosen finds that in the period studied from 1937 to 1953, 'there was no serious shortage of capital for the largest firms in India'. Gustav F. Papanek makes a similar finding for Pakistan for the period from 1950 to 1964 in a book about to be published.

4 The Uppsala internationalization process model revisited

From liability of foreignness to liability of outsidership*

Jan Johanson and Jan-Erik Vahlne

Introduction

Much has changed since our model of the internationalization process of the firm was published in the *Journal of International Business Studies* (*JIBS*) (Johanson & Vahlne, 1977). In fact, the economic and regulatory environments have changed dramatically. Company behavior is also different in some respects. The research frontier has moved too. There are some concepts and insights that did not exist when our model was published.

The Uppsala model explains the characteristics of the internationalization process of the firm. When we constructed the model there was only a rudimentary understanding of market complexities that might explain internationalization difficulties, but subsequent research on international marketing and purchasing in business markets provide us with a business network view of the environment faced by an internationalizing firm. We further develop this view and explore its implications for the internationalization process of the firm. Our core argument is based on business network research, and has two sides. First is that markets are networks of relationships in which firms are linked to each other in various, complex and, to a considerable extent, invisible patterns. Hence *insidership* in relevant network(s) is necessary for successful internationalization, so by the same token there is a *liability of outsidership*. Second, relationships offer potential for learning and for building trust and commitment, both of which are preconditions for internationalization. Before we look at this business network view in depth, we summarize our original model.

The 1977 model

In the mid-1970s, researchers in the Department of Business Studies at Uppsala University made empirical observations that contradicted the established economics and normative, international business literature of the time. According to that literature, firms choose, or should choose, the optimal mode for entering a market by analyzing their costs and risks based on market characteristics and taking into consideration their own resources (for example Hood & Young, 1979). However, our empirical observations from a database of Swedish-owned subsidiaries abroad, and from a number of industry studies of Swedish companies in international markets, indicated that Swedish companies frequently began internationalizing with *ad hoc* exporting (Carlson, 1975; Forsgren & Kinch, 1970; Hörnell et al., 1973;

Johanson, 1966; Nellbeck, 1967). They would subsequently formalize their entries through deals with intermediaries, often agents who represented the focal companies in the foreign market. Usually, as sales grew, they replaced their agents with their own sales organization, and as growth continued they began manufacturing in the foreign market to overcome the trade barriers that were still in place in the post-World War II era. We labeled this dimension of the internationalization pattern the *establishment chain*. Another feature of the pattern was that internationalization frequently started in foreign markets that were close to the domestic market in terms of *psychic distance*, defined as factors that make it difficult to understand foreign environments. The companies would then gradually enter other markets that were further away in psychic distance terms (Johanson & Wiedersheim-Paul, 1975; Vahlne & Wiedersheim-Paul, 1973). This process had its origin in the *liability of foreignness*, a concept that originally explained why a foreign investor needed to have a firm-specific advantage to more than offset this liability (Hymer, 1976; Zaheer, 1995). The larger the psychic distance, the larger the liability of foreignness.

We searched primarily in the theory of the firm for explanations of the deviations between what the extant theories prescribed and the Swedish pattern of internationalization, and developed our original model based on the work of Penrose (1966), Cyert and March (1963), and Aharoni (1966). The underlying assumptions of our 1977 model are uncertainty and bounded rationality. It also has two change mechanisms. First, firms change by learning from their experience of operations and current activities in foreign markets. Second, they change through the commitment decisions that they make to strengthen their position in the foreign market. We define commitment as the product of the size of the investment times its degree of inflexibility. While a large investment in saleable equipment does not necessarily indicate a strong commitment, unwavering dedication to meeting the needs of customers does. Experience builds a firm's knowledge of a market, and that body of knowledge influences decisions about the level of commitment and the activities that subsequently grow out of them: this leads to the next level of commitment, which engenders more learning still (Figure 4.1). Hence the model is dynamic.

The model does not specify the form that increased commitment might take. Indeed, commitment may decline, or even cease, if performance and prospects are not sufficiently promising. Contrary to the views expressed by some, the process is by no means deterministic. We assumed that the process of internationalizing will continue as long as the performance and prospects are favorable.

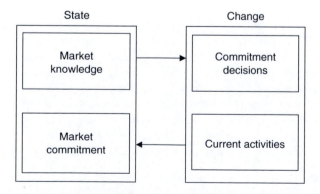

Figure 4.1 The basic mechanism of internationalization: state and change aspects (Johanson & Vahlne, 1977: 26).

We also assumed that learning and commitment-building take time. This explains why moves into more risky, but potentially rewarding, modes and moves into markets that are more distant in terms of psychic distance are made incrementally.

We considered the model to be descriptive, largely because we based it on Cyert and March (1963). It has generally been characterized in the subsequent literature as behavioral, compared with other theories that are seen as economic, such as internalization theory (Buckley & Casson, 1976), transaction cost theory (Hennart, 1982), and the eclectic paradigm (Dunning, 1980). More recent empirical studies have indicated that the internationalization process as explained by our model has a positive impact on performance (Barkema et al., 1996; Delios & Beamish, 2001; Li, 1995; Luo & Peng, 1999). Our model can therefore be considered a model of rational internationalization, and can be used for prescriptive purposes.

The firm in the market environment: a business network view

A number of studies have demonstrated the role of networks in the internationalization of firms. Coviello and Munro (1995, 1997) conducted empirical studies of the internationalization of small software firms. They found that network relationships have an impact on foreign market selection as well as on the mode of entry in the context of ongoing network processes. Their findings led them to develop a model that combines the process model and the network approach. In a study of the international expansion of Japanese suppliers of automotive components, Martin et al. (1998) found that the inter-organizational relationships of suppliers, especially those with buyers, affected their pattern of international expansion. Other researchers have looked at networks in studies of internationalization strategy (Welch & Welch, 1996), the location of foreign direct investment (Chen & Chen, 1998), the first step abroad (Ellis, 2000), SME internationalization (Chetty & Blankenburg Holm, 2000), internationalization of firms from emerging markets (Elango & Pattnaik, 2007), and rapid internationalization (Loane & Bell, 2006), to name but a few.

We conclude that our original model needs to be developed further in light of such clear evidence of the importance of networks in the internationalization of firms. The research that has been done to date generally has studied the ways in which networks influence internationalization, without discussing how those networks have been created, and without considering the network structure in the country or countries firms entered. Based on case analyses, Coviello (2006) developed a model of "how [international new venture] networks evolve" during the early phase of internationalization. Our aim differs from that of Coviello in that we focus on business networks as a market structure in which the internationalizing firm is embedded and on the corresponding business network structure of the foreign market. While our goal is to develop a more general business network model of firm internationalization, Coviello's (2006) work is of great interest, as she shows that "insidership" in networks, developed before entry into a new market, even before the foundation of the firm, is instrumental to the specific internationalization process at hand.

The studies on which the 1977 model was based indicated that the received theories of markets and marketing were not useful in trying to understand the market situation of individual firms. An international business-to-business marketing research program started in Uppsala in the mid-1970s in order to develop a better understanding of business markets and marketing. Early observations that firms develop lasting relationships with important customers were an important input into this research program (Forsgren & Kinch, 1970; Johanson, 1966). An interaction approach that focused on the adaptation and exchange between suppliers and customers was used as a theoretical framework for studies of business relationships (Håkansson & Östberg, 1975).

A large-scale empirical study of international marketing and purchasing of industrial products (the IMP project) that was carried out in the late 1970s and early 1980s by researchers from Sweden and four other European countries was based on the interaction approach (Ford, 1997; Håkansson, 1982; Turnbull & Valla, 1986). Work done during the project demonstrated that close and lasting business relationships between suppliers and customers are indeed important, be they within a given country or between countries (Hallén, 1986). A number of studies since then have shown the importance of relationships in the internationalization process, client-following strategies, for example (Bonaccorsi, 1992; Erramilli & Rao, 1990; Majkgård & Sharma, 1998; Sharma & Johanson, 1987). IMP project studies also showed that such relationships usually involve a number of managers who coordinate the activities of the different firms, and who together create interrelated routines (Cunningham & Homse, 1986). Moreover, these relationships seem to develop through social exchange processes in which the firms involved enact the relationship interactively and sequentially (Kelley & Thibaut, 1978). The result is the accumulation of knowledge and building of trust, and eventually greater commitment, as also demonstrated in channel and relationship marketing studies (Anderson & Weitz, 1992; Dwyer et al., 1987; Morgan & Hunt, 1994). In the process, weak ties and unilateral dependence can be transformed into strong relationships and bilateral interdependence, and ultimately increased joint productivity (Hallén et al., 1991; Zajac & Olsen, 1993). As with the internationalization process model, the research done in the IMP project shows that relationships develop through a process of experiential learning, whereby firms learn about the resources and capabilities of their counterparts, and gradually increase their commitments (Hägg & Johanson, 1982). There is one important difference between our model and the findings of the IMP project: relationship development is a bilateral process that involves two parties who learn interactively and make a mutual commitment to the relationship (Anderson & Weitz, 1992; Blankenburg Holm et al., 1999). When we constructed our original model we were not aware of the importance of mutual commitment for internationalization. Now our view is that successful internationalization requires a reciprocal commitment between the firm and its counterparts (Johanson & Vahlne, 1990; Vahlne & Johanson, 2002).

It takes time – some data indicate as long as five years – and managerial effort to create working relationships, many attempts fail (Hohenthal, 2001). A working relationship is the result of considerable investment and is an important firm resource (Dyer & Singh, 1998). While there may be some formal aspects, developing relationships is essentially an informal process (Powell, 1990). Intentions, expectations, and interpretations are important. Relationships are basically socially constructed. The informal and subtle nature of relationships makes it almost impossible for anyone who is not personally involved to judge the scope of the investment that has gone into building it, or its value. The larger the psychic distance, other things being equal, the more difficult it is to build new relationships. This is the effect of the liability of foreignness. Two firms that are parties to a relationship are tied to each other to some extent: they share in their mutual future development, and may exercise some degree of power over one another (Granovetter, 1985). Thus, in practice, they are not fully autonomous: they are linked by a non-trivial level of mutual control.

Research has now also shown that firms are frequently involved in a set of different, close and lasting relationships with important suppliers and customers (Cowley, 1988; Håkansson, 1989). As those firms presumably in turn are engaged in a number of additional business relationships, firms operate in networks of connected business relationships (Anderson et al.,

1994; Cook & Emerson, 1978; Hägg & Johanson, 1982). The term *connected* means that exchange in one relationship is linked to exchange in another. These webs of connected relationships are labeled *business networks*.

The firm may create new knowledge through exchanges in its network of interconnected relationships. Knowledge creation is an outcome of the confrontation between producer knowledge and user knowledge. The process of creating knowledge is not separate from the other activities in business relationships; rather it is embedded in them. Knowledge does not accrue only from the firm's own activities, but also from the activities of its partners, and since those partners also have other relationship partners with whom their activities are coordinated, the focal firm is indirectly engaged in a knowledge creation process that extends far beyond its own horizon. Thus a network of business relationships provides a firm with an extended knowledge base (Hägg & Johanson, 1982; Kogut, 2000).

Penrose (1966) and the resource-based view (RBV) (Barney, 1986) assume that resources are heterogeneous and that these idiosyncratic resource bundles lead to value creation, irrespective of market conditions. The business network view starts with these same assumptions, and adds that exchange within a network allows a firm to acquire knowledge of its relationship partners, including their resources, needs, capabilities, strategies, and other relationships. Relationship partners are therefore indirectly a source of relevant business information about their own partners and more distant actors in the network. Thus the firm commands privileged knowledge of its business network.

Based on the above, we view the firm as a business entity engaged primarily in exchange activities (Snehota, 1990); exchange, rather than production, being the distinctive feature of the firm (cf. Alchian & Allen, 1964). Indeed, the value of production is derived from exchange. While traditional economic theory defines a firm without reference to other firms, we define a firm on the basis of its exchange with specific other actors (Forsgren et al., 2005).

Johanson and Mattsson (1988) developed a network model of internationalization based on business network research. They discussed the internationalization of firms in the context of both the firm's own business network and the relevant network structure in foreign markets. In contrast to many other network studies, their model highlights the importance of the network structure outside the firm's own business network. It stresses the importance of specific business relationships in a firm's internationalization, though it lacks dynamic elements. That model provided conceptual input for our work on the mechanism of internationalization, in which we view internationalization as a multilateral network development process (Johanson & Vahlne, 1990).

A firm's success requires that it be well established in one or more networks. Anything that happens, happens within the context of a relationship, and a firm that is well established in a relevant network or networks is an "insider." As shown, it is previously through relationships that firms learn, and build trust and commitment; the essential elements of the internationalization process. We argue that insidership is a necessary but insufficient condition for successful business development.

A firm that does not have a position in a relevant network is an "outsider." If a firm attempts to enter a foreign market where it has no relevant network position, it will suffer from the *liability of outsidership* and foreignness, and foreignness presumably complicates the process of becoming an insider. Outsidership makes it impossible to develop a business, yet somehow the internationalization process begins. It might happen that a potential partner inside the target market requests a service from the focal firm, thus creating an initial insider opportunity. The learning process, and trust- and commitment-building, may then begin. It could also happen that another firm in the focal firm's home country would need to have products delivered to its own customer's new facility in a foreign market, so might ask the focal firm to do that. In that case the focal firm's existing insidership in a relevant network may help it enter a foreign market. Evidently, the process may start through efforts by the focal firm.

In our view a firm's environment is made up of networks, this has implications for the ways in which we think about learning, building trust and developing commitment, as well as about identifying and exploiting opportunities. Such activities must be understood within the context of business networks where the liability of outsidership is an impediment. In the following three sections we discuss these activities, which in simultaneity may result in business development and internationalization.

Knowledge and learning

Our original model is based on the assumption that developing knowledge is fundamental to a firm's internationalization, and in particular that knowledge that grows out of experience in current activities (operations) is crucial to the learning process. We also assumed that learning by experience results in a gradually more differentiated view of foreign markets, and of the firm's own capabilities. It is such learning that makes developing foreign operations possible. In recent decades there has been a growing interest in organizational learning in general, as well as in the context of internationalization. In this section we examine some implications of the research that has grown out of this interest for the business network view of the internationalization process.

Two reviews of our original model have been written that discuss its concepts of knowledge and learning (Forsgren, 2002; Petersen et al., 2003). Petersen et al. discuss some of the critical assumptions of our model, one of which is that market-specific knowledge is the critical kind of knowledge. A number of studies have supported this conclusion (Barkema et al., 1996; Erramilli, 1991; Luo & Peng, 1999).

In a study based on the network view, Axelsson and Johanson (1992) examined how three firms entered foreign markets. They showed that foreign market entry should not be studied as a decision about modes of entry, but should instead be studied as a position-building process in a foreign market network. Their cases revealed the complexities associated with learning when a firm enters a foreign market network. For example, firms have to identify the relevant market actors in order to determine how they are connected in often invisible complex patterns. These patterns can be identified only by the actions of the entering firm, which causes other market actors to reveal their ties to each other. The liability of outsidership must be overcome. The Axelsson and Johanson study highlights the market-specific learning process that we assumed in developing our 1977 model, and provides some input into the business network analysis of internationalization.

In their study of experiential learning in the internationalization process, Eriksson et al. (1997) found that lack of institutional market knowledge and lack of business knowledge require different amounts of time to overcome, and have dissimilar effects on the perceived cost of internationalization. A lack of institutional market knowledge, that is, lack of knowledge of language, laws and rules, has to do with factors related to psychic distance and to the liability of foreignness. Lack of business market knowledge is related to a firm's business environment that, according to the business network view, consists of the firms with which it is doing business, or trying to do business, and the relationships between firms in this environment. The lack of such market-specific business knowledge constitutes the liability of outsidership.

In developing our original model we stressed that there is general market knowledge that may be transferred between organizational units. More recent research has shown that more general internationalization knowledge, that is, knowledge that reflects a firm's resources and its capabilities for engaging in international business, is also important (Eriksson et al., 1997; Welch & Luostarinen, 1988). Furthermore, several studies have shown that a number of different aspects of general internationalization knowledge may be important as well. We believe now that the general internationalization knowledge that encompasses several kinds of experience, including foreign market entry (Sapienza et al., 2006), mode-specific (Padmanabhan & Cho, 1999), core business (Chang, 1995), alliance (Hoang & Rothaermel, 2005), acquisition (Nadolska & Barkema, 2007) and other specific kinds of internationalization experience, is probably more important than we had assumed back in 1977. It is worth noting that knowledge of internationalization does not only result from the types of learning identified above. For instance, it has been shown that internationalization knowledge is positively related to variations in the experiences a firm has in different markets (Barkema & Vermeulen, 1998).

Given the business network view, we add to our model the concept of *relationship-specific knowledge*, which is developed through interaction between the two partners; that includes knowledge of each other's heterogeneous resources and capabilities. Moreover, we expect that interaction to contribute to more general knowledge of international relationship development, also to help the partners learn about ways in which they can develop different and transferable relationships in alternative situations (cf. Hoang & Rothaermel, 2005). Indeed, variations in the character of relationships may have a positive impact on the development of *general relationship knowledge*. Furthermore, the importance of business network coordination, as we wrote in the section about the business network view, suggests that learning how to coordinate sets of relationships is important. Such learning may develop in relationships between partners that are located in different countries, for instance, suppliers in some countries and customers in others (Johanson & Vahlne, 2003).

Moreover, knowledge development in business networks is different from the kind of knowledge development we assumed in our original model. In business networks knowledge development is not only a matter of learning extant knowledge from other actors. The interaction between a buyer's user knowledge and a seller's producer knowledge may also result in new knowledge.

Prior experience with management teams may have a strong effect on internationalization, at least in new and small companies (Reuber & Fischer, 1997). This is particularly interesting, as the 1977 model says nothing about the beginnings of internationalization (Andersen, 1993). From a business network point of view it is important to emphasize that the management team's prior relationships probably provide extremely important knowledge. We return to this issue later.

Petersen et al. (2003) discuss our original model under the headings *From simplicity to complexity* and *From determinism to managerial discretion*. Under the first heading, they compare the simple view of knowledge presented in our early model with later research in knowledge and organizational learning. We agree that research on organizational learning has demonstrated that learning is much more complex than we had assumed 30 years ago. When we constructed our model we believed – and continue to believe – in a parsimonious approach to theory development. The aim of theory building is not to replicate a complex reality; it is to explain its central elements. The conclusion of subsequent research has been that experiential learning is indeed a central factor in a firm's internationalization. In his critical review of the Uppsala and the innovation models (Bilkey & Tesar, 1977; Cavusgil, 1980) of the internationalization process, Andersen (1993) noted that the Uppsala model does not consider specific situations, phases, firms or foreign markets. In Andersen's view, the model is general. Obviously a model that has general applicability cannot also consider all the kinds of knowledge and learning that might occasionally be relevant. It is likely that ways of learning other than experiential learning may be important for studies of specific internationalization episodes and situations. In his critical review of our original model, Forsgren (2002) argues that three types of non-experiential learning – the acquisition of other firms, imitation, and search – may also speed up the internationalization process. He consequently means that our model exaggerates the gradual nature of the process.

Under the heading *From determinism to managerial discretion*, Petersen et al. (2003) write that the model we developed in 1977 is deterministic, though research has demonstrated the existence of substantial managerial discretion in the internationalization of firms. We disagree with their characterization. We do not see a causal relation between experiential learning and resource commitment as deterministic. A causal relation between two variables does not mean that one determines the other; only that one influences the other, usually in combination with other variables. We do agree that managerial discretion is important, although we think that path dependence and problematic search tend to make managers prefer certain specific alternatives to other ones. We also think that the model can easily incorporate managerial discretion and strategic intentions.

In spite of these critical views, we think that empirical studies of the internationalization process demonstrate the central role of experiential learning in the process. In addition, other important research streams have stressed learning mechanisms that are consistent with our model. For example, research on learning curves highlights learning based on experience, and is one of the fundamental sub-areas within the field of learning studies (Argote, 1999). Nelson and Winter's (1982) evolutionary theory emphasizes routines developed through experience that result in behavioral continuity and limited path dependence. The concept of absorptive capacity developed by Cohen and Levinthal (1990) is a third example. Like experiential learning, absorptive capacity means that knowledge development tends to be a cumulative process.

Given all the points made, we conclude that there is good reason to retain experiential learning as a basic mechanism in the business network view of the internationalization process. Of course, experiential learning can be complemented with other ways of knowledge development.

Trust and commitment building

Our original model does not explicitly include any affective or emotional dimensions in relationships, though it can be argued that they are implicitly present in the concept of knowledge. We now think that those dimensions should be explicit. First, much has since been written on social capital, trust and similar concepts, which of course include both affective and cognitive elements. Second, we realize from empirical observation that affective dimensions are indeed important for understanding the relationships that are a critical component of our model. Third, trust plays an important part in recent research on relationship development (Morgan & Hunt, 1994) and business networks (Johanson & Mattsson, 1987). We recognized the possibility of including these aspects in our model in a later note on the Uppsala internationalization process model (Johanson & Vahlne, 2006). Building on the work of Nahapiet and Ghoshal (1998), Granovetter (1985, 1992), Madhok (1995) and others, we conclude that trust is an important ingredient for successful learning and the development of new knowledge. Trust can also substitute for knowledge, for instance, when a firm lacks the necessary market knowledge and so lets a trusted middleman run its foreign business (cf. Arenius, 2005). We also introduce in this section a definition of commitment without the tautological relationship to knowledge that, according to Andersen (1993), is a problem in the original model (cf. Hadjikhani, 1997).

Morgan and Hunt (1994) provide definitions of trust. Trust keywords and phrases include "integrity," "reliability," and that "the word ... of another can be relied upon." In short, a sense of trust implies an ability to predict another's behavior. Trust also assumes that human behavior is characterized by high ethical standards. Trust may develop into commitment if there is willingness and positive intentions. Thus trust is a prerequisite for commitment, a conclusion that is consistent with the results obtained by Morgan and Hunt. If trust does lead to commitment, it implies that there is a desire to continue the relationship, a willingness to invest in it, even recognition of the necessity of making short-term sacrifices that benefit another for reasons of long-term interest for oneself.

In a comment on his 1995 article on international joint ventures, Madhok (2006) discusses whether it makes sense to assume either trust or opportunism. His conclusion implies that there are reasons for firms to rely on the trustworthiness of their business partners. We agree, though we believe that it is unrealistic to assume that trust is permanent, or that commitment or extreme opportunism are either. It is realistic, though, to assume that an extant degree of commitment will persist and increase when partners believe that continuing a relationship is in their long-term interest. While opportunities are the key factor in making commitments, the other side of the coin is dependency. One partner may not necessarily appreciate everything the other one does, and yet some actions will be tolerated for the sake of long-term interests (Thorelli, 1986).

Trust persuades people to share information, promotes the building of joint expectations (Madhok, 1995) and is especially important in situations of uncertainty. Trust is crucial in the early phases of a relationship, and its importance may be permanent if the relationship requires continued efforts to create and exploit opportunities. Madhok's (1995) contention is that trust "induces reciprocity and coordinates action." This supports Morgan and Hunt's (1994) conclusions that "trust is a major determinant of commitment" (see also Gounaris, 2005). They go on to say that they see "relationship commitment as an exchange partner believing that an ongoing relationship with another is so important as to warrant maximum efforts at maintaining it" (1994: 23). We agree with this definition, with the caveat that we do not believe anything is ever maximized. Commitment is rather a question of more or less intensive efforts. We do, however, agree with Morgan and Hunt that "when both commitment and trust – not just one or the other – are present, they produce outcomes that promote efficiency, productivity and effectiveness" (1994: 22).

Mathieu and Zajac (1990) distinguish between calculative and affective commitment. Calculative commitment is built on cognitive assumptions. Examples include available joint opportunities. Affective commitment is based on "a generalized sense of positive regard for and attachment to the other party" (Gounaris, 2005). Affective commitment may then replace cognitive analysis. In the absence of knowledge, if the stakes are high in terms of opportunities or of switching costs, it may be rational to act on partially subjective opinions. Therefore, given the circumstances, the decision-makers in our model are rational. Clearly, knowledge is never complete. In fact, in some situations knowledge does not exist until the parties have developed it together. Nonetheless, Gounaris (2005) finds in his empirical analysis that calculative commitment has a negative impact on the parties' intentions to preserve and strengthen their relationship, and so suggests that firms may want to avoid dependence and lock-in situations. However, dependency is an unavoidable by-product of a beneficial relationship.

We agree with Madhok (2006: 7) that "trust-building is a costly and time-consuming process." Boersma et al. (2003) picture the process as a sequence of phases in which the output of one phase constitutes the input of the next. As the output from each phase consists of either an increased or a decreased level of trust, the process is not deterministic. Commitment is developed late in the process (in Boersma et al.'s analysis, this occurs after joint venture negotiations). We believe that this view applies to relationships in general, with or without negotiations, as long as firms signal their intent to commit.

Opportunity development

In our original model we assumed that market commitment and market knowledge affect "perceived opportunities and risks which in turn influence commitment decisions and current activities" (Johanson & Vahlne, 1977: 27). Moreover, we assumed "that the commitment to a market affects the firm's perceived opportunities and risk" (1977: 27). We also stated, "knowledge of opportunities or problems is assumed to initiate decisions" (1977: 27). Despite these assumptions, our model has generally been regarded as a risk (or uncertainty) reduction (or avoidance) model. We think that risk is unavoidable when embarking on a journey into the unknown, and so stated that the firm's approach to risk is complicated and variable. This assertion, however, does not imply risk avoidance, only a need for risk management. Research on business networks and entrepreneurship has made considerable progress since the publication of our original model. We recognize now that we probably did neglect the opportunity dimension of experiential learning. Still, we did write:

> An important aspect of experiential knowledge is that it provides the framework for perceiving and formulating opportunities. On the basis of objective knowledge it is possible to formulate only theoretical opportunities, experiential knowledge makes it possible to perceive "concrete" opportunities – to have a "feeling" about how they fit into present and future activities. (1977: 28)

The field of opportunity research has grown significantly. We believe that by combining findings from that research with the business network perspective on markets described in the previous section, we can take a step forward in discussing opportunities in the internationalization process.

Kirzner (1973) offers a starting point. Entrepreneurial discovery of opportunities plays a central role in his theory of the market process. He argues that opportunities exist in the market because markets are never in equilibrium. Opportunity recognition involves discovering the hitherto unknown; it is a result of entrepreneurs being alert and prepared for surprises. This view implies that opportunity recognition is associated with ongoing business activities rather than with specific opportunity-seeking activities. He also sees entrepreneurial discovery as an outcome of serendipity (Kirzner, 1997).

Following Kirzner, Shane (2000) studied the role of prior knowledge and showed that it seems to have a stronger impact on discovery than the personal characteristics of individuals do. Prior knowledge makes individuals better at discovering some opportunities, which means that opportunity-seekers should concentrate on what they know, rather than on what others say. Similarly, building on the resource-based view, Denrell et al. (2003) conclude, as Barney (1986) argued, that the firm does not have any privileged knowledge of external resources required for identifying an opportunity. Therefore, as Shane (2000) suggests, the firm should focus its opportunity analysis on its own internal resources, where it presumably has privileged knowledge. Like Kirzner (1997), Denrell et al. conclude that identifying opportunities is likely to be the result of a serendipitous strategy characterized by effort and luck, combined with alertness and flexibility.

However, according to the network view of markets, firms do have privileged access to information about their relationship partners and their business network. Moreover, opportunity recognition is likely to be an outcome of ongoing business activities that add experience to the existing stock of knowledge. An important part of that experience is knowledge of one's own firm and its resources, including the external resources that are partially available through network relationships.

Ardichvili et al. (2003) see opportunity development as the central element in their theory of entrepreneurial opportunity identification and development, and as such it should be its primary focus: "The need or resource 'recognized' or 'perceived' cannot become a viable business without this 'development'" (2003: 106). According to the network perspective on markets, opportunity development is based on interaction between partners who build knowledge together and come to trust each other as they commit themselves further to the relationship. Provided that there is some basic entrepreneurial alertness, opportunities are likely to emerge as a consequence of the privileged knowledge that the two partners develop during their interaction. This knowledge may allow them to recognize opportunities that others do not (Agndal & Chetty, 2007). Furthermore, they may identify and understand ways in which their idiosyncratic resources match those of their partner (von Hippel, 1988). The opportunity development process is similar to the internationalization process, and to the relationship development process (Ghauri et al., 2005). It is a matter of interrelated processes of knowledge development and commitment to an opportunity. The process may be unilateral, with one firm learning about another firm's needs, capabilities, markets and network, thereby identifying an opportunity. Alternatively, it may be bilateral when two firms in interaction identify an opportunity. It may even be multilateral, with several firms interacting and increasing their commitment to an idea or opportunity. In this type of multilateral opportunity development, firms that are connected to the two focal firms are likely to be involved in the process, a process that may be facilitated by trust. One would expect network configuration and relational embeddedness to influence the type of opportunity, Kirznerian or Schumpeterian, that is developed (Andersson et al., 2005). An important conclusion based on the network view is that both Kirzner (1997) and Denrell et al. (2003) exaggerate the role of serendipity.

Consistent with the view that opportunity identification is a side-effect of an ongoing business relationship, we believe that exploitation and exploration (March, 1991) overlap. Partly because of heterogeneity, and partly because of the unavailability of information, market research may be unable to identify many of the opportunities that insiders can. As a result, exploitation breeds exploration, at least for the type of opportunities that are induced by the market. While exploitation is risky, that risk can be reduced by progressing in small steps and building successive commitments.

Shane (2000) concluded that since opportunity recognition is associated with prior knowledge, it is difficult to centralize the search for opportunities. This is consistent with Bjerre and Sharma's finding "that a major portion of the knowledge in international firms is indeed local, deposited in local subsidiaries" (2003: 138), which supports our view that market-derived opportunities will be discovered and/or created at the boundary of the firms where the necessary relationship experience exists. It also supports the view that subsidiary entrepreneurial initiatives are likely to be important for the multinational enterprise (Birkinshaw, 1997).

The following two positions, which we see as being at two ends of a spectrum, are frequently mentioned in opportunity research: opportunity discovery, which assumes that there are opportunities in the market waiting to be recognized (Kirzner, 1973) and opportunity creation, which assumes that the opportunity is created and realized by one of the firms (Gelbuda et al., 2003; Schumpeter, 1934; Weick, 1995). Our position is that the process of opportunity development includes elements of both discovery and creation (Ardichvili et al., 2003). We mean that it is meaningless to say that either one is more important. Furthermore, opportunity research usually distinguishes between two stages: recognition and exploitation. Once again our position is that opportunity development is an interactive process characterized by gradually and sequentially increasing recognition (learning) and exploitation (commitment) of an opportunity, with trust being an important lubricant. It follows then that the process of opportunity identification and exploitation in the network perspective is very similar to the internationalization process and to the relationship development process.

The declining validity of the establishment chain

Most of the criticism of the internationalization process model is based on the observation that company behavior has changed since we built our model. Examples of this are that companies sometimes leapfrog over stages in the establishment chain (Hedlund & Kverneland, 1985), that they start to internationalize soon after their birth (Oviatt & McDougall, 1994), that the internationalization process proceeds more rapidly now (Oviatt & McDougall, 1994; Zahra et al., 2000) and that the order in which companies enter foreign markets no longer correlates with psychic distance (Madsen & Servais, 1997). Also, joint ventures and strategic alliances are modes that are much more commonly used today than previously. Internationalization through acquisitions has also grown enormously in terms of value (UN World Investment Report, 2000).

We do not dispute that these observations appear to be inconsistent with the establishment chain we proposed. The establishment chain implied that companies start to internationalize in neighboring markets and subsequently move further away in terms of psychic distance, and also that in each market companies begin by using low-commitment modes, such as a middleman, and subsequently switch to modes that suggest a stronger commitment, such as wholly owned subsidiaries. Some researchers who have observed company behavior that deviates from the establishment chain of internationalization pattern have occasionally used their observations to criticize our internationalization process model. We review some of those comments in the following paragraphs. We respond first, though, in pointing out that the establishment chain is not part of the model, but rather a summary of the empirical observations on which we based our inductive theoretical arguments. We also argue that for the most part changes in company behavior have more to do with changes in the international environment than with changes in internationalization mechanisms. The network view, presented earlier, also helps to explain deviations from the establishment chain.

According to a review of articles that were published during the first four years of this decade in nine important academic journals (Andall & Fischer, 2005), one of the most debated issues in internationalization research is whether the phenomena of international new ventures (Oviatt & McDougall, 1994, 2005) and born globals (Knight & Cavusgil, 1996) are consistent with our model. We think they are, to the extent that most born globals are really "born regionals," with international activities that do not really span the globe in any significant fashion (see also Rugman & Verbeke, 2007). In fact, many of the companies the internationalization pattern of which we studied (see, for example, Johanson & Wiedersheim-Paul, 1975) should be considered born regionals or international new ventures.

We use Sandvik, a well-known multinational company, as an example. In 1862, steel production was started in Sandvik to exploit the Bessemer process:

> The founder of Sandvik, G.F. Goransson, had brought the process to Sweden from the UK through contacts he had made when he was a general manager of a Swedish trading firm that had extensive international contacts. The first firm soon went bankrupt, but in 1868 the company now known as Sandvik was formed. In the same year, relationships with representatives in Denmark, Norway and the UK were established, and, one year later, in Germany. In 1870 a representative in France was linked to Sandvik. A representative in Switzerland was taken over at the start. (Vahlne & Johanson, 2002: 218)

Sandvik relied on external resources, not only for marketing and selling abroad, but also for technology. While Sandvik's subsequent internationalization process was rapid, its history does fit the establishment chain, and correlates with what we would expect in regard to psychic distance. We can agree with Oviatt and McDougall (1994) on one point: international new ventures and born regionals are old phenomena. As such firms are frequently founded by individuals with previous international experience and have established relationships with foreign companies, they do not create a problem for our model (Coviello, 2006; Reuber & Fischer, 1997). True, the knowledge and the relationships might indeed be in place prior to the formal founding of the focal firm, but that is a formality of no major significance. It is true too that having those factors already in place may accelerate the process. If a firm starts from scratch though, as we argued above, the processes of learning and building commitment will take time. A wealth of research, including Nahapiet and Ghoshal (1998), Granovetter (1985) and Ring and van de Ven (1992), supports this point. There is nothing in our model that indicates that international expansion cannot be done quickly. It can, as long as there is sufficient time for learning and relationship building (Vahlne & Johanson, 2002). Although many contextual aspects have changed since we made our observations, almost 50 years ago, the ways in which human beings learn and make decisions have not drastically changed since. Moreover, experiential learning and building trust and commitment, the basic prerequisites for developing business, hence for internationalization, certainly have not changed. Partners still have to get involved in some sort of exchange that will create experience, while these exchanges might be performed more quickly today, it still takes time, and firms still have to face the risk of failure.

We do believe that the correlation between the order in which a company enters foreign markets and psychic distance has weakened. Some companies and individuals have acquired more general knowledge of foreign environments, perhaps this instils in them greater confidence in their ability to cope with psychic distance. This does not mean that psychic distance is unimportant. However, the relationship between market entry order and psychic distance applies at the level of the decision-maker (Johanson & Vahlne, 2003; Sousa & Bradley, 2006), not at that of the firm. Johanson and Vahlne (2003) offer some examples. The chairman of a Swedish company was a visiting professor at an American university for several years before that company made its first attempt at establishing a presence abroad by entering into a joint venture with the university (2003: 87). The president of the same company knew someone from Poland who had worked with other Swedish companies for many years (2003: 88), he recruited him to establish the firm's next subsidiary in Poland. In both instances short psychic distance helped the parties recognize and implement opportunities. The impact of psychic distance on internationalization may well be indirect, but this does not mean that it has no effect on relationship building or on the processes of learning, trust building, and so on, that occur in relationships.

The domestic market may not be the most relevant unit in terms of psychic distance. The distance to, and between, cultural blocs is more relevant in many cases (Barkema & Drogendijk, 2007; Shenkar, 2001). There may be cultural differences within a country that make it logical to view parts of the country as entirely different markets with different psychic distances. Indeed, the concept of the liability of outsidership does not necessarily refer to countries. It is a firm-level concept that may relate to a network within a country, or to a wider region (cf. Rugman & Verbeke, 2007).

We think that Autio (2005: 12) makes an interesting point when he argues that our original model emphasizes constraints to internationalization whereas Oviatt and McDougall's model emphasizes enabling factors. While we make the barriers to internationalization explicit in our model, especially psychic distance, our most basic "enabler," that is, the company and its firm-specific advantages, is implicit. Oviatt and McDougall place more emphasis than we do on the factors that make internationalization possible. We do include in our model the presence of one or more entrepreneurs, which is typical of explanations of international new ventures and born regionals, who may identify, develop, and exploit opportunities, and so are obviously indispensable. Our original article assumed corporate entrepreneurship (Johanson & Vahlne, 1977), which we explicitly explored in a subsequent article (Johanson & Vahlne, 1993).

Some authors emphasize the role played by "enablers" in rapid internationalization – for example, "boldness in decision-making" (Moen & Servais, 2002). On the surface, our decision-makers, who perhaps want to expand their company's business, do not appear to be risk takers. However, in our 1977 article, we state "it is assumed that the firm strives to increase its long-term profit, which is assumed to be equivalent to growth … The firm is, though, striving to keep risk-taking at a low level" (Johanson & Vahlne 1977: 27). We do not view our model and the rapid internationalization model as essentially different on this point. Furthermore, entrepreneurs, or at least successful ones, supposedly calculate risks carefully and try to avoid taking unnecessary risks. Perhaps the propensity of firms to take bigger risks is higher today in some cases (cf. Vahlne & Johanson, 2002: 221, in the case of venture capitalists and the internationalization of IT-consultant companies). However, it would appear that neither we nor other researchers really know much about the propensity for taking risks either in the past or now. Clearly, entrepreneurs like those at Sandvik, which we mentioned previously, were taking risks when they acted on opportunities in foreign markets.

Oviatt and McDougall's model does specifically differ from ours when it comes to the choice of modes. We have observed that companies gradually enter into what could be seen as more risky, but also potentially more beneficial and controllable, modes of operation. Increased knowledge and commitment make such risk-taking desirable and possible. On the other hand, entrepreneurs behind international new ventures are expected to optimize mode choice depending on constraints on resources and outside opportunities. We believe that this may be true. Today's companies do use a wider range of modes, although we do not see more "optimization" going on in a real sense. It is often said that environmental changes, such as globalization, rapid technological change and deregulation, force companies to enter into alliances and joint ventures, because no single company owns all the resources required to exploit larger and continuously changing markets (Contractor & Lorange, 2002). If that is the case, companies may not use those modes if their resources are sufficiently large to allow them to rely on internalized activities. In fact, companies have frequently switched from relying on an agent – that is, relying on external resources – to an internal operational mode when their performance makes that possible and there are prospects for growth and better efficiency. We do not view leapfrogging or choice of modes such as joint ventures, which our establishment chain did not predict, as problematic for our model, as when we built it neither was common among the Swedish companies at which we were looking. We no longer consider the mode a reliable indicator of the level of commitment. Contextual aspects often play a more important role. For example, Hedlund and Kverneland (1985) studied Swedish companies in Japan that had to forgo the wholly owned subsidiary mode because the structure of the Japanese industry, in which they were, made it necessary to have a local partner, who was already well established in local networks.

As we have noted, acquisitions have now become the primary mode of entry in terms of value. This is a way, of course, for a resource-rich company to quickly buy itself a position in a network in a foreign market, as opposed to proceeding incrementally in smaller less risky steps. However, in the era of globalization other motives may play a role. The focal company may want to gain access to an interesting piece of technology or some other resource, or it may want to reduce the number of competitors. We have argued that, in accordance with our model, an acquisition is much more likely to be successful if it is preceded by some kind of exchange between the acquirer and the acquiree. In such exchanges firms have already acquired a body of knowledge about each other, and have perhaps established some level of commitment (Andersson et al., 1997). Without such a previous relationship the parties will have to learn about each other after the acquisition for post-acquisition integration to proceed. This process may include some conflicts, and will take time (Ivarsson & Vahlne, 2002). Hence an acquisition is not necessarily a way of rapidly building a position on a foreign market.

It is clear that one reason for the empirically driven criticism of our model is that the business world is different today from how it was when we observed patterns of internationalization. Events move more quickly and assume somewhat different forms. Nonetheless, one constant in coping with uncertainty remains: firms need to learn, and to create or strengthen relationships in order to exploit opportunities.

A business network model of the internationalization process

In light of all of this, we have developed our revised model in the following way. The firm is embedded in an enabling, and at the same time constraining, business network that includes actors engaged in a wide variety of interdependent relationships. Internationalization is seen as the outcome of firm actions to strengthen network positions by what is traditionally referred to as improving or protecting their position in the market. As networks are borderless, the distinction between entry and expansion in the foreign market is less relevant, given the network context of the revised model. The traditional view of entry, that is, overcoming various barriers, is becoming less important than internationalizing undertaken to strengthen a firm's position in the network (Johanson & Vahlne, 2003). As a result, we claim that existing business relationships, because they make it possible to identify and exploit opportunities, have a considerable impact on the particular geographical market a firm will decide to enter, and on which mode to use. This claim is also consistent with the business network view, where much is contingent on existing relationships (Håkansson & Snehota, 1995). Learning and commitment-building take place in relationships. Although our 2003 article did not highlight that particular point, this way of thinking about internationalization places the identification of opportunities at the forefront. While in our 1977 article we mention that experiential knowledge may lead to the identification of opportunities, this aspect has largely been neglected. Primarily, it has been assumed that reducing uncertainty has to do with the differences between the culture and institutions of the home country and those of the foreign country. We now have reason to believe that learning and commitment are strongly related to identifying and exploiting opportunities (Johanson & Vahlne, 2006). As some types of knowledge are not accessible to everyone, and are instead confined to network insiders, a strong commitment to partners allows firms to build on their respective bodies of knowledge, making it possible for them to discover and/or create opportunities. We believe that internationalization is contingent more on developing opportunities than on overcoming uncertainties, for example concerning institutional conditions in the foreign market (Eriksson et al., 1997).

A reviewer of this paper has made us aware of the "effectuation process" that was constructed by Sarasvathy (2001) to describe the process entrepreneurs follow as they prepare to launch a new company. According to her, the effectuation process is "useful in understanding and dealing with spheres of human action. This is especially true when dealing with the uncertainties of future phenomena and problems of existence" (2001: 250). As we have argued, internationalization resembles entrepreneurship and may be described as corporate entrepreneurship. Internationalization too is characterized by high degrees of uncertainty. The effectuation process has much in common with our internationalization process model, including similar environmental characteristics, a limited number of available options, incremental development, and an emphasis on cooperative strategies (2001: 251). However, while Sarasvathy views the actors and their characteristics as important, our model does not include this point at all. We do argue, however, that the actors are implicitly present in our model to the extent that they are the carriers of (tacit) knowledge, trust, commitment, and network relations. We therefore consider the effectuation process as developed by Sarasvathy to be fully consistent with our model. In addition, our model underlines the fact that internationalization has much in common with entrepreneurship.

As in the 1977 model, the 2009 business network model consists of two sets of variables: state variables (shown as the left-hand side of Figure 4.2) and change variables (shown as the right-hand side of Figure 4.2), or stock and flow, which are relevant to both sides in a relationship. The variables affect each other, the current state having an impact on change and vice

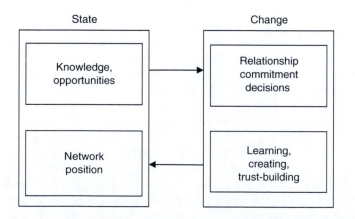

Figure 4.2 The business network internationalization process model (the 2009 version).

versa. The model depicts dynamic, cumulative processes of learning, as well as trust and commitment building. An increased level of knowledge may have a positive or a negative impact on building trust and commitment. In an extreme case scenario – which may actually not be so rare – the firm and/or the firm on the opposite side of the relationship may in fact reduce the commitment or even terminate the relationship. These processes can occur on both sides of a mutual relationship and at all points in the network in which the focal firm is a member.

Although the basic structure of the model is the same as the one we built in 1977, we have made some slight changes. We have added "recognition of opportunities" to the "knowledge" concept, as seen in the upper left-hand box of the model (see Figure 4.2). Opportunities constitute a subset of knowledge. By adding this variable, we intend to indicate that we consider opportunities to be the most important element of the body of knowledge that drives the process. Other important components of knowledge include needs, capabilities, strategies, and networks of directly or indirectly related firms in their institutional contexts. The second state variable is labeled "network position." This variable was identified in the original model as "market commitment." We now assume that the internationalization process is pursued within a network. Relationships are characterized by specific levels of knowledge, trust, and commitment that may be unevenly distributed among the parties involved, and hence they may differ in how they promote successful internationalization. Nonetheless, if the process is seen as potentially rewarding, a desirable outcome of learning, trust and commitment building will be that the focal firm enjoys a partnership and a network position.

As to the change variables, we changed the original label of "current activities" to "learning, creating and trust-building" to make the outcome of current activities more explicit. The concept of current activities, or operations, in the original model was intended to indicate that regular daily activities play an important role and lead to increased knowledge, trust and commitment. Our use of the term "learning" is at a higher level of abstraction, that is, we think of it as more than experiential learning, although we still regard that to be the most important kind of learning.

The speed, intensity and efficiency of the processes of learning, creating knowledge and building trust depend on the existing body of knowledge, trust and commitment, and particularly on the extent to which the partners find given opportunities appealing. We have made the affective dimension of trust-building more explicit than in our earlier model, as we believe it deserves a status similar to that of the cognitive dimension. In addition, we want to highlight opportunity creation, which is a knowledge-producing dimension, because we believe that developing opportunities is a critical part of any relationship. Furthermore, high levels of knowledge, trust and commitment in a relationship result in a more efficient creative process. The interplay between the processes of learning, creating opportunities, and building trust is described well by Nahapiet and Ghoshal (1998), although they use the concepts of intellectual capital and social capital.

Finally, the other change variable, "relationship commitment decisions," has been adapted from the original model. We added "relationship" to clarify that commitment is to relationships or to networks of relationships. This variable implies that the focal firm decides either to increase or decrease the level of commitment to one or several relationships in its network. In an extreme case scenario, this decision may manifest itself only on a psychological level. Usually, however, the decision will be visible through changes in entry modes, the size of investments, organizational changes, and definitely in the level of dependence. A change in commitment will either strengthen or weaken the relationship. From a network point of view, there are two kinds of decision regarding the commitment to the relationship. They may primarily be to develop new relationships, in most cases businesses, in others they may be about building bridges to new networks and filling structural holes (cf. Burt, 1992). Alternatively, they may be to protect or support the firm's existing network of strategic relationships. For example, a few years ago, Volvo demanded that some of its important Swedish suppliers develop relationships with German car manufacturers in order to demonstrate that Volvo's suppliers had the same desirable qualities and skills as those of its German competitors.

There are some implications of the revised model for the internationalization process. First, internationalization depends on a firm's relationships and network. We expect the focal firm to go abroad based on its relationships with important partners who are committed to developing the business through internationalization. These partners may be at home or abroad. The focal firm is also likely to follow a partner abroad if that partner firm has a valuable network position in one or more foreign countries. There are two possible reasons for such foreign expansion. One is the likelihood of finding interesting business opportunities. As we have said, partner bases of knowledge are interrelated, and are therefore also indirectly related to other members of the network. Relying on a related knowledge base, the focal firm may enter networks abroad, where it may be able to identify and exploit opportunities. We reiterate: mutual trust and commitment are based not on formal agreements but on a common history of at least minimally satisfactory, if not successful, joint business experiences. A second reason to go abroad occurs when a relationship partner who is going abroad, or already is abroad, wants the focal firm to follow. By following the partner abroad, the firm demonstrates its commitment to the relationship.

Where will an internationalizing company go? The general answer is: where the focal firm and its partners see opportunities. A foreign market in which the partner has a strong position is another possibility. This is not only a matter of the first step abroad. The same process may continue from market to market, depending on the actions of the focal firm's partners. If the firm has no valuable partners, it may go where it might be easy to connect with a new firm that already has a position in the foreign market. For example, it may link itself to a middleman such as an agent or a distributor. Eventually, when the focal firm has established relationships with customers, it may bypass the middleman and establish its own subsidiary. Short psychic distance will facilitate the establishment and development of relationships, which is a necessary but insufficient condition for identification and exploitation of opportunities.

How might the process start? Given the business network model's process view, any determination of a starting point will be arbitrary (cf. Coviello, 2006; Reuber & Fischer, 1997; Wiedersheim-Paul et al., 1978). Regardless of whether we consider the starting point to be the founding of the company, the first international market entry, or the establishment of a specific relationship, our process model implies that we should look for explanations in the state variables, such as knowledge, trust or commitment to the firm's specific relationships. For example, the focal firm may exploit some of its existing connections by using the trust that a partner has established with another party or parties (Larson, 1992). Increased knowledge may cause either the focal firm or its partner to become dissatisfied with the relationship. Either firm may then decide to decrease its commitment or even end the relationship.

We argued in an earlier paper that access to information is of more relevance to large companies, and that the Uppsala model is therefore more applicable to smaller firms (Johanson & Vahlne, 1990). We are now less certain about this observation, as knowledge is highly context specific. The model should be equally applicable to large and small firms (Barkema et al., 1996; Steen & Liesch, 2007). Large firms may, however, be better informed when they acquire a firm in a market in which they are already active. In such acquisitions, which are not unusual, it is more a matter of experience than of size. Such experience may also explain why international new ventures may grow very rapidly: The founding entrepreneur already has access to knowledge and relationships prior to the internationalization.

Suggested research agenda

We identify here a few of the exciting research issues that follow from our revised internationalization process model and are well worth exploring.

As a step towards formulating a more unified explanation of the emergence and growth of multinational enterprise, it could prove interesting and important to look for similarities between the internalization theory (Buckley & Casson, 1976; Hennart, 1982; Rugman, 1981) and the eclectic paradigm (Dunning, 1980) on one hand, and the business network model of the internationalization process on the other. The process of changing modes of operation is also frequently a matter of internalization or externalization. The version we propose now implicitly assumes that an internationalizing firm has access to one or more specific advantages. The original version of our model focused explicitly on location specificity as an explanation for uncertainty (Rugman & Verbeke, 2004: 12). While location specificity does matter, we now pay more attention to relational shortcomings, knowledge and commitment as reasons for uncertainty and, indirectly, for location specificity. This implies that established relationships offer a firm-specific advantage worthy of attention. We observe that Dunning's (1997) OLI paradigm has also been revised to include strategic alliances and, more recently, even broad network relationships (Dunning & Lundan, 2008). We have argued elsewhere (Johanson & Vahlne, 1990) that two large issues need to be addressed when attempting to merge the eclectic paradigm and the Uppsala model. The original version of the eclectic paradigm was rather static and rested on the behavioral assumption of strong rationality, whereas the Uppsala model is dynamic and assumes bounded rationality, a difference that has now, fortunately, largely disappeared with the latest extension of the OLI paradigm (Dunning & Lundan, 2008). To the extent that firm-specific advantages are based on Penrose and RBV thinking, the conceptual distance between the OLI paradigm and our business network model of internationalization is still further reduced. At this point the problem seems to lie primarily in the relationship to the market environment that Penrose did not consider a major issue, and about which RBV thinking says little. This is the core issue in our original model, and it is even more important in our new model, which we see as an extension of the "unknowable market" of Penrose and the RBV perspective. The remaining conceptual problem is related more to the internalization model. While that model focuses on explaining firm boundaries, our model focuses on the processes driving continuous change of those boundaries. Buckley and Casson (1998) address the evolving boundary issue, though it is unclear from their discussion whether they see it as falling within internalization theory or separate from it. In any case, organizational learning is now discussed within both lines of research (Benito & Tomassen, 2003; Kay, 2005; Pitelis, 2007).

We highlight two studies that combine the concept of firm-specific advantages with the internationalization process. Sandén and Vahlne (1976) developed the concept of an *advantage cycle* to describe how some firm-specific advantages increase over time while others decrease. The cycle is initiated by an internal firm-specific advantage that allows the MNE to develop strong positions in foreign markets. These will subsequently constitute the MNE's main firm-specific advantages. In a recent empirical study of internationalization, Hsu and Pereira (2008) develop a model in which firm-specific advantage has a direct impact on internationalization and an indirect impact on performance. In addition, organizational learning moderates the effect of internationalization on performance. Both of these studies offer opportunities for fruitful research that combines the two approaches without really integrating them.

Second, as we have argued, business relationships provide a firm with an extended and unique resource base that it only partially controls. Furthermore, exploiting the potential of such an extended resource base requires that the firm's own resources be coordinated with those of one or several of its partners. The goal of business network coordination is joint productivity of a set of relationship partners, which is difficult to implement as it involves coordinating the partners' activities (Hohenthal, 2006). When partners operate in different countries, cross-country business network coordination is also needed, and is more difficult still. How hard this will be to achieve may vary with the psychic distance between the actors. This brings to mind many interesting sub-issues, including the means of coordination and the possible allocation of coordination responsibilities between designated organizational units (Galbraith, 1973; Mintzberg, 1979). We expect that these units will be located in the strategic partners' home countries. We are convinced that international business network coordination will become an increasingly important phenomenon with strong implications for firm-specific advantage as well as for internationalization.

Third, the subtitle of this paper, *From liability of foreignness to liability of outsidership*, refers to the fact that a firm's problems and opportunities in international business are becoming less a matter of country-specificity and more one of relationship-specificity and network-specificity. For example, the problems associated with foreign market entry are largely the same as those associated with entry into any other market. The firm does not know who the business actors are, or how they are related to each other, unless it already enjoys relationships with one or several actors in that market. There is a need for research that may explain when the liability of foreignness is the main problem in foreign market entry and when the liability of outsidership is the primary difficulty. Research into ways in which the two approaches might be combined would also be interesting. For example, we suggest that studies of the impact of psychic distance on the formation and deepening of relationships, as well as of the role of relationships as vehicles in learning about institutional and cultural conditions, would both be worthwhile.

The business network model of internationalization can be used to study both resource-seeking and market-seeking internationalization. Pyndt and Pedersen (2006) found that at the resource-seeking end of the value chain the dynamics of learning and trust and commitment building lead to exploration and exploitation in the context of expanding upstream activities. As our business network model is symmetrical in terms of suppliers and customers, it can be used to analyze international sourcing and supply chain development. While there is considerable research on global supply chain development, little of it appears in international business journals compared with the number of studies on market-seeking internationalization. In recent years, however, two articles on international sourcing have been published in *JIBS* (Griffith & Myers, 2005; Murray et al., 2005). In both articles the authors study the performance of global supply relationships and alliance-based sourcing. The dynamics of the internationalization of supply networks is an increasingly important problem in international business that our model can address.

Our business network view of the firm as an exchange unit rather than a production unit, in contrast to received microeconomic theory, offers new opportunities to analyze the internationalization of companies that operate fundamentally as networks. A rapidly growing number of modern firms are built around a brand, a design or patented technology for which production and services are performed by a network of other firms (for example, Nike, IKEA). We think that the business network model will be useful in enhancing understanding of their internationalization. Trading companies are another type of network firm with a long international business tradition. Although they are very important, they have been almost entirely neglected in the international business literature, except for their recognition as more or less marginal partners to manufacturing firms. The research by Ellis (2001) is one of the few exceptions. We recommend research on these firms based on the business network model of internationalization.

Although we have avoided constructivist methodology, we believe that it does have the potential to contribute to a deeper understanding of the international network development processes that we have conceptualized in this paper. An interesting study of internationalization of professional services (Reihlen & Apel, 2005) demonstrates that this approach merits further research, possibly using longitudinal case studies. Such studies would add particularly to our understanding of the term "creating" in the business network model of the internationalization process.

Acknowledgements

The authors thank numerous colleagues, students, and authors of IB articles who through the years have contributed views and remarks, critical and encouraging. We also thank the editor, Alain Verbeke, and three anonymous reviewers who helped put this paper in a much better shape. We express gratitude to the Torsten and Ragnar Söderberg Foundations for financial assistance.

References

Agndal, H., & Chetty, S. 2007. The impact of relationships on changes in internationalisation strategies of SMEs. *European Journal of Marketing*, 41(11/12): 1449–74.

Aharoni, Y. 1966. *The foreign investment decision process*. Boston, MA: Harvard Business School Press.

Alchian, A. A., & Allen, W. R. 1964. *Exchange & production: Theory in use*. Belmont, CA: Wadsworth Publishing.

Andall, A., & Fischer, M. 2005. *The death, birth ... of internationalization: A literary review*, MSc thesis, School of Business, Economics and Law, Göteborg University.

Andersen, O. 1993. On the internationalization process of firms: A critical analysis. *Journal of International Business Studies*, 24(2): 209–32.

Anderson, E., & Weitz, B. 1992. The use of pledges to build and sustain commitment in distribution channels. *Journal of Marketing Research*, 29(1): 18–34.

Anderson, J. C., Håkansson, H., & Johanson, J. 1994. Dyadic business relationships within a business network context. *Journal of Marketing*, 58(4): 1–15.

Andersson, U., Holm, D. B., & Johanson, M. 2005. Opportunities, relational embeddedness and network structure. In P. Ghauri, A. Hadjikhani, & J. Johanson (Eds), *Managing opportunity development in business networks:* 27–48. Basingstoke: Palgrave.

Andersson, U., Johanson, J., & Vahlne, J.-E. 1997. Organic acquisitions in the internationalization process of the business firm. *Management International Review*, 37(2): 67–84.

Ardichvili, A., Cardozo, R., & Ray, S. 2003. A theory of entrepreneurial opportunity identification and development. *Journal of Business Venturing*, 18(1): 105–23.

Arenius, P. 2005. The psychic distance postulate revised: From market selection to speed of market penetration. *Journal of International Entrepreneurship*, 3(2): 115–31.

Argote, L. 1999. *Organizational learning: Creating, retaining and transferring knowledge*. London: Kluwer Academic Publishers.

Autio, E. 2005. Creative tension: The significance of Ben Oviatt's and Patricia McDougall's article "Toward a theory of international new ventures". *Journal of International Business Studies*, 36(1): 9–19.

Axelsson, B., & Johanson, J. 1992. Foreign market entry: The textbook vs the network view. In B. Axelsson & G. Easton (Eds), *Industrial networks: A new view of reality:* 218–31. London: Routledge.

Barkema, H. G., & Drogendijk, R. 2007. Internationalising in small, incremental or larger steps? *Journal of International Business Studies*, 38(7): 1132–48.

Barkema, H. G., Bell, J. H. J., & Pennings, J. M. 1996. Foreign entry, cultural barriers, and learning. *Strategic Management Journal*, 17(2): 151–66.

Barkema, H. G., & Vermeulen, F. 1998. International expansion through start-up or acquisition: A learning perspective. *Academy of Management Journal*, 41(1): 7–26.

Barney, J. 1986. Strategic factor markets: Expectations, luck and business strategy. *Management Science*, 17(1): 99–120.

Benito, G. B. G., & Tomassen, S. 2003. The micro-mechanics of foreign operations' performance: An analysis on the OLI framework. In J. Cantwell & R. Narula (Eds), *International business and the eclectic paradigm: Developing the OLI framework:* 174–99. London: Routledge.

Bilkey, W. J., & Tesar, G. 1977. The export behavior of smaller-sized Wisconsin manufacturing firms. *Journal of International Business Studies*, 8(1): 93–8.

Birkinshaw, J. 1997. Entrepreneurship in multinational corporations: The characteristics of subsidiary initiatives. *Strategic Management Journal*, 18(3): 207–30.

Bjerre, M., & Sharma, D. D. 2003. Is marketing knowledge international? A case of key accounts. In A. Blomstermo & D. D. Sharma (Eds), *Learning in the internationalisation process of firms:* 123–41. Cheltenham: Edward Elgar.

Blankenburg Holm, D., Eriksson, K., & Johanson, J. 1999. Creating value through mutual commitment to business network relationships. *Strategic Management Journal*, 20(5): 467–86.

Boersma, M. F., Buckley, P. J., & Ghauri, P. N. 2003. Trust in international joint venture relationships. *Journal of Business Research*, 56(12): 1031–42.

Bonaccorsi, A. 1992. On the relationship between firm size and international export intensity. *Journal of International Business Studies*, 23(4): 605–35.

Buckley, P. J., & Casson, M. 1976. *The future of the multinational enterprise*. New York: Holmes & Meier.

Buckley, P. J., & Casson, M. 1998. Models of the multinational enterprise. *Journal of International Business Studies*, 29(1): 21–44.

Burt, R. S. 1992. *Structural holes*. Cambridge, MA: Harvard University Press.

Carlson, S. 1975. *How foreign is foreign trade? A problem in international business research*. Uppsala: Acta Universitatis Upsaliensis. Studia Oeconomiae Negotiorum 11.

Cavusgil, S. T. 1980. On the internationalization process of firms. *European Research*, 8(November): 273–81.

Chang, S. J. 1995. International expansion strategy of Japanese firms: Capability building through sequential entry. *Academy of Management Journal*, 38(2): 383–407.

Chen, H., & Chen, T.-J. 1998. Network linkages and location choice in foreign direct investment. *Journal of International Business Studies*, 29(3): 445–68.

Chetty, S., & Blankenburg Holm, D. 2000. Internationalisation of small to medium-sized manufacturing firms: A network approach. *International Business Review*, 9(1): 77–93.

Cohen, W. M., & Levinthal, D. A. 1990. Absorptive capacity: A new perspective on learning and innovation. *Administrative Science Quarterly*, 35(2): 128–52.

Contractor, F. J., & Lorange, P. 2002. The growth of alliances in the knowledge-based economy. *International Business Review*, 11(4): 485–502.

Cook, K. S., & Emerson, R. M. 1978. Power, equity and commitment in exchange networks. *American Sociological Review*, 43(5): 721–38.

Coviello, N. E. 2006. The network dynamics of international new ventures. *Journal of International Business Studies*, 37(5): 713–31.

Coviello, N. E., & Munro, H. 1995. Growing the entrepreneurial firm: Networking for international market development. *European Journal of Marketing*, 29(7): 49–61.

Coviello, N. E., & Munro, H. 1997. Network relationships and the internationalisation process of small software firms. *International Business Review*, 6(4): 361–86.

Cowley, P. R. 1988. Market structure and business performance: An evaluation of buyer/seller power in the PIMS database. *Strategic Management Journal*, 9(3): 271–78.

Cunningham, M. T., & Homse, E. 1986. Controlling the marketing-purchasing interface: Resource development and organisational implications. *Industrial Marketing and Purchasing*, 1(2): 3–27.

Cyert, R. D., & March, J. G. 1963. *A behavioral theory of the firm*. Englewood Cliffs, NJ: Prentice Hall.

Delios, A., & Beamish, P. W. 2001. Survival and profitability: The roles of experience and intangible assets in foreign subsidiary performance. *Academy of Management Journal*, 44(5): 1028–38.

Denrell, J., Fang, C., & Winter, S. G. 2003. The economics of strategic opportunity. *Strategic Management Journal*, 24(10): 977–90.

Dunning, J. H. 1980. Towards an eclectic theory of international production: Some empirical tests. *Journal of International Business Studies*, 11(1): 9–31.

Dunning, J. H. 1997. *Alliance capitalism and global business*. London: Routledge.

Dunning, J. H., & Lundan, S. 2008. *Multinational enterprises and the global economy* (2nd ed.). Cheltenham: Edward Elgar.

Dwyer, F. R., Schurr, P. H., & Oh, S. 1987. Developing buyer–seller relationships. *Journal of Marketing*, 51(2): 11–27.

Dyer, J. H., & Singh, H. 1998. The relational view: Cooperative strategy and sources of interorganizational competitive advantage. *Academy of Management Review*, 23(4): 550–679.

Elango, B., & Pattnaik, C. 2007. Building capabilities for international operations through networks: A study of Indian firms. *Journal of International Business Studies*, 38(4): 541–55.

Ellis, P. D. 2000. Social ties and foreign market entry. *Journal of International Business Studies*, 31(3): 443–69.

Ellis, P. D. 2001. Adaptive strategies of trading companies. *International Business Review*, 10(2): 235–59.

Eriksson, K., Johanson, J., Majkgård, A., & Sharma, D. D. 1997. Experiential knowledge and cost in the internationalization process. *Journal of International Business Studies*, 28(2): 337–60.

Erramilli, M. K. 1991. The experience factor in foreign market entry behavior of service firms. *Journal of International Business Studies*, 22(3): 479–501.

Erramilli, M. K., & Rao, C. P. 1990. Choice of foreign market entry mode by service firms: Role of market knowledge. *Management International Review*, 30(2): 135–50.

Ford, D. (Ed.) 1997. *Understanding business markets*. London: The Dryden Press.

Forsgren, M. 2002. The concept of learning in the Uppsala internationalization process model: A critical view. *International Business Review*, 11(3): 257–78.

Forsgren, M., Holm, U., & Johanson, J. 2005. *Managing the embedded multinational: A business network view*. Cheltenham: Edward Elgar.

Forsgren, M., & Kinch, N. 1970. *Foretagets anpassning till förän dringar i omgivande system. En studie av massa- och pappersindustrin (The adaptation of the firm to changes in surrounding systems)*. Uppsala: Department of Business Studies.

Galbraith, J. R. 1973. *Designing complex organizations*. Reading, MA: Addison-Wesley.

Gelbuda, M., Starkus, A., Zidonis, Z., & Tamasevicius, V. 2003. *Learning in the internationalization process. A case for organizational identity and interpretative capacity*, Proceedings of the 29th EIBA Conference, Copenhagen Business School, Denmark.

Ghauri, P., Hadjikhani, A., & Johanson, J. (Eds) 2005. *Managing opportunity development in business networks*. Basingstoke: Palgrave.

Gounaris, S. P. 2005. Trust and commitment influences on customer retention: Insights from business-to-business services. *Journal of Business Research*, 58(2): 126–40.

Granovetter, M. 1985. Economic action and social structure: The problem of embeddedness. *American Journal of Sociology*, 91(3): 481–510.

Granovetter, M. 1992. Problems of explanation in economic sociology. In N. Nohria & R. G. Eccles (Eds), *Networks and organizations: Structure, form and action:* 25–56. Boston, MA: Harvard Business School Press.

Griffith, D. A., & Myers, M. B. 2005. The performance implications of strategic fit of relational norm governance strategies in global supply chain relationships. *Journal of International Business Studies*, 36(3): 254–69.

Hadjikhani, A. 1997. A note on the criticisms against the internationalization process model. *Management International Review*, 37(2): 43–66.

Hägg, I., & Johanson, J. (Eds) 1982. *Företag i nätverk (Firms in networks)*. Stockholm: SNS.

Håkansson, H. (Ed.) 1982. *International marketing and purchasing of industrial goods: An interaction approach*. Cheltenham: Wiley.

Håkansson, H. 1989. *Corporate technological behaviour: Cooperation and networks*. London: Routledge.

Håkansson, H., & Östberg, C. 1975. Industrial marketing: An organizational problem? *Industrial Marketing Management*, 4(2/3): 113–23.

Håkansson, H., & Snehota, I. (Eds) 1995. *Developing relationships in business networks*. London: Routledge.

Hallén, L. 1986. A comparison of strategic marketing approaches. In P. W. Turnbull & J.-P. Valla (Eds), *Strategies for international industrial marketing:* 235–49. London: Croom Helm.

Hallén, L., Johanson, J., & Seyed-Mohamed, N. 1991. Interfirm adaptation in business relationships. *Journal of Marketing*, 55(2): 29–37.

Hedlund, G., & Kverneland, Å. 1985. Are strategies for foreign market entry changing? The case of Swedish investments in Japan. *International Studies of Management and Organization*, 15(2): 41–59.

Hennart, J.-F. 1982. *A theory of multinational enterprise*. Ann Arbor, MI: University of Michigan Press.

Hoang, H., & Rothaermel, F. T. 2005. The effect of general and partner-specific alliance experience on joint R&D project performance. *Academy of Management Journal*, 48(2): 332–45.

Hohenthal, J. 2001. *The creation of international business relationships: Experience and performance in the internationalization process*, PhD thesis, Department of Business Studies, Uppsala University.

Hohenthal, J. 2006. Managing interdependent business relationships in SME internationalization. In A. Hadjikhani, J.-W. Lee, & J. Johanson (Eds), *Business networks and international marketing:* 209–22. Seoul: Doo Yang.

Hood, N. & Young, S. 1979. *Economics of multinational enterprise*. London: Longman.

Hörnell, E., Vahlne, J.-E., & Wiedersheim-Paul, F. 1973. *Export och utlandsetableringar (Export and foreign establishments)*. Uppsala: Almqvist & Wiksell.

Hsu, C.-C., & Pereira, A. 2008. Internationalization and performance: The moderating effects of organizational learning. *Omega*, 36(2): 188–205.

Hymer, S. 1976. *International operations of national firms: A study of foreign direct investment*. Boston, MA: MIT Press.

Ivarsson, I., & Vahlne, J.-E. 2002. Technology integration through international acquisitions: The case of foreign manufacturing TNCs in Sweden. *Scandinavian Journal of Management*, 18(1): 1–27.

Johanson, J. 1966. *Svenskt kvalitetsstål på utländska marknader (Swedish special steel in foreign markets)*, FL thesis, Department of Business Studies, Uppsala University.

Johanson, J., & Mattsson, L.-G. 1987. Interorganizational relations in industrial systems: A network approach compared with the transaction cost approach. *International Studies of Management and Organization*, 17(1): 34–48.

Johanson, J., & Mattsson, L.-G. 1988. Internationalisation in industrial systems: A network approach. In N. Hood & J.-E. Vahlne (Eds), *Strategies in global competition:* 468–86. London: Croom Helm.

Johanson, J., & Vahlne, J.-E. 1977. The internationalization process of the firm: A model of knowledge development and increasing foreign market commitments. *Journal of International Business Studies*, 8(1): 23–32.

Johanson, J., & Vahlne, J.-E. 1990. The mechanism of internationalisation. *International Marketing Review*, 7(4): 11–24.

Johanson, J., & Vahlne, J.-E. 1993. Management of internationalization. In L. Zan, S. Zambon, & A. M. Pettigrew (Eds), *Perspectives on strategic change:* 43–71. London: Kluwer Academic Publishers.

Johanson, J., & Vahlne, J.-E. 2003. Business relationship learning and commitment in the internation-alization process. *Journal of International Entrepreneurship*, 1(1): 83–101.

Johanson, J., & Vahlne, J.-E. 2006. Commitment and opportunity development in the internationaliza-tion process: A note on the Uppsala internationalization process model. *Management International Review*, 46(2): 1–14.

Johanson, J., & Wiedersheim-Paul, F. 1975. The internationalization of the firm: Four Swedish cases. *Journal of Management Studies*, 12(3): 305–22.

Kay, N. M. 2005. Penrose and the growth of multinational firms. *Managerial and Decision Economics*, 26(2): 99–112.

Kelley, H. H., & Thibaut, J. W. 1978. *Interpersonal relations: A theory of interdependence*. New York: John Wiley & Sons.

Kirzner, I. M. 1973. *Competition and entrepreneurship*. Chicago: University of Chicago Press.

Kirzner, I. M. 1997. Entrepreneurial discovery and the competitive market process: An Austrian approach. *Journal of Economic Literature*, 35(1): 60–85.

Knight, G. A., & Cavusgil, S. T. 1996. The born global firm: A challenge to traditional internationaliza-tion theory. *Advances in International Marketing*, 8: 11–26.

Kogut, B. 2000. The network as knowledge: Generative rules and the emergence of structure. *Strategic Management Journal*, 21(3): 405–25.

Larson, A. 1992. Network dyads in entrepreneurial settings: A study of the governance of exchange relationships. *Administrative Science Quarterly*, 37(1): 76–104.

Li, J. 1995. Foreign entry and survival: Effects of strategic choices on performance in international markets. *Strategic Management Journal*, 19(3): 333–52.

Loane, S., & Bell, J. 2006. Rapid internationalisation among entrepreneurial firms in Australia, Canada, Ireland and New Zealand: An extension to the network approach. *International Marketing Review*, 23(5): 467–85.

Luo, Y., & Peng, M. 1999. Learning to compete in a transition economy: Experience, environment and performance. *Journal of International Business Studies*, 30(2): 269–95.

Madhok, A. 1995. Revisiting multinational firms' tolerance for joint ventures: A trust-based approach. *Journal of International Business Studies*, 26(1): 345–69.

Madhok, A. 2006. How much does ownership really matter? Equity and trust relations in joint ventures. *Journal of International Business Studies*, 37(1): 4–11.

Madsen, T. K., & Servais, P. 1997. The internationalization of born globals: An evolutionary perspec-tive. *International Business Review*, 6(6): 561–83.

Majkgård, A., & Sharma, D. D. 1998. Client-following and market-seeking in the internationalization of service firms. *Journal of Business-to-Business Marketing*, 4(3): 1–41.

March, J. G. 1991. Exploration and exploitation in organizational learning. *Organization Science*, 2(1): 71–87.

Martin, X., Swaminathan, A., & Mitchell, W. 1998. Organizational evolution in the interorganizational environment: Incentives and constraints on international expansion strategy. *Administrative Science Quarterly*, 43(3): 566–601.

Mathieu, J. E., & Zajac, D. M. 1990. A review and meta-analysis of the antecedents, correlates and consequences of organizational commitment. *Psychological Bulletin*, 108(2): 171–94.

Mintzberg, H. 1979. *The structuring of organizations*. Englewood Cliffs, NJ: Prentice Hall.

Moen, O., & Servais, P. 2002. Born global or gradual global? Examining export behavior of small and medium-sized companies. *Journal of International Marketing*, 10(3): 49–72.

Morgan, R. M., & Hunt, S. D. 1994. The commitment–trust theory of relationship marketing. *Journal of Marketing*, 58(3): 20–38.

Murray, J. Y., Kotabe, M., & Zhou, J. N. 2005. Strategic alliance-based sourcing and market performance: Evidence from foreign firms operating in China. *Journal of International Business Studies*, 36(2): 187–208.

Nadolska, A., & Barkema, H. G. 2007. Learning to internationalise: The pace and success of foreign acquisitions. *Journal of International Business Studies*, 38(7): 1170–86.

Nahapiet, J., & Ghoshal, S. 1998. Social capital, intellectual capital and the organizational advantage. *Academy of Management Review*, 23(2): 242–67.

Nellbeck, L. 1967. *Trävaruexport – distributionsvägar och förbrukning (Wood export – distribution channels and usage)*. Stockholm: Scandinavian University Books.

Nelson, R. R., & Winter, S. G. 1982. *An evolutionary theory of economic change*. Cambridge, MA: Belknap Press.

Oviatt, B. M., & McDougall, P. P. 1994. Toward a theory of international new ventures. *Journal of International Business Studies*, 25(1): 45–64.

Oviatt, B. M., & McDougall, P. P. 2005. The internationalization of entrepreneurship. *Journal of International Business Studies*, 36(1): 2–8.

Padmanabhan, P., & Cho, K. R. 1999. Decision specific experience in foreign ownership and establishment strategies: Evidence from Japanese firms. *Journal of International Business Studies*, 30(1): 25–44.

Penrose, E. T. 1966. *The theory of the growth of the firm*. Oxford: Basil Blackwell.

Petersen, B., Pedersen, T., & Sharma, D. D. 2003. The role of knowledge in firms' internationalisation process: Wherefrom and whereto? In A. Blomstermo & D. D. Sharma (Eds), *Learning in the internationalisation process of firms:* 36–55. Cheltenham: Edward Elgar.

Pitelis, C. 2007. Edith Penrose and a learning-based perspective on the MNE and OLI. *Management International Review*, 47(2): 207–19.

Powell, W. W. 1990. Neither market nor hierarchy. *Research in Organizational Behaviour*, 12: 295–336.

Pyndt, J., & Pedersen, T. 2006. *Managing global offshoring strategies*. Fredriksberg: Copenhagen Business School Press.

Reihlen, M., & Apel, B. A. 2005. Internationalization of professional service firms as learning: A constructivist approach. *International Journal of Service Industry Management*, 18(2): 140–51.

Reuber, A. R., & Fischer, E. 1997. The influence of the management team's international experience on the internationalization behaviors of SMEs. *Journal of International Business Studies*, 28(4): 807–25.

Ring, P. S., & van de Ven, A. H. 1992. Structuring cooperative relationships between organizations. *Strategic Management Journal*, 13(7): 483–98.

Rugman, A. M. 1981. *Inside the multinationals: The economics of internal markets*. New York: Columbia University Press.

Rugman, A. M., & Verbeke, A. 2004. A perspective on regional and global strategies of multinational enterprises. *Journal of International Business Studies*, 35(1): 3–18.

Rugman, A. M., & Verbeke, A. 2007. Liabilities of foreignness and the use of firm-level versus country-level data: A response to Dunning et al. (2007). *Journal of International Business Studies*, 38(1): 200–5.

Sandén, P., & Vahlne, J.-E. 1976. *The advantage cycle*, unpublished research paper, Department of Business Studies, Uppsala University.

Sapienza, H. J., Autio, E., George, G., & Zahra, S. A. 2006. A capabilities perspective on the effects of early internationalization on firm survival and growth. *Academy of Management Review*, 31(4): 914–33.

Sarasvathy, S. D. 2001. Causation and effectuation: Toward a theoretical shift from economic inevitability to entrepreneurial contingency. *Academy of Management Review*, 26(2): 243–63.

Schumpeter, J. A. 1934. *The theory of economic development*. Cambridge, MA: Harvard University Press.

Shane, S. 2000. Prior knowledge and the discovery of entrepreneurial opportunities. *Organization Science*, 11(4): 448–69.

Sharma, D. D., & Johanson, J. 1987. Technical consultancy in internationalization. *International Marketing Review*, 4(4): 20–9.

Shenkar, O. 2001. Cultural distance revisited: Towards a more rigorous conceptualisation and measurement of cultural differences. *Journal of International Business Studies*, 32(3): 519–35.

Snehota, I. 1990. *Notes on a theory of business enterprise*. Uppsala: Department of Business Studies.

Sousa, C. M. P., & Bradley, F. 2006. Cultural distance and psychic distance: Two peas in a pod? *Journal of International Marketing*, 14(1): 49–70.

Steen, J. T., & Liesch, P. W. 2007. A note on Penrosean growth, resource bundles and the Uppsala model of internationalisation. *Management International Review*, 47(2): 193–206.

Thorelli, H. B. 1986. Networks: Between markets and hierarchies. *Strategic Management Journal*, 7(1): 35–51.

Turnbull, P. W., & Valla, J.-P. (Eds) 1986. *Strategies for international, industrial marketing*. London: Croom Helm.

United Nations. 2000. *World investment report*. Geneva: UN.

Vahlne, J.-E., & Johanson, J. 2002. New technology, new business environments and new internationalization processes? In V. Havila, M. Forsgren, & H. Håkansson (Eds), *Critical perspectives on internationalization:* 209–28. London: Pergamon.

Vahlne, J.-E., & Wiedersheim-Paul, F. 1973. Ekonomiskt avstånd: Modell och empirisk undersokning (Economic distance: Model and empirical investigation). In E. Hörnell, J.-E. Vahlne, & F. Wiedersheim-Paul (Eds), *Export och Utlandsetableringar (Export and foreign establishments):* 81–159. Uppsala: Almqvist och Wiksell.

von Hippel, E. A. 1988. *The sources of innovation*. New York: Oxford University Press.

Weick, K. E. 1995. *Sensemaking in organizations*. Thousand Oaks, CA: Sage.

Welch, D. E., & Welch, L. S. 1996. The internationalization process and networks: A strategic management perspective. *Journal of International Marketing*, 4(3): 11–28.

Welch, L. S., & Luostarinen, R. 1988. Internationalization: Evolution of a concept. *Journal of General Management*, 17(3): 333–4.

Wiedersheim-Paul, F., Olson, H.-C., & Welch, L. S. 1978. Preexport activity: The first step in internationalization. *Journal of International Business Studies*, 8(1): 47–58.

Zaheer, S. 1995. Overcoming the liability of foreignness. *Academy of Management Journal*, 38(2): 341–63.

Zahra, S. A., Ireland, R. D., & Hitt, M. A. 2000. International expansion by new venture firms: International diversity, mode of market entry, technological learning, and performance. *Academy of Management Journal*, 43(5): 925–60.

Zajac, E. J., & Olsen, C. P. 1993. From transaction cost to transactional value analysis: Implications for the study of organizational strategies. *Journal of Management Studies*, 39(1): 131–45.

5 The eclectic paradigm as an envelope for economic and business theories of MNE activity*

John H. Dunning

Introduction: the contents of the eclectic paradigm

For more than two decades, the eclectic (or OLI)[1] paradigm has remained the dominant analytical framework for accommodating a variety of operationally testable economic theories of the determinants of foreign direct investment (FDI) and the foreign activities of multinational enterprises (MNEs).[2]

The eclectic paradigm is a simple, yet profound, construct. It avers that the extent, geography and industrial composition of foreign production undertaken by MNEs is determined by the interaction of three sets of interdependent variables, which, themselves, comprise the components of three sub-paradigms. The first is the competitive advantages of the enterprises seeking to engage in FDI (or increase their existing FDI), which are specific to the ownership of the investing enterprises, i.e. their ownership (O) specific advantages. This sub-paradigm asserts that the greater the competitive advantages of the investing firms, *relative to those of other firms* — and particularly those domiciled in the country in which they are seeking to make their investments — the more they are likely to be able to engage in, or increase, their foreign production.

The second is the locational attractions (L) of alternative countries or regions, for undertaking the value-adding activities of MNEs. This sub-paradigm avers that the more the immobile, natural or created endowments, which firms need to use jointly with their own competitive advantages, favor a presence in a foreign, rather than a domestic, location, the more firms will choose to augment or exploit their O specific advantages by engaging in FDI.

The third sub-paradigm of the OLI tripod offers a framework for evaluating alternative ways in which firms may organize the creation and exploitation of their core competencies, given the locational attractions of different countries or regions. Such modalities range from buying and selling goods and services in the open market, through a variety of inter-firm non-equity agreements, to the integration of intermediate product markets, and an outright purchase of a foreign corporation. The eclectic paradigm, like its near relative, internalization theory,[3] avows that the greater the net benefits of internalizing cross-border intermediate product markets, the more likely a firm will prefer to engage in foreign production itself, rather than license the right to do so, for example, by a technical service or franchise agreement, to a foreign firm.

The eclectic paradigm further asserts that the precise configuration of the OLI parameters facing any particular firm, and the response of the firm to that configuration, is strongly

*John Dunning (2000) "The eclectic paradigm as an envelope for economic and business theories of MNE activity", International Business Review, 9(2): 163–190. Reprinted with Permission by Elsevier.

contextual. In particular, it will reflect the economic and political features of the country or region of the investing firms, and of the country or region in which they are seeking to invest; the industry and the nature of the value added activity in which the firms are engaged; the characteristics of the individual investing firms, including their objectives and strategies in pursuing these objectives; and the raison d'être for the FDI.

Regarding this last contextual variable, scholars have identified four main types of foreign based MNE activity[4]:

1   That designed to satisfy a particular foreign market, or set of foreign markets, viz. *market seeking*, or demand oriented, FDI.
2   That designed to gain access to natural resources, for example, minerals, agricultural products, unskilled labor, viz. *resource seeking*, or supply oriented FDI.
3   That designed to promote a more efficient division of labor or specialization of an existing portfolio of foreign and domestic assets by MNEs, i.e. *rationalized or efficiency seeking* FDI. This type of FDI, though related to the first or second kind, is usually sequential to it.
4   That designed to protect or augment the existing O specific advantages of the investing firms and/or to reduce those of their competitors, i.e. *strategic asset seeking* FDI.

Combining our knowledge of the individual parameters of the OLI paradigm with that of the economic and other characteristics of home and host countries, and of the investing, or potentially investing, firms, it is possible to derive a wide range of fairly specific and operationally testable *theories*. It may be hypothesized that some sectors, for example, the oil and pharmaceutical sectors, are likely to generate more FDI than others, for example, the iron and steel or aircraft sectors, because the characteristics of the former generate more unique O advantages, or because their locational needs favor production outside their home countries, or because the net benefits of internalizing cross-border intermediate product markets are greater.

Similarly, it is possible to predict that the significance of outward FDI will be greater for some countries, for example, Switzerland and the Netherlands, than for others, for example, Russia and India, simply by knowing about their economic histories, the core competencies of their indigenous firms, the size of their home markets, their experience in foreign markets, and the locational attractions of their immobile resources and capabilities, relative to those of other countries. Finally, some firms, even of the same nationality and from the same industry, are more likely to engage in FDI than others. Sometimes, this might reflect their size: on the whole, large firms tend to be more multinational than small firms; sometimes their attitude to risk, particularly those associated with foreign ventures and of foreign partnerships with foreign firms; sometimes their innovating product, marketing, locational or FDI strategies.

The extent and pattern of foreign owned production will depend on the challenges and opportunities offered by different kinds of value added activity. Thus the growth of existing, and the emergence of new, markets, for example, in China, over recent years, has led to a considerable expansion of various kinds of market seeking FDI, particularly in fast growing industries, for example, telecommunications. By contrast, the rate of expansion of several natural resource sectors has been less impressive, as many products have become less resource intensive, due, for example, to the innovation of new alloys, improved recycling techniques, the miniaturization of components, and the replacement of natural by synthetic materials. The reduction of both transport costs and artificial barriers to most forms of trade has led to more efficiency seeking FDI among developed countries and between developed and developing countries.[5] While, as some kinds of technology have become more standardized or more codifiable, licensing agreements and management contracts have replaced FDI, for example, in the hotel and fast foods sectors, in the knowledge and trade intensive indus-tries, for example, pharmaceuticals, industrial electronics and management consultancy, the economies of global integration have made for a dramatic increase in merger and acquisition (M and A) activity (UN, 1998).[6] Moreover, the advent of electronic commerce is not only heralding the end of the geography of some financial and information markets, but is revolu-tionizing the organization of intra-firm production and trade.[7]

The content and predictions of the eclectic paradigm are firmly embedded in a number of different economic and business theories. Although *taken separately*, none of these offer a comprehensive explanation of the growth and decline of MNE business activity,[8] *taken together* — i.e. as a group — they do so. Most of the theories, too, are complementary, rather than substitutable, to each other. Some focus on particular kinds of FDI, but not others. Others are designed to explain different aspects of international production, for example, its ownership, structure, its locational profile or its organizational form. Thus, location theory forms the basis of the 'where' of MNE activity; industrial organization and resource based theories of the firm offer some reasons 'why' foreign owned affiliates may have a competitive edge over their indigenous competitors; while the concept of the firm as a 'nexus of treaties' (Williamson, 1990) is critical to an understanding of the existence of MNEs, and of why firms prefer to engage in FDI rather than sell their O specific assets, or the rights to use them, to independent foreign producers.

Much of this paper will seek to demonstrate how, and in what ways, these approaches are complementary to each other; and of how the eclectic paradigm offers both an envelope of these theories, and a common analytical framework within which each can be accommodated and fully enriched in their application.[9]

Finally, the relevance of the individual components of the eclectic paradigm, and the system of which they are part, will depend on whether one is seeking to explain the static or dynamic determinants of MNE activity. For example, one of the earliest theories of FDI, viz the product cycle theory, put forward by Raymond Vernon (1966), was concerned not only with explaining the *process* by which firms deepened and widened their markets,[10] but also how their locational needs might change as they moved from the innovatory to the standardized stage of produc-tion. By contrast, much of extant location theory and internalization theory seeks to identify and explain the optimum spatial and organizational dimensions of the existing resources and capabilities of firms and nations. Knickerbocker's 'follow my leader,' and Graham's 'tit for tat' thesis (Knickerbocker, 1973; Graham, 1975) also contain a longitudinal dimension, which, for the most part, is absent in most variants of industrial organization theory, for example as originally propounded by Hymer (1960) and Caves (1971). Initially, too, the eclectic paradigm primarily addressed static and efficiency related issues (Dunning, 1977), but more recently has given attention to the dynamic competitiveness and locational strategy of firms, and particu-larly the path dependency of the upgrading of their core competencies (Dunning 1995, 1998).

The kernel of this paper is directed to examining the changes in the boundaries, constraints and structure of the eclectic paradigm over the past twenty years;[11] and those now being demanded of it by contemporary world events and scholarly thinking. In doing so, it will pay especial attention to the emergence of alliance capitalism[12] and the growth of asset augment-ing FDI (Wesson 1993, 1997; Makino, 1998; Kuemmerle, 1999). In particular, it will set its analysis in the context of four significant happenings of the 1980s and 1990s:

1   the maturation of the knowledge-based economy,[13]
2   the deepening integration of international economic and financial activity, including that fostered by electronic networks (Kobrin, 1999),

3   the liberalization of cross-border markets, and the flotation of the world's major currencies, and
4   the emergence of several new countries as important new players on the global economic stage.

The next three sections will examine how the main intellectual thrust in explaining each of the OLI triumvirate of variables has evolved over this time. In particular, it will argue that, as the dynamic composition of these variables has assumed more significance, so the value of the eclectic paradigm has increased relative to the sum of its parts, with the contribution of each becoming increasingly interdependent of each other. Finally, the paper will give especial attention to the contribution of strategic cum managerial approaches to understanding the growth and composition of MNE activity, while averring that the relevance and richness of these is enhanced if set within the overarching construct of the eclectic paradigm.

The ownership sub-paradigm

In explaining the growth of international production, several strands of economic and business theory assert that this is dependent on the investing firms possessing some kind of unique and sustainable competitive advantage (or set of advantages), relative to that (or those) possessed by their foreign competitors. Indeed, some would argue that in traditional neoclassical theory, in which the firm is a 'black box', no FDI is possible, as all firms have equal access to the same resources and capabilities *within* their own countries, while there is complete immobility of resources and capabilities *between* countries.

When the eclectic paradigm was first put forward (in 1977),[14] it was assumed that such competitive or O specific advantages largely reflected the resources and capabilities of the home countries of the investing firms; and that FDI would only occur when the benefits of exploiting, i.e. adding value to, these advantages from a foreign location outweighed the opportunity costs of so doing.

Since the 1960s, the extant literature has come to identify three main kinds of firm or O specific competitive advantages.

1   Those relating to the possession and exploitation of monopoly power, as initially identified by Bain (1956) and Hymer (1960) and the industrial organization (IO) scholars (for example, Caves 1971, 1982; Porter 1980, 1985). These advantages are presumed to stem from, or create, some kind of barrier to entry to final product markets by firms not possessing them.
2   Those relating to the possession of a bundle of scarce, unique and sustainable resources and capabilities, which essentially reflect the superior technical efficiency of a particular firm relative to those of its competitors.[15] These advantages are presumed to stem from, or create, some kind of barrier to entry to factor, or intermediate, product markets by firms not possessing them. Their identification and evaluation has been one of the main contributions of the resource based and evolutionary theories of the firm.[16]
3   Those relating to the competencies of the *managers* of firms to identify, evaluate and harness resources and capabilities from throughout the world, and to coordinate these with the existing resources and capabilities under their jurisdiction in a way which best advances the long term interests of the firm.[17] These advantages, which are closely related to those set out in (2) are especially stressed by organizational scholars, such

as Prahalad and Doz (1987), Doz et al. (1997) and Bartlett and Ghoshal (1989, 1993). They tend to be *management*, rather than *firm*, specific in the sense that, even within the same corporation, the intellectual et al., competencies of the main decision takers may vary widely.

The *relative* significance of these three kinds of O specific advantages has changed over the past two decades, as markets have become more liberalized and as wealth creating activities have become more knowledge intensive. In the 1970s, the unique competitive advantages of firms primarily reflected their ability to internally produce and organize proprietary assets, and match these to existing market needs. At the turn of the millennium, the emphasis is more on their capabilities to access and organize knowledge intensive assets from throughout the world; and to integrate these, not only with their existing competitive advantages, but with those of other firms engaging in complementary value added activities. Hence, the emergence of alliance capitalism, and the need of firms to undertake FDI to protect, or augment, as well as to exploit, their existing O specific advantages (Dunning, 1995). Hence, too, the growing importance of multinationality, per se, as an intangible asset in its own right.

The question at issue, then, is whether the changing character and boundaries of the O specific advantages of firms can be satisfactorily incorporated into the eclectic paradigm, as it was first put forward. We would argue that as long as they do not undermine the basic tenets of the paradigm, and are not mutually inconsistent, they can be, although most certainly, they do require some modification to existing sub-paradigms and theories.

In Tables 5.1 and 5.2, we set out some of the models and hypotheses which have been sought to explain the origin, nature and extent of O specific advantages. We divide these into two categories: those which view such advantages as the income generating resources and capabilities possessed by a firm, at a given moment of time, i.e. *static* O advantages; and those which treat such advantages as the ability of a firm, to sustain and *increase* its income generating assets over time, i.e. *dynamic* O advantages. Both kinds of advantage tend to be context specific, for example, with respect to industry or country; and related to the kinds of competitive advantages (as identified earlier) which firms seek to attain or sustain. While, over the past two decades, changes in the world economic scenario and knowledge about MNE activity have led to a *relative* decline in market seeking (MS) and resource-seeking (RS) FDI — both of which tend to be based on the static O advantages of the investing firms — they still help to explain a major part of first-time FDI, particularly in developing countries (Dunning, 1999).

One of the key characteristics of the last two decades has been the increasing significance of FDI based on the possession of, or need to acquire, dynamic O advantages. Thus, rationalized or efficiency seeking (ES) FDI is only viable if: (a) the investing firm is already producing in at least one foreign country and (b) both intermediate and final product, trade is relatively unimpeded by natural or artificial cross-border barriers. Strategic asset seeking (SAS) FDI is dependent on intellectual capital being located in more than one country and that it is economically preferable for firms to acquire or create these assets outside, rather than within, their home countries.

To successfully explain dynamic and alliance related O specific advantages, each of the particular theories of FDI identified in Tables 5.1 and 5.2 requires some modification. The *resource based* theory needs to reexamine the content and significance of existing resources and capabilities of the firm in terms of

Table 5.1 Theories explaining O specific advantages of firms. A: Group 1 Explaining Static O advantages[a]

	1) MS[b]	2) RS[b]	3) ES[b]	4) SAS[b]
Product cycle theory. (Vernon 1966, 1974)	• Country-specific, largely US resources and capabilities of firms • All asset exploiting FDI • Further hypothesizes that competitive advantages of firms are likely to change as product moves through its cycle		• Oa advantages based on efficiency of investing firms also described in various empirical studies from Dunning (1958) and Safarian (1966) onwards	
Industrial organization theories. (Hymer, 1960; Caves 1971, 1974; Dunning 1958, 1993; Teece 1981, 1984)	• Largely Oa advantages initiated, or protected, by entry and/or mobility barriers to product markets. These include patent protection, and marketing, production and financial scale economies • All asset exploiting FDI • Little attention paid to asset augmenting FDI			
Multinationality, organizational and risk diversification theories. (Vernon 1973, 1983; Rugman, 1979; Kogut 1983, 1985; Kogut & Kulatilaka, 1994; Doz et al., 1997; Rangan, 1998)	• Mainly Ot advantages, but also some Oa advantages arising from presence of investing firms in countries with different economic political, cultural regimes. Ot advantages include ability to access, harness and integrate differences in distribution of natural and created assets and of organizational and managerial experience related to these • Potentially could be extended to include why markets for sustaining or increasing O specific advantages are best internalized.			
Internalization theory. (Buckley & Casson, 1976, 1985, 1998a,b; Hennart 1982, 1989; Rugman 1982, 1996)	• Entirely confined to Oa and Ot advantages arising from internalization of intermediate product markets • All asset exploiting FDI • Largely, though not exclusively, a static theory, though some acknowledgment that relative transaction costs of markets and hierarchies may vary as firms seek to exploit dynamic market imperfections			

(Continued)

Table 5.1 (Continued)

	1) MS^b	2) RS^b	3) ES^b	4) SAS^b
Capital Imperfections theory. (Aliber, 1971)	• Largely independent of type of FDI. The theory argues that firms from countries with strong exchange rates, or which discount capital at higher rates of interest will be tempted to invest, often by M and As, in countries which are economically weaker. The theory, as initially put forward, has no time (t) dimension; and, in essence, is a financial variant of internalization theory			
Follow my leader, tit for tat theory. (Knickerbocker, 1973; Graham 1975, 1990; Flowers, 1976)	• Mainly concerned with explaining FDI as a space related strategy among competing oligopolists. The main hypothesis is that FDI will be bunched in particular regions or countries over time; and that there is likely to be an inter-penetration of the territories occupied by the oligopolists. Though originally applied to explain asset-exploiting FDI, it is now also being used to explain some asset augmenting FDI			

a Oa = Ownership advantage based on the possession or privileged access to a specific asset. Ot = Ownership advantages based on capabilities to organize assets, both internal and external to the investing firm, in the most efficient way.

b 1) Market seeking 2) Resource seeking 3) Efficiency seeking 4) Strategic asset seeking.

Table 5.2 Theories explaining O specific advantages of firms. B: Group 2 Explaining Dynamic O advantages[a]

	1) MS[b]	2) RS[b]	3) ES[b]	4) SAS[b]
1. Resource based theory. (Wernerfelt 1984, 1995; Conner, 1991; Helleloid, 1992; Montgomery, 1995; Conner & Prahalad, 1996)	• As initially formulated, mainly concerned with identifying and evaluating variables influencing sustainability of competitive advantages of firms. Less attention given to traditional barriers to entry and more to such variables as specificity, rareness and non-imitability of resources, and the capabilities of firms to create and utilize them. Mainly concerned with asset exploiting FDI and only limited recognition of O advantages			• FDI designed to augment domestic-based resources and capabilities (Wesson 1993, 1997; Makino, 1998; Dunning, 1996; Chen & Chen, 1999)
2. Evolutionary theory. (Nelson & Winter, 1982; Nelson, 1991; Cantwell 1989, 1994; Dosi et al., 1988, Saviotti & Metcalfe, 1991; Teece et al., 1997)	• A holistic and time related approach, mainly directed to identifying an d evaluating dynamic Oa advantages of firms. Basic proposition relates to the path dependency of accumulated competitive advantages, and that the more efficient firms are in managing these advantages, the more likely they will have the capability to engage in asset exploiting and asset augmenting FDI			
3. Organizational (management related) theories. (Prahalad & Doz, 1987; Bartlett & Ghoshal, 1989; Porter, 1991; Bartlett & Ghoshal, 1993; Doz and Santos, 1997; Doz et al., 1997)	• Essentially explain O advantages in terms of ability of managers to devise appropriate organizational structures and techniques to effectively access, coordinate and deploy resources and capabilities across the globe. These theories, in recent years, have especially focused on the cross-border sourcing of intellectual assets and the coordination of these assets with those purchased from within the MNE			

a Oa = ownership advantage based on the possession or privileged access to a specific asset. Ot = ownership advantages based on capabilities to organize assets, both internal and external to the investing firm, in the most efficient way.

b 1) Market seeking 2) Resource seeking 3) Efficiency seeking 4) Strategic asset seeking.

1   their ability to sustain and/or upgrade these advantages,
2   their ability to harness and influence the quality and price of complementary assets, and to efficiently coordinate these with their own innovating competencies and
3   their ability to locate their value added activities in countries and regions which offer the optimum portfolio of immobile assets, both for creating or acquiring new O specific advantages, and for exploiting their existing advantages. Inter alia, such immobile assets may reflect the bargaining and negotiating skills of MNEs in their dealings with foreign governments (Rugman & Verbeke, 1998).

While accepting much of the content of *resource based* theory, the *evolutionary* theory of the firm pays more attention to the *process* or *path* by which the specific O advantages of firms evolve and are accumulated over time. In contrast (or in addition) to internalization theory, it tends to regard the firm as an innovator of created assets, rather than a 'nexus of treaties'. It is, by its nature, a dynamic theory, which, like the resource based theory, accepts the diversity of competencies between firms; however, unlike the latter, it focuses on the firm's long term strategy towards asset accumulation and learning capabilities, and its implications both for established routines and the development of new ones (Nelson & Winter, 1982; Nelson, 1991; Teece et al., 1997; Foss et al., 1995).

Zeroing down to management as the unit of analysis, contemporary organizational scholars, such as Prahalad and Doz (1987), Doz et al. (1997), Bartlett and Ghoshal (1989, 1993) are paying increasing attention to the harnessing, leveraging, processing and deployment of knowledge based assets as a core competence. While the subject of interest is similar to that of the resource and evolutionary theories, the emphasis of this kind of approach is on the capabilities of management to orchestrate and integrate the resources it can internally upgrade or innovate, or externally acquire, rather than on the resources themselves. But, as with the resource based and evolutionary theories, the objective of the decision taker is assumed to be as much directed to explaining the growth of firm specific assets, as to optimizing the income stream from a given set of assets.

The question now arises. To what extent are the theories relating to the origin and content of O specific advantages, as set out in Table 5.1 — particularly their contemporary versions — consistent with, or antagonistic to, each other? Our reading is that, when the eclectic paradigm was first propounded, they were largely aimed at explaining different phenomena, or offered complementary, rather than alternative, explanations for the same phenomena. It is true the unit of analysis was frequently different; and that the underlying philosophy and some of the assumptions of industrial organization theory were different than those of resource based theories (Pauwells & Matthyssens, 1997). But, in general, within their specified analytical frameworks, the predictions of the various theories were consistent with those of a general 'envelope' paradigm, and also the more specific predictions of the O sub-paradigm about the kind of competitive advantages likely to be possessed by MNEs, and the industrial sectors and countries in which their affiliates were likely to record superior levels of performance relative to those of their indigenous competitors (Dunning, 1993; Caves, 1996).

The locational sub-paradigm of countries (and regions)

For the most part, until recently, neither the economics nor the business literature gave much attention as to how the emergence and growth of the cross-border activities of firms might be explained by the kind of location-related theories which were initially designed to explain the siting of production *within* a nation state; nor, indeed, of how the spatial dimension of FDI might affect the competitiveness of the investing entities. In the last decade or so, however, there has been a renaissance of interest by economists (for example, Audretsch, 1998; Krugman 1991, 1993; Venables, 1998), and industrial geographers (for example, Scott, 1996; Storper, 1995; Storper & Scott, 1995) in the spatial concentration and clustering of some kinds of economic activity; by economists in the role of exchange rates in affecting the extent, geography and timing of FDI (Cushman, 1985; Froot & Stein, 1991; Rangan, 1998); and by business scholars (Porter 1994, 1996; Enright 1991, 1998), in the idea that an optimum locational portfolio of assets is a competitive advantage in its own right.

The eclectic paradigm has always recognized the importance of the locational advantages of countries as a key determinant of the foreign production of MNEs (Dunning, 1998).[18] Moreover, since the 1930s, at least, there have been numerous context-specific theories of the geographical distribution of FDI and the siting of particular value added activities of firms.[19] Some of these 'partial' theories are set out in Table 5.3. They include the locational component of Vernon's product cycle theory (Vernon, 1966), and that of Knickerbocker's 'follow my leader' theory (Knickerbocker, 1973), which was one of the earliest attempts to explain the geographical clustering of FDI; and Rugman's risk diversification theory, which suggested that MNEs normally prefer a geographical spread of their foreign investments to having 'all their eggs in the same (locational) basket' (Rugman, 1979).[20]

However, for the most part, the question of *where* to locate a particular FDI, given the configuration of the O and I variables, was not thought to raise new issues of interest to students of the MNE. At the same time, throughout the last three decades, there have been many *empirical* studies on the determinants of the export and FDI choice of corporations, and the spatial distribution of MNE activity.[21]

Once again, in conformity with our earlier analysis, and as Table 5.3 shows, these explanatory variables are seen to differ according to the motives for FDI, its sectoral composition, the home and host countries of the investing firms, and a variety of firm specific considerations. But, in the main, scholarly research has extended, rather than replaced, standard theories of location to encompass cross-border value added activities. In particular, it has embraced new locational variables, for example, exchange rate and political risks, the regulations and policies of supra-national entities,[22] inter-country cultural differences; and has placed a different value of other variables common both to domestic and international locational choices.[23] However, these add-on or re-valued variables could be easily accommodated within the extant analytical structures.[24] This marked off most pre-1990 explanations of the location (L) specific advantage of nations from those of the O specific advantages of firms.

The emergence of the knowledge based global economy and asset augmenting FDI is compelling scholars to take a more dynamic approach to both the logistics of the siting of corporate activities, and to the competitive advantages of nations and regions. In the former case, firms need to take account not only of the presence and cost of traditional factor endowments, of transport costs, of current demand levels and patterns, and of Marshallian type agglomerative economies (Marshall, 1920); but also of distance related transaction costs (Storper & Scott, 1995), of dynamic externalities, knowledge accumulation, and interactive learning (Enright 1991, 1998; Florida, 1995; Malmberg, Sölvell & Zander, 1996), of spatially related innovation and technological standards (Antonelli, 1998; Sölvell & Zander, 1998), of the increasing dispersion of created assets, and of the need to conclude cross border asset augmenting or asset exploiting alliances (Dunning 1995, 1998).

Contemporary economic events are suggesting that the nature and composition of a country or region's comparative advantage, which has been traditionally based on its possession of a unique set of immobile *natural* resources and capabilities, is now more geared to its ability

Table 5.3 Theories explaining L specific advantages of countries

	1) MS	2) RS	3) ES	4) SAS
1. Traditional location theories. (Hoover, 1948; Hotelling, 1929; Isard, 1956; Losch, 1954; Lloyd & Dicken, 1977; Weber, 1929)	• Demand related variables, e.g. size, character and potential growth of local and adjacent markets • Presence of competitors	• Supply oriented variables, e.g. availability, quality and price of natural resources, transportation costs, artificial barriers to trade	• Supply oriented variables, especially those related to comparative advantages of immobile assets, e.g. labor, land and infrastructure	• Location and price of created assets, including those owned by firms likely to be acquired • Exchange rates
2. Theories related to the process of internationalization. (Anderson & Gatignon, 1986; Cavusgil, 1980; Daniels, 1971; Forsgren, 1989; Hirsch, 1976; Johanson & Vahlne 1977, 1990; Luostarinen, 1979; Vernon, 1966; Welch & Luostarinen, 1988)	• Mainly MS and RS, using traditional locational variables, but also several firm specific variables and transaction costs • Emphasis on role of psychic distance, particularly in exploiting accumulated knowledge based O advantages (Daniels, 1971; Johanson & Vahlne 1977, 1990)			• Some attention given to foli as a learning activity
3. Agglomeration theories. (Audretsch, 1998; Enright 1991, 1998; Forsgren, 1989; Krugman 1991, 1993; Malmberg et al., 1996; Porter 1994, 1996; Storper, 1995; Cantwell & Piscitello, 1997)	• Some clustering of products for convenience of consumers, including industrial consumers • Economies of scale and scope	• Supply related external economies, e g. pooled labor markets • Economies of scale and scope	• Supply related clusters, based on static external economies, e g. pooled labor • Economies of scale and scope	• Supply related clusters based on asset augmenting activities, local accumulation of knowledge, and exchange of information and learning experiences
4. Theories related to spatially specific transaction costs. (Florida, 1995; Scott, 1996; Storper & Scott, 1995)	• Given production and transport costs, external ties and scale economies, spatially related transaction costs are hypothesized to lead to a clustering of related activities. (a) to reduce overall costs and (b) to maximize benefits of inter-related innovating and learning activities			
5. Theories related to presence of complementary assets. (Teece, 1992; Teece et al., 1997; Chen & Chen, 1998, 1999)	• The presence of related activities which help lower transport costs and promote joint economics in innovation, production and marketing			• As for MS, RS and ES, but directed to asset augmenting activities, and strategic networking

Table 5.3 (Continued)

	1) MS	2) RS	3) ES	4) SAS
6. Theories related to government induced incentives. (Loree & Guisinger, 1995; UN, 1996a)	• Especially fiscal and other incentives leading to increase in demand for products of MNEs	• Supply related incentives, concessionary rights for exploitation of natural resource based sectors; intellectual property rights, tax advantages for RS and ES		• Mainly incentives to promote innovation-driven alliances, and the upgrading of existing O advantages of investing firms
7. Theories related to oligopolistic behavior and product cycle. (Graham 1975, 1998; Knickerbocker, 1973; Vernon, 1974)	• Follow my leader and other forms of oligopolistic behavior may apply to all four forms of international production, although incentives and pressures for such behavior are likely to be context specific			
8. Theories of risk diversification. (Agmon & Lessard, 1977, Rugman, 1979)	• Types of location specific risk vary with kind of FDI, but theory suggests that firm will diversify their portfolios to minimize their risk exposures, which include exchange, political and economic risks			• Risks of SAS FDI also relate to inappropriate timing (especially for M and As) and insufficient knowledge about the assets being acquired
9. Exchange rate theories. (Aliber, 1971; Cushman, 1985; Froot & Stein, 1991; Blonigen, 1997; Rangan, 1998)	• Theories which assume exchange rates or changes in exchange rates, suitably discounted for risk, capture most of the differences in cross-border locational costs, and also expectations of investors about the future course of exchange rates. These embrace all kinds of FDI, but particularly that of the timing of M and As			
10. Knowledge enhancing (dynamic) theories of location. (Dunning, 1997; Kogut & Zander, 1994; Kuemmerle, 1999; Porter 1994, 1998; Chen & Chen, 1998, 1999)	• See also SAS column, for 1–7 above. More specifically, dynamic theories are directed to explaining locational strategy in terms of sustaining and promoting location specific advantages in a world of uncertainty, learning and continuous innovation and upgrading of products. Applies especially to research and development activity of all kinds of FDI. The need to exploit dynamic locational advantage especially pronounced in high technology sectors			• Theory is that firms will invest in those countries which offer the greatest opportunities accumulated for upgrading their existing core competencies, and that such a locational strategy is path dependent

to offer a distinctive and non-imitatible set of location bound *created* assets, including the presence of indigenous firms with which foreign MNEs might form alliances to complement their own core competencies. Recent research not only reveals that some nation states are not only becoming increasingly dependent on the cross-border activities of their own and foreign based corporations for their economic prosperity (Dunning, 1996; UN, 1998);[25] but that the competitiveness of these corporations is becoming increasingly fashioned by the institutional framework within which they operate (Oliver, 1997; Doremus et al., 1998). In particular, both nation states and sub-national authorities are becoming more aware of the need to provide the appropriate economic and social infrastructure, both for their own firms to generate the O specific assets consistent with the demands of world markets, and for foreign investors to engage in the kind of value adding activities which advances the dynamic comparative advantage of the immobile assets within their jurisdiction (Porter, 1994; Peck, 1996; Dunning, 1998).

As yet, business strategists, organizational and marketing scholars have paid little attention to how their own explanations of the timing and geographical profile of international business activity need modifying in the light of the new forms of FDI and of alliance capitalism. There is, for example, little treatment of spatially related factors in either the resource based, or the evolutionary theories of the firm; although the role of spatially related agglomerative economies is being increasingly recognized as an important source of learning and innovating capabilities. Indeed, Michael Porter has gone as far as to say that, in the modern global economy, 'anything that can be moved or sourced from a distance is no longer a competitive advantage' (Porter, 1998, p. 29), and that 'the true advantages today are things that are sticky, that is not easily movable'. If this is correct, it may be inferred that as the dynamic gains from spatial clustering and network linkages become more pronounced,[26] so will the locational choice of firms become a more critical strategic variable. It also follows that national and regional authorities should pay more attention to the fostering of immobile complementary assets and cluster related public goods as part of their policies to attract and retain mobile investment.

As in the case of O specific advantages, scholarly research on the kind of L advantages most likely to explain the 'where' of international production has taken on a new trajectory over the past decade. More particularly, the dramatic increase in cross-border mergers and acquisitions,[27] has reflected the availability and price of assets that firms wish to acquire or tap into to protect or augment their competitive advantages. While the exchange rate might certainly affect a timing of the FDI, the extent to which the acquired assets — together with the business environment of which they are part — advances the competitiveness and strategic trajectories of the investing firms, are the critical locational determinants.

Finally, we would observe that, although several strands of intellectual thought contribute towards our understanding of the locational dynamics of MNE activity, these offer complementary, rather than alternative, explanations. This is not to deny that there are differences of emphasis or methodology among scholars,[28] but we believe that they are not substantive enough to preclude their incorporation into any revised paradigm of international production.

The internalization sub-paradigm

Given that a firm has a set of competitive or O specific advantages, and the immobile assets of a foreign country are such as to warrant locating value adding or asset augmenting activities there, what determines whether such activities are undertaken by the firms possessing the advantages, or by indigenous producers buying the advantage, or the right to its use, in the open market, or acquiring them by some other means?[29] Orthodox internalization theory offers a fairly straightforward answer, as long as the transaction and coordination costs of using external arm's length markets in the exchange of intermediate products, information, technology, marketing techniques, etc. exceed those incurred by internal hierarchies, then it will pay a firm to engage in FDI, rather than conclude a licensing or another market related agreement with a foreign producer. In general, the transaction costs of using external markets tend to be positively correlated with the imperfections of those markets. Over the last two decades, an extensive literature has identified a whole range of market failures, such as those associated with bounded rationality and the provision of public and jointly supplied products and common intangible assets, and which permit opportunism, information asymmetries, uncertainty, economies of scale, and externalities of one kind or another.[30]

In explaining why firms choose to engage in FDI rather than buy or sell intermediate products in some other way (the third question which any international business theorist must answer) internalization theory has provided the dominant explanation over the past two decades. Yet it has not gone unchallenged. The major criticisms have been of three kinds. The first is that it is an incomplete theory in that it ignores other functions which a firm may perform, other than those which are transaction related; and other reasons, apart from short run profit maximization, why firms may wish to engage in value added activities outside their national boundaries. For example, firms have abilities of learning, memory adaptation and the capabilities to produce, tasks which markets cannot emulate. Many cross-border M and As are undertaken to gain new resources or to access to new capabilities, markets, or to lower the unit costs of production, or to gain market power, or to forestall or thwart the behavior of competitors.

Such objectives fit less comfortably with the conception of a firm as a 'nexus of treaties', and more with that of a firm as a 'collection or bundle of resources' (Barney, 1991), or as a 'repository of knowledge and capabilities' (Kogut & Zander, 1994; Madhok, 1996). This does not destroy the validity of internalization theory per se. It does, however, suggest that its contents should be widened to incorporate *all* costs and benefits associated with corporate activities; and not only those which are transaction related![31] Contemporary writings, both by resource based and evolutionary scholars have refocused attention on the *unique* characteristics of the firm,[32] vis à vis those of other institutions; as a unit of production, whose function is to efficiently convert a given set of resources into economically rewarding products.

The second criticism of orthodox internalization theory is that it is a static theory, and gives little guidance as to how best a firm may organize its activities to create future assets, rather than optimize the use of its existing assets. The increasing role of innovation in the contemporary global economy and the need of firms to tap into, and exploit, resources and capabilities outside their home countries, is requiring a reappraisal of the rationale for, and economics of, extending the boundaries of a firm. It is also requiring scholars to judge the success of managerial strategy less on the criteria of short run profitability, and more on that of long run asset appreciation. To be relevant in a dynamic context, extant internalization theory needs to explain why firm-specific transaction costs are likely to be less than market-specific transaction costs in the *creation*, as well as in the *use*, of resources and capabilities.

Third, the growth of a range of inter-firm coalitions is resulting in de facto internalization, but without equity ownership. This is most evident in two cases. The first is where the competitive advantage of a firm is based on its ownership of a set of proprietary rights, the use of which it can effectively control and monitor through a contractual agreement. The second is that where firms engage in collaborative agreements for a very specific purpose, which is usually time limited, for example, a research and development project or a joint marketing arrangement in a particular country or region. Here, full internalization, which, in essence,

Table 5.4 Theories explaining why firms choose to own foreign value added facilities

	1) MS	2) RS	3) ES	4) SAS
1. Orthodox Internalization Theory i. Resource or productivity enhancing (Caves, 1996; Dunning, 1993) ii. Cost reduction (Anderson & Gatignon, 1986; Aoki et al., 1990; Buckley & Casson 1976, 1981, 1985, 1998a,b; Hennart 1982, 1989; Rugman 1982, 1996) iii. Risk reduction (Vernon, 1983)			• To capture coordinating and transactional benefits of common governance of related activities; to benefit (mainly through M and As), from innovating, production or marketing scale/scope economies. • To reduce transaction and coordinating costs of arm's length markets and/or non-equity contractual relations. Such costs include opportunism and shirking, and those designed to protect the reputation of the contractor. Most empirical work relates to entry modes. See, for example, Anderson and Gatignon (1986) • To reduce organizational and related risks implicit in (ii) above	
2. Dynamic Internalization Theory. (Buckley & Casson, 1998a; Ghoshal, Hahn & Moran, 1997)				• To tap into learning and experience related assets and to speed up the innovation process. To capture the advantages of Schumpeterian integration and the common governance of R&D related activities
3. Agency Theory. (Eisenhardt, 1989; Jensen & Meckling, 1976; Strong & Waterson, 1987)			• As with internalization theory, but primarily to reduce risks of external agents behaving against the interests of the principals • To reduce moral hazard and adverse selection	
4. Market Power Theories. (Cowling & Sugden, 1987; Hymer, 1960, Hymer, 1976)			• Growth by M and As intended to increase market power, rather than to upgrade efficiency	
5. Efficiency Related Theories. (Caves 1982, 1996; Liu, 1998; Teece 1981, 1984)			• To capture scale related production economies. To raise dynamic technical efficiency through shared knowledge, learning experiences and management expertise. To capture the advantages of signaling	
6. Knowledge Acquisition and Sharing Theories. (Antonelli, 1998; Kogut & Zander, 1994; Makino, 1998; Wesson 1993, 1997; Teece et al., 1997)				• To augment existing intellectual assets, thereby increasing competitive prowess • To capture synergies of knowledge creation and augmenting activities

addresses ownership issues, is not a realistic option for the participating firms. At the same time, most strategic partnerships now being formed cannot be construed as arm's length transactions as the participants have a continuing knowledge sharing relationship with each other (Dunning, 1995; UN, 1998). The advent of alliance capitalism, which may be perceived as a variant of hierarchical capitalism, offers opportunities for new interfirm organizational modalities, the rationale for which internalization theory can only partly explain.

In Table 5.4 we set out some of the mainstream theories which have attempted to explain why, given a set of O and L specific advantages, firms prefer to own their foreign value added or creating activities, rather than lease the right to use their O advantages to independently owned foreign firms. It is our contention that changing world economic events, the growing multinationality of many foreign investors, and the need for firms to engage in highly specific cross-border alliances and in asset augmenting FDI, is necessitating both a reappraisal of static organizational theories, and an integration between 'production based', 'innovation based' and 'transaction based' theories of the firm.

Again, we do not think these approaches to internalization are mutually exclusive. At the end of the day, managers will take decisions, which in any particular context (including those of competitor firms) will come closest to meeting an amalgam of short term and long term objectives. To be effective, these decisions need to take account of, and resolve in a holistic way, conflicts between very specific objectives. It is extremely unlikely, for example, that a firm will be successful, at one and the same time, in minimizing short-run transaction costs, maximizing short run and long run productive efficiency, accessing new markets, optimizing the net benefits of asset creation and asset augmenting activities, and pursuing a variety of cost-effective strategies to improve their competitive position, vis à vis that of their main rivals — all within a macro-economic environment of uncertainty and volatility.

This, then suggests that any comprehensive explanation of the existence and the growth of the contemporary MNE must almost inevitably be 'judiciously pluralistic' (Foss 1996, 1997), unless the context in which the explanation is being made is very narrowly delineated. It is a fact that most new explanations of the territorial expansion of firms tend to be incremental to extant theories, rather than a replacement of them. Any conflict between alternative theories or models is, as likely as not, to be about the relevance of, or emphasis placed on, these theories or models, rather than about their logical construction.

We would make one other point. In discussing alternative interpretations of the I component of the OLI triumvirate, organizational scholars such as Chris Bartlett, Sumantra Ghoshal, Yves Doz and C K. Prahalad, focus on the individual manager rather than on the firm as their main unit of analysis. This results in a somewhat different analytical perspective towards the rationale for existence of hierarchies and the internalization of markets, than that offered by Williamson (1985, 1986, 1990), notwithstanding the fact that, in his various writings, he incorporates the concept of managerial discretion as an explanation for the behavior of firms. Moreover, for the most part, Williamson's analysis tends to be concerned with the efficiency of asset exploitation, rather than that of asset augmentation. Because of this, his focus is more on the optimal mode of coordinating the use of existing resources and capabilities, rather than on that of upgrading such resources and capabilities, by innovating and other means.

Conclusions: the eclectic paradigm as an envelope for complementary theories of MNE activity

In the three previous sections we have suggested that, for the most part, the many and varied explanations of the extent and structure of FDI and MNE activity are complementary, rather than substitutable for, each other, and are strongly context specific. We have further observed that, as the international production by MNEs has grown and taken on new patterns, as the world economic scenario has changed, and as scholars have better understood the raison d'être for FDI, so new explanations of the phenomena have been put forward, and existing explanations have been modified and, occasionally, replaced.

According to Kuhn (1962) and Foss (1996, 1997), an existing paradigm can accommodate several contrasting theoretical models as long as these are not addressing exactly the same questions or addressing these in the same context.[33] At the same time, a paradigm that leaves no issues unresolved is of dubious value as a guide to further theorizing (Loasby, 1971). By contrast, a paradigm shift may be required when new phenomena arise which cannot be addressed within the existing paradigm, or where there are serious and irreconcilable conflicts among the theories contained in the paradigm.

However, we believe that the criteria for a successful paradigm are more demanding. More specifically, we would mention three of these. The first is that the sum of the value of the constituent theories must be greater than the whole. This suggests that there are intellectual interdependencies or externalities to each of the theories, which a paradigm can 'internalize' through its integrated approach. It follows then that the more any general paradigm of international production can advance understanding about the determinants of its constituent parts, the more successful it may be judged. Viewed in this way, we would aver that dynamizing the eclectic paradigm, and recognizing the interdependence of the OLI components not only adds value of its original conception, but helps point the way to improving a variety of the individual theories it embraces.

Second, we would aver that the strength of a paradigm also depends on the extent to which it can offer some generic hypotheses, or, indeed, predictions about the phenomena being studied. In the case of the earlier versions of the eclectic paradigm, we offered some general hypotheses about the nature of the relationship between the O L and I variables and FDI (Dunning 1977, 1980). However, we did not think it appropriate to put forward specific hypotheses about the relationship between particular OLI variables and particular kinds of FDI as the paradigm itself was not context specific.

In the case of the contemporary version of the paradigm, which embraces alliance related and asset augmenting MNE activity, even generic hypotheses are harder to make without knowing whether a firm is contemplating a FDI to exploit a competitive strength or to overcome, or counteract, a competitive weakness. Only by treating the search for, and acquisition of, competitive advantages as part of the dynamic and cumulative process of sustaining and advancing O specific advantages (rather than a discrete and once-and-for-all transaction) can this conundrum be resolved. This, then, suggests that the eclectic paradigm might better address itself to explaining the *process* of international production, than to its level and composition at a particular moment of time.

Third, a paradigm may be judged to be robust if it continues to address relevant problems and offers a satisfying conceptual structure for resolving them (Loasby, 1971); and if there are no serious contenders to it. Here, it would be foolish to deny there are not other paradigms which seek to offer general explanations of the internationalization process of firms and/or their international management strategies. But, for the most part, we would not consider these to be competing paradigms.

Managerial related paradigms, for example, are interested in explaining the behavior of managers in harnessing and utilizing scarce resources, not the overall level and pattern of FDI or MNE activity. Moreover, unlike FDI theories, they tend to be process oriented, unlike most FDI theories (Buckley, 1996). Organizational paradigms are directed to evaluating the costs and benefits of alternative institutional mechanisms for organizing a given set of resources and capabilities, independently of the location of these assets. Paradigms offered by marketing scholars usually focus on the process and/or form of international market entry and/or growth (Johanson & Vahlne, 1977; Luostarinen, 1979; Welch & Luostarinen, 1988; Anderson & Gatignon, 1986). Technologically related paradigms of international production (Cantwell 1989, 1994; Kogut & Zander, 1994) come nearest to our own approach, but cannot comfortably explain FDI in developing countries and in some service sectors. With a few exceptions (notably Gray, 1996; Markusen, 1995), modern paradigms of international trade ignore or downplay the significance of firm specific advantages. Finance related paradigms can offer only limited insights into the growth of corporate networks and cross-border strategic alliances.

We conclude, then, that an add-on dynamic component to the eclectic paradigm, and an extension of its constituent parts to embrace both asset augmenting and alliance related cross-border ventures can do much to uphold its position as the dominant analytical framework for examining the determinants of international production. We believe that recent economic events, and the emergence of new explanations of MNE activity have added to, rather than subtracted from, the robustness of the paradigm. While accepting that, in spite of its eclecticism (sic), there may be some kinds of foreign owned value added activities which do not fit comfortably into its construction, we do believe that it continues to meet most of the criteria of a good paradigm; and that it is not yet approaching its own 'creative destruction' (Foss, 1996).[34]

Acknowledgements

I am grateful to Jean Boddewyn, John Daniels, Mira Wilkins, Stephen Young and two anonymous referees for their helpful comments on an earlier draft of this article.

Notes

1 Ownership, Location and Internalization.
2 As described, for example, in Caves (1982, 1996) and Dunning (1993). For the purposes of this article we use FDI and international production, viz. production financed by FDI, as interchangeable terms.
3 As, for example, set out in Buckley and Casson (1976, 1985, 1998a), Hennart (1982, 1989) and Rugman (1982, 1996).
4 For an elaboration of these and other kinds of FDI (e.g. escape, support, and passive investments), see Dunning (1993) chapter 3, pp. 61–3.
5 The former mainly in the form of the growth of horizontal, i.e. product specialization, and the latter in the growth of vertical, i.e. process specialization.
6 Such activity is estimated to have accounted for between 55% and 60% of all new FDI flows over the period 1985 to 1997 (UN, 1998).
7 As witnessed, by the growth of intra-firm trade both of intermediate and of final products, documented, for example, by UN (1996b).
8 The explanation of foreign direct *div*estment by MNEs is exactly the reverse of that of foreign direct investment. It may be brought about by a decline in their O specific advantages and/or the L advantages of foreign countries, and/or a reduced motive by firms to internalize the cross-border market for buying or selling intermediate products (Boddewyn, 1985; Dunning, 1988).
9 Throughout our analysis, we shall proceed on the assumption that paradigmatic and model building theoretic structures to understanding international business activity are complementary rather than alternative scientific methodologies (Buckley & Casson, 1998b). While accepting the need for

rigorous theorizing and the empirical treating of specific hypotheses, we also believe that encompassing related hypotheses into an open-ended and comprehensive conceptual framework, which not only identifies and evaluates the interaction between the theories, but makes its own generic predictions, provides a useful, and in many cases, an essential, foundation to these theories. We, therefore, view the eclectic paradigm as a systemic framework which provides a set of general assumptions and boundary criteria in which operationally testable theories, germane to FDI and MNE theory, can be comfortably accommodated. It is, perhaps, the most expressive of the research tradition in international business which has evolved over the past two decades (Weisfelder, 1998). For an elaboration of the concept of a research tradition, see Laudan (1977).

10   See also the writings of the Scandinavian school on the internationalization process (e.g. Johanson & Vahlne, 1977; Luostarinen, 1979; Welch & Luostarinen, 1988).

11   For a longer term perspective, and particularly for an appreciation of the evolution of the O advantages of firms, and their changing locational patterns and organizational modalities, see two classic studies by Mira Wilkins (Wilkins 1970, 1974).

12   A generic term which suggests that the wealth of firms and countries is increasingly dependent on the kind and quality of alliances they form with other firms and countries. This concept is explored in more detail in Dunning (1995).

13   Which elsewhere (Dunning, 1997), we suggest represents a new stage in the development of market based capitalism, the previous two stages being land based and machine based capitalism.

14   The origins of the paradigm date back to 1958, when the distinction between the O advantages of firms and the L advantages of countries was first made, in a study by the present author, of American investment in British manufacturing industry (Dunning, 1958, revised 1998). The I component was not explicitly added until 1977, although some of the reasons why firms prefer to engage in FDI rather than cross-border licensing *et al* agreements were acknowledged by the author and other scholars in the early 1970s. (See the 1998 revised edition of Dunning, 1958, Chapter 11.)

15   Implicitly or explicitly, this assumes some immobility of factors of production, including created assets, and that factor markets are not fully contestable. Much earlier, several kinds of competitive advantages specific to *foreign* owned and *domestic* firms were identified by such scholars as Dunning (1958), Brash (1966) and Safarian (1966).

16   For a full bibliography, see Barney (1991), Conner (1991), Conner and Prahalad (1996), Cantwell (1994) and Dosi et al. (1988); Foss et al. (1995); Saviotti and Metcalfe (1991). See also the writings of Teece (1981, 1984, 1992) and of Teece et al. (1997).

17   Which includes minimizing the transaction costs and of maximizing the benefits of innovation, learning and accumulated knowledge.

18   Unlike with internalization theory, where the locational decision is normally taken to be independent of the modality of resource transference.

19   One of the first of these studies was that of Frank Southard in 1931 on the locational determinants of US FDI in Europe (Southard, 1931).

20   Earlier, Agmon and Lessard (1977) had suggested that US MNEs commanded a higher price than their uninational counterparts because individual investors looked on the former as a means of internationally diversifying their investment portfolios.

21   For a survey of these studies, see, for example, Dunning (1993) and Caves (1996).

22   See particularly the impact of WTO agreements and dispute settlements on the locational decisions of MNEs, as documented by Brewer and Young (1999).

23   Notably, wage levels, demand patterns, policy related variables, supply capabilities and infrastructure.

24   As set out in textbooks on location theory, e.g. Lloyd and Dicken (1977) and Dicken (1998).

25   Especially small states like Switzerland, Belgium and Sweden.

26   Chen and Chen (1998, 1999) have argued that the access to foreign located networks would both augment the O specific advantages of the investing firms, and enable firms which otherwise do not engage in FDI, so to do. The authors back up their assertion that FDI might act as a conduit for strategic linkages by drawing upon the experiences of Taiwanese firms.

27   Which, within the Triad of countries, are estimated to have accounted for around three-fifths of all new FDI between 1985 and 1995 (UN, 1998).

28   For example, there are several socio-economic and geographical theories of the rationale for industrial clustering, see, for example, Storper (1995).

29   E.g. by a subcontracting, or turn-key, agreement.

30 For two recent explanations of the various kinds of market failure and the response of firms and governments to these, see Lipsey (1997) and Meyer (1998).
31 I am grateful for one reviewer of this paper who pointed out that orthodox internalization theory addresses a single question, "where are the boundaries of the firm drawn?". I agree. But, up to now, this particular question has been approached mainly from a transaction cost perspective, which, I would argue, cannot cope with all the issues raised by it.
32 As compared with markets.
33 Thus, for example, although the transaction cost and resource based theories of the firm offer alternative predictions of the behavior of firms, they, in fact, are addressing different aspects of that behavior, e.g. the former is concerned with defining the boundaries of a firm's activities and the latter with the origins of its competitive advantages.
34 For a somewhat different, and highly refreshing, approach to some of the concepts dealt with in this paper, see a recently published article by Boddewyn and Iyer (1999).

References

Agmon, T., & Lessard, D. R. (1977). Investor recognition of corporate international diversification. *Journal of Finance*, 32, 1049–55.

Aliber, R. Z. (1971). The multinational enterprise in a multiple currency world. In J. H. Dunning, *The Multinational Enterprise* (pp. 49–56). London: Allen and Unwin.

Anderson, E., & Gatignon, H. (1986). Modes of foreign entry: transaction costs and propositions. *Journal of International Business Studies*, 17, 1–26.

Antonelli, C. (1998). Localized technological change and the evolution of standards as economic institutions. In A. D. Chandler Jr., P. Hagström, & O. Sölvell, *The Dynamic Firm* (pp. 78–100). Oxford University Press: Oxford.

Aoki, M., Gustafson, B., & Williamson, O. E. (1990). *The firm as a nexus of treaties*. London and Newbury Park (CA): Sage Publications.

Audretsch, D. B. (1998). Agglomeration and the location of economic activity. *Oxford Review of Economic Policy*, 14 (2), 18–29.

Bain, J. S. (1956). *Barriers to new competition*. Cambridge (Mass): Harvard University Press.

Barney, J. B. (1991). Firm resources and sustained competitive advantage. *Journal of Management*, 17, 99–120.

Bartlett, C. G., & Ghoshal, S. (1989). *Managing across national borders: the transnational solution*. Cambridge (Mass): Harvard Business School Press.

Bartlett, C. G., & Ghoshal, S. (1993). Beyond the M-form: towards a managerial theory of the firm. *Strategic Management Journal*, 14 (1), 23–46.

Blonigen, B. A. (1997). Firm-specific assets and the link between exchange rates and foreign direct investment. *American Economic Review*, 87 (3), 447–65.

Boddewyn, J. J. (1985). Foreign divestment theory: Is it the reverse of FDI theory? *Weltwirtschaftliches Archiv*, 119, 345–55.

Boddewyn, J. J., & Iyer, G. (1999). International business research: Beyond déjà vu. *International Management Review*.

Brash, D. T. (1966). *American investment in Australian industry*. Canberra: Australian University Press.

Brewer, T., & Young, S. (1999). The Effects on Firms' Strategic Choices of the WTO Trade Investment Regime. Paper presented to a conference on *The Locational Determinants of Multinational Firms*, Paris, June.

Buckley, P. J. (1996). The role of management in international business theory: a meta-analysis and integration of the literature on international business and international management. *Management International Review*, 36 (1, Special Issue), 7–54.

Buckley, P. J., & Casson, M. C. (1976). *The future of the multinational enterprise*. London: Macmillan.

Buckley, P. J., & Casson, M. C. (1981). The optimal timing of a foreign direct investment. *Economic Journal*, 91, 75–87.

Buckley, P. J., & Casson, M. C. (1985). *The economic theory of the multinational enterprise*. London: Macmillan.

Buckley, P. J., & Casson, M. C. (1998a). Models of the multinational enterprise. *Journal of International Business Studies*, *29* (1), 21–44.

Buckley, P. J., & Casson, M. C. (1998b). Analyzing foreign market entry strategies; extending the internalization approach. *Journal of International Business Studies*, *29* (3), 539–62.

Cantwell, J. A. (1989). *Technological innovation and multinational corporations*. Oxford: Basil Blackwell.

Cantwell, J. A. (1994). *Transnational corporations and innovatory activities, United Nations library on transnational corporations, Vol. 17*. London: Routledge.

Cantwell, J. A., & Piscitello, L. (1997). The emergence of corporate international networks for the accumulation of dispersed technological competence. Reading: Department of Economics, Discussion Paper 5 in International Investment and Management Series BX, No. 238, October.

Caves, R. E. (1971). Industrial corporations: the industrial economics of foreign investment. *Economica*, *38*, 1–27.

Caves, R. E. (1974). Causes of direct investment: foreign firms shares in Canadian and United Kingdom manufacturing industries. *Review of Economics and Statistics*, *56*, 272–93.

Caves, R. E. (1982). *Multinational firms and economic analysis*. (1st ed). Cambridge: Cambridge University Press.

Caves, R. E. (1996). *Multinational firms and economic analysis*. (2nd ed). Cambridge: Cambridge University Press.

Cavusgil, S. T. (1980). On the internationalization process of the firm. *European Research*, *8* (6), 273–81.

Chen, H., & Chen, T.-J. (1998). Network linkages and location choice in foreign direct investment. *Journal of International Business Studies*, *29* (3), 445–68.

Chen, T. J., & Chen, H. (1999). Resource Advantages and Resource Linkages in Foreign Direct Investment. Paper presented to 7th International Conference on MNEs, Taipei, Chinese Culture University, December.

Conner, K. (1991). A historical comparison of resource based theory and five schools of thought within industrial organization economics. Do we have a new theory of the firm? *Journal of Management*, *17*, 121–54.

Conner, K. R., & Prahalad, C. K. (1996). A resource based theory of the firm: knowledge versus opportunism. *Organizational Science*, *7* (5), 477–501.

Cowling, K., & Sugden, R. L. (1987). *Transnational monopoly capitalism*. Brighton: Wheatsheaf.

Cushman, D. O. (1985). Real exchange rate risk, expectations and the level of direct investment. *Review of Economics and Statistics*, *67*, 297–308.

Daniels, J. D. (1971). *Recent foreign direct investment in the United States*. New York: Praeger.

Dicken, P. (1998). *Global shift*. (3rd ed). New York and London: The Guilford Press.

Doremus, P. N., Keller, W. W., Pauly, L. W., & Reich, S. (1998). *The myth of the global corporation*. Princeton: Princeton University Press.

Dosi, G., Freeman, C., Nelson, R., Silverberg, G., & Soete, L. (1988). *Technical change and economic theory*. London: Pinter Publishers.

Doz, Y. L., Asakawa, K., Santos, J. F. P., & Williamson, P. J. (1997). The Metanational corporation. Fontainebleau, France: INSEAD Working Paper 97/60/SM.

Doz, Y. L., & Santos, J. F. P. (1997). *On the management of knowledge: from the transparency of collocation and cosetting to the quandary of dispersion and differentiation*. Fontainbleau, France: INSEAD, mimeo.

Dunning, J. H. (1958). *American investment in British manufacturing industry*. London: George Allen and Unwin. (New, revised and updated edition, London: Routledge, 1998.)

Dunning, J. H. (1977). Trade, location of economic activity and the MNE: A search for an eclectic approach. In B. Ohlin, P. O. Hesselborn, & P. M. Wijkman, *The international allocation of economic activity* (pp. 395–418). London: Macmillan.

Dunning, J. H. (1980). Towards an eclectic theory of international production: some empirical tests. *Journal of International Business Studies*, *11* (1), 9–31.

Dunning, J. H. (1988). *Explaining international production*. London: Unwin Hyman.

Dunning, J. H. (1993). *Multinational enterprises and the global economy*. Wokingham, Berkshire: Addison Wesley.

Dunning, J. H. (1995). Reappraising the eclectic paradigm in the age of alliance capitalism. *Journal of International Business Studies*, *26*, 461–91.

Dunning, J. H. (1996). The geographical sources of competitiveness of firms: the results of a new survey. *Transnational Corporations*, *5* (3), 1–30.

Dunning, J. H. (1997). Technology and the changing boundaries of firms and governments In OECD, *Industrial competitiveness and the global economy* (pp. 53–68), Paris: OECD.

Dunning, J. H. (1998). Location and the multinational enterprise: a neglected factor. *Journal of International Business Studies*, *29* (1), 45–66.

Dunning, J. H. (1999). Globalization and the theory of MNE activity. In N. Hood, & S. Young, *The globalization of multinational enterprise activity* (pp. 21–54). London: Macmillan.

Eisenhardt, K. M. (1989). Agency theory: an assessment and review. *Academy of Management Review*, *14* (1), 57–73.

Enright, M. J. (1991). *Geographic concentration and industrial organization*. Ph.D. dissertation, Harvard, Cambridge, Mass.

Enright, M. J. (1998). Regional clusters and firm strategy. In A. D. Chandler Jr., P. Hagstrom, & O. Sölvell, *The dynamic firm* (pp. 315–43). Oxford: Oxford University Press.

Florida, R. (1995). Towards the learning region. *Futures*, *27* (5), 527–36.

Flowers, E. B. (1976). Oligopolistic reaction in European and Canadian direct investment in the United States. *Journal of International Business Studies*, *7*, 43–55.

Forsgren, M. (1989). *Managing the internalization process: the Swedish case*. London and New York: Routledge.

Foss, N. J. (1996). Research in strategy, economics and Michael Porter. *Journal of Management Studies*, *33* (1), 1–24.

Foss, N. J. (1997). *Resources, firms and strategies*. Oxford: Oxford University Press.

Foss, N. J., Knudsen, C., & Montgomery, C. A. (1995). An exploration of common ground: integrating resource based and evolutionary theories of the firm. In C. A. Montgomery, *Resource based and evolutionary theories of the firm: towards a synthesis*. Boston and London: Kluwer Academic Publishers.

Froot, K. A., & Stein, J. C. (1991). Exchange rates and foreign direct investment: an imperfect market's approach. *Quarterly Journal of Economics*, *106*, 1191–217.

Ghoshal, S., Hahn, M., & Moran, P. (1997). Management competence, firm growth and economic progress. Fontainebleau, France: INSEAD Working Paper 97/21/SM.

Graham, E. M. (1975). *Oligopolistic imitation and European direct investment in the United States*. Unpublished D.B.A. dissertation, Harvard University.

Graham, E. M. (1990). Exchange of threat between multinational firms as an infinitely repeated noncooperative game. *International Trade Journal*, *4* (3), 259–77.

Graham, E. M. (1998). Market structure and the multinational enterprise: a game-theoretic approach. *Journal of International Business Studies*, *29* (1), 67–84.

Gray, H. P. (1996). *Incorporating Firm Specific Variables into Trade Theory*. Newark: Rutgers University, mimeo.

Helleloid, D. (1992). A resource based theory of the multinational enterprise. Seattle, Washington: University of Washington, mimeo.

Hennart, J. F. (1982). *A theory of multinational enterprise*. Ann Arbor, MI: University of Michigan Press.

Hennart, J. F. (1989). The transaction cost theory of the multinational enterprise. In C. N. Pitelis, & R. Sugden, *The nature of the transnational firm* (pp. 81–116). London: Routledge.

Hirsch, S. (1976). An international trade and investment theory of the firm. *Oxford Economic Papers*, *28*, 258–70.

Hoover, E. M. (1948). *The location of economic activity*. New York: McGraw Hill.

Hotelling, H. (1929). Stability in competition. *Economic Journal*, *29*, 41–57.

Hymer, S. H. (1960). *The international operation of national firms: a study of direct investment*. Ph.D. dissertation, M.I.T. (Published by M.I.T. Press in 1976).

Isard, W. (1956). *Location and the space economy*. New York: John Wiley.

Jensen, M., & Meckling, W. (1976). Theory of the firm: managerial behavior, agency costs, township structure. *Journal of Financial Economics*, *3*, 305–60.

Johanson, J., & Vahlne, J. E. (1977). The internationalization process of the firm — a model of knowledge development and increasing market commitments. *Journal of International Business Studies*, *8*, 23–32.

Johanson, J., & Vahlne, J. E. (1990). The mechanism of internationalization. *International Marketing Review*, *74* (4), 11–24.

Knickerbocker, F. T. (1973). *Oligopolistic reaction and the multinational enterprise*. Cambridge (MA): Harvard University Press.

Kobrin, S. (1999). Development after industrialization: Poor countries in an electronically integrated global economy. In: N. Hood & S. Young, *The globalization of multinational enterprise activity and economic development* (pp. 133–55). Basingstoke.

Kogut, B. (1983). Foreign direct investment as a sequential process. In C. P. Kindleberger, & D. Audretsch, *The multinational corporation in the 1980s* (pp. 38–56). Cambridge, Mass: MIT Press.

Kogut, B. (1985). Designing global strategies: profiting from operational flexibility. *Sloan Management Review*, *26*, 27–38.

Kogut, B., & Kulatilaka, N. (1994). Operational flexibility, global manufacturing and the option value of a multinational network. *Management Service*, *40* (1), 123–39.

Kogut, B., & Zander, U. (1994). Knowledge of the firm and the evolutionary theory of the multinational corporation. *Journal of International Business Studies*, *24* (4), 625–46.

Krugman, P. R. (1991). *Geography and trade*. Cambridge (MA): MIT Press.

Krugman, P. R. (1993). On the relationship between trade theory and location theory. *Review of International Economics*, *1* (2), 110–22.

Krugman, P. R. (1998). What's new about the new economic geography? *Oxford Review of Economic Policy*, *14* (2), 7–17.

Kuemmerle, W. (1999). The drivers of foreign direct investment into research and development: an empirical investigation. *Journal of International Business Studies*, *30* (1), 1–24.

Kuhn, T. S. (1962). *The structure of scientific revolutions*. Chicago: Chicago University Press.

Laudan, L. (1977). *Progress and its problems: towards a theory of scientific growth*. Berkeley (CA): University of California Press.

Lipsey, R. G. (1997). Globalization and national government policies: an economists view. In J. H. Dunning, *Governments, globalization and international business*. Oxford: Oxford University Press.

Liu, S. X. (1998). *Foreign direct investment and the multinational enterprise. A re-examination using signaling theory*. Westport, Conn: Greenwood Publishing.

Lloyd, P., & Dicken, P. (1977). *Location in space*. London: Harper and Row.

Loasby, B. J. (1971). Hypothesis and paradigm in the theory of the firm. *Economic Journal*, *81*, 863–85.

Loree, D. W., & Guisinger, S. E. (1995). Policy and non-policy determinants of US equity foreign direct investment. *Journal of International Business Studies*, *26* (2), 281–99.

Losch, A. (1954). *The economics of location*. (English translation by Woglom, W. H., & Stolper, W. F.) New Haven: Yale University Press.

Luostarinen, R. (1979). *Internationalization of the firm*. Helsinki: Acta Acadamie Oeconomicae, Helsinki School of Economics.

Madhok, A. (1996). The organization of economic activity: transaction costs, firm capabilities and the nature of governance. *Organizational Science*, *7* (5), 577–90.

Makino, S. (1998). *Towards a theory of asset seeking foreign direct investment*. Hong Kong: The Chinese University, mimeo.

Malmberg, A., Sölvell, O., & Zander, I. (1996). Spatial clustering, local accumulation of knowledge and firm competitiveness. *Geographical Annals B*, *78* (2), 85–97.

Markusen, J. R. (1995). The boundaries of multinational enterprises and the theory of international trade. *Journal of Economic Perspectives*, *9* (2), 169–89.

Marshall, A. (1920). *Principles of economics*. (8th ed). London: Macmillan.

Meyer, K. (1998). *Direct investment in economies in transition*. Cheltenham (UK), Lyme (US): Edward Elgar.

Montgomery, C. A. (1995). *Resource base and evolutionary theories of the firm: towards a synthesis*. Boston and London: Kluwer Academic Publishers.

Nelson, R. R., & Winter, S. (1982). *An evolutionary theory of economic change*. Cambridge: Belknap Press.

Nelson, R. R. (1991). The role of firm differences in an evolutionary theory of technical advance. *Science and Public Policy*, *18* (6), 347–52.

Oliver, C. (1997). Sustainable competitive advantage: combining institutional and resource based views. *Strategic Management Journal*, *18* (9), 697–713.

Pauwells, P., & Matthyssens, P. (1997). De-internationalization: a search for a theoretical framework. Paper presented at Round-table on Globalization and the Small Open Economy. Antwerp: Centre for International Management and Development, May 29.

Peck, F. W. (1996). Regional development and the production of space: the role of infrastructure in the attraction of new inward investment. *Environment and Planning Series A*, *28*, 327–39.

Porter, M. E. (1980). *Competitive strategy*. New York: Free Press.

Porter, M. E. (1985). *Competitive advantage*. New York: Free Press.

Porter, M. E. (1991). Towards a dynamic theory of strategy. *Strategic Management Journal*, *12*, 95–117.

Porter, M. E. (1994). The role of location in competition. *Journal of Economics of Business*, *1* (1), 35–9.

Porter, M. E. (1996). Competitive advantage, agglomerative economies and regional policy. *International Regional Science Review*, *19* (1/2), 85–94.

Porter, M. E. (1998). Location, clusters and the new microeconomies of competition. *Journal of Business Economics*.

Prahalad, C. K., & Doz, Y. L. (1987). *The multinational mission: balancing local demands and global vision*. New York: Free Press.

Rangan, S. (1998). Do multinationals operate flexibly? Theory and evidence. *Journal of International Business Studies*, *29* (2), 217–38.

Rugman, A. M. (1979). *International diversification and the multinational enterprise*. Lexington (MA): Lexington Books.

Rugman, A. M. (1982). *New theories of the multinational enterprise*. London: Croom Helm.

Rugman, A. M. (1996). *The theory of multinational enterprises: the selected scientific papers of Alan A. M Rugman, Vol 1*. Cheltenham: Edward Elgar.

Rugman, A. M., & Verbeke, A. (1998). Multinational enterprises and public policy. *Journal of International Business Studies*, *29* (1), 115–36.

Safarian, A. E. (1966). *Foreign ownership of Canadian industry*. Toronto: University of Toronto Press.

Saviotti, P. P., & Metcalfe, J. S. (1991). *Evolutionary theories of economic and technological change — present statistics and future prospects*. Chur: Harwood Academic Publishers.

Scott, A. J. (1996). Regional motors of the global economy. *Futures*, *28* (5), 391–411.

Sölvell, O., & Zander, I. (1998). International diversification of knowledge: isolating mechanisms and the role of the MNE. In A. D. Chandler Jr., P. Hagström, & Ö. Sölvell, *The dynamic firm* (pp. 402–16). Oxford: Oxford University Press.

Southard, F. A. Jr. (1931). *American industry in Europe*. Boston: Houghton Mifflin.

Storper, M. (1995). The resurgence of region economies: ten years later: the region as a nexus of untraded interdependencies. *European Urban and Regional Studies*, *2* (3), 191–221.

Storper, M., & Scott, A. J. (1995). The wealth of regions. *Futures*, *27* (5), 505–26.

Strong, N., & Waterson, M. (1987). Principals, agents and information. In R. Clarke, & A. McGuiness, *The economics of the firm* (pp. 18–41). Oxford: Blackwell.

Teece, D. J. (1981). The multinational enterprise: market failure and market power considerations. *Sloan Management Review*, *22*, 3–18.

Teece, D. J. (1984). Economic analysis and strategic management. *California Management Review*, *26*, 87–108.

Teece, D. J. (1992). Competition, cooperation, and innovation: Organizational arrangements for regimes of rapid technological progress. *Journal of Economic Behavior and Organization*, *18*, 1–25.

Teece, D. J., Pisano, G., & Shuen, J. (1997). Dynamic capabilities and strategic management. *Strategic Management Journal*, *18* (7), 509–33.

UN (1996a). *Incentives and foreign direct investment*. Geneva and New York: UN.

UN (1996b). *World investment report 1996: investment, trade and international policy arrangements*. Geneva and New York: UN.

UN (1998). *World investment report 1997, transnational corporations: trends and determinants*. Geneva and New York: UN.

Venables, A. J. (1998). The assessment: trade and location. *Oxford Review of Economic Policy*, *14* (2), 1–6.

Vernon, R. (1966). International investment and international trade in the product cycle. *Quarterly Journal of Economics*, *80*, 190–207.

Vernon, R. (1973). *Sovereignty at bay*. Harmondsworth: Penguin.

Vernon, R. (1974). The location of economic activity. In J. H. Dunning, *Economic analysis and the multinational enterprise*. London: Allen and Unwin.

Vernon, R. (1983). Organizational and institutional responses to international risk. In R. J. Herring, *Managing international risk*. Cambridge (MA): Cambridge University Press.

Weber, A. (1929). *The theory of location of industries, (English translation by Friedrich)*. Chicago: University of Chicago Press.

Weisfelder, C. J. (1998). Foreign production and the multinational enterprise: development of a research tradition from 1960 to 1990. Bowling Green Ohio: Bowling Green State University, mimeo.

Welch, L. S., & Luostarinen, (1988). Internationalization: evolution of a concept. *Journal of General Management*, *14* (2), 34–55.

Wernerfelt, B. (1984). A resource-based view of the firm. *Strategic Management Journal*, *5* (2), 171–80.

Wernerfelt, B. (1995). The resource based view of the firm: ten years after. *Strategic Management Journal*, *16*, 171–4.

Wesson, T. J. (1993). *An alternative motivation for foreign direct investment*. Ph.D. dissertation, Harvard University, Cambridge, Mass.

Wesson, T. J. (1997). A model of asset seeking foreign direct investment. *Proceedings International Business Division, The Administrative Sciences Association of Canada*, *18* (8), 110–20.

Wilkins, M. (1970). *The emergence of multinational enterprise: American business abroad, from the Cololian era to 1914*. Cambridge, Mass: Harvard University Press.

Wilkins, M. (1974). *The maturing of multinational enterprise, American business abroad, from 1914 to 1970*. Cambridge, Mass: Harvard University Press.

Williamson, O. E. (1985). *The economic institutions of capitalism*. New York: Free Press.

Williamson, O. E. (1986). *Economic organization: firm, markets and policy control*. Brighton: Wheatsheaf Books.

Williamson, O. E. (1990). *Organization theory*. New York: Free Press.

6 The internalisation theory of the multinational enterprise

A review of the progress of a research agenda after 30 years*

Peter J. Buckley and Mark C. Casson

The future of the multinational enterprise

This paper reviews the progress of the research agenda initiated by our book *The Future of the Multinational Enterprise* (Buckley & Casson, 1976, 2003). It centres on our joint work over the last 30 years and is in some senses a riposte to Buckley's (2002) question "Is the international business agenda running out of steam?" Its answer is firmly in the negative.

This paper is an attempt to illustrate the efforts of two researchers to progress an agenda that seemed to them to be important. It was, of course, influenced by other researchers (who, we regret, we cannot acknowledge here), but essentially it has retained a unity of purpose and a coherence over time. The pursuance of an independent research agenda has become increasingly difficult since 1976 and readers might want to question just why this should be so.

Buckley and Casson (1976) analysed the multinational enterprise (MNE) within a broad-based intellectual framework based on the pioneering work of Ronald Coase (1937). The book demonstrated how seemingly unrelated aspects of multinational operations, such as technology transfer and international trade in semi-processed products, could be understood using a single concept: the internalisation of imperfect markets.

Our book explained why MNE activity was concentrated mainly in knowledge-intensive industries characterised by high levels of research and development (R&D) expenditure and advertising expenditure, and by the employment of skilled labour. It also explained why residual MNE activity was concentrated mainly in mining and tropical agriculture.

An MNE was defined as a firm that owns and controls activities in two or more different countries. The analysis was based on the principle that the boundaries of a firm are set at the margin where the benefits of further internalisation of markets are just offset by the costs. Another principle was that firms sought out the least-cost location for each activity, taking its linkages with other activities into account. A third principle was that the firm's profitability, and the dynamics of its growth, were based upon a continuous process of innovation stemming from R&D. In this context, innovation was construed broadly, to encompass not only technology but also new products, new business methods, and other commercial applications of new knowledge. The interaction of these three principles was illustrated using a parsimonious mathematical model that was appended to Chapter 2 of the book.

The book provided a simple but radical analysis of the MNE by examining both location and internalisation strategies. Production in a multi-stage process can be characterised as

*Reprinted by permission from Macmillan Publishers Ltd: Peter J. Buckley & Mark C. Casson, "The internalisation theory of the multinational enterprise: A review of the progress of a research agenda after 30 years", Journal of International Business Studies, 40(9): 1563–1580. Copyright 2009, published by Palgrave Macmillan.

a sequence of distinct activities linked by the transport of semi-processed materials. The orthodox theory of location assumed constant returns to scale, freely available and therefore standardised technology, and that firms are price takers in all factor markets. Given such assumptions, a firm chooses its optimal location for each stage of production by evaluating regional production costs and choosing the set of locations for which the overall average cost of production is minimised. Regional production costs vary according to regional price differentials in non-tradable goods (the price of tradables is standardised by trade), the relative prices of tradables and non-tradables, and elasticities of substitution between pairs of non-tradables and between tradables and non-tradables. Overall average production costs are minimised by the correct choice of the least-cost "route" from the location of raw materials through to the destination market.

This location strategy is complicated in practice by a number of factors. First, there are increasing returns to scale in many activities. Second, modern businesses perform many activities other than routine production. Two important non-production activities are marketing, and R&D. The location strategy of a firm that integrates production, marketing and R&D is highly complex. The activities are normally interdependent and information flows as well as transport costs must be considered. Information costs that increase with distance encourage the centralisation of activities where exchanges of knowledge through teamwork are of the essence. Such activities are the "high level" ones of basic research, innovative production and the development of marketing strategy: they require large inputs of skilled labour, and the availability of skilled labour will therefore exert a significant influence on the location strategy of such firms. The third factor is that in practice firms operate largely in imperfectly competitive markets. This means that, in many cases, MNEs cannot be considered as price takers in intermediate and factor markets. Consequently, a firm that can force down input or factor prices in a particular region will tend to concentrate the production processes that are intensive in these inputs in that region. The fourth factor is government intervention. Finally, location decisions will be influenced by the extent to which the internalisation of markets in the firm modifies the above considerations.

In a situation where firms are attempting to maximise profits in a world of imperfect markets, there will often exist an incentive to bypass imperfect markets in intermediate products. The activities that were previously linked by the market mechanism are brought under common ownership and control in a "market" internal to the firm. Where markets are internalised across national boundaries, MNEs are created. Benefits of internalisation arise from the avoidance of imperfections in the external market, but there are also costs. The optimum size of firm is set where the costs and benefits of further internalisation are equalised at the margin.

Combining both internalisation and location effects allowed us to explain the division of particular markets between domestic producers, local subsidiaries of MNEs, exports from foreign-owned plants, and exports from MNEs. The division between exports and local servicing is largely the result of the economics of location. Least-cost location, influenced by regional price differentials and by barriers to trade, largely governs the proportion of a market serviced by exports. However, this is modified by the economics of internalising a market, for not only can this affect the least-cost location of any stage of protection, but also the strategy of a MNE after having internalised a market may differ from that which external market forces would dictate. Consequently, the question of servicing a final market is inextricably bound up with the nature and ownership of internal markets, which will be dictated by the costs and benefits of internalisation.

The result was a view of the firm as a complex of interdependent activities, linked by flows of knowledge and intermediate products. These internal flows were coordinated by information flows through the "internal markets" of the firm. This was a radical departure from the neo-classical economic view of the firm as a unitary "black box" devoted entirely to production, whose inputs and outputs were related by a simple production function. The new vision of the firm emphasised the internal division of labour, involving specialised functions comprising not only production but also marketing and R&D.

According to this new vision, the firm could operate multiple plants, with some plants special-ising in one type of activity and other plants in another. Different plants could be located in different countries; when different countries were involved, a multi-plant enterprise became an MNE. It was the economics of coordinating this internal division of labour, and not tech-nology, that set the limits to the boundaries of the firm. While technology might set a limit on the size of any one plant, it was diminishing returns to managerial coordination that set the limit to the size of the firm. These limits were reflected not only in the aggregate quantity of output produced by the firm, but also in the range of locations in which this output was produced and sold.

This view had an immediate impact. Previously the market entry decision had been ana-lysed as a simple choice between exporting and foreign investment, whereas afterwards it was analysed as a three-way decision between exporting, foreign investment and licensing. The speed of this transition can by appreciated by comparing a state-of-the art review of the theory produced just two years earlier (Dunning, 1974), which makes only passing reference to licensing, with a synthesis of the theory published only three years later, in which licensing plays a crucial role (Dunning, 1977). Our analysis was subsequently extended to cover other entry options such as franchising and subcontracting.

Despite this immediate impact, however, we were not fully satisfied with the way that we had developed our ideas. We were particularly keen to stress that MNEs should be viewed as part of a global system in which they both cooperated and competed with each other. This global system would comprise interdependent specialised facilities created through an inter-national division of labour. Our account of the international division of labour drew upon the classical analysis of the subject developed by Adam Smith (1776), chiefly in the context of the national economy. We encapsulated some of Smith's key insights into a schematic "global systems view" of international business.

Given a global configuration of production plants, R&D laboratories and distribution cen-tres, internalisation theory should be able to explain how the ownership of the system would be parcelled out between different firms. It would identify the external markets through which the boundaries of the firm were drawn, and the internal markets that lay within the bound-aries of particular firms. It would also predict the characteristics of the firms that internal-ised particular markets, in particular their size and nationality. Finally, it would identify the long-term factors such as entrepreneurship and technological opportunity that explain why certain types of activity are best carried out at certain types of location under the control of certain types of firm.

The power of the internalisation concept was such that we believed that, using such a global system view, it would be possible to analyse a wide range of practical issues in international business. When applied using a global systems view, internalisation theory illustrates how the activities of different MNEs interact with each other. As a result, an MNE's decisions on how to enter a particular national market are embedded within its wider global business strategy. This paper describes how we have sought to exploit potential of this way of thinking in our subsequent work.

We have not pursued our research agenda single-handed, of course. In tackling the major theoretical problems we have been able to "stand on the shoulders of the giants"; writers who have addressed big issues that transcend the specific issues in international business that have been the focus of our work. The work of some of these giants is discussed in more detail later. We have also received a lot of support from our professional colleagues in the Academy of International Business in developing specific applications of the theory, most particularly John Dunning, who was a mine of useful information on all aspects of international business, and who gave us his support throughout our careers. Many of these colleagues, notably Alan Rugman, Alain Verbeke and Niron Hashai, have introduced important extensions of the theory that complement our own work. Finally, we owe a great debt to our many doctoral students – past and present – who have worked on various aspects of the topics mentioned in this paper.

This paper does not attempt to address the impact of our research on other scholars in the field. There is no citation analysis and no attempt to identify a school of thought to which we belong. Our approach is introspective, recording our thought processes and the events that stimulated us to address particular issues. We have also tried to avoid controversy over priority with respect to the emergence of internalisation theory in the 1970s. We do not discuss in detail the work of McManus (1972), Magee (1977), Swedenborg (1979) or Hennart (1982). Nor do we offer a detailed comparison between internalisation theory and Williamson's (1975) transaction cost approach, or an assessment of the relative merits of internalisation theory and Dunning's (1977) eclectic theory. Such issues are best addressed by more disinterested parties.

The structure of this paper is as follows. The next section examines the concept of internalisation, and is followed by a discussion of the principle of rational action modelling on which internalisation theory is based. Then we examine the intellectual heritage of Ronald Coase, on which we built, and describe the historical context in which debate over MNEs emerged. The next section provides more detail on the international division of labour and the global systems view. We then review the general progress of our research, relating theoretical innovations to specific publications. We conclude with some methodological reflections, describing some of the lessons we have learned from our thirty years of research collaboration.

The concept of internalisation

Internalisation is a general principle that explains the boundaries of organisations; its application to the MNE is just one of its many spin-offs. It is a highly specialised principle, targeted specifically on explaining where boundaries lie and how they shift in response to changing circumstances. By itself, it does not explain other aspects of organisations. Progress in internalisation theory is achieved by combining this core approach with other principles to generate a wide range of predictions about different aspects of organisational behaviour. As previously indicated, it can be combined with trade theory to explain the location of the firm's operations, with organisation theory to explain international joint ventures (IJVs), and with theories of innovation to explain the kinds of industry in which a firm will operate. It applies not only to the geographical boundaries of the firm, but also to other boundaries, such as the boundary of a firm's product range, which is normally studied as a separate subject, namely product diversification. Combination with theories of entrepreneurship allows an analysis of culture to be developed by the theory.

Most organisations purchase inputs from independent suppliers and so the question naturally arises as to whether they should produce these inputs for themselves. In management studies this is often called the "make or buy decision"; in economics it is referred to as the "backward integration" issue. Backward integration by MNEs is exemplified by "resource-seeking investment".

Similarly, many organisations use independent agents to distribute their product, or to add further value to it before it is passed to the final user. This is the "forward integration" issue: in the context of distribution management, for example, it is related to the "channel leadership" issue, and in particular to whether a producer should also control the wholesalers and retailers that handle its product. In the context of international trade, the question arises as to whether producers should establish overseas sales subsidiaries to monitor and control distribution operations in foreign markets.

In general, most organisations use a range of *intermediate inputs* and generate a range of *intermediate outputs*. It is the markets for these intermediate inputs and outputs that may be internalised. Markets for factor inputs and final products cannot normally be internalised by firms, as this would be tantamount to enslaving households, but households can internalise these markets, and to some extent they do. The classic example of household internalisation is "do it yourself" production, where the owners of a household employ themselves to do a job that independent workers would normally do instead, and then purchase the output from themselves instead of selling it on to others. The popularity of the "do it yourself" principle illustrates the practical importance of internalisation decisions, not only for large MNEs, but also for individual households carrying on the ordinary business of life.

Internalisation theory assumes rational action, for the reasons set out below. Rational agents will internalise markets when the expected benefits exceed the expected costs. The profit-seeking managers of a firm will internalise intermediate product markets up to the margin where the benefits and costs of internalisation are equalised. Within this margin, firms will derive an economic rent from their exploitation of the internalisation option, equal to the excess of the benefit over the cost.

The main focus of Buckley and Casson (1976) was on a particular type of forward integration – namely forward integration into production from R&D. This approach reflected our view of knowledge as a crucial intermediate product flowing within the firm. The fact that it was intangible meant that it had been overlooked in most standard neoclassical theory.

Two distinct forms of internalisation were identified: operational internalisation, involving intermediate products flowing through successive stages of production and the distribution channel, and knowledge internalisation, the internalisation of the flow of knowledge emanating from R&D. Subsequent writers have often emphasised knowledge internalisation at the expense of operational internalisation, but we have always been clear that both forms of internalisation have a significant role in explaining the boundaries of the MNE.

The gains from knowledge internalisation can be substantial. The most important of these gains stem from what is nowadays called "asymmetric information". In particular, the "buyer uncertainty" problem means that licensees are reluctant to pay for technology that might be flawed, or that might not be so novel as is claimed. Licensors could increase the price at which they could sell the technology by providing detailed evidence to a potential licensee, but this would be tantamount to sharing the knowledge with the licensee before any contract had been made. Unless they held a patent on the knowledge, the licensee could then exploit the knowledge for free. Even if the licensor held a patent, a potential licensee might be able to "invent around" it. Furthermore, if a patent were granted, the licensee might sell the knowledge on to a third party in competition with the licensor, or might make some improvement to the technology and patent it in their own name, thereby rendering the original technology obsolete.

In the absence of such problems, licensing would be a very attractive option. A firm that employed a creative R&D team could specialise in developing new knowledge and licensing it to independent production firms that were better equipped to exploit the technology themselves. The research-oriented firm could therefore concentrate on what it did best, and avoid diversifying into complementary activities in which it had no particular skill.

By comparing the types of industry in which knowledge flows were intensive with those in which they were not, it was possible to identify a set of industries in which knowledge internalisation gains could be substantial. Within this set, it was then possible to compare types of knowledge for which internalisation gains were high, for example, unpatentable knowledge, with those in which it was low, for example patentable knowledge. It was then relatively straightforward to demonstrate that the knowledge-intensive industries with substantial internalisation gains were the ones in which MNE operations were most commonly found.

Once the general significance of internalisation issues had been grasped, lots of different specific issues quickly fell into place. These specific issues included not only the industries in which MNEs produced, but also the timing of their international expansion, the countries in which they were headquartered and the countries in which they invested.

A good example of a specific question is why the number of MNEs increased so dramatically after World War II. The answer is that after World War II opportunities for technology transfer increased dramatically. This was because many of the new technologies created through defence-related research turned out to have civilian applications. In addition, mass-production consumer goods technologies had been perfected in the US during the interwar period, and were now sufficiently well codified to be transferred overseas. Because the new technologies had potentially global application, production plants were established in many different parts of the world and MNEs proliferated as a result.

MNEs did not invest in all countries; they invested much more heavily in some countries than in others. Countries in Western Europe were very popular with MNEs, whereas others – particularly in Africa – were not. This raises another set of specific questions about the characteristics that distinguish the countries in which MNEs preferred to invest from those they tended to avoid. The literature in development economics proved useful in addressing these questions. Technology was harder to transfer to some countries because their education system was not so good; it was difficult to recruit workers who could absorb technology quickly. Political risks in post-colonial societies meant that factories were prone to nationalisation or expropriation. In some Asian countries protection for patents was weak, and so on.

The importance of these different factors depended on the industry in which the MNE was engaged and the nature of the activity in which it planned to invest. When an MNE was planning to distribute its product to local consumers, the size of the market and the local standard of living were important factors. When an MNE was planning to serve a wider market, embracing neighbouring countries, then access to a local transport hub was important. When the MNE was planning a large export-oriented production plant, then cheap labour was important.

Welfare implications were not explicitly derived in the 1976 book. It was suggested that MNEs were "a two-edged sword", improving welfare by seeking and replacing imperfect external markets with more perfect internal ones, but potentially reaping rewards by reducing competition. This assessment paid particular attention to the role of MNEs in the creation and diffusion of knowledge. The indivisibility and public good aspects of knowledge make the replication of knowledge-producing activities inefficient. In the absence of free competitive auctioning of knowledge, MNEs represent a second-best solution, but one that is likely to outperform alternative, more wasteful institutional choices.

We recognised, however, that even where efficiency gains led to overall welfare improvement, the distribution of these gains between home and host countries could be most unequal.

An MNE that monopolises a new technology for the production of a readily tradable good (for example, light, compact and high-value) has a wide choice of production locations and can therefore play off potential host countries against each other to appropriate most of the gains for itself. Conversely, if two MNEs each own a technology for producing the same product in a different way, and the product is potentially useful in just a single country, then consumers in that country can play off the firms against each other, and the gains will accrue most to the host country instead.

The welfare implications derived from internalisation theory are therefore contingent on a number of factors, which the theory itself identifies. It is therefore a mistake to claim, as some writers have done, that internalisation strategies are unambiguously "good" or "bad" from a welfare point of view.

Rational action modelling

Internalisation theory analyses the choices that are made by the owners, managers or trustees of organisations. The theory assumes that these choices are rational ones. In this context, rationality signifies that the decision-maker can identify a set of options and has an objective by which these options can be ranked, and an ability to identify the top-ranked option and select it. The assumed form of rationality is instrumental, in the sense that it concerns not the rationality of the objective, but merely the process by which the best option is identified, irrespective of the nature of the objective.

Rationality does not imply complete information. When confronted with search costs, a rational decision-maker will collect only sufficient information to make the risks surrounding the decision acceptable, recognising that mistakes are always possible. In a similar vein, the theory does not assume that the decision-makers can identify all available options; indeed, in rational action models the number of options that decision-makers consider is often restricted, in order to simplify the model. In the context of market entry, for example, only a limited number of entry strategies are usually appraised, as explained above. However, the theory always makes the set of options considered fully explicit. While rationality may be "bounded" in the sense that information is incomplete, behaviour is not irrational, in the sense that the information collected is a rational response to the information available.

Rational behaviour is not necessarily selfish, as is sometimes suggested; the decision-maker's objective may be an altruistic one. In the context of firms, internalisation theorists normally assume that the firm's objective is to maximise profit. Profit maximisation reflects the view that the shareholders are the principal stakeholders in a firm, and that the interests of other members – in particular salaried employees – are subordinated to them, and Buckley and Casson (1976) adopted this view. It is not necessary, however, to assume that shareholders are selfish: for example, an altruistic shareholder might wish the firm to maximise profit so that his own personal benevolence can be as generous as possible.

In the context of large firms, profit maximisation is a fairly robust assumption. Minor variations in the objective function, such as introducing sales maximisation as a subsidiary goal, do not materially alter the implications of the theory. Any substantial deviation from profit maximisation would endanger the firm's survival, especially in a very competitive industry. Even a modest deviation from profit maximisation could elicit a hostile takeover (except in a tightly held family firm).

Rational action modelling can generate parsimonious models that explain complex phenomena in very simple terms. Rational action models distinguish sharply between endogenous and exogenous variables. Where decision-making is concerned, the factors that influence the decision are exogenous, whereas the outcomes of the decision are endogenous. The outcomes include both the decisions themselves and their consequences for the organisation concerned.

The endogenous variables in Buckley and Casson (1976) included the growth, profitability and degree of multinationality of the firm. A substantial range of exogenous variables was introduced, including the costs of R&D, the costs of licensing, production costs at home and abroad, transport cost, tariffs, non-tariff barriers and the parameters of product demand. The exogenous variables simultaneously determined each of the endogenous variables and as a result the behavioural implications of the model were summarised by a set of simultaneous equations.

The exogenous variables in the Buckley and Casson model can be characterised as either firm-specific, industry-specific or location-specific. Firm-specific variables are exemplified by the costs of R&D, which reflect the skills of the firm's R&D team; industry-specific, factors by the costs of licensing, which reflect the nature of the knowledge used in the industry; and location-specific factors by production costs in different regions. A more refined analysis would recognise that some exogenous variables are both firm-specific and industry-specific, for example, the parameters of product demand reflect both demand conditions in an industry and customer preferences for a specific brand. Interaction variables can also be distinguished: tariff structures and trade preferences mean that levels vary according to the industry, the home-country location and the host-country location.

This classification of the exogenous variables is useful, because when data on individual exogenous variables are missing, the effect of the exogenous variables on firm behaviour can be captured by dummy variables representing industry and location characteristics, while firm-specific characteristics can be captured by residual effects estimated from regression equations.

Rational action modelling can be applied to a wide range of international business issues, including:

(1) extending the theory of the firm;
(2) dynamic market entry;
(3) IJVs;
(4) international entrepreneurship (Casson, 2000), dynamics and innovation;
(5) business culture (Casson, 1991) and strategic complexity in international business.

When internalisation theory is combined with other theories, it is necessary to ensure that these other theories are consistent with internalisation theory in their methodological approaches: otherwise, the resulting synthesis will become a confusing concoction of incompatible ideas. In particular, complementary theories must be consistent with rational action principles. Trade theory satisfies this condition, since its economics pedigree means that it has followed rational action principles from the outset. Neoclassical economic theories of innovation also satisfy this condition, although behavioural theories and sociological theories of innovation generally do not. In certain areas, such as strategic management, it is sometimes unclear whether rationality is postulated or not, and even where it is postulated it is not always clear that the postulates are consistently applied. For these reasons internalisation theorists have been circumspect in combining the internalisation principle with other bodies of theory. Rather than seeking to explain every conceivable phenomenon in international business through promiscuous liaisons with other branches of theory, they have focused on explaining those phenomena that internalisation theory and other rational action theories explain best.

As more disciplines have embraced rational action modelling, the scope of internalisation has increased, because a wider range of complementary theories has become available. Our own research agenda has exploited the increasing scope of rational action modelling in order to widen the range of issues addressed by internalisation theory.

The Coasian heritage: internalisation as a general theory of the firm

Returning to our earlier description of the interrelated activities carried out by an MNE, it might well be asked why these different activities located in different countries activities needed to be coordinated by a firm. Why not use Adam Smith's "invisible hand" to coordinate these activities through impersonal markets? Why is the "visible hand" of management preferred to the "invisible hand" of the market?

Indeed, why not coordinate the operations of an ordinary domestic firm using market forces? If a small firm employs two people, they could make contracts directly with each other instead of through a third party – their employer. Economies of internalisation provide the answer. Employment with a firm provides an independent monitor – the employer – who ensures that the workers do not impede each other. The employer has an incentive to monitor well, because the stronger is the cooperation the higher is his profit. Furthermore, the monitoring need not be intrusive; loyalty to the firm may encourage spontaneous hard work.

This is an example of operational integration in a small firm. Knowledge internalisation may be important too. The employer may have discovered a new product, and while he cannot license his knowledge of this product to his workers because they do not share his good opinion of the product, he can employ them for a wage and then direct them to produce it. Working for a fixed wage insures them against a loss should their employer's judgement turn out to be bad.

Internalisation therefore holds the key to the formation of any firm, whether multinational or not. Typically, an entrepreneur recognises a product market opportunity, hires a team of workers to exploit it (knowledge internalisation), coordinates the work of the team, possibly through a manager or supervisor (operational internalisation), and makes a profit if his judgement is correct. A team can be configured in all sorts of ways. It does not have to be concentrated in a single plant, or even a single country. The most appropriate configuration depends upon the entrepreneur's idea and the best means of exploiting it.

As indicated above, this line of argument goes back to Coase (1937). Coase had noticed that in lectures on price theory markets were said to coordinate the economy, and in lectures on business studies managers were said to coordinate the economy. Furthermore, he might have added, in lectures on socialism, planners were said to coordinate the economy. There seemed to be "overkill" where coordination was concerned. Coase concluded that, given the existence of alternative coordination mechanisms, economic principles suggested that the cheapest form of coordination would be selected in any given circumstances (Coase, 1937). In arriving at this verdict, he assumed that the economy was basically market driven, and that firms would arise only when managerial coordination proved itself superior to the market. In a similar vein, government would emerge in a free society only when state planning provided better coordination than either markets or private firms.

Following Coase's line of argument, we may therefore conclude that:

- Firms do not have to internationalise incrementally; they can be born globally. Firms are created when entrepreneurs identify profit opportunities and set up firms to exploit them. While small ideas may incubate purely local firms, big ideas will incubate multinational firms, because the knowledge possessed by the entrepreneur is of potentially global application.

• Economies of internalisation are not specific to licensing decisions nor, indeed, to the internationalisation of the firm. They provide the basic logic for the formation of the firm and remain of strategic importance throughout its life.

• The advantages exploited by multinationals are created, not endowed. They begin with the initial inspiration of the founder entrepreneur, and are refined through continuous knowledge development. This process of knowledge development involves continuous feedback effected through the circulation of information between production, marketing and R&D. In this context R&D represents any organised activity that converts ideas and experience into incremental innovations in the design, production, or marketing of the product range.

A wider point of research methodology is suggested by this view: namely that the solution to an intellectual problem – in this case explaining the international expansion of a firm – is sometimes best achieved not by breaking down the problem into a set of smaller issues, but rather by raising the level of generality and subsuming the problem under a wider issue: in this case, the rationale for the firm itself. Breaking down a problem into sub-problems can be effective when the basic intellectual framework is sound; but when the framework is too limited, or even flawed, the method is likely to fail.

A related point is that the solution to a problem is sometimes found outside the field in question – often in an apparently distinct but actually closely related field. As explained below, the theory of the firm required to address unresolved problems in the theory of the MNE was already in existence when industrial economists were addressing the issue in the 1960s, but by failing to look outside the narrow confines of their discipline they failed to exploit a theory that was ready to hand. Even today, some devotees of standard industrial economics have not yet come to terms fully with the internalisation approach and the challenge it poses to their preconception that there is something obvious about the existence of firms, rather than something fundamental that actually needs to be properly explained.

Historical context to the emergence of the theory

When economists first began to look seriously at the MNE in the early 1960s, they naturally focused on those aspects of the MNE to which existing theory drew their attention. The dominant theory in international economics at the time was Heckscher-Ohlin trade theory. According to this theory, each country had a fixed endowment of labour and capital, and specialised in producing a mix of products that made the best possible use of its endowments. Each country had access to the same technologies, and all markets worked perfectly. Countries with relatively large endowments of labour specialised in producing labour-intensive products, whereas countries with large endowments of capital specialised in producing capital-intensive products. Each country exported the products in which it specialised. There was no room in this theory for the MNE; it was purely and simply a theory of trade.

The natural way to introduce MNEs appeared to be to relax the assumption that each country had a fixed endowment of capital. MNEs would then emerge as conduits of capital flow between countries. Capital would flow from countries with a low rate of return on capital to countries with a higher rate of return on capital, and MNEs would profit from the increase in the rate of return. The problem was that, on balance, capital flows involving MNEs flowed in exactly the opposite way: from countries with a high rate of return (such as the US) to countries with a low rate of return (such as the UK). A further complication was that capital flowed between countries in both directions at once. This conflict with the evidence was fatal to the theory.

Indeed, on reflection the theory made little sense anyway, as capital could be transferred between countries very easily by the purchase and sale of bonds in the international capital markets. There was no need to route capital transfers through MNEs, especially once postwar capital exchange controls had been abolished. In modern parlance, the capital flow theory had confused indirect (or portfolio) investment with direct investments made by MNEs.

Having ruled out capital as the explanatory factor, economists turned to technology. By the 1960s a number of investigators claimed to have identified a "technology gap" between the US and other countries. Other countries needed to catch up with the US and close this gap, it was said, but they were finding it difficult to do so. This assumption of a technology gap clearly conflicted with the assumptions of Heckscher-Ohlin trade theory. Furthermore, economists who believed in perfect markets could not believe that a technology gap could persist because enormous profits could be made by closing it. In popular terminology, closing the gap looked like a "free lunch".

With trade theorists wedded to the assumption of uniform technology, it was left to industrial economists to develop the technology gap approach. The key to multinationality, they correctly argued, was technology transfer rather than capital flow. The theory of market structure, developed during the interwar period by Chamberlin (1927) and Robinson (1934) was the dominant paradigm in industrial economics, this theory argued that superior technology was a source of monopoly power. This monopoly power could be sustained in the long run if barriers to entry, such as patents or trade secrets, deterred potential competitors (Bain, 1956). Conventional industrial economists took the national market as their basic unit of analysis, however, and it was therefore a significant breakthrough when the young Canadian economist Stephen Hymer (1976) began to analyse monopoly as a global phenomenon.

The political instability of the interwar period had meant that new technologies were normally exploited globally through patent pools between "national champion" firms in the leading economies, but postwar US hegemony reduced these risks and encouraged foreign investment instead. Hymer therefore argued, correctly, that the wave of US investment in postwar Europe was a consequence of US technological supremacy, as revealed by the technology-based monopolies of its leading industrial firms.

Hymer's approach was popularised by his supervisor Charles Kindleberger (1969), who toned down the Marxist elements in Hymer's work, and diluted its intellectual force. It was common practice at that time to postulate the existence of costs of doing business abroad. Kindleberger postulated the existence of some advantage possessed by the foreign investor that more than outweighed the penalty of being foreign. In addition to Hymer's monopolistic advantage, he described other advantages, such as superior access to capital. While Hymer's advantage was specific to the firm, some of these other advantages were not; they were shared by all firms headquartered in a given country, in particular the US. Subsequently Caves (1971) suggested another source of monopolistic advantage – brands – while Aliber (1970, 1971) suggested another non-monopolistic advantage in the form of a currency premium.

The difficulty with the advantage approach, however, was that it failed to explain why firms did not license their advantage to local firms abroad, thereby generating economic rents through license fees while avoiding the costs of doing business abroad. The answer, as Buckley and Casson (1976) pointed out, was that the costs of licensing were usually even greater than the costs of doing business abroad. The industrial economists accepted this proposition as a "quick fix" for their problem, but they continued to emphasise the costs of doing business abroad, and the necessity for a compensating advantage to overcome this.

We took a different view, however. Hymer and Kindleberger, we believed, had prejudged the issue of why there was a firm to begin with. Industrial economists regarded it as self-evident that there were firms already operating in the domestic economy that had reached a point in their growth at which they sought to enter overseas markets. The costs of doing business abroad constituted a barrier to their growth, and the firms could continue to grow only if the advantages on which they were based were big enough. This view suggested that:

- firms established themselves abroad only if they were already operating at home, a view made quite explicit in Vernon's (1966) product cycle theory; there was therefore no room for "born global" firms;
- internalisation issues were important only in international expansion and had no significance for the firm's domestic operations; and
- some firms were born with advantages that would allow them to later expand abroad and others were not; however, there was no explanation of why some firms possessed such advantages and other did not, or how they were obtained.

Industrial economists, it seemed to us, were simply interested in internalisation theory as a device for patching up an unsatisfactory theory of the domestic firm in order to internationalise it. They should instead have been addressing the fundamental shortcomings of their theory by developing a general theory of the firm that encompassed both domestic and multinational firms. Such a theory was already sketched out in the work of Ronald Coase (1937), but the significance of this work was not appreciated at the time. Its significance for domestic firms was spelled out by Williamson (1975) and for multinational firms in Buckley and Casson (1976). While Williamson focused on operational integration as the key to analysing vertical integration in domestic industries, Buckley and Casson showed how both operational integration and knowledge integration worked together to explain the growth of both domestic and multinational firms. While domestic firms profited mainly from operational internalisation, as Williamson implicitly assumed, MNEs profited more from knowledge internalisation because, in general, they were more entrepreneurial and, specifically, they were more successful at organising R&D.

There were therefore three contending theories of the MNE in the mid-1970s: a trade theory with international capital movements, a monopoly theory based on industrial economics and internalisation theory. There were two main questions to be resolved:

- What explains the existence of the firm?
- What explains the existence of the MNE?

Trade theorists had no interest in the first question; they simply postulated a representative firm that operated a single plant that combined labour and capital inputs. Their failure to address the first question undermined their answer to the second; they wrongly believed that MNEs could be explained by capital mobility in a world of perfect markets.

Industrial economists were not interested in the first question either (Scherer, 1975). They took the existence of domestic firms for granted as an obvious fact that required no explanation. Once again, their failure to address the first issue undermined their ability to tackle the second issue. They treated MNEs as a special phenomenon on account of the costs of doing business abroad that they were assumed to face. They postulated a compensating advantage to explain the viability of the MNE. By the mid-1970s this advantage comprised a mixture of firm-specific and non-firm-specific advantages. But they overlooked the licensing option and turned to internalisation to patch their theory up.

Internalisation theorists regarded the first question as fundamental and the second question as derivative. By answering the first question they were able to answer the second question too. There was no need to assume special costs of doing business abroad, a significant advantage when analysing the modern globalised economy. Knowledge internalisation explained why firms were set up and how they acquired a degree of monopoly power, while operational internalisation explained why it was natural for successful firms to evolve a network of foreign subsidiaries.

Of the three strands of theory, therefore, internalisation is the only one to really "hit the nail on the head". It reveals the theory of the MNE as a special case of a general theory of the firm that embraces both domestic and multinational firms. In this theory, profit opportunities are identified by founder entrepreneurs who then build sustainable global markets supported by global production systems and a commitment to continuous R&D.

The international division of labour in a global economy: a global systems view

In the 1980s, evidence began to suggest that some MNEs were evolving systematically into global firms. Instead of serving just a selected set of overseas markets, they were beginning to serve all the markets to which foreign governments permitted access. Some writers therefore asserted that the expansion of MNEs was the cause of globalisation. Others argued that the reverse was the case and that the increasing reach of MNEs was a consequence, and not a cause, of globalisation; globalisation, they suggested, was a wider phenomenon than the growth of MNEs. Others "hedged their bets" and claimed that globalisation and MNEs were "co-evolving".

Evidence also showed that during the early 1980s many mature MNEs had begun to restructure their operations. They acquired new facilities, often through mergers and acquisitions, and divested themselves of other activities, sometimes by selling them to rival firms. How were these changes to be explained, and why they were occurring at this time? What was the link, if any, between globalisation and restructuring?

Because a number of changes were occurring simultaneously, there was plenty of scope for confusion. Unfortunately, little formal modelling was done in the international business literature, and so much of the discussion remained opaque. We therefore developed a "systems view" of international business that was designed to provide greater clarity on these issues. We visualised a world production system, based on a configuration of facilities, including R&D laboratories, production plants and distribution warehouses, spread across the world, and serving a range of different industries. Under a hypothetical socialist world system all these facilities would be owned by a single world super-state. Under the kind of free-market capitalism that characterises modern globalisation, these facilities are owned instead by a range of different firms, mostly private, but some owned by individual nation-states. Because the world is partitioned into separate states, many of these firms are MNEs, because the facilities they own are based in different countries.

Internalisation theory was then applied to explain why certain clusters of related facilities were owned by the same firm. Different clusters, owned by different firms, would interface through external markets, where different firms would trade with each other.

A key insight of this systems view was that the internalisation decisions are interdependent. Furthermore, they are interdependent in two distinct ways.

First, firms are typically involved in multiple internalisation decisions. These decisions are interdependent; the outcome of one decision cannot be fully understood without reference to other decisions. Consider, for example, an MNE that operates three facilities: R&D,

production, and marketing. Internalising one linkage, say between R&D and production, involves the firm in the ownership of two facilities, but internalising a second linkage, say between production and marketing, automatically internalises a third between marketing and R&D. While acquiring a second facility internalises only one linkage, acquiring a third facility internalises two. This demonstrates that internalisation decisions taken as part of a restructuring operation need to be analysed holistically. Focusing exclusively on a single linkage, such as the link from R&D to production, rather than the full set of linkages, can create a misleading picture.

The second interdependence concerns the internalisation decisions of different firms. From a systems perspective, a facility that is wholly owned by one firm cannot be simultaneously wholly owned by another firm, because the principle of private property does not permit this. As a consequence, if one firm internalises a linkage to a given facility, then other firms cannot internalise linkages to that facility, because to do so they would have to own it as well. They may have linkages to it, but only external ones. Thus the internalisation decisions of different firms are interdependent when they compete to internalise linkages to the same facility.

Early writers on international business ignored this interdependence because they implicitly assumed that MNEs always invested in greenfield facilities. They ignored the fact that it is not always economic to add to capacity in an industry when expanding overseas, and that for this reason it is sometimes better to make acquisitions instead. When greenfield expansion is uneconomic, firms can gain strategic advantage by being the first to acquire a target facility. A pre-emptive acquisition benefits themselves and disadvantages their rivals at the same time. Such pre-emption is possible only when greenfield investment is not an option for rival firms.

Having set out the systems view, we then examined how the forces of globalisation shaped the world production system. Following the lead of other economists, we argued that globalisation arose from a combination of exogenous factors, the most important of which were policy changes and technological improvements in international transport and communications.

Abolition of exchange controls and the deregulation of domestic capital markets encouraged international capital flows, making it easier for MNEs to borrow in one country in order to finance investment in another. Relaxation of border controls promoted migration, and gave MNEs greater freedom to post employees overseas. Most importantly, multilateral tariff reductions negotiated under UN auspices reduced the effective protection of manufacturing and encouraged the concentration of assembly in cheap-labour locations. Advances in transport reduced the cost of shipping intermediate and final products, and advances in communications made it easier to coordinate trade flows, whether internal or external to the firm. As these factors changed, so the shape of the world production system changed as well. This induced changes in internalisation, which altered the boundaries of firms.

Some exogenous changes directly affected internalisation decisions. The spread of international manufacturing standards and the strengthening of intellectual property rights improved the performance of external markets relative to internal markets and led to a significant growth in international licensing, franchising and subcontracting. These were all policies that had been considered very risky in the 1960s.

Our analysis showed how changes in the exogenous drivers of globalisation simultaneously affected the structure of the world production system and its degree of internalisation. It thereby explained both the growth and the restructuring of MNEs. It provided a logically coherent interpretation of the changing structure of the international business system from the early postwar period down to the end of the century.

According to our interpretation, the traditional high-technology MNE of the 1960s had a relatively simple structure. R&D was conducted in the home country, under the watchful eye of headquarters, and the technology generated was then diffused internally to production plants in each market. Each major market had its own production plant that used the technology in the same way, with only minor adaptations to suit local conditions. Exports from these plants were usually destined for smaller, neighbouring countries. Tariffs on finished products were generally higher than on intermediate products such as components, and finished products were often bulkier and difficult to transport as well. As a result, there was a high level of "effective protection" for assembly operations, and trade by MNEs was confined mainly to key components exported from the home country to foreign assembly plants.

By the early 1980s all this was changing, owing to these exogenous factors. The consequent rationalisation of international production led to the run-down or closure of assembly operations in some of the larger and richer countries. With fewer assembly plants, the new generation of plants exported, on average, a much higher proportion of their output. These new-generation plants helped to drive economic development in the "newly industrialising countries". Local firms in these countries began to take on component production too. South East Asia was particularly attractive to MNEs because of its good maritime links, and a well-educated non-unionised workforce with a strong work ethic. Mass production of precision components migrated from MNE home countries to specialised overseas plants.

Strategic interactions between restructuring firms help to explain some of the apparent anomalies in international business behaviour at this time, such as "follow the leader" investments. Business strategy in mature industries became concerned more with rationalising existing capacity than with building new capacity, and therefore favoured mergers and acquisitions rather than greenfield investments. The globalisation of capital markets facilitated the financing of large international mergers and acquisitions. Races therefore developed to acquire strategic facilities in newly liberalised markets, with firms acting defensively in order to avoid being locked out once all the target firms had been acquired.

During the 1980s a new elite of "systems integration" or "flagship" firms emerged in many industries. These firms expanded rapidly through merger and acquisition, building global procurement and distribution networks. These networks linked the integrator to an international supply chain of licensees and subcontractors on the one hand, and a group of distributors and resellers on the other. Sometimes described as "network" firms, or as being "hollowed out", these firms ruthlessly exploited the profit opportunities for restructuring created by globalisation. The scope of their operations, and their successful performance, are well explained by the systems view.

The progress of the research agenda

The progression of this research agenda has covered at least five key areas. These are:

(1) formalising and testing the theory;
(2) refining the analysis of foreign market entry and development strategies;
(3) IJVs;
(4) dynamics: innovation and real options; and
(5) the role of culture in international business.

Each of these areas is examined below, with particular attention to joint Buckley and Casson publications. Table 6.1 examines subsequent publications, and classifies their contribution according to the scheme above. Table 6.2 classifies papers by contribution.

Table 6.1 Buckley and Casson contributions

Date and area of contribution	Contribution
1981 2 (Entry)	A rigorous analysis of foreign market entry strategy under determinate conditions of market growth based on fixed set-up and variable operational costs predicting the timing of shifts in foreign market servicing strategy (e.g., export to licensing to foreign direct investment). The missing "short-run decision-making" chapter of *The Future of the Multinational Enterprise*.
1985 1 (Theory)	Development of theory and testing – compared and contrasted internalisation with alternative approaches to the MNE, developed comparative institutional analysis vs cartels, and integrated intermediate product trade and entrepreneurship into the theory. Reviewed the evidence on theoretical frameworks of the MNE.
1988 3 (IJVs)	The internalisation theory of IJVs. IJVs are determined by three key factors: internalisation of key markets, indivisibilities, and barriers to merger. Described JVs as "first and foremost, a device for mitigating the worst consequences of mistrust". In the language of internalisation theory, IJVs represent a compromise contractual arrangement that minimises transaction costs under given environmental constraints. JVs provide a context in which the parties to the JV can demonstrate *mutual forbearance* and build up trust. Going on from this to provide a *commitment* to cooperation strengthens the JV. These novel concepts were introduced and amplified in the paper.
1991 5 (Culture)	Multinational enterprises in less-developed countries examined the cultural and economic interaction between the MNE and the local economy. The performance of a given MNE in a given less developed country (LDC) is governed by the degree of entrepreneurship in the culture of the firm, the degree of entrepreneurship in the culture of the host country, and an interaction term. Some simple predictions about comparative economic development were derived.
1992 4 (Dynamics)	Organising for innovation was argued to be the key factor governing the long-run success of MNEs. The paper examined the pressures on managers in MNEs to innovate, and the process of innovation (from a knowledge management perspective). This was related to internalisation and to the internal organisation of skilled workers in the MNE. Source country institutions were argued to be influential in this process.
1996 3 (IJVs)	Provides a rigorous economic model of intentional JVs, using key factors suggested by internalisation theory in the strategic choice among JVs, licensing agreements and mergers. This paper explains the increasing use of IJVs in terms of the accelerating pace of technological innovation and globalisation of markets. If offered a range of predictions on the formation of IVs within and across industries, across locations and over time.
1998a 1, 4 (Theory, dynamics)	Identified flexibility as the hallmark of modelling the MNE as a response to the rationalisation and restructuring of the global economy. Flexible firms are attracted to locations with flexible host governments. Introduced the notion of "real options" into internalisation theory as a dynamic modelling technique.
1998b 2 (Entry)	A rigorous extension of the internalisation approach to foreign market entry strategy, providing a testable model of entry strategy, and identifying key parameters that determine the choice of modes of entry.
2001a 5 (Culture)	Examines the long-run development of the capitalist system, and pays particular attention to its moral basis and the problems arising from a culture of "excessive individualism" and its social costs.

Table 6.1 (Continued)

Date and area of contribution	Contribution
2001b 1, 2, 3, 4 (Theory, entry, IJVs, and dynamics)	Shows that the rational action approach can be widely applied to produce simple analytical solutions to problems alleged to be excessively complex. "Economy of coordination calls for a division of labour in information processing and this in turn calls for cooperative behaviour of a social nature". This echoes a quote from *The Future of the Multinational Enterprise* that "social interactions will follow different rules in different places".
2002 with Gulamhussen 3, 4 (IJVs and dynamics)	This paper uses the real options approach to rationalise many practical aspects of decision-making in multinationals, including information gathering, procrastination and commitment. It encompasses incremental entry (as in the Uppsala approach) as a legitimate strategic variant in internationalisation processes.
2007 1,4 (Theory and dynamics)	Provides a formal model of Edith Penrose's *Theory of the Growth of the Firm* and derives an analysis of the trade-off between product diversification and foreign market penetration that also makes a contribution to the understanding of speed of entry into foreign markets. The elaboration of Penrose's model advances our knowledge of the internationalisation of the firm by incorporating geographical expansion patterns, sequential decision-making and learning into the theory.

Area of contribution key:
1 Theory: Formalising, extending and testing the theory.
2 Entry: Foreign market entry and development strategies.
3 IJVs: International joint ventures.
4 Dynamics: Innovation and dynamics.
5 Culture: The role of culture in international business.

Table 6.2 Buckley and Casson contributions by area

1	Formalising, extending and testing the theory 1985, 1998a, 2001b, 2007
2	Foreign market entry and development strategies 1981, 1998b, 2001b
3	International joint ventures 1988, 1996, 2001b, 2002 [with Gulamhussen]
4	Innovation and dynamics 1985, 1992, 1998a, 2001b, 2002 [with Gulamhussen], 2007
5	The role of culture in international business 1991, 2001a

Formalising and testing the theory

It was always the intention to provide a theory that was testable. To this end, efforts have been made to formulate an approach that is rigorous and that can, as far as possible, be confronted with empirical data. Buckley and Casson (1985) adopted a "compare and contrast" approach to placing internalisation theory into the corpus of economics and business thinking. Chapters compared the internalisation approach with other theories of the MNE, with other forms of international cooperation (involving partial rather than full internalisation), and with international cartels. In addition, the nature of transaction costs was examined in relation to market-making, and the role of entrepreneurship was related to foreign direct investment decision-making. This emphasis on innovation – technical, managerial and entrepreneurial – is a recurring feature of the research agenda. One of the chapters presented a computable model of the behaviour of a vertically and horizontally integrated multinational operating a rationalised production system where activities are linked in a network through international trade (anticipating the "global factory" structure described by Buckley, 2007). The final chapter sought to test the predictions of the theory using extant data.

Buckley and Casson (1998a) introduced a "dynamic new agenda" for the investigation of the development of MNEs in more flexible forms. The agenda focused on: uncertainty and market volatility; flexibility and real options; cooperation through JVs and business networks; entrepreneurship and corporate culture; and organisational change including the mandating of subsidiaries and the empowerment of employees. Flexibility referred to the boundaries of the firm, which were rendered more permeable through networks and JVs, and to "flatter" organisational structures. It was noted that flexibility is not costless, in particular it increases transaction costs. This trade-off (higher flexibility vs higher transaction costs) can be reduced by engineering trust, which substitutes for monitoring expenses. This implies increased costs in promoting a corporate culture that reinforces moral values.

The links between the morality of capitalism and the theory are multiple. Modelling of the global economy is best done by postulating a set of exogenous shocks that impact on the firm. The firm's response to this increase in uncertainty can be modelled using rational action approaches; this brings in real option modelling, which explains how the firm reacts to uncertainty through information gathering and entrepreneurial decision-making. This agenda is pursued in Buckley and Casson (2001b), where the issues are firmly placed in a systems theory perspective. Rule-driven behaviour is shown to be a rational managerial response to information costs. However, in other types of environment, entrepreneurial innovation is shown to be superior. Economy of coordination calls for a division of labour in information processing, and this (again) requires cooperative behaviour of a social nature. Penrose's model is formalised in Buckley and Casson (2007). In contrasting Penrose with Buckley and Casson, a trade-off is discovered between product diversification and foreign market penetration. This formalisation incorporates geographical expansion patterns, sequential decision-making, and learning into internationalisation theory.

Foreign market entry and development

Much of international business theory has focused on the foreign market entry and development decisions of multinationals. Of crucial importance here is not only the direction of change but its timing, or what factors trigger a change in modes of foreign operation. Buckley and Casson (1981) provided a model of the timing of switches in foreign market servicing modes (export, licensing, foreign direct investment) under determinate conditions, depending on the growth of the individual foreign market and cost conditions. By positing a fixed set-up cost and differential variable costs of each entry mode, a sequential strategy is predicted.

This type of modelling was developed in Buckley and Casson (1998b). The model covered all the major market entry modes, distinguished between production and distribution, and took account of strategic interactions between the foreign entrant and its leading host country competitor. Suggestions for extending and improving the model concluded the paper.

IJVs

JVs represent a partial form of internalisation. They are popular at times of industrial restructuring, because they allow two or more firms to share access to a key resource without merging their entire business operations. The ambiguity of control involved in a JV had led some scholars to question their value. We argued, however, that the costs incurred by ambiguity of control are finite, and can be offset by a range of significant benefits. These benefits are linked to the flexibility of JVs, which is particularly valuable at times of global volatility: JVs allow firms to make incremental changes in one field of their operations without disturbing their other fields of operation. By embedding the theory of JVs within a general theory of the costs and benefits of alternative contractual arrangements we were able to show that JVs are chosen, like any other arrangement, in response to a trade-off that is governed by the same factors that affect other internalisation decisions (Buckley, 2002).

The internalisation approach to IJVs sees them as determined by three key factors: the internalisation of one or more key markets in intermediate good and services, indivisibilities in operations and barriers to merger (Buckley & Casson, 1988). In these circumstances IJVs are an optimal solution to external conditions and a vital component in international strategy. IJVs are test-beds of new concepts because they are a classic device for mitigating mistrust between the parties who are cooperating for the first time. The exercise of mutual forbearance allows the build-up of trust, which is, in itself, a transaction cost-economising investment. The venture then takes on a life of its own as a result of the mutual commitment to cooperation. Investment in cooperative behaviour can generate a reputation for cooperation, which can lead to future cooperative opportunities and enhanced value for the firm. This paper was produced (like the 1976 book) in opposition to current orthodoxy. Cynicism about cooperation was the order of the day, JVs were widely perceived to be devices to exploit partners, dupe customers and steal technology. Much of the interest of the research agenda arises because it has, at key points, challenged conventional wisdom (Davis, 1971).

This basic approach was extended and formalised in Buckley and Casson (1996). IJVs were explained in terms of the accelerating rate of technological innovation and the globalisation of markets. The strategic choice among JVs, licensing agreements, and mergers (the closest neighbours of IJVs) was explained by key factors arising from internalisation theory. A range of predications on the formation of IJVs within and across industries, across locations and over time was provided.

Dynamics: innovations and real options

Right from the inception of this research agenda, innovation has been a fundamental feature of the analytical framework. Indeed, the emphasis on innovation can be contrasted with the monopolistic returns approach derived from Hymer (Buckley, 2006; Hymer, 1976). Buckley and Casson (1992) argued that the long-run success of MNEs will be determined by their ability to cope with the accelerating pace of innovation. Top management attention needs to be shifted from the management of routines to the management of innovation. Strictly Fordist management, reliant as it is on the precise synchronisation of operations within a continuous flow process, is unable to cope with the chance and surprise that is intrinsic to the innovation process. A key success factor in innovation is a high-trust culture that reduces the costs of supervision. The managerial challenges of innovating in a global economy are highlighted in Buckley and Casson (1998a). Flexible firms are attracted to locations with flexible host governments precisely because this is the ideal context for experimentation and innovation, not just in technical aspects of operations but also in marketing and organisational arrangements. The 1992 paper argues forcefully that source-country institutions (cultural attitudes to entrepreneurship, education, and training) have an important influence on the innovative ability of the firms.

Real options are an important analytical device for the understanding of the dynamics of multinationalisation (Buckley et al., 2002). Real options reduce risk by giving decision-makers flexibility to respond to new information as it becomes available. This requires identifying information, foreseeing change, and putting into place a system that transfers information from its immediate recipients to the key decision-makers. IJVs can be identified as real investments that are contractual options for MNEs. Given that sources of supply, costs of supply, the intensity and location of demand are all uncertain, there are many states of the world where JVs (as real options) are optimal solutions to governance choices in MNEs. The modelling of such option structures explains the seeming irrationality of procrastination and delay in committing resources to new foreign ventures, and the cautious incremental approach to investment in many foreign markets.

The role of culture in international business

One of the features of this research agenda is its concerted attempt to bring a rigorous analysis of cultural differences, at both firm and national levels, into its remit. One obvious place to look for cultural differences is between MNEs from developed countries and the less-developed countries in which they invest. The remit of Buckley and Casson (1991) was to examine both cultural and economic interactions between the entrepreneurial MNE and a traditional less-developed country. This paper paid particular attention to the geographical features that influenced entrepôt potential and therefore the development prospects of the host country (including coastlines, climate, trade routes and natural endowments). This was combined with both the technical and moral elements of an entrepreneurial culture (including a scientific outlook and systems thinking) to predict comparative economic development. The dynamics of both entrepreneurship and culture are acknowledged. Globalisation modifies both entrepreneurial behaviour and culture. These interdependences were analysed by using the rational action approach to synthesise a traditional economic approach to the issues with modern sociocultural analysis.

The paper on the moral basis of global capitalism was completed just after the traumatic event of 11 September 2001 (Buckley & Casson, 2001a) and the subsequent attention to the clash of civilisations which that event brought about (Huntington, 1997). The 2001 paper investigated the view of human nature that underlies judgements of morality. It argued that morality is a vital underpinning of the efficient working of an integrated global economy, because it is a substitute for monitoring, legalism and mistrust in companies and other organizations, including government. The moral ambiguities of capitalism are still evident in 2009. Reconciliation of entrepreneurial individualism with virtue (moral behaviour) was a key project of the Scottish enlightenment, and remains so today (Herman, 2001). The analysis of international business is not, nor can it be, a purely technical matter; cultural differences, morality, and welfare issues remain at its heart.

Conclusion: the importance of multilevel analysis

This paper has reviewed the results of more than thirty years of research collaboration and has set this in the context of research in international business in general. In our first book we began with a problem: how to explain the existence of the MNE and the way that it behaves. We found an answer, in conjunction with other scholars. But the answer to that question only raised new questions. As these questions were answered, so new questions multiplied and we soon found ourselves with many more questions than we had started with.

This was progress of sorts, because the questions that we are now asking – thirty years on – are much smarter than the ones that we were asking to begin with. They are certainly more tightly focused. Instead of a single general and rather ill-defined question, we now have a set of specific, well-defined problems. The big problem has been broken down into little problems that are easier to solve. We know how to tackle the specific problems, but it still takes a long time to work through all of them.

Progress of another kind has been achieved as well. Just as every problem consists of a set of more specific problems, so that problem itself is a special case of an even bigger problem. If we can understand the bigger problem then we can solve lots of different specific problems in a single step. But how do we find out what the bigger problem is? One way is to explore analogies and metaphors. We may be able to find seemingly unrelated problems that are nevertheless fundamentally similar so far as their logic is concerned. By extracting the common logic of these problems, and examining it carefully, each individual problem can be viewed in a new light.

There are therefore two distinct problem-solving techniques: one is to break down a problem into smaller and more manageable sub-problems; the other is to embed the problem within a more general problem of which it is a special case. These two approaches are often regarded as conflicting. Thus "detail addicts" who focus on the specifics distrust "big picture thinkers" who go for generality, on the grounds that their speculations go beyond the available evidence, while big-picture thinkers distrust detail addicts on the grounds that "they cannot see for the wood for the trees".

In our view, the two approaches are complementary. It pays the problem-solver to go up to a higher level of generality in order to solve the fundamental issues, while at the same time driving down to a greater level of specificity in order to address practical outcomes. Looking at a problem simultaneously at different levels helps to put it into perspective, and thereby makes it easier to solve.

In pursuing our research agenda, we have engaged with several distinct but related problems. Each problem has been analysed as a subset of a wider problem. This produced an answer, but an answer of a very general nature. Having solved the problem in general terms, we then resolved the problem into a set of specific sub-problems that addressed particular issues arising at the empirical level. Using the solution to the general problem, these specific problems were then addressed in turn.

The careful reader of our work over the years will note that we have modified our opinions on a number of issues as we have progressed. We have not changed our views on fundamental issues, however, because we have seen no need to do so. In some respects, the theory of internalisation is quite unusual as a social science theory in the sense that it really works. There is no need to disguise weaknesses, or obfuscate difficulties; weaknesses can be acknowledged because they can be remedied, and difficulties can be recognised because they can be overcome. Failing systems of thought often degenerate through steady attrition; qualifications and complexities are added to salvage the system until it becomes more complicated than the phenomena it claims to describe, and it no longer has any heuristic value. Internalisation theory, by contrast, has, in our judgement, retained its vitality. It is as incisive today as it was when first put forward by Ronald Coase.

Acknowledgements

We would like to thank Alain Verbeke and three anonymous referees for their insightful comments on earlier versions.

References

Aliber, R. Z. 1970. A theory of foreign direct investment. In C. P. Kindleberger (Ed.), *The international corporation*, 17–34, Cambridge, MA: MIT Press.

Aliber, R. Z. 1971. The multinational enterprise in a multiple currency world. In J. H. Dunning (Ed.), *The multinational enterprise*, 49–56, London: George Allen & Unwin.

Bain, J. S. 1956. *Barriers to new competition*. Cambridge, MA: Harvard University Press.

Buckley, P. J. 2002. Is the international business research agenda running out of steam? *Journal of International Business Studies*, 33(2): 365–373.

Buckley, P. J. 2006. Stephen Hymer: Three phases, one approach? *International Business Review*, 5(2): 140–147.

Buckley, P. J. 2007. The strategy of multinational enterprises in the light of the rise of China. *Scandinavian Journal of Management*, 23(2): 107–126.

Buckley, P. J., & Casson, M. C. 1976. *The future of the multinational enterprise*. London: Macmillan

Buckley, P. J., & Casson, M. C. 1981. The optimal timing of a foreign direct investment. *The Economic Journal*, 91(361): 75–87.

Buckley, P. J., & Casson, M. C. 1985. *The economic theory of the multinational enterprise*. London; New York: Macmillan; St Martin's Press.

Buckley, P. J., & Casson, M. C. 1988. A theory of cooperation in international business. In F. J. Contractor & P. Lorange (Eds), *Cooperative strategies in international business:* 31–53. Lexington, MA: Lexington Books.

Buckley, P. J., & Casson, M. C. 1991. Multinational enterprises in less developed countries: Cultural and economic interactions. In P. J. Buckley & J. Clegg (Eds), *Multinational enterprises in less developed countries*, 27–55, London: Macmillan.

Buckley, P. J., & Casson, M. C. 1992. Organising for innovation: The multinational enterprise in the twenty-first century. In P. J. Buckley & M. C. Casson (Eds), *Multinational enterprises in the world economy: Essays in honour of John Dunning*, 212–32, Aldershot: Edward Elgar.

Buckley, P. J., & Casson, M. C. 1996. An economic model of international joint venture strategy. *Journal of International Business Studies*, 27(5): 849–876.

Buckley, P. J., & Casson, M. C. 1998a. Models of the multinational enterprise. *Journal of International Business Studies*, 29(1): 21–44.

Buckley, P. J., & Casson, M. C. 1998b. Analyzing foreign market entry strategies: Extending the internalization approach. *Journal of International Business Studies*, 29(3): 539–561.

Buckley, P. J., & Casson, M. C. 2001a. The moral basis of global capitalism: Beyond the eclectic theory. *International Journal of the Economics of Business*, 8(2): 303–327.

Buckley, P. J., & Casson, M. C. 2001b. Strategic complexity in international business. In A. M. Rugman & T. L. Brewer (Eds), *The Oxford handbook of international business:* 90–124. Oxford: Oxford University Press.

Buckley, P. J., & Casson, M. C. 2003. The future of the multinational enterprise in retrospect and in prospect. *Journal of International Business Studies*, 34(2): 219–22.

Buckley, P. J., & Casson, M. C. 2007. Edith Penrose's theory of the growth of the firm and the strategic management of multinational enterprises. *Management International Review*, 47(2): 151–173.

Buckley, P. J., Casson, M. C., & Gulamhussen, M. A. 2002. Internationalisation: Real options, knowledge management and the Uppsala approach. In V. Havila, M. Forsgen, & H. Hakansson (Eds), *Critical perspectives on internationalisation*, 229–261, Oxford: Elsevier Science.

Casson, M. 1991. *The economics of business culture*. Oxford: Oxford University Press.

Casson, M. 2000. *Enterprise and leadership: Studies on firms, networks and institutions*. Cheltenham: Edward Elgar.

Caves, R. E. 1971. International corporations: The industrial economics of foreign investment. *Economica*, 38(149): 1–27.

Chamberlin, E. H. 1927. *The theory of monopolistic competition*. Cambridge, MA: Harvard University Press.

Coase, R. H. 1937. The nature of the firm. *Economica*, 4(16): 386–405.

Davis, M. S. 1971. That's interesting! Towards a phenomenology of sociology and a sociology of phenomenology. *Philosophy of Social Science*, 1: 309–344.

Dunning, J. H. (Ed.). 1974. *Economic analysis and the multinational enterprise*. London: George Allen & Unwin.

Dunning, J. H. 1977. Trade, location of economic activity and the MNEs. In B. Ohlin, P. Hesselborn, & P. Wijkman (Eds), *The international allocation of economic activity*, 395–418, London: Macmillan.

Hennart, J. F. 1982. A theory of multinational enterprise. Ann Arbor: University of Michigan Press.

Herman, A. 2001. *The Scottish enlightenment*. London: Fourth Estate.

Huntington, S. P. 1997. *The clash of civilization and the remaking of world order*. London: Simon and Schuster.

Hymer, S. 1976. *The international operations of national firms: A study of direct investment*. Cambridge, MA: MIT Press.

Kindleberger, C. P. 1969. *American business abroad*. New Haven, CT: Yale University Press.

McManus, J. C. 1972. The theory of the multinational firm. In G. Paquet (Ed.), *The multinational firm and the nation state*, 167–182, Toronto: Collier Macmillan.

Magee, S. P. 1977. Multinational corporations, industry technology cycle and development. *Journal of World Trade Law*, 11: 297–321.

Robinson, J. V. 1934. *Economics of imperfect competition*. London: Macmillan.

Scherer, F. M. 1975. *The economics of multi-plant operation*. Cambridge, MA: Harvard University Press.

Smith, A. 1776. *An inquiry into the nature and causes of the wealth of nations*. Oxford: Clarendon Press.

Swedenborg, B. 1979. *Multinational operations of Swedish firms*. Stockholm: Almqvist & Wiskell.

Vernon, R. 1966. International investment and international trade in the product cycle. *Quarterly Journal of Economics*, 80(2): 190–207.

Williamson, O. E. 1975. *Markets and hierarchies: Analysis and anti-trust implications*. New York: Free Press.

Case study I
Internationalization of brewery companies
The case of Carlsberg

Jens Gammelgaard

The brewery industry has specific characteristics that make it worthy of a detailed analysis. It is an industry that: (a) has adopted similar technologies globally, (b) offers a homogeneous product (although differentiated by brand), (c) is dominated by a few large multinational corporations (MNCs) and (d) is highly internationalized. In addition, MNCs from what can be characterized as small or medium-sized countries, such as Heineken (the netherlands), Carlsberg (Denmark), Interbrew (now known as AB Inbev; Belgium) and SAB (now known as SAB-Miller; South Africa), have achieved the position as global market leaders through successful merger and acquisition (M&A) strategies, whereas important players from large countries, such as Anheuser Busch and Miller in the USA and Scottish & Newcastle in the UK, have become takeover targets.

This chapter analyses the internationalization paths of these companies. Investigating this industry, departing from the Uppsala approach, where companies incrementally become international in relation to geographical spread and commitment, the large brewery MNCs follow the pattern we see from other industries in relation to entry modes and governance structures. In the early stages of the internationalization process, the successful breweries concentrate on less-risky export strategies, where they often liaise with local agents and distributors. Next, international joint ventures with local breweries begin to play a significant role. Subsequently, international acquisitions increase significantly. However, some of the breweries that also tried to internationalize but later become takeover targets skipped the initial stages and started entering through acquisitions. On the other hand, the internationalization process, in relation to geographical entrance, seems to be more scattered, where entrance is not always in the next nearby country. One reason is that brewery companies seek first mover advantages and internationalize where there is a market opportunity, rather than selecting the nearby market. Further, competing breweries enter the same market, as "follow the herd" counterattacks. However, most markets soon become under pressure and there is no room for the four major brewers in each market; this leads to a scattered picture looking at the world map in relation to representation. MNC breweries are therefore challenged by global market developments. Sales have been affected by the stagnation in almost all traditional high-volume markets in the developed world with beer consumption declining recently in many of these markets (for example, in Germany, the UK and Japan). Notable growth in demand is evident in emerging economies, such as China, Russia and Brazil, but profit margins are considerably lower in these countries. Global breweries need to invest heavily in order to access distribution channels and to make their brands known in these regions, while average purchasing power (measured in GDP per capita) remains relatively low.

General internationalization patterns

Some of today's major players – especially those from small home countries – internationalized their businesses soon after their foundation. Heineken, for instance, was founded in 1863 and almost immediately began to export beer to neighbouring European countries (especially France) and to the Dutch East Indies (now Indonesia). The same is true for Carlsberg, which was founded in 1847. By 1868, the company was exporting beer to Scotland. Despite this early international trade, the overall trade of beer has never reached the levels evident among many other finished goods. Today, only about 5 per cent of global beer production is traded across national borders. This is because beer is a voluminous product that mostly consists of water, which makes its transport over large distances costly. However, the low tradability of beer has been offset by licensing agreements and, as we see today, by increasingly foreign direct investments.

Consequently, over the last two decades, the brewery industry has experienced numerous small- and medium-sized cross-border acquisitions. Heineken, the most active company in this respect, acquired no fewer than 35 smaller breweries around the world between 1990 and 2008. Often, these acquisitions involve partial shareholdings. Besides the lower risk compared to the full takeover, partial shareholdings offer the MNC a "foot in the door" in areas where a "big bang" market entry is not feasible due to market and ownership structures. Alternatively, such shareholdings may enable the MNC to enlarge its influence in a given country by gaining access to more firms in the local market. The following section will elaborate on these tendencies from one company point of view. The Danish MNC brewery is the fourth-largest brewery and is a typical example of the patterns described earlier.

Carlsberg

Carlsberg is a Danish brewery that was founded in 1847 by Carl Jacobsen. Today, Carlsberg is one of the world's leading brewers with activities in more than 150 countries, in which it markets more than 500 brands. Carlsberg's global reach has resulted in a high degree of internationalization, as expressed by the fact that foreign sales account for 92.6 per cent of total sales, though a natural outcome of being headquartered in a small country. Many minor markets are reached through export and licensing agreements. Only 29 subsidiaries are listed in the annual report as having significant operations. These subsidiaries employ most of Carlsberg's 41,000 employees.

The Carlsberg Group produces 10,895 million litres of beer annually and its net revenue was US$10,695 million (2010 figures). Carlsberg's most important brand is Carlsberg, which is also its most recognized and fastest-growing beer brand on a global basis. Other well-known brands on an international scale are Tuborg, Baltika and Kronenbourg 1664. The company has a strong market presence in Denmark, Norway, Finland, France, Russia, the UK, Laos, Nepal, Cambodia, Malaysia and Vietnam. It has a weaker presence in the Americas. The company lacks operational scale when compared to its main competitors, Anheuser-Busch InBev, Heineken and SABMiller, in terms of volume, investment in foreign acquisitions and growth in turnover. However, today it has a much stronger presence compared to ten years ago, primarily because of its market leadership in the major BRIC country Russia.

Carlsberg's internationalization process

Although Carlsberg started to export to the British market in the nineteenth century, its internationalization adventure did not take off until after the Second World War. At that time,

Carlsberg and its associated brewer Tuborg intensified their marketing campaigns abroad, which led to a tripling of exports between 1958 and 1972. In this period, the two companies also started to establish breweries around Europe and in Asia. An early investment outside Denmark was made in Malawi, although this investment led to a few licensee agreements, rather than significant internationalization in Africa.

This period was characterized by a cautious investment strategy focused on licensee arrangements and exports. In the late 1960s, Tuborg established strategic partnerships, or licensee agreements, in countries such as Turkey, Iran, Cyprus and Brazil, but many of these early engagements were later withdrawn. In the 1980s, investment was made in Asia, such as the establishment of the Carlsberg Brewery Hong Kong in 1981 and Malaysian unit in 1982. Other Asian investments include the 1991 investment in Hite Brewery, Korea's largest brewery. Carlsberg launched operations in Vietnam in 1993 through two joint ventures with Hue Brewery and SEAB. More recently, Carlsberg has acquired Chinese companies. The first entry into eastern China failed due to harsh competition on prices and expensive target prices. As a result, Carlsberg focused on breweries in western China. It now holds a controlling interest in Xinjang Wusu Beer and Dali Beer, and a minority interest in several other breweries. It also has four plants in India through a joint venture with South Asia Breweries.

Carlsberg has made major investments in the German market. In 1988, Carlsberg acquired 83 per cent of Hannen Brauerei GmbH in a follow-up to a 1977 licensee agreement with German Reemtsa group, which included Hannen Brauerei. When the licensee agreement came to an end, Carlsberg took over Hannen. One reason for doing so was the brewery's location near the Belgian border, which opened up sales opportunities in that market. In 2004, Carlsberg made further investments in the German market. Europe was the focus point for Carlsberg from 1980 onwards, takeovers were made, especially in the Nordic countries, but also in countries such as Spain, Portugal, Switzerland, Poland, Italy and Croatia.

However, Carlsberg had always paid attention to the UK markets: soon after its foundation it started to export to this region; in fact it started to export to the UK in 1868. By 1939, 55 per cent of all beer imported into the UK was from Carlsberg. Naturally, its first major foreign engagement and investment was in this market. In 1970, the company entered into a partnership with the British beer maker Watney in order to build a larger brewery in Northampton. Later, owing to some restructuring in the industry, the Danish brewery obtained 100 per cent control of this business. Furthermore, Carlsberg formed a strategic alliance with Allied-Lyons in Britain. The new firm – a 50/50 joint venture known as Carlsberg–Tetley Plc – took an 18 per cent market share. Through this alliance, Carlsberg gained access to its partner's distribution network, which included 3,500 pubs. After four years of disappointing results owing to a focus on discount brands, Allied Lyons sold its shares to Bass when the contract came to an end in 1996. In terms of turnover, the 1997 acquisition of Tetley was the largest foreign takeover by a Danish company between 1994 and 1998. Even though the British became of less importance compared to engagement in other countries, and Carlsberg faced increasing competition and decreasing sales, its latest major investment again was in the UK. This time it was the takeover of Scottish & Newcastle (S&N). This was a joint acquisition with Heineken. At the time of the takeover, S&N was considered to be a leading European brewery with operations in 15 countries. S&N's assets were divided between Carlsberg and Heineken, so that Carlsberg gained 100 per cent ownership of BBH and S&N's French (Kronenbourg), Greek (Mythos), Chinese and Vietnamese operations, whereas Heineken gained control S&N's UK, Irish, Portuguese, Finnish, Belgian, US and Indian operations. The takeover gave Carlsberg leading positions in the East European, Russian, French and Greek markets, which were expected to counter the declining beer consumption in the mature west European markets. Through the full control of BBH, Carlsberg controlled a range of subsidiaries.

This historical overview illustrates a change in Carlsberg's preferred entry mode from greenfield establishments towards acquisitions. However, it is also an overall low risk investment-profile as some of these acquisitions were partial.

Management of the acquired brewery targets

Takeovers of breweries and the immediate reorganizations of their activities illustrate Carlsberg's views on the strategic development of these acquired breweries that become subsidiaries of Carlsberg's headquarters. Carlsberg views efficiency in its production processes and distribution as key to its success. In numerous cases, old production plants have been closed and production moved to new plants. However, opposite cases can also be found, where Carlsberg upgraded the acquired local brewery. One example is Finnish Sinebrychoff, where production and administration improved after Carlsberg took full ownership. For example, new types of packaging were introduced in 2005. Many of the East European cases show similar developments, as is the case with Derbes in Kazakhstan, where major upgrades in production quality, national sales, distribution and management were evident. In fact, the upgrading of the Derbes' bottling line turned the brewery into one of the most modern in Europe.

Another integration strategy is to achieve cost reductions. This we saw in the case of a Turkish acquisition, where cost reductions were made by laying off workers in order to counteract the low sales of the local Skol brand.

Cost reductions, reorganizations, but also upgrading of technologies point to a general tendency in the brewery sector. However, what we will focus on here is the GloCal strategy of Carlsberg. This strategy is implemented in the organizational matrix structure, which is characterized by front-end localization and back-end centralization. As stated in Carlsberg's 2011 Annual Report, this entails "working closely together at a GLObal level while allowing loCAL brands and initiatives to flourish". By implementing such a matrix structure, the company aims to meet the challenges of its industry, which include considerable variations in local markets and customs, as well as significant pressure for efficiency and standard solutions arising from other major international competitors. An outcome of this strategy is evident in Carlsberg's marketing expenditure, the majority of which is devoted to local brands and directed towards emerging markets. This approach allows Carlsberg to decentralize decision-making power and resource control to its foreign subsidiaries, though often within narrowly defined value chain mandates. For example, central coordination of procurement is located in Switzerland, accounting in Poland and R&D in France. Therefore, Carlsberg appears confident that it can derive value by streamlining and centralizing across borders, while it still seems to recognize that substantial value is created locally in each individual market.

At this point, we can conclude that Carlsberg is motivated by an efficiency-seeking strategy when acquiring foreign breweries and that it creates value through such acquisitions. On the other hand, the GloCal strategy point towards simultaneous upgrades in strategic responsibilities. This mixture of different processes is investigated in three cases.

Okocim

In 1996, Carlsberg acquired a 31.8 per cent stake in the Polish brewery Okocimskie Zaklady Piwowarskie S.A. (Okocim). At the time, Poland was an interesting market for Carlsberg.

It was a major, growing beer market with 40 million inhabitants and a per capita annual demand of 40 litres. Furthermore, in this transitional period following the political and economic changes of the end of the communist regime, Polish citizens were experiencing an increase in their purchasing power and shifting their consumption preferences from spirits to beer. Carlsberg made use of its revised investment strategy and increased its ownership in the brewery to 50.1 per cent in 2001 and to 100 per cent in 2007. However, the investment in Poland was initially problematic. Carlsberg's market share fell from 8 per cent to 5 per cent. It took several years for the company to increase this share to 17 per cent, which it has achieved through additional acquisitions. In this period, Carlsberg was struggling more than other MNC breweries (Heineken and SABMiller), who had much higher market shares.

At the time of the acquisition, Okocim was an inefficient brewery and Carlsberg spent €70m to increase its efficiency, making major investments in production capacity and modernization, leading to a tripling of production capacity. Carlsberg also had staffing problems; there were frequent changes in the subsidiary's management. For example, the subsidiary was unable to keep a sales manager employed for more than a year. However, this situation improved with the replacement of the expatriate managers with local managers. This led to an improvement in managerial skills, which in turn led to the relocation of skilled managers from its Polish brewery to other subsidiaries, such as Tetley in the UK. Another example of strategic development was that the subsidiary gained an international market mandate: the Okocim brand was launched in the UK, targeting the 600,000 Polish inhabitants in the country. The Okocim brand was also launched in India.

This case illustrates the acquired firms' reorganization following the takeover, followed by the introduction of Carlsberg's best practices and control through expatriated subsidiary management. This development process is probably linked to Carlsberg's entry process, which was based on partial acquisitions of a brewery with low market power. The case also demonstrates a tendency of some of the first foreign direct investment, which for the first decade was problematic, then changed and become successful. One example is that Okocim gained responsibility for international activities over time.

Kronenbourg

Kronenbourg, a French brewery, was "indirectly" acquired by Carlsberg in 2008, when Carlsberg was involved in the Scottish and Newcastle acquisition. Carlsberg and Heineken agreed that Kronenbourg would be transferred to Carlsberg. The company had been owned by Group Danone but was taken over by S&N in 2000. At the time of its takeover by Carlsberg, Kronenbourg held a dominant position in the French market. It also had strong brands (such as 1664) and controlled important distribution networks. Furthermore, it was recognized for its innovative abilities and sophisticated approach to brewing. However, due to decreasing sales on the French market, the general international financial crisis and the increased regulation of the brewery sector, Carlsberg opted for a complete reorganization of the subsidiary. Consequently, 214 of the unit's 1,400 employees were laid off, a range of minor brands were downgraded and the subsidiary's CEO was replaced with the Swiss CEO from Feldschlösschen. After three years of restructuring, however, the company was still struggling, despite expensive marketing campaigns.

Nevertheless, the subsidiary gained a significant mandate, as the Carlsberg R&D centre dedicated to beer and packaging – a €17m investment – was located in the Obernai location. The Obernai plant already brewed and marketed several important brands, such as Kronenbourg 1664. Additional production capacity was to be added, which led to allocation of production from other Carlsberg breweries. Some of the Feldschlösschen production was to be trans-ferred to the French site, turning this site into a European cluster. There may have been several reasons for the decision to locate the R&D centre in France; one may have been Jean-Yves Malpote, who had formerly served as Subsidiary R&D CEO. After 2008, Malpote had served as Vice President for Carlsberg R&D, which implies tight and personal connec-tions with Carlsberg's top management. Another reason may have been the long tradition in brewing and R&D at this site. Finally, Kronenbourg 1664 was one of Carlsberg's strongest international brands and was distributed in more than 50 countries.

This case also illustrates that the brewery company were reorganized in some parts of their activity, while being upgraded in others. In this case, Kronenbourg controlled the resources upon which Calrsberg headquarters and other brewery subsidiaries depended, such as R&D and capacity; this is definitely a reason for the R&D mandate being gained by Kronenbourg.

Baltika breweries

The state-owned Baltika brewery was formed in 1990 and focused on quality beer from the beginning. In 1999, a modern factory was completed in St Petersburg, which was also the location of the company's headquarters. In 1992, Baltika became part of a joint venture with Orkla (named BBH, Baltic Beverages Holding), in which Carlsberg first held a 30 per cent stake, then a 50 per cent stake. In 2008, Carlsberg increased its share to 88.86 per cent as an outcome of the acquisition of S&N. Today, Baltika is the largest brewing company in the Russian Federation and in Eastern Europe. The subsidiary employs more than 9,500 individuals. Baltika is also the most well-known brand in these regions and is sold in 98 per cent of relevant stores in Russia. The brand was valued at US$2.3bn in 2010. A substantial part of Carlsberg's revenue (approximately 25 per cent) is generated by Baltika.

Baltika controls 10 subsidiaries and 12 production plants. An organization of this size is nat-urally well positioned in an MNC network, Baltika collaborates with other Carlsberg subsid-iaries to a high degree. For example, Baltika has an agreement to share marketing costs with the Finnish subsidiary Sinebrychoff Oy. It also has an agreement with Feldschlösschenin by which the two subsidiaries buy consultancy services from each other. Furthermore, Baltika builds close ties with a range of external partners. In this regard, the company emphasizes its connection with the government of St Petersburg. BBH's brand, production technologies and production capacity, and its close connections with the external environment place this unit in a favourable position. Other organizational units depend on BBH resources. In particular, the external relationships represent a type of knowledge that is difficult for headquarters or other brewery units to capture on their own, such as the importance of managing personal relationships with outside stakeholders.

From an internationalization point of view, BBH's development is of interest. Often, one would associate the international growth as an outcome of headquarters activities or decision. How-ever, much of Carlsberg's recent international growth has been driven by their Russian sub-sidiary. To give examples, since 2008, BBH has established licensee production in Japan, Uzbekistan, Australia, Kazakhstan, France, Italy and the Ukraine. Simultaneously, Baltika has launched exports to such countries as Lebanon, Vietnam, Norway, Chile, Malaysia, Guinea, Panama, Costa Rica, Congo, Syria, Mexico, Brazil, Bulgaria, Mali, Sierra Leone and Romania. In fact, the subsidiary has entered more than 60 markets since 2000.

The internationalization processes at this stage of Carlsberg's history is therefore an out-come of a decentralization of such processes. This brings a lot of power to such a subsidiary.

Debate issues

- How can it be that the major MNC breweries today are from relatively small countries (Denmark, Belgium, Holland and South Africa) and not from large countries (such as Germany, the UK, the US) which also have a long tradition of brewing?
- Carlsberg follows a typical pattern of internationalization in relation to investment (first export, then licensing, then joint ventures, then full ownership), but not in relation to geographical entrance, where the market selection seems to be scattered (for example, first foreign direct investment in Malawi). What could be the reasons for a scattered entry strategy?
- In many cases, Carlsberg enters through a partial acquisition strategy. Discuss the pros and cons of such a strategy. In comparison, what could be the advantages of entering by full ownership?
- Carlsberg is a regional player (Europe, Russia and Asia) but is hardly represented in Africa and the Americas. Can, and should, Carlsberg become a global player?
- Do you see any challenges or conflicts of being a GloCal MNC company? (Being global and local at the same time.)
- Is decentralization always beneficial or does it lead to sub-optimization of subsidiaries fighting for mandates from headquarters?
- How should a headquarters decide where to locate central value chain activities? (Such as R&D.)

Part II
Global strategy

7 Introduction

Strategy provides a plan of action to achieve certain goals and to win over competition. It goes beyond planning and day-to-day decision-making and demands consistency in objectives and actions, as well as a focussed drive and understanding of competitive conditions. In addition to this strategy formulation, an effective strategy implementation is a requisite for success.

For a successful strategy formulation, a firm should have clear goals and have necessary resources and capabilities to achieve them. At the same time, the firm should be aware of its business and its external environment, including customers, competitors and suppliers (Grant, 2002).

The knowledge of internal and external factors will enable the firm to formulate a strategy. This strategy then needs to be effectively implemented and later evaluated to see whether it has provided the desired results or not. The evaluation and lessons learned will provide feedback for the next period's strategy formulation, in addition to the new internal and external factors. This is illustrated in Figure 7.1.

The strategy is formulated at four levels: corporate level, business level, product level and brand level. Although strategy at these levels has to be interrelated and inter-dependent, they are formulated at different levels, corporate strategy is often done at top level, while business or product strategy is done at middle or divisional levels. An effective implementation of strategy is a requisite to achieve the strategic goals set out in the strategy. However, considering the dynamic nature of the external environment, it is often impossible to implement the strategy as it was formulated. According to Mintzberg, companies are always re-formulating their strategies at the implementation stage. This means that companies are always working with an "emergent" strategy (Mintzberg, 1994).

In most industries, strategy is an ongoing process and needs to be adapted according to changing environments and sometimes due to changing objectives of the firm.

Internal and external factors

The main objective of most businesses is to create value and profit for its stockholders. But to achieve that it has to achieve value for its customers, because if customers do not see any value in dealing with the firm they will not deal with the firm for a second or a third time. The product or services of the firm have to be valued by the customers. In the same way, a firm has to create value for its suppliers and employees. If the suppliers and the employees do not see value in dealing with the firm, they will not deal with it and will go to competing firms. The purpose of the firm is not only to create value for its stockholders but for its stakeholders.

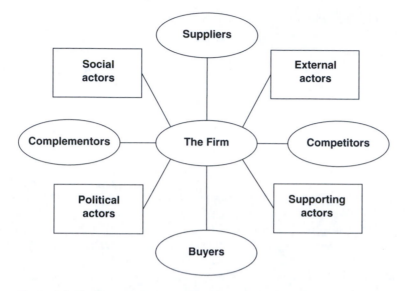

Figure 7.1 The firm and its external relationships.

This is perhaps not consistent with the belief that the main objective of the firm is to make profit for its owners advocated by many scholars (Penrose, 1958). However, considering the impact of external environment and that a firm has to create value, not only for its owners but also for other stakeholders, we believe stakeholder perspective is more relevant than stockholder perspective. This view is also supported by the increasing importance of corporate social responsibility (CSR).

Strategy is also influenced by the competitive conditions in an industry. Different factors in the industry would influence the firm and its value creation as it is trying to achieve better results than other firms in the industry. Here Porter's five forces model provides a good illustration of the competitive conditions in an industry as illustrate by Figure 7.2 (Porter 1985).

Porter's model analyzes the profitability of an industry. The strength of the five competitive forces can influence the profitability in an industry. For example, customers will not be willing to pay a high price for a product if cheaper substitutes are available, also, if an industry is making good or excessive profits, it will attract new rivals unless there are barriers to entry. For example, if an industry has very capital intensive and demand high capital investments, it will discourage new rivals, especially smaller firms, to enter the industry.

The intensity of competition (rivalry) in some industries influences the profitability and will influence the nature of competition from price-centered to non-price dimensions such as innovations and advertising. Finally, the relative power of suppliers in an industry depends upon the number of alternatives available to producers and the relative cost of switching between different suppliers.

Porter's model enables us to do an industry analysis and an investigation into how the relationships between these five forces can enable us to forecast profitability in a particular industry. This will allow a particular firm to position itself in an industry where future profitability is higher as the competitive forces are weaker (Porter, 1996). In some cases, dominant firms try to change the industry structure by weakening the forces that are too powerful to

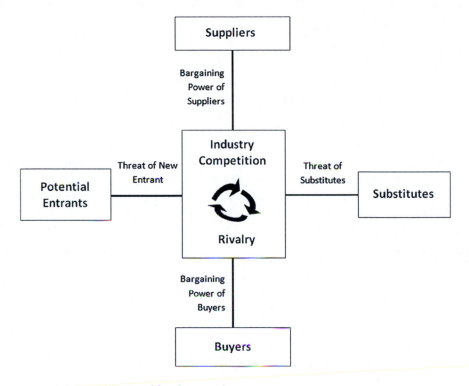

Figure 7.2 Porter's competition framework.

change the rules of the game. Finding a crucial success factor for strategic purposes is not an easy task (De Wit and Meyer, 2004).

Formulating and implementing strategy

Firms have two options for achieving the objective of making higher profits than their competitors. First, they can produce and supply a product or service by exploiting all possible means of achieving cost advantage, so they sell their product at a price that provides more value to its customers than their competitors can. It is a question not just of lowest price offering but the value as perceived by the customers. Second, a firm can adopt a differentiation strategy. They can differentiate their products and services from competitors in such a way that customers perceive them as better and are willing to pay a premier price.

In the cost advantage strategy, the firm provides similar products as its competitors but at a cheaper price. While in the differentiation strategy, the firm is perceived to provide a unique product at a premier price. In the first, the firm needs to achieve economies of scale, control overheads and often find production locations that provide considerable cost advantages. In the second, the firm focusses on branding, advertising, design and quality so customers perceive it as a premier product (Ghauri and Cateora, 2014).

Although in classical literature on strategy (for example, Porter) it is advised that companies should follow one or the other strategy, otherwise they risk being stuck in the middle, these days a number of companies have effectively combined the two strategies and are very successful (Zara, H&M and IKEA are good examples).

The purpose of strategy formulation and choosing a particular strategy is to how best to create value that is better than the competition. This can be done by being in many businesses and customer markets through diversification or by being in only one through specialization. Although many firms believe it is better to focus on the core business and specialize as it allows better resource allocation and simpler strategy formulation that is easier to implement and evaluate, our world is dominated by multi-business firms (Prahalad and Hamel 1990).

These firms are structured as multi-division firms where each division is taking care of its product market and the head office is taking care of the corporate strategy. Strategy formulation at several places leads to agency problems and have highlighted the need for better corporate governance (Grant 2002). The multi-division structure may lead to conflicts between divisions and the head office and promotes rigidities (Bartlett and Ghoshal 1989).

Strategy formulation and implementation is a daunting task, as in addition to the internal pressures, firms have to adapt continuously to societal values, expectations and turbulences (such as economic crisis) to survive and continue creating value for stakeholders.

Global strategy

There are currently few firms that can be classified as domestic firms; even if a firm is not buying and selling in cross-border markets, it is influenced by the events and competition from global environments and firms. The overall objective of the firms is thus to tackle or achieve global competitive advantage. Most firms view the world as multinational markets but are guided by a global vision. While formulating global corporate strategy, managers aim to identify and target cross-cultural similarities but are guided by the belief that each market requires its own culturally adapted strategy (Ghauri and Cateora, 2014).

Many successful firms of today are following a market-driving strategy. According to this approach, firms do not respond to different markets through adaptation. On the contrary, these firms develop a unique value proposition for customers and aim to change the behaviour of customers, competitors and other actors in the market. A market-driving firm claims to educate the market towards better value proposition and buying behaviour (Ghauri et al., 2011).

Whether a firm is following a market-driving or market-driven approach, a strategy has to be formulated at a global level. This means that firm would want to benefit from slicing its value chain into small slices, positioning each slice at the most optimal location on the globe. The firm that is able to achieve these global locational advantages will have a better competitive advantage than the firms that perform most of their value creation at home.

According to strategy literature, most firms can be categorized as pursuing one of the three strategies: global strategy, international strategy and multi-domestic strategy (Hill, 2010). Firms that follow *global strategy* aim to benefit from scale economies and experiential knowledge. These firms perform their value creation activities at a few convenient locations and tend to provide standardized products. These firms, therefore, lack in local responsiveness.

Firms following *international strategy* transfer their value creation experience and products that have been developed at home to foreign markets that lack in this experience and capabilities. Although these firms do adapt their products and strategies to local markets to some extent, these and other activities are controlled by the head office. Firms following *multi-domestic strategy* are more concerned with local responsiveness than central control. These firms adapt their products and strategy to every market and decision-making about products, value creation and marketing strategies are decentralized to local market (Prahalad and Doz, 1987). These firms benefit from local responsiveness but lack in knowledge transfer within the firm between different subsidiaries (see Figure 7.3).

Some authors have suggested a fourth strategy, *transnational strategy*, and profess that to achieve worldwide competitive advantage, cost and revenues have to be managed simultaneously and both efficiency and innovation should be integral to the strategy. The global transnational firm needs to achieve efficiency, flexibility and learning simultaneously. This requires a more sophisticated and differential configuration of competencies and resources. The firm needs to decide which key competencies should be centralized at head office and which competencies and resources should be concentrated at which unit.

This is different from decentralization; such crucial resources are centralized at one unit that is most suitable to achieve specialization. For example, manufacturing, if it is labour intensive, is specialized in a low wage emerging country such as China, and R&D can be centralized in the most suitable country, such as the UK, the USA or Germany. This will help the firm to achieve specialization as well as economies of scale in every activity and competency. This will also make the firm responsive to local capabilities and resources in each market. Other activities, where locational economies of scale are low, can be decentralized to several units to create flexibility (Bartlett et al., 2008). Table 7.1 summarizes these four strategies.

As previously mentioned, each of these strategies has its advantages and disadvantages and this creates a complex dilemma for firms. If they follow a global strategy, they can achieve cost efficiencies and better control. However, if they follow multi-domestic strategy, the firms can achieve better local responsiveness but the head office risks losing control and economies of scale. Cost pressure and a pressure for local responsiveness are opposing factors that firms need to tackle while deciding on global strategy. Some authors have suggested that it is not a question of achieving cost advantages or local responsiveness but a question of achieving the right mix, that of which value creation activities should be centralized and which should be localized, and have suggested a "Glocal" perspective on global strategy formulation (see Case Study I) (Buckley and Ghauri, 2004).

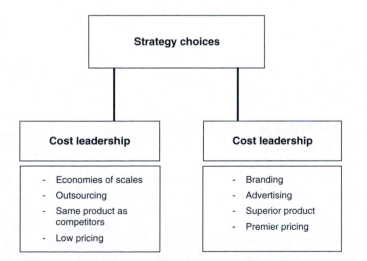

Figure 7.3 Different strategic choices.

Table 7.1 Different strategic approaches and configuration of assets and competences

	Multinational	*International*	*Global*	*Transnational*
Strategic approaches	Flexible to be able to respond to local conditions	To achieve efficiency through head office's competencies and diffusion to all units	Centralized global operations to achieve scale economies	Developing global compatibilities and efficiencies simultaneously
Configuration of assets and competencies	Decentralized and locally responsive	Core competencies centralized; others decentralized	Centralized to achieve cost advantages	Dispersed and specialized at different units

Based on Bartlett et al., 2008: p. 206.

In addition to classical views on strategy, there have been some pivotal writings on strategy and particularly on the international dimension of strategy. We have gathered some of these writings as a must-read to understand the developments in this field.

The first chapter in Part II is the seminal paper by Buckley and Ghauri that discusses the impact of globalization and the increasing importance of economic geography on the strategy of Multinational Enterprises (MNEs). The authors link the literature on ownership and location strategies to economic geography and globalization. They show how companies, through sophisticated decision-making, finely slice their value-added activities and find optimal location to perform each activity. They suggest this is deepening the international division of labour, an increase in market-based relationships and outsourcing. The location choices for different activities involve complex decision-making and considerations for geographic factors are becoming important. As a result, the relationship between MNEs and political actors is becoming complicated and is raising new questions about global capitalism.

This chapter concludes first, that the differentiated pace of globalization across capital, goods and labour markets is causing conflicts between markets and policy-makers thus creating new challenges for international institutions. Second, it shows that ownership strategies are becoming increasingly complex, creating a mixture of strategies from FDI to joint ventures and sub-contracting. Third, it stresses that lessons from economic geography are becoming more important for international business activities. Finally, the paper concludes that the globalization of production and consumption is causing new challenges and raising new questions for the justification and moral basis for global capitalism.

The second chapter, by Ghemawat, challenges the notion and extent of globalization and discusses semiglobalization and international business. The concept of semiglobalization is explained as the "incomplete cross-border integration". He draws our attention to the role played by "location-specificity" in international business strategy formulation and claims that the location-specificity has received too little attention from international business scholars. He analyses the cross-border integration during the twentieth century in terms of product, markets and in terms of various resources, such as capital, labour and knowledge.

His analysis shows that cross-border trade took off in the early twentieth century and increased substantially in the second half. FDI followed somewhat the same pattern. The capital market also increased significantly but fell short of perfection. Labour market integration on the other hand, in spite of increased migrations, has not achieved the same level of integration. For cross-border knowledge integration, although there have been substantial increases in knowledge flow across borders, it is far from complete.

Ghemawat advocates that instead of relying on changes and the speed of changes in different flows, we need to take a more measured and historically self-conscious perspective on cross-border integration. He calls for more research on the semi-globalization and local-specificity issues in international business.

The third chapter in this part, by Arregle, Miller, Hitt and Beamish, "Do regions matter? An integrated institutional and semiglobalization perspective on the internationalization of MNEs", supports the notion of regions and semiglobalization. Considering the three formal institutions: regulatory control, political democracy and capital investments, the authors examine the influence of these institutions on MNEs' location choice.

The authors are particularly concerned with factors that influence how much and where to internationalize. While traditional literature focusses on country-level institutional factors, later studies have suggested the importance of regions that leads to semiglobalization. It is suggested that regional strategy helps MNEs to coordinate their operations in different regions, exploit region-bound firm-specific advantages and be locally responsive.

They use a sample of Japanese MNEs in 45 countries and their location decisions in eight regions. Their results show that level of internationalization of these firms is influenced by country-level as well as region-level institutions. Comparing both perspectives, country factors and regional factors, their results confirm that regional institutional factors provide better explanations and thus support the "semiglobalization" perspective.

The fourth chapter, by Buckley, Devinney and Louviere, attempts to answer the question of whether managers behave the way theories suggest. They claim that most studies on FDI look at location choice and assume rules that are used by firms to make the decisions, although the decisions are made by mangers under bounded rationality.

Most MNEs have two main decisions to make: first where to go and second how to control these activities. Common theories used to study these decisions are either based on Hymer (1972) or Buckley and Casson (1976) and Dunning (1980). Another approach widely used is that of Johanson and Vahlne (1977 and 1990), which suggests that managers make incremental decisions based on limited information and risk aversion. These approaches are said to have limitations and fail to address actual issues as these are often based on panel or survey data.

These authors suggest that choice-theoretic empirical method is more suitable to capture preferences of managers for their location choice decisions. Using this method, the authors performed an empirical study to test two hypotheses: (1) Managers with more international experience will use more calculative approaches than managers with less international experience; (2) Managers with more international experience will show less risk aversion than mangers with less international experience.

They conclude that managers do follow a rational decision-making process, however, basic operational issues influence the screening method for investments and country factors play a major role. The behaviour of managers with international experience is more stable than of those with no international experience.

The final chapter in this part, by Benito, Petersen and Welch, "Towards more realistic conceptualisations of foreign operation modes", addresses the discrepancy between theories and practice regarding how firms choose their modes of operations in foreign markets. While theory suggests neat, well-specified alternatives, the practice reveals a messier picture. The problem associated with empirical studies, as most studies use cross-sectional design, have prevented the researchers from presenting deeper understanding of the choice of mode and their evolution.

Authors suggest different ways of categorizing foreign operation modes and that these modes can be assembled and packaged. This means that a firm might work with several modes simultaneously in a particular market. These multi-modes may or may not be connected or coordinated depending upon the type of activity. They define foreign operation modes as business activities that are performed in a particular location at a given time, where different roles are played by different operation modes. However, these roles might change over time as they might expand or be upgraded, for example, a joint venture might change into a licensing or exporting mode.

Their analysis shows that businesses are always struggling, not with which mode to use but which combination of modes to use in a particular market. It is also suggested that managers often fall back on their previous experience and tend to use modes that were successful in other situations, as experience with an operation mode can be seen as a unique resource on which a company can rely on in its international operations. Giving several examples, the authors demonstrate that there is a need for more research to better understand foreign operation mode choice of firms.

References

Bartlett, C.A. and Ghoshal, S. (1989), *Managing across borders*, Boston, Mass: Harvard Business School Press.

Bartlett, C., Ghoshal, S. and Beamish, P. (2008), *Transnational management*, 5th Edition, New York: McGraw-Hill.

Buckley, P. and Casson, M. (1976), *The future of the multinational enterprise*, London: Macmillan.

Buckley, P. and Ghauri, P. (2004), Globalization, economic geography and the strategy of multinational enterprises, *Journal of International Business Studies*, 35/2: 81–98.

De Wit, B.D. and Meyer, R. (2004), *Strategy: Process, content, context*, 3rd Edition, London: Thomson.

Dunning, J. (1980), Towards an eclectic theory of international production: Some empirical tests, *Journal of International Business Studies*, 11/1: 9–31.

Ghauri, P.N. and Cateora, P. (2014), *International marketing*, 4th Edition, London: McGraw-Hill.

Ghauri, P.N., Elg, U., Tarnovskaya, V. and Wang, F. (2011), Developing a marketing-driving strategy for foreign markets, *Schmalenbach Business Review*, 11/3: 1–23.

Grant, R.M. (2002), *Contemporary strategic analysis: Concepts, techniques, applications*, 4th Edition, Oxford: Blackwell.

Hill, C.L. (2010), *International business: Competing in the global marketplace*, Global Edition, London: McGraw-Hill.

Hymer, S. (1972), The multinational corporation and the law of uneven development, in J. Bhagwati (ed.) *Economics and world order from the 1970s to the 1990s*, Collier-MacMillan: New York, pp: 113–40.

Johanson, J. and Vahlne, J.-E. (1977), The internationalization process of the firm: A model of knowledge development and increasing market commitment, *Journal of International Business Studies*, 8: 23–32.

Johanson, J. and Vahlne, J.-E. (1990), The mechanism of internationalization, *International Marketing Review*, 74/4: 11–24.

Mintzberg, H. (1994), *The rise and fall of strategic planning*, New York: Free Press.

Penrose, E.T. (1958), *The theory of the growth of the firm*, New York: Wiley.

Porter, M.E. (1985), *Competitive advantage: Creating and sustaining superior performance*, New York: Free Press.

Porter, M.E. (1996), What is strategy? *Harvard Business Review*, 74/6: 61–78.

Prahalad, C.K. and Doz, Y.L. (1987), *The multinational mission: Balancing local demands and global vision*, New York: Free Press.

Prahalad, C.K. and Hamel, G. (1990), The core competence of corporations, *Harvard Business Review*, 68/3: 79–91.

8   Globalisation, economic geography and the strategy of multinational enterprises*

Peter J. Buckley and Pervez N. Ghauri

Introduction

The analysis in Buckley (2002) suggested that international business research succeeded when it focused on, in sequence, a number of big questions that arise from empirical developments in the world economy. The agenda is stalled because no such big question has currently been identified. This calls into question the separate existence of the subject area. This chapter suggests that the analysis of globalisation, with a focus on economic geography, arising from the changing strategy and the external impact of multinational enterprises (MNEs) on the world economy, can be that 'big question'. Researchers also need to take on board challenges to global capitalism and to understand the roots of current discontent.

The intention of this paper is to review the literature linking ownership and location strategies to economic geography and theories of globalisation and to explore new areas of research. The paper focuses on the relationship between the evolving strategies of MNEs, the changing economic geography of the world economy and globalisation. The first section charts the conflicts between markets and government policies as markets integrate across national borders. Markets are globalised by the actions of MNEs. This is a deliberate process, but it is proceeding at a differential pace in different types of market. The drivers of this process – the location and ownership strategies of MNEs – are examined in the second section. These strategies revolve around the ability of MNEs to subdivide their activities more precisely and to place them in the optimal location. At the same time, more sophisticated and wider control strategies ranging from full ownership to market relationships are used to coordinate global activities. This, it is argued in the third section, makes economic geography more important than ever. Where an activity is placed it interacts with its immediate hinterland and this has profound consequences for changing economic power and development. Finally, the article examines protests against globalisation that leads to the concluding research agenda.

Conflict of markets with national policies in the global economy

As Sideri (1997, 38) says, 'globalisation is essentially a process driven by economic forces. Its immediate causes are the spatial reorganisation of production, international trade and the integration of financial markets'. It is not uniform across economic space; 'the segmentation

---

of the manufacturing process into multiple partial operations, combined with the development of cheap transportation and communication networks, has brought the increasing division of production into separate stages carried out in different locations'. The strategies of multinational firms are crucial to the causes and consequences of globalisation.

We can examine globalisation as a conflict between markets and management (policies). Figure 8.1 identifies three levels of markets: financial markets, markets in goods and services and labour markets. Each of these is moving at a different speed towards global integration. Financial markets are already very closely integrated internationally, so that no individual 'national capital markets' can have a sustainable independent existence. However, attempts at national regulation do persist (Laulajainen, 2000) and the role of localities in the financial markets still provides differentiation (Berg and Guisinger, 2001; Tickell, 2000). Despite this, it is legitimate for analytical purposes to hypothesise a single integrated global capital market. Regional economic integration (REI) is becoming increasingly effective in integrating goods and services markets at the regional level. The relationship between company strategy and policy-making within regional blocs such as the EU is a fascinating area for the development of new research streams (Chapman, 1999; Raines and Wishlade, 1999; see also, Wood, 2003 on the Industrial Midwest of America). Labour markets, however, are functionally separate at the national level and here integration is largely resisted by national governments (Buckley *et al.*, 2001).

While the largest MNEs are already perfectly placed to exploit these differences in the international integration of markets (Buckley, 1997), REI offers both large and small firms the opportunity to enjoy the advantages of a large 'home' market, whether it is their native home or their adoptive home. The operation of international capital markets (which allow firms to drive their capital costs down to a minimum) has largely transcended policy on regional integration, although each region would hope to retain its own regional financial centre. It is primarily in the arena of the creation and fostering of regional goods and services markets that firms are enabled to exploit economies of scale across several countries, and

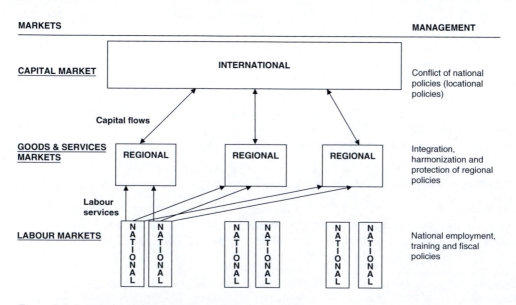

Figure 8.1 Internationalisation of firms: conflict of markets.

that REI offers the most substantial size-of-country benefits. However, regional integration that encompasses countries with differential labour markets is becoming increasingly beneficial. This regional integration enables costs to be reduced by locating the labour-intensive stages of production in the cheaper labour economies within the integrated area. Firms that serve just one regional market, as well as those that serve several of the regional goods and services markets of the world through horizontally integrated foreign direct investment (FDI), are able to complement this with vertically integrated FDI in quality-differentiated labour markets. Vertical integration also reflects the spatial distribution of supplies of key inputs and raw materials. The MNE achieves advantages through both vertical and horizontal integration. Each strategy is promoted by the 'size-of-country benefits' of REI in goods and services markets, which reduce or eliminate artificial barriers to trade between the members. This maximises the ability of firms to exploit intra-regional differences in factor abundance, including differentiated human capital.

At industry level, globalisation can be shown to have an increasing impact. Gersbach (2002) defines globalisation at the micro-level as 'the exposure of a productivity follower industry in one country to the productivity leader in another country'. The transmission mechanisms of change across country borders are trade and FDI. Gersbach found a strong relationship between globalisation and productivity differences with the most efficient producers. He concludes that globalisation matters and that its influence spreads beyond a single region (for example, Europe, North America).

More attention has been paid to vertical relationships (the supply chain). The differentiation of labour markets is most acute between advanced and less-developed countries that are typically not part of the same regional bloc. The managers of MNEs are increasingly able to segment their activities and to seek the optimal location for increasingly specialised slivers of activity. This ability to separate and relocate stages of production has led to a boom in manufacturing in China and service activities (for example, call centres) in India. MNEs are also increasingly able to coordinate these activities by means of a wide variety of mechanisms from wholly owned FDI through licensing and subcontracting to market relationships. The more precise use of location and ownership strategies by MNEs is the very essence of increasing globalisation.

In parallel with the growth of the globalisation of production, globalisation of consumption has accelerated and it is perhaps this which has excited most opposition. The alleged globalisation of tastes provokes nationalistic protectionist sentiments and is here analysed in terms of the balance of strategies within MNEs between 'local' and 'global' pressures on the firm.

The process of globalisation is not only reorganising power at world level but also at national and subnational levels (Alden, 1999; Dunning and Wallace, 1999; Graham, 2003; Mirza, 1998; Oxelheim *et al.*, 2001; Peck and Durnin, 1999; Pike, 1999; Yeung, 2003). As domestic firms move part of their production to other countries, technology, knowledge and capital become more important than land, the traditional source of state power, and this redefines the function of the state (Rosecrance, 1996; Sideri, 1997). The loss of sovereignty to supra-national regional institutions is more acceptable than to international institutions that are more remote. The EU is an example of such regional integration and governance (Bressand, 1990). Social programmes within the EU are enforcing major redistributions of revenue between the individual nations. The nation state as the possessor of the sense of identity is being replaced by subnations and internal regions as government is devolved.

A recent study by Subramanian and Lawrence (1999) found that national locations remained distinctive. Policy barriers at the borders, differences in local cultures in their widest sense and nature and geography contribute to distinctiveness. This, together with the ability of incumbents to keep outsiders at a disadvantage (Buckley *et al.*, 2001) and the first entrant benefits of local firms, reinforces the differentiation of national economies. International competition remains imperfect and international price differences persist because arbitrage is costly. Domestic market conditions largely determine prices and wages. Multinational company affiliates remain firmly embedded in their local economy and such local firms identify closely with the national government. Subramanian and Lawrence (1999) conclude that national borders still matter. Borders continue to engender and to coincide with important discontinuities stemming from government policies, geography and societal differences. The authors stress information discontinuities that coincide with national boundaries and so create search and deliberation problems for trading and manufacturing firms. These issues also account for the alleged 'home bias' of multinational firms. FDI is the key tool by which multinationals bridge cross-border discontinuities.

The two contrasting paradigms of a world made up of self-contained national economies and a 'borderless world' are incomplete and capture only part of a complex and subtle story. Lenway and Murtha (1994) examine the role of the state as a strategist along four dimensions: authority *vs* markets, communitarianism *vs* individualism, political *vs* economic objectives and equity *vs* efficiency. They state that international business scholarship 'places a benchmark value on efficient international markets and tends to regard states as causes of deviation from this ideal'.

Globalisation and corporate governance

Two key issues interact to provide governance issues arising from the globalisation of business. The first is the existence of unpriced externalities. These impose costs (for example, pollution) on the local economy and environment. The second is the remoteness of production and service activities from their ultimate owners or controllers (for example, the shareholders). These two factors interact because the mechanism for correcting negative externalities becomes difficult to implement because of remoteness and lack of immediate responsibility.

Perceived difficulties of global governance in multinational firms are exacerbated by the current crises in governance of firms in the West. The shareholder return-driven environment which prevails today is very much the creature of the merger wave of the 1980s (Buckley and Ghauri, 2002). The feeling that corporations are outside social controls and that current forms of governance benefit only executives (and owners) rather than other stakeholders contribute to the concerns outlined in the previous section.

MNE, host country relations in middle-income countries have fully emerged onto the world stage, leaving behind a group of largely inert less developed countries that have so far been bypassed by globalisation. Large, emerging countries, which contain significant middle class markets, cheaper and well-educated labour and stabilising political regimes (India, China, Brazil) are no longer seen just as new markets for old products (Prahalad and Lieberthal, 1998) but as significant locations requiring reconfigurations of the economic geography of MNE's operations. Not only do MNEs adapt products to local markets, but local markets also provide ideas for new global products (Murtha *et al.*, 2001). Increasing location 'tournaments' to attract FDI (Oxelheim and Ghauri, 2003), may have reduced the benefits to the host countries as have the increasing skill of the managers of MNEs in making their investments more 'footloose'. Corresponding skills on the part of host countries to make FDI 'sticky' are not developing at the same rate. Differences within developing countries may lead to divergence between those which can develop the velocity to catch up and those which will fall behind as the world economy becomes more interdependent.

Location and ownership strategies of multinational firms

The traditional MNE was a vertically, as well as horizontally, integrated firm. In consequence, each division of the firm was locked into linkages with other divisions of the same firm. As global competition intensified, there was growing recognition of the costs of integration of this kind. Commitment to a particular source of supply or demand of any product, intermediate good or service is relatively low cost in a high-growth scenario, since it is unlikely that any investment will need to be reversed. It is much more costly in a low-growth scenario, where production may need to be switched to a cheaper source of supply or sales diverted away from a depressed market. The desire for flexibility discourages vertical integration, whether it is backward integration into production or forward integration into distribution. It is better to subcontract production and to franchise sales instead. The subcontracting of production is similar in principle to a 'putting out' arrangement, but differs in the sense that the subcontractor is now a firm rather than just a single worker.

Disintermediation and reintermediation

Disintegration was further encouraged by a low-trust atmosphere that developed in many firms. Fear of internal monopoly became rife as explained above. Production managers faced with falling demand wished that they did not have to sell all their output through a single sales manager. Sales managers resented the fact that they had to obtain all their supplies from the same small set of plants. Each manager doubted the competence of the others and ascribed loss of corporate competitiveness to selfishness and inefficiency elsewhere in the firm. Divisions aspired to be spun off so that they could deal with other business units instead. On the other hand, managers were wary of the risks that would be involved if they severed their links with other divisions altogether. The result is that a much more complex strategy set faces decision-makers in multinational firms.

Strategy, e-commerce and networks

These changes are challenges for 'old economy' companies including the integration of online functions with existing brand and back office infrastructure. Business-to-business and building online links with suppliers and customers imply the redesign of business process networks. Smaller companies may find it easier to operate internationally because it is easier to reach customers, but there are still information problems, logistics and management control. Products still have to be delivered to customers. This is not just a matter of transport costs, but also regulatory differences between countries, cultural distance and other factors.

A natural way to cope with these pressures is to allow each division to deal with external business units, as well as internal ones. In terms of internalisation theory, internal markets become 'open' rather than 'closed'. This provides divisional managers with an opportunity to bypass weak or incompetent sections of the company. It also provides a competitive discipline on internal transfer prices, preventing their manipulation for internal political ends and bringing them more into line with external prices. There are other advantages too. Opening up internal markets severs the link between the capacities operated at adjacent stages of production. The resulting opportunity to supply other firms facilitates the exploitation of scale economies because it permits the capacity of any individual plant to exceed internal demand. Conversely, it encourages the firm to buy in supplies from other firms that have installed capacity in excess of their own needs.

The alignment of internal prices with external prices increases the objectivity of profit measurement at the divisional level. This allows divisional managers to be rewarded by profit-related pay based on divisional profit rather than firm-wide profit. Management may even buy out part of the company. Alternatively, the firm may restructure by buying in a part on an independent firm. The net effect is the same in both cases. The firm becomes the hub of a network of inter-locking joint ventures (Buckley and Casson, 1996; Buckley and Casson, 1988). Each joint venture partner is responsible for the day-to-day management of the venture. The headquarters of the firm coordinates the links between the ventures. Internal trade is diverted away from the weaker ventures towards the stronger ones, thereby providing price and profit signals to which the weaker partners need to respond. Unlike a pure external market situation, the partners are able to draw upon expertise at headquarters, which can in turn tap into expertise in other parts of the group.

A network does not have to be built around a single firm, of course. A network may consist of a group of independent firms instead (Ghauri, 1999). Sometimes these firms are neighbours, as in the regional industrial clusters described by Best (1990), Porter (1990) and Rugman *et al.* (1995). Industrial districts, such as 'Toyota city', have been hailed as an Asian innovation in flexible management, although the practice has been common in Europe for centuries (Marshall, 1919). As tariffs and transport costs have fallen, networks have become more international and 'virtual'. This is demonstrated by the dramatic growth in intermediate product trade under long-term contracts. For example, an international trading company may operate a network of independent suppliers in different countries, substituting different sources of supply in response to both short-term exchange rate movements and long-term shifts in comparative advantage.

By establishing a network of joint ventures covering alternative technological trajectories, the firm can spread its costs while retaining a measure of proprietary control over new technologies. The advantage of joint ventures is further reinforced by technological convergence, for example, the integration of computers, telecommunications and photography. This favours the creation of networks of joint ventures based on complementary technologies, rather than on the substitute technologies described earlier (Cantwell, 1995). Joint ventures are important because they afford a number of real options (Trigeorgis, 1996) which can be taken up or dropped depending upon how the project turns out. The early phase of a joint venture provides important information that could not be obtained through investigation before the venture began. It affords an opportunity later on to buy more fully into a successful venture, an opportunity that is not available to those who have not taken any stake. It therefore provides greater flexibility than does either outright ownership or an alternative involving no equity stake (Buckley *et al.*, 2002).

Global knowledge diffusion

As Buckley and Carter (2002) point out, problems in the global organisation of MNEs are frequently presented as oppositions. Typical are global *vs* local, centralise *vs* decentralise, standardisation *vs* adaptation and efficiency *vs* responsiveness. These issues are not independent of knowledge management. Global/local issues centre on the costs of managing knowledge flows and the combination of general 'company-wide' knowledge and separable, spatially fixed local-specific knowledge. Spatial questions are one part of dealing with knowledge-intensive organisations, but spatial issues are bound up with a whole set of temporal, organisational, strategic and process issues (Buckley and Carter, 2002, 46). As Murtha *et al.* (1998) show, strategy emerges from mind-sets which are changing over time; global and local issues are capable of synthesis. The role of management knowledge is a crucial and under-researched phenomenon of globalisation. Global management of knowledge does enable the separation of key activities that can therefore be managed in different ways. This has led to strategies of outsourcing, mass customisation and deduplication of functions, which can be spatially separated, bundled and differentiated and consolidated, respectively. Murtha *et al.* (2001) examine the process of global knowledge creation and dissemination in a fascinating, detailed industry case study of the type that can be replicated and extended.

The goal of a modern sourcing strategy is to obtain the optimum combination of inputs from the variety of opportunities open in the global market. Normally, this will be geographically diverse and the means of procurement will be varied. The location factor (where the inputs are acquired) and the internalisation/externalisation choice of means of procurement will vary with circumstances and will change over time. The ability of firms to 'mix and match' their sourcing strategy has been greatly enhanced by the use of the internet for procurement and the increasing use of 'outsourcing', whereby external offers can be compared to internal courses of supply, and the scope of the firm's internal activity adjusted accordingly. These strategies enable increased specialisation and localisation to enhance the division of labour globally and for individual firms to benefit from this by creating a global business network, which encompasses many locations for activities with mixed ownership/contracting modes of procurement. The reduced need for colocation locationally diversifies the firm's production base.

Similarly, the market servicing strategy comprises a mix of exporting, licensing/contracting and investment activities, again suggesting a mix of ownership and location strategies in different spatial and temporal circumstances. Here, too, different functions (more housing, distribution and advertising) can be either centrally and globally organised or differentially localised. Ownership too may be fully internal, joint venture/alliance or outsourced.

The interaction of the supply and demand side is yet to be fully studied, but it is safe to assume that large markets exercise a locational pull on inputs, and key input sources encourage local marketing. MNEs seek optimal locations for raw materials, intermediate goods, services 'brain arbitrage' and assembly plants. They also seek entry and exit strategies for markets as they wax and wane over time. This is a suitably complex subject for detailed analysis.

Global/local operations

In the strategic decisions of multinational firms, there has always been a tension between the pressures to globalise and the need to stay local and to serve individual customers (Ghauri, 1992). The advantages of global operations are cost-based, maximising economies of scale and reducing duplication, thus achieving efficiency. The advantages of localisation are revenue-based, allowing differentiation to reach all customer niches and achieving responsiveness. The tension can be summed up in the phrase 'the cost advantages of standardisation *vs* the revenue advantages of adaptation' (Table 8.1).

Much of the strategy of the multinational firm can be explained by the attempts of management to reconcile these pressures (Devinney *et al.*, 2000). Over time, firms have (been advised to) switch their organisation so as to balance these pressures; one example is the

Table 8.1 Global and local operation

Global	Local
Cost	Revenue
Efficiency	Responsiveness
Centralisation	Decentralisation
Standardisation	Adaptation
GLOCAL?	

'transnational' type of organisation advocated by Bartlett and Ghoshal (1989). However, pressures in different industries push firms towards a strategic imperative (scale in electronics, local demand differences in consumer goods) and different functions require different balances of global/local orientation (finance, production, sales functions). The 'hub and spoke' model in Figure 8.2 is a key method of attempting to reconcile these conflicts. Global and local oppositions are shown in Table 8.1. Cultural differences are of great importance in determining the extent of this balance.

The globalisation of markets has been a major factor in the growth of volatility (Buckley and Casson, 1998). A feature of many global markets is the use of regional production and distribution hubs, where several neighbouring countries are serviced from the same location. The regional hub, such as the IJV, can be understood as a strategy that offers superior flexibility. Just as an IJV offers a compromise ownership strategy, a regional hub offers a compromise location strategy. As the hub is nearer to each market that is the home location, it reduces transport costs, and offers better information capture too. Because it is close to several markets, it avoids exclusive commitment to any one. If one market declines, production can be switched to other markets instead, provided the shocks affecting the national markets are independent (or less than perfectly correlated, at any rate) and the hub provide gains from diversification. These are real gains that only the firm can achieve, as opposed to the financial gains from unrelated product diversification, which have proved disappointing in the past because they are best exploited through the diversification of individual share portfolios instead.

Location and ownership strategies revisited: 'hub and spoke' strategies

The two strategies of IJV and hub can be combined (Figure 8.2). Since one (the IJV) is an ownership strategy and the other a location strategy, they can, if desired, be combined directly in an IJV production hub. Closer examination of the issues suggests that this is not normally the best approach, however. The model suggests that a combination of a wholly owned production hub supplying IJV distribution facilities in each national market is a better solution. A hub facility is too critical to global strategy to allow a partner to become involved, because the damage they could do is far too great. Even with a wholly-owned hub facility, the combination still affords considerable flexibility to divest or withdraw from any single market. The advantage of the combination is that when divesting, the distribution facility can be sold to the partner, while the production capacity can be diverted to markets elsewhere. These options for divestment are combined with useful options for expansion too. This example illustrates the crucial role that the concepts of flexibility and volatility play in analysing foreign market entry in the modern global economy. Without these concepts it is impossible to fully understand the rationale for IJVs and production hubs. It is

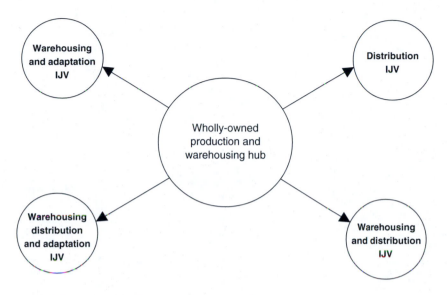

Figure 8.2 'Hub and spoke' strategies: an example.

also impossible to understand why these strategies have emerged at this particular historical juncture and not before.

Outsourcing and logistics

Many input functions are now viably outsourced, even human resource departments and procurement (The Economist, 2001a, b). Digital delivery of product is analogous on the output side. The danger is the loss of core competencies (outsourcing IT 'loses part of company's brain'). This development contributes to volatility and increases the mobility of activities internationally, as a great deal of outsourcing functions are competed for on a global basis. The policy of promoting linkages (forward as well as backward) followed by many agencies of national and local government needs to account for these changing decision-making parameters.

As is always the case, disintegration of established supply chains is followed by reintegration and consolidation. The trend to outsource (disinternalise) manufacturing by major multinationals led initially to subcontracting to independents, many of them located in South East Asia (and Mexico). Contract manufacturing (The Economist, 2000) has been growing by 20% per year in the late 1990s and early part of this century. However, contract manufacturers are rapidly consolidating, through mergers and are expected to reach an oligopolistic equilibrium, with around six firms dominating the global market. These firms are becoming supply chain managers, sometimes even organising distribution and repair. These links between customers and suppliers are, of course, facilitated by the use of the internet. Contract manufacturers, ensured of future contracts are able to achieve economies of scale and to become more capital intensive, replacing unskilled labour by high-tech capital equipment. This trend is accelerated by the competitive imperative becoming speed-to-market, rather than cost. A linked supply of available factories in different national locations mean that the contract manufacturers can switch production lines between these units. Flexibility

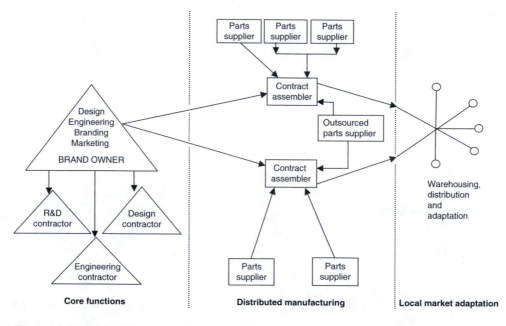

Figure 8.3 The global factory.

is achieved by moving these 'shell' factories between principals; entire production lines can be flown in from another location.

Vertical disintegration is accompanied by specialisation. The principal concentrates on R&D, design and marketing, while the contract manufacturer provides a service to the global supplier. Companies with a strong manufacturing culture, and a commitment to a fixed location, may be out-competed by more agile 'virtual' firms owning no manufacturing facilities at all.

Mass customisation is an important method of reconciling scale and differentiation (efficiency and responsiveness). An example is the textile industry where bespoke garments are ordered *en masse* from offshore sites with rapid delivery. This is associated with 'lean retailing' where distribution and design centres are linked to production centres by electronic means. Electronic ordering and automated distribution centres and inventory management systems linked to customers enable rapid response to customer needs. This combines information technology, speed and flexibility with low labour costs. So the custom-made *vs* bulk manufacture divide becomes fine. ('Cyber consumers expect to be able to customise everything'.)

Deduplication of function becomes possible where electronic links allow single locations to service the whole firm's needs. Rather than a call centre for each division or country, a single one can serve all. There is also a tendency for reintegration of the supply chain from independents back to the major manufactures or in specialist subcontracting firms as e-commerce matures.

The global factory

This review suggests that the manufacturing system of the future will use 'distributed manufacturing' (The Economist, 2002) where products are more responsive to customer needs through flexible factories. In flexible factories, all plants within the system can make all the firms' product models and can switch between models very quickly by a combination of software and robots. The global factory will be the very antithesis of 'any colour as long as it's black'. It will have a single factory design for its distributed global plants and attention to staff training so that replication and perfect substitutability between plants is achieved. Customers will be able to dictate which parts, subassemblies or 'add-ons', they require in the final assembly and the distributed manufacturing function will reassemble (Figure 8.3), where production is pushed from the hub into the spoke. Brand owners will control design, engineering and marketing while outsourcing large areas of production to parts suppliers, and they may well contract out final assembly. 'Built to order' products will be produced close to the final customer. Globalisation implies location near the customer, not a single large-scale plant. It is the high fixed costs of existing factories which compel manufacturers to achieve large-scale production and a reduction of fixed costs means that production can be more easily tailored to final demand.

Geography of globalisation

Much has been made of the 'death of distance' (Cairncross, 1997) and 'the end of geography' by authors trumpeting the importance of the internet and the ascendancy of virtual space over physical distance. Recent evidence, however, suggests that geography still matters. As Castells (2001, 209) says, 'the internet backbone is global in its reach, but territorially uneven in its layout in terms of capacity'. The internet is built on top of existing infrastructure and relies on fibre optic cables. The creation of data centres, 'web hotels' and 'server farms' has become conglomerated in key urban centres. Indeed, 49 of the servers for the top 100 web sites are colocated in Exodus Communications, Santa Clara, Cal, USA (The Economist, 2001a, b). The storage of information has become more physically concentrated, not less, and economies of agglomeration, including the need for a reliable power source, are creating these server farms, some of which come with their own power stations (iXguardian is building the biggest one in Europe just outside London, *Economist, op. cit.*). Sellers have a vested interest in determining the location of users of the internet. The difference in laws and taxes governing these consumers is determined by geography, not network topography, and firms delivering goods ordered over the internet stick with the old geographical (i.e., national) approach but are taking it online with 'geolocational services', largely using local postcodes. Web content can then be matched to the user's location. As national regulations still apply, particularly to goods such or pharmaceuticals and services, especially financial services, it is essential that companies stay within the law. So borders (national borders) are returning to the net.

Location thus becomes a search parameter for services. Filtering via precise targeting of customers (for example, through mobile phones) is possible through satellite-based global positioning systems. The Economist concludes: 'The internet means that the distance between two points on the network is no longer terribly important. However, where those points are still matters very much. Distance is dying, but geography it seems is still alive and kicking'.

Recently, technological advances have made it easier to argue for the link between geography and growth. Innovation has surged in developing links between places on the internet and real-world locations, stitching together the virtual and physical worlds (The Economist, 2003). Geolocational services are being developed both to locate end-users and to find the internet access point nearest to a particular location. Suitably equipped laptops can access wireless internet services close to a small base station (or 'hotspot'). Anyone in the locality can then avail themselves of these services. Mapping of base stations confirms that these are located in areas of highest economic activity. Again, virtual space reinforces existing spatial dispersion of activity, it does not substitute for them. Internet pages are becoming 'goecoded' or 'geotagged' to make geographical location explicit.

Deepening spatial division of labour

The evolving locational policies of MNEs have led to a deepening of the spatial division of labour. This interacts with changing ownership policies to produce radically new outcomes for the world economy (Ruigrok and Van Tulder, 1995). This section goes on to review three extant approaches to the deepening spatial division of labour (Dicken, 2003; Yeung, 2001) and then suggests future research developments.

Approach 1: The New International Division of Labour (NIDL).
The NIDL is not particularly new. It was foreshadowed by the analysis of Hymer (1972) who developed 'the law of uneven development'. Hymer envisaged a strict hierarchy in the world economy with 'higher order functions' (finance, design) being carried out in the advanced countries, with less-developed countries being relegated to the role of 'hewers of wood and drawers of water'. Frobel *et al.* (1980) foresaw the increasingly disaggregated spatial nature of production under the control of MNEs. The increasing intensity of intra-firm trade (priced at internally determined transfer prices; Emmanuel and Mehafdi, 1994; Hirshleifer, 1986; Rugman and Eden, 1985; UNCTAD, 1999), which accounts for over half of the world trade, is a concomitant of this fine spatial division. The ability of MNEs to create new specialised roles – largely corporate services – and to relocate them in favourable locations is a further innovation tracked by the NIDL approach.

Approach 2: Global Commodity Chains (GCCs).
Gereffi *et al.* (1994, 2) define GCCs as 'sets of inter-organisational networks clustered round one commodity of product, linking households, enterprises and states to one another within the world economy. These networks are situationally-specific, socially-constructed and locally-integrated, underscoring the social embeddedness of economic organisation'. Buyer-driven chains are distinguished from producer-driven chains. Buyer-driven GCCs are dominated by large retailers and brand-name manufacturers or trading companies that orga- nise decentralised production networks in developing countries for export. Typical industry settings include labour-intensive consumer goods industries organised by OEM (original equipment manufacturing) arrangements. Producer-driven GCCs are controlled by global oligopolies where TNCs control capital and knowledge-intensive production (Yeung, 2001). Empirical work on GCCs includes Dicken and Hassler (2000) and Gereffi (1999), while Jenkins (1987) applies this to development issues.

Approach 3: Regional Networks.
The role of regions and regional integration in the spatial organisation of the world economy is clearly critical as was shown above. Considerable work has been undertaken on Asian production networks which unfortunately took a wrong turn with the 'flying geese model' where it was alleged that the leading goose (Japan) would pull others in the flock (the smaller economies of Asia) along in its slipstream. Not only is this an inaccurate description of the way geese fly (different geese assume the leadership for different periods), it ignores vertical

linkages across and between these economies and those of the rest of the world, it also over-plays the benign effects of leadership and underplays power relationships (see Bernard and Ravenhill, 1995; Edgington and Hayet, 2000; Hart-Landsberg and Burkett, 1998; Hatch and Yamamura, 1996; Hill and Fujita, 1996; Tsui-Auch, 1999). There is a parallel here with the French 'filière' approach which has not permeated and influenced mainstream English language literature (Raikes *et al.*, 2000).

However, regional networks in Asia are important both theoretically (Markusen and Venables, 2000) and empirically as well (for instance, Yeung (2001) on Singapore firms in South East Asia and Ghauri and Prasad (1995) on Asian networks).

Geographical analyses of globalisation

The NIDL, global commodity chains and (regional) production networks all fit well with the international business research agenda. The progress of research in this area depends on inter-disciplinarity and connectivity.

Economic geography has a long history (Clark *et al.*, 2000; Krugman, 1991, 2000) and is currently enjoying a renaissance (Scott, 2000). The importance of the new geography is attested to by the concern for 'the new geography of competition' for mobile investment (Raines, 2003) and the increasingly complex interplay between states, economic regional blocs such as the EU and subnational regions such as states in the USA and semi-autonomous regions such as Catalonia or Scotland (Oxelheim and Ghauri, 2003; Phelps and Alden, 1999; Phelps and Rains, 2003).

Economic geographers have made many significant contributions to the analysis of globalisation that can, with profit, be noted by international business scholars. Regional integration and the division of world markets into trade and investment blocs have been extensively analysed by geographers (for summaries on Asia, North America and Europe, see Abo, 2000; Holmes, 2000; and Amin, 2000). However, the incorporation of real geographical features such as climate, coastline, river transport, soil quality and terrain has perhaps been underplayed and this represents a real opportunity for future development. This links physical geography and economic development. A research agenda of this kind is proposed by Mellinger *et al.* (2000) and Buckley and Casson (1991) included 'geographical factors that influence entrepôt potential' in their analysis of factors in the long-run economic success of a nation. The links between economic geography and development are also worthy of attention in the literature on 'spillovers' from MNEs to the local economy. Many of these spillovers are enhanced by geographical proximity (in the formation of clusters of supporting industries, for instance) and this factor is not often explicitly included in the examination of spillovers.

Aspects of the strategy of MNEs can also be enhanced by a deeper understanding of spatial issues. Geographical models can illuminate strategic decisions both through the use of models (Storper, 2000) and empirically as well (Wrigley, 2000). Local labour markets, which are a key attraction for efficiency-seeking FDI, are also geographically configured and analysis here also benefits from the insights of economic geography (Hanson, 2000). As we saw earlier, the strategy of MNEs cannot be fully comprehended without an understanding of the role of knowledge management including both its spatial and temporal aspects (Auderetsh, 2000; Schoenberger, 2000). One of the most brilliant analyses of the management of knowledge across time and space was, of course, made by Raymond Vernon (1966) in his analysis of the product cycle. There is much here for international business researchers to build on.

One of the most celebrated analyses combining economics and geography in the analysis of national economic strategies is that of Michael Porter (1990, 2000) building on a previous synthesis of work with a strong spatial element in the analysis of competitive advantage (Porter, 1985). The essence of concentrations of mutually supportive industries – clusters or industrial districts – goes back to the work of Alfred Marshall (1919, 1930) who seized on the ability of firms in close proximity to capture the external economies which might otherwise not be appropriated (Asheim, 2000). There are close connections here with mainstream work in international business notably John Dunning's OLI paradigm, with a focus on the L for location (Dunning, 2000, 1995, 1977). The ability of foreign MNEs to tap into local clusters and to create their own spatially distinct growth poles have long been a major features of international business analyses of the dynamics of growth. Perhaps the most developed of this stream of analysis is its links with 'clusters of innovation' and 'national systems of innovation' (Cantwell, 1989). The geography of innovation is an area of great potential and one to which international business scholars will continue to contribute (Antonelli, 2000; Feldman, 2000; Lundvall and Maskell, 2000; Maskell, 2000).

The geographic sources of competitiveness of international firms have attracted sporadic attention (Birkenshaw and Hood, 2000; Dunning, 1996; Frost, 2001), particularly regarding creative subsidiaries, but have not, as yet, become a mainstream preoccupation of international business theory. However, attention to foreign (decentralised) R&D and patenting activity has been studied (Almeida, 1996; Belderbos, 2001; Cantwell, 1993; Cantwell and Janne, 2000; Dalton and Serapio, 1999; Jones and Davies, 2000; Pearce, 1999) as has the internationalisation, geographic locational advantages and competitiveness of service firms (Dunning and McKaig-Berliner, 2002; Nachum, 1999).

Despite this considerable research progress in the economic geography of globalisation, there are still areas of great opportunity for further development and innovation. One of these is the geography of culture (Thrift, 2000) where international business scholars drawing on their long tradition of work in this area (Hofstede, 1997, 1980; Ronen and Shenkar, 1985) have an unrivalled ability to contribute. The spatial boundaries of 'a culture' are of enormous practical and theoretical interest, particularly with regard to their alignment or non-alignment with national, linguistic and other frontiers (Braudel, 1995; Shenkar, 2001).

A second key area of potential development is the furtherance of the research agenda of the 'Janus face of globalisation' and in particular its geographical aspects. Spatially, do the benefits of globalisation accrue to the rich (capital exporting) countries or to the poor (host) countries? (Eden and Lenway, 2001). As MNEs became more sophisticated in exploiting the spatial division of labour by slicing their activities even more finely, the question of who benefits becomes more pressing and the answer more sophisticated. The countervailing power of NGOs also requires further analysis (Doh and Teegan, 2003).

Demographic changes and migration are two of the other under-researched phenomena in examining the deepening spatial division of labour. The comparative advantage of international business scholars has always been their ability to combine different approaches and to see the big picture. This type of creative connectivity is needed in pushing forward the frontiers of research on the geography of globalisation and the role of MNEs.

Challenges to globalisation

Market capitalism, as described earlier, has inherent global tendencies. These stem directly from the central role of trade in a market system. The tendency of trade to promote globalisation can be seen in the empires of classical antiquity, as well as in the globalisation that occurred in the Age of High Imperialism before World War I (Prior, 2000). This age was the culmination of almost a millennium of incremental development, in which local markets became integrated into regional trading systems, and these trading systems were in turn integrated across continents as a consequence of trans-oceanic voyages of discovery. This integration of markets is a defining characteristic of globalisation.

Market capitalism also encourages the globalisation of finance and promotes the mobility of labour. Large financial markets offer investors greater liquidity, and more competitive pricing of stocks and shares, combined with greater legal security. This leads to the agglomeration of economic power in major metropolitan centres where financial dealings predominate. Peripheral regions of the integrated economy are plundered for their raw materials, or farmed intensively to feed the urban areas, or relegated to unskilled labour-intensive work. This is simply the imperative of efficiency seeking in a world of constant change.

This discussion provides a suitable framework for examining some of the major complaints levelled at the World Trade Organization at their 1999 Seattle meeting. The substance of the complaints appears to be that:

- the progressive reduction of trade and investment barriers leads to loss of jobs;
- an accelerating pace of technological change leads to greater insecurity of jobs and to the end of the lifetime employment system;
- inadequate environmental standards lead to increases in pollution which are incompatible with sustainable development;
- greater income inequality emerges, both within countries and between them, creating new social and political divisions;
- destruction of local communities is caused by an extension of global linkages;
- cultural diversity is reduced, because culture is homogenised by standardisation on modern Western values;
- national sovereignty is threatened, and the power of the state is undermined; and
- deregulation of industry and services leads to increased uncertainty, and to greater opportunities for stock-market speculation.

Little can be done to address some of these objections because they hit directly at the logic of the capitalist process (Rugman, 2000). For example, the dynamics of the market system mean that old jobs are destroyed at the same time that new jobs are created, and as this process accelerates, jobs become progressively more insecure. Many of these objections can be addressed fully only by changes which would dramatically reduce the long-run efficiency of the capitalist system. It is perfectly possible, for example, to insist that the metropolitan trading centres be deglomerated, thereby redistributing entrepreneurial profits to more peripheral regions. However, the costs of transporting and distributing commodities would increase, and consumers as a whole would be worse off. Similar measures could be applied to deglomerate R&D from major clusters like Silicon Valley to a host of minor ones, but again there would be efficiency losses in terms of innovations foregone. Moreover, it is likely that plans for enforced deglomeration would quickly become distorted by local politics, so that any redistribution of income would mainly favour corrupt officials.

Indeed, contrary to the claims of the Seattle protestors, globalisation confers important benefits. As Table 8.2 indicates, the opening up of trade frees domestic workers from the need to produce for subsistence and allows them to specialise, if they wish, on export production. Provided they work in a free society, they will switch to export production only if they perceive a benefit from doing so. There is little direct evidence that local producers are systematically duped into producing for export markets through selfish manipulation,

Table 8.2 Winners and losers from the globalisation of capitalism

	Winners	Losers	Factor
Labour	Labour in newly industrialising countries	Labour in mature industrial countries	Reductions in transport costs and tariffs for manufactured goods
Profit earners	Owners of successful globalised firms or of the firms that supply them	Owners of firms that fail to globalise or of firms that are dependent on them	Reduced communication costs facilitate international transfer of proprietary knowledge
Government	Non-interventionist governments with strong respect for property rights	Interventionist governments with weak respect for property rights	Reduced transport and communication costs give increased scope for international specialisation and exploitation of agglomeration economies, providing firms with a wider choice of political regimes from which to operate

Source: Buckley and Casson (2001a, p. 320).

although it is often alleged by critics of free trade that this is what local money lenders and export merchants do.

While some of the objections are invalid, others have substance to them. The moral ambiguities of the capitalist system generate a range of problems connected with negative externalities of one sort or another. No set of market contracts can cover all of the issues involved in coordinating a complex global economic system except at prohibitive transaction cost. It is wrong to suggest that nothing can or should be done about these problems. Consider, for example, the issue of financing mineral industries in developing countries. In a world where entrepreneurial greed was constrained by Protestant guilt, profits in resource-based industries would be voluntarily sacrificed to render development more sustainable. Bankers would think twice before lending large sums of money to inexperienced borrowers, such as the governments of less-developed countries. In a more secular society, issues of sustainability and manipulative lending practices can be addressed through statutory regulation, but this requires a high level of inter-governmental cooperation. The institutions of inter-governmental cooperation are often slow and bureaucratic, creating considerable impatience among activists awaiting a policy response. It is inherently wasteful to operate a capitalist system that encourages selfish profit-seeking behaviour, and to then establish a cumbersome inter-governmental bureaucracy to restrict it. Regulating profit seeking through self-restraint is, in principle, a much cheaper option, provided that the moral infrastructure is in place.

Secular ideologies provided an outlet for creative talents throughout much of the twentieth century and their demise leaves a serious vacuum. The protesters at Seattle were struggling to find a relevant language in which to express their discontent. Their demonstrations showed that they did not trust existing international institutions to make the changes that they believe are required. They sensed intuitively that there is a lack of restraint by those who hold economic power, namely by those who influence key decisions about future policy regimes in the global economy. In this sense their attitudes simply reflect the low-trust culture that modern capitalism has created.

Admittedly, many of their criticisms are not new, they echo the criticisms of international capitalism advanced by socialists in the past. Some of their claims may also be misguided. It was shown earlier that low-wage workers in developing countries can benefit substantially from global capitalism. However, there is always a tendency for people who are making a point to support their position with as many arguments as they can find: good as well as bad. Groups that wish to engage in collective action often have to promote an eclectic position in order to mobilise support as widely as possible.

The analysis in Buckley and Casson (2001a, b) suggests that the protesters' accusations of bad faith against modern capitalist enterprises may have substance. Some marketing techniques systematically probe for ignorance and lack of self-awareness among the consuming public. Popular brands are targeted at poor consumers, offering them subjective rewards, such as higher status, at a price they cannot afford to pay. Children and young people make easy targets, especially when advertisements can be skilfully designed to undermine parental veto power. When people find the time to relax, and reflect on their experience as consumers, their higher nature intuitively alerts them to the problem. However, they cannot easily articulate their feelings because they have been brought up to believe that they are rational all of the time. Even if the products they buy seem useless in retrospect, it has to be admitted that shopping for them seemed like fun at the time (see Frank, 1999). Shopping becomes an end in itself – exercising the impulse to buy being the immediate source of pleasure – and the product is just the excuse. Products have to be thrown away because otherwise storage space would limit indulgence in the shopping experience. On this view, it is when shopping palls, and the meaninglessness of the impulse to buy becomes obvious, that protests become attractive instead. People become angry when they finally have to face the fact that they have been systematically manipulated by the producers of the branded trivia of the modern capitalist system.

Moral arguments are rarely clearcut, however. Here is Lord Desai, no lover of capitalism: 'globalisation is nothing but the resurgence of capitalism in the late twentieth century. As FDI spreads to the poor countries of Asia, many of the people living there decide to quit their life of rural idiocy and join sweat shops in town. This may seem horrible to moralists of non-governmental organisations, but it is betterment for those making the decision to move. No doubt a concern for their rights in developed countries will price them out of their jobs. Thus does altruism of the rich often kill the poor by kindness' (Desai, 2003, 23).

However, it is not the poor who protest (in Seattle or elsewhere). The worry is that it is the beneficiaries of global capitalism who are its fiercest critics.

Conclusion: a research agenda

There are serious issues surrounding the notion of globalisation. There are also some myths. Empirical evidence is often disassociated from polemical writings on the subject. There is a great opportunity in front of international business scholars to confront assertions about globalisation with facts (or stylised facts).

This chapter has examined globalisation in terms of conflicts between markets and economic management and suggested that the differential pace of globalisation across markets presents a number of challenges to policy makers in local, national and regional governments and in international institutions. In examining the changing location and ownership strategies of MNEs, it has shown that the increasingly sophisticated decision making of managers in MNEs is slicing the activities of firms more finely and in finding optimum locations for each closely defined activity, they are deepening the international division of labour. Ownership strategies, too, are becoming increasingly complex, leading to a control matrix that runs from wholly-owned units via FDI through market relationships such as subcontracting, including joint ventures, as options on subsequent decisions in a dynamic pattern. The input of lessons from economic geography is thus becoming more important in understanding the key developments in international business. The consequences of the globalisation of production and consumption represent political challenges and reaction against these changes has led to a questioning of the effects of global capitalism as well as to its moral basis.

These four issues are closely intertwined and present a formidable research agenda to which the international business research community is uniquely fitted to respond. This agenda can encompass work from the empirical to the theoretical. Empirical issues include: the careful mapping and spatial analysis of FDI flows, the spatial and temporal spread of MNEs, and the geographical determinants of strategy. The underplaying of physical geography (rivers, coastlines, climate, soil types) from explanations of FDI and MNE strategies needs to be corrected. The external effects of MNEs (linkages, spillovers) need to be more closely related to the analysis of strategy so that IB researchers can contribute more to the literature on development and underdevelopment.

Theoretical avenues include the full incorporation of spatial issues in the strategy of MNEs, the integration of the role of new institutions such as NGOs and fuller attention to the political implications of the activities and changing organisation of MNEs. The management of space and time by MNEs should be in the forefront of the analysis of globalisation.

Acknowledgements

The analysis in this paper draws on three earlier pieces – Buckley and Casson (1998, 2001 a, b) and Ghauri and Buckley (2002). We are grateful for comments on an earlier version at the JIBS Conference, Duke University, NC, USA, 6–8 March 2003, from Stefanie Lenway, and from three anonymous referees and the editor of *JIBS*, Arie Lewin.

References

Abo, T. (2000) 'Spontaneous Integration in Japan and East Asia: Development, Crises and Beyond', in G.L. Clark, M.P. Feldman and M.S. Gertler (eds.) *The Oxford Handbook of Economic Geography*, Oxford University Press: Oxford, pp. 625–48.

Alden, J. (1999) 'The Impact of Foreign Direct Investment on Job Creation: The Experience of Wales', in N.A. Phelps and J. Alden (eds.) *Foreign Direct Investment and the Global Economy*, The Stationery Office: London, pp: 269–80.

Almeida, P. (1996) 'Knowledge sourcing by foreign multinationals: patent citation analysis in the US semi-conductor industry', *Strategic Management Journal* **17**(winter): 155–65.

Amin, A. (2000) 'The European Union as more than a Triad Market for National Economic Spaces', in G.L. Clark, M.P. Feldman and M.S. Gertler (eds.) *The Oxford Handbook of Economic Geography*, Oxford University Press: Oxford, pp: 671–87.

Antonelli, C. (2000) 'Restructuring and Innovation in Long-Term Regional Change', in G.L. Clark, M.P. Feldman and M.S. Gertler (eds.) *The Oxford Handbook of Economic Geography*, Oxford University Press: Oxford, pp: 395–412.

Asheim, B.T. (2000) 'Industrial Districts; The Contributions of Marshall and Beyond', in G.L. Clark, M.P. Feldman and M.S. Gertler (eds.) *The Oxford Handbook of Economic Geography*, Oxford University Press: Oxford, pp: 413–31.

Auderetsh, D.B. (2000) 'Corporate Form and Spatial Form', in G.L. Clark, M.P. Feldman and M.S. Gertler (eds.) *The Oxford Handbook of Economic Geography*, Oxford University Press: Oxford, pp: 333–51.

Bartlett, C.A. and Ghoshal, S. (1989) *Managing Across Borders: The Transnational Solution*, Hutchinson Business Books: Boston.

Belderbos, R.A. (2001) 'Overseas innovations by Japanese firms: an analysis of patent and subsidiary data', *Research Policy* **30**(2): 313–32.

Berg, D.M. and Guisinger, S.E. (2001) 'Capital Flows, Capital Controls and International Business Risk', in A.M. Rugman and T.L. Brewer (eds.) *The Oxford Handbook of International Business*, Oxford University Press: Oxford, pp: 259–81.

Bernard, M. and Ravenhill, J. (1995) 'Beyond product cycles and flying geese: regionalisation, hierarchy and industrialisation in East Asia', *World Politics* **47**(1): 171–209.

Best, M.H. (1990) *The New Competition: Institutions of Industrial Restructuring*, Polity Press: Oxford.

Birkenshaw, J. and Hood, N. (2000) 'Characteristics of foreign subsidiaries in industry clusters', *Journal of International Business Studies* **31**(1): 141–54.

Braudel, F. (1995) *A History of Civilizations*, Penguin Books: Harmondsworth.

Bressand, A. (1990) 'Beyond interdependence: 1992 as a global challenge', *International Affairs* **66**(1): 47–65.

Buckley, P.J. (1997) 'Cooperative Form of Transnational Corporation Activity', in J.H. Dunning and K.P. Sauvant (eds.) *Transnational Corporations and World Development*, Thomson: London, pp: 473–93.

Buckley, P.J. (2002) 'Is the international business research agenda running out of steam?', *Journal of International Business Studies* **33**(2): 365–73.

Buckley, P.J. and Carter, M.J. (2002) 'Process and structure in knowledge management practices of British and US multinational enterprises', *Journal of International Management* **8**(1): 29–48.

Buckley, P.J. and Casson, M. (1988) 'A Theory of Cooperation in International Business', in F. Contractor and P. Lorange (eds.) *Cooperative Strategies in International Business*, New Lexington Press: Lexington, MA, pp: 31–53.

Buckley, P.J. and Casson, M.C. (1991) 'Multinational Enterprises in less Developed Countries: Cultural and Economic Interaction', in P.J. Buckley and J. Clegg (eds.) *Multinational Enterprises in Less Developed Countries*, Macmillan: London.

Buckley, P.J. and Casson, M. (1996) 'An economic model of international joint ventures', *Journal of International Business Studies* **27**(5): 849–76.

Buckley, P.J. and Casson, M. (1998) 'Analysing foreign market entry strategies: extending the internalisation approach', *Journal of International Business Studies* **29**(3): 539–61.

Buckley, P.J. and Casson, M. (2001a) 'The moral basis of global capitalism: beyond the eclectic theory', *International Journal of the Economics of Business* **8**(2): 303–27.

Buckley, P.J. and Casson, M.C. (2001b) 'Strategic Complexity and International Business', in A.M. Rugman and T.L. Brewer (eds.) *The Oxford Handbook of International Business*, Oxford University Press: Oxford, pp: 88–126.

Buckley, P.J. and Ghauri, P.N. (2002) *International Mergers and Acquisitions*, International Thomson Business Press: London.

Buckley, P.J., Casson, M.C. and Gulamhussen, M.A. (2002) 'Internationalisation – Real Options, Knowledge Management and the Uppsala Approach', in V. Havila, M. Forsgren and H. Hakansson (eds.) *Critical Perspectives on Internationalisation*, Elsevier: Oxford, pp: 229–62.

Buckley, P.J., Clegg, J., Forsans, N. and Reilly, K.T. (2001) 'Increasing the size of the 'country: regional economic integration and foreign direct investment in a globalised world economy', *Management International Review* **41**(3): 251–74.

Cairncross, F. (1997) *The Death of Distance: How the Communications Revolution Will Change our Lives*, Harvard Business School Press: Boston, MA.

Cantwell, J.A. (1989) *Technological Innovation and the Multinational Enterprise*, Basil Blackwell: Oxford.

Cantwell, J.A. (1993) 'The internationalisation of technological activity and its implication for competitiveness', in O. Grandstand, H. Håkanson and S. Sjölander (eds.) *Technological Management and International Business*, John Wiley: Chichester, pp: 137–62.

Cantwell, J. (1995) 'The globalisation of technology: what remains of the product cycle model', *Cambridge Journal of Economics* **19**(1): 155–74.

Cantwell, J.A. and Janne, O. (2000) 'Technological globalisation and innovative centres: the role of corporate technological leadership and locational hierarchy', *Research Policy* **28**(2–3): 119–44.

Castells, M. (2001) *The Internet Galaxy*, Oxford University Press: Oxford.

Chapman, K. (1999) 'Merger/Acquisition Activity and Regional Cohesion in the EU', in N.A. Phelps and J. Alden (eds.) *Foreign Direct Investment and the Global Economy*, The Stationery Office: London, pp: 121–38.

Clark, G.L., Feldman, M.P. and Gerther, M.S. (2000) 'Economic Geography: Transition and Growth', in G.L. Clark, M.P. Feldman and M.S. Gertler (eds.) *The Oxford Handbook of Economic Geography*, Oxford University Press: Oxford, pp: 3–17.

Dalton, D.H. and Serapio, M.G. (1999) *Globalising Industrial Research and Development*, US Department of Commerce, Office of Technology Policy: Washington, DC.

Desai, M (2003) *With the Best Will in the World: Review of One World: The Ethics of Globalisation*, Times Higher Education Supplement (21.02.03). London, p: 23.

Devinney, T., Midgley, D. and Venaik, S. (2000) 'The optimal performance of the global firm: formalising and extending the integration: responsiveness framework', *Organization Science* **11**(6): 674–95.

Dicken, P. (2003) *Global Shift*, 4th edn. Sage: London.

Dicken, P. and Hassler, M. (2000) 'Organizing the Indonesian clothing industry in the global economy: the role of business networks', *Environment and Planning A* **32**(2): 263–80.

Doh, J.P. and Teegan, H. (2003) *Globalization and NGOs*, Praeger: Westport, CT.

Dunning, J.H. (1977) 'Trade, Location of Economic Activity and the MNE: A Search for an Eclectic Approach', in B. Ohlin, P.O. Hesselborn and P.M. Wijkmon (eds.) *The International Allocation of Economic Activity*, Macmillan: London, pp: 395–418.

Dunning, J.H. (1995) 'Reappraising the eclectic paradigm in the age of alliance capitalism', *Journal of International Business Studies* **26**(3): 461–91.

Dunning, J.H. (1996) 'The geographical sources of the competitiveness of firms: some results of a new survey', *Transnational Corporations* **5**(3): 1–30.

Dunning, J.H. (2000) 'The eclectic paradigm as an envelope for economic and business theories of MNE activity', *International Business Review* **9**(2): 163–90.

Dunning, J.H. and McKaig-Berliner, A. (2002) 'The geographical sources of competitiveness: the professional business services industry', *Transnational Corporations* **11**(3): 1–38.

Dunning, J.H. and Wallace, L. (1999) 'New Jersey in a Globalising Economy', in N.A. Phelps and J. Alden (eds.) *Foreign Direct Investment and the Global Economy*, The Stationery Office: London, pp: 253–69.

Eden, L. and Lenway, S. (2001) 'Introduction to the symposium, multinationals: the Janus face of globalisation', *Journal of International Business Studies* **32**(3): 383–400.

Edgington, D.W. and Hayet, R. (2000) 'Foreign direct investment and the flying geese model: Japanese electronics firms in the Asia Pacific', *Environment and Planning A* **32**(2): 281–304.

Emmanuel, C. and Mehafdi, M. (1994) *Transfer Pricing*, Academic Press: London.

Feldman, M.P. (2000) 'Location and Innovation: The New Economic Geography of Innovation, Spillovers and Agglomeration', in G.L. Clark, M.P. Feldman and M.S. Gertler (eds.) *The Oxford Handbook of Economic Geography*, Oxford University Press: Oxford, pp: 373–95.

Frank, R.H. (1999) *Luxury Fever: Why Money Fails to Satisfy in an Era of Excess*, Free Press: New York.

Frobel, F., Heinrichs, J. and Kreye, O. (1980) *The New International Division of Labour*, Cambridge University Press: Cambridge, MA.

Frost, T.S. (2001) 'The geographical source of foreign subsidiaries' innovation', *Strategic Management Journal* **22**(2): 101–23.

Gereffi, G. (1999) 'International trade and industrial upgrading in the apparel commodity chain', *Journal of International Economics* **48**(1): 37–70.

Gereffi, G., Korzeniewics, M. and Korzeniewics, R.P. (1994) 'Introduction: Global Commodity Chains', in G. Gereffi and M. Korzeniewics (eds.) *Commodity Chains and Global Capitalism*, Praeger: Westport, CT, pp: 1–14.

Gersbach, H. (2002) 'Does and how does globalisation matter at industry level?', *World Economy* **25**(2): 209–29.

Ghauri, P.N. (1992) 'New structures in MNCs based in small countries: a network approach', *European Management Journal* **10**(3): 357–64.

Ghauri, P.N. (1999) *Advances in International Marketing: International Marketing Purchasing*, JAI Press: Connecticut.

Ghauri, P.N. and Buckley, P.J. (2002) 'Globalization and the End of Competition: A Critical Review of Rent-Seeking Multinationals', in V. Havila, M. Forsgren and H. Håkansson (eds.) *Critical Research on Multinational Corporations*, Pergamon Press: Oxford, pp: 7–28.

Ghauri, P.N. and Prasad, S.B. (1995) 'A network approach to probing Asia's interfirm linkages', *Advances in International Comparative Management* **10**: 63–77.

Graham, E.M. (2003) 'Attracting Foreign Direct Investment to the United States: The Joust between the Federal Government and the States', in N.A. Phelps and P. Rains (eds.) *The New Competition for Inward Investment*, Edward Elgar: Cheltenham, pp: 61–78.

Hanson, G.H. (2000) 'Firms, Workers and the Geographic Concentration of Economic Activity', in G.L. Clark, M.P. Feldman and M.S. Gertler (eds.) *The Oxford Handbook of Economic Geography*, Oxford University Press: Oxford, pp: 477–97.

Hart-Landsberg, M. and Burkett, P. (1998) 'Contradictions of capitalist industrialization in East Asia: a critique of "flying geese" theories of development', *Economic Geography* **74**(2): 87–110.

Hatch, W. and Yamamura, K. (1996) *Asia in Japan's Embrace: Building a Regional Production Alliance*, Cambridge University Press: Cambridge.

Hill, R.C. and Fujita, K. (1996) 'Flying geese, swarming sparrows or preying hawks? Perspectives on East Asian industrialization', *Competition and Change* **1**(3): 285–98.

Hirshleifer, J. (1986) 'Internal Pricing and Decentralised Decisions', in C.P. Bonini, R.K. Jaedicke and H.M. Wagner (eds.) *Management Controls: New Directions in Basic Research*, Gartland: London, pp: 27–37.

Hofstede, G. (1980) *Culture's Consequences: International Differences in Work Related Values*, Sage: Beverly Hills, CA.

Hofstede, G. (1997) *Cultures and Organizations: Software of The Mind*, McGraw-Hill: New York.

Holmes, J. (2000) 'Regional Integration in North America', in G.L. Clark, M.P. Feldman and M.S. Gertler (eds.) *The Oxford Handbook of Economic Geography*, Oxford University Press: Oxford, pp: 649–71.

Hymer, S. (1972) 'The Multinational Corporation and The Law of Uneven Development', in J. Bhagwati (ed.) *Economics and World Order from The 1970s to the 1990s*, Collier-MacMillan: New York, pp: 113–40.

Jenkins, R. (1987) *Transnational Corporations and Uneven Development: The Internationalisation of Capital in the Third World*, Methuen: London.

Jones, G.K. and Davies, H.J. (2000) 'National culture and innovation: implications for locating global R&D operations', *Management International Review* **40**(1): 11–39.

Krugman, P. (1991) *Geography and Trade*, MIT Press: Cambridge MA.

Krugman, P. (2000) 'Where in the World is the "New Economic Geography?"', in G.L. Clark, M.P. Feldman and M.S. Gertler (eds.) *The Oxford Handbook of Economic Geography*, Oxford University Press: Oxford, pp: 49–60.

Laulajainen, R.I. (2000) 'The Regulation of International Finance', in G.L. Clark, M.P. Feldman and M.S. Gertler (eds.) *The Oxford Handbook of Economic Geography*, Oxford University Press: Oxford, pp: 215–29.

Lenway, S.A. and Murtha, T.P. (1994) 'The State as strategist in international business research', *Journal of International Business Studies* **25**(3): 513–35.

Lundvall, B.-A. and Maskell, P. (2000) 'Nation States and Economic Development: From National Systems of Production to National Systems of Knowledge Creation and Learning', in G.L. Clark, M.P. Feldman and M.S. Gertler (eds.) *The Oxford Handbook of Economic Geography*, Oxford University Press: Oxford, pp: 535–73.

Markusen, J.R. and Venables, A.J. (2000) 'The theory of endowment, intra-industry and multi-national trade', *Journal of International Economics* **52**(2): 209–34.

Marshall, A. (1919) *Industry and Trade*, Macmillan: London.

Marshall, A. (1930) *Principles ofEconomics*, 8th edn. Macmillan: London.

Maskell, P. (2000) 'Future Challenges and Institutional Preconditions for Regional Development Policy of Economic Globalisation', in I. Karppi (ed.) *Future Challenges and Institutional Preconditions for Regional Development Policy*, Nordregio: Stockholm, pp: 27–88.

Mellinger, A.D., Sachs, J.D. and Gallup, J.L. (2000) 'Climate, Coastal Proximity and Development', in G.L. Clark, M.P. Feldman and M.S. Gertler (eds.) *The Oxford Handbook of Economic Geography*, Oxford University Press: Oxford, pp: 169–95.

Mirza, H. (ed.) (1998) *Global Competitive Strategies in the New World Economy: Multilateralism, Regionalization and the Transnational Firm*, Edward Elgar: Cheltenham.

Murtha, T.P., Lenway, S.A. and Bagazzi, R.P. (1998) 'Global mind-sets and cognitive shift in a complex multinational corporation', *Strategic Management Journal* **19**(2): 97–114.

Murtha, T.P., Lenway, S.A. and Hart, J.A. (2001) *Managing New Industry Creation*, Stanford University Press: Stanford.

Nachum, L. (1999) *The Origins of the International Competitiveness of Firms: The Impact of Location and Ownership in Professional Service firms*, Edward Elgar: Cheltenham.

Oxelheim, L. and Ghauri, P.N. (eds.) (2003) *European Union and the Race for Inward FDI in Europe*, Elsevier: Oxford.

Oxelheim, L., Randoy, T. and Stonehill, A. (2001) 'On the treatment of finance-specific factors within the OLI paradigm', *International Business Review* **10**(4): 381–98.

Pearce, R.D. (1999) 'The evolution of technology in multinational enterprises: the role of creative subsidiaries', *International Business Review* **8**(2): 125–48.

Peck, F. and Durnin, J. (1999) 'Institutional Marginalisation and Inward Investment Strategies in the North of England: The Case of Cumbria', in N.A. Phelps and J. Alden (eds.) *Foreign Direct Investment and the Global Economy*, The Stationery Office: London, pp: 237–53.

Phelps, N.A. and Alden, J. (eds.) (1999) *Foreign Direct Investment and the Global Economy*, The Stationery Office: London.

Phelps, N.A. and Rains, P. (2003) *The New Competition for Inward Investment*, Edward Elgar: Cheltenham.

Pike, A. (1999) '*In situ* Restructuring in Branch Plants and their Local Economic Development Implications', in N.A. Phelps and J. Alden (eds.) *Foreign Direct Investment and the Global Economy*, The Stationery Office: London, pp: 221–37.

Porter, M.E. (1985) *Competitive Advantage: Creating and Sustaining Superior Performance*, Free Press: New York.

Porter, M.E. (1990) *The Competitive Advantage of Nationals*, Free Press: New York.

Porter, M.E. (2000) 'Locations, Clusters and Company Strategy', in G.L. Clark, M.P. Feldman and M.S. Gertler (eds.) *The Oxford Handbook of Economic Geography*, Oxford University Press: Oxford, pp: 253–75.

Prahalad, C.K. and Lieberthal, K. (1998) 'The end of corporate imperialism', *Harvard Business Review*, Vol 76, July–August 69–79.

Prior, F.L. (2000) 'Internationalisation and Globalisation of the American Economy', in T.L. Brewer and G. Boyd (eds.) *Globalising America: The USA in World Integration*, Edward Elgar: Cheltenham, pp: 1–39.

Raikes, P., Jensen, M.F. and Ponte, S. (2000) 'Global commodity chain analysis and the French filière approach: comparison and critique', *Economy and Society* **29**(3): 390–317.

Raines, P. (2003) 'Flows and Territories: the New Geography of Competition for Mobile Investment in Europe', in N.A. Phelps and P. Rains (eds.) *The New Competition for Inward Investment*, Edward Elgar: Cheltenham, pp. 119–35.

Raines, P. and Wishlade, F. (1999) 'E.C. Policy-Making and the Challenges of Foreign Investment', in N.A. Phelps and J. Alden (eds.) *Foreign Direct Investment and the Global Economy*, The Stationery Office: London, pp: 71–87.

Ronen, S. and Shenkar, O. (1985) 'Clustering countries in altitudinal dimensions: a review and synthesis', *Academy of Management Review* **10**(3): 435–454.

Rosecrance, R. (1996) 'The rise of virtual state', *Foreign Affairs* **47**(1): 45–61.

Rugman, A.M. (2000) *The End of Globalisation*, Random House: London.

Rugman, A.M., D'Cruz, J.R. and Verbeke, A. (1995) 'Internalisa-tion and De-Internalisation: Will Business Networks Replace Multinationals?', in G. Boyd (ed.) *Competitive and Cooperative Macro-management*, Edward Elgar: Aldershot, pp: 107–29.

Rugman, A.M. and Eden, L. (eds.) (1985) *Multinationals and Transfer Pricing*, Croom Helm: Beckenham.

Ruigrok, W. and Van Tulder, R. (1995) *The Logic of International Restructuring*, Routledge: London.

Schoenberger, E. (2000) 'The Management of Time and Space', in G.L. Clark, M.P. Feldman and M.S. Gertler (eds.) *The Oxford Handbook of Economic Geography*, Oxford University Press: Oxford, pp: 317–33.

Scott, A.J. (2000) 'Economic Geography: The Great Half Century', in G.L. Clark, M.P. Feldman and M.S. Gertler (eds.) *The Oxford Handbook of Economic Geography*, Oxford University Press: Oxford, pp: 483–504.

Shenkar, O. (2001) 'Cultural distance revisited: towards a more rigorous conceptualisation and measurement of cultural distance', *Journal of International Business Studies* **32**(3): 519–35.

Sideri, S. (1997) 'Globalisation and regional integration', *European Journal of Development Research* **9**(1): 38–81.

Storper, M. (2000) 'Globalization, Localization and Trade', in G.L. Clark, M.P. Feldman and M.S. Gertler (eds.) *The Oxford Handbook of Economic Geography*, Oxford University Press: Oxford, pp: 146–69.

Subramanian, R. and Lawrence, R.Z. (1999) *A Prism on Globalization: Corporate Responses to the Dollar*, Brookings Institution Press: Washington, DC.

The Economist (2000) *Factories for Hire*, London, 12 February. pp: 8.

The Economist (2001a) *Out of the Back Room*, London, 1 December, pp: 75–76.

The Economist (2001b) *Putting it in its Place – Geography and The Net*, London, 11 August. pp: 18.

The Economist (2002) *Incredible Shrinking Plants*, London, 23 February. pp: 71–73.

The Economist (2003) *The Revenge of Geography – Technology Quarterly*, London, 15 March, pp: 22–7.

Thrift, N. (2000) 'Pandora's Box? Cultural Geographies of Economies', in G.L. Clark, M.P. Feldman and M.S. Gertler (eds.) *The Oxford Handbook of Economic Geography*, Oxford University Press: Oxford, pp: 689–704.

Tickell, A. (2000) 'Finance and Localities', in G.L. Clark, M.P. Feldman and M.S. Gertler (eds.) *The Oxford Handbook of Economic Geography*, Oxford University Press: Oxford, pp: 230–51.

Trigeorgis, L. (1996) *Real Options*, MIT Press: Cambridge, MA.

Tsui-Auch, L.S. (1999) 'Regional production relationship and developmental impacts: a comparative study of three regional networks', *International Journal of Urban and Regional Research* **23**(2): 345–60.

UNCTAD (1999) *Transfer Pricing. UNCTAD Series on Issues in International Investment Agreements*, UNCTAD: Geneva and New York.

Vernon, R. (1966) 'International investment and international trade in the product cycle', *Quarterly Journal of Economics* **80**(2): 190–207.

Wood, A. (2003) 'The Politics of Orchestrating Inward Investment: Institutions, Policy and Practice in the Industrial Midwest', in N.A. Phelps and P. Rains (eds.) *The New Competition for Inward Investment*, Edward Elgar: Cheltenham, pp. 79–98.

Wrigley, N. (2000) 'The Globalization of Retail Capital: Themes for Economic Geography', in G.L. Clark, M.P. Feldman and M.S. Gertler (eds.) *The Oxford Handbook of Economic Geography*, Oxford University Press: Oxford, pp: 292–317.

Yeung, G. (2003) 'Scramble for FDI: The Experience of Guangdong Province in Southern China', in N.A. Phelps and P. Rains (eds.) *The New Competition for Inward Investment*, Edward Elgar: Cheltenham, pp: 193–212.

Yeung, H.W. (2001) *Entrepreneurship and the Internationalisation of Asian Firms: An Institutional Perspective*, Edward Elgar: Cheltenham.

9 Semiglobalization and international business strategy*

Pankaj Ghemawat

Introduction

The first of the three postulates on which Buckley and Casson (1976, 32) based their theory of the multinational enterprise was that 'firms maximize profit in a world of imperfect markets'. This structural insight has proved as fruitful in international business strategy as it has in 'mainstream' (single-country) business strategy, where it has been in circulation for even longer. What is odd is that work in this vein in international business strategy has tended to focus on the same sources of market imperfections as mainstream business strategy: small numbers and, often related, the *business/usage-specificity* of key activities, resources, competencies, capabilities, knowledge, etc., or their *firm-specificity* in the sense of being collectively held by the firm's managerial hierarchy or employee pool and inalienable from it. However, the obvious potential source of market imperfections added by the international dimension – the possibly limited cross-border integration of markets or, more generally, the possible *location-specificity* of key activities, resources, etc. – has received less attention. Location-specificity of the specific sort wrought by market segmentation at national boundaries is at the core of this paper.[1]

This paper consists of two halves. The first half contains a broad – and therefore inevitably compressed – review of the empirical evidence on the cross-border integration of markets of different types: for products (via both trade and FDI), capital, labor, and knowledge. The review points to the conclusions that, on the one hand, the observed levels of cross-border integration of these types of markets are significant and in many cases have recently reached highs without historical precedent, but that, on the other hand, the observed levels of cross-border integration are also very far from complete and, extrapolating from historical rates of increase (not to mention recent setbacks), are likely to remain that way for a long time. This condition of incomplete cross-border integration, referred to here as *semiglobalization*, is more complex than the extremes of total insulation and total integration because it involves situations in which the barriers to market integration at borders are high, but not high enough to insulate countries completely from each other. Another way of putting this is that semiglobalization covers the range – apparently broad as well as complex - of situations in which neither the barriers nor the links among markets in different countries can be neglected.

The second half of this paper can be read as a short essay on the implications of the empirical finding of semiglobalization for international business strategy. It begins by noting that semi-globalization is a sufficient condition for location-specificity to matter. Although complete market insulation also suffices, it is a less – challenging condition since, under it, international business strategy could simply be chunked up into applications of mainstream (that is, single-location) strategy, performed location by location, although some problems of coordination would still remain. Semi-globlalization is the underlying structural condition most conducive to thinking in careful ways about competing across multiple locations and how that might differ from competing at a single location. The essay elaborates on this and other, more specific, implications of the general diagnosis of semi-globalization. It discusses the balance to be struck in international business strategy between attention to location-specificity and other types of specificity, and examines the conditions under which imperfections in particular types of market (especially knowledge, which was emphasized by Buckley and Casson, 1976) should be granted elevated status. Finally, the essay highlights the scope for strategies that strive to capitalize on the (large) residual barriers to cross-border integration, as well as those that simply try to cope with such barriers. The treatment is meant as much to stimulate and direct further research as to summarize research efforts to date.

It is worth adding that the first half of this paper – the next two sections – focuses on reviewing the economic evidence about the cross-border integration of markets of different types. The economic perspective is adopted because economics offers both a relatively well-developed conceptual framework for the analysis of market integration and some empirical basis for making judgments about levels of and changes in cross-border integration of the kinds that occupy its attention. The next section of this paper looks at the cross-border integration of product markets and the section that follows at markets for various types of resource or factor: capital, labor and knowledge. The questions asked about each type of market concern changes in its level of international integration, measured in terms of quantity and price outcomes, over recent decades or the course of the twentieth century, as well as its absolute level of international integration at the millennium. For a more specific delineation of what is included in and excluded from the review, see Table 9.1. While there is arguably a logic to the pattern of inclusions and exclusions, the more fundamental point is simply that one cannot talk about everything in Table 9.1 in a paper of this scope.

Table 9.1 Dimensions of integration

Dimension	Possible emphases	
Criteria for evaluating integration	Economic	Non-economic
Key boundaries	Countries	Others
		Continents/regions
		Localities
Locus of integration	Markets	Others
		Firms
		Networks
Type of markets	Products	Factors
Input/output emphasis	Outcomes	Drivers
Outcome variables	Quantities	Prices

Dark shading = primary emphasis; gray shading = secondary emphasis.

Product market integration

This section begins by looking at the most obvious quantity measure of the cross-border integration of product markets: trade flows. It then looks at foreign direct investment (FDI) stocks and, finally and very briefly, at cross-border price integration.

Trade flows

To begin with a very long-run perspective, consider data on world exports divided by world GDP (the usual normalization) over the last two centuries based on and updated from data in Maddison (1995). As Figure 9.1 indicates, this ratio increased from about 1% at the beginning of the nineteenth century to nearly 10% towards the beginning of the twentieth century, and, despite a period of stagnation and decline bounded by the two world wars, has since managed to edge up towards 20%. Trade intensity has clearly reached new heights in the last quarter of the twentieth century.

The increase in trade intensity over the course of the twentieth century looks all the more remarkable when one accounts for the increasing share of GDP contributed, especially in developed countries, by two sectors that account for relatively little trade: services and government. One way of stripping out the effects of these 'non-traded' sectors is to remove them from the calculations and focus on the ratio of merchandise trade to merchandise value added. This leads to striking increases in measured trade exposure, as illustrated by Feenstra's (1998) sample of 11 relatively developed countries between 1913 and 1990. Over this period, the ratio of merchandise trade to merchandise value added increased for nine of these countries; the median change was +22 percentage points, compared with an initial median value of 36%, and total unweighted increases were close to 20 times as large as total unweighted decreases. The corresponding statistics for the ratio of merchandise trade to *total* GDP are increases for only six of the 11 countries, a median change of +2 percentage points from an

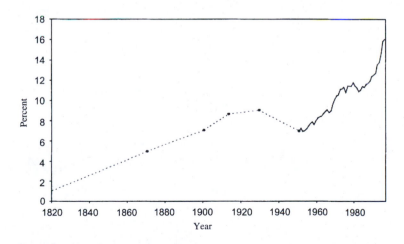

Figure 9.1 Exports divided by GDP.

Source: 1820–1992, Maddison (1995); 1993–1998, World Trade Organization and International Monetary Fund data.

initial median value of 20%, and total unweighted increases less than one-half as large as total unweighted decreases.

One interpretation of the historical patterns is that:

(1) trade had taken off in many commodities by the beginning of the twentieth century;
(2) there were substantial increases in the trade of manufactures over the course of the twentieth century, particularly its second half; and
(3) the service sector continues to be a very large bottleneck for trade-related flows even though it is growing.

Irwin's (1996) comparison of the composition of US merchandise trade over a century is suggestive in this regard: see Table 9.2. While this neat ordering of the globalization of commodities, manufactures and services is obviously an oversimplification, it is nevertheless useful.

So trade has clearly increased over the last 50, 100 and 200 years. But it is useful to supplement this observation with some data about the absolute level of integration of product markets through trade. Economists who study international trade generally do not regard trade intensity as very high in absolute terms. They tend to find the issue of why there is not much more trade more interesting than the new records being set. To see the room for increase, consider a hypothetical benchmark, suggested by Frankel (2001), in which national borders did not affect buying patterns at all. In such a situation, buyers in a particular nation would be as prone to obtain goods and services from foreign producers as from domestic ones, and the share of imports in total domestic consumption would equal 1 minus the nation's share of world product. For example, as the US economy accounts for about one-quarter of gross world product, the US import/GDP ratio would, at this benchmark, equal 1 minus the US share of world production, or 0.75, as would, under the first-order assumption of balanced trade, the US export/GDP ratio. However, the actual ratios are only about one-sixth as large as these hypothetical levels![2]

The line with slope −1 in Figure 9.2 − traces out this hypothetical benchmark of perfect product market integration as national shares of world product vary. It also plots the position of the 20 largest nations in these terms. Notice that most of the nations cluster close to the origin, and all fall well below the hypothetical maximum, including the two high-fliers, Belgium and the Netherlands.

Table 9.2 Commodity composition of US merchandise trade

Year	Percentage distribution	
	Exports	*Imports*
Agricultural goods		
1890	42.2	33.1
1990	11.5	5.6
Raw materials		
1890	36.6	22.8
1990	11.6	14.8
Manufactures		
1890	21.2	44.1
1990	77.0	79.6

Figures may not total to 100 due to rounding. Agricultural goods includes processed foods.

Source: Irwin (1996).

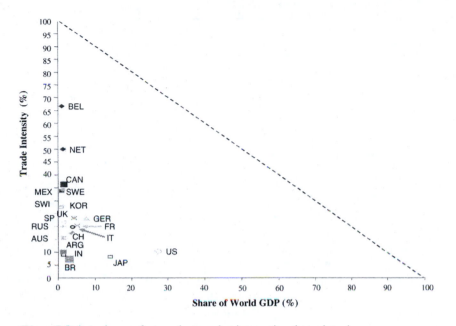

Figure 9.2 Actual *vs* perfect product market integration through trade.

Sources: GNP Rankings based on World Development Bank's World Development Indicators. 2000.Import/Export Data from WTO.

While the hypothetical benchmark suggests significant barriers to cross-border product flows, it also embodies a number of extreme assumptions. A real example that points in the same direction is provided by Canadian provinces' patterns of trade with each other compared with their trade with the USA. In addition to the fact that data for these patterns are available, they have the added advantage of involving (international) trading partners that are close to each other along a number of dimensions. As of 1988, trade linkages between Canadian provinces were 20 times as large as their linkages with the 30 US states that traded the most intensively with Canada. This was true despite the fact that Canada and the USA share a common land border and language (mostly) and have friendly relations with each other, making theirs the largest bilateral trading relationship in the world (McCallum, 1995). The free trade agreement signed in 1988 between the two countries did reduce this domestic multiple by the mid-1990s, but only to 12 (and with the multiple remaining stuck at 30–40 in the case of services) (Helliwell, 1998). Cruder data suggest a multiple of about six for trade within as opposed to between the member states of the European Union (Helliwell, 1998). Given the regionalization of world trade that has been under way, the multiples of domestic-to-international economic exchange would obviously be higher if one were comparing trade within countries with trade outside the regional blocs to which they belong.

To sum up, trade intensity has clearly reached unprecedented levels, but still reveals significant impediments to the cross-border integration of product markets.

Foreign direct investment

Trade is not the only way in which the cross-border integration of product markets might be accomplished: FDI, which involves product-specific investment across borders, is an obvious

Table 9.3 Outward FDI stock as a percentage of GDP

	1914	1938	1960	1980	1985	1990	1995	1997
France	21.1	27.8	6.8	2.7	6.0	9.2	12.0	13.6
Germany	11.1	0.8	1.1	5.3	9.7	9.2	11.1	14.4
Japan	0.8	9.9	1.2	1.9	3.3	6.9	4.7	6.5
UK	52.3	38.5	15.0	15.0	21.9	23.8	28.3	29.1
USA	7.2	8.5	6.2	8.1	6.2	7.9	10.0	10.6
World	9.0[a]	–	4.4	4.8	6.4	8.5[b]	–	11.8

Sources: 1913–1991, World Investment Report 1994; 1997, World Investment Report 1999.

a 1913 data;
b 1991 data;
Figure for 1913 is an estimate.

alternative. To start with a long-run perspective, consider data on FDI stocks divided by GDP over the last century based on calculations in *World Investment Reports* issued by the UN Center on Transnational Corporations. As Table 9.3 indicates, FDI survived the interwar years better than trade (it even came to substitute for the latter as tariff barriers rose), but did not take off again quite as rapidly in the immediate postwar years. FDI has surged, however, since 1980 and, by 1997, had come to exceed the previous (prewar) peak in its share of gross world GDP by a significant margin: 12% to 9%. Despite the declines in the ratio of outward FDI stock to GDP exhibited by the UK and France, the largest foreign investors prior to World War I, the aggregate comparison is suggestive of an increase to unprecedented levels. In sectoral terms, FDI has mirrored trade over this time period by shifting away from natural resources and raw materials (the 'primary' sector) towards manufacturing and, more recently, services.

Obviously, such historical comparisons come with some caveats. For one thing, they are affected in important ways by fundamental shifts in relative exchange rates (and purchasing power). For another, they are based on book values rather than on market values of FDI. The magnitude of this omission seems to be large: data compiled by the US Commerce Department suggest that measurement on the basis of market values rather than book values doubles the estimated values of both US FDI abroad and FDI in the USA. One could argue that this omission leads to greater underestimation of the true values of FDI stocks towards the end of the twentieth century than towards its beginning, because of higher inflation rates (until relatively recently) in the modern period and the increased importance of intangible assets that are more prone to slip through accountants' nets.

Once again, it is useful to look at the current level of integration of product markets through this channel in absolute terms, not just in relation to the levels experienced earlier. Assume, as in the analogous calculation undertaken earlier for trade, that inflows/outflows are, to a first approximation, balanced, and consider a country that accounts for $x\%$ of world investment. If national borders did not affect investment patterns at all, foreign capital would account for $(100-x)\%$ of total investment in that country. The line with slope -1 in Figure 9.3 – traces out this hypothetical benchmark of perfect integration as a function of national shares of gross fixed investment (x). It also plots the position of the 20 largest nations in these terms, based on their recorded FDI inflows. As in the case of trade, most of the nations cluster close to the origin, and all fall well below the hypothetical maximum. Also note that this broad conclusion would not be affected by looking at FDI outflows, although the positions of individual countries would shift substantially. China, for instance, would be less of a high-flier.

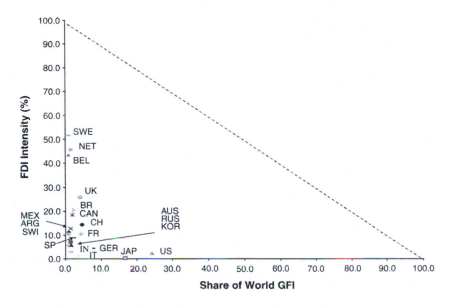

Figure 9.3 Actual *vs* perfect product market integration through FDI.

Source: EIU country data.

Overall, FDI intensity has, like trade intensity, reached unprecedented levels while continuing to fall far short of the levels that would be implied by perfect cross-border integration of product markets through this channel.

Price integration

Viewed in terms of prices rather than quantities, the ultimate in market integration is achieved when two (or more) markets are yoked together by the so-called *law of one price* (LOP), that is, prices equalize across them. Implicit in LOP is a (strong) zero-arbitrage-profits principle. Note that the degree of price integration of product markets can be high even when the quantity flows across them are limited, for example, for some commodities whose local prices are pegged to world benchmark prices, including ones with high value-to-weight ratios. As a result, economists often treat tests of market integration based on prices as being more definitive than tests based on quantities.

Quantity-based tests of cross-border market integration predominate, nonetheless, because, except for (nearly) perfect commodities, tests of price integration are generally hampered by the lack of data on local currency prices of identical products across countries. The relatively few studies of products and services that meet these objections generally indicate substantial, sustained departures from LOP. Cross-country price dispersions tend to be large and to die down at a slow pace, and there is little evidence of recent movement toward smaller dispersions or speedier dampening (Rogoff, 1996). In conjunction with the data presented earlier concerning integration through trade and FDI flows, an overall inference that product market integration has increased significantly in recent decades, while continuing to fall far short of perfection, seems most plausible.

Factor market integration

Product markets are not the only type of market whose cross-border integration one might find interesting; factor markets of various types are also candidates for attention. This section presents and discusses evidence on the extent of cross-border integration of markets for capital, labor, and knowledge, in that order. Both quantity-based and price-based measures of integration are looked at wherever possible.

Capital

The previous section's discussion of FDI can be broadened to look at international capital flows over the last 100 years.[3] Because of identities in national income accounting, countries' net capital flows can be measured as the reverse of their current account balances. Data assembled by Obstfeld and Taylor (1997) on absolute net capital flows divided by GDPs for 12 countries suggest that this index of capital mobility has increased in recent decades, but was higher still around the beginning of the twentieth century (see Table 9.4). Note that the impressive performance 100 years ago was accomplished in spite of informational and contracting problems. Such problems were, most likely, much more severe given the lack of generally accepted accounting principles and commensurately weak reporting requirements.

Of course, not all capital flows are equally important from the perspective of economic globalization. In particular, the recent period has seen a surge in short-run flows, or at least transactions, that is most strikingly evident in the volume of foreign exchange transactions, which exceeds $1 trillion *daily*. Foreign exchange trading can be regarded as a response to a source of volatility – exchange rate risk – that was mitigated significantly in the earlier period by the prevalence of the gold standard. For this reason, and because most trades of this sort seem to be purely speculative, it is problematic to use the size of foreign exchange markets today to infer a much greater level of cross-border integration of capital markets than at the beginning of the century.

This suggests focusing attention on long-run capital flows, which include portfolio investment as well as FDI. Portfolio investment has increased significantly in absolute terms in

Table 9.4 Size of net capital flows since 1870 (mean absolute value of current account as percentage of GDP, annual data)

Period	Arg	Aus	Can	Den	Fra	Cer	Ita	Jap	Nor	Swe	UK	USA	All
1870–1889	18.7	8.2	7.0	1.9	2.4	1.7	1.2	0.6	1.6	3.2	4.6	0.7	3.7
1890–1913	6.2	4.1	7.0	2.9	1.3	1.5	1.8	2.4	4.2	2.3	4.6	1.0	3.3
1914–1918	2.7	3.4	3.6	5.1	–	–	11.6	6.8	3.8	6.5	3.1	4.1	5.1[a]
1919–1926	4.9	4.2	2.5	1.2	2.8	2.4	4.2	2.1	4.9	2.0	2.7	1.7	3.1
1927–1931	3.7	5.9	2.7	0.7	1.4	2.0	1.5	0.6	2.0	1.8	1.9	0.7	2.1
1932–1939	1.6	1.7	2.6	0.8	1.0	0.6	0.7	1.0	1.1	1.5	1.1	0.4	1.2
1940–1946	4.8	3.5	3.3	2.3	–	–	3.4	1.0	4.9	2.0	7.2	1.1	3.2[a]
1947–1959	2.3	3.4	2.3	1.4	1.5	2.0	1.4	1.3	3.1	1.1	1.2	0.6	1.8
1960–1973	1.0	2.3	1.2	1.9	0.6	1.0	2.1	1.0	2.4	0.7	0.8	0.5	1.3
1974–1989	1.9	3.6	1.7	3.2	0.8	2.1	1.3	1.8	5.2	1.5	1.5	1.4	2.2
1990–1996	2.0	4.5	4.0	1.8	0.7	2.7	1.6	2.1	2.9	2.0	2.6	1.2	2.3

Source: Obstfeld and Taylor (1997).

a Average with some countries missing.

recent decades, but seems to have failed to keep pace with FDI, with its share slipping from about two-thirds of total long-run cross-border investment in the early twentieth century to about one-half today (Bloomfield, 1968). Nevertheless, the range of securities traded today across borders is much broader, in type as well as in number; a shift that, some argue, has contributed to increased cross-border integration along this dimension.

International financial crises represent the flip side of international capital mobility. Once again, historical comparisons suggest that international financial crises, particularly in emerging markets, are not without precedent. Data on the currency and banking crises experienced by 21 countries between 1880 and 1998 indicate that the most severe crises, on average, were in the interwar period, followed by the prewar period; postwar crises, in contrast, have been milder in terms of the drops in output experienced, and shorter-lived (Bordo *et al.*, 1999). Even when the sample is restricted to emerging countries, recent levels of instability do no worse than 'match' prewar levels, in which the gold standard acted as a crisis transmission belt, and emerging countries, at least, tended to lack lenders of last resort.[4]

In addition to these historical comparisons, quantity-based measures also permit some inferences about the absolute level of cross-border integration of capital markets. As in the case of trade, the professional curiosity of economists has focused on smaller-than-expected flows (or stocks). Probably the most famous 'anomaly' of this sort is the one uncovered by Feldstein and Horioka (1980), who calculated a 90% correlation between domestic savings and domestic investment across a panel of countries. Their estimate is much higher than benchmark models that assume perfect capital mobility would lead us to expect. Another anomaly that points in the same direction concerns what is called home-country bias: investors in each country hold much larger proportions of their wealth in the form of domestic securities than they would with internationally well-diversified portfolios. By one estimate, US investors should have held more than half their wealth in foreign equities in the 1980s, instead of the less than 10% that they actually held (Lewis, 1995).

Price-based measures of capital market integration – with price integration reinterpreted in terms of the equalization of rates of return on common or comparable securities across national boundaries – supply additional evidence about the continued segmentation of capital markets. One benchmark example is provided by Obstfeld and Taylor's (1997) comparison of 1-year interest rates on sterling-denominated assets sold in London and in New York over the last 100-plus years. Figure 9.4 tracks the standard deviation of differences in returns in the two cities as an inverse measure of capital market integration. The data indicate significant cross-border integration of capital markets prior to 1914, the breakdown of that integration in the interwar period, and its slow restoration in the postwar period. Qualitatively similar conclusions are suggested by comparing real rather than nominal returns, although that does increase the standard deviation of the dispersion of returns, presumably reflecting the effects of currency risk, both nominal and real.[5] At a more macro level, studies of returns, such as Bekaert and Harvey (1995), indicate that the cointegration of capital markets varies greatly in its level and extent over time.

Overall, like product market integration, capital market integration has increased significantly in recent decades, but seems to continue to fall far short of perfection.

Labor

Data on the cross-border integration of labor markets are sparser than for product or capital markets. However, they generally suggest that the number of international migrants (defined as people residing in foreign countries for more than 1 year) has grown with world

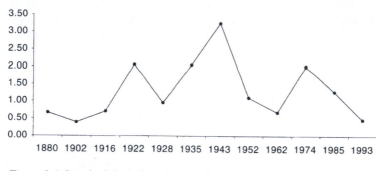

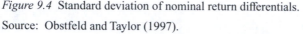

Figure 9.4 Standard deviation of nominal return differentials.

Source: Obstfeld and Taylor (1997).

population in recent decades, but represents a smaller share of world population than 100 years ago. With regard to the first point, there were, according to the World Migration Report, an estimated 150 million long-term international migrants in 2000, or 2.5% of world population (Martin, 2000). The comparable numbers for 1965 were 75 million migrants and 2.2% of world population.

Over a longer time frame, the period between 1880 and 1915/1920 stands out as the heyday of international migration. During these years, 32 million people migrated from Europe, most of them to the USA (Kenwood and Lougheed, 1989). In addition, there were 6–8 million net migrants – mostly 'coolie' or indentured labor – from India, China, and other Asian countries to the rest of the world (Held *et al.*, 1999, 293–295, 311). Adding in other cross-border movements could push the total past 45 million, or 3% of world population in 1900. Higher migration rates 100 years ago are also evident in country-level data, for example, for the largest receiver, the USA. Census data indicate that 14% of the US population was foreign-born at the turn of the century, compared with 10% today (Dune, 2001). Note that, through a substantial part of the earlier period, a number of large receivers, including the USA, placed no restrictions on immigration.

Turning from quantity-based to price-based measures, the most obvious indicator of cross-border integration of labor markets would be the cross-border convergence of wages. Data on the evolution of average per capita incomes (a rough and ready proxy for average wages) indicate that, while incomes in industrialized countries have tended to converge over the last few decades, a few Asian 'tigers' have been the only countries able to break away from the rest of the developing world and catch up with the industrialized world (see Figure 9.5).[6] More sophisticated tests confirm this conclusion, and indicate that the failure of most developing countries to catch up can be reconciled only with a weaker notion of convergence: *conditional convergence* (Barro and Sala-i-Martin, 1995). Conditional convergence allows for differences in the steady-state incomes toward which different economies are trending, based on differences along dimensions such as investment, education, and population growth. Human capital turns out, in attempts to fit conditional convergence models to the data, to have a particularly marked effect on the predicted extent of convergence.

Taking a somewhat longer view, it is worth emphasizing that the nineteenth century apparently saw a divergence, rather than a convergence, of incomes across countries that has been only partially reversed in the twentieth century (Baldwin and Martin, 1999). So, over

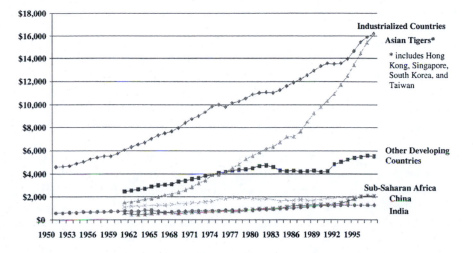

Figure 9.5 Convergence? GDP per capita across economic groups, 1950–1997 (PPP-adjusted).

Source: Scott (2000), adapted from the *Penn World Tables* and the World Bank.

that kind of time frame, the dispersion of incomes across countries increased, in net terms, instead of decreasing. This, along with the other data presented in this subsection, would seem to imply skepticism about the extent to which labor markets have integrated across national boundaries.

Knowledge

The other types of cross-border flows that have been discussed already can carry knowledge across national borders as well, since it can be congealed in products, embedded in capital equipment, vested in skilled personnel, etc. Given the topics already covered in this chapter, this subsection will focus on cross-border flows of knowledge in pure, disembodied form. In addition to rounding out the coverage, this focus has the advantage of offering a relatively simple benchmark: as disembodied knowledge has a 'non-rival' character, that is, as its use in one market, whether defined in geographic or product-related terms, should not preclude its application to others; perfect cross-border integration in this context should imply that knowledge, once developed anywhere in the world, is available everywhere else as well.

The conceptual simplicity of focusing on disembodied knowledge flows does, however, exact an empirical toll: because of their intrinsic intangibility, such flows are particularly hard to measure. The evidence presented in this subsection is correspondingly sketchy. It tentatively suggests, however, that there have been substantial increases in cross-border knowledge flows over time and, a bit more definitely, that cross-border integration in this regard nevertheless remains very incomplete. Consider these inferences in turn.

With regard to technological knowledge, cross-border licensing provides one indicator that supports the inference of increased cross-border knowledge flows over time. Such licensing is not new: international royalties accounted for a significant component of James Watt's receipts from his steam engine patents in the early nineteenth century, for example. However, the available data, along with informational and contracting problems that were even more acute early on than they are now, suggest that the voluntary transfer of knowledge across national borders is far more common than it used to be. Concerning more general managerial knowledge, the post-World War II period, in particular, has seen the development of new types of organizations and organizational forms that have also facilitated knowledge transfer. Franchising, which really emerged in its modern form in the USA in the 1950s, is one example. Management consulting firms, which began their international expansion at roughly the same time, are regarded as having evolved into major channels for the international diffusion of new managerial techniques (Micklethwait and Wooldridge, 2000). Of course, the spread of multinational enterprises, intent on applying the same technological and managerial knowledge to more and more markets, points in the same direction. So, arguably, does the explosion in cross-border information transmission capacity since the early 1980s.

These increases in cross-border knowledge flows notwithstanding, there are also numerous indications of the continued geographical localization of knowledge. The survey evidence on the size of knowledge transfer costs, although not altogether satisfying, is suggestive. An influential study by Teece (1977) concluded that transfer costs accounted for an average of 19% of total project costs – and ranged from 2% to 59% – in a sample of technology transfers in the chemicals, petroleum refining, and machinery sectors. Outcome-based perspectives that point in the same direction are numerous. Through the 1980s, nearly 90% of the US patents taken out by the world's 600 largest corporations listed the inventor as a resident of the corporation's 'home base' (Patel and Pavitt, 1994). Patents whose inventors reside in the same country are typically 30–80% more likely to cite each other than inventors from other countries, and, on average, these citations come 1 year sooner (Jaffe and Trajtenberg, 1999). A recent study of R&D and productivity spillovers across large OECD economies estimated the average elasticity of such spillovers with respect to distance as −1 to −2.4% (Keller, 2000). The importance of locally dense information flows is also evident in internationally successful geographic clusters.[7] Such perspectives remind us that, although the availability of information transmission capacity may help knowledge to travel across national borders, it is far from sufficient to make knowledge perfectly portable.

Semiglobalization as a research program

In summary, most measures of cross-border economic integration have increased significantly in the last few decades, but still fall far short of the theoretical extreme of total integration. This empirical conclusion of semiglobalization is valuable in and of itself given the ongoing debate between two polar perspectives: one maintaining that we have achieved a state of (near) globality, in which there is so much integration across national borders that the latter can, for many practical purposes, be ignored, and the other professing skepticism that there is anything fundamentally new about the levels of cross-border integration that have been achieved to date (Giddens, 1996; Held *et al.*, 1999). It seems possible to achieve some closure to this debate, at least in the economic arena.

As a bonus, semiglobalization affords – unlike alternate possibilities – room for international business strategy to have content that is distinctive from 'mainstream' (single country or location) business strategy or, for that matter, corporate strategy. To make this point as precisely as possible, it is useful to classify the field of strategy into the domains depicted in Table 9.5. Note the somewhat paradoxical character of domain 1, mainstream business strategy: by assuming total specificity, it allots the least attention to understanding either business/usage-specificity or location-specificity. As a result, we have to look to domain 2, that of mainstream corporate strategy, for interesting analyses of variations in the extent to

Table 9.5 Strategy domains

Focus		Increasing attention to business-specificity/non-specificity	
		Single business	*Multiple businesses*
Increasing attention to location-specificity/non-specificity	Single country/location	1. (Mainstream) business strategy	2. (Mainstream) corporate strategy
	Multiple countries/locations	3. International business strategy	4. International corporate strategy

which key firm activities, resources or knowledge are business-specific as opposed to generic (fungible across businesses). We must also look to domain 3, that of international business strategy, for analyses of variations in the extent to which activities, resources or knowledge are location-specific as opposed to free-flowing (fungible across locations). Domain 4, featuring international corporate strategy, purports to combine both business/usage-specificity and domain-specificity, but it is the one about which we currently know the least.

The key point to be made here is that semiglobalization and the location-specificity or geographic segmentation of markets implicit in it is critical to the possibility of domain 3 having content qualitatively distinct from domains 1 and 2. Begin by comparing domains 3 and 1. The critical role of semiglobalization can be illustrated by contrasting it with the extreme alternatives of markets totally insulated from each other by national boundaries or, at the opposite extreme, perfectly integrated with each other across them. Obviously, with complete market insulation, firms could simply decompose their choice problems into country-sized chunks. If markets were completely integrated with each other, the analysis of multiple countries could, once again, be folded back to the single-country base case that is the staple of mainstream business strategy (domain 1), as there would effectively be a single large country. Situations with intermediate levels of cross-border integration cannot be dealt with in the same way, however, in that they do not lend themselves to purely country-level analysis.[8]

Next, compare domain 3 with domain 2. The role of semiglobalization or, more precisely, location-specificity in affording scope for international business strategy to have content distinctive from mainstream corporate strategy is, perhaps, subtler but no less important than in the previous case. Specifically, note that the insights into firm boundaries and expansion derived, respectively, from Coase (1937) and Penrose (1959), were not only worked into international business strategy by Buckley and Casson (1976), among others, but also into mainstream corporate strategy by, in particular, a large body of work on corporate diversification. So, although such insights have been very valuable, they do not by themselves imply content for domain 3 that is conceptually or otherwise qualitatively distinct from that of domain 2; they are a common element of both. For that, what is needed is attention to operations across multiple locations that are distinct from, but not entirely independent of, each other.

Looking more broadly across domains 1–3, Table 9.5 indicates that location-specificity must be invoked to distinguish domain 3 from mainstream strategy of the business and corporate varieties (domains 1 and 2). Semiglobalization ensures such location-specificity, and therefore supplies a conceptually coherent foundation for further analyses at the market and firm levels.

Market/factor-level issues

The preceding argument is equivalent, in some respects, to saying that international business strategy should pay more attention to market imperfections involving location-specificity rather than business/usage-specificity. Those who work primarily on the latter are likely to be somewhat skeptical. One frequently cited concern in this context is the argument that business/usage-specificity affords more room for firm-specific advantages (and disadvantages) than location-specificity. But given complementarities among activities, resources, etc., this argument is a bit of a red herring.

To see why, consider a stylized example in which there are two factors: knowledge, denoted by N (to avoid confusion with K for capital), and labor, denoted by L, with N entirely business/usage-specific and subject to internalization pressures as a result, and L entirely location-specific. Given complementarities between L and N, profit-maximizing firms cannot afford to ignore the labor-cost differences across their various cross-border options even if their management of L itself does not offer the prospect for sustainable firm-specific advantages. In particular, if cross-border differences in the cost of L loom sufficiently large, economic viability will require either that they be capitalized on or that some powerful way of countering them be found. It is hard to see how creative thinking along either of these lines is fostered by suppressing consideration of location-specificity, even if it applies only to a 'generic' factor, L. Even if labor-cost variations cannot underpin sustained competitive advantages for the firms that exploit them because all competitors tap into them, exploitation of them may be necessary to avoid unsustainable disadvantages. The whole point of incomplete integration, after all, is that such factor price equalization will occur, if at all, only in the very long run and cannot, therefore, be assumed in decisions being made in the short-to-medium run.

Analogous points can be made in the context of K as opposed to L. Note that if capital markets were perfectly integrated, there would be one global pool of capital available to fund ventures, and decisions on whether to proceed with investments could be separated from decisions about how to finance them. Such separation of investment and financing decisions, while often assumed domestically, does not fare well in an international context. Foreign investment is, to a significant extent, financed locally in the host country. Thus Feldstein (1995) concluded that only 20% of the value of assets owned by US affiliates abroad was financed by cross-border flows of capital from the USA, with an additional 18% accounted for by retained earnings and the rest representing financing with foreign debt and equity. In such a context, it is hard to believe that MNEs allocate capital globally to equalize marginal returns on investment projects wherever they are undertaken. Instead, firms' investments in real assets seem to be affected by local financing possibilities – or wealth effects. The impact of financial variables on real ones may be more than marginal: some major merger and acquisition waves, for example, seem to have been driven, in large part, by changes in exchange rates (for example, Blonigen, 1997). This is just one of many areas for additional research related to semiglobalization, in this case, concerning segmented international markets for capital and how they interact with real (non-financial) variables.[9]

The broader point that emerges from this discussion is that semiglobalization or incomplete integration is often underplayed because of inadequate attention to the location-specificity of L and K on the grounds that they are generic factors of production incapable of sustaining firm-specific advantages. Capital also seems to get pulled down, as markets for it are supposed to be subject to a high degree of cross-border integration[10] and labor because it is seen to represent a 'low' basis for cross-border competition. In any case, whatever the precise reasoning, the effect is to devalue capital and labor for being relatively non-specialized factors and to focus attention on knowledge. This may seem a reasonable approach. However, recall that it is controverted by the evidence, summarized in the previous section, that markets for capital and labor, just like markets for knowledge, exhibit significant barriers to cross-border integration. As a result, even the apparently unspecialized factors of capital and labor are specialized at the level of location, if in no other sense. They can assume strategic importance in an international context and should be attended to.

Having said that K and L merit more attention than they have historically attracted, it must be added that this is not necessarily inconsistent with the focus of much of the relevant literature, including Buckley and Casson (1976) early on, on knowledge, or as the key factor underlying the market imperfections that are most critical for international business. Instead, what the discussion implies in this regard is that claims of special status for N as a factor in international business strategy (domain 3 in Table 9.5) have to be based on the location-specificity of N. Otherwise, international business strategy and multimarket corporate strategy will be difficult to differentiate. Also note that in some cross-border contexts, at least, considerations of location-specificity do seem to dominate in knowledge-related decision making (for example, Alcacer and Chung, 2001). Nevertheless, there would seem to be great demand for additional research on this much-discussed topic.

Firm-level issues

In addition to flagging factors/products subject to location-specificity as being salient from the perspective of international business strategy, the diagnosis of semiglobalization sheds some light on the content of such strategy at the firm (as opposed to market) level. Most broadly, semiglobalization significantly enriches the strategy space open to firms relative to the straitjacketing structural extremes of: (1) complete isolation at the borders, which would dictate localization, and (2) complete integration, which would dictate standardization. Cases intermediate to 'one country' and one world' present decision-makers with more than one obvious strategy option. These cases require some higher-level decisions about how their firms are going to compete to add value.

There are many specific ways in which firms might try to add value through cross-border operations under conditions of incomplete integration, but they can be grouped in terms of two fundamental economic functions – in the sense of mechanisms for adding value, as opposed to marketing, production, etc. – that organizations try to fulfill by crossing borders. The first function, *aggregation*, involves exploiting the similarities across countries, while somehow side-stepping the differences among them, so as to tap increasing returns to scale. The second, *arbitrage*, involves exploiting differences among countries by taking advantage of variations in absolute costs or willingness-to-pay. The prototypical aggregator is a firm that takes advantage of (partly) locationally mobile resources subject to increasing returns to perform roughly the same activities in different countries (a 'horizontal' MNE). The prototypical arbitrageur takes advantage of international differences by geographically separating activities in an integrated vertical chain (the vertical MNE).

Arbitrage was the function that dominated early international economic activity, as evident in the operations of the trading companies chartered in the sixteenth and seventeenth centuries, the whaling fleets of the eighteenth century, and the vertically integrated agricultural and extractive (mining) companies that emerged in the nineteenth century (Ghemawat, 2000). In contrast, aggregation first came to the fore – with the possible exception of a few international banking chains that emerged earlier in the nineteenth century – with the manufacturing multinationals that began to appear in the second half of the nineteenth century. Despite this late start, however, casual evidence suggests that aggregation has commandeered researchers' attention to the point where the arbitrage function is often ignored. The long-running discussion of the tensions between integration and responsiveness and their resolution is a good example (Prahalad and Doz, 1987). These issues are salient in the context of aggregation, but not in the context of arbitrage, which is often passed over in silence as a result. Note that such a bias towards aggregation would lead to suboptimal responses to conditions of incomplete integration because of an undue emphasis on treating important differences across countries as sources of difficulty to be ignored or minimized (as part of an aggregation approach) rather than as possible sources of value (as part of an arbitrage approach). To consider all possible levers of value, it is important to supplement horizontal approaches that emphasize aggregation with vertical approaches that seek to capitalize on (as opposed to merely cope with) differences, that is, that emphasize arbitrage.

Unbundling the two functions should help in this regard. To start with the one that tends to get overlooked more, arbitrage, the schema used earlier in this paper to distinguish among markets for products, capital, labor, and knowledge also suggests a correspondingly broad array of arbitrage-based mechanisms for (potentially) adding value. Firms can arbitrage the incomplete integration of product markets across borders by becoming traders. Capital market differences provide them with a strong incentive to account for international differences in the cost of capital. They can arbitrage labor cost differences by relocating labor-intensive activities to countries with low labor costs, they can try to harness knowledge differences, and more broadly, geographically dispersed knowledge by making asset-seeking (rather than asset-exploiting) investments in critical locations, a task that involves detailed coordination across multiple locations rather than, as some would have it, the death of geography.

The aggregation function also lends itself to unbundling. Here, there are continua of possibilities ranging, as noted above, from the complete localization of a business by country at one extreme to complete standardization across countries at the other. Interestingly distinct – and progressively less researched – intermediate possibilities include:

(1) adaptation, in which the business model originated in the 'home base' becomes the basis for local modification;
(2) platform or front-to-back approaches, in which certain core features of a business model (the 'platform') are preset globally, while others can be altered in light of local conditions; and
(3) clustering, which emphasizes grouping countries – regionalization is a subcase – in order to pursue commonalities more aggressively than would be possible with pure country-by-country adaptation.

Developing a contingency theory of choice that operates this level of disaggregation would seem to be a high priority.

An additional assumption that is worth discussing in this context is the textbook distinction between horizontal MNEs that emphasize aggregation and vertical MNEs that emphasize arbitrage. This dichotomy assumes that it is often possible – and useful – to distinguish firms in terms of the one function that is economically central, over long periods of time, to their strategies for adding value by competing around the world.[11] If one accepts this, then it is clear that there are two mutually exclusive approaches to achieving geographic coherence or fit, the international business analogue of mainstream business strategy's focus on internal and external fit at the level of the individual business, and corporate strategy's focus on fit or coherence across businesses. But there also seem to be indications that large multinationals engage, at least to some extent, in both aggregation and arbitrage. This naturally raises the question of the extent to which it is possible to mix and match across aggregation-oriented and arbitrage-oriented activities. Or to put matters more starkly, how feasible are transformation strategies that extensively exploit both aggregation opportunities and arbitrage possibilities?

A final question concerns whether intra-firm cross-border economic activity should be seen as a substitute for or driver of market integration. It is customary to think of (cross-border) firms as remedies for the infirmities of (cross-border) markets. However, the importance of intra-firm trade and FDI, in particular, hints that it might make sense to shift towards seeing firms as global connectors or conduits responsible, to a significant extent, for cross-border integration rather than as islands embedded in seas of market relationships. Of course, whether firms' cross-border activities substitute for or complement the cross-border integration of markets is yet another open and obviously important agenda item for future research.

Conclusions

Accounts of the cross-border integration of markets have tended to get very wrapped up in the times in which they were written, perhaps too much so. Deutsch and Eckstein (1961) emphasized that, by the 1950s, the internationalization of transactions had declined significantly since the beginning of the twentieth century, and averred that this trend was unlikely to be reversed any time soon. Contrary to their predictions, cross-border economic activity surged in the 1960s onward and, as it breached prewar records, inspired forked responses. Globalists stressed that international economic integration had reached new heights, while skeptics insisted that it had barely returned to levels experienced nearly a century earlier. Globalists gained confidence with the fall of the Berlin Wall in 1989 and the rapid growth in much of Asia through much of the 1990s. But then came the Asian financial crisis, episodes of instability in Russia and Latin America, a perceived 'globalization backlash', a global economic slowdown, and the war on global terrorism. By mid-2002, the mood, at least among practitioners, seemed to be one of skepticism rather than optimism about globalization.

The empirical evidence reviewed in this article suggests that it might be preferable to take a more measured, historically self-conscious perspective on cross-border integration instead of frequently announcing changes in its direction or speed. Specifically, the empirical review indicated that most measures of market integration have scaled new heights in the last few decades, but still fall far short of economic theory's ideal of perfect integration. Looking forward, levels of cross-border integration may increase, stagnate or even suffer a sharp reversal if the experience between and during the two world wars is any indication of the possibilities: while technological changes may be irreversible, political changes need not be. But given the parameters of the current situation, it seems unlikely that increases will any time soon yield a state in which the differences among countries can be ignored, multinationals' best efforts to connect markets across borders notwithstanding. Or that decreases could soon lead to a state in which cross-border linkages can be forgotten about. So, one does not have to make a precise forecast to diagnose that semiglobalization as a condition is sufficiently broad to persist for some time to come. Achieving similar stability in attitudes toward cross-border operations would seem preferable to manic-depressive swings in attitudes about the outlook, if only for purely pragmatic reasons.

The diagnosis of semiglobalization does more than just supply a relatively stable frame of reference for thinking about the environment of cross-border operations. Semiglobalization also calls attention to the critical role that location-specificity plays in the prospects of distinctive content for international business strategy relative to mainstream business and corporate strategy. In addition, it flags factors/products subject to location-specificity as being salient from the perspective of international business. Finally, it highlights the scope for strategies that strive to capitalize on the (large) residual barriers to cross-border integration, as well as those that simply try to cope with them.

Such considerations motivate the modest proposal that semiglobalization or location-specificity merits the status of a major research program in international business. In other words, that a significant volume of research activity should be redirected along lines that take explicit account of both the importance and the incompleteness of the integration of markets across borders. In addition to reflecting empirical reality, a research program of this sort would directly address the apparent dearth of 'big research questions' in international business. As Buckley (2002, 370) recently put it:

> International business has succeeded because it has focused on, in sequence, a number of big questions, which arise from empirical developments in the world economy. The agenda is stalled because no such big question has currently been identified. This calls into question the separate existence of the subject area. It raises the old problem of the relationship between international business and other functional areas of management and social science.

From this perspective, the issue is not whether a big research question is needed at this juncture in the development of international business, but, instead, what it should be about: semiglobalization/location-specificity or something else?

Acknowledgements

This paper has benefited from research assistance by Jamie Matthews and Raluca Lupu, helpful comments by David Collis, Beulah D'Souza, Vijay Govindarajan, Mauro Guillen, Tarun Khanna, Walter Kuemmerle, Christos Pitelis, Ravi Ramamurti, Louis T. Wells Jr., George S. Yip and, especially, Bernard Y. Yeung, as well as from presentation of material at the AIB Panel Session, in summer 2002, celebrating Buckley and Casson (1976). The Division of Research at the Harvard Business School provided financial support.

Notes

1 While location-specificity can also operate at the local or (intranational) regional level, a full treatment of it at all these levels of analyses is beyond the scope of this paper, even though many of the analytical issues that arise are similar.
2 The disparity is even greater if one recognizes that the denominator of the ratio should really be a measure of gross sales rather than a value-added measure like GDP.
3 Foreign direct investment currently accounts for roughly one-half of total foreign investment, but its share was significantly smaller at the start of the twentieth century. See Bloomfield (1968, 3–4), cited in Bordo *et al.* (1999).
4 Note that the spread of domestic safety nets does increase the likelihood that banking crises will turn into currency crises.
5 For further discussion of currency risk, see Frankel (1992).
6 Note the caveat that the extent of catch-up by the Asian tigers would look somewhat less remarkable if the data in Figure 9.5 were updated to take account of the Asian currency crisis.
7 The other (overlapping) reasons for the localization of international competitiveness identified by Porter (1990) are sophisticated local demand and the local availability of specialized inputs and complements as well as basic factors of production.

8 This point can be demonstrated formally in the context of standard supply–demand analysis. To start at one extreme, with complete insulation between two country markets, the price and quantity outcomes can be pinned down (under the assumption of atomistic competition) at the intersection of supply and demand curves in each market. At the other extreme, with complete integration, that is, zero extra costs of trading, transporting, transacting and so on across national boundaries – one could still add up the supply curves for the two markets on the one hand and their demand curves on the other and use the point of intersection of the two aggregate curves to determine the (common) prices and the quantities in the unified market. But the continuum of situations between zero and complete economic integration that I refer to as semi-globalization creates additional challenges. Given semiglobalization, the analysis of prices and quantities in the two markets cannot be reduced to supply–demand analysis of an individual market. Instead, attention has to be paid to distinct markets that are neither totally segmented nor totally integrated; an intrinsically more complex, and interesting, setup.

9 For further discussion along these lines, see Caves (1998).

10 Such integration would make access to a global pool of capital a 'given' for any worthy enterprise and thereby limit the scope for purely financial sources of advantage or disadvantage.

11 Caves (1996) also identifies a third, residual category of multinational enterprise: international diversifiers whose operations in different countries are neither horizontally nor vertically related to each other. These can be thought of as falling in domain 4 of Table 9.5 rather than domain 3.

References

Alcacer, J. and Chung, W. (2001) 'Knowledge seeking, human capital and location choice of foreign entrants in the United States', Working Paper, Stern School of Business, New York University.

Baldwin, R.E. and Martin, P. (1999) *Two Waves of Globalization: Superficial Similarities, Fundamental Differences*, National Bureau of Economic Research: Cambridge, MA, NBER Working Paper No. 6904.

Barro, R.J. and Sala-i-Martin, X. (1995) *Economic Growth*, McGraw-Hill: New York.

Bekaert, G. and Harvey, C.R. (1995) 'Time-varying world market integration', *Journal of Finance* 50(2): 403–44.

Blonigen, B.A. (1997) 'Firm-specific assets and the link between exchange rates and foreign direct investment', *American Economic Review* 87(3): 447–65.

Bloomfield, A.I. (1968) *Patterns of Fluctuation in International Finance Before 1914*, Princeton Studies in International Finance No. 21, International Finance Section, Department of Economics, Princeton University.

Bordo, M.D., Eichengreen, B. and Irwin, D.A. (1999) *Is Globalization Today Really Different than Globalization a Hundred Years Ago?*, National Bureau of Economic Research: Cambridge, MA, NBER Working Paper 7195 (Prepared for the Brookings Trade Policy Forum on Governing in a Global Economy, Washington, DC, 15–16 April 1999. Published: shorter version in Austrian Economic Papers, Vols. 1 and 2, 2000).

Buckley, P.J. (2002) 'Is the international business agenda running out of steam?', *Journal of International Business Studies* 33(2): 365–73.

Buckley, P.J. and Casson, M. (1976) *The Future of the Multinational Enterprise*, Macmillan: London.

Caves, R.E. (1996) *Multinational Enterprise and Economic Analysis*, Cambridge University Press: Cambridge.

Caves, R.E. (1998) 'Research on international business: problems and prospects', *Journal of International Business Studies* 29(1): 5–19.

Coase, R.H. (1937) 'The nature of the firm', *Economica* 4(16): 396–405.

Deutsch, K.W. and Eckstein, A. (1961) 'National industrialization and the declining share of the international economic sector, 1890–1959', *World Politics* 13(2): 267–72.

Dune, N. (2001) 'US population is now more than 10% foreign-born', *Financial Times*, 4 January 2001, The Americas, p. 4.

Feenstra, R.C. (1998) 'Integration of trade and disintegration of production in the global economy', *Journal of Economic Perspectives* **12**(4): 31–50.

Feldstein, M. (1995) 'The Effects of Outbound Foreign Direct Investment on the Domestic Capital Stock', in M. Feldstein, J. Hines and R.G. Hubbard (eds.) *The Effects of Taxation on Multinational Corporations*, University of Chicago Press: Chicago, pp: 43–63.

Feldstein, M. and Horioka, C. (1980) 'Domestic savings and international capital flows', *Economic Journal* **90**(358): 314–29.

Frankel, J.A. (1992) 'Measuring international capital mobility: a review', *American Economic Review* **82**(2): 197–202.

Frankel, Jeffrey, A. (2001) 'Assessing the Efficiency Gain from Further Liberalization', in Porter, Roger B., Pierre Sauvé, Arvind Subramanian & Americo Beviglia Zampetti (eds.) *Efficiency, Equity, and Legitimacy: The Multilateral Trading System at the Millennium*, Brookings Institution Press: Washington, DC.

Ghemawat, P. (2000) 'Global advantage: arbitrage, replication, and transformation', unpublished note, Harvard Business School, December.

Giddens, A. (1996) 'Keynote address at the United Nations Research Institute for Social Development, as excerpted in 'Essential matter'', *UNRISD News*, No. 15.

Held, D., McGrew, A.G., Goldblatt, D. and Perraton, J. (1999) *Global Transformations: Politics, Economics, and Culture*, Stanford University Press: Stanford.

Helliwell, J.F. (1998) *How Much Do National Borders Matter?*, Brookings Institution Press: Washington, DC.

Irwin, D.A. (1996) 'The United States in a new global economy? A century's perspective', *American Economic Review* **86**(2): 41–46.

Jaffe, A.B. and Trajtenberg, M. (1999) 'International knowledge flows: evidence from patent citations', *Economics of Innovation and New Technology* **8**(1–2): 105–36.

Keller, W. (2000) *Geographic Localization of International Technology Diffusion*, National Bureau of Economic Research: Cambridge, MA, NBER Working Paper No. 7509.

Kenwood, A.G. and Lougheed, A.L. (1989) *The Growth of the International Economy, 1920–1960*, Allen & Unwin: London.

Lewis, K.K. (1995) 'Puzzles in International Financial Markets', in G. Grossman and K. Rogoff (eds.) *Handbook of International Economics*, Vol. Ill, Elsevier Science: Amsterdam, pp: 1913–71.

McCallum, J. (1995) 'National borders matter: Canada – US regional trade patterns', *American Economic Review* **85**(3): 615–23.

Maddison, A. (1995) *Monitoring the World Economy: 1820–1992*, Development Centre of the Organization for Economic Cooperation and Development: Paris.

Martin, S.F. (ed.) (2000) *World Migration Report: 2000*, Copublished by the International Organization for Migration and the United Nations.

Micklethwait, J. and Wooldridge, A. (2000) *A Future Perfect: The Challenge and Hidden Promise of Globalization*, Crown Business: New York.

Obstfeld, M. and Taylor, A. (1997) *The Great Depression as a Watershed: International Capital Mobility over the Long Run*, National Bureau of Economic Research: Cambridge, MA, NBER Working Paper 5960.

Patel, P. and Pavitt, K. (1994) *National Innovation Systems: Why they are Important and How they Might be Measured and Compared*, Mimeo, Science Policy Research Unit, University of Sussex.

Penrose, E.T. (1959) *The Theory of the Growth of the Firm*, Basil Blackwell, Wiley: Oxford, New York.

Porter, M.E. (1990) *The Competitive Advantage of Nations*, Free Press: New York.

Prahalad, C.K. and Doz, Y. (1987) *The Multinational Mission: Balancing Local Demands and Global Vision*, Free Press: New York.

Rogoff, K. (1996) 'The purchasing power parity puzzle', *Journal of Economic Literature* **34**(2): 647–68.

Scott, B. (2000) *Economic Strategies of Nations*, Mimeo, Harvard Business School.

Teece, D.J. (1977) 'Technology transfer by multinational firms: the resource cost of transferring technological know-how', *The Economic Journal* **87**(346): 242–61.

UN Center on Transnational Corporations, World Investment Report (1994, 1997, 1999).

World Economic Forum, Global Competitiveness Report (various issues).

10 Do regions matter?

An integrated institutional and semiglobalization perspective on the internationalization of MNEs*

Jean-Luc Arregle, Toyah L. Miller,
Michael A. Hitt, and Paul W. Beamish

Introduction

The decision to expand operations into foreign markets, or internationalize, is one of the most important strategic decisions made by multinational enterprises (MNEs) (Goerzen and Beamish, 2003; Hitt *et al.*, 1997). As a result, factors that influence how much and where to internationalize have attracted much attention in the scholarly literature using a number of different theoretical perspectives. One perspective acknowledges the importance of institutions. Here, scholars have focused on country-level influences whereby location-specific institutional factors affect the MNE's ability to exploit its resources in host countries and thereby influence its internationalization decisions in these countries (for example, Chan *et al.*, 2008; Gaur *et al.*, 2007; Meyer *et al.*, 2009). Recently, a second stream of research has focused on MNEs' international strategy of semiglobalization. The 'semiglobalization' perspective emphasizes the importance of regions in MNEs' international strategy as their regional coordination helps them to maintain local responsiveness and exploit region-bound firm-specific advantages (Ghemawat, 2003, 2007; Rugman and Verbeke, 2004, 2005). These two streams of research have developed independently, leaving gaps in our understanding of whether and how regions matter in MNEs' international strategy. For instance, there is a need for a greater understanding of how formal institutions influence internationalization decisions at the country and regional levels (Chan *et al.*, 2008).

Accordingly, in this study we provide a multilevel rationale for MNE decisions about where and how much to internationalize (i.e., an MNE's degree of internationalization into a host country) by investigating the dual effects of formal institutions (North, 1990; Williamson, 2000) at the country and region levels. We examine the effects of three formal institutions (i.e., regulatory control, political democracy, capital investments) in the context of semiglobalization. These perspectives suggest that MNEs consider institutional environments in their decisions about where and how much to internationalize at two critical levels: selecting attractive regions and selecting attractive countries within regions. As mentioned, it is known that institutions affect the attractiveness of FDI destinations. However, we develop and test a different perspective. Countries are attractive not only because of their institutions but also because they serve as platforms for entry into their regions, enabling regional arbitrage, creating real options for regional expansion, and increasing the value of pre-existing

*'Do regions matter? An integrated institutional and semiglobalization perspective on the internationalization of MNEs', Strategic Management Journal, 34: 910–934, 10. Arregle, Jean-Luc, Toyah L. Miller, Michael A. Hitt & Paul W. Beamish.

regional investments.[1] Hence, the institutions of a region in which a country is located are an important criterion for an MNE's degree of internationalization into a country. We test these models by applying a multilevel methodology explaining the propensities of Japanese MNEs to internationalize into 45 countries located in eight geographic regions.

This study contributes in several ways to our knowledge of strategic decisions regarding foreign direct investments (FDIs), the effects of institutional environments, and a semiglobalization strategy. First, our study provides additional support for the prior arguments on the importance of regionalization (or semiglobalization). Our investigation confirms that an MNE's prior internationalization into a region has an effect on its future decisions to internationalize into a country, validating a semiglobalization approach. Second, we separate the dual effect of three formal institutions on MNEs' choices of internationalization at the region and country levels, showing the relevance of a 'semiglobalized' institutional perspective. Third, we identify the effects on internationalization decisions of the institutional environment in geographic regions and the effects of a country's institutional profile relative to other countries' profiles in the same region. Although research exists on specific regions and on effects of particular institutions (for example, Oxelheim and Ghauri, 2004; Schiavo, 2007; Seyf, 2001), little is known about how an MNE considers the attractiveness of a region and of countries within it. Finally, we further compare the traditional country-level institutional approach with the region- and country-level semiglobalized model to understand which provides a better understanding of the institutional environment's influence on MNEs' foreign market investment decisions. We complement previous studies with a more inclusive view, resulting in a new and more systematic understanding of the effects of the institutional environment on internationalization decisions.

Theoretical development

Current theoretical and empirical work on MNE internationalization emphasizes the systematic ownership and location advantages of FDI and identifies the role of institutions in motivating foreign investments into a country (for example, Delios and Henisz, 2003; Globerman and Shapiro, 2003). The institutional environment consists of those structures that form the basis for a society and constrain behavior within it (North, 1991). In addition, new institutional economists have emphasized the important role that formal institutions play in providing stability, minimizing market failures, reducing uncertainty, and alleviating information complexity in economic exchanges (North, 1990; Williamson, 2000). It is clear that institutions matter, particularly the formal institutional structures that, through written laws, regulations, policies, and their enforcement measures, prescribe the actions and behaviors of people, systems, and organizations.

The three formal institutional 'pillars'

North (1990) argued that the constraints of formal institutions occur through political, regulatory, and economic structures because of their strong and visible impact; as such, they are likely to influence localization decisions (Holmes *et al.*, 2013). The regulatory environment provides oversight and direction for the conduct of organizations. As an institution of potential coercive force, the regulatory environment influences firm actions through rule-setting, monitoring, and sanctions, thereby reducing uncertainty for the collective (North, 1991). Early institutional economists (for example, Coase, 1959) focused on the power of regulations to create and enforce property rights protections; these regulations were believed to aid market transactions under the assumption that 'government steps aside' and releases control to allow free markets after this role is fulfilled (Williamson, 2000: 598). Many attributes of the regulatory environment, such as the level of enforcement or openness of law, might also facilitate market transactions by reducing uncertainty (Globerman and Shapiro, 2003). However, Bardhan (1989) suggests that extensive governmental control or interference in business is often perceived as a hindrance to the conduct of business and may even go beyond serving its beneficiaries. For example, research has found that government regulations frequently increase the perceived transactions costs of doing business abroad and also lead to sacrifices in efficiency (Brouthers, 2002; Yiu and Makino, 2002). *Regulatory control*, that is, greater government involvement in setting rules and standards that prescribe and constrain the behavior of organizations in commerce often also imposes direct or indirect costs on the firm (i.e., the formal rules and laws that monitor and direct the conduct of firms).

Second, as an institution, *political democracy* establishes the level of checks and balances in government and reflects an ideology of how people and entities in society (for example, organizations) should be governed (Gaur *et al.*, 2007). It affects the MNE operations as political regimes can create significant uncertainty and potential costs for them. Political democracy reflects the discretion of government over its citizenry and is marked by voting rights and freedom of speech, assembly and media. While the regulatory environment focuses on the application of laws and rules in commerce, the political environment prescribes how laws and rules are created, defining the society's level of human and political rights for participation in rule-setting and freedom of expression[2] (Adam and Filippaios, 2007). As separate constructs, one captures the level of representation, participation, and freedoms available to people in voicing opinions and influencing outcomes; whereas, the other focuses on the degree of parameters for commerce resulting from legislation.

Finally, strong economic institutions serve as a formal constraint that reduces uncertainty and information asymmetries between borrowers and lenders in transactions and establishes rules in the market economy (Hodgson, 1988; North, 1990). These institutions are location specific and can facilitate as well as constrain market behaviors (Zukin and DiMaggio, 1990). Economic institutions influence the availability of financial resources and potential consumption, production, and cost of living in the country, and thus they have a strong impact on FDIs (Brouthers and Brouthers, 2000). These economic institutions are evident in a country's monetary and fiscal policies (Beck *et al.*, 2000; Lucas, 2003). Given their influence on purchasing power and investments made in labor, technology transfer, and production (Romer, 1994), a country's *capital investments*, or the commitment of capital or money to purchase assets, promote an economy's strength and liquidity, thereby increasing a location's attractiveness for MNE investment and serving as a proxy for the strength of economic institutions (Tirole, 2003).

The role of regions in semiglobalization

A focus on the globalization of international firms that solely considers effects at the level of the host country (including their institutions) may not fully or accurately represent MNEs' strategic practices (Ghemawat, 2003; Rugman and Verbeke, 2004). In response, a semiglobalization approach suggests that a firm's foreign investments follow patterns exhibiting regional aggregation and arbitrage logic to cope with the opposing pressures of globalization (i.e., integration) and local markets (i.e., localization) (Arregle *et al.*, 2009). Semiglobalization involves partial cross-border integration whereby barriers to market integration are high but not high enough to insulate countries completely from each other. These situations cannot be fully understood through purely country-level analyses but require an evaluation of operations across multiple locations (for example, within a region) that are distinct from but not entirely independent of each other (Ghemawat, 2003). Therefore, the region composed of geographically proximate countries becomes an important level of analysis when examining MNEs' internationalization and institutional influences (Arregle *et al.*, 2009; Ghemawat, 2003).

Semiglobalization mechanisms and prior regional internationalization

The semiglobalized perspective suggests that firms often seek to expand by exploiting their prior internationalization in regions and specific countries in those regions. Two key mechanisms help MNEs engage in this semiglobalization behavior: the redeployment of region-bound firm-specific advantages and organizational learning.

Region-bound firm-specific advantages

The MNE's geographic scope is a critical dimension of its international strategy and is determined by the ability to integrate firm-specific advantages (FSAs) with country-specific advantages (CSAs). As a result, 'each foreign location requires location-specific linking investments to meld existing FSAs with CSAs' (Rugman and Verbeke, 2005: 13). Asset specificity occurs within firms as they make these country-specific investments, imposing a cost and potentially limiting their redeployability. Because a particular resource may have a range of potential services (Mahoney and Pandian, 1992; Teece, 1982), its fungibility, or 'the extent to which resources can be deployed for alternative uses at low cost,' is important (Sapienza *et al.*, 2006: 924). Therefore, because internationalization is fraught with uncertainty, fungibility is important for MNEs as it provides flexibility and discretion in executing strategies and contributes to survival and growth while buffering costs (Sapienza *et al.*, 2006).

MNEs can enhance redeployability potential by developing region-bound FSAs (RFSAs) as they can be exploited successfully by a firm throughout a region rather than being restricted to one country. Firms are able to reap benefits from these regional fungible capabilities when they have expanded into countries within that region. They exist when the firm is able to integrate its foreign subsidiaries regionally while maintaining responsiveness at the country level. Therefore, RFSAs can be exploited successfully by a firm across a region through low-cost linking investments (i.e., low transaction costs) due to the relative geographic proximity of these countries and their corresponding CSAs (Rugman and Verbeke, 2005). Generally, replicating and exploiting fungible resources in foreign countries can be challenging because of their intangibility and the need to develop specific approaches to deal with the idiosyncrasies and characteristics of foreign markets (Kumar, 2009). Such processes emphasize the importance of discovering the critical traits of these markets through organizational learning.

Organizational learning and strategic options

Acquiring market- and network-specific experiential knowledge is time-consuming yet critical to internationalization success for an MNE because it must overcome its liability of foreignness or outsidership[3] (Johanson and Vahlne, 1977, 2009). Such crucial knowledge can be gained from experience in current international operations. The larger the psychic distance (i.e., 'factors that make it difficult to understand foreign environments,' [Johanson and Vahlne, 2009: 1412]) between markets, the more difficult it is for MNEs to develop such knowledge. Because of absorptive capacity (Cohen and Levinthal, 1990), a firm's knowledge development is cumulative and necessitates a certain level of proximity between old and new competences, resulting in the need for some continuity. Both psychic distance and absorptive capacity result in time compression diseconomies (Dierickx and Cool, 1989; Vermeulen and Barkema, 2002) and in limited path dependence for MNEs' international expansion. These organizational learning mechanisms explain a sequential approach to international entry as MNEs approach foreign entry with learning gained from past entry experience, gradually accumulating capabilities in relatively proximate countries and taking the best opportunities that emerge (Chang, 1995).

Prior internationalization into a region also helps MNEs in this learning process because geographic agglomeration can facilitate flows of knowledge within a firm. There are spatial aspects of knowledge, and flows of information are spatially constrained (Buckley and Ghauri, 2004; Sorenson and Baum, 2003). Geographic proximity facilitates the transmission of knowledge and organizational practices within the organization (for example, Chang and Park, 2005; Strang, 2003). Hence, the MNE's proximally close foreign subsidiaries can more easily share knowledge and organizational routines. Moreover, prior internationalization within a region can help to overcome the liability of outsidership, which is not necessarily limited to the country level but can also occur at the region level (Collinson and Rugman, 2008; Johanson and Vahlne, 2009). Due to the nature of business networks, which increasingly have a regional dimension (Buckley and Ghauri, 2004), a first FDI in a region helps the MNE to reduce this liability for its next FDIs in the same region. Finally, the similarities existing among proximate countries within a region, which result in lower psychic distances among them, allow the MNE to accumulate knowledge and to learn from its initial entries in this region. This incremental regional learning reduces the MNE's FDI expansion costs in a region and minimizes problems of absorptive capacity or time compression diseconomies in the learning of new capabilities. The result is a region-level sequential entry approach: investing in a country allows the MNE to create a 'real option' to expand in the future into other countries (Kogut, 1983; Kogut and Kulatilaka, 1994) within the same attractive region. Hence, after the MNE has established an FDI in a country within a region, it can develop RFSAs for that region providing a platform for future expansion into other countries within that region. Applying these two mechanisms, we propose the following hypothesis on MNEs' prior internationalization into a region:

Hypothesis 1: The propensity of MNEs to internationalize into a country is positively related to their prior level of internationalization into this country's region.

Semiglobalization, institutional effects, and internationalization decisions

While a firm may be more likely to expand into a country due to its prior experience within a region, such as the European Union or NAFTA, there are many choices as to which country within each region is the most attractive, and these are highly influenced by the institutional characteristics of the region and countries within it (Kreinin and Plummer, 2008; Oxelheim and Ghauri, 2004). Each geographic region can be described by the general (i.e., average) characteristics of the institutional environments of the countries within it. MNEs carefully consider the general institutional environment of a region in making location decisions because RFSAs are constrained to a specific geographic region, which establishes the boundaries for the future FDI opportunities that can be exploited. Hence, the institutional environments of countries in the region will collectively limit or increase the MNE's internationalization into a country located in that region.

As a result of possessing RFSAs, MNEs can make arbitrage decisions among countries in the same region. To do so, they compare the relative characteristics of each country to choose the most attractive environments in which to locate their subsidiaries (for example, Chung *et al.*, 2008; Ghemawat, 2003). They exploit intra-regional differences and try to benefit from these variations. A firm can choose to invest in a country based on the potential host country's institutional environment relative to the other countries in the same region, or a *country's 'region-relative' institutional environment*. This variable reflects the variations and indicates the position of a country relative to the general tendency in its region. If a country has a better (worse) region-relative institutional profile, it will attract more (less) MNEs' investments relative to these other countries in the region.

These arguments suggest that in internationalization decisions, MNEs also focus on a country's institutional environment in comparison to other countries in the same region. Next we examine the influence of regulatory, political, and economic institutions on localization decisions at the region and country levels.

Regulatory institutional environment

MNEs must conform to regulatory requirements in the host country or region and the cognitive and normative pressures that underlie them (Scott, 1995; Yiu and Makino, 2002). The adoption of organizational practices and compliance by subsidiaries imposes economic costs for implementation as well as additional risks because of the complex challenges involved in navigating rules and regulations (Eden and Miller, 2004; Tirole, 2003). However, when not burdensome, the enforcement of regulations and protections can also provide support for some business activities (Coase, 1959). For example, the development of a legal system, the openness and transparency of regulations, and regulatory enforcement (reducing uncertainty) all positively influence FDI (Bevan *et al.*, 2004; Globerman and Shapiro, 2003; La Porta *et al.*, 1998; Rammal and Zurbruegg, 2006). Government often goes beyond providing necessary protections to undergird transactions by establishing tariffs on trade in order to control such areas as market entry or expansion. In this study, we investigate a related facet of the regulatory environment, namely, the extensiveness of government control of (or interference into) commercial activity. High levels of this type of regulatory control represents a negative cost of doing business that may outweigh its related benefits.

In contrast to the freedom of an open trade environment favored by most multinationals (Globerman and Shapiro, 2003), when regulatory control increases beyond a threshold that facilitates business, it results in additional management challenges, difficult-to-predict violations, high costs, and even barriers to reaching agreements with local partners and governments. High levels of regulation increase government control over organizations, threatening their autonomy and thereby reducing incentives for MNEs to enter that country's markets (Brouthers and Bamossy, 1997; Kaufmann *et al.*, 1999). Firms must accept the costs of conforming to these local regulations and learn the regulatory requirements and policies of the new setting if they are to survive within it (Eden and Miller, 2004; Levine and Renelt, 1992). These economic costs often entail tariffs, quotas, trade barriers, entry and license fees, and costs of protecting intellectual and property rights, all of which favor local businesses (Boddewyn, 1988). Indirect costs include limits on firm actions that sometimes preclude the most efficient or desired course of action. Therefore, higher regulatory control reduces the flexibility of MNEs and may limit their strategic options, dissuading them from making investments (for example, Brouthers, 2002; Loree and Guisinger, 1995). For example, Yiu and Makino (2002) found that areas with restrictive regulatory regimes increase the liability of foreignness for foreign firms, thereby enhancing the disadvantage of foreign firms relative to local firms especially because of the difference in knowledge of how to deal with local government. Zaheer and Mosakowski (1997) found that MNEs located in countries with a greater level of regulation had higher failure rates. These findings suggest a curvilinear (inverted U-shaped) relationship between regulatory control and the propensity of MNEs to internationalize in the local market. Applying the aforementioned semiglobalization frame-work, we offer the following hypothesis:

Hypothesis 2a: A curvilinear (inverted U-shaped) relationship exists between the propensity of MNEs to internationalize into a country and the regulatory control of its region.

Hypothesis 2b: A curvilinear (inverted U-shaped) relationship exists between the propensity of MNEs to internationalize into a country and the country's 'region-relative' regulatory control.

Political institutional environment

Political democracy influences the attractiveness of internationalization into a country because it determines the risk that government leaders may change laws without proper checks and balances or input from the public (Harms and Ursprung, 2002; Jensen, 2003; Kobrin, 1979). Some research suggests that MNEs may choose to internationalize into more repressed areas under autocratic rule to obtain cost advantages in labor, reduce the risk of collective bargaining, and increase the likelihood of favorable deals with governments that allow them to exploit concentrations of power (Bucheli, 2008; O'Donnell, 1988; Rodrik, 1999). However, other studies suggest that the checks and balances of political democracy are attractive to investors because they limit unpredictable and sudden policy changes and place emphasis on the quality of human capital (Blanton and Blanton, 2007; Henisz, 2008). This is because the potential use of unilateral power and unforeseen policy changes create significant uncertainty and risk (Busse and Hefeker, 2007; Harms and Ursprung, 2002; Jensen, 2003). Where political democracy is low, government is less transparent to business and its citizens, thereby allowing the potential for autocratic control, corruption, and political instability, all of which make inward FDI less attractive (Globerman and Shapiro, 2003; Orr and Scott, 2008). For example, Jensen (2003) found that political democracies offered greater institutional stability and therefore were more likely to attract FDI. When countries or regions with low political democracy are entered, greater transaction costs are experienced by the parent firm in drafting acceptable contracts, monitoring foreign business relation-ships, and developing measures to provide a flexible exit plan (Luo, 2005; Oxley, 1999). In support of this view, Harms and Ursprung (2002) found that political and civil repression negatively influenced inward FDI. Hence, MNEs are attracted to countries with high (rather than low) political and civil rights (Busse and Hefeker, 2007; Harms and Ursprung, 2002; Jensen, 2003). These findings suggest that MNEs are more likely to internationalize into countries with greater region-relative and regional political democracy, thus increasing an MNE's degree of internationalization.

Hypothesis 3a: The propensity of MNEs to internationalize into a country is positively related to the political democracy of its region.

Hypothesis 3b: The propensity of MNEs to internationalize into a country is positively related to the country's 'region-relative' political democracy.

Economic institutional environment

Strong economic institutions represent a locational advantage that can attract FDI (Dunning, 1988). Such '[f]inancial factors are an integral part of the growth process' (Levine and Zervos, 1998: 554), which is conditioned by the capacities to produce and to consume (Lettau and Ludvigson, 2001), both requiring adequate capital. Capital investments serve as a proxy for well-developed economic institutions because the policies and actions of government, central banks, and private financial intermediaries provide for greater capital flow through capital availability and support market growth and liquidity (Agarwal, 1980; Bevan *et al.*, 2004). The decisions emanating from economic institutions promote capital availability by such activities as issuing foreign debt in order to receive an influx of capital (Tirole, 2003) and increasing budget deficits, which is an action correlating with tax cuts or increasing government spending, which infuse capital into the market (Bohn, 1991).

The role of capital investments has also been heralded as a key determinant of FDI (Agarwal, 1980) because they create spillovers for MNEs and shape demand for and supply of resources, which in turn influence firms' strategic and tactical actions (Burdekin and Weidenmier, 2001; Orphanides, 2002). Capital investments often create spillover effects from which MNEs can benefit. The economic geography literature suggests capital investments are shaped by governmental economic action and policy (Martin and Sunley, 2008; Romer, 1994). Capital investments lead to the learning and development of technology and knowledge resources, and as a result, greater capital flows in one country or region over another can explain higher concentrations of economic activity because of income differences, accessibility, infrastructure costs, and enhanced profitability (Barro, 1991; Martin and Sunley, 2008; Romer, 1994). Strong economic institutions attract more inward FDI because capital is needed by MNEs to support expansion and fund research and development, labor development, and production (Ajami and BarNiv, 1984; Beck *et al.*, 2000; Globerman and Shapiro, 2003). It is important that capital be available, cost-effective, and stable in valuation. Capital investments are also vital because they provide the potential to profit from the wealth of citizens (Meyer and Nguyen, 2005). MNEs search for markets in which investors and consumers have significant financial resources and purchasing power, thus penetrating markets that have a higher return on capital (Agarwal, 1980). Consequently, MNEs are more likely to have a higher degree of internationalization into countries with stronger region-relative capital investments and with higher capital investments in the region.

Hypothesis 4a: The propensity of MNEs to internationalize into a country is positively related to the capital investment in its region.

Hypothesis 4b: The propensity of MNEs to internationalize into a country is positively related to the country's 'region-relative' capital investment.

Method

Data source and sample

We used data from *Kaigai Shinshutsu Kiyou Souran* [Japanese Overseas Investments] which provides subsidiary-level information on the overseas activities of Japanese MNEs. The database has been found to provide reliable data for the study of Japanese FDI (for example, Delios and Henisz, 2003; Goerzen and Beamish, 2005).

We selected Japanese MNEs that had foreign subsidiaries in more than one country. Single-host country MNEs were not included because no region-level strategy for these firms could be ascertained. Moreover, including this type of firm in the sample could bias the results because it could mask potential region and corporate effects, thus creating biases in the Level-2 and Level-3 models (Bowman and Helfat, 2001; Makino *et al.*, 2004).[4] Therefore, our results are valid for MNEs with foreign subsidiaries in more than one host country. The final sample is composed of 1,076 Japanese MNEs having established 3,394 new foreign subsidiaries in 45 different countries[5] over the period 1996–2001 (see Appendix 1 for the number of new FDIs created per country and per year).

Levels of analysis

We tested our hypotheses with models measured and analyzed at three levels: firms' foreign subsidiary choices and location characteristics in a country (Level 1), firms' foreign subsidiary choices and location characteristics in a region (Level 2), and firms' corporate (headquarters) (Level 3) variables. Level 3 allows us to control for a firm's corporate-level effects.

We conceptualize regions in geographic terms and we define a region as a grouping of countries with physical continuity and proximity (Arregle *et al.*, 2009; McNamara and Vaaler, 2000; Rugman and Verbeke, 2004). While different operationalizations exist (see Aguilera *et al.*, 2007 for an extensive review), we use geographic regions because it is most consistent with the semiglobalization literature. This approach relates well to this study's focus on foreign subsidiary localization (Aguilera *et al.*, 2007) and is central to firms' international strategy (Buckley and Ghauri, 2004; McNamara and Vaaler, 2000; Rugman and Verbeke, 2007). Although regional clusters based on cultural dimensions have some value, they are less relevant for corporate strategy. Moreover, in recent years, scholars have argued for further integration of economic geography in the examination of spatial dimensions of MNE strategy (Buckley and Ghauri, 2004). Indeed, geographic proximity has been found to stimulate trade, investment, and even convergence in governance and management practices across countries (Ghemawat, 2003; Khanna *et al.*, 2006). Finally, physical distance matters for FDI and affects the way firms operate internationally (Nachum and Zaheer, 2005) and is even more important to the two primary drivers of semiglobalization (see theory sections). We therefore grouped the 45 countries used in this study into 8 geographical regions derived from the region classification proposed by the United Nations Statistics Division (2008) (see Appendices 2 and 3 for the composition of these regions and their profiles).[6]

Dependent variable

The MNE's degree of internationalization into country c is measured as: (the number of foreign subsidiaries created [i.e., inflows] by the MNE in country c over the period 1996–2001) × [their relative importance over the period 1996–2001]).
For the MNE, the score

'Relative importance over the period 1996–2001' for a country c is measured by the ratio:

$$\frac{\text{Total number of employees in new foreign subsidiaries created in country } c \text{ (1996–2001)}}{\text{Total number of employees in all of the firm's foreign subsidiaries (1996–2001)}}$$

This measure is more fine-grained than unidimensional measures and is similar to that used by others such as Hitt *et al.* (2006). Unidimensional measures (for example, number of sub-sidiaries, employees, sales) have various problems as they focus on one facet of interna-tionalization, thus only partially reflecting the MNE's internationalization (Hitt *et al.*, 1997; Sanders and Carpenter, 1998).[7] This multidimensional measure better captures the MNE's internationalization (Hitt *et al.*, 1997; Lu and Beamish, 2004) as it reflects the breadth of internationalization into a country (i.e., the number of foreign subsidiaries) and its depth (i.e., the degree of commitment to each country based on the relative number of employ-ees) simultaneously. The breadth is a measure of the structural attribute of the degree of internationalization (Sullivan, 1994) and reflects the governance and coordination costs asso-ciated with internationalization, which are compounded if an MNE expands the number of FDIs in which it operates (Hitt *et al.*, 1997; Lu and Beamish, 2004; Sanders and Carpenter, 1998). This measure is developed at the country-level because our objective is to relate the MNE's strategic investment decisions in a country to that country's institutional environment. The MNE receives a score on this variable for each one of the 45 countries in our sample. Hence, the MNE with a high score for a country on this variable indicates that it has a strong level of internationalization into this specific country.

Independent variables

We measure the MNE's *prior internationalization into a region* by the number of its prior foreign subsidiaries established in a region (1990–1995) multiplied by their relative impor-tance (1990–1995). We apply the same method as for our dependent variable but at the region level and over the period 1990–1995.

We investigate the effects of formal institutions within a country and a region, repre-senting the regulatory, political, and economic institutional environments, on an MNE's degree of internationalization into a country. We used composite measures (for example, Gaur *et al.*, 2007), created and validated by Holmes *et al.* (2013), to ensure the validity and breadth of the measures.[8] Factor scores were created based on 34 comprehensive measures of institutions in 50 countries from 1995 to 2003, which are described in more detail in Holmes *et al.* (2013). The results produced four constructs used in our two-level models: regulatory control, political democracy, capital availability, and market liquidity.[9] These factors clearly proxy three formal institutions: regulatory, political and economic and are described below.

Regulatory control

The regulatory control factor measures the degree of government involvement in business through laws, regulations, and government policies (Busenitz *et al.*, 2000), which constrain behavior through rule-setting, monitoring, and sanctions (Scott, 1995). This variable is mea-sured by a country's regulatory burden, trade policy, foreign investment restrictions, contract and property rights, government intervention in banking, informal markets, and monetary policy. All measures loaded positively (factor loadings > 0.50), reflecting greater regulatory control. A high score suggests that the country operates with broader and more restrictive regulatory oversight and involvement.

Political democracy

The political democracy factor refers to the level of discretion and power a government maintains over its citizenry, measured through the country's civil liberties, political rights, executive political restrictions, and political constraints. A high score suggests that the government is democratic, granting more rights and liberties to its citizens and having constraints to further protect these rights. Civil liberties and political rights are reverse coded in the data because higher scores indicate fewer rights; they loaded negatively on this factor (−0.76 and −0.87). Executive political restrictions and political constraints, which capture the level of checks and balances that prevent a concentration of power in government, loaded positively (0.96 and 0.68) on this dimension.

Capital investments

Two factors (3 and 4) were found that indicated prerequisites for capital investments in a country. On Factor 3, items indicating increased capital in an economy, capital investments, money supply, net reserves, nominal GDP, and total foreign debt loaded positively (loadings > 0.70). Budget balance loaded negatively (−0.73) as the balancing of a country's budget reduces the ability of the government to reinvest capital into the economy. This factor, *Capital Availability*, captures the availability of capital for domestic entities, with a higher score implying a greater availability of capital for commerce in the country.

Liabilities, exchange rate, and liquidity loaded on Factor 4, which indicates the lack of market liquidity and capital investments. Liabilities, which loaded positively on this factor (0.78), result in lower liquidity in domestic firms due to higher debt. Increases in exchange rates (factor loading of 0.64) reduce cash flow due to the depreciation of the nation's currency and result in lower liquidity (Grilli and Roubini, 1995). Liquidity loaded negatively on this factor (−0.72) as it reflects the ease of converting an asset through transactions. Factor 4 is labeled *Market Liquidity*, reflecting the degree to which a country curtails or manages the rapid expansion of its money supply and assets, with higher scores indicating lower capital investments[10] because of the lack of assets available in the market for reinvestment. Both of these economic factors are used to compute semiglobalized institutional variables (see below) to test Hypotheses 4a and 4b.

To test our hypotheses, we adapt these variables and compute two new measures for each institutional variable: *a region-level measure* of institutions and a *country-level measure* of institutions *(a region-relative variable)*. Using the eight regions specified, we calculate for each institutional variable a region-level institutional variable as the weighted average institutional score for this variable of all countries in a region. We weight the institutional scores of countries in the same region by their GDP (the ratio of a country's GDP/sum of the GDPs of countries in the same region) to take into account the different economic importance of countries in the same region (for example, Hejazi, 2007). We use this average to represent the general (central tendency) institutional environments for a region with differences taken into account by region-relative variables. The country-level region-relative variable captures a country's score on an institutional variable relative to the countries in the same region, not relative to all other countries, and is calculated as: country's original institutional score minus its respective region-level institutional score.[11] This way of analyzing institutional variables reflects the semiglobalization perspective.

Control variables

At the country level, we controlled for a firm's *prior internationalization into a country* measured with the same computation as our dependent variable but over the 1990–1995 period. A firm's *country experience* was measured by the log of the sum of subsidiary years of experience in a firm's history in the focal country (Lu, 2002). Institutional iso-morphism (mimetic) effects were estimated by *country experience of all Japanese firms* (Henisz and Delios, 2001; Lu, 2002), calculated as the log of the number of subsidiary years experience of other Japanese firms in a country. We also control for country-specific variables, and, relying on recent studies (for example, Chan *et al.*, 2006), we include *per capita income* (as the log of GDP per capita [Vaaler, 2008]), *economic growth* (the GDP per capita growth rate [Vaaler, 2008]), *population* (as the number of individuals in a country), and *cultural distance* (between a host country and Japan). Cultural distance was measured using Kogut and Singh's (1988) measure and is calculated by summing standardized differences between the cultural dimensions reported in Hofstede (1980) (for example, Gaur *et al.*, 2007).

At the firm level, we measure the firm's *total prior international experience* as the loga-rithmic transformation of the number of subsidiary years of investment in a firm's history in all countries (Delios and Henisz, 2003), the firm's *research and development intensity* (R&D expenses divided by total sales: 1990–1995 average), and *advertising intensity* (advertising expenses divided by total sales: 1990–1995 average) (Delios and Henisz, 2003). Finally, *firm size* is measured by the log of its annual sales (in 1995).

Model estimation

As preliminary analyses indicate an over-dispersion in our limited range dependent vari-able,[12] we use a negative binomial model as this is appropriate for the analysis of data with such a distribution (Cameron and Trivedi, 1998). Due to the structure of the data and the hierarchical nature of our research question, we use multilevel negative binomial models with two and three levels and analyze the data with the multilevel software SuperMix (Hedeker *et al.*, 2008).[13] Multilevel models address the potential statistical problems inherent in multi-level data and allow the identification of effects occurring at each level (country, region, and headquarters levels) and across levels (Arregle *et al.*, 2006; Hitt *et al.*, 2007). To compare and identify best models, we used the Aikake Information Criterion (AIC) and the Bayesian Information Criterion (BIC). These are the relevant statistics as they allow for the comparison of mixed models with different numbers of levels and predictors (Burnham and Anderson, 2004).[14]

Results

The intercorrelation matrix and descriptive statistics for each variable are presented in Table 10.1. The results of multilevel model predicting an MNE's degree of internation-alization into a country are presented in Models 4 and 5 in Table 10.2 (first putting in

Table 10.1 Descriptive statistics and pairwise correlations

	Variables	Mean	s.d.	1	2	3	4	5	6
	Degree of internationalization into a country	0.03	0.22						
1	Prior Internationalization —country	0.02	0.11						
2	Country experience	0.50	1.12	0.46*					
3	Cultural distance	0.50	1.12	0.04*	0.08*				
4	Population (/1,000,000)	95.60	226.86	0.08*	0.09*	−0.00			
5	Per capita income	8.86	1.33	0.09*	0.14*	0.21*	−0.47*		
6	Economic growth	0.02	0.02	0.01*	−0.07*	0.04*	0.28*	0.03*	
7	Country experience —all firms	7.04	1.87	0.27*	0.44*	0.18*	0.18*	0.30*	−0.20*
8	International experience	4.50	1.17	0.01*	0.35*	0.00	0.00	0.00	0.00
9	Advertising intensity	0.01	0.01	0.00	−0.00	0.00	0.00	0.00	0.00
10	R&D intensity	0.02	0.02	0.00	0.08*	0.00	0.00	0.00	0.00
11	Firm size	11.90	1.35	0.00	0.26*	0.00	0.00	0.00	0.00
12	Prior internationalization—region	0.29	1.02	0.21*	0.32*	0.06*	0.00	0.07*	0.01
13	Regulatory control—region	−0.08	0.74	−0.10*	−0.14*	−0.18*	0.27*	−0.72*	−0.14*
14	Capital availability —region	0.25	0.79	0.23*	0.22*	−0.01*	0.04*	0.37*	0.15*
15	Political democracy —region	−0.03	0.67	−0.05*	−0.11*	−0.04*	−0.23*	0.44*	0.20*
16	Market liquidity —region	0.27	0.56	0.10	−0.12*	−0.17*	−0.28*	0.06*	0.08*
17	Regulatory control —country's 'region relative'	−0.07	0.80	−0.06*	−0.12*	−0.11*	0.27*	−0.39*	0.15*
18	Capital availability —country's 'region relative'	−0.35	0.67	0.12*	0.12*	−0.02*	0.24**	−0.20*	−0.07*
19	Political democracy —country's 'region relative'	0.04	0.78	0.00	−0.00	−0.05*	−0.28*	0.28*	−0.16*
20	Market liquidity —country's 'region relative'	−0.22	0.63	0.05*	0.12*	−0.00	0.10*	−0.18*	−0.08*

*p < 0.05; n = 48,420 (except for correlations with R&D or Advertising n = 28,350).

**p < 0.01

7	8	9	10	11	12	13	14	15	16	17	18	19
0.00												
0.00	0.01											
0.00	0.19*	0.10*										
0.00	0.61*	0.00	0.10*									
0.14*	0.23*	0.00	0.06*	0.18*								
−0.29*	0.00	0.00	0.00	0.00	−0.13*							
0.37*	0.00	0.00	0.00	0.00	0.16*	−0.50*						
−0.10*	0.00	0.00	0.00	0.00	−0.03*	−0.51*	0.34*					
−0.50*	0.00	0.00	0.00	0.00	−0.04*	−0.18*	0.12*	0.15*				
−0.17*	0.00	0.00	0.00	0.00	0.05*	−0.22*	0.23*	0.15*	0.16*			
0.08*	0.00	0.00	0.00	0.00	−0.09*	0.38*	−0.54*	−0.29*	−0.14*	−0.29*		
−0.06*	0.00	0.00	0.00	0.00	−0.01*	−0.04*	−0.07*	−0.13*	0.23*	−.023*	0.05*	
0.31*	0.00	0.00	0.00	0.00	0.00	0.11*	−0.05*	−0.11*	−0.24*	−0.02*	0.20*	−0.23**

Table 10.2 Results of the models explaining an MNE's degree of internationalization into a country over the period 1996–2001

Variable	Model 1	Model 2	Model 3	Model 4	Model 5
Intercept	-7.94***	-4.42**	-4.10**	-4.22**	-7.21***
Level: firm's headquarters					
Advertising expense	-4.71	-4.76	-4.20	-4.18	-4.18
R&D	4.19**	4.20**	5.11**	5.05**	5.09**
Total prior international experience	-0.10	-0.09	-0.11*	-0.11*	-0.11*
Firm size	0.15***	0.16***	0.14***	0.15***	0.15***
Level: firm/country					
Regulatory control	—	-0.23	-0.24	—	—
Capital availability	—	0.38***	0.40***	—	—
Market liquidity	—	-0.28***	-0.29***	—	—
Political democracy	—	-0.22***	-0.21***	—	—
Prior internationalization in a country	0.34*	0.20	-0.03	0.03	0.04
Country experience	0.35***	0.33***	0.30***	0.30***	0.30***
Country experience of all Japanese firms	1.00***	0.84***	0.85***	0.70***	0.70***
Population (/1,000,000)	-0.00*	-0.00**	-0.00*	-0.00*	-0.00
Per capita income	0.74***	-0.94***	-0.96***	-0.85***	-0.59**
Economic growth	18.61***	15.14***	14.78***	12.41**	7.01*
Cultural distance	-0.02	-0.10	-0.09	-0.11	-0.08
Regulatory control—country's 'region-relative'	—	—	—	-0.20	0.16
(Regulatory control—country's 'region-relative')^2	—	—	—		0.18
Capital availability—country's 'region-relative'	—	—	—	0.56***	0.64***
Market liquidity—country's 'region-relative'	—	—	—	-0.23*	-0.16*
Political democracy—country's 'region-relative'	—	—	—	-0.11*	-0.09*
Level: firm/region					
Prior internationalization in a region	—	—	0.05**	0.05**	0.05**
Regulatory control—region	—	—	—	-0.72**	-0.86**
(Regulatory control—region)^2	—	—	—		0.56
Capital availability—region	—	—	—	0.25*	0.20*
Market liquidity—region	—	—	—	-0.09	0.29
Political democracy—region	—	—	—	-0.56***	-0.91**
Goodness of fit: Akaike information criterion	4,469	4,407	4,353	4,316	4,317
$\Delta = AIC_{(model)} - AIC_{(lowest AIC: Model 4)}$	153	91	37	0	1
Bayesian information criterion	4,526	4,481	4,421	4,414	4,426

***p < 0.001; **p < 0.01; *p < 0.05.

Model 4 only the first-order term for the quadratic effect in Hypothesis 2 before adding the second-order term in Model 5 (Cohen *et al.*, 2003)). To check the validity of our results, we test models without the region level in Models 1 and 2, and with the region level but without our institutional variables in Model 3. Considering the AIC and BIC, Model 4 is the best model.

First, the coefficient in Model 4 for the variable 'Prior internationalization into a region' (0.71, $p < 0.05$) shows that an MNE's prior level of internationalization into a region has a positive effect on its propensity to internationalize into a country of the region. Therefore, Hypothesis 1 receives support.

Hypotheses 2a and 2b predict an inverted U-shaped effect for (1) the region's regulatory control and (2) the country's region-relative regulatory control on the propensity of an MNE to internationalize into a country. Model 5 shows statistically nonsignificant coefficients for the squared term of country region-relative regulatory control (0.18, $p > 0.05$) and the squared term of regional regulatory control (0.56, $p > 0.05$). Neither Hypothesis 2a nor Hypothesis 2b receives support. Model 4, testing linear effects, shows a negative and statistically significant coefficient for regional regulatory control (-0.72, $p < 0.01$) and a negative but statistically nonsignificant coefficient for country region-relative regulatory control (-0.20, $p > 0.05$).

Hypotheses 3a and 3b predict a positive effect of (1) the region's political democracy and (2) the region-relative political democracy of a country on the propensity of a firm to internationalize into a country. We have intriguing results: contrary to our expectations, there is a statistically significant negative relationship between the propensity of MNEs to localize foreign investment and a region's political democracy (-0.56, $p < 0.001$) and a country's region-relative political democracy (-0.11, $p < 0.05$) in Model 4. Therefore, Hypotheses 3a and 3b do not receive support even though the importance of the region and that of the country's region-relative institutional variables are confirmed. The semiglobalization effect applies to this institutional factor but not in the expected direction.

Hypotheses 4a and 4b stated that (1) capital investments of the region and (2) the country's region-relative capital investments are positively related to a firm's propensity to internationalize in a given country. In Model 4, the effect of capital availability in a region is positive and statistically significant (0.25, $p < 0.05$). The effect of market liquidity, which reflects the *lack* of capital investments, is not statistically significant (-0.09, $p > 0.05$). Therefore, Hypothesis 4a receives partial support. The effect of region-relative capital availability is positive and statistically significant (0.56, $p < 0.001$), and the effect of region-relative market liquidity is negative and statistically significant (-0.23, $p < 0.05$). Thus, Hypothesis 4b receives support.

We know from previous research that country-level institutions affect the attractiveness of FDI destinations and the location choices of MNEs. However, for the aforementioned reasons, models reflecting the semiglobalization effect should explain *more accurately* the effect of institutional variables on MNEs' FDIs compared to a country-only approach. Hypotheses 2–4 test the value and significance of the semiglobalized institutional dimensions but do not show their *additional value* relative to the more traditional framework, which is the central contribution of this research. Therefore, we investigate whether the three-level model with regional and region-relative institutional effects (Model 4) accounts for additional variance in FDI localization decisions compared to the model with country-level institutional effects (Model 2): Model 4 clearly produces a much better explanation of internationalization (lower AIC and BIC). These results provide strong support for the notion that, compared to a country-level constrained model, a semiglobalization perspective offers a better explanation of these relationships.

Robustness checks

While the semiglobalization perspective tends to conceptualize regions in terms of geography, several other operationalizations of regions have been based on trading blocks, culture, or institutions. Therefore, we developed several models using alternative definitions of regions as *post hoc* tests to check the robustness of our results compared to other existing definitions of regions. We ran the same three-level model (i.e., Model 4) with the following definitions of regions: trading blocks, culture, and institutions. For trading blocks, we used the regions defined by UNCTAD (2001); for culture, we used two definitions: Ronen and Shenkar (1985) and GLOBE (Gupta *et al.*, 2002); for institutions, we used La Porta *et al.* (1998) (see Appendix 4). All of the alternative models show larger BIC and very large AIC differences relative to Model 4 (see Appendix 4). These differences clearly indicate that the alternative definitions of regions do not provide as good of a test of the research question as does the geographic definition of regions used in Model 4.

Discussion

This research examines the effects of the institutional environment on MNE location choices of internationalization using a more comprehensive and richer approach that complements and extends previous research. We argue for the importance of a 'semiglobalized' institutional perspective and test it by examining how MNEs implement their strategic approach to country institutional environments at the region level.

First, we present and validate the positive role of an MNE's internationalization into a region on the propensity to further internationalize into a country within this region, confirming previous semiglobalization studies (for example, Arregle *et al.*, 2009). The results also show that, central to the semiglobalization perspective, MNEs develop RFSAs, fungible at the region level, using a sequential approach with their FDIs in a region as a platform for their localization decisions of future FDIs in countries within this region. This research strongly suggests that geographic regions are an important level of analysis for MNEs' international strategy.

Additionally, and more importantly, we show that MNEs evaluate the general institutional environment of geographic regions and consider country institutions relative to those of other countries in the same region in their decisions to make foreign direct investments into a country. In other words, they view the countries' institutional environments from a regional perspective. The research provides a fine-grained and more accurate analysis of the effects of institutional environments on the foreign market investment strategies used by MNEs than the more traditional framework that considers only the country and the headquarters levels. Hence, important to the MNE is the general level of critical institutions of the regions and the country's relative institutional positions compared to other countries (except regulatory control) in the same region. However, these institutional effects vary in strength and direction across the individual formal institutions and the region and country levels. At the country level, the most important variables in receiving international investments from MNEs are not the same as at the region level: for example, the effect of capital availability is strongest at the country level. These results also provide support for Ostrom's (2005) arguments that the effects of institutions are complex; this complexity has several dimensions because there are multiple levels of institutions and each has potentially important effects.

Ignoring these regional effects can result in a partial and potentially biased understanding of MNEs' internationalization decisions and of the influence of institutional environments in these decisions as two-level models provide significant results, but the semiglobal framework (i.e., Model 4) produces a more complete explanation with different effects for the four institutional variables. Country-based models (i.e., Model 2) may provide incomplete conclusions about the role of institutions in MNEs' internationalization decisions. This outcome addresses the important question of the relevant level of analysis for examining the influence of institutions on MNE strategy, and it has major implications for both scholars and practitioners regarding the influence of institutions on MNEs. If we compare countries' institutional propensity to attract FDI obtained from the three-level model (Model 4) with the two-level model (Model 2), the average difference between them is 32 percent, which is nontrivial. For each country, we present in Figure 10.1 (left side) its score for propensity to attract MNEs' internationalization resulting from our semiglobalized institutional variables and from the traditional country-level institutions. These results in Figure 10.1 also identify countries that benefit (for example, Poland, Taiwan) or suffer (for example, Chile, Mexico) from this semiglobal assessment of their FDI attractiveness and why. This outcome for a country is explained by the complex interplay between its region's institutional attractiveness, its region-relative institutional attractiveness, and their relative values (both scores are listed in the right side of Figure 10.1).

The semiglobalization approach also produces results that reinforce the importance of the institutional environment for MNEs' FDI decisions. At the region level, regulatory control and political democracy have a negative effect on foreign investments. Alternatively, the region's capital investments motivate foreign investments. Our results on regulatory control suggest that it creates costs and overwhelms any positive effects, thereby discouraging FDI. Perhaps the threshold at which regulatory control facilitates MNE's localization is relatively low. The results for political democracy are contrary to our expectations, suggesting that MNEs may not favor democratic regions. Accordingly, lack of political democracy in a country does not appear to be a major impediment to foreign investments, but instead may encourage FDI, indicating MNEs' desire to achieve greater efficiency (Adam and Filippaios, 2007). Perhaps high levels of governmental discretion (relative to decentralized autonomy to citizens and businesses) allow MNEs to reduce the risks and costs that occur when workers collectively mobilize for such actions as protests, strikes, or litigation. While political democracy is often associated with stability, it also results in more regular regime change, thus prompting changes in policies (Jensen, 2003). Additionally, prior research suggests that some MNEs may be able to negotiate favorable terms that shield them from public demands and competition through close relationships with more autocratic governments (Fagre and Wells, 1982; Li and Resnick, 2003). Some of these agreements may be negotiated with corrupt officials who receive bribes (i.e., Bueno de Mesquita *et al.*, 2004; Jensen, 2003). In addition, fewer political and human rights afforded to citizens may result in lower workforce costs (Rodrik, 1999). The results may also suggest the need to examine further the effects of regulatory and political institutions in future research on FDI in order to understand their impact more fully. Our results are consistent with those of Li and Resnick (2003), who found that, when controlling for property rights regulations, the relationship between political democracy and FDI is negative. We believe that each explanation likely undergirds the rationales for some firms' actions. At the country level, it appears that MNEs seek out those countries in a region that have fewer constraints on business activities and more market liquidity. We also found that greater region-relative political democracy reduces the likelihood of internationalization into a country, most likely for the reasons suggested above. Alternatively, a country's higher region-relative capital investments promote greater internationalization in the country.

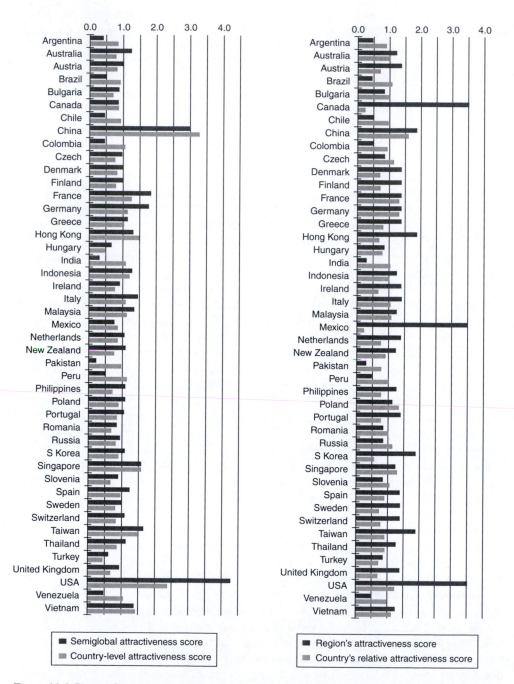

Figure 10.1 Propensity scores to internationalize into a country computed on the four institutional variables: country-level score (Model 2) vs. semiglobal score. (Model 4) (left side) and its components (right side). N.B.: as we use a negative binomial, the semiglobal institutional score (left side of the Figure) = (Region's attractiveness score) × (Country's relative attractiveness score) (right side of the Table) as Exp(a + b) = Exp(a) × Exp(b).

However, this semiglobalization behavior does not necessarily apply to all firms. If the MNE cannot use at least one of the two mechanisms related to semiglobalization (RFSAs and regional organization learning), it has few incentives to adopt a semiglobalization approach. For instance, it is possible that some MNEs might decide to locate FDIs in only · one foreign country without targeting or expanding into its corresponding region. Two main reasons could explain such behavior: the absence of regionally fungible resources[15] or an idiosyncratic desire to focus only on a certain, probably large and attractive, country.

Implications, limitations, and conclusions

Our results have five crucial implications for theory and research on international strategy. First, our study demonstrates the effects of regions on MNEs' internationalization decisions. Second, this research shows that MNEs' evaluation of institutions in their internationalization decisions (location and amount) is more comprehensive than has been suggested by prior research. MNEs appear to decide their location choices for internationalization in part based on a country's institutions relative to the institutions of other countries in the same region (i.e., in a region-relative manner). Such decisions allow firms to leverage and optimize their investments across the region, thereby controlling the risk while enhancing the benefits and returns across the countries within the region. Hence, the third contribution is the support provided for the semiglobalization perspective and its relevance to understanding institutional effects. Such an approach changes the way we measure, evaluate, and understand the institutional effects on FDI for MNEs. It indicates that future research dealing with institutions and MNE performance should consider and measure institutions differently than past research. Fourth, we found variance in the importance of different institutions at the country and region level, that is, attracting foreign investments through an institutional strategy at the region and country levels assumes different strategies with different actions at each level. Finally, our results highlight the relevance of geographic regions and the value of using multilevel models to examine important strategic decisions.

These results have important managerial and policy implications, as well. For managers of MNEs, they must be aware of institutional environments and their effects not only at the country-level but also at the region-level if they want to gain the benefits of arbitrage. This research informs the decision-making process of managers and MNE organizations by highlighting the way in which they can evaluate and coordinate the influence of specific institutional environments. For policy makers, the results of this study highlight the importance of the regional dimension of the international institutional competition to attract FDIs. Our results emphasize the potential value of collaboration among country governments across a region in their competition with other regions for foreign investments. Regional integration can be designed to increase FDI inflows to a region (Naya and Plummer, 1997) and the results in Model 4 give new and unique insights into which institutions should be considered by governments in order to attract FDI. For instance, reducing regional regulatory control may have the strongest effect[16] among region-level institutional factors. However, countries in the same region are also in competition for primary direct investments as MNEs compare their institutional environments to select the best country(ies) in the region, representing another form of *co-opetition* (Brandenburger and Nalebuff, 1996), which is likely to be challenging. Hence, cohesion within the region needs to be maintained to avoid triggering dysfunctional intra-regional competitive behaviors (Oxelheim and Ghauri, 2008). Depending on the level of changes targeted by a country, our results also provide some guidelines about whether it would be possible by repositioning the country versus its regional partners or by repositioning the region versus other regions.

As in other studies, this research has some limitations. First, its hypotheses are tested using Japanese MNEs over a specific period of time (1996–2001). The institutional environment of Japan may influence the strategies taken by these firms or the relevant definition of geographic regions, and there are opportunities for future research to study these questions with MNEs based in other regions. Second, it would be interesting to replicate this study with data for other periods of time as the institutional environments of countries and regions can change, resulting in different institutional environments. However, such potential changes do not undermine the core logic of this work or the relative superiority of the semiglobalized effects of institutional variables as hypothesized herein. Third, although we measure the effects of country-level and region-level institutions and the key role of regions, we do not consider how these different levels are integrated in the decision-making process. Do MNEs start their internationalization decision-making process from the region level, from the country level, or in tandem? Knowing that MNEs use a semiglobal institutional analysis, future research should examine the MNE decision-making process to understand its links with the firm's structure and other organizational processes. Such research will likely require data from MNE decision-makers, starting with the first decision up to the final decision to locate an FDI in a country to be able to disentangle the interactions between regional and country effects. Finally, although our approach using geographic regions provides an effective way of measuring such regions, as shown by the robustness tests, future research might explore other geographic regions, such as smaller regions within Europe.

In conclusion, this work uniquely merges traditional institutional perspectives with a semiglobalization perspective to examine the effects of the country environment and of the general institutional environment of a region on internationalization decisions. Our results suggest that the internationalization of MNEs is influenced by the general institutional environment of both countries and regions. Thus, this study introduces a new perspective regarding institutional influences on the international strategy of MNEs.

Acknowledgements

We thank our Associate Editor, Kulwant Singh, and the two anonymous reviewers for their helpful and developmental feedback. In addition, we acknowledge the helpful comments from Shih-Fen Chen, Charles Dhanaraj, Alan R. Rugman, and Laszlo Tihanyi during the development of this paper. An earlier version of this paper was presented at the Academy of Management's annual conference (2009).

Notes

1 We thank an anonymous reviewer for this idea.
2 However, we note that political structures can affect changes in regulations. For example, differing political views allowed by political democracies may slow regulatory changes (Becker, 1983; Li et al., 2005).
3 Johanson and Vahlne (2009) developed this concept of liability considering that MNEs need to enter and develop a relevant position in a network of relationships and not focus only on a specific country.
4 However, it is important to note that MNEs having subsidiaries in several countries may or may not have a region-level strategy. This sample only allows us to examine the relevance of the semiglobalization perspective by including tests for both country level and region-relative strategies.

5 These 45 countries cover 91 percent of all the international joint-ventures and FDIs made by Japanese MNEs in *Kaigai Shinshutsu Kiyou Souran* and include countries and regions commonly examined in the literature on semi-globalization or FDI activities of MNEs.

6 Because 1,960 foreign subsidiaries in our sample were located in Asia, we had to separate Asia into additional regions to achieve a more fine-grained understanding of foreign investment dynamics there. The logic used to define these Asian regions was a geographical approach based on the ASEAN region to divide Asia into three parts: 'Southeast Asia,' with countries belonging to the ASEAN trading block, 'East Asia,' with countries to the east of the ASEAN region, and 'Northwest Asia,' with countries on the northwest of the ASEAN region. This geographic approach considers a trading block as creating a geographical region with some institutional homogeneity to facilitate an institutional region-relative evaluation. Moreover, Japanese firms consider ASEAN as a relevant region for their FDI decisions in Asia (Belderbos and Zou, 2006).

7 To check the robustness of our results, we also measured an MNE's degree of internationalization into country, for our dependent and independent variables, using an MNE's number of employees and an MNE's number of FDIs. These two alternative unidimensional measures gave qualitatively the same results as those reported in this paper, confirming the stability of our results to different operationalizations of the measure of internationalization.

8 This method is similar to the procedure used by Chan *et al.* (2008) and Gaur *et al.* (2007), but more institutional characteristics were used and a different rotation technique was applied in the factor analyses.

9 The objective was to allow factors to be correlated, using oblique rotation, because theory suggests that the informal institutions shape formal institutions, suggesting they may have some common origins (see Holmes *et al.*, 2013). Oblique rotation yields information on the intercorrelations and the potential existence of hierarchical factors. In a sample of 50 countries, the highest correlation between institutional factors is between political democracy and regulatory control (-0.39, $p < 0.001$), and the lowest correlation is between capital availability and market liquidity (0.02, $p > 0.05$) and between market liquidity and regulatory control (0.02, $p > 0.05$). As reported in Holmes *et al.* (2013), these factors were stable in composition, conceptually distinct, and had a high discriminant validity and internal reliability.

10 Hence, we expect a negative coefficient for Market Liquidity to validate H4a or H4b.

11 For instance, if acountry has a Regulatory Control value of 1.2 and is in a region with a weighted average Regulatory Control value of 0.4, its value for 'Regulatory Control-Country's region-relative' score is $(1.2 - 0.4) = 0.8$.

12 A Poisson model assumes that the true variance of the dependent variable equals its mean. When the variance exceeds the mean, we have an over-dispersion that can be addressed with a negative binomial model. We tested for over-dispersion applying a Likelihood Ratio test based on a multilevel Poisson and a multilevel negative binomial (Cameron and Trivedi, 1998). Using Model 4, (Deviance of the Poisson – Deviance of the negative binomial) = 42 compared to a χ^2 critical value of 2.70 for a one-sided 0.05 test. There was an overdispersion in our data and we had to use a negative binomial.

13 We conducted a Likelihood Ratio test (on Model 4) to verify the relevance of a multilevel model versus a fixed-effects model. The result of the LR test confirmed the difference between these two types of model ($\chi^2 = 268.63$, $p = 0.000$) and the need to use a multilevel model for our data.

14 As there is a debate about the relative advantages of the BIC vs. the AIC, it is recommended to find models favored by both criteria (i.e., lowest AIC and BIC) (Kuha, 2004). Individual AIC and BIC values are not interpretable and the relevant information for selecting the best model is the difference (Δ) between a model's AIC and BIC and the AIC and BIC values of the model with the lowest AIC or BIC (Burnham and Anderson, 2004). This difference indicates the loss of information experienced if we use the model with the highest AIC or BIC compared to the (best) model with the lowest AIC or BIC.

15 MNEs internationalizing exclusively for specific resource-seeking objectives, exemplified by natural resources industries, could be such a case. Natural resources may be located in specific countries but not necessarily across geographic regions, making regional integration of FDIs irrelevant. Thus, an entry in a country does not presuppose the need to develop RFSAs.

16 As our institutional independent variables had equal variances as factor scores, the resulting coefficients largely proxy standardized coefficients in which the relative weights can be interpreted.

References

Adam A, Filippaios F. 2007. Foreign direct investment and civil liberties: a new perspective. *European Journal of Political Economy* **23**: 1038–52.

Agarwal JP. 1980. Determinants of foreign direct investment: a survey. *Review of World Economics* **16**(4): 739–73.

Aguilera RV, Flores RG, Vaaler PM. 2007. Is it all a matter of grouping? Examining the regional effect in global strategy research. In *International Strategic Management: A New Generation*, Tallman S (ed). Edward Elgar Publishers: Northampton, MA; 209–28.

Ajami R, BarNiv R. 1984. Utilizing economic indicators in explaining foreign direct investment in the U.S. *Management International Review* **24**(4): 16–26.

Arregle JL, Beamish PW, Hebert L. 2009. The regional dimension of MNE's foreign subsidiary localization. *Journal of International Business Studies* **40**(1): 86–107.

Arregle JL, Hebert L, Beamish PW. 2006. Mode of international entry: advantages of multilevel methods. *Management International Review* **5**: 557–618.

Bardhan P. 1989. The new institutional economics and development theory: a brief critical assessment. *World Development* **17**(9): 1389–95.

Barro RJ. 1991. Economic growth in a cross-section of countries. *Quarterly Journal of Economics* **106**: 407–55.

Beck T, Levine R, Loayza N. 2000. Finance and the sources of growth. *Journal of Financial Economics* **58**: 261–300.

Becker GS. 1983. A theory of competition among pressure groups for political influence. *Quarterly Journal of Economics* **1**: 371–400.

Belderbos R, Zou J. 2006. Foreign investment divestment and relocation by Japanese electronics firms in East Asia. *Asian Economic Journal* **20**(1): 1–27.

Bevan A, Estrin S, Meyer KE. 2004. Foreign investment location and institutional development in transition economies. *International Business Review* **13**: 43–64.

Blanton SL, Blanton RG. 2007. What attracts foreign investors? An examination of human rights and foreign direct investment. *The Journal of Politics* **69**(1): 143–55.

Boddewyn JJ. 1988. Political aspects of MNE theory. *Journal of International Business Studies* **19**(3): 341–63.

Bohn H. 1991. Budget balance through revenue or spending adjustments? *Journal of Monetary Economics* **27**: 333–59.

Bowman EH, Helfat CE. 2001. Does corporate strategy matter? *Strategic Management Journal* **22**(1): 1–23.

Brandenburger A, Nalebuff B. 1996. *Co-Opetition: A Revolution Mindset that Combines Competition and Cooperation*. Currency Doubleday: New York.

Brouthers KD. 2002. Institutional cultural and transaction cost influences on entry mode choice and performance. *Journal of International Business Studies* **33**(2): 203–21.

Brouthers KD, Bamossy GJ. 1997. The role of key stakeholders in international joint venture negotiations: case studies from Eastern Europe. *Journal of International Business Studies* **28**(2): 285–308.

Brouthers KD, Brouthers LE. 2000. Acquisition or greenfield start-up? Institutional cultural and transaction cost influences. *Strategic Management Journal* **21**(1): 89–97.

Bucheli M. 2008. Multinational corporations, totalitarian regimes, and economic nationalism: United Fruit Company in Central America, 1899–1975. *Business History* **50**(4): 433–54.

Buckley PJ, Ghauri PN. 2004. Globalization economic geography and the strategy of multinational enterprises. *Journal of International Business Studies* **35**(2): 81–98.

Bueno de Mesquita B, Smith A, Silverson R, Morrow J. 2004. *The Logic of Political Survival*. MIT Press: Cambridge, MA.

Burdekin RCK, Weidenmier MD. 2001. Inflation is always and everywhere a monetary phenomenon: Richmond vs. Houston in 1864. *American Economic Review* **91**(5): 1621–30.

Burnham KP, Anderson DR. 2004. Multimodel inference: understanding AIC and BIC in model selection. *Sociological Methods and Research* **33**(2): 261–304.

Busenitz LW, Gomez C, Spencer JW. 2000. Country institutional profiles: unlocking entrepreneurial phenomena. *Academy of Management Journal* **43**(5): 994–1003.

Busse M, Hefeker C. 2007. Political risk institutions and foreign direct investment. *European Journal of Political Economy* **23**(2): 397–415.

Cameron AC, Trivedi PK. 1998. *Regression Analysis of Count Data.* Cambridge University Press: Cambridge, MA.

Chan CM, Isobe T, Makino S. 2008. Which country matters? Institutional development and foreign affiliate performance. *Strategic Management Journal* **29**(11): 1179–1205.

Chan CM, Makino S, Isobe T. 2006. Interdependent behavior in foreign direct investment: the multi-level effects of prior entry and prior exit on foreign market entry. *Journal of International Business Studies* **37**(5): 642–65.

Chang SJ. 1995. International expansion strategy of Japanese firms: capability building through sequential entry. *Academy of Management Journal* **38**(2): 383–93.

Chang SJ, Park S. 2005. Types of firms generating network externalities and MNCs' co-location decisions. *Strategic Management Journal* **26**: 595–615.

Chung CC, Lu JW, Beamish PW. 2008. Multinational networks during times of economic crisis versus stability. *Management International Review* **48**(3): 279–96.

Coase RH. 1959. The federal communications commission. *Journal of Law and Economics* **2**: 1–40.

Cohen J, Cohen P, West SG, Aiken LS. 2003. *Applied Multiple Regression/Correlation Analysis for the Social Sciences* (3rd edn). Lawrence Erlbaum: Mahwah, NJ.

Cohen WM, Levinthal DA. 1990. Absorptive capacity: a new perspective on learning and innovation. *Administrative Science Quarterly* **35**: 128–52.

Collinson S, Rugman AM. 2008. The regional nature of Japanese multinational business. *Journal of International Business Studies* **39**: 215–30.

Delios A, Henisz WJ. 2003. Policy uncertainty and the sequence of entry by Japanese firms 1980–1998. *Journal of International Business Studies* **34**(3): 227–41.

Dierickx I, Cool K. 1989. Asset stock accumulation and sustainability of competitive advantage. *Management Science* **35**(12): 1504–11.

Dunning JH. 1988. The eclectic paradigm of international production: a restatement and some possible extensions. *Journal of International Business Studies* **19**(1): 1–31.

Eden L, Miller SR. 2004. Distance matters: liability of foreignness institutional distance and ownership strategy. In *The Evolving Theory of the Multinational Enterprise: Advances in International Management* (Volume **16**), Hitt MA, Cheng JAC (eds). Elsevier: Amsterdam; 187–222.

Fagre N, Wells LT. 1982. Bargaining power of multinationals and host governments. *Journal of International Business Studies* **13**(3): 9–23.

Gaur A, Delios A, Singh K. 2007. Institutional environments, staffing strategies, and subsidiary performance. *Journal of Management* **33**(4): 611–36.

Ghemawat P. 2003. Semi-globalization and international business strategy. *Journal of International Business Studies* **34**(2): 138–52.

Ghemawat P. 2007. *Redefining Global Strategy: Crossing Borders in a World Where Differences Still Matter.* Harvard Business School Press: Boston, MA.

Globerman S, Shapiro D. 2003. Governance infrastructure and US foreign direct investment. *Journal of International Business Studies* **34**(1): 19–39.

Goerzen A, Beamish PW. 2003. Geographic scope and multinational enterprise performance. *Strategic Management Journal* **24**(13): 1289–306.

Goerzen A, Beamish PW. 2005. The effect of alliance network diversity on multinational enterprise performance. *Strategic Management Journal* **26**(4): 333–54.

Grilli V, Roubini N. 1995. *Liquidity and Exchange Rates: Puzzling Evidence from the G-7 Countries.* Yale University: New Haven, CT.

Gupta V, Hanges PJ, Dorfman P. 2002. Cultural clusters: methodology and findings. *Journal of World Business* **37**(1): 11–15.

Harms P, Ursprung HW. 2002. Do civil and political repression really boost foreign direct investment? *Economic Inquiry* **40**(4): 651–63.

Hedeker D, Gibbons RD, Du Toit M, Cheng Y. 2008. *SuperMix 1.1*. Scientific Software International: Chicago, IL.

Hejazi W. 2007. Reconsidering the concentration of US MNE activity: is it global, regional or national? *Management International Review* **47**(1): 5–27.

Henisz WJ. 2008. Concentrated power, foreign direct investment, and economic growth. In *Paper Presented at the 2008 Annual Meeting of International Political Economy Society*, Philadelphia, PA. Available at: http://ncgg.princeton.edu/IPES/2008/papers/S33_paper1.pdf (accessed 5 March 2011).

Henisz WJ, Delios A. 2001. Uncertainty imitation and plant location: Japanese multinational corporations 1990–1996. *Administrative Science Quarterly* **46**(3): 443–75.

Hitt MA, Hoskisson RE, Kim H. 1997. International diversification: effects on innovation and firm performance in product-diversified firms. *Academy of Management Journal* **40**(4): 767–99.

Hitt MA, Beamish PW, Jackson SE, Mathieu JE. 2007. Building theoretical and empirical bridges across levels: multilevel research in management. *Academy of Management Journal* **50**(6): 1385–399.

Hitt MA, Bierman L, Uhlenbruck K, Shimizu K. 2006. The importance of resources in the internationalization of professional service firms: the good the bad and the ugly. *Academy of Management Journal* **49**(6): 1137–1157.

Hodgson GM. 1988. *Economics and Institutions*. Polity Press: Cambridge, UK.

Hofstede G. 1980. *Culture's Consequences: Comparing Values, Behaviours, Institutions, and Organizations Across Nations*. Sage: Thousand Oaks, CA.

Holmes RM, Miller T, Hitt MA, Salmador MP. 2013. The interrelationships among informal institutions, formal institutions, and inward foreign direct investment. *Journal of Management* **39**(2): 531–66.

Jensen NM. 2003. Democratic governance and multinational corporations: political regimes and inflows of foreign direct investment. *International Organization* **57**(3): 587–616.

Johanson J, Vahlne JE. 1977. The internationalization process of the firm: a model of knowledge development and increasing foreign market commitments. *Journal of International Business Studies* **8**(1): 23–32.

Johanson J, Vahlne JE. 2009. The Uppsala internationalization process model revisited: from liability of foreignness to liability of outsidership. *Journal of International Business Studies* **40:** 1411–31.

Kaufmann D, Kraay A, Zoido-Lobaton P. 1999. *Aggregating Governance Indicators*. Policy Research Paper No. 2195. The World Bank: Washington, DC.

Khanna T, Kogan J, Palepu K. 2006. Globalization and similarities in corporate governance: a cross-country analysis. *Review of Economics and Statistics* **88**(1): 69–90.

Kobrin S. 1979. Political risk: a review and consideration. *Journal of International Business Studies* **10**(1): 67–80.

Kogut B. 1983. Foreign direct investment as a sequential process. In *The Multinational Corporation in the 1980s*, Kindleberger CP, Audretsch D (eds). MIT Press: Cambridge, MA; 38–56.

Kogut B, Kulatilaka N. 1994. Operating flexibility global manufacturing and the option value of a multinational network. *Management Science* **40**(1): 123–39.

Kogut B, Singh H. 1988. The effect of national culture on the choice of entry mode. *Journal of Business Studies* **19**(3): 411–32.

Kreinin ME, Plummer MG. 2008. Effects of regional integration on FDI: an empirical approach. *Journal of Asian Economics* **19**(5–6): 447–54.

Kuha J. 2004. AIC and BIC: comparisons of assumptions and performance. *Sociological Methods and Research* **33:** 188–229.

Kumar MVS. 2009. The relationship between product and international diversification: the effects of short-run constraints and endogeneity. *Strategic Management Journal* **30:** 99–116.

La Porta R, López-de-Silanes F, Shleifer A, Vishny R. 1998. Law and finance. *Journal of Political Economy* **106**(6): 1113–50.

Lettau M, Ludvigson S. 2001. Consumption, aggregate wealth and expected stock returns. *Journal of Finance* **56:** 815–49.

Levine R, Renelt D. 1992. A sensitivity analysis of cross-country growth regressions. *American Economic Review* **82**(4): 942–63.

Levine R, Zervos S. 1998. Stock markets, banks, and economic growth. *American Economic Review* **88**(3): 537–58.

Li W, Qiang C, Xu LC. 2005. Regulatory reforms in the telecommunications sector in developing countries: the role of democracy and private interests. *World Development* **33:** 1307–24.

Li Q, Resnick A. 2003. Reversal of fortunes: democratic institutions and foreign direct investment inflows to developing countries. *International Organization* **57**(1): 175–211.

Loree DW, Guisinger SE. 1995. Policy and non-policy determinants of US equity foreign direct investment. *Journal of International Business Studies* **26**(2): 281–99.

Lu JW. 2002. Intra- and inter-organizational imitative behavior: institutional influences on Japanese firms' entry mode choice. *Journal of International Business Studies* **33**(1): 19–37.

Lu JW, Beamish PW. 2004. International diversification and firm performance: the S-curve hypothesis. *Academy of Management Journal* **47**(4): 598–609.

Lucas RE. 2003. Macroeconomic priorities. *American Economic Review* **93**(1): 1–14.

Luo Y. 2005. Transactional characteristics, institutional environment, and joint venture contracts. *Journal of International Business Studies* **36**(2): 209–30.

Mahoney JT, Pandian JR. 1992. The Resource-based view within the conversation of strategic management. *Strategic Management Journal* **13:** 363–80.

Makino S, Isobe T, Chan CM. 2004. Does country matter? *Strategic Management Journal* **25**(10): 1027–43.

Martin R, Sunley P. 2008. Slow convergence? The new endogenous growth theory and regional development. *Economic Geography* **74:** 201–27.

McNamara G, Vaaler P. 2000. The influence of competitive positioning and rivalry on emerging market risk assessment. *Journal of International Business Studies* **31**(2): 337–47.

Meyer KE, Nguyen HV. 2005. Foreign investment strategies and sub-national institutions in emerging markets: evidence from Vietnam. *Journal of Management Studies* **42**(1): 63–93.

Meyer KE, Estrin S, Bhaumik SK, Peng MW. 2009. Institutions resources and entry strategies in emerging economies. *Strategic Management Journal* **30**(1): 61–80.

Nachum L, Zaheer A. 2005. The persistence of distance? The impact of technology on MNE motivations for foreign investment. *Strategic Management Journal* **26**(8): 747–67.

Naya S, Plummer M. 1997. Economic cooperation after 30 years of ASEAN. *ASEAN Economic Bulletin* **14**(2): 117–26.

North DC. 1990. *Institutions Institutional Change and Economic Performance.* Cambridge University Press: Cambridge, MA.

North DC. 1991. Institutions. *Journal of Economic Perspectives* **5**(1): 97–112.

O'Donnell G. 1988. *Bureaucratic Authoritarianism: Argentina, 1966–1973 in Comparative Perspective.* University of California Press: Berkeley, CA.

Orphanides A. 2002. Monetary policy rules and the great inflation. *American Economic Review* **92**(2): 115–20.

Orr RJ, Scott WR. 2008. Institutional exceptions on global projects: a process model. *Journal of International Business Studies* **39**(4): 562–88.

Ostrom E. 2005. *Understanding Institutional Diversity.* Princeton University Press: Princeton, NJ.

Oxelheim L, Ghauri P. 2004. *European Union and the Race for Inward FDI in Europe.* Elsevier: Oxford.

Oxelheim L, Ghauri P. 2008. EU-China and the non-transparent race for inward FDI. *Journal of Asian Economics* **19**(4): 358–70.

Oxley JE. 1999. Institutional environment and mechanisms of governance: the impact of intellectual property protection on the structure of inter-firm alliances. *Journal of Economic Behavior and Organization* **38**(3): 283–309.

Rammal HG, Zurbruegg R. 2006. The impact of regulatory quality on intra-foreign direct investment flows in the ASEAN markets. *International Business Review* **15**: 401–14.

Rodrik D. 1999. Where did all the growth go? External shocks, social conflict and growth collapses. *Journal of Economic Growth* **4**: 385–412.

Romer P. 1994. The origins of endogenous growth. *Journal of Economic Perspectives* **8**(1): 3–22.

Ronen S, Shenkar O. 1985. Clustering countries on attitudinal dimensions: a review and synthesis. *Academy of Management Review* **10**(3): 435–54.

Rugman AM, Verbeke A. 2004. A perspective on regional and global strategies of multinational enterprises. *Journal of International Business Studies* **35**(1): 3–18.

Rugman AM, Verbeke A. 2005. Towards a theory of regional multinationals: a transaction cost economics approach. *Management International Review* **45**(1): 5–17.

Rugman AM, Verbeke A. 2007. Liabilities of regional foreignness and the use of firm-level versus country-level data: a response to Dunning *et al.* (2007). *Journal of International Business Studies* **38**(1): 200–05.

Sanders WMG, Carpenter MA. 1998. Internationalization and firm governance: The roles of CEO compensation, top team composition, and board structure. *Academy of Management Journal* **41**: 158–78.

Sapienza HJ, Autio E, George G, Zahra SA. 2006. A capabilities perspective on the effects of early internationalization on firm survival and growth. *Academy of Management Review* **31**(4): 914–33.

Schiavo S. 2007. Common currencies and FDI flows. *Oxford Economic Papers* **59**: 536–60.

Scott WR. 1995. *Institutions and Organizations.* Sage: Thousand Oaks, CA.

Seyf A. 2001. Can globalisation and global localisation explain foreign direct investment? Japanese firms in Europe. *International Journal of the Economics of Business* **8**(1): 137–53.

Sorenson O, Baum JAC. 2003. Geography and strategy: the strategic management of space and place. In *Advances in Strategic Management: Geography and Strategy* (Volume **20**), Baum JAC, Sorenson O (eds). JAI Press: Greenwich, CT; 1–19.

Strang D. 2003. The diffusion of TQM within a global bank. *Advances in Strategic Management* **20**: 293–316.

Sullivan D. 1994. Measuring the degree of internationalization of a firm. *Journal of International Business Studies* **25**(2): 325–42.

Teece DJ. 1982. Towards an economic theory of the multiproduct firm. *Journal of Economic Behavior and Organization* **3**(1): 39–63.

Tirole J. 2003. Inefficient foreign borrowing: a dual- and common-agency perspective. *American Economic Review* **93**(5): 1678–702.

UNCTAD. 2001. Classifications. Available at: http://unctadstat.unctad.org/UnctadStatMetadata/Classifications/UnctadStat.Countries.TradeMonetaryGroupslist.Classification_En.pdf (accessed 9 June 2008).

United Nations Statistics Division. 2008. Standard country or area codes for statistical use. Available at: http://unstats.un.org/unsd/methods/m49/m49.htm (accessed 27 March 2008).

Vaaler P. 2008. How do MNCs vote in developing country elections? *Academy of Management Journal* **51**(1): 21–43.

Vermeulen F, Barkema H. 2002. Pace rhythm and scope: process dependence in building a profitable multinational corporation. *Strategic Management Journal* **23**(7): 637–47.

Williamson OE. 2000. The new institutional economics: taking stock, looking ahead. *Journal of Economic Literature* **38**(3): 595–613.

Yiu D, Makino S. 2002. The choice between joint venture and wholly owned subsidiary: an institutional perspective. *Organization Science* **13**: 667–83.

Zaheer S, Mosakowski E. 1997. The dynamics of the liability of foreignness: a global study of survival in financial services. *Strategic Management Journal* **18**(6): 439–64.

Zukin S, DiMaggio P. 1990. *Structures of Capital: The Social Organization of the Economy.* Cambridge University Press: Cambridge, UK.

Appendices

Appendix 1 Number of new FDIs (i.e., inflows) by country and by year

Country	Number of FDIs created	
	1990–1995	*1996–2001*
Argentina	10	15
Australia	63	71
Austria	18	17
Brazil	24	42
Bulgaria	6	4
Canada	50	106
Chile	13	13
China	563	624
Colombia	5	8
Czech Republic	19	13
Denmark	7	15
Finland	10	15
France	68	48
Germany	98	85
Greece	5	12
Hong Kong	158	118
Hungary	21	15
India	25	62
Indonesia	136	162
Ireland	11	20
Italy	41	30
Malaysia	161	116
Mexico	37	124
Netherlands	83	52
New Zealand	18	19
Pakistan	7	18
Peru	7	10
Philippines	81	139
Poland	16	19
Portugal	9	13
Romania	6	4
Russia	13	17
Singapore	153	174
Slovenia	5	5
South Korea	50	106
Spain	38	31
Sweden	11	20
Switzerland	10	20
Taiwan	70	131
Thailand	204	198
Turkey	9	10

(*Continued*)

Appendix 1 (Continued)

Year	Number of new FDIs created
1990	523
1991	432
1992	393
1993	418
1994	463
1995	628
1996	799
1997	755
1998	586
1999	487
2000	505
2001	262

Appendix 2 Composition of regions

Regions	Countries	Regions	Countries
NAFTA (698 FDIs)	Canada	South America (94 FDIs)	Colombia
	USA		Venezuela
	Mexico		Peru
Europe (465 FDIs)	United Kingdom		Chile
	Netherlands		Brazil
	France		Argentina
	Germany	Oceania (90 FDIs)	Australia
	Sweden		New Zealand
	Portugal	East Asia (979 FDIs)	China
	Spain		Taiwan
	Italy		Hong Kong
	Finland		South Korea
	Austria	Northwest Asia (80 FDIs)	India
	Greece		Pakistan
	Denmark	South East Asia (901 FDIs)	Thailand
	Ireland		Singapore
	Switzerland		Vietnam
East Europe (87 FDIs)	Turkey		Malaysia
	Russia		Philippines
	Bulgaria		Indonesia
	Czech Republic		
	Hungary		
	Poland		
	Romania		
	Slovenia		

Appendix 3 Profiles of regions on the four institutional variables

Region	Weighted region-average institutional values			
	Regulatory control	Capital availability	Market liquidity	Political democracy
NAFTA	−1.13	2.90	0.87	0.50
Europe	−0.69	0.45	0.28	0.51
East Europe	0.46	−0.35	1.31	−0.43
South America	0.82	−0.10	−0.07	0.28
Oceania	−1.04	−0.17	−0.06	0.91
East Asia	0.33	0.34	−0.62	−1.40
Northwest Asia	1.63	−0.08	−0.41	0.10
South East Asia	0.27	−0.29	0.05	−0.85

Appendix 4 *Post hoc* tests—models explaining an MNE's degree of internationalization into a country over the period 1996–2001—other definitions of regions

Variable	Trading blocs	Culture (Ronen —Shenkar)	Culture (GLOBE)	Institution (La Porta et al., 1998)
Intercept	−3.26*	−5.23**	−0.41*	−3.18*
Level: firm's headquarters				
Advertising expense	−4.29	−3.80	−4.25	−4.53
R&D	4.91**	5.16**	5.05**	4.39**
Total prior international experience	−0.11*	−0.12*	−0.11*	−0.10
Firm size	0.15***	0.13**	0.13**	0.15***
Level: firm/country				
Prior internationalization into a country	−0.01	0.09	0.05	0.10
Country experience	0.30***	0.31***	0.30***	0.32***
Country experience of all Japanese firms	0.80***	0.70***	0.93***	1.01***
Population (/1,000,000)	−0.00*	−0.00	−0.00***	−0.00**
Per capita income	−1.08***	−0.71**	1.44***	1.24***
Economic growth	14.98***	12.96**	14.10**	21.77***
Cultural distance	−0.04	−0.16	−0.04	−0.07
Regulatory control—country's 'region-relative'	−0.34*	−0.06	−0.22	−0.48**
Capital availability—country's 'region-relative'	0.52***	0.41***	0.47***	0.35***
Market liquidity—country's 'region-relative'	−0.07	−0.12	−0.17	−0.25*
Political democracy—country's 'region-relative'	−0.27**	−0.17*	−0.08	−0.19**
Level: firm/region				
Prior internationalization into a region	0.05**	0.04***	0.04***	0.00
Regulatory control—region	−0.86***	−0.42	−1.32**	−2.45***
Capital availability—region	0.27**	0.70***	0.18	−0.83*
Market liquidity—region	−0.56***	−1.26**	−1.02**	0.01
Political democracy—region	−0.19*	−0.22	−0.08	−1.12*
Goodness of Fit: Akaike information criterion	4,340	4,383	4,353	4,373
$\Delta = AIC_{(model)} - AIC_{(lowest\ AIC:\ Model\ 4)}$	24	67	37	57
Bayesian information criterion	4,441	4,484	4,454	4,474

***p < 0.001; **p < 0.01; *p < 0.05.

Post hoc tests: other definitions of regions.

We used the definitions of regions proposed by the different authors. As some of our 45 countries were not always considered in these typologies, we added them as independent countries and identified them as 'other independent countries.'

Regions 'Trading blocs' (UNCTAD, 2001): EU (United Kingdom, Netherlands, France, Germany, Sweden, Portugal, Spain, Italy, Finland, Austria, Greece, Denmark, Ireland), NAFTA (USA, Canada, Mexico), MERCOSUR (Colombia, Venezuela, Peru, Chile, Brazil, Argentina), ASEAN (Thailand, Singapore, Vietnam, Malaysia, Philippines, South Korea, Indonesia), ANZCERTA (Australia, New Zealand). Other independent countries: Russia, Romania, Slovenia, Bulgaria, Czech Republic, Hungary, Poland, Romania, India, Pakistan, China, Hong Kong, Switzerland, Taiwan, Turkey.

Regions 'Culture' (Ronen and Shenkar, 1985): Anglo (Australia, Canada, Ireland, New Zealand, USA, United Kingdom), Latin Europe (France, Italy, Spain, Portugal), Nordic Europe (Denmark, Finland, Sweden), Germanic Europe (Austria, Germany, Switzerland, Netherlands), Latin America (Argentina, Chile, Mexico, etc.), Far Eastern (China, Hong Kong, Indonesia, South Korea, Malaysia, Taiwan, Thailand), Near Eastern (Greece, Turkey), Brazil, India. Other independent countries: Pakistan, Russia, Romania, Slovenia, Bulgaria, Czech Republic, Hungary, Poland, Romania.

Regions 'Culture GLOBE' (Gupta *et al.*, 2002): Anglo (Australia, Canada, Ireland, New Zealand, US, United Kingdom), Latin Europe (France, Italy, Spain, Portugal, Switzerland), Nordic Europe (Denmark, Finland, Sweden), Germanic Europe (Austria, Germany, Netherlands), Eastern Europe (Russia, Hungary, Poland, Romania, Slovenia, Bulgaria, Greece), Latin America (Mexico, Colombia, Venezuela, Peru, Chile, Brazil, Argentina), Arab culture (Turkey), Southern Asia (India, Indonesia, Philippines, Malaysia, Thailand), Confucian Asia (Taiwan, China, Hong Kong, South Korea, Singapore). Other independent countries: Pakistan.

Regions 'Institutions' (La Porta *et al.*, 1998): English-origin (Australia, HK, Canada, India, Ireland, New Zealand, Pakistan, Singapore, Thailand, United Kingdom, USA), French-origin (Argentina, Brazil, Chile, Colombia, France, Greece, Indonesia, Italy, Mexico, Netherlands, Peru, Philippines, Spain, Portugal, Turkey, Venezuela, Vietnam), German-origin (Austria, Germany, South Korea, Switzerland, Taiwan), Scandinavian-origin (Denmark, Finland, Sweden). Other independent countries: Russia, Romania, Slovenia, Bulgaria, Czech Republic, Hungary, Poland, Romania.

11 Do managers behave the way theory suggests?

A choice-theoretic examination of foreign direct investment location decision-making*

Peter J. Buckley, Timothy M. Devinney and Jordan J. Louviere

Foreign direct investment choice: theory and empirical limitations

The location and control decisions of multinational enterprises are at the core of managerial decision-making and academic theorising in international business. For each activity the firm undertakes, it has two critical decisions: (1) Where should the activity be located? (2) How should it be controlled? (Buckley, 2004). The control decision is whether to own and operate the function in house, or subcontract or outsource it to an independent company. Joint ventures are an intermediate stage between ownership and contract. Strictly speaking, foreign direct investment (FDI) implies control of the operation involving the investment, but there are many ways to control a facility beyond ownership. For example, foreign investors with minority ownership may well have power over an entity through the control of technology, management or key organisational systems.

Research in this area is derived from two intertwined theoretical traditions. The first derives from trade theory and the economics of industrial organisation, following Hymer (1960). Within the international business literature the two most dominant paradigms are those related to Dunning (1981) and Buckley and Casson (1976). According to this tradition, the choice of location for foreign investment is a deliberate, if rationally bounded, decision made with the primary goal of profitability and rent extraction, which may be combined with secondary goals of asset seeking or protection of profitability and rent. A second approach is the more loosely structured internationalisation process model associated with the 'Uppsala tradition' (for example, Johanson and Vahlne, 1977, 1990). According to this approach, managers make iterative decisions that are dominated by limited information and risk aversion. Such behaviour leads to a staged approach to entry that has specific characteristics and patterns. This approach emphasises that the subsidiary goal of 'learning to internationalise' is as important to explaining internationalisation patterns as a purely rational calculative approach.

Location decisions for FDI have received relatively little attention in the literature. Mudambi and Navarra (2003) consider location choice shortlisting to be a lacuna in the literature. It is also known that FDI is not a point-of-time 'go/no-go' decision but a process (this has been known right from the inception of studies of managerial decision-making in FDI; see the title of Aharoni's (1966) book, *The Foreign Investment Decision Process*). An examination of this process yields important changes over its duration, as we shall see.

Empirically, there has been far more work utilising and attempting to validate the economics tradition (for example, Mucchielli and Mayer, 2004; Wei *et al.*, 2005), with the more behavioural- and managerial-based internationalisation process model being relegated to case studies of small numbers of individual companies (for example, Fina and Rugman, 1996; Sarkar *et al.*, 1999; Chetty and Blankenburg Holm, 2000) or cross-sectional surveys (for example, Sullivan and Bauerschmidt, 1990; Eriksson *et al.*, 1997; Luo and Peng, 1999). However, both of these approaches have natural limitations and strong biases. The limitations of the internationalisation process model have been well documented, and are related mainly to the lack of a link between the empirical studies and a formal structural model (for example, Melin, 1992; Andersen, 1993) and concerns about the domain of the firms studied (for example, Sullivan and Bauerschmidt, 1990). But what is more worrying from our perspective are the unrecognised limitations of tests of the economics-based approach. Because most empirical FDI studies rely on panel or survey data they fail to address several issues highlighted by Devinney *et al.* (2003):

(1) The samples are based on final location choice only. Hence we do not know:

   (a) which options were considered by the firms and discarded (because they are not in the database); and
   (b) how these discarded options differed in terms of their perceived value to the managers making them.

(2) The samples are based on intra-firm choice. Hence we do not know to what extent:

   (a) the choices are idiosyncratic to the firms or managers making them (the assumption is that all managers are the same, and firm differences can be captured by covariates); and
   (b) the consideration sets of the firms differed (an implicit but binding assumption is that the choices the firms/managers are making were possible choices of the firms not making them).

In the present study we explore these issues by relying on choice-theoretic empirical methods (for example, Hensher *et al.*, 2000; Train, 2003) to capture the preference structures of managers either actively or potentially actively involved in FDI location choices. The benefit of this approach is that it allows for the examination of combinations of investment and environmental features and the relative value of each in determining the choice of managerially preferred outcomes in a more controlled setting. In addition, it allows for the direct testing of the degree of managerial variation from a purely rational model, and in this way serves as a more direct comparison between the rational calculative model and the internationalisation process model.

The next section provides a review of recent literature and then a brief summary of the economics-based calculative model and behavioural-based internationalisation process model on FDI location choice. We then move on to the heart of the paper to describe the methods and results. As this paper is aiming to present a methodology as well as some exploratory findings relating to a comparison of theories, more of the paper is devoted to a description of the methods and results than to the theories being examined. The conclusions will show that the nature of FDI investment choice is, at one and the same time, both clearer and more complex than normally discussed. We will also speculate on some of the implications of the application of experimental approaches in international business research.

Recent literature on FDI location decisions

Appendix A lists a selection of recent studies of FDI location decisions. It covers surveys of executives and managers (10 papers), secondary data including compilations of data sets at firm level (10 papers), and one survey-based Delphi study. The publication dates range from 1980 to 2006. It is natural that secondary data studies tend to emphasise 'objective' or instrumental determinants whereas surveys focus on experiential, cultural and knowledge (or information) related variables. However, the divide is not absolute. Many of the studies are of single-country outward investors (often the USA) or of single host countries.

The studies based on 'objective' firm-level data tend to adopt, consciously or unwittingly, a calculative approach to location decisions. Woodward and Rolfe (1993) find conventional results from factors such as market size, wage rates and transport costs. Barkema *et al.* (1996) find that cultural distance is a prominent factor in entry, particularly where another firm is involved, in a joint venture for example. Henisz (2000) finds that host country institutions are important, and that joint ventures are preferred when hazards in the host country are greatest. Chung (2001) finds technology factors to be important: both transfer and accession of technology show up as determinants in different contexts. Feinberg and Keane show interestingly mixed results on the impact of tariff reductions, even within narrowly defined manufacturing industries. Chung and Alcacer (2002) examine location within a single country – the USA – and find that, in addition to traditional location factors, knowledge-seeking motivations may operate through laboratories and manufacturing facilities. Mitra and Golder (2002) find that cultural distance from the home market is *not* a significant factor, but knowledge of nearby markets may have a significant effect. Zhou *et al.* (2002) find government policy initiatives to be a significant determinant of location among provinces in China for incoming FDI. Henisz and Macher (2004) find differences within semiconductor firms by level of technology, and find that firms also trade off their own experience against other firms' experience as sources of critical knowledge on foreign investment environments. Nachum and Zaheer (2005) show that industries with different levels of information intensity are driven by different investment motivations. There are rich varieties of suggested determinants in this body of literature, but equally there are sources of differences that cannot easily be reconciled.

Survey-based results are similarly heterogeneous. Davidson's (1980) pioneering study showed that corporate experience affected location decisions in two ways. First, firms preferred nations in which they were already active to those in which they were not. Second, firms with extensive international experience exhibited less preference for near, similar and familiar markets. Markets that others might perceive as less attractive because of high levels of uncertainties are given increased priority as the firm's experience rises. Crucially, for our purposes, he found that, as firms gain experience, the location of foreign activity increasingly represents an efficient response to global economic opportunities and conditions. In a single-country study, Mudambi (1998) found that firms with a longer tenure of operations are significantly more likely to invest in the host country (UK) in any given period. Brush *et al.* (1999) is a survey of plant managers in US MNEs and finds that, for this group, manufacturing strategy dominates international strategy. This is an intriguing pointer to the fact that managers may perceive location decisions differently according to where they are in the organisation. Pedersen and Petersen (2004) find that the 'shock effect' of foreign market entry develops over time (reaching its lowest level of market familiarity 8 years after entry) and supports the 'psychic distance paradox' that adjacent countries provide high levels of shock. Time periods are important in perceptions of location. Mission also reflects location, as Ambos (2005) shows for the establishment of laboratories, a complement to Kuemmerle's

(1999) argument that FDI can both augment and exploit R&D. The single Delphi study (MacCarthy and Atthirawong, 2003) found conventional results for the motivations of firms in manufacturing foreign investment location.

These results suggest that process issues in internationalisation have also been found to be significant. Learning, acculturation and cultural assimilation are variously found to be significant in different contexts, for different managers in the FDI location decision. We can oppose the two traditions – the calculative and the process – in our hypothesis construction.

The calculative vs the internationalisation process approach to FDI location choice

The calculative and internationalisation process approaches to FDI location choice have a long overlapping tradition, and comparisons between them have been attempted. However, to a greater or a lesser extent, such attempts have failed to come to any definitive conclusions, mainly because they rely on different levels of analysis, different sample domains, and different empirical traditions.

The economistic approach grew from a broadening of traditional trade-theoretic approaches to account for differences in FDI and internationalisation patterns (see the 'research forum' articles by Dunning, Devinney, Tallman, Mitchell and de la Torre in Cheng and Hitt (2004), for an overview of the some of this history). Its fundamental predictions are that firms are quasi-rational in their choices, and once the costs and benefits of specific investment opportunities are considered in light of the economic and competitive constraints operating in a market, there is little room for managerial discretion. The best managers making the most financially viable location choices ultimately out-survive those making less commercially efficacious choices. Proof of the validity of the rational calculative viewpoint is typically revealed through econometric panel data-based studies that show that firms do indeed make decisions that are rational, based on components of the fit between their firm-specific advantages and the structures and needs of the markets that they enter.

The internationalisation process model has a humbler beginning, growing out of a single-industry study of expansion by Swedish logging companies. Approaching the decision to internationalise at a more micro level, this tradition concentrates more on the issues of how firms learn as they internationalise. It proposes that specific biases exist in the nature of the decisions that they make based on their experience. One of the hallmarks of internationalisation theory is a belief that less experienced managers behave in ways that overweight specific investment characteristics (such as cultural closeness to the home country), and behave in a more risk-averse manner. Proof of the validity of the internationalisation approach is typically revealed through case studies showing how a single firm or groups of firms in the same industry follow a systematic process as they become more internationally mature.

The tradition deriving from economics makes little allowance for managerial self-interest and rent-seeking behaviour, factors given considerable latitude in the internationalisation process approach. Our experimental approach allows us both to incorporate insights from the process tradition and to highlight potential managerial biases including self-interest. As it focuses on the managers who are responsible for making the decisions it removes problems of 'the level of analysis' that bedevil comparisons of different conceptual approaches. Further, our hypotheses are framed so that we can test the degree to which final decisions over time converge on what is optimal for the firm, by gradually eliminating bias and self-interest as FDI decisions are repeated by the same manager. The effect of experience may make managerial decision-making more 'rational' from the point of view of the firm's best interest.

It would be apt to say that the debate between these two traditions is something of a dance where the partners never touch. This has been due to the inability to find a level of analysis or approach that allows for a more direct test of the tenets of the theories. However, one possibility – indeed, the approach used here – is to examine managerial decisions directly (albeit experimentally) in an attempt to address some of the areas of overlap between these two theoretical traditions. A direct test of the internationalisation process approach is to examine whether or not managers with less internationalisation experience utilise models that are distinctly different from those of more experienced managers, when facing precisely the same investment opportunities. A second test is to examine whether or not the risk profile of less experienced managers is different from the risk profile of the more experienced managers. We can state these as hypotheses:

Hypothesis 1: Managers with more internationalisation experience will use more calculative approaches than managers with less internationalisation experience.

Hypothesis 2: Managers with more internationalisation experience will show less risk aversion than managers with less internationalisation experience.

As we have shown, both these hypotheses have support in the prior literature.

Experimental methods

We applied two experimental methods in this study. The first is a variant of standard discrete choice methods (DCM) with an experimental manipulation. The second is a best-worst (BW) experiment aimed at validating the preferences extracted from the discrete choice experiment.

The sample

The subjects were active managers in the top management team of a selection of firms headquartered mainly in Australia, Denmark and the USA, where the sample was representative of three groups:

(1) local firms with international operations (managers answering here were located in the HQ);
(2) subsidiaries of multinational enterprises (managers answering here were located in the subsidiary); and
(3) managers in local firms with no international operations.

An attempt was made to match up a sufficient sample of firms in group (1) with those in group (2), for example, we sampled both the subsidiary of Danish firms in Australia and their Danish HQ. Firms in group (3) were sampled so as to approximate the size of the subsidiaries represented in group (2). Managers were approached via fax and an interview was arranged with those willing to be involved in the study.

Although an attempt was made to have a balanced and moderately representative sample, the respondents were not drawn from a large sample. The task we asked managers to complete is difficult and long (a typical interview was 1.5–2 hours), implying that many managers were unwilling to take the time to be involved. Because we are approaching the top management team at these firms, normal random sampling was abandoned for a more

Table 11.1 Sample and respondent characteristics

Headquarters location	
Australia	29.0%
Denmark	31.9%
Germany, Netherlands, Switzerland	8.6%
Japan, Malaysia, Singapore	4.2%
Singapore	2.0%
UK	2.9%
USA	23.2%
Employees (median number)	32,000
Employees (mean number)	21,147
Turnover (median range)	$500 million–$1,000 million
Median levels between respondent and CEO	1
CEOs, managing directors, CFOs	34.7%
Senior VP, directors, regional heads	33.3%
Manager personally engaged in	
Import/export	52.2%
Equity JV negotiation	50.7%
Non-equity JV negotiation	44.9%
JV or alliance	53.6%
M&A	47.8%
Traded companies	37.7%
FDI location choice (LC)	56.5%
FDI establishment (E)	59.4%
FDI operations (O)	47.8%
FDI experience (aggregation of LC or E or O)	64.1%
Number of countries in which subsidiaries operate (median)	10–25

targeted approach. That allowed us to get managers with both some and no international experience. Approximately 200 firms were approached, with a net sample of 70 respondents. The characteristics of these individuals are shown in Table 11.1. They are senior in their organisations – 35% were CEOs, MDs or CFOs – and the organisations are representative of the Fortune Global 500 plus a sample of smaller firms in many of the same industries, the median turnover was between US$500 million and US$1000 million. Given that the purpose of this paper is to highlight a method, the sample is sufficient for preliminary analysis and evaluation of the techniques. In addition to conducting the experimental exercise with these managers, each was interviewed at the time of the experiment and also in a debriefing in which their results were explained and discussed with them.

The choice experiment

The extant theories of FDI location choice were used to determine the features of investment alternatives that would be relevant to making a location choice decision. Based on pre-testing, we reduced an initial list down to 12 investment features and one size of investment condition (with three levels) and one political stability condition (with two levels). The features and the levels are shown in Table 11.2. They were aimed at capturing not just investment return but also potential opportunities, exploitation and exploration of assets, structural barriers, market inefficiencies and cultural proximity.

Theoretically, the calculative and internationalisation viewpoints would imply that specific investment attributes would be weighed more heavily or differentially. In particular, those

Table 11.2 Investment features and levels used in the choice experiment

Features of investment	Levels
The cost of operations: Choosing a specific location can lead to higher or lower costs of operation across the value chain	Decrease 10%, decrease 5%, increase 5%, increase 10%
Return on investment (ROI): Describes the rate of return expected from the investment	Less than home market and fails to meet hurdle rate, less than home market but meets hurdle rate, same as home market, greater than home market
Access to new resources, assets and technologies: Choosing a specific location can lead to greater competences being developed in the firm, through access to physical resources, organisational assets, or new technologies	No new access, access
Pre-emption of competition: Choosing a specific location can allow a firm to pre-empt competition into a location, thereby securing a first-mover advantage	Pre-emption important, pre-emption not important
Potential market size	Large relative to home market, same as home market, small relative to home market
Growth: The rate of increase in sales in the market	Decline, no growth, low growth, strong growth
The existence of established relations: Different markets will have different sets of established relationships.	No established relations, yes established relations exist
Trade and other structural barriers: Markets will have different levels of trade protection.	High barriers, no barriers
Potential for exploitation of existing resources, assets and technologies: Companies enter markets sometimes with the intent of exploiting an existing competence in a new market	No potential, potential exists
Culture/language of the new market: Indicates the natural native language used in the country	English, Arabic, Chinese, French, Portuguese, Russian, Spanish, other
Line of business: Denotes whether the new investment is in a existing, related or new line of business	Same line of business, related line of business, completely new line of business
Asset protection: Denotes whether legal structures exist for the protection of assets, both physical and intellectual	No protection, adequate/strong protection

investment attributes most readily identified with the return characteristics of the choice – the cost of operations, return on investment, potential market size, growth and access to new resources, assets and technologies – would, according to the calculative orientation, be more important. Indeed, once accounted for, the other attributes should matter little if the returns are assured. The internationalisation orientation, with its emphasis on the cognitive, learning and resource aspects of the location choice decision, would imply that managers would put differential weight on those characteristics that would reduce risk and complexity: the existence of established relations, trade and other structural barriers, the potential for exploitation of existing resources, assets and technologies, the culture/language of the market, asset protection, and whether or not the expansion was in an existing line of business. In addition, according to internationalisation theory, the size of the investment and the degree of political stability would matter more to less experienced managers. However, it should be emphasised

Table 11.3 Environment and investment level conditions

Individuals were given the following information before the choice experiment:
The investments are being made in a country that is viewed as <Insert Political Condition>. Your organisation is considering directly investing in operations in this country and the investment being made represents <Insert Investment Level Condition> of the total cash available for investment for the next three years.

Political condition	Investment-level condition
Quite politically stable in the sense that there is little likelihood of either social disturbance or political transitions other than through organised or legitimate means.	A relatively small investment totalling 10%.
	A relatively moderate investment totalling 30%.
Somewhat politically unstable in the sense that there is a not insignificant probability that social disturbances will arise or that unpredictable political transitions might occur	A relatively significant investment totalling 50%.

that the important consideration laid out in the hypotheses is not the attributes that managers take into consideration alone, but that managers with different levels of experience will make quite different decisions.

Individuals made decisions about 32 investment pairs with varying levels across the 12 investment features. Each subject was put into one of six investment-political conditions – in essence nesting the choice experiment within this investment – stability condition experiment. The investment levels varied between 10, 30 and 50% of total investment funds available, and were meant to capture the importance of the magnitude of the investment being made. The political stability levels varied between politically stable and politically unstable. Details of these conditions are presented in Table 11.3. An example of a singular choice from the experiment is presented in Figure 11.1. In all, each individual would be placed in 1 of 96 possible choice experiments × investment level × political stability conditions. Our design allowed us to test all main effects and all interaction effects; however, the size of the sample restricted us to an examination of main effects only.

In addition to the choice experiment, subjects were also asked to evaluate their organisation's most recent example of FDI (for example, establishing a call centre in New Zealand or opening a factory in China) on the 12 features presented in Table 11.2. Additional information was collected about the typicality of the most recent investment, the nature of the mode of entry, and the level of investment involved. As well as this information, standard firmographic data and information on the individual manager was collected. Information on the firm's last investment is presented in Table 11.4. It shows that 84% of the firms have engaged in FDI across a wide range of countries. In addition, it hints at what might be relevant characteristics of investment choice. The last investments show a tendency towards:

(1) markets with production cost reduction (48%);
(2) markets with larger ROI (55%);
(3) markets with larger markets (58%);
(4) markets with strong growth (66%);
(5) markets with prior investment and established relations (75%);
(6) markets where existing assets and current lines of business can be exploited (81%); and
(7) markets where they are concerned about pre-empting competitors (63%).

Features of the Investment #3	Option A	Option B
Cost of operations	Increase 10%	Decrease 10%
Return on investment (ROI)	Greater than home market	Less than home market; fails hurdle rate
Access to new resources, assets and technologies	Access	No new access
Preemption of competition	Important	Not important
Potential market size	Smaller than home market	Larger than home market
Growth	Decline	Strong growth
Existence of established relations	Yes	No
Trade and other structural barriers	No barriers	High barriers
Potential for exploitation of existing resources, assets & technologies	Potential exists	No potential
Culture/Language of the new market	Other	English
Line of business	Same	New
Asset protection	Strong	No protection
. If the investment options described above were available to your organization, which option would you recommend giving further consideration (Tick ONE box only)?	■ A	■ B
	■ Neither	
. If the investment option described above were available to your organization, which would you undertake instead of or in addition to other currently available investments (Tick ONE box only)?	■ A	■ B
	■ Neither	

Figure 11.1 Example of an investment choice option.

These items line up nicely with theory, the question we need to ask is whether they are simply a bias associated with the nature of recent opportunities or whether they are truly representative of the preferences of the managers. In other words, these are clearly factors that managers desire in the best of circumstances, but how do they make decisions when there are conflicts between these factors across investment options?

The BW experiment

To validate and further extend the models developed based on the choice-modelling experiment, we also conducted a BW experiment using the 12 features given in Table 11.2 plus four additional factors – political stability, currency value, investment assistance – and the existence of a democratic government in the host country. The use of BW scales is aimed at addressing two issues. The first is to examine any bias in the way individuals respond to the choice experiment. In theory, the DCM experiment and the BW experiments are tapping the same underlying preferences and therefore should provide confirmatory results. Second, BW experiments are relatively simple to conduct. If the results of the DCM experiment and the BW experiment are indeed equivalent, a much larger sample can be examined using the simpler method without any loss of generality of the results.

One of the biggest challenges in determining the relative importance of a set of factors in an international environment is the existence of scalar inequivalence (Cohen, 2003). Scalar inequivalence arises primarily because of differences in response styles, which are defined as 'tendencies to respond systematically to questionnaire items on some basis other than what the items were specifically designed to measure' (Paulhus, 1991: 17). There is

Table 11.4 Characteristics of last investment made

Percent with FDI	84.1%
Cost of operations[a]	
Decrease 10%	32.7%
Decrease 5%	15.4%
Increase 5%	13.5%
Increase 10%	17.3%
Not considered relevant to decision	21.1%
Return on investment[a]	
Less than home market; fails hurdle rate	12.7%
Less than home market; meets hurdle rate	12.7%
Same as home market	12.7%
Greater than home market	54.6%
Not considered relevant to decision	7.3%
Potential market size[a]	
Smaller than home market	17.5%
Same as home market	10.5%
Greater than home market	57.9%
Not considered relevant to decision	14.1%
Potential market growth[a]	
Decline or no growth	1.8%
Low growth	21.4%
Strong growth	66.1%
Not considered relevant to decision	10.7%
Established relationships existed in the market[a]	74.6%
Not considered relevant to decision	8.5%
High trade barriers existed in the market[a]	28.3%
Not considered relevant to decision	11.3%
Exploitation of existing assets important[a]	81.3%
Not considered relevant to decision	10.1%
Last market entered[a]	
China	16.3%
Other developing Asia (Vietnam, Indonesia, India, etc.)	8.4%
Developed Asia (Korea, Taiwan, etc.)	7.1%
Developed Western (EU-15, USA, etc.)	22.9%
Developing Western (E. Europe, etc.)	4.3%
Asset protection[a]	
No protection	20.8%
Weak protection	37.8%
Strong protection	32.1%
Not considered relevant to decision	9.3%
Prior investment in this market[a]	60.9%
Dominant nature of that investment	
Wholly owned subsidiary	42.9%
M&A	7.1%
Equity JV	28.6%
Non-equity alliance	7.1%
Import/export	14.3%
Compared with other investments[a]	
This was relatively routine	68.4%
This was out of the ordinary	31.6%
Compared with other investment[a]	
This amount was relatively insignificant	14.0%
This amount was normal	35.1%
This amount was significant	50.9%
Competitive pre-emption important[a]	62.7%
Not considered relevant to decision	13.6%
Same line of business entered[a]	66.7%

a These questions answered only by those whose last investment involved FDI.

Question No.	Which issue matters LEAST to you? (<u>tick ONLY ONE box</u> for each question)	Sets of social and ethical issues for you to consider	Which issue matters MOST to you? (<u>tick ONLY ONE box</u> for each question)
1	☐ ☐ ☐ ☐	Cost of operations Potential market size Growth Existence of established relations	☐ ☐ ☐ ☐
2	☐ ☐ ☐ ☐	Access to new resources Potential market size Trade and structural barriers Potential for exploitation of existing resources	☐ ☐ ☐ ☐
3	☐ ☐ ☐ ☐	Potential market size Culture/Language of market Line of business Strong asset protection	☐ ☐ ☐ ☐

Figure 11.2 Example of the best–worst experiment.

ample empirical evidence to show that individuals in different countries differ significantly in their response styles (Chen *et al.*, 1995; Steenkamp and Baumgartner, 1998; Steenkamp and Ter Hofstede, 2002), and that these differences can lead to seriously biased conclusions (Baumgartner and Steenkamp, 2001). For example, Cohen (2003) argued that differences in international market segmentation studies may be due more to differences in scale use than to true differences in consumer needs and preferences. Although most of this work is related to consumer research, there is every likelihood that similar issues arise with respect to managerial decisions as assessed by surveys.

BW scaling is a multiple-choice extension of the paired comparison approach that is scale-free and forces respondents to make a discriminating choice among the issues under consideration. As Finn and Louviere demonstrated (1992: 13), 'BW scaling models the cognitive process by which respondents repeatedly choose the two objects in varying sets of three or more objects that they feel exhibit the largest perceptual difference on an underlying continuum of interest'. Appendix B provides a detailed discussion of the logic and algebra of BW scaling. Readers are referred to Marley and Louviere (2005) for a more detailed description of the scale properties of BW experiments. BW experiments permit intra- and inter-feature comparison of levels through the use of a common interval scale (McIntosh and Louviere, 2003; Cohen and Neira, 2003). Figure 11.2 provides an example from the BW experiment.

Empirical estimation

Choice model results

Examination of the choice-modelling responses is done through a series of binary logit models. Respondents were asked to evaluate pairs of investments by indicating which of the options they (1) would 'recommend giving further consideration' and (2) 'would undertake instead of or in addition to other currently available investments'. These two decisions are akin to asking the manager a 'consideration set' question and a go/no-go, or investment, question. In this sense, they can be seen to represent nested decisions. The choices from question (2) force individuals to make a definitive decision from the set generated from decision (1).

However, before proceeding to the logit analysis, it is useful to examine the tendency of respondents to indicate whether they would consider or undertake an investment based on the characteristics of those investments. Table 11.5 indicates simply whether or not an investment was chosen (in other words, the 'neither' option was not chosen) cross-tabulated against different conditions. Overall, respondents would 'consider' 26% of the investments and 'undertake' 14%. In situations where the market was politically unstable these percentages drop to 25 and 9%, respectively. The level of the investment does not seem to reveal a consistent pattern of choices. Overall, individuals are less likely to make any choice when asked the 'would invest' question.

In addition, there are some logical patterns that arise. First, cost-of-production increases are related to a smaller likelihood of considering an investment (although not making the investment); however, the effect is not monotonic. Second, a higher ROI is positively and monotonically related to the consideration of an investment, but slightly less so in the case of the go/no-go decision. Third, access to new resources, exploitation of existing assets, pre-emption of competition, the existence of established relations in the market and avoidance of barriers to trade are all related to making or considering an investment. Fourth, market growth and market size are important to considering an investment but less so in making an investment. In both cases, large markets with strong growth are the clear choice winners. Fifth, being in the same line of business is important to considering and making an investment. Sixth, asset protection is a strong consideration factor, but less so in making the final investment. These simple results provide face validity as to the seriousness with which the managers involved considered the task.

This information provides some understanding of the nature of managerial preferences for different FDI location choices, but we need a more statistically valid approach to determine the marginal value of specific investment options. Table 11.6 presents the logit analysis for the 'consider' and 'invest' choices in the aggregate. What we see in these results is that the likelihood of considering an FDI option is more clear-cut than the likelihood of choosing the final investment, given what was considered. Ignoring the stability of the market and the level of the investment, it appears that production cost matters, as do ROI, access to resources, market size (when large), market growth, established relationships, barriers to trade, exploitation of existing assets, remaining in the same line of business, and strong asset protection. Being in an English-speaking country and not in an Arabic- or Russian-speaking country also appears as part of the criteria. When we adjust for the stability of the market and the level of the investment we find that political instability is not relevant, but small and large investment amounts are related to considering more of the investments presented. Finally, accounting for the FDI experience of the manager (FDI experience) does not matter significantly. FDI experience is defined as the manager having had experience in FDI location choice, FDI establishment or FDI operations. Sixty-four per cent of managers had FDI experience. Overall, those with no FDI experience would consider an investment 28% of the time and those with FDI experience 26% of the time.

When we move to the 'invest' model, the results are less clear-cut. Indeed, one would have to say that there is greater heterogeneity in the choices made, with political stability and the FDI experience of the managers now assuming importance. Managers with less FDI experience are more likely to make any investment choice (16% of the time *vs* 13% of the time for those with experience), all managers are less likely to make an investment when the market is politically unstable. In addition, markets with cost increases are more likely to be avoided.

Table 11.5 Propensity to choose any investment (percentage of all investments presented)

	Would consider an investment	Would invest
Overall (N = 4414 choices each)	26.0	14.0
When environment is		
Unstable (N = 2430)	25.4	8.8
Stable (N = 1984)	26.5	14.9
When investment is		
Small (N = 1408)	35.3	16.2
Medium (N = 1454)	42.4	12.6
Large (N = 1552)	37.2	13.0
Cost of production		
Declines 10%	31.8	15.2
Declines 5%	25.4	13.1
Increases 5%	20.2	8.8
Increases 10%	24.2	14.5
Return on investment		
Less than home market; fails hurdle rate	14.4	13.9
Less than home market; meets hurdle rate	21.8	10.9
Same as home market	25.7	11.2
Greater than home market	40.0	15.7
No access to new resources	23.4	13.9
Access to new resources	28.6	12.9
Pre-emption important	29.4	14.9
Pre-emption unimportant	22.7	11.9
Market size		
Smaller than home market	24.5	14.7
Same as home market	21.8	10.6
Larger than home market	32.8	15.4
Market growth		
Declining	14.9	12.9
None	18.6	10.7
Low	23.6	11.6
Strong	43.3	16.7
Established relations unimportant	21.4	11.4
Established relations important	30.7	15.4
Barriers to trade exist	21.4	12.4
Barriers to trade do not exist	30.8	14.4
No exploitation of existing assets	23.9	12.1
Exploitation of existing assets	28.1	14.7
Language		
English	24.6	12.5
Arabic	16.6	7.1
Chinese	25.4	12.3
French	23.9	9.9
Portuguese	22.0	12.8
Russian	20.1	13.1
Spanish	24.8	10.2
Other	37.4	20.7
Diversification		
Same line of business	34.9	18.3
Related line of business	24.6	10.6
New line of business	19.0	11.8
No/weak asset protection	19.9	12.1
Strong asset protection	32.4	14.8

Table 11.6 Aggregate consider and invest models

	Would consider the investment option		Would invest in the option	
Cost of production				
Declines 10%	0.328***	0.330***	0.025	0.025
Declines 5%	0.217***	0.223***	0.051	0.054
Increase 5%	0.023	0.025	−0.168**	−0.166**
Return on investment				
Less than home market; fails hurdle rate	−0.573***	−0.576***	−0.073	−0.073
Less than home market; meets hurdle rate	−0.148**	−0.149**	−0.091	−0.092
Greater than home market	0.278***	0.277***	−0.071	−0.074
No access to new resources	−0.152***	−0.154***	0.046	0.054
Pre-emption important	0.053	0.054	0.017	0.021
Market size				
Smaller than home market	−0.047	−0.047	0.080	0.081
Larger than home market	0.230***	0.233***	0.109*	0.110*
Market growth				
Declining	−0.210***	−0.208***	−0.007	−0.010
Low	0.177***	0.183***	0.044	0.040
Strong	0.674***	0.680***	0.149**	0.149**
No established relations	−0.119***	−0.121***	−0.068	−0.069
Barriers to trade exist	0.131***	−0.131***	0.048	0.048
No exploitation of existing assets	−0.141***	−0.143***	−0.109	−0.112**
Language				
English	0.084	0.098	−0.197**	−0.184**
Arabic	−0.364***	−0.354***	−0.474***	−0.458***
Chinese	−0.013	−0.003	−0.153*	−0.139
French	−0.099	−0.102	−0.286***	−0.283***
Portuguese	−0.182**	−0.173**	−0.143	−0.132
Russian	−0.233***	−0.226***	−0.118	−0.103
Spanish	−0.063	−0.068	−0.265***	−0.269***
Diversification				
Related line of business	−0.104**	−0.111**	−0.182***	−0.186***
New line of business	−0.322***	−0.329***	−0.156**	−0.162**
No asset protection	−0.259***	−0.261***	0.007	0.005
Unstable political environment		−0.037		0.127***
Level of investment				
Small investment (10%)		0.171***		0.017***
Large investment (50%)		0.076		0.009***
Manager's FDI experience		−0.084		−0.262**
−2LL	4133.00	4117.93	3349.14	3335.36
ρ^2	0.275	0.279	0.049	0.055
Percentage classified correctly	77.7	77.5	86.6	86.6

*$P < 0.10$, **$P < 0.05$, ***$P < 0.01$.

All of this indicates that managers are taking a slightly more risk-adverse stance when making the actual decision to invest, *vs* just considering an option, and that managers with less FDI experience appear even more risk-averse.

Tables 11.7 and 11.8 provide two more illustrative breakdowns in this analysis. Table 11.7 separates the analysis based on whether or not the manager in question had any prior FDI

Table 11.7 Consider and invest models split by manager's FDI experience

	Would consider option when FDI experience		Would invest in option when FDI experience	
	No	Yes	No	Yes
Cost of production				
Declines 10%	0.158	0.380***	−0.050	0.043
Declines 5%	0.154	0.249***	−0.074	0.075
Increase 5%	0.000	0.046	−0.187	−0.155*
Return on investment				
Less than home market; fails hurdle rate	−0.529***	−0.604***	0.141	−0.042
Less than home market; meets hurdle rate	−0.300**	−0.124*	0.046	−0.024
Greater than home market	0.318**	0.260***	0.004	0.081
No access to new resources	−0.175*	−0.152***	−0.103	0.082
Pre-emption important	0.150	0.028	−0.077	0.036
Market size				
Smaller than home market	−0.159	−0.010	0.178	0.068
Larger than home market	0.021	0.288***	−0.041	0.145**
Market growth				
Declining	−0.036	−0.258***	0.062	−0.006
Low	0.254*	0.170**	0.133	0.025
Strong	0.556***	0.711***	0.125	0.168**
No established relations	−0.238**	−0.094*	−0.059	−0.062
Barriers to trade exist	−0.052	−0.146***	−0.276**	0.002
No exploitation of existing assets	−0.072	−0.163***	0.061	−0.146**
Language				
English	−0.057	0.114	−0.357*	−0.161*
Arabic	−0.213	−0.388***	−0.256	−0.533***
Chinese	−0.023	−0.003	−0.351	−0.106
French	−0.108	−0.127	−0.340	−0.285**
Portuguese	−0.177	−0.180*	−0.413*	−0.076
Russian	−0.501***	−0.171*	−0.492**	−0.027
Spanish	−0.109	−0.080	−0.389*	−0.255**
Diversification				
Related line of business	0.074	−0.157***	−0.034	−0.227***
New line of business	−0.144	−0.372***	−0.038	−0.199**
No asset protection	−0.333**	−0.251***	0.016	−0.006
Unstable political environment	−0.069	−0.022	−0.456***	−0.129**
Level of investment				
Small investment (10%)	0.067	0.177***	−0.818***	0.139**
Large investment (50%)	−0.022	0.091*	0.025	0.103*
−2LL	751.14	3330.22	552.94	2688.64
ρ^2	0.262	0.294	0.099	0.074
Percent classified correctly	77.5	78.4	83.0	81.6

*$P < 0.10$, **$P < 0.05$, ***$P < 0.01$.

experience. The prior analysis allows us to see whether or not FDI experience matters to the tendency to accept any given investment, whereas this analysis asks whether or not the models of managers with or without experience are any different. As can be seen, the models for the experienced and inexperienced managers are similar, but do reveal a few differences. First, FDI-experienced managers are more likely to react positively to production cost reductions and market size, and negatively to moving out of their existing line of business. They

Table 11.8 Consider and invest models split by market stability

	Would consider option when market is		Would invest in option when market is	
	Stable	*Unstable*	*Stable*	*Unstable*
Cost of production				
Declines 5%	0.323***	0.345***	0.041	−0.027
Increases 5%	0.196**	0.253***	0.047	0.073
Increases 10%	−0.054	0.118	−0.234**	−0.101
Return on investment				
Less than home market; fails hurdle rate	−0.390***	−0.919***	0.112	−0.207*
Less than home market; meets hurdle rate	−0.192**	−0.121	0.032	−0.119
Greater than home market	0.217***	0.366***	0.078	0.058
No access to new resources	−0.156***	−0.196***	0.035	0.059
Pre-emption important	0.022	0.078	0.005	0.033
Market size				
Smaller than home market	−0.041	−0.055	0.073	0.111
Larger than home market	0.165**	0.341***	0.110	0.121
Market growth				
Declining	−0.190**	−0.255***	0.114	−0.237**
Low	0.148*	0.229**	0.085	−0.035
Strong	0.599***	0.852***	0.087	0.265**
No established relations	−0.199**	−0.047	−0.108	−0.007
Barriers to trade exist	−0.122**	−0.167**	0.034	0.091
No exploitation of existing assets	−0.181***	−0.102	−0.103*	−0.116
Language				
English	0.042	0.156	−0.213*	−0.251
Arabic	−0.224**	−0.509***	−0.372**	−0.593**
Chinese	0.091	−0.129	−0.226*	−0.072
French	−0.049	−0.170	−0.306**	−0.257*
Portuguese	−0.174	−0.181	−0.018	−0.354**
Russian	−0.148	−0.359***	−0.026	−0.246
Spanish	−0.160	0.047	−0.266**	−0.352**
Diversification				
Related line of business	−0.081	−0.162**	−0.259***	−0.111
New line of business	−0.328***	−0.317***	−0.213**	−0.092
No asset protection	−0.304***	−0.229***	0.042	−0.039
FDI experience	−0.009	−0.204	−0.139	−0.681***
Level of investment				
Small investment (10%)	0.445***	−0.067	0.462***	−0.441***
Large investment (50%)	0.378***	−0.285***	0.475***	−0.639***
−2LL	2326.97	1676.03	1945.62	1262.62
$\rho2$	0.261	0.367	0.092	0.118
Percent classified correctly	76.2	79.7	85.0	88.1

$*P < 0.10, **P < 0.05, ***P < 0.01.$

also prefer smaller investments. However, they are less concerned than inexperienced managers with the existence of established relations. When it comes to the case of the investment model we see that less experienced managers are more affected by market stability and trade barriers, whereas experienced managers prefer large markets with big growth where they can exploit existing resources and lines of business.

Table 11.8 presents an analysis based on the stability of the market experimental manipulation. What we see is that the models are quite close, particularly in the case of the 'consideration' of investments. In the investment model we see that managers are more likely to engage in avoidance behaviour, putting emphasis on avoiding low-return markets and seeking markets with high growth.

Considering the limited sample size, the choice models indicate a few things of relevance. First, which options a manager is willing to consider is quite consistent with economic-based theoretical thinking about FDI location choice, and seems unaffected by the environment in which the choice is being made. Second, the actual willingness to take on an investment is less likely to match up with the economic models, and appears much more eclectic. Part of this may be due to the stylised form of our experiments. However, it is more likely that the factors that, in the end, swing the decision toward one investment *vs* another are less obvious than we are able to discern using the investment attributes we are investigating. Even more interesting is the bias that this may introduce into the decision-making process. If managers are making a 'consideration' cut that takes into account the dominant criteria of the decision (for example, ROI) and then choosing their 'investments' conditional on this, it is hardly surprising that the marginal determinants will be the factors that were unimportant in the first stage (as these have the most variance). This is indeed confirmed by Mudambi and Navarra (2003), who show the comparability of many of the shortlists of investments investigated by firms. Third, FDI experience may be less relevant to the 'what to consider' decision and more relevant to the actual final decision being made. The implication here is that the conclusions of the internationalisation process model are less relevant for the complete investment choice decision, as even managers without much experience can make fairly rational evaluations of available alternatives.

Indeed, these conclusions appear to be the same ones that the managers involved in the experiments come to themselves. In debriefing interviews managers were shown the models that were based on their own choices (as well as the aggregate models). Invariably they reacted in two ways. One was to indicate that there are many more factors going into their decisions than our experiments capture. However, when queried about this, it turned out that the attributes we used covered almost everything they brought up. What seemed to matter to them was that the number of levels in many of the attributes was broader than we used. The second was that they felt their fiduciary responsibility to their firms was to generate broad sets of options that their board of directors could discuss in line with their overall strategy. Hence their final decision was much more one of fit with their overall strategy. This would imply that the heterogeneity seen in the 'investment' choice may be reflective of the heterogeneity of the strategies of the firms involved in the study.

BW results

The BW experiment allows for a simpler means of capturing preferences, although in a situation that is less robust than the DCM experiments presented earlier. A key methodological question we need to address is whether or not the BW experiments generate conclusions in line with the DCMs. If this is the case, then we have a means of gathering much more information from managers more quickly and for less expense than is normally the case with preference elicitation methods. Theoretically, we want to know what information these experiments reveal about the nature of managerial preferences with respect to FDI options that adds to what we have gathered from the DCMs. The BW experiment

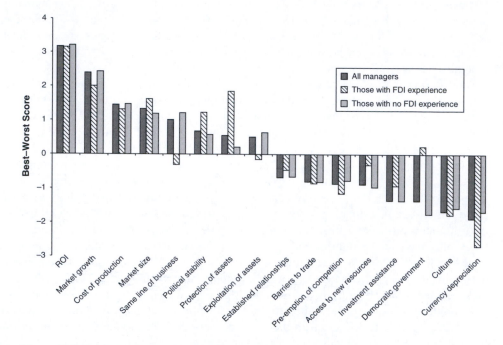

Figure 11.3 Aggregate best–worst experiment results.

used here incorporated the 12 factors in the DCM experiment along with four additional FDI determinants:

(1) investment assistance (loans, grants, rebates, etc.);
(2) the fact that the government of the country is elected in democratic fair and free elections;
(3) political stability, essentially adding in the political stability condition of the DCM experiment, and;
(4) the existence of currency depreciation.

Figure 11.3 presents the aggregate scores for the BW experiment with the 16 factors arranged from 'most important' to 'least important'. The most important items factors are (from best to worst):

(1) ROI;
(2) market growth;
(3) market size;
(4) remaining in the same line of business;
(5) market stability;
(6) exploitation of assets;
(7) asset protection; and
(8) the cost of production.

The least important factors (from worst to best) are:

(16) culture;
(15) having a democratic government;

(14) investment incentives;
(13) currency depreciation;
(12) access to new resources;
(11) pre-emption of competition;
(10) barriers to trade; and
 (9) having established relations in the market.

These factors fit nicely into the picture presented in the consideration models presented earlier.

Table 11.9 provides a simple mean comparison between managers with FDI experience and those without such experience. As in the case of the DCM analysis, we see that both groups have similar preference orderings, with a slight preference on the part of those with FDI experience to stick to the same line of business and to be slightly less concerned about asset protection, whereas those with less FDI experience favour countries with democratic governments.

Table 11.10 is perhaps the most interesting analysis as it compares the results from the BW experiment with individual-level model estimates from the DCM experiment. For each individual, the 32 'option A' and 32 'option B' responses for the 'would consider the investment' question were aggregated to form 64 pooled observations (a similar analysis could have been conducted for the 'would invest' decision but is excluded). Multi-variate ordinary least squares (OLS) regressions were estimated for each individual (estimating what is called a 'linear probability model': see Aldrich and Nelson, 1984), with the investment features used as predictors. These estimates were then correlated with the BW score from the appropriate measure. What we see is that the two sets of estimates are indeed quite well related, although in a complex way. In the case where we can make direct one-on-one comparisons

Table 11.9 Differences in individual BW scores split by manager's FDI experience

| | Manager's FDI experience | | | | | | |
| | No | | Yes | | Total | | |
	BW score	Rank	BW score	Rank	BW score	Rank	F
ROI	3.15	1	3.21	1	3.17	1	0.008
Market growth	2.00	2	2.43	2	2.39	2	0.652
Cost of production	1.31	5	1.47	3	1.45	3	0.173
Market size	1.62	4	1.19	5	1.33	4	0.376
Same line of business	−0.31	10	1.21	4	1.01	5	5.528**
Political stability	1.23	6	0.58	7	0.68	6	0.807
Protection of assets	1.85	3	0.21	8	0.55	7	5.529**
Exploitation of assets	−0.15	9	0.64	6	0.51	8	2.053
Established relationships	−0.46	11	−0.66	9	−0.68	9	0.082
Barriers to trade	−0.85	12	−0.81	11	−0.80	10	0.004
Pre-emption of competition	−1.15	14	−0.77	10	−0.86	11	0.330
Access to new resources	−0.31	10	−0.96	12	−0.88	12	1.470
Investment assistance	−0.92	13	−1.36	13	−1.35	13	0.707
Democratic government	0.23	8	−1.75	16	−1.36	14	6.821**
Culture	−1.77	15	−1.57	14	−1.67	15	0.171
Currency depreciation	−2.69	16	−1.68	15	−1.88	16	2.039

*$P < 0.10$, **$P < 0.05$, ***$P < 0.01$.

Table 11.10 Comparison between BW and individual level DCM estimates of preference ordering (absolute correlations)

Individual estimate variable	Correlation with BW variable	
	Pearson	Rank order
Cost of production		
Declines 10%	0.329***	0.268**
Declines 5%	0.096	0.082
Increase 5%	0.042	0.054
Return on investment		
Less than home market; fails hurdle rate	−0.057	−0.088
Less than home market; meets hurdle rate	−0.161*	−0.226**
Greater than home market	0.401***	0.406***
No access to new resources	−0.454***	−0.458***
Pre-emption important	0.046	0.051
Market size		
Smaller than home market	0.063	0.101
Larger than home market	0.158	0.207*
Market growth		
Declining	−0.201*	−0.129
Low	0.067	0.085
Strong	0.177*	0.244**
No established relations	−0.217**	−0.138
Barriers to trade exist	−0.176*	−0.120
No exploitation of existing assets	−0.142*	−0.145*
Language		
English	−0.177*	−0.158
Arabic	−0.280**	−0.296**
Chinese	−0.242**	−0.293**
French	−0.094	−0.142
Portuguese	−0.298***	−0.279**
Russian	−0.249**	−0.281**
Spanish	0.128	−0.153
Diversification		
Related line of business	−0.145	−0.198*
New line of business	−0.313**	−0.392***
No asset protection	−0.347***	−0.305**

*$P < 0.10$, **$P < 0.05$, ***$P < 0.01$.

(for example, barriers to trade and existence of established relations) all the variables are correlated, with the exception of the pre-emption of competition measure (which was not significant in any of the choice models). For measures with multiple levels we see that there is always some component that is correlated with the BW measure, but normally it is the most extreme measure (for example, production cost decreasing 10%, size greater than home market or operating in a new line of business). In the case of the culture measure it is related to the more extreme DCM variables, Arabic, Portuguese and Russian language countries.

Discussion

Most observational research on FDI uses actual stocks and flows and is unable to examine actual managerial decision-making because latent data (locations not chosen) are unobserved.

This chapter is an exception, because it explicitly considers hypothetical investments where we control the options being evaluated. Although this is highly stylised, it provides a unique and different window on the characteristics of managerial decision-making with respect to FDI. It also reveals the veracity of using experimental methods where previously only econometric panel data and case-theoretic methods were thought appropriate.

Our results are able to distinguish firm-focused rationality (rational from the point of view of the firm's interest as a whole) from individual-manager-focused rationality, and show an interesting interplay between these two 'rationalities'. Although it is possible that the hypothetical decision-making exercise we employed is less likely to show managerial self-interest than in actual choice situations, it does reveal a complexity that could not arise simply from managers gaming the exercise. For example, the effect of experience itself may make managerial choices more rational, and we see glimpses of this in the fact that more experience managers do indeed make different decisions. The strength of our approach is that the managers were presented with a quite complex combination of investment attributes presented in an orthogonal design. If they simply based their decisions on an overtly simple rule (choose the one with highest ROI) this would be immediately obvious in the results. Similarly, if they did not take the experiment seriously we would have found that few if any of the variables of interest were significant. Instead, we see clear, consistent patterns, both at the individual level and in the aggregate, which are confirmed by two different experimental approaches.

Our results support recent literature that has moved beyond the contrast between 'rational' and 'process' approaches to decision-making. This literature emphasises the complexity of the choices being made with respect to FDI, and we show one mechanism that may help in furthering our understanding of what managers do when faced by that complex environment. In addition, we suggest that 'when?' is as important as 'what?' in determining the outcomes of managerial decisions and their choice set. Even so, there are clearly regularities in the decision-making systems, as we suggest in the next section.

Conclusions and research implications

Our research method enables us to examine different stages of the process associated with the decision to engage in FDI (Aharoni, 1966). The first stage is the establishment of a set of potential investment destinations from a profile of attributes of alternative foreign locations that can be compared with each other across these pre-prescribed criteria. The second stage is the actual choice of an investment, either as a new investment or as an alternative to existing investments. A key conclusion from our preliminary analysis is that managers follow fairly rational rules from the point of view of the firm's interests in creating sets of investments to 'consider'. However, the choice of 'investments' in which to engage is less easy to reconcile with existing theory. One interesting conclusion that arises is that the manner in which IB researchers have analysed FDI may have introduced artefacts into their results. For example, as noted before, if managers are following a staged approach, where they narrow down investments into a smaller set and then make their final choice within that set, then it is important to understand the point in this process that is being examined. By just looking at the consideration set formation, it is likely that an investigator will walk away thinking that the rationalist theory of the firm approach is confirmed (hence rejecting Hypothesis 1 and Hypothesis 2). If one looks only at the choices within the investment model one is likely to think that the internationalisation process model is confirmed (hence accepting Hypothesis 1 and Hypothesis 2). In reality, neither is fully confirmed, because the nature of the decision-making process itself implies that factors considered in stage 1 are not going to be as relevant in stage 2.

Our results show that basic fundamental operational factors serve as the screening mechanism to determine a consideration set of investments. More country-specific factors enter the decision with higher priority when we move from 'consider' to 'invest' (a good example is host country language). Experience with FDI also figures more importantly in the 'invest' than the 'consider' decision, and perhaps this is an indication of the confidence that comes from repeating the FDI process (see also Buckley *et al.*, 1988). In addition, one can show that the models for managers with more FDI experience are more stable and have less variance around the estimates than those for less experienced managers. Variables related to host country culture play a much greater role in the 'invest' than the 'consider' decision. These are considerations that rise to prominence in the manager's mind at a late but crucial stage in the FDI process when all the more functional attributes of the investment have been accounted for.

We began this work attempting to get a better understanding of the causal mechanism by which FDI investment choice is made, and to alleviate some of the biases associated with the application of secondary data. What we see is that, just as Dunning (1981) showed that one could not understand trade without understanding the multinational enterprise, it is the case that we cannot understand FDI location choice without understanding the process used to make such choices at the level of the individual manager. Much work remains to get a fuller picture of the process by which these decisions are made and the role that the external environment plays in policing such decisions. Hence we are left with the dubious conclusion that Hypotheses 1 and 2 are both rejected and accepted. At one level our results are a 'ringing endorsement of orthodoxy', that is, managers make investment choices among a set of investments that are fundamentally driven by market characteristics, firm-specific advantages and return on investment. At another level these results indicate that managers' final investment decisions are highly idiosyncratic, and subject to biases that they might not be aware of themselves when making those decisions.

However, what our results do reveal is that structured experimentation can help to understand the complex decision-making underlying FDI. But this does not mean there are no limitations to what we have done. DCM and BW experiments are based upon random utility theoretic thinking, and suffer from all the limitations to that approach. Hence, if there are serious biases in the models used by managers, for example, if managers suffer from overconfidence bias (Camerer and Lovallo, 1999) or are using decision models that we have not designed the experiment to investigate, such as elimination by aspects (Tversky, 1972; Manrai and Sinha, 1989), our findings may have less predictive validity than we would hope (although, as McFadden (2001) notes, the models are remarkably predictive in the aggregate even in this case). Also, although our designs allow us to test interaction effects, our sample size restricts the analysis to mostly main effects. Hence, if managers are erroneously assuming related interactive structures (for example, wanting to go only into countries with high growth *and* high ROI *and* in the same line of business, but not being able to do so with the options they are given in the experiments) we would not be able to discern this with the data available here. Similarly, we have not embedded our experiments in an environment that accounts for the managers' fiduciary responsibilities. We have no way of knowing, based upon this study, how the managers' choices seen here would translate into a firm's final decision in reality, where all the complexity of ego, bonuses, financial analyst reports, institutional investment pressures and boards of directors comes into play.

Finally, our results have less than positive implications for the set of empirical findings seen in Appendix A. An examination of this research, plus much more that we could have included, shows significant sample domain issues. Most of the research examines country-out or country-in investment (for example, Taiwanese inward investment in China, or outward investment from Japan or the USA), in limited numbers of industries (for example, R&D

or semiconductors), with specific rationales that may be idiosyncratic to the circumstances being investigated. Although one can argue that 'revealed preference' data are more relevant because they represent real investment choices, they are also biased in that they may not be predictive in the sense of 'stated preference' data because they do not span the domain of possible investment options. Hence, developing a generalisable theory of FDI location choice may have been slowed by our failure to understand the extent to which we have restricted the domain of both our independent and dependent variables. However, we do not know the degree to which this is true until we attempt to re-test our findings in domains specifically structured to deal with this issue.

Future research implications

This chapter examined only one set of decisions: FDI location choice by managers. However, it also was an attempt to bring into international business an alternative approach to testing theory. In doing so, we feel there are some implications for other areas of international business research from this work. We can speculate about a few of these.

The first and most obvious implication is that other areas of firm choice behaviour can be investigated in a manner similar to what we have done. For example, the approach here can be modified to study not only entry mode type - for example, greenfield, joint venture, exporting – but also the facets of the choice of joint venture partner and the nature of the contracts with those partners. Hence we would argue that any area of location and mode choice could be studied experimentally. Furthermore, following from Roth and Kostova (2003), who argued quite elegantly that the MNE is an underutilised domain in which to study many new and interesting management phenomena, we believe that the domain of the management decision-maker is an underutilised domain in which to discover, validate and test existing and new international business theories and phenomena. However, unlike Roth and Kostova, we believe this potentially requires new theorising and new methodologies. In this regard, we are undoubtedly in line with Sullivan's (1998) call for a broader vision and more 'comprehensiveness, connectedness and complexity' (and we would add creativity) in international business research.

Second, it is clear that context matters considerably to decision-making, and this is no different and perhaps even more important in international business decisions. Indeed, the more research that is conducted, the more it is realised that simple economic rationalist *vs* behavioural internationalisation distinctions fall by the wayside. However, experimental approaches are sufficiently robust to allow for consideration of different contexts. In our experiments we examined simple issues of political stability and investment level. However, many experiments now utilise what are known as information acceleration approaches (for example, Urban *et al.*, 1997) that directly vary the context in which complex decisions are made. Although these have to date been used only in the case of technology products, there is no reason to believe that they cannot be used in more direct business contexts. Hence experiments can be conducted that look at the effects of coups, currency devaluations, and other socio-political scenarios.

Third, because experimental approaches can be designed to address issues of scale inequivalence, they are in general going to be more effective at studying cross-cultural phenomena than simple surveys. Indeed, any survey can be rewritten in a manner that mimics our BW approach, implying that one can theoretically remove all scale inequivalence from a survey instrument. For example, it would not be difficult to redevelop the Hofstede dimensions or any similar scale using this approach, theoretically generating purer measures than Likert-scale approaches alone (Hofstede, 2001).

Fourth, and most controversially, international business research has generally been limited in the approaches it has brought to bear on the phenomena under investigation. We have, to date, borrowed heavily from economics, sociology, social psychology and management but little from cognitive psychology or the rising field of experimental economics. This has limited the field in many ways, but most clearly in the study of the role of the individual decision-maker (manager, regulator, consumer). Our application shows that there are opportunities to utilise new and different methods to add insight to 'old' questions.

Acknowledgements

The authors would like to thank the three anonymous reviewers, the editor of JIBS, Arie Lewin, and the co-guest editors, Thomas Hutzschenreuter, Henk Volberda and Torben Pederson, for their comments and helpful suggestions. We would also like to thank participants at the 2004 JIBS Frontiers Conference, the 2005 AIB Conference and the 2006 Berlin ACCS Conference, and the various universities where earlier versions of this work were presented. Kristina Simkute and Natia Adamia were instrumental in the data collection effort, and their efforts are gratefully acknowledged.

References

Aharoni, Y. (1966) *The Foreign Investment Decision Process*, Harvard University Press: Boston, MA.

Aldrich, J. and Nelson, F. (1984) *Linear Probability, Logit and Probit Models*, Sage Publications: Newbury Park, CA.

Ambos, B. (2005) 'Foreign direct investment in industrial research and development: a study of German MNCs', *Research Policy* **34**(4): 395–410.

Andersen, O. (1993) 'On the internationalization process of firms: a critical analysis', *Journal of International Business Studies* **24**(2): 209–31.

Barkema, H.G., Bell, J.H.J. and Pennings, J.M. (1996) 'Foreign entry, cultural barriers and learning', *Strategic Management Journal* **17**(2): 151–66.

Baumgartner, H. and Steenkamp, J. (2001) 'Response styles in marketing research: a cross-national investigation', *Journal of Marketing Research* **38**(2): 143–56.

Brush, T.H., Maritan, C.A. and Karnani, A. (1999) 'The plant location decision in multinational manufacturing firms: an empirical analysis of international business and manufacturing strategy perspectives', *Production and Operations Management* **8**(2): 109–32.

Buckley, P. (2004) 'The role of China in the global strategy of multinational enterprises', *Journal of Chinese Economic and Business Studies* **2**(1): 1–25.

Buckley, P. and Casson, M. (1976) *The Future of the Multinational Enterprise*, Macmillan: London.

Buckley, P., Newbould, G. and Thurwell, J. (1988) *Foreign Direct Investment by Smaller UK Firms*, Macmillan: London.

Burgel, O. and Murray, G.C. (2000) 'The international market entry choices of start-up companies in high-technology industries', *Journal of International Marketing* **8**(2): 33–62.

Camerer, C. and Lovallo, D. (1999) 'Overconfidence and excess entry: an experimental approach', *American Economic Review* **89**(1): 306–18.

Chandprapalert, A. (2000) 'The determinants of US direct investment in Thailand: a survey of managerial perceptions', *Multinational Business Review* **8**(2): 82–8.

Chen, C., Lee, S. and Stevenson, H. (1995) 'Response styles and cross-cultural comparisons of rating scales among East Asian and North American students', *Psychological Science* **6**(3): 170–5.

Cheng, J. and Hitt, M. (eds.) (2004) 'Part I: Research Forum', in *Managing Multinationals in a Knowledge Economy*, Advances in International Management, Vol. **15**, Elsevier: Oxford, pp: 1–72.

Cheng, Y.-M. (2006) 'Determinants of FDI mode choice: acquisition, brownfield and greenfield entry in foreign markets', *Canadian Journal of Administrative Sciences* **23**(3): 202–20.

Chetty, S. and Blankenburg Holm, D. (2000) 'Internationalization of small to medium-sized manufacturing firms: a network approach', *International Business Review* **9**(8): 77–93.

Chung, W. (2001) 'Identifying technology transfer in foreign direct investment: influence of industry conditions and investing firm motives', *Journal of International Business Studies* **32**(2): 211–29.

Chung, W. and Alcacer, J. (2002) 'Knowledge seeking and location choice of foreign direct investment in the United States', *Management Science* **48**(12): 1534–54.

Cohen, S. (2003) *Maximum Difference Scaling: Improved Measures of Importance and Preference for Segmentation*, Sawtooth Software: Sequim, WA.

Cohen, S. and Neira, L. (2003) 'Measuring preference for product benefits across countries: overcoming scale usage bias with maximum difference scaling', Esomar 2003 Latin American Conference Proceedings, Amsterdam: ESOMAR, pp: 1–22.

Davidson, W.H. (1980) 'The location of foreign direct investment activity: country characteristics and experience effects', *Journal of International Business Studies* **11**(1): 9–22.

Devinney, T., Midgley, D. and Venaik, S. (2003) 'Managerial Beliefs, Market Contestability and Dominant Strategic Orientation in the Eclectic Paradigm', in R. Narula and J. Cantwell (eds.) *International Business and The Eclectic Paradigm*, Routledge: London, pp: 152–73.

Dunning, J. (1981) *International Production and the Multinational Enterprise*, Allen & Unwin: London.

Enright, M.J. (2005) 'Regional management centres in the Asia-Pacific', *Management International Review* **45**(1): 59–82.

Eriksson, K., Johanson, J., Majkgard, A. and Sharma, D. (1997) 'Experiential knowledge and cost in the internationalization process', *Journal of International Business Studies* **28**(2): 337–60.

Feinberg, S.E. and Keane, M.P. (2001) 'US–Canada trade liberalization and MNC production location', *The Review of Economics and Statistics* **83**(1): 118–32.

Fina, E. and Rugman, A.M. (1996) 'A test of internalization theory and internationalization theory: the Upjohn company', *Management International Review* **36**(3): 199–213.

Finn, A. and Louviere, J. (1992) 'Determining the appropriate response to evidence of public concern: the case of food safety', *Journal of Public Policy and Marketing* **11**(2): 12–25.

Henisz, W.J. (2000) 'The institutional environment for multinational investment', *Journal of Law, Economics and Organization* **16**(2): 334–64.

Henisz, W.J. and Macher, J.T. (2004) 'Firm and country level trade-offs and contingencies in the evaluation of foreign investment: the semiconductor industry, 1994–2002', *Organization Science* **15**(5): 537–54.

Hensher, D., Louviere, J. and Swait, J. (2000) *Stated Preference Modelling: Theory, Methods and Applications*, Cambridge University Press: Cambridge, UK.

Hofstede, G. (2001) *Culture's Consequences: Comparing Values, Behaviors, Institutions, and Organizations Across Nations*, 2nd edn, Sage: Thousand Oaks, CA.

Hymer, S. (1960) *The International Operations of National Firms: A Study of Direct Foreign Investment*, MIT Press: Cambridge, MA (published 1976).

Johanson, J. and Vahlne, J.-E. (1977) 'The internationalization process of the firm: a model of knowledge development and increasing foreign market commitments', *Journal of International Business Studies* **8**(1): 12–24.

Johanson, J. and Vahlne, J.-E. (1990) 'The mechanism of internationalization', *International Marketing Review* **7**(4): 12–24.

Kuemmerle, W. (1999) 'Foreign direct investment in industrial research in the pharmaceutical and electronics industries: results from a survey of multinational firms', *Research Policy* **28**(2–3): 179–93.

Louviere, J. and Woodworth, G. (1983) 'Design and analysis of simulated consumer choice or allocation experiments: an approach based on aggregate data', *Journal of Marketing Research* **20**(4): 350–67.

Luo, Y. and Peng, M. (1999) 'Learning to compete in a transition economy: experience, environment, and performance', *Journal of International Business Studies* **30**(2): 269–95.

MacCarthy, B.L. and Atthirawong, W. (2003) 'Factors affecting location decisions in international operations: a Delphi study', *International Journal of Operations and Production Management* **23**(7): 794–818.

McFadden, D. (2001) 'Economic choices', *American Economic Review* **91**(3): 351–78.

McIntosh, E. and Louviere, J. (2003) 'Separating weight and scale value: an exploration of best-attribute scaling in health economics', paper presented at Odense University, Denmark.

Manrai, A. and Sinha, P. (1989) 'Elimination-by-cutoffs', *Marketing Science* **8**(2): 133–52.

Marley, A. and Louviere, J. (2005) 'Some probabilistic models of best, and best–worst choices', *Journal of Mathematical Psychology* **49**(6): 464–80.

Melin, L. (1992) 'Internationalization as a strategy process', *Strategic Management Journal* **13**(99): 99–118.

Mitra, D. and Golder, P.N. (2002) 'Whose culture matters? Near-market knowledge and its impact on foreign market entry timing', *Journal of Marketing Research* **39**(3): 350–65.

Mucchielli, J.-L. and Mayer, T. (eds.) (2004) *Multinational Firms' Location and the New Economic Geography*, Edward Elgar: Cheltenham.

Mudambi, R. (1998) 'The role of duration in multinational investment strategies', *Journal of International Business Studies* **29**(2): 239–62.

Mudambi, R. and Navarra, P. (2003) 'Political tradition, political risk and foreign direct investment in Italy', *Management International Review* **43**(3): 247–65.

Nachum, L. and Zaheer, S. (2005) 'The persistence of distance? The impact of technology on MNE motivations for foreign investment', *Strategic Management Journal* **26**(8): 747–67.

Paulhus, D. (1991) 'Measurement and Control of Response Bias', in J.P. Robinson, P.R. Shaver and L.S. Wrightsman (eds.) *Measures of Personality and Social Psychological Attitudes*, **Vol. 1**, Academic Press: New York, pp: 17–59.

Pedersen, T. and Petersen, B. (2004) 'Learning about foreign markets: are entrant firms exposed to a "shock effect"?' *Journal of International Marketing* **12**(1): 103–23.

Roth, K. and Kostova, T. (2003) 'The use of the multinational corporation as a research context', *Journal of Management* **29**(6): 883–902.

Sarkar, M., Cavusgil, S.T. and Aulakh, P. (1999) 'International expansion of telecommunication carriers: the influence of market structure, network characteristics, and entry imperfections', *Journal of International Business Studies* **30**(2): 361–81.

Steenkamp, J. and Baumgartner, H. (1998) 'Assessing measurement invariance in cross-national consumer research', *Journal of Consumer Research* **25**(1): 78–90.

Steenkamp, J. and Ter Hofstede, F. (2002) 'International market segmentation: issues and perspectives', *International Journal of Research in Marketing* **19**(3): 185–213.

Sullivan, D. (1998) 'Cognitive tendencies in international business research: implications of a "narrow vision"', *Journal of International Business Studies* **29**(4): 837–62.

Sullivan, D. and Bauerschmidt, A. (1990) 'Incremental internationalization: a test of Johanson and Vahlne's thesis', *Management International Review* **30**(1): 19–30.

Thurstone, L. (1927) 'A law of comparative judgment', *Psychological Review* **34**: 273–86.

Train, K. (2003) *Discrete Choice Methods with Simulation*, Cambridge University Press: Cambridge, UK.

Tversky, A. (1972) 'Elimination by aspects: a theory of choice', *Psychological Review* **79**(4): 281–99.

Urban, G., Hauser, J., Qualls, W., Weinburg, B., Bohlmann, J. and Chicos, R. (1997) 'Information acceleration: validation and lessons from the field', *Journal of Marketing Research* **34**(1): 143–53.

Wei, Y., Liu, B. and Liu, X. (2005) 'Entry modes of foreign direct investment in China: a multinomial logit approach', *Journal of Business Research* **58**(11): 1495–1505.

Woodward, D.P. and Rolfe, R.J. (1993) 'The location of export-oriented foreign direct investment in the Caribbean basin', *Journal of International Business Studies* **24**(1): 121–44.

Zhou, C., Delios, A. and Yang, J.Y. (2002) 'Locational determinants of Japanese foreign direct investment in China', *Asia Pacific Journal of Management* **19**(1): 63–86.

Appendix A

Table A1 Recent literature on FDI location decisions

Author(s)	Method	Data and sample	Key variable(s)	Major results
Davidson (1980)	Survey	Foreign operations of 180 US multinationals from inception to 1975. Over 13,000 FDIs (70% of FDI by US MNEs at the time).	Entry frequencies explained by market size, corporate experience, prior presence.	Corporate experience affects location decisions in two ways: (1) firms prefer nations in which they are active to those in which they are not, and (2) firms with extensive experience exhibit less preference for near, similar and familiar markets. Markets that others might perceive as less attractive because of high uncertainty levels are given increased priority as the firms experience rises. *As firms gain experience, the location of foreign activity will increasingly represent an efficient response to global economic opportunities and conditions.*
Woodward and Rolfe (1993)	Panel	187 manufacturing investments of US companies in the Caribbean 1984–1987.	Location of export-oriented US manufacturing FDI determinants.	FDI location positively influenced by: per capita GNP, exchange rate devaluation, length of income tax holidays, size of free trade zones, and manufacturing concentration. Negative effects from wage rate, inflation rate, transport costs and restrictions on profit repatriation.
Barkema *et al.* (1996)	Panel	225 foreign entries of 13 Dutch firms.	Longevity of foreign entry.	Cultural distance is a prominent factor in foreign entry whenever this involves another firm.
Burgel and Murray (2000)	Compiled Survey	398 *export* decisions of 246 UK technology-based start-ups.	*Entry* mode of export.	Direct export or selling through intermediaries. Choice is a trade-off between resources available and support requirements of the customer.
Mudambi (1998)	Survey	MNEs in West Midlands of UK: 70 valid responses.	Length of duration of operation at a particular location (after accounting for portfolio risk).	Firms with a longer tenure of operations are significantly more likely to invest in any given period.

(Continued)

Table A1 (Continued)

Brush et al. (1999)	Survey	Contrast of manufacturing strategy: integrated or independent plant versus international strategy: locate home or abroad.	209 responses from plant managers of US MNEs.	Manufacturing choices benefit from international issues more than vice versa. Managers rank determinants associated with manufacturing strategy higher than those associated with IB.
Kuemmerle (1999)	Survey	Motives for FDI in R&D.	FDI in R&D 32 large MNEs in 4 countries.	FDI in R&D both to augment knowledge basis and to exploit it. R&D investment at home in multiple sites before venturing abroad.
Chandprapalert (2000)	Survey	Determinants of FDI in Thailand.	100 US companies with FDI in Thailand.	Firm size, market potential, investment risk key variables.
Henisz (2000)	Panel	Political and contractual hazards in host countries.	Sample of 3389 overseas manufacturing operations of 461 firms in 112 countries.	Joint ventures preferred where hazards highest. Host institutions matter.
Chung (2001)	Panel	Technology transfer, competition, productivity.	US manufacturing 1987–1991 at 4-digit SIC level.	FDI may both transfer and access technology in the host country.
Feinberg and Keane (2001)	Panel	Tariff reductions (US–Canada).	US individual foreign affiliate level data from the US Bureau of Economic Analysis.	Canadian affiliate sales to US negatively correlated with Canadian tariffs, but US parent sales to Canadian affiliates have little association with Canadian tariffs. Substantial heterogeneity to tariff changes within narrowly defined manufacturing industries.
Chung and Alcacer (2002)	Panel	Knowledge seeking (access technical capabilities in host).	1784 FDI transactions entering US 1987–1993 from OECD countries. International Trade Administration reports.	Location within USA – greater market size, lower factor costs, better access to surrounding station *and* knowledge seeking limited to research-intensive industries – manufacturing firms may seek this not only through laboratories but also through manufacturing facilities.
Mitra and Golder (2002)	Panel Compiled	Operations in similar markets on subsequent entry decisions.	19 MNEs with 722 entry operations.	Cultural distance from domestic market is *not* a significant factor. 'Near-market knowledge' and economic knowledge have significant effects.
Zhou et al. (2002)	Panel	Influence of special economic zones and opening coastal cities on inward FDI.	2933 Japanese investments in 27 provinces of China.	SEZs and OCCs have exerted periodic influences on location of Japanese FDI in China.

Table A1 (Continued)

MacCarthy and Atthirawong (2003)	Survey Delphi	Academics, consultants and government officials.	Motivations of firms to invest in manufacturing.	Top five influences: costs, infrastructure, labour characteristics, government and political factors and economic factors.
Henisz and Macher (2004)	Panel	44 semiconductor firms making 69 foreign investments in new manufacturing plants. (1994–2002).	Explanation of foreign investment in new manufacturing facility.	Firms with more advanced technological capabilities more likely to invest in countries with greater technological sophistication but not in politically hazardous countries. Less advanced technology firms more willing to trade off political hazards and technological sophistication. Firms also trade off other own versus other firms' experience as sources of critical knowledge on foreign investment environments.
Pedersen and Petersen (2004)	Survey	485 firms: 201 Denmark; 168 Sweden; 116 New Zealand.	Familiarity with local markets development over time.	'Shock effect' of foreign market entry develops over time (lowest level of market familiarity 8 years after entry), supports 'psychic distance paradox' that adjacent countries provide high levels of shock.
Ambos (2005)	Survey	HQ R&D managers. Establishment of laboratory sites of 49 German MNEs survey.	Internationalisation motives of R&D.	Resource seeking rather than market seeking is predominant. Mission affects location.
Enright (2005)	Survey	1100 MNE managers in Asia Pacific.	Regional strategies and establishment of regional management centres.	Regional structures are important in Asia-Pacific.
Nachum and Zaheer (2005)	Panel	US inward and outward FDI 1990–1998 from the US Bureau of Economic Analysis.	Cost of distance differentially affects investment motivation across industries.	Industries with different levels of information intensity are driven by different investment motivations: knowledge and efficiency seeking at high levels; market seeking at low levels.
Cheng (2006)	Survey	466 Taiwanese investors in China.	FDI mode choice (includes brownfield ventures).	FDI mode choice influenced by resources owned by investor, resources specific to host firm and risk. Incorporates brownfield investment as a choice.

Appendix B

A simple model for BW judgements

Best–worst scaling (hereafter, BWS) is a fairly general scaling method that extends Thurstone's (1927) random utility theory-based model for paired comparison judgements to judgements of the largest/smallest, best/worst, most/least, etc., items, objects or cues in a set of three or more multiple items. Specifically, BWS assumes that there is some underlying subjective dimension, such as 'degree of importance', 'degree of concern', 'degree of interest', etc., and the researcher wishes to measure the location or position of some set of objects, items, etc., on that underlying dimension. We refer to the process of assigning numerical values that reflect the positions of the items on the underlying scale as 'scaling'. The BWS approach is based on the view that such measurement arises from theory, and that theory and associated measurement are inseparable. The scale values derived from BWS are those that best satisfy a theory about the way in which individuals make BW judgements.

To begin, we assume that there is a master set of K items to be scaled, $\{I_1, I_2, ..., I_K\}$. The items are to be placed in C subsets, $\{i_1\}, \{i_2\}, ..., \{i_C\}$ and some sample of individuals of interest is asked to identify, respectively, the best and worst items in each of the subsets (or in each of some subset of the subsets). If there are K total items to be scaled, then the total number of subsets that could be presented to the individuals is 2^K, minus all subsets that are null (1), singles (K) or pairs ($K(K-1)/2$), which grows exponentially with K. Thus one needs some systematic way to pick the subsets that makes sense and as noted by Finn and Louviere (1992), constructing the sets from a 2^K orthogonal main effects design or some higher-resolution design in the 2^K family of designs is a good approach, and one that coincides nicely with previous design theory for the case of only 'best' choices (Louviere and Woodworth, 1983). There are other ways to construct appropriate sets, such as balanced incomplete block designs (BIBDs), and we illustrate the use of such designs in this paper.

BWS assumes that there is some underlying dimension of interest, and one wants to assign scale values to the K items on that single underlying dimension. It assumes that the choice of a pair of items from any subset is an indicator of that pair of items in that subset that are the farthest apart on the underlying dimension. That is, in any subset, say the cth subset, if there are P items, then there are $P(P-1)/2$ pairs of items that could be chosen best and worst, and an additional $P(P-1)/2$ pairs of items that could be chosen worst and best. For any given subset presented to an individual like the cth subset, the individual implicitly chooses from $2 \times P-1(P-1)/2$ pairs. Let us denote the quantity $2 \times P(P-1)/2$ as M, and for ease of exposition (and because it reflects the case in this paper) we assume that P is constant in every subset (for example, balanced incomplete block designs lead to subsets of fixed size, M). Now, we can formulate this choice process as a random utility model as follows:

$$D_{ij} = \delta_{ij} + \varepsilon_{ij} \tag{B.1}$$

where D_i is the latent or unobservable true difference in items i and j on the underlying dimension; δ_{ij} is an observable component of the latent difference that can be observed and measured; and ε_{ij} is an error component associated with each ij pair.

Because of the presence of the ε_{ij} component, the choice process of any individual is stochastic when viewed by the researcher, because we cannot know what the individual is thinking. We can formulate the model as a probability model to capture the probability that the individual chooses the *ij* pair in each subset:

$$P(ij|C) = P[(\delta_{ij} + \varepsilon_{ij})$$
$$> \text{all other } M - 1(\delta_{ij} + \varepsilon_{ij}) \text{ pairs]} \tag{B.2}$$

where all terms are as previously defined. This problem can be solved by making assumptions about the distribution and properties of ε_{ij}. A simple assumption that leads to a tractable model form that has seen many applications in the social and business sciences is that ε_{ij} is distributed independently and identically as an extreme value type 1 random variate (equivalently, as a Gumbel, Weibull or double exponential). It is well know that these assumptions lead to the multinomial logit (MNL) model, which is the form of analysis used in this paper. That is, the choice probabilities can be expressed as

$$P(ij|C) = \frac{\exp(\delta_{ij})}{\displaystyle\sum_{ik} \exp(\delta_{ik})} \quad \text{for all } M \; \delta_{ik} \text{ in } i_C \tag{B.3}$$

We can express δ_{ij} as a difference in two scale values, say s_i and s_j, or $s_i - s_j$. Hence we can rewrite the model as

$$P(ij|C) = \frac{\exp(s_i - s_j)}{\displaystyle\sum_{ik} \exp(s_i - s_k)} \quad \text{for all } M\{s_i, s_k\} \text{ pairs in } i_C \tag{B.4}$$

The scale values of interest are s_i and s_j, which reflect the location of each item on the underlying scale.

If the subsets are constructed in such a way that the joint probability of choosing items *i* and *j* across all subsets can be estimated independently of the marginal probabilities (for example, by using a 2^k orthogonal main effects design + its foldover, or a BIBD + its complement), then the model implied by Eq. (B.4) can be estimated directly from the observed counts associated with each best–worst, worst–best pair summed over all subsets in the experiment. If the experiment does not allow one to calculate the total choices of all implied best–worst, worst–best pairs across the subsets (for example, if one uses only the orthogonal main effects design or only the BIBD, as discussed by Finn and Louviere, 1992), one can approximate the desired scale values by taking differences in the marginal best and worst counts for each item. That is, the simple score $\delta(b_i w_i)$ = total best *i* – total worst *i* approximates the unknown difference $s_i - s_j$ for each individual or subset of individuals who exhibit the same underlying ordering of the items (apart from judgemental errors). We state this without proof, but note that one can easily see that this must be true by constructing an experiment that permits the joint choice probabilities for all the implied pairs to be estimated independently of the marginal probabilities, assuming an ordering of the items in that experiment, and simulating choices of the items with the highest and lowest rank in the order in each subset. It is easy to show that the total choices over all subsets for the implied pairs will be consistent with MNL, and once one obtains the MNL estimates, one can easily see that the best$_i$–worst$_i$ differences are perfectly proportional to the MNL estimates.

12 Towards more realistic conceptualisations of foreign operation modes*

Gabriel R. G. Benito, Bent Petersen and Lawrence S. Welch

Introduction

How do companies operate in foreign markets? That question has been at the centre of international business research for four decades (Root, 1964, 1977). Much of the early conceptualisation of how firms internationalise grew out of empirical investigations of how they change modes of operation over time (Johanson & Vahlne, 1977; Johanson & Wiedersheim-Paul, 1975; Luostarinen, 1979; Newbold et al., 1978). To some extent such a focus was inevitable, given that modes of operation in foreign markets often are the most concrete, and empirically observable, forms of international expansion. Interest has been reflected in, and possibly boosted by, theoretical developments based principally on internalisation theory (Buckley & Casson, 1976), transaction cost theory (Anderson & Gatignon, 1986; Hennart, 1982, 1989), knowledge- and resource-based perspectives (Cuervo-Cazurra et al., 2007; Kogut & Zander, 1993; Madhok, 1997; Meyer et al., 2009), and institutional theory (Kostova & Zaheer, 1999; Meyer & Peng, 2005). These approaches are usefully summarised in the ownership–location–internalisation (OLI) framework (Dunning, 2000; Dunning & Lundan, 2008). Subsequently, there has been considerable empirical research and theorising regarding various aspects of how firms choose operation modes, and the impact of such decisions on performance. At times the focus has been on specific mode forms such as joint ventures (JVs), licensing, and franchising, with a mix of cross-sectional and longitudinal investigations (for recent reviews, see Brouthers & Hennart, 2007; Datta et al., 2002; Welch et al., 2007; Zhao et al., 2004). The bulk of these empirical studies, about 100 in the past 15 years alone (Brouthers & Hennart, 2007), have used cross-sectional designs. There have been far fewer longitudinal studies because of empirical difficulties in obtaining reliable data over extended periods of time. Nevertheless, some studies have shown that mode changes occur with sufficient frequency to merit much closer investigation (Benito et al., 2005; Calof, 1993; Clark et al., 1997; Fryges, 2007).

The problems associated with empirical investigations have hampered the ability of researchers to develop deeper explanations of the choice of modes of operation and of their evolution (Benito & Welch, 1994). Although the range of modes of operation considered has been considerable, researchers have tended to see foreign operation modes as lumpy, unitary entities (Anderson & Gatignon, 1986; Hill et al., 1990). This is in contrast to the common practice of using modes in combination in individual foreign markets. For example, a study of Danish firms in Southeast Asia found that they often used packages of modes, for example by adding sales subsidiaries alongside existing arm's length distribution arrangements (Petersen et al., 2001). The experience of those firms demonstrated that, in contrast to what is predicted in much of the literature, firms incrementally changed their modes of operation by adding new modes to existing ones, creating what we can call "mode combinations". We believe that this is not reflected in the literature because it is difficult to obtain empirical detail on sometimes complex, changing mode combinations from respondent companies (Petersen & Welch, 2002). In addition, as March notes, there is a tendency to confuse measurability with importance. "Some things are more easily measured or estimated than others. Variables that can be measured tend to be treated as more 'real' than those that cannot, even though the ones that cannot be measured may be more important" (March, 2006: 203–204).

What does mode change mean in a world of mode combinations? Does dropping or adding one mode from or to a mode combination (or package) constitute a mode change? Similarly, does a reassignment of mode roles within a given package constitute mode change, and is it evidence of incremental expansion or withdrawal? In much of the IB literature, changes in foreign operation modes in a foreign market are seen as major changes in commitment to that market, especially in cases of leapfrogging over seemingly intermediate- to high-commitment modes (Barkema & Drogendijk, 2007; Hedlund & Kverneland, 1985), such as when a manufacturing company moves from a foreign agency to a manufacturing operation, skipping the more incremental step of setting up a sales subsidiary. In contrast, a more fine-grained treatment of modes might reveal a greater range of intermediate steps, for example what might be called "within-mode changes", and indicate an overall pattern of internationalisation that is far more incremental than the usual approach would seem to show. The use of foreign agents or distributors by exporters is often accompanied by substantial investments over time, to the point where the foreign intermediaries become partially internalised, and operate like quasi sales subsidiaries (Deligonul & Cavusgil, 2006). In some cases, Danish firms in Southeast Asia sent staff to work alongside the local employees of their sales agents in an effort to increase control and to develop local knowledge and networks, thereby facilitating the takeover of their agents (Petersen et al., 2001).

Despite the decades of research it appears that there is still no entirely adequate explanation of how companies operate in foreign markets. In this article we address the disconnect between the IB field view of foreign operation modes and how companies choose and modify their modes of operation. Our starting point is an investigation into the relationship between elevator manufacturers Kone and Toshiba that illustrates the complex reality of foreign operation modes, including the combination of modes in "mode packages", and switching within and between modes and modes packages.

We contribute to the literature by broadening and redefining the operation mode concept, thereby facilitating the study of the evolution and adaptation of modes, including mode dynamics, mode learning, and mode inertia. By freeing the concept of operation mode from its present unitary and static conceptualisation we take a more evolutionary perspective on mode use and change, which opens multiple avenues for future research.

Defining modes

The term foreign operation mode (or its equivalents) is generally accepted to mean a company's way of operating in foreign markets, or the "how" part of foreign operations (Welch & Luostarinen, 1988). That meaning seems now to be commonly used and accepted, whether specifically stated or not. For example, in their seminal article on the internationalisation patterns of four Swedish multinationals, Johanson and Wiedersheim-Paul (1975: 306) refer to internationalisation as "the development of operations in individual countries", as exemplified by a "sequence of stages" or "establishment chain", but there is no specific definition of "operations" or form of operations. Root (1977: 5) is more specific, defining mode as "an institutional arrangement that makes possible the entry of a company's products, technology, human skills, management or other resources into a foreign country", a definition we use as a basis for our discussion. We see foreign operation mode as the equivalent of "type of foreign operation" (Luostarinen, 1970), "foreign operation method" (Welch et al., 2007) and "foreign market servicing method" (Benito & Welch, 1994; Buckley et al., 1990), but at the same time broader than the commonly used term "entry mode" (Anderson & Gatignon, 1986), which we take to mean the mode used on entry to a foreign market but not beyond that point.

Rather than attempting to frame a formal definition, a number of researchers have defined modes (primarily entry modes) on the basis of different forms of mode classifications using various criteria. For example, Anderson and Gatignon (1986) identified 17 mode categories arranged on the basis of control, commitment, and risk. Hill et al. (1990) reduced those categories into three distinct modes of entry: licensing/franchising, JVs and wholly owned subsidiaries. Brouthers and Hennart (2007: 397) classify "modes of entry into two categories, contracts and equity" and add that "the main difference in entry modes lies in the method chosen to remunerate input providers." It should be stressed that such approaches are concerned with entry modes, which by definition block out notions of evolution in mode form through time. In addition, the categories are defined on the basis of singular modes, and qualities judged on the basis of the outcome characteristics (for example, control) of these individual modes. In contrast, we move away from a concentration on singular modes and allow for combinations or packages of modes. We therefore think of a mode, or way of operating, as part of a more encompassing concept, under which multiple mode arrangements may exist. This approach is similar to the way in which some early researchers stressed the idea of foreign direct investment (FDI) as a bundle of transfer components (Balasubramanyam, 1985; Hood & Young, 1979). Buckley and Mathew (1980: 38) go further, referring to other forms of operating in the host country apart from FDI, and note that these different types might be used "either alone or jointly". More recently, international joint venture (IJV) researchers have pointed to the broad set of mode components that may be used under an IJV umbrella, and to the way in which changes in the various components often occur over time, leaving the bare structure of the IJV in place but altering the way it functions and performs (Child, 2002; Yan & Gray, 1994; Yan & Zeng, 1999).

Our approach points to different ways of categorising foreign operation modes, depending on how the modes are assembled or packaged. For example, Petersen and Welch (2002) stress that there may be little connection between the multiple modes used by a company in a given country as a result either of geographical or other forms of market segmentation, or of the way a company is organised. For instance, the Norwegian multinational Norsk Hydro had different divisions active in India in the 1990s, but their efforts were not coordinated (Tomassen et al., 1998). Similarly, the Australian beer company Foster's kept its beer and wine operations separate in the US, in part because its wine operations came about from the acquisition of a major US wine company (Speedy, 2007).

Sometimes various modes are used simultaneously in one particular market, usually across different activities, but occasionally for the same type of activity. For example, the Israeli software firm Fundtech performed R&D in the US through a JV, a greenfield subsidiary and an acquired subsidiary, while its marketing and customer support services there were conducted through distributors, a JV, a greenfield sales office and an acquired subsidiary (Welch et al., 2007).

Multiple modes might be tightly connected, with different modes supporting each other in an overall foreign market penetration strategy. Petersen et al. (2008) use the term "mode configuration" to refer to the diverse ways in which multiple modes might be configured or arranged, to develop a configuration matrix that includes different modes categorised by (value chain) activity level, governance form, and country. In a given country, different governance forms might be used by a company to handle different parts of the value chain, for instance, R&D might be performed by a wholly owned unit, production by a JV and marketing fully outsourced. Alternatively, there might be mode packages at each activity level: R&D could involve a wholly owned unit with licensing, production via a JV with a management contract, and marketing via outsourcing of some components as well as an owned sales unit. A myriad of mode combinations is feasible. Furthermore, various mode package combinations could be categorised according to aspects such as control contribution, along the lines of previous approaches. Our conception of the term "mode", therefore, is very different from the unitary, entry mode focus of much of the existing literature, as it allows for multiple modes in various types of combinations, that is, generating greater mode diversity and a broader range of change options. We illustrate this below by looking at how the Finnish multinational Kone entered Japan and carried on operations there and elsewhere through a long-term relationship with the Japanese firm Toshiba.

To summarise, we define foreign operation modes as the organisational arrangements that a company uses to conduct international business activities. Foreign operation modes relate to the activities performed in particular locations at a given time. Our definition hence extends beyond the point of entry into a given foreign market to take into account changes made after entry. Our definition also allows for the fact that companies sometimes combine operation modes for the same types of activities and in the same locations.

Kone in Japan

We demonstrate the wide array of modes of operations that companies may use to expand in foreign markets, including forms of within-mode change, by turning to how the Finnish multinational Kone entered the Japanese market. We take an abductive inferential approach in this case: that is, we use abduction to look at the interaction between conceptual development and empirical evidence (Alvesson & Kärreman, 2007; Dubois & Gadde, 2002; Peirce, 1931–1958; Van Maanen et al., 2007).

Description[1]

We look at how the Finnish firm Kone penetrated the Japanese market as a way of clarifying what we mean by operation modes and mode combinations, and to analyse their evolution. Kone and Toshiba are both major players in manufacturing and servicing elevators and escalators, Kone across a wide array of markets and Toshiba focusing heavily on its home market. Kone and Toshiba began informal discussions in 1982. Their first major cooperative step was in 1995 when Kone began supplying hydraulic passenger elevators to Toshiba. The technical aspects of that move became the basis for ongoing cooperation. Kone competed with Toshiba in 1997 to supply elevators for a new subway line in Tokyo, and won a contract for 57 units. The two companies agreed to work together on installing and maintaining the equipment. The Kone–Toshiba relationship was further solidified in 1998 with a licensing agreement under which new elevator and crane technology that had been developed by Kone was transferred to Toshiba, and it was given exclusive marketing rights for its use in Japan. The agreement also gave Toshiba non-exclusive marketing rights in China, Hong Kong, Singapore, Malaysia, Taiwan and Indonesia. The two firms also agreed to extend technical cooperation to new product development. Despite their earlier cooperation, Kone described the move as "the first step in forging a global alliance" with Toshiba (source: Kone press release, 26 May 1998: see note 1). According to the Kone executive who spearheaded the agreement, Kone was "thinking about how to enter the Japanese market" in 1998, implying that he did not see the earlier moves by Kone as "entering" the market. He added that Toshiba did not fully appreciate the value of the licensing agreement (in 1998): "In the beginning they did not see its value" and were surprised at how commercially successful the technologies they had licensed from Kone turned out to be in Japan. However, the success of that agreement persuaded Toshiba to enter into other forms of cooperation with Kone, for example in R&D and purchasing (source: Kone interviewee: see note 1).

The alliance was extended further in 2001 when Kone took a 20% share in a newly established subsidiary, Toshiba Elevator and Building Systems Corporation (TELC), and TELC in turn purchased 5% of the shares of Kone. In addition, the 1998 licensing agreement was extended to cover elevator manufacturing and marketing rights in China using Kone's Monospace technology, and the two firms established a global alliance committee to promote ways of strengthening and deepening the alliance and extending cooperation in technology, supply and marketing. In early 2002 a seat on the Kone Board was created for TELC, and Kone was given two seats on the TELC Board.

Kone and TELC agreed to extend their technical collaboration in advanced high-rise elevator technology in 2004. TELC licensed its double-deck elevator technology to Kone, and Kone agreed to collaborate on a case-by-case basis in bidding for mega-projects in global markets. Kone and TELC then set up a 70:30 JV in China in 2005 to manufacture escalators there. The JV makes Toshiba-designed escalators that are sold by Kone and Toshiba sales companies in China under their respective brands.

Discussion

Kone's comprehensive mode package in Japan in 2005 was substantially different from the starting point in 1995, albeit that it might have been loosely described as being under an overall Kone–Toshiba alliance umbrella. Given the mix of mode changes, the within-mode changes such as reciprocal board appointments and the changes in the roles of modes both separately and collectively, it would be illogical to argue that the "operation mode" remained unchanged. There are many mode change options and they impart considerable strategic flexibility. The relative importance of Kone's individual operation modes shifted over time. At the outset, exporting was Kone's primary mode, and that defined the extent of the Kone–Toshiba relationship. This became less important as Toshiba took over more of the manufacturing, initially through licensing. The Kone–Toshiba case highlights the lack of comprehensibility in past treatments of the evolution of modes of operation. This has implications for the conclusions drawn about internationalisation and its drivers, since the original argument of the internationalisation process model was built on a study of the foreign operation modes of Swedish multinationals (Johanson & Vahlne, 1977; Johanson & Wiedersheim-Paul, 1975; Meyer & Gelbuda, 2006).

As we have seen, market penetration might be enhanced through the development of packages of operation modes, rather than by discarding an existing primary operation mode and replacing it with another. We have also seen that mode additions and deletions provide flexibility. Dislodging Toshiba from its entrenched position in the Japanese market would have been extremely difficult. Exporting to Japan alone would have been a difficult long-term penetration mode, especially without establishing maintenance facilities there. No acquisition targets were readily available at the time. At least licensing allowed Kone some access to Japanese manufacturing and service facilities, albeit with all the limitations inherent in licensing to a major competitor. The later move to a more comprehensive alliance, including an equity arrangement, gave Kone a major market penetration vehicle for Japan, some inroads into other markets, and a substantial equity stake that ensured continued involvement.

Constraints on the ability of a company to switch modes may cause it to look for ways of enhancing or buttressing the performance of its existing primary foreign operation mode with additions or deletions to the mode or through within-mode adjustments. Those constraints may be due to actual or perceived costs of changing modes, such as contract termination costs, increased competition resulting in the loss of customers and revenue losses, and the cost of setting up a new mode (Benito et al., 1999; Ellis, 2006). As a firm may view switching costs as locking it into an existing arrangement with a foreign partner, ways other than mode replacement have to be found to achieve foreign market goals (Petersen et al., 2000).

Altered roles for the different modes within the overall alliance accompanied the mode package changes by Kone. As noted earlier, adding licensing made exporting less important. Subsequently, licensing was subsumed under the reciprocal equity umbrella. At the same time, a variety of forms of cooperation in different areas were added, for example purchasing, generating subtle changes in mode roles within Kone's overall, expanding mode package. To some extent, it could be argued that the formal mode structure within the alliance became less important over time than the evolving cooperation forms that effectively extended the scope of the alliance. Kone's within-mode change enhanced the level of cooperation between the parties and the performance of the alliance. For instance, the success of the technology licensed to Toshiba led to expanded cooperation in R&D and purchasing, which in turn provided the foundation for the move to reciprocal equity arrangements in 2001. Similarly, after 2001 there were various within-mode changes such as the reciprocal board positions and extended technical and marketing collaboration that bolstered the overall alliance. A company's use of existing modes in different foreign markets will evolve in ways both large and small as its own experience develops, market circumstances change, institutions alter, and relationships with foreign parties advance. Resource commitments will be adjusted in various ways, such as when the firm appoints one of its own staff to be a "back-up agent" in the foreign market (Valla, 1986: 33).

We see within-mode change as the norm for international companies, in ways that are not reflected in the generally comparative static approach taken by most in the international business literature (Meyer & Gelbuda, 2006; Petersen et al., 2001). One exception is the work of researchers who have focused on the ways that IJVs evolve over time. They have shown that changes in partner contributions of critical resources to the IJV have a powerful impact on the functioning of the IJV, even in the absence of changes in equity positions (Ariño & de la Torre, 1998; Büchel, 2002; Child, 2002; Harrigan, 1988; Yan & Gray, 1994; Yan & Zeng, 1999). While this research focuses on IJV instability and performance, it shows that what we call within-mode changes can transform the nature of the mode itself. The net result may be to substantially ease the path to mode change, reducing the significance of the change itself.

Mode changes

Studies of changes in operation modes have tended to treat them as choices among discrete alternatives, such as moving from direct exporting to intermediaries (Fryges, 2007), from intermediaries to local sales subsidiaries (Benito et al., 2005; Calof, 1993), and from JVs to wholly owned subsidiaries (Hennart et al., 1998, 1999), or as going through a sequence of several changes, as in the original Uppsala studies (see also Clark et al., 1997). While the assumption of discrete alternatives obviously simplifies the task of researchers, business practices are somewhat more complicated.

The evolving relationship between Kone and Toshiba shows that some firms change their foreign modes of operation in ways that are not necessarily obvious when the empirical research focus is on the outer shell or a specific, seemingly dominant mode within the package, such as the FDI component. The question arises whether any and every addition to, or deletion from, an overall mode package should be defined as a change in operation mode. To what extent and in what form should within-mode adjustments be taken into account, if at all? At what point can an overall mode package be said to have been altered to an extent that it becomes a different package? For example, is it likely that a firm would see adding licensing to a mode package that includes exporting and a management contract and is dominated by a JV as "mode change"?

Our point is illustrated by Baltika Breweries' licensing of Scottish and Newcastle (S&N) to produce Baltika beer in 2007. At the time, the Russian brewery was owned by Baltic Beverages Holding (BBH), which was a 50:50 JV between Denmark's Carlsberg and S&N (S&N acquired 50% of BBH in a takeover of the Finnish firm Hartwall in 2002). Baltika Breweries had been exporting to the UK since 2003, and the goal of the licensing venture was to increase Baltika beer sales to Russians in the UK and beyond. From S&N's perspective, the mode switch from importing to licensed production within its total Russian mode package (primarily the 50% JV) was a modest extension of its Russian-based activities (Bolger, 2007). Was this, or was it not, a "mode change"?

Changes in mode roles

We have considered mode changes as additions to, and deletions from, existing operation modes, and as within-mode adjustments. We turn now to changes in the roles played by different operation modes (Petersen & Welch, 2002). Like a within-mode adjustment, a change in the role played by a mode does not necessarily involve modification of the structure of a mode package. Different parts of a mode package perform different roles in achieving a firm's foreign market penetration objectives. Kone's experience in Japan demonstrates that there can be a considerable change in the roles played by modes over time. Kone initially used licensing as a prime market penetration vehicle, and as a means of showcasing its advanced technology and technical expertise, but those roles became less important as the alliance evolved. Unlike the case of Kone, the structure of a package does not necessarily reveal the roles played by various elements of the package. For instance, JV licensing can be used to control the way technology is exploited, to limit the risk of unwanted dissemination, to generate additional revenue, to transfer profits, and to reduce tax liabilities. Exporting can also be used in the early stages of a JV to support operations in various ways. At the outset, the JV is likely to be viewed as the primary mode within the package, with licensing and exporting playing supporting roles. However, these roles might change over time in the focal market. We can expect changes in roles, some minor and subtle, others major and tantamount to an overall mode change, even though the mode package itself remains unchanged. A company might de-emphasise the importance of the JV and place greater reliance on the licensing and exporting components. We see this in the case of Hong Kong Disneyland where, despite a substantial 43% equity share, Disney appears to have structured the arrangement so that it obtains the bulk of its financial return from licensing and management fees (*Economist*, 2005; Wozniak, 2003).

Role expansion and upgrading are common when foreign market sales expand and show promise. Mode role changes are rarely observed in empirical investigations, yet they may constitute a significant change in international operation strategy. From a theoretical perspective, mode role changes are an unacknowledged manifestation of an increase or decrease in international commitment.

Interrelationships within mode combinations

The multiple modes used by a company in a foreign market are not always directly linked, as the examples we have outlined show (Petersen & Welch, 2002). The distinct modes might be employed in different product or market segments, or in different parts of the value chain. For example, the Australian brewing company Foster's licensed Molson in Canada to brew its beer for the US market, while marketing and distribution were undertaken by a JV with the American firm Miller Brewing. When Molson merged with Coors, a different US brewery, Foster's cancelled its licensing agreement with Molson and signed one for brewing, marketing and distributing beer in the US with Miller, thus generating a tighter overall mode package in an arrangement with all the hallmarks of a general strategic alliance. At the same time, all the parts of the value chain in Canada – production, marketing, and distribution – continued to be handled through a licensing agreement with the newly formed Molson Coors (Speedy, 2007). Before the new licensing agreement with Miller, Foster's used two different modes in the US in different parts of the value chain. It is precisely this kind of situation that leads us to question the validity of surveys that ask respondents to name the mode or modes that their firm uses in different markets. The mode-use picture for Foster's is further clouded by the significant and diverse activities, apart from beer, that it has in the US, particularly associated with its wine operations, including those resulting from the takeover of Beringer, one of the US's largest wine companies, in 2000.

The configuration of modes along the value chain can be still more complicated than in the case of Foster's. It is not unusual for marketing to be performed through different modes in a foreign market. Companies often use independent distributors to reach small dispersed customers while handling larger ones with their own sales staff, sometimes with the support of local sales offices (Valla, 1986). In a study of sales channels in the PC industry in Europe, Gabrielsson et al. (2002: 78) observed a number of cases where "marketing functions are shared by the producer and the channel intermediary; the former usually handles promotion and customer generation activities, whereas the intermediary is in charge of sales and distribution." It is also not unusual for sales and service functions in a foreign market to be split, with different modes used for each. An array of modes can be used along a company's value chain in a foreign market. When all the potential options for each separate part of the value chain are considered, the full range of options can be very large indeed. It can be very difficult for managers to handle such an array of choices, especially when foreign market and location options are added to the mix (Asmussen et al., 2009; Petersen et al., 2008).

Implications of altered mode perspective: mode packages and mode comparisons

Our analysis shows that businesses frequently wrestle with the question of not just which mode to use, but which combination of modes. Comparing FDI, exporting and licensing are relatively straightforward when they are treated as singular modes (see for example, Buckley & Casson, 1981), but less so when they are part of larger mode packages. The packaging of operation modes makes it far more difficult to compare the profitability, control, and resource commitment of different mode choices.

We illustrate mode comparison difficulty in Figure 12.1. For the sake of simplicity we assume that the location and scale of activities are the same for two different packages. On the surface it is difficult to determine which of the two involves greater resource commitment and control. If we were to focus on equity, it is likely that we would conclude that Package 1 represents more resource commitment and greater control, although some IJV scholars have stressed that equity level can paint a false picture of control and commitment (Child, 2002; Yan & Gray, 1994; Yan & Zeng, 1999), an argument also made in studies of transition economies (Karhunen et al., 2008). Our point is that our original impression about relative levels of control and commitment is not so clear-cut. Through licensing and a management contract, Package 2 may in fact give more control. Furthermore, while the purchase of a higher level of equity as in Package 1 may involve more financial commitment upfront, the management contract that is part of Package 2 may require a substantial level of ongoing staff support, as such contracts can be highly human-resource intensive (Welch et al., 2007). For example, the French firm that signed a management contract with the Water Authority of Jordan sent 50–60 expatriates. Six of these, each of them directors, were appointed for periods of between 2 and 4 years, with the remainder, at middle management level, appointed for more than 1 year (Al-Husan & James, 2003). Such a commitment makes a substantial demand on the resources of any firm, and those demands cannot be readily met through external hiring, because considerable internal systems and practices knowledge is needed.

From a theoretical perspective it is difficult to evaluate *a priori* the relative profitability of packages, and therefore also difficult to formulate and apply a maximisation of profit rule for mode choice (Buckley & Casson, 1981; Welch et al., 2007). Certainly it is very hard – if not impossible – to clearly see the link between expected profitability and use of a specific mode within a mode package. One might feasibly argue that a broader package, such as Package 2 in our illustration, is more profitable than a minority JV on its own. Further, it is difficult to separate out the specific contribution to profits made by each individual mode in a package, as the modes are interdependent and the whole is often different from the sum of the parts. A package cannot be classified under one specific mode, the JV component, that is in both of

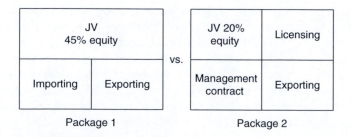

Figure 12.1 Mode comparisons?

the packages drawn in Figure 12.1 in an effort to draw any conclusions about the profitability of a JV mode relative to that of licensing or wholly owned subsidiaries or other modes.

Richer conceptualisations of operation modes and international business theories

We argue that the concept of foreign operation modes needs to be broadened and deepened if IB research is to be brought into line with how companies actually expand and operate internationally. The ideas presented in a sense are not new – there have been others pointing to different aspects of the broader mode reality (Benito & Welch, 1994; Buckley & Mathew, 1980) – but such limited forays have tended to be put aside in the interests of the development of parsimonious theories, and in the face of the empirical difficulties of obtaining more complex data, particularly in longitudinal mode studies. Our approach follows Buckley and Hashai (2004), who extend internalisation theory (Buckley & Casson, 1976) and the OLI framework (Dunning, 2000) with their analysis of the choice between ownership and contractual modes. Like Buckley and Hashai, we unlink the unit of analysis from the value chain as a whole to investigate various components, so that the explanatory factors of internalisation theory can be applied on a disaggregated level. Kone's experience in Japan also shows that a finer-grained analysis of internalisation options, combinations and paths is feasible without "combinatory explosion". A more appropriate unit of analysis improves the predictive power of internalisation theory.

Much of the IB literature focuses on international expansion. While the richer conceptualisation that we present poses theoretical and empirical challenges, it provides a better description of how firms internalise. One of the criticisms levelled at existing theories is that they approach expansion from a comparatively static perspective (Buckley, 1993; Meyer & Gelbuda, 2006; Meyer & Peng, 2005), and there are frequent calls for a greater emphasis on longitudinal processes. For example, Meyer and Gelbuda (2006: 161) point out that while existing theories regarding transition economies have "generated valuable insights ... they are less suitable to analyse dynamic processes ... Therefore we suggest to widen the conceptual domain of the internationalisation research to include new theoretical approaches that are more history, context and process-oriented ... in order to 'see' other sides of entry and adaptation processes."

The lack of dynamism in existing theoretical approaches is partly due to their restricted view of modes and mode change. Taking into account the wider range of options firms have for adjusting operation modes makes it possible to advance a more processual paradigm of international expansion and contraction. The variety of adjustments to operation modes we have described often means more frequent and more diverse forms of mode changes than a focus on individual, discrete mode change might imply. We stress three main forms of "between mode" changes that can be significant, but which fall short of involving distinctly different foreign modes: mode addition or subtraction; within-mode change; and mode role change.

Taken together, these elements of mode change provide a step towards unravelling the dynamics of companies' international business expansion. The altered perspective means more than just a finer-grained treatment of modes: it involves consideration of the nature of mode change. While internationalisation process theory has a more dynamic perspective on international expansion, like other theoretical approaches it has been developed on the basis of a limited conceptualisation of what a "mode" constitutes, closing off other potential paths of international operation development, such as we have noted. Discrete, individual mode change may reveal little about the underlying dynamics of mode change. For example, a firm's initial operation mode in a foreign market may remain unaltered for some time, implying little change. However, there might actually be continuous fine-tuning, or there might be a broader package built around it, so that eventually it ends up being substantially different from what it was initially. Emerging research on post-alliance dynamics and IJV evolution shows that alliances and IJVs evolve in response to changes affecting the foreign market and parent firms. Reuer et al. (2002) found that 44% of the alliances they studied underwent contractual alterations and governance changes after formation. That study, along with those on IJVs referred to earlier, confirm that subsequent adjustments can change the character of alliances and the way they function.

Consequently, what seems like a major change in operation mode may, because of intervening adjustments, amount to a relatively small, evolutionary, almost seamless development. For Danish companies in Southeast Asia adjustments such as sending employees from the parent firm to assist distributors were steps meant to pave the way for the ultimate mode switch (Petersen et al., 2001). Alternatively, without intent, relationships with an intermediary might evolve to such an extent that integration of the intermediary has effectively occurred before a mode switch takes place. A positive relationship with a foreign partner, intermediary, or licensee obviously is beneficial to the process (Morgan & Hunt, 1994; Wu et al., 2007) and can often prepare the ground for more concrete within-mode changes and for more substantial mode switches. Anderson and Weitz (1992: 20) use the concept of pledges, particularly so-called "idiosyncratic investments", which they describe as "specific actions binding a channel member to a relationship", to demonstrate how mutual commitment to a channel relationship may be built. Training, a common order-processing system, and sales promotions are examples of such investments. They can be viewed as forms of within-mode change, and by tying the parties together they provide a strong foundation for mode switches.

There has been considerable criticism recently of the notion of Uppsala-style incrementalism (or gradualism) in internationalisation, particularly in the entrepreneurship literature. In reviewing studies of fast internationalisers, Moen and Servais (2002: 50) argued that "the empirical results and theoretical reasoning in many of these studies question the concept of a gradual internationalization process" (see also Autio et al., 2000; Fan & Phan, 2007). Somewhat surprisingly, there has been limited treatment of operation modes in the international entrepreneurship literature (Burgel & Murray, 2000), even though it might be assumed that faster internationalisation means faster movement through modes or mode leapfrogging.

The concept of incrementalism was based on the expansion patterns of some Swedish multinationals (Johanson & Wiedersheim-Paul, 1975) and there were never any claims that it explained exactly how internationalisation does, or should, take place (Benito & Welch, 1994; Hedlund & Kverneland, 1985; Meyer & Gelbuda, 2006). Nevertheless, in explaining internationalisation aspects such as knowledge development, particularly experiential knowledge, perceived risk and uncertainty, and the need to build useful networks,[2] all of which take time, were taken into account, and so there is an implicit bias in Uppsala-type models towards incrementalism or gradualism in international expansion, or at least in its earlier stages. The richer conceptualisation of modes that we propose offers a greater set of feasible internationalisation steps, and may allow for a better description of incremental changes in modes. In a study of strategies in emerging markets, Meyer and Tran (2006) refer to the intermediate steps taken in Poland and Vietnam by the international brewer Carlsberg. Carlsberg increased its equity stakes in local breweries until its minority stakes were eventually turned into a majority stake and a full acquisition. Along the way, moves to establish control were enhanced by within-mode steps such as key personnel appointments. The experience of Konecranes, a lifting equipment manufacturer independent from Kone since 1994, is a good example of mode package development as a stepping-stone to mode switching. Konecranes penetrated Southeast Asia in the 1970s to 1990s with equipment that called for on-the-ground facilities and expertise for customisation, installation and after-sales service. The usual approach was to establish a licensing agreement with a distributor; in some markets Konecranes took a 10–15% stake in a distributor. In Singapore the arrangement ultimately led to Konecranes fully acquiring the distributor; an important, but nonetheless incremental step following licensing and partial acquisition (Loke & Ong, 2005). Kone's approach to the Japanese market, as well as its expansion into China, were both incremental, even though it was already an experienced, large multinational with one-third of the world market for elevators and escalators.

However, the world of mode change and adaptation – of *mode dynamics* – shown in the various company examples presented above indicates more than incrementalism (Zajac & Olsen, 1993). The concept of mode dynamics we advance is a wider and deeper phenomenon: "modes" evolve in response to foreign market involvement and developments over time, displaying the characteristics of evolutionary dynamics. For example, in a discussion of literature on evolutionary company change, with a focus on transition economies, Meyer and Lieb-Dóczy (2003: 466) conclude that it is "an *evolutionary process* with generation of new routines through *organizational learning* and the *context-sensitive selection* between them" (see also Lovas & Ghoshal, 2000; Meyer, 2002). Given that the change elements noted in the concept of *mode dynamics* would seem to be capable of empirical measurement, based on the level of detail attained in the Kone case and in other studies (for example, Reuer et al., 2002), there is ample scope to track how mode use evolves over time. The elements of mode change noted already are likely to be extended in further studies, but they can be viewed as part of the broader process of organisational adjustment as experience in the focal and other foreign markets evolves, incorporating learning and other change drivers that lead to the adjustment of the mode set, in smaller and larger increments. Ultimately they provide a foundation for the full mode change that is pre-eminently the focus of existing mode research.

Mode choice and change: a framework

Figure 12.2 presents a simplified dynamic model of the choice and evolution of operation modes. We insert the wider range of operation modes available to companies, recognising that the choice of modes, particularly within-mode or mode role changes, or package additions and subtractions are just as likely to be emergent responses to circumstances in the foreign market rather than deliberate policy decisions. Within-mode choices, for example extending credit to distributors, may be the result of quick responses to changes on the ground rather than something that is done after formal evaluation, but one way or another the end result might be to tie the intermediary more closely to the firm, thereby changing the mode configuration. Whereas the bulk of previous studies – especially those based on economics and strategic approaches to foreign mode choice – focus on various factors (decision drivers) influencing mode assessments and choices, and tend to treat them as basically given, the framework presented in Figure 12.2 draws on the behavioural theory of the firm, and explicitly acknowledges that decision drivers are themselves influenced by past experiences and current operations: see also Aharoni (1966) and Johanson and Vahlne (1977).

Given the considerable array of possible operation mode options, it is not surprising that managers fall back on their past experience (Ellis, 2000) and use modes that were successful in other situations (Chetty et al., 2006) or limit the choice set (Hutzschenreuter et al., 2007;

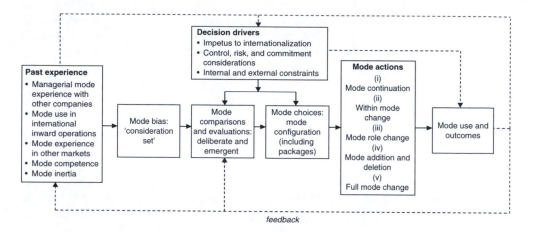

Figure 12.2 Mode choice and change.

Larimo, 1995; March & Shapira, 1987). Past experience creates its own bias (Eisenhardt & Martin, 2000), both positive and negative (see Figure 12.2). As Teece et al. (1997: 522–523) argue, "a firm's previous investments and its repertoire of routines (its 'history') constrain its future behaviour." They stress the importance of "local learning", a concept that seems particularly relevant to mode learning. Mode experience may be acquired first through international inward operations (Karlsen et al., 2003), for example, when a company accesses foreign technology via a licensing-in arrangement and subsequently uses that experience for outward foreign licensing deals (Welch & Luostarinen, 1993). Undoubtedly, bad experience with a particular mode leads to a bias against its further use (Welch et al., 2007). On the other hand, positive experience with a particular mode, and growing knowledge and confidence gained through its continued use, encourage managers to use the mode again and eventually to build competences in using a particular set of modes (Calof & Beamish, 1995). However, this may result in *mode inertia*, that is, the tendency to use an existing mode rather than looking for alternative ones. Obviously, mode inertia is a constraining factor in the evolution of firm strategies (Lovas & Ghoshal, 2000).

Experience with an operation mode can be seen as a unique resource on which the company can draw for its international operations, as argued in the internationalisation process and resource-based perspectives (Barney, 1991; Cuervo-Cazurra et al., 2007; Johanson & Vahlne, 1977; Madhok, 1997; Peteraf, 1993; Zajac & Olsen, 1993). However, the idiosyncrasies of individual markets make it difficult to use the same mode everywhere. The Australian concrete pipe manufacturer, Rocla, entered several different foreign markets through licensing, but eventually had to change its approach because of host government pressure, and so began to enter into JV arrangements (Welch et al., 2007). Such situations inevitably cause companies to consider a wider range of options, sometimes including combinations that still capitalise on existing mode competences, for example a JV with licensing as a step beyond the sole use of licensing. Companies may have to conform to internal as well as external isomorphic pressures (Davis et al., 2000) and so attempt to gain legitimacy by imitating the ways in which incumbents in given markets operate (Chan & Makino, 2007).

As we illustrate in Figure 12.2, the modes used initially by a firm in a foreign market will show some path dependence insofar as they will reflect the biases of managers. However, the initial modes considered are by definition but a starting point. The idiosyncrasies of foreign markets and the actions of potential or current partners may well bring about changes in the starting position. Sometimes, the only mode or mode package evaluated lies outside the initial consideration set when companies are approached with an offer to buy a foreign company or an offer to act as a distributor or licensee in a foreign market. In such cases there may be limited room for negotiation regarding mode form. For some time the dominant strategic mode of international expansion for Kone was making acquisitions (Marschan, 1996; Kone website: history, internationalisation: see note 1. For instance, in 2004 Kone acquired either the majority of shares in, or full ownership of, 32 companies in 17 countries (see note 1. Kone's licensing agreement with Toshiba in 1998 was unusual, but that approach was taken in light of the considerable cultural distance to be bridged, and to no small extent because there was effectively no worthwhile acquisition target (source: Kone interviewee: see note 1). Nevertheless, 3 years later Kone had taken a 20% equity share in TELC.

In the mode comparison and evaluation stage shown in Figure 12.2 we include the full potential range of mode configuration options discussed in our preceding analysis. As noted above, managers use various approaches to limit decision complexity, so that the range of mode options actually evaluated may be very limited. Mode choice and subsequent implementation (mode actions box), therefore, may involve minimal mode alteration or package change, through to full mode change or package creation. Following the mode actions there is the obvious phase of mode use and a range of outcomes that it generates, in market performance terms as well as in various forms of learning. One type of learning growing out of mode use is mode learning, which may apply across the range of mode actions, and becomes part of the mode competence base that a company can apply in future mode evaluation and action. Ultimately, as suggested by the dotted lines in Figure 12.2, these changes and outcomes feed back into a company's mode experience, bias and competence base, thereby affecting future mode decisions.

The evolving mode experience and outcomes may be seen by companies as confirming their original choices, supporting a continuation of existing mode strategy, that is, mode action (i). However, our analysis indicates that mode change is common, as shown in mode actions (ii)–(v). The richer set of mode options available to companies allow more frequent, more rapid, more varied mode change, that is more responsive to a company's internal and external circumstances, market and relational. These options represent a more substantial and varied picture of mode change than has been hitherto considered to any extent, yet they enhance our ability to depict and understand the process of internationalisation.

Managerial considerations

Mode packages will undoubtedly remain a common feature of international activity, given the range of benefits that they are potentially able to generate, especially compared with the use of a single mode. Nevertheless, it is evident that some companies are using foreign operation modes in very creative ways. The multinational express delivery firm FedEx entered into a 50:50 JV in China in 1999 as a way of upgrading its Chinese operations. Importantly, though, attached to the JV was a management contract that ensured managerial control of daily operations from FedEx's perspective (Welch et al., 2007). Licensing agreements also are sometimes used as a way of buttressing managerial control of a JV. Adding a licensing contract to a JV can provide an additional revenue stream and reduce taxes by transferring profits to countries with lower tax rates (Welch et al., 2007).

Modification of operation modes without full mode change may be particularly useful for companies that want to change the way they operate in a foreign market even though they are locked into an existing arrangement because of contractual obligations and other mode switching costs (Benito et al., 1999, 2005; Petersen et al., 2000). Adding a mode or modes to an existing contractual arrangement could be feasible in such circumstances, and if not, within-mode adjustments might be an effective alternative. It is possible to undertake a range of adjustments that eventually position the firm so that it can act alone, thereby easing the path to mode change. Some Danish firms sent their own staff to work with their distributors as a prelude to subsequently establishing a sales subsidiary (Petersen et al., 2001). The staff members were in a position to assess the value of different employees at the distributor and get close to relevant networks. In such cases the within-mode changes may be only a temporary arrangement, but important nonetheless in a key area for internationalising companies: achieving non-disruptive change, with minimal revenue losses and avoidance of excessive switching costs.

There is substantial scope for adjusting modes, but the groundwork must be laid. For companies with substantial international operations, an audit of the company's use of various modes, including where and how mode combinations are being employed, is an essential first step. Managers must also be familiar with a broad array of mode adjustment techniques. There may also be a need to counter mode bias.

Some final remarks on research issues

How do companies operate in foreign markets? The traditional answer has been that they make a strategic choice, typically a rather sticky and enduring one. They have to decide either to export or to set up a foreign subsidiary, either with a local partner or alone. The study of such "entry modes" has certainly been popular in international business research, but the research "templates" that have evolved over time have been somewhat limited when it comes to how companies really operate abroad. In this article we have argued that the literature has overlooked both the complexity and the dynamism of foreign operation modes, and we propose a re-conceptualisation in order to move the field forward.

Little is known about how managers actually choose combinations of modes and evaluate the applicability of different mode packages. Some modes are at the suggestion of a foreign partner, a potential JV or licensing partner for instance, and others a result of negotiations. The Hilton hotel chain included a minority equity investment when negotiating management contracts in Russia in the 1990s (Welch et al., 2007). However, there is little real evidence on how companies really behave on this front: that is, how many mode combination options are seriously considered? Are they proactively or reactively developed? Do decision-makers see mode combinations as a business solution?

An obvious conclusion, therefore, is that there is a need for substantial research that could lead to a better understanding of the foreign operation mode behaviour of firms. The detailed information needed is unlikely to come from large surveys. Longitudinal research is needed, be it (i) of an archival type as has been done in business history research, (ii) quantitative analyses of company panels, or (iii) qualitative in-depth studies of specific companies. In our opinion, in-depth and longitudinal qualitative studies would seem to be critical first steps. This is in line with the conclusion from a recent review of 40 years of research on the link between internationalisation and firm performance, stressing the need for more in-depth field research and clinical case studies that are longitudinal in focus (Glaum & Oesterle, 2007: 315; see also Verbeke & Brugman, 2009, for a critical review). We have shown with the

Kone–Toshiba story that it is possible to build a basic picture of mode packages and within-mode adjustments and of their evolution over time. Incorporating the points made in this article in theories of mode choice and evolution is likely to be more difficult because of the serious challenges posed to existing theoretical approaches.

Acknowledgements

We thank the *JIBS* Area Editor Alain Verbeke and three anonymous reviewers for their many constructive comments and suggestions, which have been instrumental in the development of this article, and Rebecca Piekkari for letting us use material from her research on Kone. The article also benefited from comments provided by Jean-François Hennart, Reijo Luostarinen, and other participants at the 2008 European International Business Academy Annual Conference held in Tallin, Estonia. The editorial assistance of Sondra Grace is also gratefully acknowledged.

Notes

1 Case sources: interview (7 October 2002) with the Kone executive (name confidential) responsible for the establishment of the Kone–Toshiba alliance, as part of a more general study of Kone's internationalisation, recorded at the time in Finnish by Professor Piekkari, with the relevant section translated by her into English in May 2008; frequent informal communication with Alexander Marschan, a high level executive in Kone at the time, regarding Kone's operations; Kone press releases, "Kone and Toshiba join forces in elevators and escalators", Helsinki, 26 May 1998 and "Kone and Toshiba strengthen their strategic alliance", Helsinki, 20 December 2001; Kone internal document titled "The strategic alliance between Toshiba and Kone: key dates and agreements", issued with the press release of the same date, 20 December 2001; on Kone's website: History: Toshiba alliance, accessed 10 May 2008, History: Kone China, accessed 13 May 2008; articles in Kone's internal magazine, *Kone News & Views*, "Kone and TELC increase cooperation", 2/2004, 4–6, and "Gearing up in Korea", 1/2005, 28–31; outline of an address entitled "Kone–Toshiba: Manufacturing Co-operation in China" by Kone's Senior Vice President of New Escalators, Matti Hyytiäinen, at a business seminar, Helsinki, 5 March 2007, accessed at www.finproevents.fi/tiedostot/default/finpro1000000207.pdf on 13 May 2008).
2 An emphasis on networks came somewhat later: see Johanson and Mattsson (1988) and Forsgren and Johanson (1992).

References

Aharoni, Y. 1966. *The foreign investment decision process.* Boston, MA: Harvard University Press.
Al-Husan, F. B., & James, P. 2003. Cultural control and multinationals: The case of privatized Jordanian companies. *International Journal of Human Resource Management*, 14(7): 1284–95.
Alvesson, M., & Kärreman, D. 2007. Constructing mystery: Empirical matters in theory development. *Academy of Management Review*, 32(4): 1265–81.
Anderson, E., & Gatignon, H. 1986. Modes of foreign entry: A transaction cost analysis and propositions. *Journal of International Business Studies*, 17(3): 1–26.
Anderson, E., & Weitz, B. 1992. The use of pledges to build and sustain commitment in distribution channels. *Journal of Marketing Research*, 29(1): 18–34.
Ariño, A., & de la Torre, J. 1998. Learning from failure: Towards an evolutionary model of collaborative ventures. *Organization Science*, 9(3): 306–25.
Asmussen, C. G., Benito, G. R. G., & Petersen, B. 2009. Organizing foreign market activities: From entry mode choice to configuration decisions. *International Business Review*, 18(3): 145–55.

Autio, E., Sapienza, H. J., & Almeida, J. G. 2000. Effects of age at entry, knowledge intensity, and imitability on international growth. *Academy of Management Journal*, 43(5): 909–24.

Balasubramanyam, V. N. 1985. Foreign direct investment and the international transfer of technology. In D. Greenaway (Ed.), *Current issues in international trade: Theory and policy:* 159–81. London: Macmillan.

Barkema, H. G., & Drogendijk, R. 2007. Internationalising in small, incremental or larger steps? *Journal of International Business Studies*, 38(7): 1132–48.

Barney, J. B. 1991. Firm resources and sustained competitive advantage. *Journal of Management*, 17(1): 99–120.

Benito, G. R. G., Pedersen, T., & Petersen, B. 1999. Foreign operation methods and switching costs: Conceptual issues and possible effects. *Scandinavian Journal of Management*, 15(2): 213–29.

Benito, G. R. G., Pedersen, T., & Petersen, B. 2005. Export channel dynamics: An empirical investigation. *Managerial and Decision Economics*, 26(3): 159–73.

Benito, G. R. G., & Welch, L. S. 1994. Foreign market servicing: Beyond choice of entry mode. *Journal of International Marketing*, 2(2): 7–27.

Bolger, A. 2007. West to get a taste of the great Russian beer. *Financial Times (Asia)*, *26* June: 18.

Brouthers, K. D., & Hennart, J.-F. 2007. Boundaries of the firm: Insights from international entry mode research. *Journal of Management*, 33(3): 395–425.

Büchel, B. 2002. Joint venture development: Driving forces towards equilibrium. *Journal of World Business*, 37(3): 199–207.

Buckley, P. J. 1993. The role of management in internalisation theory. *Management International Review*, 33(3): 197–207.

Buckley, P. J., & Casson, M. C. 1976. *The future of the multinational enterprise.* London: Macmillan.

Buckley, P. J., & Casson, M. C. 1981. The optimal timing of a foreign direct investment. *Economic Journal*, 91(361): 75–87.

Buckley, P. J., & Hashai, N. 2004. A global system view of firm boundaries. *Journal of International Business Studies*, 35(1): 33–45.

Buckley, P. J., & Mathew, A. M. 1980. Dimensions of the market entry behaviour of recent UK first time direct investors in Australia. *Management International Review*, 20(2): 35–51.

Buckley, P. J., Pass, C. L., & Prescott, K. 1990. Foreign market servicing by multinationals: An integrated treatment. *International Marketing Review*, 7(4): 25–40.

Burgel, O., & Murray, G. C. 2000. The international market entry choices of start-up companies in high-technology industries. *Journal of International Marketing*, 8(2): 33–62.

Calof, J. 1993. The mode choice and change decision process and its impact on international performance. *International Business Review*, 2(1): 97–120.

Calof, J., & Beamish, P. W. 1995. Adapting to foreign markets: Explaining internationalization. *International Business Review*, 4(2): 115–31.

Chan, C. M., & Makino, S. 2007. Legitimacy and multi-level institutional environments: Implications for foreign subsidiary ownership structure. *Journal of International Business Studies*, 38(4): 621–38.

Chetty, S., Eriksson, K., & Lindbergh, J. 2006. The effect of specificity of experience on a firm's perceived importance of institutional knowledge in an ongoing business. *Journal of International Business Studies*, 37(5): 699–712.

Child, J. 2002. A configurational analysis of international joint ventures. *Organization Studies*, 23(5): 781–815.

Clark, T., Pugh, D. S., & Mallory, G. 1997. The process of internationalization in the operating firm. *International Business Review*, 6(6): 605–23.

Cuervo-Cazurra, A., Maloney, M. M., & Manrakhan, S. 2007. Causes of the difficulties of internationalization. *Journal of International Business Studies*, 38(4): 709–25.

Datta, D. K., Herrmann, P., & Rasheed, A. A. 2002. Choice of foreign market entry modes: Critical review and future directions. *Advances in International Management*, 14: 85–153.

Davis, P. S., Desai, A. B., & Francis, J. D. 2000. Mode of international entry: An isomorphism perspective. *Journal of International Business Studies*, 31(2): 239–58.

Deligonul, S., & Cavusgil, S. T. 2006. Legal versus relational ordering in channel governance: The case of the manufacturer and its foreign distributor. *Advances in International Marketing*, 16: 49–79.

Dubois, A., & Gadde, L.-E. 2002. Systematic combining: An abductive approach to case research. *Journal of Business Research*, 55(7): 553–60.

Dunning, J. H. 2000. The eclectic paradigm as an envelope for economic and business theories of MNE activity. *International Business Review*, 9(1): 163–90.

Dunning, J. H., & Lundan, S. 2008. *Multinational enterprises and the global economy*, (2nd ed.) Cheltenham: Edward Elgar.

Economist. 2005. Year of the mouse. 10 September: 56.

Eisenhardt, K. M., & Martin, J. A. 2000. Dynamic capabilities: What are they? *Strategic Management Journal*, 21(10/11): 1105–21.

Ellis, P. D. 2000. Social ties and foreign market entry. *Journal of International Business Studies*, 31(3): 443–69.

Ellis, P. D. 2006. Factors affecting the termination propensity of inter-firm relationships. *European Journal of Marketing*, 40(11/12): 1169–77.

Fan, T., & Phan, P. 2007. International new ventures: Revisiting the influences behind the "born-global" firm. *Journal of International Business Studies*, 38(7): 1113–31.

Forsgren, M., & Johanson, J. 1992. *Managing networks in international business.* Philadelphia: Gordon and Breach.

Fryges, H. 2007. The change of sales modes in international markets: Empirical results for German and British high-tech firms. *Progress in International Business Research*, 1: 139–85.

Gabrielsson, M., Kirpalani, V. H. M., & Luostarinen, R. K. 2002. Multiple channel strategies in the European personal computer industry. *Journal of International Marketing*, 10(3): 73–95.

Glaum, M., & Oesterle, M.-J. 2007. 40 years of research on internationalization and firm performance: More questions than answers? *Management International Review*, 47(3): 307–17.

Harrigan, K. R. 1988. Strategic alliances and partner asymmetries. *Management International Review*, 28(SI): 53–73.

Hedlund, G., & Kverneland, A. 1985. Are strategies for foreign markets changing? The case of Swedish investment in Japan. *International Studies of Management and Organization*, 15(1): 41–9.

Hennart, J.-F. 1982. *A theory of multinational enterprise.* Ann Arbor, MI: University of Michigan Press.

Hennart, J.-F. 1989. Can the "new forms of investment" substitute for the "old forms"? A transaction costs perspective. *Journal of International Business Studies*, 20(2): 211–34.

Hennart, J.-F., Kim, D. J., & Zeng, M. 1998. The impact of joint venture status on the longevity of Japanese stakes in US manufacturing affiliates. *Organization Science*, 9(3): 382–95.

Hennart, J.-F., Roehl, T., & Zietlow, D. S. 1999. "Trojan horse" or "workhorse"? The evolution of US-Japanese joint ventures in the United States. *Strategic Management Journal*, 20(1): 15–29.

Hill, C. W. L., Hwang, P., & Kim, W. C. 1990. An eclectic theory of the choice of international entry mode. *Strategic Management Journal*, 11(2): 117–28.

Hood, N., & Young, S. 1979. *The economics of multinational enterprise.* London: Longman.

Hutzschenreuter, T., Pedersen, T., & Volberda, H. W. 2007. The role of path dependency and managerial intentionality: A perspective on international business research. *Journal of International Business Studies*, 38(7): 1055–68.

Johanson, J., & Mattsson, L.-G. 1988. Internationalization in industrial systems: A network approach. In N. Hood & J.-E. Vahlne (Eds), *Strategies in global competition:* 287–314. New York: Croom Helm.

Johanson, J., & Vahlne, J.-E. 1977. The internationalization process of the firm: A model of knowledge development and increasing foreign market commitments. *Journal of International Business Studies*, 8(1): 23–32.

Johanson, J., & Wiedersheim-Paul, F. 1975. The internationalization of the firm: Four Swedish cases. *Journal of Management Studies*, 12(3): 305–22.

Karhunen, P., Löfgren, J., & Kosonen, R. 2008. Revisiting the relationship between ownership and control in international business operations: Lessons from transition economies. *Journal of International Management*, 14(1): 78–88.

Karlsen, T., Silseth, P. R., Benito, G. R. G., & Welch, L. S. 2003. Knowledge, internationalization of the firm, and inward-outward connections. *Industrial Marketing Management*, 32(5): 385–96.

Kogut, B., & Zander, U. 1993. Knowledge of the firm and the evolutionary theory of the multinational corporation. *Journal of International Business Studies*, 24(4): 625–45.

Kostova, T., & Zaheer, S. 1999. Organizational legitimacy under conditions of complexity: The case of the multinational enterprise. *Academy of Management Review*, 24(1): 64–81.

Larimo, J. 1995. The foreign direct investment decision process: Case studies of different types of decision processes in Finnish firms. *Journal of Business Research*, 33(1): 25–55.

Loke, S., & Ong, L. 2005. *KCI Konecranes.* Melbourne: MBA company project, Mt Eliza Business School.

Lovas, B., & Ghoshal, S. 2000. Strategy as guided evolution. *Strategic Management Journal*, 21(9): 875–96.

Luostarinen, R. K. 1970. *Foreign operations of the firm.* Helsinki: HSE.

Luostarinen, R. K. 1979. *Internationalization of the firm.* Helsinki: HSE.

Madhok, A. 1997. Cost, value and foreign market entry mode: The transaction and the firm. *Strategic Management Journal*, 18(1): 39–61.

March, J. G. 2006. Rationality, foolishness, and adaptive intelligence. *Strategic Management Journal*, 27(3): 201–14.

March, J. G., & Shapira, Z. 1987. Managerial perspectives on risk and risk taking. *Management Science*, 33(11): 1404–18.

Marschan, R. 1996. *New structural forms and inter-unit communication in multinationals: The case of Kone.* Helsinki: Helsinki School of Economics and Business Administration.

Meyer, K. E. 2002. Management challenges in privatization acquisitions in transition economies. *Journal of World Business*, 37(4): 266–76.

Meyer, K. E., & Gelbuda, M. 2006. Process perspectives in international business research in CEE. *Management International Review*, 46(2): 143–64.

Meyer, K. E., & Lieb-Dóczy, E. 2003. Post-acquisition restructuring as evolutionary process. *Journal of Management Studies*, 40(2): 459–82.

Meyer, K. E., & Peng, M. W. 2005. Probing theoretically into Central and Eastern Europe: Transactions, resources and institutions. *Journal of International Business Studies*, 36(6): 600–21.

Meyer, K. E., & Tran, Y. T. T. 2006. Market penetration and acquisition strategies for emerging economies. *Long Range Planning*, 39(2): 177–97.

Meyer, K. E., Wright, M., & Pruthi, S. 2009. Managing knowledge in foreign entry strategies: A resource-based analysis. *Strategic Management Journal*, 30(5): 557–74.

Moen, Ø., & Servais, 2002. Born global or gradual global? Examining the export behaviour of small and medium-sized enterprises. *Journal of International Marketing*, 10(3): 49–72.

Morgan, R. M., & Hunt, S. D. 1994. The commitment-trust theory of relationship marketing. *Journal of Marketing*, 58(3): 20–38.

Newbold, G. D., Buckley, P. J., & Thurwell, J. 1978. *Going international.* London: Associated Business Press.

Peirce, C. S. 1931–1958. In C. Hartshorne, P. Weiss (Vols. 1–6), & A. Burks (Vols. 7–8) (Eds), *The collected papers of Charles Sanders Peirce.* Cambridge, MA: Harvard University Press.

Peteraf, M. A. 1993. The cornerstones of competitive advantage: A resource-based view. *Strategic Management Journal*, 14(3): 179–91.

Petersen, B., & Welch, L. S. 2002. Foreign operation mode combinations and internationalization. *Journal of Business Research*, 55(2): 157–62.

Petersen, B., Welch, L. S., & Nielsen, K. V. 2001. Resource commitment to foreign markets: The establishment patterns of Danish firms in South-East Asian markets. In S. Gray, S. L. McGaughey & W. R. Purcell (Eds), *Asia-Pacific issues in international business:* 7–27. Cheltenham: Edward Elgar.

Petersen, B., Welch, D. E., & Welch, L. S. 2000. Creating meaningful switching options in international operations. *Long Range Planning*, 33(5): 688–705.

Petersen, B., Benito, G. R. G., Welch, L. S., & Asmussen, C. G. 2008. Mode configuration diversity: A new perspective on foreign operation mode choice. In D. Griffith, S. T. Cavusgil, G. T. M. Hult & A. Y. Lewin (Eds), *Thought leadership in advancing international business research:* 57–78. London: Palgrave.

Reuer, J. J., Zollo, M., & Singh, H. 2002. Post-formation dynamics in strategic alliances. *Strategic Management Journal*, 23(2): 135–51.

Root, F. R. 1964. Strategic planning for export marketing. Paper Series 6, Department of International Economics and Management, Copenhagen.

Root, F. R. 1977. *Entry strategies for foreign markets: From domestic to international business.* New York: Amacon.

Speedy, B. 2007. Foster's licenses new brewer. *Australian*, 27 June: 25.

Teece, D. J., Pisano, G., & Shuen, A. 1997. Dynamic capabilities and strategic management. *Strategic Management Journal*, 18(7): 509–33.

Tomassen, S., Welch, L. S., & Benito, G. R. G. 1998. Norwegian companies in India: Operation mode choice. *Asian Journal of Business & Information Systems*, 3(1): 1–20.

Valla, J. P. 1986. The French approach to Europe. In P. W. Turnbull & J. P. Valla (Eds), *Strategies for international industrial marketing:* 11–41. London: Croom Helm.

Van Maanen, J., Sørensen, J. B., & Mitchell, T. R. 2007. The interplay between theory and method. *Academy of Management Review*, 32(4): 1145–54.

Verbeke, A., & Brugman, P. 2009. Triple-testing the quality of multinationality-performance research: An internalization theory perspective. *International Business Review*, 18(3): 265–75.

Welch, L. S., & Luostarinen, R. K. 1988. Internationalization: Evolution of a concept. *Journal of General Management*, 14(2): 32–55.

Welch, L. S., & Luostarinen, R. K. 1993. Inward-outward connections in internationalization. *Journal of International Marketing*, 1(1): 44–56.

Welch, L. S., Benito, G. R. G., & Petersen, B. 2007. *Foreign operation methods: Theory, analysis, strategy.* Cheltenham: Edward Elgar.

Wozniak, L. 2003. Crouching tiger. *Far Eastern Economic Review*, 166(3): 24–5.

Wu, F., Sinkovics, R. R., Cavusgil, S. T., & Roath, A. S. 2007. Overcoming export manufacturers' dilemma in international expansion. *Journal of International Business Studies*, 38(2): 283–302.

Yan, A., & Gray, B. 1994. Bargaining power, management control and performance in United States–China joint ventures: A comparative case study. *Academy of Management Journal*, 37(6): 1478–517.

Yan, A., & Zeng, M. 1999. International joint venture instability: A critique of previous research, a reconceptualization, and directions for future research. *Journal of International Business Studies*, 30(2): 397–414.

Zajac, E. J., & Olsen, C. P. 1993. From transaction cost to transactional value analysis: Implications for the study of interorganizational strategies. *Journal of Management Studies*, 30(1): 131–45.

Zhao, H., Luo, Y., & Suh, T. 2004. Transaction cost determinants and ownership-based entry mode choice: A meta-analytical review. *Journal of International Business Studies*, 35(6): 524–44.

Case study II
Danone

A French multinational expanding into the global market

Sylvie Hertrich, Michel Kalika and Ulrike Mayrhofer

"Bringing health through food to as many people as possible"; this is the strategic mission of the French Danone group, which has become a leading actor in the food-processing industry. Danone is the world's number one for fresh dairy products, number two for infant nutrition and bottled waters and number three for medical nutrition. These strong market positions can be attributed to the internationalization of activities. The group first developed on the European market before continuing its expansion into other geographic regions. Over the past decade, Danone has significantly strengthened its presence in emerging countries (Brazil, China, Indonesia, Russia, etc.). In 2010, the company reached the objective of achieving a balance between mature and emerging markets.

Danone's expansion into European markets

The French Danone group started its international development in Western Europe in the late 1970s, a period characterized by the increasing integration of the European Economic Area. At first, the company attempted to capture markets close to France, which offered important growth opportunities and whose distribution system was moderately concentrated, such as Italy and Spain. It then continued its international expansion into other European countries such as Germany, the UK, Belgium, Greece, Ireland and the Netherlands. The company favoured external growth operations, notably minority equity investments and acquisitions of local brands (for example, Galbani in Italy, San Miguel in Spain).

Following the fall of the Berlin Wall in 1989, which marked the end of the Soviet regime, Danone explored the possibilities of expanding to Central and Eastern European countries. It began by exporting products manufactured in Western Europe through sales subsidiaries established in the countries targeted. At the same time, joint ventures were formed with local companies in order to set up production facilities. The company later acquired some of its partners to carry out activities independently. This approach was adopted in several Central and Eastern European countries such as Hungary, the Czech Republic and Poland.

Danone's geographic diversification

From the early 1980s, Danone sought to diversify its geographic expansion. After capturing the North American and Japanese markets, the company accelerated its international development during the 1990s. The priority was given to emerging markets, and notably to countries characterized by an important population, a high growth rate and a rapidly increasing purchasing power of households. The group established itself in Southeast Asian countries (China, Indonesia, Thailand, etc.) and in Latin American countries (Argentina, Brazil, Mexico, etc.). To enter these

Table II.1 Danone's ten leading markets in 2000 and 2012

2000			2012		
Rank	Country	% of total sales	Rank	Country	% of total sales
1	France	24%	1	Russia	10%
2	Italy	11%	2	France	10%
3	United States	11%	3	United States	8%
4	Spain	8%	4	China	6%
5	China	8%	5	Spain	6%
6	United Kingdom	6%	6	Indonesia	6%
7	Argentina	5%	7	Mexico	5%
8	Benelux	3%	8	Argentina	5%
9	Mexico	3%	9	United Kingdom	5%
10	Germany	3%	10	Brazil	4%

Source: Danone (2012).

more distant markets, it engaged in export activities and carried out external growth operations, mainly through minority equity investments, joint ventures and acquisitions. Once the company had managed to establish itself in a new market, it continued developing through internal growth.

In 2012, Europe, excluding the CIS area (Commonwealth of Independent States), remained important, even if 60% of the group's total sales are developed outside the European area. Table II.1 presents the evolution of Danone's ten leading markets between 2000 and 2012. It shows that, while France represents a major market for the group, its relative importance has considerably decreased (from 24% to 10%). The company has recently defined six priority markets, Mexico, Indonesia, China, Russia, the United States and Brazil, called the MICRUB countries. This acronym includes the United States, where growth perspectives for Danone appear to be similar to emerging economies. In 2012, these six markets accounted for 39% of the group's total sales.

As shown by Table II.1, Russia has become the main market for Danone thanks to the joint venture established with the Russian Unimilk group (see Box 1).

The organizational structure of the Danone group

Figure II.1 presents the organizational structure of the group, which is based on four strategic business units (SBUs): fresh dairy products (56% of the group's total sales), bottled waters (17.2%), medical nutrition (6.2%) and infant nutrition (20.6%). This divisional structure is completed by three business functions that play a major role within the group: human resources, due to the central role of the human resource policy for the coordination of activities; finance, due to resource allocation approaches and the importance of profitability in a company listed on the stock exchange; research and development, due to its importance regarding product innovation.

In 2012, Danone had 102,401 employees working in 80 countries (with two-thirds in emerging markets), and owned 194 production sites located around the world. In each country, the organization is divided into strategic business units (SBUs) and national business managers are directly attached to the business division of the headquarters in Paris. Danone is a highly decentralized company, providing an important degree of autonomy to local subsidiaries. In accordance with its strategic mission 'bringing health through food to as many people

---

Box 1: Danone Unimilk: a Franco-Russian joint venture

In 2010, Danone decided to form a joint venture with Unimilk, the second-leading private Russian company in the field of dairy products and infant nutrition. The two partners merged their 'dairy products' activities in Russia and in several neighbouring countries (the Ukraine, Kazakhstan and Byelorussia). Danone owns 57.5% of the newly created Danone Unimilk company, while Unimilk's shareholders hold 42.5%. The joint venture is run by Andrey Beskhmelnitsky, Unimilk's former president and managing director, and managed at the operational level by Filip Kegels, the former managing director of Danone's Fresh Dairy Products activity in Eastern Europe and Central Asia.

Upon signing the agreement, both partners underlined their complementarities in regard to their geographical presence (Danone in the west and Unimilk in the east of Russia), their portfolio of products (on health segments with added value for Danone and on core market segments for Unimilk), their distribution networks (large-scale distribution for Danone and local channels for Unimilk) and their manufacturing facilities (expertise acquired by Danone and 28 manufacturing facilities owned by Unimilk in Russia, the Ukraine and Byelorussia). The Danone Unimilk company has become a leader in dairy products in the CIS area, and notably in Russia.

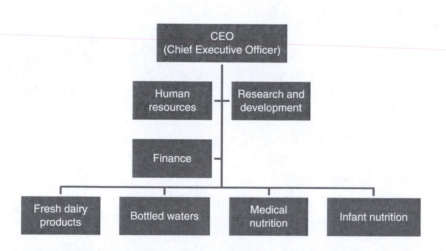

Figure II.1 The organizational structure of Danone.
Source: Danone (2012).

as possible', Danone has chosen to manufacture and market products that are part of local consumption habits and that take into account the living standards of populations. It has also set up research and development (R&D) centres in major markets in order to adapt products to the specificities of local requirements. R&D skills are grouped together within Danone Research, an organization with more than 1,500 employees, 1,000 of whom are working abroad. Considering local realities, the company also takes an interest in the 4 billion consumers who live on less than $2 a day ("BOP: Bottom of the Pyramid"). The objective is to develop economic affordability and added value ("affordvaluity").

In 2012, the Danone group achieved total sales of €20.87 billion and a net income of €1.79 billion. In the same year, 53% of the company's total sales concerned emerging markets. Danone plans to continue its expansion into all geographic regions of the world market: the priorities are to strengthen acquired positions in MICRUB countries and to develop in new markets, such as India, Ivory Coast, Cameroon and Kenya. The increasing geographic diversification of activities presents important organizational challenges for the group.

Questions

1   Evaluate the internationalization strategy developed by Danone, notably the selection of foreign markets.
2   What are the major benefits and risks associated with the organizational structure adopted by Danone?

Further reading

Danone (2012), *Annual Report.*

Hadjikhani, A., Elg, U. and Ghauri, P. (eds.) (2012), *Business, society and politics: Multinationals in emerging markets*, Howard House, Emerald Group.

Hertrich, S., Kalika, M. and Mayrhofer, U. (2011), *Danone: A world leader of the food-processing industry*, Paris, Centrale de Cas et de Médias Pédagogiques.

Mayrhofer, U. (ed.) (2012). *Management of multinational companies. A French perspective*, Palgrave Macmillan.

Part III

Organizing the multinational enterprise

13 Introduction

In international business, how firms go abroad and how they manage their international operations has been an important issue, extensively investigated. Growth of the firm is the main driver for internationalization as growth eventually leads to going beyond national borders. But how firms go abroad and how they manage their ventures and subsidiaries abroad has been subject to a lot of debate. Do firms go abroad gradually or do they leapfrog depending on their experience and size? What is the best organizational structure to manage a firm that is producing several products and is operating in many markets? We deal with these questions in this section.

One of the earlier studies (Chapter 27) presented a gradual internationalization model from no export to manufacturing subsidiaries. According to this model, firms grow at home then expand to nearby foreign markets. The obstacles to internationalization include uncertainties about risk, problems with controlling in foreign markets and psychic distance. The psychic distance (see also Chapter 29 in this book) refers to the perceived distance due to different cultural and other environmental factors. It may or may not be correlated with the geographic distance. For example, Britain and Australia are geographically far away but are close to each other due to psychic proximity (Johanson and Vahlne, 1977).

The establishment chain model of five steps of going abroad suggests that the more knowledge and experience the firms gain in a foreign market, the more it is willing to commit more resources and move to the next stage in the internationalization process. The other obstacles, the psychic distance and the need for control, also change over time and induce the firm to advance to the next stage (Ghauri and Cateora, 2014).

Depending on the objectives of internationalization, market seeking, efficiency seeking or resource seeking, firms would choose the location. Studies on the location choice decision-making process reveal that firms choose the market that can best serve its objectives. Depending on the objectives of the firm in the particular market, different characteristics of the target market become more or less important (Dunning, 2009).

For market entry, the firm also has to see whether it is going to be the first foreign firm in the market or whether it has to compete with other foreign firms. If it is the first foreign firm, then it gets first mover advantage and can gain a major proportion of the market share. However, it may lead to some additional costs to introduce the market to and convince it of the new product, while other competing firms that will enter later, need not incur these costs (Elg et al., 2008).

The first step in foreign market entry is the market opportunity assessment to make decisions such as which market is potentially attractive to enter and whether there is product and market fit and sales potential for its products or not (Cavusgil et al., 2013). For this purpose, the firm needs to go through a proactive market selection process. This is done by visiting the potential market and through market research. To gauge the attractiveness of the market, companies need to gather information on market size and growth, total and segments, as well as on cultural, legal and political environments.

At the same time, managers need to analyse the competitive conditions in that particular market. To find out the intensity of competition and to assess whether they can gain some market shares from existing competitors or not, they also have to look at their own capabilities and resources as well as product and positioning fit (Ghauri and Cateora, 2014). After a market has been selected, the next decision is about how to enter that market. Managers have many options from exporting, licensing, joint ventures to wholly owned subsidiaries. Some of the chapters in Part III deal with conditions that may lead to one or the other entry modes (Hennart, 1982).

As Kogut (1985) puts it, 'a firm's initial investments in new markets can be considered as buying the right to expand in the future' (p 19). The possibility of deferring decisions, and the ability to use the deferral period to collect information using the initial (perhaps small) investment as a 'listening post', expands the strategies open to foreign investors (Buckley and Casson, 1998). The real options view shows that the decision to undertake FDI is not a simple 'go/no go' choice but can be nuanced. Joint ventures may be a way to stage an entry and to gather information over time, although investors should be aware that it is not always possible to exit a joint venture, at least not without cost. Intermediate forms of organization – minority joint ventures, non-equity joint ventures and small initial investment – are examples of strategies that fit the real options approach and these may be of particular use in risky or volatile foreign markets.

Once a firm has established itself in a foreign market, it needs to decide how to organize, coordinate and control its operations not only in one foreign market but in all of its markets. It has to decide about formal and informal structure and control mechanisms. It has to decide whether to centralize its decision-making or to decentralize it to local units in foreign markets, or which decisions to decentralize to local units (Buckley and Ghauri, 2004).

Centralization allows better coordination, consistency in decision-making, avoids duplication and achieves economies of scales and tighter control. Decentralization, on the other hand, can release top management from routine decision-making so they can concentrate more on corporate strategic matters. Decentralization of decision-making to local managers enhances the commitment of these managers and allows rapid responses to local demands and developments. As decisions are made closer to each market, these tend to be better suited and make local managers more responsible.

From the start most firms are structured in functional structures (see Figure 13.1). As the firm grows further and begins producing several products, it is structured in a product-based structure where each product division controls its own purchasing, manufacturing and

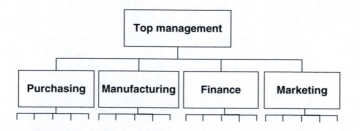

Figure 13.1 Structures based on functions.

marketing functions (Hill, 2012). Traditionally, when the firm grows further and internationalizes, an international division is added to its structure (see Figure 13.2).

These international divisions are often given responsibility for a country or a group of countries, such as Europe, the Middle East or North America. The international divisions sell the products that are produced by product divisions in the firm.

As the firm becomes a multinational it has to rethink its structure and depending on its expansion pattern, the firm moves either towards a worldwide product division or towards a global matrix (see Figure 13.3). The firms that are diversified and have product division structure at domestic level, would move towards a worldwide product division, where each worldwide product division will be self-contained and responsible for its own strategy and value creation. However, later studies (Chapter 14 by Bartlett and Ghoshal) suggest that a multinational company needs to adapt a transnational structure based on location and experience based economies simultaneously. This will allow them to achieve local responsiveness as well as capitalize on core competencies within the firm (Ghauri, 1992).

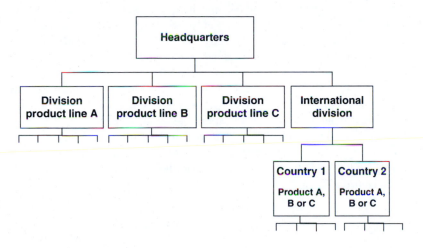

Figure 13.2 Structure based on products in an international company.

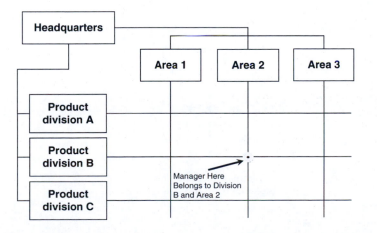

Figure 13.3 A matrix structure.

For a multinational firm, the need for coordination becomes crucial. It is easier to achieve in multinational and multi-domestic company where local managers are allowed to make decisions and are made responsible for local responsiveness. This is possible as there is less need for overall central coordination. The coordination is crucial in global firms where internal capabilities are centralized and need to be transferred to different locations and have to be combined with local experience and locational factors to create value (Hill, 2012). There are several impediments to coordination in these firms, as managers from different units may have different goals and difficulties in cross-cultural communication might be problematic.

For some important tasks, such as new product development or R&D, these firms tend to use ad hoc or permanent teams from several subunits. Other firms create matrix structures, where employees or managers report to two managers from different units to achieve high levels of coordination (see Figure 13.4). Matrix structures are difficult to manage and often lead to more conflicts than coordination (Ghauri, 1992).

To overcome these problems, Bartlett and Ghoshal proposed a network structure where managers at different units are linked directly or indirectly. This allows mangers from different units to communicate with each other. Advancement in communication technology is believed to be facilitating these direct and indirect networks. Enabling this structure to work properly, a firm needs to incorporate as any managers as possible in this network. This is normally done through information systems and extended inter-unit management development schemes (Bartlett and Ghoshal, 1989).

In addition to coordination, the goal of the top management is to control the various units of a firm. Managers achieve this through instating several types of controls, such as quality control, output and performance control. This is not an easy task, for example, if the performance of one unit is at least partly dependent on the performance of other units, or there are no clear performance measures possible (Bartlett et al., 2008). This performance ambiguity is inherent in interdependencies between different units of the firm and lead to increased cost of coordination and control.

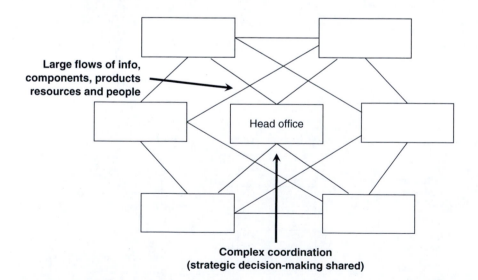

Figure 13.4 Integrated network.

Source: Based on Bartlett and Ghoshal (1993) and de Wit and Meyer (2004).

Table 13.1 Strategy, structure and control

Strategy	Structure	Control
Multinational strategy	Multi-domestic structure; local responsiveness; locally self-sufficient units/subsidiaries.	Decentralized decision-making at local units. Local responsiveness.
International strategy	International structure; transfer of core competence to local units that is centralized; R&D at head office and other important competencies centralized.	Core competence centrally controlled; adaption to parent company competencies; some core competencies decentralized.
Global strategy	Head office as centralized hub; core competencies and resources centralized. Minimum decentralization.	Central decision-making and operational control; competencies retained at the head office; subsidiaries or foreign units implement strategies directed by head office.
Transnational strategy	Specialization of different competences and different units; closely connected to the head office.	Transnational network of formal and informal communication and interdependencies.

In case each unit is totally independent, this ambiguity is low and performance can be easily controlled. But in an international firm, this is seldom the case and there is a need for overall integration and control systems. There are four types of control systems: personal control through direct supervision, cultural control through indoctrinating employees into organizations culture, output control by setting clear and objective goals for units, and bureaucratic control through system rules, regulations and procedures (Hill, 2012).

These structures and control systems are strongly connected to strategies of the firm. A multi-domestic firm normally follows a multinational structure where decision-making is decentralized to self-contained foreign subsidiaries. A firm following international strategy, normally follows international structure where the head office keeps control over the firm's core competencies, such as R&D and marketing, and all other decisions are decentralized to subsidiaries and units. Firms pursuing a global strategy normally follow worldwide product divisions as a base for their structure. Decision-making about most decisions is centralized at the head office. Finally, firms following transnational strategy often work with a matrix-type structure with product and geographic area divisions. For coordination and integration, these firms use formal and informal management systems and networks (Bartlett et al., 2008). The relationship between strategy, structure and control is summarized in Table 13.1.

As shown in Table 13.1, when deciding on strategy and structure, the main concern of the firm is to control its worldwide operations. In other words, it has to decide which functions, competencies and resources should be centralized and which should be decentralized to its units around the world.

Centralization versus decentralization

When organizing an international company, the most important decision is how to control its operations and subsidiaries; how much power and autonomy should be given to different units around the globe. The benefit of decentralized units is that decisions are made by those managers who are closest to the market. But these managers only have the perspective of their own market and subsidiary and not of the firm as a whole. On the other hand, if the decision-making is centralized at the head office, the managers making these decisions have no, or limited, knowledge of several local markets. Developments and changes taking place in different local markets cannot be considered in central decision-making.

Centralization and decentralization both have advantages and disadvantages, managers constantly struggle with the issue of which decisions are to be centralized and which are to be decentralized. Where they decentralize decision-making, the coordination becomes problematic as it is difficult to link and integrate activities of different subsidiaries and units. Managers try to achieve this coordination through structure design and through rules and procedures about formal and informal communication. Some companies also use ad hoc teams or task forces to coordinate significant decision-making, where members from different units participate.

The first chapter in this part is the seminal paper by Bartlett and Ghoshal, "Organizing for worldwide effectiveness: the transnational solution", discusses the enormous success of newcomers, Japanese companies and the way in which they have forced Western firms to rethink their organizational strategies. Managers in Japan have focussed on the forces of localization, while Western firms are worried about barriers of trade.

The growing demand of host governments for local investments and changing manufacturing technologies are making small-scale production and tailored products more feasible. The authors claim that these changes demand more than efficient central management and flexible operations. Given a number of examples from companies such as Philips, Ericsson and Matsushita, they conclude that dynamic interdependences is the basis of a transnational company, one that thinks globally and acts locally. They suggest that to deal with these new challenges, what is needed is a gradual approach that protects and builds on the company's administrative heritage plus flexible, central and local management capabilities.

The second chapter in this part, by Barney, "Firm resources and sustained competitive advantage", has been extremely influential in the field of international business, competitive advantage and strategic management. The main purpose of this chapter is to understand the sources of competitive advantage. It assumes strategic resources are heterogeneously distributed among firms and that these influence the competitive advantage over time. The resources discussed are value, rareness, inimitability and sustainability.

Barney's analysis is based on two assumptions: resources possessed by firms in an industry are heterogeneous, and these resources are not perfectly mobile across firms and thus provide a sustainable competitive advantage. Firm resources are defined as assets, capabilities, processes, attributes and knowledge controlled by the firm. But even more important are the conditions under which resources can be a source of sustained competitive advantage. This is defined as value-creating strategy that is different from other current and potential competitors. This becomes a sustainable competitive advantage when the value-creating strategy is inimitable or the competitors are unable to duplicate the benefits of that strategy.

Sustainable competitive advantage may not last forever but it is not duplicated by the competition. Changes in the environment or industry (Schumpeterian shock) may make the crucial resource that helped the firm to achieve sustainable competitive advantage lose its value and cannot be a source of advantage anymore. It is also made clear that firms cannot purchase such competitive advantage as it resides in rare and imperfectly imitable resources controlled by the firm.

The next chapter in this section, by Inkpen and Beamish, "Knowledge, bargaining power, and the instability of International Joint Ventures", has been very influential as it tackled the instability and high rate of failure of International Joint Venture (IJVs). It investigates the underlying reasons for this instability. The instability is defined as a major unexpected change from one or both parties points of view, that causes changes in bargaining power and dependencies between partners.

Several studies have found that the failure rate in IJVs is close to 50%. The type of IJVs discussed in the study are where a foreign partner seeks a presence in a country through Foreign Direct Investment (FDI), where a foreign partner normally contributes technology, management expertise and global support, while the local partner contributes local knowledge through which instability may be controlled, in addition to capital from both sides.

The authors are looking into the factors that are endogenous to IJVs and may cause instability. They claim a shift in a partner's bargaining power will eliminate the partner dependency and make the IJV bargain obsolete. This may be caused by unplanned equity changes or major re-organization and result in the termination of IJV. Based on this view and bargaining and dependence perspectives, authors present a framework to explain how this influences instability in IJVs. To explain how the model works, they present seven propositions explaining in what conditions a partner may wish to gain control or create instability.

They conclude that because many firms enter IJVs to gain knowledge, when knowledge acquisition shifts the bargaining power between partners, the cooperative basis for the cooperation erodes causing venture instability. They claim that this risk is higher in IJVs than in local or domestic joint ventures, as IJVs are built on the premise that the foreign partner wants to benefit from local partners' knowledge of local economic, political and cultural environment. Once that foreign partner has acquired this knowledge there is a greater chance of IJV instability, as the rationale for cooperation disappears.

The final chapter in this part, by Yeniyurt, Townsend, Cavusgil and Ghauri, "Mimetic and experiential effects in international marketing alliance formations of US pharmaceuticals firms: an event history analysis", argues that alliances are an indispensible tool for managers operating in global business environments, particularly for the internationalization process. It investigates the mimetic and experiential effects in international alliance formation. The novelty in this study is that it particularly looks at how mimetic behaviour and previous alliance experience mitigate uncertainty in international strategic alliances.

A co-evolutionary framework is presented to explain the alliance formation phenomenon and the process. The reading deals with questions such as how the compatriot firms influence internationalization of the firm and international alliance formation. Is cultural experience important in cross-cultural alliance formation process?

International alliances are conceptualized as non-equity collaborative ventures between partners whose head offices are located in different countries. Authors combine firm behaviour and population-related dynamics and their interdependences. Three hypotheses are developed: first, on the relationship between density of international marketing alliances and new international strategic alliances; second, on the relationship between firms alliance experience and their propensity to enter into new international strategic alliances; third, on the experience of the firm in cross-cultural alliances and its propensity to enter into new international alliances.

These hypotheses are tested by an event history analysis on 792 international strategic alliances in pharmaceutical industry. The results confirm the co-evolutionary nature of international strategic alliances among firms. It also supports the assertion that previous alliance experience facilitates future alliances formation. Moreover, it confirms that cultural experience is significantly important in forming new cross-cultural alliances. However, size of the firm is positively related to new strategic alliances.

References

Bartlett, C.A. and Ghoshal, S. (1989), *Managing across borders*, Boston, Mass: Harvard Business School Press.

Bartlett, C.A. and Ghoshal, S. (1993), Beyond the M-Form: Towards a managerial theory of the firm, *Strategic Management Journal*, 14/1: 23–46.

Bartlett, C., Ghoshal, S. and Beamish, P. (2008), *Transnational management*, 5th edition, New York: McGraw-Hill.

Buckley, P.J. and Casson, M.C. (1998), Models of multinational enterprises, *Journal of International Business Studies*, 29/1: 21–44.

Buckley, P.J. and Ghauri, P.N. (2004), Globalization, economic geography and strategy of multinational enterprise, *Journal of International Business Studies*, 35/2: 81–98.

Cavusgil, T., Ghauri, P. and Akcal, A. (2013), *Doing business in emerging markets*, 2nd edition, London: Sage.

De Wit, B. and Meyer, B. (2004), *Strategy: Process, Content, Context*, London: Thomson.

Dunning, J. (2009), Location and multinational enterprise: A neglected factor, *Journal of International Business Studies*, 40/1: 5–19.

Elg, U., Ghauri, P.N. and Tarnovskaya, V. (2008), 'The role of networks and matching in market entry to emerging retail markets', *International Marketing Review*, 25/6: 674–99.

Ghauri, P.N. (1992), New structures in MNCs based in small countries: A network approach, *European Management Journal*, 10/3: 357–64.

Ghauri, P. and Cateora, P. (2014), *International marketing*, 4th edition, London: McGraw-Hill.

Hennart, J.-F. (1982), *A theory of multinational enterprise*, Ann Arbor: University of Michigan Press.

Hill., C. (2012), *International business: Competing in the global marketplace*, Global Edition, McGraw-Hill.

Johanson, J. and Vahlne, J.-E. (1977), The internationalization process of the firms: A model of knowledge development and increasing foreign market commitments. *Journal of International Business Studies*, 8/1: 23–32.

Kogut, B. (1985), Designing global strategies: Profiting from operational flexibility, *Sloan Management Review*, 26: 27–38.

14 Organizing for worldwide effectiveness

The transnational solution*

Christopher A. Bartlett and Sumantra Ghoshal

The enormous success of Japanese companies that burst onto the international competitive arena in the 1960s and 1970s has triggered a barrage of analysis and advice in the Western business press. Most of this analysis has highlighted the convergence of consumer preferences worldwide, the impact of changing technologies and scale economies on international industry structures, and the emergence of increasingly sophisticated competitive strategies that have led to a rapid process of globalization in a large number of worldwide businesses.[1]

As Western companies have searched for the source of the newcomers' incredible ability to sell everything from automobiles to zippers, one conclusion has gained increasing credibility: companies that are unable to gain firm strategic control of their worldwide operations and manage them in a globally coordinated manner will not succeed in the emerging international economy. There are few senior managers in the West who are unaffected by the implications of this message.

The concerns of top managers in Japan have been quite different and have focused on the forces of localization that have also been gathering strength in the recent past. Like their Western counterparts, they have been sensitized, not only by their own experiences, but also by stories in the Japanese business press, which have focused on the growing barriers to trade and, most recently, the impact of a strengthening yen in offsetting the efficiencies of global-scale Japanese plants. These managers are much more sensitive to the flip side of globalization: the growing demand of host governments for local investments, the building resistance of consumers to standardized homogenized global products and the changing economics of emerging flexible manufacturing technologies that are making smaller-scale production and more tailored products feasible.

In the course of a study of some of the world's leading Japanese, European and American multinationals, we found that these globalizing and localizing forces are working simultaneously to transform many industries.[2] But for historical reasons, few companies have built the organizational capabilities to respond equally to both of these forces.

Many of the European- and American-based companies had well-established networks of fairly independent and self-sufficient national subsidiaries; 'decentralized federations' we call them. Those with such organizations had little difficulty in responding to the increased demands from their host governments or adapting to shifts in consumer preferences worldwide and their strategic posture was often literally multinational: multiple national positions,

*Bartlett, C. A. & S. Ghoshal (1999) "Organizing for worldwide effectiveness: the transnational solution", The University of California Press.

each highly sensitive to its local market. The problem with this strategy and the organizational structure that supported it was difficult to coordinate and control worldwide operations in order to respond to the global forces.

Most of the Japanese companies we studied had the opposite problem. Their operations tended to be concentrated in the home country – we term them 'centralized hubs' – and this gave them the ability to capture the opportunities presented by the global forces. Indeed, the strategic posture of these companies was literally global – the world was considered an integrated whole. Such an approach made these companies less successful in building worldwide operating units that were sensitive and responsive to the countervailing forces of localization.[3]

The constraint of a company's heritage

As the international operating environment became more complex over the past decade or so, the great temptation for companies was to try to imitate the organizational characteristics and strategic postures of their competitors. For example, in the United States, multinational managers are being advised to 'rein in far-flung autonomous subsidiaries, produce standardized global products, and pull decision-making power back to the home office', with the reminder that 'this is a formula that, not coincidentally, many Japanese companies have used for years'.[4]

But the appropriate response to the developing international demands cannot be captured in a formula, certainly not one that is imitative of companies in totally different situations. The problem is that while a company's tasks are shaped by its external environment, its ability to perform those tasks is constrained by what we term its 'administrative heritage', the company's existing configuration of assets, its traditional distribution of responsibility and its historical norms, values and management style.[5] This internal organizational capability is something that cannot be changed overnight or by decree, and one of the important lessons for management is to shift its attention from a search for the ideal organization structure to a quest for ways in which to build and leverage the company's existing capabilities to make them more responsive to the ever-changing external demands.

That is not to deny that there are lessons to be learned from other companies, indeed, our research indicates quite the opposite. However, the important lesson is that either blind imitation simply to eliminate obvious differences or wholesale adoption of another company's organizational approach or strategic posture is likely to end in failure. In the first part of this chapter, we distil some of the important transferable lessons that *can* be learned from companies that manage global coordination effectively and from those that have been most successful in developing and managing a responsive and flexible localized approach. Although the lessons are drawn from a broader study, we will emphasize the importance of a company's administrative heritage by comparing and contrasting the approaches of two leading consumer electronics companies and suggesting ways in which they can learn from each other.

But while such lessons are helpful, they do not provide the full solution. Today's operating environment in many worldwide businesses demands more than efficient central management and flexible local operations; it requires companies to link their diverse organizational perspectives and resources in a way that would allow them to leverage their capabilities for achieving global coordination and national flexibility simultaneously. In response to this need, a few companies have evolved beyond the simpler multinational or global approach to international business and developed what we term a *transnational* capability; an ability to manage across boundaries.[6] In the final part of this chapter, we will describe some of the characteristics of such an organization, and will suggest some steps that can be taken to build these capabilities.

Making central management flexible: lessons from Matsushita

For companies that expanded internationally by establishing fairly independent and self-sufficient subsidiary companies around the world, the task of imposing some kind of global direction or achieving some measure of coordination of activity is often a Herculean challenge. The problem that has confronted successive generations of top management at Philips is typical. The Dutch-based electronics giant has built a justifiable reputation as one of the world's most innovative companies, yet has continually been frustrated in its attempt to deliver its brilliant inventions to the world's markets. The recent failure of its VCR system is a classic example.

Despite the fact that it was generally acknowledged to be technologically superior to the competitive VHS and Beta formats, the Philips V2000 system failed because the company was unable to commercialize it. Within the company there is no shortage of theories to explain the failure: some suggest that those who developed the product and its competitive strategy were too distant from the market; others feel the barriers between research, development, manufacturing and marketing led to delays and cost over-runs; others point to the fact that worldwide subsidiaries were uninvolved in the project and therefore uncommitted to its success. All these explanations reflect organizational difficulties and have some element of truth.

On the other hand, Matsushita Electric Company, Philips archrival in consumer electronics, has built the global leadership position of its well-known Panasonic and National brands on its ability to control its global strategy from the center in Japan yet it has been able to implement it in a flexible and responsive manner throughout its worldwide operations. As we tried to identify the organizational mechanisms that were key to Matsushita's ability to provide strong central direction and control without becoming inflexible or isolated, three factors stood out as the most important explanations of its outstanding success:

- gaining the input of subsidiaries into its management processes;
- ensuring that development efforts were linked to market needs; and
- managing responsibility transfers from development to manufacturing to marketing.

By examining how these core mechanisms work in Matsushita, managers in other companies may see ways in which they can gain more global coordination without compromising local market sensitivity.

Gaining subsidiary input: multiple linkages

The two most important problems facing a centrally-managed multinational company are that those developing the new product or strategy may not understand market needs or that those required to implement the new direction are not committed to it. Matsushita managers are very conscious of these problems and spend much time building multiple linkages between headquarters and overseas subsidiaries to minimize their impacts. These linkages are designed not only to give headquarters managers a better understanding of country level needs and opportunities, but also to give subsidiary managers greater access to and involvement in headquarters decision-making processes.

Matsushita recognizes the importance of market sensing as a stimulus to innovation and does not want its centrally-driven management process to reduce its environmental sensitivity. Rather than trying to limit the number of linkages between headquarters and subsidiaries or to focus them through a single point (as many companies do for the sake of efficiency), Matsushita tries to preserve the different perspectives, priorities and even prejudices of its diverse groups worldwide, and tries to ensure that they have linkages to those in the headquarters who can represent and defend their views.

The organizational systems and processes that connect different parts of the Matsushita organization in Japan with the video department of MESA, the U.S. Subsidiary of the company, illustrate these multifaceted interlinkages. The vice president in charge of this department has his career roots in Matsushita Electric Trading Company (METC), the organization with overall responsibility for Matsushita's overseas business. Although formally posted to the United States, he continues to be a member of the senior management committee of METC and spends about a third of his time in Japan. This allows him to be a full member of METC's top management team that approves the overall strategy for the U.S. market. In his role as the VP of MESA, he ensures that the local operation effectively implements the agreed video strategy.

At the next level, the general manager of MESA's video department is a company veteran who had worked for 14 years in the video product division of Matsushita Electric, the central production and domestic marketing company in Japan. He maintains strong connections with the parent company's product division and is its link to the local American market. Two levels below him, the assistant product manager in the video department (one of the more junior-level expatriates in the American organization) links the local organization to the central VCR factory in Japan. Having spent five years in the factory, he acts as the local representative of the factory and handles all day-to-day communication with factory personnel.

None of these linkages are accidental. They are deliberately created and maintained and they reflect the company's open acknowledgement that the parent company is not one homogeneous entity, but a collectivity of different constituencies and interests, each of which is legitimate and necessary. Together, these multiple linkages enhance the subsidiary's ability to influence key headquarters decisions relating to its market, particularly decisions about product specifications and design. The multiple links not only allow local management to reflect its local market needs, they also give headquarters managers the ability to coordinate and control implementation of their strategies and plans.

Linking direction to needs: market mechanisms

Matsushita's efforts to ensure that its products and strategies are linked to market needs does not stop at the input stage. The company has created an integrative process that ensures that the top managers and central staff groups are not sheltered from the pressures, constraints, and demands felt by managers on the front line of the operations. One of the key elements in achieving this difficult organizational task is the company's willingness to employ 'market mechanisms' for directing and regulating the activities located at the center. Because the system is unique, we will describe some of its major characteristics.

Research projects undertaken by the Central Research Laboratories (CRL) of Matsushita fall into two broad groups. The first group consists of 'company total projects' which involve developing technologies important for Matsushita's long-term strategic position and that may be applicable across many different product divisions. Such projects are decided jointly by the research laboratories, the product divisions, and top management of the company and are funded directly by the corporate board. The second group of CRL research projects consists of relatively smaller projects which are relevant to the activities of particular product divisions. The budget for such research activities, approximately half of the company's total research budget, is allocated not to the research laboratories but to the product divisions. This creates an interesting situation in which technology-driven and market-led ideas can compete for attention.

Each year, the product divisions suggest research projects that they would like to sponsor and which would incorporate their knowledge of worldwide market needs developed through their routine multiple linkages to subsidiaries. At the same time, the various research laboratories hold annual internal exhibitions and meetings and also write proposals to highlight research projects that they would like to undertake. The engineering and development groups of the product divisions mediate the subsequent contracting and negotiation process through which the expertise and interests of the laboratories and the needs of the product divisions are finally matched. Specific projects are sponsored by the divisions and are allocated to the laboratories or research groups of their choice, along with requisite funds and other resources.

The system creates intense competition for projects (and the budgets that go with them) among the research groups, and it is this mechanism that forces researchers to keep a close market orientation. At the same time, the product divisions are conscious that it is their money that is being spent on product development and they become less inclined to make unreasonable or uneconomical demands on R&D.[7]

The market mechanism also works to determine annual product styling and features. Each year the company holds what it calls merchandising meetings, which are, in effect, large internal trade shows. Senior marketing managers from Matsushita's sales companies worldwide visit their supplying divisions and see on display the proposed product lines for the new model year. Relying on their understanding of their individual markets, these managers pick and choose among proposed models, order specific modifications for their local markets, or simply refuse to take products they feel are unsuitable. Individual products or even entire lines might have to be redesigned as a result of input from the hundreds of managers at the merchandising meeting.

Managing responsibility transfer: personnel flows

Within a national subsidiary, the task of transferring responsibility from research to manufacturing and finally marketing is facilitated by the smaller size and closer proximity of the units responsible for each stage of activity. This is not so where larger central units usually take the lead role, Matsushita has built some creative means for managing these transitions. The systems rely heavily on the transfer of people, as is illustrated by the company's management of new product development.

First, careers of research engineers are structured so as to ensure that most of them spend five to eight years in the central research laboratories engaged in pure research, then they spend another five years in the product divisions in applied product and process development, and finally they spend the rest of their working lives in a direct operational function, usually production processes, where they take up line management positions. More importantly, each engineer usually makes the transition from one department to the next along with the transfer of the major project on which he has been working.

The research project that began Matsushita's development of its enormously successful VCR product was launched in the late 1950s under the leadership of Dr Hiroshi Sugaya, a young physicist in the company's Central Research Laboratory. As the product evolved into its development stage, the core members of Dr Sugaya's team were kept together as they transferred from CRL to the product development and applications laboratory located in the product division. After a long and difficult development process, the product was finally ready for commercial production in 1977 and many of the team moved with the project out into the Okanyama plant.[8]

In other companies we surveyed, it was not uncommon for research engineers to move to development, but not with their projects, thereby depriving the companies of one of the most important and immediate benefits of such moves. We also saw no other examples of engineers routinely taking the next step of actually moving to the production function. This last step, however, is perhaps the most critical in integrating research and production both in terms of building a network that connects managers across these two functions and also for transferring a set of common values that facilitates implementation of central innovations.

Another mechanism that integrates production and research in Matsushita works in the opposite direction. Wherever possible, the company tries to identify the manager who will head the production task for a new product under development and makes him a full-time member of the research team from the initial stage of the development process. This system not only injects direct production expertise into the development team, but also facilitates transfer of the innovation once the design is completed. Matsushita also uses this mechanism as a way of transferring product expertise from headquarters to its worldwide sales subsidiaries. Although this is a common practice among many multinationals, in Matsushita it has additional significance because of the importance of internationalizing management as well as its products.

As with the multiple linkages and the internal market mechanisms, this organizational practice was a simple, yet powerful tool that seemed to be central to Matsushita's ability to make its centrally driven management processes flexible, sensitive, and responsive to the worldwide opportunities and needs. More importantly, these three organizational mechanisms are simple enough to be adopted, probably in some modified form, by other companies. They meet the needs of those trying to build an organization process that allows management at the center more influence and control over worldwide operations, without compromising the motivation or operating effectiveness of the national units.

Making local management effective: lessons from Philips

If Matsushita is the champion of efficient centrally coordinated management, its Netherlands-based competitor, Philips, is the master of building effective national operations worldwide. As surely as Philips' managers envy their Japanese rival's ability to develop products and strategies in Osaka that appear to be implemented effortlessly around the globe, their counterparts in Matsushita are extremely jealous of Philips' national organizations that are not only sensitive and responsive to their local environments, but are also highly innovative and entrepreneurial.

For example, the company's first color TV set was built and sold not in Europe, where the parent company is located, but in Canada, where the market had closely followed the U.S. lead in introducing color transmission; Philips' first stereo color TV set was developed by the Australian subsidiary; teletext TV sets were created by its British subsidiary; 'smart cards' by its French subsidiary; a programmed word processing typewriter by North American Philips; the list of local innovations and entrepreneurial initiatives in the company is endless.

While Matsushita has had no difficulty in establishing effective sales organizations and assembly operations around the world, top management has often been frustrated that its overseas subsidiaries do not exhibit more initiative and entrepreneurial spark. Despite pleas to its overseas management to become more self-sufficient and less dependent on headquarters for direction, the company has found that the decentralization of assets that accompanies its 'localization' program has not always triggered the kind of independence and initiative that had been hoped for.

Out of the many factors that drive Philips' international organization, we were able to identify three that not only appear central to the development and maintenance of its effective local management system, but also may be adaptable to other organizations that are trying to promote national innovativeness and responsiveness within a globally integrated organization:

- Philips' use of a cadre of entrepreneurial expatriates;
- an organization that forces tight functional integration within a subsidiary; and
- a dispersion of responsibilities along with the decentralized assets.

A cadre of entrepreneurial expatriates

Expatriate positions, particularly in the larger subsidiaries, have been very attractive for Philips' managers for several reasons. With only 7% or 8% of its total sales coming from Holland, many different national subsidiaries of the company have contributed much larger shares of total revenues than the parent company. As a result, foreign operations have enjoyed relatively high organizational status compared to most companies of similar size with headquarters in the United States, Japan, or even the larger countries in Europe. Because of the importance of its foreign operations, Philips' formal management development system has always required considerable international experience as a prerequisite for top corporate positions. Eindhoven, the small rural town in which the corporate headquarters is located, is far from the sophisticated and cosmopolitan world centers that host many of its foreign subsidiaries. After living in London, New York, Sydney, or Paris, many managers find it hard to return to Eindhoven.

Collectively, all these factors have led to the best and the brightest of Philips' managers spending much of their careers in different national operations. This cadre of entrepreneurial expatriate managers has been an important agent in developing capabilities of local units, yet keeping them linked to the parent company's overall objectives. Further, unlike Matsushita where an expatriate manager typically spends a tour of duty of three to six years in a particular national subsidiary and then returns to the headquarters, expatriate managers in Philips spend a large part of their careers abroad continuously working for two to three years each in a number of different subsidiaries.

This difference in the career systems results in very different attitudes. In Philips, the expatriate managers follow each other into assignments and build close relations among themselves. They tend to identify strongly with the national organization's point of view, and this shared identity makes them part of a distinct subculture within the company. In companies such as Matsushita, there is very little interaction among the expatriate managers in the different subsidiaries, most tend to see themselves as part of the parent company temporarily on assignment in a foreign country.

One result of these differences is that expatriate managers in Matsushita are far more likely to take a custodial approach which resists any local changes to standard products and policies. In contrast, expatriate managers in Philips, despite being just as socialized into the overall corporate culture of the company, are much more willing to be advocates of local views and to defend against the imposition of inappropriate corporate ideas on national organizations. This willingness to 'rock the boat' and openness to experimentation and change is the fuel that ignites local initiative and entrepreneurship.[9]

Further, by creating this kind of environment in the national organization, Philips has had little difficulty in attracting very capable local management. In contrast to the experience in many Japanese companies where local managers have felt excluded from a decision-making process that centers around headquarters management and the local expatriates only, local managers in Philips feel their ideas are listened to and defended in headquarters.[10] This too, creates a supportive environment for local innovation and creativity.

Integration of technical and marketing functions within each subsidiary

Historically, the top management in all Philips' national subsidiaries consisted not of an individual CEO but a committee made up of the heads of the technical, commercial, and finance functions. This system of three-headed management had a long history in Philips, stemming from the functional backgrounds of the founding Philips brothers, one an engineer and the other a salesman. Although this management philosophy has recently been modified to a system which emphasizes individual authority and accountability, the long tradition of shared responsibilities and joint decision-making has left a legacy of many different mechanisms for functional integration at multiple levels. These integrative mechanisms within each subsidiary in Philips enhance the efficiency and effectiveness of local decision-making and action in the same way that various means of cross-functional integration within Matsushita's corporate headquarters facilitates its central management processes.

In most subsidiaries, integration mechanisms exist at three organizational levels. First, for each product, there is an article team that consists of relatively junior managers belonging to the commercial and technical functions. This team evolves product policies and prepares annual sales plans and budgets. At times, subarticle teams may be formed to supervise day-to-day working and to carry out special projects, such as preparing capital investment plans, should major new investments be felt necessary for effectively manufacturing and marketing a new product.

A second tier of cross-functional coordination takes place at the product group level, through the group management team, which again consists of both technical and commercial representatives. This team meets monthly to review results, suggest corrective actions and resolve any interfunctional differences. Keeping control and conflict resolution at this low level facilitates sensitive and rapid responses to initiatives and ideas generated at the local level.

The highest level coordination forum within the subsidiary is the senior management committee (SMC) consisting of the top commercial, technical, and financial managers in the subsidiary. Acting essentially as a local board, the SMC provides an overall unity of effort among the different functional groups within the local unit, and assures that the national unit retains primary responsibility for its own strategies and priorities. Again, the effect is to provide local management with a forum in which actions can be decided and issues resolved without escalation for approval or arbitration.

Decentralized authority and dispersed responsibility

While Matsushita's localization program was triggered by political pressures to increase local value added in various host countries, the company had also hoped that the decentralization of assets would help its overseas units achieve a greater measure of local responsiveness, self-sufficiency and initiative. To management's frustration, such changes were slow in coming.

Philips, on the other hand, had created such national organizations seemingly without effort. The difference lay in the degree to which responsibility and authority were dispersed along with the assets. Expanding internationally in the earliest decades of the century, Philips managers were confronted by transport and communications barriers that forced them to delegate substantial local autonomy to its decentralized operating units. The need for local units to develop a sense of self-sufficiency was reinforced by the protectionist pressures of the 1930s that made cross-shipments of products or components practically impossible. During World War II, even R&D capability was dispersed to prevent it from falling into enemy hands and the departure of many corporate managers from Holland reduced parent company's control over its national operations abroad.

In the postwar boom, while corporate managers focused on rebuilding the war-ravaged home operations, managers in foreign units were able to capitalize on their well-developed autonomy. Most applied their local resources and capabilities to build highly successful national businesses, sensitive and responsive to the local needs and opportunities. In doing so, they achieved a degree of local entrepreneurship and self-sufficiency rare among companies of Philips' size and complexity.

Although it would be impossible for another company to replicate the historical events that resulted in this valuable organizational capability, the main characteristics of their development are clear. First, it must be feasible for offshore units to develop local capabilities and initiative, this requires the decentralization of appropriate managerial and technological resources along with the reconfiguration of physical assets.

While this is necessary, it is not sufficient, Matsushita and many other companies have begun to recognize. Local initiatives and entrepreneurial action must not only be feasible, they must also be desirable for local managers. This requires the legitimate delegation of responsibilities and authority that not only gives them control over the decentralized resources, but rewards them for using them to develop creative and innovative solutions to their problems.[11] Only when the decentralization of assets is accompanied by a dispersion of responsibilities can local management develop into a legitimate corporate contributor rather than simple implementers of central direction.

Building transnational capabilities: lessons from L.M. Ericsson

In multinational corporations, the location of an opportunity (or threat) is often different from where the company's appropriate response resources are situated. This is so because environmental opportunities and threats are footloose, shifting from location to location, while organizational resources, contrary to the assumptions of many economists, are not easily transferable even within the same company. The location of a company's strategic resources – plants and research centers are good examples – is related not only to actual organizational needs and intentions, but also to the idiosyncrasies of the firm's administrative history. The result is a situation of environment–resource mismatches: the organization has excessive resources in environments that are relatively noncritical, and very limited or even no resources in critical markets that offer the greatest opportunities and challenges.

Such environment–resource mismatches are pervasive in MNCs. For many historical reasons, Ericsson has significant technological and managerial capabilities in Australia and Italy, even though these markets are relatively unimportant in the global telecommunications business. At the same time, the company has almost no presence in the United States, which not only represents almost 40% of world telecommunications demand but is also the source of much of the new technology. Procter & Gamble is strong in the United States and Europe, but not in Japan where important consumer product innovations have occurred recently and where a major global competitor is emerging. Matsushita has appropriate technological and managerial resources in Japan and the U.S., but not in Europe, a huge market and home of archrival Philips.

Rectifying these imbalances in the configuration of their organization resources is taking these companies a long time; since the relative importance of different environments will continue to change, the problem will never be fully overcome. The need, therefore, is not simply to make adjustments to the geographic configuration or resources, but also to create organizational systems that allow the spare capacity and slack resources in strong operating units to be redirected to environments in which they are weak.

Simply creating effective central and local management does not solve this mismatch problem, and to succeed in today's demanding international environment, companies must develop their organizational capabilities beyond the stages described in the first part of this article. The limitation of companies with the most well-developed local and central article. The limitation of companies with even the most well-developed local and central capabilities is that the location of resources also tends to determine the locus of control over those resources, whether organizationally mandated or not, local management develops strong influence on how resources available locally are to be used. Further, organizational commitments are usually hierarchical, with local needs taking precedence over global needs. Consequently, at the core of resolving the problem of environment–resource mismatches is the major organizational challenge of loosening the bonds between ownership and control of resources within the company.

Among the companies we studied, there were several that were in the process of developing such organizational capabilities. They had surpassed the classic capabilities of the *multinational* company that operates as a decentralized federation of units able to sense and respond to diverse international needs and opportunities; and they had evolved beyond the abilities of the *global* company with its facility for managing operations on a tightly controlled worldwide basis through its centralized hub structure. They had developed what we termed *transnational* capabilities: the ability to manage across national boundaries, retaining local flexibility while achieving global integration. More than anything else this involved the ability to link local operations to each other and to the center in a flexible way, and in so doing, to leverage those local and central capabilities.

Ericsson the Swedish telecommunications company, was among those that had become most effective in managing the required linkages and processes, and we were able to identify three organizational characteristics that seemed most helpful in facilitating its developing transnational management capabilities.

- an interdependence of resources and responsibilities among organizational units;
- a set of strong cross-unit integrating devices, and
- a strong corporate identification and a well-developed worldwide management perspective.

Interdependence of resources and responsibilities

Perhaps the most important requirement of the transnational organizational is a need for the organizational configuration to be based on a principle of reciprocal dependence among units. Such as interdependence of resources and responsibilities breaks down the hierarchy between local and global interests by making the sharing of resources, idea and opportunities a self-enforcing norm. To illustrate how such a basic characteristic of organizational configuration can influence a company's management of capabilities, let us contrast the way in which

ITT, NEC and Ericsson developed the electronic digital switch that would be the core product for each company's telecommunications business in the 1980s and beyond.

From its beginnings in 1920 as a Puerto Rican telephone company, ITT built its worldwide operation on an objective described in the 1924 annual report as being 'to develop truly national systems operated by the nationals of each company'. For half a century ITT's national 'systems houses' as they were called within the company, committed themselves to integrating into their local environments and becoming attuned to national interests and market needs. All but the smallest systems houses were established as fully integrated, self-sufficient units with responsibility for developing, manufacturing, marketing, installing and servicing their own products.

With the emergence of the new digital electronic technology in the 1970s, however, this highly successful strategic posture was threatened by the huge cost of developing a digital switch. Some single systems house would be able to muster the required technological and financial resources on its own or recoup the investment from its market, the obvious solution was for ITT to make the System 12 digital switch project a corporate responsibility. Given their decade of operating independence, the powerful country unit managers were unwilling to yield the task developing the new switch to the corporate R&D group, indeed, little expertise had been gathered at the center to undertake such a task.

By exercising their considerable influence, the European systems houses were able to capture the strategic initiative on System 12, but then began disagreeing about who should take what role in this vital project. Many of the large systems houses simply refused to rely on others for the development of critical parts of the system; others rejected standards that did not fit with their view of local needs. As a result, duplication of efforts and divergence of specifications began to emerge and the cost of developing the switch ballooned to over $1 billion.

The biggest problems appeared when the company decided to enter the battle for a share of the deregulated U.S. market. Asserting its independence, the U.S. business launched a major new R&D effort, despite appeals from the chief technological officer that they risked developing what he skeptically termed 'System 13'. After further years of effort and additional hundreds of millions of dollars in costs, ITT acknowledged in 1986 it was withdrawing from the U.S. central switching market. The largest and most successful international telecommunications company in the world was blocked from its home country by the inability to transfer and apply its leading edge technology in a timely fashion. It was a failure that eventually led to ITT's sale of its European operations and its gradual withdrawal from direct involvement in telecommunications worldwide.

Its effective global innovation was blocked by the extreme independence of the organizational units in ITT, it was impeded in NEC by the strong dependence of national subsidiaries on the parent company. The first person in NEC to detect the trend toward digital switching was the Japanese manager in charge of the company's small U.S. operation. However, his role was one of selling corporate products and developing a beachhead for the company in the U.S. market. Because of this role, he had a hard time convincing technical managers in Japan of a supposed trend to digitalization that they saw nowhere else in the world.

When the U.S. managers finally were able to elicit sufficient support, the new NEAC 61 digital switch was developed almost entirely by headquarters personnel. Even in deciding which features to design into the new product, the central engineering group tended to discount the requests of the North American sales company and rely on data gathered in their own staff's field trips to U.S. customers. Although the NEAC 61 was regarded as having good hardware, customers felt its software was unadapted to U.S. needs. Sales did not meet expectations.

Both ITT and NEC recognized the limitations of their independent and dependent organizations systems and worked hard to adapt them. But the process of building organizational interdependence is a slow and difficult one that must be constantly monitored and adjusted. In our sample of companies, Ericsson seemed to be the most consistent and experienced practitioner of creating and managing a delicate balance of interunit interdependency. The way in which it did so suggests the value of a constant readjustment of responsibilities and relationships as a way of adapting to changing strategic needs while maintaining a dynamic system of mutual dependence.

Like ITT: in the 1920s and 1930s, Ericsson had built a substantial worldwide network of operations sensitive and responsive to local national environments, but like NEC, it had a strong home market base and a parent company with technological, manufacturing and marketing capability to support those companies. Keeping the balance among those units has required constant adjustment of organizational responsibilities and relationships.

In the late 1930s, management became concerned that the growing independence of its offshore companies was causing divergence in technology, duplication of effort and inefficiency in the sourcing patterns. To remedy the problem they pulled sales and distribution control to headquarters and began consolidating responsibilities under product divisions. As worldwide control improved, the divisions eventually began to show signs of isolation and short-term focus. In the early 1950s the corporate staff functions were given more of a leadership role. It was in this period that the central R&D group developed a crossbar switch that became an industry leader. As the product design and manufacturing technology for this product became well-understood and fully documented, Ericsson management was able to respond to the increasing demands of host governments to transfer more manufacturing capacity and technological know-how abroad. Once again, the role of the offshore subsidiaries increased.

This half a century of constant ebb and flow in the roles and responsibilities of various geographic, product and functional groups allowed Ericsson to build an organization in which all these diverse perspectives were seen as legitimate and the multiple capabilities were kept viable. This multidimensional organization gave the company the ability to quickly sense and respond to the coming of electronic switching in the 1970s. Once it had prevented the emergence of strong dependent or independent relationships, product development efforts and manufacturing responsibilities could be pulled back to Sweden without great difficulty. Where national capabilities, expertise, or experience could be useful in the corporate effort, the appropriate local personal were seconded to headquarters. Having established overall strategic and operational control of the digital switching strategy, corporate management at Ericsson was then willing to delegate substantial design, development and manufacturing responsibilities to its internal subsidiaries, resulting in a reinforcement of the interdependence of worldwide operations.

Sourcing of products and components from specialized plants have long provided a base on interdependence, but recently that has been extended to product development and marketing. For example, Italy is the company's center for global development of transmission system development, Finland has the leading role for mobile telephones and Australia develops the company's rural switch. Further, headquarters has given some of these units responsibility for handling certain export markets (for example, Italy's responsibility for developing markets in Africa). Increasingly, the company is moving even advanced core system software development offshore to subsidiary companies with access to more software engineers than it has in Stockholm.[12]

By changing responsibilities, shifting assets and modifying relationships in response to evolving environmental demands and strategic priorities, Ericsson has maintained a dynamic interdependence among its operating units that has allowed it to develop entrepreneurial and innovative subsidiary companies that work within a corporate framework defined by knowledgeable and creative headquarters product and functional groups. This kind of interdependence is the basis of a transnational company, one that can think globally and act locally.

Interunit integrating devices

Although the interdependence of resources and responsibilities provides a structural framework for the extensive use of interunit cooperation, there is a need for effective organizational integrating mechanisms to link operations in a way that taps the full potential of the interdependent configuration.

Compared to some companies in our study where relationships among national companies were competitive and where headquarter–subsidiary interactions were often of an adversarial nature, the organizational climate in Ericsson appeared more cooperative and collaborative. The establishment and maintenance of such attitudes was important since it allowed the company's diverse units to work together in a way that maximized the potential of their interdependent operations. We identified three important pillars to Ericsson's success in interunit integration:

- a clearly defined and tightly controlled set of operating systems;
- a people-linking process employing such devices as temporary assignments and joint teams; and
- interunit decision forums, particularly subsidiary boards, where views could be exchanged and differences resolved.

Ericsson management feels strongly that its most effective integrating device is strong central control over key elements of its strategic operation. Unlike ITT, Ericsson has not had strong or sophisticated administrative systems (it introduced strategic plans only in 1983), but its operating systems have long been structured to provide strong worldwide coordination. Knowing that local modifications would be necessary, the company designed its digital switch as a modular system with very clear specifications. National units could custom-tailor elements of the design to meet local needs without compromising the integrity of the total system design. Similarly, Ericsson's global computer-aided design and manufacturing system allowed the parent company to delegate responsibility for component production and even design without fear of losing the ability to control and coordinate the entire manufacturing system.

Rather than causing a centralization of decision-making, management argues that these strong yet flexible operating systems allow them to delegate much more freely, knowing that local decisions will not be inconsistent or detrimental to the overall interests. Rather than managing the decisions centrally, they point out they are managing the parameters of decisions that can be made by local units, thereby retaining the flexibility and entrepreneurship of those units.

But in addition to strong systems, interunit cooperation requires good interpersonal relations, Ericsson has developed these with a long-standing policy of transferring large numbers of people back and forth between headquarters and subsidiaries. It differs from the more common transfer patterns in both direction and intensity, as a comparison with NEC's transfer process will demonstrate. Where NEC may transfer a new technology through a few key managers. Ericsson will send a team of 50 or 100 engineers and managers from one unit to another for a year or two; while NEC's flow is primarily from headquarters to subsidiary, Ericsson's is a balanced two-way flow with people coming to the parent not only to learn, but also to bring their expertise; while NEC's transfers are predominantly Japanese, Ericsson's multidirectional process involves all nationalities.[13]

Australian technicians seconded to Stockholm in the mid-1970s to bring their experience with digital switching into the corporate development effort established enduring relationships that helped in the subsequent joint development of a rural switch in Australia a decade later. Confidences built when a 40-man Italian team spent 18 months in Sweden in the early 1970s to learn about electronic switching, provided the basis for the subsequent decentralization of AXE software development and the delegation of responsibility for developing the corporate transmission systems to the Italian company.

But any organization in which there are shared tasks and joint responsibilities will require additional decision-making and conflict-resolving forums. In Ericsson, often divergent objectives and interests of the parent company and the local subsidiary are exchanged in the national company's board meetings. Unlike many companies whose local boards are proforma bodies whose activities are designed solely to satisfy national legal requirements, Ericsson uses its local boards as legitimate forums for communicating objectives, resolving differences and making decisions. At least one, but often several senior corporate managers are members of each board and subsidiary board meetings become an important means for coordinating activities and channelling local ideas and innovations across national lines.

National competence, worldwide perspective

If there is one clear lesson from ITT's experience, it is that a company cannot manage globally if its managers identify primarily with local parochial interests and objectives. But as NEC has learned, when management has no ability to defend national perspectives and respond to local opportunities, penetration of world markets is equally difficult. One of the important organizational characteristics Ericsson has been able to develop over the years has been a management attitude that is simultaneously locally sensitive and globally conscious.

At the Stockholm headquarters, managers emphasize the importance of developing strong country operations, not only to capture sales that require responsiveness to national needs, but also to tap into the resources that are available through worldwide operation. Coming from a small home country where it already hires over a third of the graduate electrical and electronics engineers, Ericsson is very conscious of the need to develop skills and capture ideas wherever they operate in the world. But, at the same time, local managers see themselves as part of the worldwide Ericsson group rather than as independent autonomous units. Constant transfers and working on joint teams over the years has helped broaden many manager's perspectives from local to global, but giving local units systemwide mandates for products has confirmed their identity with the company's global operations. It is this ability for headquarters and subsidiary managers to view the issues from each other's perspective that distinguishes the company that can think globally yet act locally.

Conclusion: organizational capability is key

There are few companies that have not recognized the nature of the main strategic tasks facing them in today's complex international business environment. Philips' managers have understood for years that they need to build global scale, rationalize their diverse product lines and establish a more integrated worldwide strategy. While their counterparts at Matsushita have recently made localization a company watchword, this is just the culmination of years of effort to build more self-sufficient and responsive national subsidiaries which the company recognizes it will need to remain globally competitive. If changes have been slow in coming to both companies, it is not for the lack of strategic clarity about the need for change but for want of the organizational ability to implement the desired change.

In the course of our study, we found that managers engaged in a great deal of cross-company comparison of organizational capabilities; the managerial grass inevitably looked greener on the other side of the corporate fence. Philips' managers envied their Japanese competitors' ability to develop global products, manufacture them centrally and have them launched into markets worldwide on a time cycle that would be virtually impossible in their own organization. On the other hand, as Matsushita's managers face growing pressure from host governments worldwide, and as they feel the vulnerabilities of their central sourcing plants in an era of the strong yen, they view Philips' worldwide network of self-sufficient, well-connected and innovative national organizations as an asset they would dearly love to have. But the apparently small step from admiration to emulation of another company's strategic capabilities usually turns out to be a long and dangerous voyage.

What we suggest is that managers ignore battle cries calling for 'standardization, rationalization, and centralization' or any other such simplistic quick-fix formulas. What is needed is a more gradual approach that, rather than undermining a company's administrative heritage, protects and builds on it. Having built flexible central and local management capabilities, the next challenge is to link them in an organization that allows the company to do what it must to survive in today's international environment: think globally and act locally. For most worldwide companies it is the development of this transnational organizational capability that is key to long-term success.

Notes

1 See for example, Theodore Levitt, 'The Globalization of Markets,' *Harvard Business Review* (May/June 1983), pp. 92–102; Michael Porter, 'Changing patterns of International Competition,' *California Management Review* 28/2 (Winter 1986): 9–40: and Gary Harnel and C. K. Prahalad, 'Do You Really Have a Global Strategy,' *Harvard Business Review* (July/August 1985), pp. 139–48.
2 The research on which this article is based consisted of a three-year-long in-depth study of nine leading American, Japanese, and European multinational companies in three diverse industries. We interviewed over 235 managers in the headquarters and a number of different national subsidiaries of these companies to uncover how these companies with their diverse national backgrounds and international histories were adapting their organizational structures and management process to cope with the new strategic demands of their operating environments. The companies studied were Philips, Matsushita, and General Electric in the consumer electronics industry; Ericsson, NEC, and ITT in the telecommunications switching industry: and Unilever, Kao, and Procter & Gamble in the branded packaged products business. The complete findings of this study will be reported in our forthcoming book *Managing Across Borders: The Transnational Solution* to be published by the Harvard Business School Press.
3 For a more detailed explication of the decentralized federation and centralized hub forms of multinational organizations, see Christopher A. Bartlett. 'Building and Managing the Transnational: The New Organizational Challenge,' in Michael E. Porter, ed., *Competition in Global Industries* (Boston, MA: Harvard Business School Press, 1986).
4 'Rebuilding Corporate Empires – A New Global Formula,' *Newsweek*, April 14, 1986. p. 40.
5 The concept of administrative heritage is explained more fully in Christopher Bartlett (op. cit.) and also in Christopher Bartlett and Sumantra Ghoshal, 'Managing Across Borders: New Strategic Requirements,' *Sloan Management Review* (Summer 1987) pp. 7–17.

6 The organization we describe as the transnational has a long but discontinuous history in the international management literature. The concept of such an organizational form was manifest in Howard Perhnutter's celebrated paper. 'The Torturous Evolution of the Multinational Corporation,' *Columbia Journal of World Business* (January/February 1969). pp. 9–18. Similarly, C. K. Prahalad and Yves Doz's idea of a multifocal organization is described in *The Multinational Mission: Balancing Local Demands and Global Vision* (New York, NY: The Free Press, 1987); Gunnar Hedlund's definition of the heterarchy in 'The Hypermodern MNC: A Heterarchy,' *Human Resource Management* (Spring 1986), pp. 9–35; and Roderick White and Thomas Poyneter's description of the horizontal organization in 'Organizing for Worldwide Advantage,' presented at the seminar on management of the MNC at the European Institute for Advanced Studies in Management, Brussels, on June 9–10, 1987, are conceptually similar to what we describe as the transnational organization, though the models differ significantly in their details.

7 Westney and Sakakibara have observed a similar system of internal quasi-markets governing the interface between R&D and operating units in a number of Japanese computer companies. See Eleanor Westney and K. Sakakibara 'The Role of Japan-Based R&D in Global Technology Strategy,' *Technology in Society*, No. 7, (1985).

8 See Richard Rosenbloom and Michael Cusumano, 'Technological Pioneering and Competitive Advantage: Birth of the VCR Industry,' *California Management Review*, 29/4 (Summer 1987); 51–76, for a full description of this interesting development process.

9 See John Van Mannen and Edger H. Schein. 'Toward a Theory of Organizational Socialization,' in Barry Staw, ed., *Research in Organizational Behavior* (Greenwich, CT: JAJ Press, 1979) for a rich and theory-grounded discussion on how such differences in socialization processes and career systems can influence managers' attitudes towards change and innovation.

10 See Christopher Bartlett and Hideki Yoshihara 'New Challenges for Japanese Multinationals: Is Organizational Adaptation Their Achilles' Heel?' *Human Resource Management*, 27/1 (Spring 1988): 1–25, for a fuller discussion of some of the personnel management implications of managing local nationals in a classic centralized hub Japanese organization.

11 The need for both feasibility and desirability for facilitating innovativeness of organizations has been suggested by Lawrence Mohr, 'Determinants of Innovation in Organizations,' *American Political Science Review*, 63 (1969).

12 For a detailed discussion of how managers make such choices and how new responsibilities and relationship are developed, see Christopher Bartlett and Sumantra Ghoshal, 'Tap Your Subsidiaries for Global Reach,' *Harvard Business Review* (November/December 1986), pp. 87–94.

13 The effectiveness of personnel transfers as an integrative mechanism in multinational companies has been highlighted by many authors, most notably by E. Edstrom and J. R. Galbraith, 'Transfer of Managers as a Coordination and Control Strategy in Multinational Organizations,' *Administrative Science Quarterly* (June 1977).

15 Firm resources and sustained competitive advantage*

Jay Barney

Understanding sources of sustained competitive advantage for firms has become a major area of research in the field of strategic management (Porter, 1985; Rumelt, 1984). Since the 1960s, a single organizing framework has been used to structure much of this research (Andrews, 1971; Ansoff, 1965; Hofer & Schendel, 1978). This framework, summarized in Figure 15.1, suggests that firms obtain sustained competitive advantages by implementing strategies that exploit their internal strengths, through responding to environmental opportunities, while neutralizing external threats and avoiding internal weaknesses. Most research on sources of sustained competitive advantage has focused either on isolating a firm's opportunities and threats (Porter, 1980, 1985), describing its strengths and weaknesses (Hofer & Schendel, 1978; Penrose, 1958; Stinchcombe, 1965), or analyzing how these are matched to choose strategies.

Although internal analyses of organizational strengths and weaknesses and external analyses of opportunities and threats have received some attention in the literature, recent work has tended to focus primarily on analyzing a firm's opportunities and threats in its competitive environment (Lamb, 1984). As exemplified by research by Porter and his colleagues (Caves & Porter, 1977; Porter, 1980, 1985) this work has attempted to describe the environmental conditions that favor high levels of firm performance. Porter's (1980) "five forces model", for example, describes the attributes of an attractive industry and thus suggests that opportunities will be greater, and threats less, in these kinds of industries.

To help focus the analysis of the impact of a firm's environment on its competitive position, much of this type of strategic research has placed little emphasis on the impact of idiosyncratic firm attributes on a firm's competitive position (Porter, 1990). Implicitly, this work has adopted two simplifying assumptions. First, these environmental models of competitive advantage have assumed that firms within an industry (or firms within a strategic group) are identical in terms of the strategically relevant resources they control and the strategies they pursue (Porter, 1981; Rumelt, 1984; Scherer, 1980). Second, these models assume that should resource heterogeneity develop in an industry or group (perhaps through new entry), that this heterogeneity will be very short lived because the resources that firms use to implement their strategies are highly mobile (i.e., they can be bought and sold in factor markets) (Barney, 1986a; Hirshleifer, 1980).[1]

There is little doubt that these two assumptions have been very fruitful in clarifying our understanding of the impact of a firm's environment on performance. However, the

---

*Barney, J. (1991) "Firm resources and sustained competitive advantage", Journal of Management, 17: 99–120. Reprinted by permission of SAGE publications, Inc.

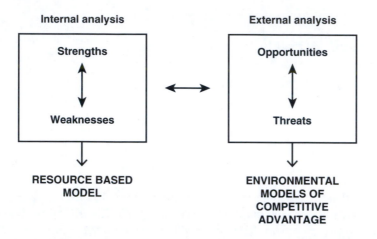

Figure 15.1 The relationship between traditional "strengths-weaknesses-opportunities-threats" analysis, the resource based model, and models of industry attractiveness.

resource-based view of competitive advantage, because it examines the link between a firm's internal characteristics and performance, obviously cannot build on these same assumptions. These assumptions effectively eliminate firm resource heterogeneity and immobility as possible sources of competitive advantage (Penrose, 1958; Rumelt, 1984; Wernerfelt, 1984, 1989). The resource-based view of the firm substitutes two alternate assumptions in analyzing sources of competitive advantage. First, this model assumes that firms within an industry (or group) may be heterogeneous with respect to the strategic resources they control. Second, it assumes that these resources may not be perfectly mobile across firms, and thus, heterogeneity can be long lasting. The resource-based model of the firm examines the implications of these two assumptions for the analysis of sources of sustained competitive advantage.

This chapter begins by defining some key terms, then examining the role of idiosyncratic, immobile firm resources in creating sustained competitive advantages. Next, a framework for evaluating whether or not particular firm resources can be sources of sustained competitive advantage is developed. As an example of how this framework might be applied, it is used in the analysis of the competitive implications of several resources that others have suggested might be sources of sustained competitive advantage. The chapter concludes by describing the relationship between this resource-based model of sustained competitive advantage and other business disciplines.

Defining key concepts

To avoid possible confusion, three concepts that are central to the perspective developed in this chapter are defined in this section. These concepts are firm resources, competitive advantage, and sustained competitive advantage.

Firm resources

In this chapter, *firm resources* include all assets, capabilities, organizational processes, firm attributes, information, knowledge, etc., controlled by a firm that enable the firm to conceive of and implement strategies that improve its efficiency and effectiveness (Daft, 1983). In the language of traditional strategic analysis, firm resources are strengths that firms can use to conceive of and implement their strategies (Learned et al., 1969; Porter, 1981).

A variety of authors have generated lists of firm attributes that may enable firms to conceive of and implement value-creating strategies (Hitt & Ireland, 1986; Thompson & Strickland, 1983). For purposes of this discussion, these numerous possible firm resources can be conveniently classified into three categories: physical capital resources (Williamson, 1975), human capital resources (Becker, 1964), and organizational capital resources (Tomer, 1987). Physical capital resources include the physical technology used in a firm, a firm's plant and equipment, its geographic location and its access to raw materials. Human capital resources include the training, experience, judgment, intelligence, relationships, and insight of *individual* managers and workers in a firm. Organizational capital resources include a firm's formal reporting structure, its formal and informal planning, controlling, and coordinating systems, as well as informal relations among groups within a firm and between a firm and those in its environment.

Of course, not all aspects of a firm's physical capital, human capital and organizational capital are strategically relevant resources. Some of these firm attributes may prevent a firm from conceiving of and implementing valuable strategies (Barney, 1986b). Others may lead a firm to conceive of and implement strategies that reduce its effectiveness and efficiency. Still others may have no impact on a firm's strategizing processes. However, those attributes of a firm's physical, human and organizational capital that do enable a firm to conceive of and implement strategies that improve its efficiency and effectiveness are, for purposes of this discussion, firm resources (Wernerfelt, 1984). The purpose of this article is to specify the conditions under which such firm resources can be a source of sustained competitive advantage for a firm.

Competitive advantage and sustained competitive advantage

In this article, a firm is said to have a *competitive advantage* when it is implementing a value-creating strategy not simultaneously being implemented by any current or potential competitors. A firm is said to have a *sustained competitive advantage* when it is implementing a value creating strategy not simultaneously being implemented by any current or potential competitors *and* when these other firms are unable to duplicate the benefits of this strategy. These two definitions require some discussion.

First, these definitions do not focus exclusively on a firm's competitive position vis-a-vis firms that are already operating in its industry. Rather, following Baumol et al. (1982), a firm's competition is assumed to include not only all of its current competitors, but also potential competitors poised to enter an industry at some future date. A firm that enjoys a competitive advantage or a sustained competitive advantage is implementing a strategy not simultaneously being implemented by any of its current or potential competitors (Barney et al., 1989).

Second, the definition of *sustained* competitive advantage adopted here does not depend upon the period of calendar time during which a firm enjoys a competitive advantage. Some authors have suggested that a sustained competitive advantage is simply a competitive advantage that lasts a long period of calendar time (Jacobsen, 1988; Porter, 1985). Although an understanding of how firms can make a competitive advantage last a longer period of calendar time is an important research issue, the concept of *sustained* competitive advantage used in this article does not refer to the period of calendar time that a firm enjoys a competitive advantage.

Rather, whether or not a competitive advantage is sustained depends upon the possibility of competitive duplication. Following Lippman and Rumelt (1982) and Rumelt (1984), a competitive advantage is sustained only if it continues to exist after efforts to duplicate that advantage have ceased. In this sense, this definition of sustained competitive advantage is an equilibrium definition (Hirshleifer, 1980).

Theoretically, this equilibrium definition of sustained competitive advantage has several advantages, not the least of which is that it avoids the difficult problem of specifying how much calendar time firms in different industries must possess competitive advantages in order for those advantages to be "sustained." Empirically, sustained competitive advantages may, on average, last a long period of calendar time. However, it is not this period of calendar time that defines the existence of a sustained competitive advantage, but the inability of current and potential competitors to duplicate that strategy that makes a competitive advantage sustained.

Finally, that a competitive advantage is sustained does not imply that it will "last forever." It only suggests that it will not be competed away through the duplication efforts of other firms. Unanticipated changes in the economic structure of an industry may make what was, at one time, a source of sustained competitive advantage, no longer valuable for a firm and not a source of any competitive advantage. These structural revolutions in an industry—called "Schumpeterian Shocks" by several authors (Barney, 1986c; Rumelt & Wensley, 1981; Schumpeter, 1934, 1950)—redefine which of a firm's attributes are resources and which are not. Some of these resources, in turn, may be sources of sustained competitive advantage in the newly defined industry structure (Barney, 1986c). However, what were resources in a previous industry setting may be weaknesses, or simply irrelevant, in a new industry setting. A firm enjoying a sustained competitive advantage may experience these major shifts in the structure of competition, and may see its competitive advantages nullified by such changes. However, a sustained competitive advantage is *not* nullified through competing firms duplicating the benefits of that competitive advantage.

Competition with homogeneous and perfectly mobile resources

Armed with these definitions, it is now possible to explore the impact of resource heterogeneity and immobility on sustained competitive advantage. This is done by examining the nature of competition when firm resources are *perfectly* homogeneous and mobile.

In this analysis, it is not being suggested that there are industries where the attributes of perfect homogeneity and mobility exist. Although this is ultimately an empirical question, it seems reasonable to expect that most industries will be characterized by at least some degree of resource heterogeneity and immobility (Barney & Hoskisson, 1989). Rather than making an assertion that firm resources are homogeneous and mobile, the purpose of this analysis is to examine the possibility of discovering sources of sustained competitive advantage under these conditions. Not surprisingly, it is argued that firms, in general, *cannot* expect to obtain sustained competitive advantages when strategic resources are evenly distributed across all competing firms and highly mobile. This conclusion suggests that the search for sources of sustained competitive advantage must focus on firm resource heterogeneity and immobility.

Resource homogeneity and mobility and sustained competitive advantage

Imagine an industry where firms possess exactly the same resources. This condition suggests that firms all have the same amount and kinds of strategically relevant physical, human, and organizational capital. Is there a strategy that could be conceived of and implemented by any one of these firms that could not also be conceived of and implemented by all other firms in this industry? The answer to this question must be no. The conception and implementation of strategies employs various firm resources (Barney, 1986a; Hatten & Hatten, 1987; Wernerfelt, 1984). That one firm in an industry populated by identical firms has the resources to conceive of and implement a strategy means that these other firms, because they possess the same resources, can also conceive of and implement this strategy. Because these firms all implement the same strategies, they all will improve their efficiency and effectiveness in the same way, and to the same extent. In this type of industry, it is not possible for firms to enjoy a sustained competitive advantage.

Resource homogeneity and mobility and first-mover advantages

One objection to this conclusion concerns so-called "first mover advantages" (Lieberman & Montgomery, 1988). In some circumstances, the first firm in an industry to implement a strategy can obtain a sustained competitive advantage over other firms. These firms may gain access to distribution channels, develop goodwill with customers, or develop a positive reputation, all before firms that implement their strategies later. First-moving firms may obtain a sustained competitive advantage.

However, upon reflection, it seems clear that if competing firms are *identical* in the resources they control, it is not possible for any one firm to obtain a competitive advantage from first moving. To be a first mover by implementing a strategy before any competing firms, a particular firm must have insights about the opportunities associated with implementing a strategy that are not possessed by other firms in the industry, or by potentially entering firms (Lieberman & Montgomery, 1988). This unique firm resource (information about an opportunity) makes it possible for the better informed firm to implement its strategy before others. However, by definition, there are no unique firm resources in this kind of industry. If one firm in this type of industry is able to conceive of and implement a strategy, then all other firms will also be able to conceive of and implement that strategy, and these strategies will be conceived of and implemented in parallel, as identical firms become aware of the same opportunities and exploit that opportunity in the same way.

It is not being suggested that there can never be first-mover advantages in industries. It is being suggested that in order for there to be a first-mover advantage, firms in an industry must be heterogeneous in terms of the resources they control.

Resource homogeneity and mobility and entry/mobility barriers

A second objection to the conclusion that sustained competitive advantages cannot exist when firm resources in an industry are perfectly homogeneous and mobile concerns the existence of "barriers to entry" (Bain, 1956), or more generally, "mobility barriers" (Caves & Porter, 1977). The argument here is that even if firms within an industry (group) are perfectly homogeneous, if there are strong entry or mobility barriers, these firms may be able to obtain a competitive advantage vis-a-vis firms that are not in their industry (group). This sustained competitive advantage will be reflected in above normal economic performance for those firms protected by the entry or mobility barrier (Porter, 1980).

However, from another point of view, barriers to entry or mobility are only possible if current and potentially competing firms are heterogeneous in terms of the resources they control *and* if these resources are not perfectly mobile (Barney et al., 1989). The heterogeneity requirement is self-evident. For a barrier to entry or mobility to exist, firms protected by these barriers must be implementing different strategies than firms seeking to enter these protected areas of competition. Firms restricted from entry are unable to implement the same strategies as firms within the industry or group. Because the implementation of strategy requires the application of firm resources, the inability of firms seeking to enter an industry or group to implement the same strategies as firms within that industry or group suggests that firms seeking to enter must not have the same strategically relevant resources as firms within the industry or group. Barriers to entry and mobility only exist when competing firms are heterogeneous in terms of the strategically relevant resources they control. Indeed, this is the definition of strategic groups suggested by McGee and Thomas (1986).

The requirement that firm resources be immobile in order for barriers to entry or mobility to exist is also clear. If firm resources are perfectly mobile, then any resource that allows some firms to implement a strategy protected by entry or mobility barriers can easily be acquired by firms seeking to enter into this industry or group. Once these resources are acquired, the strategy in question can be conceived of and implemented in the same way that other firms have conceived of and implemented their strategies. These strategies are not a source of sustained competitive advantage.

Again, it is not being suggested that entry or mobility barriers do not exist. However, it is being suggested that these barriers only become sources of sustained competitive advantage when firm resources are not homogeneously distributed across competing firms and when these resources are not perfectly mobile.

Research that has focused on the impact of opportunities and threats in a firm's environment on competitive advantage has recognized the limitations inherent in analyzing competitive advantage with the assumption that firm resources are homogeneously distributed and highly mobile. In his recent work, Porter (1985) introduced the concept of the value chain to assist managers in isolating potential resource-based advantages for their firms. The resource-based view of the firm developed here simply pushes this value chain logic further, by examining the attributes that resources isolated by value chain analyses must possess in order to be sources of sustained competitive advantage (Porter, 1990).

Firm resources and sustained competitive advantage

Thus far, it has been suggested that in order to understand sources of sustained competitive advantage, it is necessary to build a theoretical model that begins with the assumption that firm resources may be heterogeneous and immobile. Of course, not all firm resources hold the potential of sustained competitive advantages. To have this potential, a firm resource must have four attributes: (1) it must be valuable, in the sense that it exploit opportunities and/or neutralizes threats in a firm's environment; (2) it must be rare among a firm's current and potential competition; (3) it must be imperfectly imitable, and (4) there cannot be strategically equivalent substitutes for this resource that are valuable but neither rare or imperfectly imitable. These attributes of firm resources can be thought of as empirical indicators of how heterogeneous and immobile a firm's resources are and thus how useful these resources are for generating sustained competitive advantages. Each of these attributes of a firm's resources are discussed in more detail below.

Valuable resources

Firm resources can only be a source of competitive advantage or sustained competitive advantage when they are valuable. As suggested earlier, resources are valuable when they enable a firm to conceive of or implement strategies that improve its efficiency and effectiveness. The traditional "strengths-weaknesses-opportunities-threats" model of firm performance suggests that firms are able to improve their performance only when their strategies exploit opportunities or neutralize threats. Firm attributes may have the other characteristics that could qualify them as sources of competitive advantage (for example, rareness, inimitability, non-substitutability), but these attributes only become *resources* when they exploit opportunities or neutralize threats in a firm's environment.

That firm attributes must be valuable in order to be considered resources (and thus as possible sources of sustained competitive advantage) points to an important complementarity between environmental models of competitive advantage and the resource-based model. These environmental models help isolate those firm attributes that exploit opportunities and/or neutralize threats, and thus specify which firm attributes can be considered as resources. The resource-based model then suggests what additional characteristics that these resources must possess if they are to generate sustained competitive advantage.

Rare resources

By definition, valuable firm resources possessed by large numbers of competing or potentially competing firms cannot be sources of either a competitive advantage or a sustained competitive advantage. A firm enjoys a competitive advantage when it is implementing a value-creating strategy not simultaneously implemented by large numbers of other firms. If a particular valuable firm resource is possessed by large numbers of firms, then each of these firms have the capability of exploiting that resource in the same way, thereby implementing a common strategy that gives no one firm a competitive advantage.

The same analysis applies to bundles of valuable firm resources used to conceive of and implement strategies. Some strategies require a particular mix of physical capital, human capital, and organizational capital resources to implement. One firm resource required in the implementation of almost all strategies is managerial talent (Hambrick, 1987). If this particular bundle of firm resources is not rare, then large numbers of firms will be able to conceive of and implement the strategies in question, and these strategies will not be a source of competitive advantage, even though the resources in question may be valuable.

To observe that competitive advantages (sustained or otherwise) only accrue to firms that have valuable and rare resources is not to dismiss common (i.e., not rare) firm resources as unimportant. Instead, these valuable but common firm resources can help ensure a firm's survival when they are exploited to create competitive parity in an industry (Barney, 1989a). Under conditions of competitive parity, though no one firm obtains a competitive advantage, firms do increase their probability of economic survival (McKelvey, 1982; Porter, 1980).

How rare a valuable firm resource must be in order to have the potential for generating a competitive advantage is a difficult question. It is not difficult to see that if a firm's valuable resources are absolutely unique among a set of competing and potentially competing firms, those resources will generate at least a competitive advantage and may have the potential of generating a sustained competitive advantage. However, it may be possible for a small number of firms in an industry to possess a particular valuable resource and still generate a competitive advantage. In general, as long as the number of firms that possess a particular valuable resource (or a bundle of valuable resources) is less than the number of firms needed to generate perfect competition dynamics in an industry (Hirshleifer, 1980), that resource has the potential of generating a competitive advantage.

Imperfectly imitable resources

It is not difficult to see that valuable and rare organizational resources may be a source of competitive advantage. Indeed, firms with such resources will often be strategic innovators, for they will be able to conceive of and engage in strategies that other firms could either not conceive of, or not implement, or both, because these other firms lacked the relevant firm resources. The observation that valuable and rare organizational resources can be a source of competitive advantage is another way of describing first-mover advantages accruing to firms with resource advantages.

However, valuable and rare organizational resources can only be sources of *sustained* competitive advantage if firms that do not possess these resources cannot obtain them. In language developed in Lippman and Rumelt (1982) and Barney (1986a; 1986b), these firm resources are imperfectly imitable. Firm resources can be imperfectly imitable for one or a combination of three reasons: (1) the ability of a firm to obtain a resource is dependent upon *unique historical conditions*; (2) the link between the resources possessed by a firm and a firm's sustained competitive advantage is *causally ambiguous*; or (3) the resource generating a firm's advantage is *socially complex* (Dierickx & Cool, 1989). Each of these sources of the imperfect imitability of firm resources are now examined.

Unique historical conditions and imperfectly imitable resources. Another assumption of most environmental models of firm competitive advantage, besides resource homogeneity and mobility, is that the performance of firms can be understood independent of the particular history and other idiosyncratic attributes of firms (Porter, 1981; Scherer, 1980). These researchers seldom argue that firms do not vary in terms of their unique histories, but rather that these unique histories are not relevant to understanding a firm's performance (Porter, 1980).

The resource-based view of competitive advantage developed here relaxes this assumption. Indeed, this approach asserts that not only are firms intrinsically historical and social entities, but that their ability to acquire and exploit some resources depends upon their place in time and space. Once this particular unique time in history passes, firms that do not have space- and time-dependent resources cannot obtain them, these resources are imperfectly imitable.

Resource-based theorists are not alone in recognizing the importance of history as a determinant of firm performance and competitive advantage. Traditional strategy researchers (for example, Ansoff, 1965; Learned et al., 1969; Stinchcombe, 1965) often cited the unique historical circumstances of a firm's founding, or the unique circumstances under which a new management team takes over a firm, as important determinants of a firm's long term performance. More recently, several economists (for example, Arthur et al., 1987; David, 1985) have developed models of firm performance that rely heavily on unique historical events as determinants of subsequent actions. Employing path-dependent models of economic performance (Arthur, 1983, 1984a, 1984b; Arthur et al., 1984) these authors suggest that the performance of a firm does not depend simply on the industry structure within which a firm finds itself at a particular point in time, but also on the path a firm followed through history to arrive where it is. If a firm obtains valuable and rare resources because of its unique path through history, it will be able to exploit those resources in implementing value-creating strategies that cannot be duplicated by other firms, for firms without that particular path through history cannot obtain the resources necessary to implement the strategy.

The acquisition of all the types of firm resources examined in this article can depend upon the unique historical position of a firm. A firm that locates it facilities on what turns out to be a much more valuable location than was anticipated when the location was chosen possesses an imperfectly imitable physical capital resource (Hirshleifer, 1980; Ricardo, 1966). A firm with scientists who are uniquely positioned to create or exploit a significant scientific breakthrough may obtain an imperfectly imitable resource from the history-dependent nature of these scientist's individual human capital (Burgelman & Maidique, 1988; Winter, 1988). Finally, a firm with a unique and valuable organizational culture that emerged in the early stages of a firm's history may have an imperfectly imitable advantage over firms founded in another historical period, where different (and perhaps less valuable) organizational values and beliefs come to dominate (Barney, 1986b; Zucker, 1977).

The literature in strategic management is littered with examples of firms whose unique historical position endowed them with resources that are not controlled by competing firms and that cannot be imitated. These examples are the case analyses that have dominated teaching and research for so long in the field of strategic management (Learned et al., 1969; Miles & Cameron, 1982). However, the systematic study of the impact of history on firm performance is in its infancy (David, 1985).

Causal ambiguity and imperfectly imitable resources. Unlike the relationship between a firm's unique history and the imitability of its resources, the relationship between the causal ambiguity of a firm's resources and imperfect imitability has received systematic attention in the literature (Alchian, 1950; Barney, 1986b, Lippman & Rumelt, 1982; Mancke, 1974; Reed and DeFillippi, 1990; Rumelt, 1984). In this context, causal ambiguity exists when the link between the resources controlled by a firm and a firm's sustained competitive advantage is not understood or understood only very imperfectly.

When the link between a firm's resources and its sustained competitive advantage are poorly understood, it is difficult for firms that are attempting to duplicate a successful firm's strategies through imitation of its resources to know which resources it should imitate. Imitating firms may be able to describe some of the resources controlled by a successful firm. However, under conditions of causal ambiguity, it is not clear that the resources that can be described are the same resources that generate a sustained competitive advantage, or whether that advantage reflects some other non-described firm resource. Sometimes it is difficult to understand why one firm consistently outperforms other firms. Causal ambiguity is at the heart of this difficulty. In the face of such causal ambiguity, imitating firms cannot know the actions they should take in order to duplicate the strategies of firms with a sustained competitive advantage.

To be a source of sustained competitive advantage, both the firms that possess resources that generate a competitive advantage and the firms that do not possess these resources but seek to imitate them must be faced with the same level of causal ambiguity (Lippman & Rumelt, 1982). If firms that control these resources have a better understanding of their impact on competitive advantage than firms without these resources, then firms without these resources can engage in activities to reduce their knowledge disadvantage. They can do this, for example, by hiring away well placed knowledgeable managers in a firm with a competitive advantage or by engaging in a careful systematic study of the other firm's success. Although acquiring this knowledge may take some time and effort, once knowledge of the link between a firm's resources and its ability to implement certain strategies is diffused throughout competing firms, causal ambiguity no longer exists, and thus cannot be a source of imperfect imitability. In other words, if a firm with a competitive advantage understands the link between the resources it controls and its advantages, then other firms can also learn about that link, acquire the necessary resources (assuming they are not imperfectly imitable for other reasons), and implement the relevant strategies. In such a setting, a firm's competitive advantages are not sustained because they can be duplicated.

On the other hand, when a firm with a competitive advantage does not understand the source of its competitive advantage any better than firms without this advantage, that competitive advantage may be sustained because it is not subject to imitation (Lippman & Rumelt, 1982). Ironically, in order for causal ambiguity to be a source of sustained competitive advantage, *all* competing firms must have an imperfect understanding of the link between the resources controlled by a firm and a firm's competitive advantages. If one competing firm understands this link, and no others do, in the long run this information will be diffused through all competitors, eliminating causal ambiguity and imperfect imitability based on causal ambiguity.

At first, it may seem unlikely that a firm with a sustained competitive advantage will not fully understand the source of that advantage. However, given the very complex relationship between firm resources and competitive advantage, such an incomplete understanding is not implausible. The resources controlled by a firm are very complex and interdependent. Often, they are implicit, taken for granted by managers, rather than being subject to explicit analysis (Nelson & Winter, 1982; Polanyi, 1962; Winter, 1988). Numerous resources, taken by themselves or in combination with other resources, may yield sustained competitive advantage. Although managers may have numerous hypotheses about which resources generate their firm's advantages, it is rarely possible to rigorously test these hypotheses. As long as numerous plausible explanations of the sources of sustained competitive advantage exist within a firm, the link between the resources controlled by a firm and sustained competitive advantage remains somewhat ambiguous, and which of a firm's resources to imitate remains uncertain.

Social complexity. A final reason a firm's resources may be imperfectly imitable is that they may be very complex social phenomena, beyond the ability of firms to systematically manage and influence. When competitive advantages are based in such complex social phenomena, the ability of other firms to imitate these resources is significantly constrained.

A wide variety of firm resources may be socially complex. Examples include the interpersonal relations among managers in a firm (Hambrick, 1987), a firm's culture (Barney, 1986b), a firm's reputation among suppliers (Porter, 1980) and customers (Klein et al., 1978; Klein & Leffler, 1981). Notice that in most of these cases it is possible to specify how these socially complex resources add value to a firm. There is little or no causal ambiguity surrounding the link between these firm resources and competitive advantage. However, understanding that, say, an organizational culture with certain attributes or quality relations among managers can improve a firm's efficiency and effectiveness does not necessarily imply that firms without these attributes can engage in systematic efforts to create them (Barney, 1989b; Dierickx & Cool, 1989). Such social engineering may be, for the time being at least, beyond the capabilities of most firms (Barney, 1986b; Porras & Berg, 1978). To the extent that socially complex firm resources are not subject to such direct management, these resources are imperfectly imitable.

Notice that complex physical technology is not included in this category of sources of imperfectly imitable. In general, physical technology, whether it takes the form of machine tools or robots in factories (Hayes & Wheelwright, 1984) or complex information management systems (Howell & Fleishman, 1982), is *by itself* typically imitable. If one firm can purchase these physical tools of production and thereby implement some strategies, then other firms should also be able to purchase these physical tools; such tools should not be a source of sustained competitive advantage.

On the other hand, the exploitation of physical technology in a firm often involves the use of socially complex firm resources. Several firms may all possess the same physical technology, but only one of these firms may possess the social relations, culture, traditions, etc., to fully exploit this technology in implementing strategies (Wilkins, 1989). If these complex social resources are not subject to imitation (and assuming they are valuable and rare and no substitutes exist), these firms may obtain a sustained competitive advantage from exploiting their physical technology more completely than other firms, even though competing firms do not vary in terms of the physical technology they possess.

Substitutability

The last requirement for a firm resource to be a source of sustained competitive advantage is that there must be no strategically equivalent valuable resources that are themselves either not rare or imitable. Two valuable firm resources (or two bundles of firm resources) are strategically equivalent when they each can be exploited separately to implement the same strategies. Suppose that one of these valuable firm resources is rare and imperfectly imitable, but the other is not. Firms with this first resource will be able to conceive of and implement certain strategies. If there were no strategically equivalent firm resources, these strategies would generate a sustained competitive advantage (because the resources used to conceive and implement them are valuable, rare and imperfectly imitable). However, that there are strategically equivalent resources suggests that other current or potentially competing firms can implement the same strategies, but in a different way, using different resources. If these alternative resources are either not rare or imitable, then numerous firms will be able to conceive of and implement the strategies in question, and those strategies will not generate a sustained competitive advantage. This will be the case even though one approach to implementing these strategies exploits valuable, rare, and imperfectly imitable firm resources.

Substitutability can take at least two forms. First, though it may not be possible for a firm to imitate another firm's resources exactly, it may be able to substitute a *similar* resource that enables it to conceive of and implement the same strategies. For example, a firm seeking to duplicate the competitive advantages of another firm by imitating that other firm's high quality top management team will often be unable to copy that team exactly (Barney & Tyler, 1990). However, it may be possible for this firm to develop its own unique top management team. Though these two teams will be different (different people, different operating practices, a different history, etc.), they may likely be strategically equivalent and thus be substitutes for one another. If different top management teams are strategically equivalent (and if these substitute teams are common or highly imitable), then a high quality top management team is not a source of sustained competitive advantage, even though a particular management team of a particular firm *is* valuable, rare and imperfectly imitable.

Second, very *different* firm resources can also be strategic substitutes. For example, managers in one firm may have a very clear vision of the future of their company because of a charismatic leader in their firm (Zucker, 1977). Managers in competing firms may also have a very clear vision of the future of their companies, but this common vision may reflect these firms' systematic, company-wide strategic planning process (Pearce et al., 1987). From the point of view of managers having a clear vision of the future of their company, the firm resource of a charismatic leader and the firm resource of a formal planning system may be strategically equivalent, and thus substitutes for one another. If large numbers of competing firms have a formal planning system that generates this common vision (or if such a formal planning is highly imitable), then firms with such a vision derived from a charismatic leader will not have a sustained competitive advantage, even though the firm resource of a charismatic leader is probably rare and imperfectly imitable.

Of course, the strategic substitutability of firm resources is always a matter of degree. It is the case, however, that substitute firm resources need not have exactly the same implications for an organization in order for those resources to be equivalent from the point of view of the strategies that firms can conceive of and implement. If enough firms have these valuable substitute resources (i.e., they are not rare), or if enough firms can acquire them (i.e., they are imitable), then none of these firms (including firms whose resources are being substituted for) can expect to obtain a sustained competitive advantage.

Applying the framework

The relationship between resource heterogeneity and immobility; value, rareness, imitability and substitutability; and sustained competitive advantage is summarized in Figure 15.2. This framework can be applied in analyzing the potential of a broad range of firm resources to be sources of sustained competitive advantage. These analyses not only specify the theoretical conditions under which sustained competitive advantage might exist, they also suggest specific empirical questions that need to be addressed before the relationship between a particular firm resource and sustained competitive advantage can be understood. Three brief examples of how this framework might be applied are presented here.

Strategic planning and sustained competitive advantage

There is a large and growing literature on the ability of various strategic planning processes to generate competitive advantages for firms (Pearce et al., 1987). Evaluating strategic planning as a firm resource may help resolve some of the conflicting results in this literature (Armstrong, 1982; Rhyne, 1986).

It seems reasonable to expect that *formal* strategic planning systems (Lorange, 1980) are unlikely by themselves to be a source of sustained competitive advantage. Even if these planning systems are valuable, in the sense that they enable firms to recognize opportunities and threats in their environment, there is empirical evidence suggesting that many firms engage in such formal planning exercises, such planning mechanisms are not rare (Kudla, 1980). Even if in a particular industry formal planning is rare, the formal planning process has been thoroughly described and documented in a wide variety of public sources. Any firm interested in engaging in such formal planning can certainly learn how to do so, formal planning seems likely to be highly imitable (Barney, 1989b). Apart from substitutability

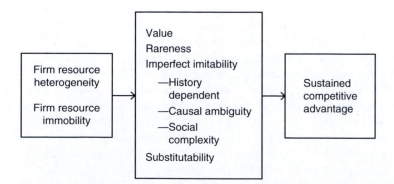

Figure 15.2 The relationship between resource heterogeneity and immobility, value, rareness, imperfect imitability, and substitutability, and sustained competitive advantage.

considerations, formal strategic planning by itself is not likely to be a source of sustained competitive advantage.

This does not mean that firms that engage in formal strategic planning will never obtain sustained competitive advantages. It may be that the formal planning system in a firm enables a firm to recognize and exploit other of its resources, some of these resources might be sources of sustained competitive advantage. However, it is probably inappropriate to conclude that the sustained competitive advantages thus created reflect the formal planning process per se. Rather, the source of these advantages is almost certainly other resources controlled by a firm.

Of course, *formal* strategic planning is not the only way that firms choose their strategies. A variety of authors have described informal (Leontiades & Tezel, 1980), emergent (Mintzberg, 1978; Mintzberg & McHugh, 1985) and autonomous (Burgelman, 1983) processes by which firms choose their strategies. To the extent that these processes suggest valuable strategies for firms, they can be thought of as firm resources, and their potential for generating sustained competitive advantage can be evaluated by considering how rare, imperfectly imitable and substitutable they are.

Those who study these informal strategy-making processes tend to agree about their rareness and imitability. Although the rareness of these informal strategy-making processes is an empirical question, current research suggests that at least some firms attempt to prevent these informal processes from unfolding (Burgelman, 1983), or ignore the strategic insights they generate (Burgelman & Maidique, 1988). In industries where most current and potential competitors either prevent or ignore these informal processes, firms that understand their potential value may possess a rare strategic resource. Moreover, because these processes are socially complex (Mintzberg & McHugh, 1985), they are also likely to be imperfectly imitable.

There is less agreement concerning possible substitutes for these informal strategy-making processes. On the one hand, some authors seem to suggest that formal planning mechanisms are strategic substitutes for informal, emergent or autonomous processes (Pearce et al., 1987). If this is true, because these formal processes are highly imitable, informal strategy making has a highly imitable substitute and is not a source of sustained competitive advantage. On the other hand, others have argued that formal and informal strategy making are not substitutes for one another, that formal processes are effective in some settings and ineffective in others, that informal processes are effective where formal processes are not and are ineffective when formal processes are effective (Fredrickson, 1984; Fredrickson & Mitchell, 1984). If these processes are not substitutes for one another, and if the conditions of rareness and imperfect imitability hold, informal strategy-making processes may be a source of sustained competitive advantage. The question of the substitutability of informal strategy making in firms needs to be resolved empirically before the impact of these firm resources on sustained competitive advantage can be fully understood.

Information processing systems and sustained competitive advantage

There is also a growing literature that focuses on information processing systems and sustained competitive advantage (O'Brien, 1983). As with strategic planning, whether or not information processing systems are a source of sustained competitive advantage depends on the type of information processing system being analyzed. If seems very unlikely that computers (of any size, no matter how they are linked or networked) by themselves, can be a source of sustained competitive advantage (Hayes & Wheelwright, 1984). Machines, be they computers or other types of machines, are part of the physical technology of a firm, and usually can be purchased across markets (Barney, 1986a). Because the machines can be purchased, any strategy that exploits just the machines themselves is likely to be imitable and thus not a source of sustained competitive advantage.

On the other hand, an information processing system that is deeply embedded in a firm's informal and formal management decision-making process may hold the potential of sustained competitive advantage. Research seems to suggest that relatively few firms have been able to create this close manager-computer interface, this kind of information processing system may be rare (Christie, 1985; Rasmussen, 1986). It is also a socially complex system and will probably be imperfectly imitable.

The question of possible substitutes for these complex machine-manager systems has not received as much attention in the literature. To specify possible strategic substitutes requires understanding what strategic benefits accrue to a firm that possesses a system where computers and managers are intimately linked. Any list of possible benefits might include an efficient flow of information among managers, the ability of consider large amounts of information quickly and the ability to share this information efficiently (O'Brien, 1983). These same benefits might accrue to a firm with a closely knit, highly experienced management team, without an information management system (Hambrick, 1987). This type of management team may be a substitute for an information-processing system embedded in a firm's informal and formal decision-making processes.

However, the existence of substitutes by itself does not mean that a particular firm resource cannot be a source of sustained competitive advantage. In addition, these substitutes have to be either not rare, or highly imitable, or both. Closely knit, highly experienced management teams for a particular set of competitors may be rare and, because they are socially complex, may be imperfectly imitable. If this is true, an embedded information-processing system may be a source of sustained competitive advantage, even if a close substitute for such a processing system (a close knit, highly experienced top management team) exists.

Positive reputations and sustained competitive advantages

Positive reputations of firms among customers and suppliers have also been cited as sources of competitive advantage in the literature (Porter, 1980). An application of the framework presented in Figure 15.2, again, suggests the conditions under which a firm's positive reputation can be a source of sustained competitive advantage. If only a few competing firms have such reputations, then they are rare. In general, the development of a positive reputation usually depends upon specific, difficult-to-duplicate historical settings. To the extent that a particular firm's positive reputation depends upon such historical incidents, it may be imperfectly imitable. In addition, positive firm reputations can be thought of as informal social relations between firms and key stakeholders (Klein & Leffler, 1981). Such informal relations are likely to be socially complex and thus imperfectly imitable.

The question of substitutes for a positive reputation is, again, more complicated. Some authors (Klein et al., 1978) have suggested that rather than developing a positive reputation, firms may reassure their customers or suppliers through the use of guarantees and other long-term contracts. These guarantees substitute for a firm's reputation. However, it is not clear that the implicit psychological contract between a firm and its stakeholders when a firm has a positive reputation is the same as the implicit psychological contract between a firm and its stakeholders when a firm uses guarantees for reassurance. If reputation and guarantees are substitutes, why is it that some firms invest both in a positive reputation and guarantees?

If these two firm resources are not substitutes, then a reputation (if it is rare and imperfectly imitable) may be a source of sustained competitive advantage.

Discussion

The brief analyses of strategic planning, information processing and a firm's reputation among customers and suppliers and sustained competitive advantage are suggestive of the kinds of analyses that are possible with the framework presented in Figure 15.2. This framework suggests the kinds of empirical questions that need to be addressed in order to understand whether or not a particular firm resource is a source of sustained competitive advantage: is that resource valuable, is it rare, is it imperfectly imitable and are there substitutes for that resource? This resource-based model of sustained competitive advantage also has a variety of implications for the relationship between strategic management theory and other business disciplines. Some of these implications are now considered.

Sustained competitive advantage and social welfare

The model presented here addresses important social welfare issues linked with strategic management research. Most authors agree that the original purpose of the structure–conduct–performance paradigm in industrial organization economics was to isolate violations of the perfectly competitive model, to address these violations in order to restore the social welfare benefits of perfectly competitive industries (Barney, 1986c; Porter, 1981). As applied by strategy theorists focusing on environmental determinants of firm performance, social welfare concerns were abandoned in favor of the creation of imperfectly competitive industries within which a particular firm could gain a competitive advantage (Porter, 1980). At best, this approach to strategic analysis ignores social welfare concerns. At worst, this approach focuses on activities that firms can engage in that will almost certainly reduce social welfare (Hirshliefer, 1980).

The resource-based model developed here suggests that strategic management research can be perfectly consistent with traditional social welfare concerns of economists. Beginning with the assumptions that firm resources are heterogeneous and immobile, it follows that a firm that exploits its resource advantages is simply behaving in an efficient and effective manner. To fail to exploit these resource advantages is inefficient and does not maximize social welfare. In this sense, the higher levels of performance that accrue to a firm with resource advantages are due to the efficiency of these firms in exploiting those advantages, rather than to the efforts of firms to create imperfectly competitive conditions in a way that fails to maximize social welfare. These profits, in a sense, can be thought of as "efficiency rents" as opposed to "monopoly rents" (Scherer, 1980).

Sustained competitive advantage and organization theory and behavior

Recently, a variety of authors have suggested that economic models of organizational phenomena fundamentally contradict models of organizations based in organization theory or organizational behavior (Perrow, 1986). This assertion is fundamentally contradicted by the resource-based model of sustained competitive advantage (Barney, 1990). This model suggests that sources of sustained competitive advantage are firm resources that are valuable, rare, imperfectly imitable and non-substitutable. These resources include a broad range of organizational, social and individual phenomena within firms that are the subject of a great deal of research in organization theory and organizational behavior (Daft, 1983). Rather than being contradictory, the resource-based model of strategic management suggests that organization theory and organizational behavior may be a rich source of findings and theories concerning rare, non-imitable and non-substitutable resources in firms. Indeed, a resource-based model of sustained competitive advantage anticipates a more intimate integration of the organizational and the economic as a way to study sustained competitive advantage.

Firm endowments and sustained competitive advantage

Finally, the model presented here emphasizes the importance of what might be called firm resource endowments in creating sustained competitive advantages. Implicit in this model is the assumption that managers are limited in their ability to manipulate all the attributes and characteristics of their firms (Barney & Tyler, 1991). It is this limitation that makes some firm resources imperfectly imitable, and thus potentially sources of sustained competitive advantage. The study of sustained competitive advantage depends, in a critical way, on the resource endowments controlled by a firm.

That the study of sources of sustained competitive advantage focuses on valuable, rare, imperfectly imitable and non-substitutable resource endowments does not suggest—as some population ecologists would have it (for example, Hannan & Freeman, 1977)—that managers are irrelevant in the study of such advantages. In fact, managers are important in this model, for it is managers that are able to understand and describe the economic performance potential of a firm's endowments. Without such managerial analyses, sustained competitive advantage is not likely. This is the case even though the skills needed to describe the rare, imperfectly imitable, and non-substitutable resources of a firm may themselves not be rare, imperfectly imitable, or non-substitutable.

Indeed, it may be the case that a manager or a managerial team is a firm resource that has the potential for generating sustained competitive advantages. The conditions under which this will be the case can be outlined using the framework presented in Figure 15.2. However, in the end, what becomes clear is that firms cannot expect to "purchase" sustained competitive advantages on open markets (Barney, 1986a, 1988; Wernerfelt, 1989). Rather, such advantages must be found in the rare, imperfectly imitable, and non-substitutable resources already controlled by a firm (Dierickx & Cool, 1989).

Notes

1 Thus, for example, Porter (1980) suggests that firms should analyze their competitive environment, choose their strategies, and then acquire the resources needed to implement their strategies. Firms are assumed to have the same resources to implement these strategies or to have the same access to these resources. More recently, Porter (1985) has introduced a language for discussing possible internal organizational attributes that may affect competitive advantage. The relationship between this "value chain" logic and the resource based view of the firm is examined below.

References

Alchian, A.A. 1950. Uncertainty, evolution, and economic theory. *American Economic Review*, 58: 388–401.

Andrews, K.R. 1971. *The concept of corporate strategy*. Homewood, IL: Dow Jones Irwin.

Ansoff, H.I. 1965. *Corporate strategy*. New York: McGraw-Hill.

Armstrong, J.S. 1982. The value of formal planning for strategic decisions: Review of empirical research. *Strategic Management Journal*, 3: 197–211.

Arthur, W.B. 1983. *Competing technologies and lock-in by historical small events: The dynamics of allocation under increasing returns*. Unpublished manuscript, Center for Economic Policy Research, Stanford University.

Arthur, W.B. 1984a. *Industry location patterns and the importance of history: Why a silicon valley?* Unpublished manuscript, Center for Economic Policy Research, Stanford University.

Arthur, W.B. 1984b. Competing technologies and economic prediction. *Options*, IIASA, Laxenburg, Austria.

Arthur, W.B., Ermoliev, Y. & Kaniovski, Y.M. 1984. Strong laws for a class of path dependent stochastic processes with applications. In Arkin, V.I., Shiryayev, A., and Wets, R. (Eds.), *Proceedings of a Conference on Stochastic Optimization, Kiev 1984:* 87–93.

Arthur, W.B., Ermolieve, Y.M., & Kaniovsky, Y.M. 1987. Path dependent processes and the emergence of macro structure. *European Journal of Operations Research*, 30: 294–303.

Bain, J. 1956. *Barriers to new competition*. Cambridge: Harvard University Press.

Barney, J.B. 1986a. Strategic factor markets: Expectations, luck, and business strategy. *Management Science*, 42: 1231–41.

Barney, J.B. 1986b. Organizational culture: Can it be a source of sustained competitive advantage? *Academy of Management Review*, 11: 656–65.

Barney, J.B. 1986c. Types of competition and the theory of strategy: Toward an integrative framework. *Academy of Management Review*, 11:791–800.

Barney, J.B. 1988. Returns to bidding firms in mergers and acquisitions: Reconsidering the relatedness hypothesis. *Strategic Management Journal*, 9: 71–8.

Barney, J.B. 1989a. Asset stock accumulation and sustained competitive advantage: A comment. *Management Science*, 35: 1511–13.

Barney, J.B. 1989b. *The context of strategic planning and the economic performance of firms*. Working paper no. 88–004, Strategy Group Working Paper Series, Department of Management, Texas A&M University.

Barney, J.B. 1990. The debate between traditional management theory and organizational economics: substantive differences or intergroup conflict? *Academy of Management Review*, 15: 382–93.

Barney, J.B., & Hoskisson, R. 1989. Strategic groups: Untested assertions and research proposals. *Managerial and Decision Economics*, 11:187–98.

Barney, J.B., & Tyler, B. 1990. The attributes of top management teams and sustained competitive advantage. In M. Lawless & L. Gomez-Mejia (Eds.), *Managing the High Technology Firm:* JAI Press, in press.

Barney, J.B., & Tyler, B. 1991. The prescriptive limits and potential for applying strategic management theory, *Managerial and Decision Economics*, in press.

Barney, J.B., McWilliams, A., & Turk, T. 1989. *On the relevance of the concept of entry barriers in the theory of competitive strategy*. Paper presented at the annual meeting of the Strategic Management Society, San Francisco.

Baumol, W.J., Panzar, J.C., & Willig, R.P 1982. *Contestable markets and the theory of industry structure*. New York: Harcourt, Brace, and Jovanovich.

Becker, G.S. 1964. *Human capital*. New York: Columbia.

Burgelman R. 1983. Corporate entrepreneurship and strategic management: Insights from a process study. *Management Science,* 29: 1349–64.

Burgelman, R., & Maidique, M.A. 1988. *Strategic management of technology and innovation*. Homewood, IL: Irwin.

Caves, R.E., & Porter, M. 1977. From entry barriers to mobility barriers: Conjectural decisions and contrived deterrence to new competition. *Quarterly Journal of Economics*, 91: 241–62.

Christie, B. 1985. *Human factors and information technology in the office*. New York: Wiley.

Daft, R. 1983. *Organization theory and design*. New York: West.

David, P.A. 1985. Clio and the economics of QWERTY. *American Economic Review Proceedings*, 75: 332–7.

Dierickx, I., & Cool, K. 1989. Asset stock accumulation and sustainability of competitive advantage. *Management Science*, 35: 1504–11.

Fredrickson, J. 1984. The comprehensiveness of strategic decision processes: Extension, observations, future directions. *Academy of Management Journal*, 27: 445–66.

Fredrickson, J., & Mitchell, T.R. 1984. Strategic decision processes: Comprehensiveness and performance in an industry with an unstable environment. *Academy of Management Journal*, 27: 399–423.

Hambrick, D. 1987. Top management teams: Key to strategic success. *California Management Review*, 30: 88–108.

Hannan, M.T., & Freeman, J. 1977. The population ecology of organizations. *American Journal of Sociology*, 82: 929–64.

Hatten, K.J., & Hatten, M.L. 1987. Strategic groups, asymmetrical mobility barriers and contestability. *Strategic Management Journal*, 8: 329–42.

Hayes, R.H., & Wheelwright, S. 1984. *Restoring our competitive edge*. New York: Wiley.

Hirshleifer, J. 1980. *Price theory and applications* (2nd ed.). Englewood Cliffs, NJ: Prentice-Hall.

Hitt, M., & Ireland, D. 1986. Relationships among corporate level distinctive competencies, diversification strategy, corporate strategy and performance. *Journal of Management Studies*, 23: 401–16.

Hofer, C., & Schendel, D. 1978. *Strategy formulation: Analytical concepts*. St. Paul, MN: West.

Howell, W.C., & Fleishman, E.A. 1982. *Information processing and decision making*. Hillsdale, NJ: L. Erlbaum.

Jacobsen, R. 1988. The persistence of abnormal returns. *Strategic Management Journal*, 9: 41–58.

Klein, B., & Leffler, K. 1981. The role of price in guaranteeing quality. *Journal of Political Economy*, 89: 615–41.

Klein, B., Crawford, R.G., & Alchian, A. 1978. Vertical integration, appropriable rents, and the competitive contracting process. *Journal of Law and Economics*, 21: 297–326.

Kudla, R.J. 1980. The effects of strategic planning on common stock returns. *Academy of Management Journal*, 23: 5–20.

Learned, E.R, Christensen, C.R., Andrews, K.R., & Guth, W. 1969. *Business policy*. Homewood, IL: Irwin.

Leontiades, M., & Tezel, A. 1980. Planning perceptions and planning results. *Strategic Management Journal*, 1: 65–79.

Lieberman, M.B., & Montgomery, D.B. 1988. First mover advantages. *Strategic Management Journal*, 9: 41–58.

Lippman, S., & Rumelt, R. 1982. Uncertain imitability: An analysis of interfirm differences in efficiency under competition. *Bell Journal of Economics*, 13: 418–38.

Lorange, P. 1980. *Corporate planning: An executive viewpoint*. Englewood Cliffs, NJ: Prentice-Hall.

McGee, J., & Thomas, H. 1986. Strategic groups: Theory, research and taxonomy. *Strategic Management Journal*, 7: 141–60.

McKelvey, W. 1982. *Organizational systematics: Taxonomy, evolution, and classification*. Los Angeles: University of California Press.

Mancke, R., 1974. Causes of interfirm profitability differences: A new interpretation of the evidence. *Quarterly Journal of Economics*, 88: 181–93.

Miles, R., & Cameron, K. 1982. *Coffin nails and corporate strategy*. Englewood Cliffs, NJ: Prentice-Hall.

Mintzberg, H. 1978. Patterns in strategy formation. *Management Science*, 24: 934–48.

Mintzberg, H., & McHugh, A. 1985. Strategy formation in adhocracy. *Administrative Science Quarterly*, 30: 160–97.

Nelson, R., & Winter, S. 1982. *An evolutionary theory of economic change*. Cambridge: Harvard University Press.

O'Brien, J. 1983. *Computers and information processing in business*. Homewood, IL: Irwin.

Pearce, J.A., Freeman, E.B., & Robinson, R.B. 1987. The tenuous link between formal strategic planning and financial performance. *Academy of Management Review*, 12: 658–75.

Penrose, E.T. 1958. *The theory of the growth of the firm*. New York: Wiley.

Perrow, C. 1986. *Complex organizations: A critical essay* (3rd ed.). New York: Random House.

Polanyi, M. 1962. *Personal knowledge: towards a post critical philosophy*. London: Routledge.

Porras, J., & Berg, P.O. 1978. The impact of organizational development. *Academy of Management Review*, 3: 249–66.

Porter, M. 1980. *Competitive strategy*. New York: Free Press.

Porter, M. 1981. The contributions of industrial organization to strategic management. *Academy of Management Review*, 6: 609–20.

Porter, M. 1985. *Competitive advantage*. New York: Free Press.

Porter, M. 1990. *Why are firms successful*. Paper presented at the Fundamental Issues in Strategy Conference, Napa, CA.

Rasmussen, J. 1986. *Information processing and human machine interaction*. New York: North Holland.

Reed, R., & DeFillippi, R. 1990. Causal ambiguity, barriers to imitation, and sustainable competitive advantage. *Academy of Management Review*, 15: 88–102.

Rhyne, L.C. 1986. The relationship of strategic planning to financial performance. *Strategic Management Journal*, 7: 423–36.

Ricardo, D. 1966. *Economic essays*. New York: A.M. Kelly.

Rumelt, R. 1984. Towards a strategic theory of the firm. In R. Lamb (Ed.), *Competitive Strategic Management:* 556–570. Englewood Cliffs, NJ: Prentice-Hall.

Rumelt, R., & Wensley, R. 1981. In search of the market share effect. In K. Chung (Ed.), *Academy of Management Proceedings 1981:* 2–6.

Scherer, F.M. 1980. *Industrial market structure and economic performance* (2nd ed.). Boston: Houghton-Mifflin.

Schumpeter, J. 1934. *The theory of economic development*. Cambridge: Harvard University Press.

Schumpeter, J. 1950. *Capitalism, socialism, and democracy* (3rd ed.). New York: Harper.

Stinchcombe, A.L. 1965. Social structure and organizations. In J.G. March (Ed.), *Handbook of Organizations:* 142–193. Chicago: Rand-McNally.

Thompson, A.A., & Strickland, A.J. 1983. *Strategy formulation and implementation*. Dallas: Business Publications.

Tomer, J.F. 1987. *Organizational capital: The path to higher productivity and well-being*. New York: Praeger.

Wernerfelt, B. 1984. A resource based view of the firm. *Strategic Management Journal*, 5: 171–80.

Wernerfelt, B. 1989. From critical resources to corporate strategy. *Journal of General Management*, 14: 4–12.

Wilkins, A. 1989. *Developing corporate character*. San Francisco: Jossey-Bass.

Williamson, O. 1975. *Markets and hierarchies*. New York: Free Press.

Winter, S. 1988. Knowledge and competence as strategic assets. In D. Teece (Ed.) *The Competitive Challenge*. Cambridge: Ballinger. 159–84.

Zucker, L. 1977. The role of institutionalization in cultural persistence. *American Sociological Review*, 421: 726–43.

16 Knowledge, bargaining power, and the instability of international joint ventures*

Andrew C. Inkpen and Paul W. Beamish

As competition increasingly becomes more global, many firms are using alliances to enter new markets, obtain new skills and share risks and resources. Despite the surge in their popularity, international alliances are often described as inherently unstable organizational forms. Porter (1990), for example, observed that alliances involve significant costs in terms of co-ordination, reconciling goals with an independent entity and creating competitors. Porter suggested that these costs make many alliances transitional rather than stable arrangements and, therefore, alliances are rarely a sustainable means for creating competitive advantage. Supporting this argument, authors of several empirical studies of alliances have found instability rates of close to 50 per cent (for example, Bleeke & Ernst, 1991; Kogut, 1988). Based on the finding that 24 of the 49 international alliances they studied were considered failures by one or both partners, Bleeke and Ernst (1991) suggested that most alliances will terminate, even successful ones.

Alliances also have been described as a race to *learn*, and the partner that learns the fastest dominates the relationship (Hamel, 1991). According to this scenario of inevitable instability, there are clear winners and losers. However, some international alliances survive and prosper for many years and both sides become more competitive through a win-win relationship. This example raises the issue of why some international alliances are more stable than others. We address this issue by examining equity-based international joint ventures (IJVs). An equity-based JV is an alliance that combines resources from more than one organization to create a new organizational entity (the "child"), which is distinct from its parents. Equity-based JVs are considered hierarchical because they more closely replicate some of the features associated with organizational hierarchies than do other alliances (Gulati, 1995). Siecor, an alliance between Siemens and Corning, provides an example. In this JV, the partners brought together their complementary capabilities in telecommunications and glass technology to build an independent organization with its own headquarters, CEO, board of directors, and staff. An IJV is a JV with two or more parents of different nationality. Our focus is on IJVs based in the home country of one of the partners, which we call the *local partner*. The partner operating outside its country of domicile is referred to as the *foreign partner*.

A variety of strategic objectives have been suggested to explain firms' motives for the formation of IJVs (Contractor & Lorange, 1988; Hennart, 1991; Kogut, 1988). A firm that enters a foreign market for the first time is likely to use a joint venture; this is also true for

*Republished with permission of Academy of Management, from A. Inkpen & P. Beamish (1997) "Knowledge, bargaining power and the instability of international joint ventures". Academy of Management Review, 22(1): 177–202; permission conveyed through Copyright Clearance Centre Inc.

the foreign firm that seeks to obtain access to resources controlled by local firms (Hennart, 1991). In both situations, IJVs are often chosen because the alternatives of replicating a complete operation via full acquisition or greenfield investment are too costly and because the local partner controls resources deemed useful to the foreign partner. An IJV may be designed to market a product in the local market, or it may be involved in the sourcing of materials, components, or technology, possibly for use in the foreign partner's home market. IJVs are widely used as a mode of direct foreign investment. For example, Makino (1995) found that almost 70% of Japanese direct investments in manufacturing in Asia as of 1991 were via IJVs.

Regardless of the specific venture objective, our primary interest, like that of Yan and Gray (1994) and Parkhe (1991), is IJVs in which the foreign partner seeks a viable long-term presence in a country via direct investment. In this type of IJV, it would be unusual for the local partner not to contribute some local knowledge. The primary knowledge contribution of foreign partners generally involves technology, management expertise, and global support (Yan & Gray, 1994). Note that we are not suggesting that the only contribution of a local partner is local knowledge. In another section of this chapter, we suggest that if local partners take steps to ensure that their roles encompass more than a one-time contribution of local knowledge, instability may be controllable. Nevertheless, even when technology sourcing or risk sharing are important objectives of the foreign partner, if the venture is international, it is likely that the local partner possesses important local knowledge.[1]

Unlike alliances such as R&D partnerships or licensing agreements, contracts between IJV partners are often executed under conditions of high uncertainty, therefore, it is highly unlikely that all future contingencies in an IJV can be anticipated at the outset. As IJVs grow, they may develop an identity and a culture distinct from that of the partners, adding to problems of coordination. Also, the collaborative motives for IJVs are often different from other alliances; therefore, statements generalizing about the instability of alliances should be interpreted carefully.[2] The factors associated with instability of IJVs are not necessarily the same as those for all types of alliances.

In the literature on JV instability, various factors have been identified as causes of instability, including changes in partners' strategic missions (Harrigan & Newman, 1990), changes in importance of the JV to the parents (Harrigan & Newman, 1990), increases in the competitive rivalry between partners (Kogut, 1989), the foreign investment climate of the host country (Blodgett, 1992) and the existence of prior relationships between the partners (Blodgett, 1992). Although these factors may be associated with instability, and in some cases provide a strong indication that instability is imminent, they provide incomplete explanations for the instability of IJVs.

Our interest is instability that results from factors endogenous to the IJV relationship. Figure 16.1 illustrates the boundaries of the article and the conceptual orientation. Factors creating instability as a result of reasons exogenous to IJVs (for example, changes in foreign country investment or ownership regulations; shifts in political regimes) are for the most part not controllable by managers of IJVs and are outside the scope of this article. We argue that the primary factor contributing to instability, and a factor that can be controlled by firms in IJVs, is a shift in partner bargaining power associated with the acquisition of knowledge and skills that allows a firm to eliminate a partner dependency. With a few exceptions (Hamel, 1991; Parkhe, 1991; Yan & Gray, 1994), the literature on IJVs has not addressed this issue in detail. Thus, the departure in this article is the focus on factors that *enable* firms to make the IJV bargain obsolete. We explore the question of how IJV firms, and in particular foreign partners, are able to create an unstable environment.

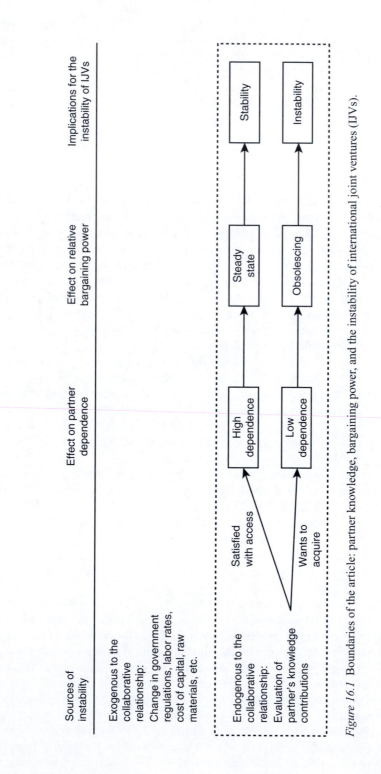

Figure 16.1 Boundaries of the article: partner knowledge, bargaining power, and the instability of international joint ventures (IJVs).

Firms contribute various types of knowledge and skills to their IJVs. For local partners, a critical knowledge contribution revolves around an understanding of local market, cultural and environmental conditions. Although the foreign partner does not necessarily enter the IJV with the specific objective of knowledge acquisition, *access* to knowledge originating in the local country is an important factor in motivating the foreign partner to choose an IJV investment rather than full ownership. We propose that as the foreign partner's local knowledge and its commitment to acquire local knowledge increase, the probability of the instability of the IJV also increases because of changes in partner dependency. We also argue that the acquisition of technology-based knowledge by the local partner, although possible, is less likely to be a factor in creating instability than is the foreign partner's acquisition of knowledge.

The local knowledge argument complements the well-developed theme in the international management literature concerning the frequent conflict between global and local optimization of strategy (for example, Bartlett & Ghoshal, 1989; Franko, 1971). Given these conflicting demands, two closely related questions are addressed in this article. First, when a multinational enterprise (MNE) involved in an IJV as a foreign partner decides to pursue a localization strategy (i.e., a strategy of operating autonomously in the local environment), how can it happen? We argue that the MNE's acquisition of local knowledge *enables* the MNE to make the transition from an IJV to a subsidiary. We also suggest that an important distinction has to be made between the effect that local knowledge has on stability and the decision to acquire the knowledge. For example, an MNE may decide that its IJV should be a wholly owned subsidiary. Unless the MNE has acquired the local knowledge necessary to manage the venture autonomously, a wholly owned subsidiary is not a viable option. The acquisition of local knowledge can facilitate the transition to a subsidiary, and it is a necessary factor in the decision.

The second and equally important question involves the factors that influence the foreign partner's decision and ability to acquire local knowledge. In some IJVs, the foreign partner may choose not to pursue a localization strategy. In other IJVs, localization may not be possible because the local partner outlearns the foreign partner, which becomes the basis for an obsolete bargain. An examination of these questions requires an analysis of the dynamics of collaborative relationships, so that we can develop a comprehensive framework of the instability of IJVs.

Definitions and theoretical underpinnings

Local knowledge

To establish an operational presence in a country, a firm must access local knowledge as a means of overcoming market uncertainties (Stopford & Wells, 1972). IJVs provide low-cost, fast access to new markets by "borrowing" a partner's already-in-place local infrastructure (Doz et al., 1990). This infrastructure includes sales forces, local plants, market intelligence and the marketing presence necessary to understand and serve local markets. Local knowledge also relates to cultural traditions, norms, values and institutional differences. For example, when Kentucky Fried Chicken entered China, a local partner was considered essential because of the complexities associated with obtaining operating licenses and leases, negotiating employment contracts, and interpreting investment regulations. When a foreign firm does not have local knowledge, as in the case of Kentucky Fried Chicken, an IJV can be used to gain quick access to a local partner's knowledge base. Yan and Gray (1994: 1492) quoted a U.S. manager in a U.S.-China IJV: "We have the technology and certain know-how. The Chinese partner knows how to make things happen in China. You put the two together right, it works."

Instability of IJVs

As indicated previously, the primary factor contributing to instability is a shift in partner bargaining power. Several definitions of instability have been used in the JV literature. Franko (1971) defined a JV as *unstable* when parent holdings changed to include 50% or 95% ownership, a parent sold its JV interest, or the venture was liquidated. Killing (1983) considered both a shift in JV control and venture termination as evidence of instability. Other researchers have adopted a narrower view. For example, Kogut (1989) used venture termination as the sole indicator of instability. However, as Kogut indicated, a JV cannot be considered unstable simply because its lifespan is short. All relationships between firms face challenges that threaten to change or terminate the basis for cooperation. Sometimes terminations are planned and anticipated by the involved parties. Ventures also may be terminated as a matter of policy when there is a change in the ownership or management of the parent. In other cases, difficulties associated with ending a relationship may create a rationale for maintaining an existing JV that would otherwise be terminated.

We maintain that instability should be linked with *unplanned* equity changes or major reorganizations. Usually, instability will result in premature termination of a JV, either when one partner acquires the JV business or the venture is dissolved. A complicating factor is that termination of a JV will not always be a mutual decision (Hamel, 1991; Parkhe, 1991). The premature termination of a JV may be precipitated by the actions of one partner. For example, when one firm is trying to learn from its partner in order to reduce its dependency, the partner that is doing the learning may have very different longevity objectives than the partner that is providing the knowledge. In this scenario, a terminated relationship would be classified as unstable, because termination was premature from the perspective of the partner that is providing the knowledge. If at least one of the partners anticipates a long-term relationship, premature termination of the venture would constitute instability. When both partners plan for termination at the time the JV is formed, instability will not be an issue unless termination occurs prematurely.

In keeping with the previous arguments, JV *instability* is defined as a major change in relationship status that was *unplanned* and *premature* from the perspective of either one or both partners. In most JVs, the partners do not have a specific plan for the termination of their ventures.[3] The premature termination of a JV can be traumatic for the venture partners. However, it is important to emphasize that we do not equate JV longevity with JV success. Many firms view JVs as intentionally temporary and recognize that their ventures will not last indefinitely. If a JV termination is an orderly and mutually planned event, the JV may well be evaluated as extremely successful. A JV that is prematurely terminated also may be evaluated as successful, depending on the criteria used to evaluate its performance.[4]

If an unstable JV involves changes in relationship status, a stable JV, by definition, must be one without unplanned changes in relationship status. However, stable JVs may be terminated when the strategic needs of the partners change. For example, in 1995, Chrysler announced that it was winding down its 25-year alliance with Mitubishi Motors (Templin, 1995). One of Chrysler's objectives in the relationship was access to a source of small cars for the U.S. market. Because Chrysler developed an internal supply of cars, the rationale for the relationship with Mitsubishi was no longer present.

A further consideration is that stability carries a positive connotation. In the opening section of this chapter, we linked stability with a win-win relationship. In our view, a stable JV is one in which the partners believe the benefits to the relationship exceed the costs of termination. Nevertheless, a JV may have the outward appearances of stability; however, one partner may view it as unsuccessful because the balance of power has shifted to a degree that is undesirable. In another section of this article, we discuss how the acquisition of knowledge by one partner in what looks like a stable JV can create the potential for instability.

Theoretical underpinnings

Our framework is conceptually grounded in a bargaining power and dependence perspective. This perspective was developed by Emerson (1962) and was generalized to the organizational level in Pfeffer and Salancik's (1978) resource dependence model. The essence of the model is that the possession or control of key resources by one entity may make other organizations dependent on that entity. According to this notion of resource fit, relationships are terminated for the inverse of the reasons for which they were formed (Seabright et al., 1992). Young and Oik (1994) found support for this argument in a study of U.S.-based R&D consortia. In this study, alliance firms that had gained knowledge as a result of membership in the consortium were more likely to leave the alliance.

In a cooperative relationship, dependence can be a source of power for the firm controlling key resources, because, to some degree, each firm can increase or withhold resources that are attractive to its partner (Bacharach & Lawler, 1980). When one firm controls an "irreplaceable" JV resource or input, a dependency situation is created (Hamel, 1991). Although dependency is voluntary when firms choose to form JVs, once the JV is operational, firms depend on their partners for specific resources and inputs. A firm that has the option to contribute or withhold an important resource or input can use that option as leverage in bargaining with its partner (Pfeffer, 1981).

The notion of "cooperative" may seem at odds with dependence and power. However, the key point is that at the time an IJV is formed, each partner is dependent on the other(s) for critical inputs. The firms must cooperate to ensure that these critical inputs are transformed into a productive entity (i.e., the IJV). Over time, the dependence may change, and as a result, the bargaining power of one partner may be enhanced. When that happens, the JV partner with the increased bargaining power has access to more partners and options, including terminating the venture, compared to the partner with limited bargaining power (Yan & Gray, 1994).

The bargaining power perspective is particularly appropriate for the examination of the stability of JVs, because all JVs involve a negotiated bargain between the partners. At a general level, bargaining power in JVs is based on the relative urgency of cooperation, available resources, commitments, other alternatives, and the strengths and weaknesses of each partner (Schelling, 1956). Focusing mainly on domestic JVs, Harrigan and Newman (1990) adopted the view that the relative bargaining power of potential JV partners is determined primarily by what each partner brings to the venture. Rarely will these contributions be symmetrical, because each partner views the potential costs and benefits of cooperating differently. As partners' strategic missions, expectations, loyalties and resource mixes change, the balance of bargaining power in the JV shifts (Harrigan & Newman, 1990). When the balance of power shifts, and inevitably it will, the need for cooperation between the partners may diminish or disappear. At this point, the parent may decide to undertake all activities that were previously performed by the JV (Harrigan, 1986).

Yan and Gray's (1994) inductive study, perhaps the most systematic exploration of the concept of bargaining power in IJVs to date, identified resource-based and context-based components of bargaining power. The context-based components, although important, are only indirectly related to the dynamics of the IJV relationship. Given our primary interest in shifts in partner bargaining power associated with the acquisition of knowledge, the resource-based components are of particular interest. The resources and capabilities committed by the partners to the JV were a major source of bargaining power. Expertise in areas such as local sourcing, domestic distribution, and personnel management was the main resource contributed by the local partners (Yan & Gray, 1994). For the foreign partners, resource contributions included expertise and technology for production management and global support.

To link the partner resource contributions directly to bargaining power and to understand the process of bargaining power shifts, concepts of organizational knowledge management must be incorporated in the framework. The pace of knowledge acquisition by one IJV partner is an important process dimension, because, as Hamel (1991) argued, this dimension is very much within the firm's control. Therefore, Hamel identified learning as the most important element in determining relative bargaining power. Substantial knowledge acquisition by one partner over time can erode the value of the knowledge contributed by the other partner, breaking down the bargaining relationship between the partners. This argument forms the fundamental conceptual premise of this article: The acquisition of knowledge and skills can shift an IJV partner's bargaining power and may enable the firm to eliminate its dependency on its partner.

Partners in IJVs acquire knowledge and skills through a process of knowledge management and creation. Although still rather small, there is a growing body of theoretical (Kogut, 1988; Parkhe, 1991; Pucik, 1991; Westney, 1988) and empirical studies (Dodgson, 1993; Hamel, 1991; Inkpen, 1995a; Inkpen & Crossan, 1995; Simonin & Helleloid, 1993) addressing the issue of JVs and alliances as mechanisms for gaining access to partners' knowledge and skills. When a JV is created, organizational boundaries become permeable. This permeability provides firms with a "window on their partners' broad capabilities" (Hamel et al., 1989: 134). Consequently, knowledge creation and learning should be viewed as potential strategic benefits of joint venturing.

By forming a JV, partner firms may gain access to the embedded knowledge of other organizations and, therefore, to new organizational skills and capabilities. Through their involvement in the operation of the JV, firms can learn from their partners. Huber (1991) called this *grafting*, the process by which firms internalize knowledge not previously available within the organization. Knowledge perceived as potentially useful for the organization may be acquired by individual managers or organizational subunits, such as a JV (Inkpen, 1995b). This knowledge has the potential to be shared and distributed within the organization, and through processes of amplification and interpretation, the knowledge is given shared organizational meaning (Daft & Weick, 1984; Nonaka, 1994). The translation of new knowledge into organizational action is the basis for creating new skills that underpin a firm's competitive advantage. Of particular interest in this article is the knowledge that enables firms involved in IJVs to eliminate dependencies on their partners.

A framework of instability in IJVs

Through a focus on partner knowledge acquisition that shifts bargaining power, Figure 16.2 illustrates the framework of the instability of the IJV. As discussed in the previous section, the initial balance of power between partners of the IJV will inevitably shift. In the next sections,

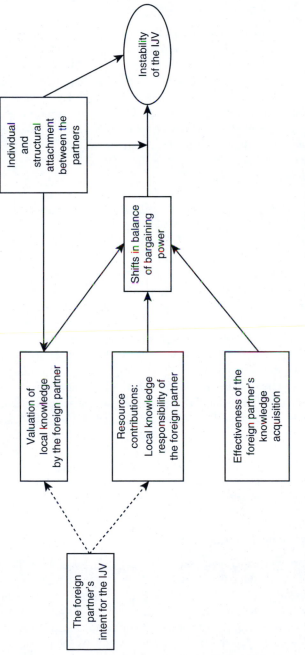

Figure 16.2 Instability of the International Joint Ventures (IJVs) and the foreign partner's bargaining power.

we examine the factors associated with these shifts in bargaining power, and from this discussion, we generate specific propositions.

Knowledge acquisition by the foreign partner

Knowledge of the local environment is usually a key resource of local partners; it is also a key source of bargaining power, because it makes the foreign partner dependent on the local partner (Yan & Gray, 1994). As a foreign partner increases its knowledge of the local market, instability of the IJV relationship becomes more probable, because the foreign partner gains bargaining power. When the JV was formed, local knowledge may have contributed to the mutual needs of the partners (Beamish, 1988). When the need dissipates, and the foreign partner acquires local knowledge, the foreign partner may view a JV as unnecessary. In effect, over time, the unique domain of the local partner shifts from being complementary to the foreign partner to being undistinguished (Ring & Van de Ven, 1994). This line of reasoning leads to the following proposition:

> *Proposition 1: As the foreign partner's local knowledge increases, the foreign partner's dependence on the local partner decreases, leading to a shift in bargaining power and greater likelihood of the instability of the IJV.*

A reduction in the foreign partner's commitment to the IJV and need for its partner need does not always mean the foreign partner will acquire the IJV business or establish a subsidiary. As the foreign partner increases its local knowledge, various outcomes are possible. For example, an increase in knowledge that erased a partner dependency plus a desire to maintain a presence in the local market were the circumstances prompting Ralston Purina, Bayer AG, Monsanto Co. and Sandoz to convert alliances to subsidiaries in Japan (Ono, 1991).[5] In Ralston Purina's case, the firm ended its 20-year venture with Taiyo Fishery Company and established a wholly owned Japanese subsidiary. After gaining experience in Japan, Ralston Purina's management apparently decided that a Japanese partner was no longer necessary.

Alternatively, as the foreign partner learns about local market realities, it may decide to withdraw from the market. In contrast, the foreign partner may seek a more prominent role in the management of the JV, leading to conflict over the division of control, which in turn could lead to an unstable relationship. Finally, as we discuss in another section, the embedded history of prior relationships between the partners may be a stabilizing factor that counterbalances shifts in bargaining power.

Knowledge acquisition by the local partner

In contrast to the foreign partner's building of a local knowledge base, the local partner may acquire the skills of its foreign partner, making the IJV redundant, because the foreign partner's skill-based resource contributions are no longer needed. In their study of U.S.-China JVs, Yan and Gray (1994) found that for Chinese firms in IJVs, the overwhelming goal in cooperating with Western firms was to learn the more advanced Western technology. The Chinese partners fully expected that management would shift from the foreigners to them. However, Yan and Gray (1994) concluded that the Chinese partners did not significantly gain bargaining power through knowledge, because the U.S. partners protected their technologies. Also, the U.S. partners were able to maintain the original balance of bargaining power by making additional resource commitments to their technological capabilities.

Even if local partners have unhindered access to the foreign partner's skills, the knowledge required to eliminate a foreign dependency is usually more difficult to acquire for the local partner than for the foreign partner. The New United Motor Manufacturing Inc. (NUMMI) JV in California between General Motors and Toyota illustrates this point. Because NUMMI had been managed by Toyota, Toyota's managers were forced to learn how to work with American workers and labor unions. Toyota has deployed its new knowledge in a wholly owned plant in Georgetown, Kentucky. As described by a senior manager at Toyota, that knowledge came directly from Toyota's NUMMI experience (Sasaki, 1993).

Hedlund (1994) distinguished among three forms of knowledge: (a) cognitive knowledge in the form of mental constructs, (b) skills and (c) knowledge embodied in products and well-defined services. Hedlund suggested that embodied knowledge was the easiest to transfer, followed by cognitive knowledge, skills were most difficult to transfer. Skills, such as complex engineering processes, are highly embedded in organizational routines (Nelson & Winter, 1982) and, therefore, are difficult to extract from another firm. Also, the foreign partner can take explicit measures to protect the transparency of its skills, particularly if the skills comprise explicit knowledge held by a few "experts" (for example, Kentucky Fried Chicken's secret recipe of herbs and spices). Local knowledge, such as investment regulations, supplier practices, labor laws and cultural traditions, can be classified primarily as cognitive knowledge. Cognitive knowledge is usually easier to transfer than skills because it is not as sensitive to team embeddedness (Zander, 1991, cited in Hedlund, 1994). In many cases, it is tacit knowledge (Polanyi, 1966) that is highly contact dependent; for IJVs, the context is the local environment. Because this knowledge often comes packaged in the form of individuals (Hedlund, 1994), foreign partners can gain access to the knowledge through active managerial involvement in the IJV process. In other words, the experience of the managers in an IJV is the key to acquiring this type of knowledge (Nonaka & Takeuchi, 1995).

The skills provided by the foreign partner, such as how to manufacture high-precision products, will consist of a combination of both tacit and explicit, or codifiable, knowledge. The explicit knowledge that can be expressed in schemata, diagrams and charts is relatively easy to transfer, although as Zander (1991) found, codifiability does not necessarily lead to faster competitor imitation. Because tacit and explicit knowledge are mutually complementary (Nonaka & Takeuchi, 1995), there will be a strong tacit dimension associated with how to use and implement the explicit knowledge. This tacit and difficult dimension is the "glue" that holds together the organizational routines associated with the foreign partner's skills.

Empirical evidence supports the previous arguments. Hamel (1991) found that market intelligence was transfered between alliance partners more easily than knowledge of leading-edge manufacturing skills. The local partners in Yan and Gray's (1994) study encountered significant difficulty in learning from their U.S. partners. When successfully implementing a local strategy in the United States, Toyota's executives needed only to learn how to transfer an existing management process to North America. For General Motors to reduce its dependency on Toyota, changes in very fundamental operating philosophies were required (Badaracco, 1991; Sasaki, 1993). The local knowledge that Toyota needed was more accessible and easier to internalize than the knowledge base that General Motors had to build. Finally, Hennart et al. (1995) studied Japanese JVs in the United States and found that when JVs were terminated, the more common scenario involved the Japanese partner acquiring the JV business, and by implication, the local knowledge necessary to run the business.

In summary, knowledge acquisition by either partner has the potential to shift the balance of bargaining power that, in turn, could lead to the initiation of changes in the partner relationship. This is illustrated in Figure 16.3. To the extent that the balance of power shifts

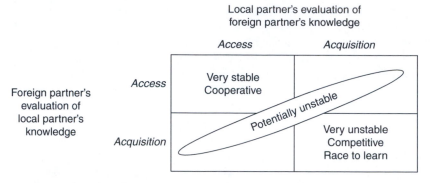

Figure 16.3 Knowledge acquisition and instability.

sufficiently to lead to instability, it is more likely that the underlying cause is knowledge acquisition by the foreign partner compared to knowledge acquisition by the local partner. We also expect that the "skilling" of the local partner (leaking the foreign partner's skills to the local partner) should be less likely in IJVs than in other types of alliances, most notably technology-sharing relationships or R&D alliances. This is because a JV is a separate entity, in which the local partner may have difficulty penetrating the venture's boundaries to gain access to the foreign partner's skills. The foreign partner may put up barriers to keep the local partner outside specific skill areas. In contrast, there are fewer boundaries in a technology-sharing relationship, which increases the risk that organizational skills may be appropriated by a partner (for a discussion of learning in R&D alliances from a domestic perspective, see Young & Oik, 1994). There is little question that particularly in the 1960s, many Japanese firms used licensing arrangements as a source for learning their partner's skills (Reich & Mankin, 1986).

The value of local knowledge

The preceding discussion focused on the *effect* of IJV stability posed when partner knowledge acquisition leads to changes in partner dependency. An equally important issue is why, in some IJVs, foreign partners aggressively seek to acquire local knowledge, but in other IJVs, they do not. We examine this question by starting with a key assumption: When an IJV is formed, the contribution of local knowledge by the local partner has strategic value to the foreign partner (Yan & Gray, 1994). Until the foreign partner acquires sufficient local knowledge to operate autonomously, the foreign partner will continue to depend on its local partner.

The foreign partner's valuation of local knowledge involves two stages. The first stage occurs prior to the formation of the IJV when the foreign partner considers the value associated with gaining access to a potential partner's local knowledge. If gaining access to a partner's local knowledge satisfies the foreign partner's resource requirements, an IJV may result. The second stage occurs after the formation of the IJV, when the foreign partner gains access to local knowledge. The question for the foreign partner now becomes: "Is access sufficient, or should the knowledge be acquired?"

A foreign firm involved in an IJV can choose what resources and how much it can devote to gaining local knowledge acquisition. Acquiring local knowledge *enables* a foreign partner to reduce its commitment to collaboration. If a foreign partner places high strategic value on access to and acquisition of local knowledge, shifts in bargaining power become more likely, because it is likely that the foreign partner will not be content with access alone. Thus, Figure 16.2 shows a direct relationship between the valuation of local knowledge and shifts in the balance of the bargaining power.

> *Proposition 2: The strategic value of local knowledge to the foreign partner will be positively related to shifts in IJV bargaining power.*

Proposition 2 is a refinement of Proposition 1. Proposition 1 suggests that the foreign partner's knowledge of local conditions will inevitably increase over time, simply because the foreign partner is in the host country. This process represents passive knowledge acquisition. Proposition 2 implies active knowledge acquisition by the foreign partner that can shift the JV bargaining power away from the local partner.

Why would a foreign partner actively seek to acquire local knowledge? The critical factor is the strategic intent of the foreign partner. Firms often utilize IJVs as an entry mode in an effort to balance their desire for international product/market diversification and growth with their perceived need for control. The subsequent desire to acquire local knowledge will be driven by various strategic factors. The decision to acquire local knowledge may reflect a desire to increase control over the IJV because of a shift in the strategic importance of the venture (Harrigan & Newman, 1990) or because of the increased importance of the local market. Alternatively, a foreign partner's increased concerns about leaking proprietary technology to the local partner may result in its acquiring local knowledge.

A partner's decision not to acquire local knowledge may reflect the cost of this acquisition. Previously, we used the example of Kentucky Fried Chicken. In order for Kentucky Fried Chicken to eliminate a dependency in China, the firm would have to learn many complex investment regulations, local operating laws, and so on. Although this knowledge was possible, it could be very expensive and there was no guarantee of success. Finally, acquiring local knowledge may be in response to the foreign partner's recognition that the original IJV agreement was an obsolescing bargain (Vernon, 1977), because the local partner has little to contribute on an ongoing basis.

Factors influencing acquisition of local knowledge

When a foreign partner has a strategic objective of acquisition and proprietary control over local knowledge, the speed of knowledge acquisition that is necessary to shift bargaining power will be influenced by two key factors: (a) the foreign partner's effectiveness in acquiring local knowledge, and (b) the initial resource contributions of the partners.

Effectiveness in acquiring local knowledge. Although a foreign partner's acquisition of local knowledge can occur passively over time, explicit efforts to acquire this knowledge are of greater interest. This leads to the premise that knowledge acquisition is an organizational process that can be managed by the foreign partner (Hedlund & Nonaka, 1993; Nonaka, 1994). The process of acquiring knowledge that originates with an IJV partner is, in effect, the process of creating organizational knowledge (Nonaka, 1994). Creating organizational knowledge is not simply a matter of learning from others or acquiring knowledge from outside (Nonaka & Takeuchi, 1995). It is a complex organizational process involving various organizational levels and actors. Through this process, specific knowledge becomes amplified throughout the organization. To capture the dynamic movement of knowledge across various organizational levels, Nonaka (1994) developed the concept of a spiral of knowledge creation. In the spiral, knowledge moves upward in an organization; it begins at the individual level, moves to the group level, and finally moves to the firm level. As the knowledge spirals upward in the organization, individuals interact with each other and with their organizations.

In an IJV, managers assigned to the venture from the foreign parent will be exposed to various aspects of local knowledge. Clearly, these managers will develop new ideas about conducting business in the local environment. However, in order for that local knowledge to be internalized at the parent organizational level, there must be knowledge connections among the various organizational levels to create the potential for individuals to share their observations and experiences (Von Krogh et al., 1994). These knowledge connections provide a basis for transforming individual knowledge into organizational knowledge. An organization's set of internal managerial relationships facilitates the sharing and communicating of new knowledge.

Although the process of knowledge creation is nonlinear and interactive, specific organizational conditions can be identified that promote this process (Nevis et al., 1995; Nonaka & Takeuchi, 1995). Drawing on Nonaka and Takeuchi's (1995) work, empirical researchers using the JV context have identified several key factors that contribute to the ability of firms to acquire knowledge associated with their IJVs (Inkpen, 1997). These factors include partner intention, top management commitment, and tolerance for information redundancy. The absence of these factors creates obstacles to knowledge creation. Although a detailed examination of these factors is beyond the scope of this article, it is important to recognize that the foreign partner's effectiveness in acquiring knowledge will influence its bargaining power. If a foreign partner is ineffective at knowledge creation (and more specifically at acquiring local knowledge), it will not be able to reduce its dependency on the local partner.

Proposition 3: There will be a positive relationship between the foreign partner's effectiveness in acquiring local knowledge and shifts in bargaining power.

Resource contributions of the partners. When a JV is formed, the partners must allocate responsibility for various decision areas (Geringer & Hebert, 1989; Killing, 1983). This allocation of responsibility is the basis for determining the resources and capabilities committed by the partners to the JV (Yan & Gray, 1994). These resource contributions are negotiated by the partners and they are an important factor in determining the initial balance of power.

In an IJV, the local partner is usually expected to contribute important local knowledge. However, this does not mean that the foreign partner cannot contribute resources associated with local management. For example, in many of the Japanese-American JVs formed to supply U.S.-based automotive transplants, the Japanese partners controlled local marketing functions (Womack, 1988). Therefore, the American partners contributed local knowledge confined to areas such as legal process, workforce management, and some supplier management. Without control over local marketing, American partners were in a vulnerable position should their Japanese partners seek to acquire further local knowledge.

Initial resource contributions of the partners, as determined by the allocation of strategic responsibilities, will play an important role in stability of the IJV, because of their influence on the complexity of the foreign partner's knowledge acquisition task. By relinquishing local responsibilities to the foreign partner when the venture is formed, the local partner provides the foreign partner with an incentive to gain complete local knowledge and, hence, to increase its bargaining power. The acquisition of local knowledge by the foreign partner also is simplified if the JV starts out with the responsibility for key local knowledge belonging to the foreign partner.

Thus, we predict that initial resource contributions made to an IJV will influence subsequent shifts in bargaining power. It has already been established that firms will differ in how effective they will be at acquiring knowledge. The foreign partner's responsibility for local knowledge at the time the IJV is formed will determine the nature of the knowledge-acquisition task necessary to reduce a partner dependency. If the foreign partner views the task as complex, it may be dissuaded from acquiring additional knowledge. In contrast, if the foreign partner views the task as relatively simple, it is likely that it will acquire more knowledge and likelihood for shifts in bargaining power will be greater. The foreign partner's responsibility for local knowledge will be related to the likelihood of shifts in bargaining power.

Proposition 4: The greater the responsibility for local knowledge initially allocated to the foreign partner, the more likely that the foreign partner will seek additional local knowledge from the local partner and the more likely that bargaining power will shift.

Regardless of the speed of local knowledge acquisition, it is important to emphasize that when a foreign partner has the explicit intent to gain knowledge, the local partner is in a vulnerable position. In IJVs in developing countries, the vulnerability of the local partners can be high if the local partner is not a competitive threat to the foreign partner outside the IJV's country of domicile. In this case, the foreign partner is usually larger and has greater international scope; therefore, local partners may not be able to prevent a foreign partner from increasing its local knowledge. It is also unrealistic to expect foreign partners to complacently ignore the opportunity to increase their local knowledge. However, as Dymsza (1988) noted, the foreign firm's contribution may become less important over time if the firm from the developing country is committed to increasing its skills.

Furthermore, if the value of local knowledge declines, in terms of either access or acquisition, the foreign partner may choose to end the venture. For example, local knowledge may decline in value if changes in local regulations open up a previously closed economy to greater competition.

Attachment between the partners

Attachment is the binding of one party to another (Salancik, 1977). Attachment between partners develops through experience in the collaborative relationship and through investments the partners make in the relationship over time (Seabright et al., 1992). When the partners have developed a strong attachment, inertial forces may block the pressures for change in the relationship (Blau, 1964; Salancik, 1977). If firms have worked together in the past, they will have a basic understanding about each other's skills and capabilities (Heide & Miner, 1992). The partners may have developed commitments to each other because of a relationship that existed prior to forming the JV. According to Parkhe (1993a: 803): "The older a relationship, the greater the likelihood it has passed through a critical shakeout period of conflict and influence attempts by both sides."

Because of prior relationships, firms often form JVs with firms with whom they have transacted in the past. For example, in a study of 40 IJVs, Inkpen (1995a) found that in 24 cases, the partners had previously worked together. An MNE's knowledge about its local partner, generated through previous interactions, also can play an important role in determining its equity position in the host country (Sohn, 1994).

Attachments in collaborative relationships may be the result of individual or structural ties that reflect the prior history of the relationship (Seabright et al., 1992). Individual attachment reflects the socialization by individuals during their involvement in exchange activities. Seabright and colleagues (1992) suggested that individual attachments are important early in a relationship but that they diminish in significance as the relationship persists. In IJVs, individual attachment may be represented by personal relationships between partners' managers. Such managers may initiate a relationship based on personal knowledge and trust that in the early years of the JV provides a buffer against the normal pressures of collaboration. It is common in IJVs for a partner's senior managers to take an active interest in the JV process and make a commitment to working with top managers from the other partner(s). Ring and Van de Ven (1994) suggested that personal bonds of friendship can lead to norms of group inclusion and escalate the commitment by parties to a cooperative relationship. They proposed that the likelihood of termination of inter-organizational relationships decreased over time, because economic exchanges become transformed into socially embedded relationships.

Individual attachments are closely related to the tenure of individual boundary-spanning managers involved in the IJV (Seabright et al., 1992). A high turnover of managers can lead to a loss of relationship continuity and a reduction of individual attachment. Structural attachment reflects the history of organizational investments made since the formation of the IJV (Seabright et al., 1992). Structural attachments should increase with the duration of the relationship as formalized procedures replace some of the coordination of IJV activities through personal contact (Van de Ven, 1976).

Continuing business relationships often become overlaid with social content that generates strong expectations of trust and forbearance (Granovetter, 1985). Attachment can lead to the formation of JVs that have an existing stock of "relationship assets" (Fichman & Levinthal, 1991) and a high degree of interpartner trust (Gulati, 1995). Parkhe (1991) suggested that the unplanned termination of an IJV is more likely when firms are working together for the first time. Kogut (1989) found that structural ties between JV partners were negatively related to JV dissolution. Kogut's variable for structured ties was a composite of three types of relationships: supply, other JVs and licensing agreements. We predict that attachment exerts a main effect on the likelihood of instability.

Proposition 5: The greater the individual or structural attachment between the IJV partners, the lower the likelihood of IJV instability.

The central theme of this article is that shifts in partner bargaining power are the underlying cause of instability in IJVs. As a firm acquires knowledge that reduces its dependency on its IJV partner, the likelihood of instability increases. As we argued previously in the case of the foreign partner, knowledge of local conditions will inevitably increase over time, simply because the foreign partner is now located in the host country. An IJV partner also may actively engage in acquiring knowledge, which results in reduced partner dependency and a shift in bargaining power. However, because of attachment, the shift in bargaining power associated with knowledge acquisition will not necessarily lead to instability in IJVs.

Blau (1964) and Cook (1977) argued that attachment can lead to maintaining a relationship that provides fewer of the needed resources than it originally did. Seabright and colleagues

(1992: 123) suggested that attachment "constitutes a counterforce to change rather than a pressure for change. . . In this manner, attachment may attenuate the effects of changes affecting resource fit on the likelihood of a relationship dissolving." This discussion suggests that attachment can moderate the effects of shifts in bargaining power. Thus, the effect of shifts in bargaining power on the likelihood of instability decreases as attachment increases.

> *Proposition 6: The greater the individual and structural attachment between IJV partners, the lower the effect of shifts in bargaining power on the likelihood of IJV instability.*

The argument that relationship investments and attachments can moderate the forces of shifts in bargaining power may appear counter to the previous discussion on resource fit and the termination of relationships for the inverse of the reasons for which they were formed. IJVs involve many layers of interfirm complexity (Harrigan & Newman, 1990). Our view is that in any IJV, there will be both resource fit and attachment implications, which may exert opposing forces on the stability of the relationship. The forces may lead to what we term dormant *instability*.[6] When the foreign partner acquires sufficient local knowledge to destabilize the IJV, a situation of dormant instability (or superficial stability from the opposite perspective) results. The foreign partner may choose to reorient or restructure the relationship, or, because of attachment, it may be willing to let the potential instability lie dormant. In any event, once the local knowledge is acquired by the foreign partner, the balance of power between the partners has shifted. This dormant instability may ultimately have a destabilizing impact on the IJV, because both partners now understand that the foreign partner's voluntary dependence on the local partner's knowledge contributions may not last. This situation may also lead to resentment by the local partner, which in itself is a source of instability.

Attachment and the valuation of knowledge. Our proposed framework incorporates the dynamic nature of IJVs. A foreign partner's valuation of local knowledge will be influenced by both strategic factors and by the strength of the partner relationship. This valuation is represented in Figure 16.2 by the feedback loop from attachment to the valuation of local knowledge by the foreign partner. Attachment is the result of an evolving history of partner interactions. When an IJV is formed, attachments may be present that may have developed either through prior interfirm relationships or during the negotiation stage. As the duration of an IJV increases, structural attachments will likely continue to develop. Individual attachments may increase or decrease, depending on the continuity of managers involved in the IJV. As the level of attachment changes, we predict that this shift will influence the foreign partner's evaluation of the strategic value associated with its partner's local knowledge.

> *Proposition 7: Changes in individual and structural attachment between IJV partners will lead to updating of the foreign partner's valuation of local knowledge.*

Managerial implications

For a foreign firm that is interested in maintaining a stable, long-term IJV relationship, this chapter has several implications. First, explicit attempts to build knowledge of the local country by capitalizing on the local partner's experience are usually transparent and may be interpreted by local partners as competitive rather than collaborative in nature. Second, IJV partners may have to let their IJV develop its own culture and systems. General Electric has followed this strategy with its successful Japanese JVs. GE has leveraged its Japanese partners' names to recruit personnel for its JVs and allowed its JVs to develop into independent companies without interference from the parents in day-to-day management (Turpin, 1993). Third, continuity in the personal relationships between the top management of both partners can be an important source of attachment between the partners. Without continuity, there is the risk of "corporate amnesia", whereby managers in the parent companies forget their original motivation for this alliance and the past lessons from their relationship (Turpin, 1993).

Toppan Moore, a JV between Toppan Printing of Japan and Moore Corporation (Moore) of Canada, provides a good example of a stable, long-lasting collaboration (Beamish & Makino, 1994). With 1994 revenues of more than $1.5 billion and more than 3,000 employees, Toppan Moore was Japan's largest company that produced business forms and its third largest printing company. In this, Moore contributed manufacturing and product technologies, and the Japanese partner assumed initial responsibility for sales, distribution and local marketing support.[7] Over time, the JV modified products to meet the requirements of Japanese customers and developed its own production capabilities, reducing its day-to-day dependence on Moore. Moore maintained its bargaining power by continuing to make technological and marketing contributions. Although the Japanese partner's immediate operational need for Moore lessened, access to future technological developments remained an important aspect of the relationship. Consequently, the advantages of collaboration for Moore and Toppan Printing continued to outweigh the need for competition.

Local partners and the control of instability. When a local partner is interested in stability, it should consider several ideas associated with controlling IJV stability and minimizing the foreign partner's acquisition of local knowledge. First, the local partner can discourage the foreign partner from sending large numbers of managers to the venture. As we indicated previously, knowledge creation in organizations begins with individuals. The greater the number of foreign managers at the IJV, the greater the foreign partner's access to local knowledge. Second, the local partner can continue to actively invest in local knowledge. In other words, the local partner should not treats its knowledge contributions passively, but it should continue to upgrade the value of the knowledge to the foreign partner. Third, the local partner can consider the track records of potential partners, particularly how long other IJVs that they were a part of have survived. This record should provide an indication of the foreign partner's expectations regarding the role of the local partner. Finally, the local partner can bargain for greater responsibility in managing the JV and, in effect, increase the importance of its role in the venture's success.

Conclusion

When JVs are formed to exploit interfirm differences in skills, there is always the risk that one partner may acquire knowledge that it lacked when the alliance was formed (Parkhe, 1993b). In fact, many firms enter JVs with the objective to gain explicit knowledge (Hamel, 1991; Inkpen, 1995a). When knowledge acquisition shifts the balance of bargaining power between partners, the cooperative basis for the JV may erode and venture instability may result. Even though this argument applies to any JV in which partner knowledge contributions create a dependency, the focus in this article was on IJVs and the specific nature of local knowledge. When a JV is international and the foreign partner seeks to expand its geographic scope of operations, the local partner's knowledge of local economic, political and cultural environments will be a key contribution to the JV. Our main argument is that once the venture is formed, if the foreign partner attaches a high value to the acquisition of local knowledge and has the ability to acquire the knowledge, the probability of JV instability increases. Once the foreign partner has acquired local knowledge, unless the local partner is contributing other valuable and nonimitable skills to the JV, the rationale for cooperation will be eliminated. Instability may be the result, although attachment between the partners may moderate the shifts in bargaining power. Thus, the acquisition of local knowledge is an enabling device for the foreign partner to operate autonomously.

Although some ventures are formed in which the partners agree on a termination plan, this article was focused on instability as an undesirable event for one or all partners. Given its undesirability, if a local partner takes steps to ensure that its role encompasses more than simply contributing local knowledge, instability may be controllable. A foreign partner may also choose as a viable strategy access of local knowledge rather than acquisition of the knowledge. Consequently, IJVs can be stable and sustainable arrangements for creating competitive advantage.

Notes

The authors thank Steve Currall, Charles Hill, and *AMR*'s five anonymous reviewers for their help in developing this article.

1 When government legislation prohibits wholly owned subsidiaries, silent partners that contribute little more than a means to bypass legislation may be used. Also, if a foreign partner cannot legally become sole owner of the JV, our stability arguments do not hold. However, as trade and investment opportunities have become more liberal, particularly in developing countries, few countries continue to mandate the use of JVs for foreign investment.

2 For example, licensing agreements and arrangements for sharing technology have gained notoriety as vehicles for licensee firms to build their own skill base and shift the alliance of power in their favor. An article that describes the competitive implications of sharing technology with a potential competitor was written by Reich and Mankin (1986). These authors focused on high-technology agreements in which the U.S. partner acquired and distributed Japanese products (in effect, outsourcing relationships). Note that these are not JVs according to our definition.

3 A seldom used option is to incorporate "fade-out" provisions in the JV agreement. This type of venture has been used in China, but it has been largely discontinued. If longevity is not a goal, another option is "contractual" JVs that include a specific termination date. Also, JV agreements sometimes include a specific period of time during which the partners have the option to either renegotiate or modify their agreement.

4 This definition of instability raises some interesting methodological questions. Specifically, how can the pre-JV motives of the JV partners be measured accurately? A longitudinal approach beginning at, or ideally before, the time of JV formation would provide the richest insights into the collaborative process.

5 A popular stereotype is that of a "naive" U.S. firm contributing technology and a Japanese firm contributing local knowledge to a Japan-based JV. After several years of operation, the Japanese company is familiar with the technology and no longer needs the JV, whereas the U.S. firm has gained nothing in the local market. There is no systematic evidence to support this argument. Many technology-licensing arrangements in Japan have ended this way, but these were not JVs designed to enter the Japanese market. As the Purina, Monsanto, Bayer and Sandoz cases suggest, foreign firms in Japan are capable of making their local partners obsolete. According to Jones and Shill (1993), the survival record of Western-Japanese alliances in Japan is very good. These authors studied 200 alliances that were terminated and found that, on average, the alliances lasted 20 years.

6 Our thanks to an anonymous reviewer for suggesting this point.

7 Given the difficulty in penetrating Japanese markets, it is unlikely that Moore was in a position to control sales and distribution in the JV when it was formed. However, the examples of Ralston Purina, Bayer AG, and Monsanto Co. suggest that foreign firms can acquire local marketing knowledge over time.

References

Bacharach, S., & Lawler, E. J. 1980. *Power and politics in organizations*. San Francisco: Jossey-Bass.

Badaracco, J. 1991. *The knowledge link*. Boston: Harvard Business School Press.

Bartlett, C. A., & Ghoshal, S. 1989. *Managing across borders: The transnational solution*. Boston: Harvard Business School Press.

Beamish, P. W. 1988. *Multinational joint ventures in developing countries*. London: Routledge.

Beamish, P. W., & Makino, S. 1994. Toppan Moore. In P. W. Beamish, J. P. Killing, D. Lecraw, & A. Morrison (Eds.), *International management* (2nd ed.): 388–402. Burr Ridge, IL: Irwin.

Blau, P. M. 1964. *Exchange and power in social life*. New York: Wiley.

Bleeke, J., & Ernst, D. 1991. The way to win in cross-border alliances. *Harvard Business Review*, 69(6): 127–35.

Blodgett, L. L. 1992. Factors in the instability of international joint ventures: An event history analysis. *Strategic Management Journal*, 13: 475–81.

Contractor, F. J., & Lorange, P. 1988. Why should firms cooperate: The strategy and economics basis for cooperative ventures. In F. Contractor & P. Lorange (Eds.), *Cooperative strategies in international business:* 3–30. Lexington, MA: Lexington Books.

Cook, K. 1977. Exchange and power in networks of interorganizational relations. *Sociological Quarterly*, 18: 62–82.

Daft, R. L., & Weick, K. E. 1984. Toward a model of organizations as interpretation systems. *Academy of Management Review*, 9: 284–95.

Dodgson, M. 1993. Learning, trust, and technological collaboration. *Human Relations*, 46: 77–95.

Doz, Y., Prahalad, C. K., & Hamel, G. 1990. Control, change, and flexibility: The dilemma of transnational collaboration. In C. Bartlett, Y. Doz, & G. Hedlund (Eds.), *Managing the global firm:* 117–143. London: Routledge.

Dymsza, W. A. 1988. Successes and failures of joint ventures in developing countries: Lessons from experience. In F. Contractor & P. Lorange (Eds.), *Cooperative strategies in international business:* 403–24. Lexington, MA: Lexington Books.

Emerson, R. M. 1962. Power dependence relationships. *American Sociological Review*, 27(February): 31–41.

Fichman, M., & Levinthal, D. A. 1991. Honeymoons and the liability of adolescence: A new perspective on duration dependence in social and organizational relationships. *Academy of Management Review*, 16: 442–68.

Franko, L. 1971. *Joint venture survival in multinational companies*. New York: Praeger.

Geringer, J. M., & Hebert, L. 1989. Control and performance of international joint ventures. *Journal of International Business Studies*, 20: 235–54.

Granovetter, M. 1985. Economic action and social structure: The problem of embeddedness. *American Journal of Sociology*, 78: 481–510.

Gulati, R. 1995. Does familiarity breed trust? The implications of repeated ties for contractual choice in alliances. *Academy of Management Journal*, 38: 85–112.

Hamel, G. 1991. Competition for competence and inter-partner learning within international strategic alliances [Special Issue]. *Strategic Management Journal*, 12: 83–104.

Hamel, G., Doz, Y. L., & Prahalad, C. K. 1989. Collaborate with your competitors—and win. *Harvard Business Review*, 67(1): 133–9.

Harrigan, K. R. 1986. *Managing for joint venture success*. Lexington, MA: Lexington Books.

Harrigan, K. R., & Newman, W. H. 1990. Bases of interorganizational cooperation: Propensity, power, persistence. *Journal of Management Studies*, 27: 417–34.

Hedlund, G. 1994. A model of knowledge management and the N-form corporation. *Strategic Management Journal*, 15: 73–90.

Hedlund, G., & Nonaka, I. 1993. Models of knowledge management in the West and Japan. In P. Lorange, B. Chakravarthy, J. Roos, & A. Van de Ven (Eds.), *Implementing strategic processes: Change, learning, and cooperation:* 117–144. Oxford: Basil Blackwell.

Heide, J. B., & Miner, A. S. 1992. The shadow of the future: Effects of anticipated interaction and the frequency of contact on buyer–seller cooperation. *Academy of Management Journal*, 35: 265–91.

Hennart, J. F. 1991. The transactions cost theory of joint ventures: An empirical study of Japanese subsidiaries in the United States. *Management Science*, 37: 483–97.

Hennart, J. F., Roehl, T., & Zietlow, D. S. 1995. *"Trojan horse" or "workhorse"? The evolution of U.S.–Japanese joint ventures in the United States*—Revised. CIBER Working paper 95–103, College of Commerce and Business Administration, University of Illinois, Urbana-Champaign, IL.

Huber, G. P. 1991. Organizational learning: The contributing processes and a review of the literatures. *Organization Science*, 2: 88–117.

Inkpen, A. C. 1995a. *The management of international joint ventures: An organizational learning perspective*. London: Routledge.

Inkpen, A. C. 1995b. Organizational learning and international joint ventures. *Journal of International Management*, 1: 165–98.

Inkpen, A. C. 1997. An examination of knowledge management in international joint ventures. In P. W. Beamish & J. P. Killing (Eds.), *Cooperative strategies: North American perspectives*. San Francisco: New Lexington Press.

Inkpen, A. C, & Crossan, M. M. 1995. Believing is seeing: Joint ventures and organization learning. *Journal of Management Studies*, 32: 595–618.

Jones, K. K., & Shill, W. E. 1993. Japan: Allying for advantage. In J. Bleeke & D. Ernst (Eds.), *Collaborating to compete: Using strategic alliances and acquisitions in the global marketplace*: 115–44. New York: Wiley.

Killing, J. P. 1983. *Strategies for joint venture success*. New York: Praeger.

Kogut, B. 1988. Joint ventures: Theoretical and empirical perspectives. *Strategic Management Journal*, 9: 319–22.

Kogut, B. 1989. The stability of joint ventures: Reciprocity and competitive rivalry. *Journal of Industrial Economics*, 38: 183–98.

Makino, S. 1995. *Joint venture ownership structure and performance: Japanese joint ventures in Asia*. Unpublished doctoral dissertation. University of Western Ontario, London, ON.

Nelson, R. R., & Winter, S. G. 1982. *An evolutionary theory of economic change*. Cambridge, MA: Harvard University Press.

Nevis, E. C, DiBella, A., & Gould, J. M. 1995. Understanding organizations as learning systems. *Sloan Management Review*, 23(2): 73–85.

Nonaka, I. 1994. A dynamic theory of organizational knowledge. *Organization Science*, 5: 14–37.

Nonaka, I., & Takeuchi, H. 1995. *The knowledge-creating company: How Japanese companies create the dynamics of innovation*. New York: Oxford University Press.

Ono, Y. 1991. Borden's breakup with Meiji Milk shows how a Japanese partnership can curdle. *Wall Street Journal*, February 21: Bl, B6.

Parkhe, A. 1991. Interfirm diversity, organizational learning, and longevity in global strategic alliances. *Journal of International Business Studies*, 22: 579–602.

Parkhe, A. 1993a. Strategic alliance structuring: A game theoretic and transaction cost examination of interfirm cooperation. *Academy of Management Journal*, 36: 794–829.

Parkhe, A. 1993b. "Messy" research, methodological predispositions, and theory development in international joint ventures. *Academy of Management Review*, 18: 227–68.

Pfeffer, J. 1981. *Power in organizations*. New York: Pitman.

Pfeffer, J., & Salancik, G. R. 1978. *The external control of organizations: A resource dependence perspective*. New York: Harper and Row.

Polanyi, M. 1966. *The tacit dimension*. London: Routledge & Kegan Paul.

Porter, M. E. 1990. *The competitive advantage of nations*. New York: Free Press.

Pucik, V. 1991. Technology transfer in strategic alliances. Competitive collaboration and organizational learning. In T. Agmon & M. A. Von Glinow (Eds.), *Technology transfer in international business*: 121–38. New York: Oxford University Press.

Reich, R., & Mankin, E. 1986. Joint ventures with Japan give away our future. *Harvard Business Review*, 64(2): 78–86.

Ring, P. S., & Van de Ven, A. 1994. Developmental processes of cooperative interorganizational relationships. *Academy of Management Review*, 19: 90–118.

Salancik, G. R. 1977. Commitment and the control of organizational behavior and belief. In B. M. Staw & G. R. Salancik (Eds.), *New directions in organizational behavior:* 1–54. Chicago: St. Clair Press.

Sasaki, T. 1993. What the Japanese have learned from strategic alliances. *Long Range Planning*, 26(6): 41–53.

Schelling, T. C. 1956. An essay on bargaining. *American Economic Review*, 46: 281–306.

Seabright, M. A., Levinthal, D. A., & Fichman, M. 1992. Role of individual attachments in the dissolution of interorganizational relationships. *Academy of Management Journal*, 35: 122–60.

Simonin, B. L., & Helleloid, D. 1993. Do organizations learn? An empirical test of organizational learning in international strategic alliances. In D. Moore (Ed.), *Academy of Management Best Paper Proceedings:* 222–6.

Sohn, J. H. D. 1994. Social knowledge as a control system: A proposition and evidence from the Japanese FDI behavior. *Journal of International Business Studies*, 25: 295–324.

Stopford, J. M., & Wells, L. T. 1972. *Managing the multinational enterprise*. New York: Basic Books.

Templin, N. 1995. Strange bedfellows: More and more firms enter joint ventures with big competitors. *Wall Street Journal*, November 1: A1, A6.

Turpin, D. 1993. Strategic alliances with Japanese firms: Myths and realities. *Long Range Planning*, 26(5): 11–16.

Van de Ven, A. H. 1976. On the nature, formation, and maintenance of relations among organizations. *Academy of Management Review*, 1: 24–36.

Vernon, R. 1977. *Storm over multinationals*. Cambridge, MA: Harvard University Press.

Von Krogh, G., Roos, J., & Slocum, K. 1994. An essay on corporate epistemology. *Strategic Management Journal*, 15: 53–71.

Westney, D. E. 1988. Domestic and foreign learning curves in managing international cooperative strategies. In F. Contractor & P. Lorange (Eds.), *Cooperative strategies in international business:* 339–46. Lexington, MA: Lexington Books.

Womack, J. P. 1988. Multinational joint ventures in motor vehicles. In D. Mower (Ed.), *International collaborative ventures in U.S. manufacturing:* 301–48. Cambridge, MA: Ballinger.

Yan, A., & Gray, B. 1994. Bargaining power, management control, and performance in United States-China joint ventures: A comparative case study. *Academy of Management Journal*, 37: 1478–1517.

Young, C., & Oik, P. 1994. Why dissatisfied members stay and satisfied members leave: Options available and embeddedness mitigating the performance commitment relationship in strategic alliance. *Academy of Management Best Papers Proceedings:* 57–61.

Zander, U. 1991. *Exploiting a technological edge—Voluntary and involuntary dissemination of technology*. Unpublished doctoral dissertation, Institute of International Business, Stockholm.

17 Mimetic and experiential effects in international marketing alliance formations of US pharmaceuticals firms

An event history analysis*

Sengun Yeniyurt, Janell D. Townsend,
S. Tamer Cavusgil and Pervez N. Ghauri

Introduction

Collaborative ventures are an indispensable tool for managers in the quest to achieve a sustainable competitive advantage in the marketplace. International business scholars have a strong tradition of studying inter-organizational relationships, from which the study of international alliances is a fundamental derivative. A large body of literature exists with respect to international collaborative ventures, with previous research elucidating facets of the phenomenon such as antecedents of alliance formation (Glaister & Buckley, 1996; Rothaermel, 2001; Sarkar et al., 1999), partner selection (Beckman et al., 2004; Elg, 2000; Lavie & Rosenkopf, 2006), governance structures (Hagedoorn & Narula, 1996; Osborn & Baughn, 1990; White, 2005), organizational learning (Beckman & Haunschild, 2002; Grant & Baden-Fuller, 2004) and performance implications (Fey & Beamish, 2001; Heimeriks & Duysters, 2007; Park & Ungson, 1997, 2001; Rothaermel et al., 2006; Sarkar et al., 2001; Saxton, 1997). This area remains important for academics and practitioners alike for a number of reasons that relate to firm and environmental gaps in our knowledge.

As firms cope with the complexity and costs of doing business in a global marketplace, marketing alliances are no longer a luxury, but a necessity (Ohmae, 1989a). This is because firms must find ways to participate in more geographically and culturally diverse country markets. Nevertheless, entering foreign markets adds inherent risk and uncertainty with new and relatively unknown surroundings (Astley & Brahm, 1989). Since a firm's knowledge of a new market is limited, the degree of perceived risk is greater and management may be cautious about committing scarce resources to the foreign market (Erramilli & Rao, 1990; Johanson & Vahlne, 1977). A means to overcoming this lack of knowledge and perceived risk is to pursue international marketing alliances. This complex phenomenon encompasses dynamic aspects of the competitive environment and various perspectives of firm behavior. On the one hand, as firms collaborate to compete in global markets (Ohmae, 1989b), there is a readily discernible mimetic effect as executives use competitor actions as a mean to learn about global markets, by following their lead into markets and copy the mode of entry employed (Pangarkar & Klein, 1998). On the other hand, there are competitive effects that can also be observed since the relative population of potential partner firms remains

*Reprinted by permission from Macmillan Publishers Ltd: Yeniyurt, S., Janell, D. Townsend, S. Tamer-Cavusgil & Pervez N. Ghauri, "Mimetic and experiential effects in international marketing alliance formations of US pharmaceuticals: An event history analysis", Journal of International Business Studies, 40: 301–320. Copyright 2009, published by Palgrave Macmillan.

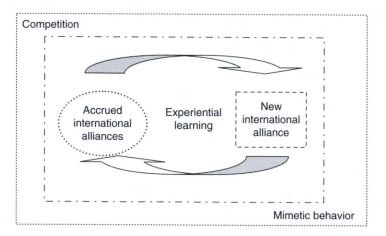

Figure 17.1 Conceptual framework.

somewhat static over time, eventually leading to competition for collaboration in an industry and a net reduction in the number of marketing alliances formed across borders.

At the same time, the ability to gain knowledge about foreign markets and organizational forms is a function of a firm's ability to learn (Huber, 1991; Sinkula, 1994) and is fundamentally important for the ability to conduct international operations effectively (Cavusgil, 1980; Johanson & Vahlne, 1977). Among the most important skills considered in the international literature is that of learning with respect to psychic distance. It is interesting, though, that while the literature generally proposes cultural distance as a significant factor in the internationalization process (Johanson & Vahlne, 1977; Johanson & Weidersheim-Paul, 1975; Kogut & Singh, 1988), recent findings do not necessarily support this proposition (Mitra & Golder, 2002; Ruigrok & Wagner, 2003; Tihanyi et al., 2005; Zhao et al., 2004).

International alliance formation involves complexity due to environmental uncertainty and requires significant organizational learning, but there are other means besides experience by which firms learn. An alternate approach to dealing with uncertainties related to the outcomes of strategic actions is by mimicking competitor actions (Greve, 1998). To account for this variety of environmental and firm-level issues, the present study contributes to the literature by providing a novel approach that reconciles previous perspectives of learning and experience on international marketing alliance formations. Specifically, we focus on mimetic and experiential learning, with respect to the propensity to engage in international marketing alliances. In order to achieve integration of these multivariate effects, we employ a co-evolutionary framework to explain the alliance formation phenomenon in a way that incorporates both aggregate-population-level (mimetic effects) and firm-level (experiential effects) simultaneously. A visual depiction of the phenomenon studied is illustrated in Figure 17.1. This approach enables us to address specific issues and contribute to the literature on a number of fronts, particularly:

- How do the actions of compatriot firms affect the internationalization process of a firm in terms of its international alliance formation?
- What is the role of previous international alliance formation experience in initiating future alliances?

- Are there diminishing returns from alliance formation with respect to learning?
- Do firms become more proficient at forming international alliances by learning to cope with cultural differences in their partnerships?
- Is cultural experience more important when forming alliances with partners from culturally distant countries?

These research questions are tested within the context of the global marketing alliances of US pharmaceutical firms over two decades.

The remainder of this chapter is organized in the following way. First, the co-evolutionary nature of international marketing alliances is explored. Next, hypotheses are developed. The data are then presented and a hazard rate model is employed to test the hypotheses. Finally, a discussion of the findings is offered, along with limitations and directions for future research.

Co-evolution of international marketing alliances

Over the last few decades, cross-border business has experienced phenomenal growth. This escalation is due to a combination of factors: advances in communication, information and transportation technologies; a shift toward market economies; privatization and deregulation in emerging markets; the emergence of the global consumer; the availability of transnational media; and the proliferation of global products (Zou & Cavusgil, 2002). The literature has captured this phenomenon, conceptualizing the transformation of leading business organizations from multinational enterprises to those with broad global scale and scope (Ghoshal, 1987; Perlmutter, 1969). To a large extent, the trend has been rationalized as an extension of the process of global integration as nation-states break down barriers to international trade and consumer preferences converge (Douglas & Craig, 1989; Levitt, 1983; Ohmae, 1989b). It is implied that the globalization of the firm provides greater means for achieving comparative and competitive advantages. As is evidenced by the structures assumed by such global firms as Coca-Cola and General Motors, firms with global reach engage in many different forms of business integration. International marketing alliances are among the strategic tools available to create a global entity through quasi-forms of governance (Ohmae, 1989b).

With this in mind, we explore the dynamic nature of international marketing alliance formations. There are a broad range of names used to identify collaborative ventures, which have been derived from a myriad of terms including versions of symbiotic marketing, collaboration, consortia, joint ventures, linkages, alliances, networks and partnerships (Varadarajan & Cunningham, 1995; Williams et al., 1998). Collaborative ventures can be broadly grouped into two categories: equity-based joint ventures and non-equity alliance arrangements. Alliance arrangements are agreements between firms that cooperate in some way; however, they do not involve the creation of new entities (Contractor & Lorange, 1988; Glaister & Buckley, 1996). In this study we conceptualize alliances as *non-equity collaborative ventures*. International alliances are constituted by partners whose parent companies reside in different countries. When the parties of the alliance who are from different national markets engage in joint marketing programs or licensing, the partnership is defined as an *international marketing alliance*.

Cross-border partnership formation is a key decision in the internationalization process of the firm that is dependent on the internal characteristics of the firm and the actions of competitor firms. Employing a co-evolutionary framework allows us to examine the phenomenon of international marketing alliance formation in a dynamic and interdependent way. This is because co-evolution posits a broad relationship between several units of analysis, each of which tends to have its own theoretical perspective. The macro environment includes such theories as organizational ecology and institutionalization, while the firm-level theories include foundations such as organizational learning and the resource-based view (Volberda & Lewin, 2003: 2113). We incorporate the environmental perspectives of organizational ecology and the firm perspectives of experiential learning in the internationalization process into the framework employed for this study.

This approach assimilates both firm behavior and population-related dynamics, focusing on the interdependencies between the two, and presents a compelling foundation to understand the relationship between factors affecting international alliance formations. It provides the means for incorporating multivariate analysis of firm-level behavior (managerial adaptation) and population ecology (environmental selection) within a competitive environment (Volberda & Lewin, 2003: 2113). Alliance formations in the global marketplace occur as the result of a complex set of factors, a basic environmental consideration of which can be represented by the pool of potential international partners. Deliberate actions based on experience allow managers to develop anticipatory models and systems of control in order to act in advance of blind environmental selection (Volberda & Lewin, 2003). This implies that firms will modify their alliance activities based on their understanding of the competitive dynamics of the industry population of global partners. Clearly, coping with a global marketplace and developing the skills necessary to implement structural transformation to include international marketing alliances is a complex adaptive process.

Therefore, international marketing alliance formation embodies a co-evolutionary process of change, where managerial adjustment is based on environmental factors, as well as on experience and learning. Organizational capability is coupled with geographic market and partner selection to represent an innovative means of adaptation. Population ecology suggests that mimetic behavior and competition can be explained and predicted through the consideration of relative niche density. Managers typically have knowledge of the actions of other organizations in their own industry, and the awareness of other firm's approaches to given situations appears to drive managers to imitate the actions of their competitors (Haveman, 1993). This type of mimicking effect can be captured by analyzing the density dependence of new international alliance formations in an industry. From a firm-level perspective, learning and adaptation can be investigated using experiential effects. Previous international alliance activities have been shown to be opportunities for experiential learning that will influence future activities (Robson & Katsikeas, 2005). In order to investigate these effects in an interdependent manner, density dependence and previous alliance experience are among the key factors considered in this study with respect to international alliance formations.

Hypothesis development

Mimetic effects in international alliance formation

International marketing alliances of companies in a specific industry, which vie for resources in the same competitive domain, can be regarded as a population that strives for survival in the global market. A population is defined by a collection of entities with a similar degree of environmental dependence, common reliance on certain resources and limits to the range of activities and structures assumed (Hannan & Freeman, 1977). Therefore, the environmental level of co-evolution can be employed to study the effects of changes in the density of the international alliance population on the likelihood of a new cross-border alliance being initiated.

Assessing the dynamics of competition for resources and how constraints in the environment affect relative sizes of different populations is one means of explaining and predicting outcomes (Hannan & Freeman, 1977). While there are a number of important considerations when entering international markets through alliance relationships, perhaps the most significant is the choice of partner firms: the pool of potential collaborators is a fundamental resource. New international marketing alliance formations are constrained by the availability of foreign partners as well as by regulatory, geographic and other socio-economic factors.

The size of the population from which appropriate partners can be found is limited to the size of the industry population, effectively establishing it as a niche parameter. This is not to say that the total number of potential partners is fixed over time; it is static only at any given point in time. The total density of the population is a function of the carrying capacity of the niche, which represents an upper bound of the aggregate activity that can be performed by an organizational form (Boone & Witteloostuijn, 1995). Density dependence describes the consequences of competition within a population: the size of a population at any time affects the rate of birth and death from the population (Hannan & Carroll, 1992). At low density levels, legitimation of the population occurs as new entities are formed.

Efforts to establish legitimacy are a function of a firm's intentions to reflect characteristics congruent with prevailing institutional norms (Oliver, 1990). Since managers tend to be aware of organizations in their own industry, they are inclined to mimic the actions of other firms within their competitive group (Haveman, 1993). The tenets of mimetic isomorphism (DiMaggio & Powell, 1983) provide a means to elucidate the growth of the international alliance formations in this stage of population development. Conceptually, this is considered to be a contagion effect, where trendy ideas proliferate from one organization to another (Haveman, 1993; March, 1981; Rogers, 1962). What emerges is a mimetic process where organizations adopt innovations as a function of the degree to which other firms in their industry have already adopted them. Cycles occur when increases in the number of adopters raise mimetic pressures and these pressures cause the number of adopters to grow (Abrahamson & Rosenkopf, 1993). The mimetic effect – operationalized as the proportion of competing firms engaged in alliances in the previous year – has been shown to influence the probability that a firm will engage in a new international alliance (Pangarkar & Klein, 1998). As firms in an industry enter alliances, other firms are compelled to act in a similar manner.

The literature suggests a non-monotonic relationship between the density of a population and the rate of formation of new entities (Carroll & Hannan, 1989). While at low density levels the growth of density legitimates the population and the organizational form it uses, at high density levels scarce resources give rise to more intense competition. The competition for resources fosters a situation in which density increases have a negative effect on new formations. When considering international marketing alliances, a key resource is available partners and projects. As competition for attractive partners and projects becomes increasingly intense, the number of new alliances will begin to decline. Essentially, owing to increased competition for partners, density is likely to have a curvilinear effect on the propensity to engage in new international marketing alliances (Carroll & Hannan, 1989). Therefore, as can be anticipated through the tenets of the environmental elements of the co-evolutionary framework we employ, we expect a strong interdependence between population density and new alliance formations:

Hypothesis 1: The density of international marketing alliances in an industry has a non-monotonic (inverted U shape) effect on the rate of new international alliance formations initiated by the firm.

The role of experiential learning in global collaboration

The acquisition of knowledge is an important assumption of the internationalization process, as the understanding necessary to operate a global environment can be gained only through international market experience (Johanson & Vahlne, 1977). Market knowledge, in and of itself, can be considered a resource vested in the firm's decision-making system, with components that include both general knowledge, distinguished by marketing methods and common characteristics that are irrespective of geographic location, and market-specific knowledge, characterized by knowledge about a specific national market. In the context of this study the concern is for effects of the acquisition of general knowledge regarding international alliance formation that is utilized commonly across global markets (i.e., the development of an understanding of the processes required for engaging in alliances with foreign partners). Thus, we examine the impact of successive international marketing alliances on the propensity to engage in future alliance activity.

Conceptually, this can be explained through the tenets of a co-evolutionary framework in that organizational learning, or the development of insights, knowledge and associations between past actions, the effectiveness of those actions and future actions (Fiol & Lyles, 1985) has to take place for adapting to changing environmental conditions (Volberda & Lewin, 2003). From a learning perspective, experience is a pattern of recognition, a repetition of activity that has been undertaken previously, while future actions become a function of the accumulated memory of the firm (Sinkula, 1994; Slater & Narver, 1995). Organizational memory is the collective beliefs, behavioral routines, or physical artifacts that vary in their content, level of dispersion, and accessibility (Moorman & Miner, 1997). Organizational routines, procedures and structures are vital components for controlling the behavior of the organization, and are accumulated over time, establishing conditions for subsequent firm actions and activities (Cyert & March, 1963; March, 1981). Consequently, organizational learning is a function of age and experience (Sinkula, 1994). How a firm applies experiential knowledge to its activities is a major source of capability (Grant, 1996).

Experiential knowledge is critical for successful international operations (Eriksson et al., 1997). As firms gain experience and confidence in their ability to form international marketing alliances, they build on past experience and engage in further alliance activity in other markets. Robson and Katsikeas (2005) found that previous inter-firm international alliance experience had an effect on a firm's willingness to invest in future alliances. Additionally, direct experience provides input for market selection (Davidson, 1983), supporting the argument that experiential knowledge will allow firms to be driven by economic opportunity (Davidson, 1983). As firms globalize, the geographic scope of international business operations enhances the accumulation of experiential knowledge (Eriksson et al., 2000).

Over time, organizations develop greater competency in alliance management; there is evidence to support the idea that firms become better at managing alliances as they gain experience (Anand & Khanna, 2000). Further, as alliances go through distinct stages, learning is a function of these stages as well as of the particular strategic and organizational contexts facing the partners at a given time (Newman, 1995). It has been shown that the longevity of a foreign collaborative venture is positively related to a firm's previous foreign expansion experience (Barkema et al., 1996). Moreover, companies with extensive networking relationships are more likely to implement innovation activities with strategic partners. In addition, the cumulative number of inter-organizational actions increases the probability of undertaking collaborative ventures in the future (Pennings & Harianto, 1992). The experiential effect is expected to be significant in international marketing alliance formations, as it is for other collaborative venture forms.

As companies continue to internationalize, entry forms of greater intensity and investment are observed (Cavusgil, 1980; Johanson & Vahlne, 1977) and the propensity to use alliances as an entry form will diminish as alternate forms are chosen. This position is supported by findings which indicate that, as firms acquire greater degrees of experiential knowledge, they are more inclined toward selecting wholly owned subsidiaries (Davidson, 1983; Gatignon & Anderson, 1988). The previous number of a company's international marketing alliances is expected to have a curvilinear positive impact that company's propensity to engage in new international alliances. The effect is expected to increase over time, at a decreasing rate, with the learning accrued from each successive alliance diminishing in effect (Rothaermel, 2001), until the firm-level benefits are saturated. Additional alliances beyond the saturation point will not have a learning benefit, resulting in an inverted U shaped effect on new alliance formations. Therefore we predict:

Hypothesis 2: A firm's existing portfolio of alliances has a non-monotonic (inverted U shape) effect on its propensity to enter into additional international partnerships.

The role of inter-cultural experience

Research related to the internationalization process suggests that firms internationalize gradually as the perceived risk of foreign markets decreases (Cavusgil, 1980; Czinkota, 1982; Johanson & Vahlne, 1977; Johanson & Weidersheim-Paul, 1975). Identifying alliance opportunities and establishing collaborative relationships is an integral component of this progression. A major assumption is that firms enter markets that are psychically close to their home market first and then gradually expand into other markets with a higher degree of psychic distance from the home market (Johanson & Vahlne, 1977; Johanson & Weidersheim-Paul, 1975). Psychic distance has therefore been posited to be one of the most important factors in company internationalization (Nordstrom & Vahlne, 1994).

In this study we employ cultural distance as a proxy for psychic distance: this is consistent with previous research in international business (Benito & Gripsrud, 1992; Kogut & Singh, 1988; O'Grady & Lane, 1996). Capturing all the possible components of psychic distance is difficult, so cultural distance is often employed as a proxy (Nordstrom & Vahlne, 1994; O'Grady & Lane, 1996). For the purpose of this investigation, cultural distance is being calculated through the adoption of the method used by Contractor and Lorange (1988), Kogut and Singh (1988), and Nordstrom and Vahlne (1994), and relies on computations derived primarily from Hofstede's (1980, 1991) cultural dimension scores.

The difficulties associated with developing and maintaining successful alliances are amplified with increased cultural distance and appear to be mitigated through increased cultural experience. Cultural differences remain an important component of doing business internationally, since cultural norms and beliefs shape manager's perceptions, dispositions, and behaviors (Markus & Kitayama, 1991; Triandis, 1989). Barkema et al. (1996) found that cultural distance is a significant factor when firms engage in foreign entry with a partner firm. Further, the role of cultural distance is important factor in market selection (Erramilli, 1991; Erramilli & Rao, 1993; Kogut & Singh, 1988), and experiential knowledge about culture plays a role in market selection (Davidson, 1983). Findings by Delios and Henisz (2003) indicate that international experience decreases sensitivity to market uncertainties. These studies have primarily considered the effect of culture distance experience in specific markets, as opposed to the impact of the variety of cultural distance experiences on an organization's inclination toward future actions.

In aggregate, these previous studies suggest that engaging in alliances with companies based in other cultures requires a unique set of competencies, which accrue with the frequency of engagement. This set of competencies would be accumulated via previous experiences with partners from culturally distant countries, and is essential for co-evolution to occur. It should be expected that individual alliances with culturally distant experiences would provide a cumulative learning effect over time, regardless of the country context of an alliance. This experiential effect should provide for the average cultural distance of previous alliances to have a positive effect on the propensity to engage in a new alliance. Using co-evolutionary tenets, it can be postulated that firms which have greater experience in dealing with culturally diverse partners are more likely to have a competitive advantage in the race for global cooperation from their previous experiential learning.

> **Hypothesis 3:** The greater the experience of a firm with culturally distant partners, the higher its propensity to enter into additional international partnerships.

When firms undertake international operations, it is generally held that they are more likely to enter markets that are culturally familiar first (Johanson & Vahlne, 1977; Johanson & Weidersheim-Paul, 1975) and will be more aggressive in committing resources to culturally similar markets (Erramilli & Rao, 1993; Kogut & Singh, 1988). Yet Benito and Gripsrud (1992) found this is not necessarily true for FDI forms of entry, and Mitra and Golder (2002) found that culture distance is not a significant factor with respect to market entry timing. In this study, our interest is in how a firm's culture distance experience will impact on marketing alliances with culturally similar or culturally distant markets.

If firms do learn from previous cross-cultural experiences then the result of the learning should be the ability to transfer the knowledge gained from this experience to other collaborative ventures in incrementally further markets. The implementation of an alliance in a culturally distant country will theoretically require a greater degree of past learning. Engaging in alliances in culturally close markets requires less experience with culturally diverse environments. The similarities to the home country make understanding the idiosyncrasies of the infrastructure and partner firm more straightforward and the process is simpler to navigate. The effects of previous cultural experiences should have a lesser impact on the propensity to engage in alliances in culturally close markets.

> **Hypothesis 4:** A firm's experience with culturally distant partners has a greater effect on its propensity to enter into culturally distant partnerships than in culturally close ventures.

The empirical study

The study context and data

We analyzed the international marketing alliance formations of all US-based pharmaceutical companies from 1 January 1984 to 1 January 2003. The pharmaceutical industry represents an interesting context for this study, for a number of reasons. First, the intensive international marketing alliance formation activity reported suggests an industry that employs this form of collaborative venture as part of its globalization efforts. This is further evidenced by the accelerated globalization of the industry during the time frame examined, which is also in line with the data requirements for this study. Finally, the pharmaceutical industry has been the contextual domain of a number of similar academic studies (Hoang & Rothaermel, 2005; Madhok & Osegowitsch, 2000). The data were extracted from the Thomson Financial Security Database, as compiled in the SDC Platinum database. This source contains comprehensive alliance-specific and participating-party-specific information. It provides data back to the date when the first international alliance formation was announced, as well as the date when the partnership became effective. This dataset is adequate for testing the hypotheses, as the history of the international marketing alliances in the industry is complete, not exhibiting any left-censoring. We also have no reason to suspect sample selection bias, given that all the announcements of alliance formations are recorded. The precise recording of the timing of effects enabled us to accurately analyze the dynamics of new international marketing alliance formations.

Using the information extracted from this data-set, an event history was constructed for each US pharmaceutical company, starting with the date of its first international marketing alliance. The data were arranged into yearly spells (i.e., observation periods) that are updated when an event occurred and at the end of each year to account for the changes in variables. Each company is considered at risk the day after its last event (the day an international marketing alliance becomes effective) and until the next event. The spell is considered right-censored if the company does not have a new alliance until 1 January 2003.

The original sample includes 793 alliances from 317 US pharmaceutical companies (an average of 2.5 international marketing alliances per firm). The effective date was missing for two alliances, but in one case the date when the alliance was planned for engagement was used; the second case was dropped because similar information was not available.

Cultural distance was computed in the conventional manner using Kogut and Singh's (1988) approach of averaging the deviations in Hofstede's (1991) cultural scores, after adjusting for the differences in variations of each of the four dimensions.

$$\text{Cultural distance}_j = \frac{1}{4} \sum_{i=1}^{4} \left(\frac{I_{ij} - I_{iu}}{V_i} \right) \tag{1}$$

where I_{ij} stands for the cultural score of the ith dimension in the jth country, V_i is the variance of the ith dimension and u indicates the US home market. The cultural distance values calculated for the sample are presented in the Appendix.

Further, we differentiate between international alliances with companies from culturally close countries and those from culturally distant countries. Although the average of the cultural distance values of the countries in the sample is 1.78, a clear discontinuity exists between Sweden (Cultural distance = 1.99) and Hong Kong (Cultural distance = 2.42). Hence countries with cultural distance scores equal or higher to 2.42 have been selected as culturally distant, resulting in 524 and 268 international marketing alliances classified as culturally close and distant, respectively. Next, the events of the dataset were categorized as culturally close and culturally distant, according to the cultural distance of the home country of the partner.

Independent variables

The independent variables include the density of international marketing alliances and international alliance experience. Also, firm size and age are included as control variables.

Density. The density of international marketing alliances of US pharmaceutical companies was measured using the cumulative number of previous alliance formations that were still active at the observation time (Carroll & Hannan, 1989). The cumulative number of alliances was computed at the end at each year and assumed constant during the next year. The spells were split at the beginning of each year and the previous year's density values were updated. To test for the expected negative effects of high levels of density, the square of density was also included in the specifications.

Experience. International alliance experience was measured by the cumulative number of previous international marketing alliances engaged. To test the diminishing effects of alliance formation experience, the square of this term was also included in the specification. To capture the experience of the company with culturally distant partners, the average cultural distance of previous international marketing alliances of the company was recorded as an independent variable. Hence:

$$\text{Cultural distance experience}_t = \frac{\sum_{k=1}^{n_t} \text{CD}_k}{n_t} \tag{2}$$

where n_t denotes the number of international alliances a company has been part of at time t, and CD_k stands for the cultural distance of the partner company's home country, relative to the US.

Control variables

A positive relationship has been noted between firm size and the propensity to invest in foreign markets (Horst, 1972; Li & Guisinger, 1992). Therefore, the number of employees of each firm was utilized as a time-varying indicator for company size, and included as a control variable in the model. These figures were available only for a limited number of observations, so some of the missing observations were completed from the Donovan Dun & Bradstreet Million Dollar Database, which increased the availability to 2143 spells. The size variable was then adjusted for normality by taking the natural logarithm. Finally, the age of the company was defined as the time elapsed since the company was founded and was controlled for. The inclusion of this variable decreased the number of available spells to 1967.

Method

A continuous time event history analysis with time-varying covariates is employed in order to estimate the effects of the independent variables on the probability of a company engaging in a new international alliance. This type of model provides the best tool to analyze time-based phenomena such as the co-evolutionary events (Blossfeld & Rohwer, 2002). The technique is similar to multi-variate regression but the dependent variable is the unobserved probability of an event occurring at a specific point in time. In our case, the dependent variable is "the propensity to engage in a new international marketing alliance". The significance of the estimates can be analyzed using conventional hypothesis testing (Tuma & Hannan, 1984).

The determination of the probability distribution function of the transition rate over time is a critical decision in event history analysis. There are two basic approaches to modeling time dependence: parametric (Tuma & Hannan, 1984) and semi-parametric (Cox, 1975). Parametric methods assume a specific distribution of hazard rate over time. While the exponential model assumes constant hazard rates over time; Gompertz, Makeham, and Weibull models assume a monotonically increasing or decreasing rate over time (Blossfeld & Rohwer, 2002). The non-monotonic time dependence with a single hump can also be modeled using parametric methods such as the log-logistic (Bruderl & Schussler, 1990) or log-normal distribution

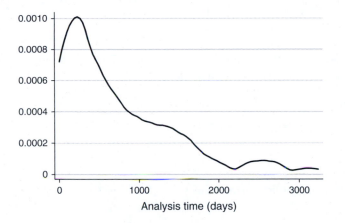

Figure 17.2 Smoothed hazard rate estimates.

(Levinthal & Fichman, 1988). On the other hand, semi-parametric methods such as the Cox (1972) model make very few assumptions regarding the distribution of the hazard rate over time, by allowing for a salient base rate function that is identical for all the members in the population, yet does not follow any prescribed shape (Blossfeld & Rohwer, 2002).

Figure 17.2 shows the smoothed hazard rate estimates of a US-based pharmaceutical firm to engage in a new international marketing alliance since the time of its last international alliance. The smoothed hazard indicates that a firm is most likely to engage in a new international marketing alliance approximately a year after its last alliance formation. The likelihood of new alliance activity is relatively high for two to three years after a similar action, after which the likelihood diminishes considerably and approaches zero.

The shape of the curve suggests that the exponential distribution has to be eliminated from the pool of potential models that can be employed. Additionally, there is no theoretical justification to assume a constant hazard rate distribution over time. If a Gompertz or Weibull distribution were to be employed, given that the maximum of the curve is very close to the origin of the time axis, they will tend to estimate a monotonically decreasing function, overlooking the hump. Ordinary log-normal or log-logistic models would either force the curve to start from the origin or estimate a curve similar to the Gompertz and Weibull, with a monotonically declining shape. Therefore, ordinary parametric models do not seem adequate for our purpose.

The semi-parametric Cox model does not assume an *a priori* shape of hazard rate distribution over time and is thus appropriate for this analysis. The Cox model utilizes partial likelihood maximization by sorting the data according to the event times. Given that the data provide the event times up to the day of engagement, the results of the partial likelihood estimation are reliable. Moreover, a relatively large portion of our observations (41%) are right-censored, which does not create any difficulty for the estimation of the Cox model, such observations being included in the risk set at the event time.

Pooled model

The propensity to engage in an alliance at time t given that the company's previous alliance was formed at time t_n can be defined as a continuous time hazard rate:

$$\lambda(t \mid t_n) = \lim_{\Delta t \to 0} \frac{P(t_n \leq T < t_n + \Delta t \mid T \geq t_n)}{\Delta t} \tag{3}$$

That is, the hazard rate is defined as the limit as Δt approaches zero of the probability of engaging in a new international marketing alliance in the interval of time between the previous alliance (t_n) and $t_n + \Delta t$. This approach of resetting the time axis after each event is very similar to the clock reset model employed by Amburgey, Kelly, and Barnett (1993).

In line with similar studies (Carroll & Hannan, 1989; Mitra & Golder, 2002), we employ the Cox model to identify the effects of different covariates on the hazard rate:

$$\lambda(t \mid t_n) = h(t - t_n) \exp[\beta X(t)], \quad t > t_n \tag{4}$$

where $h(t - t_n)$ is the unspecified baseline hazard and $X(t)$ is the vector of covariates evaluated at t.

Results of pooled model

The descriptive statistics and the correlations between the independent variables are presented in Table 17.1. Stata 9's survival time module was utilized to perform the analyses. The effects of the covariates on the hazard rate were estimated using the Efron (1977) partial likelihood approximation method to deal with the event time ties. The standard errors were adjusted for clustering on each company. The estimated effects of the independent variables are presented in Table 17.2. All three specifications have Wald χ^2 statistics statistically significant at the 0.001 confidence level, indicating good overall fit to the data. Despite the limitations of the sample size in the more complete model specifications, the coefficients of the variables are relatively stable in terms of magnitude and significance, indicating that the results are robust. The density variable has a very stable effect over different specifications of the model, with a statistically significant ($p < 0.001$) positive linear effect and a statistically significant ($p < 0.001$) negative quadratic effect. Therefore, Hypothesis 1 is strongly supported. The linear effect relates to a 0.43% ($e^{0.004} = 1.0043$) increase per unit change in density and the quadratic effect relates to a 0.09% ($e^{-0.0009} = 0.9991$) decrease per 100 units change in squared density. The effect is positive at the low levers of density, increasing at a decreasing rate, and after reaching a maximum it decreases and becomes increasingly negative. Further, a visual representation of the effects can be seen in Figure 17.3.

The estimates of the pooled model also suggest that the cumulative number of previous alliances of the company has a significant positive effect ($p < 0.001$) on the propensity to form a new alliance, even after controlling for the size and age of the company. The effect is negative and statistically significant ($p < 0.05$) in the case of the squared number of previous alliances, indicating a non-monotonic effect. The magnitude of the quadratic coefficient is relatively stable over the alternative specifications, although the significance level changes. Hence Hypothesis 2 is supported. One unit increase in the previous alliances of the company has a linear effect of a 26.26% increase in the likelihood of engaging in a new international marketing alliance, when controlling for the size and age of the company. On the other hand, the squared effect relates to a 1.08% decrease in the hazard rate per unit change. The shape of the effect is similar to the effect of density and can be seen in Figure 17.3.

The cultural distance experience from a company's previous alliances has a positive effect on new international alliance formation. The effect is statistically significant in two of the three model specifications. One unit change in the cultural distance experience relates to

Table 17.1 Descriptive statistics

Covariate	Mean	s.d.	Correlation					
			1	*2*	*3*	*4*	*5*	*6*
1. International alliance density	543.04	237.21						
2. (International alliance density)^2/100	3511.46	2147.71	0.978*					
3. International alliance experience	2.61	2.66	0.096*	0.075*				
4. (International alliance experience)^2	13.89	38.84	0.083*	0.069*	0.909*			
5. Cultural distance experience	1.30	0.95	−0.121*	−0.106*	0.020	0.010		
6. Firm size	5.94	2.49	−0.148*	0.131*	0.269*	0.301*	0.168*	
7. Firm age	25.25	33.22	−0.042*	−0.022	0.316*	0.272*	0.252*	0.687*

*p < 0.05.

Table 17.2 Partial likelihood estimates of covariate effects on the propensity to engage in a new international alliance

Covariate	Alternate specifications		
International alliance density			
B	0.0041***	0.0039***	0.0043***
Robust s.e.	(0.0008)	(0.0009)	(0.0010)
(International alliance density)^2/100			
B	−0.0009***	−0.0008***	−0.0009***
Robust s.e.	(0.0001)	(0.0001)	(0.0001)
International alliance experience			
B	0.2917***	0.2621***	0.2332***
Robust s.e.	(0.0326)	(0.0505)	(0.0526)
(International alliance experience)^2			
B	−0.0092***	−0.0120**	−0.0109*
Robust s.e.	(0.0016)	(0.0041)	(0.0043)
Cultural distance experience			
B	0.0888*	0.1034*	0.0605
Robust s.e.	(0.0413)	(0.0442)	(0.0493)
Firm size			
B		0.0547**	0.0563
Robust s.e.		(0.0213)	(0.0305)
Firm age			
B			0.0022
Robust s.e.			(0.0020)
Log pseudo-likelihood	−2795.61	−1911.00	−1824.75
χ^2	232.00***	215.09***	240.29***
d.f.	5	6	7
Observations	3126	2143	1967
Events	475	347	336

***p < 0.001; **p < 0.01; *p < 0.05 (two-tailed test).

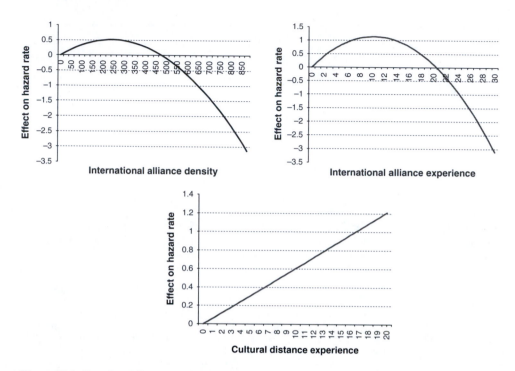

Figure 17.3 Covariate effects on pooled hazard rate.

a 26.26% increase in the likelihood of engaging in a new international marketing alliance, when size and age are controlled for. Overall, Hypothesis 3 is partially supported. A visual representation of the mono-tonic positive effect of cultural distance experience on the likelihood of new alliance formation can be seen in Figure 17.3.

Organizational size has a positive effect on the propensity to engage in a new international marketing alliance. The effect of size is significant in only one of the specifications, and relates to a 5.79% increase in the likelihood of engaging in a new international marketing alliance, per unit change. The effect of age is positive but statistically insignificant.

Competing risks model

In order to identify the differences in the effects of the covariates on the probabilities of engaging in culturally distant or culturally close international alliances, a semi-parametric Cox model with competing risks was employed. It should be noted that a non-sequential decision is assumed in building this model (Hachen, 1988). Considering the idiosyncratic difficulties of engaging in business relations with companies from culturally distant countries, the decision to engage in an alliance is highly dependent on identification of the proper partner. Hence these two actions are assumed to be concomitant. In order to estimate the competing risks model, the overall hazard rate was broken down into two rates (Hachen, 1988):

$$\lambda_j(t \mid t_n) = \lim_{\Delta t \to 0} \frac{P(t_n \leq T < t_n + \Delta t, J = j \mid T \geq t_n)}{\Delta t}$$
$$J \in \{1, 2\}$$

(5)

where $j = 1$ indicates culturally close alliance formations and $j = 2$ indicates culturally distant alliance formations, as per the criteria previously established. As such, the two types of event are mutually exclusive and collectively exhaustive, with

$$\sum_j \lambda_j(t \mid t_n) = \lambda(t \mid t_n) \tag{6}$$

The effects of the independent variables on the competing hazards were estimated using alternate specifications similar to the pooled model. The Efron (1977) partial likelihood approximation method was employed to estimate the effects of the covariates on each of the competing hazard rates independently (Hachen, 1988). Also, the standard errors were adjusted for clustering on each company.

Results of the competing risks model

The estimated coefficients, the robust standard errors, the significance levels, and the exponential of the coefficients are presented in Tables 17.3 and 17.4 for the propensity to engage in culturally close and culturally distant alliances, respectively. The model fit is satisfactory across all the specifications and the two different hazard rates, with the Wald χ^2 statistic significant at the 0.001 confidence level. The coefficients are relatively stable across specifications

Table 17.3 Partial likelihood estimates of covariate effects on the propensity to engage in a new culturally close international alliance

Covariate	Alternate specification		
International alliance density			
B	0.0041***	0.0043***	0.0047***
Robust s.e.	(0.0010)	(0.0012)	(0.0013)
(International alliance density)²/100			
B	−0.0009***	−0.0009***	−0.0009***
Robust s.e.	(0.0001)	(0.0002)	(0.0002)
International alliance experience			
B	0.2749***	0.2616***	0.2281***
Robust s.e.	(0.0429)	(0.0622)	(0.0640)
(International alliance experience)²			
B	−0.0083***	−0.0114**	−0.0104*
Robust s.e.	(0.0020)	(0.0043)	(0.0045)
Cultural distance experience			
B	−0.1123	−0.0740	−0.1068
Robust s.e.	(0.0585)	(0.0626)	(0.0651)
Firm size			
B		0.0208	0.0248
Robust s.e.		(0.0246)	(0.0337)
Firm age			
B			0.0019
Robust s.e.			(0.0026)
Log pseudo-likelihood	−1898.57	−1264.20	−1202.02
χ^2	143.76***	130.76***	147.59***
d.f.	5	6	7
Observations	3126	2143	1967
Events	322	229	221

***p < 0.001; **p < 0.01; *p < 0.05 (two-tailed test).

Table 17.4 Partial likelihood estimates of covariate effects on the propensity to engage in a new culturally distant international alliance

Covariate		Alternate specification	
International alliance density			
B	0.0038*	0.0034	0.0036*
Robust s.e.	(0.0017)	(0.0018)	(0.0018)
(International alliance density)^2/100			
B	−0.0008***	−0.0007***	−0.0008***
Robust s.e.	(0.0002)	(0.0002)	(0.0002)
International alliance experience			
B	0.3601***	0.2882**	0.2401*
Robust s.e.	(0.0593)	(0.1034)	(0.1060)
(International alliance experience)^2			
B	−0.0123***	−0.0144	−0.0125
Robust s.e.	(0.0034)	(0.0089)	(0.0089)
Cultural distance experience			
B	0.4533***	0.3928***	0.3436***
Robust s.e.	(0.0640)	(0.0775)	(0.0811)
Firm size			
B		0.1171***	0.1318**
Robust s.e.		(0.0312)	(0.0469)
Firm age			
B			0.0009
Robust s.e.			(0.0028)
Log pseudo-likelihood	−882.72	−635.51	612.16
x^2	153.06***	108.15***	109.19***
d.f.	5	6	7
Observations	3126	2143	1967
Events	153	118	115

***$p < 0.001$; **$p < 0.01$; *$p < 0.05$ (two-tailed test).

in terms of magnitude. Small differences in the significance levels can be attributed to the change in the number of available observations.

In the case of the propensity to engage in a new alliance with a company from culturally close countries (Table 17.3), density has a non-monotonic effect across all three specifications. The effect of density is positive and significant and the effect of the squared density is negative and statistically significant at 0.001 confidence level. The linear effect relates to a 0.47% increase per unit change in density, and a quadratic effect relates to a 0.09% decrease per 100 units change in squared density on the propensity to engage in a new alliance after controlling for size and age (Table 17.5). Hence the international marketing alliance density has a positive impact in the earlier stages. This effect is a diminishing one, becoming negative at increased density levels.

The number of previous alliances of the company also indicates a non-monotonic effect. The linear term is significant at the 0.001 confidence level across all specifications and the quadratic term is statistically significant at the 0.05 confidence level when controlled for firm size and age. One unit change in the number of previous alliances of the focal company relates to a linear effect of a 25.62% increase, and a quadratic effect of 1.3% decrease in the propensity to engage in a new international marketing alliance, per unit change. Hence, earlier alliances have a positive effect on new alliance formations, yet this effect diminishes

Table 17.5 Exponentially transformed estimates

Covariates	Hazard rate (%)		
	New international alliance	New culturally close alliance	New culturally distant alliance
International alliance density	+0.43	+0.47	+0.36
(International alliance density)^2/100	−0.09	−0.09	−0.08
International alliance experience	+26.26	+25.62	+27.14
(International alliance experience)^2	−1.08	−1.03	−1.24
Cultural distance experience	+6.24	−10.13	+41.00
Firm size	+5.79	+2.51	+14.09
Firm age	+0.22	+0.19	+0.09

with increased levels of alliance formations for each company, becoming negative once a critical mass of alliances is accrued. While the cultural distance experience has a negative statistically insignificant effect, organizational size and age have positive and statistically insignificant coefficients in all of the alternate specifications.

In the case of the propensity to engage in culturally distant international marketing alliances (Table 17.4), density has a statistically significant non-monotonic effect ($p < 0.05$ for the linear and $p < 0.001$ for the quadratic component). While the linear effect relates to a 0.36% change in the hazard rate per unit change in density, the quadratic effect is of a 0.08% decrease per 100 units change in density squared (Table 17.5). Hence the effect of international marketing alliance density is relatively stable across the models employed in this study. The effect follows the hypothesized shape, being positive in the earlier stages and negative at increased levels of population density.

International alliance experience also has a significant positive linear effect ($p < 0.05$) and a statistically insignificant negative quadratic effect on the hazard of engaging in culturally distant alliances when firm size and age are controlled for. One unit increase in the alliance experience of a company increases the hazard of engaging in a culturally distant alliance by 27.14%. The quadratic effect decreases the hazard rate by 1.24% per unit change (Table 17.5).

The cultural distance experience of past alliances has a very strong positive effect across all specifications ($p < 0.001$). After firm size and age are controlled for, one unit increase in cultural distance experience relates to a 41.00% increase in the likelihood of engaging in a new international marketing alliance with a company from a culturally distant country. Considering that cultural distance experience has a strong positive effect on engaging in culturally distant alliances, but an insignificant negative effect on engaging in culturally close alliances, Hypothesis 4 is strongly supported.

Finally, size has a significant positive effect that relates to a 14.09% increase per unit change in the likelihood of engaging in a new international marketing alliance with a company from a culturally distant country. Age does not have a significant effect on the hazard rate.

Discussion

The present study provides an interesting platform for empirically verifying the co-evolutionary nature of international alliances among firms from the US pharmaceutical sector. It represents a significant complement to the theoretical literature on co-evolution by presenting convincing findings on the relevance of dynamic events in this industry. The study is novel in at least three respects. First, it examines the behavior of alliance formation over a fairly long period of time (which coincides with a flurry of alliance formation in this industry). Second, the particular statistical method employed – event history analysis – is able to reveal complex, dynamic, non-linear relationships among the phenomena of interest. Third, this study reveals that there are limits to the mimetic and learning effects. Specifically, mimetic effects, although positive, diminish at an increasing rate. Fourth, this study provides fresh perspectives on the internationalization process framework by suggesting that firms are able to leverage the knowledge and experience they derive from an individual alliance to successive international alliance endeavors.

The results sustain the assumptions of co-evolution, extending the framework to the global context of international inter-firm relationships. Density of international marketing alliances in the industry has a non-monotonic effect on a company's propensity to engage in new international marketing alliances. Particularly important to the literature is that strong mimetic and competitive effects are clearly present, with companies appearing to exhibit an eagerness to follow their competitors in the early stages of industry-level internationalization, utilizing marketing alliances as a mode of entry; yet, as can be seen in Figure 17.2, once a critical mass of international marketing alliances is attained in the industry (the evidence suggests that this critical mass is approximately 244), the propensity to seek new alliances declines. This supports the arguments of mimetic effects and competition for collaboration, and implies that managers will have a better selection of alliance partners earlier in the globalization of an industry with an increasing competitive effect. In an industry environment with a finite number of potential partners and partnering synergies, the industry as a whole reaches the limits of new alliance creation. Companies may search for additional partners in key markets, but find that the opportunities are not there.

The smoothed hazard rate estimates indicate that the likelihood of new alliance formation is highest within a year from the time a firm engages in an international marketing alliance. Beyond that, the likelihood declines and within three years rapidly diminishes, approaching a zero probability. Hence it can be postulated that the learning benefits may be highest within the early years of alliance formation activity; the motivation and ability to engage in further international partnerships will be higher within this limited period of time.

The findings provide support for the assertion that current international alliance experience facilitates future alliance formations. Further, the results of this study imply that the benefits of international alliances are limited once a firm achieves a critical number of alliances. The threshold appears to be approximately nine international alliances; presumably organizations reach a limit where they can no longer initiate and actively manage more alliances. The evidence suggests that, as firms build up alliance experience, they become even more likely to engage in new alliances; however, the likelihood of new partnership formation decreases at an increasing rate. The coordination costs of a large number of global partners could be one of the reasons why the alliance formation activity slows down. Apparently firms become more proficient at establishing new alliances until they reach a critical number, at which point there would appear to be a diminishing return in the value of these relationships to managers responsible for international marketing alliance formation. The effect of the alliance portfolio of a company on new alliance formation is non-monotonic, implying a decreasing return of international marketing alliances to the focal organization. It can also be inferred that as firms gain international experience they choose alternative, and presumably, more intense, forms of international entry.

Previous research has shown that direct experience provides input for market selection (Davidson, 1983); a firm's previous foreign expansion experience is positively related to the longevity of a foreign collaborative venture (Barkema et al., 1996); and the cumulative number of inter-organizational actions increases the probability of undertaking collaborative ventures in the future (Pennings & Harianto, 1992). The present study is the first reported investigation that substantiates the diminishing effects of experiential learning on future international marketing alliance activity. Hence it can be concluded that companies learn from their international alliance formations, especially in the early stages of internationalization.

Contrary to earlier findings suggesting that cultural distance experience in a given market is not a significant factor in market entry timing (Mitra & Golder, 2002; Tihanyi et al., 2005), the present research suggests that cultural distance experience increases the likelihood that a company will engage in a future international marketing alliance. This finding is in line with the internationalization process literature, suggesting that cultural distance is a significant factor in the process of searching for and engaging in international marketing alliances on a global basis. It is also consistent with findings that cultural distance is a significant factor in the longevity of an international market entry undertaken with a partner firm (Barkema et al., 1996). The important difference is that extant studies considered the effect of cultural distance experience in specific markets, as opposed to the impact of the richness of cultural distance experiences on an organization's inclination toward future actions. Illustrating that cross-cultural experience is a significant factor in the propensity to engage in international marketing alliances is an important contribution to the literature. The study is convincing in the sense that individual alliance experiences tend to have a cumulative learning effect over time regardless of the country context of an alliance. Firms are able to leverage the knowledge and experience they derive from an individual alliance to successive ones.

The cultural distance experience effect is substantially stronger in the case of engaging in international alliances with companies from culturally distant countries, but not significant in the case of establishing alliances with partners that are culturally close. Therefore these findings contribute to the debate regarding the effect of the cultural distance in the internationalization process of companies, indicating that cultural experience is less important in the case of engaging in international activities in culturally similar markets, yet extremely significant when engaging in activities with partners from culturally distant countries. The implication is that firms will find it easier to engage in alliances with partners from distant cultures once they acquire cross-cultural experience closer to home.

Finally, firm size has a positive effect on new alliance formation, suggesting perhaps that larger companies are more likely to possess the resources required to find and engage partners. This effect is stronger in the case of culturally distant alliances, implying that a greater resource base may enable a greater degree of collaboration on a global scale.

Limitations and future research directions

Although the present research contributes to the literature in several ways, some limitations can be overcome in future investigations. First, the focus of this study is non-equity, international marketing ventures. Past research evaluates the trade-off between equity-based ventures and non-equity-based alliances in the market entry decisions. Future research should examine the interaction between the company experience with each specific type of collaboration and market entry, organizational resources, overall globalization strategy, and the final decision of the managerial team. Also, a company's international activities, other than its inter-organizational relationships, provide opportunity to gain international experience.

Future scholarly work should consider incorporating additional variables such as the proportion of international sales into the analysis. Additionally, managerial cognition has a significant effect on a company's international activity patterns. The effects of cognitive factors such as the global mindset (Kedia & Mukherji, 1999; Murtha et al., 1998) and global orientation (Townsend et al., 2004; Workman et al., 1998; Zou & Cavusgil, 2002) of the managerial team should be subject to investigation with respect to international patterns of market entry.

Several previous works analyzed the factors affecting foreign market entry decisions, with some noting the importance of country-specific variables, such as economic (Mitra & Golder, 2002), political and geographic characteristics (Delios & Henisz, 2003). This study did not examine such country-specific variables. In this article, the unit of analysis and the agent at risk is the organization itself. The organization-specific and industry-specific time-varying factors have been incorporated in the analysis, with the primary concern being to capture the co-evolutionary effects on organizational behavior. To investigate the effects of country-level variables on the likelihood of choosing a partner from a specific country, the agent at risk can be denoted as the two-dimensional variable firm–country (see Delios & Henisz, 2003; Yeniyurt et al., 2007). Such a definition and operationalization would allow for the inclusion of country-specific, time-varying covariates such as culture and cultural distance, economic factors, demand conditions and competition intensity, regardless of whether the firm enters the country or not (Blossfeld & Rohwer, 2002). In a study of this nature, the effects of market-specific experience on market entry, partner selection and subsequent performance could be compared with the effects of general international experience (for example, Yeniyurt et al., 2007).

Hofstede's dimensions of culture were used to operationalize psychic distance in this study. Although this is common practice in international literature, it does present a limitation owing to the restrictive range of psychic distance concepts captured by culture alone. Also, there have been a number of criticisms of Hofstede's measures of culture, based on the nature of the study from which the factors were derived. However, it is common for international marketing studies to employ these measure (e.g., Soares et al., 2007; Steenkamp et al., 1999; Yeniyurt & Townsend, 2003). Therefore future research should incorporate additional measures of psychic distance and alternative measures of culture, including the potential for a non-monotonic relationship between culture and the likelihood of engaging in a new international marketing alliance.

The present empirical study did not reveal a statistically significant relationship between firm age and the probability of engaging in future alliances. Nevertheless, it has been shown that some companies engage in international operations very early, becoming born-globals (Knight & Cavusgil, 2004). Therefore, the relationship between the age of the organization and its international alliance formations requires further attention. Future studies may consider organizational age as a moderator, since it is probable that young and dynamic firms may benefit from their international experiences. Further, the product portfolio of the company may increase its attractiveness to potential alliance partners and have a positive effect on new international alliance formations (Rothaermel & Deeds, 2004; Rothaermel et al., 2006) and should be considered by future studies.

Overall, this study extends the co-evolutionary framework to the context of international marketing alliances, suggesting that this approach provides plausible explanations for exploring the international alliance formation of firms. There is substantial evidence that firms are influenced by the internationalization endeavors of their competitors, and utilize their accrued international experiences in adapting and responding to the challenges associated with cross-border operations. It is hoped that the findings presented here will prompt other researchers to continue this work.

Acknowledgements

The valuable comments of Professor Henrich R Greve and participants at the Applied Event History Modeling Workshop at Fuqua School of Business, Duke University, on earlier versions of this paper are gratefully acknowledged by us. We sincerely appreciate the valuable comments received from the anonymous *JIBS* reviewers.

References

Abrahamson, E., & Rosenkopf, L. 1993. Institutional and competitive bandwagons: Using mathematical modelling as a tool to explore innovation diffusion. *Academy of Management Review*, 18(3): 487–517.

Amburgey, T. L., Kelly, D., & Barnett, W. P. 1993. Resetting the clock: The dynamics of organizational change and failure. *Administrative Science Quarterly*, 38(1): 51–73.

Anand, B. N., & Khanna, T. 2000. Do firms learn to create value? The case of alliances. *Strategic Management Journal*, 21(3): 295–315.

Astley, W. G., & Brahm, R. 1989. Organizational designs for post-industrial strategies: The role of interorganizational collaboration. In C. Snow (Ed.), *Strategy, organization design, and human resource management:* 233–70. Greenwich, CT: JAI Press.

Barkema, H. G., Bell, J. H., & Pennings, J. M. 1996. Foreign entry, cultural barriers, and learning. *Strategic Management Journal*, 17(2): 151–66.

Beckman, C. M., & Haunschild, P. R. 2002. Network learning: The effects of partners' heterogeneity of experience on corporate acquisitions. *Administrative Science Quarterly*, 47(1): 92–124.

Beckman, C. M., Haunschild, P. R., & Phillips, D. J. 2004. Friends or strangers? Firm-specific uncertainty, market uncertainty, and network partner selection. *Organization Science*, 15(3): 259–75.

Benito, G., & Gripsrud, G. 1992. The expansion of foreign direct investments: Discrete rational location choices or a cultural learning process? *Journal of International Business Studies*, 23(3): 461–76.

Blossfeld, H.-P., & Rohwer, G. 2002. *Techniques of event history modeling new approaches to causal analysis*. Mahwah, NJ: Lawrence Erlbaum Associates.

Boone, C., & van Witteloostuijn, A. 1995. Industrial organization and organizational ecology: The potentials for cross-fertilization. *Organization Studies*, 16(2): 265–698.

Bruderl, J., & Schussler, R. 1990. Organizational mortality: The liabilities of newness and adolescence. *Administrative Science Quarterly*, 35(3): 530–47.

Carroll, G. R., & Hannan, M. T. 1989. Density dependence in the evolution of populations of newspaper organizations. *American Sociological Review*, 54(4): 524–41.

Cavusgil, S. T. 1980. On the internationalization process of firms. *European Research*, 8(6): 273–81.

Contractor, F., & Lorange, P. 1988. Why should firms cooperate? In F. Contractor & P. Lorange (Eds), *Cooperative strategies in international business:* 3–30. Lexington, MA: Lexington Books.

Cox, D. R. 1972. Regression models and life tables. *Journal of the Royal Statistical Society*, 34(2): 187–220.

Cox, D. R. 1975. Partial likelihood. *Biometrica*, 62(2): 269–76.

Cyert, R. M., & March, J. G. 1963. *A behavioral theory of the firm*. New York: Prentice-Hall.

Czinkota, M. R. 1982. *Export development strategies: US promotion policy*. New York: Praeger.

Davidson, W. H. 1983. Market similarity and market selection: Implications for international marketing strategy. *Journal of Business Research*, 11(4): 439–56.

Delios, A., & Henisz, W. J. 2003. Political hazards, experience, and sequential entry strategies: The international expansion of Japanese firms, 1980–1998. *Strategic Management Journal*, 24(11): 1153–64.

DiMaggio, P. J., & Powell, W. W. 1983. The iron cage revisited: Institutional isomorphism and collective rationality in organizational fields. *American Sociological Review*, 48(2): 147–60.

Douglas, S. P., & Craig, C. S. 1989. Evolution of global marketing strategy: Scale, scope, and synergy. *Columbia Journal of World Business*, 24(3): 47–59.

Efron, B. 1977. The efficiency of Cox's likelihood function for censored data. *Journal of the American Statistical Association*, 72(359): 557–65.

Elg, U. 2000. Firms' home market relationships: Their role when selecting international alliance partners. *Journal of International Business Studies*, 31(1): 169–77.

Eriksson, K., Johanson, J., Majkgard, A., & Sharma, D. D. 1997. Experiential knowledge and cost in the internationalization process. *Journal of International Business Studies*, 28(2): 337–61.

Eriksson, K., Majkgard, A., & Sharma, D. D. 2000. Path dependence and knowledge development in the internationalization process. *Management International Review*, 40(4): 307–29.

Erramilli, M. K. 1991. The experience factor in foreign market entry behavior of service firms. *Journal of International Business Studies*, 22(3): 479–501.

Erramilli, M. K., & Rao, C. P. 1990. Choice of foreign market entry modes by service firms: Role of market knowledge. *Management International Review*, 30(2): 135–50.

Erramilli, M. K., & Rao, C. P. 1993. Service firms' international entry-mode choice: A modified transaction-cost analysis approach. *Journal of Marketing*, 57(3): 19–38.

Fey, C. F., & Beamish, P. W. 2001. Organizational climate similarity and performance: International joint ventures in Russia. *Organization Studies*, 22(5): 853–82.

Fiol, C. M., & Lyles, M. A. 1985. Organizational learning. *Academy of Management Review*, 10(4): 803–13.

Gatignon, H., & Anderson, E. 1988. The multinational corporations' degree of control over foreign subsidiaries: An empirical testofa transaction cost explanation. *Journal of Law, Economics and Organization*, 4(2): 305–35.

Ghoshal, S. 1987. Global strategy: An organizing framework. *Strategic Management Journal*, 8(5): 425–40.

Glaister, K. W., & Buckley, P. J. 1996. Strategic motives for international alliance formation. *Journal of Management Studies*, 33(3): 301–32.

Grant, R. M. 1996. Toward a knowledge-based theory of the firm. *Strategic Management Journal*, 17(Winter Special Issue): 109–22.

Grant, R. M., & Baden-Fuller, C. 2004. A knowledge accessing theory of strategic alliances. *Journal of Management Studies*, 41(1): 61–84.

Greve, H. R. 1998. Managerial cognition and the mimetic adoption of market positions: What you see is what you do. *Strategic Management Journal*, 19(10): 967–88.

Hachen Jr, D. S. 1988. The competing risks model: Amethod for analyzing processes with multiple types of events. *Sociological Methods & Research*, 17(1): 21–54.

Hagedoorn, J., & Narula, R. 1996. Choosing organizational modes of strategic technology partnering: International and sectoral differences. *Journal of International Business Studies*, 27(2): 265–84.

Hannan, M. T., & Carroll, G. R. 1992. *The dynamics of organizational populations*. New York: Oxford University Press.

Hannan, M. T., & Freeman, J. 1977. The population ecology of organizations. *American Journal of Sociology*, 82(5): 929–64.

Haveman, H. A. 1993. Follow the leader: Mimetic isomorphism and entry into new markets. *Administrative Science Quarterly*, 38(4): 593–627.

Heimeriks, K., & Duysters, G. 2007. Alliance capability as a mediator between experience and alliance performance: An empirical investigation into the alliance capability development process. *Journal of Management Studies*, 44(1): 25–49.

Hoang, H., & Rothaermel, F. T. 2005. The effect of general and partner-specific alliance experience on joint R&D project performance. *Academy of Management Journal*, 48(2): 332–45.

Hofstede, G. 1980. *Culture's consequences: International differences in work-related values*. Beverly Hills, CA: Sage Publications.

Hofstede, G. 1991. *Cultures and organizations: Software of the mind*. New York: McGraw-Hill.

Horst, T. 1972. Firm and industry determinants of the decision to invest abroad: An empirical study. *Review of Economics and Statistics*, 54(3): 258–66.

Huber, G. P. 1991. Organizational learning: The contributing processes and the literatures. *Organization Science*, 2(1): 88–115.

Johanson, J., & Vahlne, J.-E. 1977. The internationalization process of the firm: A model of knowledge development and increasing foreign market commitments. *Journal of International Business Studies*, 8(1): 23–32.

Johanson, J., & Weidersheim-Paul, F. 1975. The internationalization of the firm: Four Swedish cases. *Journal of Management Studies*, 12(3): 305–22.

Kedia, B. L., & Mukherji, A. 1999. Global managers: Developing a mindset for global competitiveness. *Journal of World Business*, 34(3): 230–51.

Knight, G. A., & Cavusgil, S. T. 2004. Innovation, organizational capabilities, and the born-global firm. *Journal of International Business Studies*, 35(2): 124–41.

Kogut, B., & Singh, H. 1988. The effect of national culture on the choice of entry mode. *Journal of International Business Studies*, 19(3): 411–32.

Lavie, D., & Rosenkopf, L. 2006. Balancing exploration and exploitation in alliance formation. *Academy of Management Journal*, 49(4): 797–818.

Levinthal, D. A., & Fichman, M. 1988. Dynamics of inter-organizational attachments: Auditor–client relationships. *Administrative Science Quarterly*, 33(3): 345–69.

Levitt, T. 1983. The globalization of markets. *Harvard Business Review*, 61(3): 92–102.

Li, J., & Guisinger, S. 1992. The globalization of service multinationals in the 'triad' regions: Japan, Western Europe and North America. *Journal of International Business Studies*, 23(4): 675–96.

Madhok, A., & Osegowitsch, T. 2000. The international biotechnology industry: A dynamic capabilities perspective. *Journal of International Business Studies*, 31(2): 325–35.

March, J. G. 1981. Decisions in organizations and theories of choice. In A. H. Van de Ven & W. F. Joyce (Eds), *Perspectives on organization design and behavior:* 205–44. New York: Wiley.

Markus, H. R., & Kitayama, S. 1991. Culture and the self: Implications for cognition, emotion and motivation. *Psychological Review*, 98(2): 224–53.

Mitra, D., & Golder, P. N. 2002. Whose culture matters? Near-market knowledge and its impact on foreign market entry timing. *Journal of Marketing Research*, 39(3): 350–65.

Moorman, C., & Miner, A. S. 1997. The impact of organizational memory on new product performance and creativity. *Journal of Marketing Research*, 34(1): 91–106.

Murtha, T. P., Lenway, S. A., & Bagozzi, R. P. 1998. Global mindsets and cognitive shift in a complex multinational corporation. *Strategic Management Journal*, 19(2): 97–114.

Newman, W. H. 1995. Stages in cross-cultural collaboration. *Journal of Asian Business*, 11(4): 69–94.

Nordstrom, K. A., & Vahlne, J.-E. 1994. Is the globe shrinking? Psychic distance and the establishment of Swedish sales subsidiaries during the last 100 years. In M. Landeck (Ed.), *International trade: Regional and global issues:* 41–56. New York: St Martin's Press.

O'Grady, S., & Lane, H. W. 1996. The psychic distance paradox. *Journal of International Business Studies*, 27(2): 309–33.

Ohmae, K. 1989a. The global logic of strategic alliances. *Harvard Business Review*, 67(2): 143–55.

Ohmae, K. 1989b. Managing in a borderless world. *Harvard Business Review*, 67(3): 152–61.

Oliver, C. 1990. Determinants of interorganizational relationships: Integration and future directions. *Academy of Management Review*, 15(2): 241–65.

Osborn, R. N., & Baughn, C. C. 1990. Forms of interorganizational governance for multinational alliances. *Academy of Management Journal*, 33(3): 503–19.

Pangarkar, N., & Klein, S. 1998. Bandwagon pressures and interfirm alliances in the global pharmaceutical industry. *Journal of International Marketing*, 6(2): 54–73.

Park, S. H., & Ungson, G. R. 1997. The effect of national culture, organizational complementarity, and economic motivation on joint venture dissolution. *Academy of Management Journal*, 40(2): 279–307.

Park, S. H., & Ungson, G. R. 2001. Interfirm rivalry and managerial complexity: A conceptual framework of alliance failure. *Organization Science*, 12(1): 37–53.

Pennings, J. M., & Harianto, F. 1992. Technological networking and innovation implementation. *Organization Science*, 3(3): 356–82.

Perlmutter, H. V. 1969. The tortuous evolution of the multinational corporation. *Columbia Journal of World Business*, 4(1): 9–18.

Robson, M. J., & Katsikeas, C. S. 2005. International strategic alliance relationships within the foreign investment decision process. *International Marketing Review*, 22(4): 399–419.

Rogers, E. M. 1962. *Diffusion of innovations*. New York: Free Press.

Rothaermel, F. T. 2001. Incumbent's advantage through exploiting complementary assets via interfirm cooperation. *Strategic Management Journal*, 22(6/7): 687–99.

Rothaermel, F. T., & Deeds, D. L. 2004. Exploration and exploitation alliances in biotechnology: A system of new product development. *Strategic Management Journal*, 25(3): 201–21.

Rothaermel, F. T., Hitt, M. A., & Jobe, L. A. 2006. Balancing vertical integration and strategic outsourcing: Effects on product portfolio, product success, and firm performance. *Strategic Management Journal*, 27(11): 1033–56.

Ruigrok, W., & Wagner, H. 2003. Internationalization and performance: An organizational learning perspective. *Management International Review*, 43(1): 63–83.

Sarkar, M. B., Cavusgil, S. T., & Aulakh, P. S. 1999. International expansion of telecommunication carriers: The influence of market structure, network characteristics, and entry imperfections. *Journal of International Business Studies*, 30(2): 361–81.

Sarkar, M. B., Echambadi, R., Cavusgil, S. T., & Aulakh, P. S. 2001. The influence of complementarity, comparability, and relationship capital on alliance performance. *Journal of the Academy of Marketing Science*, 29(4): 358–73.

Saxton, T. 1997. The effects of partner and relationship characteristics on alliance outcomes. *Academy of Management Journal*, 40(2): 443–61.

Sinkula, J. M. 1994. Market information processing and organizational learning. *Journal of Marketing*, 58(1): 35–45.

Slater, S. F., & Narver, J. C. 1995. Market orientation and the learning organization. *Journal of Marketing*, 59(3): 63–74.

Soares, A. M., Farhangmehr, M., & Shoham, A. 2007. Hofstede's dimensions of culture in international marketing studies. *Journal of Business Research*, 60(3): 277–84.

Steenkamp, J.-B. E. M., ter Hofstede, F., & Wedel, M. 1999. A cross-national investigation into the individual and national cultural antecedents of consumer innovativeness. *Journal of Marketing*, 63(2): 55–69.

Tihanyi, L., Griffith, D. A., & Russell, C. J. 2005. The effect of cultural distance on entry mode choice, international diversification, and MNE performance: A meta-analysis. *Journal of International Business Studies*, 36(3): 270–83.

Townsend, J. D., Yeniyurt, S., Deligonul, S., & Cavusgil, S. T. 2004. Exploring the marketing program antecedents of performance in a global company. *Journal of International Marketing*, 12(4): 1–24.

Triandis, H. C. 1989. The self and social behavior in differing cultural contexts. *Psychological Review*, 96(3): 506–20.

Tuma, N. B., & Hannan, M. T. 1984. *Social dynamics: Models and methods*. New York: Academic Press.

Varadarajan, P. R., & Cunningham, M. H. 1995. Strategic alliances: A synthesis of conceptual foundations. *Journal of the Academy of Marketing Science*, 23(4): 282–96.

Volberda, H. W., & Lewin, A. Y. 2003. Co-evolutionary dynamics within and between firms: From evolution to co-evolution. *Journal of Management Studies*, 40(8): 2111–36.

White, S. 2005. Cooperation costs, governance choice and alliance evolution. *Journal of Management Studies*, 42(7): 1383–412.

Williams, J. D., Han, S.-L., & Qualls, W. J. 1998. A conceptual model and study of cross-cultural business relationships. *Journal of Business Research*, 42(2): 135–43.

Workman Jr, J. P., Homburg, C., & Gruner, K. 1998. Marketing organization: An integrative framework of dimensions and determinants. *Journal of Marketing*, 62(3): 21–41.

Yeniyurt, S., & Townsend, J. D. 2003. Does culture explain acceptance of new products in a country? An empirical investigation. *International Marketing Review*, 20(4): 377–96.

Yeniyurt, S., Townsend, J. D., & Talay, M. B. 2007. Factors influencing brand launch in a global marketplace. *Journal of Product and Innovation Management*, 24(5): 471–85.

Zhao, H., Luo, Y., & Suh, T. 2004. Transaction cost determinants and ownership-based entry mode choice: A meta-analytical review. *Journal of International Business Studies*, 35(6): 524–44.

Zou, S., & Cavusgil, S. T. 2002. The GMS: A broad conceptualization of global marketing strategy and its effects on firm performance. *Journal of Marketing*, 66(4): 40–56.

Appendix

Table A1 Cultural distance for the home countries of the foreign partners

Home countries	Cultural distance
Australia	0.02
United Kingdom	0.08
Canada	0.10
New Zealand	0.26
South Africa	0.33
Switzerland	0.34
Ireland	0.34
Germany	0.42
Italy	0.55
Czech Republic	0.65
Finland	1.09
Netherlands	1.25
Hungary	1.30
Austria	1.43
France	1.50
Belgium	1.50
India	1.60
Argentina	1.61
Israel	1.64
Denmark	1.71
Spain	1.74
Norway	1.74
Sweden	1.99
Hong Kong	2.42
Japan	2.44
Chile	2.68
Taiwan	2.86
Thailand	2.98
Costa Rica	3.00
Portugal	3.02
Mexico	3.12
Philippines	3.15
China	3.38
South Korea	3.40
Indonesia	3.42
Greece	3.46
Singapore	3.51

Case study III
Renault–Nissan–Daimlar

A global strategic alliance

Christoph Barmeyer and Ulrike Mayrhofer

In 2010, three leading actors of the global automobile industry, the French company Renault, its Japanese partner Nissan and the German Daimler group, announced the creation of a strategic alliance. The cooperation is formalized by a contractual agreement with mutual minority equity stakes. The main objectives of this trilateral partnership are to save costs and to develop synergies, while keeping brand and corporate identities. The fields of collaboration cover supply, R&D, production, enlargement of product lines and human resources.

The formation of the trilateral alliance

The strategic alliance between Renault, Nissan and Daimler was announced in April 2010. The agreement was signed between the Renault–Nissan alliance, formed in 1999, and the Daimler group. It is important to mention that the Renault–Nissan alliance has proved to be highly successful: specialists consider the partnership as one of the most productive and longest-lasting international cooperations among car manufacturers. Following cost savings and synergies developed within their bilateral alliance (see Box 1), Renault and Nissan searched to enlarge their cooperation to a third partner. Negotiations were first undertaken with the American General Motors group, but they failed in 2006. Daimler had merged with the American Chrysler company in 1998, but the two companies did not reach their objectives and thus separated in 2007. Daimler was then looking for a new partner in order to reach a critical size in the world market. Negotiations with several car manufacturers like its German competitor BMW did not come to an end (Mayrhofer and Urban, 2011).

Box 1: The Renault–Nissan alliance

The alliance signed by Renault and Nissan is often mentioned as an example of successful collaboration in the automobile industry. Both companies have been saving significant costs and developing important synergies, notably in the fields of supply, R&D, production, logistics, information systems, marketing and sales. The Renault–Nissan Purchasing Organization (RNPO), the alliance's largest common organization, negotiates prices among suppliers on behalf of both partners. Since 2009, joint purchasing represents 100 per cent of alliance purchases, compared to 30 per cent in 2001. Shared platforms and common parts have contributed to increase economies of scale and to reduce development and production costs. The launch of the Renault Pulse and Nissan Micra models in India in 2011–2012 marked the alliance's most important passenger-car

---

platform-sharing project. The companies have recently adopted a new approach, called "Common module Family" (CmF), which is a system where different sets of parts and derivatives can be applied to various car models and powertrains. The two partners have also capitalized on their powertrain expertise: they co-develop common engines and gearboxes; Renault specializes in diesel engines and manual transmissions, while Nissan specializes in gasoline engines and automatic transmissions. Powertrain synergies represented 280 million euros in 2011. In the field of logistics, a unified team has commonized packing, shipping and other functions, thus saving more than 220 million euros in 2011. Another team has been working on the reduction of customs duties and administrative costs concerning trade, with cost savings of at least 50 million euros per year. Renault and Nissan also share common information systems, data centres and licenses. Concerning marketing and sales, the partners won their first fleet contracts in 2012 for the worldwide supply of more than 15,000 vehicles to the French Danone group. Finally, the cooperation has also reinforced the presence of the two groups in international markets and accelerated their expansion in emerging markets.

Sources: Barmeyer and Mayrhofer (2009); Renault Nissan (2013).

The organizational structure of the alliance

The partnership signed between Renault, Nissan and Daimler takes the form of a contractual agreement, which is accompanied by minority equity investments. As shown by Figure III.1, both Renault and Nissan acquired a 1.55 per cent equity stake in the capital of Daimler, and Daimler bought a 3.1 per cent stake in Renault (owned at 15 per cent by Nissan) and a 3.1 per cent stake in Nissan (owned at 43.4 per cent by Renault). These cross-shareholdings should ensure the mutual self-interest of the three partners and encourage strategies that benefit each of them.

The cooperation between Renault, Nissan and Daimler is governed by the Alliance Board, set up by Renault and Nissan, and managers of the Daimler group. As indicated by Figure III.2, the Renault–Nissan Alliance Board is composed of three Renault and three Nissan senior executives. The board is chaired by Renault–Nissan Alliance Chairman and Chief Executive

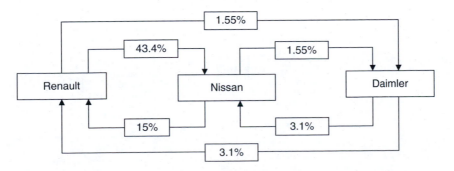

Figure III.1   Minority equity stakes of the Renault–Nissan–Daimler alliance.

Source: Renault Nissan (2013).

Officer Carlos Ghosn, who has played an important role for both companies as well as for their cooperation. After having started his career at the French Michelin group, Carlos Ghosn joined Renault in 1996 and became the number two of the group, reporting directly to CEO Louis Schweitzer. In 1999, he was nominated Chief Operating Officer at Nissan before being appointed the company's CEO two years later. Renowned as a "cost killer" with a strong leadership, Carlos Ghosn succeeded the recovery of the financial situation for both companies and brought them back to profitability. In 2005, he was also nominated Chairman and CEO of Renault (Barmeyer and Mayrhofer, 2009). The Alliance Board, which is supported by the Executive Committees of Renault and Nissan, focuses on strategic direction, new opportunities for collaboration, and the progress of the alliance relative to industry benchmarks. Alliance board meetings concern major topics associated with the collaboration: mid-term plan progress, validation of product plans, commonality of products and powertrains, strategic investments impacting the alliance and strategic partnerships with third parties. The Alliance Board thus also manages joint projects developed with Daimler within the trilateral agreement.

The cooperation with Daimler also involves managing directors that were nominated for the Renault–Nissan alliance. In 2009, the Renault–Nissan alliance decided to create a team of dedicated alliance directors (see Box 2) in order to accelerate synergies and best-practice sharing between the two companies. The alliance managing directors are responsible for the operations of alliance functions and advice project teams in both companies. They may oppose measures taken by Renault or Nissan that do not contribute to the development of synergies, referring the matter to the executive committee of the company concerned or even to the Alliance Board. It seems interesting to note that one managing director has been working for both Renault and Nissan, five of them come from Renault, six from Nissan and two were recruited without prior experience in any of the partner companies.

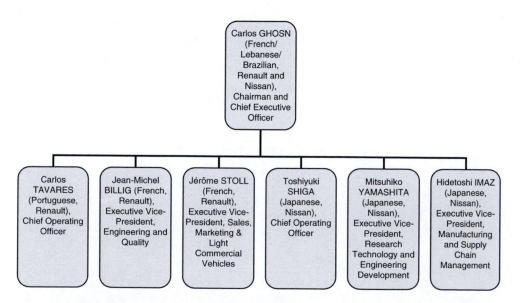

Figure III.2 Presentation of the Alliance Board of Renault–Nissan (in 2013).

Source: Renault Nissan (2013).

Box 2: List of alliance managing directors of Renault–Nissan (in 2013)

Gérard DETOURBET (French, Renault): Managing Director, A-Segment development unit

Celso GUIOTOKO (Brazilian with family of Japanese origin, Nissan): Managing Director, Information Systems & Technologies

Rachel KONRAD (American): Communication

Christian MARDRUS (French, Renault): Managing Director, Office & Logistics

Toshiaki OTANI (Japanese, Nissan): Managing Director, Battery Business

Jérémie PAPIN (French/American): Finance

Alain RAPOSO (French, Renault): Powertrain Planning

Minoru SHINOHARA (Japanese, Nissan): Research & Development

Hiromi TAKAOKA (Japanese, Nissan): Industrial Sourcing

Christian VANDENHENDE (Belgian, Renault): Alliance Director, Global Purchasing & RNPO Managing Director, Purchasing

Jacques VERDONCK (French, Renault): Daimler Coordination

Isabelle VIEUILLE (French, Renault and Nissan): Economic Advisor

Hideaki WATANABE (Japanese, Nissan): Managing Director, ZE (Zero Emission, all-electric) Vehicles

Tsuyoshi YAMAGUCHI (Japanese, Nissan): Platforms & Parts

Source: Renault Nissan (2013).

The outcomes of the alliance

Since the creation of the Renault–Nissan–Daimler alliance in 2010, several major projects have been conducted:

* the development and production of Renault Twingo and Daimler's Smart models, including electric versions (the Smart plant in Hambach, France, is chosen as the production location for the two-seater versions, and the Renault plant in Novo Mesto, Slovenia, is the production location for the four-seater versions);
* Citan, a new light commercial vehicle under the Mercedes-Benz vans brand, based on Renault technology and produced in Renault's plant in Maubeuge (France);
* low-consumption diesel and gasoline engines, including a Renault-produced diesel engine for the Mercedes A-Class;
* production of Mercedes-Benz four-cylinder gasoline engines at Nissan's powertrain assembly plant in Decherd (Tennessee);
* cross-supply of Mercedes Canter – Nissan Atlas trucks in Japan;
* a "premium entry" car for Infiniti co-developed on a Mercedes platform;
* research and development on next-generation fuel-cell vehicles.

The three partner companies have also been exploring other areas of potential collaboration, including regional cooperation agreements in the Americas, China and Japan.

Table III.1 indicates some key figures concerning the three companies in terms of number of employees, revenues, net income and portfolio of brands. It shows that Renault, Nissan and Daimler achieved net profits in 2012, despite the global economic crisis which has

Table III.1 Key figures of Renault, Nissan and Daimler (2012)

	Renault	*Nissan*	*Daimler*
Number of employees	127,086	157,365	275,087
Revenues	41.3 billion €	90.2 billion €	114.3 billion €
Net income	1.7 billion €	3.2 billion €	6.5 billion €
Major brands	Renault, Dacia, Renault Samsung Motors	Nissan, Infiniti, Datsun	Mercedes, Smart

Sources: Renault, Nissan and Daimler websites.

deeply affected the automobile industry. Cost savings and synergies developed within their trilateral alliance have undoubtedly contributed to these positive results.

The Renault–Nissan–Daimler alliance seems to have benefited to all three partners. Renault, Nissan and Daimler continue their cooperation and target to achieve a 10 per cent market share in all markets, with accelerated growth in emerging markets, notably in BRIC (Brazil, Russia, India, China) countries, which offer interesting growth perspectives for the automobile industry (Mayrhofer, 2013).

Questions

1. What are the main factors that explain the success of the Renault–Nissan–Daimler alliance?
2. How far does the adopted organizational structure facilitate the outcomes of this trilateral alliance?

Further reading

Barmeyer, C. and Mayrhofer, U. (2009), Management interculturel et processus d'intégration: une analyse de l'alliance Renault–Nissan. *Management & Avenir*, 22, 109–131.
Mayrhofer, U. (ed.) (2013), *Management of Multinational Companies: A French Perspective*. Basingstoke: Palgrave Macmillan.
Mayrhofer, U. and Urban, S. (2011), *Management international. Des pratiques en mutation*. Paris: Pearson Education.
Renault Nissan (2013), *Alliance Facts & Figures 2012–2013*, Paris.

Part IV

External relationships

18   Introduction

With an increasing level of interdependences between firms and their environments and also between different firms, it is clear that a firm cannot achieve excellence on its own and sustain competitive advantage. The main reason for this is that a firm cannot own all crucial resources that are needed to grow and perform successfully. The earlier view that a firm can own all or most of the unique resources through internalization is proving to be somewhat misleading (Hennart, 2009). It has now been established that a firm cannot own many of these unique resources and has to collaborate with other firms and even non-business actors in order to achieve its goals (Deligonul et al., 2013). Firms are therefore bound to cooperate with other firms and organizations who own the resources that are external to their own organization.

Companies do not develop their strategies in isolation and have to collaborate with other firms to develop these strategies (Jack and Anderson, 2002). Several studies on networks and on interaction between businesses and political actors stress that it is beneficial for firms to engage in collaborative relationships with other firms and organizations (Johanson and Vahlne, 2009). Although some of these relationships evolve over time without clear strategic intentions, most firms consider external relationships to be an integral part of strategy formulation.

A firm is believed to have a network of relationships with business actors that are directly related to its daily business and routines as well as with non-business actors that are indirectly related to its operations, as illustrated in Figure 18.1 (De Wit and Meyer, 2004).

Actors directly related to the firm

A number of external business actors are directly related to the firm and its value creation or value consumption. These actors include suppliers, competitors, buyers and complementors.

Suppliers are those actors that provide several types of input to the firm's value creation activities. They may provide raw materials, components, operational support services or any other production factors. They can also include landlords from whom the firm has rented the premises or contractors who provide the focal firm with temporary staff or labour. These suppliers are often referred to as upstream vertical relations (Hadjikhani et al., 2008).

Competitors are the actors who provide similar products or services that directly compete with the focal firm's products or services. These actors are often referred to as horizontal industrial relations.

Buyers are vertical downstream relationships that exist between a seller of a product or service and its customers. They may or may not be actual buyers or users and may include distributors or agents who sell the firm's products or services to final consumers.

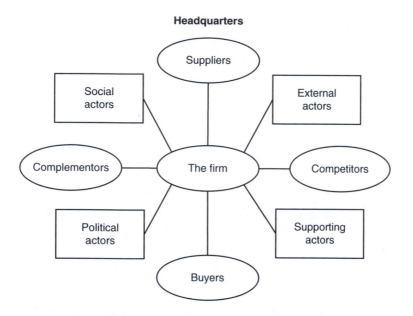

Figure 18.1 Interaction between MNEs and socio-political actors.

Source: Based on Hadjikhani et al., 2012.

Complementors are the actors who are not direct competitors of the firm but those who manufacture or provide complementary products or services. These relationships are important as they can be used as barriers of entry for new entrants. Tyres and battery producers are good example of complementors for the auto industry. These relationships can also be useful if a firm wants to diversify. They are considered horizontal relationships.

Actors indirectly related

Social actors are individuals and organizations that are important members of a society. They may include media, non-government organizations (NGOs), religious groups and sports clubs. As these actors play an important role in the society and form public opinion, more and more companies are interacting with them. They can support or alienate a firm's operations, in a particular market that can have a long-lasting impact on its success.

Political actors are the members of the government and international institutions, such as the WTO and local regulatory authorities. Most firms have to deal with these actors directly or indirectly through agents or lobbyists.

Economic actors refer to actors that play an important role in a market and indirectly interact with local as well as foreign firms. They may include tax authorities, labour unions, stock exchanges and import or export regulators.

Supporting actors are several authorities and institutions that grant different types of permissions and permits, such as patent office and standards-setting institutions. These actors may also include research institutes and universities that can be of assistance to a firm in its activities for value creation.

In many markets, such as the European Union, firms need to adhere to certain rules and regulations. In emerging markets, firms try to negotiate their entry conditions with the local governments or seek support from other social organizations such as NGOs (Hamel and

Prahalad, 1994). In some cases, such as approval of standards in the European Union, firms work together with other firms to influence decision-making and standards-setting in their industry (Johanson and Vahlne, 2009).

According to the network approach, it is in the interest of the firms to cooperate with each other and build a network of relationships. The main idea is that no firm can own all necessary resources for a sustainable competitive advantage and should build relationships with other firms or actors who have complementary resources. All members of the network have the same objectives and accrue benefits from each other's resources (Kelley and Thibaut, 1978). Moreover, as network partners, they can improve the pool of joint resources, which would not be possible individually for any of them. In other words, they learn from each other and support each other through collaborative activities.

In global markets there are more and more networks that compete with other networks of companies. This means that to be competitive at a global level, firms need to be members of a network. The importance of external relationships in the internationalization process is now well established. These relationships are developed through active social exchange processes and are more behaviour-based than the common economic-based theories, or theories based on transaction cost economics (Hennart, 1982).

Jointly, members of networks create new knowledge and provide the focal firm with an extended knowledge base. This is referred to as relationship-specific knowledge, which is developed through international relationships with external partners. Companies in a network coordinate and collaborate their activities without hierarchical order and may not even have contractual relationships or equity ownership in each other. They seek common and mutual efficiencies and specializations. These relationships are based on reciprocal respect, trust and commitments. One drawback of these networks is that more powerful members of the network might benefit more than the weaker members (De Wit and Meyer, 2004).

MNEs and socio-political actors

Some scholars have taken the network approach further to also include socio-political actors as members of the network (Hadjikhani et al., 2008). These studies stress that business firms need to manage their political market as well as the business market. Increasingly, scholars have suggested inter-dependencies between business actors and political actors. While business actors seek support and endorsements of political actors, the aim of political actors is to increase employment, social welfare and growth for the society. This cannot be achieved without the business actors' success and growth.

For management of political environment, the social interaction through formal and informal networking and lobbying gain influence on political units (Boddewyn, 1988). Scholars envisage lobbying as the creation of specific pressure on political units for unique gains. Numerous studies have noted a lack of research concerning the mutual dependency between MNCs and political and social organizations (Stafford and Hartman, 1996).

Indifferent to business firms that have pure business construction, social organizations may or may not be financed by private groups and individuals, the state or MNEs. These organizations voluntarily challenge and/or seek to protect issues such as the environment, human rights, corruption and society's welfare. Greenpeace, the World Wildlife Fund, Amnesty International, Human Rights Watch and Transparency International are all well-known NGOs. During the 1990s, NGOs increasingly began to affect companies in issues pertaining to the environment and human rights.

The terminology for such cooperation between society and the firm varies in the literature: it is sometimes referred to as a 'green alliance' or a 'social alliance' (Christmann and Taylor, 2002). One underlying reason for such cooperation is the immense complexity of some of the major problems facing companies. There are for example environmental issues many actors are involved in. These actors have a variety of sometimes conflicting interests. The aim of these actors is to strengthen their own legitimate position and knowledge of future developments (Doh and Teegen, 2002). Interaction with NGOs has therefore gained importance for MNEs during the last decade to safeguard the interest of society towards issues concerning corporate social responsibility.

Many scholars believe that such cooperation should be viewed as an opportunity for MNEs, states and society for mutual gains. MNEs manage their relationships with business, social and political units engaged in different markets to achieve their strategic goals. As shown in Figure 18.2, MNEs act in different markets with differentiated needs and aims. The fundamental concern of MNEs is to undertake legitimate actions to alter the coercive actions of the society and political organizations to supportive one. Therefore, association with society not only improves the company's and the state's image and reputation, but also the status of members of society.

MNEs can have access to social actors' networks and technological knowledge and can achieve a legitimate position in society. Social actors also make demands on MNEs to improve the well-being of society, which increases the speed of knowledge development and innovation. MNEs' cooperation with social units can be assumed as a management tool to gain legitimacy and support from society and political organizations. This cooperation can influence the future formulation of legislation and standards.

Close relationships with socio-political actors may make it possible to avoid scandals that have to do with employee conditions, or environmental pollution that can harm a firm's reputation worldwide (Elg et al., 2008). Some scholars note that MNEs can reduce their transaction costs by including NGOs in their development strategies, especially in markets that differ significantly from the home market (Vachani et al., 2009).

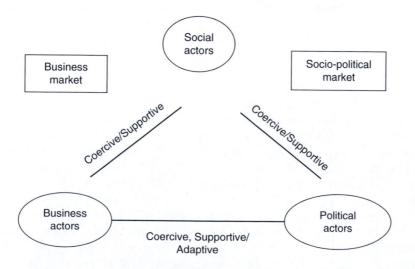

Figure 18.2 The firm and its external relationships.

The first reading in this part is a groundbreaking piece by Zaheer, 'Overcoming the liability of foreignness'. It addresses whether firms in a competitive global environment face a liability of foreignness and how these firms can overcome this liability. Several earlier studies have pointed out costs related to foreignness for firms going into new markets and how these costs can be met through firm-specific advantages (FSAs) such as organizational or management capabilities. Many of these studies have argued that foreign firms normally mimic the organizational practices of local successful firms. This chapter addresses the question of whether it is better for the firm to import their own organizational capabilities or to imitate local organizational practices to deal with this liability of foreignness.

The author presents two hypotheses to study this issue. In horizontal MNEs, MNEs whose units abroad are replicas to each other to manufacture and distribute goods and services and are not vertically integrated with other foreign units. The liability of foreignness is particularly acute in market-seeking horizontal MNEs. Hypotheses are tested with empirical data from 28 financial trading rooms from Western and Japanese markets.

The study concludes that a liability of foreignness does exist. It also confirms that firm-specific advantages may be a more effective way to overcome this liability than imitating local practices, because the effect of imitation of local practices on the liability of foreignness varies in different industries and market practices.

The next chapter in this section, by Hennart, 'Down with MNE-centric theories: market entry and expansion as the bundling of MNE and local assets', challenges existing theories of internationalization process of the firm. The author claims that establishment chain (Uppsala model) and OLI assume that internationalization decisions, how MNEs choose the mode of entry, are made solely by MNEs' internal capabilities and assets that are controlled by the firm, such as company- and country-specific assets. Establishment chain model advocates that MNEs make these decisions based on their tolerance for risk or need for control, while OLI suggests that MNEs bundle their FSAs with location- or country-specific advantages (CSAs) while making these decisions.

What these theories fail to recognize is that these CSAs are not owned by the firm but by the outsiders. Therefore, the best mode of entry should be that which satisfies the firm and those outside owners of CSAs. The author aims to present models for the optimal mode of foreign market entry that maximizes the benefits of both sides.

Based on earlier literature (for example, Hennart 1982), the author develops a model for optimal foreign entry mode that explains whether MNEs will choose a wholly owned subsidiary (WOS) or an equity joint venture. The model also attempts to explain whether an MNE will go for an acquisition or a greenfield investment for WOS. The author concludes that MNEs that enter foreign markets have to bundle their FSAs with local complementary assets. This means that entry mode is decided not only by MNEs but by MNEs and owners of local assets. The mode that is chosen will be that which satisfies the party whose behaviour is most difficult to constrain. In case behaviour of both parties is equally constrained, then an equity joint venture (EJV) will be chosen.

The next chapter, on firms external relationships, by Hadjikhani, Lee and Ghauri, 'Network view of MNCs' socio-political behavior', is a good example of MNEs and their relationship-building with non-business actors in society and politicians. The authors aim to understand how MNEs manage and use their relationships with non-business actors. They develop a theoretical view that firms and other actors are striving for legitimacy, commitment and trust in society, which means that they are mutually interdependent.

The authors propose a model based on these three concepts and the network approach, which is tested through two in-depth case studies: Daewoo motor company, a Korean MNE from the automobile industry, and Vattenfall, a Swedish MNE from the power generation industry. It is proposed that there are two parallel markets: business market and socio-political market, working side by side. All actors, MNEs, politicians and social actors, have to manage both of these markets and are dependent on each other.

The case studies show how Daewoo developed relationships with EU politicians, trade unions and with local society. For example, by providing doctors and nurses in the market they enter (Poland), arranging festivals for children and supporting a local football team. Vattenfall developed strong relationships with EU politicians to influence energy policy and rules on environment. They prepared cases for several EU committees and opened an office in Brussels to handle these relationships.

This study concludes that although there are differences in MNE behaviour as to type and amount of resources they spent on socio-political networking, the behaviour of both firms was quite similar as both were trying to enhance their legitimacy and trustworthiness through showing commitments to society.

The last reading in this section by Bouquet and Birkinshaw, 'Weight versus voice: how foreign subsidiaries gain attention from corporate headquarters' deals with the strategies that foreign subsidiaries use to get attention and critical resources from the top executives at head office. This is a unique piece as it focuses on the foreign units and not the head office, and their behaviour and strategies in deciding which issues to focus on. As MNEs are highly diversified in business portfolio and markets, it is difficult and complex for top executives to pay full attention to all the subsidiaries in the world. It thus becomes the responsibility of the managers in subsidiaries to attract the attention of head office. The main idea is to identify the factors that influence the attention of head office that is given to subsidiaries.

Based on archival data and a survey of 283 MNE subsidiaries, the analysis reveals three main factors that influence the level of attention from head office to subsidiaries: (1) the structural position of the subsidiary in the overall corporation system, in other words the 'weight' a subsidiary carries in the whole system; (2) whether the subsidiary uses its 'voice' to attract the attention from head office or not; (3) whether the head office listens to this voice depends upon the subsidiary's historical position, geographic distance and downstream competencies. The attention of head office refers to a positive conscious involvement of head office executives in the issues related to the subsidiary that are forward-looking and value enhancing.

The results of their empirical investigation reveal that the attention given to a subsidiary is not only influenced by the structural position (weight) but the voice of the subsidiary is also crucial in attracting the head office's attention. They also explain that in some situations it is more likely that the voice of the subsidiary will create a positive outcome. The authors triangulate their findings by interviewing 24 executives and conclude that the positive attention of the head office has three dimensions: supportive, visible and relative. That head office is supportive of subsidiary's efforts to achieve its goals, it is visible as the head office openly or publicly expresses appreciation for the subsidiary and it is relative in the way the head office treats this subsidiary compared with other subsidiaries in its portfolio.

References

Boddewyn, J. (1988), "Political aspects of MNE theory", *Journal of International Business Studies*, Vol. 19, No. 3, pp. 341–63.

Christmann, P. and Taylor, G. (2002), "Globalization and the environment: Strategies for international voluntary environmental initiatives", *The Academy of Management Executive*, Vol. 16, No. 3, pp. 121–36.

De Wit, B. and Meyer, B. (2004), *Strategy: Process, content, context*, London: Thomson.

Deligonul, S., Elg, U., Cavusgil, T. and Ghauri, P.N. (2013), Developing strategic supplier networks: An institutional perspective, *Journal of Business Research*, 66/4: 506–15.

Doh, J. and Teegen, H. (2002), "Nongovernmental organizations as institutional actors in international business: Theory and implications", *International Business Review*, Vol. 11, No. 6, pp. 665–84.

Elg, U., Ghauri, P.N. and Tarnovskaya, V. (2008). "The role of networks and matching in market entry to emerging retail markets." *International Marketing Review*, Vol. 25, No. 6, pp. 674–99.

Hadjikhani, A., Elg, U. and Ghauri. P.N., (eds) (2012), *Business, society and politics: Multinationals in emerging markets,* Bingley: Emerald.

Hadjikhani, A., Lee, J.-W. and Ghauri, P.N. (2008), A network view of MNCs socio-political behaviour, *Journal of Business Research,* 61/3: 912–24.

Hamel, G. and Prahalad, C.K. (1994), *Competing for future*, Boston MA: Harvard Business School Press.

Hennart, J.-F. (1982), *A theory of multinational enterprise,* Ann Arbor: University of Michigan Press.

Hennart, J.-F. (2009), Down with MNE-centric theories: Market entry and expansion as the bundling of MNE and local assets, *Journal of International Business Studies*, 40: 1432–54.

Jack, S.L. and Anderson, A.R. (2002), The effect of embeddedness in the entrepreneurial process, *Journal of Business Venturing,* 17: 467–87.

Johanson, J. and Vahlne, J.-E. (2009), The Uppsala internationalization process model revisited: From liability of foreignness to liability of outsidership, *Journal of International Business Studies*, 40: 1411–31.

Kelley, H.H. and Thibaut, J.W. (1978), *Interpersonal relations: A theory of interdependence*, New York: John Wiley & Sons.

Stafford, E. and Hartman, C. (1996), "Green alliances: strategic relations between businesses and environmental groups", *Business Horizons*, Vol. 39, no. 2, pp. 50–59.

Vachani, S., Doh, J.P. and Teegen, H. (2009), "NGOs influence on MNEs social development strategies in varying institutional contexts: A transaction cost perspective", *International Business Review*, Vol. 18, pp. 446–56.

19 Overcoming the liability of foreignness*

Srilata Zaheer

Researchers in international business have long theorized that multinational enterprises (MNEs) doing business abroad face costs (Hymer, 1976; Kindleberger, 1969) arising from the unfamiliarity of the environment, from cultural, political and economic differences, and from the need for coordination across geographic distance, among other factors. This liability of foreignness has been the fundamental assumption driving theories of the multinational enterprise (Buckley & Casson, 1976; Caves, 1982; Dunning, 1977; Hennart, 1982). Further, it has been argued that to overcome the liability of foreignness and compete successfully against local firms, MNEs need to provide their overseas subunits with some firm-specific advantage, often in the form of organizational or managerial capabilities (Buckley & Casson, 1976; Caves, 1982; Dunning, 1977; Hennart, 1982). Resource-based views of strategy (Barney, 1991; Lippman & Rumelt, 1982; Winter, 1991) have also stressed the importance of firm-specific resources and organizational capabilities in providing sustainable competitive advantage to firms. These theories suggest that multinationals' subunits will try to overcome the liability of foreignness by importing capabilities embodied in the organizational practices of their parent enterprises, particularly if the subunits are competing in an undifferentiated product market in which other sources of imported competitive advantage, such as a brand name, a superior technology, or factor-cost advantages, have little role to play.

Drawing from institutional theory (DiMaggio & Powell, 1983; Scott, 1987; Zucker, 1988), writers in international organization theory (Powell & DiMaggio, 1991; Rosenzweig & Nohria, 1994; Rosenzweig & Singh, 1991) have argued that MNE subunits are most likely to attend to the demands of their local, host country environments and that their organizational practices will tend to become similar, or isomorphic, to the practices of local firms. In particular, institutional theory would lead one to predict that, if local firms are the best-performing exemplars in the immediate local environment of an MNE subunit, it will attempt to mimic their organizational practices in its bid to better its performance (DiMaggio & Powell, 1983).

The puzzle that emerges from these two theories is this: If in fact MNE subunits face a liability of foreignness, does importing firm-specific organizational practices or imitating local organizational practices better help them overcome this liability and compete successfully against purely local firms? This is the question addressed here and tested in an industry context in which organizational capabilities, rather than product differentiation or product–market fit considerations, provide an important source of competitive advantage.

I addressed this research question by studying one industry, foreign exchange trading, in depth through observation, interviews and multiple-respondent surveys conducted in a paired sample of the trading rooms of a set of U.S. and Japanese banks in New York and Tokyo. I defined local trading rooms as those in banks that were substantially owned by individuals or firms from the country in which the rooms were located and foreign trading rooms as those in banks that were substantially owned by individuals or firms from countries other than the country of the trading rooms' location. Specific organizational practices on which the Western trading rooms in New York differed most from the Japanese trading rooms in Tokyo were identified. I then tested to what extent the competing theories of local isomorphism and imported firm-specific advantage explained the difference between the performance of the foreign and local trading rooms.

This study is of interest for both theory and practice. It sought to establish whether there are costs to doing business abroad, an assumption that, although largely untested, is critical to theories of multinational enterprise. I also attempted to test the performance implications for firms of two sets of alternative theories, the resource-based and the institutional. The study also has implications for the question of how integrated or responsive a company can or should be in its organizational practices (Prahalad & Doz, 1987) as it pursues an international strategy.

Theory and hypotheses

The liability of foreignness

In the literature on multinational enterprises (Hymer, 1976; Kindleberger, 1969), the liability of foreignness—the costs of doing business abroad that result in a competitive disadvantage for an MNE subunit—have been broadly defined as all additional costs a firm operating in a market overseas incurs that a local firm would not incur. In general, the liability of foreignness can arise from at least four, not necessarily independent, sources: (1) costs directly associated with spatial distance, such as the costs of travel, transportation, and coordination over distance and across time zones; (2) firm-specific costs based on a particular company's unfamiliarity with and lack of roots in a local environment; (3) costs resulting from the host country environment, such as the lack of legitimacy of foreign firms and economic nationalism; (4) costs from the home country environment, such as the restrictions on high-technology sales to certain countries imposed on U.S.-owned MNEs. The relative importance of these costs and the choices firms can make to deal with them will vary by industry, firm, host country and home country. Whatever its source, the liability of foreignness implies that foreign firms will have lower profitability than local firms, all else being equal, and perhaps even a lower probability of survival.

The liability of foreignness is likely to be particularly acute in a simple, market-seeking, horizontal MNE (Caves, 1982), which is a multinational whose subunits are essentially replicas of each other that manufacture or distribute goods and services in different markets around the world. Such operations essentially compete on a local-for-local basis (Bartlett & Ghoshal, 1989). A vertical multinational enterprise, which uses its geographically dispersed subunits as stages in a globally integrated value-adding system in which it can exploit economies of global scale or scope, or a networked MNE, whose subunits have differentiated roles and levels of integration, may feel the liability of foreignness less (Ghoshal & Nohria, 1989).

The foreign exchange trading rooms of major multinational banks approximate horizontal MNEs in the financial services industry as they are essentially simple stand-alone operations in each of the locations they operate in, mandated to turn a profit by speculating on global currency markets and by providing currency exchange services to local customers. The product is undifferentiated. The bulk (over 85%) of banks' trading in currency markets appears to be driven by speculation on short-term trends in currencies (Bank for International Settlements, 1993; Lyons, 1993; Ohmae, 1990). Information—on trends in the demand for various currencies, on market expectations of price movements and on likely policy outcomes—is critical to running a successful speculative trading operation. The rest of the trading is business conducted for bank customers, which tends to be competitively priced and may even be offered at no profit as a service to important customers (Eccles & Crane, 1988). However, the customer-related business is still valued as the flow of customer orders provides important advance information to trading rooms about the demand for different currencies, thereby acting as a leading indicator of potential price movements and facilitating the rooms' speculative operations. Further, currency trading rooms are legally allowed to "trade ahead" of customer orders, and large customer orders can contribute to speculative profit making (Lyons, 1993; Zaheer, 1992) even if the orders are not themselves particularly profitable. Although the speculative portion of trading may take place across international borders, the customer-based business of currency trading rooms tends to be largely local (Bank for International Settlements, 1993). Perhaps institutional relationships or cost and convenience lead customers to contact trading rooms in the country in which they are located for quotes on currencies, rather than trading rooms overseas.

In this context, foreign trading rooms' liability of foreignness is likely to arise from the fact that the local trading rooms in a given location are better integrated into local information networks and perhaps also have a larger customer base than the foreign trading rooms in that location. Further, local trading rooms may have better connections to the local central bank and to other policy makers who influence the exchange rates of the local currency. German banks in Germany might have a better feel for whether the Bundesbank is going to lower interest rates within the next 24 hours than might British banks located in Germany. Information of this type is critical to running a successful trading operation; thus,

> *Hypothesis 1: Foreign trading rooms will be less profitable than local trading rooms in the same location, ceteris paribus.*

Firm-specific advantage versus local isomorphism

To overcome the liability of foreignness and compete with local firms, a multinational enterprise needs to either bring to its foreign subunit resources or capabilities specific to the firm (firm-specific advantages) or attempt to mimic the advantages of successful local firms. The costs that contribute to creating a liability of foreignness do not directly point to which of these options an MNE might prefer. An MNE might attempt to reduce the costs of coordination directly by giving total autonomy to a foreign subunit allowing it to behave like a local firm by, for instance, performing all value-adding stages in the foreign location. Or the parent might attempt to compensate for distance-related costs through scale economies or the premium attached to a brand name imported from the home country. Researchers studying international strategy and organization (Bartlett & Ghoshal, 1989; Porter, 1986; Prahalad & Doz, 1987) have suggested a range of industry-specific factors that might influence the extent of "local responsiveness" required from an MNE subunit, which in turn could affect the subunit's degree of similarity to local firms. Rosenzweig and Singh (1991) suggested that

MNE subunits in multidomestic industries might be much more prone to local isomorphism than those in global industries.[1]

In general, firm-specific advantage can be derived from traditional sources of competitive advantage, such as cost savings derived from economies of scale or scope (Porter, 1986), or exploiting location-based cost advantages (Dunning, 1977), or such resources as a brand name or a differentiated product. Competitive advantage can also be derived from organizational capabilities such as the ability to learn or to transfer organizational practices and managerial skills across a multinational network (Bartlett & Ghoshal, 1989; Kogut, 1993).

In foreign exchange trading, the products are undifferentiated commodities, practically any trading room anywhere in the world can satisfy a particular customer's requirements for most currencies. The technology in use in the large multinational banks' trading rooms is also fairly standard, as there are essentially three major global technology suppliers to this industry. In this context, the traditional sources of competitive advantage are likely to be of little or no consequence. Therefore, the transfer of firm-specific managerial or organizational skills, as embodied in organizational routines, is likely to be critical in compensating for the liability of foreignness. Thus,

> *Hypothesis 2a: Foreign trading rooms whose organizational practices more closely resemble those of their firms' domestic trading rooms will show less evidence of the liability of foreignness.*

In discussing and testing the hypotheses, I use the difference between a foreign trading room's profitability and the average profitability of the local trading rooms in a particular location as an indicator of the foreign firm's liability of foreignness.

However, as discussed earlier, an alternative hypothesis is plausible. Writers in international organization theory (Arias & Guillen, 1991; Powell & DiMaggio, 1991; Rosenzweig & Nohria, 1994; Rosenzweig & Singh, 1991) have argued that MNE subunits are most likely to attend to the demands of their local environments. Others (Westney, 1988, 1993; Zaheer, 1992) have argued for the existence of multiple isomorphic pulls on MNE subunits, and Rosenzweig and Nohria (1994) suggested a number of factors that, across industries or practices, might moderate the extent of local isomorphism. The assumption behind the arguments for local isomorphism in these models is that an MNE subunit operating in a particular local environment (say, a subsidiary of an American multinational in Germany) will tend to follow local practices either because of coercive isomorphism (caused by the requirements of German regulations, for example), normative isomorphism (caused by professionally imposed requirements), or mimetic isomorphism (imitation caused by the success of local exemplars; DiMaggio & Powell, 1983). Mimetic isomorphism is likely to be particularly important in areas of free and unregulated economic competition, where firms will try to adopt the practices of others that appear to be the most successful in a given environment.

These arguments suggest that if local firms are generally more profitable than foreign firms in an industry (that is, if Hypothesis 1 is supported), the pressures of mimetic isomorphism would lead MNE subunits to mimic the organizational practices of local firms and that those that do so will be more successful and show less evidence of the liability of foreignness than those that do not. Thus,

> *Hypothesis 2b: Foreign trading rooms whose organizational practices more closely resemble the practices of local trading rooms in their location will show less evidence of the liability of foreignness.*

Market and bureaucratic controls

Two criteria were used in selecting the organizational practices to be studied. First, the chosen practices had to be very different in the two sets of local trading rooms—those in the Western banks in New York and the Japanese banks in Tokyo—as only in that case would I be able to separate the effects of local isomorphism from the effects of imported firm-specific advantage. In addition, the practices needed to have some influence on trading room performance.

An exploratory phase of the study eliminated several organizational practices and pointed toward others. For example, formal structure was identical in all the trading rooms in New York and Tokyo and was therefore inappropriate for the purposes of this study. Every trading room had interbank traders dealing with currency pairs (dollar–mark traders and dollar–yen traders, for example), a smaller number of customer traders who executed orders from corporate clients and a back office that confirmed deals and wired payments. Even the physical layout of trading desks tended to be fairly similar in both sets of local rooms, although a few of the Western banks in New York had island-shaped layouts rather than the less space-consuming straight-line layouts common in both New York and Tokyo. I eliminated both formal structure and physical layout as organizational practices worth comparing.

The one area in which the Western trading rooms in New York differed markedly from the Japanese trading rooms in Tokyo was in their control systems, which can be viewed as made up of market and bureaucratic controls.[2]

Market controls. When an organization employs a market mode of control, it "can simply reward each employee in direct proportion to his contribution" (Ouchi, 1979: 835). Organizational practices associated with market-type controls, such as basing a high proportion of traders' total incomes on performance-linked bonuses, hiring experienced traders from the external labor market and high turnover among traders, were prominent in Western banks in New York. The Japanese banks in Tokyo showed little evidence of these practices. Other writers have noticed these differences between Japanese and Western organizations (for example, Aoki, 1988; Beechler, 1990; Ouchi, 1981).

What makes market-based controls particularly interesting in this context are the possible links between incentive-based compensation of traders, which is likely to result in better individual performance, and trading room performance. Profits in interbank foreign exchange trading in the major multinational banks tend to be driven largely by taking speculative positions in different currencies (Lyons, 1993; Ohmae, 1990; Zaheer, 1992) rather than by providing service to customers. As a room's speculative profits depend on the ability and efforts of individual traders, tying traders' compensation to their profit performance could lead both to a self-selection process, in which high-quality traders are attracted to market-controlled organizations, and to traders being motivated to put more effort into trading as they have high personal stakes in outcomes (Nalbantian, 1987). A trading room's profit largely depends on the aggregate profits of its individual traders, so individual and organizational performance are closely linked. This discussion suggests that market control will be positively associated with trading room performance.

Bureaucratic microcontrols. Bureaucratic control, which has been extensively discussed in the organization theory literature (for example, Crozier, 1964; Meyer, 1990; Thompson, 1967; Weber, 1978), is a system of control based on rules and on the legitimacy of authority rather than on prices (market control) or on socialized commitment (clan control). There were striking variations in the type and extent of bureaucratic control exercised in the Japanese trading rooms in Tokyo and Western trading rooms in New York. These differences were most pronounced in an aspect of bureaucratic control unique to the trading environment, "microcontrols". These involve firms' setting detailed limits on intraday and overnight open positions[3] by currency and by trader in an attempt to micromanage speculation by individual traders. Although some Western banks in New York also had such limits, the limits were much more rigid and appeared to be taken far more seriously by the Japanese banks in Tokyo. Again, other researchers studying Japanese organizations have commented on the tight bureaucratic control exercised in Japanese organizations (Beechler, 1990).

Further, bureaucratic controls are also likely to influence performance in a speculative profit-making context. Successful speculation in the currency markets depends on a trader's being able to accurately gauge market expectations of short-term price movements. To do so, the trader needs to be intensely engaged in trading and in seeking market information on the direction of trades and who is buying or selling particular currencies. Further, the trader has to make decisions within seconds on what prices to quote and whether to go long (buy) or go short (sell) a particular currency. Only the trader on the spot has all the information required to make good decisions. Even a trading room manager who is watching the monitor on which banks display indicative prices from time to time does not have the intense engagement in the market required to sense and "ride" on short-term market trends, especially as when the market is busy, the prices shown on the monitor tend to lag behind the actual action (Lyons, 1993). In such a situation, attempts to micromanage trading through strict limits on risk positions and rules on the levels at which losses and profits have to be realized are likely to constrain traders' abilities to take full advantage of profit opportunities as they arise and are therefore likely to have a negative impact on trading room profitability.

The extents of these two organizational practices, use of market controls and of bureaucratic microcontrols, were examined to test the alternative Hypotheses, 2a and 2b. However, I decided to test for the effect of firm-specific advantage and local isomorphism on the liability of foreignness separately for each practice as I expected them to influence performance in different directions, with market controls having a positive impact on profits per trader and bureaucratic controls having a negative impact. Not just the absolute distance, but the direction in which a particular trading room's practices differed from local or from home country practices, was likely to make a difference to its performance.

The results of a one-way analysis of variance and of a Scheffé test confirmed that market control was significantly different ($p < .01$) and bureaucratic control marginally different ($p < .10$) between the Japanese foreign exchange trading rooms in Tokyo and the Western rooms in New York.

Methods

An initial exploratory study, which consisted of observation and interviews conducted at eight foreign exchange trading rooms of U.S. and Japanese banks in New York and in Tokyo, was used to identify the organizational practices that appeared most different in U.S. trading rooms in New York and Japanese trading rooms in Tokyo. This initial phase was followed by two surveys: the first, given to all foreign exchange traders in each room, asked about room-level practices (the independent variables); the second, given to the head of each trading room, assessed the dependent variable, trading room performance. Use of these two respondent groups was designed to eliminate common method bias.

Data

The full sample consisted of 28 trading rooms, 13 in New York and 15 in Tokyo, belonging to eight Western and eight Japanese banks. Surveys were returned by 198 traders in the 28 rooms, for a 79 percent response rate, 63 percent in New York and 92 percent in Tokyo. The tests of isomorphism and firm-specific advantage were carried out on a subset of this sample, a paired sample of 24 trading rooms, 12 in New York and 12 in Tokyo, belonging to six Western and six Japanese banks. Each pair consisted of a trading room in Tokyo and a trading room in New York belonging to the same parent bank. The number of traders answering the survey in the paired sample was 174; numbers in each trading room subsample were as follows: Japanese rooms in Tokyo, 51; Japanese rooms in New York, 31; Western rooms in Tokyo, 53; Western rooms in New York, 39.

The banks were selected as follows: Using the list of foreign banks in Tokyo published by the Federation of Bankers Associations of Japan (Zenginkyo, 1989) and the Hambros Bank's (1989) *Foreign Exchange and Bullion Dealers Directory* as a guide, I identified nine New York-based U.S. commercial and investment banks as having operations and being authorized foreign exchange banks in Tokyo. The managers of six of the nine banks agreed to participate, but one bank had to be dropped as it did not have a full-fledged interbank currency-trading operation in Tokyo. Ten Japanese commercial and wholesale banks were identified as having trading operations in New York and Tokyo, and the managers of eight of these agreed to participate in the study. However, the New York operations of two of these banks could not be surveyed within this study's time frame because the heads of these rooms were away. Further, to increase the number of non-Japanese banks in the sample, I decided to include one American–European joint venture that had trading operations in New York and Tokyo. The banks studied were all prominent players in the global foreign exchange market. Ten of the 12 banks appeared on a list of the top 50 worldwide foreign exchange dealers over the 1979–91 period (*Euromoney*, 1991).

Questionnaires

I administered the questionnaires to all foreign exchange traders at each trading room and gave a separate questionnaire to the head of the trading room, who was also interviewed. The traders' aggregated responses were used in the analyses. Although the full sample consisted of only 28 trading rooms, the room-level measures aggregated from the responses of 198 traders were remarkably robust and free from position bias (Phillips & Bagozzi, 1982). A Japanese version of the traders' questionnaire, which went through translation, back-translation, and pretesting, was used in Tokyo. To verify the accuracy of the translation, I calculated the reliability of all the constructs separately for the Japanese and English questionnaires and found them to be stable ($\alpha = .65$–95; results are available upon request).

Variables

I checked the basic variables from the trader's questionnaires for inter-rater reliability and for the existence of room-level effects and aggregated them for each room. I further checked the room-level measures for correlation with the responses of the heads of the trading rooms. The variables were then converted into distance measures, which are described below.

The liability of foreignness. For the foreign trading rooms (the Japanese trading rooms in New York and the Western trading rooms in Tokyo), the dependent variable was measured as the difference between the average profits per trader of all local trading rooms and the foreign room's profits per trader in the same city. For example, the liability of foreignness of a Japanese trading room in New York is the difference between the average profits per trader of all Western trading rooms in New York and the actual profit per trader of that particular Japanese trading room in New York. As the profits per trader of the local rooms were higher than those of the foreign rooms in *most cases*, the liability of foreignness was typically positive (though I did not constrain it to be so), with higher values implying a higher liability.

Profits per trader was derived from the questionnaire given to the trading room heads. I used a logarithmic transformation of this variable as it was a dollar figure.

Perceived room performance. In addition, a perceptual measure of room performance was constructed from the aggregated responses to four questions. Traders were asked if their rooms had "some of the best traders in the city" and were "among the most profitable rooms in the city" (1 = strongly disagree to 7 = strongly agree). They also rated total room profit and profits per trader. The reliability of this construct ranged from .93 to .95 across the subsamples. A high correlation with the trading room heads' ratings of profit per trader ($r = .65$, $p < .01$) provided an external check on the perceptual measure of room performance.

Some data on the basic dependent variable, profits per trader, were missing as only 18 heads of trading rooms reported this figure. This level of missing data (for 10 rooms across all subsamples) is understandable, given that this information is not publicly available, and it is remarkable that this study generated the level of support and confidence it did from the trading room heads who did report profits per trader.

The question then arose of whether to proceed using only the perceptual measure of performance. Although the perceptual measure is a good measure, I decided that the 18 data points on actual profits per trader were too valuable to ignore. The missing data were therefore estimated from the perceptual data, and a derived variable, profit per trader, was created, which consists of actual profits per trader for the 18 cases and predicted profits per trader for the other 10 cases ($R^2 = .29$, $F = 10.56$, $p = .003$, $\beta = .54$, $t = .003$). Some of the heads of trading rooms whom I was subsequently able to contact on the phone confirmed that the estimated figures were approximately correct. This estimated measure is at least as good as the perceptual measure on which it is based, and it benefits from including the available hard data on actual profits per trader.

Age and size. In testing Hypothesis 1 for the existence of a liability of foreignness, I controlled for trading room age, derived for most of the rooms from the Hambros Bank's directories, which commenced publication in 1960, and in two cases, from interviews with long-tenured staff in the trading rooms. Trading room size, defined as number of traders, was drawn from the trading room heads' questionnaire.

Extent of local isomorphism. For each of the two organizational practices of interest, extent of market controls and extent of bureaucratic microcontrols, I measured the distance of a foreign room from the average value for that practice for the local rooms in the same city. These measures, signed distance on market controls and signed distance on microcontrols, captured both the degree of similarity and its direction, or whether the foreign rooms' use of the practices exceeded or fell short of local average use. I also measured absolute distance on both sets of practices, taking just the absolute values of the signed distance measures. For example, the extent of local isomorphism in market control for a particular Western trading room in Tokyo was the absolute value of the difference between its use of market controls and the average value of market control use for all Japanese trading rooms in Tokyo. The smaller this difference, the greater the extent of local isomorphism. A point to note here is that the reliability of a difference score on a construct is the square of the reliability of the underlying construct. As the reliabilities of the basic constructs being "differenced" for the full sample were .83 for market control and .92 for bureaucratic microcontrol, the reliabilities of the calculated difference scores are reasonably good (.69 and .85).

Firm-specific advantage. As in the case of local isomorphism, a separate measure of imported firm-specific advantage was created for each practice. Two measures, signed distance from home market controls and signed distance from home microcontrols, capturing both distance and the direction of firm-specific advantage, were calculated for each foreign trading room as the difference between the value of that practice for that room and the value of that practice for its paired room in the home country. As with the local isomorphism measures, I also calculated nondirectional measures of firm-specific advantage, capturing only how close a focal room's practices were to those of its home counterpart, without considering whether the values were larger or smaller. All the distance measures were based on the following measures of bureaucratic and market controls.

Bureaucratic microcontrols. Most empirical studies (for example, Ghoshal & Nohria, 1989; Khandwalla, 1976) have defined bureaucratic control as formalization, centralization, and standardization, after the Aston studies (Pugh et al., 1969). However, as discussed earlier, in foreign exchange trading the major source of variation in bureaucratic controls is the extent to which different trading rooms set detailed limits on open positions. These microcontrols are related to the concepts of centralization, standardization and formalization, but the focus on controlling and dictating individual behavior is perhaps unique to trading environments. I used four questions to capture the existence of microcontrols, asking traders if their rooms employed overnight position limits by currency, intraday position limits by currency, overnight position limits by trader and intraday position limits by trader (yes or no; $\alpha = .92$, full sample).

Market control. Trading rooms that rely on the market to control their employees tend to pay for performance, are likely to hire traders from the external labor market and are likely to sustain a fair amount of turnover because traders leave if they perceive their market price as higher (or are asked to leave if their market price is lower). Market control was therefore measured as the average for a trading room of responses on three questions capturing the extents of pay for performance, outside hiring and turnover on seven-point Likert-type scales ($\alpha = .83$, full sample).

Control variable: Actual risks taken. Since foreign exchange trading profits are closely tied to risks taken (Ohmae, 1990), I controlled for actual risk taking in the trading rooms, measuring the difference in risk taking between each foreign room and the average risk taking of the local rooms.

In foreign exchange trading, risk is easily measured as the size of the net open position, as all trading rooms face the same exogenous volatility in currencies. This definition is analogous to viewing risk as bet-size (March & Shapira, 1992) when odds are the same. Further, individual traders have a good sense of what overnight positions each of them and their currency groups as a whole usually hold. This information and an indicator of the level at which individual traders usually took their losses were aggregated for each room and used to form an index of actual risk taking in that room. This index had high reliability ($\alpha = .83-.93$) across the subsamples and was a reasonable proxy for the rooms' net open positions. This measure also had a high correlation ($.63$, $p < .01$) with trading room heads' ratings of risk taking, providing an independent check on the measure's validity.

Results

Caveats

Some caveats about interpreting the results of the data analysis are in order. Although the sample is small, the measures reflect an aggregation of the responses of 174 traders, so the reported correlations are ecological (Hofstede, 1980), or correlations of means. Regression analyses of such measures tend to have high explanatory power because of the robustness of the underlying measures and their low variance. Second, the sample consists of carefully matched pairs and contains a large proportion of the population I sought to represent (the nine U.S. and ten Japanese banks that had full-fledged currency-trading operations in both New York and Tokyo).

The problem of small numbers will affect nearly any study that attempts to look in depth at cross-national matched pairs of subunits of the same firm in any single industry. Without a doubt, one should treat findings based on small numbers as suggestive rather than definitive. But comparing local isomorphism with imported firm-specific advantage requires studies that control for industry and firm because specific organizational practices differ in their importance and impact across different industries, and both isomorphism and competitive advantage are subtle concepts that benefit from exploration through combined field and survey methods.

A further caveat is that performance could only be measured once. However, the heads of the trading rooms did not consider the period during which the survey was given to be atypical.

Subsample descriptive statistics

Table 19.1 gives descriptive statistics for the four subsamples. Profits per trader, which ranged from $0.95 million for the Japanese trading rooms in New York to $1.88 million for the Japanese trading rooms in Tokyo, with the Western rooms in Tokyo and in New York in between, and the index of actual risk taking were not significantly different across the four subsamples. However, the subsamples differed significantly on market control, age, and size ($p < .05$), and bureaucratic control was marginally higher ($p = .07$) in the Japanese rooms in Tokyo than in the Western rooms in New York. In terms of age, the Western trading rooms in New York had been in the business of interbank currency trading longest, averaging 24 years in 1991, and were significantly older than all three other groups. The average age of the Japanese rooms in Tokyo, 12 years, was not significantly different from the average age of all the foreign rooms (8 years). In terms of number of traders, the Japanese rooms in Tokyo, with an average 82 traders each, were twice the size of all the other rooms, which averaged between 31 and 43 traders.

The liability of foreignness

In testing, I controlled for age to ensure that the liability of foreignness was not just a liability of newness (Carroll, 1983; Freeman et al., 1983), or a parent bank's lack of experience in a particular location in this line of business. I also controlled for trading room size. A one-way analysis of variance comparing profits per trader in the foreign and local rooms, with the age and the size of the trading room as covariates, yielded a cell mean of 13.9 for foreign trading rooms and 14.42 for local rooms ($F = 7.5$, $p < .05$). These results support Hypothesis 1, which predicts that trading rooms operating overseas will be less profitable than rooms operating in their home country.

Further, neither the age nor size of a trading room was significantly related to profits per trader. Size did not matter perhaps in part because these were all large rooms of major international banks, the only banks to trade out of both New York and Tokyo. Age may not be significant in explaining performance in this industry because, although some trading rooms have been providing customer service for over 30 years, the industry changed dramatically in the late 1970s and early 1980s after the Jamaica agreement of 1976 formalized the break

Table 19.1 Descriptive statistics for subsamples[a]

Variables	1. Western trading rooms in New York	2. Western trading rooms in Tokyo	3. Japanese trading rooms in New York	4. Japanese trading rooms in Tokyo	F[b]	F[c]
Profit per trader	$1.76 million	$1.23 million	0.95 million	1.88 million		
Profit per trader (log)						
Mean	14.38	14.03	13.76	14.45	2.13	
s.d.	0.70	0.75	0.32	0.38		
Risk taking						
Mean	1.32	1.23	1.37	1.69	1.81	
s.d.	0.48	0.43	0.36	0.09		
Market controls						
Mean	1.87	1.99	1.66	0.92	12.81**	26.87**
s.d.	0.45	0.22	0.48	0.17		
Bureaucratic microcontrols						
Mean	2.51	2.87	3.79	3.51	2.63†	4.05†
s.d	1.21	1.21	0.33	0.51		
Age[d]						
Mean	24.14	7.86	7.67	11.75	9.84**	
s.d.	9.77	3.53	5.09	5.73		
Size						
Mean	43.14	31.43	42.00	82.13	6.77**	
s.d.	28.16	25.09	21.08	19.45		
N	7	7	6	8		

a Superscripts indicate which other subsamples a given subsample is significantly different from ($p < .05$).
b Across all four subsamples.
c Subsamples 1 and 4 only
d Age is in years.
† $p < .10$
** $p < .01$

from fixed exchange rates (Daniels & Radebaugh, 1994). As a result, it is possible that length of experience is not as important in this industry as it may be in some others. Since age and size showed no relationship to the relative profitability of local and foreign trading rooms in this group of firms, I omitted them from the regression analyses reported below.

The finding that a liability of foreignness exists even in a highly competitive, global industry such as foreign exchange trading, where the product is undifferentiated and the costs of operating across borders should be minimal, lends strong support to Hymer's (1976) primary argument that there are always costs to doing business abroad.

Local isomorphism versus firm-specific advantage

Correlation matrixes of all variables used in the subsequently reported hypothesis tests, including a variable for location, appear in Table 19.2 for the signed measures and in Table 19.3 for the absolute measures of isomorphism.

For both market controls and microcontrols, local isomorphism and firm-specific advantage were negatively correlated, though the relationship was significant only for market controls (Pearson's $r = -.87$, $p < .01$). Also, location (New York or Tokyo) significantly affected both the extent to which the market control practices of foreign firms were similar to local market control practices ($r = .80$, $p < .01$) and the extent to which they imported such practices from home ($r = -.65$, $p < .01$); however, location was unrelated to microcontrols. Among the foreign trading rooms in Tokyo, local isomorphism in market control was low and imported practices were high. This finding has considerable face validity, for it is the foreign firms in Tokyo that have been introducing market control practices such as performance-linked compensation into the Japanese foreign exchange trading industry. The direction of the relationships in microcontrols is just the opposite, with foreign rooms in Tokyo showing greater distance from their home rooms, though this relationship is not significant.

Table 19.4 shows the results of regression analyses using both the absolute values of distance from local and home practices (the measures of isomorphism and firm-specific advantage, respectively) and the signed directional measures.

Table 19.2 Descriptive statistics and correlations of signed distance measures

Variables	Means	s.d.	1	2	3	4	5	6
1. Liability of foreignness	0.45	0.62						
2. Distance from local rooms, microcontrols	0.17	1.45	.43					
3. Distance from home rooms, microcontrols	0.05	0.67	−.16	.12				
4. Distance from local rooms, market controls	0.44	0.77	−.07	−.64*	.24			
5. Distance from home rooms, market controls	0.39	0.58	.58*	.72**	−.07	−.38		
6. Distance from local rooms, risk	−0.21	0.48	−.30	.52	.09	−.65*	.24	
7. Location[a]		1.50	−.28	−.80**	.12	.88**	−.75**	−.57

a New York = 1, Tokyo = 2.
* p < .05
** p < .01

Table 19.3 Descriptive statistics and correlations of absolute distance measures

Variables	Means	s.d.	1	2	3	4	5	6
1. Liability of foreignness	0.45	0.62						
2. Distance from local rooms, microcontrols	0.16	0.82	.42					
3. Distance from home rooms, microcontrols	0.44	0.49	−.17	−.14				
4. Distance from local rooms, market controls	0.73	0.47	−.17	−.28	.26			
5. Distance from home rooms, market controls	0.54	0.43	.29	.18	−.33	−.87**		
6. Distance from local rooms, risk	−0.21	0.48	−.30	.09	−.11	−.18	−.04*	
7. Location[a]	1.50		−.28	−.15	.33	.80**	−.65**	−.57

a New York = 1, Tokyo = 2.
* $p < .05$
** $p < .01$

Table 19.4 Results of regression analyses for liability of foreignness

Variables	Absolute distances		Signed distances	
	Microcontrols	Market controls	Microcontrols	Market controls
Distance from local practice	−0.47[†]	1.01	0.79[†]	−2.24[†]
Distance from home practice	−0.08	0.03	−0.19	2.06*
Distance from local rooms, risk	−0.67*	−1.08*	−0.71*	−0.59*
Location[a]	−0.71*	−1.68*	−0.03	2.90[†]
R^2	0.61	0.64	0.60	0.72
Adjusted R^2	0.39	0.44	0.37	0.56
F	2.78	3.15	2.63	4.49
P	0.11	0.09	0.13	0.04

a New York = 1, Tokyo = 2.
† $p < .10$
* $p < .05$

Results on the absolute measures suggest that the most important finding is that local isomorphism and imported firm-specific advantage have different effects on the liability of foreignness for the two sets of organizational practices. For microcontrols, foreign trading rooms that are distant from local practice show less evidence of the liability of foreignness (they perform better), but this is not true of market control. Previous studies have established that local isomorphism varies across organizational practices (Rosenzweig & Nohria, 1994; Zaheer, 1992). This study attempted to take those findings a step further by relating the extent of local isomorphism and imported firm-specific advantage to the difference in performance between local and foreign subunits.

In results for the signed difference measures, the differing effects on the liability of foreignness of market controls and of microcontrols is more marked. The higher the extent of market control compared to local norms, the lower a trading room's liability of foreignness. Whether a trading room is in New York or in Tokyo, strong market-based controls relative to the local average are likely to lead to better performance. The opposite appears to be the case with microcontrols, whose extensive use appears to depress performance.

As for imported firm-specific advantage, the closeness (the absolute distance) to home practices does not have a significant relationship to the liability of foreignness for bureaucratic or for market control, but the direction in which the extent of market control differs from practices at home does have an effect: the higher the extent of market control in a focal unit compared to practices at home, the greater the liability of foreignness.

The combination of that finding with the earlier finding, that high market control compared to local practice is linked to better performance, has some very subtle implications regarding firm-specific advantage. Although it is clear that high use of market-based control relative to local practice enhances performance, subunits of firms whose home trading rooms do not use high levels of market control (and whose foreign rooms have higher levels of market control than their counterparts at home) suffer in performance. This result may occur because the firms lack the internal expertise needed to implement market controls. This finding reinforces the idea that firms find it difficult to implement practices with which they are unfamiliar and that their administrative heritage can facilitate or constrain their performance (Bartlett & Ghoshal, 1989). It also supports the idea that the mimicking of organizational routines across firms is an imperfect process, but that "a firm with an established routine possesses resources on which it can draw very helpfully in the difficult task of attempting to apply that routine on a larger scale" (Nelson & Winter, 1982: 119). In other words, for a multinational enterprise trying to establish organizational routines (such as market controls) in a subsidiary, experience with those routines in the home office can provide significant firm-specific advantage. In contrast, attempting to copy the practices of efficient local organizations in areas in which the home office has no expertise may depress performance at the subunit level.

Follow-up interviews with the heads of some of the Japanese trading rooms in New York and in Tokyo further supported this finding. Almost without exception, the heads of these rooms (all Japanese nationals) felt that market-based controls could help improve performance among their traders, given the nature of trading, and some of them were trying to implement performance-based compensation plans, particularly in their New York offices. However, the lack of expertise in the parent banks in this area appeared to hinder their efforts to implement effective plans, some of them mentioned their continuing struggles and experimentation with different types of performance-based plans.

Specific examples of foreign rooms that were high and low performers will illustrate some of the issues raised. Most of the Japanese trading rooms in New York attempted to differentiate some of their organizational practices from those of the local rooms by being even more bureaucratic than their Tokyo siblings, while still attempting to copy local New York practices in market control; the extent of market control in these rooms was, however, lower than that of the average Western bank in New York. But the worst-performing Japanese trading room in New York was less differentiated from the local rooms on bureaucratic control than the other New York-based Japanese trading rooms, and in trying to copy local practices, it ended up more market-oriented in its control than the average Western bank in New York. This attempt to outdo the locals in what they were good at was clearly not working for this trading room, and perhaps in the process, it lost distinctive organizational competence that might have been available to it as a result of its administrative heritage.

In contrast, the two best-performing Western trading rooms in Tokyo (which, incidentally, were the best-performing foreign rooms in the sample) were both more driven by market control than even their siblings at home in New York, thus differentiating themselves substantially from the local rooms in Tokyo. One of the two was also lower on bureaucratic controls (it had no limits or rule-based controls at all) than its sibling in New York and substantially lower on bureaucratic controls than the local rooms in Tokyo, and the other was sightly more bureaucratic than its home-based sibling in New York, while still significantly less bureaucratic than the average Japanese trading room in Tokyo.

Implications

The reported results imply that, when the major source of firm-specific advantage lies in organizational capabilities, foreign subunits may be better off sticking with routines imported from home than attempting to completely mimic local practices with which their parent organizations have little experience. This result supports the role of administrative heritage in providing competitive advantage to multinational subunits (Bartlett & Ghoshal, 1989) and offers evidence of the difficulty firms face in copying organizational routines from other firms (Lippman & Rumelt, 1982; Nelson & Winter, 1982).

Although the results generally support the role of firm-specific advantage as embodied in imported organizational practices over local isomorphism as an effective way for MNE subunits to overcome the liability of foreignness, this finding needs to be interpreted with caution. In particular, it is possible that in industries in which firm-specific advantage is embodied in technology, brand name, scale, or some other resource, rather than in organizational capabilities, local isomorphism in organizational practices may not hurt and may even help subunit performance.

Overall, the influence of isomorphism and of firm-specific advantage on the organizational practices of multinational subunits as they try to overcome their liability of foreignness is complex and often practice-dependent. Certain practices—for example, the formal structure of a trading room—are globally isomorphic, driven by practicality and efficiency considerations: any caller from anywhere in the world wanting to trade can ask for the dollar-mark trading desk and be assured that there will be one. Deviation from such global norms would likely be a source of competitive disadvantage as such a structure would ignore the demands of the global environment (Lawrence & Lorsch, 1967). Again, certain practices may be isomorphic with those of the local environment, but not because of the regulatory influences of coercive isomorphism, or because of the professional norms of normative isomorphism, or because of deliberate mimetic behavior, but because of economic considerations alone. For instance, even those Western trading rooms in Tokyo whose home offices in New York have island layouts have little choice but to adopt a tightly packed, straight-line layout, given the high price of real estate in the downtown Ohtemachi district of Tokyo. Some theorists, notably Westney (1988, 1993), have begun to deal with some of the complexity in the issue of isomorphism in multinational subunits by discussing the pressures for isomorphism from the multiple "organizational fields" (DiMaggio & Powell, 1983) to which a multinational subunit belongs.

The results of this study also suggest a different way of looking at the issue of integration versus responsiveness (Prahalad & Doz, 1987) for different elements of value-adding activity in multinational enterprises and may offer a way to integrate the theory of multinational enterprise (Buckley & Casson, 1976; Dunning, 1977; Hymer, 1976) with theories of multinational strategy and organization (Bartlett & Ghoshal, 1989; Prahalad & Doz, 1987). For instance, one could speculate that value-adding activities that provide a multinational corporation with its firm-specific advantage are best carried out in a globally integrated manner (whether the integration happens through centralization or through coordination or through the systematic replication of the source of the advantage across all of the MNE's subunits) but that other value-adding activities, those in which the multinational has no particular advantage over local firms (or even faces a disadvantage), are best left to the discretion of the subunit. Of course, an MNE may have different advantages over its competitors in various markets, a factor that shifts the choice from the simple one of whether a particular activity should be managed in an integrated or responsive fashion, to the more complex issue of the transnational management (Bartlett & Ghoshal, 1989) of networks of subunits. Perhaps groups of subunits that share similar advantages over their competitors could be managed as an integrated cluster. Cross-subunit learning could be encouraged if a particular subunit develops expertise that may be valuable for another subunit facing a different type of competitor in another local market. If, for example, the Japanese trading rooms in New York gradually became more adept in implementing market controls, they might be in a position to transfer their skill in this area to their sister rooms in say, France, where such skill might provide a competitive advantage over French trading rooms.

This study suggests several possible directions for future research. The issue of the liability of foreignness itself opens up a range of possible research questions and suggests a need for both longitudinal and cross-sectional empirical work in different industries with different types of firms. How does the liability of foreignness behave in different industries and over time? As a foreign firm gains experience in a particular location, does its liability of foreignness decline? As industries globalize, does foreignness continue to carry costs? What aspect of foreignness matters most: a unit's ownership, the location of its head office, or the perception that its parent is foreign? Does variation in the legitimacy of foreign firms in different countries influence the liability of foreignness?

The study also suggests a need to empirically compare strategic choice-based theories of competitive advantage to institutional theories, even in nonforeign situations. Further, researchers need to understand what influences successful intra- and interfirm replication of organizational practices.

Conclusions

This study established that a liability of foreignness exists in a competitive industry, foreign exchange trading, and examined whether local isomorphism or imported capabilities better explained the difference in the profitability of local and foreign trading rooms in international banks. The results suggest that firm-specific advantage, as embodied in imported organizational practices, may be a more effective way for multinational enterprises' subunits to overcome the liability of foreignness than imitation of local practices. Although local isomorphism was related to differences in profitability, the relationship was not always in the direction predicted by institutional theory. For example, greater distances from local practice in the area of market controls were related to better performance. Further, the effect of imitation of local practices on the liability of foreignness varied by practice. It became apparent in this in-depth study of one industry that a multinational subunit trying to overcome its liability of foreignness is likely to be drawn toward models both from its local and its home environment in complex and subtle ways, with its administrative heritage influencing the effectiveness with which it can implement certain organizational practices overseas. The study also suggested a way of integrating the theory of multinational enterprise with theories of international strategy and organization.

Notes

I thank Kathleen Sutcliffe, Andrew Van de Ven, Akbar Zaheer, and two anonymous reviewers for comments on earlier versions of this article. This study was supported in part by the International Financial Services Research Center at the Sloan School of Management, Massachusetts Institute of Technology.

1 In multidomestic industries, competition in each country is essentially independent of competition in other countries (Porter, 1986); this is not so in global industries.

2 I did not use clan controls, which Ouchi (1981) noted as distinguishing Japanese and Western organizations, for two reasons: first, a construct of clan control based on variables drawn from previous research had low reliability across the subsamples (ranging from 0.35 to 0.62); second, the literature on clan controls would lead one to predict a relationship between clan controls and speculative profit making in currency trading only if they reduced costs by acting as a substitute for other forms of control. However, that was not the case in this sample, as the Japanese banks were high on both clan and bureaucratic control.

3 An open position is the stock of a particular currency held by a trader in anticipation of a price change.

References

Aoki, M. 1988. *Information, incentives and bargaining in the Japanese economy.* Cambridge: Cambridge University Press.

Arias, M. E., & Guillen, M. F. 1991. *The transfer of organizational management techniques across borders: Combining neo-institutional and comparative perspectives.* Paper presented at the INSEAD conference, Fontainebleau, France, November 1991.

Bank for International Settlements. 1993. *Central bank survey of foreign exchange market activity in April 1992.* Basel, Switzerland: Bank for International Settlements.

Barney, J. B. 1991. Firm resources and sustained competitive advantage. *Journal of Management*, 17: 99–120.

Bartlett, C, & Ghoshal, S. 1989. *Managing across borders: The transnational solution.* Boston: HBS Press.

Beechler, S. L. 1990. *International management control in multinational corporations: The case of Japanese consumer electronics subsidiaries in Southeast Asia.* Unpublished doctoral dissertation, University of Michigan, Ann Arbor.

Buckley, P. J., & Casson, M. C. 1976. *The future of the multinational enterprise.* London: Macmillan.

Carroll, G. R. 1983. A stochastic model of organizational mortality: Review and reanalysis. *Social Science Research*, 12: 303–29.

Caves, R. E. 1982. *Multinational enterprise and economic analysis.* New York: Cambridge University Press.

Crozier, M. 1964. *The bureaucratic phenomenon.* Chicago: University of Chicago Press.

Daniels, J. D., & Radebaugh, L. H. 1994. *International business: Environments and operations.* Reading, MA: Addison-Wesley.

DiMaggio, P. J., & Powell, W. W. 1983. The iron cage revisited: Institutional isomorphism and collective rationality in organizational fields. *American Sociological Review*, 48: 147–60.

Dunning, J. H. 1977. Trade, location of economic activity and the MNE: A search for an eclectic approach. In B. Ohlin, P. O. Hesselborn, & P. M. Wijkman (Eds.), *The international allocation of economic activity:* 395–418. New York: Holmes & Meier.

Eccles, R. G., & Crane, D. B. 1988. *Doing deals: Investment banks at work.* Boston: Harvard Business School Press.

Euromoney. 1991. Annual survey of foreign exchange dealers. May: 81–102.

Freeman, J., Carroll, G. R., & Hannan, M. T. 1983. The liability of newness: Age dependence in organizational death rates. *American Sociological Review*, 48: 692–710.

Ghoshal, S., & Nohria, N. 1989. Internal differentiation within multinational corporations. *Strategic Management Journal*, 10: 323–37.

Hambros Bank. 1989. *Foreign exchange and bullion dealers directory.* London: Hambros Bank.

Hennart, J. F. 1982. *A theory of multinational enterprise.* Ann Arbor: University of Michigan Press.

Hofstede, G. 1980. *Culture's consequences: International differences in work-related values.* Beverly Hills, CA: Sage.

Hymer, S. H. 1976. *The international operations of national firms: A study of direct investment.* Cambridge, MA: MIT Press.

Khandwalla, P. 1976. *The design of organizations.* New York: Harcourt Brace Jovanovich.

Kindleberger, C. 1969. *American business abroad.* New Haven, CT: University Press.

Kogut, B. 1993. Learning, or the importance of being inert: Country imprinting and international competition. In S. Ghoshal & D. E. Westney (Eds.), *Organization theory and the multinational corporation:* 136–54. New York: St. Martin's Press.

Lawrence, P. R., & Lorsch, J. 1967. *Organization and environment.* Cambridge, MA: Harvard University Press.

Lippman, S., & Rumelt, R. 1982. Uncertain imitability: An analysis of interfirm differences in efficiency under competition. *Rell Journal of Economics*, 13: 418–38.

Lyons, R. U. 1993. *Tests of microstructural hypotheses in the foreign exchange market.* Working paper no. 4471, National Bureau of Economic Research, Cambridge, MA.

March, J. G., & Shapira, Z. 1992. Variable risk preferences and the focus of attention. *Psychological Review*, 99: 172–83.

Meyer, M. W. 1990. The growth of public and private bureaucracies. In S. Zukin & P. DiMaggio (Eds.), *Structures of capital: The social organization of the economy:* 153–72. Cambridge: Cambridge University Press.

Nalbantian, H. R. 1987. *Incentives, cooperation and risk taking.* Totowa, NJ: Rowman & Littlefield.

Nelson, R. R., & Winter, S. G. 1982. *An evolutionary theory of economic change.* Cambridge, MA: Belknap Harvard.

Ohmae, K. 1990. *The borderless world.* New York: Harper Business.

Ouchi, W. G. 1979. A conceptual framework for the design of organizational control mechanisms. *Management Science*, 25: 833–49.

Ouchi, W. G. 1981. *Theory Z.* Reading, MA: Addison-Wesley.

Phillips, L. W., & Bagozzi, R. P. 1982. *On measuring organizational properties: Methodological issues in the use of key informants.* Working paper, Stanford University Graduate School of Business, Stanford, CA.

Porter, M. 1986. *Competition in global industries.* Boston: HBS Press.

Powell, W., & DiMaggio, P. 1991. *The new institutionalism in organizational analysis.* Chicago: University of Chicago Press.

Prahalad, C. K., & Doz, Y. 1987. *The multinational mission.* New York: Free Press.

Pugh, D., Hickson, D. J., & Hinings, C. R. 1969. The context of organization structures. *Administrative Science Quarterly*, 14: 91–114.

Rosenzweig, P. M., & Nohria, N. 1994. Influences on human resource management practices in multinational corporations. *Journal of International Business Studies*, 25: 229–52.

Rosenzweig, P. M., & Singh, J. V. 1991. Organizational environments and the multinational enterprise. *Academy of Management Review*, 16: 340–61.

Scott, R. W. 1987. The adolescence of institutional theory. *Administrative Science Quarterly*, 32: 493–511.

Thompson, J. D. 1967. *Organizations in action.* New York: McGraw-Hill.

Weber, M. 1978. Bureaucracy. In G. Roth & C. Wittich (Eds.), *Economy and society*, vol. 2: 956–1005. Berkeley: University of California Press.

Westney, D. E. 1988. *Isomorphism, institutionalization and the multinational enterprise.* Paper presented at the annual meeting of the Academy of International Business, San Diego.

Westney, D. E. 1993. Institutionalization theory and the multinational corporation. In S. Ghoshal & D. E. Westney (Eds.), *Organization theory and the multinational corporation:* 53–76. New York: St. Martin's Press.

Winter, S. G. 1991. Why are firms different and why does it matter? *Strategic Management Journal*, 12: 61–74.

Zaheer, S. 1992. *Organizational context and risk-taking in a global environment: A study of foreign-exchange trading rooms in the United States and Japan.* Unpublished doctoral dissertation, Massachusetts Institute of Technology, Cambridge, MA.

Zenginkyo. 1989. *The banking system in Japan.* Tokyo: Federation of Bankers Associations of Japan.

Zucker, L. G. 1988. (Ed.). *Institutional patterns and organizations: Culture and environment.* Cambridge, MA: Ballinger.

20 Down with MNE-centric theories

Market entry and expansion as the bundling of MNE and local assets*

Jean-François Hennart

Introduction

Anderson and Gatignon's (1986) "Modes of foreign entry" and the Uppsala internationalization model (Johanson & Vahlne, 1977, 1990) have both played an influential role in shaping the way international business (IB) scholars look at how the multinational enterprise (MNE) chooses its initial mode of entry into a foreign market and subsequently decides whether to increase its involvement there. For those authors, MNEs make these decisions unilaterally, based on a tradeoff between their need for control and their tolerance for risk (Anderson & Gatignon, 1986), with the latter a function of their degree of familiarity with the host country (Johanson & Vahlne, 1977, 1990).

In contrast, OLI and internalization scholars have stressed that, in order to operate in a foreign country, MNEs need to bundle two sets of assets, firm-specific advantages (FSAs) on one hand, and location, or country-specific advantages (CSAs), such as natural resources and low-cost labor, on the other (Dunning, 1988; Dunning & Lundan, 2008; Rugman & Collinson, 2006; Rugman & Verbeke, 1990; Verbeke, 2009). Accordingly, the relative strength of these CSAs determines whether firms will serve foreign markets through exports from the home country or through local production, and in the latter case, which markets they will decide to enter. But these models pay little attention to the conditions under which MNEs can access such CSAs, and how those conditions may affect their initial mode of foreign entry and subsequent operation.

A few authors have recognized that CSAs have owners, that the optimal mode of entry must be one that maximizes the welfare of those owners as well as that of the MNE (Chen, 2005; Hennart, 1988, 1989, 2000; Yeung & Mirus, 1989), and that the end result may be that those local owners end up with the bulk of the profits (Teece, 1986). I build on this literature to develop a model of the optimal mode of MNE foreign market entry. The model yields a number of new insights. Unlike some studies of entry modes that have focused on an MNE's choice between a wholly owned subsidiary (WOS) and an equity joint venture (EJV), but have not included the licensing alternative (for example, Gatignon & Anderson, 1988; Hennart, 1991), or that have focused on the choice between licensing proprietary assets or integrating into WOSs, but have excluded the EJV option (for example, Arora & Fosfuri, 2000; Davidson & McFetridge, 1984), I am able to consider licensing, EJVs, and WOS simultaneously. Furthermore, looking at the relative efficiency of the different markets in which MNE and complementary local assets are traded, and at how these assets match, allows me to explain an MNE's establishment mode, that is, its choice between greenfields, brownfields, and acquisitions. The model also offers an interesting perspective on the evolution of the MNE footprint in host countries and on the emergence of Dragon MNEs.

I start by reviewing Anderson and Gatignon's (1986) model of the determinants of modes of entry, the Uppsala model of the dynamics of modes of operation in a host market (Johanson & Vahlne, 1977, 1990), as well as OLI and internalization theories of foreign production (Dunning, 1988; Dunning & Lundan, 2008; Rugman & Verbeke, 1990) and of entry dynamics (Buckley & Casson, 1981; Rugman, 1981). I show that these theories are by and large MNE-centric, because they tend to overlook the role played by owners of complementary local assets. I then review two seminal articles that took, early on, a different tack, and set the foundations on which to model the role played by those assets: Hennart's (1988) transaction cost theory of joint-ventures (EJV), and Teece's (1986) model of who profits from technological innovations.

After a short discussion of the three alternative markets in which exchange can take place, and of the role of apportionment of equity in maximizing the rents derived from exchange, I integrate the Hennart and Teece insights into a model of the MNE's mode of entry, its establishment mode, and the trajectory taken by its expansion in a given market. I conclude by discussing the implications of the model for the impact of institutional contexts on foreign market entry, and whether and how the rise of emerging market MNEs calls for a revision of extant theories of the MNE.

MNE-centric theories of initial and subsequent entry mode choices

A long-accepted strand in the IB literature has modeled the choice of mode of entry as unilaterally determined by MNEs. Anderson and Gatignon's (1986) theoretical framework states that MNEs "trade various levels of control for reduction of resource commitments in the hope of reducing some forms of risk while increasing their returns". Their first proposition is that MNEs should insist on a WOS when exploiting highly proprietary products and processes abroad, but choose EJVs when their products and processes are not proprietary, while in their sixth proposition they argue that when MNEs have considerable international experience they should also choose a WOS. Anderson and Gatignon's framework is widely used by IB scholars studying the choice between WOSs and EJVs. Padmanabhan and Cho (1996: 47), for example, write that the choice "involves tradeoffs related to the [MNE's] level of resource commitment, the degree of control, the specification and assumption of risks and returns, and the degree of global rationalization", while Brouthers (1995: 11) states that "in selecting the appropriate entry mode firms have to answer two questions: (1) what level of resource commitment are they willing to make? (2) What level of control over operations do they desire?" Similar statements are also found in Ahmed et al. (2002); Wei et al. (2005), and Sanchez-Peinado and Pla-Barber (2006), among others.

Other IB models of the evolution of an MNE in a host country also see it as determined primarily by the MNE itself, with owners of complementary local assets playing no explicit role in the outcome. The Uppsala internationalization model (Johanson & Vahlne, 1977, 1990) predicts that an MNE will progressively deepen its commitment to a specific market, moving from contractual entry to EJV and to WOS as it gains additional experience from its current activities in the host market. Other authors have argued that MNEs unilaterally choose between greenfield entry and acquisition based on their international experience (Barkema & Vermeulen, 1998; Vermeulen & Barkema, 2001) or mode-specific experience

(Padmanabhan & Cho, 1999). Similarly, complementary local assets play no part in Buckley and Casson's (1981) model of the evolution of MNE entry modes from exports to licensing to foreign production, which they see as driven by differences in the level of fixed costs between these modes.[1]

Dunning's (1988) OLI paradigm of the MNE does take local complementary assets into account, since it states that firms will serve foreign markets through exports when their FSAs are best exploited in conjunction with home factors of production, and will engage in foreign production when such exploitation requires complementary inputs that are located outside their own country. The quality and quantity of these host-country assets, called location advantages by Dunning (1988), and CSAs by Rugman and Verbeke (1990), determine an MNE's choice between exports and foreign production. Rugman and Verbeke (1990) develop a matrix of how FSAs and CSAs interact to determine an MNE's global strategy and its chances of survival. MNEs will survive if they have strong FSAs and/or if they are located in home and host countries with strong CSAs. None of these authors explicitly consider the transactional characteristics of CSAs that may influence whether and how they can be accessed by MNEs. As I will show, the level of transaction costs involved in accessing these complementary local assets impacts the MNE's mode of entry and its subsequent footprint in the host country.

This almost exclusive focus on the MNE, and the relative neglect of the role played by local complementary assets, may account for the lack of consistent empirical support for some of the hypotheses presented above (Brouthers & Hennart, 2007). Contrary to the prediction of Gatignon and Anderson (1988) that firms with highly proprietary assets will seek WOSs, Gomes-Casseres (1989) in the case of US firms and Hennart (1991) in that of Japanese ones found that R&D-intensive MNEs did not show a greater probability of choosing WOSs than their less R&D-intensive counterparts (in the Japanese case the results were robust to different measures of research intensity), while Kogut and Singh (1988) found that R&D-intensive firms preferred entry through EJVs. Similarly, Vermeulen and Barkema's (2001) hypothesis that experienced MNEs will choose greenfields over acquisitions has received mixed support (Slangen & Hennart, 2007). The same is true for the predictions of Johanson and Vahlne (1977) and Anderson and Gatignon (1986) that, as firms gain more experience in a particular target country, they will increase their commitment to that country. Millington and Bayliss (1990) found that UK MNEs set up plants in other European Union (EU) countries without previous experience in those countries. Hennart (1991) and Delios and Beamish (1999) found that MNEs with host-country experience were more likely to choose WOSs over EJVs, but this was not supported by Gomes-Casseres (1989) and Padmanabhan and Cho (1996).

The extant asset-bundling literature

In contrast to those basically MNE-centric views, a number of authors have taken what I call an asset-bundling approach in which the initial entry mode and its subsequent evolution are determined by the transactional characteristics of the assets being bundled. In their empirical studies of the choice between WOSs and EJVs, Gomes-Casseres (1989), Hennart (1991), and Delios and Beamish (1999) argue that MNEs are more likely to opt for EJVs when venturing abroad in resource-based industries because local firms often enjoy privileged access to natural resources. Hennart and Reddy (1997) find that the organizational structure of the US firms that hold the complementary assets needed by Japanese entrants explains whether the latter will enter the US through greenfield EJVs or through acquisitions. Eapen (2007) shows that the absorptive capacity of Indian technology recipients determines whether technology transfer to India will take the form of a licensing agreement or that of an EJV. Chen (2005) models the choice between Original Equipment Manufacturer (OEM), licensing and vertical integration as a function of the level of transaction costs in the markets for two complementary assets, technology and manufacturing. Chi (1994) investigates the trading of imperfectly imitable and mobile resources between firms and analyzes the choice between acquisitions of whole firms, parts of firms and cooperative ventures, which he defines as both contracts and EJVs. Yeung and Mirus (1989) look at the mode of market entry and the evolution of that mode as an equilibrium contract between the MNE and local factor owners. Hennart (1988) develops a theory of EJVs as resulting from the interaction between at least two owners of complementary assets. Teece (1986) models whether innovators will capture the profits from their innovations based on the nature of their interaction with owners of complementary assets. In this chapter I review, integrate and extend the insights of Hennart (1988, 2000) and Teece (1986), which, to the best of my knowledge, other authors have kept entirely separate, and show that they can provide the foundations of a more complete theory of the role of complementary local assets in foreign market entry. I start by briefly outlining the main contribution of both works before combining them into a model of the modes of foreign market entry and expansion.

Hennart (1988, 2000)

The goal of Hennart (1988) is to show that transaction cost theory can be used to describe the necessary and sufficient conditions for the choice of EJVs as a first-best strategy, with EJVs defined as both greenfield joint ventures and partial acquisitions. I argue that vertical integration (i.e., owning equity in an activity) is used to bypass high-transaction-costs markets. EJVs will arise when at least two owners hold complementary assets that they want to bundle, and the market sale of those assets would incur high information, bargaining, and enforcement costs. To illustrate the argument, I consider the case where efficient production requires the combination of two types of complementary knowledge held by firms A and B. I use a 2×2 matrix (reproduced as Figure 20.1) to show that EJVs occur whenever the knowledge contributed by both A and B is subject to high information, bargaining and enforcement costs, and licensing when this is the case for only the knowledge held by A or that held by B.

| | | Firm A | |
		Marketable know-how	Non-marketable know-how
Firm B	Marketable know-how	1. Indeterminate	3. B licenses A
	Non-marketable know-how	2. A licenses B	4. A joint ventures with B

Figure 20.1 Hennart's (1988) model of equity joint ventures.

In the second part of my argument, I investigate the circumstances under which bundling the services of assets through EJVs is preferable to bundling them in the market for assets or asset services through greenfields, or in the market for firms through acquisitions. I argue that EJVs are preferable to acquisitions whenever bundling the assets via the market for firms would incur higher information, bargaining, and enforcement costs than other options. Besides cases where acquisitions are illegal, or would lead to ill will, EJVs are preferable to full acquisitions when the assets that each party needs are a subset of the assets held by the respective firms, but are hard to separate from the assets that are not needed. Bundling the service of assets through EJVs is preferable to bundling assets through greenfields whenever assets can be shared by many users without reducing the amount available to each (they are what economists call "public goods"), since in that case it is cheaper to obtain access to an existing asset than to replicate it.

In Hennart (2000) I suggest how my 1988 2 × 2 matrix could be adapted to describe an MNE's mode of entry. If firm A is the MNE, and firm B is a local firm, then cell 2 in Figure 20.1 corresponds to a wholly owned local firm, cell 3 to a wholly owned MNE subsidiary, and cell 4 to an EJV between the two (Hennart, 2000: 98). This reasoning is used to predict when the so-called "new forms of investment" (Oman, 1984) are likely to be efficient.[2] But there is no systematic analysis of the role played by complementary local assets and there are no implications for MNE survival.

Teece (1986)

Teece (1986) shows that when imitation is relatively easy, the profits from innovations may accrue to the owners of certain complementary assets rather than to the innovators. He illustrates this point with the story of the CAT scanner developed by the UK firm EMI. Eight years after EMI introduced its scanner in the US, it conceded that market to General Electric (GE) and exited the business altogether. EMI failed because it did not invest in the service network needed to train users.[3] GE, as a highly reputed distributor of medical equipment to hospitals, did have such a network, and after having successfully reverse-engineered the scanner, put EMI out of the scanner business.

Teece argues that whether innovators (for example, EMI) or imitators (for example, GE) capture the fruits of innovation hinges on three factors:

(1) the appropriability regime;
(2) the dominant design paradigm;
(3) the nature of complementary assets.

The appropriability regime refers to the extent to which an innovator can prevent imitation: this depends on the nature of the technology and on the efficacy of the legal systems of protection. The emergence of a dominant design makes it easier for imitators to compete with the innovator. In almost all cases, successful commercialization of innovations requires that they be combined with other assets such as manufacturing, distribution, after-sales services or complementary technologies. These complementary assets can be generic, in the sense that they do not need to be tailored to the innovation, or non-generic, that is, specialized or co-specialized with the innovation, as in the case of container ships and container terminals.

The interaction of appropriability regime and complementary assets determines who profits from innovations. Innovators with strong appropriability are almost sure to gain. They will license owners of generic assets, and integrate into specialized assets. If innovators do not enjoy high appropriability, then everything hinges on the terms under which they can access complementary assets. If such assets are generic, the innovator can contract for them. If they are specialized, then access to them will become a key success factor. If innovators are unable to access such assets in due time, then owners of complementary factors may end up capturing most of the gains of the innovation, as in the case of EMI and GE.

With its focus on innovations, Teece's framework is less general than Hennart's, which can be applied to any combination of assets. Teece is somewhat vague about the precise strategies to be used by innovators to integrate into complementary assets. His model is set in a domestic context, and his seminal contribution has not, to the best of my knowledge, been applied to foreign market entry and post-entry growth. Nevertheless, it is clear that the Hennart and Teece frameworks are complementary. In the following pages I combine them into a general theory of the forms of market entry, and of their evolution post-entry.

A bundling model of foreign market entry mode

Figure 20.2 modifies Hennart's (1988) original 2×2 matrix (Figure 20.1) to address the optimal way in which two parties, a foreign firm seeking to exploit innovations (an MNE) on one hand, and a local owner of complementary resources on the other, combine their assets in order to undertake value-adding activities in a foreign market. In the rest of this chapter I will assume that knowledge is the main FSA that MNEs seek to exploit in foreign markets. I adopt a wide definition of knowledge, which includes ideas, information of various types, new management techniques, business models, and new products and processes. The axes in Figure 20.2 refer to the transaction costs that are incurred in selling knowledge and complementary local assets in the markets for the services of assets, in the market for assets, and in the market for firms owning the assets. I start by developing two fundamental concepts:

(1) the relationship between markets for the service of assets, markets for assets, and markets for firms;
(2) the role of residual claimancy (the apportionment of equity) in maximizing rents from the exchange.

| | | Knowledge assets held by the MNE | |
		Easy to transact	Difficult to transact
Complementary assets held by local owners	Easy to transact	1. Indeterminate	3. MNE is sole residual claimant = wholly owned affiliate of the MNE
	Difficult to transact	2. Local firm is sole residual claimant = wholly owned operations of local firm	4. Joint venture between MNE and local firm

Figure 20.2 Optimal mode of foreign market entry.

I then develop the model.

Interactions between economic agents can take place in three markets: the market for the services of assets, the market for assets, and the market for firms owning the assets. An MNE eager to exploit its knowledge has three choices: (1) sell it on the *market for asset services* by licensing a foreign manufacturer, (2) access the *market for assets*, by bundling its know-how directly with a variety of purchased assets and incorporating all of these into goods and services, thereby engaging in exporting or producing abroad close to the foreign customer; (3) access the *market for firms*, by selling itself or parts of itself to another firm. Likewise, a local firm that owns land that is needed by an MNE can rent it in the market for land services, sell title to it in the market for land, or sell itself to the MNE, and *ipso facto* transfer its land.

When one market is subject to high transaction costs, agents may switch to another (Alchian & Allen, 1977). As the theory of the MNE tells us (Buckley & Casson, 1976; Dunning, 1988; Hennart, 1982), foreign production in MNE subsidiaries corresponds to the special case where production takes place in a foreign country and firms find it more efficient to sell their knowledge incorporated in products and services than in the market for the services of their knowledge assets (licensing), or in that for firms (selling themselves to other firms).

What is the most efficient way to bundle the services of complementary assets when their sale is subject to positive transaction costs? Property rights theory (Barzel, 1989; Chi, 1996; Eswaran & Kotwal, 1985) states that the party who should be the residual claimant, i.e., who should be entitled to what remains after all contractual payments to owners of collaborating factors of production have been made, should be the one whose behavior is the most difficult to monitor, or, in other words, whose behavior can potentially impose the highest cost on the other parties. Equity is the right to the residual income of a business, and hence should be given to the party whose output is the most difficult to measure, or, in other words, who incurs the highest transaction costs, because by becoming equity owner her performance does not have to be monitored. She will make a fixed payment to the other party whose performance is relatively easier to measure and will keep the residual gain or loss of the venture.[4] Note that the model predicts the most efficient way to bundle assets, not necessarily the way economic agents will always end up doing it. Agents will make mistakes, but we would expect that inefficient arrangements would not survive in the long run.

Let us now examine the two axes of Figure 20.2: the transaction costs involved in transferring knowledge from MNEs to owners of complementary assets, and those of transferring local complementary assets to MNEs. I begin by discussing what determines whether the transfer of knowledge incurs high or low transaction costs, before investigating the determinants of transaction costs in the transfer of complementary local assets.

Markets for knowledge and appropriability

The columns of Figure 20.2 refer to the costs incurred in transferring knowledge from MNEs to local owners of complementary assets. To simplify, I put these costs into two categories: high and low. Also for simplicity, the MNE stands here for innovators based outside the host country. I describe below the various alternative markets in which knowledge can be traded, and show that the efficiency of its transfer varies significantly across knowledge types and institutional environments.

Knowledge is sometimes available on the licensing market. In that market, it is put into a patent and its use licensed to others. The efficiency of that market is impaired by factors that have been extensively discussed elsewhere (Hennart, 1982, 1989; Teece, 1986). Some types of knowledge, such as formulae for chemicals and pharmaceuticals, can be efficiently transferred through licensing, but others cannot (Arora et al., 2001; Levin et al., 1987). In some cases, knowledge is easily available in the market for consulting services: specialized engineering firms are routinely hired to design and construct chemical plants (Arora & Gambardella, 1998) and best-practice management and advertising skills can often be bought from professional service firms (Zeng & Williamson, 2007).

Knowledge can be tacit and consequently embedded in individuals. It can then be accessed in the employment market. Pearl River Piano, the Chinese firm that is the world's largest piano maker, was able to obtain the knowledge it needed by hiring "more than ten world-class consultants to assist in improving every aspect of piano making, from design to production to final finish" (Zeng & Williamson, 2007: 52). Tacit knowledge that resides in a group of workers or in firm routines is hard to separate from the firm in which it has been developed. If such knowledge is difficult to obtain through technical assistance agreements, an alternative is to take over the firm that owns it, or to joint-venture with it. The Chinese firm Huawei built up its expertise in optical network technologies by buying OptiMight and Cognigine, two small high-tech US firms (Zeng & Williamson, 2007: 141). Accessing knowledge by hiring experts or by taking over firms that employ them requires sophisticated management skills, because employees are free to defect at any time (Verbeke, 2009).

Finally, knowledge is sometimes embedded in products. By buying components, laptop PC assemblers can access up-to-date PC technology and incorporate it into products sold to final users. Manufacturing technology can also be obtained by purchasing equipment and being trained in its use (Mathews, 2002). To sum up, knowledge can be accessed on three alternative markets, and at transaction costs that range from low to high.

Markets for complementary local assets

The rows of Figure 20.2 refer to complementary local assets. MNEs that integrate into foreign markets need access to such assets, such as manufacturing and distribution. Manufacturing and distribution, in turn, require land, utilities, and labor and managerial services. Contrary to the implicit assumptions of OLI and internalization theories, these local complementary assets (country-specific assets or location advantages) are not always freely accessible to MNEs. In some cases, contracting for the services of these local assets, for the assets themselves, or for the firms that hold them, will incur high transaction costs. A joint examination of the transactional characteristics of both MNE and local complementary assets is needed to explain the choice of mode of entry.

As examples of markets for local complementary assets, I will focus on just one physical asset, land, and one human asset, distribution skills. I show below that:

(1) complementary physical assets can be transacted on a variety of markets, while the employment market and the market for firms are alternative ways of obtaining the services of human assets;
(2) the efficiency by which these markets can transfer complementary local assets varies with the type of asset and the host country's institutional environment.

In some cases, all markets will fail and MNE entry will not be possible.

Let's consider first land. Land services can often be accessed in rental markets. This poses problems when there is site specificity, i.e., when the value of land is affected by the actions of the renter (Williamson, 1985). When this is the case, renters are exposed to the possible expropriation of their quasi-rents through the *ex post* abrogation or renegotiation of their lease. If consumers, for example, come regularly to a specific location to shop, the store will lose part of its goodwill if its lease is canceled and it has to relocate elsewhere.

Similar problems arise in the case of mineral deposits. In many countries, resources below land surface are government property and hence cannot be owned by MNEs. Then MNEs that make site-specific investments to develop the resource are vulnerable to being held up, and to having their quasi-rent confiscated by governments, a process Vernon (1971) has called the "obsolescing bargain."

When rental contracts fail because of site specificity, one alternative is for MNEs to buy the land on which they want to establish their business. This may be difficult if there are no private property rights in land, if land titles are insecure owing to non-existent or poorly kept land registers, or if they are not fully transferable, for example, because they are subject to zoning laws. Wal-Mart left Germany because it could not acquire fast enough the large parcels of land it needed for its stores (Verbeke, 2009). A third solution is to acquire the firms that occupy the desired land.[5] This is not always fail-safe, because it still exposes the MNE to expropriation in countries without enforceable property rights. Hence the ability and the method chosen by MNEs to access the land they need are likely to depend on the foreign country's institutional environment.

Distribution is one asset that MNEs entering a foreign country need to access to commercialize their innovations. Logistical services can usually be bought in competitive markets. However, if consumers rely on distributors for advice, demonstration, and repair, effective distribution may require that distributors make significant physical (warehouses and repair facilities), intellectual (understanding the product) and relational investments (understanding customer needs). Independent distributors may refuse to make the optimal amount of investments if they see them as specific to particular manufacturers, for fear of being held up by those manufacturers. Distribution contracts may also fail when the successful sale of a product requires its adaptation to local conditions. Independent distributors may resist providing marketing feedback if they fear that by doing so they run the chance of being replaced by employees of the manufacturer. A third reason distribution contracts may incur high transaction costs is that successful sales sometimes require the joint effort of manufacturers and distributors, so that buyers cannot easily separate their respective contributions and may blame one for the failings of the other. Manufacturers can in principle solve this problem by putting behavioral constraints on distributors, requiring them to make the necessary investments in stores, equipment and stock, and to undergo proper training, but this works only if these measures are reliably correlated with performance (Hennart, 2000).

Whenever contracting for distribution services experiences these types of problems, MNEs will have to integrate into local distribution (Anderson & Coughlan, 1987; Hennart, 2000; Klein et al., 1990), either by hiring their own sales force or by taking over existing distributors. This can be quite difficult. In some countries, MNEs are prohibited from establishing a local distribution network. Even when permitted, it can be a difficult and lengthy process, as local customers may have formed strong bonds with existing local distributors. Taking over these distributors may be blocked by host-country governments. If allowed, it may require sophisticated post-integration management skills. Hence access to host-country distribution is often a challenge, and, as we will see later, the inability of MNEs to do so has often hampered their entry and jeopardized their survival. To sum up, MNEs can access complementary local assets on alternative markets, but it cannot be assumed that there will always be one efficient market where they can obtain the services of these assets.

Determinants of MNE equity levels

I now turn to the cells in Figure 20.2. Take the case of an American MNE that has developed a new technological process that can profitably be used in Japan. Figure 20.2 shows that there are three possibilities. First, the American innovator could set up a WOS in Japan (cell 3), either a greenfield subsidiary firm (this means that it will contract for the services of all the complementary assets, land, permits, etc., or acquire them, and strike employment contracts with human assets, so as to build and operate the needed manufacturing and distribution facilities), or by acquiring an existing Japanese firm and transferring its new process technology internally to the new acquisition. Second, a local Japanese firm that owns complementary local assets may be able to acquire the knowledge developed by the American MNE by taking a technology license from it, by purchasing equipment from it, by hiring away key personnel from it, or by buying the American MNE in the market for firms (cell 2). Third, the American firm and the local Japanese firm that owns complementary assets may jointly own the operation, the US MNE contributing its process, and the Japanese firm local complementary assets (cell 4). This can be the result of the American firm taking a partial stake in an existing Japanese firm, or from both firms setting up a new greenfield EJV. I do not differentiate between the greenfield and the acquisition versions of these three basic scenarios at this point, as I will deal with this issue later.

Figure 20.2 makes it clear that Anderson and Gatignon (1986), Dunning (1988), and Rugman (1981) focus only on the columns of the matrix: that is, on the absolute level of transaction costs affecting the knowledge services of MNEs, with MNEs licensing local firms when knowledge is easy to transact, and integrating vertically into the local production of goods and services incorporating their know-how when it is not. For Anderson and Gatignon and Johanson and Vahlne, an MNE's choice between a WOS (cell 3) or an EJV (cell 2) will then depend only on its level of commitment and its appetite for risk.

My bundling model shows, however, that the choice of mode of entry depends on a comparison of the costs that MNEs must incur to obtain access to the complementary assets necessary to incorporate their knowledge into locally produced goods and services relative to those that local owners of complementary assets incur in accessing knowledge on all of its markets. If the market sale of the knowledge held by the MNE is subject to high transaction costs, but the MNE can acquire complementary local assets on efficient markets, then the MNE could potentially inflict higher costs on local owners of complementary assets than those owners could inflict on the MNE. The solution that maximizes the total rents from the bundle of assets is then to give the MNE the right to the residual, and have it contract for the complementary assets. The MNE will then enter with a WOS (cell 3). Inversely, if the market for knowledge is efficient, and so knowledge sellers can be expected to reliably deliver as promised, but, because of inefficient markets for complementary assets, their owners cannot be expected to behave as reliably, then the best solution is to have those owners hold the equity. This is the case when an MNE finds it very difficult to contract with local distributors, or to manage them as employees. The optimal solution for both parties is then to have local distributors hold the equity and obtain knowledge on relatively efficient markets, for example, by taking a license from an MNE, by hiring its employees, or through the purchase of parts or components incorporating the needed knowledge (cell 2).

Cell 4 corresponds to the case where the knowledge held by the MNE and the services of complementary local asset owned by the local firm are costly to access on the market for assets and asset services, or on that for firms owning the assets. The solution that maximizes total rents is then to have each input provider become a residual claimant, that is, to have the operation jointly owned by the MNE and the local owner of complementary assets. It is easy to see why such an arrangement is efficient. If the market for its knowledge is inefficient, then the MNE needs to internalize the transaction by integrating into foreign manufacturing. Otherwise, significant costs would be imposed on the owners of complementary local assets. If the market for local complementary assets is also inefficient, then local owners of such assets must also integrate into making the products that make use of their difficult-to-sell assets. Otherwise they would impose significant costs on the MNE. Hence both parties must simultaneously own equity, and the best solution is therefore a "residual sharing arrangement" (Hennart, 1988). In that case, giving reduced incentives to both parties is preferable to allocating higher incentives to either party. Examples of such arrangements are greenfield EJVs, partial acquisitions, partnerships, and sharecropping, among others.

Looking at market entry from the point of view of both MNEs and local owners of complementary assets allows us to use a single framework to model the choice of MNEs between licensing their FSAs, integrating vertically into WOSs, or integrating into EJVs. Our approach also shows that a failure of the market for the MNE's FSAs is not sufficient to explain the form taken by market entry, because it cannot discriminate between a WOS and a partially owned affiliate of the MNE. This may be the reason, as noted earlier, empirical research fails to support a clear connection between an MNE's R&D intensity and its preference for WOSs. If complementary assets are sold on inefficient markets, then the MNE will have to enter into a joint-venture to access them.

A bundling approach also makes it clear that the distinguishing characteristic of EJVs is the method it uses to reward input suppliers. In contrast to market contracts, where one of the interacting parties is paid a fixed amount *ex ante* and the other keeps the residual, the owners of complementary assets in an EJV are paid for their contribution through a share of the residual, in other words they are joint residual claimants. This differs from the view that EJVs are efficient because the equity stakes taken by the EJV partners provide mutual hostages (Kogut, 1988), or because they allow for greater administrative controls than market transactions because EJV parents have the right to monitor and control each other through the EJV board of directors (Oxley, 1997). Because in an EJV input suppliers are residual claimants, they will also demand residual control rights. This sharing of residual control rights in EJVs can lead to better decisions, but can also be a source of serious problems if the parties have conflicting goals.

Another implication of the model is that there is no theoretical reason to reserve the term "EJV" to, as Das and Teng put it, "new legal entities that are created separately from but jointly owned by the partner firms" (Das & Teng, 2002: 453; see also Oxley, 1997: 390). Both jointly owned new legal entities (greenfield joint ventures) and partial acquisitions should be called EJVs, because they have the same basic incentive structure and the same efficiency properties. I discuss the differences between these two types of EJV in the next section.

Williamson (1996: 51) and some transaction cost theorists believe that governance forms can be placed along one dimension, usually called "hierarchical intensity", and that EJVs are halfway along that continuum (Gulati & Singh, 1998; Oxley, 1997). In other words, EJVs are hybrids of market and hierarchy (Boerner & Macher, 2003; Kreps, 1990). Oxley (1997: 390), for example, calls EJVs "the classic form of hybrid organization". My analysis, however, shows that EJVs are not hybrids, at least not in the way I define them in Hennart (1993), that is as institutions where agents are simultaneously subject to both behavior and price constraints, as in the case of franchising where outlets owners are subject to price constraints because they are the residual claimants, but are also subject to behavior constraints imposed by their franchisor (Brickly & Dark, 1987). By contrast, individuals working for an EJV are either employees of the EJV or employees of the parents, but in either case there is no reason to believe that they are subject to more behavior constraints at the EJV than colleagues working directly for the parent firms.[6] The essence of EJVs, along with partnerships, sharecropping and other residual sharing contracts, is joint hierarchy.

Because Williamson (1991) has argued that hybrids are chosen when both asset specificity and uncertainty are at intermediate levels, some authors, for example, Erramilli and Rao (1993) and Brouthers et al. (2003), have modeled the choice between WOSs and EJVs in terms of differing levels of asset specificity. My model shows that this choice is not one between an intermediate and a full-level hierarchy, and hence does not depend on the level of asset. My model shows that this choice is not one between an intermediate and a full-level hierarchy, and hence does not depend on the level of asset specificity. Rather it is one between two types of hierarchy, joint vs unitary.

Greenfields, brownfields, acquisitions, and EJVs

I have argued in the previous section that the optimal choice of entry mode depends on the relative efficiency of markets for both imported and local inputs: hence Figure 20.2, where I predicted whether the optimal entry mode would be a WOS of a foreign MNE, a wholly owned local firm, or an EJV between a local firm and a foreign MNE. But I did not predict whether these wholly owned firms would be established by bundling disembodied inputs obtained in markets for asset services or assets, i.e., through a greenfield operation, or by buying the firms that control these needed inputs, that is, through an acquisition. I now address this issue. To simplify, I set aside two other important determinants of the choice between greenfield entry and acquisitions, the differential speed of entry afforded by these two modes, and their differing impact on installed production capacity, and hence on competition (Caves & Mehra, 1986; Hennart & Park, 1993). In the following developments the term "acquisition" means a full acquisition, and the term "greenfield" means a fully owned greenfield, whereas the term "EJV" refers to both a partial acquisition and a greenfield EJV.

Figure 20.3 summarizes the argument, and shows that the choice between greenfields and acquisitions depends on how efficient the markets for asset and asset services are relative

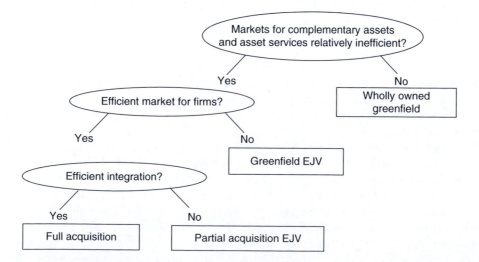

Figure 20.3 Greenfields, acquisitions and joint ventures.

to those for firms, in other words, on the extent to which assets are more easily available in disembodied form than embedded in firms. Acquisitions will be the most efficient solution when:

(1) assets are embedded in firms, and accessing them by acquiring the firms that hold them is efficient, because
(2) the market for firms is efficient, and
(3) their access through acquisitions involves low management costs.

Firm embeddedness

The first thing to be determined is whether the market for assets or asset services is efficient. If markets for assets and asset services are efficient, then the MNE will be able to access them in disembodied form on these markets, and will enter through a greenfield investment. Whenever markets for assets or for asset services are inefficient, assets will be embedded in firms, that is, they will be owned by firms and bound to them. Then it may be easier to access them by acquiring all or part of the firm that owns them, or by setting up a greenfield joint venture with that firm.

We have seen earlier that knowledge is often embedded in firms. This is also the case with complementary local assets. When there is site specificity, owning the land becomes crucial. When land titles are insecure, the most efficient way to acquire land may be to acquire the firms already sitting on it (Estrin et al., 1997). Permits, licenses, and quotas may also not be tradable, and the only way to acquire them may be to acquire, or joint-venture with, the firm that holds them. Meyer and Møller (1998) cite the acquisition by Danisco, a Danish sugar producer, of eight small and technologically obsolete East German sugar refineries that had been given non-tradable sugar quotas by the EU when East Germany joined the EU. The only way Danisco could expand was by acquiring the firms that held the quotas, or by joint-venturing with them.

There are also less obvious cases of firm-embedded assets, i.e., of assets that cannot be acquired separately from the firm to which they are bound. In some cases customers are mobile, and MNEs can pry them away from local firms through marketing effort. But when customers have made physical or relational investments that are specific to a particular man-ufacturer, they become tied to it and the easiest way to obtain them is to buy the firm to which they are tied. Efficient printing, for example, requires tight coordination between printers and ink manufacturers. Given high customer-switching costs, the most efficient way manu-facturers of printing ink can gain customers is by buying other printing ink manufacturers. This is the reason Japanese ink makers entered the US in the 1970s through the acquisition of US firms, even though this was a mode of entry with which they were unfamiliar, since acquisitions were then relatively uncommon at home (Ikeda, 2007). Customers may also have strong emotional attachment to existing brands, as seems to be the case with beer. The easiest way to obtain customers is to acquire the firms that own the brands. This may explain why entry in the beer industry often takes the form of acquisitions (Marinov & Marinova, 1998).[7]

Managerial resources may also be embedded in firms if employees face substantial costs in changing employers. Until recently, Japanese managers in large firms were assured of permanent employment in their firm. The downside was that those who lost their jobs in mid-career had little chance of finding new employment. Experienced managers were there-fore extremely reluctant to change employer, and especially to work for an unproven foreign

MNE. In other words, the Japanese lifetime employment system embedded managers and skilled workers into Japanese firms. Because of this embeddedness, MNEs entering Japan through greenfields found it difficult to hire experienced managers (Jones, 1991).

Embeddedness is a question of degree. It increases the cost of acquiring resources in the market for asset services or in that for assets relative to that of acquiring firms or joint-venturing with them. We must therefore also consider the costs involved in accessing the service of assets through the purchase of firms.

The costs of accessing assets embedded in firms

The costs of accessing assets embedded in firms fall into two categories: (1) those of carrying out acquisitions (i.e., is the market for firms efficient?), and those of accessing the services of the acquired assets after the acquisition has taken place: in other words, (2) is integration efficient?

What makes the market for firms efficient? The costs of carrying out acquisitions are the costs of finding, evaluating, and taking over firms. Those costs vary across countries and industries. In some, acquisitions are barred or frowned upon by national authorities. Where acquisitions are allowed, the market for firms is more efficient if their shares are quoted on stock exchanges and their ownership is widely dispersed, something that occurs in very few countries (Healy & Palepu, 1993). In most countries there are structural barriers to acquisitions, such as family or government ownership, cross-shareholdings, and exceptions to the one share, one vote rule (Pedersen & Thomsen, 1997; Slangen & Hennart, 2007).

Embedded assets and a relatively efficient market for firms are not sufficient conditions for acquisitions to be the preferred mode of entry. The costs to the acquirer of accessing the services of the acquired assets must also be sufficiently low. These costs are essentially management costs, because many of the capabilities sought through an acquisition are controlled by the employees of the target firm. The level of management costs depends on:

(1) the degree to which the acquired assets match those of the acquirer, which itself depends on the modularity of the acquired assets; and
(2) the incentive losses that come from having the acquirer appropriate the residual claims held by the owners of the target firm.

Everything else constant, acquisitions will be preferred to EJVs when the acquired assets are modular, and when the resulting incentive losses are minimal.

Modularity

Modularity means that the assets that are embedded in acquired firms can be easily integrated with other assets held by the acquirer. This was the case for many of the acquisitions of Eastern European food companies made by Western MNEs in the 1980s and 1990s. The acquired assets were usually modular, because MNEs could superimpose their superior advertising and distribution skills over local manufacturing facilities and locally-established brand names without having to make substantial changes to these assets (Estrin et al., 1997; Marinov & Marinova, 1998).

Acquisitions will be chosen over greenfields and EJVs even if the needed assets embedded in a local firm make up a relatively small part of the total assets acquired, as long as the acquired assets are modular, in the sense that the desired assets can be easily separated from the non-desired ones without reducing the value of the latter. In that case, the acquirer may thoroughly restructure the acquisition, sometimes fully replacing its plant and equipment, its employees, and even its products, without damaging the value of the retained assets. This type of acquisition has been called "brownfield" because of its similarity to greenfield investment (Meyer & Estrin, 2001). It occurs whenever there is a critical local asset that can be more efficiently acquired in the market for firms than in that for the asset itself, even though that asset makes up a rather limited part of the package of assets needed for local production. This was the case in the Danisco acquisitions mentioned above: Danisco needed to acquire the firms to get the sugar quotas, but was subsequently able to close all the acquired plants and to transfer the quotas to one of its large modern plants.

Meyer and Estrin (2001) wonder whether brownfields are specific to emerging markets, but there is no good reason why this should be the case. Indeed, the brownfield acquisitions made by Western MNEs in Eastern and Central Europe have their parallel in some of the recent Chinese acquisitions of US and European firms. Just as Western MNEs bought Central European firms for some of their assets, and then sold or closed off the parts they did not need, Chinese firms have acquired Western firms for their technology, brands and customers. They have transferred these assets to their Chinese operations and closed or sold the acquired manufacturing facilities. Wanxiang, a Chinese maker of universal joints, bought its US competitor Schiller in 1998 for its brand, patents, and US distribution channels. It was able to separate these from Schiller's US manufacturing plants, which it did not want because of their high costs. It sold the plants to a US firm and is filling all US orders from its low-cost Chinese facilities (Zeng & Williamson, 2007: 45).

Whenever acquired assets are not modular, and hence the integration of acquisitions would be costly, MNEs will favor greenfields if asset services can be accessed in non-embedded forms, and EJVs if they cannot. The Japanese manufacturers of automobiles, tires, televisions and bearings that entered the US in the 1980s are a good example of the first case. Their main competitive advantage was superior quality, obtained through sophisticated shop-floor, factory and corporate management practices. These practices, which are based to a large extent on employee commitment and discipline, have been called the "Japanese management system", or JMS (Liker et al., 1999). Greenfield entry has allowed Japanese entrants to carefully select and train a labor force that is receptive to these practices (Kenney & Florida, 1993). Entering through acquisitions, on the other hand, has required retraining the workforce to make them unlearn many of their existing practices so as to allow them to learn new ones. This is difficult, because practices reflect values, and values are hard to change. As a result, the Japanese firms relying on JMS that have entered the US through acquisitions have experienced serious problems. Brannen et al. (1999) describe the difficulties the Japanese firm NSK experienced in transferring its practices to the Ann Arbor plant it acquired from Hoover. NSK later established a greenfield factory in Clarinda, Iowa, and in 2005 closed the Ann Arbor plant to consolidate production in Clarinda. Of the 14 television plants established by Japanese manufacturers in the United States in the 1980s, two – Matsushita's Franklin Park and Sanyo's Forrest City – were acquisitions; the others were greenfields. In contrast to the greenfield plants, both acquisitions experienced serious labor problems (Kenney, 1999).

EJVs will be the most efficient choice whenever desired assets are embedded, and hence are costly to access in disembodied form, but are not modular, and hence cannot be separated from non-desired assets. Consider, for example, a local manufacturer of household appliances who is vertically integrated into distribution because distribution assets are

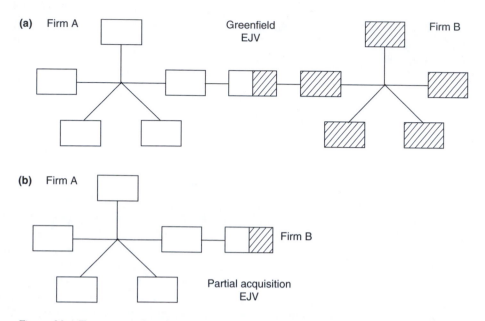

Figure 20.4 Two types of equity joint ventures: (a) greenfield equity joint ventures; (b) partial acquisition equity joint ventures.

firm-specific. An MNE eager to sell personal computers (PCs) in that market might be able to use that channel at very low marginal cost. Acquiring the local firm would, however, propel the computer MNE into the manufacture of household appliances, thus raising management costs. But because of high transaction costs in the market for distribution services, the computer MNE would find it difficult to sell the household appliances plants without giving the buyer of these plants an equity stake in the distribution assets. Figure 20.4a illustrates this case: firm A is the computer-manufacturing MNE and firm B is the local manufacturer of household appliances. Figure 20.4a shows that the most efficient solution is a greenfield EJV between the computer MNE and the local household appliance manufacturer, by which the two parties co-own the distribution assets (Hennart & Reddy, 1997; Kay, 1999). Note that an EJV solves the modularity problem by making the services of the distribution assets modular, in the sense that sharing their use with the MNE does not reduce the value of the local firm's other assets.

Incentive loss

In contrast to acquisitions, greenfield EJVs make it possible for an MNE to access the local complementary assets it needs without removing them from the ownership of the local firm and transferring them to itself. Accessing assets without owning them is efficient when the needed assets are tied to unneeded ones (Figure 20.4a). There is, however, another reason why EJVs may be efficient, and that is when the target firm possesses embedded assets that are difficult to replicate through greenfield entry, but a full acquisition would lead to a loss of motivation on the part of the owner-managers or employees of the acquired firm (Figure 20.4b). When a firm is acquired, its owner-managers, who were previously self-motivated because they were being paid out of the residual, become employees of the acquirer. The greater the tacit knowledge held by these owner-managers, the more important it is to elicit their cooperation. One way to do this is to leave a part of the residual to them, that is, to do a partial acquisition EJV (Hennart, 1988; Ichikawa, 2009). The argument can be extended to employees if these employees value their independence. Then a partial acquisition may encourage them to continue to provide the needed services, while a full acquisition might lead to a mass exodus, as has occurred in so many cases of full acquisitions of high-technology or professional firms (Inkpen et al., 2000).

Everything else constant, the cost of managing integration will be a function of the degree of post-acquisition integration that the MNE needs to bundle assets efficiently. The greater the required degree of integration, the greater the management costs of implementing it, and the more attractive EJVs, both greenfield joint ventures and partial acquisitions, relative to full acquisitions.

To illustrate the preceding discussion, consider the case of Western MNEs entering Japan in the 1980s. They needed a local manufacturing base, but Japanese managers were embedded in firms, making greenfield entry difficult. Acquiring a local firm was made difficult by cross-shareholding between Japanese firms, and by considerable public resistance to acquisitions. Given this, the most efficient mode of entry was a greenfield EJV, and Western firms continued to use this mode even after the Japanese government lifted restrictions on foreign WOSs (Jones, 1991).

This analysis may explain why most studies have found that MNEs that are product-diversified prefer acquisition over greenfield entry (Slangen & Hennart, 2007: Table 20.3), since such firms can easily superimpose their marketing and general management skills over local manufacturing and distribution assets without the need to thoroughly modify the latter. It also explains why Vermeulen and Barkema's (2001) hypothesis that internationally experienced firms will opt for greenfields has not been empirically supported (Slangen & Hennart, 2007: Table 20.3), since MNE experience has no direct bearing on the match between local and imported assets.

Chen (2008) argues that, in contrast to full acquisitions, partial-acquisition EJVs are not motivated by capability procurement, but by other strategic motives. My model and Figure 20.4 show that this is not the case, as both types of EJVs are undertaken to bundle MNE and local assets, in other words to acquire complementary capabilities, but that greenfield EJVs are undertaken when an acquisition would substantially increase management costs by adding to the size and complexity of the combined firm (Figure 20.4a), whereas partial acquisitions EJVs are chosen when a full acquisition would not necessarily lead to that outcome, but might reduce the motivation of the target's owners and key employees (Figure 20.4b). Greenfield EJVs will be chosen when the target is large and non-divisionalized, so that the parts of the potential target that the MNE wants cannot be separated from the parts it does not want, while partial-acquisition EJVs will be sought when it is important to safeguard the motivation of the managers of the acquired firm, for example in the case of acquisitions of high-technology firms.

Harzing (2001) has hypothesized that the strategy followed by MNEs is an important determinant of their choice between greenfield and acquisition entry. Based on extant arguments (for example, Hennart & Park, 1993: 1056) that MNEs find it easier to transfer their routines to greenfield affiliates than to acquisitions, she argues that MNEs that follow global strategies will choose greenfields, whereas those that opt for multidomestic strategies will enter through acquisitions. MNEs follow global strategies because their investments in intangibles, both knowledge and reputation, are subject to economies of scale and need to be amortized through a high volume of internationally homogeneous output. Greenfield plants are supposed to facilitate such strategies because of their compatibility to the parent. My bundling model shows, however, that the match between global strategies and greenfields on one hand, and multidomestic strategies and acquisitions on the other, is not a perfect one, since some firms following global strategies may still choose acquisitions. While the Japanese case described above shows that it may be necessary to set up greenfield plants to exploit innovations based on human resource management, the case of Western investments in Eastern Europe indicates that the international exploitation of product innovations or of reputation is compatible with acquisitions, because it requires only limited changes to the target. Hence, what matters is not so much whether MNEs follow global or local strategies, but rather the specific match between local and MNE assets.

This view gets some support from the fact that Japan and Germany, two countries known for producing high-quality products based on superior human resources, seem to have an unusually high proportion of greenfield entries. While the evidence is limited, data in Kogut and Singh (1988) show that the percentage of WOSs in the US that were greenfields was 44% for German and 48% for Japanese affiliates, compared with 12% for UK affiliates and 22% for Dutch ones.

The dynamics of foreign expansion

What happens after entry? We have seen that both Anderson and Gatignon (1986) and the Uppsala internationalization model (Johanson & Vahlne, 1977, 1990) predict that as MNEs accumulate experience in a host market they will move from licensing to EJV and to WOS, but that no robust large-sample empirical evidence supports these claims.[8] Figure 20.2 shows why.

Both Anderson and Gatignon and Johanson and Vahlne's Uppsala internationalization model predict that MNEs will move from cell 2 (licensing or contractual sale of technology to wholly-owned local firm) to cell 4 (EJV with local firm) and finally to cell 3 (WOS). Figure 20.2 clearly shows that such an evolution is only one of many that are possible, and suggests that a necessary condition for a move from cell 2 (licensing) to cell 4 (EJV) is that the complementary assets held by the local firm remain difficult to transact, while those held by the MNE change from easy to transact to difficult to transact. Likewise, Figure 20.2 tells us that for MNEs to move from cell 4 to cell 3, and hence to take over their local EJV partner and transform their EJV into a WOS, the market for the complementary assets held by local firms must become more competitive, while the technological advantages held by the MNE must remain difficult to sell.

But divergent evolutions are possible. For example, it may be that with the passage of time the efficiency of the market for MNE knowledge improves faster than that for local complementary assets, with knowledge moving from difficult to transact to easy to transact while complementary assets remain difficult to transact. Then the evolution will not conform to Anderson and Gatignon, nor to the Uppsala internationalization model. The MNE footprint will shrink rather than expand, with MNEs switching from EJVs (cell 4) to contractual relationships with local asset owners (cell 2) rather than to WOSs (cell 3). In spite of their greater experience of the host country, MNEs will switch from *high* (wholly-owned affiliates) to *low* control modes (licensing or other forms of contractual technology transfer).

This is not an unusual pattern. Consider the experience of Borden in Japan. Borden, a US manufacturer of dairy products, entered the Japanese market in 1971 by licensing Meiji Milk to make and sell ice cream (cell 2). The following year the two companies formed a 50/50 greenfield EJV, Meiji-Borden, to produce and market cheese, margarine, and ice cream (cell 4). Meiji was a major Japanese milk producer, with an extensive distribution network, but, as with other milk producers in Japan, had no experience processing cheese and ice cream, which were then still unfamiliar to Japanese consumers (Ono, 1991). Borden helped Meiji-Borden manufacture these two products in a factory leased from Meiji, with the output distributed through Meiji's vast distribution network. Together the partners created a market for premium ice cream, and their brand, Lady Borden, had by 1990 a 70% market share in that product segment (Yuasa, 1990).

In 1990, Borden decided to go on its own, and attempted to buy back Meiji's share of the EJV to form a WOS (cell 3). The partners were not able to come to an agreement, and the EJV was dissolved. As a result, Meiji was faced with the loss of the Lady Borden brand name and of Borden's technical help, while Borden lost access to Meiji's factories and distribution system. As in the EMI–GE case, local complementary assets proved to be harder to replace than MNE knowledge. Meiji quickly came up with two competing premium ice creams, Aya and Breuges (Ono, 1991). Borden began importing Lady Borden ice cream from Australia and New Zealand, and enlisted Meiji's rival, Morinaga, and Mitsui Trading to distribute it (Yuasa, 1990). But while Meiji was able to capitalize on its extensive distribution system, and quickly gained market share for its premium ice creams, Borden's strategy of enlisting Morinaga and Mitsui backfired. In 1994, Borden left Japan, licensing the technology, formulation, and trademark of Lady Borden to Lotte, a Japanese firm, and hence moving back to cell 2. Not surprisingly, industry observers attributed Borden's exit to its failure to build its own distribution (Kilburn, 1994).

The story of what happened to Borden shows that the increased MNE footprint predicted by MNE-centric theories is far from inevitable. When distribution is manufacturer-specific, its contractual purchase will be inefficient. If vertical integration into distribution is not possible, the MNE will be shut out from distribution. It will then revert to licensing its FSA if appropriability is strong, or, as in the EMI case, will lose the business if it is weak.

China's PC industry provides another example. In 1992, the two largest sellers of PCs in China were AST, with 27% of the market, and Compaq, with an 18% market share. Today Lenovo is the market leader in China, with one-third of the market, well ahead of Hewlett-Packard and Dell (Xie & White, 2004). Lenovo started in 1987 as Legend, a distributor of AST and other foreign-branded PCs and peripheral products (Chen et al., 2001; Pan, 2005; Xie & White, 2004). At that time foreign-owned PC makers were not allowed to own their own distribution in China. In 1988, Legend started to manufacture motherboards and add-on cards in Hong Kong, and in 1991 its own PCs, which it sold under its own brand in mainland China (Xie & White, 2004). Through its experience distributing PCs for others, Legend was able to gain an in-depth knowledge of the requirements of Chinese consumers, and to respond quickly to changes by offering customized products (Pan, 2005; Xie & White, 2004). By 1997, Legend was China's top PC seller, a position it has been able to hold onto up to this day. The bundling model shows why. In the PC industry, technology is basically embedded in components and in manufacturing equipment, which are available on competitive markets (Xie & White, 2004). In other words, knowledge is easy to transact. On the other hand, Lenovo's first-mover advantage in setting up what is the largest and most efficient dealer network in the IT industry in China is harder to imitate. According to Guo Wei, the architect of Legend's distribution network, "the distribution business in China is not as scalable as outsiders might think: it will take many years for any international player to develop such a network" (Chen et al., 2001: 14). Lenovo's position in cell 2, a wholly owned local firm, and its dominance of the Chinese market, can be explained by the fact that its main asset, control of Chinese distribution, is harder for foreign MNEs to access than it is for Lenovo to access the knowledge necessary to compete in the industry.

By considering both MNE and local resource owners, I have shown that the evolution of MNE presence in a specific industry in a specific country will hinge on the relative change in the level of transaction costs for the assets held by *both* MNEs and local firms, and not only on that for MNEs assets, as predicted by extant theories. The bundling model suggests that if the FSAs held by MNEs become increasingly available on the market or easier to imitate, while MNEs still experience difficulty in acquiring complementary assets held by local firms, the MNE footprint in the foreign market may shrink, either because the MNE ends up selling its knowledge through licensing contracts or embedded in exports, or because local firms will copy it and the MNE will lose the market. The result is that firms with access to distribution will end up owning the equity, because it is harder for technology- or reputation-exploiting MNEs to control the performance of distributors than it is for local distributors to control the performance of the MNEs that sell them technology, or license them their brand names.[9]

The bundling model also shows that, just as in the EMI domestic case studied by Teece (1986), the possession of hard-to-access complementary assets, such as distribution, is an important advantage that can allow local firms to defend their home turf successfully against attacks by MNEs. These local firms can later consolidate their initial position by accessing the necessary knowledge assets, whether in the market for machinery or components, or in the market for knowledge services through licensing or technical assistance contracts, or in the market for firms.

Such attempts by emerging-market firms to acquire the firms that hold the technological inputs that complement their own firm-specific distribution assets is ostensibly behind some of the increase in outward foreign direct investment flows by emerging countries (Goldstein, 2007; Mathews, 2002; Morck et al., 2008; Narula, 2006; Zeng & Williamson, 2007). Some of those investments involve the acquisition of technology-intensive or brand-intensive Western firms by emerging market firms that have a strong hold on their domestic markets (Zeng & Williamson, 2007: 5). Besides Lenovo's acquisition of IBM's PC division, Chinese firms have made numerous acquisitions of German, American and Korean high-tech firms (Zeng & Williamson, 2007). Huawei has bundled its strong Chinese distribution assets (Rui & Yip, 2008) with technology acquired through the purchase of two US optical network leaders and an investment in a third (Zeng & Williamson, 2007). The bundling model suggests that this combination of strong domestic market position and easy-to-transact complementary knowledge is behind the growth of MNEs from emerging markets, the Dragon MNEs (Mathews, 2002; Zeng & Williamson, 2007).

The model also suggests that the outcome of the competition behind Western and Dragon MNEs is likely to hinge on the relative cost incurred by the Dragons in acquiring advanced technology and brand names vs that which Western MNEs will face in obtaining access to emerging market distribution. As my earlier developments suggest, a number of factors may work out to the Dragons' advantage. First, the increased codification and modularity of technology and the emergence of a global market for experts have reduced the transaction costs involved in acquiring technology (Zeng & Williamson, 2007). The part of Western technological knowledge that is tacit and embedded in firms can be acquired in the market for firms, and here also the Dragons are at an advantage. Recall that assets end up embedded in firms when the market for them, or for their services, is inefficient. The greater efficiency of markets for assets and asset services in developed economies makes Western firms less diversified, and hence their assets more modular. This facilitates their integration. The Dragons are able to access the knowledge they need by taking over small or middle-sized R&D-intensive Western firms without the major management problems involved in acquiring unneeded vertically linked assets. One major challenge the Dragons still face is that of managing the integration of their high-technology acquisitions (Zeng & Williamson, 2007), a task that has proven difficult even for the more managerially competent European acquirers of Silicon Valley firms (Inkpen et al., 2000).

At the same time the in-depth knowledge of emerging market consumers and of their changing needs that is held by local distributors is likely to remain tacit, and hence difficult for MNEs to access through contract (Arora et al., 2001). As we have seen, often the only way to access such knowledge is to take over the firms that hold it. Here Western MNEs are at a disadvantage. Markets for firms in emerging countries are often embryonic, and the acquisition of local firms is frequently discouraged or prohibited by host governments. Furthermore, inefficient markets for assets and asset services cause firms there to be vertically integrated (Fan et al., 2007; Silver, 1984). Their assets are therefore less modular, and more difficult for MNEs to integrate. Joint-venturing with local distributors may then be the next best solution, but this solution has its own problems, as shown by the Meiji/Borden case discussed earlier.

Conclusion

MNEs that enter foreign markets to exploit their FSAs must bundle those advantages with local complementary assets. Hence one would expect the entry mode used, and what happens afterwards, to be simultaneously determined by the MNE and the owners of these local complementary assets. In other words, whether MNEs enter through a licensing agreement, an EJV, or a WOS, and whether they find it efficient to acquire the necessary complementary assets already bundled up in an existing firm or in disembodied form in competitive markets, should be the equilibrium outcome of their own decisions and of those of owners of local complementary assets. Furthermore, whether MNEs continue to expand their host-market activities after entry or subsequently reduce their footprint should also depend on both their own actions and those of owners of local complementary assets.

Surprisingly, this is not the way extant theories model market entry. Anderson and Gatignon (1986) and the Uppsala internationalization school (Johanson & Vahlne, 1977, 1990) see the choice of initial mode of foreign market entry and its subsequent evolution as unilaterally determined by MNEs. For Anderson and Gatignon it is the result of a tradeoff between an MNE's desire for control and its appetite for risk, and for Johanson and Vahlne it is determined by the MNE's host-country experience. Dunning's OLI paradigm (Dunning, 1988) and the internalization school (Rugman, 1981; Rugman & Verbeke, 1990) recognize the importance of complementary local assets, which Dunning calls "location advantages" and internalization scholars call "CSAs". But they do not explicitly recognize that the transactional characteristics of those assets affect whether, and how, they can be accessed by MNEs, and hence influence the MNE's mode of entry and subsequent expansion.

In this chapter I argue that the choice between different modes of market entry is essentially one of different assignments of residual rights between MNEs and local resource owners, and that the configuration eventually chosen will be the one that maximizes total potential rents by assigning residual rights to the party whose behavior is the most difficult to constrain. When both behaviors are equally difficult to constrain, the outcome will be an EJV.

This formulation clarifies the connection between transaction costs, property rights and agency theory: high information and measurement costs in the sale of asset services make it possible for sellers to inflict substantial costs on buyers. Giving sellers title to the residual of the joint buyer–seller output saves on the costs that buyers would have to incur to measure the seller's output. Hence when parties bundle complementary assets, the one who will take the residual will be the one whose output is the most difficult to measure. The residual claimant will then contract with the other party or parties. For example, whenever knowledge is tacit and there is a high degree of information asymmetry between knowledge sellers and potential buyers (knowledge is difficult to transact), but the services of complementary assets such as land and labor can be contracted for on efficient markets (they are easy to transact), giving title to the residual of the joint product of the bundle to the knowledge seller will yield a higher level of rents than the alternative of giving the residual to owners of local complementary resources, or that of sharing the residual between these owners and the knowledge owner. What drives our model is the relative level of transaction costs in the markets for all necessary inputs. Note that having title to the residual is a mixed blessing, since it entails getting both the upside and the downside of the venture.

The model builds on Teece (1986) and Hennart (1988). I apply to foreign market entry Teece's insight that owners of specialized complementary assets play a much greater role than generally acknowledged by the literature on innovation, and that they may end up capturing the bulk of the profits from the introduction of the innovation if the innovator's knowledge suffers from poor appropriability. I combine this insight with Hennart's (1988) model of EJVs as resulting from high market transaction costs in the sale of complementary inputs. I use this model to predict how the relative efficiency of all markets for knowledge and complementary local assets can explain how equity rights will be apportioned between a MNE contributing technology and a local firm controlling complementary assets, that is, whether the optimal solution will be a WOS of the MNE, a wholly-owned local firm obtaining knowledge from the MNE through markets or contracts, or an EJV between the MNE and a local firm. This yields some interesting insights into the nature and properties of EJVs, for example that EJVs are not hybrids.

I also expand on Hennart's (1988) treatment of the choice between EJVs, wholly-owned greenfields, and acquisitions, and show how the choice between these modes depends on the relative level of transaction costs for both knowledge and complementary local assets in three alternative markets: the markets for assets, for asset services, and for the firms holding the assets. I argue that even when markets for firms are efficient, greenfields and EJVs may be chosen when there is a mismatch between the assets of the acquirer and those of the potential target. I also show that brownfields are a special type of acquisition, and not solely a product of the East European institutional environment.

Finally, I use the model to predict how entry modes will evolve over time. I show that the predictions of Anderson and Gatignon and of the Uppsala internationalization model that MNEs gradually deepen their commitment with experience all rest on the very specific assumption that, with the passage of time, the market for complementary local assets becomes more efficient while that for MNE FSAs remains inefficient. I use the examples of Borden and Lenovo to show that the reverse can also occur. When it is more difficult for MNEs to access distribution, or to garner local market knowledge, than it is for local distributors to acquire technological knowledge, local distributors will end up owning the equity, and the MNE footprint in the host market will contract rather than expand. If the MNEs' FSAs have poor appropriability, they will be imitated by local firms. If they enjoy strong appropriability, local distributors will access them through the purchase of parts and machinery, through licensing and technical assistance contracts, or through the acquisition of the firms that possess these FSAs. Acquisitions of foreign technology-intensive firms by emerging market firms with a strong domestic market position are, in part, behind the recent surge in foreign direct investment from developing countries and the emergence of the so-called Dragon MNEs.

Like Chi (1994), I explain modes of entry as the outcome of the optimal apportionment of residual rights, but there are important differences between Chi's model and mine. One of them is that I take an explicit IB perspective. Another is that while Chi analyses the choice between acquisitions of full or parts of firms vs collaborative ventures (EJVs and contracts), I compare wholly-owned acquisitions, wholly-owned greenfields, partial acquisitions and greenfields EJVs. Chen (2005), building on Chen and Hennart (1997), also sees the choice of optimal governance structure as determined by interactions between MNEs and local actors, but in contrast to the present model, where I look at how the optimal bundling of MNE knowledge and local complementary assets determines the level of equity and the choice between greenfields and acquisitions, he analyzes the choice between licensing, OEM, foreign direct investment, and various marketing arrangements. Finally, along with Yeung and Mirus (1989), I am, as far as I know, among the first to show how a bundling approach can explain the evolution of the various modes of MNE operation in host countries.

This bundling model is only a first pass, and the evidence put forward is only illustrative. Much more work is required to fully assess its relevance and applicability. Looking at acquisitions as favored when assets are both embedded in firms and modular may account for unexplained regularities in the relative use of greenfield and acquisitions across industries and parent MNEs, but this clearly deserves further study.

Nevertheless, the bundling model has a number of interesting implications for IB theory and practice. The model suggests that practitioners should take into account the goals and interests of owners of complementary local assets when setting up MNE strategy. The most obvious implication for IB theory is that all IB phenomena should be analyzed from the point of view of all parties involved. For instance, one cannot model foreign market entry and expansion, and more generally the role played by local and foreign firms in a host-country industry, without considering the transactional structure of complementary local assets. Predicting whether it will be the MNE or the local owners of complementary assets who will end up owning the equity of local businesses requires the simultaneous consideration of the level of transaction costs in various substitute markets in which MNE FSAs and local complementary assets can be transacted. The familiar case of the MNE establishing an overseas greenfield WOS corresponds to the special one where knowledge is imperfectly appropriable, so innovators need to incorporate it into products and services; and where exports are not possible, so access to local complementary assets is necessary and the foreign firm is able to access them on efficient local markets. My bundling model shows that many other cases are possible. Acquisitions of local firms will be the preferred mode of entry when an MNE's FSAs have poor appropriability so that operation in the foreign market is necessary, complementary local assets are embedded in local firms, the market for these firms is efficient and the assets they hold are modular. But if appropriability is strong, MNEs may be able to exploit their FSAs without the need to set up manufacturing operations in foreign countries. Instead, they will sell their knowledge to foreign owners of complementary assets incorporated into machinery and components or through licenses or technical services agreements.

The model also has implications for the debate on how institutional contexts affect both the ability of MNEs to enter foreign countries and the modes that they will choose to do so (Gaur & Lu, 2007; Wright et al., 2005). The specialized complementary assets an MNE needs to access will vary across industries. Their transactional characteristics are likely to hinge on the specific regime of property rights in that host-country industry. Hence the evaluation of the impact of host-country institutions on MNE entry requires going beyond macro country factors, such as political or social institutions, and needs to focus more on the detailed study of the actual barriers that MNEs face when accessing these needed specialized complementary assets. Germany has highly developed institutions, yet local barriers to the acquisition of sufficiently large plots of land have discouraged Wal-Mart from doing business there (Verbeke, 2009). All possible markets for complementary local assets should also be considered, since MNEs shut out from the market for complementary asset services or from that for complementary assets may, for example, access them in the market for firms.[10]

The model also throws light on the recent debate on the rise of Dragon MNEs (Mathews, 2002, 2006). Mathews claims that "their sudden appearance cannot be explained by conventional multinational strategies" and that "the Dragon multinationals help to expose the weaknesses and limits of traditional accounts of MNEs and of existing theories and framework of international business", because, contrary to the predictions of OLI theory that MNEs expand abroad based on intangible-based FSAs, the Dragons started without initial technology resources (Mathews, 2006: 8). Mathews proposes instead that the Dragons' expansion is driven by resource linkage, leverage and learning, a framework he contrasts with OLI. Nonetheless, Mathews does not make a break with the dominant IB viewpoint that assumes that a firm's internalization is driven by its transferable knowledge and reputation assets (its FSAs), while complementary local resources (CSAs) are implicitly assumed to be freely available, and hence do not provide any advantages to local firms. As I have shown, an explicit consideration of the transactional characteristics of complementary local assets suggests that control of such assets, distribution, for example, may in fact endow the Dragons with strong advantages, which they can leverage in order to access the technology that they need. Both the local-asset seeking investments of Western MNEs and the knowledge-seeking investments of their Dragon counterparts thus fit comfortably within my bundling model.

Acknowledgements

I owe special thanks to Departmental Editor Alain Verbeke for his guidance. I also thank the three *JIBS* referees, Alex Eapen, Tom Roehl and Manuel Bueno for their useful comments. Valuable comments were also received at seminars at Baruch College, City University of New York, the University of Calgary, the University of Sydney, the University of Newcastle, Hong Kong University of Science and Technology, Keio Business School, and at the Graduate School of International Strategy at Hitotsubashi University. Financial support from the Japan Society for the Promotion of Science, Osaka City University and the Japan Foundation is gratefully acknowledged.

Notes

1 This is not strictly true in the case of Rugman (1981), who models the evolution of entry modes on the relative cost of exporting, licensing, and running foreign operations. Owners of local complementary factors play a limited role in that model, since the cost of licensing is that of running the risk of having the licensee resell the licensor's knowledge to third parties.
2 In the 1970s and 1980s a number of authors, such as Oman (1984), argued that contractual arrangements between MNEs and host countries could always advantageously substitute for equity control by MNEs. Hennart (1989) argues against this point of view.
3 Bartlett and Ghoshal (1986) argue that EMI's over-centralized and UK-centric organizational structure explains why it was late in recognizing GE's threat and in setting up an adequate distribution system in the US.

4 The reasoning is similar to the property rights theory of vertical integration, which discusses the allocation of residual rights of control (Grossman & Hart, 1986; Hart & Moore, 1990). In fact, it makes sense for residual claimancy and residual rights of control to be aligned. I thank an anonymous referee for help on this point.

5 On the premise that "possession is nine-tenths of the law".

6 One could argue, however, that in an EJV both parents impose behavioral rules on each other, and that in that sense they are hybrids. I am indebted to an anonymous referee for this insight.

7 Leasing a brand is also possible, but the lessee runs the risk that some of the goodwill investments it makes to build the brand will be held up by the lessor at contract renewal time.

8 In contrast to Anderson and Gatignon (1986) and Johanson and Vahlne (1977), who model the switch from licensing to EJVs to WOSs, both Rugman (1981) and Buckley and Casson (1981) model the evolution from exports to licensing and to foreign production, but do not consider EJVs. For the sake of comparability I focus on the comparison between the first two theories and my model.

9 Morck et al. (2008) argue along similar lines, but for them equity ends up being vested in Chinese firms because their skills in manufacturing and cost control are less contractible and more crucial to creating value than the MNE's technology or brand names.

10 Wal-Mart's initial entry into Germany was through the acquisition of 21 Wertkauf stores and 74 Interspar hypermarkets, but these acquisitions were insufficient to provide the volume Wal-Mart needed to be profitable (Verbeke, 2009).

References

Ahmed, Z., Mohamad, O., Tan, B., & Johnson, J. 2002. International risk perceptions and mode of entry: A case study of Malaysian multinational firms. *Journal of Business Research*, 55(10): 805–14.

Alchian, A., & Allen, W. 1977. *Exchange and production: Competition, coordination, and control*, (2nd ed.) Belmont: Wadsworth.

Anderson, E., & Coughlan, A. 1987. International market entry and expansion via independent or integrated channels of distribution. *Journal of Marketing*, 51(1): 71–82.

Anderson, E., & Gatignon, H. 1986. Modes of foreign entry: A transaction cost analysis and propositions. *Journal of International Business Studies*, 17(3): 1–26.

Arora, A., & Fosfuri, A. 2000. Wholly owned subsidiary vs technology licensing in the worldwide chemical industry. *Journal of International Business Studies*, 31(4): 555–72.

Arora, A., & Gambardella, A. 1998. Evolution of industry structure in the chemical industry. In A. Arora, R. Landau & N. Rosenberg (Eds), *Chemicals and long-term economic growth*: 379–414. New York: John Wiley.

Arora, A., Fosfuri, A., & Gambardella, A. 2001. Markets for technology and their implications for corporate strategy. *Industrial and Corporate Change*, 10(2): 419–51.

Barkema, H., & Vermeulen, F. 1998. International expansion through start-up or acquisition: A learning perspective. *Academy of Management Journal*, 41(1): 7–26.

Bartlett, C., & Ghoshal, S. 1986. Tap your subsidiaries for global reach. *Harvard Business Review*, 64(6): 87–94.

Barzel, Y. 1989. *Economic analysis of property rights*. Cambridge: Cambridge University Press.

Boerner, C., & Macher, J. 2003. Transaction cost economics: An assessment of empirical work in the social sciences. Working Paper, Georgetown University.

Brannen, M., Liker, J., & Fruin, W. M. 1999. Recontextualization and factory-to-factory knowledge transfer from Japan to the United States: The case of NSK. In J. Liker, W. M. Fruin & P. Adler (Eds), *Remade in America*: 117–53. New York: Oxford University Press.

Brickly, J., & Dark, F. 1987. The choice of organizational form: The case of franchising. *Journal of Financial Economics*, 18(2): 401–20.

Brouthers, K. 1995. The influence of international risk on entry mode strategy. *Management International Review*, 35(1): 7–28.

Brouthers, K., & Hennart, J.-F. 2007. Boundaries of the firm: Insights from international entry mode research. *Journal of Management*, 33(3): 395–425.

Brouthers, K., Brouthers, L., & Werner, S. 2003. Transaction cost-enhanced entry mode choices and firm performance. *Strategic Management Journal*, 24(12): 1239–48.

Buckley, P., & Casson, M. 1976. *The future of the multinational enterprise.* London: Macmillan.

Buckley, P., & Casson, M. 1981. The optimal timing of a foreign direct investment. *Economic Journal*, 91(361): 75–87.

Caves, R., & Mehra, S. 1986. Entry of foreign multinationals into US manufacturing industries. In M. Porter (Ed.), *Competition in global industries:* 449–81. Boston: Harvard Business School Press.

Chen, H., Qin, H., Ye, G., & Yin, G. 2001. *A technology legend in China.* Harvard Business School case 9-701-52.

Chen, S.-F. 2005. Extending internalization theory: A new perspective on international technology transfer and its generalization. *Journal of International Business Studies*, 36(2): 231–45.

Chen, S.-F. 2008. The motives for international acquisitions: Capability procurements, strategic considerations, and the role of ownership structures. *Journal of International Business Studies*, 39(3): 454–71.

Chen, S.-F., & Hennart, J.-F. 1997. When is original equipment manufacture the most efficient way to source foreign-made products? Paper presented at the Academy of International Business Annual Meetings, Monterrey.

Chi, T. 1994. Trading in strategic resources: Necessary conditions, transaction cost problems, and choice of exchange structure. *Strategic Management Journal*, 15(4): 271–90.

Chi, T. 1996. Performance verifiability and output sharing in collaborative ventures. *Management Science*, 42(1): 93–109.

Das, T. K., & Teng, B. S. 2002. A social exchange theory of strategic alliances. In F. Contractor & P. Lorange (Eds), *Cooperative strategies and alliances:* 439–60. Amsterdam: Pergamon.

Davidson, W., & McFetridge, D. 1984. International technology transactions and the theory of the firm. *Journal of Industrial Economics*, 32(3): 253–64.

Delios, A., & Beamish, P. 1999. Ownership strategy of Japanese firms: Transactional, institutional, and experience influences. *Strategic Management Journal*, 20(10): 915–33.

Dunning, J. 1988. The theory of international production. *The International Trade Journal*, 3(1): 21–66.

Dunning, J., & Lundan, S. 2008. *Multinational enterprises and the global economy.* Cheltenham: Edward Elgar.

Eapen, A. 2007. Essays on international market entry: Strategic alliance governance and product segment entry. PhD Dissertation, Tilburg University.

Erramilli, M., & Rao, C. 1993. Service firms' international entry mode choice: A modified transaction-cost analysis approach. *Journal of Marketing*, 57(3): 19–38.

Estrin, S., Hughes, K., & Todd, S. 1997. *Foreign direct investment in Central and Eastern Europe.* London: Pinter.

Eswaran, M., & Kotwal, A. 1985. A theory of contractual structure in agriculture. *American Economic Review*, 75(3): 352–67.

Fan, J., Huang, J., Morck, R., & Yeung, B. 2007. *Institutional determinants of vertical integration: Evidence from China*, Unpublished manuscript.

Gatignon, H., & Anderson, E. 1988. The multinational corporation's degree of control over foreign subsidiaries: An empirical test of a transaction cost explanation. *Journal of Law, Economics, and Organization*, 4(2): 305–36.

Gaur, A., & Lu, J. 2007. Ownership strategies and survival of foreign subsidiaries: Impacts of institutional distance and experience. *Journal of Management*, 33(1): 84–110.

Goldstein, A. 2007. *Multinational companies from emerging economies.* New York: Palgrave.

Gomes-Casseres, B. 1989. Ownership structures of foreign subsidiaries: Theory and evidence. *Journal of Economic Behavior and Organization*, 11(1): 1–25.

Grossman, S., & Hart, O. 1986. The costs and benefits of ownership: A theory of vertical and lateral integration. *Journal of Political Economy*, 94(4): 691–719.

Gulati, R., & Singh, H. 1998. The architecture of cooperation: Managing coordination costs and appropriation concerns in strategic alliances. *Administrative Science Quarterly*, 43(4): 781–814.

Hart, O., & Moore, J. 1990. Property rights and the nature of the firm. *Journal of Political Economy*, 98(6): 1119–58.

Harzing, A. 2001. Acquisitions versus greenfield investments: International strategy and management of entry modes. *Strategic Management Journal*, 23(3): 211–27.

Healy, P., & Palepu, K. 1993. International corporate equity acquisitions: Who, where and why? In K. Froot (Ed.), *Foreign direct investment:* 231–54. Chicago: University of Chicago Press.

Hennart, J.-F. 1982. *A theory of multinational enterprise.* Ann Arbor: University of Michigan Press.

Hennart, J.-F. 1988. A transaction costs theory of equity joint ventures. *Strategic Management Journal*, 9(4): 361–74.

Hennart, J.-F. 1989. Can the 'new forms of investment' substitute for the 'old forms'? A transaction costs perspective. *Journal of International Business Studies*, 20(2): 211–33.

Hennart, J.-F. 1991. The transaction costs theory of joint ventures: An empirical study of Japanese subsidiaries in the United States. *Management Science*, 37(4): 483–97.

Hennart, J.-F. 1993. Explaining the swollen middle: Why most transactions are a mix of 'market' and 'hierarchy'. *Organization Science*, 4(4): 529–48.

Hennart, J.-F. 2000. Transaction costs theory and the multinational enterprise. In C. Pitelis & R. Sugden (Eds), *The nature of the transnational*, (2nd ed.) 72–118. London: Routledge.

Hennart, J.-F., & Park, Y. R. 1993. Greenfield vs. acquisition: The strategy of Japanese investors in the United States. *Management Science*, 39(9): 1054–70.

Hennart, J.-F., & Reddy, S. 1997. The choice between mergers/ acquisitions and joint ventures: The case of Japanese investors in the United States. *Strategic Management Journal*, 18(1): 1–12.

Ichikawa, T. 2009. Chairman, Toyo Cotton (Japan) Co. personal interview, Osaka, Japan, 23 March.

Ikeda, K. 2007. Deputy general manager, corporate marketing and development division. Sakata Inx, personal interview, Osaka, Japan, 17 May.

Inkpen, A., Sundaram, A., & Rockwood, K. 2000. Cross border acquisitions of US technology assets. *California Management Review*, 42(3): 50–71.

Johanson, J., & Vahlne, J. 1977. The internationalization process of the firm: A model of knowledge development and increasing market commitments. *Journal of International Business Studies*, 8(1): 23–32.

Johanson, J., & Vahlne, J. 1990. The mechanism of internationalization. *International Marketing Review*, 7(4): 11–24.

Jones, K. 1991. The dilemma of foreign-affiliated companies: Surviving middle age in Japan. In J. Bleeke & D. Ernst (Eds), *Collaborating to Compete:* 145–63. New York: Wiley.

Kay, N. 1999 (Ed.). Collaborative strategies of firms. *The Boundaries of the Firm:* 177–98. Basingstoke: Macmillan.

Kenney, M. 1999. Transplantation? A comparison of Japanese television assembly plants in Japan and the United States. In J. Liker, W. M. Fruin & P. Adler (Eds), *Remade in America:* 256–93. New York: Oxford University Press.

Kenney, M., & Florida, R. 1993. *Beyond mass production.* New York: Oxford University Press.

Kilburn, D. 1994. Borden's hopes melt in Japanese market. *Advertising Age*, 18 July.

Klein, S., Frazier, G., & Roth, V. 1990. A transaction cost analysis model of channel integration in international markets. *Journal of Marketing Research*, 27(2): 196–208.

Kogut, B. 1988. Joint ventures: Theoretical and empirical perspectives. *Strategic Management Journal*, 9(4): 319–32.

Kogut, B., & Singh, H. 1988. The effect of national culture on the choice of entry mode. *Journal of International Business Studies*, 19(3): 411–32.

Kreps, D. 1990. *A course in microeconomic theory.* Princeton, NJ: Princeton University Press.

Levin, R., Klevorick, R., Nelson, R., & Winter, S. 1987. Appropriating the results from industrial research and development. *Brookings Papers on Economic Activity*, 18(3): 783–820.

Liker, J., Fruin, W. M., & Adler, P. 1999. Bringing Japanese management systems to the United States: Transplantation or transformation? In J. Liker, W. M. Fruin & P. Adler (Eds), *Remade in America:* 3–35. New York: Oxford University Press.

Marinov, M., & Marinova, S. 1998. Investor strategy development and adaptation: The case of Interbrew. *European Management Journal*, 16(4): 400–11.

Mathews, J. 2002. Competitive advantages of the latecomer firm: A resource-based account of industrial catch-up strategies. *Asia Pacific Journal of Management*, 19(4): 467–88.

Mathews, J. 2006. Dragon multinationals: New players in 21st century globalization. *Asia Pacific Journal of Management*, 23(1): 5–27.

Meyer, K., & Estrin, S. 2001. Brownfield entry in emerging markets. *Journal of International Business Studies*, 32(3): 575–84.

Meyer, K., & Møller, I. 1998. Managing deep restructuring: Danish experiences in Eastern Germany. *European Management Journal*, 16(4): 411–21.

Millington, A., & Bayliss, B. 1990. The process of internationalization: UK companies in the EC. *Management International Review*, 30(2): 151–61.

Morck, R., Yeung, B., & Zhao, M. 2008. Perspectives on China's outward foreign direct investment. *Journal of International Business Studies*, 39(3): 337–50.

Narula, R. 2006. Globalization, new ecologies, new zoologies, and the purported death of the eclectic paradigm. *Asia Pacific Journal of Management*, 23(2): 143–51.

Oman, C. 1984. *New forms of international investment in developing countries.* Paris: OECD. Ono, Y. 1991. Corporate divorce, Japanese style. *The Globe and Mail*, 23 February.

Oxley, J. 1997. Appropriability hazards and governance in strategic alliances: A transaction cost approach. *Journal of Law, Economics and Organization*, 13(2): 387–409.

Padmanabhan, P., & Cho, K. 1996. Ownership strategy for a foreign affiliate: An empirical investigation of Japanese firms. *Management International Review*, 36(1): 45–65.

Padmanabhan, P., & Cho, K. 1999. Decision specific experience in foreign ownership and establishment strategies: Evidence from Japanese firms. *Journal of International Business Studies*, 30(1): 25–44.

Pan, Y. 2005. *Lenovo: Countering the Dell challenge.* Asia Case Research Center case 905-020-1.

Pedersen, T., & Thomsen, S. 1997. European patterns of corporate ownership: A twelve-country study. *Journal of International Business Studies*, 28(4): 759–78.

Rugman, A. 1981. *Inside the multinational: The economics of internal markets.* New York: Columbia University Press.

Rugman, A., & Collinson, S. 2006. *International business*, (4th ed.) Harlow: Prentice Hall.

Rugman, A., & Verbeke, A. 1990. *Global corporate strategy and trade policy.* London: Routledge.

Rui, H., & Yip, G. 2008. Foreign acquisitions by Chinese firms: A strategic intent perspective. *Journal of World Business*, 43(2): 213–26.

Sanchez-Peinado, E., & Pla-Barber, J. 2006. A multidimensional concept of uncertainty and its influence on the entry mode choice: An empirical analysis in the service sector. *International Business Review*, 15(3): 215–32.

Silver, M. 1984. *Enterprise and the scope of the firm.* Oxford: Martin Robertson.

Slangen, A., & Hennart, J. F. 2007. Greenfield or acquisition entry: A review of the empirical foreign establishment mode literature. *Journal of International Management*, 13(4): 404–29.

Teece, D. 1986. Profiting from technological innovation: Implications for integration, collaboration, and public policy. *Research Policy*, 15(6): 285–305.

Verbeke, A. 2009. *International business strategy.* Cambridge: Cambridge University Press.

Vermeulen, F., & Barkema, H. 2001. Learning through acquisitions. *Academy of Management Journal*, 44(3): 457–76.

Vernon, R. 1971. *Sovereignty at bay.* New York: Basic Books.

Wei, Y., Liu, B., & Liu, X. 2005. Entry modes of foreign direct investment in China: A multinomial logit approach. *Journal of Business Research*, 58(11): 1495–1505.

Williamson, O. 1985. *The economic institutions of capitalism.* New York: Free Press.

Williamson, O. 1991. Comparative economic organization: The analysis of discrete structural alternatives. *Administrative Science Quarterly*, 36(2): 269–96.

Williamson, O. 1996. Economic organization: The case for candor. *Academy of Management Review*, 21(1): 48–57.

Wright, M., Filatotchev, I., Hoskisson, R., & Peng, M. 2005. Strategy research in emerging economies. *Journal of Management Studies*, 42(1): 1–33.

Xie, W., & White, S. 2004. Sequential learning in a Chinese spin-off: The case of Lenovo Group Limited. *R&D Management*, 34(4): 407–22.

Yeung, B., & Mirus, R. 1989. *On the mode of international expansion: The role of agency costs in an expanded framework*, Unpublished manuscript.

Yuasa, K. 1990. Meiji Milk, Borden to end tie. *Japan Economic Journal*, 23 June.

Zeng, M., & Williamson, P. 2007. *Dragons at your door: How Chinese cost innovation is disrupting global competition.* Boston, MA: Harvard Business School Press.

21 Network view of MNCs' socio-political behavior*

Amjad Hadjikhani, Joong-Woo Lee and Pervez N. Ghauri

Introduction

While the growing interest of researchers in business networks focuses on inter-firm rela-tionships, the issue of business–government relationships in international market attracts less attention (Boddewyn, 1988; Hadjikhani and Thilenius, 2005; Ring et al., 1990; Welch and Wilkinson, 2004). Some studies, such as those of Welch and Wilkinson (2004) and Jacob-son et al. (1993), highlight the failure to incorporate socio-political issues into the business network marketing texts. In the absence of much research in this area, this study attempts to offer an answer to the inquiry of researchers like Welch and Wilkinson (2004), Hadjikhani and Thilenius (2005), and Ghauri and Holstius (1996). This chapter simply raises the question of how firms manage their relationship with socio-political organizations in international market and why there is heterogeneity in their behaviors.

According to Welch and Wilkinson's (2004) studies, despite a large volume of interna-tional news published in the mass media and an extensive general public discussion, this research topic seldom attracts researchers in business relationships. In contrast to this devel-opment, the issue occupies the attention of researchers in other theoretical fields. The rising interest since the 1980s in fields like political risk (Ahmed et al., 2002; Lenway, 1985; Miller, 1992; Poynter, 1985), in lobbying (Fabella, 1991; Hoffman, 2005; Lagerlöf, 1997), in bar-gaining and bargaining power (Chae and Heidhues, 2004; Dell'Arringa, 2001; Moon and Lado, 2000; Nomden et al., 2003), in political market (Bonardi et al., 2005; O'Cass, 1996) and in political strategy (Butler and Collins, 1996; Shaffer and Hillman, 2000; Taylor et al., 2000) increases understanding of these research fields. However, unfortunately, researchers in business relationship and networks are less inclined to develop theoretical tools for further understanding of the MNCs' socio-political behavior.

Business firms need to manage their socio-political market as well as the business market. As a consequence of this, socio-political actors and business firms have relationships with each other and are directly or indirectly interdependent (Boddewyn, 1988; Hadjikhani and Ghauri, 2001; Ring et al., 1990). In this relationship, business firms' aim is to gain support and stability and the aim of socio-political units is to increase employment and social welfare of the society. Both parties can benefit from the relationship, which they perceive is of mutual interest. In order to achieve a deeper understanding of the management of this relation-ship, the study develops a conceptual view about the interaction between these two different units. Knowledge of MNCs' political behavior can also aid business firms when developing

---

*Republished with permission, Hadjikhani, Amjad, Joong-Woo Lee & Pervez N. Ghauri. (2008) "Network view of MNCs' socio-political behaviour" Journal of Business Research 61: 912–924.

strategies towards political and social organizations (Buckley and Ghauri, 1999; Ghauri and Buckley, 2004; Hadjikhani, 2000; Ring et al., 1990).

The view here contains the three interrelating relationship concepts of commitment, trust (Morgan and Hunt, 1994), and legitimacy (Hadjikhani and Sharma, 1999). The concepts of commitment and trust describe the behavior of these units in developing their legitimate position. The proposition is that business firms have a heterogeneous behavior towards the actors in the socio-political market, which relates to their business goals in the particular market. These three conceptual elements enable the study to understand the varieties in the firms' managerial behavior. The proposition is that these theoretical tools facilitate the analysis and the understanding of the variety in the management behavior of MNCs in socio-political market. These concepts are used to examine the behavior of two MNCs with different management strategies. The comparison of the cases will also manifest the variety in the behavior of one MNC which aims to penetrate into a new market compared with another MNC which aims to expand in a market. The comparison by means of these theoretical tools can shed new light on similarities and differences in the behavior of firms.

Earlier research

The attempts of the earlier researchers, along the same lines as this study, can in a broad sense be grouped into two categories; hierarchical or interaction views on MNEs and political actors (Hadjikhani and Thilenius, 2005). In the first group, researchers like Ahmed et al. (2002) and Miller (1992) elaborate thoughts on hierarchical power of the political institutions and firms' adaptive action concerning political risk which then turns to risk management (Keillor et al., 2005; Keillor and Hult, 2004). A large number of researchers in political science (Maddison, 1991; Nowtotny et al., 1989) also adopt the hierarchical view. In this view, the socio-political units gain their power from their legitimacy in the market that they achieve through establishing a trustworthy position (Hadjikhani and Sharma, 1999). Implicitly, firms demonstrate their commitment by their actions in terms of management of risk (Ahmed et al., 2002; Miller, 1992), risk in international operations (Keillor et al., 2005), development of structures to fit with the regulations (Buckley and Ghauri, 2004; Cosset and Roy, 1991; Spencer et al., 2005) or corporate structure (Murtha, 1991; Lenway and Murtha, 1994). Researchers in this field are uncomfortable with the views concerning relationship mutuality.

Researchers concentrating on governance (see for example, Fligstein, 1990; Streeck, 1992), problems when encountering rules (Chaudri and Samson, 2000), impact of government on competition (Ramaswamy and Renforth, 1996) and heterogeneity of the firms' and industrial policy (Barros and Nilssen, 1999) question the hierarchical power of political units and are more reliant on behavior theory. They elaborate concepts like political legitimacy and proclaim the dependency of political actors on the other actors in the surrounding region, like business firms and people.

Business studies' researchers examining interaction and dyadic relationships view the strategy of firms as cooperative and adaptive towards socio-political actors (Ring et al., 1990; Taylor et al., 2000). The interactions between the two provide benefits for both parties (see Boddewyn, 1988; Hadjikhani, 1996; Jacobson et al., 1993). Business scholars have recently turned their attention to studying both political and business actors in a political market (Baines and Egan, 2001; O'Shaughnessy, 2001) and that firms are having parallel business and political objectives (Bonardi et al., 2005; Kotler, 1999; Kotler, and Andreason, 1991).

One research track that deals with the specific actions of the firms is bargaining; researchers paid considerable attention to this over the last two decades. The main standpoint is specificity and heterogeneity in the impact of the governmental decisions on business firms and the firms' bargaining strategy (Crawford, 1982; Poynter, 1985). Some researchers, such as Dell'Arringa (2001) and Nomden et al. (2003) relate bargaining to the collective actions ofthe interest groups; others like Crystal (2003) specifically relate the firms' resources and strategy towards host government (Conner, 1991; Crystal, 2003; Kim, 1988; Korbin, 1982; Moon and Lado, 2000). In their conceptual development, some such as Moon and Lado (2000) propose resource-based theory for the study of bargaining power. They stress the specificity in the firms' resources and their relationship with host governments. However, they have no concern with views like legitimacy, which has its base in political science. Against the hierarchical view with adaptive commitment towards the socio-political organizations, bargaining power studies elaborate conceptual tools such as cooperation and influence. The implication is that commitment influences actions. Taylor et al. (2000), for example, stress bargaining power as using proper resources, Hoffman (2005) and Lagerlöf (1997) expand further and elaborate behavioral views on trust in negotiations for lobbying the non-business actors.

Researchers on political strategy (Andersen and Eliassen, 1996) and on lobbying (Bolton, 1991; Hoffman, 2005; Lagerlöf, 1997; Lenway et al., 1990) consider views of the interest groups in order to study business influences. In this field, while some like Lagerlöf (1997) and Pecorino (1998) pay attention to topics like influence and interest groups and firms' interaction with host government (Andersen and Eliassen, 1996; Potters, 1992) and pressure groups (Kroszner and Stratmann, 1998), others connect the influence and relationship to illegitimate means such as bribery (Fredrikson and Svensson, 2003). While these researchers, similar to the bargaining group, put stress on firms' commitment actions, researchers in social responsibility connect the issue of firms' and non-business actors' relationships to involve parties' mutual gains (Crane and Desmond, 2002; Follows and Jobber, 2000; Hadjikhani and Ghauri, 2001; O'Shaughnessy, 1996). Researchers such as Crane and Desmond (2002) follow the theoretical view of Boddewyn (1988) and pursue an interesting discussion on dividing the market into two interrelated business and socio-political markets. However, instead of business network they employ concepts like legitimacy and influence for a dyadic view.

The theoretical view

The theoretical view in this study goes beyond the mainstream in business network and assumes that enterprises are interwoven in a network containing business and nonbusiness actors (Hadjikhani and Ghauri, 2001; Keillor and Hult, 2004). Similar to the business market, researchers explain that the socio-political market has a heterogeneous nature and that firms undertake strategic actions in order to gain specific support from the socio-political units (Dixon, 1992; Ghauri and Holstius, 1996). Such a view relies on a relationship explanation between MNCs and socio-political actors, firms depend on the socio-political units because these units, by their legitimate position in the society, can support MNCs or act against them. At the same time, socio-political units depend on MNCs because their investments create jobs that affect the economy as a whole. That, in turn, affects groups like the media and the public at large, on which the social and political actors depend (Hadjikhani, 1996, 2000; Jacobson et al., 1993). This gives rise to the explanation that these actors have interdependent relationships and their interplay is embedded in a network with a set of business and socio-political (non-business) actors.

Business relationship with socio-political actors

Researchers in business network stress the two conceptual elements of commitment and trust as vital for understanding the business relationship (Hausman, 2001; Morgan and Hunt, 1994; Walter and Ritter, 2003) and also the relationship between business and political units (Hadjikhani and Thilenius, 2005; Welch and Wilkinson, 2004). Besides these two concepts, researchers such as Boddewyn (1988) pinpoint the view that exchange relationship in political market is dissimilar to that in business markets. Technological or knowledge interdependency which construct the fundamental bonds in business markets, do not have the same function in socio-political market. Researchers such as Higgins and Morgan (2006), Mobus, (2005) and Warren (2003) refer to the concept of legitimacy since the relationship among these actors does not necessarily require exchange of monetary or technological resources. Consequently, these three relationship elements – legitimacy, commitment and trust – are the foundations of the theoretical view in this study (see Figure 21.1).

Legitimacy is a perception or assumption that the actions of an entity are appropriate within a socially constructed system of values and beliefs (Mobus, 2005; Schwarz and Schuman, 1997). Accordingly, legitimacy is the position recognized by the surrounding actors in a network of relationships. This legitimacy depends on the type and strength of values and beliefs developed by interrelated surrounding actors towards an actor. The higher the nature of appropriate business and socio-political commitment, the higher can be the trust and the stronger will be the legitimate position. Legitimacy of an actor is constructed on the surrounding actors' knowledge on how an actor's performance preserves the rule of mutuality and maintains its own interest and that of others. While business legitimacy primarily consists of evaluation by connected suppliers, customers, etc., having business exchange, political legitimacy relies on how business and social actors perceive the act of political actors (Hadjikhani and Sharma, 1999). In this context, publicity can, for example, provide socio-political legitimacy mediated through the commercial text. Political actors gain legitimacy when they can manifest cooperation with MNCs that have created new jobs and increased economic prosperity. In terms of their penetration strategy and creation of a position, MNCs may not necessarily behave in a similar way.

Commitment actions can be explained in terms of the size of investment and actions towards the counterpart alone or towards the connected actors (Denekamp, 1995; Scott, 1994). These actors can be political or business. Commitment can require, for example, the establishment of a political unit in the firms' organizations or investing in lobbying organizations and units

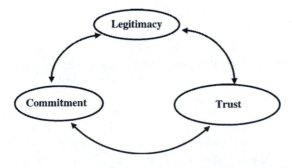

Figure 21.1 A conceptual view of socio-political behavior of MNCs.

414 Hadjikhani et al.

outside the organization. Naturally, the level of resource commitment varies depending on the firms' market strategy. On occasions when firms aim to penetrate into a new international market, they need to commit a high level of resource into a variety of relationships.

Trust as the driving force for commitment or as an outcome of the commitment, is defined as the benevolence of the counterpart's actions towards the achievement of mutuality (Morgan and Hunt, 1994) between business and socio-political actors. Trust in business relationships generally contains the nature of specificity (Boersma et al., 2003). Trust in socio-political relationship, besides the nature of specificity, can also have a general dimension that directly affects the commitment and legitimacy. Any actions of political actors affect their legitimacy in the society, as the actions are always valuable to members in the society and create an attitude, even among those not directly affected by the political decisions. Distrust of people towards politicians, for example, does not necessarily have its nature in a specific relationship but affects people's decisions towards the political actors. Business actors also use their means to develop trust in the society and reach the political actors in order to gain specific treatment (Hadjikhani and Ghauri, 2001). The variations in the degree of firms' socio-political commitment and trust explain differences in relationship interdependency and managerial behavior (Egelhoff, 1988; Keillor et al., 1997; Lee, 1991). Naturally, building new trustful relationships, for example, for starting from scratch, is more complex than maintenance of existing trustful relationships.

Business network in the context of socio-political interactions

As Brunsson (1986) and Hadjikhani and Ghauri (2001) note, socio-political actors have to try to satisfy different actors with complementary or conflicting demands. Political actors have connections to actors like media, voters, unions, people (customers): all of whom drive their actions in different directions. The strategy of MNCs is to strengthen the relationships with these socio-political actors. In this vein, firms' commitment of resources and trust building towards political and social actors are the means to exercise influence without which they would become dependent on these actors (Hanf and Toonen, 1985; Rehbein and Lenway, 1994).

The view that business firms embed in a network implies, for example, that the media can provide socio-political legitimacy that can benefit/harm or support/coerce both political actors and MNCs. With positive publicity, political actors can manifest to the connected actors the benefit of cooperation with an MNC undertaking its social responsibility. Gains in employment and economic prosperities lead to public trust, which is essential for political actors to keep their political legitimacy. Any action from the two focal actors is modified and reported to others like trade unions, the media and the public. Political actors' strategy is to gain legitimacy from all the groups to whom they are connected. This interdependency determines the types of strategy that socio-political actors undertake towards business firms. In this network, as Figure 21.2 illustrates, political actors' strategy towards MNCs is either coercive or supportive and MNCs' socio-political strategy can be supportive (influence) or adaptive. Supportive action is composed of relationship mutuality resulting in cooperation and negotiation and coercive is the opposite. In the same manner, social actors can be supportive and influential towards both the political actors and business actors.

Marketing researchers make claims for strategic actions to convert adaptation to influence, that is changing coercive actions of political or social actors to supportive ones (Crespin-Mazet and Ghauri, 2007; Ford, 1990). Coercive actions of social or political units can, for example, force firms to change their strategy, or exit from the market, or resort to bribery.

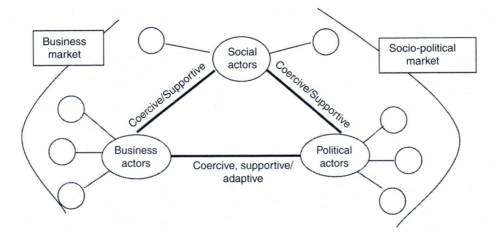

Figure 21.2 Socio-political behavior – gaining legitimacy.

Firms lacking resources to change coercive actions, in severe cases, file for bankruptcy. A highly coercive impact generates high adaptation cost (Forsgren et al., 1995). On the other hand, the higher the firms' resource commitment and knowledge, the higher is the influence and the lower will be the adaptation cost. The higher the influence, the more specific and heterogeneous is the impact of the government on different firms and the stronger is the firm's legitimate market position. The strategy for specific support is to strengthen the market position as compared to competitors. Thus, *supportive* actions can be of a *specific* or a *general* nature. To alter the coercive to supportive and specific relationship, firms undertake resource commitment and trust-building actions in a variety of ways. The proposition is that the variation relates to firms' business strategy. While firms aiming to build a new legitimate position acquire a high level of input towards socio-political relationships, firms' input is naturally lower when aiming to keep or strengthen the existing socio-political relationships.

Method

The propositions connected to the theoretical framework contain the two simple conditions of socio-political behavior for penetration and maintenance of legitimate position. The research needed at least two cases to manifest these behaviors and their varieties (Yin, 2003). In the following sections, the empirical facts for the two case studies make use of both primary and secondary data. The first case is that of the Korean MNC, Daewoo Motor Company (DMC) which penetrates into a new market, the second case is that of Vattenfall (a Swedish MNC) which aimed to strengthen and keep its market position. Access and background location of researchers in Sweden and Korea were also influencing factors (Ghauri and Grønhaug, 2005).

When collecting information, the critical problem was the topic of the research. The subject of the firms' relationship with "socio-political actors" tended to be a sensitive area. The managers were therefore, unwilling to disclose all their information for public scrutiny and for competitors who could counter-act. The two cases in this study had reached different development stages at the time of the interviews. While it became easier to gain access to very detailed information in the case of Daewoo Motor Company (DMC), information collection faced some difficulties in the case of Vattenfall.

The total number of in-depth interviews included 72 directors and managers of DMC, and Vattenfall in the countries of Poland, Sweden, Korea, and their subsidiaries and production units in Germany and Brussels, as well as politicians in these countries. The number of politicians interviewed was 16, consisting of 6 Polish, 5 Korean and 5 Swedish politicians in the Commission. The rest (56) included interviews with managers in the political units, bureaucrats, trade unions and marketing and production units of the two companies. Interviews also took place with intermediary organizations, public (like Euro Trade Association) and private commercial consulting companies and hybrid organizations, such as the Export Commission in the countries involved in the cases. Brochures and information released by these firms in these countries provided the secondary data. Considering the nature of the study, and in order to achieve a holistic view, a semi-structured interview guide provided the means to collect the primary data. The data is analyzed through pattern matching and through systematic case comparison (Ghauri, 2004; Ghauri and Grønhaug, 2005).

Case 1: Daewoo Motor Company

Daewoo Motor Company (DMC) with 250,000 employees is one of the major Korean MNCs specializing in the manufacturing and marketing of motor vehicles and is one of the largest companies in the Daewoo Group. DMC has a 28% market share in Korea and its production capacity in a couple of decades has skyrocketed from 180,000 units per annum to 1.92 million units in 2000, valued at (US$) 40 billion. The Group has 454 operating subsidiaries with worldwide branch offices, of these 60 subsidiaries were obtained by acquisitions. The political activities of the firm form the discussion in the following four sections: (a) interaction between Top Managers and Top Politicians, (b) DMC's interaction with trade unions, (c) interaction with EU automotive manufacturing association and (d) interaction with socio-cultural organizations in Poland.

Relationship between top managers and top politicians

The foreign expansion of Korean DMC played a key role in the modernization of the automobile industry in Poland. In the 1990s, Poland had a strong interest in establishing a strategic position in the automobile market. One of the major political issues was the creation of a balance between foreign and local firms. In this context, the visit by the Polish president to Korea in 1992 was crucial in developing a relationship between Daewoo and the firms in the Polish automobile industry. President Walesa visited the Bupyung manufacturing plant of DMC to observe the modern production system. He also met the chairman of Daewoo Group, Woo-Chung Kim, to discuss the development of the automobile industry. In the same year, the Warsaw sales office of Daewoo Corporation was established. Under the direction of the director Byung-Il Chun, and with the business report received from him, DMC began to show an interest in investing in a manufacturing plant in Poland in 1993.

Daewoo Group had also employed two former American foreign ministers (Henry Kissinger and Alexander Haig) in 1994 to function as business advisers in the matter of socio-political activities in Europe. In total, the firm had engaged twelve people for this function, three of whom were located in Warsaw, six in Korea and the rest in other European countries. The task of the advisor unit in Korea and the European HQ of Daewoo Group in Germany was to assist the unit in Warsaw by, for example, providing information or by negotiating with the Polish politicians involved in the political decisions of the two factories, FSL (Fabryka Samochodow Lublin) and FSO (Fabryka Samochodow Osobowych) about privatization.

At the end of 1994, DMC decided to establish a sales unit in Warsaw to collect information on strategic issues such as privatization, modernization and liberalization, which had started at the beginning of the 1990s. These include: (a) the rules applying to the merger and acquisition (M&A) of Polish automobile firms, and (b) EU's harmonization of product standards. One person with experience at the headquarters of the Daewoo Group in Europe was responsible for dealing with these issues. He cooperated with almost all of the European market coordinators and experts who possessed the relevant technical and market knowledge. The director's political task was: (a) creating and maintaining relationships with the EU's political units responsible for automobile market, (b) mobilizing resources in DMC when a political proposal or decision was undertaken. He divided the activities into internal (within DMC) and external ones. The director studied official journals, financial releases and reports on the European automobile industry. This task took up more than 15% of the director's time. A part of the remaining time was devoted to studying protocols and collecting information on media, competition and consumers. One fundamental area mentioned by the director dealt with building and maintaining social relationships. These duties had a social nature: they covered areas such as engagement in social arrangements and meetings specifically arranged for people from Poland and other EU countries. The time spent in social and official meetings was 50%, and phone calls took up 10–15% of the time.

DMC's relationship with trade unions

In 1995–1999, DMC invested (US$) 829.8 million in Daewoo-FSO (the joint venture company in Poland), (US$) 101 million in Daewoo Motor Poland (DMP) and (US$) 6.2 million in ANDORIA (a diesel engine manufacturing company), thus the company invested a total of (US$) 937 million in Poland during that time. The size of the investment was more than twice that of the total amount of the planned contractual investment (with the Polish government). The investment of 22 component JV firms was included in the sum of total investment. DMC had thus invested a total amount of (US$) 2.27 billion in their Polish subsidiaries by 2001. The investment plans focused on developing a central position for the European business headquarters of DMC in Poland, as the base for implementing the European strategy of the Daewoo Group. These were important for both government and trade unions. Trade unions, for example, increased: (a) the employment and th e number of members, (b) the income from the fees that members paid and (c) their power both in Poland and the EU.

Traditionally, Poland has strong trade unions. It was essential that DMC cooperated with the leaders of trade unions. Issues under discussion were, for example, the symbolic flag of Daewoo-FSO and the modernization plan of Daewoo-FSO. The first issue was the design of the company flag, which involved creative discussions. DMC suggested an alternative design for the flag based on both a symbolic flag of the Daewoo Group and the traditional flag of FSO. DMC had a more strategic approach than FSO to achieve a high degree of respect from the members of trade unions and from the Polish consumers. The flag of the Daewoo Group, for example, has the symbolic blue color of the brand mixed with a white color base. However, the flag of Daewoo-FSO was determined as a symbolic dark red color mixed with a light red color base, as a reference to the previous flag of FSO.

In 1998, the newly employed Korean CEO of the component JV firm introduced a rationalization program to reduce the number of employees from 389 to 251 people. The members of the trade unions demonstrated strongly and the protest from the labor movement spread seriously throughout all the JV firms. The CEO of Daewoo-FSO and a few directors immediately consulted with the leaders of trade unions and the Ministry of Labor. As a result, the CEO of the JV firm resigned and the problems were resolved.

Relationship with the EU Automotive Manufacturing Association (AMA)

In 1995, DMC established an informal political unit engaging 3 people. This unit cooperated with units in at least four countries. The main interest of the CEO was to cover political issues such as: (a) rules and regulations about manufacturing plant and R&D to develop new products, (b) deregulation and harmonization of the market, (c) the White Paper, explaining the automobile manufacturing policy for the year 2020, (d) technological questions like the reduction of air-pollution (CO_2) in Europe, (e) technological standardization, especially ISO 9002, (f) the EU Automotive Manufacturing Association (AMA)'s technological certificate, and even general social and economic questions such as employment. The sections in the Commission that the DMC managers were to deal with were Directorates, DGXII for R&D, DGXVI for energy and DGXIV for public procurement.

One issue that strengthened the DMC's relationship with government was that of the development of Polish industry, Daewoo-FSO had to maintain a 60% component of 'local' and EU producers (local content rule suggested by the EU AMA). The rest, 40%, was to be imported from component producers in Korea or elsewhere. This meant that Daewoo-FSO had to build up a large number of relationships with component suppliers both in Poland and nearby European countries.

The task of the political unit in Daewoo-FSO was to collect the market, technological and political information needed to make proposals to the EU. The first important knowledge concerned the EU's bureaucratic function, i.e., the position of different people. Questions discussed in the media included those such as air-pollution risks or alternative energy using hydroelectric motors and bio/natural gas resources. The unit used to check public opinion in the media in order to give strength to the proposals passed on to the Commission. The task of the unit was to gain support, not only in the Commission, but also in the EU AMA. The effort was always to engage in meetings. According to the directors, this social investment was necessary in the periods both before and during negotiations. They intensified when there was, or there expected to be, a project.

Daewoo had 28% share of passenger cars and 78% share of commercial vehicles in the market in 1998. The strategy involved various kinds of marketing activities. The company created an image of reasonable price and high technical quality. One social commitment that was very successful was the slogan, "a new life begins with a Reganza car" which initially was the suggestion of the sales subsidiary of DMC in Germany. The social marketing was a great success in building up marketing networks (585 units: 203 dealers and 382 after sales, A/S centers) for the customers in Poland and enabled the firm to show its commitment and establish a trustworthy position in the market.

Social activities towards intermediaries

DMC gained a significant marketing support by sending 72 medical staff (doctors and nurses) from Aju University Hospital to Daewoo Motors Poland (DMP) in Lublin. The medical service teams stayed at DMP to perform medical services for people living in different districts of Lublin. This action made it clear that DMC wanted to manifest that it did not only look for short-term business profit. The firm wanted to strengthen its legitimacy by convincing Polish society that it would take care of people's health. This might have led to more potential for Polish people to become familiar with DMC's brand name in Poland. Moreover, DMC arranged various kinds of cultural activities, such as a "Festival for Children Day" on 5th May and an annual fashion show. The children's day included the performance of several

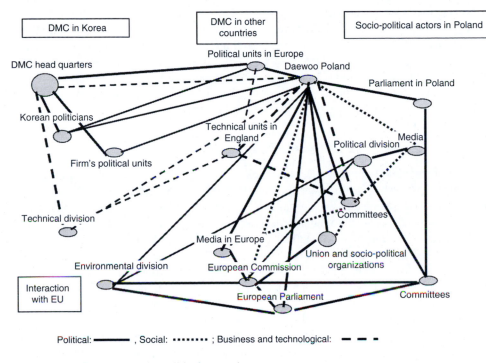

DMC in Korea	DMC in other countries	Socio-political actors in Poland

Political units in Europe

DMC head quarters

Daewoo Poland

Parliament in Poland

Korean politicians

Technical units in England

Political division

Media

Firm's political units

Technical division

Committees

Media in Europe

Union and socio-political organizations

Environmental division

European Commission

Interaction with EU

European Parliament

Committees

Political: ——— , Social: •••••••• ; Business and technological: ▬ ▬ ▬

Figure 21.3 DMC in its socio-political network.

interesting shows and game programs in which Korean and Polish families and children participated. The festival of children's day and other cultural activities also appeared on Polish TV and were organized through cooperation between DMC and the Korean–Polish culture association.

In another social commitment, DMC acquired a professional football team, Legia, which achieved first place in the Polish football league. DMC strongly attempted to promote its brand image by cooperation with the football league, as Polish people very much liked to support their best football team. Therefore, the activities of DMC were building up a friendly image among Polish people. Figure 21.3 illustrates DMC's business, social and political networking in Europe.

Daewoo-FSO activities, which manifest its social responsibility, had strengthened DMC's market position. These investments facilitated the firm's contacts and cooperation with the political and social-cultural units in Poland. One major task of the directors was to identify and explain the sociopolitical benefits of the proposals. In the case of "Successful establishment of Daewoo-FSO", for example, the technical solutions, along with the political and socio-economical applications of the proposal, ensured that DMC succeeded in receiving permission to increase production capacity and ISO 9002 from EU AMA.

Case 2: Vattenfall

Vattenfall is the largest electric power company in Sweden, with a turnover of more than (US$) 11 billion and 33,000 employees. The company has decades of experience in the energy generation industry. The liberalization policy of the EU affected Vattenfall in a sense that it increased its foreign operations in European countries. Recently, Vattenfall made large investments in countries such as Germany and Poland. More than 60% of total sales come from countries like Germany, Finland and Poland. In Germany, for example, Vattenfall has more than 21,000 employees. After liberalization, the firm competes with competitors such as Sydkraft in the Swedish market, Preussen Elektra, EdF Electricité de France, IMO, the Finnish electric power plant, the Norwegian Statkraft and Statoil and the German RVF that are all extensively active in the European market. The intensive competition makes the political activities more necessary, in order to gain specific support.

Interaction with socio-political actors in the EU

Vattenfall's managers stated that one crucial area, which concerns not only Vattenfall's activity, but also that of other firms in this market, is the EU's rules on environment. All information about environmental issues is vital for the firm. Therefore, they keep up to date with committees dealing with environmental issues. The manager responsible for the political issues stated that any political decision affects not only Vattenfall, but also other firms especially those highly dependent on energy.

Since the political decisions have a large impact on the firm, Vattenfall established a unit to take care of relationships with politicians and the media. The number of people working with these issues varies depending on the project. The minimum number at the office is three. This group then involves both internal and external people when necessary. This section in Brussels is active since spring 1996. Their first mission was to provide proposals and comments on environmental issues and evaluate whether EU committees were willing to cooperate with Vattenfall. The managers stated that they regarded the office as being a signal amplifier, in the sense that they can receive the most indistinct signals from politicians and inform the whole organization. Grasping the context and to learn what signals were important.

As far as the contacts with different units in the EU were concerned, it was above all contacts with Directorates DG17 and DG11, which dealt with energy, that were of prime importance. This network continued even if they did not have any specific project to discuss. The managers engaged in social meetings to keep the relationship alive. The projects, the manager explained, were about environmental protection in the production of energy. In its proposals, Vattenfall's aim was to manifest how its competencies in technology and market arenas could assist committees to reach their aims. For instance, in the choice of technology, Vattenfall chose to express its vision on the impact of environmental issues on customer demands and the economy in a macro perspective (like employment opportunities). The intention was that the politicians together with the company could keep the balance between these different interests. However, it was the politicians who gave the consent and the company that developed the proposal who ultimately benefited both sides. Vattenfall valued technological or economic competence as less important than the competence to be sensitive to the customer's needs and demands and to have a mutually beneficial relationship with politicians.

The manager explained that besides cooperation with the energy sections in the EU, contacts with the Swedish cabinet had been a good asset in establishing a legitimate position. The embassy also played an important role indirectly influencing the council. Cooperation with other companies, especially those doing research in electro-magnetic fields was also vital. Issues of interest were lifecycle analysis within the nuclear power fields and development of new products. This was to convince the EU politicians and also the general public regarding the environmental awareness and trustworthiness of the firm. Lifecycle analysis and manifestation of a more conscious action was to influence political actors, such as

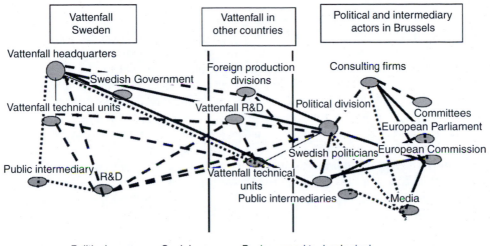

Figure 21.4 Vattenfall in its EU, socio-political network.

committees for energy production in the EU, Swedish representatives in the EU, media and consumers and also firms in the industry. Influencing the Swedish representatives was easier than other actors because, previously, Vattenfall was a large state-owned firm. However, the most important actors to lobby were the committees, as they provided the proposals for the decision makers in the EU. Figure 21.4 shows Vattenfall's social, political and business inter-actions with respective partners.

Vattenfall's managers focused on two general issues: deregulation of the electric power market and detailed issues such as the use of Poly Colored Biphenyl (PCB) in transformer-oil. Issues on the agenda included the Rio-convention about the so-called "Integrated Resource Planning" program. This program concerned electricity and gas, where the EU had aimed to have a steering function. EU politicians stated the limits for what ranges of actions were possible. But Vattenfall believed that it was more important to take the consumers and suppliers into consideration. The information provided to the committee strengthened Vattenfall's position in the negotiations and finally the political decisions. According to the managers, in order to achieve such a position, it required a great deal of effort to keep up the network of contacts with politicians, Swedish suppliers, industry organizations, various power plant associations, electricity producers and also to gather knowledge about the consumers. Within these contact networks, the manager stated that the Swedish cabinet had been a good asset ever since Sweden joined the EU. In social gatherings or representations, Vattenfall could lobby the council indirectly. The network important for political networking, the manager explained, could be split up into three groups. The first group was a minority of about 30 people, who made the final decisions. The second group was the so-called VIPs (Very Important Persons) that took part in the decision processes but did not take part in the final decisions. The final group, of about 200–250, consisted of people who were handling officers and specialists and were involved at different levels. It was definitely the personal contacts either in a meeting or when bumping into each other in corridors and receptions that were most important.

Discussion

This section contains the analysis of the socio-political behavior of the firms in the two cases and the varieties and similarities in connection with the three theoretical elements of legitimacy, commitment and trust. Firms had their own specific strategy in the market. Both firms with their resource commitment and trust-building activities were able to gain or strengthen a legitimate position in their socio-political market. In this market, the relationships are explained to be embedded in a network in which the actors directly and indirectly are interdependent on each other. In both firms, but specifically DMC which aimed to penetrate into the market, the resource commitment and trust building were directed not only towards the political actors but also towards other actors in the network. The behavior of Vattenfall was slightly different as the firm was already in the market and its aim was to strengthen its position. This paper analyzes the behavior of these two firms under two different themes of: (a) heterogeneity in socio-political relationship and (b) commitment, trust and legitimacy dimensions.

Heterogeneity in socio-political relationship

In traditional studies, firms are generally seen as homogeneous units constrained by governments (Jansson et al., 1995; Rogers et al., 2005). However, in line with researchers in bargaining (Crystal, 2003) and political strategy (Hoffman, 2005; Lenway et al., 1990), the two case studies present a completely different picture: (a) firms' socio-political relationships are specific, and therefore, (b) the relationships have a heterogeneous nature. In the case of DMC, the focused and assertive commitment actions towards the socio-political actors took place in order to influence the political units. The well-elaborated liberalization plan defined by Vattenfall was also designed to gain specific support but of a different kind. However, firms' socio-political behavior is specifically connected to their market strategy. The trust-building actions towards social community varied for these two firms. DMC devoted a large amount of resources for building trust with people but Vattenfall did not.

In their relationships with political actors, actions were sometimes geared towards influencing the decisions before they were actually made. In their relationships, the firms had a specific concern in using negotiation and cooperation tactics. While in DMC, for example, ministers were actively involved in negotiations, ministers in Vattenfall case had a very passive role and were not so active. Traditional studies claim that the aspect of specificity includes activities for measuring and avoiding the risk (Miller, 1992; Shubik, 1983) or for understanding the firm/state interdependence. In the case of this study, the specificity relates particularly to the firms' resource commitment and trust-building actions, which were connected to the firms' business strategy. In their relationships with social and production units, the firms in these cases managed their relationships differently. As illustrated in Table 21.1, they had, for example, different types of socio-political questions, different administrative commitment, and were connected to different groups of actors. DMC, for example, invested resources needed for social projects like participation in football leagues and the opening of a medical centre but Vattenfall did not follow the same path.

Commitment, trust and legitimacy dimensions

The view in the model relies on the proposition that there are two types of business and socio-political networks. The cases manifest interdependency between the two networks and

Table 21.1 A summary of the firms' political activities

	DMC	Vattenfall
Major questions	Market penetration, and increasing market share in the vehicle market. Activity is how to adapt production activities to the rules of EU.	Influence the political decisions, market liberalization environment.
Organization for political action	Top managers in Korea, and Poland, a number of people in Brussels, Paris, Munich and Warsaw. Contacts and negotiations with the ministers, commission, committees and Parliament in a matter of modernizing, privatizing and harmonizing the industry.	Top managers in both Sweden and Brussels, minimum three persons in Brussels.
Place of action Establishment in Brussels Forms of behavior	Poland, Korea, European countries. In 1990 via Poland, 1996 in Brussels. Alone. Frequent contacts and negotiations with the leaders of trade unions to convince of its guarantee of maintaining the current number of 20,000 employees, and no strikes during the five years. The effort was to gain their trust. Connect the business commitment and trust with the socio-political actors.	Mainly Brussels and Sweden 1996 in Brussels. Alone and ad hoc. Connect the business commitment and trust with the socio-political actors.
Major source in EU	Polish government, EU committees and commission, trade union, social groups like football teams and media.	Committees and Parliament
Interaction with intermediaries	Building medical centers, sport engagement, cultural and fashion festivals, cultural units, membership cards and cars for new married couples; trade unions, discussion with socio-political actors and also trade union for issues like the flag of the company. The strategy was to build trust and legitimacy.	Media, interaction with social groups to understand the needs. The strategy was to strengthen trust and legitimacy

that the actions in one have an impact on the other. For example, the result of actions towards trust transfers or diffuses from the socio-political relationship to the business relationship and vice versa. In other words, actions have side effects because of the interdependency between the relationships in the two networks. The two cases epitomize the specificity and varieties in the trust relationship. While some are concerned with social trust, which embodies the trust of the public (consumers) and trade unions, others relate to the political trust connected to political actors. Investments in hospitals or football league are among some of the commitments for building social trust. Political trust relates to the promises of, for instance, Polish government support for DMC business and DMC's statement for employment. Both types of trust are essential for business relationship trust and finally commercial activities. Commitments towards social groups, for example, develop social trust and thereby legitimacy. In this vein, the "firm's legitimacy" is an accumulation of the firm's business, social and political legitimacies. In the Vattenfall case, the firm's legitimacy and relationship trust contained a more general nature. Vattenfall, for example, besides its actual business, strengthened its trust by referring to its reputation in business and also developed trust in the relationship with political actors and intermediaries which affected the firm's legitimacy. In reaching social trust, DMC committed much larger resources. DMC invested hundreds of millions US$ to integrate several social units. DMC's commitments towards the sport activities and social arrangements like festivals, flag of the company, social clubs and fashion shows were to develop and maintain social trust.

In this vein, DMC used its retention and employment of labor, which essentially is a business issue, to reach both social and political trust to strengthen its market legitimacy. The crucial reason for the firm's investment in social activities is not just that it had become a social or political organization but its belief that the social trust transfers to other types of relationships, that builds and strengthens the trust in business or political relationships. Firms aim to generate profit and an investment in socio-political network is put in place in order to strengthen the business relationship and ultimately legitimacy. Interrelationship between these two networks is the reason that researchers imply that the investment in socio-political responsibility (Crane and Desmond, 2002; Follows and Jobber, 2000) is a marketing investment.

These two firms devoted different types and size of resources to influence the socio-political actors. Commitments like administrative, social and technological commitments and also trust-building actions towards units like business, social and political units can easily be separated.

There are also similarities in the behavior of DMC and Vattenfall. Both have a high level of experience in selecting managementactions and strengthening the firms' legitimacy and trust worthiness. For the internal organizations, one major effort of the managers was to find out and understand the timing and the reasons for discussions and decisions. The new rules were either coercive or supportive. If a crucial political decision were coercive, DMC, for example, had an obligation to contact and change the organization of 585 intermediary dealers and A/S centers, in order to take the adaptive measures.

As Table 21.1 illustrates, DMC and Vattenfall recognized socio-political activities as a critical part of their international market activities. In the case of DMC, for example, the required resources were not only to handle political and social groups in Warsaw, but also groups in Brussels, Paris and Munich. DMC had organized groups and individuals in several foreign countries. Both cases manifest how political units, in their relationships with politicians, mobilized both internal and external resources to affect political decisions in matters like privatizing, production, harmonizing and rules for JVs. The business commitment of Vattenfall and DMC became an idiosyncratic investment leading to, for example, increase in trust and reputation.

The difference in the level of investment is related to three major factors of: (1) the physical distance, country of origin of the firm and the country it aims to operate in (Johanson and Vahlne, 1990). DMC has its origin in Asia with experience from that region and Vattenfall is from Sweden, located within EU; (2) the firms' strategy had a deceptive role in the content of relationship element. DMC had a more specific strategy, which was penetration into a new market. DMC's strategy was aimed towards a specific country, as compared to Vattenfall, which had a more general approach. While DMC had the strategy of penetration, the aim of Vattenfall was comparatively less clear-cut as it was rather generally interested towards getting favorable rules regarding environmental issues. DMC therefore interacted with a larger number of actors compared with Vattenfall; (3) DMC's socio-political investment aimed to develop legitimacy and its social and political trust-building activities intended to manifest that the firm's aim was to undertake its socio-political responsibility in Poland. Vattenfall on the other hand was a well-known firm in the European market and already enjoyed legitimacy and actions undertaken were to strengthen the position. These differences lay the ground for the varieties in the level of investment and also the complexity in their network relationships.

For the relationship with the social actors, DMC with its large industrial investment (more than (US$) $2 billion) made clear to trade unions and politicians its specific contribution to the labor market, car industry and technology development in Poland and EU. This investment was to manifest where the firm's legitimacy should be positioned. Arrangements of social events for children and married couples, close cooperation with trade unions and the media and also the involvement of ministers and high level executives and opening a medical center involving 72 medical personnel (managers estimated that the costs were more than (US$) 50 million required a much higher level of investments as compared with Vattenfall. The firm welcomed the high level of investment in these relationships, as it facilitated market penetration and expansion. For these activities, DMC also developed organizational units absorbing a high level of internal resources. While socio-political actors in Europe had knowledge and experience about Vattenfall and recognized the firm as trustworthy, DMC was obliged to devote a high level of resources to build a legitimate and trustworthy image not only towards politicians, but also towards intermediary organizations and consumers.

Conclusions

The study extends the perceptual boundary of the business network and presented a theoretical tool to understand the interaction of non-business actors with business actors. The two case studies develop and examine the theoretical view building from the three relationship elements of trust, commitment, and legitimacy. In spite of the limitations of having only two case studies or weak connections to theories other than business network, the results contribute towards theory development in this field.

The relationships between business and socio-political actors have a long-term and mutual nature. However, contrary to business-to-business relationships, the relationship mutuality did not have a financial exchange or profit base. Actors in the social and political market, because of their legitimacy, ground their relationships on socio-political values. This chapter draws the conclusion that the nature of the trust, resource commitment and legitimacy in the business market and socio-political market is different. A further conclusion is that these elements in these two markets are interdependent. Business trust, for example, diffuses and transfers to socio-political relationships, as illustrated by Figure 21.5. Commitment towards socio-political actors aims to build and maintain social and political trust, which subsequently is to be spread to the firms' business relationships. Socio-political commitment strengthens firm's business relationship trust and legitimacy in the market.

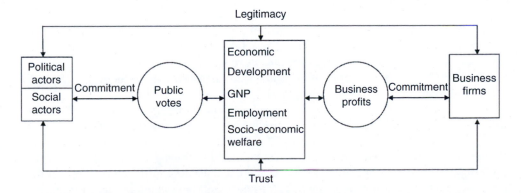

Figure 21.5 Mutual interdependence between business and socio-political actors.

The study manifests that MNCs, in reaching their business goals, undertake actions to convert the coercive actions of socio-political actors to supportive relationships. Coercive actions of socio-political actors can, as for DMC's relationship with the union, harm the commercial activities. The conclusion emerges that supportive socio-political relationships coexist with mutuality which is not necessarily gained with direct exchange relationships.

Concerning the proposition for heterogeneity, the empirical cases disclose several other interesting issues. One reflects the impact of the firms' strategy in these elements. In the case of DMC's penetration strategy, there was a higher level of activities in socio-political network as compared to the other case, which had an expansion strategy as objective. The aspect of heterogeneity also relates to earlier experience of the firms from that specific market. The conclusion is that the more experience and knowledge a firm has in its international socio-political market, the lower is the resource commitment to build supportive relationships. Further, while a strategy like penetration demands a high degree of input to build a new network of socio-political relationships, strategy to maintain legitimacy and trust requires a lower level of input. This conclusion is close to the view of internationalization process for business market wherein firms' penetration and expansion are analyzed by relationship commitment and experiential knowledge (see also Hadjikhani and Ghauri, 2001 and Johanson and Vahlne, 1990). Further research on internationalization in socio-political market and also differences/similarities for different kinds of strategy can promote the understanding of socio-political networks.

The study also reveals another interesting aspect, which is about the heterogeneity in the content of the relationship elements. Each of these relationship elements contains at least two or three dimensions. As discussed in the theoretical framework, commitment, for example, can have a business or social nature. Trust can be related to socio-political actors or can directly be aimed towards development of business trust. The cases demonstrated that these dimensions of trust, commitment and legitimacy are interrelated. Producing good cars, for example, increased the DMC's trust relationship not only with consumers, but also with the labor union and the government in Poland. This conclusion has both theoretical and managerial implications. Trust and legitimacy in socio-political network should support business activities. A deeper and more constructive study on these dimensions and their connections can aid further understanding of socio-political market.

A general conclusion from the empirical evidence is that MNCs' socio-political activities are simply connected to the firms' business activities. In this vein, the study gives some reasons to draw this general conclusion that there is a mechanism of parallel existence of the two interconnected networks of business and socio-political actors. The study also pinpoints that any action in one affects the other (see also Hadjikhani and Thilenius, 2005; Welch and Wilkinson, 2004). The socio-political activities are an essential and distinguishable part, which supplements the business activities. These two types of networks are complementary and exist side by side. The element of legitimacy, trust and commitment in one diffuses and affects the other. Further research on the connection between the two networks can aid a deeper understanding of types and strength of the bridges between the two.

The study presents several managerial implications. The emphasis on socio-political actors, instead of socio-political environment offers some ideas for the management of socio-political markets. Against the earlier studies, that MNCs should obey and adapt to the political rules and regulations in the foreign markets, the results show that managers can undertake actions to manage their socio-political environment. The understanding of the connection between the strategies in these two different markets, business and socio-political, can encourage the managers to exploit their competencies for strengthening their socio-political legitimacy and to achieve business objectives. This view puts stress on the management of socio-political environment at a different level. The strategy involves managers from headquarter and subsidiaries and is more beneficial in the long run. The differentiation of social and political trust, commitment, and legitimacy and learning how such differentiations combine to achieve business goals are contributions of this study.

References

Ahmed ZU, Mohamad O, Tan B, Johnson JP. International risk perceptions and mode of entry: a case study of Malaysian multinational firms. J Bus Res 2002; 55:805–13.

Andersen S, Eliassen KA. The European Union: how democratic is it? London: Sage; 1996.

Baines PR, Egan J. Marketing and political campaigning: mutually exclusive or exclusively mutual?, Qualitative Market Research: An International Journal, 2001;4(1):25–33.

Barros PP, Nilssen T. Industrial policy and firm heterogeneity. Scand J Econ 1999;101(4):597–616.

Boddewyn JJ. Political aspects of MNE theory. J Int Bus Stud 1988;14(3): 341–62.

Boersma M, Buckley PJ, Ghauri PN. Towards a model of trust in international joint venture relationships. J Bus Res 2003;56:1031–42.

Bolton G. A comparative model of bargaining: theory and evidence. Am Econ Rev 1991;81:1096–136.

Bonardi J-P, Hillman AJ, Keim GD. The attractiveness of political markets: implications for firm strategy. Acad Manage Rev 2005;30(2):397–413.

Brunsson N. Industrial policy as implementation or legitimacy. In: Wolf R, editor. Organizing industrial development, Berlin, De Gryyter; 1986. p. 137–56.

Buckley PJ, Ghauri PN. The global challenge for multinational enterprises: managing increasing interdependence. Amsterdam: Pergamon; 1999.

Buckley P, Ghauri PN. Globalisational, economic geography and strategy of multinational enterprises. J Int Bus Stud 2004;35(2):81–98.

Butler P, Collins N. Strategic analysis in political markets. Eur J Mark 1996;13(10/11):25–36.

Chae S, Heidhues P. Buyers' alliances for bargaining power. J Econ Manage Strategy 2004;13(4):731–54.

Chaudri V, Samson D. Business–government relations in Australia: cooperating through task forces. Acad Manage Exec 2000;14(3):19–29.

Conner KR. A historical comparison of resource-based theory and five schools of thoughts within industrial organization economics. J Manage 1991;17:121–54.

Cosset J-C, Roy J. The determinants of country risk ratings. J Int Bus Stud 1991;22(1):135–42.

Crane A, Desmond J. Societal marketing and morality. Eur J Mark 2002;36(5/6):548–69.

Crawford V. A theory of disagreement in bargaining. Econometrica 1982;50:607–37.

Crespin-Mazet F, Ghauri PN. Co-development as a marketing strategy in construction industry. Ind Mark Manage 2007;36:158–72.

Crystal J. Bargaining in the negotiations over liberalizing trade in services: power, reciprocity and learning. Rev Int Polit Econ 2003;10/3:552–78.

Dell'Arringa C. Reforming public sector labour relations. In: Dell'Arringa C, Della Rocca G, Keller B, editors. Strategic choices in reforming public service employment. An international handbook, Basingstoke, Palgrave, 2001.

Denekamp J. Intangible assets, internationalization and foreign direct investment in manufacturing. J Int Bus Stud 1995;26(3):493–504.

Dixon DF. Consumer sovereignty, democracy and the marketing concept. Can J Adm Sci 1992;9(2):116–25.

Egelhoff WG. Strategy and structure in multinational corporations: a revision of the Stopford and Wells model. Strateg Manage J 1988;9:1–14.

Fabella Raul V. The bias in favor of pro-tariff lobbies. J Public Econ 1991;44:87–93.

Fligstein N. The transformation of corporate control. Cambridge, Mass.: Harvard University Press; 1990.

Follows SB, Jobber D. Environmentally responsible purchase behaviour. Eur J Mark 2000; 34(5/6):723–46.

Ford D, editor. Understanding business market: interaction, relationships, networks. London: Academic Press; 1990.

Forsgren M, Hägg I, Hàkansson H, Johanson J, Mattsson L-G. Firms in networks. A new perspective on market power. Acta Universitatis Upsaliensis Stockholm: SNS Press; 1995.

Fredrikson PG, Svensson J. Political instability, corruption and policy formation: the case of environmental policy. J Public Econ 2003; 87:1383–405.

Ghauri PN. Designing and conducting case studies in international business research. In: Marchan-Piekkari R, Welch C, editors. Handbook of qualitative research methods for international business. Cheltenham: Edward Elgar; 2004. p. 109–24.

Ghauri PN, Buckley PJ. Globalization and end of competition: a critical review of rent-seeking multinationals. In: Buckley PJ, editors. The challenge of international business. Basingstoke: Palgrave, 2004; p. 83–100.

Ghauri PN, Grønhaug K. Research methods in business studies: a practical guide. 3rd Edition. London: Pearson; 2005.

Ghauri PN, Holstius K. The role of matching in the foreign market entry process in the Baltic States. Eur J Mark 1996;30(2):75–88.

Hadjikhani A. Sleeping relationship and discontinuity in project marketing. Int Bus Rev 1996;5(3): 319–37.

Hadjikhani A. The political behaviour of business actors. Int Stud Manage Organ 2000;30(1):95–119.

Hadjikhani A, Ghauri PN. The internationalization of the firm and political environment in the European Union. J Bus Res 2001;52(3):263–75.

Hadjikhani A, Sharma DD. A view on political and business actions. In: Ghauri PN, editor. International marketing and purchasing: advances in international business and marketing. New York: JAI Press; 1999. p. 243–57.

Hadjikhani A, Thilenius P. The impact of horizontal and vertical connections on relationships' commitment and trust. J Bus Ind Mark 2005;20/3:136–47.

Hanf K, Toonen TAJ, editors. Policy making in federal and unitary systems. Dordrecht: Kluwer; 1985.

Hausman A. Variations in relationship strength and its impact on performance and satisfaction in business relationships. J Bus Ind Mark 2001;16(7):600–16.

Higgins ERE, Morgan JW. Stakeholder salience and engagement in political organizations. Who and what really counts? Soc Bus Rev 2006;1(1):62–76.

Hoffman MES. Discretion, lobbying and political influence in models of trade policy. J Policy Reform 2005;8(3):175–88.

Jacobson CK, Lenway SL, Ring PS. The political embeddedness of private economic transactions. J Manage Studies 1993;30(3):453–78.

Jansson H, Dagub M, Sharma DD. The state and transnational corporations. Cheltenham: Edward Elgar; 1995.

Johanson J, Vahlne J-E. The mechanism of internationalization. Int Mark Rev 1990;7(4):11–24.

Keillor BD, Boller GW, Ferrel OC. Firm-level political behaviour in the global market place. J Bus Res 1997;40:113–26.

Keillor BD, Hult TM. Predictors of firm-level political behaviour in the global business environment. Int Bus Rev 2004;13(3):309–29.

Keillor BD, Wilkinson TJ, Owens D. Threats to international operations: dealing with potential risk at the firm level. J Bus Res 2005;58:629–35.

Kim WC. The effects of competition and corporate political responsiveness on multinational bargaining power. Strateg Manage J 1988;9:289–95.

Korbin S. Managing political risk assessment: strategic responses to environmental changes. Berkeley, CA: University of California Press; 1982.

Kotler P. How to create, win and dominate markets. New York, NY: Free Press; 1999.

Kotler P, Andreason AR. Strategic marketing for nonprofit organizations. 4th (ed.). Englewood Cliffs NJ: Prentice-Hall; 1991.

Kroszner RS, Stratmann T. Notes on evolution of the congressional committee system in the twentieth century. Corporate campaign contributions, legislator reputation, and political ambiguity. Mimeo, University of Chicago, June 1998.

Lagerlöf J. Lobbying, information, and private and social welfare. Eur J Polit Econ 1997;13:615–37.

Lee J-W. Swedish firms entering the Korean market—position development in distant industrial networks, Dissertation, Department of Business Studies, Uppsala University, 1991.

Lenway SA. The politics of U.S. international trade: protection, expansion and escape. Boston: Pitman Publishing Co; 1985.

Lenway SA, Murtha T. Country capabilities and the strategic state: how national political institutions affect multinational corporations' strategies. Strateg Manage J 1994;15:113–29.

Lenway SA, Jacobson CK, Goldstein J. To lobby or to petition: the political environment of U.S. trade policy. J Manage 1990;16(1):119–34.

Maddison A. Dynamic forces in capitalist development, a long-run comparative view. Oxford: Oxford University; 1991.

Miller KD. Industry and country effects on managers' perspective of environmental uncertainties. J Int Bus Stud 1992;24(1):693–714.

Mobus JL. Mandatory environmental disclosures in a legitimacy theory context. Account Audit Account J 2005;18(4):492–517.

Moon CW, Lado AA. MNC-host government bargaining power relationship: a critique and extension within the resource-based view. J Manage 2000;26(1):85–117.

Morgan RM, Hunt SD. The commitment–trust theory of relationship marketing. J Mark 1994;58(3):20–38.

Murtha TP. Surviving industrial targeting: state credibility and public policy contingencies in multinational subcontracting. J Law Econ Organ 1991;7(1):117–43.

Nomden K, Farnham D, Onnee-Abbruciati M-L. Collective bargaining in public services. Some European comparisons. Int J Public Sector Manage 2003;16(6):412–23.

Nowtotny K, Smith DB, Trebling HM, editors. Public utility regulation: the economic and social control of industry. Boston: Kluwer; 1989.

O'Cass A. Political marketing and the marketing concept. Eur J Mark 1996;30(10/11):37–53.

O'Shaughnessy N. Social propaganda and social marketing: a critical difference. Eur J Mark 1996;10/11:54–67.

O'Shaughnessy N. The marketing of political marketing. Eur J Mark 2001;35(9/10):1047–57.

Pecorino P. Is there any problem in lobbying? Am Econ Rev 1998;2(2):167–81.

Potters J. Lobbying and pressure. Amsterdam: Tinbergen Institute; 1992. Poynter TA. Multinational enterprises and government intervention. New York, NY: St. Martin's Press; 1985.

Ramaswamy K, Renforth W. Market intensity and technical efficiency in public sector firms: evidence from India. Int J Public Sector Manage 1996;9(3):4–17.

Rehbein K, Lenway S. Determining an industry's political effectiveness with the U.S. International Trade Commission. Bus Soc 1994;33(3):270–92.

Ring PS, Lenway SA, Govekar M. Management of the political imperative in international business. Strateg Manage J 1990;11:141–51.

Rogers H, Ghauri PN, George K. The impact of market orientation on internationalisation of retailing firms. Int Rev Retail Distrib Consum Res 2005;15(1):53–74.

Schwarz N, Schuman H. Political knowledge, attribution, and inferred interest in politics: the operation of buffer items. Int J Public Opin Res 1997;9(2):191–5.

Scott J. Social network analysis, a handbook. London: Sage; 1994.

Shaffer B, Hillman A. The development of business–government strategies by diversified firms. Strateg Manage J 2000;21(2):175–90.

Shubik M. Political risk, analysis, process and purpose. In: Herring RJ, editor. Managing international risk. New York: Cambridge University Press; 1983. p. 109–38.

Spencer JW, Murtha TP, Lenway SA. How government matter to new industry creation. Acad Manage Rev 2005;30(2):321–37.

Streeck W. Social institutions and economic performance: studies of industrial relations in advanced capital economics. London: Sage; 1992.

Taylor CR, Zou S, Osland GE. Foreign market entry strategies of Japanese MNCs. Int Mark Rev 2000;17(2):146–63.

Walter A, Ritter T. The influence of adaptations, trust and commitment on value-creating functions of customer relationships. J Bus Ind Mark 2003;18(4/5):353–65.

Warren RC. The evolution of business legitimacy. Eur Bus Rev 2003;15(3):153–63.

Welch C, Wilkinson I. The political embeddedness of international business network. Int Mark Rev 2004;21(2):216–31.

Yin R. Case study research. (3rd ed.). Thousand Oaks, CA: Sage Publications; 2003.

22 Weight versus voice

How foreign subsidiaries gain attention from corporate headquarters*

Cyril Bouquet and Julian Birkinshaw

The attention of executives at corporate headquarters is recognized to be a scarce and critical resource (Cyert & March, 1963; Simon, 1947). The choices senior executives make about which organizational units or issues to focus on have profound implications for the strategic direction of an organization, and for its ability to respond effectively to emerging opportunities (March & Olsen, 1976; Ocasio & Joseph, 2005). Researchers have begun to study the role that formal structures play in directing investments of managerial attention toward the most attractive opportunities (Ocasio, 1997). There is also research on how individual players within an organization can access or get around these structures to more effectively capture the attention of executives at the top (Dutton, 1997; Dutton & Ashford, 1993; Hansen & Haas, 2001).

In this study, we utilized and built on the latter stream of research by theorizing further on the strategies that organizational *units* deploy to attract headquarters' attention. Existing research has primarily focused on the packaging and selling of specific issues or projects (Dutton & Ashford, 1993; Morrison & Phelps, 1999). Fewer studies have examined organizational units themselves as meaningful entities that may capture (or fail to capture) attention from headquarters executives (Morrison & Milliken, 2000: 707). One notable exception is the research conducted by Galunic and Eisenhardt (1996, 2001). Those authors found that organizational units have longer-lived and more "path-dependent" connections with executives at headquarters than do specific issues, which are typically short-lived and linked to key individuals. Their qualitative studies of divisional charter gains and losses suggested that the factors shaping organizational unit attention may be somewhat different from those observed in the issue-selling literature and perhaps may involve a combination of individual initiative *and* aspects of a unit's historical situation.

Although such findings are informative, multinational enterprises (MNEs) provide a fascinating context for exploring this issue further. The distinctive features of MNEs are high levels of geographical and cultural diversity coupled with complex portfolios of businesses, functions and markets. This diversity and complexity make it impossible for executives at corporate headquarters to give full attention to all subsidiary units around the world (Bouquet, 2005; Levy, 2005). Rather, their attention is typically divided among subsidiaries in ways that do not give an equal hearing to all parties (Prahalad & Doz, 1987). So for the individuals managing a specific subsidiary, a key question becomes how they can gain the

*Republished with permission of Academy of Management, from 22. Bouquet, C., & J. Birkinshaw, (2008) "Weight Versus Voice: How Foreign Subsidiaries Gain Attention for Corporate Headquarters", Academy of Management Journal, 51(3): 577–601; permission conveyed through Copyright Clearance Centre Inc.

necessary levels of headquarters' attention to deliver on their potential and contribute to their MNE's long-term success (Birkinshaw et al., 1998).

MNE researchers have observed for many years that it is important for corporate head-quarters to be alert to their promising subsidiaries (Bartlett & Ghoshal, 1986; Doz et al., 2004) and for subsidiaries to be vocal in support of their own achievements (Birkinshaw, 2000; Dutton, 1997). However, there are still plenty of examples of subsidiaries that struggle to gain even the smallest amounts of interest or investment from headquarters, often result-ing in missed opportunities for the parent company. For example, one of our interviewees, the chief executive of Dun & Bradstreet (D&B) Australia, took the highly unusual step of using private equity backing to buy the subsidiary from its American parent company, after realizing that its low ranking in the D&B world was preventing additional investment. The business subsequently doubled in three years and the profits grew tenfold.

Our objective in this study was to uncover the factors that affect the level of attention given by corporate headquarters executives (hereafter, "headquarters' attention") to a subsidiary unit.[1] We address two specific questions: The first question is, "How should the construct of headquarters' attention be operationalized to have both practical and theoretical value?" The existing literature on attention suggests disparate points of view (Moray, 1969; Ocasio, 1997). In the context of an MNE, for example, attention can evoke images of corporate staff seeking to coerce a subsidiary into complying with global policies, or it can suggest a more developmental relationship, in which headquarters is seeking to identify and build on new ideas (Chandler, 1991; Rugman & Verbeke, 2001). We adopt the latter point of view on attention and conceptualize it as a largely "positive" form of parental intervention and, more specifically, as a meta-construct that consists of three interrelated and reinforcing dimensions (Law et al., 1998). We then validate this operational approach in our empirical study.

The second research question is, "What are the key factors that shape headquarters' attention for a subsidiary unit?" We argue that two sets of factors are at work. Theories of intraorganizational power suggest that the structural configuration of an MNE network (Ghoshal & Bartlett, 1990; Nohria & Ghoshal, 1997)—in our terms, a subsidiary's *weight* in a system—influences headquarters' attention. A relational process in which the subsidi-ary's *voice* (Hirschman, 1970; Morrison & Phelps, 1999) is used to emphasize its existing or potential contribution to the MNE as a whole (Birkinshaw, 2000) also shapes head-quarters attention. In this chapter we integrate these perspectives to develop theoretically grounded predictions regarding the attention that subsidiaries receive from headquarters. Further, we investigate the possibility of moderating influences. In particular, we develop the reasoning that the voice of a subsidiary becomes increasingly important as a means for capturing attention when the subsidiary is at a risk of strategic isolation (Monteiro et al., 2007). Subsidiaries prone to strategic isolation are those that are a long way from headquarters and those whose competencies are largely anchored in the downstream part of the value chain. We make this logical extension to our framework to determine whether important aspects of a subsidiary's situation interact with relational processes to impact headquarters' attention.

We believe this study has theoretical implications for several important domains of interna-tional management and organization theory. In terms of international management, although many studies have examined the potential value of subsidiary-level initiatives in MNEs (for example, Birkinshaw, 2000; Ling et al., 2005; O'Donnell, 2000), none of them has demon-strated how that potential is realized. This study represents the missing link in the chain in that it shows the conditions under which entrepreneurial efforts by subsidiary managers can influence headquarters' attention, which in turn may result in significant changes to the roles of particular subsidiaries and a rethinking of the broader priorities of an MNE (Birkinshaw & Hood, 1998). In doing so, we provide a careful operationalization of headquarters' attention in an MNE context.

In terms of organization theory, our research contributes to a deeper understanding of how the allocation of attention can influence a broader realignment of priorities and investments within a multiunit organization. That is, we see the shifting level of attention given to a particular organizational unit as an important *mechanism* through which its role or charter evolves to reflect changes in the organization's operating environment (Galunic & Eisenhardt, 2001). In sum, this article develops new theoretical ideas about the allocation of attention in large multiunit organizations, and to our knowledge it is also the first to empirically test such issues in the specific context of MNEs.

The concept of headquarters' attention

Attention constitutes a broad field of research that spans several disciplines (Jones, 2005; Thornton, 2004) and fields of inquiry.[2] For most organizational scholars, attention refers to the set of elements (events, trends, ideas and, in our case, foreign subsidiaries) that occupies the consciousness of managers (Dutton et al., 1989; Fiske & Taylor, 1984). The emerging attention-based view of the firm (Ocasio, 1997; Ocasio & Joseph, 2005) portrays attention as a meta-construct describing the noticing, encoding, and interpreting of available stimuli and the accompanying focusing of time and effort. To develop an appropriate conceptualization of attention for this research, we supplemented our review of the organizational and international management literature with an exploratory round of research interviews with 24 subsidiary executives. Appendix A describes this approach in detail. This research highlighted the multifaceted nature of attention in an MNE and the need to define the term in a very precise way to avoid confusing it with related notions of control and compliance. We focused on a positive form of headquarters' attention that is value-enhancing and forward-looking (Chandler, 1991). Specifically, we introduce the concept of "positive headquarters' attention" and define it as the *extent to which a parent company recognizes and gives credit to a subsidiary for its contribution to the MNE as a whole*. The definition has three important elements: it portrays attention as a largely positive thing that can facilitate a subsidiary's future development (rather than as a form of corporate interference or control); it puts the granting of attention into the hands of the parent company as a whole (rather than the CEO or a particular subset of executives); and it is achieved on the basis of the subsidiary's contribution to the MNE as a whole (rather than its contribution to a local market). Moreover, our interviews suggested that positive headquarters' attention can be broken down into three subconstructs, which will now be discussed.

Subconstructs of positive attention

Relative attention. This is the perceived level of recognition and credit given to a focal subsidiary relative to the level given to other subsidiaries in an MNE. Many of the subsidiary managers we interviewed saw attention as a competitive process resembling the zero-sum games described in agenda-setting research (Dutton, 1997; Jones & Baumgartner, 2005). For example, one individual we spoke to had responsibility for the entire Asian region in his company. He described attention as a scarce commodity that needed to be allocated across a portfolio of countries. In his opinion, the headquarters were "overinvested" in mainland China, "radically underweight in Japan" and "uncertain" about India, which he felt was "a real wild card". He also acknowledged that the smaller countries (the "poor cousins") were typically not getting much interest from parent executives.

Supportive attention. This is the provision by a corporate parent of discretionary resources as a way to facilitate a subsidiary's development (Luo, 2003; Rugman & Verbeke, 2001). MNE theorists (Bartlett & Ghoshal, 1989; Doz et al., 2001) and scholars interested in the function of corporate headquarters (Chandler, 1991; Goold et al., 1994) have described attention as a kind of "emotional energy" (Collins, 1998) that underpins the value-added interventions of parent executives. Our interviewees adopted a similar point of view, often describing attention as a gateway to the best practices, technologies, people, and career opportunities available in the corporate world, many of which are in limited supply.

Visible attention. This describes explicit recognition from its corporate parent of a subsidiary's existence and achievements, expressed in media that are transmitted to a broad body of stakeholders. In particular, and building on the assumption that language and thoughts are closely related (Huff, 1990), numerous studies have suggested that annual reports depict the major topics that a parent company attends to (Cho & Hambrick, 2006; D'Aveni & MacMillan, 1990; Levy, 2005), partly because such reports reflect the perception and in put of many individuals at the top. Our interviewees echoed this viewpoint, often alluding to the symbolic value of annual reports, which they believed send strong signals as to who the winners and losers are in their firms' systems.

Positive attention as an aggregate multidimensional construct

These three dimensions are conceptualized as forming an overall representation of how much positive attention a subsidiary receives from its parent company. However, it makes little sense to argue that there exists a higher-order latent construct called positive attention that can be manifested solely in terms of any one dimension, for example visibility. Instead, we view attention as an aggregate multidimensional construct (Law et al., 1998) that is formed as the composite of three sub-constructs, which may or may not covary. In other words, changes in the visible dimension of our core construct will not necessarily lead to changes in the supportive or relative dimensions. Rather, lack of any single dimension will decrease but not totally eliminate the amount of positive attention that a subsidiary receives from its corporate parent.

Before proceeding, we also need to clarify the relationship between positive headquarters' attention and strategic role. A long tradition of research examines the causes and consequences of subsidiaries' strategic roles in MNEs (for example, Bartlett & Ghoshal, 1986; Jarillo & Martinez, 1990; White & Poynter, 1984). *Strategic role* is defined as the activities a subsidiary performs and has responsibility for within an MNE (Birkinshaw & Hood, 1998: 782); it is typically established over a number of years, is widely communicated and understood in the organization and changes relatively rarely (Galunic & Eisenhardt, 1996). The concept of positive attention, as we have defined it, is an indicator of the current level of recognition and credit accorded to the subsidiary by headquarters executives, and as such positive attention is likely to be more subjective and less stable than a subsidiary's strategic role. Of course, we would expect a subsidiary's strategic role to correlate with the attention it receives from headquarters, but we would also expect there to be occasions when a subsidiary receives more or less attention than would be expected in view of its formal role within the MNE, perhaps because of recent changes in the subsidiary's marketplace, or because of the specific initiatives it is pursuing. By focusing on attention, rather than strategic role, this study opens up several new avenues for research into the dynamics of headquarters–subsidiary relationships.

Theory development

Two theoretical perspectives inform our model of corporate attention allocation in MNEs. Figure 22.1, which graphically presents the conceptual framework for our study, delineates these two perspectives on the left. The structural perspective, which can be seen as representing the baseline perspective for this study, embraces ideas from theories of intraorganizational power (Benson, 1975; Hickson et al., 1971; Lawrence & Lorsch, 1967). It suggests that headquarters' attention is fundamentally determined by the internationally differentiated positions that foreign subsidiaries occupy in the corporate system of an MNE (Ghoshal & Bartlett, 1990; Nohria & Ghoshal, 1997). According to this perspective, an MNE is a value-maximizing entity that functions according to criteria of proven strategic significance. The positive attention a subsidiary receives is therefore based on its *weight* in the global ordering of power. Prior studies suggest that key components of a subsidiary's weight are the strategic significance of its local market (Hypothesis 1a) and the strength of the subsidiary within the MNE network (Hypothesis 1b) (Bartlett & Ghoshal, 1986; Jarillo & Martinez, 1990).[3]

Although this line of thinking is by far the most established in MNE literature, it has its limitations. Often, indicators of weight concern how successful a subsidiary has been in the past or convey something about the received view of the subsidiary's marketplace (usually from external sources). But decision-making heuristics tend to be relatively biased and simple-minded (Cyert & March, 1963), so without any evidence to the contrary, arguments centered on the notion of weight suggest that parent company executives will continue to allocate attention to subsidiaries in the way they have always done.

The *relational* perspective, to which this study seeks to contribute, is grounded upon the issue-selling literature (Dutton, 1997; Dutton & Ashford, 1993; Dutton et al., 2001) to highlight the possibility that headquarters executives do not see the world simply in this

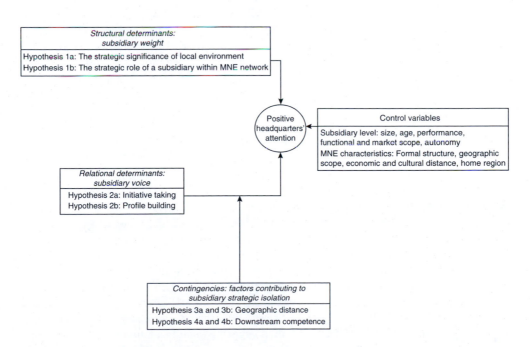

Figure 22.1 Conceptual framework.

hierarchical manner. Combining the issue-selling literature with related research in organizational behavior (Hirschman, 1970; Morrison & Phelps, 1999) and unit-level studies of divisional charter gains and losses (Galunic & Eisenhardt, 1996, 2001), we suggest that *headquarters' attention can also be viewed as the outcome of a bottom-up process* (Birkinshaw & Hood, 1998; Birkinshaw et al., 1998; Ling et al., 2005). That is, foreign subsidiary units have voices of their own that they can use in their relationships with headquarters to more effectively position their achievements within a corporate system, irrespective of current weight considerations.

With our model, we build on this relational perspective to develop theoretically grounded, unit-level predictions regarding the components of subsidiary voice. In this regard, we view MNEs as complex organizational systems characterized by a dual (and sometimes contradictory) logic of action (Luo, 2005). On the one hand, an MNE is an economically integrated economic institution that encourages members to continuously justify their existence within an emerging global hierarchy, so taking the initiative is important (Hypothesis 2a) because it may lead to the acquisition of specialized resources that offer future competitive advantages. On the other hand, an MNE is also a socially constructed community of subsidiary members that can only advance their cause with corporate headquarters if they are believed to adhere to a common set of strategic goals, norms and values (Bartlett & Ghoshal, 1994; Galunic & Eisenhardt, 1996). So although taking the initiative is important, so are the concrete actions undertaken by host country managers to build a subsidiary's profile with headquarters executives (Hypothesis 2b) and reinforce their perception that it is a reliable citizen of the MNE family.

We further expand the relational perspective by also exploring whether there are conditions that moderate the strength of our voice arguments. Two variables—geographic distance and downstream competence—have often been described as contributing to the strategic isolation of a subsidiary (Ghemawat, 2001; Mudambi & Navarra, 2004), although these links have not always been supported empirically (Monteiro et al., 2007). The third part of our model addresses the extent to which geographic distance (Hypotheses 3a and 3b) and "downstream competence" (Hypotheses 4a and 4b) act as moderator variables for the hypothesized effects of initiative taking and profile building on the positive attention that subsidiary units receive from corporate headquarters. We now develop each of these hypotheses in detail.

Structural determinants of attention: the weight of a subsidiary

The task of allocating attention over an entire portfolio of subsidiary units is complex. But strategic management requires that headquarters executives make some choices rather than try to allocate their limited attention in a uniform manner, as if all subsidiary units were equally critical to MNE success (Prahalad & Doz, 1987: 150–152). No simple formula exists, yet a large number of prior studies have suggested that headquarters executives use relatively objective criteria to categorize subsidiaries; they assess the strategic significance of a local market as well as the strength of the subsidiary operations within the MNE network. By gaining weight along such dimensions, subsidiary units increase the likelihood that headquarters executives know of their accomplishments in the firm system, and therefore the units increase the amount of positive attention that actually flows in their direction.

Local market strategic significance. This dimension reflects the perception that the particular market in which a subsidiary operates is critical to the performance of its parent MNE. In this respect, previous researchers have often suggested that headquarters managers flock toward those subsidiary markets that provide the greatest sales opportunities, relative to those available elsewhere in their corporation (for example, Christensen, 1997). The presence of other foreign multinationals in a local market may also trigger positive headquarters' attention because it typically signals the availability of critical location-specific advantages that can improve the competitiveness of an MNE (Dunning, 1998). Alternatively, it may also indicate agglomeration effects (such as rapid technological advances and improved competitive practices) from which the MNE can derive benefits. These effects, which were originally described by Marshall (1920), typically emerge through the clustering of related activities and specialized support services, which, as Porter (2000) described, typically act as magnets for the allocation of attention in MNEs.

Hypothesis 1a. The strategic significance of its local market is positively related to the positive attention that a subsidiary receives from corporate headquarters.

Subsidiary strength within an MNE network. This dimension is defined as the extent to which a subsidiary undertakes activities upon which sister subsidiaries depend. For example, a subsidiary might have responsibility for manufacturing a product on behalf of its entire MNE, or it might be designated as a "center of excellence" that other subsidiaries can learn from (Ghoshal & Bartlett, 1990; Nohria & Ghoshal, 1997). Building on well-established theories of intraorganizational power (Benson, 1975; Hickson et al., 1971; Lawrence & Lorsch, 1967), we argue that the higher the level of dependence of other subsidiaries on a focal subsidiary, the more powerful the focal subsidiary is likely to be and, consequently, the greater the amount of attention it is likely to receive from corporate headquarters.

Hypothesis 1b. The strength of a subsidiary within an MNE network is positively related to the positive attention that the subsidiary receives from corporate headquarters.

Relational determinants of attention: the voice of a subsidiary

Initiative taking. This dimension refers to the conscious and deliberate actions of subsidiary managers in their marketplace (Birkinshaw & Hood, 1998; Birkinshaw et al., 1998). Initiative taking is similar to other forms of "taking charge" behavior (Morrison & Milliken, 2003; Morrison & Phelps, 1999) in that it is voluntary (not formally required by headquarters) and change-oriented (that is, aimed at improving a subsidiary's status and perceived significance in a corporate system). Subsidiary initiatives are typically directed toward new products or services, or new market opportunities. They usually represent an extension to or departure from the subsidiary's established mandate. Evidence from a variety of sources highlights the potential value of subsidiary initiatives for a firm as a whole (Rugman & Verbeke, 2001), but their outcomes are uncertain and to some degree embedded in their local market contexts, so the effectiveness of subsidiary initiatives as attention-capturing tools is ambiguous (Schulz, 2001). Birkinshaw (2000) argued that many MNEs are intolerant of ideas and proposals that have not been directly solicited from the top and that, as a result, subsidiary managers are sometimes reluctant to fully exert their entrepreneurial influence.

In this study, we argue that initiative taking can generate flows of positive attention from parent companies both directly and indirectly. The direct effect is likely to be experienced during routine visits to a subsidiary operation. Consider an example from our research interviews: when the CEO of ABB, a Swiss-Swedish engineering group, visited the managers of its Czech subsidiary, he discovered that they had come up with the rather ingenious idea of linking the company's administrative computers at night (when they were not used) to leverage their combined processing capacity. This meta-network, which allowed the company to more quickly run R&D algorithms with a particular mathematical structure, gave unprecedented recognition and support to the Czech subsidiary. The indirect effect takes two forms: either headquarters executives see the early-stage results of a subsidiary initiative in the form of increased revenues or higher profitability, or the individuals behind the initiative develop a reputation across the MNE for their actions and subsequently come to the attention of headquarters executives.

Hypothesis 2a. Initiative taking by a subsidiary's managers is positively related to the positive attention that the subsidiary receives from corporate headquarters.

Profile building. This dimension refers to the broad set of efforts undertaken by subsidiary managers to improve their image, credibility and reputation within their parent MNE. If initiative taking is fundamentally about action taken in the local subsidiary context, profile building is the complementary set of activities focused on the corporate network. The logic stems from the argument that for a subsidiary's current status and growth plans to influence parent company attention, the managers running the subsidiary have to work hard to shape the corporate agenda (Dutton & Ashford, 1993) and to build perceptions that their activities and operations are strategically important and supportive of established corporate goals, norms, and values. In this respect, Galunic and Eisenhardt's (1996, 2001) studies of divisional charter gains and losses emphasized the importance of a subsidiary's being seen as a reliable citizen of the corporate community. As one manager whom these authors interviewed related: "Omni [the parent corporation] knows we deliver, and we've had a great reputation for that. I cannot remember not delivering" (Galunic & Eisenhardt, 2001: 1238).

Our review of the MNE literature suggested that profile building consists of three main factors. The most important factor is probably the subsidiary's *track record*, that is, "the extent to which it has delivered, over the years, results at or above the expectations of the parent company" (Birkinshaw & Hood, 1998: 788).[4] A solid track record helps to build confidence that the subsidiary is a reliable and trustworthy actor within the firm network.[5] The subsidiary's *commitment to the parent company* constitutes a second important factor. As Galunic and Eisenhardt noted, headquarters executives can seldom "ignore a widely felt need to reward good citizenship" (2001: 1238), perhaps because a strong sense of affiliation serves to reduce goal conflict and the likelihood that subsidiaries will pursue actions detrimental to overall corporate objectives (Black & Gregersen, 1992; Gregersen & Black, 1992; Roth & O'Donnell, 1996). A third factor is related to the *impression management* (Gardner & Martinko, 1988; Schlenker, 1980) efforts by which a subsidiary is able to more effectively emphasize its contributions and strategic proposals (Dutton & Ashford, 1993). Such efforts may involve working with headquarters to demonstrate strategic alignment, or simply maintaining exposure and connections with power brokers at head office.[6]

Hypothesis 2b. Profile building by a subsidiary's managers is positively related to the positive attention that the subsidiary receives from corporate headquarters.

Contingencies: contributors to subsidiary strategic isolation

Geographic distance. Even in an era of global economic interdependence, as Helliwell observed, "being further from home usually means being less well connected to local networks, less able to understand local norms, and less able to be sure how much to trust what people may say" (2002: 21). All else being equal, headquarters executives understand the subsidiaries in their corporate network that are the furthest away less well than they understand the closer ones, which in turn means that the executives are more likely to fall back on simple heuristics (rather than deep personal knowledge) to evaluate distant subsidiaries. This formulation suggests that distant subsidiaries are therefore at a greater risk of capturing low levels of attention than those closer to home. Findings in related areas support this argument. For example, studies of knowledge transfers in MNEs have shown that transfers between units drop off dramatically with increasing distance (Buckley & Carter, 2004; Hansen & Lovas, 2004; Monteiro et al., 2007) and puzzling stories of "home bias" in the patterns of trade flows and capital investments between countries offer parallel findings (Ricart et al., 2004).

If this logic is correct, there is also reason to believe that, by more fully exerting their voice (i.e., through initiative taking and profile building), a subsidiary's managers can improve the quality and quantity of information that parent company executives have at their disposal, which in turn increases the likelihood that the attention afforded to the subsidiary is a fair reflection of its actual activities and capabilities. Subsidiaries close to headquarters have various informal and ad hoc mechanisms for achieving this objective of gaining attention, whereas those further away have no choice but to be proactive in initiative taking and profile building. This statement would suggest that voice-based mechanisms for channeling positive levels of headquarters' attention are likely to become increasingly important as geographic distance increases (see Agrawal et al., 2006 study of the Indian diaspora).

Hypothesis 3a. Geographic distance strengthens the relationship between initiative taking and positive headquarters' attention.

Hypothesis 3b. Geographic distance strengthens the relationship between profile building and positive headquarters' attention.

Downstream competence. Although subsidiary units are nodes in a network from which headquarters executives potentially have much to learn (Bartlett & Ghoshal, 1986), the extent to which the particular initiative-taking and profile-building efforts of managers elicit positive attention from headquarters may vary according to the kind of activity that underpins subsidiary competence. In particular, we suggest that a subsidiary with a downstream competence, by which we mean a unit responsible for activities mostly confined to product sales, service or marketing, is generally more likely to fall out of the loop than a subsidiary with an upstream competence, such as manufacturing, R&D, or strategic support services (see Mudambi and Navarra [2004] for a recent review of this issue). This expectation prevails because some subsidiary advantages are location-bound: although occasional examples of subsidiaries developing global centers of excellence in downstream functions exist (Frost et al., 2002), downstream assets usually lead to the creation of competencies and insights that cannot be "leveraged into" other distant markets (Forsgren, 2000; Hu, 1995) and are therefore viewed as less important to corporate headquarters (Schulz, 2001). A downstream competence can also exacerbate concern at an MNE's head office that a subsidiary is engaging in opportunistic "empire-building" behavior that may destroy value for the MNE (Williamson, 1975), diminishing the flow of positive attention to the subsidiary.

But again, there is reason to believe that subsidiary managers can, through their initiatives in particular, channel information to parent company executives that facilitates their understanding of how the subsidiary's knowledge or expertise in downstream activities can contribute to the rest of the MNE (Monteiro et al., 2007). The maintenance of a good profile can also create perceptions of trust and commitment that strengthen the exchange relationships between headquarters and their marketing affiliates (Hewett & Bearden, 2001; Morgan & Hunt, 1994). We expect that voice mechanisms become increasingly important as vehicles for capturing attention when a subsidiary's competencies are confined to the downstream part of the value chain.

Hypothesis 4a. A downstream competence strengthens the relationship between initiative taking and positive headquarters' attention.

Hypothesis 4b. A downstream competence strengthens the relationship between profile building and positive headquarters' attention.

Methods

Sample and data collection

The study involved 283 foreign subsidiaries of large MNEs in Australia, Canada and the United Kingdom (U.K.). These countries were considered appropriate domains of study in this research because they all have substantial populations of foreign-owned affiliates with similarities along two dimensions: (1) they constitute a relatively homogeneous cultural group that shares a common language, thus mitigating the issue of measurement equivalence and (2) all three have established histories of inward investment, thus offering an interesting context for the study of how subsidiaries may succeed in attracting attention. Foreign subsidiaries, defined as local affiliates whose parent companies held at least 51 percent of their ownership, were identified in each country through a slightly different sampling methodology because of the nature of the available databases. In Australia, we used the membership listing of the International CEO Forum, a leading industry association (whose members are exclusively foreign-owned subsidiaries), to compile our selection of foreign subsidiaries. In Canada and the U.K., a random sample was drawn up from the *Directory of Corporate Affiliations*. The initial set consisted of 1,400 subsidiaries for which the names of CEO contacts could be identified, excluding operating branches without a significant level of strategic decision making. To reduce problems associated with common methods variance, we collected data from primary and secondary sources. Secondary data were collected for one dimension of the dependent variable (i.e., visible attention) and for several independent, moderating and control variables. Since the focus of our investigation was on privately held subsidiary companies, it was impossible to get consistent public-record data on other aspects of internal subsidiary activities.

We mailed questionnaires to the managing directors of the selected subsidiaries, using local sponsors in each case. This study received the generous support of reputable local organizations, namely the International CEO Forum, the Social Sciences and Humanities Research Council of Canada and the Advanced Institute of Management Research in the U.K. Clearly identifying these endorsements in our communications with subsidiary executives may have helped to build trust that our data collection effort was legitimate and useful. Specific steps were also taken to maximize response rate (Dillman, 2000; Fowler, 1993): (1) requests for participation in the mail survey engaged the respondents' natural interest in the topic of "attention", (2) we provided stamped return envelopes and offered access to a summary report of the study's findings, and (3) about three weeks after the initial mailing, we sent non-respondents a second letter with a new questionnaire. In total, 286 subsidiary CEOs responded, providing a response rate of 20 percent, which is satisfactory for research of this type (Harzing, 2000). After eliminating three questionnaires with missing data, we ended up with 283 usable responses that were used in all subsequent analysis.

We developed the questionnaire in three stages. First, we asked three academics to review the initial draft instrument to identify questions that were vague, ambiguous or sources of possible bias. Through this feedback, we eliminated or modified some of the initial survey items and added others to the revised instrument. Second, we attempted to minimize consistency artifacts by keeping the questionnaire short (four pages), varying the scale formats and scattering same-construct questions throughout the questionnaire. Third, we tackled the risk of social desirability bias by asking informants to answer survey questions in an indirect way, from the perspective of a group of managers rather than from their own individual points of view (Fisher, 1993). We also maintained the confidentiality of informants and used serial numbers on the mail survey to keep track of respondents and nonrespondents (Sharma, 2000).

The distribution of the respondents was as follows: 101 foreign subsidiaries in Australia, 96 in Canada and 86 in the U.K. The mean annual revenues of the sample were $412 million (in U.S. dollars), with a range from $2 million through to $6 billion (s.d. = $752 million). The subsidiaries represented 246 different corporate parents whose sales ranged from $12 million to $92 billion, with the average parent sales being $3.2 billion (s.d. = $7.5 billion). The most common parent company nationality by far was the United States (96), followed by France (31), Germany (30), Japan (25) and the United Kingdom (21). To estimate the likelihood of nonresponse bias, we examined whether respondents and non-respondents differed significantly on parent nationality, but no significant difference was found. We also used a Kolmogorov-Smirnov two-sample test to examine differences of central tendency, dispersion and skewness in the distribution of respondents and nonrespondents related to size, using the logarithm of total subsidiary sales, but no significant differences were found. A nonsignificant time trend extrapolation test (Armstrong & Overton, 1977) provided further confidence that our sample was representative.

Measuring attention

Procedures. To construct a clear understanding of how to apply scholarly views of the attention concept (Ocasio, 1997; Thornton, 2004) to the study of parent-subsidiary relationships in an MNE context,[7] we conducted a preliminary set of face-to-face interviews. This approach, which led to the identification of three unifying themes corresponding to the *relative*, *supportive* and *visible* aspects of attention, is described in Appendix A. It should be noted that some of the interviewees described more negative forms of attention that we later determined (on closer inspection in the course of analyzing this content) actually referred to issues of corporate control, that is, procedures undertaken by headquarters managers to monitor and evaluate subsidiary activities. We felt it was more appropriate to label these activities "headquarters' control". However, for the sake of completeness, we performed some additional post hoc analysis to investigate the impact of our independent variables on headquarters' control.

Multidimensional scales. We measured *relative attention* by asking respondents to answer three questions on a scale ranging from 1 ("much lower") to 4 ("about the same") to 7 ("much higher"). Our abbreviations for the items follow their descriptions to facilitate interpretation of the relevant confirmatory factor analysis results): "The amount of attention paid to us relative to key Asian markets (for example, China) is . . ." (AT1), "The amount of attention paid to us relative to comparatively sized markets in the region is . . ." (AT2), and "The amount of attention paid to us relative to comparatively sized markets in other parts of the world is ...” (AT3) *Supportive attention* items used a three-item scale ranging from 1 (“strongly disagree”) to 7 (“strongly agree”). Respondents were asked to assess the value-added aspects of the attention they received from corporate headquarters by indicating the extent to which they agreed with the following: “Corporate headquarters provide cash bonuses and career opportunities to our people” (AT4), “Parent companies want to learn more about our local market and products” (AT5), and “The head-office helps diffuse our best practices across the firm’s global network” (AT6).

Finally, we followed D’Aveni and MacMillan’s (1990) recommended procedures to assess *visible attention* in terms of the content of an MNE’s annual report. We calculated three ratios using data averaged over two years (2003–04). These ratios were computed as the total number of times a subsidiary country location was mentioned in the annual report (excluding references to currency and accounting standards) divided by the total number of words used in the annual report (AT7), the total number of times a subsidiary country location was mentioned divided by the total number of references made to the parent company’s nationality (AT8), and the total number of times a subsidiary country location was mentioned divided by the total number of references made to China (AT9). The use of China as a country comparator provided a realistic and objective sense of the relative attention afforded to a focal subsidiary in the MNE corporate world. We converted all three measures to logarithms to correct for their non-normal distributions.

Psychometric properties. We used confirmatory factor analysis (CFA) with AMOS version 5 and maximum-likelihood estimation to evaluate whether attention could be conceptualized as a higher-order construct represented by nine items loading on three first-order dimensions. Here we followed Kline’s (2005: 134) recommendation in reporting a minimal set of fit indexes that included: (1) the model chi-square, (2) the Steiger-Lind root-mean-square-error of approximation (RMSEA), (3) the Bentler comparative fit index (CFI), and (4) the standardized root-mean-square residual (SRMR). As shown in Table 22.1, the hypothesized CFA model provided a very good fit to the data ($\chi^2[25, n = 283] = 33.94, p > .01$; RMSEA = .04, with a 90% confidence interval of .00–.06; CFI = .99; SRMR = .04). Each indicator variable loaded significantly on its respective factor, as expected.

For completeness, we compared this higher-order, three-factor model structure to one- and two-factor structures, using the chi-square difference test to compare these models (Bollen, 1989; Kline, 2005). The single-factor model inadequately accounted for the observed covariances ($\chi^2[27, n = 283] = 248.92, p < .01$; RMSEA = .17 with a 90% confidence interval of .15–.19; CFI = .79; SRMR = .14). When we examined whether attention could be modeled as two correlated factors (one of which corresponded to the items representing visible attention), we found that the fit associated with this model ($\chi^2[26, n = 283] = 97.14$, $p < .01$; RMSEA = .10 with a 90% confidence interval of .08–.12; CFI = .93; SRMR = .08) was significantly decreased compared to the higher-order, three-factor structure. Indeed, the chi-square difference of 63.18 between these two models was highly significant ($\Delta df = 2$, $p < .001$). Taken together, these analyses suggested that attention was best captured as a meta-construct of three first-order dimensions. Table 22.1 gives the statistical values resulting from our CFA assessing the fit of our attention-getting model.

Independent variables

The strategic significance of a local market. We measured this construct using two separate indicators, both computed at the North American Industry Classification Index (NAICS)

Table 22.1 Results of CFA model for attention[a]

Construct/indicator	Standardized loading	Z	Composite reliability (AVE)[b]
Relative			.80 (.57)
AT1	.68		
AT2	.62	6.77***	
AT3	.53	5.38***	
Supportive			.84 (.63)
AT4	.55		
AT5	.62	7.49***	
AT6	.75	7.56***	
Visible			.98 (.95)
AT7	.94		
AT8	.96	20.58***	
AT9	.82	30.34***	
Attention			.74 (.51)
Relative	.61	4.89***	
Supportive	.59	4.42***	
Visible	.48	5.49***	

a For spell-outs of the abbreviations for the individual items, see the text. Zs (critical ratios) were set to 1.00 to establish scale.
b "AVE" is average variance extracted.
***$p < .001$

three-digit-industry level of analysis. The first indicator captured the size of the local subsidiary market. *Local market* size was calculated as the proportion of worldwide industry sales realized in a given subsidiary's host country. We used data reported in Compustat Global Vantage to compute this first item. The second indicator captured the presence of multinationals in a local subsidiary market (*presence of MNEs in local market*), which, as indicated earlier, may indicate the presence of location-specific advantages or agglomeration effects from which a parent company can learn. We calculated this indicator as the ratio of foreign direct investment (FDI) inflows to FDI outflows over the most recent previous ten years, using data from the United Nations 2005 *World Investment Report*.

The strength of a subsidiary in its MNE network. This construct captures the idea that a subsidiary's activities are central to its MNE system. It was measured with a scale adapted from O'Donnell (2000) that asked respondents to indicate (1 = "to a very little extent" to 7 = "to a great extent") whether: (1) "the activities of this subsidiary influence the outcomes of other subsidiaries", (2) "work in this subsidiary is connected to the work of other subsidiaries", (3) "the activities of other subsidiaries influence the outcomes of this subsidiary", and (4) "this subsidiary depends on the effective functioning of other subsidiaries to keep performing its own tasks effectively". The final measure was calculated as follows:

$$\text{Subsidiary strength in MNE network} = \frac{\text{Item a}}{\text{Average of (item b, item c and item d)}}.$$

Initiative taking. We measured this construct using a four-item scale from Birkinshaw et al. (1998) tapping various aspects of subsidiary initiatives. The items were all preceded by the stem, "How often have any of the following activities occurred over the previous five years?" The items were: "new products developed in [the host-market] and then sold internationally", "successful bids for corporate investments in [the host market]", "new corporate investments in R&D or manufacturing attracted by host-country management", and "proposals to transfer manufacturing to [the host market] from elsewhere in the corporation" (1 = "never" to 7 = "plentifully").

Profile building. Our composite measure of profile building captured the track record of a subsidiary, its commitment to its parent company, and the impression management efforts of subsidiary managers. *Track record* was operationalized with items based on the work of Birkinshaw and Hood (1998). The items were: "The subsidiary has a history of delivering what it has promised to the parent company" (PF1), "The subsidiary has a history of strong, internationally-respected leaders" (PF2), and "The credibility of subsidiary top management is high" (PF3). The notion of subsidiary *commitment* was assessed with a three-item scale used by Gregersen and Black (1992) and Roth and O'Donnell (1996). The items were: "Subsidiary managers care about the fate of the parent company" (PF4), "What this parent company stands for is important to our subsidiary managers" (PF5), and "Subsidiary managers feel a strong sense of affiliation with the multinational corporation as a whole" (PF6). Finally, to measure *impression management*, we developed a three-item scale based on the work of Bartlett and Ghoshal (1989). The items were: "We work with head-office managers to focus the subsidiary's efforts towards meeting corporate goals and values (therefore maintaining strategic alignment)" (PF7), "We involve the parent company in our business and welcome their input" (PF8) and "We spend time developing connections with people in positions of authority at corporate headquarters" (PF9).

As we did for attention, we used CFA to assess the fit of the hypothesized profile-building structure; Table 22.2 presents relevant statistics. The initial model provided a reasonable fit to the data (χ^2[26, n = 283] = 65.57, p > .01; RMSEA = .07 with a 90% confidence interval of .05–.10; CFI = .95; SRMR = .06), but further inspection of the output helped determine that large correlation residuals existed between item PF6 (sense of affiliation to MNE as a whole) and other factors. Dropping this item and reestimating the CFA model significantly improved fit (χ^2[19, n = 283] = 29.66, p < .05; RMSEA = .05 with a 90% confidence interval of .00–.07; CFI = .98; SRMR = .04). This revised model provided superior fit to one-factor and two-factor models, so we retained the reduced set of items for all subsequent tests.

Moderating variables

Geographic distance. We applied the great-circle distance formula to the latitude and longitude coordinates of the city locations of both subsidiary and corporate headquarters to precisely calculate physical distance in kilometers. An application of this approach can be found in Coval and Moskowitz (1999). All distances were computed with a calculator available at www.mapcrow.info

Subsidiary downstream competence. Following established approaches (Hewett et al., 2003; White & Poynter, 1984), we assessed each subsidiary's downstream competence by asking respondents to indicate which value-added activities it performed. We listed eight activities: Four corresponded to downstream parts of the value chain (product sales and after-sales service, marketing, sale of professional services, and logistics/distribution); four involved the upstream part (manufacturing, provision of strategic services [regional headquarters], R&D, and "back office" support). Our measure of a downstream competence was the number of downstream activities divided by the total number of subsidiary activities.

Table 22.2 CFA Model for Profile Building[a]

Construct/indicator	Standardized loading	Z	Composite reliability (AVE)[b]
Track record			.81 (.60)
PF1	.50		
PF2	.81	7.61***	
PF3	.60	7.50***	
Commitment to parent company			.93 (.87)
PF4	.81		
PF5	.93	9.24***	
PF6[c]			
Impression management			.84 (.63)
PF7	.57		
PF8	.82	8.44***	
PF9	.65	8.29***	
Profile building[d]			.75 (.52)
Track record	.50		
Commitment to parent company	.75	3.63***	
Impression management			
	.58	3.64***	

a For spell-outs of the abbreviations for the individual items, see the text. Zs (critical ratios) were set to 1.00 to establish scale.
b "AVE" is average variance extracted.
c This item was dropped from the measurement model because of high cross-loadings on other constructs.
d Hypothesized second-order model with residual variances constrained to be equal.
***$p < .001$

Control variables

We controlled for several factors that had potential to confound the study's hypotheses. Appendix B describes our operationalizations of these control variables. At the subsidiary level of analysis, we included a measure of subsidiary *size*, because large subsidiaries often possess a form of administrative heritage that commands attention in an MNE system (Bartlett & Ghoshal, 1989). To reflect the possibility that subsidiaries might attract more attention at both the early and late stages of their strategic development, as well as when they experienced extreme levels of performance, we also controlled for the nonlinear effects of subsidiary *age* and *performance*. The *functional scope* and the *market scope* of a subsidiary's activities and the strategic *autonomy* of the subsidiary were also included as controls because such variables are often assumed to shape the broad role and mandate of subsidiary actors within an MNE network (Jarillo & Martinez, 1990; White & Poynter, 1984). MNE characteristics were also included as controls. In particular, we controlled for considerations of formal structure, which may affect the attention routinely allocated to country affiliates (Galbraith, 2000), using the dichotomous variables *matrix structure* and *geographic area structure*. We also coded the *geographic scope* of a parent company, which determines the number of subsidiary actors that compete for the same finite pool of attention resources (Miller & Eden, 2006). We controlled for the *cultural distance* between an MNE's headquarters and a subsidiary and for the *parentage* (home region) of the MNE when testing our hypotheses to account for the possibility of attentional differences resulting from broad differences in mind-sets (Perlmutter, 1969).

Additional validity tests

We estimated a CFA model that included all of the study's latent constructs—attention, initiative taking, profile building, subsidiary size, performance and autonomy—and in which the factor scores obtained for the first-order dimensions of profile building and attention were used as manifest indicators of their higher-order constructs. This model was a good fit to the data ($\chi^2[155, n = 283] = 274.80, p < .01$; RMSEA = .05 with a 90% confidence interval of .04–.06; CFI = .95; SRMR = .06). In addition, all the parameters loaded significantly on their respective constructs ($p > .001$, critical value = 2.58, all Zs > 4). The average variance extracted exceeded .5 in all cases, providing good evidence of convergent validity. The correlations between latent constructs, shown in Table 22.3, were not particularly high, indicating adequate discriminant validity (Anderson & Gerbing, 1988; Bagozzi & Phillips, 1982). The composite reliabilities ranged from .72 to .92, indicating that the measures were reliable.

We also tested for the possibility of common method bias among survey variables. This was done by estimating a CFA model in which all survey items for the constructs described in this study were loaded on a common "method" factor. This model demonstrated poor fit to the data ($\chi^2[104, n = 283] = 868.45, p < .01$; RMSEA = .16 with a 90% confidence interval of .15–.17; CFI = .45; SRMR = .15), indicating the absence of a single general factor. Additional exploratory factor analysis on attention, initiative-taking, and profile-building items clearly replicated the factor structure we intended to use in the tests of hypotheses. Items loaded on the intended factors, all of which had eigenvalues greater than 1.0, as was consistent with the measurement model. Importantly, this analysis did not reveal significant cross-loadings that would suggest the presence of substantial common method variance. In addition, common method bias was unlikely to explain the hypothesized interaction effects between voice variables, geographic distance, and downstream competence as the survey respondents would have been unlikely to hypothesize interactions (Aiken & West, 1991; Evans, 1985.)

Results

Tests of hypotheses

We used hierarchical ordinary least square (OLS) regression analysis to test the study's hypotheses. Table 22.4 contains the results of these analyses. We centered component variables used for square terms or interactions to reduce possible problems of multicollinearity. All variance inflation factors (VIFs) had values lower than 5, suggesting that multicollinearity did not threaten parameter estimates. Model 1 presents the control coefficients predicting attention.

In model 2, we present results of the multiple regression analysis pertaining to Hypothesis 1a. Our prediction that the importance of the local market in which a subsidiary is located would be positively associated with headquarters' attention is supported. Indeed, the coefficients indicating the presence (through FDI) of MNEs in the subsidiary market and the relative size (as a proportion of worldwide industry sales) of this market, were both positive and significant. In model 3, a similar pattern of results emerged to support Hypothesis 1b. The coefficient measuring the strength of a subsidiary within its MNE network was positive and significant. Taken together, considerations of weight accounted for 20 percent of the explained variance in attention, compared to 12 percent for the baseline controls included in model 1.

Table 22.3 Means, standard deviations, and correlations[a]

Variables[b]	Mean	s.d.	1	2	3	4	5	6	7	8	9	10	11	12	13	14	15	16	17	18	19
1. Positive headquarters' attention	0.00	1.00																			
2. Subsidiary size	0.00	1.00	.13																		
3. Subsidiary age	33.94	29.12	-.02	.25																	
4. Subsidiary autonomy	3.39	0.94	.11	.18	.01																
5. Subsidiary performance	0.00	1.00	.07	.05	.06	.09															
6. Subsidiary functional scope	3.95	2.10	-.07	.23	.23	.01	.14														
7. Subsidiary market scope	19.84	24.10	.12	-.04	-.05	-.02	-.11	.00													
8. Geographic area structure	0.18	0.39	.10	-.29	-.12	-.16	-.08	-.04	.14												
9. Matrix structure	0.63	0.48	-.01	.18	.17	.02	.04	.05	-.02	-.61											
10. Geographic scope	14.17	16.05	-.09	.20	.28	-.06	.01	.18	-.03	-.13	.22										
11. Asia-Pacific parentage	0.32	0.93	-.04	-.13	-.07	-.08	-.06	-.10	.06	-.01	.05	-.17									
12. North American parentage	0.36	0.48	.02	.18	.10	.02	.05	.16	.02	-.03	-.04	-.05	-.26								
13. Headquarters–subsidiary cultural distance	0.92	1.02	-.03	-.30	-.11	-.09	-.08	-.21	.01	.01	.14	-.04	.56	-.62							
14. Presence of MNEs in local market	1.34	2.06	.18	.03	.01	-.04	-.03	.09	.06	.15	-.06	.02	.04	.05	-.01						
15. Local market size	2.21	3.09	.10	.09	-.04	.10	-.01	-.14	-.01	-.06	.02	-.09	.00	.06	-.07	-.04					
16. Subsidiary strength within MNE network	0.94	0.44	.27	.09	-.05	.10	.04	.07	.06	.02	-.02	-.02	.03	.06	-.04	.09	-.02				
17. Subsidiary initiative taking	2.78	1.32	.18	.31	.06	.22	.03	.32	.19	-.07	.07	.10	-.14	.16	-.19	.13	.04	.09			
18. Subsidiary profile building	0.00	1.00	.30	.14	.06	.03	.20	.11	.03	.02	.08	.13	-.03	.10	-.12	.02	-.03	.09	.10		
19. Headquarters–subsidiary geographic distance	8,027.98	6,243.81	-.08	.09	.00	.13	.11	.18	-.01	.07	-.10	.03	.06	.11	-.08	.22	-.16	-.04	-.01	.04	
20. Subsidiary downstream competence	0.51	0.27	-.05	-.12	-.02	-.04	.00	-.19	.01	.00	.12	-.02	.15	-.07	.12	-.01	.00	.01	-.10	.02	-.06

a $n = 283$; correlations above .15 are significant at the .01 level, and those above .12 are significant at the .05 level (two-tailed tests).

b "Subsidiary size" is the factor score of three items assessing total subsidiary sales, number of employees, and number of officers in the subsidiary's top management team. "Geographic area structure," "matrix structure," "Asia-Pacific parentage," and "North American parentage" are dichotomous variables and refer to the MNE level. "Local market size" is measured as sales. "Geographic distance" is computed in kilometers from the latitudes and longitude coordinates of headquarters and subsidiary city locations.

Table 22.4 Results of OLS regressions analyses[a]

Variables	Model 1		Model 2		Model 3		Model 4		Model 5		Model 6		Model 7	
Constant	-.37*	(.19)	-.52	(.19)	-.46**	(.19)	-.41*	(.19)	-.32*	(.18)	-.36*	(.18)	-.41*	(.18)
Subsidiary size	.19**	(.07)	.17**	(.07)	.15**	(.06)	.12*	(.07)	.09†	(.06)	.12*	(.06)	.11*	(.06)
Subsidiary age centered	-.01*	(.00)	-.01*	(.00)	-.01*	(.00)	-.00†	(.00)	-.00	(.00)	-.00	(.00)	-.00	(.00)
Subsidiary age squared	.00**	(.00)	.00**	(.00)	.00**	(.00)	.00**	(.00)	.00*	(.00)	.00*	(.00)	.00*	(.00)
Subsidiary autonomy	.07†	(.06)	.07	(.06)	.05	(.06)	.02	(.06)	.02	(.06)	.04	(.06)	.04	(.06)
Subsidiary performance	.10*	(.06)	.01*	(.06)	.10†	(.06)	.10	(.06)	.06	(.06)	.06	(.06)	.05	(.06)
Subsidiary performance squared	-.02	(.04)	-.02	(.04)	-.02	(.04)	-.02	(.04)	-.00	(.04)	.01	(.04)	.01	(.04)
Subsidiary functional scope	-.09†	(.06)	-.09†	(.06)	-.10*	(.06)	-.14*	(.06)	-.15***	(.06)	-.12*	(.06)	-.13*	(.06)
Subsidiary market scope	.01*	(.00)	.01*	(.00)	.00*	(.00)	.00†	(.00)	.00†	(.00)	.00	(.00)	.00†	(.00)
Geographic area structure	.49**	(.20)	.40*	(.20)	.36*	(.19)	.36*	(.19)	.24†	(.19)	.30*	(.18)	.31*	(.18)
Matrix structure	.22†	(.16)	.19	(.16)	.16	(.15)	.15	(.15)	.07	(.15)	.08	(.14)	.10	(.15)
Geographic scope	-.01**	(.00)	-.01*	(.00)	-.01*	(.00)	-.01*	(.00)	-.01***	(.00)	-.01*	(.00)	-.01**	(.00)
HQ Asia-Pacific parentage	-.07	(.08)	-.08	(.08)	-.10	(.07)	-.09	(.07)	-.11†	(.07)	-.08	(.07)	-.06	(.07)
HQ North American parentage	-.07	(.16)	.04	(.16)	.01	(.15)	-.01	(.15)	-.03	(.14)	.00	(.14)	-.01	(.14)
HQ–subsidiary cultural distance	.08	(.09)	.08	(.09)	.09	(.09)	.09	(.09)	.11†	(.08)	.11†	(.08)	.10	(.08)
H1a: Presence of MNEs in local market			.09*	(.03)	.08**	(.03)	.07***	(.03)	.07**	(.03)	.07**	(.03)	.08**	(.03)
H1a: Local market size			.04*	(.02)	.04*	(.02)	.04*	(.02)	.04*	(.02)	.03*	(.02)	.04*	(.02)
H1b: Subsidiary strength within MNE network					.50***	(.13)	.49***	(.13)	.46***	(.12)	.43***	(.12)	.41***	(.12)
H2a: Subsidiary initiative taking							.12**	(.05)	.11*	(.05)	.10*	(.05)	.09*	(.05)
H2b: Subsidiary profile building									.26***	(.06)	.27***	(.06)	.29***	(.06)
HQ–subsidiary geographic distance											-.02*	(.01)	-.02*	(.01)
H3a: Initiative taking × geographic distance											.01†	(.01)	.01*	(.01)
H3b: Profile building × geographic distance											.02**	(.01)	.02**	(.01)
Subsidiary downstream competence													-.11*	(.05)
H4a: Initiative taking × downstream competence													-.08*	(.04)
H4b: profile building × downstream competence													.09*	(.05)
R^2 (adjusted R^2)	.12	(.07)	.16	(.11)	.20	(.15)	.22	(.17)	.28	(.23)	.31	(.25)	.34	(.27)
R^2 (adjusted R^2)			.04	(.04)	.04	(.04)	.02	(.02)	.06	(.04)	.03	(.02)	.03	(.02)
F	2.43**		6.28**		14.84***		5.93**		22.09***		3.82**		3.13*	

a Unstandardized coefficients are reported; the figures in parentheses are standard errors; $n = 283$ for all models. Component variables used for square terms or interactions were centered to reduce possible problems of multicollinearity. "HQ" is "headquarters," and "H" is hypothesis.

† $p < .10$, * $p < .05$, ** $p < .01$, *** $p < .001$, One-tailed tests.

Supporting our predictions, initiative taking (model 4), and profile building (model 5), were both positively related to positive headquarters' attention and accounted for an additional 8 percent of unique variance explained. Therefore, Hypotheses 2a and 2b are supported, though it is worth noting that the effect of profile building on attention is qualitatively much stronger than the effect of initiative taking.

The results presented in model 6 support Hypotheses 3a and 3b. The main effect for the geographic distance variable was negative and statistically significant, and the interaction between profile building and geographic distance has a positive and significant ($p < .01$) coefficient, as we expected. The increase in the explained variance was also significant. The interaction between subsidiary initiative taking and geographic distance only marginally significant ($p < .10$), but it was also positive, as we expected. Following the procedures outlined by Jaccard and colleagues (Jaccard et al., 1990), decomposition of these interaction terms revealed that the simple effects of the two variables representing subsidiary voice were a positive and increasing function of geographic distance, as we predicted. Figure 22.2 is a graphic depiction of this moderating effect. It can be seen that the effect of voice becomes stronger as geographic distance increases, as Hypotheses 3a and 3b predict. Stated differently, although geographic distance tends to decrease the attention that a subsidiary receives from headquarters, this negative effect slowly diminishes with increasing levels of initiative taking and profile building. A subsidiary's voice can be used to neutralize or defeat the effect of geographic distance.

The results presented in model 7 provide mixed support for the final hypotheses. Indeed, the main effect for the downstream competence variable was negative and statistically significant and the interaction between profile building and geographic distance was positive and significant ($p < .05$), as we expected. However, the interaction between initiative taking and a downstream competence was negative and significant ($p < .05$). Therefore, Hypothesis 4b is supported but Hypothesis 4a is not. Figure 22.3 is a graphic depiction of the contrasting moderating effects associated with this pattern of results. In contrast to profile building, initiative taking does not seem to constitute a particularly effective mechanism for capturing positive headquarters attention when a subsidiary's competence (as well as its perceived competences and contributions to an MNE network) is confined to the downstream part of the value chain. As Figure 22.3 indicates, initiative taking is perhaps better suited to those subsidiary units

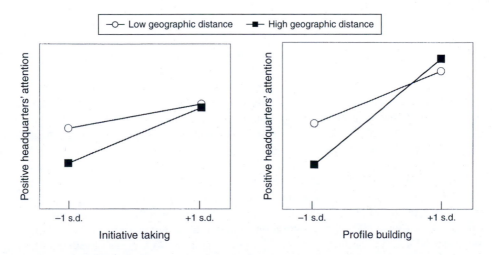

Figure 22.2 Moderating effect of geographic distance.

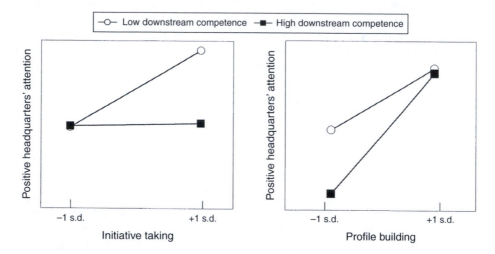

Figure 22.3 Moderating effect of downstream competence.

that have "evolved" toward competences that extend to such activities as manufacturing, R&D, and strategic support activities.

Although these interaction effects were contributing about 6 percent of additional variance in total, they were significant even after we controlled for many important characteristics operating at multiple levels of analysis. In particular, it would appear that the geographic scope of an MNE, the way it is structurally organized (its geographic area orientation) and specific attributes of its local context (the age and size of a subsidiary) all have significant bearing on a subsidiary's capacity to effectively capture positive attention from headquarters. We also conducted additional analyses to determine if joint interactions existed between structural and relational determinants, but these supplemental analyses yielded no significant results.

Post hoc analyses

To further verify our findings and gain additional insight into the details of our statistical analysis, we estimated two additional regression models. First, we used a general linear model (GLM) multivariate procedure to predict the relative, supportive, and visible aspects of attention as a joint set of three related dimensions. The significant multivariate effect was consistent with those reported above for our OLS regressions, in which we treated attention as a composite variable. With respect to structural determinants, the measures indicating the presence of multinationals within a local subsidiary market and subsidiary strength within its MNE network offered by far the best indicators of weight. Both variables were significantly related to all three attention subconstructs. In this model, we also found that if initiative taking represented a useful voice strategy for earning attention, this effect was primarily gained through the relative dimension. Profile building, on the other hand, was found to exert a much more robust influence on attention. It had a direct and significant relationship with both relative attention and supportive attention, as well as a link to visible attention through a significant and positive interaction with geographic distance.

Because attention may not always correspond to a desirable state, we estimated an additional statistical model in which the dependent variable was headquarters control, measured as the average of a six-item scale ($\alpha = .74$) assessing the frequency (from less than once a year, to monthly, weekly and daily) with which corporate headquarters reviewed subsidiary actions and decisions (for example, operating expenditures, quality control assessments, budgeting process, resource allocation, capital equipment purchases and strategic business plans) (O'Donnell, 2000). Of our predictor variables, subsidiary initiatives was positively related to headquarters control ($p < .005$) and distance was negatively related to it ($p < .001$). Also, a downstream competence was positively related to headquarters control ($p < .005$), bringing some support to the empire-building arguments evoked in Hypothesis 4b. The interaction between initiative taking and a downstream competence was positive and significant. This represents a particularly interesting finding, in terms of the key arguments in this article, as it would appear that *initiative taking only attracts positive headquarters' attention when a subsidiary's competence extends to the upstream part of the value chain*. When a subsidiary's competence involves more location bound assets, initiative taking is likely to result in greater control from headquarters. Subsidiaries in this position may benefit from strong track records, as additional analysis revealed that this particular dimension of profile building was negatively related to headquarters control. In terms of the control variables, the geographic scope of an MNE ($p < .005$), subsidiary autonomy ($p < .001$) and the square term for subsidiary age ($p < .005$) were negatively related to headquarters control, but subsidiary size was positively related to headquarters control ($p < .005$).

Discussion

In this study, we adopted a multimethod approach to understanding how foreign subsidiary units gain positive attention from headquarters while also generating new insights into the mechanisms and processes at work in the sample MNEs. We found strong evidence that the attention given to a foreign subsidiary is not simply influenced by structural considerations of weight; the voice of a subsidiary critically matters. In addition, our study also identifies a relevant set of contingencies that contribute to improving researchers' understanding of when being vocal is most likely to generate positive outcomes for a subsidiary. This study raises important issues for both theory and practice.

Implications for theory

We make several contributions to the understanding of "attention markets" in organizations (Dutton & Ashford, 1993; Hansen & Haas, 2001; Ocasio, 1997). First, we provide a careful operationalization of attention in an MNE context. Despite the considerable amount of research on attention management in recent years, there have been few serious attempts to operationalize the core construct. We therefore adopted a grounded approach to this research by interviewing 24 executives and then pulling together their responses and reconciling them with concepts from previous research before ending up with our multidimensional construct. As a result of our research, we can state that the positive attention of an MNE has three elements: a supportive element, expressed in the ways headquarters executives interact with and help a subsidiary's managers achieve their goals; a visible element, expressed in the public statements headquarters executives make about how the subsidiary is doing; and a relative element, expressed in the subsidiary's perceived status vis-à-vis other subsidiaries in the corporate network. Conceptualized in this broadly positive way, attention is distinct from headquarters control and compliance, which have negative connotations. Parenthetically, it is also interesting to observe that a subsidiary may receive *too much* attention. As we discovered during our research interviews, many managers of Chinese subsidiaries have found themselves in this position in recent years; the result is high and often unreasonable expectations for subsidiary performance and a constant drain on time from visits of corporate executives.

The second major contribution of our study is to provide a general model of how subsidiaries gain the attention of MNE executives that integrates several important theoretical perspectives found in the pertinent literature. In particular, our research highlights two complementary processes through which headquarters' attention is shaped. There is a *top-down structural process* whereby attention is allocated according to a subsidiary's weight in an MNE, and there is a *bottom-up relational process* whereby attention is earned according to the subsidiary's voice in the MNE. This model has obvious parallels with Burgelman's (1983) process theory of strategy, but it adds a layer of precision in one important respect. Specifically, Burgelman (1983) adopted a very broad view of an organization's "strategic context"; the political process through which bottom-up, or "autonomous", behavior gets rationalized and translated into changes in corporate strategy. Our approach to headquarters' attention can be viewed as one way of operationalizing strategic context. It is certainly narrower in scope than Burgelman's definition, but it has the important advantages of being both measurable and meaningful to practicing managers.

Third, we consider the strategies that organizational units deploy to attract headquarters' attention. Although the notion of voice has been discussed elsewhere (for example, Morrison & Phelps, 1999), as far as we know our study constitutes the first empirical attempt to directly extend this line of thinking to the level of the subsidiary *unit* itself. It is clear from the statistical analysis described earlier, and from our conversations with executives, that initiative taking and profile building constitute important drivers of MNE attention, particularly for those subsidiaries located far away from headquarters. In this respect, it is interesting to observe that the ability to capture attention is by no means straightforward. Taking the initiative—perhaps by pursuing opportunities in emerging market segments that no other subsidiary is pursuing—works best for a subsidiary that has developed competencies in upstream parts of the value chain (such as R&D and manufacturing). Profile-building activities have a more robust impact on headquarters' attention, but their deployment requires a subsidiary to be committed to an integrated set of priorities. Our findings suggest that, to be successful in shaping the perception that it is a reliable, credible, and trustworthy actor in an MNE organization, a subsidiary not only needs to maintain a basic track record of success, but also needs to reaffirm its commitment to the parent's objectives; then it needs to take deliberate steps to manage impressions with power brokers at the head office. Achieving all three sets of objectives is by no means straightforward.

Finally, our findings hint at some important issues in the dynamics of change for multiunit organizations. The concept of attention potentially represents a "missing link" between studies of unit-level entrepreneurship (for example, Birkinshaw, 2000) and resource-based notions of competitive advantage. Although multiunit organizations such as MNEs may generate advantages through the heterogeneous bundles of assets and capabilities that exist in their networks of subsidiaries, very little research has been concerned with *how* subsidiary-specific advantages get transformed into firm-specific assets (Rugman & Verbeke, 2001). Our focus on attention highlights one important mechanism by which this transformation is achieved. Specifically, we suggest that subsidiary voice is an internally generated stimulus for changing headquarters' attention (there could also be externally generated stimuli, such as media interest in a particular market), that in turn influences the internal strategic context for decision making in an MNE (Burgelman, 1983) and therefore influences choices about which markets to invest in and focus on. These choices can, over time, result in significant changes to the weight of a subsidiary, or its strategic role, within the MNE's portfolio. So although the level of headquarters' attention will not always be directly aligned with the strategic role of a subsidiary, it plays an important part in influencing any long-term changes to that role.

Implications for practice

The practical implications of this research should be immediately apparent. For managers of foreign subsidiaries, attention is a vital commodity. With a few notable exceptions, such as subsidiary managers in China and India at the moment, most subsidiary managers would argue they do not get the level of attention they need or deserve. What emerges from this research is clear evidence that headquarters priorities can be influenced from the bottom up. To be clear, this is not an entirely surprising finding, because many researchers over the years have argued that subsidiaries need to be vocal in support of their own achievements. But it is important nonetheless, because it provides clear evidence that parent companies can view initiative-taking and profile-building efforts positively (rather than as unnecessary or annoying lobbying). The results suggest three specific things subsidiary managers can do. First, a manager can develop a position of strength within the MNE network for his or her subsidiary (by, for instance, undertaking activities upon which sister subsidiaries are dependent; most likely in the upstream part of the value chain); a key part of the job of country managers is to take initiatives that contribute to nurturing and augmenting this position of strength. Second, the manager can view the foreign subsidiary itself as a nexus of relationships: significant value can be generated over time in the course of maintaining a good profile.[8] Third, attention is a key mechanism for influencing the priorities of headquarters executives and—as we just explained—the future role of the subsidiary company. When an executive finds ways to manage attention that are to his or her subsidiary's advantage, the subsidiary can become a more salient entity within its corporate system.

For headquarters executives, the research highlights the need to be open to stimuli from multiple sources when assessing the capabilities and potential of subsidiary companies. Most MNEs are highly effective at using their standard reporting tools to monitor past and current performance, and they implicitly allocate attention according to those measures. This research highlights, in addition, the importance of careful market intelligence, often gained through external sources and internal representations from the individuals running subsidiaries around the world, as inputs into the strategic priorities of MNEs. There is no simple way of weighing the relative importance of these different sources of information, but at the very least it is important that multiple "attention channels" exist if important new insights are to emerge.

Limitations and extensions

This study has several limitations that we should acknowledge. First, although the sample extends the scope of research to subsidiary units based in Australia, Canada and the United Kingdom, the results could be moderated by the noted propensity of organizations in these countries to innovate as a way to more rapidly increase their influence in the corporate world (Birkinshaw, 2000). Future research could provide insight into the applicability of this study's results for samples drawn from other host country settings. Second, we conducted our study with measures derived from archival sources (i.e., the visible aspects of attention expressed in the firms' annual reports) and survey measures compiled at the subsidiary level. A useful extension would be to capture the point of view of headquarters respondents. The possibility of common method bias is a concern (Podsakoff et al., 2003), yet the careful design procedures adopted in the construction and administration of our survey questionnaire and the statistical CFA tests reported earlier, provide reinsurance that the observed findings are not common methods artifacts. Two key findings in this study are interaction effects, which are unlikely to be the spurious result of correlated measurement errors (Aiken & West, 1991: 155; Evans, 1985). Further evidence is found in the results of our post hoc analyses. Common method bias would have produced consistent effects of the profile-building and initiative-taking variables on the three types of dependent variables measuring attention, yet slightly different effects were observed. Ordinary forms of common method bias are not consistent with this pattern.

Third, although we examined two important sets of factors—weight and voice—critical to attention decisions in MNEs, we did not view our framework as comprehensive. In fact, our statistical analysis reveals that the way an MNE is organized (for example, its formal structure and geographic scope) creates strict constraints on the allocation of headquarters' attention that certainly transcend weight and voice considerations. The interviews we conducted also revealed that companies are managing headquarters' attention through different types of organizational design approaches. Some are trying to improve the ease of attention flows by promoting communal types of bonds throughout their worldwide organizations.[9] Others are adding regional headquarters to their organizational charts, only to find out this additional layer of complexity can in fact cause a lot of grief. A grand theory of attention decisions in MNEs would include organizational design factors in addition to the ones included in our study. Moreover, we also limited our conceptualization of voice to an examination of initiative-taking and profile-building activities. Research in organizational behavior suggests that effective voice strategies may sometimes include certain shades of "silence" (Milliken & Morrison, 2003). Reflecting this point of view, our interviews revealed instances in which keeping a low profile led to clear practical advantages.[10] Presumably, headquarters executives do not need to know about all subsidiary developments because the sheer volume of inputs would be quite overwhelming. Future studies could examine the functionality of subsidiary silence in an MNE, rather than simply assume that silence always reduces influence. One could also argue that receiving attention is not always a desirable state from a subsidiary's viewpoint. One company that we surveyed for this study, 3M, recently reacted to the disappointing results of its Canadian subsidiary by almost completely replacing local management. Four out of five vice presidents were let go; the Canadian CEO who completed our survey was moved to a lesser position in the United States; and a substantial number of middle-level managers were replaced. The conditions leading to such drastic interventions on the part of headquarters managers are yet to be fully understood. Studies attempting to operationalize the concept "negative headquarters' attention" would be a useful extension to the present study.

Finally, our research design did not, of course, allow us to test causality. Our expectation is that most of the observed relationships exhibit reciprocal causality, so that, for example, initiative taking and profile building lead to more positive attention, while at the same time higher levels of positive attention likely increase a subsidiary's level of initiative taking and profile building (a form of "Hawthorne effect"). But this reciprocal relationship is unlikely to be entirely symmetrical. Recall that our conceptualization of attention suggests a high level of inertia in how attention is allocated among subsidiaries. Absent major changes at a geopolitical level (such as the opening up of China to foreign investment), the attention allocated to a subsidiary from above changes very slowly, so it is unlikely to be the stimulus for dramatic changes in initiative taking or profile building by subsidiary managers. Rather, the evidence collected in this and earlier work is that these activities are the internal stimuli for change. They typically lead to increases in attention from a subsidiary's parent company, which in turn reinforce the efforts of subsidiary managers in taking initiative and promoting their efforts. Of course it would be useful for research to examine these issues on a longitudinal basis to establish clearly the causal nature of the relationships we observed, but for the moment this logical inference is as far as we can go.

In conclusion, the purpose of this study was to use the concept of attention to shed new light on the dynamics of headquarters–subsidiary relationships in MNEs. This fresh approach allowed this study to develop rich insights into the mechanisms by which subsidiaries actively gain or lose the positive attention of their parent companies, in contrast to previous studies, such as those rooted in agency theory or control theory, whose authors have assumed that such choices are driven exclusively from above. The current research therefore helps to explain how a subsidiary company can take charge of its own destiny and how corporate headquarters managers can more effectively allocate their attention and efforts across their portfolio of international operations.

Notes

We would like to thank Duane Ireland, two anonymous *AMJ* reviewers, Tina Ambos, Jean-Philippe Bo-nardi, Lex Donaldson, Moshe Farjoun, Tony Frost, Anoop Madhok, Allen Morrison, Charles McMillan and Bernie Wolf, as well as the organizers and participants of the "New Perspectives on Subsidiary Management Research" workshop in Newcastle, Australia, for their very helpful suggestions on drafts. Tina Ambos, Hamid Hak-bari, Liza Mercier (from York's Institute for Social Research), Yesim Ozalp, and Serdar Yaruz also helped with data collection. Support from the Advanced Institute of Management Research (AIM), the Social Sciences and Humanities Research Council of Canada (Grant #4102005-2079), and International Management Australia is gratefully acknowledged.

1 Many MNEs have distributed headquarters operations, with some executives in the global office and others in regional headquarters. Although we conceptualized headquarters as the set of executives with central (non-business-specific) responsibilities, in practice we operationalize the concept as the corporate or global (rather than regional) set of executives. We did this to avoid any confusion among respondents, some of whom had regional headquarters and some of whom did not.

2 In psychology, for example, William James wrote: "Every-one knows what attention is. It is the taking possession by the mind in clear and vivid form of one out of what seem several simultaneous objects or trains of thought" (1890: 403–4). Yet Moray (1969) proposed seven distinct uses of the term, which included the concentration of mental resources as a way to improve task performance; the act of vigilance, in which a person monitors the environment in the hope of detecting something; selective filtering; oriented search; activation; and set, whereby an attending actor demonstrates a readiness to respond in a certain way.

3 These two dimensions can be interpreted as constituting the subsidiary's *strategic role* in its MNE, though as noted earlier we prefer not to use the term "strategic role" as it is sometimes confused with attention. Other variables are also sometimes used to define subsidiary roles, such as "level of autonomy" and "size," and these are controlled for in the analysis.

4 This concept is distinct from that of subsidiary performance, which we include as a control variable.

5 For example, one subsidiary president observed: "Getting attention is about establishing credibility and it doesn't happen within a short period of time. People need time to evaluate how you run a business. If you demonstrate predictability and results over time, you start to build a confidence that ultimately works in your favor."

6 One manager we interviewed commented: "In terms of getting attention, there's an enormous amount of pre-selling that goes on. For example, if we have a project which we know we're going to put up the line, I will go out and pre-sell this to my boss, I'll pre-sell it to the business development people or the worldwide marketing teams, so by the time it gets to discussion at the executive team, we already have a number of support pillars in place. It's unusual at that stage that people turn around and say, 'I didn't know about this,' or, 'I don't feel comfortable with this,' because you've already had that discussion."

7 In the specific context of an MNE, attention is often evoked in general terms as a type of parental intervention by which headquarters executives are able to recognize and support promising subsidiary developments, such as new technologies and emerging customer needs in various parts of the world (e.g., Rugman & Verbeke, 2001). The limited attention of decision makers at headquarters typically means that subsidiaries compete for this scarce resource, a challenge often described as particularly daunting for subsidiaries, particularly those located at the periphery of the world economy (Doz et al., 2001).

8 Several of the subsidiary executives we spoke to had specific advice on how impressions get formed. One talked a great deal about the pre-selling process—getting all the interested parties involved at an early stage and "oiling the wheels" of the organization so that when the formal proposal is presented it encounters no resistance. Another talked about the importance of timing: "If you tell the story too early, you risk getting shot down or building up unreasonable expectations; if you tell it too late, and they get mad, you will struggle to get support." Much of this, of course, is common sense to a seasoned executive, but it is interesting to observe the amount of careful planning that often goes into a successful campaign to exert the subsidiary voice.

9 One individual we interviewed observed: "Australia is a really pretty small fry, a spoke in a big wheel, but it is amazing how much attention we get. You could walk into any office around the world and know you're in a [company X] office. You talk the same language. There is very much a family culture right throughout the world, and no matter how big or small the operation is, you get attention."

10 The following interview segment illustrates this line of thinking: "You are naive if you don't keep some things up your sleeve. You have to manage expectations, which involves not telling the whole story until you are ready. So I act as a buffer."

References

Agrawal, A., Kapur, D., & McHale, J. 2006. How do spatial and social proximity influence knowledge flows? Evidence from patent data. *Journal of Urban Economics*.

Aiken, L. S., & West, S. G. 1991. *Multiple regression: Testing and interpreting regressions*. London: Sage.

Anderson, J. C., & Gerbing, D. W. 1988. Structural equation modeling in practice: A review and recommended two-step approach. *Psychological Bulletin*, 103: 411–23.

Armstrong, J. S., & Overton, T. S. 1977. Estimating non-response bias in mail surveys. *Journal of Marketing Research*, 14: 396–402.

Bagozzi, R. P., & Phillips, L. W. 1982. Representing and testing organizational theories: A holistic construal. *Administrative Science Quarterly*, 27: 459–89.

Bartlett, C., & Ghoshal, S. 1986. Tap your subsidiaries for global reach. *Harvard Business Review*, 64(6): 87–94.

Bartlett, C. A., & Ghoshal, S. 1989. *Managing across borders: The transnational solution*. Boston: Harvard Business School Press.

Bartlett, C. A., & Ghoshal, S. 1994. Changing the role of top management: Beyond strategy to purpose. *Harvard Business Review*, 72(6): 79–88.

Benson, J. K. 1975. Interorganizational network as a political economy. *Administrative Science Quarterly*, 20: 229–49.

Birkinshaw, J. M. 2000. *Entrepreneurship in the global firm*. London: Sage.

Birkinshaw, J., & Hood, N. 1998. Multinational subsidiary evolution: Capability and charter change in foreign-owned subsidiary companies. *Academy of Management Review*, 23: 773–95.

Birkinshaw, J., Hood, N., & Jonsson, S. 1998. Building firm-specific advantages in multinational corporations: The role of subsidiary initiative. *Strategic Management Journal*, 19: 221–41.

Black, J. S., & Gregersen, H. B. 1992. Serving two masters: Managing the dual allegiance of expatriate employees. *Sloan Management Review*, 33(4): 61–71.

Bollen, K. A. 1989. *Structural equations with latent variables*. New York: Wiley.

Bouquet, C. 2005. *Building global mindsets: An attention perspective*. London: Palgrave Macmillan.

Buckley, P., & Carter, M. I. 2004. A formal analysis of knowledge combination in multinational enterprises. *Journal of International Business Studies*, 35: 371–84.

Burgelman, R. A. 1983. A model of the interaction of strategic behavior, corporate context, and the concept of strategy. *Academy of Management Review*, 8: 61–70.

Butterfield, K. D., Trevino, L. K., & Ball, G. A. 1996. Punishment from the manager's perspective: A grounded investigation and inductive model. *Academy of Management Journal*, 39: 1479–512.

Chandler, A. D. 1991. The functions of the HQ unit in the multibusiness firm. *Strategic Management Journal*, 12: 31–50.

Cho, T. S., & Hambrick, D. C. 2006. Attention as the mediator between top management team characteristics and strategic change: The case of airline deregulation. *Organization Science*, 17: 453–69.

Christensen, C. 1997. *The innovator's dilemma*. Boston: Harvard Business School Press.

Collins, R. 1998. *The sociology of philosophies: A global theory of intellectual change*. Cambridge, MA: Belknap.

Coval, J. D., & Moskowitz, T. J. 1999. Home bias at home: Local equity preference in domestic portfolios. *Journal of Finance*, 54: 2045–73.

Cyert, R. M., & March, J. G. 1963. *A behavioral theory of the firm*. Englewood Cliffs, NJ: Prentice-Hall.

D'Aveni, R., & MacMillan, I. C. 1990. Crisis and the content of managerial communications: A study of the focus of attention of top managers in surviving and failing firms. *Administrative Science Quarterly*, 35: 634–57.

Delios, A., & Beamish, P. W. 1999. Geographic scope, product diversification, and the corporate performance of Japanese firms. *Strategic Management Journal*, 20: 711–27.

Dillman, D. A. 2000. *Mail and Internet surveys: The tailored design method* (2nd ed.). New York: Wiley.

Doz, Y. L., Santos, J., & Williamson, P. 2001. *From global to metanational: How companies win in the knowledge economy*. Boston: Harvard Business School Press.

Doz, Y. L., Santos, J., & Williamson, P. J. 2004. Marketing myopia re-visited: Why every company needs to learn from the world. *Ivey Business Journal*, 68(3): 1–6.

Dunning, J. H. 1998. Location and the multinational enterprise: A neglected factor. *Journal of International Business Studies*, 29: 45–66.

Dutton, J. E. 1997. Strategic agenda building in organizations. In Z. Shapira (Ed.), *Organizational decision making*: 81–105. Cambridge, U.K.: Cambridge University Press.

Dutton, J. E., & Ashford, S. J. 1993. Selling issues to top management. *Academy of Management Review*, 18: 397–428.

Dutton, J. E., Ashford, S. J., O'Neill, R., & Lawrence, K. A. 2001. Moves that matter: Issue selling and organizational change. *Academy of Management Journal*, 44: 716–36.

Dutton, J. E., Walton, E. J., & Abrahamson, E. 1989. Important dimensions of strategic issues: Separating the wheat from the chaff. *Journal of Management Studies*, 26: 379–96.

Evans, M. G. 1985. A Monte Carlo study of the effects of correlated method variance in moderated multiple-regression analysis. *Organizational Behavior and Human Decision Processes*, 36: 305–23.

Fisher, C. D. 1993. Boredom at work. *Human Relations*, 46: 395–417.

Fiske, S. T., & Taylor, S. 1984. *Social cognition*. New York: Random House.

Forsgren, M., & Pedersen, T. 2000. Subsidiary influence and corporate learning: Centers of excellence in Danish foreign-owned firms. In U. Holm & T. Pedersen (Eds.), *The emergence and impact of MNC centers of excellence*: 68–78. London: Macmillan.

Fowler, F. J. 1993. *Survey research methods* (2nd ed.). Newbury Park, CA: Sage.

Frost, T., Birkinshaw, J. M., & Ensign, S. 2002. Centers of excellence in multinational corporations. *Strategic Management Journal*, 23: 997–1018.

Galbraith, J. R. 2000. *Designing the global corporation*. San Francisco: Jossey-Bass.

Galunic, D. C., & Eisenhardt, K. M. 1996. The evolution of intracorporate domains: Divisional charter losses in high-technology, multidivisional corporations. *Organization Science*, 7: 255–82.

Galunic, D. C., & Eisenhardt, K. M. 2001. Architectural innovation and modular corporate forms. *Academy of Management Journal*, 44: 1229–49.

Gardner, W. L., & Martinko, M. J. 1988. Impression management in organizations. *Journal of Management*, 14: 321–38.

Ghemawat, P. 2001. Distance still matters—The hard reality of global expansion. *Harvard Business Review*, 79(8): 137–47.

Ghoshal, S., & Bartlett, C. A. 1990. The multinational corporation as an interorganizational network. *Academy of Management Review*, 15: 603–25.

Glaser, B. G., & Strauss, A. L. 1967. *The discovery of grounded theory*. Chicago: Aldine.

Goold, M., Alexander, M., & Campbell, A. 1994. *Corporate-level strategy creating value in the multibusiness company*. New York: Wiley.

Gregersen, H. B., & Black, J. S. 1992. Antecedents to commitment to a parent company and a foreign operation. *Academy of Management Journal*, 35: 65–90.

Hansen, M. T., & Haas, M. R. 2001. Competing for attention in knowledge markets: Electronic document dissemination in a management consulting company. *Administrative Science Quarterly*, 46: 1–28.

Hansen, M. T., & Lovas, B. 2004. Leveraging technological competences. *Strategic Management Journal*, 25: 801–22.

Harzing, A. W. 2000. Cross national industrial mail surveys: Why do response rates differ between countries. *Industrial Marketing Management*, 29: 243–54.

Helliwell, J. F. 2002. *Globalization and well-being*. Vancouver: UBC Press.

Hewett, K., & Bearden, W. O. 2001. Dependence, trust, and relational behavior on the part of foreign subsidiary marketing operations: Implications for managing global marketing operations. *Journal of Marketing*, 65: 51–66.

Hewett, K., Roth, M. S., & Roth, K. 2003. Conditions influencing headquarters and foreign subsidiary roles in marketing activities and their effects on performance. *Journal of International Business Studies*, 34: 567–85.

Hickson, D. J., Hinings, C. R., Lee, C. A., Schneck, R. E., & Pennings, J. M. 1971. A strategic contingencies' theory of intraorganizational power. *Administrative Science Quarterly*, 16: 216–29.

Hirschman, A. O. 1970. *Exit, voice, and loyalty: Responses to decline in firms, organizations, and states*. Cambridge, MA: Harvard University Press.

Hofstede, G. 1991. *Culture and organizations*. New York: McGraw-Hill.

Hu, Y. S. 1995. The international transferability of the firm's advantages. *California Management Review*, 37(4): 73–88.

Huff, A. S. 1990. *Mapping strategic thought*. Chichester, U.K.: Wiley.

Jaccard, J., Turrisi, R., & Wan, C. K. 1990. *Interaction effects in multiple regression*. Newbury Park, CA: Sage.

James, W. 1890. *The principles of psychology*. New York: Dover.

Jarillo, J. C., & Martinez, J. I. 1990. Different roles for subsidiaries—The case of multinational corporations in Spain. *Strategic Management Journal*, 11: 501–12.

Jones, B. D., & Baumgartner, F. R. 2005. *The politics of attention: How government prioritizes problems*. Chicago: University of Chicago Press.

Kline, R. B. 2005. *Principles and practice of structural equation modeling* (2nd ed.). New York: Guilford Press.

Law, K. S., Wong, C.-S., & Mobley, W., H. 1998. Toward a taxonomy of multidimensional constructs. *Academy of Management Review*, 23: 741–55.

Lawrence, P. R. & Lorsch, J. W. 1967. Differentiation and integration in complex organizations. *Administrative Science Quarterly*, 12: 1–47.

Levy, O. 2005. The influence of top management team attention patterns on global strategic posture of firms. *Journal of Organizational Behavior*, 26: 797–819.

Ling, Y., Floyd, S. W., & Baldridge, D. C. 2005. Toward a model of issue-selling by subsidiary managers in multinational organizations. *Journal of International Business Studies*, 36: 637–54.

Luo, Y. 2003. Market-seeking MNEs in an emerging market: How parent–subsidiary links shape overseas success. *Journal of International Business Studies*, 34: 290–309.

Luo, Y. D. 2005. Toward coopetition within a multinational enterprise: A perspective from foreign subsidiaries. *Journal of World Business*, 40(1): 71–90.

March, J. G., & Olsen, J. P. 1976. *Ambiguity and choice in organizations.* Bergen, Norway: Universitetsforlaget.

Marshall, A. 1920. *Principles of economics.* London: Macmillan.

Miller, S. R., & Eden, L. 2006. Local density and foreign subsidiary performance. *Academy of Management Journal*, 49: 341–56.

Milliken, F. J., & Morrison, E. W. 2003. Shades of silence: Emerging themes and future directions for research on silence in organizations. *Journal of Management Studies*, 40: 1563–68.

Monteiro, F., Arvidsson, N., & Birkinshaw, J. M. 2007. Knowledge flows in multinational corporations: Explaining subsidiary isolation and its performance implications. *Organization Science*, 19: 90–107.

Moray, N. 1969. *Listening and attention.* Harmondsworth, U.K.: Penguin.

Morgan, R. M., & Hunt, S. D. 1994. The commitment–trust theory of relationship marketing. *Journal of Marketing*, 58(3): 20–38.

Morrison, E. W., & Milliken, F. J. 2000. Organizational silence: A barrier to change and development in a pluralistic world. *Academy of Management Review*, 25: 706–25.

Morrison, E. W., & Milliken, F. J. 2003. Speaking up, remaining silent: The dynamics of voice and silence in organizations—Guest editors' introduction. *Journal of Management Studies*, 40: 1353–58.

Morrison, E. W., & Phelps, C. C. 1999. Taking charge at work: Extrarole efforts to initiate workplace change. *Academy of Management Journal*, 42: 403–19.

Mudambi, R., & Navarra, P. 2004. Is knowledge power? Knowledge flows, subsidiary power and rent-seeking within MNCs. *Journal of International Business Studies*, 35: 385–406.

Nohria, N., & Ghoshal, S. 1997. *The differentiated network: Organizing multinational corporations for value creation.* San Francisco: Jossey-Bass.

Ocasio, W. 1997. Towards an attention-based view of the firm. *Strategic Management Journal*, 18 (summer special issue): 187–206.

Ocasio, W., & Joseph, J. 2005. An attention-based theory of strategy formulation: Linking micro- and macroperspectives in strategy processes. *Advances in Strategic Management: Strategy Process*, 22: 39–61.

O'Donnell, S. W. 2000. Managing foreign subsidiaries: Agents of headquarters, or an interdependent network? *Strategic Management Journal*, 21: 525–48.

Perlmutter, H. V. 1969. The tortuous evolution of the multinational corporation. *Columbia Journal of World Business*, 4(1): 9–18.

Podsakoff, P. M., MacKenzie, S. B., Lee, J. Y., & Podsakoff, N. P. 2003. Common method biases in behavioral research: A critical review of the literature and recommended remedies. *Journal of Applied Psychology*, 88: 879–903.

Porter, M. E. 2000. Location, competition, and economic development: Local clusters in a global economy. *Economic Development Quarterly*, 14(1): 15–34.

Prahalad, C. K., & Doz, Y. L. 1987. *The multinational mission.* New York: Free Press.

Ricart, J. E., Enright, M. J., Ghemawat, P., Hart, S. L., & Khanna, T. 2004. New frontiers in international strategy. *Journal of International Business Studies*, 35: 175–200.

Roth, K., & O'Donnell, S. 1996. Foreign subsidiary compensation strategy: An agency theory perspective. *Academy of Management Journal*, 39: 678–703.

Rugman, A. M., & Verbeke, A. 2001. Subsidiary-specific advantages in multinational enterprises. *Strategic Management Journal*, 22: 237–50.

Schlenker, B. R. 1980. *Impression management*. Monterey, CA: Brooks/Cole.

Schulz, M. 2001. The uncertain relevance of newness: Organizational learning and knowledge flows. *Academy of Management Journal*, 44: 661–81.

Sharma, S. 2000. Managerial interpretations and organizational context as predictors of corporate choice of environmental strategy. *Academy of Management Journal*, 43: 681–97.

Simon, H. A. 1947. *Administrative behavior: A study of decision-making processes in administrative organizations* (2nd ed.). New York: Macmillan.

Thornton, P. H. 2004. *Markets from culture: Institutional logics and organizational decisions in higher education publishing*. Stanford: Stanford Business Books.

White, R. E., & Poynter, T. A. 1984. Strategies for foreign-owned subsidiaries in Canada. *Business Quarterly*, 49(2): 59–69.

Williamson, O. E. 1975. *Markets and hierarchies: Analysis and antitrust implications*. New York: Free Press.

Appendix A: Preliminary field research

We focused our preliminary interviews on the Australian affiliates of some major MNEs. This particular group was well suited for the generation of a rich set of ideas and insights: the population of established subsidiary units from which to solicit interviews was large and many seemed to operate in a position of strength within their firm system; at the same time there are also good publicized examples of "isolated" subsidiaries that continuously struggled to attract the interest of strategic headquarters. To improve access, we solicited and secured the help of the International CEO Forum, the Australian partner of the U.K.-based Economist Group, which provides comprehensive business briefing and networking services for about 200 country managers, chief financial officers (CFOs) and other senior executives of subsidiary companies operating in Australia. The Forum regularly holds high-level round-tables among its members to discuss particular sets of competitiveness issues. In the summer of 2004, we utilized the Economist Group's contacts to organize two roundtables around the topic "managing headquarters' attention". Table A1 lists all participating senior executives.

We found it necessary to organize eight additional interviews; these were with the regional president (Australia, Middle East and Africa) of Abott Laboratories; the respective CEOs of Yum! Restaurants International (YRI), Australia, Dun & Bradstreet, Australia, Mercer, Australia, and Siemens, Australia; the managing director of Oracle, Australia; the president and

Table A1 Interview participants

Roundtable 1	Roundtable 2
Managing director and chief executive officer, 3M President and chief executive officer, ABB Chief executive officer, Alcatel	Chairman and chief executive officer, ATOFINA Managing director, Henkel Group vice president, Illinois Tool Works
Country president and managing director, Alstom	Construction Products Chief executive officer, Cargill
Managing director, Dupont	Managing director, PZ Cussons
Chief executive officer, HSBC Bank	Chairman and managing director, Robert Bosch
Managing director, Manpower Services	Managing director, Sara Lee Household and Body Care
Chief financial officer, ABN Amro	Managing director, STIHL

CEO of Unilever, Canada; and the vice president for corporate development of ABB. These interviews provided further insights that helped to refine our conceptualization of attention and the emerging framework for the present study.

A semistructured format (Butterfield et al., 1996; Glaser & Strauss, 1967) was followed for all interviews. After briefly introducing the research project, we asked interviewees to describe their views and company experiences on the relevant set of issues. We found it frequently necessary to probe for additional comments, illustrations, and insights along the following question lines:

1   How would you describe the main changes underway in the global organization?
2   How do they affect your subsidiary unit? Are you seeing a reduction in the power base that you have?
3   What does the term "attention" mean to you? Are you getting all the attention you need from HQ?
4   What are you doing about it? Are there things that you can do to improve your status within the firm system?

All interviews were about an hour and a half long and were audiotaped and transcribed. The information obtained through these interviews generated several recording units (relevant and coherent interview segments for which a single meaning structure could be generated) on the forms that headquarters' attention could take. These insights were then organized into three unifying themes, corresponding to the *relative*, *supportive* and *visible* aspects of attention. One of us returned to Australia to debrief a broader audience of subsidiary executives at one of the international CEO forums on the study's findings. This additional step allowed us to build further face validity into our conceptual framework and ensure the insights we present are useful both for theory and practice.

Appendix B: Operationalization of control variables

Subsidiary-level factors

For *subsidiary size*, we considered total sales, total number of employees and the size of the top team and found high correlations among these variables (greater than .50). All three variables loaded on one factor with a high eigenvalue, high explained variance (72 percent), and high interitem reliability ($\alpha = .86$). We used the corresponding factor score as our measure of subsidiary size. *Subsidiary age* was measured in years with data from the *Directory of Corporate Affiliations*. For *subsidiary performance*, respondents were asked to rate, on a seven-point Likert scale, their subsidiary's performance relative to their corporation as a whole over the past five years. We used four items: market share, return on investment, profit and cash flow from operations. All three variables loaded on one factor with a high eigenvalue and high explained variance (70 percent); interitem reliability was good ($\alpha = .85$). We used the corresponding factor score to measure subsidiary performance.

Subsidiary autonomy was measured with five items: "discontinuing a major existing product or product line", "investing in major plant or equipment to expand manufacturing capacity", "formulating and approving your subsidiary's annual budgets", "increasing (beyond budget) expenditures for research and development" and "subcontracting out large portions of the manufacturing (instead of expanding the subsidiary's own facilities)". These were measured on a five-point scale as follows: 1 = "the subsidiary's opinion is not asked; decision is explained to subsidiary by corporate headquarters", 2 = "proposal by corporate headquarters, but the subsidiary's opinion carries little weight", 3 = "proposal by corporate headquarters, and the subsidiary's opinion carries a lot of weight", 4 = "proposal by the subsidiary, decision made jointly by you and corporate headquarters", 5 = "decision made by the subsidiary without much consultation with headquarters".

For the *functional scope* of a subsidiary's activities, respondents were asked to indicate how many of the following eight activities the subsidiary performed: product sales and after-sales service, manufacturing, marketing, sales of professional services, provision of strategic services (regional headquarters), logistics/distribution, R&D and "back office" support. Greater functional scope might indicate the possibility of a "miniature replica" that makes few strategic contributions to an MNE (White & Poynter, 1984); conversely, a narrow set of value-added activities sometimes corresponds to a more specialized subsidiary mandate that warrants positive attention from the top. The *market scope* of a subsidiary's activities was measured as the percentage of subsidiary sales realized in foreign markets.

MNE characteristics

To assess *formal MNE structure*, we used the company hierarchy provided by the *Directory of Corporate Affiliations* and determined whether subsidiaries belonged to an MNE that was configured into geographic divisions, worldwide business units, or a matrix. We treated a product orientation as the base case, creating dummy variables for other types of structures. The *geographic scope of the parent company* was measured as the number of countries in which the MNE had foreign subsidiaries (Delios & Beamish, 1999).

We calculated a Euclidian index of *cultural distance* using Hofstede's (1991) indexes of power distance, uncertainty avoidance, individualism, and masculinity.

In assessing *home region*, we treated European parentage as the base case. All MNEs in the sample were headquartered in North America, Europe, or the broad Asia-Pacific region. Dummy variables were created for the two other regions.

Case study IV
Axis communications

Building the global market for network surveillance cameras

Ulf Elg and Janina Schaumann

Axis Communications was founded in 1984 in Lund, Sweden, and is the global market leader within the area of network/IP-based surveillance cameras. In 1996, the firm was the first in the world to launch a network camera. A main ambition is to drive the market from analogue technologies to IP-based solutions. Axis is established in 40 countries and is present in 179 others through partners. Today, the firm works with more than 45,000 partners worldwide. The products and solutions that Axis works with are mainly developed in-house. They are based on innovative, open technology platforms especially aimed to support security surveillance and remote monitoring. Axis' strive to drive the market for network cameras has been successful with an average increase in sales of 26 per cent during the last five years. The firm has also received several international awards for its innovative products and solutions in the field of network video.

Axis is a strong driving force behind the technological development in the industry, with unique products in terms of innovativeness and quality. In the headquarters in Lund, about 550 engineers work with technology development. A major effort is put into educating customers and other stakeholders, and explaining the advantages of IP technology over analogue solutions. In 2012 the sales increased by 17 per cent globally. Today, the market is rapidly shifting in favour of digital technology and the future growth opportunities appear to be substantial.

Corporate global strategy

Eight business areas are especially targeted by Axis: education (universities, schools, education institutes), banking and finance (banks, post offices, insurance companies), retail (stores, gas stations, supermarkets), industrial (process industries, engineering, construction, pharmaceutical, energy companies), transportation (airports, railways, harbours, traffic surveillance, toll stations), government (authorities, police, military, health care, prisons, museums, casinos), city surveillance and healthcare.

Applying an indirect business model can be regarded as a strategic cornerstone for Axis. This means that Axis never sells products directly to any end users, instead relying on having a strong network of close collaborations with different partners based on loyalty and long-term cooperation. The network includes distributors responsible for the physical transfer of products and system integrators and resellers that usually are the main coordinators of the projects Axis are involved in, reaching the final users. Axis has also developed partnerships with other IT companies so that the market can be offered a full network security solution based on the core competencies of the different partners. One example is that a software company may develop a certain programme that can be combined with the network cameras and that directly fits the need of a certain end user.

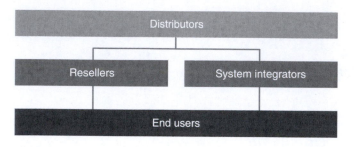

Figure IV.1 The indirect business model used by Axis communications.

Competition in the network camera segment is increasing as more and more firms realize that this is likely to be the future of the industry. However, the main competitors are manufacturers that still put some emphasis on analogue cameras, such as Panasonic, Samsung and Sony. These firms offer network cameras as well as traditional, analogue solutions. While overall being considerably larger than Axis, they are still ranked below when it comes to network and security cameras. Here, Axis has the position as global market leader. In total, there are around 300 brands in the world offering network cameras of varying quality. Many of them are relatively local players. Axis is positioned as a high-price/high-quality product for elite segment and offers the same product range all over the world, without making any local adaptations. In some price-sensitive emerging markets such as India, this positioning can be a challenge for Axis as well as for its business partners. Until now, the firm has consistently decided not to make any local adaptations and not to develop less-advanced camera alternatives that can be sold at a lower price on certain markets.

The Axis brand

Axis is putting a major effort into developing and strengthening the corporate brand and building a global identity that is based on its technically advanced, high-quality products and the reputation as an innovator in the industry. This work targets the internal organization and external actors, including business partners in the value chain but also different types of experts and consultants. The aim has been to create a consistent and recognizable image that represents the vision and the values that Axis stands for. A major goal with this has been to align employees as well as business partners to the brand and to make them committed to support building the Axis brand and the values it represents.

The brand development work was carried out mainly at the global headquarter in Lund, but it was based on a large number of seminars and meetings with employees from different parts of the organization. The brand vision of Axis was formulated as "Everything can communicate over intelligent networks" while the mission was described as "To be the driving force in bringing customers the full benefits of intelligent network video solutions". Furthermore, three brand values have been developed as the cornerstones and as a clarification of the firm's way of gaining a long-term competitive advantage.

"Leading Expert" communicates that Axis should always be in the forefront of the business, being innovative and offering new solutions to increase customer value. Customers should always be able to rely on Axis for the best possible solutions in network video.

Figure IV.2 Axis logo.

"Dedicated" stresses that Axis is really passionate about network video. The firm should be prepared to do everything to support loyal customers and partners, offering expertise and enhancing trust and mutual benefits within the partner network.

"Open" refers to an ambition to always be approachable and accessible for customers, partners and other important actors. It also refers to an ambition to have a mind that is open for new ideas, to be willing to listen and to search for new, future needs.

A brand platform was also developed as a support in marketing and positioning of the Axis brand. This includes a graphic identity manual, information tools and marketing material. It was also made clear that all types of local communication and marketing should be based on the material available from head office and should comply with the image and identity standards established for the Axis brand.

Political and societal aspects

The firm views political factors and legal requirements regarding surveillance as a threat as well as an opportunity. In some markets, such as Axis' home market in Sweden, the regulations are strict and limit the use of camera monitoring in cities and public places. At the same time in other markets, strict regulations require camera monitoring. One example is that a public authority may require that dispensing counters for medicines should be monitored. The firm also perceives a growing acceptance of surveillance cameras that can be a driver of the market. In many societies it is regarded as a basic right for citizens to feel safe and secure, and this may be facilitated by surveillance cameras.

Many political contacts regarding a certain project are normally handled on the local level and through the different business partners responsible for a project where Axis is involved. However, on a global level, Axis is still an active part in driving the international opinion in a direction from analogue towards IP technology. This is done mostly by PR and events, or by collaborating with other parties in order to educate decision-makers. In emerging markets government is often an important part in big projects requiring a security surveillance solution and often influences decisions regarding technology standards more generally. Axis has taken the initiative to establish a standardization committee for driving the opinion regarding standards for network video called ONVIF. The committee also includes companies such as Sony and Bosch.

One additional challenge for Axis is that there are a number of ethical aspects that can be brought to the fore when it comes to surveillance. For example, Axis cameras are today used for the surveillance of Tiananmen Square in Beijing, China. The firm also sees substantial future opportunities in selling network cameras for city surveillance in China. However, according to the Swedish newspaper *Sydsvenskan* (14 October 2010), Amnesty International raised concerns and argued that this type of surveillance may assist totalitarian regimes in violating human rights. As a response to these views, Axis at the corporate level works with CSR issues and in presenting the Axis brand as socially responsible and ethical. This is done, for example, through relationships with NGOs such as Amnesty International and membership of the UN Global Compact. The aim is to show that Axis is not involved in any ethically questionable surveillance. Profiling Axis this way also helps in developing government relationships.

Managing challenges in India

The Indian market provides an example of the challenges that Axis can meet when developing the business in an emerging market. India can be characterized as a technology-friendly and progressive culture. However, a main challenge for Axis is to influence the opinion to go from the earlier established analogue technology towards modern, IP-based technology. In India, many businesses have already invested in analogue technology and are reluctant to move to an alternative solution. For Axis, a central part of driving the business has been to apply its indirect sales model. The partner network handles most direct contacts with end customers, meaning that Axis can also draw on the reputation that partners already have on the market. As a complement, Axis strives to influence opinions about IP technology as well as the Axis brand through educational programmes targeting different decision-makers and by PR and events. In many important big projects requiring a security surveillance solution, business and political actors are involved as customers. Therefore, it is important for Axis to influence their view of technical standards more indirectly. Educational programmes that are in collaboration with other IT firms are a part of this.

Managing competitive and infrastructural factors

Axis is still a comparatively small player on the Indian market. It entered in 2007 and in early 2012 the firm had twelve employees. At the same time, the firm is growing rapidly at a rate of about 30–35 per cent a year. There are a number of competitors, including Axis, with similar market shares of around 10 per cent. These competitors would include firms such as Bosch, Pelco and Sony. In early 2012 Axis covered the whole of India with three sales managers responsible for different regions. In line with the indirect sales strategy, the main responsibility of these managers is to establish relationships with partners involved in major projects with large customers.

The historically weak infrastructure is a major opportunity for Axis. India is currently in a strong development phase when it comes to infrastructure. A substantial number of major public projects are under development that also require security solutions. This includes airports, administration buildings, hospitals, subways and highways. Typically, the government is either the main customer or an actor with a substantial influence. Other areas with substantial investments, mainly under the influence of political actors, are city surveillance, large defence projects and power plants. It is of critical importance to have partners that support the developments towards digital solutions and at the same time provide access to big infrastructural development projects, such as the building of new airports and city surveillance.

Though having the final say, the political actors in these projects typically do not possess the technical know-how to specify the kind of surveillance solution that ought to be required. Therefore, they often hand over the main influence to external consultants and design institutes. These actors will decide the standards and specifications that are required for the project, suggest the kind of equipment needed the specification for that equipment, the quantities, etc. Being a premium player in the price-quality segment, it is essential for Axis that the specifications do not open up for low price competition, but that they instead stress quality aspects and a need for the type of features offered by the Axis cameras. A part of the strategy has thus been to develop specially tailored education programmes that demonstrate and teach these experts the values of the solutions offered by Axis. Events and training programmes are organized where those identified as key influencers are invited to participate. These events are also perceived as valuable by the target groups because they offer new, frontline knowledge. The education programmes are usually carried out in collaboration with business partners that bring solutions, such as specially designed software programmes, that complement the use of the surveillance cameras and increase the customer value. One example is a programme designed for registering the number of cups served in a coffee shop and calculating the pilferage. Axis offers this type of training in most major cities during the year. On top of this, the regional sales managers strive to develop their own individual relationships with the most influential consultants and engineers.

However, the high price positioning is a challenge in India, where some customer segments are price-sensitive. One example is retailers and smaller local business, but even large government projects sometimes have to manage considerable budget constraints. Customers, partners and some local employees have sometimes stressed that an adapted product range with less-advanced cameras and a lower price would help to increase the market share of Axis. At the same time, it is recognized that such adaptations could damage the firm's brand positioning and the consistency in the global strategy.

Navigating the administrative complexities

Axis' political actors and various regulations and tax issues on different levels are also a critical factor. India is perceived to be complicated in several ways. First, there are several political decision levels which require multiple contacts with central as well as regional and local authorities. Second, India is considered to have a particularly complicated, complex and bureaucratic administrative structure. At the same time, Axis is hesitant to take any actions to initiate changes at this point in time, and instead tries to adapt to existing conditions. However, some managers feel a more proactive approach will soon become necessary. At the same time, it can be a problem if Axis is too critical and offensive in questioning established norms and routing decision-makers on different levels. This may jeopardize the relationships that the firm is trying to build.

Axis also gets assistance and help from business partners in coping with regulative issues. One particularly important area is taxation and customs. As stressed in the literature, Indian tax laws are something of a jungle. For example, Axis has to pay a tax of 30% for importing complete cameras, while by importing the cameras in two parts and assembling them locally the tax can be reduced to 8%. However, this requires substantial investments in a new assembling facility. It is difficult to assess whether such an investment is justified from a long-term perspective. The political and administrative context is uncertain and there is always a possibility that rules and taxation levels may change; that would have an impact on Axis' prices.

Another taxation issue is that in India, each province has a local tax that is added on and that can vary considerably. Furthermore, by sending a bill to a customer between two states the firm will give rise to an additional interstate tax of 4%. Axis' network of partners can be a substantial help in these matters. In particular, the distributors are critical in guiding Axis in how to minimize product taxes. On the positive side for Axis, it can be mentioned that the

Indian government has recently made it mandatory for all public places – including retail outlets of all sizes – to have a surveillance system. This is due to the fact that the Indian population in general, as well as public figures and government officials more specifically, are becoming increasingly aware of and exposed to terrorist threats and problems related to political instability.

Political actors can often also play a decisive role in setting or influencing different industry standards. This may happen through recommendations or by formal regulations. For example, Axis experienced how political representatives decided to require that all the cameras considered during the development of a high court building had to be under certification from the American organization UL. Because Axis is certified by the European testing company, EN, but not UL-certified, this created a major problem. This also illustrates how a public policy-maker can unintentionally create a threat through a relatively uninformed recommendation. Most experts appear to view these two certifications as being equal. In more general terms, respondents also discussed the recommendations and broad guidelines developed especially for government bodies by the National Informatics Centre in Delhi are especially influential. When it comes to this type of national political actor, Axis normally acts in collaboration with business partners or trade associations such as the international standardization board discussed earlier.

Future prospects

The rapid growth rate of the leading emerging markets, accompanied by major investments in infrastructure is likely to continue to offer new business opportunities for Axis. Most of the firm's strategic customer segments also continue to grow. The demand for network cameras increased in all regions and for all end customers segments in 2011. The growth rate was especially strong within transportation, retail and city surveillance.

While Axis is to some extent still learning how to compete and to adapt to the challenges of emerging markets, it is clear that the firm has gained a well-recognized and highly regarded reputation within the industry. One example of these is that as the website IFSEC Global published a ranking of the world's most influential people in the security and fire industries in early 2013, Axis co-founder and board member Martin Gren ended up in first place. In 2012, Axis also received the Wall Street Journal Technology Innovation Award for its Lightfinder technology in the Physical Security category. This technology was found to enable 'outstanding performance in network cameras during difficult light conditions, specifically low light'.

Questions

1   How can Axis meet the demand for a low-price solution while the Axis brand is positioned as a high-price/high-quality product?
2   Do you think that it is ethical for a firm such as Axis to help a government to spy on its citizens? What arguments, for and against, can you think of?
3   Analyse the role that political and societal factors have for Axis. Do you think that Axis is tackling these factors efficiently? What advice can you give in this respect?
4   Discuss the special cultural challenges that the Indian market has for Axis. What actions can be taken in order to ensure long-term success?
5   What do you think will be the main threats and opportunities for Axis in the future? Globally? In India?

References

Axis: more information available at www.axis.com

Budhwar, P. (2001). Doing business in India. *Thunderbird International Business Review*, 43(4): 549–68.

Iyer, G.R., Sheth, J.N. and Sharma, A. (2012). The resurgence of India: Triumph of institutions over infrastructure? *Journal of Macromarketing*, 32(3): 309–18.

Prater, E., Swafford, P.M. and Yellepeddi, S. (2009). Emerging economies: Operational issues in China and India. *Journal of Marketing Channels*, 16(2): 169–87.

Quer, D., Claver, E. and Rienda, L. (2010). Doing business in China and India: A comparative approach. *Asia-Pacific Journal of Business Administration*, 2(2): 153–66.

Ray, G. (2011). Doing business in India: Opportunities and challenges. *Journal of Marketing Development & Competitiveness*, 5(4): 77–95.

Rienda, L., Claver, E. and Quer, D. (2011). Doing business in India: A review of research in leading international journals. *Journal of Indian Business Research*, 3(3): 192–216.

Venkatesh, A. (2012). Special issue on India: Macromarketing perspectives. *Journal of Macromarketing*, 32(3): 247–51.

Part V

Culture and international business

23   Introduction

Herodotus, writing in the fifth century BC, has an early account of cultural differences and their importance. One might recall in particular, an account told of Darius. When he was King of Persia, he summoned the Greeks, who happened to be present at his court, and asked them what it would take for them to eat the bodies of their fathers. They replied that they would not do it for all the money in the world. Later, in the presence of the Greeks, and through an interpreter so that they could understand what was said, he asked some Indians of the tribe called Callatiae, who do in fact eat their parents' bodies, what they would take to burn them. They uttered a cry of horror and forbade him to mention such a dreadful thing. One can see by this what custom can do, and Pindar, in my opinion, was right when he called it "king of all" (Herodotus, 1972: p. 187).

This is a powerful statement of the importance of culture and that cross-cultural analysis is faced with challenges arising from the difficulty of distinguishing the universal from the particular.

Hofstede (1980) refers to culture as "software of the mind". There is no doubt that people wired differently need to be managed in a fashion that accords with their culturally programmed behaviour. Multinational enterprises must adapt their strategy to different cultural values in the areas in which they operate, just as they adapt their production strategies to different costs arising from locational factors. Negotiation styles, decision-making processes, recruitment, selection, training, marketing and performance measurement are among the operational factors that need to account for cultural differences among the workforce, customers, suppliers and partners with which the MNE deals. The influence of culture on policy-making is uncontested. How to do this is problematic, not least because the concept of culture is nebulous and is itself contested.

There is considerable division in the literature between those who see culture as a measurable entity and those who feel that only the most trivial of cultural differences are captured by assigning numeric scales to amorphous and ill-defined notions such as "national cultures". The work of Hofstede (1980) has excited interest among researchers and the Hofstede dimensions have collectively and severally been the focus of a great deal of imitation and extension, notably in the single indicator "Kogut and Singh index". Such measures can be defended as proxies, but Shenkar (2012, p. 16) calls them, "questionable and frankly indefensible proxies". These arguments are presented in Chapter 24.

We should be aware of equating "culture" with "national culture". This is typical of the methodological nationalism that is frequently endemic in international business research. As well as a national dimension, culture can also be examined within a sub-region of a country (cities within large countries such as India, China and the USA are often different in a large number of ways), within a firm (the differences in cultures within companies are often seen as competitive advantages and as sources of pride. or indeed of shame), within an industry, a profession, a religion, a gender or a myriad of other subgroupings. Generalization is dangerous and we should be aware of attributing too much to cultural differences. Cultural differences can be overestimated or even underestimated (when a too-easy assumption of similarity is made, for example, between UK and Australia) (Buckley et al., 2003) when only national factors are considered. There is no substitute, in research or in management for a deep understanding and investigation of "cultural differences".

Culture and international business

The fundamental study by Hofstede (1980) emphasized the importance of culture on international business in the next chapter. He distinguished national cultures from organizational cultures. Using a huge database from fifty countries, he discussed the validity of management theories across borders. A special emphasis was given to East Asian cultures explaining the recent economic growth of these countries. The four dimensions are discussed at length: power distance, individualism, masculinity and femininity and uncertainty avoidance. A fifth dimension, long-term or short-term orientation, is introduced to explain East Asian cultures. The study concluded that existing management theories have a limited validity across cultures, not only because many companies operate in different countries, but also because they operate in different lines of businesses. The managers have to see the relativity of their own cultural framework with that of others. Hofstede's studies called for improved inter-cultural management skills focussing on working rather than on living in other countries.

Oded Shenkar's 2001 article from the *Journal of International Business*, is a critical response to the concept of "cultural distance". It is a challenge to the "hidden assumptions" of the notion of cultural distance and it takes issue with the theoretical base and methodological properties of the concept. Shenkar deconstructs the conceptual properties of cultural distance in terms of the illusion of symmetry (cultural distance A to B is not equal to B to A), the illusion of stability, the illusion of linearity, the illusion of causality and the illusion of discordance. In methodological properties, Shenkar questions the assumptions of corporate homogeneity, spatial homogeneity and the assumption of equivalence. He explores other elements of "distance" and introduces the important alternative metaphor of "friction" (see also Shenkar et al., 2008). The piece ends with a series of recommendations as to future developments in theory and measurement. Shenkar (2012) has suggested that research should be redirected away from the static cultural distance construct towards the dynamic interaction of the actual entities that come into contact in international business.

Chapter 25 by Cuervo-Cazurra and Genc examines the interesting case of developing country MNEs in the least developed countries. It is often taken for granted that cultural distance is measured from "the West" (usually the USA). Cultural differences thus take "Western culture" as the norm and see others as deviating from this. Chapter 25 uses a different context and therefore alerts us to the fact that all cultures have distinctive elements. The key to building strategy is to identify those aspects of a host country's "culture" that are relevant to doing business in that setting. This will affect not only marketing, but all aspects of operation including HR and management styles.

Brannen and Peterson (Chapter 26) show the impact of cross-cultural work alienation on the success and failure of cross border mergers and acquisitions (M&As). This is an important study not only in its examination of the role of culture in a specific mode of doing international business (acquisitions) but also because a great deal of current research in M&As focusses on post-merger integration as a key success element. Cross-cultural interorganizational relations are critical in the success of all modes of conducting international business, from long-term contracting to alliances, joint ventures and mergers. This study identifies 'pockets of alienation' and shows how these can disrupt successful integration in a post M&A context. This chapter is an example of use of theory in analysing international business problems and moving from this to suggesting practical strategies to avoid and to remedy these problems. Another example of empirical evidence on the linkage between national cultures and the institutional structure of firms, with strategy implications is provided by Witt and Redding (2009).

Chapter 27 by Hallén and Wiedersheim-Paul, deals with psychic distance and buyer–seller interaction. The authors claim that the gap between buyers and sellers is two-dimensional. First, the 'hard' dimension, such as the physical distance and second, the soft dimension connected with differences in attitudes and perceptions caused, for example, by differences in cultural environments (in a wide sense) between buyers and sellers. Although the reading addresses buyers and sellers, the approach is wide-ranging and can be applied to comparative management and management in multinational firms. The 'soft' dimension of distance is of particular importance in international marketing and management. As inter-firm relationships (such as that between head office and subsidiary) develop, mutual understanding between the units reduces this psychic gap. This is a fundamental chapter in building our knowledge of cultural distance.

References

Buckley, P.J., Fenwick, M. and Edwards, R.W. (2003). 'Is cultural similarity misleading? The experience of Australian manufacturers in Britain', *International Business Review*, 12 (3): 297–309.

Herodotus (1972). *The Histories*, translated by Aubrey de Selincourt (revised edition. London. Penguin).

Hofstede, G. (1980). *Culture's consequences: International differences in work-related values*. Beverly Hills: Sage Publications.

Shenkar, O. (2001) 'Cultural distance revisited: Toward a more rigorous conceptualization and measurement of cultural differences', *Journal of International Business Studies*, 32(3): 519–535.

Shenkar, O. (2012). 'Beyond cultural distance: Switching to a friction lens in the study of cultural differences', *Journal of International Business Studies*, 43: 12–17.

Shenkar, O., Luo, Y. and Yeheskel, O. (2008). 'From "distance" to "friction": Substituting metaphors and redirecting intercultural research', *Academy of Management Review* 33(4): 905–923.

Witt, M.A. and Redding, G. (2009) 'Culture, meaning and institutions: Executive rationale in Germany and Japan', *Journal of International Business Studies*, 40(4): 859–885.

24 Cultural distance revisited

Towards a more rigorous conceptualization and measurement of cultural differences*

Oded Shenkar

Few constructs have gained broader acceptance in the international business literature than cultural distance (CD). Presumably measuring the extent to which different cultures are similar or different, the construct has been applied to most business administration disciplines, i.e., management, marketing, finance and accounting. In management, CD has been used as a key variable in strategy, management, organization behavior and human resource management. The construct has been applied to a multitude of research questions, from innovation and organizational transformation to foreign expansion and technology transfer (Gomez-Mejia and Palich, 1997) and from affiliate performance to expatriate adjustment (Black and Mendenhall, 1991). It is in the area of foreign direct investment (FDI) that the construct has had its greatest impact.

To understand the appeal of the CD construct, it is useful to recall the nature of the phenomenon it is set to capture. Complex, intangible and subtle, culture has been notoriously difficult to conceptualize and scale (Boyacigiller et al., 1996). Establishing a measure gauging the "distance" between cultures has understandably presented an even greater challenge. By offering a seemingly simple and standardized measure of cultural differences, the CD construct offered a tangible and convenient tool with which to bypass the complexities and intricacies of culture, yielding a quantitative measure to be employed in combination with other "hard" data (see Kogut and Singh, 1988).

The appeal of the CD construct is, unfortunately, illusory. It masks serious problems in conceptualization and measurement, from unsupported hidden assumptions to questionable methodological properties, undermining the validity of the construct and challenging its theoretical role and application. Those problems, their implications and their remedies are the focus of the present paper.

Cultural distance in the foreign investment literature

For almost three decades, CD and its proxies have been applied to multiple areas of business, from strategy to organization behavior to accounting and auditing, in both domestic and international contexts. The construct found its most loyal following in international business, where it has been used in such realms as foreign direct investment (FDI), headquarter–subsidiary relations, and expatriate selection and adjustment. By and large, FDI represents the most popular arena for the application of the CD construct, most often in the form of an index compiled by Kogut and Singh (1988) from Hofstede's (1980) cultural dimensions.

In the FDI literature, CD has had three primary thrusts. The first thrust has been to explain the foreign market investment location and especially the sequence of such investment by multinational enterprises (MNEs). The second, to predict the choice of mode of entry into foreign markets. A third application has been to account for the variable success, failure and performance of MNE affiliates in international markets. A brief review of each of those three thrusts follows.

Cultural distance and the launch/sequence of foreign investment

The first use of CD in the FDI literature has been to account for the very decision of firms to invest in a foreign country. A theory of familiarity emerged, arguing that firms were less likely to invest in culturally distant markets. Yoshino (1976) and Ozawa (1979) viewed Japan's CD from Western nations as a constraint on Japanese FDI in the West. In a similar vein, Davidson (1980) attributed the large US investment in Canada and the UK – well beyond what their market size, growth, tariffs and proximity would have predicted – to cultural similarity. Dunning (1988), in contrast, argued that larger CD between home and host markets rather encouraged FDI as a way of overcoming transactional and market failures.

A related and eventually more influential use of the CD construct within the expansion stream has been to predict the sequence of multiple foreign entries. This work is closely associated with Johanson and Vahlne (1977), who observed that Swedish firms progressively expanded from their home base into countries with greater "psychic distance". This thesis has later become known as the Uppsala process model, or the "Scandinavian school" (Johanson and Wiedersheim-Paul, 1975; Luostarinen, 1980; Engwall, 1984; Welch and Luostarinen, 1988; Forgsren, 1989; Axelsson and Johanson, 1992). Support for the Scandinavian thesis has been limited (Turnbull, 1987; Engwall and Wallenstal, 1988). Both Benito and Gripsrud (1992) and Sullivan and Bauerschmidt (1990) failed to find CD to be a predictor of FDI sequence per the Johanson and Vahlne thesis.

Cultural distance and entry mode

The Scandinavian school also predicted an incremental increase in investment commitment from exports into FDI. It was not clear whether the two trends – incremental distance and incremental commitment – were to occur in tandem, however, a first of many omissions in the area. Eventually, the thesis predicting relationship between CD and FDI mode has become synonymous with transaction cost theory (Williamson, 1985). The higher the CD, the more control the MNE was likely to maintain over its foreign operations (Root, 1987; Davidson and McFeteridge, 1985; Kim and Hwang, 1992). Control was phrased as a choice between licensing and FDI but more often between the wholly-owned subsidiary (WOS) and the partially controlled international joint venture (IJV) (Agarwal, 1994; Cho and Padmanabhan, 1995; Erramilli, 1991; Erramilli and Rao, 1993; Kogut and Singh, 1988; Larimo, 1993; Padmanabhan and Cho, 1994).

The loosening of control in culturally distant locations was seen as a way of reducing uncertainty and information costs (Alpander, 1976; Richman and Copen, 1972). As Goodnow and Hansz (1972, p. 46) put it, "degree of control declines as the environment becomes less favorable". In predicting entry mode, transaction cost theorists associate higher distance with a higher cost of transaction due to information costs and the difficulty of transferring competencies and skills (Buckley and Casson, 1976; Vachani, 1991). In transaction costs, internalization is imperative when market agents are likely to take advantage of a firm's limited knowledge and when future transaction contingencies could not be specified because of uncertainty or complexity (Williamson, 1985; Beamish and Banks, 1987). In the absence of internalization, it will not be possible to verify claims by agents and reduce operational uncertainty or reverse the investment all together (Williamson, 1985).

The underlying though implicit assumption in incorporating CD into the transaction costs argument is that international operations are highly uncertain. Presumably, it will be more difficult to verify claims by culturally distant agents, since the agents will make claims rooted in an unfamiliar environment while buffered from enforcement by an MNE. Roth and O'Donnell (1996) argue that agency costs increase as a function of CD because complete and accurate information on agents' (subsidiaries') performance becomes more difficult and more costly to obtain, resulting in higher dependence of headquarters upon the subsidiary.

Gatignon and Anderson (1988) acknowledge that CD does not fit very well within the transaction costs argument. Logically, the theory can accommodate opposite predictions of the CD–control mode relation. A firm may prefer low control to compensate for its lack of knowledge in high CD situations, relying on a local partner to contribute local knowledge. Or, it may opt for high control, i.e., a WOS, as a way of reducing dependence upon agents whose actions are poorly understood. Anderson and Gatignon (1986) suggest that high control is perhaps more efficient when the entrant's methods confer a transaction-specific advantage that cannot be easily imitated by other firms. "On occasion, operation methods that do not fit local culture will constitute the necessary advantage that enable foreigners to compete with locals on their home ground" (Anderson and Gatignon, 1986, p. 18). Indeed, from a resource-based perspective (Barney, 1991), the very ability to bridge CD confers a unique advantage.

Empirical results regarding the impact of CD on entry mode are mixed (Benito and Gripsrud, 1992; Padmanabhan and Cho, 1994). Erramilli and Rao (1993) found that low CD resulted in low control, though the relationship was mediated by level of experience and asset specificity. Pan (1996) found that the larger the CD, the more likely it was for a foreign partner to have an equal or a majority stake in their Chinese IJV. Boyacigiller (1990) found that CD was positively related to control (defined as the proportion of US nationals in the foreign affiliate). On the other hand, Kogut and Singh (1988) and Kim and Hwang (1992) report low control modes at high CD levels. Kogut and Singh (1988) found that greater CD increased the likelihood of green-field IJVs over both green-field WOSs and the acquisition of a controlling stake in an existing operation. While the contradictory results can be partially attributed to the firms studied (the service firms examined by Erramilli and Rao and Boyacigiller could have lower control costs than the manufacturing enterprises researched by Kim and Hwang and Kogut and Singh), this is unlikely to explain the full spectrum of inconsistent results.

Cultural distance and affiliate performance

In this third application, CD has largely been taken to represent a hindrance to the performance of the MNE and its affiliates. According to Chang (1995), CD limits the ability of a MNE to generate rent when entering new domains. Empirical results have been mixed. Li and Guisinger (1991) found that US affiliates whose foreign partners came from culturally dissimilar countries were more likely to fail. Barkema et al. (1997) found that firms which have gradually ventured into more culturally distant locations were less likely to have their affiliates terminated prematurely; controlling for experience, IJV longevity decreased with the CD to the host country. Johnson et al. (1991) reported that "cultural congruence" between IJV partners had no effect on the Japanese partner's perceptions of success, and Park and Ungson (1997) found that a larger CD was actually associated with lower rate of JV dissolution.

Hidden assumptions in the cultural distance construct

The inconsistent results obtained for the three FDI thrusts may be the result of the conceptual or methodological properties of the CD construct. In this section, these properties are culled from an extensive review of the literature applying the CD construct to the domain of FDI and enriched with insights from the broader literature on culture, FDI and related areas. The properties are presented in the form of hidden assumptions that largely go unnoticed but are not supported by either logic or empirical evidence.

The hidden assumptions appear in two clusters, one emanating from the conceptual properties of the construct, the other from its methodological properties. Conceptual properties produce illusions that are the core of the CD construct and undermine its validity within the context of FDI theories. Methodological properties present instrumentation and measurement biases that distort the accurate measurement of cultural differences; they are most closely associated with the Kogut and Singh (1988) index but address broader measurement issues as well. While the two sets of properties are intertwined, they represent distinct sets of problems that require different sets of remedies and are hence presented in separate clusters.

Conceptual properties

The Illusion of Symmetry. "Distance", by definition, is symmetric: The distance from point A to point B is identical to the distance from point B to point A. CD symmetry is however difficult to defend in the context of FDI. It suggests an identical role for the home and host cultures, for instance, that a Dutch firm investing in China is faced with the same CD as a Chinese firm investing in the Netherlands. There is no support for such an assumption. Numerous studies have shown the importance of investor culture in predicting investment, entry mode and performance (for example, Pan, 1996; Kogut and Singh, 1988; Tallman, 1988). Other studies have shown a role for the host culture. However, there are no studies showing symmetry between the two nor is there a reason to assume one. On the contrary, home and host country effects are different in nature, the former being embedded in the firm while the latter is in a national environment.

The Illusion of Stability. Measured at a single point in time, CD is implicitly assumed to be constant. Cultures change over time, however. The culture measured at market entry time may have changed by the time performance is measured. Further, a convergence thesis (Webber, 1969) would predict CD narrowing over time as more investors flock into the market and local employees become knowledgeable of MNE management methods (Richman and Copen, 1972). As firms learn more about a market, their CD to that market decreases. Stopford and Wells (1972) found that when a firm had more experience in a country, it was more likely to choose a WOS that an IJV (see also Dubin, 1975). Hennart (1991) found that experience in the US has led Japanese firms to look more favorably at a WOS than at an IJV. International experience may also lead firms to prefer acquisition to green-field investment (Caves and Mehra, 1986), a preference which is not captured by the control thesis yet significantly influences the availability of WOS versus IJV investment.

The Illusion of Linearity. Also embedded in the distance metaphor is the assumption of linear impact on investment, entry mode and performance. The higher the distance between cultures, the higher the likelihood that (a) investment will occur at a later stage in the investment sequence, (b) a less controlling entry mode will be chosen and (c) the worse the performance of foreign affiliates will be. These are all questionable assumptions. The Scandinavian school acknowledges that the time lag between expansion waves will vary due to differences in learning curves. Erramilli (1991) showed that CD and experience interacted to influence ownership in a nonlinear fashion. Davidson (1980) suggested that firms taking their first investment steps were more likely to prefer culturally similar countries than those in an advanced stage of internationalization (see also Bilkey, 1978). Pan (1996) found that foreign partners who already held a majority equity stake in a JV were not interested in further increasing this stake when CD was large.

Parkhe (1991) points out that CD, like other "diversity variables", plays a different role at the strategic choice and operational phases. At the strategic phase, cultural differences may be a basis for synergy while at the operational phase they may erode the applicability of the parent's competencies (see also Brown et al., 1989; Chowdhury, 1992; Gomes-Casseres, 1989; Harrigan, 1985, 1988; Hergert and Morris, 1988; Lorange and Roos, 1991). The expatriate literature suggests that adaptation to a foreign culture may be U-shaped (Black and Mendenhall, 1991) and reports that adjustment to a relatively similar culture is often as difficult as adjustment to a "distant" one because differences are not anticipated (for example, Brewster, 1995; O'Grady and Lane, 1996).

The Illusion of Causality. An implicit assumption in much of the literature is that CD has a causal effect on FDI pattern, sequence and performance. The connotation is that culture is the only determinant of distance with relevance to FDI. Earlier work has been tuned to the problem and attempted to compensate by incorporating non-culture variables in a broader "distance" measure. Johanson and Vahlne's (1977) definition of "psychic distance" refers to the "sum of factors" affecting information to the market. Goodnow and Hansz (1972) treat "geocultural distance" as one of a number of variables (also including level of development, political stability), making a country a "hot" or "cold" investment opportunity. Richman and Copen's (1972) measure of "socio-cultural distance" includes such variables as the foreign education of local executives.

As Boyacigiller (1990, p. 363) offers, "key characteristics of nations such as dominant religion, business language, form of government, economic development and levels of emigration to the US indicate a country's cultural distance from the US". Factors such as language (Buckley and Casson, 1976, 1979) political instability (Thunnell, 1977), level of development, market size and sophistication (Davidson and McFetridge, 1985) all play a role in establishing "distance". Barkema et al. (1997), in their study of the FDI of Dutch firms, found the effect of CD to be significant for IJVs in developing countries, but not for IJVs in developed countries. A similar point is made by Beamish (1993) vis-a-vis investment in China's transitional economy. Brown et al. (1989) argue that the combination of economic and cultural factors creates firm specific assets, which can cause failure.

The Illusion of Discordance. The implicit assumption that differences in cultures produce lack of "fit" and hence an obstacle to transaction is questionable. First, not every cultural gap is critical to performance. As Tallman and Shenkar (1994, p. 108) note, "different aspects of firm culture may be more or less central, more or less difficult to transmit, and more or less critical to operations". Second, cultural differences may be complementary and hence have a positive synergetic effect on investment and performance. For instance, as global cooperation demands both concern for performance (masculine) and concern for relationships (feminine), the two may be mutually supportive (Hofstede, 1989; Haspeslagh and Jemison, 1991). Similar evidence can be found in the FDI (Barkema and Vermeulen, 1998), merger and acquisition (for example, Haspeslagh and Jemison, 1991; Morosini, 1998) and IJVs literature (Shenkar and Zeira, 1992).

Methodological properties

The Assumption of Corporate Homogeneity. The CD index used to measure the construct relies on national culture measures and implicitly assumes lack of corporate culture variance, an assumption that lacks support (for example, Hofstede et al., 1990). Laurent (1986) proposes that corporate culture can modify the behavior and beliefs associated with national culture, a proposition confirmed by Weber et al. (1996) for international mergers. Corporate culture alters the dynamics of national CD though not necessarily in the way of reducing its impact. As Schneider (1988) notes "national culture may play a stronger role in the face of a strong corporate culture. The pressures to conform may create the need to reassert autonomy and identity, creating a national mosaic rather than a melting pot".

The Assumption of Spatial Homogeneity. Measuring distance from one national culture to another, the CD index assumes uniformity within the national unit. Quite to the contrary, evidence suggests that intra-cultural variation explains as much if not more than inter-cultural variation (Au, 2000). Neither the spatial location of the firm in the home or host country nor the actual physical distance between the locations, have an impact upon the CD measure calculated. This masks actual investment conditions, for instance a "border effect" formed across contiguous regions divided by a national border (Mariotti and Piscitello, 1995). A somewhat similar argument can be made regarding the variable location of industries from the cultural milieu, as, for instance, in the case of "cultural industries".

The Assumption of Equivalence. The Kogut and Singh (1988) index is a rather simplistic aggregate of Hofstede's (1980) dimensions and is hence liable to the same criticism leveled against Hofstede, for example, non-exhaustiveness, reliance on single company data, and the like (for example, Schwartz and Bilsky, 1990; Schwartz, 1994; Drenth, 1983; Goodstein and Hunt, 1981). The index amplifies the problems associated with the Hofstede framework in two important ways, however.

First, the index has not been updated to incorporate latter work by Hofstede and others, for instance, the fifth dimension of Confucian dynamism or Long Term Orientation (LTO) (Hofstede and Bond, 1988). Derived from a Chinese instrument, this dimension captures a facet that is critical to corporate strategy. Because of its relationship to Confucianism, CD measures involving East-Asian countries, for instance, those used in studies of Japanese FDI (for example, Yoshino, 1976; Ozawa, 1979; Li and Guisinger, 1991), are especially open to challenge.

The second and most important way in which the Kogut & Singh's measure amplifies the measurement problems associated with Hofstede is by making an invalid assumption of equivalence. Hofstede (1989) offers that some cultural gaps are less disruptive than others, and that differences in uncertainty avoidance are potentially the most problematic for international cooperation due to their correlates in terms of differential tolerances towards risk, formalization, and the like. Kogut and Singh (1988) themselves examined the role of uncertainty avoidance separately from their index. Both Barkema et al. (1997) and Barkema and Vermeulen (1998) supported Hofstede's (1989) contention and found that uncertainty avoidance was more important than other cultural dimensions in predicting FDI success. Other studies have shown individualism to have a special effect on FDI (for example, Hamel et al., 1989; Shane, 1992; Dickson and Weaver, 1997). The aggregate measure may hence provide false readings regarding meaningful cultural differences.

Integration and construct development

The significant conceptual and methodological inadequacies relating to the CD construct carry important implications for theory and research. For example, the illusion of symmetry pinpoints divergent transaction costs and the prospect of conflict between partners as each seeks to minimize its cost of the transaction regardless of the cost incurred by the other party; necessitating convergence of transaction and bargaining models. By showing that certain cultural combinations possess synergetic rather than disruptive potential, the illusion of discordance may explain the inconsistent results obtained for the transaction cost argument regarding control and performance. The illusion of causality may explain the inconsistent results obtained for CD and FDI sequence. For instance, Benito and Gripsrud (1992) proposed that their lack of support for the gradual expansion thesis might have been the result of similarity in labor costs among countries within the same cultural cluster. The assumption of spatial homogeneity may explain obtaining inconsistent results for the same pair of countries.

In the following pages, an integrative framework for the treatment of CD construct is developed. In a departure from the existing metaphor that is focused on what sets cultures apart, we also consider mechanisms closing CD. Then, we incorporate a crucial yet missing element in the current conceptualization of CD, namely the interface among transacting parties and its accorded friction. Taken together, the two serve to form a basis from which a comprehensive framework for the treatment of the CD construct is launched.

Closing cultural distance

A product of the use of a metaphor can be the framing of one's frame of reference (Morgan, 1986). In the case of CD, the "distance" metaphor is translated into a focus on what sets cultures apart but not on what might bring them together. A balanced analysis of the relations between social entities should however consider both opening and closing mechanisms. A number of key mechanisms with the potential of closing cultural distance follow.

Globalization and Convergence. Increased communication and interaction bridge CD by encouraging the convergence of cultural systems (Webber, 1969). This implies a trend towards lower CD over time albeit at different paces across the globe. The *World Competitiveness Yearbook* (2000) publishes an index of openness to foreign influences showing substantial differences between relatively open countries such as the Netherlands to closed countries such as France and Korea.

Geographical proximity. Often confused with CD (as in the case of Canada as a first foreign investment for East- and Mid-West US firms), geographic proximity reduces entry barriers (Buckley and Casson, 1979; see also Mariotti and Piscitello, 1995), subject to transportation and information processing requirements. Geographical proximity lowers the costs of managerial coordination and control and reduces the cost of monitoring agents' behavior. It can also facilitate the personal contact that is necessary for effective transfer of knowledge and other resources (Vachani, 1991).

Foreign Experience. The literature acknowledges the importance of foreign experience as a CD closing mechanism. It is not always clear however whether it is international experience per se or experience in the host culture and to what extent the experience of individual managers can substitute for corporate experience, a point that would be especially important to smaller firms (see also acculturation).

Acculturation. Acculturation has been defined (Berry, 1980) as "changes induced in systems as a result of the diffusion of cultural elements in both directions". Acculturation can generally be assumed to reduce the CD to the host country. It is interesting that in explaining one exception to the pattern of gradual involvement they observed (the establishment of a sale subsidiary in a new market), Johanson and Vahlne (1977) explain that the decision-maker in that case was partly educated in the other country. Nor is acculturation dependent upon actual experience. Black et al. (1991, p. 310) suggest that "individuals make anticipatory adjustments before they actually encounter the new situation". Corporations may do the same, in effect closing the CD to a country even prior to the establishment of operations there. Another intriguing question is whether the reentry syndrome described by Adler (1981) would apply at the corporate level.

Cultural Attractiveness. Certain cultures are considered attractive to other cultures. A foreign culture's perceived attributes may be a major reason for the preferences expressed by potential partners and host countries (Gould, 1966). From a cognitive perspective (Sackmann, 1983; Boyacigiller et al., 1996), even when attractiveness is absent, adjustment to a relatively similar culture is often as difficult as adjustment to a "distant" one. This is explained by the expatriate literature in that expatriates do not expect differences in relatively similar cultures (for example, Brewster, 1995; O'Grady and Lane, 1996).

Staffing. Staffing is not only a means of control but also a venue through which groups and individuals bring their cultural properties into a system. Shenkar (1992) discusses the role of employee groups as mechanisms affecting the national and corporate CD in an IJV. For instance, foreign parent expatriates bring with them both the national and corporate culture of the parent while third country nationals recruited by the foreign parent will likely bring the parent firm's culture into the venture, but less of its national culture. The M&A literature make the point that such senior managers have a major influence on the motivation of the other employees and play the most significant role in shaping and transmitting corporate culture signals to the broader membership (see Weber et al., 1996). Bicultural individuals play an especially important role in closing the CD between the foreign and host countries. By virtue of their familiarity with both cultures, such individuals bring the two countries together by serving as emissaries and interpreters of culturally embedded signals and behaviors. The presence of such individuals in a company, especially in senior positions, may hence serve as a mechanism closing CD.

Cultural interaction as friction

While the existence of mechanisms opening and closing CD can be accommodated within the "distance" metaphor, a closer look into the reality of FDI points at interaction as the key issue. After all, how different one culture is from another has little meaning until those cultures are brought into contact with one another. Hence, we suggest replacing the "distance" metaphor with that of "friction", the term used by Williamson (1985) in his original treaty on transaction costs theory. By friction, we mean the scale and essence of the interface between interacting cultures, and the "drag" produced by that interface for the operation of those systems.

As an example, let us consider the difference in the cultural interface between an IJV and an international M&A. An IJV is, by definition, an entity separate from its parent firms. While the parents maintain direct contact as well, the bulk of the interaction is mediated by the IJV whose activities remain compartmentalized from those of the parents. The cultural differences between the parent firms produce friction only to the extent of their involvement with the new entity. Individuals and units in the parent firms who are not involved with the IJV operations do not produce friction. In contrast, a merger brings together the entire set of operations on both sides, producing, at least on the onset, much greater friction. In many M&As, integration is a key goal (see Weber et al., 1996, for a summary). The intense inter-action makes it more dramatic, and the ensuing conflict makes differences salient (Sales and Mirvis, 1984). Weber et al. (1996) found that the top managers in acquired firms have made anticipatory adjustment towards the acquiring organization. In contrast, officers of the acquiring firm may find little reason to do the same.

Obviously, friction varies within the M&A population as well. Where the acquiring firm determines goals, strategic choices and other operations for the acquired company, more friction can be initially expected, but such friction may decline faster than where each firm retains its autonomy. "Modes of acculturation", such as integration, assimilation, separation and deculturation (Nahavandi and Malekzadeh, 1988) will hence influence friction levels. For similar reasons, friction is also likely to differ between acquisition and green-field investment. In an acquisition, the potential friction is greater, because the acquired firm has already a cor-porate culture in place. Indeed, lower CD was found to increase the rate of acquisitions over green-field investments (Dubin, 1975), while high CD has been suggested as a reason why Jap-anese investors in the US prefer green-field investments and partial over complete acquisitions (Hennart, 1991). Li and Guisinger (1991), among others, report that foreign acquisitions of US firms tend to fail more than green-field investment, possibly the result of cultural friction.

The friction among cultural systems is also the product of strategic objectives, that is, how closely do firms want the other system to be positioned vis-à-vis their own. The tighter the control to be maintained, the greater the friction potential. Hence, control (and, in exten-sion, entry mode) is not only the product of cultural "distance", it is also a potential trigger of cultural friction. Further, culture itself is a means of control (Schneider, 1988). A strong corporate culture could, in theory, lower the transaction cost as the subsidiary becomes sim-ilar to the parent, though results by Laurent (1986) suggest that corporate culture actually accentuates national culture differences.

Recommendations

While the theory development effort delineated earlier will eventually result in new CD mea-sures, a number of key steps can be taken now, as follows. First, the Kogut and Singh (1988) index must be supplemented by Long Term Orientation (Confucian Dynamism) especially where East-Asian countries are involved. The use of the aggregate index must be theoretically justified and where appropriate, substituted by CD measures calculated separately for one or more of the five dimensions as necessitated by theoretical and domain considerations. Both aggregate and one-dimensional measures should also be drawn from alternative classifica-tions, for example, Schwartz' (1994) with multiple measures employed wherever possible.

Second, measures of general cultural similarity such as Ronen and Shenkar's (1985, for applications see Barkema et al., 1997; Park and Ungson, 1997; Vachani, 1991), which do not assume linearity, additivity and normal distribution should be used in conjunction with other measures. Findings showing relationship between CD and governance for select coun-try clusters (for example, Gatingnon and Anderson, 1988) suggest supplementing those approaches with measures of cultural diversity such as Gomez-Mejia and Palich's (1997) indices of inter-cluster and intra-cluster diversity.

Third, national-level data should be supplemented by cognitive CD measures (for example, Sullivan and Bauerschmidt, 1990). An example can be found in Boyacigiller (1990), where executives were asked to rank adjustment difficulties in countries where they had served in the past. Retrospective data should be considered in deriving such cognitive measures. Evidence suggests such data do not become less accurate over time periods as long as ten years (Finkelstein, 1992; Huber and Power, 1985) and are especially helpful when anchored in dramatic events such as mergers that tend to make culture and cultural differences more salient. A recent example can be found in Veiga et al. (2000a; see also Veiga et al. 2000b). Qualitative, emic data should be added wherever feasible.

Fourth, control for closing distance mechanisms such as cultural attraction, acculturation and foreign experience, geographical distance (Balabanis, 2000), language, level of development, home market and company size (Erramilli, 1996) which have already been found to correlate with CD or to mediate or moderate its impact on FDI. Control for CD at the corporate level using the wide repertoire of corporate culture instruments while remaining aware of both instrument design (Geringer, 1998) and interaction effects (Weber et al., 1996) across the two levels.

Fifth, consider CD not only as an independent variable predicting FDI governance, sequence and performance (or other variables as the case may be) but also as a dependent variable. CD is as much the product as the consequence of entry mode, and FDI sequence and even performance may have an impact on the perceived distance. Consider culture also as a quasi-moderator variable altering the form if not the strength of the relationship between environmental and strategic variables.

Finally, consider cultural differences as having the potential for both synergy and disruption (Morosini, 1998; Parkhe, 1991). This point cannot be overstated as it lies at the intersection of strategic logic and operational challenges that underline the FDI, expatriate adjustment, auditing and other international business issues. Replacing the "distance" with "friction" as the underlying metaphor for cultural differences is a natural step from there. Not merely semantic, this implies focusing on the interface between transacting entities rather on the void between them.

References

Adler, N. J. 1981. Re-Entry: Managing Cross-Cultural Transitions. *Group and Organization Studies*, 6: 341–56.

Agarwal, S. 1994. Socio-Cultural Distance and the Choice of Joint Ventures: A Contingency Perspective. *Journal of International Marketing*, 2(2): 63–80.

Alpander, G.G. 1976. Use of Quantitative Methods in International Operations by U.S. vs. Overseas Executives. *Management International Review*, 16(1): 71–77.

Anderson, E. & H. Gatignon. 1986. Modes of Foreign Entry: A Transaction Cost Analysis and Propositions. *Journal of International Business Studies*, 17(2): 1–26.

Au, K.Y. 2000. Inter-Cultural Variation as Another Construct of International Management: A Study Based on Secondary Data of 42 Countries. *Journal of International Management*, 6, 217–38.

Axelsson, B. & Johanson, J. 1992. Foreign Market Entry–The Textbook Versus the Network View. In. B. Axelsson & G. Easton (eds.), *Industrial Networks: A New View of Reality.* London, UK: Routledge, 218–34.

Balabanis, G. I. 2000. Factors Affecting Export Intermediaries' Service Offerings: The British Example. *Journal of International Business Studies*, 31(1) 83–99.

—— & Vermeulen, F. 1998. International Expansion through Start-Up or Acquisition: A Learning Perspective. *Academy of Management Journal*, 41(1): 7–26.

Barkema, H., Shenkar, O., Vermeulen, F. & Bell, J.H. 1997. Working Abroad, Working with Others: How Firms Learn to Operate International Joint Ventures. *Academy of Management Journal*, 40(2), 426–442.

Barney, J. B. 1991. Firm Resources and Sustained Competitive Advantage. *Journal of Management*, 17(1): 99–120.

Beamish, P. 1993. The Characteristics of Joint Ventures in the People's Republic of China. *Journal of International Marketing*, 1(2): 29–48.

—— & Banks, J.C. 1987. Equity Joint Ventures and the Theory of the Multinational Enterprise. *Journal of International Business Studies* (summer), 1–16.

Benito, R.G. & Gripsrud, G. 1992. The Expansion of Foreign Direct Investments: Discrete Rational Location Choices or a Cultural Learning Process? *Journal of International Business Studies*, 3, 461–76.

Berry, J.W. 1980. Social and Cultural Change. In Triandis H.C. & Brislin R.W. (Eds.), *Handbook of Cross-Cultural Psychology* (Volume 5, pp. 211–79). Boston: Allyn & Bacon.

Bilkey, W.J. 1978. An Attempted Integration of the Literature on the Export Behavior of Firms. *Journal of International Business Studies*, 9, 33–46.

Black, J.S. & Mendenhall, M. 1991. The U-Curve Adjustment Hypothesis Revisited: A Review and Theoretical Framework. *Journal of International Business Studies*, 22(2): 225–47.

——, ——, & Oddou, G. 1991. Toward a Comprehensive Model of International Adjustment: An Integration of Multiple Theoretical Perspectives. *Academy of Management Review*, 16, 291–317.

Boyacigiller, N. 1990. The Role of Expatriates in the Management of Interdependence. *Journal of International Business Studies*, 21(3): 357–81.

——, Kleinberg, M.J., Philips, M. & Sackmann, S. 1996. Conceptualizing Culture. In B.J. Punnett & O. Shenkar, *Handbook for international Management Research*. Cambridge, MA: Blackwell.

Brewster, C. 1995. Effective Expatriate Training. In Selmer, J. (Editor), *Expatriate Management: New Ideas for International Business*. Westport, CN: Quorum.

Brown, L. T., Rugman, A. M. & Verbeke, A. 1989. Japanese Joint Ventures with Western Multinationals: Synthesizing the Economic and Cultural Explanations of Failure. *Asia Pacific Journal of Management*, 6: 225–42.

Buckley, P.J. & M. Casson. 1976. *The Future of the Multinational Enterprise*. London: Macmillan.

—— & ——1979. A Theory of International Operation. In J. Leontiades & M. Ghertman (eds), *European Research in International Business*. Amsterdam/London: North-Holland.

Caves, R.E. & Mehra, S.K. 1986. Entry of Foreign Multinationals into U.S. Manufacturing Industries. In Michael E. Porter, editor, *Competition in Global Industries*. Boston: Harvard Business School.

Chang, S.J. 1995. International Expansion Strategy of Japanese Firms: Capability Building through Sequential Entry. *Academy of Management Journal*, 38, 383–407.

Cho, K.R. & P. Padmanabhan. 1995. Acquisition Versus New Venture: The Choice of Foreign Establishment Mode by Japanese Firms. *Journal of International Management*, 1(3): 255–85.

Chowdhury, J. 1992. Performance of International Joint Ventures and Wholly Owned Foreign Subsidiaries: A Comparative Perspective. *Management International Review*, 32(2): 115–33.

Davidson, W.H. 1980. The Location of Foreign Direct Investment Activity: Country Characteristics and Experience Effects. *Journal of International Business Studies*, 11(2): 9–22.

—— & McFetridge, D.J. 1985. Key Characteristics in the Choice of International Technology Transfer Mode. *Journal of International Business Studies*, 16 (Summer), 5–22.

—— 1980. The Location of Foreign Direct Investment Activity: Country Characteristics and Experience Effects. *Journal of International Business Studies*, 11(2): 9–22.

Dickson, P.H. & Weaver, K.M. 1997. Environmental Determinants and Individual-Level Moderators of Alliance Use. *Academy of Management Journal*, 40(2): 404–25.

Drenth, P.J.D. 1983. Cross-Cultural Organizational Psychology: Challenges and Limitations. In Irvine, S.H., & Berry, J.W. (Eds.), *Human Assessment and Cultural Factors*. New York: Plenum press.

Dubin, M. 1975. Foreign Acquisitions and the Spread of the Multinational Firm. D.B.A. thesis, Graduate School of Business Administration, Harvard University.

Dunning, J.H. 1988. The Eclectic Paradigm of International Production: A Restatement and Some Possible Extensions. *Journal of International Business Studies*, 19, 1–31.

Engwall, L. 1984 (ed.). *Uppsala Contributions to Business Research.* Uppsala, Sweden: Acta Universitatis Upsaliensis.

—— & Wallenstal, M. 1988. Tit for Tat in Small Steps: The Internationalization of Swedish Banks. *Scandinavian Journal of Management*, 4(3/4): 147–55.

Erramilli, M.K. 1991. The Experience Factor in Foreign Market Entry Behavior of Service Firms. *Journal of International Business Studies*, 22(3): 479–501.

—— 1996. Nationality and Subsidiary Patterns in Multinational Corporations. *Journal of International Business Studies*, 27, 225–48.

—— & CP. Rao. 1993. Service Firms' International Entry Mode Choice: A Modified Transaction–Cost Analysis Approach. *Journal of Marketing*, 57(July): 19–38.

Finkelstein, S. 1992. Power in Top Management Teams: Dimensions, Measurement, and Validation. *Academy of Management Journal*, 35: 505–38.

Forgsren, M. 1989. *Managing the Internationalization Process: The Swedish Case.* London, UK: Routledge.

Gatignon, H. & E. Anderson. 1988. The Multinational Corporation's Degree of Control over Foreign Subsidiaries: An Empirical Test of a Transaction Cost Explanation. *Journal of Law, Economics, and Organization*, 4(2): 305–36.

Geringer, J.M. 1998. Assessing Replication and Extension. A Commentary on Glaister and Buckley: Measures of Performance in UK International Alliances. *Organization Studies*, 19(1): 119–38.

Gomes-Casseres, B. 1989. Ownership Structures of Foreign Subsidiaries: Theory and Evidence. *Journal of Economic Behaviour and Organization*, 11: 1–25.

Gomez-Mejia, L.R. & Palich, L. 1997. Cultural Diversity and the Performance of Multinational Firms. *Journal of International Business Studies*, 309–35.

Goodnow, J.D. & Hansz, J.E. 1972. Environmental Determinants of Overseas Market Entry Strategies. *Journal of International Business Studies*, 3, 33–50.

Goodstein, L. D. & Hunt, J.W. 1981. Commentary: Do American theories Apply Abroad? *Organizational Dynamics*, 10(1): 49–62.

Gould, P. 1966. On Mental Maps. Discussion paper No 9, Department of Geography, University of Michigan.

Hamel, G., Doz, Y.L. & Prahalad, C.K. 1989. Collaborate with Your Competitors – And Win. *Harvard Business Review*, 67(1): 133–9.

Harrigan, K.R. 1985. *Strategies for Joint Ventures.* Lexington, MA: Lexington Books.

—— 1988. Strategic Alliances and Partner Asymmetries. In F.J. Contractor & P. Lorange (eds.). *Cooperative Strategies in International Business.* Lexington, MA: Lexington Books, 205–26.

Haspeslagh, P. C. & Jemison, D. B. 1991. *Managing Acquisitions: Creating Value Through Corporate Renewal.* New York: Free Press.

Hennart, J.-F. 1991. The Transaction Costs Theory of Joint Ventures: An Empirical Study of Japanese Subsidiaries in the United States. *Management Science*, 37(4): 483–97.

Hergert, M. & D. Morris. 1988. Trends in International Collaborative Agreements. In F.J. Contractor & P. Lorange (eds.). *Cooperative Strategies in International Business.* Lexington, MA: Lexington Books, 99–110.

Hofstede, G. 1980. *Culture's Consequences.* New York: Sage.

—— 1989. Organizing for Cultural Diversity. *European Management Journal*, 7(4): 390–7.

—— & Bond, M.H. 1988. The Confucius Connection: From Cultural Roots to Economic Growth. *Organizational Dynamics*, 16(4): 4–21.

——, Neuijen, B., Ohavy, D. D., and Sanders, G. 1990. Measuring Organizational Cultures: A Qualitative and Quantitative Study Across Twenty Cases. *Administrative Science Quarterly*, 35: 386–96.

Huber, G.P. & Power, D.J. 1985. Retrospective Reports of Strategic Level Managers: Guidelines for Increasing their Accuracy. *Strategic Management Journal*, 6: 171–80.

Johanson, J. & J.E. Vahlne. 1977. The Internationalization Process of the Firm: A Model of Knowledge Development and Increasing Foreign Market Commitments. *Journal of International Business Studies*, 8(Spring/Summer): 23–32.

—— & F. Wiedersheim-Paul. 1975. The Internationalization of the Firm: Four Swedish Cases. *Journal of Management Studies*, 12(3): 305–22.

Johnson, J. L., Cullen, J. B. & Sakano, T. 1991. Cultural Congruency in International Joint Ventures: Does it Matter? *Proceedings of the Eastern Academy of Management Fourth Biennial International Conference*, Nice, France (June).

Kim, W.C. & Hwang, P. 1992. Global Strategy and Multinational Entry Mode Choice. *Journal of International Business Studies*, 23(1): 29–53.

Kogut, B. & Singh, H. 1988. The Effect of National Culture on the Choice of Entry Mode. *Journal of International Business Studies*, 19(3): 411–32.

Larimo, J. 1993. *Foreign Direct Investment Behaviour and Performance: An Analysis of Finnish Direct Manufacturing Investments in OECD countries.* Acta Wasaensia, no. 32. Faasa, Finland: University of Vaasa.

Laurent, A. 1986. The Cross-Cultural Puzzle of International Human Resource Management. *Human Resource Management*, 25(1): 91–102.

Li, J.T. & S. Guisinger. 1991. Comparative Business Failures of Foreign-Controlled Firms in the United States. *Journal of International Business Studies*, 22(2): 209–24.

Lorange, P. & J. Roos. 1991. Why Some Strategic Alliances Succeed and Others Fail. *Journal of Business Strategy*, (January/February): 25–30.

Luostarinen, R. 1980. *Internationalization of the Firm.* Helsinki: Helsinki School of Economics.

Mariotti, S. & Piscitello, L. 1995. Information Costs and Location of FDIs within the Host Country: Empirical Evidence from Italy. *Journal of International Business Studies*, 26(4): 815–41.

Morgan, G. 1986. *Images of Organization.* Beverly Hills: Sage Publications.

Morosini, P. 1998. *Managing Cultural Differences.* UK: Pergamon.

Nahavandi, A. & Malekzadeh, A. 1988. Acculturation in Mergers and Acquisitions. *Academy of Management Review*, 13, 79–90.

O'Grady, S. & Lane, H.W. 1996. The Psychic Distance Paradox. *Journal of International Business Studies*, 27(2): 309–33.

Ozawa, Terutomo. 1979. International Investment and Industrial Structure: New Theoretical Implications from the Japanese Experience. *Oxford Economic Papers*, 31(1): 72–92.

Padmanabhan, P. & Cho, K.R. 1994. Ownership Strategy for a Foreign Affiliate: An Empirical Investigation of Japanese Firms. *Management International Review*, 36(1): 45–65.

Pan, Y. 1996. Influences on Foreign Equity Ownership Level in Joint Ventures in China. *Journal of International Business Studies*, 77(1): 1–26.

Park, S.H. & Ungson, G.R. 1997. The Effect of National Culture, Organizational Complementarity, and Economic Motivation on Joint Venture Dissolution. *Academy of Management Journal* 40, 2, 279–307.

Parkhe, A. 1991. Interfirm Diversity, Organizational Learning, and Longevity in Global Strategic Alliances. *Journal of International Business Studies*, 22(4): 579–600.

Richman, B.M. & Copen, M. 1972. *International Management and Economic Development.* New York: McGraw-Hill.

Ronen, S. & Shenkar, O. 1985. Clustering Countries on Attitudinal Dimensions: A Review and Synthesis. *Academy of Management Review*, 10(3): 435–54.

Root, F. 1987. *Entry Strategies for International Markets.* Lexington, MA: Lexington Books.

Roth & O'Donnell. 1996. Foreign Subsidiary Compensation Strategy: An Agency Theory Perspective. *Academy of Management Journal*, 39(3): 678–703.

Sackmann, S.A. 1983. Organizationskltur-Die Unsichtbare Einflussgrosse (Organizational Culture – The Invisible Influence). *Gruppendynamick*, 14: 393–406.

Sales, M.S. & Mirvis, P.H. 1984. When Cultures Collide: Issues in Acquisitions. In J.R. Kimberly & R.E. Quinn (Eds), *Managing Organizational Transitions.* Homewood, IL: Irwin.

Schneider, S.C. 1988. National vs. Corporate Culture: Implications for Human Resource Management. *Human Resource Management*, 27: 231–46.

Schwartz, S.H. & Bilsky, W. 1990. Toward a Theory of the Universal Content and Structure of Values: Extensions and Cross-Cultural Replications. *Journal of Personality and Social Psychology*, 58(5): 878–91.

—— 1994. *Beyond Individualism/Collectivism: New Cultural Dimensions of Values. Individualism and Collectivism: Theory, Method, and Applications* (p. 85–119). Oaks, CA: Sage.

Shane, S.A. 1992. The Effect of National Cultural Differences in Perceptions of Transaction Costs on National Differences in the Preferences for Licensing. *Academy of Management Best Papers Proceedings.*

Shenkar, O. 1992. The Corporate/National Culture Matrix in International Joint Ventures. Paper presented at the AIB annual meeting. Brussels, Belgium.

—— & Zeira, Y. 1992. Role Conflict and Role Ambiguity of Chief Executive Officers in International Joint Ventures. *Journal of International Business Studies*, 23: 55–75.

Stopford, J.M. & L.T. Wells Jr. 1972. *Managing the Multinational Enterprise: Organisation of the Firm and Ownership of the Subsidiaries.* New York: Basic Books.

Sullivan, D. & Bauerschmidt, A. 1990. Incremental Internationalization: A Test of Johanson and Vahlne's Thesis. *Management International Review*, 30, 19–30.

Tallman, S. B. 1988. Home Country Political Risk and Foreign Direct Investment. *Journal of International Business Studies*, 19(2): 219–34.

—— & Shenkar, O. 1994. A Managerial Decision Model of International Cooperative Venture Formation. *Journal of International Business Studies*, 25(1), 91–114.

Thunnell, L. H. 1977. *Political Risk in International Business.* New York: Praeger.

Turnbull, P.W. 1987. A Challenge to the Stages Theory of the Internationalization Process. In Reid, S. & Rosson, P. (eds.). *Managing Export Entry and Expansion*, New York: Praeger, p. 21–40.

Vachani, S. 1991. Distinguishing Between Related and Unrelated International Geographic Diversification: A Comprehensive Measure of Global Diversification. *Journal of International Business Studies*, 22(2): 307–22.

Veiga, J., Lubatkin, M., Calori, R. & Very, P. 2000a. Measuring Organizational Culture Clashes: A Two-Nation Post-Hoc Analysis of Cultural Compatibility Index. *Human Relations*, 53(4): 539–57.

——, ——, Calori, R., Very, P. & Tung, Y.A. 2000b. Using Neutral Network Analysis to Uncover the Trace Effects of National Culture. *Journal of International Business Studies*, 31(2): 223–38.

Webber, R. 1969. Convergence or Divergence? *Columbia Journal of World Business*, 4, 3.

Weber, Y., Shenkar, O. & Raveh, A. 1996. National and Corporate Cultural Fit in Mergers & Acquisitions: An Exploratory Study. *Management Science*, 42(8): 1215–27.

Welch, L.S. & Luostarinen, R. 1988. Internationalization: Evolution of a Concept. *Journal of General Management* 14(2): 34–55.

Williamson, O. 1985. *The Economic Institutions of Capitalism.* New York: Free Press.

World Competitiveness Yearbook. 2000.

Yoshino, Michael Y. 1976. *Japan's Multinational Enterprises.* Cambridge, MA: Harvard University Press.

25 Transforming disadvantages into advantages

Developing-country MNEs in the least developed countries*

Alvaro Cuervo-Cazurra and Mehmet Genc

Introduction

Sarik Tara, chairman of Enka Holding, Turkey's biggest construction company, has learnt to search for contracts in difficult places. "I am stamped 'Made in Turkey', not 'Made in Germany'," says Mr. Tara. "I have to try harder. No one is going to ask me to build anything in the Champs Elysees. I have to go to difficult countries where it is easier for me to win contracts."

The collapse of communism opened a new chapter for Enka. Its first job was the restoration of the Petrovsky Passage, a shopping arcade in Moscow, in 1988. Through Mosenka, the company's Russian arm, Enka has become the biggest private real-estate owner in Moscow, and one of the city's leading developers. It has also completed more than 60 projects within the Russian Federation. (Munir, 2002: 2)

The story of Enka illustrates the disadvantages and advantages of developing-country multinational enterprises (MNEs) in comparison with developed-country MNEs. Compared with developed-country MNEs, developing-country MNEs tend to be of smaller size (Wells, 1983) and to possess technology that is less cutting-edge (Lall, 1983; Wells, 1983) and resources that are less sophisticated (Bartlett & Ghoshal, 2000; Dawar & Frost, 1999). Additionally, country-of-origin effects may create a disadvantageous image among potential clients (Bilkey & Nes, 1982). These factors compound the difficulties these companies suffer as a result of operating in a home country characterized by a difficult institutional environment and inefficient or missing market mechanisms (Ghemawat & Khanna, 1998; Khanna & Palepu, 1997, 2000).

Nevertheless, developing-country MNEs can be successful abroad, despite these disadvantages. Their ability to manage in difficult institutional conditions, a capability they were required to foster in their home countries to survive and be successful there, may be useful in other developing countries that also have difficult conditions and therefore present similar problems. They would be at less of a disadvantage and in some cases may even have an edge over their developed-country counterparts. This is the central argument of our paper. In other words, although both sets of foreign firms will face difficulties in their internationalization (Cuervo-Cazurra et al., 2007) that put them at a disadvantage in relationship to local competitors (Zaheer, 1995), when developing-country MNEs are operating in third countries with

*Reprinted by permission from Macmillan Publishers Ltd: Cuervo-Cazurra, A., & M. Genc, 'Transforming disadvantages into advantages: developing-country MNEs in the least developed countries', Journal of International Business Studies, 39 (6): 957–979. Copyright 2008, published by Palgrave Macmillan.

difficult institutional conditions, they may face fewer difficulties than developed-country MNEs thanks to their ability to manage under difficult conditions. As a result, developing-country MNEs become more prevalent among the largest foreign firms there. We discuss these ideas in the context of the least developed countries (LDCs): countries with very low income, weak human capital and high economic vulnerability (UNCTAD, 2004: xiv).

The arguments presented in this chapter contribute to three streams of literature: one focusing on institutions and MNE behavior, a second on competitive advantage and disadvantage and a third on developing-country MNEs. First, we discuss how *home* country institutions and *similarity* between home and host country institutional environments influence the competitive behavior of MNEs abroad. This complements the majority of studies in the international management literature that have focused on studying the influence of *host* country institutions on the entry of foreign MNEs (for example, Bevan et al., 2004; Henisz, 2000). Second, we argue that suffering from the disadvantage of having a home country with poor institutions can become a competitive advantage abroad. This complements the argument that advantages at one point in time can become disadvantages at a later point in time (Leonard-Barton, 1992). Third, this chapter is the first to analyze competition between developing- and developed-country MNEs in multiple host countries: the LDCs. This complements existing analyses of the behavior of developed-country MNEs in developed (Tallman, 1991) and developing countries (Rangan & Drummond, 2004), as well as competition between developed and developing countries in the home markets of the latter (Dawar & Frost, 1999).

A better understanding of where developing-country MNEs can be relatively more successful is important for managers. It can help managers of developing-country MNEs better select countries into which to expand their firms. It also helps dispel the assumption held by many of these managers that their firms will always be at a disadvantage relative to developed-country MNEs. Developing-country MNEs can have an advantage, at least in some countries.

The rest of the chapter is organized as follows. In the following section we review existing literature on developing-country MNEs' advantages and disadvantages relative to developed-country MNEs. We then provide a short description of LDCs, discussing their importance as an empirical setting and appropriate laboratory to test our arguments. After this we build on the resource-based theory to elaborate the arguments presented to explain how more difficult governance conditions in LDCs would lead to the prevalence of developing-country MNEs among the largest affiliates of foreign firms there. A discussion of the research design follows. Next, we present the results of the empirical analysis and discuss their implications. We conclude by outlining the contributions of the present study to existing knowledge.

Disadvantages and advantages of developing-country MNEs in comparison with developed-country MNEs

Although there was some interest in and research on developing-country MNEs in the late 1970s and early 1980s (for example, Kumar & McLeod, 1981; Lall, 1983; Lecraw, 1977; Wells, 1983), there has been a lull in research in this area (Lecraw, 1993: 589) despite the large gaps in our knowledge (Wells, 1998). Attention to this topic is starting to resurface, in part as a result of the increased interest in emerging markets (for example, Amsden, 2001; Hoskisson et al., 2000; Wright et al., 2005), and in part because developing-country firms are quickly catching up and internationalizing (for example, Aulakh et al., 2000; Cuervo-Cazurra, 2007, 2008a; del Sol & Kogan, 2007; Lecraw, 1993; Young et al., 1996; see the special issues edited by Aulakh, 2007 and by Luo & Tung, 2007). As a result, these countries and firms are becoming an important research topic in international business (Buckley, 2002).

Within the study of developing-country MNEs (for reviews, see Yeung, 1994, 1999), we focus on the narrower topic of advantages and disadvantages of these companies compared with developed-country MNEs when both operate in a third country. Our study therefore complements the limited research on competition among foreign firms from different countries in a single host market (Rangan & Drummond, 2004; Tallman, 1991). Tallman (1991) analyzes strategic groups of foreign firms in the automobile industry in the USA; his account of their activities and performance is informed by the resource-based view. Rangan and Drummond (2004) analyze foreign firms in Brazil, and argue that those coming from countries with strong ties to Brazil dominate others, unless the foreign firm is the leader in the competitor's country of origin. We build on these studies by analyzing competition across multiple countries, comparing firms from developed countries with firms from developing countries and explaining why developing-country MNEs can become prevalent in other countries despite their relative disadvantages.

Disadvantages of developing-country MNEs in comparison with developed-country MNEs

Although both have their respective advantages, it is generally accepted that developing-country MNEs are at a disadvantage relative to developed-country MNEs. Both developed- and developing-country MNEs have ownership advantages from firm-specific resources that help them internationalize (Dunning, 1977; Dunning et al., 1998; Hymer, 1976; Rugman & Verbeke, 1992; Tallman, 1992; see Cuervo-Cazurra & Un, 2004a, for a review of advantages of MNEs). However, developed-country MNEs tend to have stronger ownership advantages in areas such as branding and advertising (Lall, 1983) and technology (Bartlett & Ghoshal, 2000; Dawar & Frost, 1999; Wells, 1983). Moreover, host governments favor the establishment of developed-country MNEs, which is believed to bring more advanced technology to the country (Stopford & Strange, 1992), while individual consumers often prefer products that are provided by foreign firms from developed countries (Bilkey & Nes, 1982). Finally, MNEs from developing countries often find themselves in the position of late movers, competing against well-seasoned and well-heeled developed-country MNEs as well as local firms with superior knowledge of their home turf (Bartlett & Ghoshal, 2000).

These perceived relative disadvantages are evident in the prevalence of developing-country MNEs among the largest firms in the world. Although developing-country MNEs have increased in numbers in recent years, they still constitute only a minute fraction of the largest firms. Table 25.1 summarizes the evolution of developing- and developed-country MNEs in the 1990s and early 2000s.[1] First, we analyze the prevalence of developing-country firms among the *Fortune Global 500,* which are the largest public firms in the world ranked by revenue. Although their numbers have increased, developing-country firms account for only between 5 and 8.4 percent of the largest public firms. Moreover, they tend to be present at the lower end of the ranking. For example, in 2003, the first developing-country firm appeared in position 46. Among the top 200 there are 13 developing-country firms, while among the bottom 200 there are 21. Second, we study the prevalence of developing-country MNEs among transnational firms, as reported by the United Nations Conference on Trade and Development (UNCTAD). UNCTAD compiles a list of transnationals, which it defines as firms with assets outside their home country. Developing-country firms have increased in number, moving from representing less than one eighth of all transnationals in 1991 to representing over one quarter in 2003. This increase took place at the same time that the overall number of transnationals in the world almost doubled, increasing from 35,000 in 1991 to 61,582 in 2003. However, despite these increases, developing-country firms are not prevalent

Table 25.1 Evolution of developing-country MNEs, 1990–2003

Year	Percentage of developing-country firms		
	Among the largest 500 public firms in the world[a]	Among all transnational firms in the world[b]	Among the largest 100 transnational firms in the world[c]
1990	5.0	NA	0
1991	5.4	11.7	NA
1992	5.1	8.5	0
1993	5.0	8.7	0
1994	4.4	10.9	0
1995	5.0	11.7	2
1996	6.2	18.3	2
1997	5.8	19.2	2
1998	5.2	17.1	1
1999	6.8	24.6	3
2000	7.0	22.6	5
2001	7.4	22.2	4
2002	7.0	23.2	4
2003	8.4	26.8	4

NA: not available.

a *"Source:* Computed using data from *Fortune Global 500* (Fortune, 1995–2004) and *Fortune Global Industrial 500* (Fortune, 1991–1994a) and *Fortune Global Service 500* (Fortune, 1991–1994b). The largest public firms are ranked by revenue. The *Global 500* includes industrial and service firms for 1994–2003. Between 1990 and 1993, there are two rankings, one for industrial firms and another for service firms. The data presented for these years are the number and percentage of developing-country firms among the largest 1000 industrial and service firms.

b *Source:* Computed using data from UNCTAD (1992–2005), number of parent corporations by region and economy. The number of developing-country MNEs was computed by deducting the developed-country MNEs from the total number of transnational firms. The number of transnational firms is based on national sources that vary in their definition and year of collection, resulting in an underestimation of the numbers (UNCTAD, 1992: 13). For more information regarding the limitations of the database, please see the original source.

c *Source:* Computed using data from UNCTAD (1992–2005), the top 100 transnational corporations ranked by foreign assets. Data on the top transnational firms are provided with a 2-year lag. There are no data for 1991 because the 1993 report provides the top 100 firms using 1990 data, while the 1994 report provides the top 100 firms using 1992 data.

among the largest transnationals. In the early 1990s, no developing-country firms appeared among the largest 100 transnationals. By 2002, there were only four firms.

Advantages of developing-country MNEs in comparison with developed-country MNEs

We argue that, as well as experiencing disadvantages, developing-country MNEs also experience some advantages. These enable them to compete at home against larger developed-country MNEs (Dawar & Frost, 1999). In their home countries, developing-country firms know their clients better and have production facilities and distribution networks that are better adapted to the conditions of the country (Lall, 1983). They also know how to operate in the challenging institutional environment – comprising an imperfect contracting environment, less-developed market mechanisms, an inefficient judiciary, unpredictable and burdensome regulations, heavy bureaucracy, political instability or discontinuity in government policies – that characterizes developing countries (Ghemawat & Khanna, 1998; Khanna & Palepu, 1997). On some occasions, they are even supported by their governments (Aggarwal & Agmon, 1990). Additionally, developed-country MNEs face difficulties in their internationalization in developing countries (Cuervo-Cazurra & Un, 2004b). The absence of a well-established infrastructure, well-developed market mechanisms and a well-developed contracting and intellectual property rights regime creates difficulties for developed-country MNEs, which are not used to such conditions (Prahalad & Lieberthal, 1998).

Moreover, developing-country MNEs also have advantages that enable them to compete in other developing countries against developed-country MNEs and become leading investors there: this is the focus of the present paper. Both types of MNE face difficulties in their internationalization (Cuervo-Cazurra et al., 2007; Eden and Miller, 2004). However, developing-country MNEs may face fewer difficulties than their developed-country counterparts when expanding into other developing countries because of their familiarity with the more difficult institutional conditions of developing countries and their expertise in managing in such environments. As a result, they become leading investors in those countries.

There is some anecdotal evidence that developing-country MNEs may have an edge in other developing countries thanks to their ability to manage there, although this has not been formally tested. The 2005 World Bank's *Global Development Finance Report* indicates that companies from China, India, Malaysia, Russia and South Africa are becoming important investors in many developing countries (World Bank, 2005: 99). The report suggests that these firms have comparative advantages, in the form of greater experience with the economic and political conditions of the host country, lower overhead costs, managers who are indigenous to the region, geographical proximity, and cultural similarities. These render coordination of foreign operations less expensive. The World Bank's report cites the example of Uganda's mobile-phone market, as reported by Goldstein (2004). Celtel, a subsidiary of Britain's Vodafone, once enjoyed a comfortable monopoly. South Africa's MTN entered the market and built a subscriber base 22 times larger thanks to its expertise in dealing with the economic and political risks.

The least developed countries

We analyze in detail and test the argument that developing-country MNEs may have an edge over developed-country MNEs in other developing countries by analyzing the prevalence of developing-country MNEs among the largest foreign firms in the Least Developed Countries (LDCs). These countries have very challenging environments, as they are at the bottom of the development scale among developing countries; they provide a natural setting to test our arguments. By choosing an extreme research setting, we can provide a reliable test of our arguments where the ability to manage in a difficult environment takes prevalence over other advantages, such as technology or marketing. In other words, if we argue that governance quality, or lack thereof, is a determining factor in the success of developing-country firms, we would want to test this in countries with very poor governance, where the ability to manage the institutional environment would be crucial to success. In other parts of the world this particular capability would still be useful, but it could be overshadowed by other capabilities.

The United Nations defines an LDC as a country that fulfills three criteria (UNCTAD, 2004: xiv). First, it is low-income, as measured by gross national income per capita. Second, it suffers human resources weaknesses, as measured by a composite index of per capita intake of calories, child mortality rate, secondary school enrollment, and adult literacy. Third, it has high economic vulnerability, measured by a composite index of instability in agricultural production, instability in exports of goods and services, the share of manufacturing and services in GDP, merchandise export concentration, and population.

According to the United Nations' classification, 50 countries in the world qualify as LDCs (UNCTAD, 2001b, 2004). They represent a total population of 703 million inhabitants (11.2 percent of the world's population) and a total GDP of only US$224 billion (0.6 percent

Table 25.2 Selective descriptive statistics for the least developed countries

Country	GDP[a] (US$m)	Population[b] (1,000s)	GNI per capita[c] (US$)	Life expectancy[d] (years)	Adult literacy[e] (% adults)
Afghanistan	11,704.5	28,766.0	406	43.2	36.0
Angola	13,189.2	13,522.0	740	46.7	42.0
Bangladesh	51,897.3	138,066.0	400	62.1	41.1
Benin	3498.8	6720.0	440	52.7	39.8
Bhutan	645.0	874.0	660	63.2	47.0
Burkina Faso	4181.9	12,109.0	300	42.9	12.8
Burundi	669.2	7206.0	100	41.7	50.4
Cambodia	4299.2	13,404.0	310	54.0	69.4
Cape Verde	831.1	470.0	1490	69.1	75.7
Central African Republic	1198.2	3881.0	260	42.1	48.6
Chad	2647.6	8582.0	250	48.4	45.8
Comoros	322.7	600.0	450	61.4	56.2
Congo, Dem. Republic	5600.2	53,153.0	100	45.3	62.7
Djibouti	625.0	705.0	910	43.5	65.5
East Timor	314.5	810.0	430	57.4	43.0
Equatorial Guinea	2894.0	494.0	930	51.7	84.2
Eritrea	734.2	4389.0	190	51.1	56.7
Ethiopia	6637.8	68,613.0	90	42.1	41.5
Gambia	386.3	1421.0	310	53.4	37.8
Guinea	3625.7	7909.0	430	46.2	41.0
Guinea-Bissau	235.7	1489.0	140	45.4	39.6
Haiti	2744.8	8440.0	380	52.0	51.9
Kiribati	58.4	96.0	880	62.8	NA
Laos	2035.5	5660.0	320	54.5	66.4
Lesotho	1135.3	1793.0	590	37.9	81.4
Liberia	442.2	3374.0	130	47.1	54.0
Madagascar	5458.8	16,894.0	290	55.5	67.3
Malawi	1731.2	10,962.0	170	37.5	61.8
Maldives	695.8	293.0	2300	69.2	97.2
Mali	4326.0	11,652.0	290	40.9	19.0
Mauritania	1127.6	2693.1	430	51.0	41.2
Mozambique	4320.4	18,791.0	210	41.1	46.5
Myanmar	12,905.7	49,362.0	261	57.2	85.3
Nepal	5834.9	24,660.0	240	59.9	44.0
Niger	2729.7	11,762.0	200	46.2	17.1
Rwanda	1637.3	8251.0	220	39.8	69.2
Samoa	322.6	178.0	1600	69.4	98.7
Sao Tome & Principe	53.7	157.0	320	65.8	83.1
Senegal	6496.4	10,048.0	550	52.3	39.3
Sierra Leone	793.3	5337.0	150	37.4	36.0
Solomon Islands	256.7	457.0	600	69.3	76.6
Somalia	1772.4	9626.0	184	47.4	24.0
Sudan	17,793.2	33,546.0	460	58.4	59.9
Togo	1758.9	4861.0	310	49.6	59.6
Tuvalu	13.9	10.5	1323	NA	NA
Uganda	6197.7	25,280.0	240	43.1	68.9
United Rep. of Tanzania	9871.8	35,889.0	290	43.1	77.1
Vanuatu	283.3	210.0	1,180	68.5	34.0
Yemen	10,830.6	19,173.0	520	57.4	49.0
Zambia	4298.9	10,403.0	380	36.9	79.9

(*Continued*)

Table 25.2 (Continued)

Country	GDP[a] (US$m)	Population[b] (1,000s)	GNI per capita[c] (US$)	Life expectancy[d] (years)	Adult literacy[e] (% adults)
Averages					
Least developed countries	4481.3	14,060.8	487.0	51.3	54.6
Other developing countries	69,261.3	36,925.8	4072.4	69.0	88.7
Developed countries	1,110,756.9	28,164.4	26,200.8	78.1	99.0

Source: Created using data from the UNCTAD and World Development Indicators databases.

NA: not available.

a Gross domestic product in millions of current US$, 2003 or latest available year. Data for Myanmar are in PPP terms.
b Population in thousands of individuals, 2003 or latest available year.
c Gross national income per capita in US$ following the Atlas method (average exchange rate of the last 3 years), 2003 or latest available year. Data for Myanmar are available only in PPP terms.
d Life expectancy (years expected to live from birth) in years, 2002 or latest available year.
e Adult literacy as percentage of adult population (15 years or older), 2002 or latest available year.

of world total). Table 25.2 provides a list of LDCs and basic information about each. Comparing the averages of selected indicators, we note that LDCs have an average GNI per capita of less than $500, a life expectancy of a little over 50 years and an adult literacy rate of less than 60 percent. This contrasts not only with developed countries, which have an average GNI per capita of over $26,000, life expectancy close to 80 years and a fully literate population, but also with other developing countries, which have an average GNI per capita of over $4000, life expectancy of almost 70 years, and an adult literacy rate of almost 90 percent.

These countries are an interesting research setting, not only because of our limited knowledge about them, but also because a better understanding can help move these countries out of poverty. FDI can play an important role in the economic growth and development of LDCs (UNCTAD, 2002: 1). At the same time, these countries can be important sources of revenue for MNEs (Prahalad, 2004). For example, mobile telephony has grown faster in Africa than in any other region of the world in the period 1996–2003, with an average growth rate of 78 percent a year. Although the initial base was very small, it has overtaken fixed lines, which have traditionally been provided by inefficient state-owned monopolies. This expansion of telephony has been led by MNEs, many of them African ones (White, 2003).

Converting a disadvantage into an advantage: developing-country MNEs in the least developed countries

The institutional environment of a given country refers to the set of rules and regulations that govern economic activity in that country (North, 1990). Managers develop the ability to manage in a particular institutional environment over time in a learning-by-doing manner (Eriksson et al., 1997; Johanson & Vahlne, 1977). They generate assumptions and attitudes that influence the way in which the firm governs its relationships with its external environment.

In the case of developing-country MNEs, these firms emerge in countries that are characterized by poorer governance compared with developed countries. As the firm internationalizes, its managers will be able to maneuver more easily in other countries that also have poor governance conditions, because they understand the norms for conducting business there: for example, they know the norms regarding corruption (Cuervo-Cazurra, 2006). In contrast, managers of developed-country MNEs, who are used to operating in countries with better governance and institutions, face the challenge of altering their deep-seated assumptions about the institutional environment (Prahalad & Hammond, 2002). They will also be hampered by inefficient markets that make their technological and other firm-specific resources less valuable, because these resources require the presence of relatively well-developed markets and a stable contracting environment.

Hence we expect developing-country MNEs to be more prevalent in LDCs with worse institutional conditions, because managers of developing-country MNEs can more easily understand and adapt to these poor conditions than can their developed-country counterparts. That said, however, we do not argue that MNEs from developed countries cannot successfully operate in these countries. As we indicate later in our discussion, many developed-country MNEs are present in LDCs and in many LDCs they constitute the majority of the largest affiliates. What we claim is that the poorer the quality of governance in a country, the higher the number of developing-country MNEs among the largest subsidiaries in that country.

Governance refers to the institutions and traditions by which authority is established in a country and which affect the rules and regulations according to which economic activity is undertaken. Following research conducted at the World Bank (Kaufmann et al., 2003; Kaufmann et al., 1999) we discuss six dimensions: voice and accountability, political stability and absence of violence, government effectiveness, regulatory quality, rule of law, and control of corruption. These six dimensions correspond to three aspects of governance. The first two, voice and accountability, and political stability and absence of violence, reflect the process by which governments are selected, monitored and replaced. The second two, government effectiveness and regulatory quality, represent the capacity of the government to effectively formulate and implement sound policies. The final two, rule of law and control of corruption, reflect the respect of the state and its citizens for the institutions that govern the social and economic interactions among them.

Not all of these dimensions have the same importance for MNEs. For example, as we will discuss further, the existence of government accountability to citizens is less likely to affect the behavior of foreign MNEs. In contrast, the absence of rule of law, or a poorly developed, stifling regulatory environment in which regulations do not apply equally to all, may discourage all foreign firms from investing in the country. Despite the greater importance of certain dimensions, in the current study all six are analyzed, in order to provide a comprehensive analysis of governance. The empirical test will reveal the dimensions that are relevant in explaining the prevalence of developing-country MNEs in LDCs.

Voice and accountability

Voice and accountability represent the ability of citizens to participate in the selection of their governments, in terms of the political process, civil liberties, and political rights (Kaufmann et al., 2003). Although voice and accountability are important features of the governance environment of the country, they tend to matter less to foreign investors than other governance dimensions. MNEs will still invest in a country where the citizens cannot affect the political process if there are good business opportunities. The recent inflows of FDI into China illustrate this. By 2003, China, which has an authoritarian regime, had become the second largest recipient of FDI inflows in the world, with $53 billion.

Nevertheless, developing-country MNEs may have a slight edge in LDCs with poor voice and accountability because they should be more adept at dealing with this. Managers of developing-country MNEs may have learned how to interact with dictators or authoritarian regimes because of their experience in dealing with current or past totalitarian regimes in their country of origin. Additionally, some developed-country MNEs face pressures from non-governmental organizations and home country governments that limit their operations in total-itarian regimes. For example, US firms were pressed to limit their operations in South Africa in the 1980s when the country was under the apartheid regime. Thus we hypothesize that:

> **Hypothesis 1:** The lower the voice and accountability in an LDC, the higher the prevalence of developing-country MNEs among the largest subsidiaries of foreign firms in that country.

Political stability and the absence of violence

The dimension of political stability and the absence of violence refers to the idea that the quality of governance in a country can be jeopardized by the probability of sudden changes in government, which can disrupt existing policies and limit the ability of citizens to select and replace government peacefully (Kaufmann et al., 2003). Foreign firms are concerned about political stability in the host country because sudden changes of politicians may lead to changes in policies with regard to foreign investors, and even reneging upon existing con-tracts (Henisz & Williamson, 1999). For example, the financial crisis in Argentina in late 2001, which resulted in the collapse of the economy and the change of government three times in two weeks, also resulted in new legislation against foreign investors, especially those in utilities and energy (*Economist*, 2005a).

All foreign investors can potentially suffer from political instability, but developing-country MNEs may be better at dealing with it because they are used to political instability and violence in their home countries. For example, Turkish firms have experienced several epi-sodes of high political instability in the past. As a result, they have internationalized into countries in the Middle East and in the former Soviet Union with high success, partly because of their ability to manage in such difficult conditions, as the opening example illustrated. Additionally, in the case of political crises, foreign firms, particularly those from developed countries, become the target of attacks, as happened in Argentina in late 2001 and early 2002. Developed-country MNEs are branded as instruments of imperialistic rule and are subjected to political risks (Fitzpatrick, 1983; Kobrin, 1979) that may reduce their willingness and ability to become large players in politically volatile countries. Therefore we contend that:

> **Hypothesis 2:** The lower the political stability in an LDC, the higher the prevalence of developing-country MNEs among the largest subsidiaries of foreign firms in that country.

Government effectiveness

Government effectiveness refers to the quality of the "inputs" required by the government to implement good policies and deliver public goods. It represents the quality of the bureau-cracy and of public service provisions, the competence of civil servants, the independence of civil servants from political pressures, and the credibility of the government's commitment to policies (Kaufmann et al., 2003). Government effectiveness is important for foreign investors in the sense that they do not have to invest to cover for the deficiencies in the provision of public goods by the government.

Although governmental inefficiency harms all foreign firms, developing-country MNEs may be able to deal with it better because they are used to doing so at home. Developing-country MNEs come from countries that have lower government effectiveness, and are therefore more used to dealing with a slow, politically dependent bureaucracy and lack of high-quality public goods (Ghemawat & Khanna, 1998). As a result, they are also more experienced in investing in the provision of public goods because their home governments do not supply these (Fisman & Khanna, 2004). Thus developing-country MNEs may face less difficulty in LDCs than developed-country MNEs because the former take into account the inefficiency of the government in their decision to enter and invest in the country. In contrast, developed-country MNEs may not have planned for the ineffectiveness of the government and may become laden with unexpected costs that limit their operations in the country. Therefore we hypothesize that:

> **Hypothesis 3:** The lower the government effectiveness in an LDC, the higher the prevalence of developing-country MNEs among the largest subsidiaries of foreign firms in that country.

Regulatory quality

Regulatory quality refers to the existence of market-unfriendly policies such as price controls or poor bank supervision, as well as perceptions of excessive regulation in areas such as business development, entry and obtaining licenses, or foreign trade; it also refers to whether regulations are applied uniformly or in a discretionary fashion (Kaufmann et al., 2003). Few companies like regulations, because these limit their freedom of operation. However, managers may be more concerned about the quality of the regulations than their level. A highly regulated industry constrains the firm but increases the certainty of operations. In contrast, a poorly designed regulatory framework introduces distortion into investments and increases the uncertainty of operation (Laffont & Tirole, 1995). In response, firms limit their investments, particularly large fixed ones such as production plants.

Developing-country MNEs may be better positioned to deal with poor regulation in LDCs and more willing to undertake large investments than developed-country MNEs. Developing-country MNEs emerge in countries where there is more political intervention in the economy in general. Managers of developing-country firms are likely to develop skills to cope with bureaucratic constraints at home (Ghemawat & Khanna, 1998) that can give their firms an edge when they expand into other developing countries (Lall, 1983: 63). These managers understand not only how to establish relationships with government officials, but also the way in which these relationships are altered with changes in the government or in the "mood" of government officials (Wells, 1983). These companies operate in expectation of such changes, understand the timing of these changes and develop flexible strategies to deal with them when they occur. In contrast, developed-country MNEs come from countries with better-defined rules of the game in industry, and where government has a reduced presence in the economy. These firms may become more reluctant to undertake large investments in a country where there are excessive regulations, or where regulations can vary unpredictably. Hence we argue that:

> **Hypothesis 4:** The lower the regulatory quality in an LDC, the higher the prevalence of developing-country MNEs among the largest subsidiaries of foreign firms in that country.

Rule of law

The rule of law refers to the success of a society in creating an environment in which fair and predictable rules form the basis for economic and social interactions, and, importantly, the extent to which property rights are enforced (Kaufmann et al., 2003). MNEs are less likely to invest in countries where there is poor rule of law, because they fear having their investments expropriated by the government (Fitzpatrick, 1983; Kobrin, 1979). They also fear the opportunistic behavior of business partners such as joint-venture partners, suppliers or clients, without the ability to use the judicial system to solve the contractual problems (Henisz, 2000). For example, the lack of good protection of private property rights in Russia, highlighted by the prosecution of the former owner of the oil firm Yukos in 2004, reduced foreign investment (*Economist*, 2005b).

Developing-country MNEs may still be more adept at managing in such conditions than developed-country MNEs. They operate in home countries with poorer rule of law. Their managers may be more flexible with regard to the application of the law, and more used to managing outside the realm of contractual relationships (de Soto, 2000). They will also be more careful in choosing the right partners, because contractual disputes are unlikely to be resolved efficiently in courts. In contrast, developed-country MNEs are used to operating with stable institutions that clearly establish property rights and limit the ability of the government to alter its policies at will (World Bank, 2002). They are more likely to trust that they can recoup their losses through the judicial system if their partner reneges on the contract. Their inability to do so in LDCs will limit their willingness to have large investments there. Thus we contend that:

Hypothesis 5: The lower the rule of law in an LDC, the higher the prevalence of developing-country MNEs among the largest subsidiaries of foreign firms in that country.

Control of corruption

Corruption refers to the exercise of public power for private gain. The existence of corruption indicates a lack of respect for the rules that govern economic interactions in the society. It refers to the need to make additional, irregular payments to get things done, or to state capture by elites (Kaufmann et al., 2003). Corruption increases the difficulty of operating in the country (Shleifer & Vishny, 1993). It decreases foreign direct investment (FDI) and alters its composition (Wei, 2000; Smarzynska & Wei, 2000) and mode of entry (Rodriguez et al., 2005).

Developing-country MNEs are more used to dealing with corruption and face fewer constraints in the use of bribes than developed-country MNEs. Managers in developing countries are more used to facing corruption at home, especially low-level corruption in the form of small payments made in order to expedite procedures. Public employees' low salaries, as well as high levels of regulation and red tape, are common in developing countries, and provide fertile ground for such practices. As a result, developing-country MNEs are more used to paying in order to secure permits and win contracts, which can help them achieve an edge in LDCs with high corruption (Cuervo-Cazurra, 2006). In contrast, developed-country MNEs are less used to dealing with corruption at home. They are even constrained in bribing officials abroad because there are laws in their home country that explicitly forbid them from giving bribes to gain business abroad (Cuervo-Cazurra, 2008b). Moreover, non-governmental organizations closely monitor the behavior of developed-country MNEs, further constraining their ability to pay bribes in LDCs. As a result, these firms may not be able to secure key contracts or permits needed to operate in the country. We thus propose that:

Hypothesis 6: The lower the control of corruption in an LDC, the higher the prevalence of developing-country MNEs among the largest subsidiaries of foreign firms in that country.

Research design

We test our hypotheses on a database of the largest affiliates of foreign firms in LDCs. We know little about LDCs, particularly because of the difficulty of finding information about them. This is a challenge common to analyses of developing countries (for example, Aykut & Ratha, 2004; Booth et al., 2001; Wells, 1983). We rely on data collected by UNCTAD on LDCs. UNCTAD has published two reports on FDI in LDCs (UNCTAD, 2001a, 2002), with data for 1999 and 2001, for 49 countries. These are the only sources of data at the company level in LDCs that we could find, and are the most comprehensive listings on these countries. We use these lists, as well as additional data on each country from the World Bank, in our analysis of the factors that influence the prevalence of developing-country MNEs in LDCs.

Variables and measures

Table 25.3 summarizes the variables, measures, and data sources. The dependent variable is the prevalence of developing-country MNEs among the largest foreign firms in LDCs. We measure it as the share of developing-country MNE affiliates among all the largest affiliates of foreign MNEs in the country. To construct the measure, we used the list of the largest affiliates of foreign firms in each country that appear in the UNCTAD reports (2001a, 2002) and coded the affiliates into two groups based on their country of origin (developed or developing country) according to the UNCTAD (2004) classification of countries. We then divided the number of affiliates of developing-country MNEs by the total number of foreign affiliates and multiplied the resulting number by 100. We use a count rather than a sales proportion because the database does not provide sales information for many of the firms. Such a measure is in line with studies of the turnover among the largest firms over time (for example, Stonebraker, 1979). Additionally, we computed variations of the dependent variable to conduct robustness tests. In the first test, we excluded affiliates of firms in natural resource industries: agriculture, forestry, fishing, cattle, oil, and mining. We identified the industry of operation using the information on the industry provided in UNCTAD's list. In the second test, we excluded affiliates of former colonial powers. We identified the former colonial power using the CIA's (2005) indicator of independence, corroborating it with information from *Encyclopedia Britannica* (2005).

The independent variables of interest are the six governance dimensions discussed above: voice and accountability, political stability and absence of violence, government effectiveness, regulatory quality, rule of law, and control of corruption. For these, we use the indicators of the World Bank, described in detail in Kaufmann et al. (2003). Kaufmann et al. (1999) first identified the indicators for 1998 and created six composite aggregate indicators. Later, Kaufmann et al. (2003) revised the previous work and extended it to cover 199 countries for four time periods: 1996, 1998, 2000, and 2002. The use of these composite indicators reduces the limitations of using single measures. To facilitate interpretation, we modified their original spread of -2.5 to 2.5 to a spread of 0 to 5 by adding 2.5 to each score. This does not alter the statistical significance of the coefficients.

The differences in quality of governance across the three groups of countries – LDCs, other developing countries and developed countries – are significant. Looking at the most recent indicators of governance, the averages for LDCs are 1.85 for voice and accountability, 1.89 for political stability and absence of violence, 1.73 for government effectiveness, 1.70 for regulatory quality, 1.76 for rule of law, and 1.81 for control of corruption. This is in contrast to other developing countries, which have the following scores: 2.43 for voice and accountability, 2.48 for political stability and absence of violence, 2.43 for government effectiveness,

Table 25.3 Variables, measures, and sources of data

Variable	Measure	Source
Dependent variables		
Prevalence of developing-country MNEs	Number of largest affiliates of MNEs from developing countries divided by total number of largest affiliates of foreign firms and multiplied by 100	Computed using data from FDI in LDCs in UNCTAD (2001a, 2002)
Prevalence of developing-country MNEs excluding firms in natural resource industries	Number of largest affiliates of MNEs from developing countries, excluding those in natural resource industries (agriculture, fishing, forestry, cattle, oil, mining), divided by total number of largest affiliates of foreign firms, excluding those in natural resource industries, and multiplied by 100	Computed using data from FDI in LDCs in UNCTAD (2001a, 2002)
Prevalence of developing-country MNEs excluding firms from former colonial power	Number of largest affiliates of MNEs from developing countries divided by total number of largest affiliates of foreign firms, excluding firms from former colonial power, and multiplied by 100	Computed using data from FDI in LDCs in UNCTAD (2001a, 2002) and information on the colonial power from CIA (2005) and *Encyclopedia Britannica* (2005)
Independent variables of interest		
Voice and accountability	Indicator of accountability of government, from 0 to 5	Data from aggregate governance indicators database, Kaufmann et al. (2003)
Political stability and absence of violence	Indicator of political stability and absence of violence in the country, from 0 to 5	Data from aggregate governance indicators database, Kaufmann et al. (2003)
Government effectiveness	Indicator of effectiveness of government, from 0 to 5	Data from aggregate governance indicators database, Kaufmann et al. (2003)
Regulatory quality	Indicator of quality of regulation, from 0 to 5	Data from aggregate governance indicators database, Kaufmann et al. (2003)
Rule of law	Indicator of rule of law, from 0 to 5	Data from aggregate governance indicators database, Kaufmann et al. (2003)
Control of corruption	Indicator of control of corruption, from 0 to 5	Data from aggregate governance indicators database, Kaufmann et al. (2003)
Control variables		
GNI per capita	Gross national income divided by number of inhabitants, in US$	Data from World Development Indicators database, World Bank (2004)
Roads paved	Kilometers of roads paved as percentage of total kilometers of roads	Data from World Development Indicators database, World Bank (2004)
Phones per capita	Number of fixed-line and mobile telephones per 1,000 inhabitants	Data from World Development Indicators database, World Bank (2004)
Geographic proximity	Dummy indicator of existence of a firm from a country with common border with the LDC among the largest affiliates of foreign firms in the country, 0 or 1	Computed using data from FDI in LDCs in UNCTAD (2001a, 2002) and list of neighboring countries from CIA (2005)
Colonial link	Dummy indicator of the existence of a firm from the former colonial power of the LDC among largest affiliates of foreign firms in the country, 0 or 1	Computed using data from FDI in LDCs in UNCTAD (2001a, 2002) and information on the colonial power from CIA (2005) and *Encyclopedia Britannica* (2005)

2.47 for regulatory quality, 2.43 for rule of law, and 2.39 for control of corruption. Developed countries have much higher scores in all dimensions: 3.85 for voice and accountability, 3.56 for political stability and absence of violence, 4.12 for government effectiveness, 3.98 for regulatory quality, 4.06 for rule of law, and 4.14 for control of corruption.

Additional influences: economic, geographic and cultural factors

In addition to governance, other characteristics of the host country can play a role in the increased prevalence of developing-country MNEs in LDCs. A country's environment can be analyzed in four dimensions (Ghemawat, 2001): cultural, administrative, geographic and economic (CAGE). These can be viewed as roughly corresponding to four disciplines that focus on a country's environment: sociology, political economy, geography and economics. Although Ghemawat (2001) proposed this CAGE framework to analyze distance between countries, we believe that it is a useful tool to analyze the country environment in general. In the hypothesis development we focused on governance, which can be viewed as the administrative dimension. We now describe how we controlled for economic, geographical and cultural dimensions.

Economic environment: wealth and infrastructure. Developing-country MNEs may be better adapted to operate in countries with poorer customers. They are better positioned to serve the needs of poor people in LDCs because they emerge in countries where citizens have lower average levels of wealth, and where the distribution of wealth is more skewed than in developed countries (World Bank, 2002). The knowledge and resources developed to serve customers who have low income are equally valuable in LDCs. In contrast, developed-country MNEs may struggle to understand consumers' preferences in LDCs and have to undertake additional investments to adapt their products and ways of dealing with poor clients, such as reducing the size of the product, using less expensive ingredients, or providing financing to enable the purchase (Prahalad & Hammond, 2002; Yunus, 1999). We measure wealth using GNI per capita.

Developing-country MNEs are also likely to be better adapted to the poor infrastructure of LDCs. Developing-country MNEs are used to operating in countries with less developed infrastructure, adapting their technology and managerial skills to these conditions (Lall, 1983). In contrast, developed-country MNEs are used to being supported by well-established infrastructures and developing ownership advantages built on that external infrastructure. These firms face a challenge when moving into LDCs because much of the infrastructure with which they are used to working in their home country, such as nationwide distribution channels, transportation networks and high-capacity communication networks, is absent in these markets (Prahalad & Lieberthal, 1998; Prahalad & Hammond, 2002). We measure infrastructure in two ways: communication infrastructure, measured as the number of fixed line and mobile phones per thousand people; and transportation infrastructure, measured as the percentage of kilometers of roads that are paved, divided by the total number of kilometers of roads in the country.

Geographic environment: proximity. Developing-country MNEs may have an edge in LDCs thanks to the geographic proximity between home and host country. Geographic distance, or proximity, alters the attractiveness of host countries and affects the ease of trading and operating across countries (Ghemawat, 2001; Johanson & Vahlne, 1977; Johanson & Wiedersheim-Paul, 1975). The addition of foreign operations and their physical distance requires the firm to deal with additional transportation, communication, and coordination (Hitt et al., 1997; Vernon, 1977). Developing countries are often closer to each other; there are few common borders between developed and developing countries. Proximity of other developing countries to LDCs can give developing-country MNEs a natural advantage. For example, India and China account for more than half of the FDI in Nepal: India in hotels and manufacturing and China in manufacturing (World Bank, 2005: 99). Geographic proximity was measured using a binary indicator of the existence of a common border between the home country of a firm listed among the largest foreign affiliates, and the host LDC.

Cultural environment: colonialism. The cultural environment may influence the operations of developing-country MNEs in LDCs, but, unlike other dimensions, there is no clear advantage over developed-country MNEs in this regard. One cannot establish a clear distinction in terms of culture between developed- and developing-country MNEs that influences their operations in LDCs. Culture alone may not yield significant differences in the dominance of one or another type of foreign investor (Rangan & Drummond, 2004), as it masks too many underlying assumptions (Shenkar, 2001). Cultural similarities among countries can be traced back to the transfer of the culture through population movements. These have been particularly important in the case of colonization, where the colonial power imposes upon its colonies its language and religion, as well as norms of behavior such as the legal system (La Porta et al., 1998). A common colonial past results in a commonality in cultural attitudes across countries that are far apart and have not had direct ties of their own. For example, there are high cultural similarities between Australia, Canada, Ireland, New Zealand, South Africa and the United States (Hofstede, 1980); all were former colonies of Great Britain. However, such similarity in culture is not assured; there are few cultural similarities between these countries and other former colonies of Great Britain such as India, Myanmar, or Kenya, nor between the latter three. Nevertheless, firms from the former colonial power may still benefit from the direct ties and transfer of values established at the time of the colonial relationship (Rangan & Drummond, 2004): we thus control for their presence. We measure colonial links using an indicator of the existence of MNEs from the former colonial power among the largest affiliates of foreign firms in the LDC.

Method of analysis

We used a Tobit model to test the hypotheses, because the dependent variable is constrained to an interval of 0 to 100. Since the error term is truncated, the use of regression would yield biased results (Maddala, 1983; Tobin, 1958). Since we have data for two time periods, we were able to control for other unobserved characteristics that may influence the dependent variable by using a cross-sectional panel. The results report the feasibility of using a random effect cross-sectional panel Tobit by comparing it with the pooled panel Tobit. We use the following specification:

> Prevalence of developing-country MNE affiliates among the largest affiliates of foreign firms in the LDC
> $= \beta_0 + \beta_1$ Voice and accountability
> $+ \beta_1$ Political stability and absence of violence
> $+ \beta_2$ Government effectiveness
> $+ \beta_3$ Regulatory quality $+ \beta_4$ Rule of law
> $+ \beta_5$ Control of corruption $+ \beta_6$ Wealth

$+ \beta_7$ Transportation infrastructure
$+ \beta_8$ Communication infrastructure
$+ \beta_9$ Geographic proximity
$+ \beta_{10}$ Colonial link $+ \varepsilon$

The hypotheses are supported if the coefficients of β_1 to β_6 are negative and statistically significant.

Results

Table 25.4 provides the summary statistics and correlation matrix. Many of the variables show high correlation. This is to be expected, because all of these countries share low levels of economic and human development. We checked for the possibility of collinearity among independent variables by running a variance inflation matrix analysis. The result is a maximum value of 3.92 and an average value of 2.73, which are lower than the accepted value of 30 that indicates problems of collinearity (StataCorp, 2001).

Prevalence of developing-country MNEs among the largest foreign firms in LDCs

We test the influence of the governance characteristics of LDCs on the prevalence of developing-country MNEs among the largest foreign investors by means of a Tobit analysis. Developing-country MNEs represent 10 per cent of the 30 largest MNEs in LDCs, which contrasts with 4 per cent among the largest 100 transnationals in the world (UNCTAD, 2002). Hence developing-country MNEs are relatively more prevalent among the largest subsidiaries in LDCs than one would otherwise expect. The governance characteristics of LDCs may explain why this is the case.

Table 25.5 presents the results of the analyses examining the prevalence of developing-country MNEs among the largest foreign firms in LDCs. We discuss the results of Model 1b, which is the full model. The results support the idea that developing-country MNEs tend to be more prevalent in LDCs with poorer governance. The coefficients of regulatory quality and control of corruption are negative and statistically significant, the coefficient of rule of law is positive and statistically significant, and the coefficients of the other variables are not statistically significant. These results support Hypotheses 4 and 6, are contrary to Hypothesis 5, and do not provide support for Hypotheses 1–3. In other words, the prevalence of developing-country MNEs among the largest foreign affiliates is, as expected, negatively related to regulatory quality and the control of corruption, but, contrary to expectations, positively related to the rule of law. As we noted, some of these variables were not expected to affect the prevalence of developing-country MNEs.

These results imply that, although developing-country MNEs may have an edge in LDCs because they know how to deal with the poorer regulatory quality and lower control of corruption that is prominent in developing countries, they nevertheless prefer LDCs where the rule of law applies and property rights are protected. Managers of developing-country MNEs may be more adept at dealing with corruption and with imperfect and changing regulation, but still prefer respect for rules and enforceable contracts. An example that illustrates this point is the case of a Taiwanese firm investing in Vietnam: the firm "was so frustrated by corrupt customs officials who failed to do what they had been bribed to do that it tried to sue one of them for breach of contract" *(Economist,* 2000).

Table 25.4 Summary statistics and correlation matrix

Variable	Mean	Std. dev	1	2	3	4	5	6	7
1. Prevalence of developing-country MNEs	11.444	20.639	1						
2. Prevalence of developing-country MNEs excluding firms in natural resource industries	12.372	22.569	0973***	1					
3. Prevalence of developing-country MNEs excluding firms from former colonial power	16.466	27.363	0.849***	0.824***	1				
4. Voice and accountability	1.938	0.858	-0.219*	-0.216*	-0.131	1			
5. Political stability and absence of violence	1.954	0.992	-0.085	-0.058	-0.072	0.538***	1		
6. Government effectiveness	1.856	0.677	0.003	-0.034	0.077	0.371***	0.591***	1	
7. Regulatory quality	1.837	0.826	-0.225*	-0.231*	-0.091	0.474***	0.563***	0.704***	1
8. Rule of law	1.743	0.507	-0.179†	-0.186†	-0.100	0.498***	0.603***	0.725***	0.766***
9. Control of corruption	1.855	0.501	-0.316**	-0.337***	-0.224*	0.351***	0.579***	0.723***	0.589***
10. GNI per capita	450.089	398.443	0.253*	0.251*	0.159	0.391***	0.465***	0.361***	0.177†
11. Roads paved	21.251	18.694	-0.185†	-0.186†	-0.203†	0.252*	0.412***	0.202†	0.109
12. Phones per capita	16.542	25.113	0.124	0.123	0.048	0.359***	0.462***	0.409***	0.238*
13. Geographical proximity	0.082	0.275	0.304**	0.303**	0.296**	-0.025	-0.077	0.100	0.124
14. Colonial link	0.612	0.490	-0.101	-0.111	0.080	0.119	-0.112	0.016	0.239*

Table 25.4 (Continued)

Variable	Mean	Std. dev	8	9	10	11	12	13
1. Prevalence of developing-country MNEs	11.444	20.639						
2. Prevalence of developing-country MNEs excluding firms in natural resource industries	12.372	22.569						
3. Prevalence of developing-country MNEs excluding firms from former colonial power	16.466	27.363						
4. Voice and accountability	1.938	0.858						
5. Political stability and absence of violence	1.954	0.992						
6. Government effectiveness	1.856	0.677						
7. Regulatory quality	1.837	0.826						
8. Rule of law	1.743	0.507	1					
9. Control of corruption	1.855	0.501	0.650***	1				
10. GNI per capita	450.089	398.443	0.251*	0.230*	1			
11. Roads paved	21.251	18.694	0.286**	0.398***	0.390***	1		
12. Phones per capita	16.542	25.113	0.429***	0.317**	0.765***	0.598***	1	
13. Geographical proximity	0.082	0.275	0.059	-0.122	-0.140	-0.177†	-0.112	1
14. Colonial link	0.612	0.490	0.041	-0.067	-0.245*	-0.174	-0.252*	0.237*

†p < 0.1; *p < 0.05; **p < 0.01; ***p < 0.001.

Table 25.5 Results of random-effect Tobit analyses of determinants of prevalence of developing-country MNEs among largest affiliates of foreign firms in LDCs

	All subsidiaries		Excluding firms in natural source industries		Excluding firms from former colonial power	
	Model 1_a	Model 1_b	Model 2a	Model 2b	Model 3a	Model 3b
Independent variables of interest						
Voice and accountability	—	-6.756	—	-7.409	—	0.904
		(5.321)		(5.238)		(7.262)
Political stability and absence of violence	—	-3.105	—	-2.563	—	**-19.242****
		(4.477)		(4.374)		(6.910)
Government effectiveness	—	1.797	—	2.392	—	**20.794***
		(6.278)		(6.026)		(8.338)
Regulatory quality	—	**-16.672****	—	**-15.724****	—	**-24.820*****
		(5.375)		(5.059)		(7.637)
Rule of law	—	**20.882***	—	**22.274***	—	**36.540****
		(9.208)		(8.928)		(13.765)
Control of corruption	—	**-27.706****	—	**-29.514*****	—	**-44.473*****
		(9.456)		(9.068)		(12.715)
Controls						
GNI per capita	0.050***	0.068***	0.023*	0.071***	0.028*	0.078***
	(0.009)	(0.012)	(0.010)	(0.012)	(0.014)	(0.017)
Roads paved	-0.497	-0.113	-0.258	-0.074	-0.401	1.196*
	(0.332)	(0.277)	(0.338)	(0.271)	(0.331)	(0.466)
Phones per capita	-0.190	-0.179	-0.123	-0.179	-0.205	-0.350
	(0.262)	(0.288)	(0.280)	(0.284)	(0.376)	(0.418)
Geographic proximity	52.603***	52.057***	50.946***	54.021***	83.394***	154.44***
	(8.042)	(6.831)	(7.600)	(6.732)	(12.326)	(20.504)
Colonial link	16.684*	5.985	14.675*	5.149	—	—
	(6.508)	(6.912)	(6.383)	(6.718)		
Constant	-30.458***	17.681	-30.244**	13.179	-19.379†	-54.707*
	(8.751)	(14.683)	(9.011)	(14.738)	(11.452)	(24.694)
N	44	42	44	42	44	42
Chi-squared	61.62***	106.46***	60.25***	119.97***	63.61***	84.94***
Log likelihood	-189.585	-161.035	-185.323	-160.385	-184.790	-152.885
Test random *vs* pooled model	35.74***	25.24***	36.38***	28.17***	39.00***	44.47***

†$p < 0.1$; *$p < 0.05$; **$p < 0.01$; ***$p < 0.001$. Numbers in bold indicate statistical significance.

The coefficients of the control variables show that the prevalence of developing-country MNEs is positively related to GNI per capita and to geographic proximity. First, developing-country MNEs are more prevalent in LDCs where citizens have higher average income. Consumers in an LCD with a high per capita GDP are much more similar to consumers in developing countries than to consumers in developed nations. Therefore the developing-country MNE will truly know how to serve consumers in these LDCs, because they will have an economic profile similar to consumers at home. It is also possible that in LDCs with very low per capita income, investments are concentrated on exporting industries (such as natural resources) or on serving foreign clients (such as in hospitality services) rather than serving the home market, which is where the developing country MNE would be stronger. Second, developing-country MNEs are more prevalent in countries that are more geographically proximate to their home country. The reduced geographical distance provides an advantage to developing-country MNEs in terms of transfer of resources and coordination. It is important to note that the results of analyzing the governance conditions are significant after controlling for this variable.

Robustness tests and alternative explanations

We check for the robustness of these results and the existence of alternative explanations that may account for the findings by running additional analyses.

The influence of natural resource industries. An argument that may account for some of the observed behavior is that developed-country MNEs invest in LDCs only to obtain access to natural resources rather than to sell to consumers in those countries, while developing-country MNEs invest in LDCs in order to sell to consumers there. If this is the case, comparing these two groups of MNEs would be like comparing apples and oranges. Developed-country MNEs have to invest in LDCs because these countries have some desired natural resources, whereas developing-country MNEs choose to invest in LDCs because these countries can be profitable markets. Hence we check for the robustness of the previous results by excluding firms in natural resource industries: agriculture, fishing, forestry, cattle, oil and mining.

The results of our analysis examining the prevalence of developing-country MNEs excluding firms in natural resource industries are in line with the previous findings. First, although much of the FDI in LDCs is in extractive industries (UNCTAD, 2001a, 2002; World Bank, 2005), both developed- and developing-country MNEs invest in those industries. For example, Indian and South African companies have invested in the Zambian mining sector alongside firms from Switzerland and the United States. The idea that developed-country MNEs invest in LDCs only to access natural resources while developing-country MNEs invest in LDCs only to serve clients is not borne out by the data. After excluding affiliates in natural resource industries, developed-country MNEs still account for over 83% of all the largest affiliates of foreign firms in LDCs. Second, the results of the test excluding firms in natural resources (Model 2b) point toward similar conclusions to the previous test. The coefficients of regulatory quality and control of corruption are negative and statistically significant, the coefficient of rule of law is positive and statistically significant and the coefficients of voice and accountability, political stability and absence of violence and government effectiveness are not statistically significant. In other words, after excluding firms in natural resource industries, developing-country MNEs are more prevalent in LDCs with poorer quality of regulation, lower control of corruption, and higher rule of law.

The influence of firms from the former colonial power. The influence of firms from former colonial powers could also affect the results. West European MNEs historically undertook much of the FDI in LDCs, especially in Africa, because of colonial history and post-colonial ties (UNCTAD, 2001a: 10). Some of the foreign affiliates from these countries have been in the LDCs for a long period of time. Therefore, although they qualify as developed-country MNEs in our data, in practice they have already developed the ability to manage in the "difficult" institutional environment of the LDC. Moreover, they benefit from the historical links and similarity in the environment imposed by the colonial power (Ghemawat, 2001; Johanson & Wiedersheim-Paul, 1975; La Porta et al., 1998; Rangan & Drummond, 2004). The presence of such firms places a downward bias on our results.

Model 3b presents the results after excluding firms from the former colonial power. In this analysis we do not control for the colonial link, because we are excluding firms that have such a link. The results are similar to the ones presented previously, with additional variables gaining statistical significance. The coefficients of political stability and absence of violence, regulatory quality, and control of corruption are negative and statistically significant, the coefficients of government effectiveness and rule of law are positive and statistically signifi-cant, and the coefficient of voice and accountability is not statistically significant. In sum, the results support Hypotheses 2, 4 and 6, are contrary to Hypotheses 3 and 5, and do not provide support for Hypothesis 1. After excluding firms from the former colonial power, developing-country MNEs are more prevalent in LDCs with lower political stability, lower regulatory quality, and less control of corruption, as expected. However, contrary to expectations, they are also more prevalent in LDCs with better government effectiveness and better rule of law.

However, although significance is gained in some of the variables, this is an imperfect test. By excluding all MNEs from a former colonial power we also censor the more recent entries by MNEs from those countries that would still face difficulties in managing there. A better test would require us to exclude only those firms that had been there for longer than a specified period of time. This test cannot be conducted, unfortunately, because we lack the establishment dates for many foreign affiliates.

Lack of investment by developed-country MNEs in LDCs. A third argument that may account for the results is that MNEs from developing countries become prevalent in LDCs not because they are more adept at managing under poor governance conditions, but because developed-country MNEs do not invest in LDCs. Developed-country MNEs may have a higher return on their ownership advantages in other developed nations, where the quality of governance, consumer purchasing power, or infrastructure is similar to their home market. Since LDCs would not provide better returns for these firms, they avoid expanding into these countries. We treat this alternative explanation as an empirical question and explore in the results section whether or not developed-country MNEs invest in LDCs.

The analysis of data on the largest affiliates of foreign firms (Table 25.6) does not support this competing argument. In 2001, the most recent year for which we have data, 44 of the *Fortune 500* firms had invested in 31 LDCs (UNCTAD, 2002: 8). All of these *Fortune 500* firms except for one originated in developed countries. This tells us that developed-country MNEs do invest in LDCs. However, the *Fortune 500* firms are rarely, if at all, among the largest subsidiaries in LDCs, proving our point that they are not as large and successful as in other countries. Moreover, on average, developed-country MNEs constitute 87% of the largest affiliates of foreign firms in LDCs. We also observe that, in 22 LDCs, all the largest foreign firms are developed-country MNEs, again proving that developed-country MNEs do invest in LDCs and can become successful (as measured by their size). In contrast, developing-country MNEs represent half or more of the largest foreign affiliates only in four LDCs. One might argue that this shows that developed-country MNEs dominate in LDCs

Table 25.6 Foreign direct investment in the least developed countries

Country	FDI inflows[a] ($USm)	Fortune 500[b]	Largest affiliates of foreign firms[c]		
			All	Developing country	Developed country
Afghanistan	0.1	0	3	3	0
Angola	1312.1	10	25	3	22
Bangladesh	45.2	7	25	3	22
Benin	41.0	3	10	0	10
Bhutan	0.3	1	NA	NA	NA
Burkina Faso	8.2	1	10	2	8
Burundi	0.0	0	3	0	3
Cambodia	53.8	2	3	0	3
Cape Verde	13.9	0	NA	NA	NA
Central African Rep.	4.3	3	5	0	5
Chad	900.7	1	4	0	4
Comoros	1.5	0	1	0	1
Congo, Dem. Rep.	31.9	3	5	1	4
Djibouti	3.5	1	7	1	6
East Timor	NA	NA	NA	NA	NA
Equatorial Guinea	323.4	1	2	1	1
Eritrea	21.0	0	NA	NA	NA
Ethiopia	75.0	4	17	1	16
Gambia	42.8	1	6	0	6
Guinea	30.0	3	11	2	9
Guinea-Bissau	1.0	0	1	0	1
Haiti	5.7	0	7	0	7
Kiribati	0.5	0	1	0	1
Laos	25.4	0	2	0	2
Lesotho	24.4	0	2	0	2
Liberia	−65.1	5	29	0	29
Madagascar	8.3	4	27	3	24
Malawi	0.0	0	1	0	1
Maldives	12.3	1	3	2	1
Mali	102.2	3	7	0	7
Mauritania	12.0	2	2	1	1
Mozambique	405.9	1	26	6	20
Myanmar	128.7	5	24	3	21
Nepal	9.0	2	7	0	7
Niger	7.9	1	7	0	7
Rwanda	2.6	2	2	0	2
Samoa	1.3	2	8	0	8
Sao Tome & Principe	1.8	0	1	0	1
Senegal	93.3	7	38	1	37
Sierra Leone	4.7	1	3	0	3
Solomon Islands	−6.6	0	19	5	15
Somalia	−0.2	0	NA	NA	NA
Sudan	681.0	1	5	1	4

(Continued)

Table 25.6 (Continued)

Country	FDI inflows[a] ($USm)	Fortune 500[b]	Largest affiliates of foreign firms[c]		
			All	Developing country	Developed country
Togo	74.7	1	8	1	7
Tuvalu	0.1	0	NA	NA	NA
Uganda	274.8	4	38	16	22
U. Rep. of Tanzania	240.4	7	38	9	29
Vanuatu	15.0	7	24	3	21
Yemen	64.3	3	7	0	7
Zambia	197.0	8	34	3	31

Source: Created using data from UNCTAD (2002) and World Bank (2004). East Timor joined the list of LDCs in December 2003; data on its FDI inflows and the largest affiliates of foreign firms are not available.

NA: not available.

a Foreign direct investment inflows in millions of US$, 2002 or latest available year.

b Number of *Fortune 500* firms present in the country from the list of global 500 companies in *Fortune*, 23 July 2001. Although 7% of the *Fortune 500* companies are developing-country firms, only one appears as an investor in LDCs.

c Largest affiliates of foreign firms from the UNCTAD FDI/TNC database, based on *Who owns Whom* CD-ROM (London: Dun and Bradstreet Ltd, 2002) and national sources. Only majority-owned (above 50%) affiliates are considered.

and that this evidence goes counter to our core proposition. However, it should be remembered that we are not claiming that developing-country MNEs will *always* be prevalent in LDCs. Rather, our core proposition is that the poorer the governance conditions are in an LDC, the higher the proportion of developing-country MNEs among the largest subsidiaries in that country. We should also emphasize that, although developed-country MNEs constitute 87 per cent of the largest subsidiaries in LDCs, overall they constitute 96 per cent of the largest 100 TNCs list and 91.6 per cent of the *Fortune 500* global list; both higher than the 87 per cent we see in LDCs.

A variant of this competing argument is that the data say more about MNEs from developing countries doing poorly in developed countries than about their prowess in LDCs.[2] We would argue that this is simply a restatement of our central argument. That is, developing-country MNEs' skills in managing difficult institutional environments are useful when operating in LDCs with poor governance environments. Since we have shown that developed-country MNEs operate side by side with their developing-country counterparts in LDCs, there must be some factor(s) explaining why the latter are represented more heavily among the largest subsidiaries in LDCs than they are in the developed world, or why they comprise an even higher percentage of largest affiliates in LDCs with poorer governance quality. We argue that in developed countries these skills are not as valuable, which makes them less prevalent there. Simply put, in the absence of difficult institutional environments, developing-country MNEs are robbed of a major advantage.

Finally, a third variant of the competing argument is that developed-country MNEs serve LDCs using trade, while developing-country MNEs prefer to use FDI. However, data on trade patterns presented in UNCTAD (2004: 339) do not support this idea. In 2002, imports from developed countries represented 39.0 per cent of all imports into LDCs, while imports from developing countries accounted for 57.1 per cent, and 3.9 per cent were unallocated amounts. Even after excluding imports from OPEC countries, which are primarily energy resources, imports into LDCs from developing countries still accounted for 50.1 per cent of total imports. These figures contrast with the distribution of imports into all developing countries, where 50.7 per cent came from developed countries, 46.9 per cent from developing countries and 2.5 per cent were unallocated.

Limitations of the empirical analysis

Although our results are robust to inclusion and exclusion of several relevant variables representing alternative explanations, there are several limitations that we would like to point out. One issue is the lack of data for LDCs, which is a standard problem in firm-level studies in developing countries (for example, Aykut & Ratha, 2004; Booth et al., 2001; Wells, 1983). This precludes a more complete analysis. First, lack of data already reduces the effective sample to those countries for which data are available. Second, it constrains the classification of firms into two types: developed-country MNEs and developing-country MNEs. In making this classification, we are implicitly assuming a degree of homogeneity among firms within each group. We acknowledge that there are variations within a group of firms and that competition occurs among firms in each group. However, the groups also have widely accepted commonalities, which constitute our object of analysis. Third, we do not have firm-level data other than home country and industry of operation, making it impossible to delve into the resources and capabilities possessed by each firm. Hence we cannot definitively show that it is the capability to operate under poor governance conditions that makes the developing-country MNEs prevalent in the LDCs. Moreover, we cannot directly control for the experience of operating in developing countries. Experience in other developing countries may help developed-country MNEs in LDCs, rendering country of origin less important. Additionally, we do not have data on profitability. We acknowledge that being among the largest foreign subsidiaries in an LDC does not necessarily imply above-average profitability. Theoretically, we used as many examples from the popular press and academic literature as we could to present evidence supporting our argument. Empirically, we imperfectly control for these additional variables through the panel specification. However, lacking detailed resource profiles of individual firms in a country, we can only state that the results are consistent with our theoretical argument (and inconsistent with several competing arguments). Fourth, we cannot prove beyond doubt that the distribution of developing- *vs* developed-country MNEs is different in LDCs than elsewhere in the world without data for all countries. However, we do show that developing-country MNEs are less prevalent among the largest transnationals around the world than they are in LDCs (see Table 25.1). We hope to address these issues when more data becomes available.

Second, it may not be possible to replicate our results in more developed countries. We deliberately selected LDCs because these countries provide a unique research setting to test our arguments. Developing-country MNEs invest in developed and developing countries and can be successful in both. We focus on the more "difficult" countries to illustrate the theoretical arguments, where the developing-country MNEs not only are successful, but can also become the largest foreign firms thanks to their ability to manage under poor governance conditions.

Third, the analysis is a cross-sectional panel. As with any cross-sectional study, it has limited power in establishing causality relationships. We partially overcome this limitation by lagging the independent variables by one year and using a panel data specification. However, we have only two years of data available and 50 potential data points in each, with 42 usable ones after accounting for missing data. This limits our ability to introduce additional controls and study longer temporal patterns. Nevertheless, we make the most of the available data on LDCs.

Discussion

The empirical analysis reveals three findings. First, developing-country MNEs are more prevalent among the largest foreign firms in LDCs than among the overall population of largest public firms or transnationals in the world. Whereas developing-country MNEs tend to have a relative disadvantage in that they come from countries with poor institutions and are much smaller than developed-country MNEs, they can nevertheless possess an advantage and have relatively large operations in LDCs. A source of relative disadvantage – having a home country with poorly developed institutions – becomes a source of relative advantage when the MNE moves into other countries with poor institutional environments. This argument complements the idea that the value of resources is contingent on time and location (Amit & Schoemaker, 1993; Brush & Artz, 1999; Hu, 1995; Tallman, 1992) and specifically the idea that a source of advantage may later become a source of disadvantage (Leonard-Barton, 1992).

Second, the prevalence of developing-country MNEs among the largest affiliates of foreign firms in LDCs varies with prevailing governance conditions in the country, especially governance indicators relating to the efficiency and smooth functioning of markets. In particular, developing-country MNEs are more prevalent in LDCs with worse regulatory quality and with more corruption. However, they are also more prevalent in LDCs with better rule of law and a relatively higher per capita income. Managers of developing-country MNEs may be more used to high uncertainty and be more flexible in dealing with unpredictable regulatory agencies and corrupt government officials. However, they still prefer to operate in countries where the rule of law applies and property rights are protected. In other words, developing-country MNEs need the basic protection of the rule of law to become successful. But they seem to have ability in managing several market inefficiencies such as poor regulatory quality (for example, discretionary regulation) or corruption. In contrast, and as we suspected, political governance quality does not seem to have an effect on whether the largest firms are from developing or developed countries. This idea complements extant literature on institutions and MNEs, which has focused primarily on understanding how the conditions of *host* countries influence the behavior of foreign MNEs (for example, Bevan et al., 2004; Henisz, 2000). We add to this literature by showing how the conditions of the *home* country influence the behavior of MNEs and how *similarity* between home and host country institutional environments influences MNE performance in the host market.

Third, contrary to popular belief, developed-country MNEs do invest in LDCs, not only to obtain natural resources but also to sell to clients there. They constitute the majority of the largest foreign firms in LDCs. The fact that even LDCs can become markets for developed-country MNEs provides further support for the idea that the bottom of the pyramid is a valuable market for developed-country MNEs (Prahalad, 2004).

These results are valid even after accounting for geographic, economic and cultural factors. However, the relative advantage of developing-country MNEs over developed-country MNEs when both operate in LDCs with poor governance conditions cannot be taken for granted. Developed-country MNEs learn to operate in the LDC over time and gradually change their attitudes as they gain knowledge about the characteristics of the LDC (Johanson & Vahlne, 1977), thus reducing their relative liability of foreignness (Zaheer & Mosakowski, 1997). Developed-country MNEs may even try to rapidly surmount the challenge of operating in LDCs with poor governance conditions by hiring local managers. However, this may not fully eliminate the difficulty of operating in LDCs. Such an option may not be available because of the lack of trained managers in LDCs. Additionally, local managers still have to deal with managers in the regional or global headquarters, who may not be receptive to their ideas because of their attitudes towards international markets (Perlmutter, 1969). This difficulty is not situated at the local level, but rather in headquarters and in the assumptions of its managers regarding the potential of developing countries (Prahalad & Lieberthal, 1998).

Conclusions

We discussed the disadvantages and advantages of developing-country MNEs in comparison with developed-country MNEs. Despite being smaller, having less sophisticated resources and coming from problematic home markets with poorly developed governance environments, developing-country MNEs can still be successful in their internationalization. The ability to manage in a challenging governance environment, which they have developed at home, can help them become leading firms in LDCs by reducing their difficulties in internationalization.

This chapter makes several contributions to the literature. First, we focus on the capability to manage the institutional environment, as opposed to more conventional resources and capabilities necessary to compete in an industry (for example, Barney, 1991; Peteraf, 1993). We argue that having a home country with poor institutions, which creates disadvantages in the firm's operations at home, can become a relative advantage when the firm moves into other countries with even more difficult governance conditions. Hence, when analyzing internationalization, we need to broaden our attention from those resources that help the firm compete, including resources that help the firm operate in an institutional environment. Both can support the firm's advantage abroad.

Second, we provide a statistical test to complement anecdotal evidence and prior case-based analyses of competition between developing- and developed-country firms (Bartlett & Ghoshal, 2000; Dawar & Frost, 1999). In so doing, we add to the trailblazing single-country analyses of competition among foreign firms in third countries (Rangan & Drummond, 2004; Tallman, 1991) by studying the prevalence of developing-country MNEs in multiple countries. Our study highlights how variation in the institutional conditions of the host country affects the nature of the largest foreign firms. Competition among MNEs can be based on resources that help firms compete in an industry as well as those that help firms operate in an institutional environment.

Finally, this is the first paper to investigate the phenomenon of MNEs in LDCs. These countries are in particularly dire need of foreign firms to contribute to their growth, and yet attract the least FDI (UNCTAD, 2002; World Bank, 2005). The present paper sheds light on the nature of foreign investors in these countries, dispelling previous assumptions. Both developed- and developing-country MNEs invest there, not only to extract resources but also to serve clients there. LDCs can be attractive markets despite their challenging institutional conditions.

Acknowledgements

The comments of the Associate Editor Pankaj Ghemawat, anonymous reviewers, Jim Hagen, Tom Murtha, Steve Tallman and participants at the Strategic Management and Organization Seminar at the University of Minnesota and the Academy of International Business Annual Meeting helped us improve previous versions of the chapter. It was developed while the first author was an Assistant Professor and the second author was a PhD student at the University of Minnesota. The first author would like to thank the University of Minnesota International Programs for financial support and the Applied Economics and Management Department at Cornell University for its hospitality during the revision of the manuscript. The second author would like to thank the Carlson School of Management Dissertation Fellowship for financial support. All errors remain ours.

Notes

1 We follow UNCTAD's (2004) classification of countries into developed and developing. Developed countries are: Canada, United States, Andorra, Austria, Belgium, Denmark, Finland, France, Germany, Greece, Iceland, Ireland, Italy, Liechtenstein, Luxembourg, Malta, Monaco, Netherlands, Norway, Portugal, San Marino, Spain, Sweden, Switzerland, United Kingdom, Israel, Japan, Australia and New Zealand. All other countries are classified as developing countries.
2 We would like to thank an anonymous referee for bringing this to our attention.

References

Aggarwal, R., & Agmon, T. 1990. The international success of developing country firms: Role of government-directed comparative advantage. *Management International Review*, 30(2): 163–80.

Amit, R., & Schoemaker, P. J. H. 1993. Strategic assets and organizational rents. *Strategic Management Journal*, 14(1): 33–46.

Amsden, A. H. 2001. *The rise of "the rest": Challenges to the west from late-industrializing economies*. New York: Oxford University Press.

Aulakh, P. S. 2007. Emerging multinationals from developing economies: Motivations, paths and performance. *Journal of International Management*, 13(3): 235–40.

Aulakh, P. S., Kotabe, M., & Teegen, H. 2000. Export strategies and performance of firms from emerging economies: Evidence from Brazil, Chile and Mexico. *Academy of Management Journal*, 43(3): 342–61.

Aykut, D., & Ratha, D. 2004. South-South FDI flows: How big are they? *Transnational Corporations*, 13(1): 149–76.

Barney, J. B. 1991. Firm resources and sustained competitive advantage. *Journal of Management*, 17(1): 99–120.

Bartlett, C. A., & Ghoshal, S. 2000. Going global: Lessons from late movers. *Harvard Business Review*, 78(2): 132–42.

Bevan, A. A., Estrin, S., & Meyer, K. 2004. Foreign investment location and institutional development in transition economies. *International Business Review*, 13(1): 43–64.

Bilkey, W. J., & Nes, E. 1982. Country-of-origin effects on product evaluations. *Journal of International Business Studies*, 13(1): 89–99.

Booth, L., Aivazian, V., Demirguc-Kunt, A., & Maksimovic, V. 2001. Capital structures in developing countries. *Journal of Finance*, 56(1): 87–130.

Brush, T., & Artz, K. 1999. Toward a contingent resource-based theory: The impact of information asymmetry on the value of capabilities in veterinary medicine. *Strategic Management Journal*, 20(3): 223–50.

Buckley, P. J. 2002. Is the international business research agenda running out of steam? *Journal of International Business Studies*, 33(2): 365–74.

CIA 2005. *World factbook*. www.cia.gov/library/publications/the-world-factbook Accessed 7 January 2005.

Cuervo-Cazurra, A. 2006. Who cares about corruption? *Journal of International Business Studies*, 37(6): 803–22.

Cuervo-Cazurra, A. 2007. Sequence of value-added activities in the multinationalization of developing country firms. *Journal of International Management*, 13(3): 258–77.

Cuervo-Cazurra, A. 2008a. The internationalization of developing country MNEs: The case of Multilatinas. *Journal of International Management*, Forthcoming.

Cuervo-Cazurra, A. 2008b. The effectiveness of laws against bribery abroad. *Journal of International Business Studies*, 39(4): 634–51.

Cuervo-Cazurra, A., & Un, C. A. 2004a. Firm-specific and non-firm-specific sources of advantages in international competition. In A. Ariño, P. Ghemawat, & J. Ricart (Eds) *Creating and appropriating value from global strategy*: 78–94. New York: Palgrave Macmillan.

Cuervo-Cazurra, A., & Un, C. A. 2004b. The bald eagle cannot find its way in the rainforest: Sources and solutions to the difficulties in the internationalization of developed country MNEs into developing countries. In S. B. Prasad & P. N. Gauri (Eds) *Global firms and emerging markets in the age of anxiety*: 13–36. Westport, CT: Praeger.

Cuervo-Cazurra, A., Maloney, M., & Manrakhan, S. 2007. Causes of the difficulties in internationalization. *Journal of International Business Studies*, 38(5): 709–25.

Dawar, N., & Frost, T. 1999. Competing with giants: Survival strategies for local companies in emerging markets. *Harvard Business Review*, 77(2): 119–29.

de Soto, H. D. 2000. *The mystery of capital: Why capitalism triumphs in the West and fails everywhere else.* New York: Basic Books.

del Sol, P., & Kogan, J. 2007. Regional competitive advantage based on pioneering economic reforms: The case of Chilean FDI. *Journal of International Business Studies*, 38(6): 901–27.

Dunning, J. H. 1977. Trade, location of economic activity and the MNE: A search for an eclectic approach. In B. Ohlin, P. O. Hesselborn, & P. M. Wijkman (Eds) *The international allocation of economic activity*: 395–418. London: Macmillan.

Dunning, J. H., Van Hoesel, R., & Narula, R. 1998. Third world multinationals revisited: New developments and theoretical implications. In J. H. Dunning (Ed.) *Globalization, trade and foreign direct investment*: 255–95. Oxford: Elsevier.

Economist 2000. Foreign direct investment: Goodnight, Vietnam. 8 January: 65–66.

Economist 2005a. Business in Argentina: Getting serious. 21 May: 76.

Economist 2005b. The Khodorkovsky case: The tycoon and the president. 21 May: 24.

Eden, L., & Miller, S. R. 2004. Distance matters: Liability of foreignness, institutional distance and ownership. *Advances in International Management*, 16: 187–221.

Encyclopedia Britannica 2005. www.britannica.com Accessed 15 January 2005.

Eriksson, K., Johanson, J., Majkgard, A., & Sharma, D. D. 1997. Experiential knowledge and cost in the internationalization process. *Journal of International Business Studies*, 28(2): 337–60.

Fisman, R., & Khanna, T. 2004. Facilitating development: The role of business groups. *World Development*, 32(4): 609–28.

Fitzpatrick, M. 1983. The definition and assessment of political risk in international business: A review of the literature. *Academy of Management Review*, 8(2): 249–55.

Fortune, 1991–1994a. *Fortune Global Industrial 500.* www.fortune.com Accessed 1 May 2004.

Fortune, 1991–1994b. *Fortune Global Service 500.* www.fortune.com Accessed 1 May 2004.

Fortune, 1995–2004. *Fortune Global 500.* www.fortune.com Accessed 1 May 2004.

Ghemawat, P. 2001. Distance still matters. *Harvard Business Review*, 79(8): 137–45.

Ghemawat, P., & Khanna, T. 1998. The nature of diversified business groups: A research design and two case studies. *Journal of Industrial Economics*, 46(1): 35–61.

Goldstein, A. 2004. *Regional integration, FDI, and competitiveness in Southern Africa.* Paris: OECD.

Henisz, W. J. 2000. The institutional environment for multinational investment. *Journal of Law, Economics and Organization*, 6(2): 334–64.

Henisz, W. J., & Williamson, O. E. 1999. Comparative economic organization – within and between countries. *Business and Politics*, 1(3): 261–76.

Hitt, M. A., Hoskisson, R. E., & Kim, H. 1997. International diversification: Effects on innovation and firm performance in product-diversified firms. *Academy of Management Journal*, 40(4): 767–98.

Hofstede, G. 1980. *Culture's consequences: International differences in work-related values.* Beverly Hills, CA: Sage.

Hoskisson, R. E., Eden, L., Lau, C. M., & Wright, M. 2000. Strategy in emerging economies. *Academy of Management Journal*, 43(3): 249–67.

Hu, Y. S. 1995. The international transferability of the firm's advantages. *California Management Review*, 37(4): 73–88.

Hymer, S. 1976. *The international operations of national firms: A study of direct investment.* Cambridge, MA: MIT Press.

Johanson, J., & Vahlne, J. E. 1977. The internationalization process of the firm: A model of knowledge development and increasing foreign market commitments. *Journal of International Business Studies*, 8(1): 23–32.

Johanson, J., & Wiedersheim-Paul, F. 1975. The internationalization of the firm: Four Swedish cases. *Journal of Management Studies*, 12(3): 305–22.

Kaufmann, D., Kraay, A., & Zoido-Lobaton, P. 1999. *Governance matters.* Working Paper 2196, World Bank, Washington, DC.

Kaufmann, D., Kraay, A., & Mastruzzi, M. 2003. *Governance matters III: Governance indicators 1996–2002.* Working Paper 3106, World Bank, Washington, DC.

Khanna, T., & Palepu, K. 1997. Why focused strategies may be wrong for emerging markets. *Harvard Business Review*, 75(4): 41–51.

Khanna, T., & Palepu, K. 2000. The future of business groups in emerging markets: Long-run evidence from Chile. *Academy of Management Journal*, 43(3): 268–85.

Kobrin, S. J. 1979. Political risk: A review and reconsideration. *Journal of International Business Studies*, 10(1): 67–80.

Kumar, K., & McLeod, M. G. (Eds) 1981. *Multinationals from developing countries.* Lexington, MA: Lexington Books.

Laffont, J. J., & Tirole, J. 1995. *A theory of incentives in procurement and regulation.* Cambridge, MA: MIT Press.

Lall, S. 1983. *The new multinationals: The spread of third world enterprises.* New York: Wiley.

La Porta, R., Lopez-de-Silanes, F., Shleifer, A., & Vishny, R. W. 1998. Law and finance. *Journal of Political Economy*, 106(6): 1113–55.

Lecraw, D. 1977. Direct investment by firms from less developed countries. *Oxford Economic Papers*, 29(3): 445–57.

Lecraw, D. J. 1993. Outward direct investment by Indonesian firms: Motivation and effects. *Journal of International Business Studies*, 24(3): 589–600.

Leonard-Barton, D. 1992. Core capabilities and core rigidities: A paradox in managing new product development. *Strategic Management Journal*, 13(5): 111–26.

Luo, Y., & Tung, R. L. 2007. International expansion of emerging market enterprises: A springboard perspective. *Journal of International Business Studies*, 38(4): 481–98.

Maddala, G. S. 1983. *Limited-dependent and qualitative variables in econometrics.* New York: Cambridge University Press.

Munir, M. 2002. Survey – Turkey: Infrastructure & investment: Builder of troublesome projects in difficult places. *Financial Times*, 26 March: 2.

North, D. C. 1990. *Institutions, institutional change, and economic performance.* New York: Cambridge University Press.

Perlmutter, H. 1969. The tortuous evolution of the multinational corporation. *Columbia Journal of World Business*, 4(1): 8–18.

Peteraf, M. A. 1993. The cornerstones of competitive advantage: A resource-based view. *Strategic Management Journal*, 14(3): 179–91.

Prahalad, C. K. 2004. *The fortune at the bottom of the pyramid: Eradicating poverty through profits.* Philadelphia, PA: Wharton School Publishing.

Prahalad, C. K., & Hammond, A. 2002. Serving the world's poor, profitably. *Harvard Business Review*, 80(9): 4–11.

Prahalad, C. K., & Lieberthal, K. 1998. The end of corporate imperialism. *Harvard Business Review*, 76(4): 68–78.

Rangan, S., & Drummond, A. 2004. Explaining outcomes in competition among foreign multinationals in a focal host market. *Strategic Management Journal*, 25(3): 285–93.

Rodriguez, P., Uhlenbruck, K., & Eden, L. 2005. Government corruption and the entry strategies of multinationals. *Academy of Management Review*, 30(2): 383–96.

Rugman, A. M., & Verbeke, A. 1992. A note on the transnational solution and the transaction cost theory of multinational strategic management. *Journal of International Business Studies*, 23(4): 761–71.

Shenkar, O. 2001. Cultural distance revisited: Towards a more rigorous conceptualization and measurement of cultural differences. *Journal of International Business Studies*, 32(3): 519–35.

Shleifer, A., & Vishny, R. W. 1993. Corruption. *Quarterly Journal of Economics*, 108(3): 599–617.

Smarzynska, B. K., & Wei, S. J. 2000. *Corruption and composition of foreign direct investment: Firm-level evidence.* NBER Working Papers 7969, National Bureau of Economic Research, Cambridge, MA.

StataCorp 2001. *Stata Statistical Software: Release 7.0.* College Station, TX: Stata Corporation.

Stonebraker, R. J. 1979. Turnover and mobility among the 100 largest firms: An update. *American Economic Review*, 69(5): 968–973.

Stopford, J., & Strange, S. 1992. *Rival states, rival firms: Competition for world market shares.* Cambridge: Cambridge University Press.

Tallman, S. B. 1991. Strategic management models and resource-based strategies among MNEs in a host market. *Strategic Management Journal*, 12(4): 69–82.

Tallman, S. B. 1992. A strategic management perspective on host country structure of multinational enterprises. *Journal of Management*, 18(3): 455–71.

Tobin, J. 1958. Estimation of relationships for limited dependent variables. *Econometrica*, 26(1): 24–36.

UNCTAD 1992–2005. *World investment report.* New York: United Nations.

UNCTAD 2001a. *FDI in the least developed countries at a glance.* New York: United Nations.

UNCTAD 2001b. *Statistical profile of the least developed countries at a glance.* New York: United Nations.

UNCTAD 2002. *FDI in the least developed countries at a glance.* New York: United Nations.

UNCTAD 2004. *The least developed countries report.* New York: United Nations.

Vernon, R. 1977. *Storm over the multinationals: The real issues.* Boston, MA: Harvard University Press.

Wei, S. J. 2000. How taxing is corruption on international investors? *The Review of Economic and Statistics*, 82(1): 1–11.

Wells, L. T. 1983. *Third world multinationals.* Cambridge, MA: MIT Press.

Wells, L. T. 1998. Multinationals and the developing countries. *Journal of International Business Studies*, 29(1): 101–14.

White, D. 2003. How Africa joined the new wireless world. *Financial Times*, 23 November: 8.

Wright, M., Filatotchev, I., Hoskisson, R. E., & Peng, M. W. 2005. Strategy research in emerging economies: Challenging the conventional wisdom. *Journal of Management Studies*, 42(1): 1–33.

World Bank 2002. *World development report: Institutions for markets.* New York: Oxford University Press.

World Bank 2004. *World development indicators.* www.worldbank.org/data Accessed 7 December 2004.

World Bank 2005. *Global development finance: Mobilizing finance and managing vulnerability.* Washington, DC: World Bank.

Yeung, H. W. C. 1994. Third World multinationals revisited: A research critique and future agenda. *Third World Quarterly*, 15(2): 297–317.

Yeung, H. W. C. 1999. Competing in the global economy: The globalization of business firms from emerging economies. In H. W. C. Yeung (Ed.) *The globalization of business firms from emerging economies:* xiii–xlvi. Cheltenham: Edward Elgar.

Young, S., Huang, C. H., & McDermott, M. 1996. Internationalization and competitive catch-up processes: Case study evidence on Chinese multinational enterprises. *Management International Review*, 36(4): 295–314.

Yunus, M. 1999. *Banker to the poor: Micro-lending and the battle against world poverty.* New York: Public Affairs.

Zaheer, S. 1995. Overcoming the liability of foreignness. *Academy of Management Journal,* 38(2): 341–63.

Zaheer, S., & Mosakowski, E. 1997. The dynamics of the liability of foreignness: A global study of survival in financial services. *Strategic Management Journal,* 18(6): 439–53.

26 Merging without alienating

Interventions promoting cross-cultural organizational integration and their limitations*

Mary Yoko Brannen and Mark F. Peterson

Introduction

As multinational firms race for the future while racing for the world, motivated by the promise of scale economies in globalizing industries, they are doing so increasingly by means of cross-border mergers and acquisitions (M&As) (Shimizu et al., 2004; Stahl et al., 2005). Technological advancement, knowledge-scanning opportunities, and competitive pressures to consolidate industries and regions have all contributed to a recent surge in worldwide M&As (Hitt et al., 2001a, b; Vermeulen & Barkema, 2001). Of the different forms of foreign direct investment (FDI) throughout the world, Japanese investment in the United States has been among the most substantial (JETRO, 2007), even despite the Asian financial crisis. New Japanese FDI (with M&A being the main entry mode) has been in the range of $7 billion–$14 billion per year, and has been showing an increasing trend since the latter half of 2003. Cumulatively, over the last two decades, Japanese-owned investment in the United States has grown to reach a total of $148 billion.

Whereas there has been a significant amount of research on the economic motivations for and entry modes of Japanese FDI in the United States, the social, intraorganizational aspects of Japanese or any other incoming FDI has been inadequately studied (Bhagat et al., 2002; Hitt et al., 2001a, b). On the other hand, there have been many compelling yet unsubstantiated accounts of working for foreign-owned firms (especially Japanese-owned ones) in the popular literature. While a few of these accounts are favorable, in particular those that report bottom-line profitability turnarounds in M&As, the majority tell of a darker social side to working for foreign-owned firms (Thiederman, 2003). For example, the 1990s surge in Japanese FDI spawned notorious reports of working for "Japan, Inc." in the popular business press, news media and film; the satirical comedy *Gung Ho* being a poignant case in point. Chinese-owned FDI has come under similar scrutiny, with reports of unfavorable hiring biases, limited promotion opportunities, etc. (Wong, 1990; Yeung, 2000). Despite the negative press regarding careers in foreign-owned companies, with very few exceptions (Brannen, 1994; Kleinberg, 1989; Peterson et al., 1999), academic studies have not assessed individual-level outcomes of FDI. US academe has been criticized for being sluggish in paying attention to even the most pressing domestic US cross-cultural issues such as cultural diversity, let alone to cross-cultural interactions between United States and foreign parties (Adler, 1983; Boyacigiller & Adler, 1991; Gelfand et al., 2007).

---

*Reprinted by permission from Macmillan Publishers Ltd: Brannen, M.Y. & M. Peterson, "Merging without alienating: Interventions promoting cross-border organizational integration and their limitations". Journal of International Business Studies, 40: 468–489. Copyright 2009, published by Palgrave Macmillan.

Given that the failure rates of international M&As are between 50 and 83% (Lee, 2003; Stahl et al., 2005), that cultural distance is the often attributed yet unsubstantiated cause of failure (Uhlenbruck, and that recent literature suggests that integration is the critical link in realizing M&A success (Bijlsma-Frankema & Costa, 2005; Schweiger & Lippert, 2005), there is a pressing need to respond to this research lacuna. By combining qualitative and quantitative methods this study makes a strong empirical contribution towards understanding both the potential individual-level outcomes from the fallout of poorly managed cross-cultural integration and the intraorganizational mechanisms by which successful integration can be achieved in cross-border M&As.

Indeed, the potentially alienating stressors of FDI in the United States, including but not solely associated with Japanese investors, continues not only to be reflected in the subjective accounts of the popular press, but also to be objectively documented in the large number of labor-related judgments against foreign-owned as compared with domestically owned firms in the United States (Mezias, 2002; Very et al., 1997). These include ongoing litigation of individual-level grievances, such as sexual harassment (Mitsubishi in rural Illinois), ethnocentric favoritism in promotion ("rice-paper ceiling" at Daiwa Bank in New York, reported in Kopp, 1994) and perceived entitlement to "lifetime employment" in Japanese-owned concerns in the United States that have continued since the late 1970s to the staggering costs of over $5 million a claim (cf. Marubeni Corporation of America, reported in Glater, 2005).

In sum, while FDI, especially in the form of M&As, in the United States and throughout the industrial world continues to grow, the academic research – especially in regard to individual-level outcomes of such strategic activity – has not been forthcoming. Whereas there has been some important research on firm-level issues and there is recent movement toward understanding post-merger integration processes in cross-border M&As (Child et al., 2001; Shimizu et al., 2004), the work is fragmented across various disciplines and belies a paucity of research on individual-level outcomes. Further, despite contradictory empirical findings, the conceptual research on FDI largely focuses on the effect of cross-cultural issues such as cultural distance on performance (cf. Datta & Puia, 1995; Kanter & Corn, 1994; Markides & Ittner, 1994; Morosini et al., 1998). The consulting literature echoes this focus. According to a telling KPMG study, "83% of all cross-border M&As failed to produce any benefit for the shareholders and over 50% actually destroyed value", and interviews with over 100 senior executives involved in 700 cross-border M&A deals over a 2-year period disclosed that the single biggest perceived cause for failure was cultural differences (cited in Lee, 2003).

The problems that expatriate decision-makers face when managing host-country employees need to be elaborated beyond a general nod toward cross-cultural differences or cultural distance, and distinguished from general post-acquisition challenges. While there is much popular business press and some academic support for national cultural differences in M&A producing increased stress, negative attitudes toward the merger, less cooperation, lower commitment and executives with negative experiences quitting their jobs (Krug & Hegarty, 2001; Very et al., 1996; Weber et al., 1996), there has been no in-depth academic study that fleshes out the nature and parameters of such negative individual-level outcomes, or assesses possible integrative interventions in cross-border M&As. In cases such as this, where there are unsubstantiated suppositions and few or no studies of a newly emerging organizational phenomenon, in-depth, single-site studies are useful to advance theory (Eisenhardt, 1991). By combining qualitative findings from a larger, 5-year ethnographic study of one such occurrence of cross-border M&A with a quantitative triangulation of the results, this chapter takes a significant step towards filling this individual-level research gap in the

FDI literature, distinguishing between cross-cultural and general post-acquisition issues and providing direction for future research.

In this study we first use the results of the ethnography to trace and examine the process of post-acquisition integration. We then employ the constant comparative method (Glaser & Strauss, 1967) to surface and develop in-depth understanding of the salient issues that emerged, particularly feelings of cross-cultural work alienation. Alienation emerged as a central and much talked-about concern early on in the post-acquisition period as a condition of malaise that employees felt owing to a sense of not feeling integrated into the dominant culture of the post-merger organization that echoed the popular cultural reports of negative individual-level outcomes associated with working in foreign-owned concerns. We then used a quantitative triangulation and ongoing qualitative follow-up interviews to check and counter-check the conclusions drawn in the initial ethnographic fieldwork. Since alienation is a multifaceted concept, we selected established organizational behavioral constructs to represent its various facets and designed other new measures to reflect aspects that the ethnography suggested were particularly important at the field site.

Such between- and within-methods triangulations are critical to ascertain whether seemingly "big", vocal and emotional issues such as alienation are indeed representative of the general population, or whether they are eclipsing other intraorganizational outcomes from coming into clear view. As we show in this chapter, our triangulation served various research objectives: to discon-firm cross-cultural work alienation as the general state of the post-acquisition organization; to confirm the substantial success of particular interventions that management implemented to promote cross-cultural integration; to refine our understanding of cross-cultural work alienation at the plant as particular hierarchical and functional area "pockets" of alienation that emerged over time; and to provide a framework for selecting and developing a set of measures that cover a broad range of cross-cultural work alienation indicators for future studies of post-M&A integration.

Conceptual background and theoretical overview

Part of the significance of this particular analysis lies in its position as an in-depth study of individual-level outcomes, especially of Japanese M&A in the United States and more broadly of the social side of FDI in general. The basic idea of work alienation comes from the recognition that separating the doing of work by less powerful parties from the control of work by more powerful parties can generate a host of attitudinal and social dysfunctions (for example, Blauner, 1960; Durkheim, 1933). Similarly, cross-cultural work alienation, the central post-acquisition intraorganizational issue that emerged in the ethnographic study, has been known to arise when the power to influence an organization's culture is distributed (oftentimes unequally) between two distinct cultural groups (Middleton, 1963; Zurcher et al., 1965), in this case American and Japanese. In Japanese-owned FDI concerns, Japanese are formally empowered by their role as owners, and whereas the Americans at the plant have "field power", in that the FDI operates within the legal and social context of the United States, the foreign ownership has intraorganizational "arena" power and thereby provides the possibility for a sense of loss of control and alienation (Brannen & Fruin, 1999).

Alienation theory

The idea of cross-cultural work alienation draws from a long tradition of alienation research and theory. Karl Marx (1897) viewed work alienation as an objective condition of late eighteenth- and nineteenth-century industrial practices that separated the laborer from the ownership of the means and fruits of production. Marx refers to the emotional and collective behavioral reactions of laborers to alienation by using ideas that suggest excessive routine and lack of control. However, he did not have available the sort of organizational behavior constructs that we can use to understand work alienation today. Emile Durkheim's (1933) view of work alienation places greater stress on individuals' subjective experience of alienation than does Marx's view. He treats it as a subjective condition of modern urbanization in which the laborer experiences psychological separation because of detachment between the self and work. Again, his work suggests ideas later included in organizational behavior theories about job design, autonomy and control, yet such theories rarely acknowledge a Durkheim heritage.

Seeman (1959), one of the first organizational alienation scholars who focused on individual-level issues, exposed the complexity and multidimensional nature of work alienation in a comprehensive discussion that was then built upon by Blauner (1964). Blauner (1964) outlined four facets of this complex condition:

(1) *impotence* – lack of control over pace, methods, and content of work;
(2) *disconnectedness* – not understanding how one's own work is linked to organizational processes;
(3) *social isolation* – lack of integration in the work community; and
(4) *self-estrangement* – viewing work as a means to an end rather than a self-fulfilling end.

As we will explain, we found Blauner's four facets of alienation to provide a particularly useful way to frame alienation issues for application to international M&As.

Aiken and Hage (1966) discovered alienation in welfare agencies, hospitals and schools. Most importantly, their study suggested that organizations were not inherently alienating, but that they could be structured and managed to either exacerbate or ameliorate alienation. They supported the significance of two of Blauner's (1964) facets of alienation by finding that work alienation and alienation from expressive relations are distinct forms of alienation that are common in highly centralized and formalized organizational structures. They began to link alienation to organizational behavior issues by showing that participation in decision-making (an aspect of decentralization) and a high degree of job codification and rule observation (aspects of formalization) have strong, independent effects on the degree of work alienation.

Research and theory about alienation, particularly the four facets identified by Blauner (1964) and the relationships to organizational behavioral variables noted by Aiken and Hage (1966), strongly suggest that FDIs have a potential to create work alienation among employees. Working for an owner from a culturally and geographically distant society has the potential to make the objective separation of laborers from owners particularly salient to employees (Kopp, 1994). Managers who represent headquarters in the overseas facility face problems of stereotyping and potentially a stigma of being foreign in the eyes of local employees (Harvey et al., 2005). Management and human resources practices by owners who have very different understandings and expectations of how things should be done in organizations from US organizational culture norms are thus likely to have many of the qualities that Aiken and Hage (1966) and their successors suggest will create the experience of work alienation to which Blauner (1964) drew attention. Gardberg and Fombrun (2006) explain that organizations working across boundaries between nations showing substantial institutional difference should create programs to promote citizenship that balance the legitimacy of the overseas partner with the need for localization. Their conceptualization of citizenship is in many respects successful integration and the converse of the sorts of work alienation issues to which international M&As are particularly susceptible, and which became evident in the present study of a Japanese acquisition in the United States.

Post-merger integration challenges in cross-border M&As

Successful integration is essential to realize the business potential of acquisitions, whether domestic or cross-border (Child et al., 2001). Scholars have identified three integration challenges:

(1) national and organizational cultural differences between acquired and acquiring firms (Chaterjee et al., 1992; Nahavandi & Malekzadeh, 1988; Shimizu et al., 2004);
(2) managers from different countries who are accustomed to different control systems (Barkema et al., 1996; Calori et al., 1994); and
(3) acquirer's nationality effects on the integration procedures introduced in the acquired firm (Barkema et al., 1996).

Further, in domestic M&As, organizational cultural differences have been shown to substantially affect stress, attitudes, behavior and turnover (Marks, 1982; Marks & Mirvis, 1985). Although most of the research on cultural differences in M&As refers to organizational rather than national culture, this research identifies multiple facets of cultural integration in M&A contexts. Weber et al. (1996) found that negative individual-level outcomes are particularly prevalent in the employees and managers of acquired companies in domestic and international M&As. Very et al. (1996) found an outcome with much in common with the current study's notion of cross-cultural work alienation termed "acculturative stress". They found that this type of intraculturally generated stress was even more likely to occur in cross-border acquisitions than in domestic acquisitions. Such acculturative stress was associated with lower commitment and cooperation on the part of the acquired firm employees, thereby increasing turnover.

In regard to cross-cultural differences in the social construction of control, Calori et al. (1994) showed that French acquiring firms rely more on managerial transfer and use more strategic control than do British firms. Child et al. (2001) call American acquirers "absorbers", Japanese acquirers "preservers", and French acquirers "colonialists". Successfully implementing cross-culturally distinct controls relies heavily on the way that the control systems are managed (Child et al., 2001; Larsson & Lubatkin, 2001), communicated (cf. Xu & Van de Vliert, 2004; Zhu et al., 2004) and, in sum, mindfully integrated into the newly formed organization.

The setting and ethnographic background

Ethnography – comprising two essential elements, fieldwork and participant observation – is the method of choice for gaining insights into micro-level, intraorganizational, multifaceted cultural phenomena, especially in cases where little is known about the research phenomenon (Van Maanen, 1992). The ethnographer combined focus group interviews, in-depth structured and informal interviews, and participant observation at the US facility and in Japan at both the home office and Japanese plant locations. A detailed methodology of the ethnography is provided elsewhere (Brannen, 1994, 1996). The following is a summary of the ethnographic setting of the research presented here.

During the zenith of Japanese FDI in the United States, in December 1986, a western Massachusetts paper-converting plant was acquired by Japanese management. The original US plant was founded in 1916. The plant was run like a family business, with benevolent yet authoritative leaders. For example, employees enjoyed a Christmas party, a spring "thawing-out" party and a summer barbecue each year. As a result of mergers during the mid-1950s, a new corporation was formed with a total of six manufacturing plants. Between 1954 and the mid-1970s the plant experienced much growth but it began to decline in productivity. It was the town's second largest employer, and in 1979 it grossed $20 million dollars in sales. By then corporate headquarters operated the facility on an extremely tight budget, "only spending money on equipment if it was broken".

From 1981 on there were no social gatherings, hourly workers were regularly laid off and many of the office staff members were terminated. The management was characterized by a hierarchical structure, with senior and middle managers supervising a unionized workforce made up of 120 second- and third-generation workers of mostly Polish or French-Canadian ancestry. The most common metaphor used by the hourly workers to describe the American management style was "hammer and sickle". The management–union relationship had deteriorated: grievances were up to an average of 12 per month, ultimately leading to a strike vote that closed the plant for 6 weeks.

In 1983 the plant was sold to a holding company. From 1983 until the Tomioka Paper Company's (TPC – a pseudonym for the Japanese company that acquired the plant) acquisition of the plant in 1986, the predominant concern of the employees was job security. During these 3 years the plant was operated on an intermittent 3-days-a-week schedule, hourly workers were laid off for an average of 12 weeks per year and more office workers were terminated. Management continued its notoriously bad relationship with the United Paper Makers' Union, as indicated by a reported average of three formal grievances a month. When the sale was final, the new Japanese management rehired approximately 170 of the 216 blue- and white-collar workers from the previous company (the remaining 36 employees were transferred by choice as an entire division to another plant of the former owner). At the time of the acquisition, there were 271 US employees at the plant: 122 office workers and 149 hourly workers. There were nine Japanese employees, three of whom were in top plant management positions.

The new management's main reason for purchasing the plant was the pre-existing equipment (albeit in much need of adjustment) and the already trained workforce. A greenfield venture would have cost much more than the acquisition price, and it would have taken up to 2 years longer to get a new plant operating smoothly.

TPC took special care to gain the goodwill of both the community and the employees during this changeover time, many of whom were World War II veterans or had relatives who had lost their jobs to "oriental labor" when whole local industries went bankrupt owing to foreign wage competition. The summer before the takeover, TPC hosted a "Get Acquainted" picnic in the parking lot of the factory for the community. The new president personally introduced himself to each employee with a handshake and a word of goodwill. The only setback during the takeover was the collective bargaining agreement outcome with the union. Hourly workers were embittered because they each lost an average of two weeks of paid vacation leave as well as the portability of their pension plan.

After the acquisition, the new Japanese management replaced the former leadership while retaining the middle management and hourly workers. Three years after the acquisition, the plant was operating 7 days a week, there had been no layoffs or terminations of employees and grievances were down to an unprecedented two in all of 1989. In addition, the plant underwent a $40 million expansion to house a state-of-the-art thermal coating machine, which increased total plant capacity by more than 200% and provided approximately 100 new jobs.

Constructs and hypotheses

A number of locally significant aspects of cross-cultural work alienation were induced from the ethnography. Several issues related to alienation theory surfaced early on and throughout the ethnography that are commonly represented in organizational behavior survey research. A theme that integrates the four facets of alienation that Blauner identifies – impotence, disconnectedness, social isolation and self-estrangement – is the issue of separation. The ethnographic data suggested that some plant employees experienced what Blauner called *impotence* and *disconnectedness* in that the outcome of meetings was seemingly mysteriously settled among the Japanese managers in advance, and the employees' participation was not really valued. The ethnography also suggested that *social isolation* was experienced by some, in that Japanese work-related values were very different from the personal values of the predominantly French-Canadian and Polish-American employees at the plant, and that supervisors did not accept them as genuinely important organization members. These particular individual-level alienation outcomes resulted directly from cross-cultural differences in expectations of the way meetings are conducted and how participation is valued. Whereas in US organizations meetings are typically forums to make decisions, in Japanese organizations formal meetings are typically called to confirm and consensually acknowledge that a decision has been made (Lebra, 1976; Rohlen, 1974). Individual input into decisions is generally gathered informally on a one-on-one basis in order to save face and limit interpersonal conflict (Doi, 1971; Ohnuki-Tierney, 1984). The common practice of Japanese managers conducting side-bar conversations in Japanese during meetings was also prevalent at the plant, this only added to their alienating capability, especially among monolingual employees. Interestingly, employees who grew up in bilingual households (some of the French-Canadians and Polish-Americans) were less likely to take issue with this.

Blauner's idea of *self-estrangement* is the opposite of commitment in the OB literature; the sharing of values, a heart-felt effort to contribute, and an interest in remaining a part of an organization. Work satisfaction and life satisfaction are related constructs. In addition, a significant characteristic of alienation theory is that pay attitudes are theoretically distinct from other work attitudes. In fact, staying in an organization simply for reasons of satisfactory pay can be an element in a larger syndrome of alienation. That is, given a lack of viable options, employees sometimes stay in an alienating job only for financial reasons. Work alienation is then evident when the other measures that we use to represent Blauner's aspects of alienation outcomes decline without a decline in pay satisfaction.

The ethnographic analysis suggested several additional measures and hypotheses to quantitatively evaluate the prevalence of cross-cultural work alienation that some employees had expressed. Engaging in an FDI reflects an expectation by the acquiring managers that the acquisition itself will promote the success of the acquired plant. Similarly, the specific steps that management takes to promote an acquisition's acceptance by employees reflect a management prediction that these steps will limit the alienating conditions of impotence, disconnectedness, social isolation, and self-estrangement. These managerial expectations require empirical testing. However, the alternative hypothesis also needs to be considered based on the ethnographic analysis summarized here, which showed signs of cross-cultural work alienation.

Hypothesis 1a: Owing to employee dissatisfaction with the state of affairs prior to the acquisition and the interventions that the new management took to promote the acquisition's success, work alienation will decrease over time on average for employees.

Hypothesis 1b: Work alienation will be shown by a decrease in positive attitudes that employees report between the pre-acquisition and the later acquisition periods.

The unique characteristics of the particular interventions as they unfolded also resulted in observations that required additional quantitative research.

Cross-cultural work alienation emerged early in the research process as an issue that at least some employees, particularly middle managers, found personally salient. The Japanese management, in a purposeful gesture to build trust in the workforce and community, rehired all the employees who had worked under the previous management. New management teams frequently "clean house" by not hiring or terminating employees with low performance records. Instead, TPC management dealt with poor performers in a typically "Japanese" fashion by relocating them to new positions within the plant; a practice referred to as creating a *madogiwazoku* (by-the-window tribe), meaning the workers sent there would have nothing better to do than look out the window. This practice is both consistent with Japanese "lifetime employment" principles (Rohlen, 1974) and TPC management's desire to harbor goodwill. All those who were relocated had been shopfloor supervisors in the functional areas of key strategic concern to the acquisition, thermal paper coating. In interviews of non-management employees, these managers were described as behaving in stereotypic Theory X terms (McGregor, 1960). For example, they treated their subordinates as if they were lazy, irresponsible and needing coercion to perform. These managers (five in all) were given positions where they supervised special projects in such areas as environmental concerns, expansion planning and technical support to sales. In all five cases the manager's span of control was trimmed down to zero. While this practice is consistent with Japanese management norms, and would have been appreciated and seen as a benevolent gesture in Japan (Lincoln & Kalleberg, 1990), in the US context this practice produced feelings of alienation consistent with negative individual-level outcomes associated with feelings of disempowerment (Spreitzer, 1996).

Indeed, some research points out the vulnerability of middle managers to work alienation even in monocultural settings. Spreitzer (1996) relates social–cultural characteristics of work units to individual-level perceptions of role ambiguity, span of control, sociopolitical support and access to information and resources, as well as to work unit climates that make the manager feeling increasingly disempowered. Downsizing that leaves middle managers having to do more with substantially fewer resources can also produce a feeling of disempowerment (Alvesson & Sveningsson, 2003; Holden & Roberts, 2004). Organizational anthropology evidence documents the alienating effects of globalization on MNE middle managers as more and more of their work is done virtually over distance (Hassard et al., 2007; Peltonen, 2007).

Although work alienation appeared to be acute in the five cases, mentioned previously, interviews showed that certain symptoms of this condition were more widely spread among other middle managers not put into by-the-window positions. Early indicators of other types of cross-cultural work alienation included the following:

(1) One middle manager who had worked at the plant for 10 years quit his job in frustration because he felt he was being discriminated against by having reduced influence in decision-making and a smaller span of control.

(2) An article in *Business Month* (September 1988) on similar Japanese FDI-related cross-cultural work alienation experiences entitled "A matter of control" was sent anonymously to the ethnographer. Certain managers had taken to whiting out the names in the original article and substituting their own in a non-too-subtle act of victim identification.

(3) Informants told the ethnographer that certain middle managers were "acting differently – bored ... they say they have nothing to do now".

(4) Two managers in the finance area complained that no matter how early they came nor how late they left, their Japanese boss was always there and that this made them feel hopeless, as though they just could not compete.

(5) A significant group of middle managers, already flagged in the ethnographic study as crossculturally alienated, refused to go to the company Christmas party, citing excuses such as "what do Japanese know about Christmas?" and "It just seems weird to celebrate with people who don't give a damn about you".

(6) A high frequency of verbal indicators of cross-cultural work alienation came up in the ongoing content analyses of interview transcripts. The following flag-words were used to code the condition: impotent, eunuch, go fish, fishing expedition, by-the-window tribe, useless, bored and *gaijin* (foreigner, a Japanese word used ironically by Americans to describe their feelings of being outcasts on their own home ground). Each of these accounts also found support during participant observation and ongoing within-methods triangulation of interview data during the 5-year time period over which the ethnography was conducted.

These expressions of cross-cultural work alienation occurred in the context of an overall response of the workforce to the new management that appeared on the surface to be quite favorable. The Japanese management, after all, turned around a severely faltering plant. The question remained, though, of which sentiment was more widespread: *did expressions of cross-cultural work alienation by a few reflect the hidden sentiments of many, or were those who expressed such alienation an outspoken minority?*

Consequently, the quantitative portion of the project was conducted to clearly identify the portions of the workforce that reacted positively to the Japanese acquisition, as distinct from the portions that experienced cross-cultural work alienation. The qualitative work suggested that alienation was more likely among middle managers than among lower-level workers and that they were generally managers in production areas directly related to the strategic focus of the new management.

> *Hypothesis 2:* Middle managers will be more prone to experience alienation than will lower-level employees.

Larsson and Lubatkin (2001) provide evidence that an acquiring company's use of several social control practices tends to promote successful acculturation in international M&As. Aware of the negative stereotype of working for "Japan, Inc." cultivated in the media around the time of the acquisition, the acquiring company engaged in two practices that were designed to manage the social side of the transition and limit cross-cultural alienation. One was to send 20 employees to Japan for on-site training in the way things were done in the home organization (Japanese parent organizational culture). The intent was to promote deeper contextual understanding and, in Blauner's framework, to manage *disconnectedness* by showing how the acquired facility was connected to Japan. The hope was that not only would the experience be a positive one for these particular employees but also that they would express positive attitudes and explain distinctions of the Japanese organizational culture to their colleagues after their return. The people sent to Japan were chosen on the basis of functional position and criticality to implementing technology introduced by the expansion rather than on their personal attitudes or background.

The second practice was to bring a number of supervisors from Japan in order to guide and put in place best practices during the expansion. Whereas many practices of Japanese acquirers have been described as having the sole purpose of transferring shopfloor procedures (Peterson et al., 1999), the intent in this case was also to improve cross-cultural understanding and thereby limit what Blauner's model would describe as US employees' social isolation and self-estrangement from working for a culturally and physically distant owner.

> *Hypothesis 3:* Employees who are sent to Japan for cultural training (3a) and those who have experience of working with Japanese supervisors (3b) will show less alienation than will others.

Method

The ethnography

The ethnography used the primary data collection methods of participant observation and in-depth interviews as well as secondary data collection of in-house documents and articles in the popular press (Figure 26.1).

The ethnography was conducted at an average of 10 h per week on-site for 5 years. Formal meetings, quality control group discussions and two collective bargaining sessions were observed; in-depth interviews were conducted. Follow-up interviews were also conducted at the US plant, and at corporate headquarters and three sister plants in Japan. The participant observer process in the United States and in Japan generated 1635 pages of field

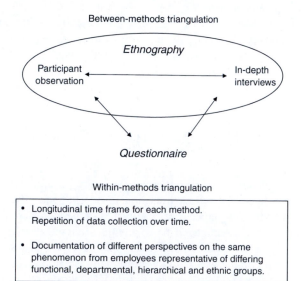

Figure 26.1 Qualitative/quantitative data collection method.

Source: adapted from Brannen (1996).

notes, which were accompanied by ongoing informal journal entries in an ethnographer's log kept throughout the study. The in-depth interviewing process was conducted in three steps: preliminary focus group interviews, follow-up structured interviews and ongoing informal, unstructured dialogue. The data from these interviews took the form of 2896 pages of interview transcripts. The field notes and interview transcripts were entered into semantic analysis software called Hypercard to facilitate the content analysis to identify key constructs and themes.

As Figure 26.1 outlines, the ethnographic portion of the study included several within-method triangulations for validation:

(1) the use of multiple data collection methods for primary and secondary data;
(2) the documentation of different perspectives by conducting formal and informal interviews with key informants from differing functional, hierarchical, departmental and national groups; and
(3) the repetition of data collection over time using each method.

This third strategy was operationalized by conducting prolonged participant observation at the site and by interviewing the same informants at different time periods throughout the course of study.

The quantitative triangulation: the survey

Questionnaires were administered on-site in the final year of the 5-year ethnographic study. The questionnaire was administered as a sit-down census to the entire workforce, including management and blue-collar workers. The total size of the workforce during survey data collection was 229 employees, 138 of whom were blue-collar workers. The attrition rate since the change in management had been less than 0.8 per year.

Research design and time periods. The questionnaire was designed to be retrospective. It asked respondents to answer parallel questions about their attitudes and perceptions during three distinct time periods. These were identified in the survey as follows:

(1) "the period of time up to the acquisition (September 1981–December 1986)";
(2) "the period of time between the acquisition and the expansion (December 1986–September 1989)"; and
(3) "the period of time since the expansion (September 1989–Present)."

Identifying these three time periods fitted well with highly salient, clearly demarcated events in the organization's collective memory. The transition from the prior owners to the Japanese acquirers was emotionally meaningful to all concerned. The period after the acquisition was marked by the $40 million dollar expansion described earlier and was commonly viewed as the zenith of the company's success. The present time for these respondents meant a recent situation in which the company had endured its first layoffs in the wake of a severe downturn in the industry.

The retrospective survey design was not intended to provide the kind of quantitative basis for assessing the effects of change that is sometimes done in quasi-experimental organizational change research. Instead, it was intended to provide a way for all organization members to structure their accounts of what had happened, and to triangulate with the ethnography. The ability of a respondent to recall his or her true feelings after a period of 5 years is, of course, somewhat limited. However, we expected that the relatively clear demarcation of periods and the emotional significance of the changes within them to respondents' lives would promote greater than usual accuracy. Retrospective research has been occasionally used with success in the past (Butterfield & Farris, 1972). As the results will show, the respondents did in fact differentiate the three periods and their questionnaire responses converge in reasonable ways with the ethnographic analysis.

Respondents. The workforce at the time of the surveys consisted of 229 employees, of whom 138 were blue-collar workers. Of these 229 eligible respondents, 203 provided usable surveys. Of these, 85 had been at the site since before the Japanese acquisition (Time A as described above) 47 had been hired during the subsequent expansion period (Time B above) and 71 were more recent hires (Time C above). In order to focus on the experiences of the same people as they went through the full cross-cultural experience, hypothesis tests were based on the 85 respondents who had been at the site during all three phases of the change. In instances where significant changes were found over time, these respondents were then compared with the others who were hired through Time B and Time C.

Measures. As previously articulated, the measures selected reflect Blauner's alienation concepts as well as the ethnographic analysis of the present organization. Blauner's idea of *self-estrangement* was represented by established organizational behavior measures of commitment and satisfaction. Organizational commitment was measured using five items that Lincoln and Kalleberg (1990) had adapted from the Organization Commitment Questionnaire (Mowday et al., 1979) for use in Japan. Pay satisfaction, work satisfaction, and life satisfaction were each measured using four-point Likert scales headed by: "How satisfied are you with". The pay satisfaction measure used three items, including: "your pay compared to what others in this company earn". The work satisfaction measure included four items, such as: "your job in general". The life satisfaction measure was a single item: "your life in general". A number of items in each of these measures had been used by Lincoln and Kalleberg (1990) in a comparative study of US and Japanese manufacturing organizations.

We created several new measures for this project, based on cross-cultural alienation issues that arose in the ethnography. Blauner's (1964) idea of *social isolation* was represented by measures of supervisor acceptance and Japanese values. Supervisor acceptance consisted of three items beginning with "Your supervisor" and including the following: "Makes you feel like a valued group member". Japanese values was a single-item measure: "Do you feel that your work values are not so different than the work values of the Japanese employees?" Blauner's ideas of *impotence* and *disconnectedness* were represented by measures of participation valued and meetings pre-settled. Participation valued was also a single-item measure (coded 1=no, 3=yes): "When you attend a meeting at the request of your supervisor, do you feel that your participation is seriously valued?" Meetings pre-settled was represented by a single item (coded 1=no, 3=yes): "Do you feel that the outcome of a meeting is already set before it begins?"

Unless noted otherwise, responses for each question were provided on five-point Likert scales, with the adjectives in the response alternatives phrased to correspond with the content of the particular question (see Brannen, 1994: 245–275 for details). High values on an item denoted high levels of the construct measured. The tense of each question was adjusted as appropriate to past or present, depending on the time period about which the question asked.

For example, one question asked "The chances for promotion are/were good on my job" and asked respondents to answer the question separately for each of the three time periods noted above. (The item examples noted above all use present-tense phrasing.)

Several predictors are categorical variables. Hierarchy is represented as an item that contrasts managers with other employees. Time is coded as a three-category variable corresponding to the three phases noted above. The interventions are coded as whether a respondent had been "sent to Japan" (1) or not (0), whether a respondent had a "Japanese supervisor" at Time B (1) or not (0) and also at Time C (1) or not (0).

Means, standard deviations and alpha coefficients for each of the measures are provided in Table 26.1. For the scales taken from prior research, the measures were generally reliable. Measure construction for the new measures went through a refinement step prior to the descriptive statistics shown in Table 26.1. The new items designed particularly for this project were analyzed using exploratory factor analysis to determine whether scales could be created (results available from the authors). Preliminary scaling choices were made based on the factor analysis and the concepts intended by each question. These scales were then assessed for reliability using alpha reliability estimates and item-to-total correlations.

Data analysis. One set of analyses testing Hypothesis 1 was a set of repeated-measures MANOVAs to assess overall change in attitudes over the three time periods. For attitudes in which significant changes are found, ANOVA was then used to determine whether the reports of Time A pre-acquisition attitudes of the most experienced employees also differed from the attitudes of the more recently hired respondents at Time C, as detailed in the results shown. Other analyses used hierarchy as a two-category between-subjects factor that contrasted managers with other employees and time as a within-subjects factor that contrasted reported perceptions over the three time periods. The interaction of time with hierarchy was used to test Hypothesis 2. Repeated-measures MANOVAs were similarly used to test Hypothesis 3 about change over time for respondents who participated in one of the interventions. Since the respondents who had a Japanese supervisor at Time B overlapped with those who had a Japanese supervisor at Time C and the number of respondents was relatively low (85), one set of analyses is reported for each criterion using the "Sent to Japan" predictor and the "Japanese supervisor at Time C" predictor, and a second is reported for each criterion using the "Sent to Japan" and "Japanese supervisor at Time B" predictor.

Table 26.1 Measures indicating alienation: veterans

Measure	Mean			SD			Alpha		
	C	B	A	C	B	A	C	B	A
Supervisor acceptance	3.38	3.32	3.21	0.84	0.86	0.92	0.64	0.71	0.80
Participation valued	2.45	2.23	2.12	0.80	0.86	0.80	—	—	—
Meetings pre-settled	2.09	2.01	2.07	0.91	0.88	0.83	—	—	—
Organization commitment	3.54	3.46	3.27	0.75	0.69	0.69	0.78	0.74	0.68
Pay satisfaction	2.78	2.73	2.65	0.88	0.81	0.83	0.92	0.92	0.92
Work satisfaction	3.23	3.16	3.10	0.56	0.54	0.61	0.76	0.72	0.75
Life satisfaction	3.38	3.34	3.23	0.64	0.78	0.77	—	—	—

Notes: Time C: since the company's recent expansion; Time B: during acquisition by Japanese company; Time A: just before the Japanese acquisition.
$N = 82-85$ depending on missing data for a particular measure.

Results of quantitative triangulation

Overall changes

Hypothesis 1a suggests that the intervention will be successful, as indicated by increasingly positive attitude means over time, while Hypothesis 1b recognizes that the ethnographic analysis suggested that alienation might be prevalent. The means shown in Table 26.1 indicate that respondents generally reported that their attitudes became more positive in later years than they were before the acquisition. Table 26.2 shows the results of significance tests applied to these means using repeated-measures MANOVA predicting each criterion from time. Hypothesis 1a is supported for two measures. Respondent's reports became significantly more positive over time for their sense that participation was valued by their superiors (participation valued) and for their commitment to the organization (organization commitment). In contrast, no changes were found in pay attitudes.

In order to assess whether these two changes were unique to the 85 people who had been in the plant since before the Japanese takeover, or whether they were also reflected in the attitudes of respondents hired at the two later points noted before, additional analyses of the participation valued and organizational commitment measures were conducted (details available from the authors). For these two measures, the Time C attitudes of the 117 employees hired during Time B and Time C were compared with the Time A attitudes reported by the 85 employees hired before the Japanese acquisition. ANOVAs showed more positive Time C attitudes for the more recent hires than for the Time A attitudes reported by the employees who had been at the plant prior to the acquisition for both participation valued ($F = 6.21$, d.f. = 1, 198, $p < 0.05$, two-tailed) and organizational commitment ($F = 4.07$, d.f. = 1, 198, $p < 0.05$, two-tailed). Since the more recent hires had no memory of the previous management regime, they serve as a control in that their responses were not colored by improvement or deterioration in alienation due to better or worse management. All these newly hired employees knew was that they were joining a firm with Japanese management, so their responses reflect their perceptions of working in the post-acquisition organizational culture alone. These results of the control group comparison support the conclusion that the changes over time in these two attitudes for the employees who remained with the plant during all three time periods generalize for these individual-level outcomes throughout the plant.

Differences in change over time by hierarchical level. Hypothesis 2 follows the results of the ethnography by suggesting that managers will be more prone to experience alienation than will lower-level employees. Table 26.3 reports the repeated-measures MANOVA

Table 26.2 Repeated-measures MANOVA predicting attitudes from time

	Wilks' lambda	*F*	*d.f.*
Supervisor acceptance	0.97	2.00	2, 162
Participation valued	0.87	6.83**	2, 166
Meetings pre-settled	0.99	0.37	2, 162
Organization commitment	0.94	3.93*	2, 162
Pay satisfaction	0.98	1.38	2, 162
Life satisfaction	0.96	2.32	2, 162
Work satisfaction	0.96	1.95	2, 162

*p < 0.05; **p < 0.01.

Table 26.3 Repeated-measures MANOVA predicting from hierarchy and time

| | Hierarchy | | Time | Hierarchy × Time | |
	F	d.f.	F	F	
Supervisor acceptance	7.50**	1, 78	0.03	0.59	2, 2, 156
Participation valued	8.94**	1, 80	1.15	1.16	2, 2, 160
Meetings pre-settled	0.30	1, 78	0.18	0.16	2, 2, 156
Organizational commitment	2.52	1, 78	0.28	0.61	2, 2, 156
Pay satisfaction	5.99**	1, 78	0.94	0.13	2, 2, 156
Life satisfaction	0.08	1, 78	0.69	2.43	2, 2, 156
Work satisfaction	0.74	1, 78	0.40	1.94	2, 2, 156

*$p < 0.05$; **$p < 0.01$.

predicting each criterion from time, hierarchy and the interaction of time and hierarchy. The results show the typical effects of hierarchy, reflecting the generally higher sense by managers that superiors show acceptance of opinions and value participation more when it comes from managers than from lower-level employees (group means available from the authors). The significant pay satisfaction differences between the hierarchical level groups reflect highest pay satisfaction by managers and union workers and lowest by office workers (group means available from the authors). However, the results show none of the significant interactions of hierarchy with time that would reflect higher alienation among managers that are predicted in Hypothesis 2 based on the ethnography.

Differences in change over time based on interventions. Hypothesis 3 suggests that individuals who have gone to Japan for training (Hypothesis 3a) and those who have experience working with Japanese supervisors (Hypothesis 3b) will show more positive attitude change than will others. The hypotheses are tested in the "Intervention effects by time" columns of Table 26.4. These results indicate that supervisor acceptance, organizational commitment, and work satisfaction show different changes for those who went to Japan than for others. Means for the two subgroups indicate that the changes are more positive for those who went than for others. Consistent with the ethnography, Hypothesis 3a is generally supported.

The results testing the hypothesis about the effects of having a Japanese boss are provided separately for respondents who reported having a Japanese boss at the time data were collected (at Time C) and for those who had a Japanese boss during the period of expansion (at Time B). Two attitudes, life satisfaction and work satisfaction, show differences indicating more positive attitude change between respondents with Japanese supervisors as at Time B compared with others. Table 26.4 shows other effects not associated with Hypothesis 3. The significant coefficients in the "intervention effects" columns do not correspond with any of the significant intervention by time effects, and so do not confound these effects. The main effects noted in the "Time" column largely reflect the results noted for Hypothesis 1.

Adjustment and alienation in specific departments. The overall results indicated that alienation did not permeate the plant. Nevertheless, the ethnographic results indicated pockets of alienation scattered throughout the organization that still might appear in attitudes expressed within particular departments. The number of respondents in specific departments, however, is too small to test for differences statistically. Means for each department at the three time points are provided in Table 26.5.

Table 26.4 Repeated-measures MANOVA predicting from having a Japanese supervisor at Time B, Time C, and being sent to Japan: all three times

	Interventions			Interventions by time			
	Sent to Japan	Japanese supervisor	d.f.	Time	Sent to Japan	Japanese supervisor	d.f.
Supervisor acceptance							
Supervisor Time C	2.70	1.82	1, 1, 79	3.19	6.88**	1.64	2, 2, 2, 158
Supervisor Time B	1.20	7.83**	1, 1, 79	8.58**	6.11**	0.47	2, 2, 2, 158
Participation valued							
Supervisor Time C	5.22*	2.34	1, 1, 81	5.66**	1.07	0.17	2, 2, 2, 162
Supervisor Time B	3.78	4.11*	1, 1, 81	6.97**	0.56	1.35	2, 2, 2, 162
Meetings pre-settled							
Supervisor Time C	0.77	3.57	1, 1, 79	0.71	0.23	0.87	2, 2, 2, 158
Supervisor Time B	0.77	1.21	1, 1, 79	1.04	0.08	1.81	2, 2, 2, 158
Organizational commitment							
Supervisor Time C	2.82	0.59	1, 1, 79	10.45**	7.25**	0.10	2, 2, 2, 158
Supervisor Time B	1.77	2.55	1, 1, 79	13.45**	5.27**	2.88	2, 2, 2, 158
Pay satisfaction							
Supervisor Time C	0.07	2.17	1, 1, 79	2.03	0.74	0.19	2, 2, 2, 158
Supervisor Time B	0.17	0.18	1, 1, 79	3.56*	0.23	2.31	2, 2, 2, 158
Life satisfaction							
Supervisor Time C	1.24	1.33	1, 1, 79	2.67	0.03	1.35	2, 2, 2, 158
Supervisor Time B	0.85	0.16	1, 1, 79	4.80**	0.12	4.20*	2, 2, 2, 158
Work satisfaction							
Supervisor Time C	0.07	1.47	1, 1, 79	8.11**	6.29**	0.96	2, 2, 2, 158
Supervisor Time B	0.15	1.57	1, 1, 79	16.19**	3.37*	9.84**	2, 2, 2, 158

*p < 0.05;** p < 0.01.

Notes: Time C: since the company's recent expansion; Time B: during acquisition by the Japanese company. For each criterion, the first row is for the repeated-measure MANOVA for having a Japanese supervisor at Time C, and the second row is for having a Japanese supervisor at Time B.

Frequencies for veterans: Japanese supervisor at Time C – No: 65, Yes: 20; Japanese Supervisor at Time B – No: 73, Yes: 12; Sentto Japan – No: 68, Yes: 17.

Discussion

The response of the popular press to globalization as MNEs strive to use the world as their playing field through FDI and international M&As suggests the emergence of a new variation on work alienation. The present project thus drew from a 5-year ethnography of one such instance of a cross-border M&A and existing alienation theory to compile a set of measures to empirically test and systematically build theory in this regard. In the discussion section, we will first consider how the quantitative results guided us to reconsider some of the initial ethnographic evidence for alienation. We then consider implications for alienation theory in general, for theories of culture and biculturalism, for research about M&As and for international research in general. We conclude the section by considering the project's limitations.

Between-methods contradictions, tensions and synergistic discovery

The quantitative results complement the ethnographic results by suggesting that the approach the company took in the acquisition overcame much of the risk of alienation for the employees in general. The alienation that appeared in the qualitative analysis turns out to have been localized, rather than widespread. The quantitative analysis also indicated that the positive

Table 26.5 Departmental means at three time points: searching for pockets of alienation

	Time	Department										
		Coating	Converting	Engineering	Finance	HR	Maintenance	Mixing	Other production	Purchase	RRD/QC	Salary
Supervisor acceptance	C	3.55	2.64	3.67	3.00	5.00	3.11	4.50	3.29	4.33	4.00	3.67
	B	3.44	2.69	3.67	3.33	5.00	2.67	4.00	3.38	4.67	3.89	3.33
	A	3.14	2.90	3.33	4.42	2.67	2.56	4.33	3.33	4.67	2.56	3.13
Participation valued	C	2.33	2.15	3.00	2.50	3.00	2.67	3.00	2.25	3.00	3.00	3.00
	B	2.14	2.08	3.00	2.25	3.00	1.83	2.00	2.13	3.00	2.67	2.40
	A	1.95	2.15	3.00	2.75	1.00	2.00	1.00	2.00	1.00	1.33	2.40
Meetings pre-settled	C	2.10	1.75	1.00	2.00	3.00	2.00	3.00	2.13	1.00	2.33	2.20
	B	2.10	1.58	1.00	1.25	3.00	1.83	3.00	2.00	3.00	2.33	2.00
	A	1.90	1.92	3.00	2.50	1.00	2.00	3.00	2.25	1.00	1.00	2.20
Organization commitment	C	3.71	3.22	3.20	2.75	5.00	3.37	4.10	3.30	3.80	4.07	4.00
	B	3.57	3.22	3.20	2.90	5.00	3.23	3.60	3.23	3.80	4.00	3.80
	A	3.20	3.10	3.00	4.00	1.40	3.17	3.80	3.06	3.80	3.00	3.52
Pay satisfaction	C	3.29	2.44	3.00	1.75	3.33	2.83	3.50	2.54	1.00	2.44	2.47
	B	3.19	2.41	3.00	1.67	3.33	2.72	3.50	2.48	1.00	2.33	2.47
	A	3.20	2.36	3.00	2.50	1.67	2.78	3.50	2.19	3.00	1.78	2.60
Work satisfaction	C	3.27	2.85	2.75	2.69	4.00	3.17	3.75	3.13	3.00	3.67	3.45
	B	3.23	2.79	3.25	2.88	4.00	3.08	3.38	3.00	3.00	3.50	3.30
	A	3.08	3.00	3.00	3.81	2.00	3.33	3.50	2.82	3.50	2.42	3.20
Life satisfaction	C	3.36	3.38	2.00	3.00	4.00	3.33	3.50	3.25	4.00	4.00	3.80
	B	3.52	3.38	3.00	3.25	4.00	3.17	2.50	3.14	3.00	4.00	3.60
	A	3.19	3.54	3.00	3.75	3.00	3.33	3.50	3.29	2.00	3.33	3.40

effects of the interventions were somewhat stronger for the employees who directly participated in them. Further, the quantitative analysis helped to pinpoint potential pockets of cross-culturally alienated employees among the managers distinguishable by hierarchy, by functional area, and by whether or not their direct supervisor was Japanese. The ethnographic results reported previously showed frequent complaints that a number of employees were not included in the actual decision-making process, suffered through meetings conducted mostly in Japanese, and perceived a foreign "shadow management" rendering home-country managers powerless. They also had limited advancement potential, received few or no performance reviews, and were given the opportunity to participate only in matters of trivial significance. The quantitative results, however, suggested that these individuals might have been an outspoken alienated minority in the larger context of an organization that was functioning effectively.

The between-methods triangulation, though ultimately helpful in putting the emergent issue of cross-cultural alienation in the context of the larger organizational climate, generated many challenges and qualifications to the ethnographic findings. This overall discursive research logic of tensions, contradictions, and synergistic learning that resulted from the between-methods triangulation is outlined in Figure 26.2.

Even while the general theme of cross-cultural alienation was not found in the results of the questionnaire analysis, the condition continued to surface in localized situations over the 5-year time period over which the ethnography was conducted. Two additional middle managers quit their job, citing "unfair Japanese management practices" and "bamboo ceiling" as reasons. Several others were shuffled into what they called "just some more by-the-window slots." A group of hourly workers and foremen reporting directly to Katsan – a Japanese expatriate promoted to plant manager 2 years after the acquisition – formed the GROK club (Get Rid of Katsan club). An old-timer who was asked to take an early retirement filed an age discrimination suit against the Japanese management. While the ethnography found cross-cultural alienation to be a prominent narrative theme, analysis of the questionnaire

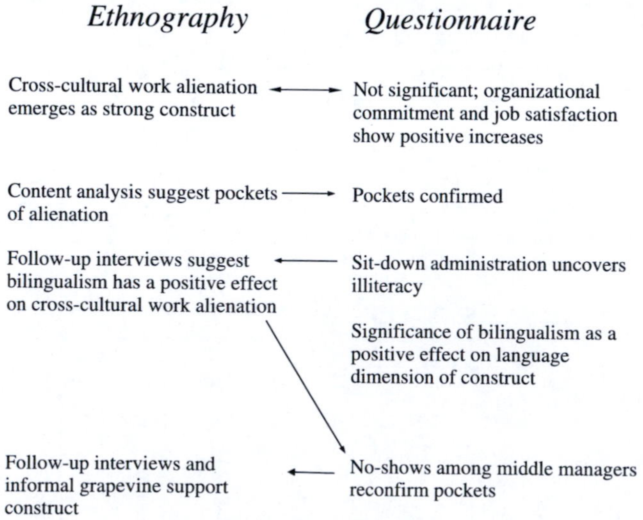

Ethnography	*Questionnaire*
Cross-cultural work alienation emerges as strong construct	←——→ Not significant; organizational commitment and job satisfaction show positive increases
Content analysis suggest pockets of alienation	——→ Pockets confirmed
Follow-up interviews suggest bilingualism has a positive effect on cross-cultural work alienation	←—— Sit-down administration uncovers illiteracy
	Significance of bilingualism as a positive effect on language dimension of construct
Follow-up interviews and informal grapevine support construct	←—— No-shows among middle managers reconfirm pockets

Figure 26.2 Between-methods triangulation: tensions, contradictions and synergies.

Source: adapted from Brannen (1996).

results indicated rather that this might have been appearing more as localized alienation, even in the context of a generally positive response to the acquisition.

The synergistic discovery of pockets of alienation. This partial contradiction in the findings of the ethnography and questionnaire led to the re-examination of both data sets. The means in Table 26.5 suggest that we should look carefully at interview data for explanations of the apparent decline in attitudes in the conversion/product finishing, finance and engineering departments, and the relative lack of improvement over time in a few others. The ethnographic data suggested that the type of employees susceptible to cross-cultural work alienation tended to be middle managers in the production areas most directly connected to the $40 million expansion. These areas were the mixing, coating and finishing departments. Because these departments were at the core of the strategic operations focus of the new management, they had a higher concentration of Japanese expatriates as well as Japanese outside contractors. In addition, control was centered more firmly in Japanese hands in these areas during the first few years of the acquisition, because the success of the venture rested on the successful implementation of these technologies.

Two middle managers from these departments declined to take the questionnaire. When asked about this they explained that they felt awkward taking it because their boss and long-time friend, a senior executive, had just been asked to take an early retirement by the Japanese president. This senior executive was upset about the forced early retirement, and was threatening to sue the Japanese management for age discrimination. The two subordinate managers felt a conflict of interest in taking the questionnaire, because although they wanted to help the ethnographer out, their boss had made it clear that he was not going to take the questionnaire, and they did not want to do something that would make their boss feel they were unsympathetic. The follow-up interviews discovered more data to support the presence of cross-cultural alienation, even while the loss of these three respondents might have contributed to the lack of evidence for alienation in the analysis of the questionnaire.

These ethnographic observations informed further analysis of the quantitative data to look for differences on cross-cultural alienation scores across various departments, levels of hierarchy and union membership. This subsequent quantitative analysis then uncovered specific pockets of alienation among managers in the mixing, coating and finance departments. The evidence in Table 26.5 of pockets of alienation among middle managers in mixing and coating confirmed the ethnographic findings. Again, these findings make sense conceptually, because these functional areas had the key technologies to ensure the profitability of the plant and thus received the most intervention efforts by new management. Indeed, it was from these departments that managers were taken and put into "by-the-window" positions devoid of formal authority. However, alienation of middle managers in finance was unexpected.

Again, the ethnographic data were re-examined to make sense of this new quantitative finding. The ethnographic secondary data, in the form of organizational charts, showed that finance was the only department in which there was a Japanese departmental head but where no systematic acculturation occurred in the form of Japan on-site training or ongoing cross-cultural consulting support. In addition, the department head, being a senior Japanese manager, exhibited the most "hyper"-normal (meaning stereotypically "Japanese"; cf. Brannen & Salk, 2000) Japanese organizational cultural behavior. For example, being senior, he was expected to come to work earlier and to work later than the other Japanese at the plant (Lebra, 1976). This behavior, as already noted in the ethnographic results, was particularly worrisome to the American managers who were his direct reports, as they would try without success to impress him by coming earlier or working later. What they did not know was that his behavior was dictated by Japanese organizational norms and that their Japanese supervisor was expected culturally to be the first in and last out of the organization daily. Had the managers undergone Japanese cultural training, this negative spiral of perceptual imputation might have been circumvented. In this case, the contradictions between the findings generated by the two methods were catalysts for the re-examination and re-analysis of both data sets, out of which came new insights into both analyses and a more accurate understanding of the post-merger dynamics.

The multi-method research approach thus indicates several advantages of combining ethnographic with quantitative methods, especially when researching complex cultural phenomena. It also identifies several possible new directions for the survey components of research about FDI, cross-border M&As, and cross-cultural work alienation.

Implications for alienation research

One contribution of our project has been to introduce a set of measures that can be used to represent individual-level alienation outcomes, particularly outcomes that are relevant to cross-border M&A. This endeavor complements projects that have sought to design measures of initial cultural incompatibility between M&A partners (for example, Veiga et al., 2000). The measures chosen are linked to Blauner's (1964) ideas of impotence, disconnectedness, social isolation and self-estrangement. These measures included established measures of commitment and satisfaction, and new cross-culturally related aspects of alienation suggested by the ethnographic analysis. A new measure of supervisor acceptance was created. Individual items reflecting the potential dissonance between the national cultural work-related norms of the acquiring firm and the local employees were developed, such as whether participation was valued and whether outcomes of meetings were predetermined. These culture-specific measures showed divergence from the other measures, suggesting that cross-cultural work alienation is indeed a distinct variation on work alienation. Their single-item nature is a limitation for the present study, but the results support the value of designing multiple-item measures for future alienation research in international business. Future research that builds on the alienation theme could also develop implications of Blauner's alienation concepts for each of the moderately correlated aspects of commitment that have been identified in other research (Meyer & Allen, 1991). The study also showed change over time in these variables and the effects of various interventions that can be viewed as targeted at ameliorating Blauner's four aspects of alienation and preventing cross-cultural work alienation itself.

Cross-cultural work alienation and the concept of culture in international M&As

While there is not a large base of established research on cross-cultural work alienation, the construct has been identified in the social psychology literature as a condition that can arise when an organization's power base is split between two distinct cultural groups that have different modal values (Zurcher et al., 1965). Studies of equity or justice issues in M&A (for example, Lipponen et al., 2004) also touch on topics related to alienation, although equity and justice issues focus more narrowly on ethical aspects of how a more powerful party deals with a less powerful party than does alienation.

Several social psychology studies of work alienation in different country contexts (cf. Kanungo, 1984, 1990; Misra et al., 1985) highlight distinct antecedents of work alienation based on the particular national cultural attributes of the originating contexts. Although this work has helped to point out cultural differences in the causes and manifestations of work alienation, because the studies have focused on single country, single organizational contexts, they only indirectly help our understanding of the dynamics of intraorganizational cross-cultural work alienation that we find in international M&As.

As is often the case in the international business literature, culture in the studies cited above was taken as national culture. Despite this pervasive and often imprecise usage, in the current study the word "culture" without a descriptive adjective designating a specific kind of culture (as in "Japanese national culture") refers to "culture" as the system of shared behaviors, values, and meanings of a designated group of individuals (Fine, 1984; Geertz, 1973). In this view, the negotiated culture of the organization is a dynamic amalgam of various cultural spheres of influence, including but not limited to national cultures of origin of the acquirers and the local employees in the acquired facility (Brannen & Salk, 2000; Strauss, 1982). As such, cross-cultural alienation can stem from cultural differences at the national, organizational and even occupational cultural level in the acquired entity. In this vein, another body of research in organization studies based in sociology and urban anthropology has focused on the related issue of marginalization in domestic organizations that have more than one dominant culture.

Biculturalism research: African-American, bicultural integration and the negotiated culture literature in organization studies and anthropology

Cross-border M&As are complex organizational phenomena in which organizational culture, national culture, and cultural change are in a constant dynamic interplay (Ong, 1987). Consistent with the negotiated culture view, the biculturalism literature in organizational studies is the only stream of work that takes up intraorganizational individual-level outcomes similar to cross-cultural work alienation. The concept of biculturalism first emerged in the organizational studies literature for describing the experience of African-American organizational participants in the white-dominated work culture of the United States (Bell, 1990; Dill, 1979; Valentine, 1971). This work documents how African-Americans must daily negotiate a path between two distinct cultural realities: the African-American community in which they live, and the white organizational community in which they work. Scholars of biculturalism describe this sort of social marginality as a condition in which a person lives on the boundaries of two distinct cultures and feels disconnected from both (Mann, 1958; Stonequist, 1937). Although significantly different in many respects, the bicultural experiences of African-American organizational participants and US employees of Japanese-owned companies are similar, in that both must negotiate their organizational lives in a cultural milieu distinct from their own, a milieu with the potential to make them feel neither fully integrated nor completely valued.

More recent work on bicultural identity integration in organizations strives to understand individuals who negotiate between their disparate cultural identities in response to varying cultural cues (Benet-Martinez & Haritatos, 2005; Benet et al., 2002; Cheng et al., 2006). While this work does not deal directly with cross-cultural work alienation, it does focus on understanding the marginalized nature of non-integrated biculturals (similar to Blauner's concept of self-isolation).

The kind of biculturalism that might emerge in cross-border post-acquisition situations would of course be distinct from either of these types of biculturalism. However, the theory generated on biculturalism and biculturals offers important insights into understanding the individual-level outcomes in the Japanese-American organizational case as studied here and cross-cultural work alienation more generally.

To summarize, our conceptualization of cross-cultural work alienation draws from these two distinct bodies of research – work alienation and marginalization in bicultural contexts – and seeks to link them to individual-level organizational behavior concepts. We follow Blauner's (1964) adaptation of Marx's view of societal alienation by treating it as a manageable characteristic of relationships within particular organizations. We add to this literature both by integrating it with the literature on biculturalism and marginalization and by viewing cross-cultural work alienation as a distinct and increasingly relevant form of societal alienation and marginalization.

Theories of alienation largely precede the theories and measures that have come into common use in organizational behavior, and are rarely explicitly invoked in organizational theory development. Nevertheless, the ongoing ethnographic portion of the present project suggested that a number of the organizational behavior measures that we had selected for the assessment process could be better understood theoretically, better linked to the interventions used by management, and more readily linked to the ethnographic field notes by viewing them as reflecting aspects of work alienation that Blauner (1964) had identified. It is our hope that the research presented here will guide the development of a set of measures that will cover the full range of issues that constitute cross-cultural work alienation. For example, we included measures of whether or not participation was valued and of whether or not meetings were only a formality at which predetermined decisions were ceremonially announced that are linked to Blauner's idea of *impotence*. Our measure of respondents' sense of whether their supervisor accepted them as an important member of the work group is related to the idea of *social isolation* and a measure of organizational commitment is related to successful avoidance of *self-estrangement*. In addition to links of our survey measures to Blauner's concepts, several of the interventions that the company used to enhance cross-cultural integration are related to aspects of alienation. In particular, arranging for employees to visit the parent company in Japan had the potential to reduce *disconnectedness* by showing how activities in the US facility were intimately linked to work in the Japanese facilities. It also had the potential to reduce *social isolation* by humanizing the Japanese owners and workers to the US workers through direct contact. Transferring some supervisors from Japan to the United States also had the potential for similar effects.

Implications for the alienating potential of cross-border M&As and for limiting cross-cultural work alienation in M&As

Another contribution has been to explain why alienation can arise in cross-border M&As and how it can be managed. The organization studied faced a potential alienation problem in an acquisition situation that is at once quite stressful and quite commonplace. Any unique FDI is likely to have distinctive features, but the experience studied here shows some possible ways of successfully avoiding the all too frequent experience that an acquisition that makes financial sense on paper fails owing to social issues in implementation. Although generalization from a single case is difficult, our sense is that the success that this company had from exposing employees of the acquired organization to the culture of the acquiring company is likely to have value in many settings.

Alienation theory suggests that cultural and geographic separation should create problematic disconnectedness and social isolation, so interventions that connect employees to the acquirer's culture directly address these sorts of separation. The basic logic of having a supervisor for a period of time from the acquirer's home country and visiting the acquirer's home company makes sense on these grounds. Much learning is described in philosophy as tacit learning (Polanyi, 1966), in psychology as automatic or schema-based learning (Markus & Zajonc, 1985) and is generally recognized as intuitive and difficult to learn even from the most careful explanation. Communication scholars refer to a *social presence* that comes from direct exposure and which can promote the development of social bonds (Fairclough, 1995). This sort of learning and bonding is likely to be more difficult if the acquirers remain distant. Developing this sense of social presence should reduce the sense of social isolation. Interventions such as sending people from the acquired company to the acquirer's home and sending supervisors as part of a transition, should promote this sort of tacit learning and bonding (cf. Nonaka & Takeuchi, 1995) and reduce the sense of disconnectedness. The particular national cultural work-related differences that might cause cross-cultural work alienation and the interventions used to circumvent its occurrence would need to be fitted to the idiosyncratic cultural dynamics between the particular cultures of the acquiring and acquired firms in question.

Implications for international research methods

Another contribution has been to show what can be learned by multiple-method triangulation. Our triangulation served various research objectives: to disconfirm cross-cultural work alienation as the general state of the post-acquisition organization; to confirm the substantial success of particular interventions that management implemented to promote cross-cultural integration; to refine our understanding of cross-cultural work alienation at particular hierarchical and functional area pockets of alienation that emerged over time; and to provide a framework for developing a set of measures that cover a broad range of cross-cultural alienation indicators for future studies of post-M&A integration. Neither method alone would have given the full picture of this post-acquisition experience. The ethnography by itself would have given an account skewed toward negative individual-level outcomes with alienation at center stage. The quantitative survey would have been significantly less rich without the information provided by the qualitative data. Further, without the iterative theory development provided by utilizing both methods, we would not have been able to fully understand the nature and pervasiveness of the cross-cultural work alienation construct, nor clearly identify the type of employee (job-role, position, etc.) who is particularly susceptible to this type of alienation.

Limitations

The research has a number of limitations in the nature of both the ethnographic and the questionnaire aspects of the research. As an internal facilitator of the change, the ethnographer was exposed to a considerable amount of information. This information was not neutral and unbiased, but was affected by the priorities of informants. The informants who were in greatest contact with the ethnographer gave a greater sense of alienation than the survey indicated was prevalent. The within-methods triangulation used by the ethnographer to systematically interview the entire population of managers served to correct this bias, as did the survey results themselves. In addition, the facilitator stance of the ethnographer also made it possible to overcome a bias in the survey results that would ordinarily be missed. Specifically, non-response was not random, but was systematically due to the non-participation of many of the managers who had individually expressed alienation outside the survey setting. While the survey change assessment, guided by direct knowledge of where to look for alienation, was able to identify it, the survey research underestimates the extent of alienation among a particular set of middle managers.

A source of measurement error for analysis of temporal changes across the three time periods is that we assessed responses retrospectively across the three time periods. It would be more appropriate to take responses at each point of time than retrospectively. The findings indicating that changes in the attitudes of the employees who had been with the company during the complete transition process are reflected in the attitudes of the more recent hires strengthen the conclusion that a genuine change occurred throughout the plant. The number of respondents was also smaller than one would like, although sufficient to identify the main effects of some of the interventions the company used to overcome alienation. Nevertheless, the combination of ethnographic and survey methods helped identify the location and extent of alienation.

The research also has the limitations of any single case study. While our study surfaces an important new variation on work alienation and provides preliminary scale-building aids in the form of cross-cultural work alienation and post-cross-border M&A integration measures to include in future research, only a large, cross-sectional study including multiple cross-cultural situations that vary in the degree of cultural difference between parties could determine the prevalence of this new form of alienation in FDI. A specific limitation is that this method does not make it possible to determine whether or not all the efforts of managing alienation that were used in the present site would be necessary if cultural differences were smaller, or whether they would be adequate if cultural differences were greater. Given the theoretical basis of much of alienation theory in identity and control rather than cultural difference, on conceptual grounds we expect that alienation is likely to need considerable attention even in cross-cultural situations involving culturally similar nations.

Further, a limitation of our analysis is shared with any quasi-experimental project. The interventions are complex. Through the ethnographic analysis, we are able to describe aspects of the change process that would have been useful regardless of the nationality of the acquirer, such as the investment in new equipment. We also describe aspects of the change process that were distinctly related to the Japanese culture of the acquirer, such as the example of arrival time and the use of the "by-the-window tribe". The ethnography goes beyond what could be inferred from the quantitative results by suggesting that the positive response to the changes was due to successful management in general and to successful management of cross-cultural integration.

Conclusion

The present case suggests that, even in the climate of general success in developing cross-cultural interorganizational relations, pockets of alienation can remain and deserve attention. The idea of pockets of alienation is different from alienated individuals. It was not just isolated people in the present case who showed alienation, but groups of people. Was the alienation spawned by interaction between discontented people, or by characteristics of the work situations these people faced that made them unlike others in their workplace? Our study suggests that a certain positional profile of employee is most vulnerable to such alienation, but answers to these questions remain speculative, even after a combination of personal contact with the ethnographer and careful survey data analysis.

While the discrepancy in findings on cross-cultural alienation generated by the two distinct methods upsets the nomothetic theory-building agenda of between-methods triangulation, the disparate results are not altogether surprising. Ethnographic inquiry under the best of conditions produces richly textured descriptions of organizational realities. Informants tell tales of their realities to the researcher, who then captures the essence of these tales in the actual writing-up of the account. Sometimes informants tell third-person tales of organizational scenarios: that is, they give accounts of what they see or feel happening to others in the setting. These third-person accounts not only help to further deepen the texture of the accounts, they also serve as a within-methods validity check in ethnographic research. In the case of the cross-cultural work alienation construct, although there were first-person testimonials to the construct, many informants engaged in such third-person accounts. Often, whereas they would have many examples of cross-cultural alienation at the plant, they claimed that they themselves were not suffering from an analogous condition. It could be that because the construct captures the dark side of what was, overall, a successful acquisition, people were curious about it and vigilant in noticing its many manifestations. It could also be that they were themselves alienated but did not want to align themselves directly with a subgroup at odds with current management. Whatever the case may be, ethnographic inquiry attempts to capture the intricate nature of such recurrent themes that emerge as central issues in the cultural schema of an organization. Individuals who gave vivid, third-person accounts of cross-cultural work alienation as related by the ethnography might not have themselves responded affirmatively to questions about alienation as it pertained to their own experience at the plant.

The increasing number of cross-border M&As and their importance in the globalization strategies of multinational firms create tremendous challenges, particularly at the post-merger stage and dictate a better understanding of the difficulties and opportunities for positive integration interventions. This study provides a strong foundation for future research in this domain, including a set of measures of individual-level outcomes particularly germane to cross-border M&A, examples of positive integration practices that can help prevent such negative outcomes and a powerful methodology for researching complex cultural phenomena in international business.

Acknowledgements

The authors would like to thank Kanzaki Specialty Papers for their support for this research, especially in terms of ongoing access to the Massachusetts site for the principal researcher for 5 years. Thanks also go to Abhijit Sanyal, who helped in the initial quantitative analysis, Julie Bae for research assistance, Harry Lane for encouraging us to submit to *JIBS* and the thoughtful guidance of our editor Charles Galunic and two anonymous reviewers.

References

Adler, N. J. 1983. Cross-cultural management research: The ostrich and the trend. *Academy of Management Review*, 8(2): 226–32.

Aiken, M. T., & Hage, J. 1966. Organizational alienation: A comparative analysis. *American Sociological Review*, 31(4): 497–507.

Alvesson, M., & Sveningsson, S. 2003. Managers doing leadership: The extra-ordinarization of the mundane. *Human Relations*, 56(12): 1435–59.

Barkema, H. G., Bell, H. J., & Pennings, J. M. 1996. Foreign entry, cultural barriers, and learning. *Strategic Management Journal*, 17(2): 151–66.

Bell, E. L. 1990. The bicultural life experience of career-oriented black women. *Journal of Organizational Behavior*, 11(6): 459–77.

Benet-Martinez, V., & Haritatos, J. 2005. Bicultural identity integration (BII): Components and psychological antecedents. *Journal of Personality*, 73(4): 1015–50.

Benet-Martinez, V., Leu, J., Lee, F., & Morris, M. 2002. Negotiating biculturalism: Cultural frame switching in biculturals with oppositional versus compatible cultural identities. *Journal of Cross-Cultural Psychology*, 33(5): 492–516.

Bhagat, R. S., Kedia, B. L., Harveston, P. D., & Triandis, H. C. 2002. Cultural variations in the cross-border transfer of organizational knowledge: An integrative framework. *Academy of Management Review*, 27(2): 204–22.

Bijlsma-Frankema, K., & Costa, A. C. 2005. Understanding the trust-control nexus. *International Sociology*, 20(3): 259–82.

Blauner, R. 1960. Work satisfaction and industrial trends in modern society. In W. Galenson & M. S. Lipset (Eds), *Labor and trade unionism:* 339–60. New York: John Wiley.

Blauner, R. 1964. *Alienation and freedom: The factory worker and his industry.* Chicago: University of Chicago Press.

Boyacigiller, N., & Adler, N. J. 1991. The parochial dinosaur: Organizational science in a global context. *Academy of Management Review*, 16(2): 1–32.

Brannen, M. Y. 1994. *Your next boss is Japanese: Negotiating cultural change at a Western Massachusetts paper plant.* Unpublished Dissertation, University of Massachusetts, Amherst.

Brannen, M. Y. 1996. Ethnographic international management research. In B. J. Punnet & O. Shenkar (Eds), *Handbook for international management research:* 115–43, Cambridge: Blackwell.

Brannen, M. Y., & Fruin, W. M. 1999. Cultural alienation in today's multinational work arenas: Behavioral fallout from globalization. In T. Hamada (Ed), Anthropologists and the Globalization of Business, Special Issue of *Practicing Anthropology*, Vol. 21(4) Fall.

Brannen, M. Y., & Salk, J. E. 2000. Partnering across borders: Negotiating organizational culture in a German-Japanese joint-venture. *Human Relations*, 53(4): 451–87.

Butterfield, D. A., & Farris, G. F. 1972. *The Likert organizational profile: Methodological analysis and test of system 4 theory in Brazil.* Sloan School of Management Working Paper No. 608–72.

Calori, R., Lubatkin, M., & Very, P. 1994. Control mechanisms in cross-border acquisitions: An international comparison. *Organizational Science*, 15(3): 361–79.

Chaterjee, S., Lubatkin, M. H., Schweiger, D. M., & Weber, Y. 1992. Cultural differences and shareholder value in related mergers: linking equity and human capital. *Strategic Management Journal*, 13(5): 319–34.

Cheng, C.-Y., Lee, F., & Benet-Martinez, V. 2006. Assimilation and contrast effects in cultural frame switching: Bicultural identity integration and valence of cultural cues. *Journal of Cross-Cultural Psychology*, 37(6): 742–60.

Child, J., Falkner, D., & Pitkethy, R. 2001. *The management of international acquisitions.* Oxford: Oxford University Press.

Datta, D. K., & Puia, G. 1995. Cross-border acquisitions: an examination of the influence of relatedness and cultural fit on shareholder value creation in US acquiring firms. *Management International Review*, 35(4): 337–59.

Dill, B. T. 1979. The dialectics of black womanhood. *Signs*, 4(3): 543–55.

Doi, T. 1971. *Amae no kozo (The structure of amae).* Tokyo: Kobundo.

Durkheim, E. 1933. *The division of labor in society.* New York: Free Press.

Eisenhardt, K. 1991. Better stories and better constructs: The case for rigor and comparative logic. *Academy of Management Review*, 16(3): 620–27.

Fairclough, N. 1995. *Critical discourse analysis: The critical study of language.* London: Longman.

Fine, G. A. 1984. Negotiated orders and organizational cultures. *Annual Review of Sociology*, 10: 239–62.

Gardberg, N. A., & Fombrun, C. J. 2006. Corporate citizenship: Creating intangible assets across institutional environments. *Academy of Management Review*, 31(2): 329–46.

Geertz, C. 1973. *The interpretation of cultures.* New York: Basic Books.

Gelfand, M. J., Erez, M., & Aycan, Z. 2007. Cross-cultural organizational behavior. *Annual Review of Psychology*, 58: 479–514.

Glaser, B. G., & Strauss, A. L. 1967. *The discovery of grounded theory: Strategies for qualitative research.* New York: Gruyter.

Glater, J. D. 2005. Suit by two employees in US accuses Japanese company of bias. *New York Times.* newyorktimes.com, January 20.

Harvey, M., Novicevic, M. A., Buckley, A. R., & Fung, H. 2005. Reducing inpatriate managers' "liability of foreignness" by addressing stigmatization and stereotype threats. *Journal of World Business*, 40(3): 267–80.

Hassard, J., McCann, L., & Morris, J. 2007. At the sharp end of new organizational ideologies. *Ethnography*, 8(3): 324–44.

Hitt, M. A., Harrison, J. S., & Ireland, R. D. 2001a. *Mergers and acquisitions: A guide to creating value for stakeholders*. New York: Oxford University Press.

Hitt, M. A., Ireland, R. D., Camp, S. M., & Sexton, D. L. 2001b. Strategic entrepreneurship: Entrepreneurial strategies for wealth creation. *Strategic Management Journal*, 22(6–7): 479–91.

Holden, L., & Roberts, I. 2004. The depowerment of the European middle-managers: Challenges and uncertainties. *Journal of Managerial Psychology*, 19(3): 269–87.

JETRO (Japan External Trade Relations Organization). 2007. Japanese trade and investment statistics. http://www.jetro. go.jp/en/stats/statistics/.

Kanter, R. M., & Corn, B. I. 1994. Cultural changes during the integration process of acquisitions: A comparative study between German-Korean acquisitions. *International Journal of International Relations*, 31(5): 591–604.

Kanungo, R. 1984. *Work alienation: An integrative approach*. New York: Praeger.

Kanungo, R. 1990. Work alienation: A pan-cultural perspective. *Journal of Cross-Cultural Psychology*, 21(2): 232–48.

Kleinberg, J. 1989. Cultural clash between managers: America's Japanese firms. *Advances in International Comparative Management*, 4: 221–43.

Kopp, R. 1994. *The rice paper ceiling: Breaking through Japanese corporate culture*. Berkeley, CA: Stone Bridge Press.

Krug, J. A., & Hegarty, W. H. 2001. Predicting who stays and leaves after an acquisition: A study of top managers in multinational firms. *Strategic Management Journal*, 22(2): 185–96.

Larsson, R., & Lubatkin, M. 2001. Achieving acculturation in mergers and acquisitions: An international case survey. *Human Relations*, 54(12): 1573–607.

Lebra, T. S. 1976. *Japanese patterns of behavior*. Honolulu: University of Hawaii Press.

Lee, S. 2003. *Global acquisitions: Strategic integration and the human factor*. New York: Palgrave Macmillan.

Lincoln, J. R., & Kalleberg, A. L. 1990. *Culture, control, and commitment*. Cambridge: Cambridge University Press.

Lipponen, J., Olkkonen, M. E., & Moilanen, A. 2004. Perceived procedural justice and employee responses to an organizational merger. *European Journal of Work and Organizational Psychology*, 13(3): 391–413.

McGregor, D. 1960. *The human side of enterprise*. New York: McGraw-Hill.

Mann, J. 1958. Group relations and the marginal personality. *Human Relations*, 11(1): 77–92.

Markides, C., & Ittner, C. D. 1994. Shareholder benefits from corporate international diversification: Evidence from US international acquisitions. *Journal of International Business Studies*, 25(2): 343–60.

Marks, M. L. 1982. Merging human resources: A review of current research. *Mergers and Acquisitions*, 17(2): 50–55.

Marks, M. L., & Mirvis, P. 1985. Merger syndrome: Stress and uncertainty. *Mergers and Acquisitions*, 20(2): 50–55.

Markus, H. R., & Zajonc, R. B. 1985. The cognitive perspective in social psychology. In G. Lindzey & E. Aronson (Eds), *Handbook of social psychology* (3rd ed.). Vol. 1: 137–230. New York: Random House.

Marx, K. 1897. *Capital*, Vol. 1. (Trans. 1967), New York: New World Paperbacks.

Meyer, J. P., & Allen, N. J. 1991. A three-component conceptualization of organizational commitment. *Human Resource Management Review*, 1(1): 61–89.

Mezias, J. 2002. Identifying liabilities of foreignness and strategies to minimize their effects: The case of labor lawsuit judgments in the United States. *Strategic Management Journal*, 23(3): 229–44.

Middleton, R. 1963. Alienation, race and education. *American Sociological Review*, 28(6): 973–7.

Misra, S., Kanungo, R., Von Ronsenstiel, L., & Stuhler, E. 1985. The motivational formulation of job and work involvement: A cross-national study. *Human Relations*, 33(6): 501–18.

Morosini, P., Shane, S., & Singh, S. 1998. National cultural distance and cross-border performance. *Journal of International Business Studies*, 29(1): 137–58.

Mowday, R. T., Steers, R. M., & Porter, L. W. 1979. The measurement of organizational commitment. *Journal of Vocational Behavior*, 14: 224–47.

Nahavandi, A., & Malekzadeh, A. R. 1988. Acculturation in mergers and acquisitions. *Academy of Management Review*, 13(1): 79–90.

Nonaka, I., & Takeuchi, H. 1995. *The knowledge creating company.* New York: Oxford University Press.

Ohnuki-Tierney, E. 1984. *Illness and culture in contemporary Japan.* Cambridge: Cambridge University Press.

Ong, A. 1987. *Spirits of resistance and capitalist discipline: Factory women in Malaysia.* Albany: State University of New York Press.

Peltonen, T. 2007. In the middle of managers' occupational communities, global ethnography and the multinationals. *Ethnography*, 8(3): 346–60.

Peterson, M. F., Peng, T. K., & Smith, P. B. 1999. Using expatriate supervisors to promote cross-border management practice transfer: The experience of a Japanese electronics company. In J. K. Liker, W. M. Fruin, & P. S. Adler (Eds), *Remade in America: Transplanting and transforming Japanese management systems:* 294–327. New York: Oxford University Press.

Polanyi, M. 1966. *The tacit dimension.* New York: Doubleday.

Rohlen, T. 1974. *For harmony and strength: Japanese white-collar organization in anthropological perspective.* Berkeley: University of California Press.

Schweiger, D. M., & Lippert, R. L. 2005. Integration: The critical link in M&A value creation. In G. Stahl & M. Mendenhall (Eds), *Mergers and acquisitions:* 17–46. Stanford: Stanford University Press.

Seeman, M. 1959. On the meaning of alienation. *American Sociological Review*, 24(6): 783–91.

Shimizu, K., Hitt, M., Vaidyanath, D., & Pisano, V. 2004. Theoretical foundations of cross-border mergers and acquisitions: A review of current research and recommendations for the future. *Journal of International Management*, 10(3): 307–53.

Spreitzer, G. M. 1996. Social structural characteristics of psychological empowerment. *Academy of Management Journal*, 39(2): 483–504.

Stahl, G., Mendenhall, M., Pablo, A., & Javidan, M. 2005. Sociocultural integration in mergers and acquisitions. In G. Stahl & M. Mendenhall (Eds), *Mergers and acquisitions:* 3–16. Stanford: Stanford University Press.

Stonequist, E. V. 1937. *The marginal man: A study in personality and culture conflict.* New York: Russell & Russell.

Strauss, A. L. 1982. Interorganizational negotiation. *Urban Life*, 11(3): 350–67.

Thiederman, S. 2003. *Making diversity work: 7 steps for defeating bias in the workplace.* Chicago: Dearborn Trade Publishing.

Uhlenbruck, K. 2004. Developing acquired foreign subsidiaries: The experience of MNEs in transition economies. *Journal of International Business Studies*, 35(2): 109–23.

Valentine, C. 1971. Deficiency, difference and bicultural models. *Harvard Educational Review*, 41(2): 137–57.

Van Maanen, J. 1992. Displacing Disney: Some notes on the flow of culture. *Qualitative Sociology*, 15(1): 5–35.

Veiga, J. F., Lubatkin, M. H., Calori, R., & Very, P. 2000. Measuring organizational culture clashes: A two-nation post-hoc analysis ofa cultural compatibility index. *Human Relations*, 53(4): 539–57.

Vermeulen, F., & Barkema, H. 2001. Learning through acquisitions. *Academy of Management Journal*, 44(3): 457–76.

Very, P., Lubatkin, M., Calori, R., & Veiga, J. 1996. Cross-national assessment of acculturative stress in recent European mergers. *International Studies of Management and Organization*, 26(1): 59–88.

Very, P., Lubatkin, M., Calori, R., & Veiga, J. 1997. Relative standing and the performance of recently acquired European firms. *Strategic Management Journal*, 18(8): 593–615.

Weber, Y., Shenkar, O., & Raveh, A. 1996. National and corporate cultural fit in mergers/acquisitions: An exploratory study. *Management Science*, 42(8): 1215–27.

Wong, N. 1990. *A studyofthe specialeconomiczones andcoastal open cities in China*, Research report on investment environment of Mainland China (6). Taipei: Investment Department, Ministry of Economy.

Xu, H., & Van de Vliert, E. 2004. Job level and national culture as joint roots of job satisfaction. *Applied Psychology*, 53(3): 329–48.

Yeung, H. W. C. 2000. State intervention and neoliberalism in the globalising world economy: Lessons from Singapore's regionalization programme. *The Pacific Review*, 13(1): 133–62.

Zhu, Y., May, S., & Rosenfeld, L. 2004. Information adequacy and job satisfaction during merger and acquisition. *Management Communication Quarterly*, 18(2): 241–70.

Zurcher Jr, L. A., Meadow, A., & Zurcher, S. L. 1965. Value orientation, role conflict, and alienation from work: A cross-cultural study. *American Sociological Review*, 30(4): 539–48.

27 Psychic distance and buyer–seller interaction*

Lars Hallén and Finn Wiedersheim-Paul

Introduction

There is always a distance between a selling and a buying organization, in a geographical and in a mental sense. There are distances also in the dimensions between actors in the same organization. These distances will cause difficulties for the different types of flows between buyer and seller: flows like information, products, and money. Disturbances in the flows of products and money have been discussed by several authors, but less so factors disturbing or preventing the flows of information. In this article we will formulate definitions of different types of psychic distance and also state a dynamic model of psychic distance and its development.

Psychic distance is particularly important in the interaction approach to the study of marketing exchanges, where the creation and maintenance of long lasting links between buyer and seller are basic assumptions.

In this chapter we will discuss some aspects of this distance or closeness between buyers and sellers. The idea of closeness in industrial markets is seen as connected with the situation (or 'atmosphere') within specific buyer-seller dyads. The concept has also been analysed and defined on more general levels. Our discussion will be focused on distance at different levels of specificity, i.e. with respect to the degree of individualization of the identification of the parties.

Psychic distance: definition and examples

The internationalization of firms often takes place gradually. When the need to go beyond the local market develops, expansion is often initiated by selling to customers that are situated closely to the local market. Initially the growth is a type of 'internationalization at home', i.e. a domestic expansion process. Later on, exports will occur.

It is not just the geographical distance but also other factors that are of importance when measuring distance. On an inter-country level concepts and measurements have been developed by Vahlne and Wiedersheim-Paul (1973, Chs 3 and 4). They use the term 'psychic distance' to denote those factors which inhibit trade between countries in a wide sense. As indicators they have used the level of development and its difference to the selling country, the level of education and its difference to the selling country and the difference in business and everyday languages. These factors have been selected due to the observation that the levels of development and education must have reached a certain minimum level in order to allow trade to take place. Furthermore it has been observed that trade

*Republished with permission from the authors. Hallén, Lars & Wiedersheim-Paul, Finn (1999) "Psychic distance and buyer–seller interaction".

is favoured between countries of roughly the same level of development (Burenstam-Linder, 1961), i.e. the difference between them should not be too big and this is also the case regarding the effects of the language differences. By means of statistical analysis a great number of countries have been ranked with respect to this psychic distance from Sweden.

So far we have not made a strict definition of psychic distance. In order to do so we first need a definition of marketing. We define marketing in a general sense as the activities used for 'bridging the gap' between buyer and seller. This gap can be defined in several ways. We have chosen to utilize *different perceptions*:

1   the buyer's perception of his own need (i.e. 'ideal solution');
2   the buyer's perception of the seller's offer;
3   the seller's perception of his own offer;
4   the seller's perception of the buyer's need.

In these definitions we have assumed that the different perceptions do exist, i.e. seller has a perception (a picture) of the buyer's need in a specific situation. The 'perception' is really a package of perceptions in different dimensions such as product quality, service, price and ability to deliver.

We have not assumed that the buyer's and the seller's perception packages will contain the same dimensions. Rather incongruity between the packages will be an important feature of the gaps discussed below.

This means that Figure 27.1 is only intended as a very simple illustration of the rare case when the perceptions only exist in one common dimension or when it has been possible to translate them to one dimension.

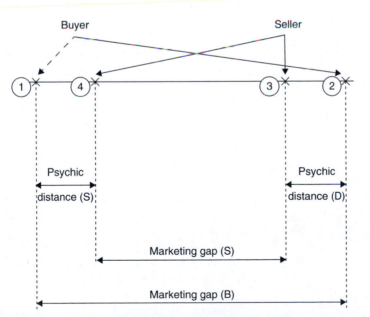

This figure illustrates the very specific situation where the perceptions can be transformed to one dimension. In all real situations a multidimensional illustration would be necessary. The numbers refer to the four different perceptions defined in the text.

Figure 27.1 Illustration of gaps between perceptions.

Using the four definitions of perceptions given in Figure 27.1 we can now define two types of gaps:

- *marketing gap* (S) which denotes the difference between perceptions 3 and 4 and indicates the gap between buyer and seller as perceived by the seller;
- *marketing gap* (B) which denotes the difference between perceptions 1 and 2 and indicates the gap between buyer and seller as perceived by the buyer.

Marketing gap (S) will form the basis for the seller's marketing behaviour. It is not a correct basis, because the buyer's buying behaviour will be influenced by marketing gap (B).

In this article we are not going to discuss these marketing gaps and their consequences for marketing behaviour in any detail. Instead we will concentrate on the 'marketing disturbance component' labelled psychic distance. The difference between the two marketing gaps is explained by the psychic distance which is defined as consisting of two components:

Different perception of needs

The difference between the seller's perception of the buyer's need and the buyer's perception of his own need (4 and 1).

This is psychic distance with particular relevance for the seller, *psychic distance (S)*.

Different perception of offers

The difference between the buyer's perception of the seller's offer and the seller's perception of his own offer (2 and 3).

This is psychic distance with particular relevance for the buyer, *psychic distance (B)*.

It will be obvious from these definitions that psychic distance is a measure of the difficulty a seller has to perceive or estimate the needs of a buyer or the corresponding difficulty a buyer experiences in perceiving the seller's offer.

Psychic distance (S) and psychic distance (B) will be labelled *inter-firm distances*. On the analogy of their definition we will also create two other measures:

- *inter-country distances*, which will denote the psychic distance between two countries, i.e. the difference between the perceptions of an average firm in one country as seen by foreign and by domestic businessmen.
- *intra-firm distances* which will denote the psychic distances between any two actors in each of the organizations, i.e. the difference between the perceptions of a counterpart as seen by different people in the same firm.

It should be observed, that psychic distances will occur within organizations as well as between organizations. This follows from the fact that we have defined psychic distance as a difference in perceptions.

These three definitions of psychic distance will later in this article form the basis for a dynamic model of psychic distance. But let us first give some more examples of psychic distance in action, which will indicate the type of factors causing psychic distances to occur.

Inter-country and inter-firm distances: an example

Within the framework of established international buyer–seller relationships there is not necessarily a correspondence between the intercountry psychic distance and the distance or closeness that characterizes the inter-firm relationship. The relationship between a Swedish equipment producing firm and its French supplier of a certain quality of steel may exemplify this. Compared to other major countries in Western Europe France is perceived by many Swedish businessmen as a country which is difficult to deal with. There are not only language difficulties (Swedes seldom speak French and Frenchmen often give the impression of reluctantly accepting languages other than their own), but there are also differences in business culture (for example, Frenchmen are believed to favour centralized and formal procedures, whereas Swedes are seen to be more flexible and informal). Furthermore, both the Swedish and the French sometimes have a tendency to consider their own technical standards self-evidently superior to foreign ones and consequently mistrust other solutions (see Hallén 1980).

The Swedish firm of our example has bought its raw material from the French supplier – one of the major French steel works – since the mid 1960s. On average one third of the Swedish firm's needs has been covered by deliveries from the French steel works, but lately it has expanded its share of the Swedish firm's needs to 100 per cent. This is against the will of the French firm: they want to reduce their share to 50 per cent in order not to make the Swedish firm too dependent. The relationship runs extremely smoothly: the Swedes have almost never made any complaints, deliveries arrive regularly every month and there are good personal contacts both between the marketers and purchasers and between the technical and laboratory personnel of the two firms. There has been a long-term contract between the firms since 1974, but previously there were no contracts. The purchasing manager of the Swedish firm considers this contract unnecessary, which means that the situation could be handled as well prior to the contract being concluded. 'Contracts', he said, 'are papers that are intended for people who are not honest. Instead of legal procedures we rely upon common sense.' The inter-firm atmosphere thus renders the cultural differences unimportant. 'We do not speak French', the Swedish purchasing manager said. 'We can just say, "je t'aime", and that is sufficient.'

Inter-country distance: the firm-to-country difference

The method of analysis used by Vahlne and Wiedersheim-Paul (1973) implies that the study focuses on the impact on company behaviour of conditions on the national level. This approach is of special interest when the analysis is concerned with processes that cover long time spans, for example, the internationalization process of Swedish firms in the twentieth century. The inter-firm differences are suppressed in the analysis and this may be a correct way of handling the problem given that no crucial inter-firm differences are present. This is in a way so: looking at a long perspective it is clear that once a firm had, for example, no exporting experience, which makes it comparable to other inexperienced firms in that respect.

Utilizing the measures developed by Vahlne and Wiedersheim-Paul (1973), the internationalization process of individual firms, i.e. the order in which establishments of selling and producing subsidiaries have taken place in various countries, has been compared to the computed values of psychic distance to the countries in question. Similarities and dissimilarities in the internationalization process of individual firms were observed and analysed (see Johanson and Wiedersheim (Paul, 1975).

Håkansson and Wootz (1975) have examined the selection of suppliers in an international context. Purchasers have chosen suppliers for certain products in a quasi-experimental situation. The suppliers have been identified with information about size and address, etc., and based on the purchasers' decisions conclusions have been made regarding the tendency to select suppliers from countries at different psychic distances when certain variations in price and quality separate the offers from each other. The psychic distance between the purchasing firms in Sweden and their foreign suppliers is analysed on the company level, but it is only the buying firms, i.e. the firms where the participants of the experiment are to be found, that are actual ones: the counterpart is an abstraction, with whom the buyers thus have no personal experience. The analysis of the psychic distance is inferred from the purchasers' reactions to the relative importance of price and quality differences when buying from abroad. Their behaviour is considered to be based upon their general experience of foreign suppliers. It can thus be argued that the analysis is made on the company level as seen from the buying side but on the country level as seen from the selling side.

The conclusions of the study by Håkansson and Wootz are compatible with Vahlne and Wiedersheim-Paul's results in so far as the domestic market and Britain/Germany were considered to be closer to Sweden than France/Italy. This is what might have been expected, as the counterpart is defined abstractly, although using different indicators.

Inter-firm distances and total image

The interaction approach to the study of buyer–seller relationships in industrial markets implies that there is an interaction process between individual identified parties. This forms the buying and the selling behaviour. The trust that may have developed between the parties within a specific relationship due to previous contacts in connection with deliveries or other activities before or after earlier transactions has a profound influence on behaviour. These process have been studied in an international setting by the researchers participating in the IMP Project (see Håkansson, 1980). The distance between sellers and buyers are here studied at two different levels. Firstly, the opinions of counterparts in general in five Western European countries are mapped. Second, the relation to one specific supplier or purchaser is investigated. The number of relationships mapped in this way exceeds 900.

An analysis of distance between buyers and sellers based on the first of the two approaches that are used in the IMP Project is reported by Hallén (1980). In contrast to the mentioned studies by Vahlne and Wiedersheim-Paul (1973) and Håkansson and Wootz (1975) the analysis here deals with actual firms on the perceiving as well as on the perceived side. But as the respondents have expressed their opinions of their actual suppliers or customers in general, total images are obtained. The experience of incidents and episodes within one specific buyer–seller relationship, which certainly has formed the opinion to a large extent, still cannot be observed directly. The counterpart is an aggregate, although of actual firms.

A rather crude measure has been applied in the determination of the psychic distance in this context. The respondents' opinions of difficulties in communication due to language problems, of difficulties to make friends with the personnel in the other firm, and their feeling of being understood by their customers/suppliers in the other country were expressed on a five-point scale and added with each other into an index. The five-country design of the study gives the opportunity to analyse this distance also from other viewpoints than Sweden. This analysis shows that some countries seem to be more 'distant' than others both according to their own opinions and according to the opinion of their foreign business partners. Thus Italy seems to be the most isolated country of the group of five countries (Sweden, W. Germany, Britain,

France and Italy), and Sweden actually seems to be most integrated in the group, although the other four are members of the European communities and Sweden is not. Another observation from the analysis is that purchasers generally consider the distance to be shorter than the marketers. A possible reason for this is that marketers more often take upon them the task to bridge the gap between buyer and seller than purchasers do, which might make the marketers more aware of the distance that may exist. Also, the observation stresses the important fact that psychic distance between two parties is asymmetrical.

Inter-firm distance and atmosphere

For a deeper understanding of the psychic distance in an international setting it is probably necessary to conduct the analysis on a firm-to-firm level. The interaction between buyer and seller leads to the development of an 'atmosphere', which can be described in terms of closeness/distance, conflict/cooperation and power/dependence. The closeness or distance between the parties in a buyer–seller dyad is conditioned by characteristics of the interacting firms and the interaction processes as well as environmental factors. In the approaches previously described, these environmental factors have played quite a dominating role, but their importance in the company-specific analysis is reduced to one factor group among others. Its importance for the development of an atmosphere characterized by 'closeness' between the parties is often secondary to the effects of the interaction processes, for example, the adaptations and the role institutionalization that takes place within an ongoing relationship. A Swedish firm may experience a greater distance to another Swedish firm than to an established British supplier, in spite of the language and spatial gaps between Sweden and Britain. The access to informal communication channels to the foreign firm may be an indication of such 'closeness'.

Interaction processes between marketers and purchasers of the two firms in a buyer–seller dyad may bring these individuals together in a way that makes them feel as representatives of a common buying–selling organization rather than of their respective firms. The inter-firm distance, i.e. the distance between the two firms, in certain situations is shorter than the intra-firm distance between the selling or buying function and other involved functions of the concerned firms. The phenomenon of 'side-changing' mentioned by Ford (1980) where employees of one company in a buyer–seller dyad act in the interest of the other company may be seen as an extreme example of short inter-firm distance coupled with certain intra-firm distances.

Inter-firm and intra-firm distances: an example

In order to further clarify the various concepts of distance we will use a case description of the relations between a Swedish firm ('Nya Mekaniska Verkstaden', NMV) and a large French mining company, which we may call 'Union des Montagnes Métallifères', UMM. The Swedish firm is rather small and is specialized in the production of capital equipment for use in the mining industry. In 1962 the first drilling equipment was sold by NMV to UMM as a result of an ambitious campaign by NMV to establish itself as a company with worldwide sales. Based on advertising in professional journals all over the world NMV wanted to create a basis for expanded production by means of acquiring sales in other countries than the domestic market, to which most of its sales had gone before. This general approach to export marketing turned out to be too resource demanding, and therefore NMV decided to concentrate its marketing efforts to some ten countries. One of these countries was France, where a sales subsidiary was established in order to take care of contacts with prospective buyers of NMV's products. As the number of mining companies in France is rather limited (NMV believes that there are about 50 firms) contacts have been established with almost all of them, and about 20 firms in France more or less regularly buy NMV's drilling equipment. But a very large share of NMV's total sales to the French firms is bought by its largest French customer: UMM. Between 25 and 50 per cent of NMV's French sales have during the last years gone to UMM.

From the very beginning NMV tried to deal with technicians and production managers in UMM rather than to negotiate through UMM's purchasing department. NMV considers its product to have two major advantages compared to competing equipment: it considerably improves the working environment for the miners and it increases the speed of the operations. Both these arguments impress upon production managers, NMV believes.

During the period between 1962 and 1975 NMV thus established what they considered to be a strong position as a supplier of mining equipment and spare parts to UMM. But during 1975 and 1976 production costs rose in Sweden and NMV raised their prices by more than 80 per cent during the three years 1975/77. This did not at all please the purchasing department at UMM. As far as NMV was able to find out, a decision was made centrally by the top management at UMM that NMV should be 'blacklisted', i.e. nothing was to be bought from NMV, neither complete units nor spare parts.

This decision created problems for two of the involved parties. First of all it naturally worried the marketers at NMV. But it also annoyed the production department at UMM. They needed spare parts from NMV for their equipment, and they did not want to change from NMV's equipment to substitutes as UMM's technicians considered those inferior. Therefore, they continued to order from NMV, and after some time they also resumed purchasing new equipment. The blacklisting may still formally be in force, but it seems to have turned into a dead letter. At present, UMM buys two or three units of equipment every year from NMV, and there are good relations between the firms, particularly between NMV's marketers and UMM's technicians. NMV tries to obtain a situation where decisions are made at the purchasing department in UMM, but as a NMV marketer put it: 'We would not make any extreme efforts in order to get hold of one of their purchasers.'

An analysis of this mini-case shows us that factors relating to 'distance' have been of importance in several instances. First, there is the inter-country distance. The Swedish firm NMV did not inform UMM in advance of their plans to raise prices and they also let these prices rise so as to compensate Swedish cost increases fully. It did not occur to the Swedes to negotiate this with the French purchasing unit, probably because they felt that the 'real' decision-makers in the French firm were not the purchasers but the production engineers. The Swedish marketers characterized the French purchasers of UMM as 'very French Frenchmen', by which they meant that they found them aloof and secretive. There are clear differences in behaviour and expectations between the Swedes and the French, which may have been one of the major reasons behind the blacklisting.

Second, there is the inter-firm distance: the state of the inter-firm relationship in terms of conflict/cooperation, closeness/distance and power/dependence. The production engineers of UMM seemed to consider themselves to have interests that were compatible with NMV's, and they were also dependent on NMV for spare parts for uninterrupted production.

In terms of closeness/distance UMM's production unit can be said to be rather close to NMV, as five to ten or so persons from UMM with regular contacts with NMV were technicians. Only one regular contact came from UMM's purchasing unit. The total atmosphere of the relationship was characterized not only by cultural differences but also by similarities in terms of perceived needs of cooperation and of dependence. The inter-firm distance was shorter than the inter-country distance.

Third, the case gives an example of the difference between intra-firm and inter-firm distances. As seen from NMV (which is the source of information) the purchasing department of UMM had not very good contacts with their own production people, although the purchasing unit was believed to have a high status in the French firm. The outcome of the crisis seems to indicate that the purchasing unit of UMM with its 'blacklisting' were more distant from the actual decision-making and actions of their own organization than NMV's marketers were.

A dynamic model of psychic distance

We are now in a position to develop a model of psychic distance and its implications for firms, based on the definitions and the different examples presented earlier. In this model we will study the changing impact of psychic distance in the development process of a buyer–seller relation where the parties are located in different environments. In order to simplify the discussion we assume that these environments are two different countries. The development of different types of psychic distance is of course a continuous process but in order to simplify the discussion we have chosen to identify the following three stages:

- pre-contact stage;
- initial interaction stage;
- maturing interaction stage.

During the first stage the seller has not yet any contacts with the buyer. In the extreme case when the seller is in the position to enter the export market for the first time the inter-country distance will be the relevant measure of psychic distance. This means that the difference between the buyer's and the seller's perception of the relevant need of the buyer (psychic distance (S)) will mainly be determined by factors on a national level, for example, differences in language, level of development and level of education between the countries in question.

The same would be true for a potential buyer; his perception of the unknown seller's offer would be determined by his perception of the seller's country of origin (unless the buyer has some previous experience of other seller in this country).

In those cases where the seller has exported to the specific country or to other countries the psychic distance will consist not only of the intercountry component but also to some extent of distance more on the interfirm level. Two cases would be rather common:

- The seller has other customers in the specific country. In this situation a kind of *halo* effect will occur; the new customer belongs to the same family, as it were.
- The seller has a representative/agent selling to the specific country. In this case much of the psychic distance between seller and potential customer will consist of the inter-firm distance between seller and representative/agent.

This latter case contains a number of sub-cases: the representative/agent is located in the same country as the seller or the representative/agent is located in the specific foreign market. These situations will reflect a choice, intentional or unintentional, in locating the psychic distance. In the first situation most of the psychic distance will occur between representative/agent and the market, in the second situation most of the distance will occur between seller

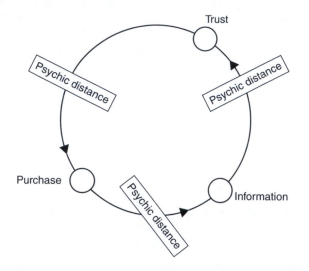

Figure 27.2 Interaction and psychic distance.

and representative/agent. It is of course impossible to state *the* best solution, but the discussion in Johanson (1972) will give some indication.

A related case is when the seller uses a representative in a third country for marketing in a specific country. An example would be the use of trading houses in London for approaching present or former Commonwealth countries. It is to be expected that this deviation via a third country would result in a shorter psychic distance than if a representative in the seller's or the buyer's country were chosen.

In the initial interaction phase there has been a first contact between seller and buyer and this contact has resulted in a purchase. The psychic distance between the two firms will consist of a mixture of inter-country and inter-firm distances. The impact of the inter-country distance will still be comparatively strong but the importance will gradually shift to the inter-firm distance at the same time as this factor changes. The process is illustrated in Figure 27.2.

According to this illustration the interaction between buyer and seller may start with any of the factors: purchase, information or trust. A 'normal' course of events would perhaps start with information, leading to trust, leading to purchase. The psychic distance plays different roles in this process. Apart from disturbing or preventing the start of the process, it slows down or prevents information from resulting in trust and trust in leading to purchase. But if the barrier between information and trust or between trust and purchase has been passed it will in itself be changed.

In some cases the psychic distance will increase, causing the interaction process to end. In other cases it will decrease leading to a more intensive interaction process. The development of the inter-firm psychic distance will also have an impact on the inter-country distance: the 'image' of a country will improve if there are improving relations with a firm in that country.

If the initial contacts between two firms will develop into an interaction process, and if so, at what speed also depends on the buyer's perception of the initial state and the subsequent changes of the uncertainty variables: need uncertainty, market uncertainty, and transaction uncertainty (Håkansson *et al.* 1977). High need uncertainty, indicating a considerable perceived difficulty for the buyer to interpret the exact nature of the need for which a functional solution is required, would mean a large initial inter-firm psychic distance and a slow decrease in this distance. We will not discuss these problems here, however.

If the relations between buyer and seller continue, they will gradually move into the maturing interaction stage. In this phase, it is assumed that the elements that are exchanged within the transaction episodes (the product or service, the information, the means of payment, the social elements) eventually will lead to adaptations between the parties in terms of e.g. product modifications, special inventories, changed administration routines or the establishment of informal communication channels and the development of liking and trust between individuals of the concerned firms. This development will cause the inter-firm distance between buyer and seller to decrease but other effects will also occur. The informal contacts and the trust that may be present within well-established relations often have the effect of raising barriers to entry against new partners, i.e. the inter-firm distances towards these potential sellers will increase.

The close relation between buyer and seller may result in the intra-firm distances becoming important, for example, employees in the selling firm working in close contact with the buying firm may feel split loyalties between the two parties. In this maturing interaction stage the different perceptions illustrated in Figure 27.1 tend to be close together but not totally coinciding. A coincidence would be impossible due to differences between individuals and the continuous change in the problem situation.

Concluding remarks

Our discussion of the different 'levels' or 'approaches' to the concept of inter-country and inter-firm psychic distance and degree of closeness in the interaction atmosphere is intended to illuminate when these differently defined concepts are applicable. In this concluding section we will focus upon two categories of marketing situations: (1) the differences between the marketing of consumer goods and the marketing of industrial goods and (2) the difference between the initiation and the continuation of buyer–seller relationships in markets for producer goods.

The inter-country differences are likely to be more important in consumer goods marketing than in industrial marketing, whereas the inter-firm distance to a higher extent affects industrial marketing. Cultural idiosyncrasies probably are of considerable importance for the purchasing decisions of household and other end-consumers. Here subtle aspects of marketing such as design, ways of distribution and 'image' may mean the difference between success and failure and it may be difficult to operate in a culturally distant market. As mass marketing is the norm for consumer goods, the necessary 'feeling' for the right approach to the market cannot be replaced by the development of special relations to selected customers. For an analysis of consumer goods situations the concept of 'psychic distance' on the inter-country level thus may prove useful.

It is an oversimplification, however, to state that the dividing line between the applicability of the 'general' level of distance as opposed to the 'specific' distance within the framework of a buyer–seller dyad coincides with the dividing line between marketing to individual end consumers and marketing to organizations. The interaction approach to marketing deals primarily with the development of existing customer relations; the initiation of a relationship is seen as a 'special case'. Before there is any relation between the firms, there is no 'atmosphere' that may act to compensate for cultural differences between the seller and his prospective buyer. The general concept of 'psychic distance' also is applicable for the analysis of the industrial marketing problem in new markets. The studies of the internationalization process of Swedish firms mentioned above take as a starting point the situation when most firms were domestically oriented and the gradual penetration of foreign markets is analysed against the background of inter-country differences. This first phase of future interaction processes with customers abroad is often approached with marketing tools that can be classified as belonging to the marketing mix 'tool kit'. The Swedish firm NMV of our final example above approached the French market with advertisements in professional journals. Here the psychic distance in a general sense may affect the outcome of the attempts to market entry. But in later stages of buyer–seller relationships the inter-firm aspects may turn into the dominant feature of the distance/closeness question. Here an analysis of the marketing problems may better be conducted using the interaction approach.

The ongoing discussion in Sweden of whether Swedes are bad international marketers is to a large extent a question of psychic distance between Swedish marketers and their foreign customers. Consequently, the discussion would improve if a distinction was made between the ability to create a new relation and the ability to maintain a stable relation. According to recent studies (Philips-Martinsson, 1979 and Hallén, 1980) the first-mentioned ability is perhaps inferior to the second one. If this is correct it may cause considerable difficulties in the long run, as the ability to create new relations may become comparatively more important. This is one aspect of the domain problem of the firm, i.e. the problem to select the directions of future expansion: new customers, new knowledge, new products or what? (Wiedersheim-Paul and Erland, 1979; Wiedersheim-Paul, 1979).

New types of distance problems may develop: the perception of possible internal distances within each firm. The institutionalization of roles, for example, the boundary-spanning roles of the purchasers and marketers of the two organizations involved in a transaction, may create a feeling that they represent their common 'buyer–seller unit' rather than their respective firms. A reduction of inter-company distance may be obtained at the expense of intra-firm distances.

References

Burenstam-Linder, S. (1961), *An Essay on Trade and Transformation.* Almqvist and Wiskell. Uppsala.

Ford, D. (1980), Developing Buyer-Seller Relationships in Export Marketing. *Organization.* Marknad och Samhälle, Vol. 16, No. 5.

Håkansson, H., (ed.). 1980. *Industrial Marketing and Purchasing in Europe. An Interaction Approach.* Forthcoming.

Håkansson., H. and Wootz. B. (1975), Supplier Selection in an International Environment. *Journal of Marketing Research*, Vol. XII (Feb), pp. 46–51.

Håkansson., H., Johanson, J. and Wootz, B. (1977), Influence Tactics in Buyer–Seller Processes. *Industrial Marketing Management*, Vol. 5, pp. 319–32.

Hallén, L. (1980), Sverige pä Europamarknaden. *Studentlitteratur*, Lund.

Johanson, J., (1972), Fasta affärsförbindelser vid export. En jämförelse mellan olika exportkanaler. In: Johanson. J. (ed), *Exportstralegiska problem.* Stockholm.

Johanson, J. and Wiedersheim-Paul. F. (1975), The Internationalization of the Firm Four Swedish Cases. *Journal of Managemnt Studies.* October.

Philips-Martinsson, J. (1979), *Cross-Cultural Relations in International Marketing.* Stockholm.

Vahlne, J.-E. and Wiedersheim-Paul, F. (1973), Ekonomiskt avstånd model loch empirisk undersökning. In: Hörnell, E., Vahlne, J.-E. and Wiedersheim-Paul, F. *Export och utlandsetableringar.* Almqvist and Wiksell, Stockholm.

Wiedersheim-Paul, F. (1979), Towards a Model of International Marketing. In: Ståhl, I. (ed.), *Forskning, utbildning, praxis.* EFI, Stockholm.

Wiedersheim-Paul, F. and Erland, O. (1979), Technological Strategies and Internationalization. In: Mattsson, I.-G. and Wiedersheim-Paul, F. (eds.), *Recent Research on the Internationalization of Business.* Almqvist and Wiksell, Uppsala.

Case study V
UniCredit Group

A bank goes East[1]

Stefan Schmid, Dennis J. Wurster and
Thomas Kotulla

Currently operating in twenty countries with more than 9,200 branches and over 150,000 employees, UniCredit Group is one of Europe's largest banks. The former local player from North Italy occupies a dominant position in Central and Eastern Europe (CEE), a region with promising growth prospects not only for the financial industry. The cross-border merger between the Italian UniCredit Group and the German HVB Group in 2005 was essential for the leading role in these markets.[2] Even before 2005, both banks' growth strategies had been characterized by numerous mergers and acquisitions. These transactions laid the foundation for the firm's thriving expansion into the CEE region.

UniCredit Group's market entries in Central and Eastern Europe

When investigating UniCredit Group's successful expansion into the CEE markets, the timing and chronology of the bank's market entries are of particular interest. Even before its merger in 2005, UniCredit Group had taken on a pioneering role in CEE countries, primarily targeting the retail banking segment. In contrast, the world's largest banking groups at that time, such as Citigroup, HSBC and Bank of America, and even European-headquartered banks, such as Barclays, Deutsche Bank and UBS, were hardly present in CEE markets until a few years ago. Figure V.1 illustrates UniCredit Group's first-time market entries in the CEE region, differentiating between the Italian UniCredit Group and the German HVB Group, including their respective predecessor institutions.

One of HVB Group's predecessor institutions, Austrian Creditanstalt, entered the Hungarian market as early as 1975. Therefore, the bank can be regarded as a first mover to CEE, as compared to other foreign competitors. In 1987, after a decade of halt, HVB Group established itself in Bulgaria, the Czech Republic and Russia. These entries took place within a short period of time. This was the starting point for a sequential timing strategy. From then on, HVB Group continued its expansion cautiously and stepwise into Slovenia, Poland and Slovakia, followed by two subsequent waves of four market entries, one taking place in 1997 and the other one in 2001. When analysing the market entries into the CEE region, HVB Group can not only be characterized as a first and early mover compared to international competitors in general, but also compared to its merger partner, UniCredit Group.

In contrast with the HVB Group, UniCredit Group pursued a (slightly) different timing strategy for its market entries in the CEE region. Indeed, with its entry in the Polish market in 1999, UniCredit Group can still be described as an early mover to this country. Apart from Turkey and Bosnia and Herzegovina, all CEE markets entered by UniCredit Group had already been occupied by HVB Group, a competitor at that time, for several years.

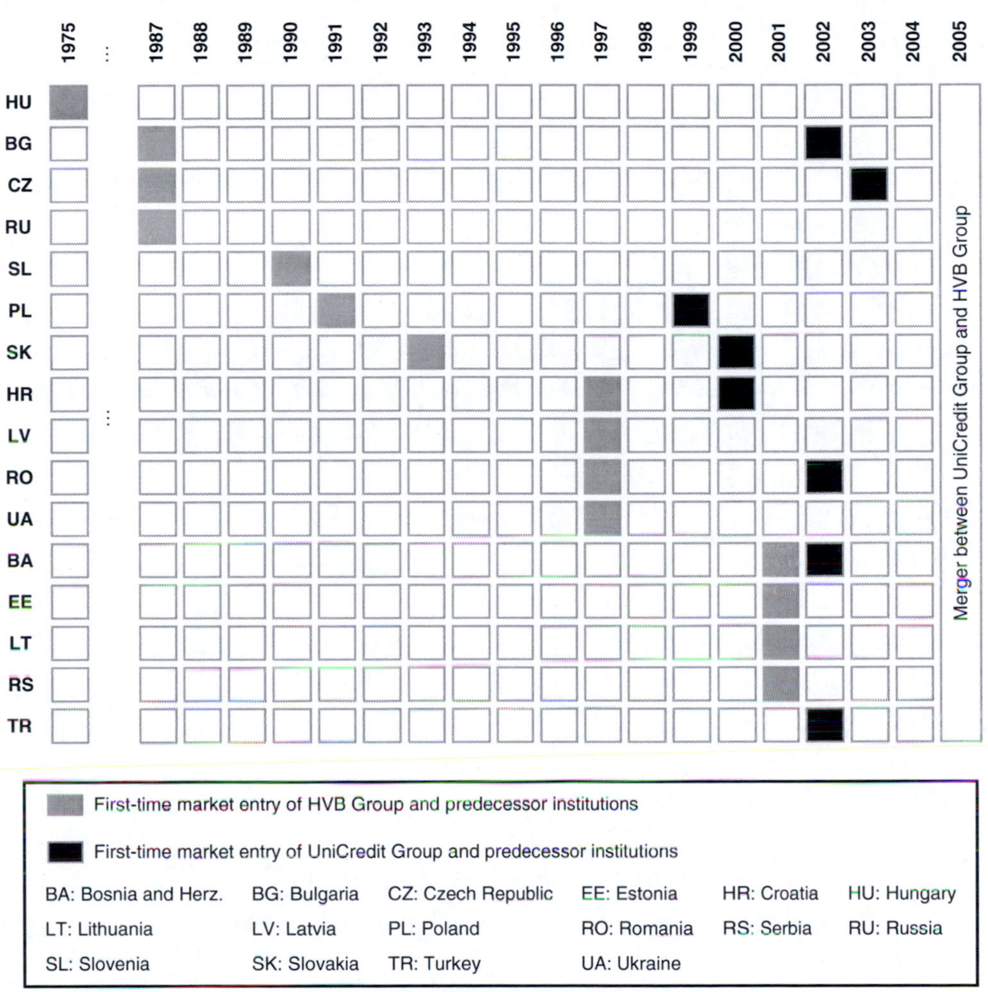

Figure data — First-time market entries (G = First-time market entry of HVB Group and predecessor institutions; B = First-time market entry of UniCredit Group and predecessor institutions):

Country	1975	1987	1988	1989	1990	1991	1992	1993	1994	1995	1996	1997	1998	1999	2000	2001	2002	2003	2004	2005
HU	G																			
BG		G															B			
CZ		G																B		
RU		G																		
SL					G															
PL						G								B						
SK								G								B				
HR												G				B				
LV												G								
RO												G					B			
UA												G								
BA																G	B			
EE																G				
LT																G				
RS																G				
TR																	B			

Merger between UniCredit Group and HVB Group

Legend:
- First-time market entry of HVB Group and predecessor institutions
- First-time market entry of UniCredit Group and predecessor institutions

BA: Bosnia and Herz. BG: Bulgaria CZ: Czech Republic EE: Estonia HR: Croatia HU: Hungary
LT: Lithuania LV: Latvia PL: Poland RO: Romania RS: Serbia RU: Russia
SL: Slovenia SK: Slovakia TR: Turkey UA: Ukraine

Figure V.1 First-time market entries of UniCredit Group, HVB Group and their predecessor institutions in CEE.

Furthermore, UniCredit Group's market entries took place within a relative short time span of only five years. Between 1999 and 2003, the bank established itself in eight CEE countries; a resource-intensive approach also called 'parallel strategy' in international business and marketing literature.

UniCredit Group: a market leader with a strong European focus

When UniCredit Group and HVB Group merged in 2005, they gave birth to the largest banking group operating in the CEE region. In view of the threatening market power of this newly formed institution, antitrust agencies had imposed some restrictions on the approval of the merger, such as the divestment of stakes in Croatian banks. Despite these restrictions the new market leader was more than twice as large as its biggest competitor in the CEE region,

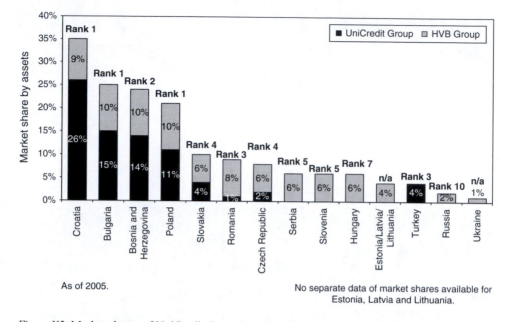

Figure V.2 Market shares of UniCredit Group in major CEE countries after the merger.

the Austrian Erste Bank. In Croatia, Bulgaria, Bosnia and Herzegovina and Poland very high market shares were reached in 2005, in some countries amounting to more than 20%. This is also depicted in Figure V.2.

Today's relevance of CEE markets for UniCredit Group

Already during the financial crisis, which commenced in autumn 2008, UniCredit Group's expansion towards the East has proven vital for the bank's situation. Poland, for example, was the only country within the European Union not to suffer from a recession in 2009. In the following year, Poland experienced a GDP growth of almost 4 per cent, surpassed by Turkey being the fastest-growing economy in Europe with an increase in GDP of about 9 per cent. In the following years, it was mainly UniCredit Group's business in Poland, Turkey and Russia that contributed to the bank's stability which was called into question during the euro crisis. Tensions on financial markets, loan defaults as well as good-will impairments due to the economic recession and the macroeconomic situation in Italy and other European countries led to a loss of about €10 billion in the third quarter of 2011.

Today, UniCredit Group operates more than 1,000 branches in Poland and holds a strategic position in this market. In 2012, the Polish retail banking business yielded more than €400 million operating profit, representing the group's second profitable market after Italy in this segment. However, not only the Polish market but also the remaining CEE countries contribute substantially to UniCredit Group's bottom line. With over €2.5 billion, the CEE region (Poland excluded) was responsible for about 25 per cent of the consolidated group's total operating profit in 2012. Besides retail banking, corporate lending is seen as a promising business segment in this region, owing to the revived economic growth in some CEE countries that is expected to outperform that of core Western countries in the next years.

Table V.1 UniCredit Group's leading position in CEE countries in 2012

Bank (home country)	Total assets in CEE countries €bn	Number of branches in CEE countries	CEE countries of presence*	CEE % share in group revenues
UniCredit Group (Italy/Germany)	140	3,793	19	24
Raiffeisen Bank (Austria)	87	3,141	19	78
Erste Bank (Austria)	84	2,072	7	58
Société Générale (France)	72	2,626	18	14
KBC Bank (Belgium)	71	1,522	13	37
Intesa Sanpaolo (Italy)	41	1,343	11	10
OTP Bank (Hungary)	35	1,419	9	–

* Including direct and indirect presence in the 25 CEE countries, excluding representative offices.

However, UniCredit Group's business in the CEE region is not spared from adverse effects of the euro crisis. 80 per cent of the revenues in the CEE region are created in no more than five countries: Poland, Turkey, Russia, the Czech Republic and Croatia. 'In the future, we will have to focus on countries in which we are strong and we will have to rethink our market presence in the other CEE countries', said Frederico Ghizzoni, the bank's CEO, in 2012. Meanwhile, the bank has begun to consolidate its business in the Baltic States (Estonia, Latvia and Lithuania) by concentrating operations in Latvia. The foreign subsidiaries in the Czech Republic and Slovakia were merged. In doing so, synergy effects will be achieved and the cost structure optimized.

Nevertheless, UniCredit Group holds a leading position in the CEE region that is based on various reasons. With regard to the entire region, the bank not only capitalizes on its timing strategy, but also on a high market penetration as compared to its main competitors which is reflected in the amount of total assets (€140 billion), the number of branches (3,793) and the strong presence in 19 CEE countries in 2012 (see Table V.1).

In addition, strong brand recognition and an appropriate allocation strategy have helped UniCredit Group to become the leading bank in the CEE region. Whereas certain functions, such as planning, finance & administration, risk management and legal and compliance, are mainly centralized in headquarters, others are decentralized in the host countries to ensure customer proximity. For instance, by granting high responsibility and autonomy with respect to marketing activities including the product portfolio, pricing and communication strategy, country-specific client segments in the retail banking business can be targeted efficiently. As a result, the CEE region represents an important pillar of UniCredit Group's portfolio and complements the bank's core markets in Italy, Germany and Austria.

Questions

1 In Central and Eastern Europe, UniCredit Group and HVB Group can be characterized as first-early movers compared to their international competitors.

a   Discuss – regardless of this particular case – the general benefits and drawbacks that can be inherent in a first-/early mover market entry strategy, as opposed to a follower/late-mover market entry strategy.

b   Considering the banking industry, and in particular, the retail banking segment, do you think the timing of the first-time market entry in a foreign country plays a crucial role in gaining competitive advantage? Give a detailed reasoning for your answer.

2   The timing strategies UniCredit Group and HVB Group pursued for entering CEE markets before their merger in 2005 differ.

a   What advantages and disadvantages could have been behind the parallel strategy and the sequential strategy chosen by both banks?

b   Do you think that pursuing a particular timing strategy for several countries (parallel strategy and sequential strategy) influences the choice of market entry strategy (for example, exporting, international joint venture, international merger or international greenfield investment)?

3   UniCredit Group has chosen numerous adjacent target markets and has driven its expansion towards the East. Would you support the proposition that geographic proximity can contribute to the success of market entries?

Notes

1 The material for this short case was drawn from a variety of published sources. All sources are also cited in detail in a more comprehensive version of this case which is available in German in the following: Schmid, Stefan/Kotulla, Thomas (2013): UniCredit Group. Vom Local Player aus Norditalien zum Marktführer in Osteuropa, in: Schmid, Stefan (ed.): Strategien der Internationalisierung. Fallstudien und Fallbeispiele. 3rd Edition, Oldenbourg, Munich, 2013, pp. 495–529. The version in German contains an extensive list of references and further readings in English as well as in German language.
2 Since the merger between UniCredit Group and HVB Group in 2005, the newly formed institution has been operating under the name of UniCredit Group.

References

Korth, K. (2013). Unicredit geht im Baltikum auf Rückzugskurs. Handelsblatt, 21, p. 26.
Menzel, S. (2013). Zurück zu Brot und Butter. Handelsblatt, 41, p. 30.
Schmid, Stefan/Kotulla, Thomas (2013). UniCredit Group. Vom Local Player aus Norditalien zum Marktführer in Osteuropa. In Schmid, Stefan (ed.) Strategien der Internationalisierung. Fallstudien und Fallbeispiele. 3rd Edition, Oldenbourg, Munich, 2013, pp. 495–529.
UniCredit Group (2011). Consolidated reports and accounts 2010, Milan.
UniCredit Group (2012). Consolidated reports and accounts 2011, Milan.
UniCredit Group (2013a). Consolidated reports and accounts 2012, Milan.
UniCredit Group (2013b). UniCredit profile – focus on Central and Eastern Europe. UniCredit Group CEE Identity and Communications, Milan.
Welp, C. (2012). Wir müssen sehr vorsichtig sein. Wirtschaftswoche, 66(7), pp. 63–65.

Part VI

Emerging markets

28 Introduction

The terms "emerging markets" and "emerging countries" are perhaps a little anachronistic, as it can be argued that several of them have long since emerged as global economic powers. The mismatched quartet (or quintet) of BRIC(S) (Brazil, Russia, India, China and South Africa) are mixed on any indicator that can be used to measure their global presence except growth, which has been rapid – for many varied reasons – for all of them over the past decade. The current selection of papers in this section is similarly varied. The first examines an important phenomenon: outward investment from emerging countries in the case of China. The second paper looks at an industry that is emerging as a global competitor: the Indian pharmaceutical sector. The final two papers examine the stance of foreign multinational enterprises in emerging countries, focussing on emerging strategies and the hidden risks. The challenge of doing business "at the bottom of the pyramid" (Prahalad, 2010) is a central one for all firms, whether local businesses or foreign multinationals.

Emerging markets are broadly identified with those middle-income countries that have liberalized, reformed and opened up their internal markets to foreign trade and investment. They have welcomed and fostered the import and investment in high technology methods of production (there has been less liberalization and reform of the services sector, notably banking and retailing). Many emerging markets have become significant locations for foreign direct investment in "offshore" facilities and in larger markets to serve their growing middle classes. They are characterized by high growth and expanding influence in world politics and the international institutions. Emerging countries have made special efforts to improve infrastructure, reduce transaction costs and reduce the risks of doing business (see the World Bank's Annual Report, "Doing business in 2014"). Emerging markets have led to a rebalancing of economic power and many leading emerging countries are becoming major outward foreign investors, both in portfolio investments (notably through Sovereign Wealth Funds) and direct investors through greenfield investments and acquisitions of western companies and brands (Cavusgil et al., 2013).

An important subset of the emerging countries are BRICs (O'Neill, 2001) covering Brazil, Russia, India and China (and sometimes South Africa). These are the large, rapidly growing and politically powerful producers and consumers. It will be noted, of course, that this subset of countries (like emerging markets overall) are highly heterogeneous, being united only by size and rapid growth. This has been a useful mnemonic, focussing attention on the growth of economic power and influence of these countries. No serious international strategy would treat them similarly because of the differences in economic structure, culture, demography and political economy amongst them.

Emerging markets need to be considered as current markets, production bases, competitors and sources of future opportunity in areas such as services. It is increasingly important that this be built into the strategies of multinational companies and that SMEs consider the potential of these countries. SMEs from emerging markets have opportunities to join the value chains of MNEs, but sometimes may wish to avoid being "locked in" to these chains in positions of subservience. This is a difficult strategic choice, one that is time dependent. It may often be a good strategy to join such a value chain dominated by a "global factory" (Buckley and Ghauri, 2004, Buckley 2004, 2007, 2009, 2010, 2011a, 2011b, 2011c), to learn and establish own brands. This is a difficult manoeuvre and lock in may prevent its execution.

Multinationals from emerging countries

Emerging country-originated multinational enterprises (EMNEs) are a major new phenomenon in the global economy. They are important not only because they raise new issues of competition for established firms and because their management styles are allegedly different from "western" multinationals, but also because they represent a challenge to the established theory of the multinational enterprise. When new phenomena arise, there is always the question of whether existing explanations can accommodate them or whether new phenomena require new theory. This has generated considerable controversy in the international business literature.

A question at issue is whether EMNEs possess competitive advantages or "ownership advantages". It will be remembered that Dunning's eclectic paradigm conceived three sections of explanation for foreign direct investment: locational advantages (L), internalization advantages (I) and ownership advantages (O). Ownership advantages are necessary according to Dunning (Hymer, [1960] 1976) and Kindleberger (1969) to overcome the "liability of foreignness" (Zaheer, 1995), which describes the disadvantages that foreign companies face when entering an unfamiliar, alien and possibly discriminatory host country. Much of the research on EMNEs has been the search for "O" advantages (Williamson et al., 2013, Deng, 2012). Others, taking a more purist view of internalization theory, have denied that "O" advantages are an essential theoretical component and that if "I" is interpreted correctly, it is logically redundant (Buckley and Hashai, 2014). Moreover, in practice, "O" advantages need to be defined for a limited period as they atrophy and are competed away, unless further investment in the relevant area takes place. This technology, brands, marketing and organizational skills, management techniques and business models can be copied, stolen or overtaken over time. In part, this question has transformed into the question "can EMNEs innovate?" (Williamson et al., 2013). This puts the question into a longer timespan and focusses attention on macrofactors; on country specific advantages (CSAs) rather than firm specific areas (FSAs). Indeed, the EMNEs question also calls into question the relationship between CSAs and FSAs. Several analysts (such as Rugman, 2009) have argued that EMNEs rely on home country generated CSAs such as low-cost labour, government subsidies and natural resource endowments for their competitive abilities. A variety of channels are used to transform these CSAs into FSAs, such as government ownership, favouritism through support for selected companies (or oligarchs or owning families), through capital market distortions or forced surpluses. EMNAs have also focussed attention on the relationship between CSAs and FSAs on theoretical and empirical planes.

It is clear that the strategies of EMNEs differ from conventional multinationals. This arises partly because of different circumstances. First, EMNEs are in a "catch-up" situation and often have to break into industry structures dominated by established MNEs. Second, they are newcomers and have to learn about the pitfalls and opportunities of doing business abroad from scratch. All newcomers often make mistakes because of a misreading of risks, we should expect this of EMNEs. Third, and positively, they are entering a global economy that is much more open than their earlier internationalizers. Fourth, they operate in a world where the value chain, rather than the individual firm, is the key unit of competition. They can therefore join established value chains, or establish new ones, or a combination of both, in sequence or in parallel. Finally, and again, positively, EMNEs have the potential to learn from established MNEs, either indirectly by observation or study or directly by hiring experienced executives and consultants.

One key manifestation of these factors is the preference of EMNEs for acquisition as a mode of entry and operation in key foreign markets. Acquisition enables EMNEs to "jump start" their operations (obviating start-up problems) and to acquire key embedded assets such as brands, technology and experienced managers. The importance of this mode of operation, particularly for Indian EMNEs, has frequently been noted.

China is the most rapidly growing foreign direct investor and source country for an increasing number of multinationals (World Investment Report, 2013). It is also a country where firm-level data is hard to come by. The study by Buckley et al. (Chapter 29) uses a unique project-level database of Chinese outward investment and subjects it to quantitative analysis. Many standard theoretical explanations for outward FDI performance vary in explaining Chinese FDI. It is remarkable that a theory developed in the mid-1970s to explain largely western, privately owned multinationals, performs well in the twenty-first century to explain state-owned MNEs from an emerging country (Buckley and Casson, 1976). However, Chinese OFDI is foreign direct investment with Chinese characteristics; some of the decision-making captured in this article is idiosyncratic to China. Of particular importance is the perverse behaviour of the "country risk" variable that shows other things being taken into account by other variables, that Chinese firms prefer higher-risk locations. The argument that the authors use to explain this is that capital market imperfections in China channel capital to state-owned firms such that these firms ignore macro-risk variables. It is also possible to argue that political motives favour "risky" countries or that Chinese MNEs are seeking out locations with low levels of (foreign-owned) competition because western firms avoid these risky or "pariah" countries. Apart from this fascinating conundrum, Chinese OFDI is surprisingly conventional in terms of its motivation and location selection.

Global value chains

Internationalization is bound with the growth and deepening of global value chains (as Chapters 8, 9 and 22 also show). Upgrading of these value chains and an improved position in them are vital goals for emerging countries (Gereffi and Memedovic, 2003, Gereffi et al. 2005). Chapter 30 examines the "global sourcing networks" of MNEs and shows the importance of value chains to the focal firm and to all the participants. Global value chains have immense importance for trade, investment, employment and development.

Emerging markets and global strategy

Chapter 31 is an analysis of the key factors underlying successful strategies in emerging markets by Khanna, Palepu and Sinha. Institutional voids occur because of the absence of specialized intermediaries, regulatory systems and contract-enforcing mechanisms in emerging markets. Khanna et al. see these voids as crucial impediments to the globalization strategies of MNEs. This chapter suggests that MNEs need to develop strategies that differ from those in advanced markets. Understanding these problems at a practical, micro level is crucial in designing entry and development paths in such markets and the authors provide a checklist to identify the key institutional voids likely to be encountered in key emerging markets. They advise that MNEs approach different markets as part of a system and recommend that value chain design (see Chapter 6) should reflect the realities on the ground in emerging markets.

Chapter 32 cautions against taking emerging markets at face value. Henisz and Zelner see immature and volatile political systems underlying hidden risks in emerging markets. Just as with Chapter 30, they do not believe that aggregate "country risk" indices capture these risks. Astute political strategies are required that use modern communications technology, social networking and an understanding of game theory if multinationals are to protect their interests in these environments. The final chapter reiterates a key lesson of the book, that an analytical approach towards strategy and the understanding of the external environment is vital to a successful internationalization process.

References

Buckley, P.J. 2004. The role of China in the global strategy of multinational enterprises. *Journal of Chinese Economic and Business Studies*, 2/1, 1–25.

Buckley, P.J. 2007. The strategy of multinational enterprises in the light of the rise of China. *Scandinavian Journal of Management*, 23/2, 107–26.

Buckley, P.J. 2009. The impact of the global factory on economic development. *Journal of World Business*, 44/2, 131–43.

Buckley, P.J. 2010. The role of headquarters in the global factory. In U. Andersson and U. Holm (Eds.), *Managing the Contemporary Multinational*. Cheltenham: Edward Elgar, pp. 60–84.

Buckley, P.J. 2011a. (Ed.) *Globalization and the Global Factory*. Cheltenham: Edward Elgar, pp. 634.

Buckley, P.J. 2011b. The impact of globalisation and the emergence of the global factory. In R. Ramamurti and N. Hashai, (Eds.), *Research in Global Strategic Management Volume 15, The Future of Foreign Direct Investment and the Multinational Enterprise*. Emerald Books, pp. 213–49.

Buckley, P.J. 2011c. International integration and coordination in the global factory. *Management International Review*, 51/2, pp. 269–83.

Buckley, P.J. and Casson, M. 1976. *The Future of the Multinational Enterprise*. London: Macmillan.

Buckley, P.J. and Ghauri, P.N. 2004. Globalisation, economic geography and the strategy of multinational enterprises. Journal of International Business Studies, 35/2, pp. 81–98.

Buckley, P.J. and Hashai, N. 2014. Is competitive advantage a necessary condition for the emergence of the Multinational Enterprise? *Global Strategy Journal*, Vol. 1 February (forthcoming).

Cavusgil, S.T., Ghauri, P.N. and Akcal, A.A. 2013. *Doing Business in Emerging Markets*, Second Edition, London: SAGE Publications.

Deng, P. 2012. The internationalization of Chinese firms: A critical review and future research. *International Journal of Management Reviews*, 14(4): 408–27.

Gereffi, G. and Memedovic, O. 2003. The Global Apparel Value Chain: What Prospects for Upgrading by Developing Countries? Vienna: UNIDO.

Gereffi, G., Humphrey J. and Sturgeon, T. 2005. The governance of global value chains. *Review of International Political Economy*, 12(1): 78–104.

Hymer, S.H. 1976. *The International Operations of National Firms: Study of Foreign Direct Investment*. Cambridge, MA: MIT Press. Originally published 1960.

Kindleberger, C.P. 1969. *American Business Abroad*. New Haven: Yale University Press.

O'Neill, J. 2001. Dreaming with BRICs: The Path to 2050. Goldman Sachs. Global Economics Paper No. 99.

Prahalad, C.K. 2010. *The Fortune at the Bottom of the Pyramid: Eradicating Poverty through Profits*. Upper Saddle River, NJ: Wharton School Publishing.

Rugman, A. 2009. How global are TNCs from emerging countries? In Sauvant, K.P. 2008. (Ed.) The *Rise of Transnational Corporations from Emerging Countries: Threat or Opportunity*? Cheltenham: Edward Elgar.

Williamson, P.J., Ramamurti, R., Fleury, A. and Fleury M.T.L. 2013. *The Competitive Advantage of Emerging Market Multinationals*. Cambridge: Cambridge University Press.

World Investment Report 2013. UNCTAD, New York and Geneva, 2010.

Zaheer, S. 1995. Overcoming the liability of foreignness. *Academy of Management Journal*, 38: 341–63.

29 The determinants of Chinese outward foreign direct investment*

Peter J. Buckley, L. Jeremy Clegg, Adam R. Cross,
Xin Liu, Hinrich Voss and Ping Zheng

Introduction

This paper investigates the determinants of foreign direct investment (FDI) by Chinese multinational enterprises (MNEs) over the period 1984 to 2001.[1] The process of China's deepening reintegration with the global economy began, in the modern era, with the 'Open Door' policies of the late 1970s, and accelerated with accession to the World Trade Organisation (WTO) in 2001. Studies of this process examine China in terms of its position in global trade flows (for example, Lall and Albaladejo, 2004); its comparative advantage as a manufacturing location (for example, Chen *et al.*, 2002; Rowen, 2003); and in the volume, distribution and impacts of *inbound* FDI (for example, Buckley et al., 2002; Buckley, 2004b).[2] In contrast, understanding of a further dimension to this process – the rise in Chinese outward direct investment (ODI) – remains incomplete. One reason is the paucity of sufficiently disaggregated data to permit formal analysis of the forces shaping Chinese ODI. The result has been a preponderance of descriptive research on FDI trends (for example, Taylor, 2002; Deng, 2003, 2004; Wong and Chan, 2003; Buckley et al., 2006) coupled with in-depth case studies on a small number of high-profile Chinese MNEs (for example, Liu and Li, 2002; Warner *et al.*, 2004).

Using official data from one of the key agencies concerned with China's investment approval process, the State Administration for Foreign Exchange (SAFE), this exploratory study is, to our knowledge, one of the first to model formally the forces driving Chinese ODI. Our focus is on FDI determinants and the extent to which established theoretical explanations of the MNE (much of which concentrates on industrialised country, and especially US, investors) can explain FDI from an emerging economy like China. China is a particularly good test case for the general theory of FDI as it presents many special conditions rarely encountered in a single country.

Several indicators point to a strengthening of China's role as an investor country in recent years. By 2004, China was the eighth most important FDI source among developing countries, behind economically more advanced economies such as Hong Kong SAR (Special Administrative Region), South Korea, Republic of China (Taiwan) and Singapore (UNCTAD, 2005a). A recent survey of national investment promotion agencies predicts that China will become a top four source country of FDI over the period 2005–2008 (UNCTAD, 2005b), with African and Asia-Pacific country agencies in particular highlighting the dominant role expected of China, placing it second to South Africa and the USA in each region, respectively.

*Reprinted by permission from Macmillan Publishers Ltd: Buckley, Peter J., J. Clegg, A. Cross, P. Zheng, H. Voss & X. Liu, 'The determinants of Chinese outward foreign direct investment', Journal of International Business Studies, 38 (4): 499–518. Copyright 2007, published by Palgrave Macmillan.

There is every indication that China will contribute increasingly to global FDI flows over the coming years. These indicators highlight the timeliness of this study.

Chinese outward investors can be regarded as being state-owned in the period under study, as private firms were legally prohibited from investing abroad prior to 2003. Since 1979, when ODI was formally permitted under the 'Open Door' policies, the internationalisation of Chinese firms has been tightly controlled by national and provincial government, either directly, by administrative fiat, or indirectly, through economic policy and other measures designed to advance the economic development agenda (Buckley *et al.*, 2006). Initially, ODI was permitted on a selective basis. However, in recent years administrative controls have been relaxed, approval processes and procedures streamlined, and the ceiling raised on the amount of foreign exchange that can be committed to individual investment projects (Sauvant, 2005). The process of accelerated outward investment liberalisation and growth can be traced from Deng Xiaoping's tour of South China in 1992 through to the government-led 'go global' (*zou chu qu*) initiative, which was instigated in 1999. This initiative aims to promote the international competitiveness of Chinese firms by further reducing or eliminating foreign-exchange-related, fiscal and administrative obstacles to international investment (Sauvant, 2005). In order to properly understand Chinese ODI, it is therefore important that formal empirical analysis takes full account of this changing institutional context and the idiosyncratic response by Chinese firms that it might engender. In other words, it is necessary to understand the extent to which the investment location decisions of Chinese MNEs, when considered in aggregate, are explicable by received theory, or whether the context and institutional environment of the home country exerts a distinctive effect. Such distinctiveness might be a consequence of the continued pursuit of national economic imperatives, for instance, with state-owned enterprises (SOEs) employed as an instrument of policy.

The paper is organised as follows. First, we review the general theory of FDI and discuss the extent to which it holds for an emerging economy like China, where central planning has greatly influenced the development of the external sector. We do this by considering three potential arguments (capital market imperfections, special ownership advantages and institutional factors) for a special theory to be nested within the general theory. We then describe a number of economic and policy variables proposed in the literature to have a significant influence on (industrialised country) FDI flows, and hypothesise on their ability to explain Chinese ODI patterns. We go on to test the special theory in a model of Chinese ODI using official data on individual approved Chinese FDI projects. We find that Chinese ODI is indeed distinctive in certain respects that have implications for theory, particularly the finding for political risk, but that familiar explanations of FDI are relevant, too. We conclude by recommending and commenting on future research directions.

The general theory of FDI

The general principles of the theory of FDI are twofold (Buckley and Casson, 1976): (1) firms internalise missing or imperfect external markets until the costs of further internalisation outweigh the benefits and (2) firms choose locations for their constituent activities that minimise the overall costs of their operations. Expansion by the internalisation of markets means that firms use FDI to replace imperfect external markets in intermediate products and knowledge (as exemplified by exporting and licensing) and appropriate the profits from so doing. In the case of emerging economy MNEs, there are likely to be particular imperfections in home country capital markets that may require special applications of the theory, and this, as we will see, is true of China.

The location aspect of the mainstream or general theory, as encapsulated in Dunning's eclectic paradigm, suggests three primary motivations (Dunning, 1977, 1993):

- foreign-market-seeking FDI;
- efficiency-seeking (cost reduction) FDI;
- resource-seeking FDI (including a subset that is known as strategic-asset-seeking FDI).

The general theory of FDI has been built largely on the experience of industrialised country investors. In certain respects this can be readily applied to emerging economy investors, however there are inevitably gaps. Here, we look critically at the applicability of the general theory. Market-seeking FDI will be undertaken by emerging economy firms for traditional trade supporting reasons: to access distribution networks, to facilitate the exports of domestic producers, and to enhance exports from the host country to other large and rapidly growing markets. Efficiency-seeking FDI will occur when outward investors seek lower-cost locations for operations, in particular in the search for lower-cost labour. Given China's comparatively low labour cost levels this motivation is unlikely, and is not explicitly considered here. Resource-seeking FDI from emerging economies occurs to acquire or secure the supply of raw materials and energy sources in short supply at home. This may well involve Chinese ODI in relatively high-income countries that have significant energy reserves and raw material deposits (for example, Australia and Canada). It may also involve the search for specific assets such as R&D capacity and output, design facilities and brand names that are embedded in advanced country firms and that can usually be accessed only by takeover of these firms or subdivisions of them (Dunning, 2001).

Various studies also identify an incremental or stages process to firm internationalisation that is linked to geographic and psychic distance (for example, Johanson and Vahlne, 1977), with firms beginning their international operations in locations geographically close to the home market and in (psychically close) countries where knowledge, relationships and experience have already been established through prior trade business and other interactions. Examples of such behaviour are to be found in work on MNEs from Hong Kong (Lau, 1992, 2003), South Korea (Erramilli *et al.*, 1999), India and Argentina in the 1980s (Ferrantino, 1992; Pradhan, 2003), Brazil (Villela, 1983) and Malaysia (Zin, 1999).

A special theory for Chinese ODI?

The question then arises of whether FDI from emerging economies and, specifically, from China requires a special theory nested within the general theory above. There are three potential arguments: capital market imperfections, the special ownership advantages of Chinese MNEs and institutional factors.

Capital market imperfections

Capital market imperfections in emerging economies such as China may require a special application of the general theory. Such imperfections may mean that capital is available at below-market rates for a considerable period of time, creating a semipermanent disequilibrium in the capital market that (potential) outward investors can exploit. In this sense, market imperfections may be transformed into ownership advantages by emerging economy firms (Buckley, 2004a). This ability may arise from a number of particular and interrelated imperfections:

(1) state-owned (and state-associated) firms may have capital made available to them at below-market rates (for example, in the form of soft budget constraints) (for example, Lardy, 1998; Scott, 2002; Warner *et al.*, 2004);

(2) inefficient banking systems may make soft loans to potential outward investors, either as policy or through inefficiency (for example, Warner *et al.*, 2004; Child and Rodrigues, 2005; Antkiewicz and Whalley, 2006);

(3) conglomerate firms may operate an inefficient internal capital market that effectively subsidises FDI (for example, Liu, 2005 on the diversified Chinese conglomerate Haier); and

(4) family-owned firms may have access to cheap capital from family members (for example, Tsai, 2002; Child and Pleister, 2003; Erdener and Shapiro, 2005).

There are good grounds for believing that all four of these imperfections exist in China. State-sponsored soft budget constraints make acquisition by Chinese enterprises a 'normal' mode of entering and penetrating a host economy (Warner *et al.*, 2004). Over-bidding by Chinese MNEs is attributed to the absence of private shareholders and sanguine views of the associated technical, commercial and political risks, to limited fear of failure, close government support and low cost of capital (Ma and Andrews-Speed, 2006).[3] Indeed, the survival of inefficient Chinese firms in general is attributed to the pervasive nature of soft budget constraints promoted by local government and party officials, resulting in the inability of banks and other financial institutions to impose either restructuring or exit on firms (Lardy, 1998). The 'sizeable venture capital' afforded to SOE is exemplified by the State Council's provision to the China International Trust and Investment Corporation (CITIC) when it was instructed to explore overseas investment opportunities in priority resource sectors (Zhang, 2003). The State Council also directed the transfer of the China Investment and Trust Corporation for Foreign Economic Cooperation and Trade (FOTIC, previously the financial arm of MOFTEC) to the Sinochem Group, effectively giving it an 'internal bank' (Zhang, 2003), while the Beijing steel producer, Shougang Group, was granted the right to start and own a bank, virtually guaranteeing the lifting of a hard budget constraint (Steinfeld, 1998). The acquisition of IBM's personal computer business by Lenovo (concluded in 2005) was regarded to have been underwritten by the Chinese government, who at the time held a stake of 57% in the company (*Business Week*, 2004). From this discussion, it appears possible that capital market imperfections may account for the ease with which natural-resource-seeking FDI (typically in energy and raw materials sectors) and strategic-asset-seeking FDI might be undertaken by Chinese MNEs.

Imperfections in the capital market would become evident if Chinese MNEs had a distinctive foreign investment strategy in terms of location, as exemplified by a perverse reaction to risk and return not predicted by studies on the FDI motivations of industrialised country firms. In the current study, we test for this by including political risk in our determinants of Chinese ODI after controlling for the risk premium, which is proxied by market size and market growth.

Ownership advantages of Chinese MNEs

There is an argument that emerging economy MNEs have developed ownership advantages that allow them to operate certain types of activity in foreign countries more effectively than local firms and industrialised country MNEs. These advantages may include flexibility (Wells, 1983), economising on the use of capital (or resources), benefits accruing from home country embeddedness (i.e., prior familiarity of operating within an emerging market context), and the ability to engage in beneficial relations with firms and other actors in order to provide access to resources controlled by others. The latter advantage, which some term a relational asset (Dunning, 2002; Erdener and Shapiro, 2005), may be revealed as networking skills and may be linked to the Chinese diaspora in the case of Chinese firms.[4] Where these conditions are relatively long-lasting then they provide the case for semi-permanent 'owner-ship advantages' of emerging economy MNEs, the third element of Dunning's eclectic theory after internalisation and location factors (Dunning, 1993). This argument is less easy to test using aggregate FDI data, however.

Extant theory asserts that the early investments of firms frequently occur in countries with similar cultural background to the home country (Johanson and Vahlne, 1977) or where rela-tional assets in the form of ethnic or familial ties with a specific minority population in the host country can be exploited (Lecraw, 1977; Wells, 1983; Lau, 2003). Within such a network, market information about the most suitable and profitable investment opportunities can circu-late with ease, and fruitful commercial relationships can be established that facilitate market entry and development. Investment and commercial risk can be reduced as a consequence (Lecraw, 1977; Zhan, 1995). The importance of networking skills as a special ownership advantage of Chinese firms would be evident if Chinese ODI was associated positively with host countries endowed with relevant location-specific relational advantages, such as the presence of an appreciable ethnic Chinese population.

Institutional factors influencing Chinese ODI

The institutional fabric of an emerging economy can determine the ability and will of domestic firms to invest abroad. A straightforward, consistent and liberal policy towards outward FDI will encourage it, while a discretionary and frequently adjusted policy may do the opposite. There is an emerging body of theoretical work that concerns the institution-based view of strategy, or institutional theory for short (North, 1990; Peng, 2002; Meyer and Nguyen, 2005; Wright *et al.*, 2005). This has the potential to help explain distinctiveness in the behaviour of outward-investing Chinese firms. The basic thrust of this contribution is that firms' strategy is shaped by the home institutional environment (more colloquially 'the rules of the game'), which is formally and informally enforced by government and its agents (Scott, 2002) and which bears upon the norms and cognitions that influence investment, including foreign investment, behaviour. High levels of government support, typically in the form of privileged access to raw materials and other inputs, low-cost cap-ital (discussed earlier), subsidies and other benefits help emerging country firms to offset ownership and location disadvantages abroad (Aggarwal and Agmon, 1990). On the other hand, such investors also often encounter highly bureaucratic and burdensome adminis-trative FDI approval procedures as government, at various levels, seeks to influence the amount, direction and scope of outward capital flows. If this is combined with discrimi-natory policy tools against certain industries and ownership forms, flows of ODI can be distorted. In such instances, FDI through informal or illegal routes may occur (or indeed be tacitly encouraged).

Given the extent of state control of the Chinese economy (Scott, 2002), the institutional environment is likely to have had far-reaching and profound effects on the internationalisation decision of Chinese firms. Key periods in the evolution of China's FDI approval process are presented in Table 29.1. Because various agencies within the state administration have been required to approve every outward FDI project from China (predominantly through the control

Table 29.1 Key stages in Chinese ODI policy development

1979–1985	**Stage 1: Cautious internationalisation** With the 'open-door' policy, Chinese ODI is identified by government as one means of opening and integrating China into the world economy. Chinese state-owned firms start to set up their first international operations. Only state-owned trading corporations under MOFERT (later MOFCOM or the Ministry of Commerce) and provincial and municipal 'economic and technological cooperation enterprises' under the State Economic and Trade Commission (now part of the National Development and Reform Commission [NDRC]) are allowed to invest abroad. Some 189 projects are approved, amounting to around US\$197m in value.
1986–1991	**Stage 2: Government encouragement** The government liberalises restrictive policies and allows more enterprises to establish foreign affiliates, provided they have sufficient capital, technical and operational know-how and a suitable joint venture partner. Approval is granted to 891 projects, totalling some US\$1.2bn.
1992–1998	**Stage 3: Expansion and regulation** Encouraged by domestic liberalisation, initiated by Deng Xiaoping's journey to the South and the incorporation of enterprise internationalisation into the national economic development policy, subnational-level authorities actively promote the international business activities of enterprises under their supervision, especially in Hong Kong to engage in real estate and stock market speculation. The Asian crisis in 1997 and the subsequent collapse of some enterprises slow down this development. Latterly, concerns about loss of control over state assets, capital flight and 'leakage' of foreign exchange lead to a tightening of approval procedures, notably for projects of US\$1m or more. Individual ODI project activity declines, despite an increase of total ODI of US\$1.2bn in value terms.
1999–2001	**Stage 4: Implementation of the 'go global' policy** Contradictory policies characterise this period. Further measures to control illicit capital transfers and to regularise ODI towards genuinely productive purposes are introduced. By contrast, ODI in specific industries is actively encouraged with export tax rebates, foreign exchange assistance and direct financial support, notably in trade-related activities that promoted Chinese exports of raw materials, parts and machinery and in light industry sectors like textiles, machinery and electrical equipment. In 2001 this encouragement is formalised in the 10th five-year plan which outlines the 'going global' or *zou chu qu* directive. Total approved ODI rises by US\$1.8bn, with an average project value of US\$2.6m.
Since 2001	**Stage 5: Post-WTO period (included here for completeness)** Heightened domestic competitive pressures, owing to the opening of once protected industries and markets to foreign and domestic competitors, forces some Chinese firms to seek new markets abroad. In the 11th five-year plan the Chinese government stresses again the importance of zou chu qu for Chinese firms and the Chinese economy. Although the approval system is decentralised and streamlined to become less burdensome, contradictory regulations still prevail. Direct, proactive support of ODI continues to be limited, aimed mainly at preventing illegal capital outflows and loss of control of state assets.

Sources: Yu et al. (2005), Zhang (2003), Wong and Chan (2003), Wu and Chen (2001), Guo (1984), Ye (1992), Ding (2000).

of foreign exchange), this evolution is likely to have influenced strongly the development, strength and orientation of Chinese MNEs. To illustrate, extant research portrays Chinese ODI of the 1980s and early 1990s as having been directed by government towards supporting the export function of state-owned manufacturers; towards providing stability to the supply of domestically scarce natural resources; and towards the acquisition of information and learning on how to operate at an international level (Ye, 1992; Zhan, 1995; Liu and Li, 2002). In particular, FDI in the energy and minerals sectors was encouraged to meet growing needs at home (Lawrence, 2002). In this sense, China has 'built' some of its MNEs, as did Singapore, South Korea and Malaysia (Heenan and Keegan, 1979; Yeung, 1998; Wang, 2002; Dicken, 2003). FDI, and especially natural resources-oriented FDI, was concentrated by value in the developed countries (Buckley *et al.*, 2006) (see Table 29.2). There is some evidence that latterly Chinese MNEs have internationalised to gain better access to foreign proprietary technology, strategic assets and capabilities (brands, distribution channels, foreign capital markets, etc.), often by acquisition; to exploit new markets; and to diversify business activities in a manner that seeks to improve their international competitiveness (Taylor, 2002; Deng, 2003; Zhang, 2003, Buckley *et al.*, 2006). This development, which has occurred in conjunction with increasing policy openness and liberalisation over the period under study (Sauvant, 2005), has seen Chinese ODI dispersed more widely, especially among the developing countries (see Table 29.2), with defensive (import-substituting and quota-hopping) and offensive (developing new markets) market-seeking FDI increasingly undertaken (Buckley *et al.*, 2006). This is in addition to the continuance of natural resources-oriented FDI, which now increasingly encompasses developing countries. The promotion of exports and export-oriented FDI also continues. For example, direct government support in the form of export tax rebates, foreign exchange assistance and financial support was introduced in 1999 to foster FDI in trade-related activities and to promote Chinese exports, especially in the textiles, machinery and electrical equipment sectors (Wong and Chan, 2003). The effect of home country institutions on the investment behaviour of Chinese MNEs would be evidenced by a correlation between a key policy change and a change in the amount or distribution of Chinese ODI, or both.

The determinants of Chinese ODI: hypotheses

We now review the determinants of FDI derived from theory and hypothesise on their ability to influence the distribution of Chinese ODI.

Market-seeking FDI

Host market characteristics, such as market size, are recognised as a significant determinant of FDI flows: as markets increase in size, so do opportunities for the efficient utilisation of resources and the exploitation of economies of scale and scope through FDI (UNCTAD, 1998). Numerous studies (surveyed by Chakrabarti, 2001) show that FDI flow and market size are associated positively. Recent work points to the rise of offensive market-seeking motives driving Chinese MNEs (Taylor, 2002; Zhang, 2003; Deng, 2004; Buckley *et al.*, 2006) and posits that this activity may increasingly be directed towards large markets. Theory suggests that market-oriented, horizontal FDI will be associated positively with growth in demand. The market growth hypothesis holds that rapidly growing economies present more opportunities for generating profits than those that are growing more slowly or not at all (Lim, 1983). We therefore derive the following three hypotheses:

Hypothesis 1a: Chinese ODI is associated positively with absolute host market size.

Hypothesis 1b: Chinese ODI is associated positively with host market size per capita.

Hypothesis 1c: Chinese ODI is associated positively with host market growth.

Table 29.2 Approved Chinese FDI outflows, by host region and economy, 1990–2003 (US$10,000 and %)

	Annual average of ODI stock (%)				
	1990–1992	*1993–1995*	*1996–1998*	*1999–2001*	*2002–2003*
Total Chinese ODI (US$10,000)	133,847.53	176,010.77	235,466.77	377,761.70	1,038,208.76
Percentage distribution by region:					
Developed countries	69.44	64.12	49.95	36.11	22.60
Western Europe	2.62	2.63	2.21	1.72	4.15
European Union	2.29	2.38	2.01	1.58	4.08
(15 countries)					
Other Western Europe	0.33	0.25	0.20	0.14	0.07
(3 countries)					
North America	41.59	39.86	31.25	23.67	12.82
Other developed countries	25.22	21.63	16.49	10.71	5.62
Developing countries	30.56	35.88	50.05	63.89	77.40
Africa	4.03	5.18	11.02	16.07	8.40
North Africa	0.20	0.19	0.76	1.13	0.85
(6 countries)					
Other Africa	3.83	4.99	10.27	14.93	7.55
(46 countries)					
Latin America and the	4.87	4.96	10.04	13.83	7.13
Caribbean					
South America	3.64	3.19	8.40	8.89	4.18
(12 countries)					
Other Latin America and	1.23	1.78	1.64	4.94	2.95
Caribbean (18 countries)					
Central and Eastern Europe	4.17	5.76	4.85	4.44	4.62
(18 countries)					
Asia	16.61	18.71	22.22	27.87	56.60
West Asia (Middle East)	1.09	1.17	0.98	1.61	1.46
(12 countries)					
Central Asia (8 countries)	0.09	0.26	0.49	1.50	0.91
South, East and SE Asia	15.42	17.28	20.74	24.75	54.22
(20 countries)					
The Pacific (9 countries)	0.88	1.27	1.92	1.69	0.67

Source: Calculated from MOFCOM Almanac of China's Foreign Relations and Trade (various years) and China Commerce Yearbook 2004 (2004).

Note: The total number of recipient countries per region is shown in the region heading. Regions are as per UNCTAD (2003).

Natural resource endowment

The Chinese government has used ODI to ensure the supply of domestically scarce factor inputs as the Chinese economy has grown (Ye, 1992; Zhan, 1995). Key sectors include minerals, petroleum, timber, fishery and agricultural products (Cai, 1999; Wu and Sia, 2002). Purchases of stakes in Australian mineral and food companies by CITIC and the acquisition of Canada-based PetroKaz by China National Petroleum Corporation (CNPC) are examples (Wu and Sia, 2002). Internalisation theory asserts the importance of equity-based control in the exploitation of scarce natural resources, so a positive association between the natural resources endowment of countries and Chinese ODI is expected (Buckley and Casson, 1976). Thus:

Hypothesis 2: Chinese ODI is associated positively with host country endowments of natural resources.

Asset-seeking FDI

Chinese ODI has been directed to the acquisition of information and knowledge of how to operate internationally, especially in the 1980s (Ye, 1992; Zhan, 1995; Buckley *et al.*, 2006). In recent years, an expressed goal of state-directed Chinese ODI has been to access advanced proprietary technology, immobile strategic assets (for example, brands, local distribution networks) and other capabilities abroad (Taylor, 2002; Deng, 2003; Zhang, 2003; Warner *et al.*, 2004), through greenfield entry and acquisition. It is expected that Chinese MNEs would direct such asset-seeking ODI towards economies with significant levels of human and intellectual capital, and in particular the industrialised countries, to help them to strengthen their competitiveness elsewhere (Dunning et al., 1998; Dunning, 2006). It is worth noting that many acquisitions by Chinese firms, especially in Europe and the USA, have involved a target company that was ailing or insolvent. Proprietary ownership advantage endowments can be proxied by the rate of patenting in the host country. Thus:

Hypothesis 3: Chinese ODI is associated positively with host country endowments of ownership advantages.

Political risk

Internalisation theory predicts that in countries experiencing high political risk, market-oriented firms will tend to substitute arm's length servicing modes (exporting or licensing) for directly owned local production, and that resource-oriented firms are discouraged from committing substantial sunk costs in the form of FDI projects (Buckley and Casson, 1981, 1999). Thus, high political risk is associated with low values of FDI inflow, *ceteris paribus* (Chakrabarti, 2001). The use of a risk index on its own would beg the question of the return on investment. If higher risk host countries also offer higher returns, then FDI will still flow to them, and an increasing relationship between risk and FDI will be observed. In this study, the role of returns is approximated (as it is in many studies on country risk) by market-related variables, so we can argue that returns of a market-related nature have been controlled for. Similarly, the scope for returns on Chinese investment in natural resources (the most likely motive for investment in risky countries of Central Asia and Africa) is controlled for by the natural resources variable. Because the measure of political risk we use assigns higher values to greater political stability, the general theory of FDI would predict a positive relationship between the dependent and independent variables. Thus:

Hypothesis 4: Chinese ODI is associated negatively with rising levels of host country political risk.

Cultural proximity

The Chinese diaspora is acknowledged to have contributed to the integration of China into the world economy since 1979, especially in positively influencing inbound FDI from Singapore, the Republic of China (Taiwan) and Hong Kong (Henley *et al.*, 1999; Yeung, 1999; Sikorski and Menkhoff, 2000; Ng and Tuan, 2002).[5] Strong economic connections among overseas Chinese and the importance of *guanxi* (the ancient system of personal relationships and social connections based on mutual interest and benefit) in Chinese business dealings may also influence patterns of Chinese ODI (Luo, 1997; Standifird and Marshall, 2000; Tong, 2003). A number of scholars argue that ethnic and family *guanxi* networks constitute a firm-specific advantage for Chinese MNEs because these help to reduce the business risk and transaction costs (Sung, 1996; Braeutigam, 2003; Erdener and Shapiro, 2005) associated with the identification of business opportunities in certain foreign markets (Zhan, 1995). These networks may also compensate Chinese MNEs for their relatively late entry into international markets (Li, 2003).

This argument suggests that Chinese firms will invest in countries with a large resident population of ethnic Chinese. Such countries are mostly to be found in Asia, which accounts for some 88% of all ethnic Chinese living outside China. In 1990 there were about 37 million overseas Chinese, with the majority (66%) distributed more or less evenly among Indonesia, Thailand, Hong Kong SAR and Malaysia. A further 8% lived in North and South American countries, 2% in European countries and 1% each in Oceania and on the African continent (Poston *et al.*, 1994). Thus:

> **Hypothesis 5:** Chinese ODI is associated positively with the proportion of ethnic Chinese in the host population.

Policy liberalisation

From the discussion above, it is clear that policies on international capital transfers are likely to have greatly influenced patterns and trends in Chinese ODI. Although it is important for completeness that any formal model of Chinese ODI incorporates a policy dimension, lack of transparency in the application of regulations and incentive policies experienced by investors (Wong and Chan, 2003) makes this a difficult aspect to capture. Deng Xiaoping's South China Tour in 1992 was associated with significant domestic market liberalisation. In response to this, numerous subnational-level authorities allowed enterprises under their supervision to internationalise, especially towards Hong Kong SAR, in order to engage in real estate and stock market speculation (Wong and Chan, 2003). Therefore, to investigate the role of institutional liberalisation towards ODI, we introduce a time dummy for 1992. Thus:

> **Hypothesis 6:** Liberalisation of Chinese FDI policy in 1992 increased Chinese ODI.

We control for a number of conventional variables from standard theory to specify correctly the estimated equation, and so reveal the effects of the main variables, including those to test the special theory applied to Chinese ODI.

Exchange rate

A low or undervalued exchange rate encourages exports but discourages outward FDI (Kohlhagen, 1977; Logue and Willet, 1977; Stevens, 1993). As the home country exchange rate appreciates, more profitable opportunities for outward FDI will occur as foreign currency denominated assets become cheaper. It is possible that a rapid appreciation of the exchange rate, from a low or undervalued position, will more than proportionately increase outward FDI. For this reason, the exchange rate is included as a control variable. An appreciation of the home country's currency *vis-à-vis* other countries should increase ODI into these countries as it is effectively a depreciation in the host country's currency (Scott-Green and Clegg, 1999). In the case of China, the yuan Renminbi (RMB) was *de facto* pegged to the US dollar at a constant nominal level over the period under study (Roberts and Tyers, 2003; Hall, 2004). However, the RMB peg against the US dollar allowed for revaluation of the yuan RMB against other currencies so the real effective exchange rate of the yuan RMB appreciated by more than 20% between 1995 and 2002 (Hall, 2004). Thus:

> **Hypothesis 7:** A relative depreciation of the host country's currency leads to an increase in Chinese ODI.

Host inflation rate

Volatile and unpredictable inflation rates in a host country discourage market-seeking FDI by creating uncertainty and by making long-term corporate planning problematic, especially with respect to price-setting and profit expectations. High rates of inflation may also lead to domestic currency devaluation, which in turn reduces the real value of earnings in local currency for market-seeking inward-investing firms. High inflation rates tend to check the export performance of domestic and foreign investors and thereby discourage export-oriented FDI by increasing the prices of locally sourced inputs, making it harder to maintain a cost advantage in third markets. We therefore expect a negative relationship between Chinese ODI and host country inflation. Thus:

> **Hypothesis 8:** Chinese ODI is associated negatively with host country inflation rates.

Exports and imports

Exports from China proxy the intensity of trade relations between home and host country by capturing the market-seeking motive of Chinese firms. During the 1980s and early 1990s, much Chinese ODI took place to provide a local support function for domestic Chinese exporters and to help them increase their hard currency earnings (Wu and Sia, 2002). Typically, such investments were small scale, with local subsidiaries providing information, international trade, transportation and financial services to their Chinese principals and other Chinese firms (Ye, 1992; Zhan, 1995). In some cases, these were vanguard operations for later and more substantial investment. Thus:

> **Hypothesis 9:** Chinese ODI is associated positively with Chinese exports to the host country.

Imports to a home country from a host country also capture the intensity of trade relations. As they are an indication of the importance of the resources transferred, we would expect home country firms to internalise these strategic flows using outward FDI as the key mechanism (Buckley and Casson, 1976). Thus:

> **Hypothesis 10:** Chinese ODI is associated positively with Chinese imports from the host country.

Geographic distance from China

Internalisation theory predicts that market-seeking firms are more likely to serve geographically proximate countries through exports and more distant markets through FDI (Buckley

Table 29.3 The determinants of Chinese ODI

Hypotheses and number	Proxy	Expected sign	Theoretical justification	Main or control variable	Data source
FDI (dependent variable)	Annual outflow of Chinese FDI (see text)				State Administration for Foreign Exchange
Host market characteristics (I): absolute market size (H1a)	LGDP: Host country GDP	+	Market seeking	Main	World Bank Development Indicator (2005)
Host market characteristics (II): relative market size (H1b)	LGDPP: Host country GDP per capita	+	Market seeking	Alternative main (I)	World Bank Development Indicator (2005)
Host market characteristics (III): market growth (H1c)	LGGDP: Annual percentage increase in GDP	+	Market seeking	Alternative main (II)	World Bank Development Indicator (2005)
Natural resource endowment (H2)	LORE: the ratio of ore and metal exports to merchandise exports of host country	+	Resource seeking	Main	World Bank Development Indicator (2005)
Asset-seeking FDI (H3)	LPATENT: Total (resident plus nonresident) annual patent registrations in host country	+	Strategic asset seeking	Main	World Intellectual Property Organisation (2006)
Political risk (H4)	LPOLI: Host country's political risk rating (higher values indicate greater stability)	+	Transaction costs	Main	International Country Risk Guide (2005)
Cultural proximity to China (H5)	CP: = 1 when percentage of ethnic Chinese in total population is >1%	+	Region-specific transaction costs	Main	Ohio University (2006); Ma (2003); Kent (2003);
Policy liberalisation (H6)	TD92: Influence of Deng's South China tour (1992)	+	Institutional factors	Main	United Nations Statistics Division (2006)
Exchange rate (H7)	LERATE: Host country official annual average exchange rate against RMB (fixed to dollar)	+	Domestic currency price of foreign assets	Control	World Bank Development Indicator (2005)
Host country inflation rate (H8)	LINF: Host country annual inflation rate	−	Macroeconomic conditions	Control	IMF: World Economic Outlook Database (2005)
Exports (H9)	LEXP: China's exports to the host country	+	Market seeking	Control	China Statistical Yearbook (2005)
Imports (H10)	LIMP: China's imports from the host country	+	Trade intensity	Control	China Statistical Yearbook (2005)
Geographic distance from China (H11)	LDIS: Geographic distance between host and home country (capital)	−	Spatial costs	Control	Calculated using www.geobytes.com
Openness to FDI (H12)	LINFDI: Ratio of inward FDI stock to host GDP	+	Investment policy	Control	UNCTAD FDI database (2006)

Note: all monetary values are in constant (2000) US$ prices.

and Casson, 1981). This suggests a substitution of FDI for other modes as distance increases. However, our dependent variable is in the form of the annual flow of Chinese FDI alone (i.e., not in the form of a ratio with exports). As we predict the flow of FDI to be greatest to nearby countries, so we would expect to capture a negative effect of distance on the flow of FDI (Loungani *et al.*, 2002). A physical distance variable is therefore needed to complement our cultural proximity variable, to isolate its effect. We incorporate distance as a control. Thus:

> **Hypothesis 11:** Chinese ODI is associated negatively with geographic distance from China.

Openness to FDI

The more open a country is to international investment, the more attractive it is likely to be as a destination for FDI (Chakrabarti, 2001). We include openness to FDI in our investigation, as a control:

> **Hypothesis 12:** Chinese ODI is associated positively with the degree of openness of the host economy to international investment.

Our hypotheses, their theoretical justification, the proxies we use and the expected signs are detailed in Table 29.3 with our data sources. We expect the distinctive nature of the factors influencing Chinese ODI to be captured by the collective significance in the main variables that we identify in the table.

The model

Our discussion suggests the following log-linear model:

$$LFDI = \alpha + \beta_1 LGDP + \beta_2 LGDPP + \beta_3 LGGDP + \beta_4 LORE + \beta_5 LPATENT$$
$$+ \beta_6 LPOLI + \beta_7 CP + \beta_8 TD92 + \beta_9 LERATE + \beta_{10} LINF + \beta_{11} LEXP$$
$$+ \beta_{12} LIMP + \beta_{13} LDIS + \beta_{14} LINFDI + \varepsilon_{it} \tag{1}$$

The data are transformed into natural logarithms as we expect non-linearities in the relationships on the basis of theory and previous empirical work.

Data and method

Our dependent variable is the total amount of foreign exchange approved by SAFE during the project investment process. This includes pre-approved reinvested earnings and intra-company loans, plus in-kind investment up to the total authorised value of a given project, in addition to equity capital.[6] Forty-nine countries are host to Chinese ODI in our data set, of which 22 are members of the Organisation for Economic Co-operation and Development (OECD) and 27 are not (see Appendix).

Two statistical models were used to estimate Eq. (1): pooled ordinary least squares (POLS) and the random effects (RE) generalised least squares method. A fixed effects (FE) model cannot be used since Eq. (1) includes a time dummy variable. A Lagrangian multiplier (LM) test was conducted to identify whether POLS or RE furnished the better model. A value for the LM test that is significantly different from zero means that RE estimation is preferable to that of POLS.

To investigate heterogeneity within the data we employ a structural break framework. First, we investigate the impact of significant changes in the policy regime dating from 1992. These changes might influence the decision-making of investors across all the variables. Therefore, we divide the period into two phases: 1984–1991 and 1992–2001. Second, and as our discussion above has indicated, China's preference to invest in developing countries may indicate a different model of investment behaviour arising from state policy. To investigate this possibility we draw a distinction between developed and developing hosts using their OECD membership status.

Results and discussion

In preliminary regressions, two of the three alternative measures of host market size (growth in GDP and GDP per capita) never attained significance and were therefore not included in the final specification, this is reported in Table 29.6. The absolute host market size variable is retained to capture the market-seeking motive (Hypothesis 1a) and to act as a control (for market returns) in the estimation of the relationship between Chinese ODI and host country risk. The empirical results obtained from the POLS and the RE equations are similar. However, the large and significant LM value indicates in favour of the RE and therefore only the results from RE are discussed. Tables 29.4 and 29.5 present the correlation matrix and variance inflation factor (VIF) test results, which indicate that there are no general problems with the data.

We first discuss the results of the RE model for the main variables (column 2, Table 29.6). We find that host market characteristics (measured by absolute size of economy, *LGDP*), cultural proximity (*CP*) and policy liberalisation (*TD*92) are all significant and correctly signed. These findings support Hypotheses 1a, 5 and 6. By contrast, political risk (*LPOLI*) is found to be significant but with a sign contrary to expectation as predicted in Hypothesis 4. We find that natural resource endowments (*LORE*) and asset-seeking FDI (*LPATENT*) are both insignificant. Therefore, Hypotheses 2 and 3 are not supported. We now discuss each of these main findings in more detail.

Absolute host market size (*LGDP*) has a positive influence on Chinese FDI outflows, with a 1% rise in the variable increasing Chinese ODI by 0.35%. This indicates that market seeking was a key motive for Chinese ODI in the period under study (Hypothesis 1a). Cultural proximity (*CP*) is found to have a highly significant and positive effect on Chinese ODI (Hypothesis 5). This result suggests that the presence of ethnic Chinese people in the host country has promoted inward investment by Chinese firms. The policy liberalisation variable (*TD*92) is also positive and significant. This supports the argument that the qualitative changes in Chinese policy that took place in 1992, the year of Deng Xiaoping's visit to the southern provinces, did mark a significant step towards liberalisation in a number of ODI-related areas, and positively influenced the value of approved Chinese ODI for that year (Hypothesis 6). Our interpretation is that policy changes freed SOEs to invest abroad for reasons other than the promotion of exports; they were able to service foreign markets directly.

A major finding is that the coefficient on the index of political risk (*LPOLI*) indicates an increasing relationship between host country political risk levels and Chinese ODI. We find that a 1% increase in the host country risk index (i.e., a decrease in risk) is associated with a decrease in Chinese ODI of 1.8%. Thus we find no evidence to support Hypothesis 4. This runs counter to the normal findings for this variable, and requires discussion. In line with theory advanced in this paper, capital market imperfections and institutional factors in China may have induced a perverse attitude to risk, which contrasts with that found among

Table 29.4 Correlation matrix

	LFDI	LGDP	LORE	LPATENT	LPOLI	LERATE	LINF	LEXP	LIMP	LDIS	LINFDI
LFDI	1.0000										
LGDP	0.2188	1.0000									
LORE	0.0044	0.0274	1.0000								
LPATENT	0.0691	0.6684	0.1918	1.0000							
LPOLI	−0.0432	0.4851	0.1789	0.4618	1.0000						
LERATE	0.0745	−0.2606	−0.1282	−0.2237	−0.2760	1.0000					
LINF	−0.0019	−0.2879	0.1739	−0.1421	−0.4528	−0.0978	1.0000				
LEXP	0.4428	0.6565	−0.1286	0.3747	0.3516	0.0414	−0.3952	1.0000			
LIMP	0.3580	0.7282	0.0881	0.4587	0.4022	−0.1296	−0.3211	0.8545	1.0000		
LDIS	−0.1767	−0.0368	0.2335	−0.0844	−0.0098	−0.3316	0.1982	−0.4947	−0.4217	1.0000	
LINFDI	0.1826	−0.2559	−0.1238	−0.2632	0.1313	−0.0067	−0.1856	0.1248	−0.0073	0.0868	1.0000

Table 29.5 Variance inflation factor test

Variable	VIF	1/VIF
LGDP	7.12	0.140471
LORE	1.58	0.632445
LPATENT	2.18	0.458703
LPOLI	2.02	0.494854
CP	2.17	0.459989
TD92	1.05	0.948919
LERATE	1.47	0.682196
LINF	1.64	0.611576
LEXP	6.61	0.151327
LIMP	7.59	0.131727
LDIS	2.89	0.345584
LINFDI	2.43	0.410728

industrialised country firms. In other words, Chinese foreign investors seem not to perceive risk in the same way as industrialised country firms. There are a number of reasons Chinese firms may not behave in the conventional manner. First, Chinese state-owned firms may not be profit-maximisers, or may be maximising subject to government-led institutional influences. Second, the bulk of Chinese FDI is in developing countries (see Table 29.2), and these are precisely the countries that, as a group, record higher levels of political risk. Much of this investment may have been promoted by political affiliations and connections between China and the developing host country government concerned. The bargaining position of the Chinese government and Chinese firms may have been further strengthened *vis-à-vis* governments in those host countries that attract only modest amounts of investment from the industrialised nations. Third, China's political and ideological heritage in the modern era may have led to Chinese ODI being preferentially directed to fellow communist or ideologically similar countries, many of which also record higher levels of political risk. Fourth, home country embeddedness (i.e., in the current context, the knowledge of operating in an emerging country environment characterised by tight, centralised economic planning) may have provided Chinese firms with ownership advantages that enable them to mitigate the risk associated with operating in equivalent environments abroad. Fifth, Chinese firms may also be prepared to invest in countries generally avoided by industrialised country firms for ethical (for example, human rights) reasons, with Sudan being an example. Sixth, we should finally note that the relative inexperience of some Chinese firms concerning the establishment and management of large-scale operations abroad may have led to FDI projects being undertaken with insufficient due diligence and attention to associated risks (Wong and Chan, 2003; Ma and Andrews-Speed, 2006). Our finding for risk also highlights potential shortcomings in familiar measures of political risk, which are typically calculated from the point of view of industrialised country firms (World Bank, 2006). Such indices may need to be recalculated to better capture the perceptions of firms from emerging economies like China. Given that our regression specification controls for market returns, it does appear that Chinese behaviour towards conventionally measured host political risk differs from that of developed country investors. In line with the theory put forward earlier, the evidence suggests that capital market imperfections play a role.

Of the main variables we examine, we find no support for Hypothesis 3. The asset-seeking variable (*LPATENT*) in the RE model is insignificant, which suggests that Chinese firms have not been motivated to acquire strategic intellectual capital assets over the period under study.

We now discuss the results for our six control variables. The finding for exports (*LEXP*) is significant and correctly signed, supporting Hypothesis 9. By contrast, we find that infla- tion (*LINF*) and imports (*LIMP*) are significant but with signs contrary to expectation as predicted in Hypotheses 8 and 10. Our findings for the exchange rate (*LERATE*), geographic distance (*LDIS*) and market openness (*LINFDI*) are all insignificant. In short, we find no support for Hypotheses 7, 11 or 12.

The two trade-related variables, *LEXP* and *LIMP*, when viewed together, indicate that Chinese ODI has a conventional and an idiosyncratic nature. As expected, *LEXP* positively affects FDI, which is the conventional finding that FDI follows exports. It also supports the market-seeking motive (Hypothesis 9). This finding concurs with the view that one of the key motivations of Chinese investment has been to promote domestic exports. We find that *LIMP* is also a significant determinant of Chinese ODI but, against expectations (Hypothesis 10), has a negative effect. A 1% increase in China's imports from a host country is associated with a 0.25% reduction in Chinese ODI. This result could be generated by the practice of Chinese investors relocating production from China to other developing countries. In this account, imports of intermediate products to China for processing and re-export are reduced when Chinese firms relocate processing abroad through FDI. By value, most Chinese ODI is in the developing countries (see Table 29.2), and outward investment to these countries to circumvent trade barriers in third markets may have been a motive. It is possible that some Chinese ODI substitutes for intermediate imports to China.

The coefficient on inflation (*LINF*) is significant and positive, indicating that a 1% increase in the variable is associated with an increase in Chinese ODI of 0.19%. This is contrary to expectation (Hypothesis 8). Such an association might suggest that countries with moderate demand inflation are more attractive to Chinese investors. This link between the variables would be reasonable on the assumption that moderate demand inflation accompanies eco- nomic growth. It may also support the view that the investment decisions of Chinese firms are unusually tolerant of less-stable countries with respect to local economic conditions. This contrasts with the normal behaviour of profit-maximising industrialised country firms, and again suggests that Chinese firms may be influenced strongly by home country capital market failure and institutional factors.

Changes over time

In order to investigate whether Chinese FDI has changed in character over the period in question, we divide our data into two time periods around 1992. This procedure is borne out by the results in columns 3 and 4 of Table 29.6, which contrast sharply. These indicate that different locational determinants and motivations apply over time. Of our main variables, we find that market size (*LGDP*) and cultural proximity (*CP*) were important determinants of Chinese ODI for the period prior to 1991; in the later time period (post-1992), natural resource endowment (*LORE*), political risk (*LPOLI*), cultural proximity (*CP*) and policy liberalisation (*TD*92) are instead significant determinants. We also detect differences across time among the control variables. Before 1991, inflation (*LINF*), geographic distance (*LDIS*) and market openness (*LINFDI*) were important determinants of Chinese ODI, but post-1992 only the two trade-related variables, exports (*LEXP*) and imports (*LIMP*), are significant. These findings are in agreement with the earlier discussion that there has been a significant change in the foreign investment behaviour of Chinese enterprises over time, and that this is at least partly due to the variable policy regime, as suggested by our finding for the policy liberalisation variable (*TD*92), which indicates a surge in ODI for the year 1992. Arguably, this provides further substantiation for the notion that institutional factors have influenced patterns of Chinese ODI. We find that, over the period under study, Chinese firms have moved away from undertaking mainly market-seeking strategies in nearby foreign markets towards the securing of raw materials in riskier markets. These findings reinforce the view that the securement of natural resources has become an imperative in more recent years, in line with Chinese domestic growth, and that this investment has been directed to countries with higher levels of political risk (by Western standards). The fact that *LDIS* is significant and negative for the earlier period but not for the later one shows that geographic proximity of host countries to China was a positive influence only on early Chinese ODI. This development may be an outcome of the growing maturity of Chinese market-seeking investors and the increasing propensity for Chinese firms to engage in natural resources in more spatially distant markets.

The highly significant and positive coefficient for cultural proximity (*CP*) in both time periods (columns 3 and 4) supports our hypothesis that familiarity between populations is important in the flow of Chinese FDI. The facilitating role of the Chinese diaspora persists throughout the period under study, as expected, and suggests that relational assets indeed constitute an ownership advantage for Chinese firms when they invest in countries with a significant Chinese population. In the later period only, ODI is positively associated with Chinese exports, indicating that a significant part of FDI has followed export trade. These results are consistent with a 'stages approach' to internationalisation being applicable to Chinese ODI, and further research is required.

Host country level of development

Theory suggests that home country market imperfections can exert a significant impact on the decisions of foreign investors. It follows that Chinese government policy may have led to a distinctive pattern of outward FDI by host country. Here, we test this for developed and developing countries by comparing results for the subsamples of OECD and non-OECD countries in columns 5 and 6 of Table 29.6, respectively. Looking at the main variables, we see that market size (*LGDP*) is a significant determinant of Chinese ODI within the OECD group: Chinese investors preferentially seek out larger markets within the OECD countries. This is a conventional result, and captures that part of Chinese FDI that is market seeking. Also significant is the cultural proximity variable (*CP*). This variable appears to be capturing the tendency for Chinese firms to invest in OECD countries where a sizeable population of ethnic Chinese can be found. The highly significant and positive policy liberalisation variable for OECD countries alone (*TD*92 in column 5 of Table 29.6) again yields insight into the relatively undeveloped state of the FDI decision process by Chinese investors. The policy change in 1992 is associated with a large increase in FDI to the developed world. This implies that the decision to invest was previously tightly circumscribed by government, and this may be the reason a full and conventional pattern of significance is not observed. However, the pattern of investment flows to the developed economies fits with Chinese government priorities during liberalisation.

It is clear that Chinese ODI in non-OECD countries is not motivated by host market size, and that other motives must therefore be at play. Looking at the control variables, the positive significance of the *LEXP* variable applies to OECD and non-OECD countries. This suggests that Chinese ODI follows trade for both categories of country. The strong result for *LEXP* captures FDI that follows Chinese exports, and is an indicator of the role of host market

Table 29.6 Results for the determinants of Chinese ODI

	POLS (1)	REs (2)	REs 1984–91 (3)	REs 1992–01 (4)	REs OECD (5)	REs Non-OECD (6)
LGDP (H1a)	0.3463 (0.1249)***	0.3448 (0.1640)**	0.5085 (0.2787)*	0.2448 (0.2009)	0.6674 (0.3650)*	0.3472 (0.2238)
LORE (H2)	0.1713 (0.0742)**	0.1447 (0.1057)	0.1039 (0.1654)	0.2253 (0.1206)*	−0.0138 (0.3906)	0.1820 (0.1144)
LPATENT (H3)	0.0223 (0.0309)	0.0363 (0.0359)	0.0794 (0.0605)	0.0516 (0.0439)	0.0752 (0.0773)	0.0262 (0.0447)
LPOLI (H4)	2.4762 (0.5822)***	1.7997 (0.6974)**	0.7347 (1.0846)	2.6308 (0.9750)***	1.8973 (1.8807)	1.4560 (0.8903)
CP (H5)	1.4779 (0.2588)***	1.4929 (0.4276)***	1.4520 (0.6059)**	1.5338 (0.4634)***	2.0464 (0.8415)**	0.8414 (0.6563)
TD92 (H6)	0.6595 (0.2698)**	0.6961 (0.2534)***		0.8033 (0.3002)***	0.9489 (0.3178)***	0.4104 (0.4021)
LERATE (H7)	0.0471 (0.0337)	0.0688 (0.0463)	0.1032 (0.0638)	0.0246 (0.0618)	0.2319 (0.1866)	0.0142 (0.0540)
LINF (H8)	0.2406 (0.0628)***	0.1891 (0.0734)**	0.4664 (0.1167)***	0.1323 (0.0896)	0.3487 (0.1579)**	0.1320 (0.0914)
LEXP (H9)	0.6934 (0.1084)***	0.6153 (0.1291)***	0.2731 (0.2094)	0.8275 (0.1803)***	0.4062 (0.2053)**	0.8375 (0.1964)***
LIMP (H10)	0.2601 (0.0931)***	0.2544 (0.1027)**	0.3087 (0.2061)	0.3098 (0.1204)**	0.1914 (0.1898)	0.3677 (0.1374)***
LDIS (H11)	0.1905 (0.2035)	0.1554 (0.2972)	0.9266 (0.4794)*	0.2885 (0.3400)	0.7452 (0.7360)	0.0171 (0.4259)
LINFDI (H12)	0.0927 (0.0886)	0.0510 (0.1244)	0.3294 (0.1562)**	0.0589 (0.0439)	0.1181 (0.2480)	0.1218 (0.1546)
N	402	402	116	286	198	204
LM test	$\chi^2(1) = 15.43$***					
Adj. R²	0.3642	0.6019	0.6142	0.6024	0.5763	0.6737

Notes: Standard errors are in parentheses. ***, **, and * indicate that the coefficient is significant at the 1, 5 and 10% levels, respectively.

demand. As we would expect from the argument above concerning the mechanism through which the Chinese import variable (*LIMP*) associates with Chinese ODI, it is the non-OECD group of hosts that records a negative effect. These results indicate that it is specifically those developing countries from which China imports least to which Chinese investors have been attracted. Inflation (*LINF*) is significant for OECD countries only. This suggests that moderate inflation is a characteristic of those buoyant markets that attracted Chinese firms.

One of the most compelling earlier findings – that our main variable political risk (*LPOLI*) is significant – is lost in both estimations (5) and (6). From this, we infer that, while Chinese ODI is associated with higher levels of host country political risk, the difference in risk in the data is primarily that between developed and developing countries, rather than within these two country groupings. The apparent preference for less developed and risky host countries compared with developed hosts is consistent with our argument on the lower cost of capital enjoyed by SOEs, as well as with the relatively unsophisticated country risk evaluation processes of Chinese investors. This result supports our theoretical contention that capital market imperfections in China have been crucial to outward FDI over the period in question.

Conclusions

This paper is one of the first attempts to formally model Chinese ODI. Our motivation is to test the extent to which the mainstream theory that explains industrialised country FDI is applicable to emerging country contexts, and whether special explanations nested within the general theory are needed. We develop a theoretical framework that draws on this body of theory but which allows for conventional and novel hypotheses to be tested. This is done within a well-specified model using previously unexamined official data on Chinese ODI and by employing a wide range of main and control variables. We find that Chinese ODI has a conventional and an idiosyncratic dimension.

In terms of our main variables, we find a conventional result for market size. We infer from the significant role played by host country natural resource endowments that the institutional environment has strongly shaped Chinese ODI, leading to significant natural resources-seeking FDI. We also find that policy liberalisation has had a positive influence in stimulating Chinese ODI. This is further evidence of a distinctive explanation, to the extent that home country institutions have played a significant role in determining the flow and direction (OECD compared with non-OECD) of Chinese ODI. Viewed together, these findings are in agreement with the well-publicised expansion of natural resources-seeking activities of Chinese MNEs in recent years, especially to the industrialised countries, in response primarily to domestic economic imperatives (Taylor, 2002; Deng, 2003, 2004). Although there are indications that Chinese firms have become increasingly acquisitive in recent years, we find that, prior to 2001 (when our data end), ODI was not driven by the motive to acquire strategic assets. Arguably, the asset-seeking hypothesis is more likely to be supported on data for more recent years: for example, as China's 'go global' policy becomes fully implemented and acted upon by firms.

Cultural proximity is found to be a significant factor, indicating that reduced transaction costs and network effects are important in attracting Chinese investors, and that relational assets constitute a special ownership advantage, even for state-owned firms. This supports a role for reduced psychic distance in explaining Chinese ODI. When we examine differences over time, we find that market size, geographic proximity, inflation and market openness are important locational determinants for the period 1984 to 1991, with the distance variable suggesting that the Chinese diaspora and market familiarity have positively influenced the destination of earlier

Chinese investment outflows. However, the finding that the cultural proximity variable does not change over time suggests that Chinese ODI is still in an early stage of development, and that more familiar cultures in host countries continue to help promote Chinese inward investment. These findings warrant further investigation on a longer time series of data.

More challenging is the unprecedented finding that Chinese ODI is attracted, rather than deterred, by political risk (as measured conventionally and with market returns controlled for by market size). This suggests that Chinese firms do not perceive or behave towards risk in the same way as do industrialised country firms. In accordance with our theory, we attribute this to the low cost of capital that Chinese firms (for the most part SOEs) enjoy as a consequence of home country capital market imperfections. Indeed, state ownership can be considered a firm-specific advantage for many Chinese MNEs in this context (Ding, 2000). However, the experience of operating in a highly regulated and controlled domestic environment (i.e., home-country embeddedness) may also be relevant. This experience may have equipped Chinese MNEs with the special ownership advantages needed to be competitive in other emerging economies. Moreover, further augmentation of the ownership advantages of Chinese firms is likely to occur as Chinese MNEs become more experienced internationally (Deng, 2004) and as the Chinese government and its agencies continue to provide political, financial and other support, as implied by our discussion of institution-based theory.

Our study of Chinese outward FDI offers the opportunity to examine how a country with distinctive home country institutions fits with the emerging body of theoretical work on the 'institution-based view of strategy'. Chinese firms that invest abroad have to straddle environments, institutions and rules that differ probably more than for any other outward-investing country in the world. In this paper we have expected contrasts with the conventional model, and we have found evidence for these. Theorising on the strategy of firms, especially those from emerging countries, needs to pay greater attention to the influence of home country institutions. It is arguable that Chinese firms seek foreign investment opportunities in environments that resemble their home environment. Further, it is tenable that Chinese investors are unconstrained by the ethical and governance obligations that are normally expected of Western MNEs today. If so, they may resemble outward investors from the West in an earlier period, and future changes in Chinese firms' behaviour and location decisions can be envisaged, contingent upon the evolution of institutions and rules of the game at home. For the present, Chinese outward investors clearly present marked contrasts from the conventional model in key respects.

There are implications of this research for our understanding of the outward FDI strategies of firms from other emerging markets, such as the other 'BRICs' (Brazil, Russia and India). First, state direction over firms (whether formal or informal) is likely to generate a signature in the locational pattern of outward investment that would not be predicted by the general theory of FDI, which assumes that firms are profit maximisers. The second implication is that liberalisation is a very powerful instrument for emerging economies. This does not mean trade liberalisation, but includes the whole range of internal liberalisations possible for countries with a significant state sector or dominant (private or public) firms, or both. The behaviour of domestic firms changes dramatically once competition, or its prospect, is introduced. Firms that performed a social role, such as the SOEs, once divested of this, are able to seek growth. However, China remains distinctive from other emerging economies in that many of its MNEs remain in state hands, even though corp-oratised in order to focus on commercial objectives. State direction means that these firms still align their operations, whether at home or abroad, with the five-year plans and national imperatives. This is a model that is not replicated, in any general way, in any of the other leading emerging economies.

With respect to further work, an issue requiring investigation, possibly of a qualitative nature, is whether and how Chinese investors are influenced (as are industrialised country firms) by concerns of due diligence, risk evaluation and ethical considerations in host countries. Similarly, how patterns of FDI are affected by formal and informal political links between China and other countries (i.e. the supranational institutional framework) also merits further examination.

Acknowledgements

We thank Mark Casson for important comments, Tim Rose for his supportive work, and the referees and Focused Issue editors for their insightful and helpful comments.

Notes

1 In this paper, we take the standard UNCTAD definition of FDI as being an investment involving a long-term relationship and reflecting a lasting interest and control by a firm in an enterprise resident in a foreign country (UNCTAD, 2005a). FDI normally has three components: (1) equity capital (the purchase of shares in the foreign enterprise); (2) reinvested earnings (those earnings not distributed as dividends by foreign affiliates or remitted to the investor enterprise); and (3) intra-company loans or debt transactions (borrowing and lending between parent and foreign affiliate enterprises) (UNCTAD, 2005a).
2 In this study, the terms 'China' and 'Mainland China' are used interchangeably to refer to the People's Republic of China (PRC). For our purposes, the PRC excludes the special autonomous regions of Hong Kong and Macau, unless specifically stated. The Republic of China (Taiwan) is treated as a separate economy. Regions with disputed borders (e.g., the Spratly Islands) are excluded from our definition of the PRC.
3 Although it postdates the time frame of the current study, the establishment of a special state fund (valued by some at around US$15bn) available to qualifying Chinese firms for the acquisition of foreign brands and companies underscores these points (Swystun *et al.*, 2005).
4 We are grateful to one of the reviewers for this point.
5 Overseas Chinese are defined by Poston *et al.* (1994: 633) as 'all Chinese living outside mainland China and Taiwan, including *Huaqiao* (Chinese citizens residing abroad), *Huaren* (naturalized citizens of Chinese descent) and *Huayi* (descendants of Chinese parents)'.
6 This also reflects the regulatory framework of Chinese ODI over the majority of the period under study. Until quite recently, Chinese firms were obliged to repatriate overseas earnings to financial authorities at home, while the ability to make inter-company loans was highly restricted under China's foreign exchange controls.

References

Aggarwal, R. and Agmon, T. (1990) 'The international success of developing country firms: role of government-directed comparative advantage', *Management International Review* **30**(2): 163–80.
Antkiewicz, A. and Whalley, J. (2006) 'Recent Chinese buyout activities and the implications for global architecture', National Bureau of Economic Research (NBER) Working Paper 12072, NBER, Cambridge, MA.
Braeutigam, D. (2003) 'Close encounters: Chinese business networks as industrial catalysts in Sub-Saharan Africa', *African Affairs* **102**(408): 447–67.
Buckley, P.J. (2004a) 'Asian network firms: an analytical framework', *Asia Pacific Business Review* **10**(3/4): 254–71.
Buckley, P.J. (2004b) 'The role of China in the global strategy of multinational enterprises', *Journal of Chinese Economic and Business Studies* **2**(1): 1–25.
Buckley, P.J. and Casson, M. (1976) *The Future of the Multinational Enterprise*, Macmillan: London.

Buckley, P.J. and Casson, M. (1981) 'The optimal timing of a foreign direct investment', *Economic Journal* **91**(361): 75–87.

Buckley, P.J. and Casson, M. (1999) 'A Theory of International Operations', in P.J. Buckley and P.N. Ghauri (eds.) *The Internationalization Process of the Firm: a Reader*, 2nd edn, International Business Thomson: London, pp: 55–60.

Buckley, P.J., Clegg, L.J. and Wang, C. (2002) 'The impact of inward FDI on the performance of Chinese manufacturing firms', *Journal of International Business Studies* **33**(4): 637–55.

Buckley, P.J., Cross, A.R., Tan, H., Voss, H. and Liu, X. (2006) 'An investigation of recent trends in Chinese outward direct investment and some implications for theory', Centre for International Business University of Leeds Working Paper.

Business Week (2004) 'Big Blue's Bold Step into China', 20 December: 33–4.

Cai, K.G. (1999) 'Outward foreign direct investment: a novel dimension of China's integration into the regional and global economy', *China Quarterly* **160** (December): 856–80.

Chakrabarti, A. (2001) 'The determinants of foreign direct investments: sensitivity analyses of cross-country regressions', *Kyklos* **54**(1): 89–114.

Chen, X., Yung, R.L. and Zhang, B. (2002) *China Manufacturing*, BNP Paribas Peregrine Economics/ Sector Update April 2002.

Child, J. and Pleister, H. (2003) 'Governance and management in China's private sector', *Management International* **7**(3): 13–24.

Child, J. and Rodrigues, S.B. (2005) 'The internationalization of Chinese firms: a case for theoretical extension?' *Management and Organization Review* **1**(3): 381–410.

Deng, P. (2003) 'Foreign direct investment by transnationals from emerging countries: the case of China', *Journal of Leadership and Organizational Studies* **10**(2): 113–24.

Deng, P. (2004) 'Outward investment by Chinese MNCs: motivations and implications', *Business Horizons* **47**(3): 8–16.

Dicken, P. (2003) *Global Shift: Reshaping the Global Economic Map in the 21st Century*, 4th edn, Sage: London.

Ding, X.L. (2000) 'Informal privatization through internationalization: the rise of *nomenklatura* capitalism in China's offshore business', *British Journal of Political Science* **30**(1): 121–46.

Dunning, J.H. (1977) 'Trade, Location of Economic Activity and the MNE: A Search for an Eclectic Approach', in B. Ohlin, P.O. Hesselborn and P.M. Wijkmon (eds.) *The International Location of Economic Activity*, Macmillan: London, pp: 395–418.

Dunning, J.H. (1993) *Multinational Enterprises and the Global Economy*, Addison-Wesley: Wokingham.

Dunning, J.H. (2001) 'The eclectic (OLI) paradigm of international production: past, present and future', *International Journal of the Economics of Business* **8**(2): 173–90.

Dunning, J.H. (2002) 'Relational Assets, Networks, and International Business Activities', in F.J. Contractor and P. Lorange (eds.) *Cooperative Strategies and Alliances*, Pergamon: Amsterdam, pp: 569–93.

Dunning, J.H. (2006) 'Comment on dragon multinationals: new players in 21st century globalization', *Asia Pacific Journal of Management* **23**(2): 139–41.

Dunning, J.H., van Hoesel, R. and Narula, R. (1998) 'Third World Multinationals Revisited: New Developments and Theoretical Implications', in J.H. Dunning (ed.) *Globalization, Trade and Foreign Direct Investment*, Elsevier: Amsterdam and Oxford, pp: 255–85.

Erdener, C. and Shapiro, D.M. (2005) 'The internationalization of Chinese family enterprises and Dunning's eclectic MNE paradigm', *Management and Organization Review* **1**(3): 411–36.

Erramilli, M.K., Srivastava, R. and Kim, S.-S. (1999) 'Internationalization theory and Korean multinationals', *Asia Pacific Journal of Management* **16**(1): 29–45.

Ferrantino, M.J. (1992) 'Transaction costs and the expansion of third-world multinationals', *Economic Letters* **38**(4): 451–56.

Guo, H. (1984) 'On Establishment of Joint Ventures Abroad', *Almanac of China's Foreign Economic Relations and Trade*, Ministry of Commerce: Beijing, pp: 652–4.

Hall, T. (2004) 'Controlling for risk: an analysis of China's system of foreign exchange and exchange rate management', *Columbia Journal of Asian Law* **17**(2): 433–81.

Heenan, D.A. and Keegan, W.J. (1979) 'The rise of third world multinationals', *Harvard Business Review* **57**(1): 101–9.

Henley, J., Kirkpatrick, C. and Wilde, G. (1999) 'Foreign direct investment in China: recent trends and current policy issues', *The World Economy* **22**(2): 223–43.

International Monetary Fund (IMF) (2005) *World Economic Outlook Database*, www.imf.org/external/pubs/ft/weo/2005/01/data/dbcsubm.cfm. (accessed 26 September 2006).

Johanson, J. and Vahlne, J.-E. (1977) 'The internationalization process of the firm: a model of knowledge development and increasing foreign market commitments', *Journal of International Business Studies* **8**(1): 23–32.

Kent, R.B. (2003) 'A Diaspora of Chinese Settlement in Latin America and the Caribbean', in L.J.C. Ma and C. Cartier (eds.) *The Chinese Diaspora: Space, Place, Mobility, and Identity*, Rowman & Littlefield: Lanham, pp: 117–38.

Kohlhagen, S.W. (1977) 'The Effects of Exchange-Rate Adjustments on International Investment: Comment', in P.B. Clark, D.E. Logue and R. Sweeney (eds.) *The Effects of Exchange Rate Adjustments*, US Government Printing Office: Washington, DC, pp: 194–7.

Lall, S. and Albaladejo, M. (2004) 'China's competitive performance: a threat to East Asian manufactured exports?' *World Development* **32**(9): 1441–6.

Lardy, N.R. (1998) *China's Unfinished Economic Revolution*, Brookings Institution: Washington, DC.

Lau, H.-F. (1992) 'Internationalization, internalization, or a new theory for small, low-technology multinational enterprise?' *European Journal of Marketing* **26**(10): 17–31.

Lau, H.-F. (2003) 'Industry evolution and internationalization processes of firms from a newly industrialized economy', *Journal of Business Research* **56**(10): 847–52.

Lawrence, S.V. (2002) 'Going global', *Far Eastern Economic Review* **165**(12): 32.

Lecraw, D.J. (1977) 'Direct investment by firms from less developed countries', *Oxford Economic Papers* **29**(3): 442–57.

Li, P.P. (2003) 'Toward a geocentric theory of multinational evolution: the implications from the Asian MNEs as latecomers', *Asia Pacific Journal of Management* **20**(2): 217–42.

Lim, D. (1983) 'Fiscal incentives and direct investment in less developed countries', *Journal of Development Studies* **19**(2): 207–12.

Liu, H. and Li, K. (2002) 'Strategic implications of emerging Chinese multinationals: the Haier case study', *European Management Journal* **20**(6): 699–706.

Liu, L. (2005) *China's Industrial Policies and the Global Business Revolution: The Case of the Domestic Appliance Industry*, RoutledgeCurzon: London.

Logue, D.E. and Willet, T.D. (1977) 'The Effects of Exchange-Rate Adjustments on International Investment', in P.B. Clark, D.E. Logue and R. Sweeney (eds.) *The Effects of Exchange Rate Adjustments*, US Government Printing Office: Washington, DC, pp: 137–50.

Loungani, P., Mody, A. and Razin, A. (2002) 'The global disconnect: the role of transactional distance and scale economies in gravity equations', *Scottish Journal of Political Economy* **49**(5): 526–43.

Luo, Y. (1997) 'Guanxi: principles, philosophies, and implications', *Human Systems Management* **16**(1): 43–51.

Ma, L.J.C. (2003) 'Space, Place, and Transnationalism in the Chinese Diaspora', in L.J.C. Ma and C. Cartier (eds.) *The Chinese Diaspora: Space, Place, Mobility, and Identity*, Rowman & Littlefield: Lanham, pp: 1–4.

Ma, X. and Andrews-Speed, P. (2006) 'The overseas activities of China's national oil companies: rationale and outlook', *Minerals and Energy* **21** (1): 17–30.

Meyer, K.E. and Nguyen, H.V. (2005) 'Foreign investment strategies and sub-national institutions in emerging markets: evidence from Vietnam', *Journal of Management Studies* **42**(1): 63–93.

MOFCOM (various years) *Almanac of China's Foreign Relations and Trade*, Ministry of Commerce (MOFCOM): Beijing.

MOFCOM (2004) *China Commerce Yearbook* [Zhongguo shang-wu nianjian] Ministry of Commerce (MOFCOM): Beijing.

National Bureau of Statistics (2005) *China Statistical Yearbook 2005*, China Statistics Press: Beijing.

Ng, L.F.Y. and Tuan, C. (2002) 'Building a favourable investment environment: evidence for the facilitation of FDI in China', *The World Economy* **25**(8): 1095–114.

North, D.C. (1990) *Institutions, Institutional Change and Economic Performance*, Cambridge University Press: Cambridge.

Ohio University (2006) *Distribution of the Ethnic Chinese Population Around the World*, University Libraries, Ohio University http://cicdatabank.library.ohiou.edu/opac/population.php. (accessed 17 May 2006).

Peng, M.W. (2002) 'Towards an institution-based view of business strategy', *Asia Pacific Journal of Management* **19**(2/3): 251–67.

Political Risk Services (PRS) (2005) *International Country Risk Guide* (ICRG), www.prsgroup.com/ICRG.aspx (accessed April 2005).

Poston Jr, D.L., Mao, M.X. and Yi, M.-Y. (1994) 'The global distribution of overseas Chinese around 1990', *Population and Development Review* **20**(3): 631–45.

Pradhan, J.P. (2003) 'Outward foreign direct investment from India: recent trends and patterns', Jawaharlal Nehru University Working Paper Series, Jawaharlal Nehru University, New Delhi.

Roberts, I. and Tyers, R. (2003) 'China's exchange rate policy: the case for greater flexibility', *Asian Economic Journal* **17**(2): 155–84.

Rowen, H.S. (2003) 'Will China take over world manufacturing?' *The International Economy* **17**(1): 72.

Sauvant, K. (2005) 'New sources of FDI: The BRICs. Outward FDI from Brazil, Russia, India and China', *Journal of World Investment and Trade* **6**(October): 639–709.

Scott, W.R. (2002) 'The Changing World of Chinese Enterprises: An Institutional Perspective', in A.S. Tsui and C.-M. Lau (eds.) *Management of Enterprises in the People's Republic of China* Kluwer Academic Press: Boston, pp: 59–78.

Scott-Green, S. and Clegg, L.J. (1999) 'The determinants of new FDI capital flows into the EC: a statistical comparison of the USA and Japan', *Journal of Common Market Studies* **37**(4): 597–616.

Sikorski, D. and Menkhoff, T. (2000) 'Internationalisation of Asian business', *Singapore Management Review* **22**(1): 1–17.

Standifird, S.S. and Marshall, R.S. (2000) 'The transaction cost advantage of *guanxi*-based business practices', *Journal of World Business* **35**(1): 21–42.

Steinfeld, E.S. (1998) *Forging Reform in China: The Fate of State-Owned Industry*, Cambridge University Press: Cambridge.

Stevens, G.V.G. (1993) 'Exchange rates and foreign direct investment: a note', International Finance Discussion Papers, April, No. 444, Board of Governors of the Federal Reserve System, Washington, DC.

Sung, Y.-W. (1996) 'Chinese outward investment in Hong Kong: trends, prospects and policy implications', OECD Development Centre Technical Papers, No. 113, Organisation for Economic Cooperation and Development, Paris.

Swystun, J., Burt, F. and Ly, A. (2005) *The Strategy for Chinese Brands: Part 1 – The Perception Challenge*, [www document] http://www.interbrand.com. (accessed 11 January 2006), Interbrand White Paper, Interbrand, New York.

Taylor, R. (2002) 'Globalization strategies of Chinese companies: current developments and future prospects', *Asian Business and Management* **1** (2): 209–25.

Tong, S.Y. (2003) 'Ethnic Chinese networking in cross-border investment: the impact of economic and institutional development', Hong Kong Institute of Economics and Business Strategy (HIEBS) Working Paper, University of Hong Kong, Hong Kong.

Tsai, K.S. (2002) *Back-Alley Banking: Private Entrepreneurs in China*, Cornell University Press: Ithaca.

UNCTAD (1998) *World Investment Report 1998: Trends and Determinants*, United Nations: New York and Geneva.

UNCTAD (2003) *World Investment Report 2003: FDI Policies for Development: National and International Perspectives*, United Nations: New York and Geneva.

UNCTAD (2005a) *World Investment Report 2005: Transnational Corporations and the Internationalization of R&D*, United Nations: New York and Geneva.

UNCTAD (2005b) *Prospects for Foreign Direct Investment and the Strategies of Transnational Corporations, 2005–2008*, United Nations: New York and Geneva.

UNCTAD (2006) 'FDI/TNC database', http://stats.unctad.org/fdi (accessed 09 May 2006).

UN Statistics Division (2006) *UN Demographic Yearbook Special Census Topics*, [preliminary release 27 March 2006] http://unstats.un.org/unsd/demographic/products/dyb/dybcens.htm (accessed 17 May 2006).

Villela, A.V. (1983) 'Transnationals from Brazil', in S. Lall (ed.) *The New Transnationals: The Spread of Third World Transnationals*, John Wiley: Chichester, pp: 220–49.

Wang, M.Y. (2002) 'The motivations behind Chinese government-initiated industrial investments overseas', *Pacific Affairs* **75**(2): 187–206.

Warner, M., Hong, N.S. and Xu, X. (2004) 'Late development experience and the evolution of transnational firms in the People's Republic of China', *Asia Pacific Business Review* **10**(3/4): 324–45.

Wells, L.T. (1983) *Third World Multinationals: The Rise of Foreign Investments from Developing Countries*, MIT Press: Cambridge, MA.

Wong, J. and Chan, S. (2003) 'China's outward direct investment: expanding worldwide', *China: An International Journal* **1**(2): 273–301.

World Bank (2005) *World Development Indicators* (WDI) April 2005, ESDS International, (MIMAS) University of Manchester.

World Bank (2006) *Indicators of Governance and Institutional Quality*, http://siteresources.worldbank.org/INTLAWJUSTINST/Resources/IndicatorsGovernanceandInstitutionalQuality.pdf (accessed 16 January 2006).

World Intellectual Property Organisation (2006) 'Who files the most PCT patent applications?', WIPO world: The Hague.

Wu, F. and Sia, Y.H. (2002) 'China's rising investment in Southeast Asia: trends and outlook', *Journal of Asian Business* **18**(2): 41–61.

Wu, H.-L. and Chen, C.-H. (2001) 'An assessment of outward foreign direct investment from China's transitional economy', *Europe-Asia Studies* **53**(8): 1235–54.

Wright, M., Filatotchev, I., Hoskisson, R.E. and Peng, M.W. (2005) 'Strategy research in emerging economies: challenging the conventional wisdom', *Journal of Management Studies* **42**(1): 1–33.

Ye, G. (1992) 'Chinese transnational corporations', *Transnational Corporations* **1**(2): 125–33.

Yeung, H.W.-C. (1998) 'The political economy of transnational corporations: a study of the regionalization of Singaporean firms', *Political Geography* **17**(4): 389–416.

Yeung, H.W.-C. (1999) 'The internationalisation of ethnics Chinese business firms from Southeast Asia: strategies, processes and competitive advantages', *International Journal of Urban and Regional Research* **23**(1): 88–102.

Yu, A., Chao, H. and Dorf, M. (2005) 'Outbound investments by Chinese companies: the Chinese government approval regime', Topics in Chinese Law, O'Melveny&Myers Research Report, November 2005.

Zhan, J.X. (1995) 'Transnationalization and outward investment: the case of Chinese firms', *Transnational Corporations* **4**(3): 67–100.

Zhang, Y. (2003) *China's Emerging Global Businesses: Political Economy and Institutional Investigations*, Palgrave Macmillan: Basingstoke.

Zin, R.H.M. (1999) 'Malaysian reverse investments: trends and strategies', *Asia Pacific Journal of Management* **16**(3): 469–96.

Appendix

Countries host to Chinese ODI in the data set

OECD countries
Australia, Austria, Canada, Czech Republic, Denmark, Finland, France, Germany, Greece, Hungary, Italy, Japan, Mexico, Netherlands, New Zealand, Poland, Portugal, South Korea, Spain, Sweden, United Kingdom, United States.

Non-OECD countries
Algeria, Argentina, Armenia, Brazil, Bulgaria, Chile, Colombia, Croatia, Cyprus, Ecuador, Egypt, Ghana, Hong Kong SAR, India, Indonesia, Israel, Malaysia, Morocco, Nigeria, Philippines, Russia, Singapore, South Africa, Sudan, Thailand, Ukraine, Venezuela.

30 Market driving multinationals and their global sourcing network*

Pervez N. Ghauri, Veronika Tarnovskaya and Ulf Elg

Introduction

The market driving approach is gaining increasing attention in marketing and management literature (Harris and Cai, 2002; Jaworski *et al.*, 2000; Kumar *et al.*, 2000; Narver *et al.*, 2004; Tuominen *et al.*, 2004). It developed as a reaction to the more general research on market orientation that has dominated the marketing area for almost 20 years (Greenley, 1995; Homburg and Pflesser, 2000; Kohli and Jaworski, 1990; Matsuno and Mentzer, 2000; Narver and Slater, 1990). The market orientation approach was claimed to promote a view of firms as actors that passively respond to current market trends and existing customer preferences (Christensen and Bower, 1996; Kumar, 1997; Slater and Narver, 1998).

Among other things, market driving firms are characterized by an ability to develop unique internal business processes for the radically new value propositions to customers (Kumar *et al.*, 2000). In order to create a leap in customer value, they shape the market structure and behaviours of different market actors (Jaworski *et al.*, 2000). A market driving approach usually also requires that the firm is innovative in restructuring the activities in the value chain. Previous studies further indicate that strong supplier relationships are important (Martin and Grbac, 2003; Tuominen *et al.*, 2004). However, we still need a more detailed insight into how supplier relationships can be developed in order to provide support for the market driving strategy. The reconfiguration of roles and relationships in the value chain is needed to match the capabilities of different actors and the customer value opportunities in the best possible way (Carrillat *et al.*, 2004).

The importance of close partnerships with actors in the value chain also suggests a link between market driving research and the network perspective (Elg, 2007). The theoretical view in the network approach is that firms develop long-lasting relationships with other actors in the market (such as suppliers, distributors, etc.) thereby using each other's resources for a joint competitive position (Håkansson and Snehota, 1995). Having its origin in social network and behavioural theory, the approach is now extensively used in the fields of business-to-business marketing (Crespin-Mazet and Ghauri, 2007; Alajoutsijarvi *et al.*, 2001; Ghauri, 1999), in internationalisation studies (Buckley and Ghauri, 1999; Chetty and Blankenburg Holm, 2000; Ghauri and Fang, 2001) and in MNE–government relationships (Hadjikhani *et al.*, 2008). The network approach also stresses the critical role of supplier relationships and purchasing (Gadde and Håkansson, 2001). It is particularly relevant to our study as we combine the buyer–supplier relationships with the internationalisation strategies.

*Reprinted with permission from Emerald Publishing group. Ghauri, P.N., V. Tarnovskaya & U. Elg, (2008) "Market driving multinationals and their global sourcing networks", International Marketing Review, 25(5): 504–519.

The concept of a market driving supplier strategy is defined as a proactive approach of a firm to its supplier relationships, with the goal of mobilizing suppliers in creating a leap in customer value, and in influencing the customers' behaviour and the market structure in general. The market driving supplier strategy is also expected to change the suppliers' roles in the value chain in a way that creates a better fit with the firm's value proposition to customers, as well as a change in the suppliers' competitive positions. We will especially discuss how such supplier relationships can be developed and maintained, based on how central actors carry out different types of activities and the exchange of a number of critical resources.

Our aim is therefore to contribute to the integration of the market driving approach and the network perspective by investigating how the reconfiguration of relationships and roles in the supplier network supports the market driving strategy, and by identifying critical mechanisms that stimulate the supplier development. We have conducted a case study of IKEA's corporate activities in order to develop a strong supplier base, as well as relationships to four specific suppliers representing different stages of development and types of relationships. The literature often refers to IKEA as a good example of a market driving firm (Carrillat *et al.*, 2004; Jaworski *et al.*, 2000; Kumar, 1997; Kumar *et al.*, 2000).

Theoretical background

Since the late 1980s, market orientation (Kohli and Jaworski, 1990; Narver and Slater, 1990) has been a central research area (Stoelhorst and van Raaij Erik, 2004). Numerous studies have investigated various aspects of market orientation (Cadogan *et al.*, 1999; Hooley *et al.*, 2000; Jaworski and Kohli, 1993; Liu *et al.*, 2003; Pitt *et al.*, 1996; Ruekert, 1992). Some authors have also stressed the importance of inter-firm relationships to market orientation in general, showing that inter-firm cooperation can influence market orientation (Elg, 2007; Grunert *et al.*, 2005; Langerak, 2001; Siguaw *et al.*, 1998). As already mentioned, the market orientation perspective has also been criticized (Christensen and Bower, 1996; Day, 1999; Slater and Narver, 1998), and a market driving, proactive strategy has been presented (Jaworski *et al.*, 2000; Kumar, 1997; Kumar *et al.*, 2000; Narver *et al.*, 2004). According to Kumar *et al.* (2000), successful market driving firms have developed a unique internal business system that offers customers a leap in the value proposition in terms of, for example, new price points or a superior service level. Jaworski *et al.* (2000) stress the external activities, arguing that a market driving firm can reshape the value chain through eliminating players (deconstruction), adding players (construction) or by changing their functions (re-construction). Market driving firms may also shape the behaviour of key actors such as customers or competitors by educating them or influencing their incentives and preferences.

Kumar *et al.* (2000) claim that market driving firms have introduced innovative distribution and channel management practices in their industries. Harris and Cai (2002) studied de Beers in China, and showed how cooperative retailer-supplier relationships were a key element in the firm's success. This is remarkable when considering that cultural differences make the development of buyer–supplier relationships especially challenging (Mathyssens and Faes, 2006). Tuominen *et al.* (2004) also found that a market driving approach requires collaborative learning and close partnership with important actors in the vertical chain. This finding is confirmed by Berghman *et al.* (2006), they argue that in business-to-business markets, collaboration and partnership with leading customers constitute a critical supply chain/network competence of a market driving firm. For example, product development, preserving quality in the value chain, human resource and category management are critical parts of the interactions within the supply chain (Fernie and Leigh, 1998; Gadde and Håkansson, 2001; Saunders, 1997).

We argue that a market driving supplier strategy is based on collaborative relationships with suppliers that include different mechanisms required to drive these relationships, as well as different implications for the involved parties. The outcome for suppliers in terms of the perceived value is also important to consider because they indirectly affect the customer value. Furthermore, companies regarded as market driving appear to be almost exclusively global or at least international firms, but this dimension is not discussed explicitly in the literature. In addition, the general understanding of the nature of global supplier relationships is still limited and there is a need of further research (Quintens *et al.*, 2006). We therefore aim to contribute further by discussing market driving retailer–supplier relationships from an international perspective.

Considering the business-to-business nature of this study, we use the network approach. The network emerged out of industrial marketing and purchasing group's studies in industrial marketing (Ghauri, 1999). This view was further developed from a dyadic relationship (interaction approach) to a multi-actor (network) relationship. The network approach has also been used in previous studies to analyse reciprocal relationships between suppliers and retailers (Håkansson and Snehota, 1995), international business exchange and the specific nature of relationships between buyers and suppliers from culturally different markets (Ghauri and Holstius, 1996). The logic and dynamics of network relationships can be further understood by identifying the critical actors, activities and resources and by analysing their role within the exchange (Cova and Salle, 2000). The actor dimension refers to the role and identity of the interacting actors in relation to each other. Activities refer to the critical tasks that need to be performed and coordinated for the exchange to provide additional values. The resource dimension focuses on the critical resources that are exchanged. By combining critical resources, the parties gain additional values and advantages.

As Figure 30.1 shows, we adopt these tenets of the network approach and intend to integrate them with the market driving approach in analysing international market driving buyer–supplier

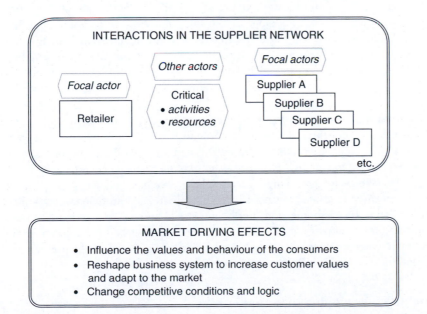

Figure 30.1 A model based upon market driving and networking factors.

relationships. The model introduced above should be regarded as a preliminary framework intended to guide our empirical study.

Research method

The research is based on in-depth case-studies of IKEA and its four suppliers at corporate level and its local market activities in Russia and Poland. With its global supply base of 1,300 suppliers in more than 50 countries, IKEA represents a typical market driving company, and it induces suppliers to introduce changes to their production and delivery systems and sometimes even re-configure their whole business system. This fits into the 'talking pig' analogy suggested by (Siggelkow, 2007) and agrees with his arguments for the 'nonrepresentativeness' (a small sample) in case study research. The choice of IKEA as a market driving firm is thus justified. However, we are going beyond a single case, as we are studying four of IKEA's supplier relationships, thus allowing us to seek patterns for drawing conclusion from these four cases.

We considered several factors in selecting cases. First, we have limited our study to suppliers supplying to the same company (IKEA) to minimise extraneous variation (Eisenhardt, 1989). Second, we have selected cases from two markets, Russia and Poland, to allow adequate variation. Third, we have selected cases that granted us full access. Fourth, we have selected suppliers that have been supplying for different time periods, to capture the differences in their relationship with IKEA (Yan and Gray, 1994). Russia is a new purchasing country (less than 1 per cent of the global output) with just 50 suppliers mostly in the solid wood industry and a great untapped potential as a major purchasing country. Poland is IKEA's oldest purchasing country producing about one-third of all products from the range (12 per cent of the global output) and with about 135 suppliers in various industries.

Overall, the cases were chosen to generate insights into 'how' a global retailer develops supplier relationships to support its market driving strategy. The design allowed us to illuminate some critical issues (Yin, 2003). In-depth interviews were used as the major data collection technique, supported by an extensive use of secondary sources and observations (Eisenhardt, 1989; Ghauri, 2004). A key approach to interviews was to use numerous and highly knowledgeable informants who viewed the market driving phenomenon from different perspectives (Eisenhardt and Graebner, 2007). This allowed us to triangulate the information received and check for accuracy in historical and current information (Miles and Huberman, 1994). On the corporate level, four interviews were conducted with purchasing managers responsible for Europe and Russia and business area managers. Four interviews were conducted in Russia with purchasing managers, new product development managers, trading managers and technicians and three interviews in Poland with trading and environmental managers as well as technicians. In addition, three Russian and two Polish suppliers were studied. These interviews involved factory directors, marketing managers and technicians.

We conducted interviews in three languages: English, Swedish and Russian. In most cases, the respondents' mother tongue was used, given the researchers' proficiency in all three languages. We kept on asking sub-questions until comparable and equivalent answers were received (Neuman, 2002; Sinkovics *et al.*, 2005). Each interview lasted for approximately one and a half hours in accordance with a general interview guide based on the preliminary theoretical framework.

IKEA's strategy for developing the supplier base

In 2006 IKEA had 46 trading offices in 32 countries. The company's top five purchasing countries are China (18 per cent), Poland (12 per cent), Sweden (8 per cent), Italy (7 per cent) and Germany (6 per cent).[1] The company also has 28 distribution centres in 16 countries that supply to IKEA stores. The rationale of IKEA's relationships with suppliers lies in the company's business idea of producing low-price products in a socially responsible way. All IKEA products are manufactured in accordance with a specially designed code of conduct 'The IKEA Way on Purchasing Home Furnishing Products' (IWAY), which also provides a basis for the company's supplier relationships. All IKEA suppliers must fulfil basic requirements regarding legal issues, working conditions, prevention of child labour, external environment and forestry management. Suppliers also have to prepare an action plan for meeting the other criteria of IWAY demands. Representatives from IKEA's Trading offices are in charge of looking for new suppliers in their respective markets as well as developing personal relationships with the existing suppliers.

In Russia, first contacts with suppliers were made in the mid 1980s by Ingvar Kamprad (the Chairman and owner of IKEA). Since then, the search for new potential partners has never stopped. It has proven to be a hard endeavour according to managers, there is still a lack of local managers with 'the right management style' and 'right spirit'. The process of finding new partners in Russia was described by one respondent as 'vacuum cleaning Russia' in order to find the entrepreneurs.

The relationships were built on a personal level, with IKEA representatives becoming actively involved in different issues of factories' production, supply and sometimes even human resource management. These relationships always reflected the principles of the code of conduct and the overall status of a local supplier here. As most suppliers only satisfied Steps 1 and 2 of the four-step IWAY process, the respondents were talking about 'pushing' Russian suppliers to increase their general standards.

Supplier 1 (Konakovo factory) established a relationship with IKEA in 1999. It manufactured different types of products, often designed in-house and hand made and produced in small volumes. The exchange with IKEA has developed slowly but successfully. At the time of our study, the firm had become IKEA's principal supplier of ceramics in Russia ('Every fifth plate produced in Russia is from Konakovo!') and it had also started to export to other IKEA markets. The production for IKEA constituted only 2 per cent of the factory's total turnover, but IKEA was nevertheless one of the factory's biggest clients and the share was expected to increase to 10 per cent in the near future. However, the Director expressed concerns about becoming too dependent and the risk that the factory would lose its historical profile. This could lead to a social catastrophe in the small town and for the employed staff. At the same time, relationship with IKEA was marked by a very good contact on a personal level. The supplier had qualified for the Level 1 of IKEA's Code of Conduct at the time of our study.

The relationship with Supplier 2 (Priozersk) started in the 1970s, in the Soviet era. IKEA was the biggest client and in 2004 the supplier produced five chair models. IKEA had always been actively involved in the production process. The first chair produced by the factory was manufactured in accordance with IKEA's sketches, and the Director stated that his factory almost reproduced IKEA's business idea of flat package production and delivery. The factory had significantly increased its production volumes in order to meet the demands of four newly opened IKEA stores. It mainly supplied Russian stores, although some products were exported to other IKEA markets. The factory qualified to Level 2 of IKEA's Code of Conduct and its management was proud of its high-quality standards. However, the long IKEA relationship had not been without friction. Serious problems in communications between the owner and IKEA representatives that concerned the supplier's overall dissatisfaction in IKEA's pricing and HR policy as well as the lack of mutual understanding had affected further plans to increase production. The supplier also actively looked for other clients in Russia and abroad.

Supplier 3 (Lenrauma) had a relationship with IKEA dating back to 1994 that had also gone through different phases. It was temporarily terminated but resumed in 2003. The reason behind the decision to terminate the relationship was the incompatibility with IKEA's low-price policy. After the firm later decided to apply IKEA's principle and tie its price to the volume, the negotiations with IKEA re-started and resulted in about 40 per cent of all factory products being produced for IKEA. During this time, the factory was restructured with regards to production and delivery processes and was now a modern production plant planned for IKEA. According to the director, the enterprise was backed with Russian capital to 100 per cent, but nevertheless, 'a westernized enterprise'. In 2004, the goal was to make IKEA the biggest client by increasing the share of the volume to 60 per cent. The relationship was based on a good personal understanding. IKEA was perceived as a 'role model' of a modern Western company with a strong concept, and the supplier strived to copy almost all elements of IKEA's business concept. The factory had also reached Level 2 of IKEA's Code of Conduct and its management was enthusiastic to further improve the standards.

Poland was IKEA's first purchasing market outside Sweden, dating back to 1961. The IKEA Group's own Swedwood factories were also well represented in Poland. According to the respondents, these factories were to provide good examples for suppliers in other markets. All IKEA's Polish suppliers were internationally competitive and exported to other IKEA markets. The goal for Poland was to decrease the number of suppliers, leaving only the largest, most committed and price-competitive ones. Giving more responsibility to existing suppliers was also a major issue in relationships between IKEA Trading organisation and Polish suppliers. One of the key issues with Polish suppliers was also helping them to switch to a direct stores delivery system. Supporting suppliers in these new challenges, IKEA managers offered them help with efficiency training and access to the company's electronic data bases. A strong focus was also on training of IKEA's own business developers who would, in their turn, develop local suppliers. Similar to the situation in Russia, IKEA was carrying out the project called 'Push Poland'; 'trying to purchase local articles at a good price to help our Retail organisation to be competitive in the market'.

Supplier 4 (PROFIm) established a relationship with IKEA in 1997, regarded by the Director as 'promising'. IKEA was the biggest customer and accounted for 20–30 per cent of the total output. The supplier produced three types of office chairs for IKEA, and had two production plants and a total output of more than 70,000 chairs a month. About 50 per cent of these were exported on the European market. In 2004, Supplier 4 became the main manufacturer of office chairs in Poland. The supplier's brand had also become well known in the industry and recognized as a guarantee of high quality. The relationship with IKEA was marked by a good understanding between the parties at local level, but there were some problems with the corporate IKEA. The latter factor caused a cautious approach to be taken by the factory's management. It otherwise demonstrated a proactive position, striving for a shared responsibility for the production process and a pursuit of mutual interests. The supplier also had developed a unique quality-testing laboratory, initiated by the cooperation with IKEA. Supplier 4 was the first Polish office chair manufacturer to receive a quality certificate compatible with ISO 9001 standards in 2000, which corresponded to Level 4 of IKEA's code of conduct.

A network of relationships

The empirical findings have helped us to identify critical actors, activities and resources actively used in the retailer–supplier relationships. The activities and resources used by corporate managers have been compared with those used by suppliers to identify those most critical for successful market driving relationships. Table 30.1 summarises the main characteristics of the four supplier relationships. They are further elaborated upon below.

As relationships with suppliers were a primary responsibility of IKEA Trading organisation, local trading and supply managers were among the most important actors involved in the day-to-day interactions. Often, a trading manager supervised several local suppliers within a specific area. IKEA technicians were also involved in the support and control through regular visits. They were often referred to as the most trustworthy people with a lot of expertise. In new markets like Russia, where the search for suppliers was an ongoing process, the higher level managers such as the country manager and even Mr Kamprad, the company's founder, were sometimes involved at earlier stages of relationships. Thus, Kamprad's contacts with Soviet and Russian officials were invaluable for building up contacts in this market. In Poland, managers stressed the role of business developers: people combining knowledge in product development, finance and logistics.

Among reported activities, the respondents stressed the importance of building up personal relationships based on a shared understanding of each other's vision and business idea, which is typical for market driving and market driven activities. The extensive exchange of the norms and standards in accordance with the code of conduct and control of the progress were characteristic of all relationships. In Russia, IKEA managers described how cooperation with other international retailers increased the local production standards. That was considered an important trigger for local industry development as certain environmental or technological standards were still much lower. In Poland, standards were higher and managers cooperated with other professional firms to help suppliers to further increase their efficiency. Both these examples contradicted the normal rules of competition in the retail sector, due the market driving firm's ultimate goal of a higher customer value, which could only have been achieved through intensifying the local industry development.

While the relationships between technicians were in all cases functioning well, that was not always the case between factory management and IKEA Trading. This created a strong feeling of dissatisfaction for Supplier 2. One of the reasons was the perceived lack of expertise on IKEA's side resulting from the company's practice of appointing 'people from the street' to deal with suppliers. The common IKEA practice of staff rotation was also mentioned by Supplier 2 as affecting the continuity and quality of relationships. All suppliers have mentioned the involvement of factory workers in the relationship with IKEA. Although workers were not directly involved in interactions, they were aware of the importance of IKEA as a customer as well as of the requirements set up by IKEA. For example, Supplier 3 stressed that 'every worker knows what is required of him. Because the worker works better, if he knows it. If he comes to work with a purpose'. The involvement of workers was highest at those suppliers who reported strongly shared vision and values (Supplier 3 and 4).

Among major resources, the respondents mentioned technology, new environmentally friendly materials, expertise in flat-pack production and delivery, quality testing and control, training, global network of suppliers and financial support. All suppliers reported certain technological changes that took place at their factories. Thus, all had adopted IKEA's packaging and delivery systems, and some of them started the direct delivery to stores. This was considered important in spite of the 'headache' it brought about for the workers at production sites. In most cases, IKEA's products were also slightly modified in size and shape, while in other cases some locally produced items were used to support IKEA's local assortment. Most suppliers expressed the desire to participate more in the product development together with IKEA, however, only two suppliers (3 and 4) reported positive results.

Table 30.1 Critical network factors in developing the market driving supplier relationships

Network factor	Actors	Activities	Resources
Organization			
IKEA corporate and local organisations	Founder Country manager Functional managers Specialists	Explaining vision and key core values Initiate changes to fit IKEA's business idea Apply new technological solutions Develop personal relationships with staff Assist with HR issues Training at Swedwood and IKEA of Sweden	Knowledge in product technology and production process Environmentally friendly materials Flat pack packaging, delivery and logistics Quality testing and control Global network of sub-suppliers Loans and lease of equipment
Supplier 1	Director Technicians Workers	Learn IKEA's vision of 'pushing' customers Resist adapting to IKEA concept at the expense of quality Informal, close interaction with contact person at IKEA Educate workers about IKEA concept	Knowledge of local customer needs and local contacts transferred from supplier to IKEA Technology and know-how transferred from IKEA to supplier
Supplier 2	Director Technicians Workers	Questions IKEA's vision, strategy and training Opposes IKEA's pricing policy and lack of local adaptation Change of contact person undermines personal ties	Knowledge of local market situation, local norms and industry standards transferred from supplier to IKEA Financial help transferred from IKEA to supplier, but reduced due to problems in relationship
Supplier 3	Director Technicians Workers	Adapts to IKEA mission of large volume at low price Modifies IKEA's product design to cut prices Introduce own products that fit IKEA's style Inform workers about IKEA principles	Production technologies, know-how and financial help transferred from IKEA to supplier
Supplier 4	Manager Director Technicians Workers	Shared responsibility in production Joint product development Cooperate in building new assembling unit for several factories working with IKEA Close interaction with local IKEA contacts Lack of communication with corporate IKEA Staff trained at Swedwood and IKEA of Sweden	Product ideas, technical solutions, price calculations, info on local market, customers and sub-suppliers transferred from supplier to IKEA Production technologies, know-how transferred from IKEA to supplier

While the Code of Conduct constituted the basis for all relationships, the achieved level of technical standard and motivation to go further with it were very different. Thus, Supplier 1 mentioned the improved working conditions and safety standards; Supplier 3 appreciated new technologies and environmentally "pure" materials while Supplier 4 talked about the quality-testing laboratory "borrowed" from IKEA. This laboratory and the exchange of expertise in quality testing allowed this supplier to reach the status of a high-quality office chair producer in Poland and abroad. This supplier also mentioned the impact of cooperation on new materials that his factory started to use due to IKEA. It is interesting that Supplier 2, who had also introduced many of IKEA's quality and environmental standards, talked about them with a great deal of scepticism, which shows how personal relationships affect other aspects of cooperation.

A major result of the extensive technology exchange was the substantial improvement of the standards at suppliers. In many cases, this led to their improved image among their existing customers, increased attractiveness for new customers, addition of new products to the range, and improved competitiveness in their markets. For example, Supplier 1 reported the increasing number of orders from its customers of "IKEA-style" products and the factory's recognition in Europe as IKEA supplier. Even Supplier 2, which was rather unsatisfied, used IKEA as a reference for its diversification efforts. The motivation on the suppliers' side to further increase their standards differed from a proactive desire to go forward at Supplier 4 to a strong motivation to increase standards at Supplier 1 and 3 and a deep scepticism of the relevance of IKEA's rules at Supplier 2.

All respondents also discussed the financial support received by factories from IKEA. The important feature of this support is that it was always tied to the supplier's general compliance with the Code of Conduct and, thus, functioned as a motivational tool. Three of the suppliers had already received a lot of support in loans while Supplier 1 was still aiming at getting the support. For Supplier 2, it "helped the factory to survive all crises" during the turbulent perestroika times in Russia in the 1990s. Supplier 4 stressed the importance of a joint investment into new projects with IKEA. This factory was preparing a business plan for a new assembly unit that would increase efficiency not only for this supplier but also for other IKEA furniture producers in Poland and neighbouring markets. On the contrary, the problems perceived by Supplier 2 hindered this factory from receiving the planned loans. As explained by the Director, "the unfortunate situation with IKEA personnel" forced his factory to find another investor.

As far as training at IKEA facilities was concerned, all suppliers reported participating in courses at IKEA of Sweden, Swedwood or at their own premises. Although appreciating the possibility to get training for management and workers, some suppliers expressed the wish that IKEA should adjust it more to the factories' real needs and conditions: "Training and learning should be down here, on the spot, in the specific situation!" (Supplier 2).

Discussion

The discussed actors, activities and resources were critical in terms of their impact on the relationship in terms of long-term collaboration, trust, motivation, and in terms of the change of suppliers' business systems and capabilities and their roles in the retailer's supply chain. Figure 30.2 shows the main variables identified and how they interact with each other. This is in line with Ghauri *et al.* (2005) and Håkansson and Johanson (1992).

All successful relationships were characterised by a strong personal bonding and an extensive exchanges of vision and business ideas, technology, and, in some cases, finances, as

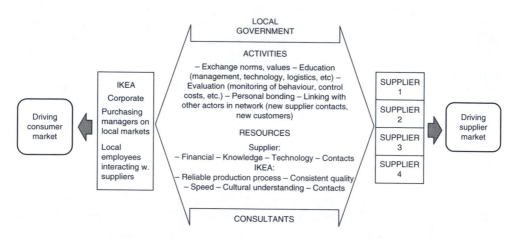

Figure 30.2 A conceptual model of market driving firm and its relationship with suppliers.

suggested by Tuominen *et al.* (2004). It is clear that personal bonding and the suppliers' satisfaction with it has played a crucial role in the speed of development process and the technical level achieved by the suppliers.

The most shared vision and business ideas were exhibited by Suppliers 3 and 4, only partly by Supplier 1, and very little by Supplier 2. The effectiveness of sharing depended on the regularity and stability of the parties' contacts. In the more successful relationships both partners shared a desire to pursue mutual interests. This led to a feeling of trust and motivated suppliers to invest more internal resources into the cooperation, confirming Ghauri and Holstius (1996) and Gadde and Håkansson (2001).

As the network approach suggests (Hadjikhani and Ghauri, 2001; Håkansson and Johanson, 1992) the exchange of resources was most crucial. It especially stressed product technologies, materials, knowledge of production process, quality issues, capital and lease of equipment. Among the least effective ones were training and global network of partners. Those resources were under-used because suppliers perceived difficulties to adjust them to local conditions. Among the local suppliers' resources, the most eagerly shared with IKEA were knowledge of the local market, local technologies, contacts and capital. Still, they were not always fully used by IKEA. For example, local contacts and local industry norms and standards were frequently under-used by the retailer leading to a certain lack of local cultural sensitivity. This is in line with Harris and Cai (2002) arguing that cultural differences may create hindrances to a market driving strategy. It might be summarised that a retailer was 'driving' its suppliers through personal bonding, share of ideas, principles and technology, using the code of conduct as guidelines while the suppliers were trying to make this strategy more locally sensitive with local knowledge and contacts.

Conclusions and implications

This study enhances our understanding about the international market driving firms' strategies and confirms our proposition that development of a long-lasting and trustworthy relationship with suppliers is an important factors. This also enabled us to further develop the ideas presented by earlier studies on market driving strategies (Jaworski *et al.*, 2000; Kumar *et al.*, 2000). In all cases, the relationships between suppliers and the market driving firm were built up over several (3–5) years and developed on a very personal level. The continuity and regularity of relationships were mentioned by several respondents as being very important. When the relationship was marked by occasional contacts, changing contact persons, formality and the lack of trust, other issues of the factory relationships with IKEA were also directly affected (Mathyssens and Faes, 2006). For example, a perceived lack of dialogue with central IKEA resulted in the supplier's cautious approach to increase production.

It is interesting to note that the most developed relationships (Suppliers 3 and 4) were marked by good understanding and even adoption of IKEA's vision and mission. Thus, Supplier 3 explained that the factory had gone "from no mission to IKEA's mission of saturation of the market with high quality and inexpensive goods" and that closeness of goals was decisive for a successful relationship. On the other hand, the less successful relationship marked by opportunistic behaviour of Supplier 2 was characterised by a strong scepticism towards IKEA's vision and environmental strategy referred to as "marketing tricks".

As far as IKEA's auditing and control work with the code of conduct was concerned, most suppliers recognized the relevance of this practice. However, not all were satisfied by the way the auditing and control was done. In most cases, a feeling of dissatisfaction was caused by a perceived inefficiency of auditors' visits and the unwillingness on IKEA's part to take into account the existing industry norms and standards adopted by the supplier.

In general, it appears that top management from both sides need to be involved in developing marked driving supplier relationships. IKEA has been has successful in conveying and convincing its suppliers to follow its values, visions and business ideas. IKEA has also provided financial support and training, which of convinced suppliers of its long-term commitment in the relationship (Hadjikhani and Ghauri, 2001). However, the suppliers' perspective that there was a lack of understanding suppliers' specific situations in the industry and market are important factors. By increasing the understanding of suppliers' conditions, a retailer can make better use of its own resources invested in the relationships as well as activate and utilize the suppliers' resources for mutual benefit.

Our results provide certain implications for managers of a retailing company and their local suppliers. First managers need a better understanding of the local conditions under which the suppliers operate, which can be achieved by establishing good personal relationships built on regular contacts, trust and expertise. Second, they need to decide early in the relationship what model of relationship with a particular supplier is optimal for both parties. Our study shows that some relationships appeared to suffer from a lack of mutual understanding. It is thus important for the retailer to establish contacts required to understand the supplier's level of development, market strategy and expectations. For example, a less-developed supplier can be expected to be more willing to receive a high level of support and at the same time to adopt the retailers values and market strategy. On the other hand, a more advanced supplier may expect a more "equal" relationship. Here, the retailer should also recognize the value of different competencies and resources offered by the supplier. Our study indicates that gaining a proper understanding of the suppliers position and expectations can be a critical and difficult task that requires a certain cultural understanding.

This study reveals that in global markets, adaptation and market orientations are not the only success factors. Companies can be market driving, thus making the markets adapt to their products and strategies. However, for this strategy to work fully, the companies need to be consistent in their networking, backward and forward as suggested also by Crespin-Mazet and Ghauri (2007). Moreover, they need to convince the market and educate their suppliers that they are providing extra value, in comparison to competing offers.

Note

1   The IKEA Group in brief, 2005.

References

Alajoutsijarvi, K., Eriksson, P. and Tikkanen, H. (2001), "Dominant metaphors in the imp network discourse: 'the network as a marriage' and 'the network as a business system'", *International Business Review*, Vol. 10 No. 1, pp. 91–107.

Berghman, L., Matthyssens, P. and Vandenbempt, K. (2006), "Building competences for new customer value creation: an exploratory study", *Industrial Marketing Management*, Vol. 35 No. 8, p. 961.

Buckley, P.J. and Ghauri, P.N. (Eds) (1999), *The Internationalization of the Firm: A Reader*, 2nd ed., International Thompson Business Press, London.

Cadogan, J.W., Diamantopoulos, A. and de Mortanges, C.P. (1999), "A measure of export market orientation: scale development and cross-cultural validation", *Journal of International Business Studies*, Vol. 30 No. 4, pp. 689–707.

Carrillat, F.A., Jaramillo, F. and Locander, W.B. (2004), "Market-driving organizations: a framework", *Academy of Marketing Science Review*, Vol. 4, available at: www.amsreview.org/articles/carrillat 05-2004.pdf

Chetty, S. and Blankenburg Holm, D. (2000), "Internationalisation of small to medium-sized manufacturing firms: a network approach", *International Business Review*, Vol. 9 No. 1, pp. 77–93.

Christensen, C.M. and Bower, J.L. (1996), "Customer power, strategic investment, and the failure of leading firms", *Strategic Management Journal*, Vol. 17 No. 3, pp. 197–218.

Cova, B. and Salle, R. (2000), "Rituals in managing extra business relationships in international project marketing: a conceptual framework", *International Business Review*, Vol. 9 No. 6, pp. 669–85.

Crespin-Mazet, F. and Ghauri, P. (2007), "Co-development as a marketing strategy in the construction industry", *Industrial Marketing Management*, Vol. 36 No. 2, pp. 158–72.

Day, G.S. (1999), "Misconceptions about market orientation", *Journal of Market-Focused Management*, Vol. 4 No. 1, p. 5.

Eisenhardt, K.M. (1989), "Building theories from case study research", *Academy of Management Review*, Vol. 14 No. 4, pp. 532–50.

Eisenhardt, K.M. and Graebner, M.E. (2007), "Theory building from cases: opportunities and challenges", *Academy of Management Journal*, Vol. 50 No. 1, pp. 25–32.

Elg, U. (2007), "Market orientation as inter-firm cooperation: an international study of the grocery sector", *European Management Journal*, Vol. 25 No. 4, pp. 283–97.

Fernie, J. and Leigh, S. (1998), *Logistics and Retail Management: Insights into Current Practice and Trends from Leading Experts*, Kogan Page, London.

Gadde, L-E. and Håkansson, H. (2001), *Supply Network Strategies*, Wiley, Chichester.

Ghauri, P.N. (1999), "From mass marketing to relationships and networks", in Ghauri, P.N. (Ed.), *Advances in International Marketing*, JAI Press, Greenwich, CT, pp. 1–17.

Ghauri, P.N. (2004), "Designing and conducting case studies in international business research", in Marschan-Piekkari, R. and Welch, C. (Eds), *Handbook of Qualitative Research Methods for International Business*, Edward Elgar, Cheltenham, pp. 109–24.

Ghauri, P.N. and Fang, T. (2001), "Negotiating with Chinese: a socio-cultural analysis", *Journal of World Business*, Vol. 36 No. 3, pp. 303–25.

Ghauri, P.N. and Holstius, K. (1996), "The role of matching in the foreign market entry process in the Baltic states", *European Journal of Marketing*, Vol. 30 No. 2, pp. 75–88.

Ghauri, P.N., Hadjikhani, A. and Johanson, J. (Eds) (2005), *Managing Opportunity Development in Business Networks*, Palgrave Macmillan, Basingstoke.

Greenley, G.E. (1995), "Forms of market orientation in UK companies", *Journal of Management Studies*, Vol. 23 No. 1, pp. 47–66.

Grunert, K.G., Jeppesen, L.F., Jespersen, K.R., Sonne, A.-M., Hansen, K., Trondsen, T. and Young, J.A. (2005), "Market orientation of value chains: a conceptual framework based on four case studies from the food industry", *European Journal of Marketing*, Vol. 39 No. 5, pp. 428–55.

Hadjikhani, A. and Ghauri, P.N. (2001), "The behaviour of international firms in socio-political environments in the European Union", *Journal of Business Research*, September, Vol. 61, pp. 912–24.

Hadjikhani, A., Lee, J.W. and Ghauri, P.N. (2008), "Network view of MNC's socio-political behavior", *Journal of Business Research*, Vol. 13 No. 1, pp. 5–18.

Håkansson, H. and Johanson, J. (1992), "A model of industrial networks", in Axelsson, B. and Easton, G. (Eds), *Industrial Networks: A New View of Reality*, Routledge, London, pp. 28–34.

Håkansson, H. and Snehota, I. (1995), *Developing Relationships in Business Networks*, International Thomson Business Press, London.

Harris, L.C. and Cai, K.Y. (2002), "Exploring market driving: a case study of De Beers in China", *Journal of Market-Focused Management*, Vol. 5 No. 3, pp. 171–96.

Homburg, C. and Pflesser, C. (2000), "A multiple-layer model of market-oriented organizational culture: measurement issues and performance outcomes", *Journal of Marketing Research*, Vol. 37 No. 4, pp. 449–62.

Hooley, G., Cox, T., Fahy, J., Shipley, D., Beracs, J., Fonfara, K. and Snoj, B. (2000), "Market orientation in the transition economies of central Europe: tests of the Narver and Slater market orientation scales", *Journal of Business Research*, Vol. 50 No. 3, pp. 273–85.

Jaworski, B.J. and Kohli, A.K. (1993), "Market orientation: antecedents and consequences", *Journal of Marketing*, Vol. 57 No. 3, pp. 53–70.

Jaworski, B., Kohli, A.K. and Sahay, A. (2000), "Market-driven versus driving markets", *Journal of the Academy of Marketing Science*, Vol. 28 No. 1, pp. 45–54.

Kohli, A.K. and Jaworski, B.J. (1990), "Market orientation: the construct, research propositions and managerial implications", *Journal of Marketing*, Vol. 54 No. 2, pp. 1–18.

Kumar, N. (1997), "The revolution in retailing: from market driven to market driving", *Long Range Planning*, Vol. 30 No. 6, pp. 830–5.

Kumar, N., Scheer, L. and Kotler, P. (2000), "From market driven to market driving", *European Management Journal*, Vol. 18 No. 2, pp. 129–42.

Langerak, F. (2001), "Effects of market orientation on the behaviors of salespersons and purchasers, channel relationships, and performance of manufacturers", *International Journal of Research in Marketing*, Vol. 18 No. 3, pp. 221–34.

Liu, S.S., Luo, X. and Shi, Y-Z. (2003), "Market-oriented organizations in an emerging economy: a study of missing links", *Journal of Business Research*, Vol. 56 No. 6, pp. 481–91.

Martin, J.H. and Grbac, B. (2003), "Using supply chain management to leverage a firm's market orientation", *Industrial Marketing Management*, Vol. 32 No. 1, pp. 25–38.

Mathyssens, P. and Faes, W. (2006), "Managing channel relations in china: an exploratory study", *Advances in International Marketing*, Vol. 16, p. 187.

Matsuno, K. and Mentzer, J.T. (2000), "The effects of strategy type on the market orientation-performance relationship", *Journal of Marketing*, Vol. 64 No. 4, pp. 1–16.

Miles, M.B. and Huberman, A.M. (1994), *Qualitative Data Analysis: An Expanded Sourcebook*, Sage, Thousand Oaks, CA.

Narver, J.C. and Slater, S.F. (1990), "The effect of a market orientation on business profitability", *Journal of Marketing*, Vol. 54 No. 4, pp. 20–35.

Narver, J.C., Slater, S.F. and MacLachlan, D.L. (2004), "Responsive and proactive market orientation and new product success", *Journal of Product Innovation Management*, Vol. 21 No. 5, pp. 334–47.

Neuman, W.L. (2002), *Social Research Methods: Qualitative and Quantitative Approaches*, 5th ed., Allyn and Bacon, Boston, MA.

Pitt, L., Caruana, A. and Berthon, P.R. (1996), "Market orientation and business performance: some European evidence", *International Marketing Review*, Vol. 13 No. 1, pp. 5–18.

Quintens, L., Pauwels, P. and Matthyssens, P. (2006), "Global purchasing: state of the art and research directions", *Journal of Purchasing & Supply Management*, Vol. 12 No. 4, pp. 170–81.

Ruekert, R.W. (1992), "Developing a market orientation: an organizational strategy perspective", *International Journal of Research in Marketing*, Vol. 9, pp. 225–45.

Saunders, M. (1997), *Strategic Purchasing & Supply Chain Management*, 2nd ed., Financial Times, London.

Siggelkow, N. (2007), "Persuasion with case studies", *Academy of Management Journal*, Vol. 50 No. 1, pp. 20–4.

Siguaw, J.A., Simpson, P.M. and Baker, T.L. (1998), "Effects of supplier market orientation on distributor market orientation and the channel relationship: the distributor perspective", *Journal of Marketing*, Vol. 62 No. 3, pp. 99–111.

Sinkovics, R.R., Penz, E. and Ghauri, P.N. (2005), "Analysing textual data in international marketing research", *Qualitative Market Research: An International Journal*, Vol. 8 No. 1, pp. 9–38.

Slater, S.F. and Narver, J.C. (1998), "Customer-led and market-oriented: let's not confuse the two", *Strategic Management Journal*, Vol. 19, pp. 1001–6.

Stoelhorst, J.W. and van Raaij Erik, M. (2004), "On explaining performance differentials: marketing and the managerial theory of the firm", *Journal of Business Research*, Vol. 57 No. 5, pp. 462–77.

Tuominen, M., Rajala, A. and Möller, K. (2004), "Market-driving versus market-driven: divergent roles of market orientation in business relationships", *Industrial Marketing Management*, Vol. 33 No. 3, pp. 207–17.

Yan, A. and Gray, B. (1994), "Bargaining power, management control, and performance in United States–China joint ventures: a comparative case study", *Academy of Management Journal*, Vol. 37 No. 6, pp. 1478–517.

Yin, R.K. (2003), *Case Study Research: Design and Methods (Applied Social Research Methods Series)*, 3rd ed., Sage, Thousand Oaks, CA.

Further reading

Ghauri, P.N. and Grønhaug, K. (2005), *Research Methods in Business Studies: A Practical Guide*, 3rd ed., Financial Times/Prentice-Hall, London.

Hills Stacey, B. and Sarin, S. (2003), "From market driven to market driving: an alternate paradigm for marketing in high technology industries", *Journal of Marketing Theory and Practice*, Vol. 11 No. 3, pp. 13–24.

31 Strategies that fit emerging markets*

Tarun Khanna, Krishna G. Palepu and Jayant Sinha

CEOs and top management teams of large corporations, particularly in North America, Europe and Japan, acknowledge that globalization is the most critical challenge they face today. They are also keenly aware that it has become tougher during the past decade to identify internationalization strategies and to choose which countries to do business with. Still, most companies have stuck to the strategies they've traditionally deployed, which emphasize standardized approaches to new markets while sometimes experimenting with a few local twists. As a result, many multinational corporations are struggling to develop successful strategies in emerging markets.

Part of the problem, we believe, is that the absence of specialized intermediaries, regulatory systems and contract-enforcing mechanisms in emerging markets, "institutional voids," we christened them in a 1997 HBR article, hampers the implementation of globalization strategies. Companies in developed countries usually take for granted the critical role that "soft" infrastructure play in the execution of their business models in their home markets. But that infrastructure is often underdeveloped or absent in emerging markets. There's no dearth of examples. Companies can't find skilled market research firms to inform them reliably about customer preferences so they can tailor products to specific needs and increase people's willingness to pay. Few end-to-end logistics providers, which allow manufacturers to reduce costs, are available to transport raw materials and finished products. Before recruiting employees, corporations have to screen large numbers of candidates themselves because there aren't many search firms that can do the job for them.

Because of all those institutional voids, many multinational companies have fared poorly in developing countries. All the anecdotal evidence we have gathered suggests that since the 1990s, American corporations have performed better in their home environments than they have in foreign countries, especially in emerging markets. Not surprisingly, many CEOs are wary of emerging markets and prefer to invest in developed nations instead. By the end of 2002, according to the Bureau of Economic Analysis, an agency of the U.S. Department of Commerce, American corporations and their affiliate companies had $1.6 trillion worth of assets in the United Kingdom and $514 billion in Canada but only $173 billion in Brazil, Russia, India and China combined. That's just 2.5 per cent of the $6.9 trillion in investments American companies held by the end of that year. Although U.S. corporations' investments in China doubled between 1992 and 2002, that amount was still less than 1 per cent of all their overseas assets.

Many companies shield away from emerging markets when they should have engaged with them more closely. Since the early 1990s, developing countries have been the fatest-growning market in the world for most products and services. Companies can lower costs by setting up

*Reprinted with permission from Harvard Business Review. Khanna, T., K. Palepu & J. Sinha (2005) "Strategies that fit emerging markets", Harvard Business Review, 83(6) June: 63–76.

manufacturing facilities and service centers in those areas, where skilled labor and trained managers are relatively inexpensive. Moreover, several developing-country transnational corporations have entered North America and Europe with low-cost strategies (China's Haier Group in household electrical appliances) and novel business models (India's Infosys in information technology services). Western companies that want to develop counter-strategies must push deeper into emerging markets, which foster a different genre of innovations than mature markets do.

If Western companies don't develop strategies for engaging across their value chains with developing countries, they are unlikely to remain competitive for long. However, despite crumbling tariff barriers, the spread of the Internet and cable television and the rapidly improving physical infrastructure in these countries, CEOs can't assume they can do business in emerging markets the same way they do in developed nations. That's because the quality of the market infrastructure varies widely from country to country. Advanced economies have large pools of seasoned market intermediaries and effective contract-enforcing mechanisms, whereas less-developed economies have unskilled intermediaries and less-effective legal systems. Because the services provided by intermediaries either aren't available in emerging markets or aren't very sophisticated, corporations can't smoothly transfer the strategies they employ in their home countries to those emerging markets.

During the past ten years, we've researched and consulted with multinational corporations all over the world. One of us led a comparative research project on China and India at Harvard Business School and we have all been involved in McKinsey & Company's Global Champions research project. We have learned that successful companies work around institutional voids. They develop strategies for doing business in emerging markets that are different from those they use at home and often find novel ways of implementing them, too. They also customize their approaches to fit each nation's institutional context. As we will show, firms that take the trouble to understand the institutional differences between countries are likely to choose the best markets to enter, select optimal strategies, and make the most out of operating in emerging markets.

Why composite indices are inadequate

Before we delve deeper into institutional voids, it's important to understand why companies often target the wrong countries or deploy inappropriate globalization strategies. Many corporations enter new lands because of senior managers' personal experiences, family ties, gut feelings or anecdotal evidence. Others follow key customers or rivals into emerging markets; the herd instinct is strong among multinationals. Biases, too, dog companies' foreign investments. For instance, the reason U.S. companies preferred to do business with China rather than India for decades was probably because of America's romance with China, first profiled in MIT political scientist Harold Isaac's work in the late 1950s. Isacs pointed out that partly as a result of the work missionaries and scholars did in China in the 1800s, Americans became more familiar with China than with India.

Companies that choose new markets systematically often use tools like country portfolio analysis and political risk assessment, which chiefly focus on the potential profits from doing business in developing countries but leave out essential information about the soft infrastructures there. In December 2004, when the McKinsey Global Survey of Business Executives polled 9,750 senior managers on their priorities and concerns, 61 per cent said that market size and growth drove their firms' decisions to enter new countries. While 17 per cent felt that political and economic stability was the most important factor in making those decisions, only 13 per cent said that structural conditions (in other words, institutional contexts) mattered most.

The trouble with composite indices

Companies often base their globalization strategies on country rankings, but on most lists, it is impossible to tell developing countries apart. According to the six indices below, Brazil, India and China share similar markets while Russia, though an outlier on many parameters, is comparable to the other nations. Contrary to what these rankings suggest, however, the market infrastructure in each of these countries varies widely, and companies need to deploy very different strategies to succeed.

	Brazil	Russia	India	China
Growth Competitiveness Index ranking* (out of 104 countries; for 2003)	57	70	55	46
Business Competitiveness Index ranking* (out of 103 countries; for 2003)	38	61	30	47
Governance indicators (percentile rankings)** (out of 199 countries; for 2002)				
Voice and accountability	58.1	33.8	60.2	10.1
Political stability	48.1	33.0	22.2	51.4
Government effectiveness	50.0	44.3	54.1	63.4
Regulatory quality	63.4	44.3	43.8	40.2
Rule of law	50.0	25.3	57.2	51.5
Control of corruption	56.7	21.1	49.5	42.3
Corruption Perceptions Index rankings*** (out of 145 countries; for 2004)	59	90	90	71
Composite Country Risk Points**** (for January 2005; the larger the number, the less risky the country)	70	78	72	76
Weight in Emerging Markets Index (%)***** (for February 2004; out of 26 emerging markets)	6.96%	5.16%	5.02%	4.76%

Sources:
* World Economic Forum, "Global Competitiveness Report" 2004–2005
** World Bank Governance Research Indicator Country Snapshot 2002
*** Transparency International, Corruption Perceptions Index 2004
**** The PRS Group, *International Country Risk Guide*, January 2005
***** Barclays Global Investors, iShares "2004 Semi-Annual Report to Shareholders"

Just how do companies estimate a nation's potential? Executives usually analyze its GDP and per capita income growth rates, its population composition and growth rates, and its exchange rates and purchasing power parity indices (past, present and projected). To complete the picture, managers consider the nation's standing on the World Economic Forum's Global Competitiveness Index, the World Bank's governance indicators, and Transparency International's corruption ratings; its weight in emerging market funds investments; and, perhaps, forecasts of its next political transition.

Such composite indices are no doubt useful, but companies should use them as the basis for drawing up strategies only when their home bases and target countries have comparable institutional contexts. For example, the United States and the United Kingdom have similar product, captial and labor markets, with networks of skilled intermediaries and strong regulatory systems. The two nations share an Anglo-Saxon legal system as well. American companies can enter Britain, comfortable in the knowledge that they will find competent market research firms, that they can count on English law to enforce agreements they sign with potential partners, and that retailers will be able to distribute products all over the country. Those are dangerous assumptions to make in an emerging market, where skilled intermediaries or contract-enforcing mechanisms are unlikely to be found. However, composite indices don't flash warning signals to would-be entrants about the presence of institutional voids in emerging markets.

Composite index–based analyses of developing countries conceal more than they reveal (see the exhibit "The Trouble with Composite Indices"). In 2003, Brazil, Russia, India and China appeared similar on several indices. Yet despite the four countries' comparable standings, the key success factors in each of those markets have turned out to be very different. For instance, in China and Russia, multinational retail chains and local retailers have expanded into the urban and semi-urban areas, whereas in Brazil, only a few global chains have set up shop in key urban centers. In India, the government prohibited foreign direct investment in the retailing and real estate industries until February 2005, so mom-and-pop retailers dominate. Brazil, Russia, India and China may all be big markets for multinational consumer product makers, but executives have to design unique distribution strategies for each market. That process must start with a thorough understanding of the differences between the countries' market infrastructures. Those differences may make it more attractive for some businesses to enter, say, Brazil than India.

How to map institutional contexts

As we helped companies think through their globalization strategies, we came up with a simple conceptual device – the five contexts framework – that lets executives map the institutional contexts of any country. Economics 101 tells us that companies buy inputs in the product, labor, and capital markets and sell their outputs in the products (raw materials and finished goods) or services market. When choosing strategies, therefore, executives need to figure out how the product, labor, and capital markets work – and don't work – in their target countries. This will help them understand the differences between home markets and those in developing countries. In addition, each country's social and political milieu – as well as the manner in which it has opened up to the outside world – shapes those markets, and companies must consider those factors, too.

The five contexts framework places a superstructure of key markets on a base of sociopolitical choices. Many multinational corporations look at either the macro factors (the degree of openness and the sociopolitical atmosphere) or some of the market factors, but few pay attention to both. We have developed sets of questions that companies can ask to create a map of each country's context and to gauge the extent to which businesses must adapt their strategies to each one (see the exhibit "Spotting Institutional Voids"). Before we apply the framework to some developing countries, let's briefly touch on the five contexts.

Political and social systems

Every country's political system affects its product, labor and captial markets. In socialist societies like China, for instance, workers cannot form independent trade unions in the labor market, which affects wage levels. A country's social environment is also important. In South Africa, for example, the government's support for the transfer of assets to the historically disenfranchised native African community – a laudable social objective – has affected the development of the captial market. Such transfers usually price assets in an arbitrary fashion, which makes it hard for multinationals to figure out the value of South African companies and affects their assessments of potential partners.

The thorny relationships between ethnic, regional and linguistic groups in emerging markets also affects foreign investors. In Malaysia, for instance, foreign companies should enter into joint ventures only after checking if their potential partners belong to the majority Malay community or the economically dominant Chinese community, so as not to conflict with the government's longstanding policy of transferring some assets from Chinese to Malays. This policy arose because of a perception that the race riots of 1969 were caused by the tension between the Chinese haves and the Malay have-nots. Although the rhetoric has changed somewhat in the past few years, the pro-Malay policy remains in place.

Executives would do well to identify a country's power centers, such as its bureaucracy, media and civil society, and figure out if there are checks and balances in place. Managers must also determine how decentralized the political system is, if the government is subject to oversight and whether bureaucrats and politicians are independent from one another. Companies should gauge the level of actual trust among the populace as opposed to enforced trust. For instance, if people believe companies won't vanish with their savings, firms may be able to raise money locally sooner rather than later.

Openness

CEOs often talk about the need for economics to be open because they believe it's best to enter countries that welcome direct investment by multinational corporations, although companies can get into countries that don't allow foreign investment by entering into joint ventures or by licensing local partners. Still, they must remember that the concept of "open" can be deceptive. For example, executives believe that China is an open economy because the government welcomes foreign investment but that India is a relatively closed economy because of the lukewarm reception the Indian government gives multinationals. However, India has been open to ideas from the West, and people have always been able to travel freely in and out of the country, whereas for decades, the Chinese government didn't allow its citizens to travel abroad freely, it still doesn't allow many ideas to cross its borders. Consequently, while it may be true that multinational companies can invest in China more easily than they can in India, managers in India are more inclined to be market oriented and globally aware than managers are in China.

The more open a country's economy, the more likely it is that global intermediaries will be allowed to operate there. Multinationals, therefore, will find it easier to function in markets that are more open because they can use the services of both the global and local intermediaries. However, openness can be a double-edged sword: A government that allows local companies to access the global capital market neutralizes one of foreign companies' key advantages.

The two macro contexts we have just described – political and social systems and openness – shape the market contexts. For instance, in Chile, a military coup in the early 1970s led to the establishment of a right-wing government, and that government's liberal economic policies led to a vibrant captial market in the country. But Chile's labor market remained underdeveloped because the government did not allow trade unions to operate freely. Similarly, openness affects the development of markets. If a country's captial markets are open to foreign investors, financial intermediaries will become more sophisticated. That has happened in India, for example, where captial markets are more open than they are in China. Likewise, in the product market, if multinationals can invest in the retail industry, logistics providers will develop rapidly. This has been the case in China, where providers have taken hold more quickly than they have in India, which has only recently allowed multinationals to invest in retailing.

Product markets

Developing countries have opened up their markets and grown rapidly during the past decade, but companies still struggle to get reliable information about consumers, especially those with low incomes. Developing a consumer finance business is tough, for example, because the data sources an credit histories that firms draw on in the West don't exist in emerging markets. Market research and advertising are in their infancy in developing countries, and it's difficult to find the deep databases on consumption patterns that allow companies to segment consumers in more-developed markets. There are few government bodies or independent publications, like *Consumer Reports* in the United States, that provide expert advice on the features and quality of products. Because of a lack of consumer courts and advocacy groups in developing nations, many people feel they are at the mercy of big companies.

Labor markets

In spite of emerging markets' large populations, multinationals have trouble recruiting managers and other skilled workers because the quality of talent is hard to ascertain. There are relatively few search firms and recruiting agencies in low-income countries. The high-quality firms that do exist focus on top-level searches, so companies must scramble to identify middle-level managers, engineers, or floor supervisors. Engineering colleges, business schools and training institutions have proliferated, but apart from an elite few, there's no way for companies to tell which schools produce skilled managers. For instance, several Indian companies have sprung up to train people for jobs in the call center business, but no organization rates the quality of the training it provides.

Capital markets

The capital and financial markets in developing countries are remarkable for their lack of sophistication. Apart from a few stock exchanges and government-appointed regulators, there aren't many reliable intermediaries like credit-rating agencies, investment analysts, merchant bankers, or venture capital firms. Multinationals can't count on raising debt or equity capital locally to finance their operations. Like investors, creditors don't have access to accurate information on companies. Businesses can't easily assess the creditworthiness of other firms or collect receivables after they have extended credit to customers. Corporate governance is also notoriously poor in emerging markets. Transnational companies can't trust their partners to adhere to local laws and joint venture agreements. Since crony capitalism thrives in developing countries, multinationals can't assume that the profit motive alone is what's driving local firms.

Several CEOs have asked us why we emphasize the role of institutional intermediaries and ignore industry factors. They argue that industry structure, such as the degree of competition, should also influence companies' strategies. But when Harvard Business School professor Jan Rivkin and one of the authors of this article ranked industries by profitability, they found that the correlation of industry rankings across pairs of countries was close to zero, which means that the attractiveness of an industry varied widely from country to country. So although factors like scale economies, entry barriers, and the ability to differentiate products matter in every industry, the weight of their importance varies from place to place. An attractive industry in your home market may turn out to be unattractive in another country. Companies should analyze industry structures – always a useful exercise – only after they understand a country's institutional context.

Applying the framework

When we applied the five contexts framework to emerging markets in four countries – Brazil, Russia, India and China – the differences between them became apparent (see the exhibit "Mapping Contexts in Brazil, Russia, India and China"). Multinationals face different kinds of competition in each of those nations. In China, state-owned enterprises control nearly half the economy, members of the Chinese diaspora control many of the foreign corporations that operate there, and the private sector brings up the rear because entrepreneurs find it almost

---

Mapping contexts in Brazil, Russia, India and China

The five contexts (below) can help companies spot the institutional voids in any country. An application of the framework to the four fastest-growing markets in the world reveals how different those countries are from developed nations and, more important, from one another.

Political and social system

U.S./EU	Brazil	Russia	India	China
Political structure				
Countries have vibrant democracies with checks and balances. Companies can count on rule of law and fair enforcement of legal contracts.	The democracy is vibrant. Bureaucracy is rampant. There are pockets of corruption in federal and state governments.	A centralized government and some regional fiefdoms coexist. Bureaucracy is stifling. Corruption occurs at all levels of government.	The democracy is vibrant. The government is highly bureaucratic. Corruption is rampant in state and local governments.	The Communist Party maintains a monopoly on political power. Local governments make economic policy decisions. Officials may abuse power for personal gain.
Civil society				
A dynamic media acts as a check on abuses by both companies and governments. Powerful nongovernmental organizations (NGOs) influence corporate policies on social and environmental issues.	Influential local media serves as a watchdog. The influence of local NGOs is marginal.	The media is controlled by the government. NGOs are underdeveloped and disorganized.	A dynamic press and vigilant NGOs act as checks on politicians and companies.	The media is muzzled by the government, and there are few independent NGOs. Companies don't have to worry about criticism, but they can't count on civil society to check abuses of power.

Openness

U.S./EU	Brazil	Russia	India	China
Modes of entry				
Open to all forms of foreign investment except when governments have concerns about potential monopolies or national security issues.	Both greenfield investments and acquisitions are possible entry strategies. Companies team up with local partners to gain local expertise.	Both greenfield investments and acquisitions are possible but difficult. Companies form alliances to gain access to government and local inputs.	Restrictions on greenfield investments and acquisitions in some sectors make joint ventures necessary. Red tape hinders companies in sectors where the government does allow foreign investment.	The government permits greenfield investments as well as acquisitions. Acquired companies are likely to have been state owned and may have hidden liabilities. Alliances let companies align interests with all levels of government.

Product markets

U.S./EU	Brazil	Russia	India	China
Product development and intellectual property rights (IPR)				
Sophisticated product design capabilities are available. Governments enforce IPR and protect trademarks, so R&D investments yield competitive advantages.	Local design capability exists. IPR disputes with the United States exist in some sectors.	The country has a strong local design capability but exhibits an ambivalent attitude about IPR. Sufficient regulatory authority exists, but enforcement is patchy.	Some local design capability is available. IPR problems with the United States exist in some industries. Regulatory bodies monitor product quality and fraud.	Imitation and piracy abound. Punishment for IPR theft varies across provinces and by level of corruption.
Supplier base and logistics				
Companies use national and international suppliers. Firms outsource and move manufacturing and services offshore instead of integrating vertically. A highly developed infrastructure is in place, but urban areas are saturated.	Suppliers are available in the mercosur region. A good network of high-ways, airports, and ports exists.	Companies can rely on local suppliers for simple components. The European region has decent logistics networks, but trans-Ural Russia is not well developed.	Suppliers are available, but their quality and dependability varies greatly. Roads are in poor condition. Ports and airports are underdeveloped.	Several suppliers have strong manufacturing capabilities, but few vendors have advanced technical abilities. The road network is well developed. Port facilities are excellent.

Product markets (Continued)

U.S./EU	Brazil	Russia	India	China
Brand perceptions and management				
Markets are mature and have strong local and global brands. The profusion of brands clutters consumer choice. Numerous ad agencies are available.	Consumers accept both local and global brands. Global as well as local ad agencies are present.	Consumers prefer global brands in automobiles and high tech. Local brands thrive in the food and beverage businesses. Some local and global ad agencies are available.	Consumers buy both local and global brands. Global ad agencies are present, but they have been less successful than local ad agencies.	Consumers prefer to buy products from American, European, and Japanese companies. Multinational ad agencies dominate the business.

Labor markets

U.S./EU	Brazil	Russia	India	China
Markets for managers				
A large and varied pool of well-trained management talent exists.	The large pool of management talent has varying degrees of proficiency in English. Both local and expatriate managers hold senior management jobs.	The large pool of management talent has varying degrees of proficiency in English, and it is supplemented by expatriate managers. Employment agencies are booming.	The country has a highly liquid pool of English-speaking management talent fueled by business and technical schools. Local hires are preferred over expatriates.	There is a relatively small and static market for managers, especially away from the eastern seaboard. Many senior and middle managers aren't fluent in English. A large number of managers are expatriates. Some members of the Chinese diaspora have returned home to work.
Workers market				
The level of unionization varies among countries. Industrial actions take place in Europe, especially in the manufacturing and public sectors, but not in the United States.	Trade unions are strong and pragmatic, which means that companies can sign agreements with them.	Trade unions are present, but their influence is declining except in certain sectors, such as mining and railways.	The trade union movement is active and volatile, although it is becoming less important. Trade unions have strong political connections.	Workers can join the government-controlled All-China Federation of Trade Unions. Historically, there were no industrial actions, but there have been recent strikes at HongKong- and Taiwan-owned manufacturing facilities.

Capital markets

U.S./EU	Brazil	Russia	India	China
Debt and equity				
Companies can easily get bank loans. The corporate bond market is well developed. The integration of stock exchanges gives companies access to a deep pool of investors.	A good banking system exists, and there is a healthy market for initial public offerings. Wealthy individuals can invest in offshore accounts.	The banking system is strong but dominated by state-owned banks. The consumer credit market is booming, and the IPO market is growing. Firms must incorporate local subsidiaries to raise equity capital.	The local banking system is well developed, Multinationals can rely on local bank for local needs. Equity is available to local and foreign entities.	The local banking system and equity markets are underdeveloped. Foreign companies have to raise both debt and equity in home markets.
Venture capital (VC)				
VC is generally available in urban areas or for specific industry clusters. VC is not as readily available in southern Europe.	A few private equity players are active locally.	Only companies in the most profitable businesses, such as real estate development and natural resources, can access VC.	VC is available in some cities and from the Indian diaspora.	VC availability is limited.
Accounting standards				
Apart from off-balance-sheet items, a high level of transparency exists. In the European Union, accounting practices should become more uniform after 2005 because of new norms.	The financial-reporting system is based on a common-law system and functions well.	The modified Soviet system of financial reporting works well. Banks are shifting to international accounting standards.	Financial reporting, which is based on a common-law system, functions well.	There is little corporate transparency. China's accounting standards are not strict, although the China Securities Regulatory Commission wants to tighten disclosure rules.
Financial distress				
Efficient bankruptcy processes tend to favor certain stakeholders (creditors, labor force, or shareholders) in certain countries.	Processes allow companies to say in business rather than go out of business. Bankruptcy processes exist but are inefficient.	Bankruptcy processes and legislation are fully developed. Corruption distorts bankruptcy enforcement.	Bankruptcy processes exist but are inefficient. Promoters find it difficult to sell off or shut down "sick" enterprises.	Companies can use bankruptcy processes in some cases. Write-offs are common.

Source: Media reports and interviews with academics and businesspeople.

Spotting institutional voids

Managers can identify the institutional voids in any country by asking a series of questions. The answers – or sometimes, the lack of them – will tell companies where they should adapt their business models to the nation's institutional context.

Political and social system

1. To whom are the country's politician accountable? Are there strong political groups that oppose the ruling party? Do elections take place regularly?
2. Are the roles of the legislative, executive, and judiciary clearly defined? What is he distribution of power between the central, state, and city governments?
3. Does the government go beyond regulating business to interfering in it or running companies?
4. Do the laws articulate and protect private property rights?
5. What is the quality of the country's bureaucrats? What are bureaucrats' incentives and career trajectories?
6. Is the judiciary independent? Do the courts adjudicate disputes and enforce contracts in a timely and impartial manner? How effective are the quasi-judicial regulatory institutions that set and enforce rules for business activities?
7. Do religious, linguistic, regional, and ethnic groups coexist peacefully, or are there tensions between them?
8. How vibrant and independent is the media? Are newspapers and magazines neutral, or do they represent sectarian interests?
9. Are nongovernmental organizations, civil rights groups, and environmental groups active in the country?
10. Do people tolerant corruption in business and government?
11. What role do family ties play in business?
12. Can strangers be trusted to honor a contract in the country?

Openness

1. Are the country's government, media, and people receptive to foreign investment? Do citizens trust companies and individuals from some parts of the world more than others?
2. What restrictions does the government place on foreign investment? Are those restrictions in place to facilitate the growth of domestic companies, to protect state monopolies, or because people are suspicious of multinationals?
3. Can a company make greenfield investments and acquire local companies, or can it only break into the market by entering into joint ventures? Will that company be free to choose partners based purely on economic considerations?
4. Does the country allow the presence of foreign intermediaries such as market research and advertising firms, retailers, media companies, banks, insurance companies, venture capital firms, auditing firms, management consulting firms, and educational institutions?
5. How long does it take to start a new venture in the country? How cumbersome are the government's procedures for permitting the launch of a wholly foreign-owned business?
6. Are these restrictions on portfolio investments by overseas companies or on dividend repatriation by multinationals?
7. Does the market drive exchange rates, or does the government control them? If it's the latter, does the government try to maintain a stable exchange rate, or does it try to favor domestic products are imports by propping up the local currency?
8. What would be the impact of tariffs on a company's capital gods and raw materials imports? How would import duties affect that company's ability to manufacture its products locally versus exporting them from home?
9. Can a company set up its business anywhere in the country? If the government restricts the company's location choices, are its motives political, or is it inspired by a logical regional development strategy?

Openness (Continued)

10. Has the country signed free-trade agreements with other nations? If so, do those agreements favor investments by companies from some parts of the world over others?
11. Does the government allow foreign executives to enter and leave the country freely? How difficult is it to get work permits for mangers and engineers?
12. Does the country allow its citizens to travel abroad freely? Can ideas flow into the country unrestricted? Are people permitted to debate and accept those ideas?

Product markets

1. Can companies easily obtain reliable data on customer tastes and purchase behaviors? Are there cultural barriers to market research? Do world-class market research firms operate in the country?
2. Can consumers easily obtain unbiased information on the quality of the goods and services they want to buy? Are there independent consumer organizations and publications that provide such information?
3. Can companies access raw materials and components of good quality? Is there a deep network of suppliers? Are there firms that assess supplier's quality and reliability? Can companies enforce contracts with suppliers?
4. How strong are the logistics and transportation infrastructures? Have global logistics companies set up local operations?
5. Do large retail chains exist in the country? If so, do they cover the entire country or only the major cities? Do they reach all consumers or only wealthy ones?
6. Are there other types of distribution channels, such as direct-to-consumer channels and discount retail channels, that deliver products to customers?
7. Is it difficult for multinationals to collect receivables from local retailers?
8. Do consumers use credit cards, or does cash dominate transactions? Can consumers get credit to make purchases? Are date on customer creditworthiness available?
9. What recourse do consumers have against false claims by companies or defective products and services?
10. How do companies deliver after-sales services to consumers? Is it possible to set up a nationwide service network? Are third-party service providers reliable?
11. Are consumers willing to try new products and services? Do they trust goods from local companies? How about from foreign companies?
12. What kind of product-related environmental and safety regulations are in place? How do the authorities enforce those regulations?

Labor markets

1. How strong is the country's education infrastructure, especially for technical and management training? Does it have a good elementary and secondary education system as well?
2. Do people study and do business in English or in another international language, or do they mainly speak a local language?
3. Are data available to be help sort out the quality of the country's educational institutions?
4. Can employees move easily from one company to another? Does the local culture support that movement? Do recruitment agencies facilitate executive mobility?
5. What are the major postrecruitment-training needs of the people that multinationals hire locally?
6. Is pay for performance a standard practice? How much weight do executives give seniority, as opposed to merit, in making promotion decisions?

Labor markets (Continued)

7. Would a company be able to enforce employment contracts with senior executives? Could it protect itself against executives who leave the firm and then compete against it? Could it stop employees from stealing trade secrets and intellectual property?
8. Does the local culture accept foreign managers? Do the laws allow a firm to transfer locally hired people to an other country? Do managers want to stay or leave the nation?
9. How are the rights of workers protected? How strong are the country's trade unions? Do they defend workers' interests or only advance a political agenda?
10. Can companies use stock options and stock-based compensation schemes to motivate employees?
11. Do the law and regulations limit a firm's ability to restructure, downsize, or shut down?
12. If a company where to adopt its local rivals' or suppliers' business practices, such as the use of child labor, would that tarnish its image overseas?

Capital markets

1. How effective are the country's banks, insurance companies, and mutual funds at collecting savings and channeling them into investments?
2. Are financial institutions managed well? Is their decision making transparent? Do noneconomic considerations, such as family ties, influence their investment decisions?
3. Can companies raise large amounts of equity capital in the stock market? Is there a market for corporate debt?
4. Does a venture capital industry exist? If so, does it allow individuals with good ideas to raise funds?
5. How reliable are sources of information on company performance? Do the accounting standards and disclosures regulations permit investors and creditors to monitor company management?
6. Do independent financial analysts, rating agencies, and the media offer unbiased information on companies?
7. How effective are corporate governance norms and standards at protecting shareholder interests?
8. Are corporate boards independent and empowered, and do they have independent directors?
9. Are regulators effective at monitoring the banking industry and stock markets?
10. How well do they courts deal with fraud?
11. Do the laws permit companies to engage in hostile takeovers? Can shareholders organize themselves to remove entrenched managers through proxy fights?
12. Is there an orderly bankruptcy process that balances the interests of owners, creditors, and other stockholders?

impossible to access capital. India is the mirror image of China. Public sector corporations, though important, occupy nowhere near as prominent a place as they do in China. Unlike China, India is wary of foreign investment, even by members of the Indian diaspora. However, the country has spawned many private sector organizations, some of which are globally competitive. It's difficult to imagine a successful business in China that hasn't had something to do with the government; in India, most companies have succeeded in spite of the state.

Brazil mixes and matches features of both China and India. Like Chine, Brazil has floated many state-owned enterprises. At the same time, it has kept its doors open to multinationals, and European corporations such as Unilever, Volkswagen and Nestlé have been able to build big businesses there. Volkswagen has six plants in Brazil, dominates the local market, and exports its Gol model to Argentina and Russia. Brazil also boasts private sector companies that, like Indian firms, go head-to-head in the local market with global firms. Some Brazilian companies, such as basic materials company Votorantim and aircraft maker Embraer, have become globally competitive.

Russia is also a cross between China and India, but most of its companies are less competitive than those in Brazil. A few multinationals such as McDonald's have done well, but most foreign firms have failed to make headway there. There are only a few strong private sector companies in the market, such as dairy products maker Wimm-Bill-Dann and cellular services provider VimpelCom. The Russian government is involved, formally and informally, in several industries. For instance, the government's equity stake in Gazprom allows it to influence the country's energy sector. Moreover, administrators at all levels can exercise near veto power over business deals that involve local or foreign companies, and getting permits and approvals is a complicated chore in Russia.

One level deeper, the financial markets in Brazil, Russia, India and China vary, too. In Brazil and India, indigenous entrepreneurs, who are multinationals' main rivals, rely on the local capital markets for resources. In China, foreign companies compete with state-owned enterprises, which public sector banks usually fund. The difference is important because neither the Chinese companies nor the banks are under pressure to show profits. Moreover, financial reporting in China isn't transparent even if companies have listed themselves on stock exchanges. State-owned companies can for years pursue strategies that increase their market share at the expense of profits. Corporate governance standards in Brazil and India also mimic those of the West more closely than do those in Russia and China. In Russia and China, multinationals can't count on local partners' internal systems to protect their interests and assets especially their intellectual property.

The three strategy choices

When companies tailor strategies to each country's contexts, they can capitalize on the strengths of particular locations. Before adapting their approaches, however, firms must compare the benefits of doing so with the additional coordination costs they'll incur. When they complete this exercise, companies will find that they have three distinct choices: They can adapt their business model to countries while keeping their core value propositions constant, they can try to change the contexts, or they can stay out of countries where adapting strategies may be uneconomical or impractical. Can companies sustain strategies that presume the existence of institutional voids? They can. It took decades to fill institutional voids in the West.

Adapt your strategies

To succeed, multinationals must modify their business models for each nation. They may have to adapt to the voids in a country's product markets, its input markets, or both. But companies must retain their core business propositions even as they adapt their business models. If they make shifts that are too radical, these firms will lose their advantages of global scale and global branding.

Compare Dell's business models in the United States and China. In the United States, the hardware maker offers consumers a wide variety of configurations and makes most computers to order. Dell doesn't use distributors or resellers, shipping most machines directly to buyers. In 2003, nearly 50 per cent of the company's revenues in North America came from orders placed through the Internet.

The cornerstone of Dell's business model is that it carries little or no inventory. But Dell realized that its direct-sales approach wouldn't work in China, because individuals weren't accustomed to buying PCs through the Internet. Chinese companies used paper-based order processing, so Dell had to rely on faxes and phones rather than online sales. Several Chinese government departments and state-owned enterprises insisted that hardware venors make their bids through systems integrators. The upshot is that Dell relies heavily on distributors and systems integrators in China. When it first entered the market there, the company offered a smaller product range than it did in the United States to keep inventory levels low. Later, as its supply chain became more efficient, it offered customers in China a full range of products.

Smart companies like Dell modify their business model without destroying the parts of it that give them a competitive advantage over rivals. These firms start by identifying the value propositions that they will not modify, whatever the context. That's what McDonald's did even as it comprehensively adapted its business model to Russia's factor markets. In the United States, McDonald's has outsourced most of its supply chain operations. But when it tried to move into Russia in 1990, the company was unable to find local suppliers. The fast-food chain asked several of its European vendors to step up, but they weren't interested. Instead of giving up, McDonald's decided to go it alone. With the help of its joint venture partner, the Moscow City Administration, the company identified some Russian farmers and bakers it could work with. It imported cattle from Holland and russet potatoes from America, brought in agricultural specialists from Canada and Europe to improve the farmers' management practices, and advanced the farmers money so that they could invest in better seeds and equipment.

Then the company built a 100,000 square-foot McComplex in Moscow to produce beef, bakery, potato, dairy products, ketchup, mustard and Big Mac sauce. It set up a trucking fleet to move supplies to restaurants and financed its suppliers so that they would have enough working capital to buy modern equipment. The company also brought in about 50 expatriate managers to teach Russian employees about its services standards, quality measurements and operating procedures and sent a 23-person team of Russian managers to Canada for a four-month training program. McDonald's created a vertically integrated operation in Russia, but the company clung to one principle: It would sell only hamburgers, fries and Coke to Russians in a clean environment – and fast. Fifteen years after serving its first Big Mac in Moscow's Pushkin Square, McDonald's has invested $250 million in the country and controls 80 per cent of the Russian fast-food market.

Change the contexts

Many multinationals are powerful enough to alter the contexts in which they operate. The products or services these companies offer can force dramatic changes in local markets. When Asia's first satellite TV channel, Hong Kong–based STAR, launched in 1991, for example, it transformed the Indian marketplace in many ways. Not only did the company cause the Indian government to lose its monopoly on television broadcasts overnight, but it also led to a booming TV-manufacturing industry and the launch of several other satellite-based channels aimed at Indian audiences. By the mid-1990s satellite-based TV channels had become a vibrant advertising medium, and many organizations used them to launch products and services targeted at India's new TV-watching consumer class.

The entry of foreign companies transforms quality standards in local product markets, which can have far-reaching consequences. Japan's Suzuki triggered a quality revolution after it entered India in 1981. The automaker's need for large volumes of high-quality components roused local suppliers. They teamed up with Suzuki's vendors in Japan, formed quality clusters, and worked with Japanese experts to produce better products. During the next two decades, the total quality management movement spread to other industries in India. By 2004, Indian companies had bagged more Deming prizes than Firms in any country other than Japan. More important, India's automotive suppliers had succeeded in breaking into the global market, and several of them, such as Sundram Fasteners, had become preferred suppliers to international automakers like GM.

Companies can change contexts in factor markets, too. Consider the capital market in Brazil. As multinationals set up subsidiaries in those countries, they needed global-quality audit services. Few Brazilian accounting firms could provide those services, so the Big Four audit firms – Deloitte Touche Tohmatsu, Ernst & Young, KPMG and Pricewaterhouse-Coopers – decided to set up branches there. The presence of those companies quickly raised financial-reporting and auditing standards in Brazil.

In a similar vein, Knauf, one of Europe's leading manufacturers of building materials, is trying to grow Russia's talent market. During the past decade, the German giant has built 20 factories in Russia and invested more than $400 million there. Knauf operators in a people-intensive industry; the company and its subsidiaries have roughly 7,000 employees in Russia. To boost standards in the country's construction industry, Knauf opened an education center in St. Petersburg in 2003 that works closely with the State Architectural and Construction University. The school acts both as a mechanism that supplies talent to Knauf and as an institution that contributes to the much-needed development of Russian architecture.

Indeed, as firms change contexts, they must help countries fully develop their potential. That creates a win-win situation for the country and the company. Metro Cash & Carry, a division of German trading company Metro Group, has been changed contexts in a socially beneficial way in several European and Asian countries. The Düsseldorf-based company – which sells everything to restaurants from meats and vegetables to napkins and toothpicks – entered China in 1996, Russia in 2001, and India in 2003. Metro has pioneered business links between farmers and small-scale manufacturers in rural areas that sell their products to small and midsize urban companies.

For instance, Metro invested in a cold chain in China so that it could deliver goods such as fish and meats from rural regions to urban locations. That changed local conditions in several important ways. First, Metro's investment induced farmers in China to invest more in their agricultural operations. Metro also lobbied with governments for quality standards to prevent companies from selling shoddy produce to hapless consumers. By shifting transactions from roadside markets to computerized warehouses, the company's operations brought primary products into the tax net. Governments, which need the money to invest in local services, have remained on the company's side. That's a good thing for Metro since, in developing markets, the jury is always out on foreign companies.

Stay away

It may be impractical or uneconomical for some firms to adapt their business models to emerging markets. Home Depot, the successful do-it-yourself U.S. retailer, has been cautious about entering developing countries. The company offers a specific value proposition to customers: low prices, great service and good quality. To pull that off, it relies on a variety of U.S.-specific institutions. It depends on the U.S. highways and logistical management systems to minimize the amount of inventory it has to carry in its large, warehouse-style stores.

It relies on employee stock ownership to motivate shop-level workers to render top-notch service. Its value proposition takes advantage of the fact that high labor costs in the United States encourage home owners to engage in do-it-yourself projects.

Home Depot made a tentative foray into emerging markets by setting up two stores in Chile in 1998 and another in Argentina in 2000. In 2001, however, the company sold those operations for a net loss of $14 million. At the time, CEO Robert Nardelli emphasized that most of home Depot's future growth was likely to come from North America. Despite that initial setback, the company hasn't entirely abandoned emerging markets. Rather, it has switched from a greenfield strategy to an acquisition-led approach. In 2001, Home Depot entered Mexico by buying a home improvement retailer, Total Home, and the next year, it acquired Del Norte, another small chain. By 2004, the company had 42 stores in Mexico. Although Home Depot has recently said that it is exploring the possibility of entering China, perhaps by making an acquisition, it doesn't have retail operations in any other developing countries.

Home depot must consider whether it can modify its U.S. business model to suit the institutional contexts of emerging markets. In a country with a poorly developed capital market, for example, the company may not be able to use employee stock ownership as a compensation tool. Similarly, in a country with a poorly developed physical infrastructure, Home Depot may have difficulty using its inventory management systems, a scenario that would alter the economics of the business. In markets where labor costs are relatively low, the target customer may not be the home owner but rather contractors who serve as intermediaries between the store and the home owner. That change in customer focus may warrant an entirely different marketing and merchandising strategy, one that Home Depot isn't convinced it should deploy yet.

While companies can't use the same strategies in all developing countries, they can generate synergies by treating different markets as part of a system. For instance, GE Healthcare (formerly GE Medical Systems) makes parts for its diagnostic machines in China, Hungary and Mexico and develops the software for those machines in India. The company created this system when it realized that the market for diagnostic machines was small in most low-income countries. GE Healthcare then decided to use the facility it had set up in India in 1990 as a global sourcing base. After several years, and on the back of borrowed expertise from GE Japan, the India operation's products finally met GE Healthcare's exacting standards. In the late 1990s, when GE Healthcare wanted to move a plant from Belgium to cut costs, the Indian subsidiary beat its Mexican counterpart by delivering the highest quality at the lowest cost. Under its then-CEO, Jeff Immelt, GE Healthcare learned to use all its operations in low-income countries – China, Hungary, Mexico and India – as parts of a system that allowed the company to produce equipment cheaply for the world market.

Parent company GE has also tapped into the talent pool in emerging markets by setting up technology centers in Shanghai and Bangalore, for instance. In those centers, the company conducts research on everything from materials design to molecular modeling to power electronics. GE doesn't treat China and India just as markets but also as sources of talent and innovation that can transform its value chain. That's how multinational companies should engage with emerging markets if they wish to secure their future.

32 The hidden risks in emerging markets*

Witold J. Henisz and Bennet A. Zelner

When a firm with a value-generating technological or managerial capability invests abroad, its shareholders and the host country's citizens both stand to benefit. But no matter how good the apparent fit between what foreign companies offer and what host countries need, success is far from assured. Elections and other political events, economic crises and changing societal attitudes can disrupt the best-laid plans in both emerging and advanced economics. The interplay of these forces—and the implications for the political choices that multinational firms make—will become especially prominent as national governments chart an uncertain course toward stabilization following the global financial meltdown.

Issues such as taxation of executive compensation, the proper scope of financial regulation, and international M&A have come to the foreground in the wake of crisis, and stark international differences in opinions and policies on these matters are already evident. The differences will only become more pronounced as discussions about the appropriate near-term policy response to the crisis give way to debates about who should pay and how much. Politicians will struggle to balance popular demands to punish those perceived as responsible against fears of stymied innovation and the flight of human and financial capital. Broader domestic economic concerns, for example, protectionist sentiment in response to the realignment of economic power in favor of emerging nations such as China and India, will inevitably affect the debate as well. The multinational firms best able to anticipate and manage the related risks and opportunities will have the strongest competitive edge.

Historically, the biggest risks faced by foreign investors were in developing countries with immature or volatile political systems. The chief concern was "expropriation risk", the possibility that host governments would seize foreign-owned assets. Today, this risk has largely disappeared. Stronger international law and the symbiotic nature of growth in emerging and developed economics reduced asset seizures to nearly zero during the 1980s. However, as interest in emerging markets has soared, host countries have learned, according to George Chifor at the University of Windsor in Canada, "that more value can be extracted from foreign enterprises through the more subtle instrument of regulatory control rather than outright seizures". The risk that a government will discriminatory change the laws, regulations, or contracts governing an investment—or will fail to enforce them—in a way that reduces an investor's financial returns is what we call "policy risk".

Although the data on policy risk are less clear-cut than the hard numbers on direct seizures, press mentions of policy risk (using terms such as "political risk", "political uncertainty",

*Reprinted with permission from Harvard Business Review. Henisz, Witold J. & Bennet A. Zelner (2010) "The Hidden Risks in Emerging Markets", Harvard Business Review April: 88–95.

"policy risk", "policy uncertainty", "regulatory risk" and "regulatory uncertainty") indicate that it has risen dramatically as seizure risk has fallen. (See the exhibit "The changing face of risk in emerging markets.") Press mentions of actual seizure have also increased somewhat since 2001, but that does not reflect a broad-based resurgence in seizures.

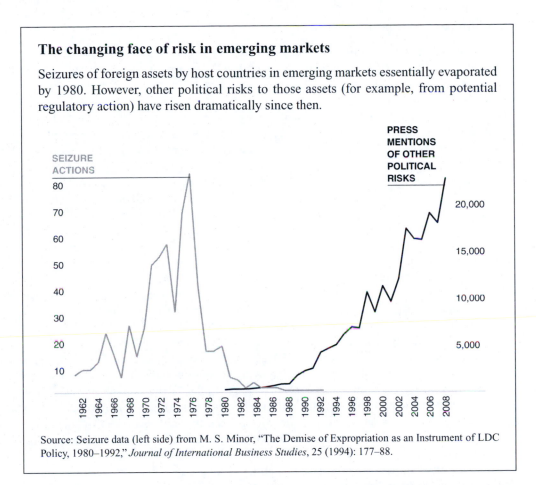

The changing face of risk in emerging markets

Seizures of foreign assets by host countries in emerging markets essentially evaporated by 1980. However, other political risks to those assets (for example, from potential regulatory action) have risen dramatically since then.

Source: Seizure data (left side) from M. S. Minor, "The Demise of Expropriation as an Instrument of LDC Policy, 1980–1992," *Journal of International Business Studies*, 25 (1994): 177–88.

Other recent data are consistent with the finding that policy risk has increased greatly. A 2001 PriceWaterhouseCoopers study concluded that an opaque policy-making environment is equivalent to at least a 33% increase in taxation. A World Bank study in 2004 revealed that 15–30% of the contracts covering $371 billion of private infrastructure investment in the 1990s were subject to government-initiated renegotiations or disputes. A 2009 survey by the Multilateral Investment Guarantee Agency and the Economist Intelligence Unit found that multinational enterprises considered breach of contract, restrictions on the transfer and con-vertibility of profits, civil disturbance, government failure to honor guarantees and regulatory restrictions all to be more significant risks than the potential seizure of assets.

Unfortunately, the traditional financial and contractual mechanisms that firms use to assess and mitigate business risks have limited value. Therefore, investors must develop proactive political-management strategies that lessen government officials' incentives to divert investors' returns. In this article, we explore the experiences of multinational investors as they confront these issues in variety of industries and countries, and we offer best-practice guidelines for assessing the political landscape and for modeling political decision making. As with the management of any risk or uncertainty, political mastery can become a source of competitive advantage in addition to a means of avoiding losses.

Its's hard to hedge policy risk

Firms engaged in international business often use some combination of legal contracts, insurance, and trade in financial instruments to protect the income streams from their investments against currency or price swings. These approaches, however, offer little protection against policy risk.

For starters, legal contracts are useful only if they are enforced, and shifting laws and regulations can render them void. In the 1990s many Southeast Asian governments wooing private power investors offered contracts that insulated the investors from risks related to lower-than-expected demand, fuel supplies, exchange rates, currency conversions, regulations and political force majeure. The Asian financial crisis in 1997 brought those investors' favorable treatment into sharp relief as currency values, share prices and electricity demand all plummeted. Political officials had to choose between honoring the contracts, at the risk of compromising their own popular support and renegotiating them in order to maintain that support. In the end, many career-minded public officials in Southeast Asia chose to renegotiate or cancel scores of contracts.

Even when contracts can be legally enforced, experience shows that inventive politicians can circumvent them, through a wide variety of means other than changing laws. For example, in 1998, when U.S.-based AES Corporation—then the world's largest independent power company—acquired the Georgian electricity distribution company Telasi, high-priced lawyers constructed an ironclad set of guarantees that allowed AES-Telasi to pass the costs of policy and other risks on to Georgian consumers. One analyst remarked to us: "If you believed the contract, AES was guaranteed a 20% return on its investment." The Georgian government actually never interfered formally with AES-Telasi's ability to pass costs on to consumers. However, the venture was doomed by public officials' inaction, for instance, their failure to terminate supply to nonpaying industrial consumers, to supply fuel to AES-Telasi and to keep the government's own account current, and by the government's demand for tax payments on electricity for which the company had never been paid. The result was that AES's "guaranteed" 20% return became a shareholder losses of $300 million.

Insurance offers limited protection against policy risk because a firm's exposure is largely determined by its own ability to manage the policy-making process. In the words of one insurer: "I prefer to focus on what my assured [customer] can bring to risk. My reasoning is that if you back the right assured, you can usually keep problems from occurring in the first place—and if they do happen, you have an excellent chance of mitigating your loses." It is very difficult for insurers to know who the "right assured" is, and the firms with the greatest risk exposure are often those most likely to seek insurance in the first place. As a result, underwriters price their products extremely high, offer very short-term coverage, or don't offer any coverage, or don't offer any coverage at all.

Financial hedges have limited value for similar reasons. Instruments for hedging against risks in specific emerging markets—such as exchange-rate, market and credit risks—are ubiquitous because multiple parties are willing to participate. The project- and firm-specific nature of policy risk, however, renders conventional hedging strategies infeasible.

Some of the more-inventive instruments are based on the average risk premium associated with existing companies in a given country—but they give false comfort. Because the baseline risk premiums are those of firms that are actively participating in a given market (and that often have their risk-mitigation strategies in place), new entrants are likely to face far greater exposure. Foreign investors who focus on constructing financial hedges at the expense of developing their own risk-mitigation strategies may increase their exposure. It is therefore not surprising that, despite the ability to calculate residual risk premiums, no financial institutions have used such premiums to price an instrument that pays out money when a policy risk is realized.

The new risk-management playbook

Given the difficulty of constructing hedges against policy risk through contracts, insurance, or financial risk-management tools, foreign investors must accept the responsibility for directly managing the risk themselves. For many companies, that means rewriting the playbook. Instead of looking for immediate ways to improve operations, managers have to move beyond the quick cost–benefit analyses that they usually undertake and think more about how they can frame and shape public debate. And they must learn how to apply political pressure, either individually or as part of a coalition.

Investing in goodwill

In the developed world, managers spend a great deal of time and energy on improving efficiency. When companies move into less developed markets, they often expect huge, instant efficiency gains from exploiting the technologies, business models and practices that they have managed to hone in their home markets. Unfortunately, the political costs of such practices may outweigh those gains.

Consider the 1997 Christmas blackout in large parts of Brazil, including Rio de Janeiro. The then recently privatized electric utility Light (in which AES held a 13.75% stake) faced record-high outdoor temperatures that week, and it was already struggling with poorly maintained equipment that had deteriorated before privatization. However, the press and the public focused on the 40% reduction in personnel, combined with the utility company's record profits, to paint a picture of an exploitative foreign investor. The negative sentiment toward foreign firms in general and AES in particular contributed to the awarding of a 900-megawatt energy-supply contract the following spring to a joint venture led by Brazilian firms (Votorantim Group, Bradesco Group and Camargo Corrêa) rather than consortia led by AES and British Gas.

A smarter approach was used by Italian state-owned oil company Eni. After the 1998 devaluation of the *real*, when many companies put their investment plans on hold or even exited Brazil, Eni's then-CEO, Franco Bernabe, visited Rio de Janeiro to announce a $500 million investment. He proclaimed: "Now is the time to show that Petrobras [the state-owned oil company] has long-term friends." Eni and Petrobras have collaborated closely ever since.

Framing the debate

When companies enter new countries, they often engage in extensive PR campaigns that amount to little more than advertisements for the brand and specific commercial ventures. Instead, firms need to master the art of political spin. Presenting a venture as "fair", "equitable", or "growth enhancing" is often a simpler and more powerful means of securing political support than providing a cost–benefit analysis. The precise meaning attributed to such labels varies depending on a firm's market position. New entrants garner support for policies that favor them over incumbents by citing the abuse of monopoly power. Conversely, domain firms appeal to "fairness" by arguing that smaller entrants cannot survive without the government's helping hand.

This type of debate played out in the South Korean wireless market. LG Telecom—the third entrant, behind the much larger SK Telecom and Korea Telecom—made repeated calls for "asymmetric" government regulation of the market leaders in order to "level the playing field". As the *Korea Times* reported, "The defining question is whether the government will back new entrants in the name of encouraging fair competition, or limit the pool to experienced players". LG ultimately prevailed: In May 2001 the South Korean government announced that it would "guarantee a market share of at least 20% for a third major telecom operator through asymmetric regulation on Korea Telecom and SK Telecom".

Finding political pressure points

The network of relationships in a society greatly influences policy outcomes, especially in countries with weak legal systems. To turn these networks to their advantage, international investors must identify and engage local politicians' power bases. Once again, Eni has shown the way, this time in Kazakhstan. Through its subsidiary Agip KCO, Eni has adopted a business model that responds to the former Soviet republic's economic and social needs. The company favours Kazakh over non-Kazakh suppliers, and it conducts knowledge-transfer, training, and development seminars for them. At least 60% of local employees are Kazakh citizens. The company also funds the construction of various public works, including the national library, the prime minister's residence, schools, computer labs, and multifamily housing units for the poor. As a result, many Kazakh officials now have a stake in Eni's success.

For the vast majority of organizations—which do not possess enough leverage to influence the full range of relevant actors on their own—a crucial component of an effective strategy is to assemble a coalition of interests. In the South Korean wireless battle, LG Telecom benefited from the influence of upstream suppliers. The major Korean carriers wanted to shift to the globally favored WCDMA standard for the newest generation of cellular service, but domestic champion Samsung had developed a global leadership position in the competing CDMA2000 technology. Under pressure from Samsung, the government insisted that one of the new 3G licenses be awarded to LG Telecom in return for its promise to adopt CDMA2000.

An international investor's home government can also be a powerful channel of influence. Observers in central Europe have noted the lobbying success of the German and French governments on behalf of national champions in countries seeking EU membership. However, the use of "foreign influence" may create a perception of meddling, can stoke nationalism and is generally less likely to have a lasting impact. There's also the risk that your home government will sacrifice your needs in order to gain traction on another issue.

Taking these pages out of the political playbook requires building the sorts of capabilities in intelligence gathering and analysis that are familiar to politicians, spies, and journalists. Managers must begin by understanding the attitudes, opinions and positions of relevant actors toward their firm, the industry in which the firm operators and any specific actions that the firm might take to influence outcomes on the playing field.

Tapping the right flow of data

Traditionally, managers who have undertaken political analysis in a host country have directly consulted employees, local business partners, and supply chain partners. The information-gathering process varies in intensity and structure, ranging from surveying radio and newspaper stories to conversing with locals to computerized contact-management systems. Some firms rely almost exclusively on informal chats, whereas others favor more-formal Delphi (iterative expert survey) methods. (See the sidebar "Why country risk ratings don't work.")

Why country risk ratings don't work

When it comes to assessing levels of policy risk, managers are far too quick to rely on the subjective ratings of country "experts". One popular index focuses on asset-seizure and contract-repudiation risks. Ratings are incorporated, in the form of country risk premiums, into the discount rates used to evaluate investment opportunities. This approach appears to have the formal rigor of financial risk management, but it is actually inadequate.

To begin with, such ratings usually fail to account for the fact that the levels of policy risk vary among different investors in a country, some of whom may adapt their business practices to local norms and lobby key policy makers better than others do. Also, policy-risk exposure is to some extent contingent on the relative importance of the proposed investment to the two parties (how easy is it for the firm to walk away and how badly does the local government want the deal?). Finally, country risk ratings are usually retrospective, reflecting past policy outcomes. To assess the correlation with current policy risk, an analyst needs to determine how similar the past and present policy-shaping factors actually are.

Even as purely country-level measures, most political risk scorecards are woefully short on analysis, as an example from Chile and Indonesia clearly shows. In 1997, one risk index ascribed an identical score to those two countries. The measure took no account of the significant institutional differences between them. Faced with violent citizen demands to redistribute investor returns in the wake of the 1997 Asian financial crisis, Indonesia's longtime military dictator, General Suharto, renegotiated contracts with foreign investors that were unaffiliated with his family or close friends. After he was ousted in a coup, the previously favored companies experienced a backslash as the successor government renegotiated their contracts.

Chile, in contrast, had a democratic multiparty system and possessed a well-respected independent judiciary, a further check against arbitrary policy change. Pressures in Chile to enhance equity and social cohesion culminated in the 2000 election of socialist Ricardo Lagos as president. He shifted some discretionary spending toward social programs but also respected the rule of law and existing commercial contracts. Underlying risks in Chile and Indonesia were therefore very different, but the country-level ratings didn't reflect those distinct realities.

Although these sources provide valuable conventional input, they can require more time and money than such small, subjective, potentially biased snapshots might merit. Moreover, given the availability of multiple real-time indicators and metrics in functional areas such as finance, marketing and human resources, CEOs and boards of directors increasingly demand similar real-time data on the preferences of key players. This human intelligence can be effectively and continuously incorporated into enterprise risk-management models and frameworks.

To broaden their perspectives, more and more companies are reaching out to nonbusiness organizations that can help them anticipate and preempt consumer concerns about environmental, health and safety issues. For example, after a bruising experience over the disposal of its Brent Spar oil-drilling platform in 1995, Royal Dutch Shell now routinely includes Greenpeace in substantive environmental discussions. Some companies also consult professional experts, ranging from well-positioned ex-government officials operating on retainer; to the stringers who write for the Economist Intelligence Unit, Stratford and Oxford Analytica; to global political consultancies, such as Political Risk Services or Eurasia Group. Although employees, suppliers and activists may have access to better information, they lack the specialized training that these advisors bring to the table.

Of increasing importance is the vast amount of information emanating from third-party sources—primarily the mainstream news media, but also bloggers and other observers—that routinely monitor the policy-making process in various countries. The large volume and relatively unfocused nature of the material make it hard to synthesize, digest and act upon effectively, even if a company has substantial resources for this activity. However, with information-extraction software, it's now possible to identify the relevant political and social actors on a given issue and their intensity of interest in it.

One approach, known as data mining, relies on the coincident location of words to derive information about key players' preferences. For example, the occurrence of "Russia",

Are the locals hostile to you?

Information-extraction software can capture changes in attitudes toward a business venture by syntactically analyzing the content of media reports about it. This example compares the total number of sentences in an article about Gabriel Resources' plan to develop the Rosia Montana gold mine in Romania with the percentage of sentences indicating NGO opposition to the plan.

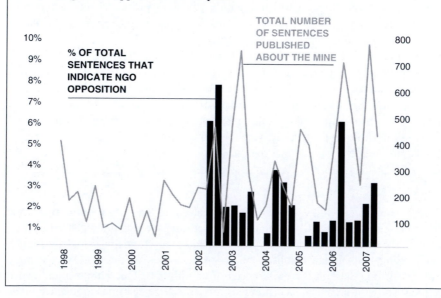

"AES-Telasi" and "protest" in the same sentence implies a negative sentiment in the relationship between Russia and the electricity investor AES-Telasi. Another tool, called natural language parsing (NLP) software, facilities more-refined sentence-level inferences by syntactically distinguishing among subjects, verbs, and objects, thereby identifying the orientation of actions or preferences. Consider this possible sentence: "The Union of Consumers of Georgia is outraged by the AES-Telasi American company proposal to increase the tariff on electric energy." NLP software would recognize the precise grammatical relationship among "Union of Consumers of Georgia", "is outraged by" and "AES-Telasi...proposal", pointing to a strong negative sentiment toward the U.S. company. NLP software can also gauge the intensity of sentiment. If the verb phrase in the sentence had been "objects to" instead of "is outraged by", the software would have recognized that the sentiment of the Union of Consumers of Georgia toward AES was negative, but less so.

Similarly, information-extraction tools can readily and objectively highlight shifts in an actor's preferences over time. For example, a coalition of local and international activists sharply contested the plan by Canadian mining company Gabriel Resources to develop the Rosia Montana gold mine in Romania. The exhibit "Are the Locals Hostile to You?" plots the frequency in the worldwide media of sentences mentioning statements or actions against the mine by nongovernmental organizations through 2007, relative to the total number of sentences in articles about the mine during the same period. The data show that NGOs were relatively indifferent to the issue until mid-2002, when negative reports increased sharply.

The "tummy test" and other models

With data about political actors and their level of interest in hand, managers must then synthesize that information into a model of the policy-making process. At the informal end of the synthesis spectrum is the "tummy test", in which a decision-maker who has spoken with or been briefed about relevant sources draws upon his or her own knowledge of similar cases to make an educated guess about the likely policy outcome. The accuracy of this technique clearly varies enormously according to the skill set of the decision maker and the relevance of his or her past experience to the current situation. To improve the accuracy of such judgments, managers can also involve specialized consultancies that draw upon a more diverse set of experiences from multiple firms and industries in the target country or a comparable one.

A sophisticated extension of the tummy test is the "war room", in which managers come together for a one-off meeting or a series of brainstorming sessions. Sessions may be scheduled regularly or triggered by a shock or event that requires a strategic response. "Influence maps" are used to depict each politically relevant actor as a bubble arrayed in space according to the player's position on a given issue, with the size of the bubble proportional to the player's power. Linkages across actors or clusters of actors can be indicated by either location or connecting lines. Although no formal analytic tools are used, the maps can help guide discussion o action scenarios: What happens if we target actor X? What if we break the link between X and Y? What if we try to reduce Z's power? The insights produced by this approach are, of course, only as good as the information brought into the room and the quality of the team assembled.

The most formal tool for modeling the policymaking process is the dynamic expected utility model, which is based on game theory. It assumes that, in each of several time periods, every actor (an individual or an organization) with a vested interest in an issue has a choice of three possible alternatives: proposing a policy, opposing a proposed policy, or doing nothing. Each actor chooses the alternative that maximizes his, her, or its expected utility in each period. The selection depends on the direction and intensity of the actor's preferences, the salience of the issue, the cost of proposing or opposing a policy and similar information about other actors. The combined actions of all the actors result in a likely policy outcome. The sensitivity of the outcome to various assumptions and parameters can then be calculated, helping to identify which actors are so pivotal that a change in their preferences, power, or salience would have a large impact on policy.

Models like this are widely used by the intelligence community and by specialist consulting groups such as Mesquita & Roundell, Sentia Group, the Probity Group, and Commentrix. A growing number of multinational corporations are also adopting these tools. A large British company, for example, used such a model to decide how to influence the climate change debate in the European Union. Analysts first identified which actors were most commonly cited in the press and whom these actors referenced in their speeches and writings. The analysts then constructed a network of key "influencers" and modeled various points of entry into this system to identify the target areas and the messages that would maximize their effect on the climate change debate.

Although the integration of automated data collection, dynamic expected utility modeling, and influence-map visualizations remains in its infancy, the potential applications are broader than the management of policy risk alone. Marketing research, financial analysis, operations, and human resources all could benefit from a richer analysis of the best ways to affect stakeholders' options.

Of course, the risks of investment may simply be too great to justify entry into certain political zones. But in many cases investors who explicitly recognize the dynamism of the environment and implement appropriate strategies to address it will find the risks quite manageable. By combining data-mining and modeling technologies with traditional approaches, as we've described, they can start the journey forward, moving from "tummy tests" toward an analytically oriented, defensible system for managing policy risk that will greatly expand their investment options. At its heart, this system will always retain elements of tacit knowledge and experience, and not all managers and firms will be able to master its intricacies. But those that do will find it a powerful source of competitive advantage.

Case study VI
Internationalization of Indian pharmaceutical multinationals

Surender Munjal

Introduction

The growth of the Indian pharmaceutical industry has impressed the world; Indian pharmaceutical multinationals are 'admired and reviled' for producing low-cost generic versions of patented medicines. However, these multinationals are slowly shedding their copycat image (*Financial Times* 2013). The industry is growing at an average rate of 15–20 per cent per annum and is expected to grow at similar rates in the near future. The industry has several internationally known players, for example, Dr Reddy's Laboratories, The Chemical, Industrial and Pharmaceutical Laboratories (CIPLA), Sun Pharma, Lupin and Wockhard.

Industry overview

The Indian pharmaceutical industry is ranked second (by volume) and thirteenth (by revenue) in the world (CARE 2013). The industry has seen a major transition since the introduction of a new institutional regime brought in by the introduction of the New Patent Act in 2005, India's accession to the Trade Related Aspects of Intellectual Property Rights (TRIPS) and the World Trade Organization (WTO). Earlier, Indian pharmaceutical multinationals gained worldwide popularity for their ability to reverse engineer innovations and drugs discovered by western multinationals. Many Indian pharmaceutical multinationals reinvented the wheel by modifying the process of production because previously they were allowed to patent the process of production rather than the end product.

Indian pharmaceutical multinationals did face challenges in the international courts, particularly in the USA for breaching patent protection. However, the proposition of reverse engineering was tempting. Many Indian pharmaceutical companies could not resist the temptation to reverse engineering patented drugs until the law changed at home. Production of generic drugs using reverse engineering methods significantly reduces the cost of production because it saves on the huge spending involved in undertaking the research and development (R&D) of new drugs.[1]

Most generic drugs produced through reverse engineering are exported by Indian multinationals to third-world countries where consumers' and the state's ability to buy original (expensive) drugs are limited. For obvious reasons, poor developing states welcome generic drugs. Indian pharmaceutical multinationals argue that they did a socialistic act by making life-saving drugs available at lower prices, however, these multinationals pilfer the intellectual property developed by other multinationals who have spent huge money on R&D.

Due to the large volume of generic exports, India's trade balance in the pharmaceutical industry has been positive for a long time. However, in the new institutional regime, India's exports of pharmaceuticals have fallen slightly. Now, generic drugs can only be produced for the off-patent drugs. In response to the institutional changes, Indian pharmaceutical multinationals have increased their spending on their R&D (see Table VI.1) as their business model of producing generic drugs based on reengineering is no longer valid.

Though the transition into the new institutional regime was not welcomed by the Indian pharmaceutical industry, the Indian government was committed to the change. They viewed active engagement in R&D as likely to make Indian pharmaceutical multinationals internationally competitive. Notably, few multinationals have already shown signs of success in original drug search. Recently Zydus Cadila, a family-owned Indian pharmaceutical firm, made a breakthrough by discovering a new drug for diabetes called 'Lipaglyn'. This drug can control cholesterol and high blood sugar. It is claimed to have been discovered and developed entirely in India (*Financial Times* 2013).

Active engagement in R&D has also provided opportunities for Indian pharmaceutical multinationals to form joint ventures with foreign multinationals. For instance, Glenmark Pharma has a joint research programme with Sanofi, a French firm, and with Forest Laboratories of the USA.

Pharma Vision 2020

In order to foster R&D in the pharmaceutical industry so that it becomes internationally competitive and India becomes one of the leading destinations for drug discovery and innovation, the Department of Pharmaceuticals, Government of India, has prepared a strategy document called 'Pharma Vision 2020'.

The aim of Pharma Vision 2020 is to make India a pharmaceutical innovation hub by 2020, with one out of every five drugs discovered worldwide originating in India. To fulfil this aim, the Indian government is providing world-class infrastructure and venture capital to the industry. The supply of internationally competitive scientists, such as chemists and pharmacologists, is promoted through enhancing the number and quality of educational institutions in India.

The Indian government also provides fiscal incentives in the form of tax breaks and tax-free zones to promote Indian pharmaceutical firms. In order to promote R&D, Indian income tax law provides a weighted deduction of up to 150 per cent of expenditure incurred on R&D, including capital expenditure to pharmaceutical companies in India. These incentives are available to foreign and Indian pharmaceutical companies of all sizes – small, medium and large – operating from India.

Main players

The Indian pharmaceutical industry has more than 10,000 small, medium and large firms (PWC 2010). Table VI.1 shows the Top 10 Indian pharmaceutical multinationals and their size, measured in terms of market capitalization, sales and total assets. The table shows that Dr. Reddy's Laboratories, CIPLA and Lupin are the three largest pharmaceutical companies in India when ranked by sales. These companies are also the most profitable Indian pharmaceutical companies.

From these three companies, the next section illustrates the business model and internationalization strategies of CIPLA and Dr. Reddy's Laboratories. These firms sharply differ from each other. CIPLA focusses more on the generic drug business and Dr. Reddy's Laboratories on new drug discovery. CIPLA's approach for international business is mainly based

Table VI.1 Top 10 Indian pharmaceutical multinationals (in Indian Rupees (billion)) for the financial year 2012–13

Name	Market capitalisation	Sales	Net profit	Total assets
Dr. Reddy's Labs	378.31	84.34	12.65	93.73
CIPLA	345.70	82.02	15.07	98.35
Lupin	374.63	71.23	12.60	54.02
Ranbaxy Labs*	134.77	63.04	−1.62	66.86
Zydus Cadila	137.52	33.64	4.67	36.53
GlaxoSmithKline	199.30	26.30	5.77	20.14
Divis Labs	130.37	21.29	6.11	25.86
Glenmark	144.26	19.49	3.86	28.32
Sun Pharma	1,167.31	16.58	1.33	78.32
Piramal	104.00	16.20	−2.32	123.33

Source: Moneycontrol.com

*Ranbaxy is no longer an Indian pharmaceutical company. It was acquired by Daiichi Sankyo, a Japanese multinational, in June 2008.

on indirect exports while Dr. Reddy's Laboratories has expanded internationally through foreign direct investment.

CIPLA

CIPLA is the most profitable, and the second largest (by sales) pharmaceutical company in India. The company exports more than 51 per cent of its output. CIPLA was founded in 1935 by Dr. Khwaja A. Hamied, with a vision of making India self-reliant in healthcare. To a large extent, CIPLA has remained successful in its mission; India is self-reliant and self-sufficient in healthcare. Today, patients from around the word visit India for treatment for a variety of diseases.

Until recently, the company was led by Dr Yusuf K. Hamied, son of Dr Khwaja A. Hamied, who stepped down on 6 February 2013. Dr Yusuf K. Hamied extended the company vision to societal care for all by making affordable world-class medicines available. CIPLA has an annual turnover of about US$1.35 billion and employs 20,000 people, which makes it India's leading pharmaceutical company.

The caring manifest has also provided a basis for CIPLA's organization culture, which values safety and equal opportunity in the workplace and fosters innovation for a healthier world. It also brings the confidence of supplying world-class quality drugs at competitive prices to its business partners.

Dr Yusuf K. Hamied provides great leadership in management and research for the company. He spends about five hours every day reading the latest research and subscribes to about 400 journals. He says that he does so 'because he sees things in totality'.

CIPLA's achievements have been acknowledged though conferring India's national honour '*Padam Bhushan*' to Dr. Yusuf K. Hamied in 2005 by the then President of India Dr A.P.J. Abdul Kalam and by the Thomson Reuters Innovation Award in 2012 (see Exhibit 2 in Appendix VI for CIPLA's awards and honours). In 1939, Mahatma Gandhi visited CIPLA and expressed his delight. He wrote, 'I was delighted to visit this Indian enterprise'.

CIPLA's business model is largely based on the production of generic drugs; it is one of the world's largest generic drug producers. CIPLA has core competency in adopting and cross-pollinating diverse technologies to provide new solutions. The company offers more than 2,000 products. Notably, the company has its entire manufacturing base in India. It has about 40 state-of-the-art manufacturing facilities all of which are approved by major international regulatory agencies including WHO, US FDA and MHRA, UK. CIPLA has technically competent human resources that follow the highest standards of medical research and environmentally green and clean processes.

CIPLA has a long contribution in laying the foundation of the Indian pharmaceutical industry. In the 1960s, CIPLA laid the basis for the bulk drug industry in India by becoming expert in the area of pharmaceutical ingredient manufacturing. CIPLA also provided the foundation for the generic drugs business to the Indian pharmaceutical industry by gathering the momentum for the Patent Act of 1970 (this legislation allowed patenting of the production process until recently when it was replaced by the New Patent Act of 2005).

The company engages in R&D and offers technical consultancy services. CIPLA's R&D focuses on innovation, both product and process, that results in cost and time saving. CIPLA has gained expertise in producing generics of very complex molecules. The company has given many generic solutions to India and to the world.

In 2012, CIPLA made a breakthrough in reducing the prices of an off-patent cancer drug, making world-class medicines affordable, while in 2005, during the outbreak of avian influenza, they produced an anti-flu drug within three months, compared with the normal development time of three years. Against the general notion of cost and quality trade-off, CIPLA is known for maintaining quality standards in its production worldwide.

In 2001, the company produced an antiretroviral, a drug for HIV-positive patients, called 'Triomune' by combining three generic medicines. The drug was priced at US$300 per year (less than a dollar per day), compared with the price of US$12,000 charged for the same medicines by western multinationals. This innovation made the medicine accessible to millions of HIV patients in poor African countries. CIPLA was heavily criticized for producing Triomune because it breached three existing patents.

CIPLA provides consulting, commissioning, plant engineering, technical know-how transfer and support to many developing countries. CIPLA also has partnerships and alliances for product development, technical support and marketing, especially with firms from countries that have a quest for self-reliance. Medpro Pharmaceuticals, South Africa's first generic drug producer, was extensively helped by CIPLA. According to Medpro's website, the companies formed a strategic alliance. Medpro Pharmaceuticals is currently the third-largest South African pharmaceutical company. This strategic alliance gave CIPLA a trusted partner and an outlet to sell its products in African markets. The strategic alliance was later converted into a joint venture. In July 2013, Medpro Pharmaceuticals was acquired by CIPLA for US$440 million and the company is now known as CIPLAMedpro.

Apart from Medpro's acquisition, CIPLA grew organically and avoided mergers and acquisitions (M&As). The company has always expanded organically. Arguably, CIPLAMedpro is not totally inorganic given CIPLA's prior involvement with Medpro.

Except Medpro, CIPLA's physical expansion took place within India. This may be because any expansion outside India might have made CIPLA vulnerable for legal suites for the previous breach of intellectual property rights. Therefore, while operating from India, CIPLA conducted its international business through indirect exports. However, the company hopes that it will not face too many challenges when it moves abroad in the near future because it has partners worldwide with whom it has long-standing relationships (*Business Today* 2013).

CIPLA is currently one of the world's largest generic pharmaceutical companies with products sold in more than 180 countries. So far, the main mode of international business is exports of formulations, pharmaceutical ingredients, prescription and over-the-counter drugs and veterinary products. However, going forward, CIPLA is looking to make a shift in its business model.

After Dr Yusuf K. Hamied stepped down, the company hired professionals from the world's leading pharmaceutical multinationals, such as Novartis and Teva. They are aiming for a direct presence in the USA, Europe, Japan and Africa. It appears that in the near future, they are planning to undertake foreign direct investment for expansion. The expansion is most likely to be a forward expansion as the company aims to build marketing and sales networks abroad. CIPLA is looking for target firms that can be acquired in Brazil, Turkey and Japan (*Business Today* 2013).

CIPLA has core competencies in product development skills and manufacturing capabilities, but not in marketing. However, the company aims to build marketing capabilities that are associated with its future expansion plans; they understand the need to iron out issues before undertaking any further expansion abroad.

Dr. Reddy's Laboratories

Dr. Reddy's Laboratories is the leading Indian pharmaceutical company. It ranks first in terms of sales. The company was founded in 1984. Dr. Reddy's Laboratories has an annual turnover of about US$1.4 billion and employs more than 16,000 employees. It is recognized as India's first pharmaceutical company to take up drug discovery programmes. Unlike other Indian pharmaceutical companies, the company choose to not to pursue copying patented drugs. In 1993, the company established Dr. Reddy's Foundation, a research unit that works on drug discovery programmes in the country. Later in 2007, in order to foster cutting-edge research in life science, Dr. Reddy's Laboratories formed the 'Institute of Life Science' with the help of the government of Andhra Pradesh, where they are domiciled. Dr. Reddy's Institute of Life Science is an initiative of public–private partnership launched under the government's 'Pharma Vision 2020' programme.

Over the years, Dr. Reddy's Laboratories has made significant investments in R&D. In 1994, in order to finance its research programmes, the company raised US$34 million from the capital markets in Europe by issuing the Global Depository Receipts (GDR). According to Dr. Satish Reddy, managing director and chief operating officer of Dr. Reddy's Laboratories, financing through the GDR has "brought in an international profile of investors and gave us great visibility in the international financial community."

Dr. Reddy's Laboratories R&D efforts paid off in 1997, when it discovered one of the most potent chemical molecules that can help in producing more efficient diabetic drugs. The molecule was licensed to Novo Nordisk, a Danish multinational which pioneered drug development for diabetes. This made Dr. Reddy's Laboratories the first Indian pharmaceutical company to out-license an original molecule to a western multinational. This is recognized as a momentous occasion for Dr. Reddy's Laboratories and a milestone in the history of the Indian pharmaceutical industry.

Dr. Reddy's Laboratories also focusses on producing affordable generic drugs. In 1986, the second year of operation, the company became international by starting the export of generic drugs to West Germany, Yugoslavia, Bangladesh, Kenya and Canada. Recognizing the company's pioneering success in exports, the Indian Chemical Manufacturers Association (ICMA) gave an award for ICMA best export performance to the company (see Exhibit 3 in Appendix VI for Dr. Reddy's Laboratories awards and honours).

The company got its first US FDA approval in 1987 and showed that not only is it capable of producing drugs at affordable prices but can also do it credibly. After getting the US FDA approval, the company became a global supplier for bulk pharmaceutical ingredients. In 1989, Dr. Reddy's Laboratories became the largest Ibuprofen exporter to many countries including the USA, Spain, Italy and Japan. In 1990, Dr. Reddy's Laboratories also became the first Indian pharmaceutical company to export Norfloxacin and Ciprofloxacin to Europe and the Far East. Dr. Reddy's Laboratories was also among the first Indian Pharmaceutical companies to enter the Russian market for prescription drugs in 1991.

Unlike CIPLA and many other Indian pharmaceutical companies, Dr. Reddy's Laboratories started building brands for drugs from its early years. This strategy fits with the new product development undertaken by the company. Generally, branding and promotion does not fit with the generic drugs business where the products are uniform and cost reduction is the key. However, in 2003, Dr. Reddy's Laboratories launched its generic product for Ibuprofen under its own label. This is a contradiction, however, Dr. Reddy's Laboratories is such a big producer and exporter of Ibuprofen that it resorted to branding a generic drug. The company saw this as a significant event that helped build its business in the USA.

The company also has some internationally known brands, for example, "Omez", an omeprazole drug used to treat acid-peptic disorders. According to the company website, Omez is a top brand in eleven countries in the world and has achieved a valuation of US$20 million. In order to boost the marketing activities, Dr. Reddy's established sales subsidiaries in the USA and Europe in early 1990s.

In order to build competitiveness in marketing and R&D, Dr. Reddy's acquired a number of companies in India and abroad. In 2002, it acquired BMS Laboratories Limited and its marketing and distribution subsidiary, Meridian Healthcare (UK) Limited, for about US$14 million. This was the first foreign acquisition by Dr. Reddy's Laboratories. This acquisition allowed Dr. Reddy's to expand in the UK and other European markets.

In 2005, Dr. Reddy's Laboratories acquired the pharmaceutical ingredients business of the Mexico-based subsidiary of US multinational Roche for US$59 million. In this acquisition Dr. Reddy's Laboratories got a state-of-the-art manufacturing site in Cuernavaca, including all employees and the business supply contracts of Roche. This strategic acquisition helped

Dr. Reddy's Laboratories to expand its custom pharmaceutical business from US$10 million to US$100 million in a period of just 18 months.

The acquired custom pharmaceutical business involved manufacturing and sale of active pharmaceutical ingredients including intermediates to Roche and other innovator companies. This acquisition added to the manufacturing capabilities of Dr. Reddy's Laboratories. Notably, the Cuernavaca site was approved by US FDA and other international regulatory agencies. After this acquisition, Dr. Reddy's Laboratories emerged as a leading player in the custom pharmaceutical business. As a result, the company is seen as a valuable supplier by many research active global pharmaceutical multinationals.

In 2009, GlaxoSmithKline (GSK) signed a strategic alliance with Dr. Reddy's Laboratories. The partnership aimed to develop and market select products across emerging markets outside India. Through this alliance, GlaxoSmithKline got access to Dr. Reddy's Laboratories product portfolio and future pipeline of more than 100 branded pharmaceuticals and Dr. Reddy's Laboratories obtained global legitimacy and access to R&D programmes of GlaxoSmithKline.

Dr G.V. Prasad, chairman and CEO of Dr. Reddy's Laboratories said,

> we are extremely pleased to combine forces with GSK, a global leader, to fully realize the potential of our strengths in technology, product development and manufacturing across a range of high growth emerging markets. We hope to take our purpose of providing affordable and innovative medicines to a much wider population through this partnership.

In 2006, Dr. Reddy's Laboratories acquired Betapharm, the fourth largest generic pharmaceuticals company in Germany, for over US$600 million. To date, it is the largest foreign acquisition ever made by an Indian pharmaceutical company. Dr. Reddy's Laboratories see the acquisition of Betapharm as the key strategic initiative that made it a true global pharmaceutical company with a strong presence in different pharmaceutical businesses and a strong presence in Europe. As a result, Dr. Reddy's Laboratories revenues passed US$1.5 billion in 2007 and it became the top pharmaceutical company in India in terms of sales.

In 2008, Dr. Reddy's Laboratories acquired the small molecules business of Mirfield (UK) and Cambridge (UK) based Dowpharma. The research facilities of Dowpharma provided Dr. Reddy's Laboratories with proprietary technology and a team of chemists of exceptional quality. Their highly specialised knowledge has created immense value for Dr. Reddy's Laboratories. Dowpharama was US FDA and UK MHRA approved with customers in North America, Europe and Japan.

In 2008, Dr. Reddy's Laboratories also acquired the contract manufacturing business of Louisiana (USA) based BASF, a world-leading chemical company with more than 110,000 employees and revenue over US$50 billion. This acquisition gave Dr. Reddy's Laboratories a product portfolio and manufacturing facility for the prescription and over-the-counter drugs for the North American market. It also strengthened Dr. Reddy's Laboratories supply chain in the North America.

The acquisitions also gave Dr. Reddy's Laboratories a connection with US government agencies because BASF was a supplier to them. This provided additional growth opportunities and linkages with other generic companies in the network of BASF.

In 2011, Dr. Reddy's Laboratories founder Dr Anji K. Reddy also received the national honour '*Padam Bhushan*' award by the then President of India, Mrs Pratibha Patil for his outstanding contribution to the pharmaceutical industry.

Conclusion

Indian Pharmaceutical multinationals have made a big impact on the global pharmaceutical industry and on international society. In many ways they have changed how the industry operates. Now, in the new institutional regime, Indian multinationals are finding ways to upgrade their own international competitiveness in production and marketing of pharmaceuticals.

Indian multinationals are also upgrading their business models from pure generics and bulk drug manufacturing to new drug discovery. In-house activity and collaboration with foreign multinationals are actively sought by Indian multinationals. Acquisitions of business units of foreign multinationals in western countries are also often undertaken as a strategy for chasing global competition. However, Indian pharmaceutical multinationals also have an outstanding issue of legitimization in the international market.

Understanding the importance of pharmaceutical industry for the Indian economy, the Government of India is also making significant efforts to make the pharmaceutical industry in India a global hub for innovation. The Pharma Vision 2020 programme is good testament of this.

Questions

1. To what factors do Indian pharmaceutical multinationals owe their success?
2. Does the case on Indian pharmaceutical multinationals show that the internationalisation of multinationals does or does not possess firm-specific advantages? Present reasoned arguments for or against the proposition that emerging market multinationals have firm specific advantages that underpin their internationalisation.
3. What future strategies do you advocate for Indian pharmaceutical multinationals? Do you suggest further internationalisation for these firms? If so, what directions should this take? Does your proposed strategy include foreign acquisitions?

Notes

1 As per an estimate, an average cost of producing a new drug is about US$5 billion (Herper 2013).

References

CARE (2013). Indian Pharmaceutical Industry, Credit Analysis & Research: Mumbai.
CIPLA (2013). www.cipla.com (accessed 16 September 2013).
CIPLAMedpro (2013). www.ciplamedpro.co.za (accessed 16 September 2013).
Dr. Reddy's Laboratories (2013). www.drreddys.com (accessed 16 September 2013).
Financial Times (2013). Indian pharmaceutical groups shed copycat image, 22 July 2013.
Herper, M. (2013). The cost of creating a new drug now $5 billion, pushing Big Pharma to change. Forbes 11 August 2013.
PWC (2010). India Pharma Inc.: Capitalising on India's growth potential, Pricewaterhouse Cooper: Mumbai.
Rath, B.N. (2009). Does R&D intensity matter for trade performance in case of Indian pharmaceutical industry? ICRIER: New Delhi.

Appendix VI

Exhibit 1

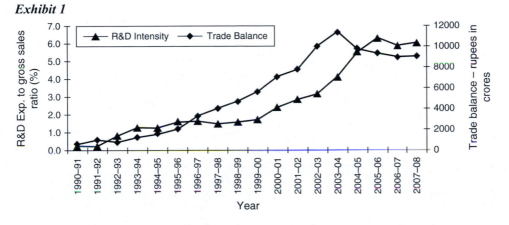

Source: Rath (2009).

Exhibit 2

Awards and honours: CIPLA

- Padam Bhushan conferred to Dr Y.K. Hamied, CMD of CIPLA (2005).
- Dun & Bradstreet American Express Corporate Award (2006).
- Scrip Award for Best Company in Emerging Market (2006).
- Outstanding Exporter Award (2006).
- Best under a Billion Award, Forbes Asia Award (2007).
- Most Trusted Pharmaceutical Brand in the Brand Trust Report – India Study (2011).
- Platinum Award from Pharmaceutical Export Promotion Council of India (2012).
- Conscious Capitalist Award at Forbes India Leadership award (2012).
- Thomson Reuters Innovation Award (2012) recognizing CIPLA's contribution to innovation through R&D.

Source: Compiled from CIPLA (2013).

Exhibit 3

Awards and honours : Dr. Reddy's Laboratories

- ICMA Award for Export of Chemical Products (1986).
- Department of Scientific and Industrial Research award for R&D efforts in (1994).
- FICCI Award in recognition of DRF's initiative in Research in Science and Technology (1997).
- ISO 9001 certification for design manufacture and supply of bulk pharmaceutical ingredients.
- Padam Bhushan conferred to Dr A.K. Reddy, CMD of Dr. Reddy's Laboratories (2011).

Source: Compiled from Dr. Reddy's Laboratories (2013).

Index

Page numbers in **bold** refer to figures, page numbers in *italic* refer to tables.